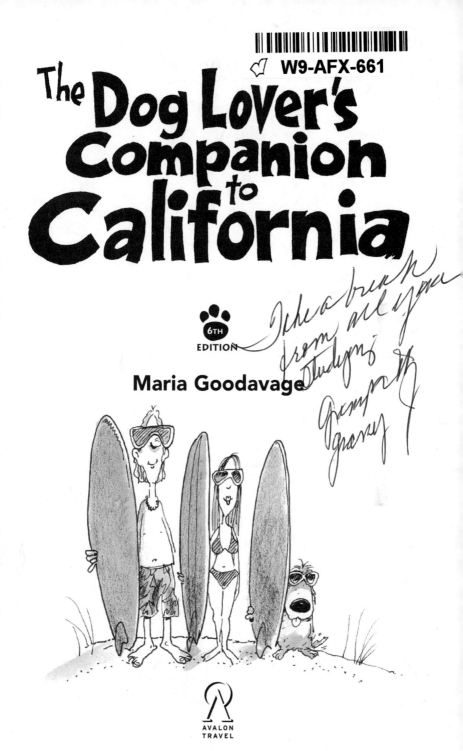

The Dog Lover's Companion to California

6TH EDITION

Maria Goodavage

Take a break from all your studying

AVALON TRAVEL

THE DOG LOVER'S COMPANION TO CALIFORNIA
THE INSIDE SCOOP ON WHERE TO TAKE YOUR DOG

Published by
Avalon Travel
a member of the Perseus Books Group
1700 Fourth Street
Berkeley, CA 94710, USA

Printing History
1st edition—1993
6th edition—May 2008
5 4 3 2 1

ISBN-10: 1-59880-020-5
ISBN-13: 978-1-59880-020-3
ISSN: 1086-7856

Editor: Shaharazade Husain
Copy Editor: Valerie Sellers Blanton
Designer: Jacob Goolkasian
Graphics Coordinator: Elizabeth Jang
Production Coordinator: Elizabeth Jang
Map Editor: Albert Angulo
Cartographers: Kat Bennett, Hank Evans, Chris Markiewicz, Ben Pease, Shizue Seigel
Proofreader: Deana Shields
Indexer: Jean Mooney

Cover and Interior Illustrations by Phil Frank

Printed in United States of America by RR Donnelley

ABOUT THE AUTHOR

Jake the Yellow-Lab-sort-of-dog and Maria Goodavage have traveled throughout the state to check out some of the most dog-friendly parks, beaches, lodgings, and restaurants in the world. As part of their research, they've ridden on ferries, horse-drawn carriages, cable cars, gondolas, and steam trains. They've visited chichi art galleries, dumpy drive-in movies, kitschy tourist attractions, dog-friendly wineries, high-end  stores, ski resorts, major-league ballgames, and even had high tea together. They've eaten at restaurants where dogs are treated almost like people (except they never get the bill). They've stayed at the best hotels, the worst flea-bitten motels, and everything in between. Jake's favorite saying: "You're not really gonna leave the house without me, are ya?" (This is usually accompanied by all his extra folds of neck skin drooping forward into his face, his floppy ears hanging especially low, his tail sagging dejectedly, and his big seal-like eyes looking wet and wide and oh-so-woeful.)

Since Jake still doesn't have a driver's license after all these years, he relies on Maria, former longtime *USA Today* correspondent, to be his chauffeur. Maria is well qualified—she started chauffeuring dogs nearly 20 years ago, when her intrepid Airedale, Joe, joined her during some of her travels for the newspaper. With all of their experiences on the road, it was only a matter of time before a book was born, followed by a series of books. Both *The Dog Lover's Companion to California* and *The Dog Lover's Companion to the San Francisco Bay Area* are now in their sixth editions.

Jake gets a little restless when not traveling around the state, so he has helped Maria and a small crew of video professionals launch Smiling Dog Films (www.smilingdogfilms.com). They make really cool broadcast-quality videos of dogs and their people (or if a dog prefers, dogs and no people). Jake encourages people to look at the website's samples page because one of the short videos—under "Custom Creations"—stars his big, blond, and beautiful self.

Jake lives near the beach in San Francisco with Maria, her husband, and their daughter. He encourages his fans to write to him, care of Maria (who won't let him online anymore—long story), and tell him about new dog-friendly places he should sniff out for this book's next edition. You can find contact info at www.caldogtravel.com.

CONTENTS

Sacramento County 365

Contra Costa County 379

Alameda County. 397

Marin County 421

San Francisco County 457

Riverside County 907

Imperial County 935

RESOURCES. 941

National Forests and Wilderness Areas. 942

INDEXES 947

Accommodations Index 948

Restaurant Index 957

General Index. 963

CALIFORNIA

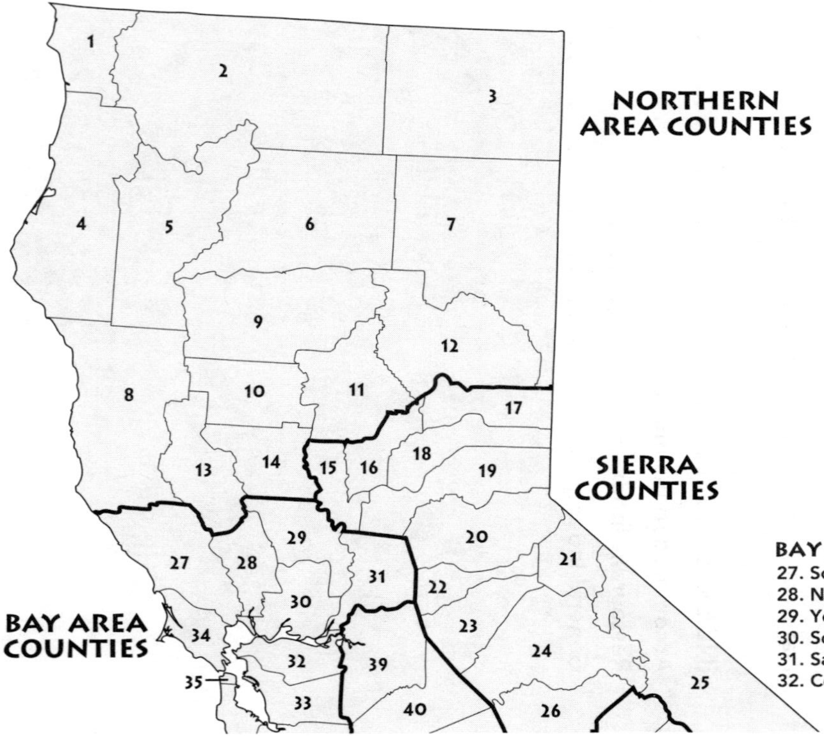

NORTHERN AREA COUNTIES
SIERRA COUNTIES
BAY AREA COUNTIES
1
2
3
4
5
6
7
8
9
10
11
12
13
14
15
16
17
18
19
20
21
22
23
24
25
26
27
28
29
30
31
32
33
34
35
39
40

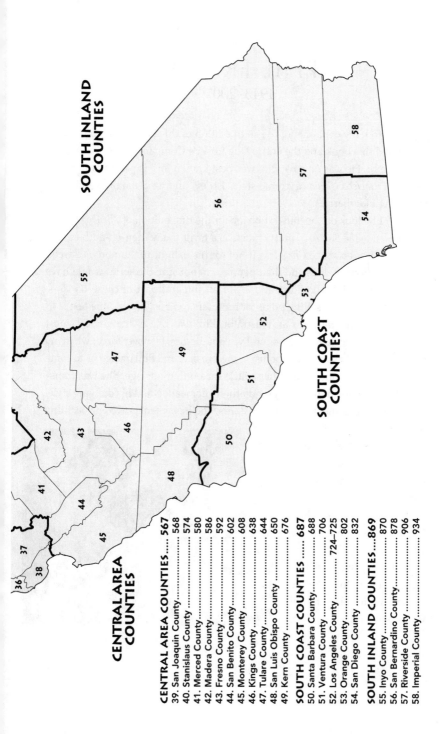

SOUTH INLAND
COUNTIES

SOUTH COAST
COUNTIES

CENTRAL AREA
COUNTIES

In Memoriam

PHIL FRANK
1943–2007

Just before my deadline for the sixth edition of this book, Phil Frank, who illustrated this book and the entire Dog Lover's Companion series, died of a brain tumor. He was only 64. Phil was best known for his perennially popular *San Francisco Chronicle* comic strip, Farley, and a nationally syndicated strip, The Elderberries.

In 1991 he took on the illustration job for the first edition of *The Dog Lover's Companion to the Bay Area* pretty much as a favor to my then-co-author, Lyle York, a colleague at the *Chronicle*. If not for his delightful, humorous, sweet, fun illustrations of dogs and their people, I'm not sure the series would have taken off as it did. His illustrations are an integral part of these books— sometimes the main selling point for browsers too busy to read the text.

But beyond his talent as an illustrator, Phil was one of the kindest, most humble, most decent human beings I've come across. I'll never forget when my daughter was an aspiring cartoonist at the age of 6, and Phil invited us to come to his Sausalito studio to give her a little cartooning tutelage. She was transfixed by his gentle humor, his grandfatherly demeanor, and his drawing style. They worked together for nearly two hours, and he invited us to come back any time she needed a refresher.

Sadly, life got busy, and although we emailed a few times, that was the last time I saw him.

I am comforted that Phil's illustrations—and thus a part of him—will live on in these books. But I wish he were still here to make the world a better place for all who knew him.

Introduction

Now, Charley is a mind-reading dog. There have been many trips in his lifetime, and often he has to be left at home. He knows we are going long before the suitcases come out, and he paces and worries and whines and goes into a state of mild hysteria, old as he is.

John Steinbeck, *Travels with Charley*

There was a time when dogs could go just about anywhere they pleased. Well-dressed dogs with embarrassing names attended afternoon teas, while their less-kempt counterparts sauntered into saloons without anyone's blinking a bloodshot eye.

No one thought it strange to see a pug-nosed little snookum-wookums of a dog snuggled on his mistress's lap on a long train journey. Equally accepted were dogs prancing through fine hotels, dogs at dining establishments, and dogs in almost any park they cared to visit.

But then there came a time (a period perhaps best referred to as the Doggy Dark Ages) when dogs came to be seen as beasts not fit for hotels, restaurants, or even many parks. The world was getting more crowded, patience growing thinner; there was only so much room, and, dangit, four-legged varmints weren't going to be sharing it. They were just *dogs* after all—animals who eat from bowls on the floor and lick their heinies at unfortunate moments. Dogs were for the house, the backyard, sidewalks (with canines being "curbed"), and some tolerant parks. So we got used to leaving our dogs behind when we took off for an afternoon, or for a road trip. It hurt—oh, how it hurt—but what could you do?

Many of us know that guilt too well. The guilt that stabs at you as you push your dog's struggling body back inside the house and tug the door shut can be so painful that sometimes you just can't look back. Even a trip to the grocery store can become a heart-wrenching tale of woe. A survey by the American Animal Hospital Association shows that the vast majority of us feel guilty when leaving pets at home. Thirty-nine percent of pet people call to talk to their pets when they're away. I've tried that, but it always made me feel even worse.

Joe, the Airedale terrier who inspired not only this book but the entire *Dog Lover's Companion* series, was born with an unparalleled gift for making people feel guilty—and not your ordinary, run-of-the-mill guilt where you smart for a couple of hours after seeing your dog's moping eyes follow your car as you speed away. It's that deep-in-the-gut-for-days guilt, where the sight of that pouting snout, those drooping ears, and that tail lowered to half-mast hangs with you until you return home.

John Steinbeck's blue poodle, Charley, was a master of powerful pleas that were carefully designed to allow him to accompany his people on trips. Eventually, his hard work paid off and he won himself a seat in Steinbeck's brand-new truck/house on their epic journey across America. They sought and found the heart of this country in their adventures across 34 states.

Joe's guilt-inducing expertise won him a spot in my rusty, beat-up, hiccupping pickup truck in our sporadic little journeys around the Bay Area, and later, California. We sought and found thousands of dog-friendly places in our adventures and misadventures.

Joe and I were frequently joined by two other experts in the field of rating parks and sniffing out good dog attractions. Nisha, our old-lady springer spaniel, insisted on standing in the back of the truck, under the camper top, madly wagging her tail for hours on end as we drove and drove and drove. She was a real asset to have around when it came to checking out beaches, lakes, rivers, and ponds—any area with water. (Joe hated to get his paws wet, so he couldn't be impartial in his rating of watery attractions.)

Bill, a big, lovable galoot of a dog, was my other original canine researcher. I found him partway through my travels. He was trembling in the middle of a Northern California road, with a big chain tight around his neck. He'd evidently broken loose, because the last link of the thick chain was mauled. I came to find out that his owner beat him regularly. Bill went back to San

Francisco with me that afternoon. During the months when I was looking for the perfect home for him (oh, and did he ever get the perfect home!), he became one of the friendliest, most outgoing dogs I've ever had the pleasure to meet. His presence during my journeys was invaluable. He lifted my spirits when I was tired, and his 85 pounds of muscle kept away bad spirits when we visited questionable areas.

Time marches on. All journeys have to end someday. Joe, Nisha, and Bill have gone to that giant off-leash beach in the sky. They're dearly missed, but their legacy—that of helping other dogs lead better lives by sniffing out places they're allowed to go with their humans—lives on. I'm pretty sure that now Joe is chasing—and finally catching—cats (in Dog Heaven, in case you didn't know, all cats are slow), and eating all the horse manure he wants.

Before I choke up, I'd like to introduce you to a dog you'll be seeing plenty of throughout this book. His name is Jake, and we figure he's about 97 percent yellow Lab, leaving 3 percent hound or Great Dane or some other big thing with short fur. When he was about six months old, we were asked to foster him for a week. That was a few years ago.

Jake now weighs a big 95 pounds and is one of the sweetest, most noodley dogs I've ever met. When we're home, he can usually be found reposing on his chair (despite our best attempts to keep him off it, the big comfy IKEA chair is now referred to as "Jake's chair"), jowls sprawled over the windowsill (which is half chewed away from his younger days—a very attractive sight), big brown eyes staring off into the distance as if longing for another road trip.

We've had some terrific trips together. Since traveling with a giant furry termite is a bad idea, I waited until his penchant for chewing furniture, windowsills, and floorboards had disappeared. Then we hit the road, enjoying dog-friendly lodgings, restaurants, and parks around California.

As a water dog, he excels at checking out liquidy attractions, from wading pools at dog parks to ponds, lakes, and beaches. Fortunately, I never have to worry about him going after ducks, per his breed's instinct. For some reason, when swimming ducks see him dogpaddling, they make a beeline right for him. This gives Jake the creeps, and he swims away, with the ducks fast on his tail. It's a sight that would make a duck hunter cry.

On a similar note, he's always glad when we visit a dog park that has a separate section for small dogs. Tiny dogs become giants with Jake, yapping a couple of times while giving him the chase. He tucks his tail between his legs and runs away, glancing nervously behind him to make sure he's escaped before relaxing enough to be his big doggy self again.

Jake and I (the "we" you will be reading about throughout the book) are happy to announce that the sixth edition of the book finds the Doggy Dark Ages further behind us than ever. Dog travel is scorching hot. Everyone's getting in on it. For many reasons, dogs have become a real part of our families ("fur kids" is a common name for their status), and businesses have seen the golden opportunities. Witness the dog travel agents, dog road-trip accessories, and even an upstart doggy airline (which has yet to get off the ground).

Many lodgings, from the humblest cabins to the most regal luxury suites and chichi vacation rentals, are now allowing dog guests. "If we have a house that doesn't permit dogs, they're just not going to do very well," a Sonoma County vacation rental agent told me. A Bay Area innkeeper's policy sums up this dog-loving travel trend: "Come here with a young child, I'll probably turn you away. Come here with a dog, I go all gaga."

Many upscale chains have taken the dog-friendly policy all the way. Loews has its "Loews Loves Pets" program. Kimpton hotels all welcome dogs, and most provide them some sort of VIP package. And Starwood Hotels, one of the leading hotel companies in the world, started its Starwood LTD (Love That Dog) program in its Sheraton, Westin, and W hotels in the United States and Canada.

"Dog owners are a market niche that's been underserved by the travel industry," a Starwood press release announced. And Barry Sternlicht, Starwood's founder, chairman, and CEO, has lofty goals for Starwood. "We intend to become the most dog-friendly hotel company in the land, and not just allow dogs to stay, but actually pamper and spoil them," says Barry, who has two dogs of his own.

The vacation industry is truly going to the dogs. And California is rife with dog-friendly destinations.

We've tried to find the very best of everything you can do with your dog in California, so you'll never again have to face the prospect of shutting the door on your dog's nose. This book is crammed to the breaking point with descriptions of thousands of dog-friendly parks, restaurants with outdoor tables, and lodgings. The book also describes dozens of unusual adventures you and your dog can share. You can ride on steam trains, cable cars, gondolas, houseboats, canoes, and surreys. You can sip wine at dozens of vineyards where dogs are adored, attend a professional baseball game, go cross-country skiing, hit a nightclub, go to church, enjoy concerts by world-renowned performers, watch plays, sniff around bookstores, check out art galleries, and shop at high-fashion stores.

The sixth edition of this book is the most fun-packed yet. We've added countless new places to go with your dog, many of them discovered through readers whose dogs insist on writing to tell us about their favorite new park, cool eatery, or pooch-loving hotel. We're so grateful to these dogs that, whenever possible, we acknowledge them under the new listing. (See the imprint page for easy ways to get in touch with us with your hot dog tips. Better yet, go to my website, www.caldogtravel.com, and click on the "contact" button.)

California dogs are lucky dogs indeed: Since the fifth edition, oodles more dog parks have sprung up. Dog parks are a huge trend, one that shows no signs of slowing. We personally prefer being out of the confines of a fenced area, and on a leash-free beach or trail, but these parks do put a wag in many a dog's tail. Dog parks run the gamut from very basic (often just bones city governments throw to appease their dog-bearing constituents) to gorgeous, perfectly manicured, custom-designed doggy playgrounds.

A traveling dog's life has changed significantly from the days when John Steinbeck and Charley traversed the country together. Dogs have less freedom, but, ironically, more choices.

And you can pretty much rest assured that no one will look askance when he or she realizes that your traveling companion is none other than the furry beast at your side. "Used to be odd when someone wanted a room to stay in with their dog," says a rural innkeeper. "Now it doesn't even make us blink."

The Paws Scale

At some point, we've got to face the facts: Humans and dogs have different tastes. We like eating oranges and smelling lilacs and covering our bodies with soft clothes. They like eating roadkill and smelling each other's unmentionables and covering their bodies with horse manure.

The parks, beaches, and recreation areas in this book are rated with a dog in mind. Maybe your favorite park has lush gardens, a duck pond, a few acres of perfectly manicured lawns, and sweeping views of a nearby skyline. But unless your dog can run leash-free, swim in the pond, and roll in the grass, that park doesn't deserve a very high rating.

The very lowest rating you'll come across in this book is the fire hydrant symbol 🔥. This means the park is merely "worth a squat." Visit one of these parks only if your dog just can't hold it any longer. These parks have virtually no other redeeming qualities for canines.

Beyond that, the paws scale starts at one paw 🐾 and goes up to four paws 🐾🐾🐾🐾. A one-paw park isn't a dog's idea of a great time. Maybe it's a tiny park with few trees and too many kids running around. Or perhaps it's a magnificent-for-people park that bans dogs from every inch of land except paved roads and a few campsites. Four-paw parks, on the other hand, are places your dog will drag you to visit. Some of these areas come as close to dog heaven as you can imagine. Many have lakes for swimming or zillions of acres for hiking. Some are small, fenced-in areas where leash-free dogs can tear around without danger of running into the road.

This book is *not* a comprehensive guide to all of the parks in California. If I included every single park, it would be ridiculously unportable. Instead, I tried to find the best, largest, and most convenient parks—and especially parks that allow dogs off leash. Some counties have so many wonderful parks that I had to make some tough choices in deciding which to include and which to leave out. Other counties have such a limited supply of parks that, for the sake of dogs living and visiting there, I ended up listing parks that wouldn't otherwise be worth mentioning.

I've provided specific directions to the major parks and parks near highways. Other parks are listed by their cross streets. If you don't have GPS, I highly recommend checking an Internet map site such as Mapquest.com or picking up detailed street maps from the AAA—California State Automobile Association (maps are free for members)—before you and your dog set out on your adventures.

He, She, It

In this book, whether neutered, spayed, or au naturel, dogs are never referred to as "it." They are either "he" or "she." I alternate pronouns so no dog reading this book will feel left out.

To Leash or Not to Leash...

This is not a question that plagues dogs' minds. Ask just about any normal, red-blooded American dog whether she'd prefer to visit a park and be on leash or off, and she'll say, "Arf!" No question about it, most dogs would give their canine teeth to frolic about without a cumbersome leash.

Whenever you see the running dog symbol ![running dog] in this book, you'll know that under certain circumstances, your dog can run around in leash-free bliss. Fortunately, California is home to hundreds of such parks. The rest of the parks demand leashes. I wish I could write about the parks where dogs get away with being scofflaws. Unfortunately, those would be the first parks the animal control patrols would hit. I don't advocate breaking the law, but if you're going to, please follow your conscience and use common sense.

Also, just because dogs are permitted off leash in certain areas doesn't

necessarily mean you should let your dog run free. In large tracts of wild land, unless you're sure your dog will come back when you call or will never stray more than a few yards from your side, you should probably keep her leashed. An otherwise docile homebody can turn into a savage hunter if the right prey is near. Or your curious dog could perturb a rattlesnake or dig up a rodent whose fleas carry bubonic plague. In pursuit of a strange scent, your dog could easily get lost in an unfamiliar area. (Some forest rangers recommend having your dog wear a bright orange collar, vest, or backpack when out in the wilderness.)

There's No Business Like Dog Business

There's nothing appealing about bending down with a plastic bag or a piece of newspaper on a chilly morning and grabbing the steaming remnants of what your dog ate for dinner the night before. It's disgusting. Worse yet, you have to hang onto it until you can find a trash can. And how about when the newspaper doesn't endure before you can dispose of it? Yuck! It's enough to make you wish your dog could wear diapers. But as gross as it can be to scoop the poop, it's worse to step in it. It's really bad if a child falls in it, or—*gasp!*—starts eating it. And have you ever walked into a park where few people clean up after their dogs? It's so whiffy even the dogs look vaguely discomfited.

Unscooped poop is one of a dog's worst enemies. Public policies banning dogs from parks are enacted because of it. And not all poop woes are outside. A dog-loving concierge at an upscale hotel told us that a guest came up to her and said there was some dirt beside the elevator. The concierge sent someone to clean it up. The dirt turned out to be dog poop. The hotel, which used to be one of the most elegant dog-friendly hotels around (it even had a Pampered Pet Program), now bans dogs. (There were other reasons, including a new boss, but the poop was the last straw.)

Just be responsible and clean up after your dog everywhere you go. (And obviously, if there's even a remote chance he'll relieve himself inside, don't even bring him into hotels or stores that permit dogs!) Anytime you take your dog out, stuff plastic bags in your jacket, purse, car, pants pockets—anywhere you might be able to pull one out when needed. Or, if plastic isn't your bag, newspapers will do the trick. If it makes it more palatable, bring along a paper bag, too, and put the used newspaper or plastic bag in it. That way you don't have to walk around with dripping paper or a plastic bag whose contents are visible to the world. If you don't enjoy the squishy sensation, try one of those cardboard or plastic bag pooper-scoopers sold at pet stores. If you don't feel like bending down, buy a long-handled scooper. There's a scooper for every taste.

This is the only lecture you'll get on scooping in this entire book. To help keep parks alive, I should harp on it in every park description, but that would take another 100 pages—and you'd start to ignore it anyway. And, if I mentioned it in some park listings but not others, it might imply that you don't have to clean up after your dog in the parks where it's not mentioned.

A final note: Don't pretend not to see your dog while he's doing his bit. Don't pretend to look for it without success. And don't fake scooping it up when you're really just covering it with sand. I know these tricks because I've been guilty of them myself—but no more. I've seen the light. I've been saved. I've been delivered from the depths of dog-doo depravity.

Etiquette Rex:
The Well-Mannered Mutt

While cleaning up after your dog is your responsibility, a dog in a public place has his own responsibilities. Of course, it really boils down to your responsibility again, but the burden of action is on your dog. Etiquette for restaurants and hotels is covered in other sections of this chapter. What follows are some fundamental rules of dog etiquette. I'll go through it quickly, but if your dog's a slow reader, he can read it again: no vicious dogs; no jumping on people; no incessant barking; no leg lifts on surfboards, backpacks, human legs, or any other personal objects you'll find hanging around beaches and parks; dogs should come when they're called; dogs should stay on command.

Joe Dog managed to violate all but the first of these rules at one point or another. (Jake followed in his pawsteps to an amazing extent, considering he never even met Joe.) Do your best to remedy any problems. It takes patience, and it's not always easy. For instance, there was a time during Joe's youth when he seemed to think that human legs were tree trunks. Rather than pretending I didn't know the beast, I strongly reprimanded him, apologized to the victim from the depths of my heart, and offered money for dry cleaning. Joe learned his lesson—many dry-cleaning bills later.

Safety First

A few essentials will keep your traveling dog happy and healthy.

Heat: If you must leave your dog alone in the car for a few minutes, do so only if it's cool out and if you can park in the shade. *Never, ever, ever* leave a dog in a car with the windows rolled up all the way. Even if it seems cool, the sun's heat passing through the window can kill a dog in a matter of minutes. Roll down the window enough so your dog gets air, but not so much that there's danger of your dog getting out or someone breaking in. Make sure your dog has plenty of water.

You also have to watch out for heat exposure when your car is in motion.

Certain cars, such as hatchbacks, can make a dog in the backseat extra hot, even while you feel OK in the driver's seat.

Try to time your vacation so you don't visit a place when it's extremely warm. Dogs and heat don't get along, especially if the dog isn't used to heat. The opposite is also true. If your dog lives in a hot climate and you take him to a freezing place, it may not be a healthy shift. Check with your vet if you have any doubts. Spring and fall are usually the best times to travel.

Water: Water your dog frequently. Dogs on the road may drink even more than they do at home. Take regular water breaks, or bring a heavy bowl (the thick clay ones do nicely) and set it on the floor so your dog always has access to water. I use a nonspill bowl, which comes in really handy on curvy roads. When hiking, be sure to carry enough water for you *and* a thirsty dog.

Rest Stops: Stop and unwater your dog. There's nothing more miserable than being stuck in a car when you can't find a rest stop. No matter how tightly you cross your legs and try to think of the desert, you're certain you'll burst within the next minute... so imagine how a dog feels when the urge strikes, and he can't tell you the problem. There are plenty of rest stops along the major California freeways. I've also included many parks close to freeways for dogs who need a good stretch with their bathroom break.

How frequently you stop depends on your dog's bladder. If your dog is constantly running out the doggy door at home to relieve himself, you may want to stop every hour. Others can go significantly longer without being uncomfortable. Watch for any signs of restlessness and gauge it for yourself.

Car Safety: Even the experts differ on how a dog should travel in a car. Some suggest doggy safety belts, available at pet-supply stores. Others firmly believe in keeping a dog kenneled. They say it's safer for the dog if there's an accident, and it's safer for the driver because there's no dog underfoot. Still others say you should just let your dog hang out without straps and boxes. They believe that if there's an accident, at least the dog isn't trapped in a cage. They say that dogs enjoy this more, anyway.

I'm a follower of the last school of thought. Jake loves sticking his snout out of the windows to smell the world go by. The danger is that if the car kicks up a pebble or angers a bee, his nose and eyes could be injured. So far, he's been OK, as has every other dog who has explored the Golden State with us, but I've seen dogs who needed to be treated for bee stings to the nose because of this practice. If in doubt, try opening the window just enough so your dog can't stick out much snout.

Whatever travel style you choose, your pet will be more comfortable if he has his own blanket with him. A veterinarian acquaintance brings a faux-sheepskin blanket for his dogs. At night in the hotel, the sheepskin doubles as the dog's bed.

The Ultimate Doggy Bag

Your dog can't pack his own bags, and even if he could, he'd probably fill them with dog biscuits and chew toys. It's important to stash some of those in your dog's vacation kit, but here are other handy items to bring along: bowls, bedding, a brush, towels (for those muddy days), a first-aid kit, pooper-scoopers, water, food, prescription drugs, tags, treats, toys, and—of course—this book.

Make sure your dog is wearing his license, identification tag, and rabies tag. Bringing along your dog's up-to-date vaccination records is a good idea, too. If you should find yourself at a park or campground that requires the actual rabies certificate, you'll be set. In addition, you may unexpectedly end up needing to leave your dog in a doggy day care for a few hours so you can go somewhere you just can't bring your dog. A record of his shots is imperative. (You'll also have to get him a kennel-cough shot if boarding is a possibility.)

It's a good idea to snap a disposable ID on your dog's collar, too, showing a cell phone number or the name, address, and phone number either of where you'll be vacationing or of a friend who'll be home to field calls. That way, if your dog should get lost, at least the finder won't be calling your empty house. Paper key-chain tags available at hardware stores offer a cheap way to change your dog's contact info as often as needed when on vacation. Dog-book author and pet columnist Gina Spadafori advises always listing a local number on the tag. "You'd be surprised how many people don't want to make a long-distance phone call," she writes in her book *Dogs for Dummies*.

Some people think dogs should drink only water brought from home, so their bodies don't have to get used to too many new things. I've never had a problem giving my dogs tap water from other parts of the state, nor has anyone else I know. Most vets think your dog will be fine drinking tap water in most U.S. cities.

"Think of it this way," says Pete Beeman, a longtime San Francisco veterinarian. "Your dog's probably going to eat poop if he can get hold of some, and even that's probably not going to harm him. I really don't think that drinking water that's OK for people is going to be bad for dogs." (Jake can attest to the poop part. But let's not talk about that.)

Bone Appétit

In some European countries, dogs enter restaurants and dine alongside their folks as if they were people, too. (Or at least they sit and watch and drool while their people dine.) Not so in the United States. Rightly or wrongly, dogs are considered a health threat here. But many health inspectors I've spoken with say they see no reason why clean, well-behaved dogs shouldn't be permitted inside a restaurant. "Aesthetically, it may not appeal to Americans," an environmental specialist with the state Department of Health told me. "But the truth is, there's no harm in this practice."

Ernest Hemingway made an expatriate of his dog, Black Dog (a.k.a. Blackie), partly because of America's restrictive views on dogs in dining establishments. In "The Christmas Gift," a story published in *Look* magazine in 1954, he describes how he made the decision to take Black Dog to Cuba, rather than leave him behind in Ketchum, Idaho.

> This was a town where a man was once not regarded as respectable unless he was accompanied by his dog. But a reform movement had set in, led by several local religionists, and gambling had been abolished and there was even a movement on foot to forbid a dog from entering a public eating place with his master. Blackie had always tugged me by the trouser leg as we passed a combination gambling and eating place called the Alpine where they served the finest sizzling steak in the West. Blackie wanted me to order the giant sizzling steak and it was difficult to pass the Alpine .... We decided to make a command decision and take Blackie to Cuba.

Fortunately, you don't have to take your dog to a foreign country to eat together at a restaurant. The state is full of restaurants with outdoor tables, and hundreds of them welcome dogs to join their people for an alfresco experience. The law on outdoor dining is somewhat vague, and each county has different versions of it. In general, as long as your dog doesn't go inside a restaurant

(even to get to outdoor tables in the back) and isn't near the food preparation areas, it's probably legal. The decision is then up to the restaurant proprietor.

The restaurants listed in this book have given us permission to tout them as dog-friendly eateries. But keep in mind that rules can change and restaurants can close, so I highly recommend phoning before you set your stomach on a particular kind of cuisine. Since some restaurants close during colder months, phoning ahead is a doubly wise thing to do. (Of course, you can assume that where there's snow or ultracold temperatures, the outdoor tables will move indoors for a while each year.) If you can't call first, be sure to ask a server or the manager for permission before you sit down with your sidekick. Remember, it's the restaurant proprietor, not you, who will be in trouble if someone complains to the health department.

Some basic rules of restaurant etiquette: Dogs shouldn't beg from other diners, no matter how delicious their steaks look. They should not attempt to get their snouts (or their entire bodies) up on the table. They should be clean, quiet, and as unobtrusive as possible. If your dog leaves a good impression with the management and other customers, it will help pave the way for all the other dogs who want to dine alongside their best friends in the future.

One day, well-behaved California dogs may find themselves treated much like their European counterparts. A couple of restaurants in upscale hotels here have already figured out a way around the no-dogs-inside law. They simply set up tables in the hotel lobby, just outside the official restaurant.

People with dogs get table service as if they were in the restaurant itself, and everyone is happy. It's a toe in the door, at least.

In our neighbor to the north, Oregon state lawmaker Brian Clem (D-Salem) has sponsored a bill that would allow well-behaved dogs inside restaurants that want to let them in. The bill hasn't exactly been well received by state health officials, whom the Associated Press quoted as arguing that dogs are "quite naturally a vector for a variety of pathogens, including salmonella and campylobacter." (Er, raw meat is a major vector for these organisms, and I don't see health officials running to ban this in restaurants. Health officials I've talked with said it would be "extremely difficult" to get these germs from a dog.) If Clem's bill makes it one day, it could lead the way to the Europeanization of restaurants. Until then (and don't hold your breath) enjoy all the dog-friendly alfresco eateries the Golden State offers.

A Room at the Inn

Good dogs make great hotel guests. They don't steal towels, and they don't get drunk and keep the neighbors up all night. California is full of lodgings whose owners welcome dogs. This book lists dog-friendly accommodations of all types, from motels to bed-and-breakfast inns to elegant hotels—but the basic dog etiquette rules are the same everywhere.

Dogs should never be left alone in your room. Leaving a dog alone in a strange place invites serious trouble. Scared, nervous dogs may tear apart drapes, carpeting, and furniture. They may even injure themselves. They might also bark nonstop and scare the daylights out of the housekeeper. Just don't do it.

Only bring a house-trained dog to a lodging. How would you like a houseguest to go to the bathroom in the middle of your bedroom?

Make sure your pooch is flea-free. Otherwise, future guests will be itching to leave.

It helps to bring your dog's bed or blanket along for the night. Your dog will feel more at home and won't be tempted to jump on the hotel bed. If your dog sleeps on the bed with you at home (as 47 percent do, according to the American Animal Hospital Association survey), bring a sheet and put it on top of the bed so the hotel's bedspread won't get furry or dirty.

Don't wash your dog in the hotel tub. "It's very yucky," I was told by one motel manager who has seen so many furry tubs that she's thinking about banning dogs.

Likewise, refrain from using the ice bucket as a water or food bowl. Bring your own bowls, or stay in a hotel that provides them, as many of the nicer ones do these days.

After a few days in a hotel, some dogs come to think of it as home. They get territorial. When another hotel guest walks by, it's "Bark! Bark!" When the housekeeper knocks, it's "Bark! Snarl! Bark! Gnash!" Keep your dog quiet, or you'll both find yourselves looking for a new home away from home.

For some strange reason, many lodgings prefer small dogs as guests. All I can say is, "Yip! Yap!" It's really ridiculous. Large dogs are often much calmer and quieter than their tiny, high-energy cousins.

If you're in a location where you can't find a hotel that will accept you and your big brute (a growing rarity these days), it's time to try a sell job. Let the manager know how good and quiet your dog is (if he is). Promise he won't eat the bathtub or run around and shake all over the hotel. Offer a deposit or sign a waiver, even if they're not required for small dogs. It helps if your sweet, soppy-eyed dog is at your side to convince the decision-maker.

In the early days of my exploring California with dogs, I sometimes had to sneak dogs into hotels because so few allowed them. I don't recommend it. A lodging might have a good reason for its rules. Besides, you always feel as if you're going to be caught and thrown out on your hindquarters. You race in and out of your room with your dog as if ducking sniper fire. It's better to avoid feeling like a criminal and move on to a more dog-friendly location. With the numbers of lodgings that welcome dogs these days, you won't have to go far.

The lodgings described in this book are for dogs who obey all the rules. I list a range of rates for each lodging, from the least expensive room during low season to the priciest room during high season. Most of the rooms are doubles, so there's not usually a huge variation. But when a room price gets into the thousands of dollars, you know we're looking at royal suites.

Many lodgings charge extra for your dog. If you see "Dogs are $10 (or whatever amount) extra," that means $10 extra per night. Some charge a fee for the length of a dog's stay, and others ask for a deposit. These details are also noted in the lodging description. A few places still ask for nothing more than your dog's promise that she'll be on her best behavior. So, if no extra charge is mentioned in a listing, it means your dog can stay with you free.

Ruffing It Together

Whenever we go camping, big Jake insists on sleeping in the tent. He gets in before we do, sprawls out and doesn't budge until morning. The dog of our camping buddies keeps guard over their tent nearby while Jake dreams sweet doggy dreams about his cozy chair at home.

It may not be the most macho place to be, but Jake has the right idea. Your tent or vehicle is the safest place for a dog at night. Some experts say it's dangerous to leave even a tethered dog outside your tent at night. The dog can escape or become a late dinner for some hungry creature.

All state parks require dogs to be kept in a tent or vehicle at night. Some county parks follow suit. Other policies are more lenient. Use good judgment.

If you're camping with your dog, chances are you're also hiking with him. Even if you're not hiking for long, watch out for your dog's paws, especially those who are fair of foot. Rough terrain can cause a dog's pads to become raw and painful, making it almost impossible for him to walk. Several types of dog boots are available for such feet. It's easier to carry the booties than to carry your dog home.

Be sure to bring plenty of water for you and your pooch. Stop frequently to wet your whistles. Some veterinarians warn against letting your dog drink out of a stream because of the chance of ingesting giardia and other internal parasites, but it's not always easy to stop a thirsty dog.

A Dog in Need

If you don't have a dog but could provide a good home for one, or if you have a dog but you're thinking of getting another, I'd like to make a plea on behalf of all the unwanted dogs who will be euthanized today—and tomorrow, and the day after that, and the day after that. Animal shelters are overflowing with dogs who would devote their lives to being your best buddy, your faithful traveling companion, and a dedicated listener to all your tales of bliss and woe.

If you can't adopt a dog, consider fostering one. Most shelters and rescue groups are in great need of people who can foster dogs until the dog is adopted, or ready for adoption. (Beware, fostering is how we originally got hold of Jake. You may not be able to say good-bye once you say hello.)

You may have read about a rent-a-dog business that's popped up in Los Angeles and San Diego, with plans to open soon in San Francisco. These

doggy timeshares are terrible for the dogs and send a message that dogs are just fashionable accoutrements that can be shifted in and out of people's lives with no ill effects on the dogs. The concept is deplorable. What's next, "rent a baby?"

Fostering is free (unlike the $1,400 or so annually the doggy timeshare business charges clients), fun, and fulfilling. Go ahead. Pick up the phone and call a shelter or rescue group and find out how you can get a dog into your life. You'll be giving a dog life in return.

Keep in Touch

Our readers mean everything to us. We explore California so you and your dogs can spend true quality time together. Your input to this book is very important. In the last few years, we've heard from many wonderful dogs and their people about new dog-friendly places or old dog-friendly places we didn't know about. If you have any suggestions or insights to offer, please contact us using the information listed in the front of this book, or via my website, www.caldogtravel.com. If your tip pans out and becomes a listing, we'll try to give you and/or your dog credit in the next edition.

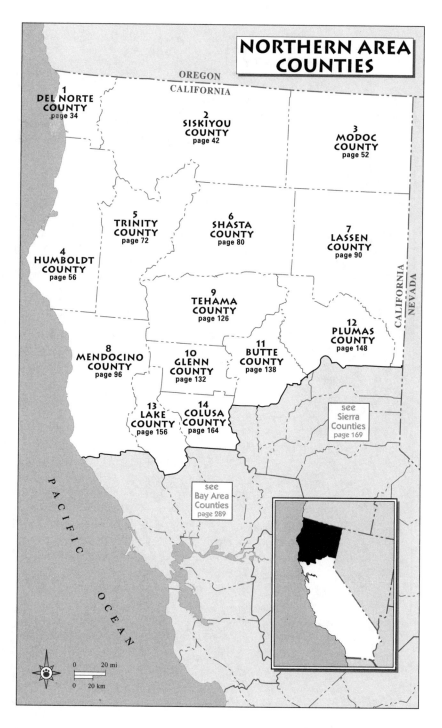

NORTHERN AREA COUNTIES

OREGON
CALIFORNIA

**1
DEL NORTE
COUNTY**
page 34

**2
SISKIYOU
COUNTY**
page 42

**3
MODOC
COUNTY**
page 52

**5
TRINITY
COUNTY**
page 72

**6
SHASTA
COUNTY**
page 80

**7
LASSEN
COUNTY**
page 90

**4
HUMBOLDT
COUNTY**
page 56

**9
TEHAMA
COUNTY**
page 126

**12
PLUMAS
COUNTY**
page 148

**8
MENDOCINO
COUNTY**
page 96

**10
GLENN
COUNTY**
page 132

**11
BUTTE
COUNTY**
page 138

CALIFORNIA
NEVADA

**13
LAKE
COUNTY**
page 156

**14
COLUSA
COUNTY**
page 164

see
Sierra
Counties
page 169

see
Bay Area
Counties
page 289

PACIFIC

OCEAN

0   20 mi

0   20 km

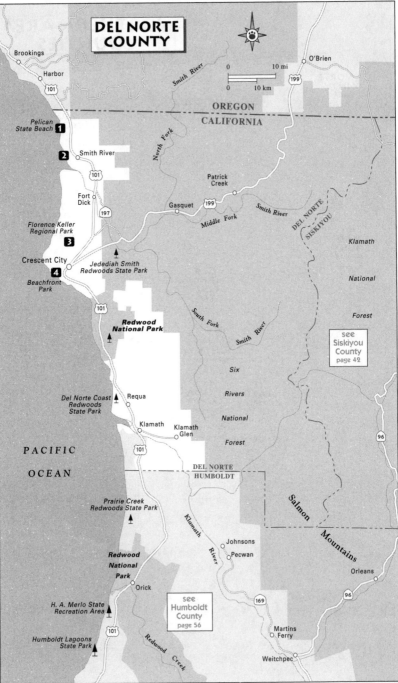

DEL NORTE COUNTY

Brookings

Harbor

101

Smith River

O'Brien

199

0   10 mi
0   10 km

OREGON
CALIFORNIA

Pelican
State Beach **1**

2   Smith River

101

North Fork

Patrick
Creek

Gasquet   199

Smith River

DEL NORTE

SISKIYOU

Fort
Dick

197

Middle Fork

Florence Keller
Regional Park

Klamath

3

Crescent City

National

4

Jedediah Smith
Redwoods State Park

Beachfront
Park

101

Forest

**Redwood
National Park**

South Fork

Smith River

see
Siskiyou
County
page 42

Six

Rivers

Del Norte Coast
Redwoods
State Park

Requa

National

Klamath

101

Klamath
Glen

Forest

96

DEL NORTE
HUMBOLDT

PACIFIC

OCEAN

Prairie Creek
Redwoods State Park

Salmon

Johnsons

Pecwan

Klamath River

**Redwood
National
Park**

Orick

Mountains

Orleans

96

H. A. Merlo State
Recreation Area

see
Humboldt
County
page 56

169

101

Humboldt Lagoons
State Park

Redwood Creek

Martins
Ferry

Weitchpec

CHAPTER 1

Del Norte County

Don't call this beautiful coastal redwood empire "Del Nort-ay" County, as many Californians do because of all the Spanish influence in this state. It's as much of a giveaway that you're from out of town as pronouncing the next state north "Or-ih-gohn" instead of "Or-ih-ghin." Pronounce this county "Del Nort," even if it reminds you of something Ralph Kramden would say.

If you want a real coastal getaway, you couldn't ask for a more beautiful, remote area. Part of the reason so few Californians know the local pronunciation of this county is because it's so out of the way that we don't often hear about the place.

As one of the state's best-kept secrets, it's a gem for people vacationing with a dog. While there are plenty of leash laws, there are also many places where civilization hasn't yet encroached sufficiently to make leashes a mandatory part of a dog's attire. The 305,000-acre Smith River National Recreation Area in the Six Rivers National Forest makes up the majority of this county and allows dogs off leash everywhere except in campgrounds!

PICK OF THE LITTER—DEL NORTE COUNTY

BEST WILD AREA
Six Rivers National Forest (page 36)

BEST HOMEMADE JAM
Glen's Bakery, Crescent City (page 39)

BEST KITSCHY ATTRACTION
Trees of Mystery, Crescent City/Klamath (page 38)

The climate in Del Norte County is very mild, with coastal temperatures generally ranging 65–75°F. That's good news for dogs who don't like temperature extremes. But this region is also known for its rain. One hundred inches a year here is common, making outdoor cafés almost nonexistent. The forests here are actually rainforests. They're lush and verdant. They're also often wet. Some dogs and people prefer this to the desert scenarios in other parts of the state. With a slicker, a dog towel, and a love of the outdoors, you and your dog could be very happy here. (While here, be sure to catch up with Paul Bunyan and ride a gondola 571 feet up a mountain—with your dog! See the Diversion *Have a Great Big Time.*)

NATIONAL FORESTS

The *National Forests and Wilderness Areas* resource at the back of this book has important information and safety tips on visiting national forests with your dog and has more background on the Six Rivers National Forest.

Six Rivers National Forest
🐾🐾🐾🐾🐕

This county is green thanks in great part to the lush 305,000-acre Smith River National Recreation Area, which is part of Six Rivers National Forest. The U.S. Forest Service has been designated as the steward of this fairly new national recreation area, and that's fantastic for dogs. The Wild and Scenic River, the 65 miles of trails, and the seven distinct plant communities can all be enjoyed by off-leash dogs, as long as they're obedient.

Smith River

PARKS, BEACHES, AND RECREATION AREAS

1 Pelican State Beach

🐾🐾🐾🐾 (See Del Norte County map on page 34)

It's only five acres, but that's plenty of running room for a dog who's been cooped up in the car all day. Pelican State Beach is actually a few miles north-west of Smith River, the closest California city to the Oregon border. It seems to be a popular stop for folks who've just come from or are about to visit our northern neighbor. Dogs are supposed to be leashed, but they love sniffing around the beach for the driftwood that's so plentiful here.

The beach is just west of U.S. 101, five miles south of the Oregon border. 707/464-6101.

2 Mouth of the Smith

🐾🐾🐾🐾 (See Del Norte County map on page 34)

This beautiful park, right on the mouth of the Smith River, is part of the state's Wild and Scenic River system. It's a great place to relax on the pebbly beach and take in the sights, or walk to Pyramid Point and do a little bird-watching with your leashed dog. It's also a popular backdrop for photographs. If your dog wants to be in pictures, this might be the place to snap away.

The park is at the end of Smith River Road. 707/464-7230.

PLACES TO STAY

Ship Ashore Best Western: If yours is a teeny-weeny dog, she can stay here with you. The weight limit for pets is 10 pounds. Fortunately, there is no weight limit for human guests. But in case you need the exercise, there's a pooch path on the premises. Rates are $54–140. 12370 U.S. 101 North 95567; 707/487-3141 or 800/487-3141.

Crescent City

This 1.25-square-mile coastal city was devastated by a giant tsunami in 1964. A series of waves about 12 feet high rushed inland as far as 1,600 feet, destroying 29 downtown blocks and killing 11 people. The city has since rebuilt, and the beach the tsunami washed over is now awash with happy dogs. Although the city itself has no leash law, it follows the county's leash law, so pooches must be appropriately attired.

DIVERSION

Have a Great Big Time! A visit to the campy but fascinating **Trees of Mystery** between Crescent City and the next town along U.S. 101, Klamath, will be a visit you and your canine buddy will never forget. This is the most dog-friendly, fun roadside attraction we've ever come across.

From the moment you step out of your car, your kitschy adventure begins. A 50-foot-tall statue of Paul Bunyan greets patrons in the parking lot. He really talks to you. He'll greet your dog by name, too. This literally scares the pee out of a few dogs, but usually dogs just look at the giant wooden man as if he's just a big weird tree with a voice—and what's so unusual about that?

When you pay your admission fee, you'll have access to a nature trail that takes you through some of the world's oldest and largest trees. But these are no ordinary trees! These are the Trees of Mystery. We won't ruin the many surprises that await you, but let's just say you'll definitely want a camera with a wide-angle lens. Boy dogs are especially fond of the trees here.

You can also go on a terrific 10-minute gondola ride 571 feet up the mountain. Although the altitude at the top is only 742 feet, you get a stunning view of the Pacific on one side and mountains on the other. You can sniff around once you disembark at the top and either ride or walk back down. (Those afraid of heights might want to walk.) The rides are included in your entry fee, and you can go up and down as many times as you want.

Our dog friend Fergus wasn't into the views up there but was very interested in the Trees of Mystery gift store. The people who work here adore dogs. Four Great Pyrenees pooches strolled in one day and "we just about went crazy over them," says Joan, one of the dog-lovers who works here. "They better be prepared to spend extra time here getting lots of love." Not only do they get love, but they also get a free dog biscuit. Humans get a free sample of delectable fudge. (They make 30 pounds of the stuff here daily.) The gift shop is also the place where you can borrow a leash if your dog is normally the naked type.

And finally, your dog can join you at The End of the Trail Museum, which adjoins the gift shop. The fascinating museum houses one of the largest private collections of Native American artifacts in the United States. We applaud the museum for welcoming well-behaved dogs.

Admission to the museum is free. The entry fee to the Trees trails and gondola is $13.50 for adults, $10 for seniors, and $6.50 for children ages 4–10. Dogs get in free, as do kids under four. 15500 U.S. 101, Klamath; 707/482-5613 or 800/638-3389; www.treesofmystery.net.

PARKS, BEACHES, AND RECREATION AREAS

3 Florence Keller Regional Park

🐾🐾🐾 (See Del Norte County map on page 34)

This 30-acre county park is one big redwood grove with space carved out for trails, playing fields, and playgrounds. It's a good balance of wild and civilized, if you need that kind of balance. Dogs have to be leashed. There are no showers here, so bring extra deodorant, or all the dogs in camp may follow you home. Camping at any of the 50 sites costs $10 a night.

Exit U.S. 101 at Cunningham Lane and follow the signs to the park. 707/464-7230.

4 Beachfront Park

🐾🐾🐾🐾 (See Del Norte County map on page 34)

Pooches are supposed to be leashed at this often-empty 80-acre beach/grassy park, but that doesn't stop them from having a ball here. They run and roll and do some mighty fine beachcombing. They stretch out beside their people in the charming gazebo, and they even manage to do the dog paddle when the surf is down. (Watch out for Elk Creek, which empties into the harbor here. Occasionally it can be too swift for even the strongest canine swimmer.)

If dogs aren't the only people in your life, this is an especially fun park to visit. Children can check out the playground, while anglers can make the acquaintance of fish at the 850-foot public fishing pier.

From U.S. 101, go west on Front Street. The park is at Front Street between B and F Streets. 707/464-9507.

PLACES TO EAT

Beacon Burger: This place truly is a beacon for dogs and their people. People often place food orders for their dogs, who get a big bowl of water if they're thirsty. If you want to make your dog very happy, try the namesake burger, which is a half-pounder with bacon and cheese. The view from the outdoor tables is terrific. 160 Anchor Way; 707/464-6565.

Glen's Bakery: The folks here make their own jam at this bakery. Add it to the fresh-baked bread, and you and your dog can feast. Try the clam chowder if you're in the mood for something hot. Dine with doggy at the outdoor bench. 722 3rd Street; 707/464-2914.

PLACES TO STAY

Best Value Inn: Good news for some dogs: No cats allowed! Bad news for some dogs: No cats allowed. They prefer dogs up to 40 pounds here. Rates are $58–115. Dogs are $10 extra. 440 U.S. 101 North 95531; 707/464-4141.

Gardenia Motel: This is your typical decent little motel. Dogs are allowed in some rooms. Rates are $50–55. Dogs are $5 extra. 119 L Street 95531; 707/464-2181.

Del Norte Coast Redwoods State Park: Dogs aren't allowed on the trails here, but they can sleep in one of the 245 campsites under a grove of redwoods. Rates are $19. The campground is about 10 miles southeast of Crescent City, just off U.S. 101. For park info, phone 707/464-6101. For reservations, call 800/444-PARK (800/444-7275) or go to www.reserveamerica.com.

Klamath

If you and your dog are sniffing out the marvelous Trees of Mystery (see the Diversion *Have a Great Big Time!*) and need a place to spend the night, Klamath offers a couple of good lodging choices.

PLACES TO STAY

Camp Marigold Garden Cottages: The cottages here were built in 1939 and are rustic, but not too much so: A poodle we know who recently stayed here gives it two paws up. Camp Marigold's cottages are set on four acres of grass and gardens, but it's the cottages' proximity to the Six Rivers National Forest that's the biggest hit with dogs. The place backs up right to the national forest, with plenty of excellent hiking trails to explore together.

Rates are $55–72. If you're throwing a big bash and want to rent Camp Marigold's recently remodeled large lodge, which sleeps up to 15 and is also dog-friendly, you'll pay $350 per night. 16101 U.S. 101 95548; 707/482-3585 or 800/621-8513.

Motel Trees: If the talking Paul Bunyan at the Trees of Mystery made your dog's hair stand on end, you might want to choose another lodging: Motel Trees is directly opposite the Trees of Mystery, and there's no escaping the scary giant man. Most dogs do just fine here and enjoy being able to look at the Trees of Mystery from their motel window. Rates are $55–65. Dogs are $10–20 extra, depending on their size. 15495 U.S. 101 North 95548; 707/482-3152.

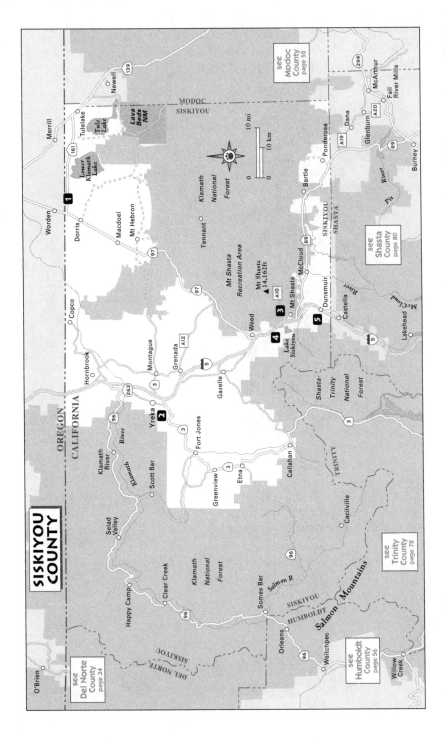

SISKIYOU COUNTY

OREGON
CALIFORNIA

MODOC
SISKIYOU

SISKIYOU
SHASTA

TRINITY

SISKIYOU
HUMBOLDT

DEL NORTE
SISKIYOU

see Del Norte County page 34

see Humboldt County page 56

see Trinity County page 72

see Shasta County page 80

see Modoc County page 52

O'Brien

Worden
Merrill
Newell
Tulelake
Tule Lake
Lava Beds NM
Lower Klamath Lake
Dorris
Macdoel
Mt Hebron
Copco
Hornbrook
Montague
Grenada
Gazelle
Yreka
Fort Jones
Scott Bar
Greenview
Etna
Callahan
Ceciville
Selad Valley
Clear Creek
Happy Camp
Somes Bar
Orleans
Weitchpec
Willow Creek

Klamath National Forest

Tennant
Mt Shasta Recreation Area
Mt Shasta 14,162ft
Weed
Lake Siskiyou
Mt Shasta
McCloud
Dunsmuir
Castella
Lakehead

Shasta-Trinity National Forest

Salmon Mountains
Salmon R

Ponderosa
Bartle
McArthur
Fall River Mills
Glenburn
Dana
Burney

Klamath River
Scott River
Salmon River
McCloud River
Pit River

10 mi
10 km

Highways: 139, 161, 97, 3, 263, 96, 12, A12, 5, 89, A10, 299, A20, A19

1 2 3 4 5

CHAPTER 2

Siskiyou County

The visual highlight of Siskiyou County is towering Mt. Shasta, but there's so much beauty here that almost anywhere you go, something's bound to impress your senses. Two national forests make up a big part of the large county. As you travel on Highway 96, you'll find dozens of places to pull off and explore the Klamath River in the Klamath National Forest. If you stop at a wide river access point that's far from the road, your dog can trot around off leash while you fish or soak your weary legs. Be careful, though—the current can really rip in some spots.

Two unique places to spend the night and have howling good views of Mt. Shasta are former fire lookouts in the Shasta-Trinity National Forest. (See *Girard Ridge Lookout* in the *Dunsmuir* section.) The price is right and the experience is one you and your dog won't soon forget. (Plus you get to bond, because, like your dog, you also must go outside when you have to go to the bathroom. At least you'll have an outhouse.)

PICK OF THE LITTER—SISKIYOU COUNTY

BEST FRESH DRINKING WATER
City Park, Mount Shasta (page 47)

BEST HIGH-ALTITUDE DIGS
Girard Ridge Lookout, Dunsmuir (page 50)

BEST CHOO CHOOS FOR POOCHOOS
Blue Goose Steam Excursion, Yreka (page 46)
Railroad Park Resort, Dunsmuir (page 51)

NATIONAL FORESTS

The *National Forests and Wilderness Areas* resource at the back of this book has important information and safety tips on visiting national forests with your dog and has more background on the national forests listed below.

Klamath National Forest
🐾🐾🐾🐾🐕

Shasta-Trinity National Forest
🐾🐾🐾🐾🐕

Dorris
PARKS, BEACHES, AND RECREATION AREAS

❶ Lower Klamath National Wildlife Refuge
🐾🐾🐾🐾🐕 (See Siskiyou County map on page 42)

This 54,000-acre waterfowl haven is home to what may be the largest wintering concentration of bald eagles in the lower 48 states. Dogs are allowed off leash only if they're helping you during waterfowl and pheasant hunting seasons. Otherwise, they have to be leashed at all times to protect this important nesting and migration area.

Lower Klamath Lake and the surrounding marshy area and uplands are a bird-watcher's paradise. During summer you'll see avocets, grebes, herons, white pelicans, black-necked stilts, and killdeers. Nearly one million waterfowl use this and nearby Tule Lake during fall migration. Keep those binoculars peeled.

The refuge has many entrances. From U.S. 97 at the Oregon border, head east on Highway 161. The refuge's entrances will be on your right in a few miles. Call 530/667-2231 for information and directions to other areas of the refuge.

Yreka

Yreka, Eureka, Ukiah, Arcata. Traveling in Northern California can be confusing, with cities whose names sound like bad Scrabble hands. But here's an easy way to have Yreka (why-REE-kuh) stick out in your mind: When you're here, just look south. See spectacular, snowy Mt. Shasta in the distance? *Yreka* is an Indian word for White Mountain. The "Y" in Yreka sounds sort of like the "white" in white mountain. Got it?

This is the county seat of Siskiyou County, and it's an attractive, historic place on the eastern edge of a huge section of the Klamath National Forest. Dogs prefer to run around unleashed in the forest, but there's a city park in town where they can enjoy a more civilized walk. And if your dog is small, he can have a roaring good time aboard the Blue Goose Steam Train (see the Diversion *Choo Choo with Your Poochoo*).

DIVERSION

Choo Choo with Your Poochoo: Put on your engineer caps and get ready to ride along a short-line railroad that's been in continuous operation since 1889. Dogs who stay out of the aisle, whether on your lap or at your feet, are allowed to accompany you on the **Yreka Western Railroad Blue Goose Steam Excursion** for a magical three-hour tour from Yreka east through Shasta Valley. You'll pass lumber mills, cross the Shasta River, and chug along through beautiful cattle country—all with majestic Mt. Shasta in the background.

The 1915 Baldwin steam engine stops for 1.5 hours in the old cattle town of Montague, where you can picnic in the park and afterward visit the old-fashioned soda fountain or take a wagon ride.

You can choose among an open car, two 1920s cars, and a couple of vintage 1948 passenger cars. Unless your dog doesn't like the wind in his face or the sound of steam rushing skyward, the open cars are the best ones for canines. Just keep hold of that leash.

The train runs from Memorial Day weekend through the last Sunday of October. Rates are $18 adults, $12 seniors, $9 kids, and dogs travel free. Fees are slightly higher for caboose rides. (Except for the dogs, who still travel free.) If your dog is too big, ask if she can stay in the manager's office. (A sad note: Longtime dog-friendly railway manager Larry Bacon passed away since the last edition of this book. He will be missed.)

Exit I-5 at the Central Yreka exit. The depot is just east of the freeway, at 300 East Miner Street. 530/842-4146 or 800/973-5277; www.yrekawesternrr.com.

PARKS, BEACHES, AND RECREATION AREAS

② Miner Park

🐾🐾 (See Siskiyou County map on page 42)

This small city park is conveniently located near the historic district of Yreka. Dogs like it just fine, as long as they don't mind a leash. The grass is green and the shade trees are big. There's also a playground and a ball field so the kids can work off their energy while the dog explores.

From Highway 3, drive west about six blocks on West Miner Street. The park is on your left, at Gold and West Miner streets. 530/841-2386.

PLACES TO STAY

Economy Inn: There's plenty of land around here for a little romping with your pooch. Rates are $53–58. Dogs are $8–15 extra, depending on their size. 526 South Main Street 96097; 530/842-4404.

Rodeway Inn: This bright inn has interesting knotty pine furniture. Rates are $40–80. Dogs are $5 extra. 1235 South Main Street 96097; 530/842-4412.

Mount Shasta

This small town sits under the watchful eye of the mighty mountain that goes by the same name. It can provide a quick highway rest stop for the weary or an enchanting place to unwind for days. Some who have come for a few days end up spending the rest of their lives here. Mount Shasta has the best of all worlds—it's remote and wildly natural, yet civilized to the point of being the area's cultural hub. Even dogs like the combination.

PARKS, BEACHES, AND RECREATION AREAS

🐾 City Park
🐾🐾🐾 (See Siskiyou County map on page 42)

We have to stop here every time we pass Mt. Shasta. We bring a couple of empty water bottles and a big thirst, since this fairly small city park is actually home to the headwaters of the Sacramento River. The crystal-clear, cold water comes bubbling down the rocks of a couple of small streams that become the Sacramento. It's the best water we've ever tasted, and it's free! There are no rules yet on how much water people can take, but there may be in the future if people abuse the privilege. Don't be a glutton and you'll be dipping your cup into eternity.

Dogs have to be leashed at this shady park, but they don't seem to mind. This is a relaxing place, where you have the chance to sit under a tree in a green meadow or under the gazebo and tune out the world for a while. Bring a picnic and toast your favorite dog with your favorite water at one of the riverside picnic tables. If your dog needs to stretch his legs more, there's a wide trail that starts in the area behind the stream. But do keep him out of the water. Dog hair doesn't go well with bottled water.

From I-5, take the Mount Shasta Boulevard exit and head southeast. Turn right within a half mile at Nixon Road and bear right into the park. 530/926-2494.

🐾 Lake Siskiyou
🐾🐾🐾 (See Siskiyou County map on page 42)

This man-made reservoir, created solely for recreational use, sits in the morning shadow of awesome Mt. Shasta. Trout fishing is one of the big draws—the lake is stocked with 20,000 trout each year! But you can also have a great vacation just camping and hiking in the area surrounding this 437-acre lake. Leashed dogs may go pretty much everywhere except the swimming beach and the picnic area.

Several trails wind through the ponderosa pines and cedars that encircle much of the lake. You can actually leave the campground and walk around the entire lake with your dog, as long as you don't mind hoofing it across a small section of the Sacramento River.

The day-use fee is $1 per human, but since dogs have to stay out of the water and away from the picnic tables, rangers tend to discourage day use with doggies. Too many people have left dogs in cars on warm days. Rangers here are so adamantly against people leaving dogs in their cars during the day that they'll flat out turn you back if they catch you. It's a good, lifesaving policy. Dogs don't pay anything during the day, but it costs $2 extra per night if your dog camps with you. There are 367 sites with fees ranging $20–29. From I-5, take the Central Mount Shasta exit, turn left at the stop sign, and follow the signs west on W. A. Barr Road to the lake. 530/926-2610; www.lakesis.com.

PLACES TO STAY

Dream Inn Bed and Breakfast: You and your dog have a choice of rooms in two very different houses when you stay here: a 1904 Victorian home or 1938 Spanish-style home. The Victorian home frightens Jake the Dog with all its breakable old lamps, plates, glassware, and frilly doodads. (Less waggy and klutzy dogs will do fine here.) Dogs of Jake's ilk might feel more comfortable in the Spanish-style home, just next door. It's got a kind of Spanish/American West/1970s thing going on, without all the antiques and breakables. The homes are surrounded by 176 rose bushes, myriad flower beds, and even a couple of big apple trees. If you're lucky, you'll be greeted by Noel, a sweet 14-year-old black Lab with a very graying head. (In the last edition, it was just his chin that was gray.) Rates are $70–190. 326 Chestnut Street 96067; 530/926-1536 or 877/375-4744; www.dreaminnmtshastacity.com.

Mountain Air Lodge: If your dog likes a little grass around his lodgings, he'll enjoy a night or two here. Rates are $50–79. Dogs are $7 extra. 1121 South Mount Shasta Boulevard 96067; 530/926-3411.

Mount Shasta Ranch Bed and Breakfast: A stay at this elegant two-story ranch house puts you up close and personal with Mt. Shasta. This historic inn offers spacious suites, a quaint vacation cottage, a large fireplace, an outdoor spa, and a tasty country-style breakfast. Dogs will enjoy the good dog-walking trails nearby. Your dog's requirement: He has to be flea-free to stay. Rooms are furnished with Oriental rugs and antiques, and a flea infestation would not be a good thing. And even squeaky-clean dogs are not allowed on the beds, so be sure to bring a bed your dog can call her own. Rates are $70–125. Dogs are $10 extra for the length of their stay. 1008 W. A. Barr Road 96067; 530/926-3870; www.beststayinshasta.com.

Swiss Holiday Lodge: Sleep here and watch the sun rise on Mt. Shasta right from your window. Rates are $55–75. Dogs are $8 extra. 2400 South Mount Shasta Boulevard 96067; 530/926-3448.

Tree House Best Western: There's no tree house here, but at least some of the rooms have views of Mt. Shasta. The maximum dog size allowed is 60 pounds. Rates are $101–199. Dogs are $10 extra. 111 Morgan Way 96067; 530/926-3101.

Dunsmuir

When I first visited this old town on the Sacramento River, it was July of 1991 and I was covering the toxic metal sodium spill that wiped out river life and made residents ill. The sign at the town's entrance, Dunsmuir—Home of the Best Water on Earth, was nothing but a sad irony and a good line for an article.

But these days, the river is clean and burgeoning with life again. The sign at the town's entrance is no longer incongruous. Check out the crystal-clear water from City Park while you and your leashed dog picnic along the river. It's so nice not to have bright green clouds of toxic pesticides floating by while you're trying to eat.

PARKS, BEACHES, AND RECREATION AREAS

⑤ City Park

🐾🐾🐾 (See Siskiyou County map on page 42)

This is not your typical, well-groomed city park. It's wild, woodsy, and full of trails winding up and down hills surrounding the Sacramento River. It's almost completely shaded here, keeping it cool during all but the hottest days of summer. If it's a particularly sticky day, you and your panting pooch can dip your toes in the always-cool river. If your dog is a landlubber like Joe was, he may want to hang out near the shaded picnic tables, so be sure to pack a little snack.

Take the Central Dunsmuir exit off I-5 and go north on Dunsmuir Avenue. The park will be on your left. 530/235-4740.

PLACES TO EAT

Café Maddalena: The best way to characterize the cuisine at this upscale-yet-casual restaurant in the heart of Dunsmuir's historic district is Italian/Spanish/North African/Southern French. Actually, the best way to describe it takes only one word: delicious. If you've got a vegetarian in you just hankering to come out, this is a good place to start. Try the butternut squash risotto or the spiced lentils with roasted veggies. If meat is your dish, Jake the Dog swears

by the café's rib eye steak with shallot butter. Actually, he swears at it, because anytime a waiter brings one to the outdoor eating area, it's never for our table. 5801 Sacramento Avenue; 530/235-2725.

Cornerstone Bakery and Cafe: Everything here is made fresh. Enjoy the veggie focaccia bread or a roasted turkey breast sandwich at the umbrella-topped tables outside. 5759 Dunsmuir Avenue; 530/235-4677.

PLACES TO STAY

Girard Ridge Lookout: You and your dog may have stayed at fancy hotels, rustic cabins, and cute inns, but you've probably never seen a lodging quite like this. Imagine sleeping in a place that has only one room, and that room is perched on a 12-foot-tall base and is walled by glass, with crystal-clear views of Mt. Shasta and Castle Crags. There are no neighbors to keep you up at night, no managers watching over you to make sure your dog behaves himself. On the flipside, there are no bathrooms (just an outhouse), you have to bring your own sleeping bags, and you can't head downstairs to an antique-festooned dining room for a piping hot breakfast in the morning.

But spending the night in a U.S. Forest Service lookout such as Girard Ridge is an experience not to be missed if you don't mind roughing it a little. You bring everything you'd bring if you were going camping (except for the tent), but you're protected from the elements, and you'll have plenty of privacy at night.

At Girard Ridge, you get to drive right up to the lookout (as do other people, who will undoubtedly think you're a fire-watch ranger and ask you how you get such a magnificent job), so there's no lugging of equipment. But—joy of joys!—you're in the middle of the Shasta-Trinity National Forest, and the Pacific Crest Trail runs right by here, so you and your dog can explore from dawn 'til dusk.

The rate is $35. Girard Ridge is about 10 miles from Dunsmuir. Another lookout, Little Mt. Hoffman Lookout, is truly in the middle of nowhere, at an elevation of 7,000 feet, on the border of Siskiyou and Modoc counties. It has magnificent 360-degree views that include Mt. Shasta and Mt. Lassen. It's so high on a peak that it doesn't have to be on a man-made perch. The rate is also $35. Call 530/964-2184 to reserve either and get directions.

Dunsmuir Lodge: Guests—both canine and human—are warmly welcome at this immaculate motel. As owners John and Donna say, "Once a guest, always a friend." You and your dog are free to enjoy the designated areas of the four acres of meadow and lawn here. Big trees are plentiful here, which is nice for dogs of the male persuasion. The location provides great views of the nearby forest and canyon area. And if you're fishing, the motel has a fish-cleaning station, plus barbecues for those fresh river trout or the burgers you brought along as backup.

Rates are $69–79. Dogs are $8 extra. 6604 Dunsmuir Avenue 96025; 530/235-2884 or 877/235-2884; www.dunsmuirlodge.net.

Railroad Park Resort/Caboose Motel: Stay here in a caboose that was once an important part of any of several major rail lines, including the Santa Fe. These restored caboose cars are intriguing places to hang your leash with your good dog, who is welcome as long as you call ahead and get the OK. The owners prefer dogs to bring their own beds. Humans get comfy beds and cushy armchairs. If you stay in the deluxe boxcar, you'll get your own wet bar and your tub will have claw feet (dogs can relate). The rooms have no kitchens, but a terrific restaurant in the dining car makes up for this (no dogs in the restaurant, though). You can also stay at one of the resort's four very cozy cabins or motel rooms. The grounds of the resort are like a park, with plenty of places to walk a dog, and killer views of the surrounding crags and mountains. Pooches have to stay off landscaped areas and out of the pool. Rates are $90–110. Dogs are $10 extra. 100 Railroad Park Road 96025; 530/235-4440; www.rrpark.com.

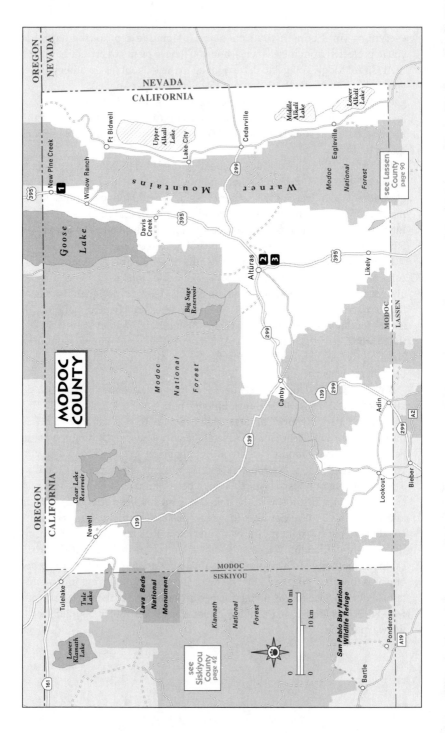

MODOC COUNTY

see Lassen County page 90

see Siskiyou County page 42

OREGON
NEVADA

NEVADA
CALIFORNIA

OREGON
CALIFORNIA

MODOC
SISKIYOU

MODOC
LASSEN

New Pine Creek

Ft Bidwell

Upper Alkali Lake

Lake City

Cedarville

Middle Alkali Lake

Lower Alkali Lake

Willow Ranch

W a r n e r   M o u n t a i n s

Modoc National Forest

Eagleville

Davis Creek

Goose Lake

Alturas

Big Sage Reservoir

Likely

Modoc National Forest

Canby

Adin

Lookout

Bieber

Clear Lake Reservoir

Newell

Tulelake

Tule Lake

Lava Beds National Monument

Klamath National Forest

Lower Klamath Lake

San Pablo Bay National Wildlife Refuge

Ponderosa

Bartle

395

299

395

299

139

299

139

139

161

A2

A19

10 mi

10 km

0

CHAPTER 3

Modoc County

Not too many people or dogs venture to the far northeast reaches of the state, but those who do find dog heaven. About 90 percent of this county is made up of Modoc National Forest and other public lands. That means years of off-leash walks for you and your pooch.

Many folks travel through here on U.S. 395 on the way from the Pacific Northwest to Reno. Alturas is a popular stopping point. But check out the numerous entrances to the eastern chunk of Modoc National Forest. Just north of Alturas you can follow Highway 299 east into the Cedar Mountain area, where there are a couple of primitive campgrounds. Closer to the town of Likely, you can head east and enter the South Warner Wilderness for access to numerous lakes, streams, and trails.

Alturas, the county seat and the only town of notable size, has a population of 3,000. That should tell you all you need to know about this get-away-from-it-all county.

PICK OF THE LITTER—MODOC COUNTY

BEST PEACEFUL LAKES
Cave Lake/Lily Lake, New Pine Creek (page 54)

NATIONAL FORESTS

The *National Forests and Wilderness Areas* resource at the back of this book has important information and safety tips on visiting national forests with your dog and has more background on the Modoc National Forest.

Modoc National Forest
🐾🐾🐾🐾🐕

The South Warner Wilderness, about 14 miles east of the town of Likely in the Modoc National Forest, is a serene place to visit. Clear little lakes abound, as do the creeks that feed them.

New Pine Creek

PARKS, BEACHES, AND RECREATION AREAS

1 Cave Lake/Lily Lake
🐾🐾🐾🐾🐕 (See Modoc County map on page 52)

You can't get much more remote than this in California. These small, trout-filled lakes are on the Oregon border, and it takes a six-mile drive up a fairly steep gravel road to get there. You probably won't find any people here, but you'll find all the peace you need. The world is truly hushed at this 6,600-foot elevation.

Dogs love it because they're allowed to hike leash-free. The campground at Cave Lake has six sites, each available on a first-come, first-served basis. Leash your dog if anyone else is camping here. The campground is free and is open July–October.

From U.S. 395 in New Pine Creek, take unpaved Forest Service Road 2 east about six long, uphill miles. The campsites are just after the Lily Lake picnic area. 530/233-5811.

Alturas

PARKS, BEACHES, AND RECREATION AREAS

2 Modoc National Wildlife Refuge

🐾🐾🐾🐕 (See Modoc County map on page 52)

The only dogs allowed off leash here are bird hunters, and only during the appropriate seasons. Otherwise, dogs have to wear leashes in the Dorris Reservoir area of the refuge. Sections of the reservoir are closed during nesting season, but you can usually take your leashed dog on a hike on the horse trail that goes across the top of the dam and down to the surrounding land. The bird-watching is excellent in the late fall and early winter. Bring your binoculars and get up close and personal with tundra swans, Canada geese, and cinnamon teal. Earthbound residents include coyotes, antelope, and rabbits. It's hard to hold binoculars while your dog is tugging at the leash, but make sure your pooch doesn't get away.

From Alturas, drive about three miles east on Parker Creek Road. Call 530/233-3572 for dates and restrictions.

3 Veteran's Memorial Park

🐾🐾 (See Modoc County map on page 52)

About the size of a city block, this park is chock-full of trees on one side and covered with grass on the other. Picnic tables dot the grounds. This is a good place to bring your lunch so you can break bread with your pooch. Dogs must be leashed.

The park is on County Road 56 and U.S. 395. 530/233-6403.

PLACES TO EAT

The Munch Box: Eat decent lunch grub with your pooch at any of the five outdoor iron tables here. 431 Highway 395 North (Lakeview Highway); 530/233-2426.

PLACES TO STAY

Best Western Trailside Inn: Rates are $72–88. Dogs are $10 extra, and there's a limit of one dog per room. 343 North Main Street 96101; 530/233-4111.

Essex Motel: You and your dog will feel right at home here, because the new owner, Steve, loves dogs. "We're very pet friendly," he says. And if your dog likes to surf the Internet, he'll happy to know that there's now free DSL here. Rates are $59–65. 1216 North Main Street 96101; 530/233-2821.

Frontier Motel: There's a big backyard behind the motel, and good dogs are allowed to check it out. Rates are $40–49. 1033 North Main Street 96101; 530/233-3383.

Rim Rock Motel: This one's surrounded by cattle property, which will make your dog's nose very happy, depending on which way the wind blows. Rates are $50–54. Small dogs are preferred, "but it's not written in stone" says a front-desk rep. Dogs are $10 extra. 395 Lake View Road 96101; 530/233-2428.

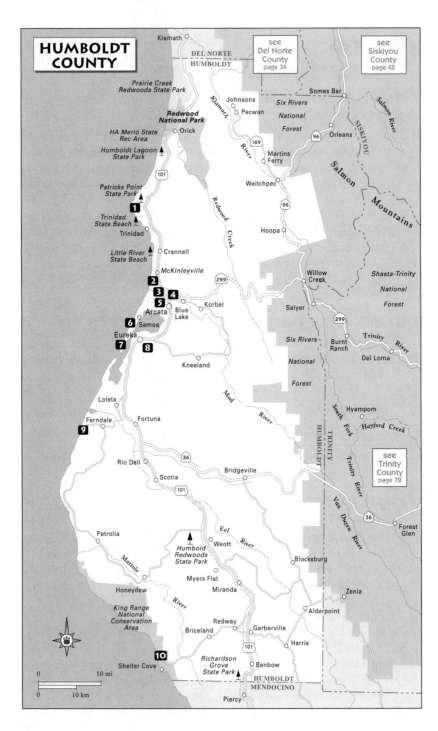

HUMBOLDT COUNTY

Klamath

DEL NORTE
HUMBOLDT

see
Del Norte
County
page 34

see
Siskiyou
County
page 42

Prairie Creek
Redwoods State Park

Somes Bar

Johnsons

Six Rivers

Pecwan

National

**Redwood
National Park**

Orick

Forest

Orleans

SISKIYOU

HA Merlo State
Rec Area

169

Martins
Ferry

96

Salmon River

Humboldt Lagoon
State Park

Weitchpec

101

96

Patricks Point
State Park

1

Hoopa

Salmon

Trinidad
State Beach

Redwood

Trinidad

Creek

Mountains

Little River
State Beach

Crannell

McKinleyville

Willow
Creek

Shasta-Trinity

2

299

National

3 **4**

Korbel

Salyer

Forest

5

Arcata

Blue
Lake

299

6

Samoa

Trinity

River

7

Eureka

Six Rivers

Burnt
Ranch

8

National

Del Loma

Kneeland

Forest

Mad

Loleta

River

Hyampom

Ferndale

Fortuna

HUMBOLDT

Hayford Creek

9

TRINITY

South Fork

36

see
Trinity
County
page 72

Rio Dell

Bridgeville

Trinity River

101

Scotia

Van Duzen River

36

Forest
Glen

Eel

River

Petrolia

Weott

**Humbold
Redwoods
State Park**

Blocksburg

Myers Flat

Miranda

Zenia

Honeydew

River

Alderpoint

Mattole

King Range
National
Conservation
Area

Redway

Garberville

Briceland

Harris

101

10

Richardson
Grove
State Park

Shelter Cove

Benbow

HUMBOLDT
MENDOCINO

Piercy

0   10 mi

0   10 km

CHAPTER 4

Humboldt County

Bigfoot. Giant redwoods. Fog. Off-leash beaches. Humboldt County is home to many of the magical, mythical wonders of Northern California. Dogs love them all, with the possible exception of Bigfoot. Jake, however, would undoubtedly adore getting a whiff of the enormous hairy creature's reputedly rotten body odor, but so far, the only big, smelly, hairy creature he's seen up this way has been in a mirror.

The coast here is one of the best in the state, as far as dogs are concerned. A few beaches and one 62,000-acre coastal park allow your dog to strip and go leashless. (Many of the county beaches are leashes-optional, but the rules are complex and vary by beach; don't assume that when you see a county beach you can let your dog run free.)

Sun worshipers won't share a dog's excitement about the coast. If fog is a four-letter word to you, try another county, or at least drive inland a bit. The fog can be so thick in Arcata that you'll have a hard time seeing your dog on the beach. But then as you drive east on mountainous Highway 299, the fog gives

PICK OF THE LITTER—HUMBOLDT COUNTY

BEST BEACHES
Mad River County Park, Arcata (page 60)
Samoa Dunes Recreation Area, Eureka (page 62)

BEST SWEEPING COASTAL PARK
King Range National Conservation Area, Shelter Cove
(page 69)

MOST DOG HEAVENLY EATERY
Angel of the Sea Coffee House, Shelter Cove (page 70)

MOST DOG-FRIENDLY VICTORIAN
Collingwood Inn Bed and Breakfast, Ferndale (page 65)

BEST GIANT TREES
Shrine Drive-Thru Tree, Myers Flat (page 68)

way a little at a time. As you reach higher elevations, white mist swirls around the taller trees, and on the way downhill on the other side, it's suddenly gone. You're free to frolic in the sun, but your beaches will be far behind.

No visit to Humboldt County is complete without a drive down the Avenue of the Giants. This world-famous 31-mile scenic drive between Redway and Pepperwood will take you past some of the biggest and most magnificent redwoods in the world. Just about all the adjectives for "really old" have been used to name the giants in this area. You can visit the Grandfather Tree, the Eternal Tree, and the Immortal Tree, to name a few of the elderly stars appearing on The Strip.

NATIONAL FORESTS

The *National Forests and Wilderness Areas* resource at the back of this book has important information and safety tips on visiting national forests with your dog and has more background on the national forests listed below.

Shasta-Trinity National Forest
🐾🐾🐾🐾🐕

Six Rivers National Forest
🐾🐾🐾🐾🐕

Trinidad

This small coastal town, complete with its own white lighthouse and rocky outcroppings, is like a Mendocino that hasn't been taken over by tourists and artists. Visit before your dog spreads the word about this well-kept secret spot.

PARKS, BEACHES, AND RECREATION AREAS

🐾 Moonstone Beach

🐾🐾🐾🐾🐾 (See Humboldt County map on page 56)

Well-behaved dogs can throw their leashes to the wind when they visit this popular county-run beach. Jake loves the surf here (as do the many surfers who were riding the waves when we visited). But wannabe water dogs can also enjoy Moonstone Beach's wet stuff: Creek waters flow out to sea, making a decent swimming hole for more landlubbing breeds. We've seen dogs who were petrified of swimming in the ocean delight in splashing through the calm waters of the creek.

On sunny days, this is one of the more popular beaches in the area, so if your pooch has a proclivity toward poaching picnics, chasing horses, or sniffing toddlers' diapers, you may want to try a more isolated beach. Note that between March 1 and September 15, dogs must be on leash from the parking area to the high-tide line, because this is a prime nesting ground of the snowy plover. (A big thanks to Woody and Katy Dog, and their human, Debra Roby, for helping us sniff out this gem.)

From Trinidad's Main Street, turn left on Scenic Road and follow it to Moonstone Beach Road, which will take you to the beach's free parking lot. 707/445-7651.

PLACES TO STAY

Bishop Pine Lodge: Most of the rustic, wood-paneled cottages here have kitchens, but does your dog care? Not unless you happen to be cooking a burger with his name on it. Dogs care much more about what's outside the cozy cabins at this very dog-friendly lodge. And what's outside is sure to put a smile on even the most somber snout. The lodge is on five acres of tree-studded land, which you're welcome to use as long as your dog is leashed and you clean up after him. The owner is so tired of off-leash dogs whose poop is left hither and thither that he's considering not allowing dogs anymore, so let's not let that happen. Rates are $100–180. Dogs are $15 extra. 1481 Patrick's Point 95570; 707/677-3314; www.bishoppinelodge.com.

Trinidad Inn: At this small, pleasant motel, you and your dog can walk right outside your door and find a trail leading to the woods nearby. But don't expect to walk to the beach; there are some mighty big cliffs around here. Rates are

$95–155. Dogs are each $10 extra. 1170 Patrick's Point 95570; 707/677-3349; www.trinidadinn.com.

Arcata

For a university town, Arcata is a mellow place. But dogs who want to have a wild time have ample opportunity. Although canines are not permitted in the lush green park in the old town square, they're allowed off leash at a couple of really prime areas, and on leash in a few more magical spots. For added dog pleasure, it's usually cool and foggy here, so it's a wonderful place to visit when the rest of the state is broiling.

PARKS, BEACHES, AND RECREATION AREAS

2 Clam Beach County Park
🐾🐾🐾🐾 🐕 (See Humboldt County map on page 56)

The winds of leash-law change have settled down a bit, and dogs are still permitted off-leash here but with a big restriction: They can be leash-free only on the "wave slope" area. This is the area wetted by the last high tide. In other words, you're up a creek if you come at high tide. If you want to visit and walk on the biggest swatch of sand possible, get yourself a tidebook for the area and look for a major high tide and a major low tide on the same day. Get here at low tide on one of those days, and the beach is your oyster!

Speaking of mollusks, Clam Beach is a good clamming area, as even your dog might have guessed from the park's name. Some dogs like to help you dig for your bivalve supper, which you can cook at the campground here. (Note that between March 1 and September 15, dogs must be on leash from the parking/camping area to the high-tide line, because this area is a prime nesting ground of the snowy plover.) There are 12 tent sites in sand dunes, available on a first-come, first-served basis. Sites are $10. Dogs are $1 extra.

From U.S. 101, about seven miles north of Arcata, take the Clam Beach Park exit west a couple of miles. 707/445-7651.

3 Mad River County Park
🐾🐾🐾🐾 🐕 (See Humboldt County map on page 56)

As you drive to this park past old barns and huge green fields full of grazing cows, you'll feel as though you're in the English countryside, especially if it's foggy. Dogs are delirious about the rural five-mile drive from Arcata.

Better yet is that once you get to this magnificent beach, leashes are no longer the law for dogs under voice control! The beach is wide, long, and desolate. Beachcombing is fun, and there's plenty of driftwood to keep your dog intrigued. The only other people we've ever seen here have been old men with metal detectors, hippies who sometimes spend the night, and dedicated dog owners willing to make the labyrinthine drive from town. Here, unlike Clam Beach, dogs aren't relegated to a narrow strip of beach. (However, between March 1 and September 15, dogs must be on leash from the parking area to the high-tide line, because that's a prime nesting ground of the snowy plover.)

From U.S. 101, exit west on Giuntoli Lane and go right almost immediately onto Heindon Road. Follow the signs to the park. On the way, you'll pass one end of the Hammond Trail, a scenic hiking/biking coastal trail between Arcata and McKinleyville. It's an invigorating walk. Once at the Mad River, you'll see a sign leading you to the right for fishing access. That's where you can launch your boat on the river, but chances are your dog would prefer to run on the beach, so keep going straight until you hit the small parking lot at the end of the road. 707/445-7651.

4 Arcata Community Forest/Redwood Park
🐾🐾🐾🐾 (See Humboldt County map on page 56)

Just a couple of minutes away from the quaint old downtown area of Arcata, this 620-acre park offers 17 trails with 10 miles of hiking for you and your leashed dog. Mornings are enchanting here. Songbirds come to life, and the earth and the redwoods smell fresh in the damp, foggy air.

From U.S. 101, exit at Samoa Boulevard and drive east. At Union Street, go north a few blocks and make a right onto 14th Street. Drive into the forest and park in the large lot. Several trailheads start here. 707/822-7091.

5 Arcata Marsh and Wildlife Sanctuary
🐾🐾🐾 (See Humboldt County map on page 56)

Formerly a sanitary landfill, this 154-acre model restoration project has three freshwater marshes, a brackish lake, and one saltwater marsh. Together, they attract about 200 species of birds, as well as critters such as river otters and muskrats. To add to your dog's joy, treated wastewater helps in wetlands restoration here.

Dogs must be leashed, for obvious reasons. Bird-watchers come from all over the state to view a vast array of fine-feathered friends, including Iceland gulls, old-squaws, bald eagles, and endangered brown pelicans. Despite Joe's exemplary behavior on his last visit, he got the evil eye from a couple of people who were chirping to some birds hidden in a tree. I found that walking around with binoculars helps these avid folks realize you're just like them, except you have a dog who wants to share in the wonders of our winged friends. If you've got a yapper dog, take him somewhere else.

Exit U.S. 101 at Samoa Boulevard and drive west, following the coastal access signs. Turn left on I Street and drive about a mile. The parking lot is on your right. Once in the marsh area, bear right at the wood-chip trail for the best walk possible. You can get a map and guide to the area by calling 707/822-7091.

PLACES TO EAT

Hole in the Wall: This is a popular pooch hangout. Dogs enjoy intermingling and catching sandwich crusts in the semi-enclosed outdoor area. 590 G Street; 707/822-7407.

Los Bagels: We like grabbing a bagel here before we start on our day's adventures. Nosh with your dog at the outdoor tables. 1061 I Street; 707/822-3150.

PLACES TO STAY

Hotel Arcata: Dogs seem to sense the history at this refurbished 1915 hotel. When Joe visited, all he could do was stick his snout around the baseboards and snort in the scents. Rates are $84–155. Dogs are $5 extra. 708 9th Street 95521; 707/826-0217 or 800/344-1221; www.hotelarcata.com.

Motel 6: This one is right beside U.S. 101, and the staff will often put dogs and their human companions in the rooms closest to the highway because there's a little on-leash dog-relief area there. The constant drone of cars can actually be soothing at 3 A.M. when your dog decides to start scratching himself. Rates are $46–51. 4755 Valley West Boulevard 95521; 707/822-7061.

Quality Inn–Mad River: There's a pretty beach next door where leashed dogs like to roam. Rates are $59–135. Dogs are $10 extra and require a $100 deposit. 3535 Janes Road 95521; 707/822-0409.

Eureka

This is the county seat of Humboldt, and it's a bustling small city. Fortunately, it also has some Victorian charm, as well as the ocean and Humboldt Bay, so it's not a typical center of commerce.

PARKS, BEACHES, AND RECREATION AREAS

6 Samoa Dunes Recreation Area

🐾🐾🐾🐾 🐕 (See Humboldt County map on page 56)

Does your dog like sand, sand, and more sand? How does 300 acres of coastal dunes between the Pacific and Humboldt Bay sound? How about boundless, fairly calm ocean? Cool breezes year-round?

If your dog isn't salivating about this park yet, here's the clincher: Well-behaved dogs can run off leash everywhere except the established trails at this Bureau of Land Management park! While you cast for surfperch, hunt for driftwood, or just relax and listen to the foghorns and gulls, your dog is free to run around, as long as he'll come when you call.

We learned about the vital importance of voice control when we spotted an injured duck waddling along the shore. Another dog, a retriever type, scooped up the bird in her mouth and brought it back to her owner. Fortunately, Joe was well leashed by the time he decided he'd like to look into a duck dinner. And even more luckily, once the bird overcame its fear, it got up and continued wad-dling down the beach as if nothing had happened.

The retriever's owner was shocked that her dog had taken off. "She's so obedient. She always comes when I call," she explained after severely repri-manding her dog. It just goes to show that even the most obedient dogs can get out of hand in tempting situations, so even if you've got a voice-control champ, keep a close eye on him when he's off leash.

This area is actually for off-highway vehicles to enjoy, and we hear it can get very crowded with ATVs, but we saw none on our visits. The place was deserted, except for a few beachcombers, a couple of dogs, and a kayaker. But keep in mind that your peace might be shattered by the roar of engines. The drivers of these noisy vehicles may not always be looking out for dogs, so make sure you and your dog are looking out for them. Also be aware that cars are allowed on the beach, but they tend to drive very slowly. There's ample room for vehicles, people, and dogs.

From Eureka, turn west on Highway 255 and cross the Samoa Bridge. Once on the Samoa Peninsula, turn left on New Navy Base Road. The park is about five miles south of the bridge, on the right side of the street. There are also several small access points along the road, but it's best to start from the main lot here. 707/825-2300.

⑦ Samoa Boat Ramp County Park

🐾🐾🐾🐾 (See Humboldt County map on page 56)

If you own a boat and a dog, and you've got them both with you, you'll be glad to know about this small park. Not only is there a launch ramp into the south end of Humboldt Bay, but there's also a small beach here so your dog can run around (leash free!) and stretch his legs before he becomes your crewmate during a cruise on the bay. (Be sure to keep your dog leashed from the parking area to the high-tide line March 1–September 15. This is snowy plover nesting land, and dogs need to steer clear in spring and summer.)

A large, open parking area here serves as a campground, but it's much better for RVs than for tents. Sites are $14, and dogs are $1 extra.

From Eureka, turn west on Highway 255 and cross the Samoa Bridge. Once on the Samoa Peninsula, turn left on New Navy Base Road. The park is about five miles south of the bridge, on the left side of the street. 707/445-7651.

⑧ Sequoia Park

🐾🐾🐾🐾 (See Humboldt County map on page 56)

This 75-acre beauty is essentially a redwood park. What could be better for dogs? A duck pond, you say? How convenient—there's one on the property. But if your dog is daffy for ducks, it's best to keep her away from the pond so you won't ruffle any feathers. Leashed dogs are allowed on the trails that meander through the giant redwoods and dense fern undergrowth and across meadows. (No dogs at the adjacent Sequoia Park Zoo, though.)

Exit U.S. 101 at Harris Street and drive east about two miles to W Street (after T, U, and V streets, if you get the picture). Turn right. The park is immediately on your right. 707/441-4226.

PLACES TO STAY

Say it ain't so! We're told the beautiful Eureka Inn, which during the last edition of this book was closed for extensive refurbishing, won't be reopening as a hotel unless a minor miracle happens. Dogs had been welcomed at this national historic landmark for decades. Now they just shake their heads as they pass by this poor locked-up Tudor. Fortunately, there are other plenty of other dog-friendly rooms to be had in Eureka, but we'll miss that grand inn.

Best Western Bayshore Inn: It's clean, it's comfortable, and, for people who like to eat in the room with their dogs, it's convenient: Each room has a fridge and a microwave. Some rooms even come with a fireplace and a whirlpool tub, should you hanker for extra relaxation. Rates are $84–119. Each dog in your party pays a $40 fee for the length of her stay. 3500 Broadway 95503; 707/268-8005 or 888/268-8005; www.bwbayshoreinn.com.

Eureka KOA: The "Kamping Kabins" here, with their cozy wood interiors and Old West bunk-style bed arrangements, are great fun for dogs, and the price is right. Rates are $45–65. Dogs are $3 extra and are allowed in four of the 10 cabins. 4050 North U.S. 101 95503; 707/822-4243 or 800/562-3136; www.koa.com.

Halcyon Inn Bed and Breakfast: Dogs under 35 pounds traveling with their people (no size limit for the humans) are allowed to stay at the Rose Room in this 1920s home that's been converted into a lovely inn. The furnishings here are antique but not in a kitschy or dark way. They're simple, tasteful, and attractive. The Rose Room even has a restored bathroom with an antique tub, fir floors, and some bath salts thrown in for good measure. (Not for your dog, should she read this and panic about the "b" word.)

The innkeepers, Mary and Ike Floyd, adore having dogs as guests and have two rescued racing whippets themselves. (Yes, whippets still do race in some parts.) "We love dogs," says Mary, one of the nicest innkeepers you'll ever meet and who makes a scrumptious breakfast to boot. Sadly, large dogs have proven too big for the Rose Room, so they have to sniff out other locales. Rates are $115–135. Dogs are $20 extra. (They steam clean the rug after each doggy visitor.) 1420 C Street 95501; 707/444-1310 or 888/882-1310; www.halcyoninn.com.

Old Town Bed and Breakfast Inn: This sweet old house, built in 1871, is about as welcoming as inns get. Since it's often cool and overcast in Eureka, a cozy breakfast is served near a blazing fireplace, with added light from oil lanterns. The house itself is cheery and airy and offers four nicely appointed guest rooms. Jake's favorite is the Lavender Room, which comes with its own wood stove.

Dogs feel at home here and are allowed to stay with you in any of the guest rooms. Innkeeper Karen Albright, who has a Kerry blue terrier, says that people who travel with dogs make the best guests. The inn has a wide front porch where dogs are welcome to repose while their people eat breakfast. They can also run around the fenced front yard, although the fence is only three feet high, which may be too tempting for escape artists. I can picture Jake thinking to himself, "Hey, I'm not getting any French toast from this place. Lemme see if I can find another joint that'll give me some," and hopping neatly over the whitewashed wood to pursue his doggy dreams. Rates are $130–150. Dogs pay a $15 one-time charge. 1521 3rd Street 95501; 707/443-5235; www .oldtownbnb.com.

Ferndale

This sweet Victorian town is so historically and architecturally authentic that the entire village is a state historic landmark. You and your dog can savor a walk down Main Street, where you're sure to pass at least a few other dogs with their people. It's so old and refined that it looks as if it could be the model for Disneyland's Main Street.

PARKS, BEACHES, AND RECREATION AREAS

🖸 Centerville County Beach

🐾🐾🐾🐾🐕 (See Humboldt County map on page 56)

This beach isn't exactly right in the middle of downtown Ferndale. In fact, it's not exactly right in the middle of anywhere, which is why Jake's tail wags nonstop when we visit. "The remoter the better" is his mantra. His favorite activity here is beachcombing: He's known for trotting merrily down the beach with pieces of driftwood longer than our car.

The county section of this desolate beach is miles long and comfortably wide at low tide. You'll want to get here during a fairly low tide, because dogs are allowed off leash here only on the "wave slope," which is the area that got wet from the last high tide. Come here at high tide and your dog will give you a look you won't soon forget. (Note that March 1–September 15, dogs must be on leash from the parking area to the high-tide line, because this is a prime nesting ground of the snowy plover.)

Head west on Main Street and take a right at Centerville Road. The beach is in about four miles. 707/445-7651.

PLACES TO STAY

Collingwood Inn Bed & Breakfast: This grand, elegant Victorian manor is one of the most beautiful and dog-friendly inns we've come across. If you're venturing anywhere near Ferndale with your dog, this is a must-stay kind of place. (You should actually be willing to drive well out of your way to stay here. It's that wonderful. In fact, Inn Traveler has rated it the "Most Elegant" with the "Best Hospitality."

The inn was built in 1885, and both the exterior and interior still have the look and grace of long ago, but with updates that make it charming, relaxing, and perfect for a 21st-century guest. Three of the inn's five guest rooms are pet-friendly. Our favorite is the Hart Room, with its plush red drapes that frame the room's large windows, and its elegant featherbed, fireplace, clawfoot tub for two (and we're not talking you and your dog), sunny stained glass, wide-board hardwood floors, and private sitting porch with a garden view.

All the inn's rooms come with featherbeds, house-made soaps and bubble bath, a fruit basket, and fresh flowers. You get free Wi-Fi too, if you just can't leave your laptop far behind.

Breakfast is to drool for, with items like hot fruit compote with red wine and nutmeg, homemade apple crisp, and "Eggs Collingwood," the signature dish of one of the innkeepers. You'll see why Inn Traveler has bestowed another rating on the Collingwood: "Best Breakfast in the West." In the afternoon, enjoy an English tea, served with cookies, scones, and little cakes.

These features are delectable for humans, but what about dogs? Innkeepers Chris and Peter make sure that dogs who lead their humans to the inn get treated very well indeed. "We like our four-legged guests to be as happy as our two-legged guests," says Chris. There's a dog run in the back of the house, and dog-sitting is available for an extra fee. Chris and Peter will be happy to point you in the direction of a pristine beach not too far away. They also supply dogs who stay here with dishes for food and water, doggy blankets, special treats, and poop bags. (The dishes and blankets are loaners. The poop bags you can keep.)

Rates for all this are $145–300. Dogs are $25 extra per night each. 831 Main Street 95536; 707/786-9219 or 800/469-1632; www.collingwoodinn.com.

Redcrest

You want redwood gifts? This is your town. The few stores in this tiny community along the Avenue of the Giants carry every redwood gift imaginable, most of no practical value. From redwood burl wall clocks to giant redwood Indians, they've got it all.

PLACES TO EAT

Eternal Tree Cafe: Dine on big old redwood tables under the shade of big old redwoods. (Is this like eating a hamburger in front of a cow?) The giant

Eternal Tree House is right behind the café. 26510 Avenue of the Giants; 707/722-4247.

PLACES TO STAY

Redcrest Motor Inn Resort: Dog guests and their people who used to stay here were always greeted by Mandy, an affable golden retriever who was so thrilled to see you that her tail was often in danger of wagging off. She was so beloved she was even listed as one of the owners on Redcrest's brochure. Sadly, she has gone to Dog Heaven. But her spirit lives on: "We LOVE dogs!" exclaims one of the human owners of the lodging. The owners here can't wag their tails, but they'll be thrilled to see you step out of your car with a pooch at your side. Cabins are $55–130, with kitchens available in some cabins. Dogs are $6 extra. There's also a vacation home on the property if you need bigger digs, and rates are $150–175. 26459 Avenue of the Giants 95569; 707/722-4208; www.redcrestresort.com.

Petrolia

If you plan to get lost on the Lost Coast, this little hamlet offers an interesting place to spend a night or a week.

PLACES TO STAY

Mattole River Organic Farm's Country Cabins: The name doesn't exactly roll off the tongue, but dogs don't care: How often does a pooch get to stay at a remote mountain getaway that specializes in organic pickled peppers and pears, and not have to worry about a guy named Peter Piper?

The small working farm here has a veggie garden, plenty of peppers, and a pear and apple orchard. Guests who stay at the cabins can sample some of the pickings with the OK of the owners, but keep in mind the harvest season is as late as August in these climes.

Big trees surround the five cabins, which are simple and rustic. (They have full kitchens, so you're not exactly camping.) The cabins are just a little hike to the Mattole River, where the swimming is mighty refreshing on a hot summer afternoon. Rates are $65–100. 42354 Mattole Road 95558; 707/629-3445 or 800/845 4607.

Miranda

PLACES TO STAY

Miranda Gardens Resort: Trees, trees, trees. Trees, trees, trees. That's what your boy dog will see when you stay at this resort's quaint, attractive cottages. After all, the resort is on the Avenue of the Giants, and there's no shortage of old-growth redwoods on the property.

DIVERSION

Give Him the Ultimate Tree Experience: Most dogs love to relax in the shade of trees or sniff at trees for hints of other dogs. But how many dogs know they can actually drive smack through the center of a tree? Few trees oblige such a fantasy, so the **Shrine Drive-Thru Tree** in Myers Flat north of Miranda is a real find. Dogs seem to enjoy riding through the car-sized hole in the 275-foot-tall redwood's 21-foot-diameter base. But, to be honest, they seem to prefer the adjacent picnic area, where sticky droplets of ice cream from the kitschy but fun gift shop hide in the grass.

A sign says the tree is 5,000 years old, but the folks around here say that it's more like 2,000 years. It doesn't really matter. It's big and it's old and it's dog-friendly. "We get lots of dogs coming through here. They like the whole tree thing," says a Shrine Drive-Thru Tree employee.

It costs $2 per person for folks over 9 years old. Dogs, regardless of age, go free, but they must be leashed. 13078 Avenue of the Giants, Myers Flat; there's no phone here, so if you have questions, call the Humboldt County Convention & Visitors Bureau, 800/346-3482.

But while the trees are the high point for pooches and many people (for different reasons, fortunately), there's much more to ogle here than the arbors. The flowering gardens around the cottages are lush. The gazebos are lovely. The cottages are homey and comfortable—a bit more upscale than most typical California rural resorts. Dogs can't do the dog paddle in the heated swimming pool here, but well-behaved leashed dogs are welcome to attend the nightly campfires hosted by the resort in the summer. Stay here May through October and you'll get a complimentary continental breakfast.

Note: Dogs need to bring their own beds (and sleep in them) to be allowed to stay here. Rates are $105–265. There's a $150 deposit for dogs, and a $15 charge per pooch. 6766 Avenue of the Giants, P.O. Box 186 95553; 707/943-3011; www.mirandagardens.com.

Shelter Cove

This coastal community is in the heart of the Lost Coast area of California. It's known for its pristine beauty and prime fishing. But dogs like it because it's surrounded by the King Range National Conservation Area. Three areas of this privately owned planned community provide ocean access. We like the Little Black Sand Beach, just off Dolphin Drive.

PARKS, BEACHES, AND RECREATION AREAS

🔟 King Range National Conservation Area

🐾🐾🐾🐾🐕 (See Humboldt County map on page 56)

We came upon this magnificent 62,000-acre coastal area by accident, and all Joe Dog could do was thank the Great Dog in the Sky. This primitive region, which constitutes a good chunk of the Lost Coast, has everything a dog desires deep in his heart: ocean, grassy flats, sandy beaches, trees galore, and best of all, leash-free living.

In less than a three-mile stretch, the King Range rises from sea level to 4,087 feet. The topography is rugged but far from impassable. Several trails take you across some of the most unspoiled coastal territory in California.

A few Indiana Jones–like dogs can handle the 26-mile wilderness trek along the Lost Coast Trail. Most of the trail is along the beach, and in the mornings you'll likely come to know one of the reasons this area is called the Lost Coast. The fog sometimes gets so thick that even the gulls are silent. But when it lifts, what spectacular sights you'll see! You and your dog will traverse green meadows, Douglas fir groves, and many streams. The terrain is fairly flat, so the real challenge is its length—don't forget, there's always the walk back! Most people prefer to leave a car at one end to make the round-trip easier. You should also keep in mind that this trail can be tough on "house dog" paws. Rangers advise dog booties for parts of the trail.

Joe was the kind of soft-pawed pooch who preferred trails such as the Lightning Trail. It's the shortest and shadiest route to King's Peak. Joe approved of the sparkling mountain streams, the shade from the firs, and the brushy meadowland where he could roll like a fool. He especially liked the trail's length—a mere 2.5 miles. The view from the top is hard to beat.

During your hikes, you may run into deer, cattle, sheep, horses, rattlesnakes, and poison oak, so if you let your dog off leash, do so only if she's under excellent voice control. And be sure to keep your pooch very far away from the marine mammals who clamber onto the beaches and rocks. This is a popular rookery, and dogs and sea critters do not mix.

You may camp anywhere you please for no fee, but you need a permit for campfires. Dogs must be leashed in designated campgrounds. It's a good idea to leash your dog at night anyway. Many dogs feel even safer in your tent. You'll pay $5–8 to camp in a designated campground.

Exit U.S. 101 at Redway and follow Briceland Thorne Road west to this Bureau of Land Management area. For more specific directions to your exact destination in this sprawling conservation area, contact the Bureau of Land Management, Arcata Field Office, 707/825-2300; or The King Range Project Office, 707/986-5400.

PLACES TO EAT

Angel of the Sea Coffee House: This dog-friendly café has several outdoor tables, some where you can look right out at the Pacific Ocean. Owner Susan puts dog treats in a jar and supplies thirsty pooches with water. Humans have it even better: The food is a delight. For breakfast, try the broccoli-brie quiche. Dogs can dine with you at the outdoor tables or the Adirondack chairs on the deck of the restaurant. The café is on the ground floor of the Inn of the Lost Coast, at 205 Wave Drive; 707/986-7888.

PLACES TO STAY

Inn of the Lost Coast: Stay here and you'll be atop a cliff overlooking the beautiful Pacific Ocean. All rooms at this two-building lodging have direct ocean views. You might even be able to see a gray whale passing by from your own patio, so don't forget the binoculars. Dogs enjoy going outside here, where the salty breeze ruffles their hair as they explore the bluffs. "Loads of dogs were just wandering around the property with me," writes Fergus, a well-informed canine correspondent. The inn even has its own dog-friendly restaurant. Room rates are $125–250. Dogs are $10 for the length of their stay. 205 Wave Drive 95589; 707/986-7521 or 888/570-9676; www.innofthe lostcoast.com.

Garberville

PLACES TO STAY

Benbow Lake State Recreation Area: Of the 975 acres here, dogs are relegated to the campground areas and the paved roads. We've seen some people fishing with their dogs down by the South Fork of the Eel River, but rangers differ about whether or not that's OK. The park is just off U.S. 101, about two miles south of Garberville. Follow the signs. Campsites are $20–28. To reserve one of the 75 sites, call 800/444-PARK (800/444-7275) or go to www.reserveamerica.com. For park information, phone 707/923-3238 in summer or 707/247-3318 in winter.

Best Western Humboldt House Inn: This is one of the better places to spend the night around here. Dogs have to stay in smoking rooms, but the complimentary wine and cheese every afternoon helps make up for the slightly ciggy ambience. Rates are $89–129. Dogs are $5 extra. 701 Redwood Drive 95542; 707/923-2771.

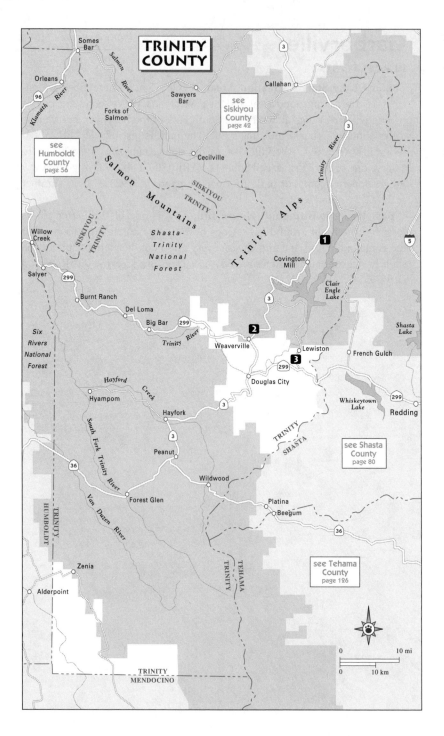

TRINITY COUNTY

Somes Bar

Orleans

96

Klamath River

Salmon River

Sawyers Bar

Callahan

3

see Siskiyou County page 42

Forks of Salmon

Cecilville

see Humboldt County page 56

Salmon Mountains

SISKIYOU TRINITY

Trinity River

Trinity Alps

Willow Creek

SISKIYOU TRINITY

Shasta- Trinity National Forest

1

Covington Mill

5

Salyer

299

Burnt Ranch

Clair Engle Lake

Shasta Lake

Del Loma

Big Bar

299

Trinity River

3

2

Weaverville

Lewiston

French Gulch

Six Rivers National Forest

299

3

Douglas City

Whiskeytown Lake

299

Redding

Hayford

Creek

Hyampom

Hayfork

3

TRINITY SHASTA

see Shasta County page 80

South Fork Trinity River

Peanut

36

Wildwood

Van Duzen River

Forest Glen

Platina

Beegum

36

TRINITY HUMBOLDT

Zenia

TEHAMA TRINITY

see Tehama County page 126

Alderpoint

0   10 mi

0   10 km

TRINITY MENDOCINO

CHAPTER 5

Trinity County

Think about this place we call dog heaven. What are some of the ingredients your dog would desire in his elysian ideal? Besides having you at his side without a leash, he'd want lots of trees, that's for sure. Rivers. Lakes. The scents of nature and rich earth. And maybe some decaying woodland critter to roll on.

Trinity County has all a dog could ever want in heaven or on earth. Joe even managed to find that decaying woodland critter when we last visited, and he rolled all over it and then came running up to me to spread the good news all over my jeans. When I walked into a store to buy some supplies later that day, the clerk and all the customers started asking each other if they smelled a mighty bad stench. I joined them in wrinkling my nose and nodding my head, praying no one would figure out my guilt until I was long gone.

The county has a couple of charming old towns, but the real charm here for dogs and their people is that more than 90 percent of the land is part of the national forest system. When driving from just about any location to just about any other location in the county (other than the few main towns on the east

PICK OF THE LITTER—TRINITY COUNTY

MOST ALPINE LAKE
Trinity Lake, Trinity Center (page 75)

MEATIEST RESTAURANT
Bear's Breath Bar and Grill, Trinity Center (page 75)

LODGING DOGS LOVE MOST
Old Garrett Ranch, Hyampom (page 77)

BEST WATER ADVENTURE
Trinity Lake houseboats, Trinity Center (page 76)

side), there are countless places where you can pull your car over and take your obedient dog for a leash-free hike. As long as you're in a national forest and away from houses and developed areas, it's generally OK.

While here, you mustn't miss the magnificent Trinity Alps. You'll feel as if you're in Switzerland, only your dog won't have to deal with plane tickets and passports! The only paper you'll need to hike the Trinity Alps Wilderness is a permit from the U.S. Forest Service.

NATIONAL FORESTS

The *National Forests and Wilderness Areas* resource at the back of this book has important information and safety tips on visiting national forests with your dog and has more background on the national forests listed below.

Shasta-Trinity National Forest
🐾🐾🐾🐾🐾🐕

Six Rivers National Forest
🐾🐾🐾🐾🐾🐕

Trinity Center

This tiny community is the home, in spirit if nothing else, of the giant and breathtaking Trinity Lake. It's also quite close to the breathtaking Trinity Alps Wilderness, where dogs can hoof it off leash.

PARKS, BEACHES, AND RECREATION AREAS

1 Trinity Lake

🐾🐾🐾🐾🐾 (See Trinity County map on page 72)

Even the national forest staff here call this place dog heaven. One dog-friendly ranger told me, "You just take your boat, pull up to just about any bank, and say, 'Okay, Fido, let's get a little exercise. No leashes required!'" But do this only if your dog isn't a chaser, and, as another ranger told me, "is under strict verbal command." I like the idea of my dog being under verbal command. Nouns will be next!

Your best bet is to take your dog to the more remote parts of the lake. And the best way to get there is by boat. If you don't have one, why not rent one? And what better boat to rent than a houseboat?

Mid-June to mid-July is the best time of year to come here. Snow still covers the peaks of the glorious Trinity Alps (which you can see in all their glory from almost anywhere on the lake), but the weather at the lake is great. So is the fishing. It's not nearly as crowded as Lake Shasta to the east, so you can fish without worrying about too many loud personal watercraft or fast boats.

The south end of the lake is 14 miles north of Weaverville on Highway 3. Call the Shasta-Trinity National Forest District Office at 530/623-2121 for more details and suggestions on which area would best suit your purposes.

PLACES TO EAT

Bear's Breath Bar and Grill: Well, that name sure leaves you hankering for a big chunk o' beef, doesn't it? What it lacks in romanticism, the Bear's Breath makes up for in pure charm and dog-friendly atmosphere. The restaurant has a patio and outdoor tables overlooking the Trinity River, and dogs are welcome to join you for some prime rib, steaks, chicken, tasty pasta dishes, or salad. (Jake says I should strike that last item.) The Bear's Breath is at the Trinity Alps Resort, 1750 Trinity Alps Road; 530/286-2205.

PLACES TO STAY

There are campgrounds all around Trinity Lake. Most are concentrated on the lake's south side, but a couple of the more secluded ones are toward the north. Below we've listed one on each side of the lake. Dogs must be leashed at all campgrounds. Call the Shasta-Cascade Wonderland Association at 800/326-6944 or go to www.shastacascade.org for more information on cabins and other lakeside lodgings.

Trinity Lakes Resort at Cedar Stock: This is a great place to enjoy a vacation at Trinity Lake. The cabins are rented by the week during the busy season, with costs ranging $504–1,890. Daily rentals are available in slower times of years. Dogs are $25 extra (daily), or $100 per week. And if you're in the mood

DIVERSION

Float in a Houseboat: Renting a houseboat is the ultimate human-dog vacation. Houseboats can be small and simple or large and fairly luxurious. (OK, OK, they usually do look like mobile homes, but they are comfortable.) As long as you pull up to shore enough for her to exercise and do her thing, she's going to be one happy pooch. The lake is pretty much surrounded by national forest land, where your dog can exercise leash-free. Make sure you keep an eye on her, though, and don't forget about her while you're inside making a soufflé.

One of the largest and most dog-friendly houseboat rental companies is **Trinity Lakes Resort at Cedar Stock.** "Dogs are just as much a part of the family as everyone else. They can't miss a vacation like this," says Steve, one of the resort's managers. Bringing a dog along will cost you $25 extra nightly, or $100 weekly. The houseboats here run $1,695–5,795 weekly, with big off-season discounts. The smaller ones fit up to six, and the larger ones can stash all your relatives.

The Cedar Stock Resort's houseboat headquarters is 15 miles north of Weaverville on Highway 3. The mailing address is HCR 1, Box 510, Lewiston, CA 96052; 530/286-2225. For other companies, call the Trinity County Chamber of Commerce at 530/623-6101. Be sure to reserve early. Sometimes summer rentals are completely booked by April! Houseboat "high season" is usually April–November.

---

for a nautical stay, call for information on houseboat rentals. The resort is 15 miles north of Weaverville. 45810 State Highway 3 96091; 530/286-2225.

Ripple Creek Cabins: The Trinity River runs right by these cozy, homey housekeeping cabins. You'll have no shortage of outdoor adventures to share with your dog here. Each cabin has a woodstove and electric heat. This is helpful, because unlike most other resorts in the area, Ripple Creek is open year-round. If he's around, the friendly owner, Jim Coleman, will make you and your pup feel right at home. Rates are $84–169. Dogs are charged a $10 per-stay fee. The address is HCR2 Box 4020 96091; 530/266-3505 or 510/531-5315; www.ripplecreekcabins.com.

Trinity Alps Resort: This is a fantastically dog-friendly place to stay. "More than 80 percent of the families who come here bring their dog," says a manager. The 43 housekeeping cabins here were built in the 1920s, and they're clean and comfy, with real wood paneling and large sleeping verandas overlooking the Stuart Fork of the Trinity River.

The resort is on 90 acres and is surrounded by 500,000 acres of Shasta-Trinity National Forest. The folks here welcome dogs. "We consider dogs part of the family," the manager said. There's even a dog-friendly eatery on the premises. Rates are $655–1275. 1750 Trinity Alps Road 96091; 530/286-2205; www.trinityalpsresort.com.

Hyampom

Don't worry if you're a native Californian and you've never heard of Hyampom. Some folks in adjacent towns have never heard of it either. Hyampomeranians (OK, that's not what they call themselves, but Jake forced me to write this) identify their location by telling you they're "about 20 miles west of Hayfork." Well, now, that certainly settles things. Dogs like it because there's plenty of national forest land around the area, and the people who live here (250 on a very good day) seem to have a big place in their hearts for dogs.

PLACES TO STAY

Old Garrett Ranch: Dogs, sit down when you read this: If you talk your folks into coming here, you'll get to stay in an old cowboy cabin on 225 acres! And those 225 acres are bordered on three sides by the Shasta-Trinity National Forest! And it's on the banks of the South Fork Trinity River! We can't say it's all yours, because there's also a dog-friendly rentable duplex at the ranch, plus horses, chickens, turkeys (at least before Thanksgiving), dogs, and the ranch's owners, Ebbe and Uschi Schneider. "This is dog heaven here!" says Ebbe. "We love dogs, and they have the time of their lives here."

As the Schneiders are fond of reminding guests, this beautiful property is home to mountain lions and bears (oh my!). Please remember this if you plan to let your dog roam leash-free with you. That's absolutely allowed here, but your dog really must be under excellent voice control if you don't want to end up giving a new meaning to dog food.

The one-bedroom cowboy cabin, officially known as the Birdwatcher's Cabin, isn't fancy, but it's cozy, with an open-beam ceiling and a woodstove, which is the cabin's only heat source. It also has a living room, a little kitchen, a deck, and in case you were wondering just how rustic it is—a bathroom. The two two-bedroom units in the duplex are more modern, and the bottom unit is wheelchair-accessible.

The Schneiders also run a dog-boarding service and train dogs, so if you're in need of either, it's right here in your own very large backyard.

Please bring a blanket or bed for your dog. Rates are $75–85. Weekly rates are $450–520. The mailing address is P.O. Box 155 96046; 530/628-4569.

Weaverville

This is the gateway to the Trinity Alps, and what a gateway it is. It's a former boomtown with a Main Street that's almost unchanged from the 1850s, complete with spiral staircases and brick facades.

About 2,500 Chinese immigrants were among the miners who came here during the Gold Rush. The Joss House State Historic Park contains the oldest active Chinese temple in California. Dogs aren't allowed inside, but as you're driving to the adjacent Lee Fong Park on Main Street, you can take a gander at it.

PARKS, BEACHES, AND RECREATION AREAS

2 Lee Fong Park

🐾🐾🐾 (See Trinity County map on page 72)

Set on the land once owned and farmed by a prominent local Chinese family, this magnificent park still has the appeal of an old-time farm. It even has several apple and pear trees that still bear fruit—but don't steal from the branches. (We were told that it's OK to pick up a piece of fruit from the ground, though.)

The park is undeveloped and fairly large. It's far from the paved road, but leashes are the law here anyway. A dirt path will take you around the park's perimeter in about 10 minutes if you want a fast walk, but most people who come here like to stop and smell the fresh and fruity air. You can pretend it's your own orchard, and chances are good that no other park user will stop by and ruin your fantasy. For some reason, the place gets very little use.

Dogs seem to love this park. Joe and Bill had a field day sniffing the freshly fallen fruit and checking out what was lurking in the tall grass. Each walked away with a fairly mushy apple in his mouth.

The park is on Main Street/Highway 299 just south of the historic part of town. It will be on your right as you're driving south. Although a small sign points to the park, the bigger farmers market sign is actually a better landmark. Turn right and drive a few hundred feet to the dirt parking lot. When you see the bathroom in front of you and the old ranch house on your left beyond some trees, you'll know you're in the right place. 530/623-5925.

PLACES TO STAY

Best Western Weaverville Victorian Inn: This is a modern, decent-looking motel, but you might run into an attitude problem, depending on who you deal with here. We haven't stayed here yet, but we've heard from a couple of people who have had problems with the management, so make sure you know what you're getting into when you reserve your room with a credit card deposit. I've also been given the "rooditude" (my term for rude attitude, which we don't see much

when researching these books; when we see it we generally note it) when calling regarding dog policies and rates. You might prefer the 49er Gold Country Inn, which treats its guests like guests. Rates are $89–110. 1709 Main Street 299 West, P.O. Box 2400 96093; 530/623-4432.

49er Gold Country Inn: The management here is a breath of fresh air after dealing with the Best Western. "We're family owned and operated, and we like people who have nice dogs," said a friendly manager. The rooms are basic, clean motel rooms. Leashed dogs are welcome to sniff out the lawn and trees but need to steer clear of the pool, no matter how their water-dog eyes plead. Rates are $50–95. 718 Main Street 96093; 530/623-4937; www.goldcountryinn.com.

Lewiston

This is a tiny, historic mining town that has so few tourists, you'll think you're in a time warp. What's really great about a visit to Lewiston is that there's plenty of access to the Trinity River. Just look around and it's there. The area off Rush Creek Road at Lewiston Road is a popular access point.

PARKS, BEACHES, AND RECREATION AREAS

◨ Community Park
🐾 (See Trinity County map on page 72)
You may as well take your dog on a walking tour of this quaint town, because you'll definitely cover more land, and you'll surely see more grass, trees, and bushes than you will in this small park. It's a pretty spot for humans, but only about one of its two acres is accessible right now. Dogs may find it a little restricting, but if your leashed dog just needs to stretch her legs, it's not a bad place to sit a spell.

On Lewiston Road at Viola Lane, the park is run entirely through volunteer efforts by the residents of this small community, so there's no phone number for it.

PLACES TO STAY

Lakeview Terrace Resort: If you ever wanted a place to call your own right on fishable, swimmable Lewiston Lake, this is about as close as you'll come (unless you call the local real estate agent). You and the dog of your choice get to stay in your very own, very clean, air-conditioned housekeeping cabin. The owners of the cabins are sweet people who love dogs. They'll be happy to point you to some good on-leash walking areas around the grounds. Boat rentals are available.

Rates are $72–190. Dogs are $10 extra. RVs can stay here for $26. 2001 Trinity Dam Boulevard 96052; 530/778-3803; www.lakeviewterraceresort.com.

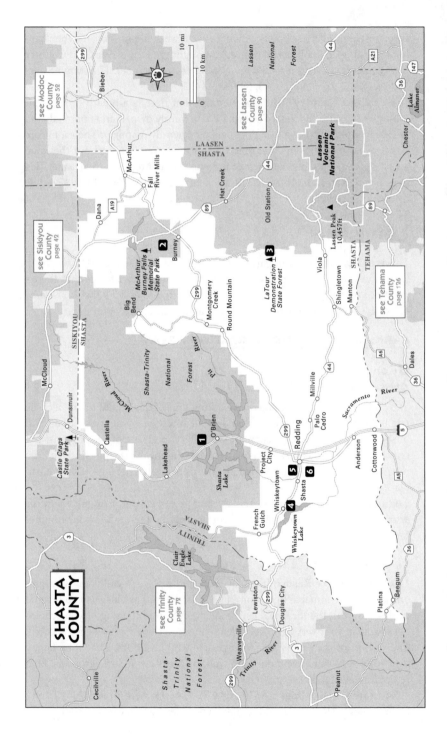

SHASTA
COUNTY

see Modoc
County
page 52

see Siskiyou
County
page 42

see Lassen
County
page 90

see Tehama
County
page 126

see Trinity
County
page 72

10 mi
10 km

Lassen National Forest

LAASEN
SHASTA

Lassen
Volcanic
National Park

Lassen Peak
10,457ft

SHASTA
TEHAMA

Bieber

McArthur

Fall
River Mills

Dana

A19

Hat Creek

44

A21

147

36

Lake
Almanor

Chester

89

89

Old Station

Viola

Shingletown

Manton

McArthur-
Burney Falls
Memorial
State Park

Burney

Big
Bend

299

Montgomery
Creek

Round Mountain

LaTour
Demonstration
State Forest

SISKIYOU
SHASTA

McCloud

Dunsmuir

Castle Crags
State Park

Castella

Lakehead

Shasta-Trinity

National

Forest

Pit River

McCloud River

Shasta Lake

O'Brien

Millville

44

Palo
Cedro

299

Redding

Anderson

Cottonwood

A6

36

Dales

A5

5

Sacramento River

Project
City

Whiskeytown

Shasta

French
Gulch

Whiskeytown
Lake

SHASTA
TRINITY

Clair
Engle
Lake

Lewiston

Douglas City

299

3

Weaverville

Shasta-
Trinity
National
Forest

Trinity River

36

Platina

Beegum

Peanut

Cecilville

3

299

CHAPTER 6

Shasta County

If you and your dog are aching to get away from city life, have we got a county for you! See that leash draped over your banister? You'll have to bring it, but you won't have to use it much.

Between the national forests, a state forest, and even a small city park, your obedient pooch can get all the leash-free exercise she needs. She'll go home with a wide grin on her snout. Your snout will be smiling, too.

NATIONAL FORESTS

The *National Forests and Wilderness Areas* resource at the back of this book has important information and safety tips on visiting national forests with your dog and has more background on the national forests listed below.

PICK OF THE LITTER—SHASTA COUNTY

BEST SWIMMING HOLE
Shasta Lake, Lakehead (page 82)

BEST FOREST HIKING
Latour Demonstration State Forest, Burney (page 85)

BEST WATER ADVENTURE
Shasta Lake houseboats, Lakehead (page 84)

Lassen National Forest
🐾🐾🐾🐾🐕

Shasta-Trinity National Forest
🐾🐾🐾🐾🐕

The forest pretty much surrounds beautiful, fish-filled Shasta Lake. If it's not too snowy before Christmas, you and your dog can pay $10 and go find yourselves a Christmas tree. Not many people have hundreds of thousands of acres of Christmas tree lots.

NATIONAL PARKS

Lassen Volcanic National Park
🔥

Dogs are barely allowed to set paw in this fascinating park. (For more details on what you and your dog are not missing if you stay away from this national park, see the description in the *Lassen County* chapter.)

Lakehead

PARKS, BEACHES, AND RECREATION AREAS

❶ Shasta Lake
🐾🐾🐾🐾 (See Shasta County map on page 80)

At 29,500 acres, this is California's largest man-made lake. If you and your dog fish, swim, or watch waterfowl, you'll be in heaven here. When full, it has 370 miles of shoreline—more than San Francisco Bay.

The lake is surrounded by national forest land. More than 30 miles of trails travel into the nearby forest. Depending on where you hike, you'll pass all kinds of natural wonders, from wooded flats and secluded creeks to rocky mountains and gushing waterfalls. Keep in mind that even though this is a northern lake, it can still get mighty toasty in the summer, so try to bring your dog here at a cooler time of year. And these days, leashes are the law, no matter how remote you get.

The U.S. Forest Service manages 380 sites at 21 campgrounds. Some are very primitive, while others seem like minimotels. Sites cost $18. The lake is one of the few in California where you and your dog can camp along the shore. If your pooch has been extra good, he deserves to "ruff" it at one of these sites. About a quarter of the sites are available on a first-come, first-served basis; the rest must be reserved.

A first visit to Shasta Lake can be a confusing experience. The lake has so many arms and so many trails that it's hard to know where to go. The trails at Jones Valley, Packers Bay, Bailey Cove, Shasta Dam, and Hirz Bay not only make for excellent woodland hiking, but they provide good access to shoreline fishing. (The lake can get very crowded during the summer, so be prepared to sacrifice solitude for the sounds of loud boats and personal watercraft, too many of which sound like mosquitoes on steroids.)

There's also such a variety of campsites that it can make your head ache just thinking about the possibilities. And who needs that just before a four-paw vacation?

Here's a suggestion: Get a map or a brochure of the lake and a little advice from a ranger. The folks at the visitor center are very helpful. Or Google "Shasta Lake campground locations" and you'll go to a U.S. Forest Service site that has the locations and descriptions of all campgrounds, and even the campsites. To get to the visitors center, take the Mountain Gate–Wonderland Boulevard exit off I-5 about four miles south of the lake. Follow the signs. For info, phone 530/275-1587 or 530/226-2500. Call 877/444-6777 for campsite reservations, or go to www.recreation.gov.

PLACES TO STAY

Sugarloaf Cottages Resort: The comfortably furnished cottages are just a Frisbee's throw from the lake. We've really enjoyed our sojourns to these modern but cozy cabins. If you visit at the right time, you'll be stunned at the peace and quiet. We stayed here once in April, and boy, was it ever quiet. Of course, it was freezing cold and pouring rain, so maybe that had something to do with it. But the comfy cabins were sure good to come home to after a long day of wet outdoor fun.

The folks who run this place have two wonderful dogs of their own, and they have the run of the place. Don't be surprised to see Bailey or Indiana's big, friendly yellow Lab faces at your front door for a pat on the head.

DIVERSION

Chuck the Dramamine: Shasta Lake is bliss for anyone of the seasick persuasion. The best way to experience this calm lake is to **rent a houseboat** for a few days. The only thing that may make you nauseated is having to go home at the end of your floating vacation.

Imagine waking up in a secluded cove, taking your dog for a lakeside hike and a brief swim, and then sitting down to a big breakfast cooked in your boat's well-equipped kitchen before setting off to cruise around the lake. (Joe, the landlubbing Airedale, would say pass the bacon but forget about the swim.)

Several local houseboat outfitters permit pooches on their boats. Weekly rates are $1,800–7,895. You can rent some for just two or three days, if that's more within your budget. Although houseboats are meant to be shared with friends, you won't want to fill the boat to capacity if you're bringing your dog along. Two big people, one or two kids, and a dog on a boat that sleeps six gives you plenty of paw room.

Three dog-friendly outfitters are Seven Crown Resorts, 800/752-9669, www.sevencrown.com; Antlers Resort, 800/238-3924, www.shastalakevacations.com; and Holiday Harbor, 800/776-BOAT (800/776-2628), www.lakeshasta.com. Check out www.houseboats.com for other Shasta houseboat getaways.

Daily rates Labor Day–Memorial Day are $102–225. During the rest of the year, the cabins must be rented by the week, and they cost $1,100–2,400. Only one dog per cabin, please. 19667 Lakeshore Drive 96051; 530/238-2448; www.shastacabins.com.

Tsasdi Resort: Many of the 20 housekeeping cabins at Tsasdi (SAUZ-dee, which owner David says is a Wintu Indian word meaning "white mountain") have decks overlooking Shasta Lake, which is just a long staircase down the hill. The cabins, built in the 1960s, are attractive and comfortable, and a forest of black oaks surround them—a big plus on a hot summer day.

Rates are $95–210. Dogs are $12 extra. During summer, rentals are by the week only and cost $990–2125. 19990 Lakeshore Drive 96051; 530/238-2575 or 800/995-0291; www.shastalakecabins.com.

Burney

This scenic mountain community is an excellent place to get away from urban life without getting carried away with the idea. There's enough civilization here to please even the primmest poodle.

PARKS, BEACHES, AND RECREATION AREAS

You won't find many community-style parks in these parts. What you will find are forests everywhere—many thousands of acres. Much of the surrounding land is public land, and people and their pooches just have to pull off the road for a fun little hike. But make sure you're not treading on private property first. Just ask around town and you'll get so much help from the dog-friendly folks here that you'll have a hard time deciding which piece of dog heaven to visit.

For a great hiking experience in a place with well-defined dog rules (off leash!) and boundaries, take your dog to the Latour Demonstration State Forest.

2 McArthur–Burney Falls Memorial State Park

🐾🐾🐾 (See Shasta County map on page 80)

This park is home to breathtaking 129-foot Burney Falls, which Theodore Roosevelt once dubbed "the eighth wonder of the world." Dogs can get a glimpse of this wonder from "The Overlook" at the top of the falls, next to the parking lot. Don't be surprised if your pooch gets that "I gotta go to the bathroom" look while gazing at the falls. About 100 million gallons of icy water cascade daily. It's enough to make a grown dog cross his legs.

And there's some great news, especially since this is a state park: A one-mile trail, called Cemetery Trail (you'll see why, but don't worry, it's from the 1800s), allows leashed dogs to walk down to the lake! It starts around campsite number 75. Water dogs can even swim in the lake near the dirt parking lot where the boat trailers are parked (but not at Swim Beach).

You can camp at one of the park's 128 sites with your pooch. Rates are $20. The day-use rate is $6 per car. From Burney, drive about five miles northeast on Highway 299, then go north on Highway 89 about another six miles to the park. Call 800/444-PARK (800/444-7275) for reservations. For park information, call 530/335-2777.

3 Latour Demonstration State Forest

🐾🐾🐾🐾 🐕 (See Shasta County map on page 80)

This 9,033-acre forest provides sweeping vistas of the Cascade Range. The 67 miles of logging roads are open to people and their leash-free pooches. But don't take your dog off leash unless she's 101 percent obedient, since the park is home to bobcats and mountain lions, who can get revenge on dogs on behalf of their city cat cousins. "Be careful, because there are critters that would make a nice meal of your pet," says Ben Rowe, assistant manager of the forest.

Firs, pines, mountain shrubs, and delicate wildflowers abound. You don't have to stay on the logging roads to enjoy the forest. Because of the sustainable-yield forestry practiced here, it's not a dense forest. For a fun day hike, set off alongside either of the two main creeks that run through here.

Camping is terrific and fairly primitive. About a dozen campsites, available on a first-come, first-served basis, are spread throughout four campgrounds in the forest. And there's no fee. The forest is off-limits through the winter, unless your dog knows how to use a snowmobile.

From Highway 299 just west of Burney, drive south on Tamarack Road. In about 10 miles, Tamarack will fork. Take the road that keeps going straight, Jack's Backbone Road/Road 16. In about six more miles, you'll see a sign for the forest. Turn right and drive to the forest headquarters to pick up a map. The park is also accessible from Redding. Call 530/225-2508 for directions or information.

PLACES TO STAY

Charm Motel: Rates are $61–67. Dogs are $5–10 extra, depending on size. (Eighty-five-pound Jake Dog thinks the big dogs should pay less than the tiny ones.) 37363 Main Street 96013; 530/335-2254; www.charmmotel.com.

Green Gables Motel: You won't find Anne (of Green Gables) around here, but you will find yourself feeling at home at this little motel nestled in pine-studded surroundings. It's conveniently situated for fishing. All rooms come with coffeepots, microwaves, and refrigerators. Rates are $57–108. Dogs are $7. 37385 Main Street 96013; 530/335-2264; www.greengablesmotel.com.

Fall River Mills

PLACES TO STAY

Fall River Hotel: As long as dogs go in through the side door (there's a good, flea-free restaurant and bar in the front) and they're not too big, they're very welcome at this historic, friendly 15-room hotel. Between the brass beds, antique furnishings (including quaint Victorian lampshades for dogs who are Martha Stewart fans), and handmade quilts, a stay at this lodging, built in 1935, makes you feel as if you've stepped back in time. Some rooms have private baths, and one even has its own kitchen. The hotel also offers a "fun package," which includes a gourmet dinner and a terrific country breakfast. The cost for two is $155.

Room rates are $70–95. Dogs are $10. The hotel is near a PGA-rated golf course (call for golf package info) and some world-class fishing, and it's about halfway between Lassen Volcanic National Park and Mt. Shasta. 24860 Main Street, P.O. Box 718 96028; 530/336-5550; www.fallriverhotel.com.

Whiskeytown

PARKS, BEACHES, AND RECREATION AREAS

4 Whiskeytown Lake

🐾🐾🐾🐾 (See Shasta County map on page 80)

Many miles of trails await you and your leashed, four-legged beast at this 42,500-acre segment of the Whiskeytown-Shasta-Trinity National Recreation

unit. The lake has 36 miles of shoreline for great fishing and pooch swimming (as long as the dog-paddling isn't at designated beaches), but most dogs seem to like to hang out here with all four feet planted on terra firma.

Dogs are allowed on 90 percent of the trails here. You can get a map and a little advice from a ranger about your hiking options.

For pooches who like to sleep all day, the camping is divine. Sites are on a first-come, first-served basis Labor Day–Memorial Day, but reservations are needed during the busy summer months. Call 877/444-6777 or go to www .recreation.gov. Sites are $16–18. There's a $5 day-use fee per vehicle.

From Redding, drive about eight miles west on Highway 299. The information center and overlook is at Highway 299 and Kennedy Memorial Drive. It's not far from Dog Gulch, in case your dog was asking. 530/246-1225.

Redding

It may be full of franchise motels and restaurant chains, but this city is the hub of the northern reaches of California. It's an excellent base for exploring the surrounding wildlands.

PARKS, BEACHES, AND RECREATION AREAS

Dogs have their own park here and they're allowed to hike on the Sacramento River Trail. Other than that, city parks are off-limits to pooches.

5 Sacramento River Trail

🐾🐾🐾 (See Shasta County map on page 80)

This 6-mile paved trail follows the wide and wonderful Sacramento River, leading you and your leashed dog through riparian terrain and rolling hills. It's best to visit on weekdays or uncrowded weekends, because on some days your dog can get the feeling of being mighty squished with the masses who like to hike and bike through here.

Bill Dog loved to take a dip in the water when we visited. He could lie in the Sacramento all day, but he hated the idea that he was missing out on sniffing the scents left by other dogs. When he was in the river, he was constantly looking to see who passed on the trail. When he was on the trail, he always kept one eye on the beckoning river. It was a real doggy dilemma, but he managed.

From Market Street/Highway 273, go west on Riverside Drive (just south of the river). Head west to the parking area. There are many other access points, and several trails that branch off from the main trail. Call 530/224-6100 for details.

⑥ Benton Airpark Park
🐾🐾🐾🐕 (See Shasta County map on page 80)

Joe's eyes opened wide and he stood utterly still for a few moments when he first saw this park. Somehow, although there were no dogs in it at the time, it seemed he could tell that this was a place of great dog happiness. He sniffed that joyous dog smell in the air, his tail started twitching, and he began paw-ing the gate to get in.

Once inside this large, completely fenced dog park, he rolled for several minutes. He rolled underneath the cold aluminum picnic table. He rolled on the mud around the water fountain. He rolled in the grass on the park's east side, and then in the grass on the west side. He stopped rolling only when another dog came in to share the park with him. They chased each other around like fiends for 30 seconds. Then he started rolling again, this time on the grass in the north side of the park. He was in heaven.

The fact that there are only a couple of small trees here doesn't seem to bother dogs. If they want shade, they can go under the picnic tables. If they need to lift a leg, there's always a fence post.

From I-5, exit at Highway 299 and go west for about two miles, following Highway 299 through a couple of turns in central Redding. At Walnut Street, turn left. Drive five blocks and turn right on Placer Street. You'll see the park in one block, at the corner of Placer Street and Airpark Drive, adjacent to the Benton Airpark (where the airplane activity provides amusement for bird dogs here). 530/224-6100.

PLACES TO EAT
Danburger: Sit on the patio with your favorite well-behaved dog and eat the classic burgers. The place has been here since 1938. 1320 Placer Street; 530/241-0136.

Wall Street Pizza: The pizza is tasty here, but the garlic rolls are decadently delicious. Share one with your pooch at the picnic tables outside. 1165 Hartnell Avenue; 530/221-7100.

PLACES TO STAY

Thanks to the very dog-friendly new manager of several motels around town, Redding is an easy, convenient place to spend the night with your traveling pooch.

Best Western Hospitality House: Rates are $79–95. Dogs are $10 extra. 532 North Market Street 96003; 530/241-6464 or 800/700-3019.

Best Value Ponderosa Inn: Rates are $50–75. Dogs are $10 for the first day, $5 for each day after. Inquire about rates for more than one dog. 2220 Pine Street 96001; 530/241-6300.

Motel 6 Redding Central: This is one of four Motel 6s in Redding. One pooch per room is permitted. Rates are $46–56. 1640 Hilltop Drive 96002; 530/221-1800.

Quality Inn: Rates are $90–106. Dogs are $15 extra for the length of their stay. 2059 Hilltop Drive 96002; 530/221-6530 or 800/4CHOICE (800/424-6423); www.choicehotels.com.

Red Lion Hotel: The folks here identify this pleasant hotel as "a pet-friendly establishment." Rates are $90–120. Dogs are $20 extra. 1830 Hilltop Drive 96002; 530/221-8700; www.redlion.com.

River Inn: This sweet motel backs up to a little lagoon where you and your leashed dog can try to catch some fish. If your angling is successful, you can grill your catch at the motel's barbecues and eat it at the picnic tables. Then the human people in your group can go for a swim in the motel's heated pool. (Dog people can't go in the pool.) Rates are $64–78. Dogs are $6. 1835 Park Marina Drive 96001; 530/241-9500 or 800/995-4341; www.reddingriverinn.com.

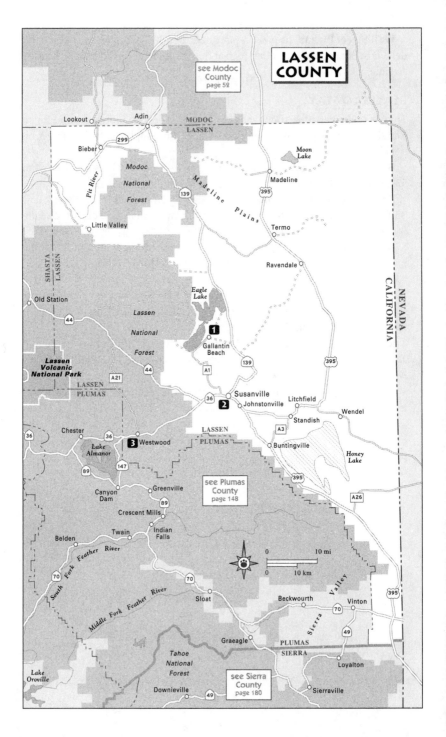

LASSEN COUNTY

see Modoc
County
page 52

Lookout

Adin

MODOC
LASSEN

299

Bieber

Pit River

Modoc

National

Forest

Moon
Lake

Madeline

395

Madeline Plains

139

Little Valley

Termo

Ravendale

SHASTA
LASSEN

Old Station

44

Lassen

National

Forest

Eagle
Lake

1

Gallantin
Beach

Lassen
Volcanic
National Park

A21

44

A1

139

395

LASSEN
PLUMAS

36

Susanville

2

Johnstonville

Litchfield

Wendel

Standish

A3

36

Chester

36

3 Westwood

LASSEN
PLUMAS

Buntingville

Honey
Lake

Lake
Almanor

89

147

395

A26

Canyon
Dam

Greenville

89

see Plumas
County
page 148

Crescent Mills

Belden

Twain

Indian
Falls

South Fork Feather River

70

70

Middle Fork Feather River

0   10 mi

0   10 km

Sloat

Beckwourth

Vinton

70

49

Lake
Oroville

Tahoe

National

Forest

Graeagle

PLUMAS
SIERRA

Loyalton

Downieville

49

see Sierra
County
page 180

Sierraville

NEVADA
CALIFORNIA

Sierra Valley

CHAPTER 7

Lassen County

There's not much civilization around here, so you and your dog may have to be content with hiking, camping, and spending quality time at the Lassen and Modoc National Forests. Most dogs could think of worse things to do.

NATIONAL FORESTS

The *National Forests and Wilderness Areas* resource at the back of this book has important information and safety tips on visiting national forests with your dog and has more background on the national forests listed below.

Lassen National Forest
🐾🐾🐾🐾🐕

They're a little more sticky about off-leash dogs here than at most national forests. Dogs are allowed sans leash, but rangers say they're quick to bow to the

PICK OF THE LITTER—LASSEN COUNTY

BEST LAKE
Eagle Lake, Susanville (page 93)

MOST INTERESTING HIKE
Biz Johnson Rail Trail, Susanville (page 93)

county leash law if there's any complaint. This could be because the forest surrounds Lassen Volcanic National Park, which has extremely strict dog laws.

Modoc National Forest
🐾🐾🐾🐾🐕

NATIONAL PARKS

Lassen Volcanic National Park
🐾

Don't get your hopes up about enjoying this gorgeous national park with your dog. Pooches are all but banned from this geological wonderland and its 150 miles of trails. Here's the long and exciting list of places they're allowed to visit: parking lots, paved main roads, and a few campgrounds.

Granted, the paved roads can provide beautiful views of the Cascades and surrounding scenery, but it's very limited, and too much of a tease. If you want to check out Lassen, by all means come on in with your dog. But don't expect to explore it beyond what your car can do.

Dogs are permitted, on leash, at the four campgrounds that are accessible by car. There are a total of 357 campsites, many on a first-come, first-served basis, but some are reservable. Sites are $14–18 and are in both Shasta and Lassen counties. Call 530/595-4444 for information. For reservations: 877/444-6777 or go to www.recreation.gov.

Susanville

Susanville is the second-oldest town in the western Great Basin, and a stroll through the historic uptown area with the city's free "Come Walk with Us" guide will fill you with all the historical knowledge you and your dog could ever need. But quite frankly, your dog will probably enjoy romping outdoors in this area much better than boning up on the local lore.

PARKS, BEACHES, AND RECREATION AREAS

🐾 Eagle Lake

🐾🐾🐾🐾 (See Lassen County map on page 90)

Tired of all those look-alike man-made reservoirs and lakes? Here's a lake that's large and natural. In fact, at 42 square miles, Eagle Lake is the second-largest natural lake in California. Better yet, it's also one of the state's cleanest and least crowded lakes.

The northern end of this clear blue lake is characteristic of high desert country, with sage and juniper, rocky shoreline, and reed patches. There's plenty of open land where you and your dog can dillydally the day away. The land leading down to the south shore is a drastic contrast, with lush pine forests and mountains of green.

Dogs should be leashed, because critters as various as deer, pronghorn antelope, and bald eagles are quite common here.

The U.S. Forest Service runs four campgrounds here, with a total of 325 sites. Fees range $18–33. Call 877/444-6777 for reservations or go to www.recreation.gov. The Bureau of Land Management's North Eagle Lake Campground has some rugged sites on the north end of the lake. BLM sites are $8 per night, and they're available on a first-come, first-served basis. Call 530/257-0456 for BLM camping information.

From Susanville, drive 2.5 miles west on Highway 44, and then turn north at County Road A1. After about 16 miles, you'll reach the south shore campgrounds. Watch for signs. For more information, call Lassen National Forest at 530/257-2151, or the Eagle Lake ranger district at 530/257-4188.

🐾 Biz Johnson Rail Trail

🐾🐾🐾🐾🐕 (See Lassen County map on page 90)

Whether your dog is a couch poochtato or a super athlete, this trail is bound to become a favorite. The wide trail winds more than 25 miles from Susanville to Mason Station and then follows existing roads another 4.5 miles into Westwood. You'll know you're there when you see the 25-foot carved redwood statue of Paul Bunyan and Babe the Blue Ox. (Boy dogs, please have some respect for this folklore hero and fight the temptation to do leg lifts on him and his bovine buddy. This is his "birthplace," and they say his ghost doesn't take kindly to such indiscretions.)

With 11 bridges and two tunnels, the trail follows the Fernley and Lassen Railway line, built in 1914 to serve the world's largest pine mill. As you hike,

GRRRRR

you'll find signs marking the locations of a 300-man logging camp, freight and passenger stations, and logging spur lines. The place is popular in the warmer months. Obedient dogs are allowed off leash, but beware of fast mountain bikes. In winter, it's a cross-country skier's heaven. Leashless dogs love charging through the white powder at your side.

If your dog prefers his hikes or ski jaunts to be short, you can use any of six trailheads and flip around when he's looking bored or bedraggled. If he's a rugged outdoor kind of guy, you'll want to consider hiking longer sections of the trail and camping along the way. Primitive sites are open year-round along the very scenic Susan River, and there's no fee. It's advisable to pack your own water or treat the river water before you drink it.

From Susanville, follow Highway 36 to South Lassen Street at the western end of town. Go left on South Lassen Street for four blocks to the trail. Call the Bureau of Land Management's Eagle Lake Resource Area at 530/257-0456 for directions to other trailheads and for pocket-sized trail guides and plant identification keys. Some of the land here is also under the management of Lassen National Forest. Call its headquarters at 530/257-2151.

PLACES TO STAY

America's Best Inns: It's your basic one-story type of motel, but it serves house-baked muffins in the morning, which makes the place smell most inviting. Rates are $60–75. Dogs are $10 extra. 2705 Main Street 96103; 530/257-4522.

River Inn Motel: The River Inn Motel happens to be right by the river (go figure!). There's a nice trail you can examine with your dog. Rates are $58–64. Dogs are $11 extra. 1710 Main Street 96130; 530/257-6051.

Westwood

PARKS, BEACHES, AND RECREATION AREAS

🖪 Biz Johnson Rail Trail

🐾🐾🐾🐾🐾 (See Lassen County map on page 90)

See the *Susanville* section for trail information. The Westwood section of the trail starts at Ash Street near 3rd Street and follows Ash Street and County Road A21 four miles to the Mason Station trailhead, where the main part of the trail begins.

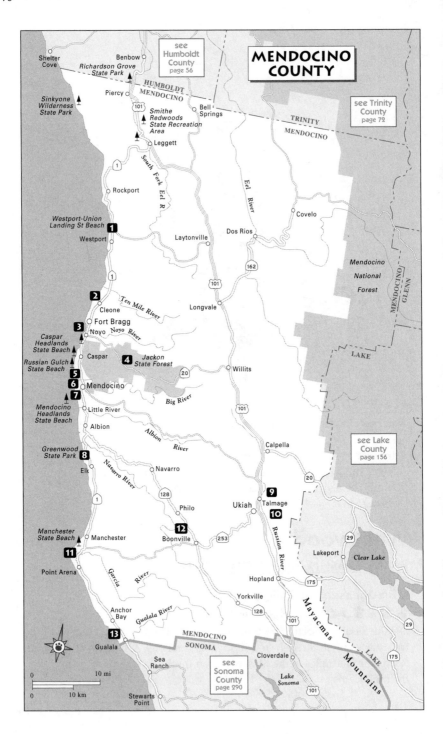

MENDOCINO COUNTY

see Humboldt County page 56

see Trinity County page 72

see Lake County page 156

see Sonoma County page 290

Shelter Cove

Benbow

Richardson Grove State Park

Piercy

HUMBOLDT
MENDOCINO

Sinkyone Wilderness State Park

Smithe Redwoods State Recreation Area

Bell Springs

TRINITY
MENDOCINO

Leggett

Rockport

South Fork Eel R.

Westport-Union Landing St Beach

Westport

Laytonville

Dos Rios

Covelo

Eel River

Mendocino National Forest

MENDOCINO
GLENN

162

Cleone

Ten Mile River

Fort Bragg

Noyo

Noyo River

Caspar Headlands State Beach

Caspar

Jackon State Forest

Russian Gulch State Beach

Mendocino

Little River

Mendocino Headlands State Beach

Albion

Albion River

Greenwood State Park

Elk

Navarro River

Navarro

Longvale

Willits

LAKE

Big River

Calpella

Philo

128

Manchester State Beach

Manchester

Boonville

253

Point Arena

Garcia River

Ukiah

Talmage

Russian River

Lakeport

Clear Lake

29

Hopland

175

Anchor Bay

Gualala River

Yorkville

128

Mayacmas

Gualala

MENDOCINO
SONOMA

Sea Ranch

Cloverdale

Lake Sonoma

101

Stewarts Point

0   10 mi

0   10 km

CHAPTER 8

Mendocino County

When people from out of town think of Mendocino County, they often think of quaint inns, sweeping seascapes, and perfect little coastal villages teeming with artists and tourists. But there's one vital image missing, that of a nosy dog sniffing about, exploring forests and fields, oceans and rivers, and some of the most dog-friendly inns in the state.

Many incredibly wonderful lodgings welcome dogs, and at two restaurants, The Ravens and The Restaurant at Stevenswood, dogs can actually dine inside. These more European (and very legal) dining setups are a first in the state, and we hope not the last.

While the coast of Mendocino County attracts most visitors, dogs have much more freedom inland, where they're allowed to run off leash in three very large parcels of land. But there's still something magical about the Mendocino coast. Although it offers just two leash-free areas, dogs thrive on the ever-cool climate and the salty air. Joe once perched himself on a Mendocino bluff top for a solid hour and sat utterly still, except for his flaring nostrils. For

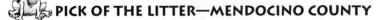

PICK OF THE LITTER—MENDOCINO COUNTY

BEST COASTAL WALKS
Mendocino Headlands State Park/Big River Beach, Mendocino (page 107)
Stornetta Public Lands, Point Arena (page 119)

BEST (ONLY) INDOOR DOGGY DINING IN THE STATE
The Ravens, Mendocino (page 107)
Restaurant at Stevenswood, Little River (page 113)

MOST DOG-FRIENDLY PLACES TO STAY
Delamere Cottages, Fort Bragg (page 104)
Abigail's, Mendocino (page 108)
MacCallum House, Mendocino (page 109)
Stanford Inn by the Sea, Mendocino (page 111)
Inn at Schoolhouse Creek, Little River (page 113)
Little River Inn, Little River (page 114)
Stevenswood Spa Resort, Little River (page 114)
Highland Ranch, Philo (page 116)

BEST PLACE TO STAY WITHOUT A MAN
Sallie & Eileen's Place, Mendocino (page 111)

BEST CANINE HOSTS/GREETERS
Zachary, at Stevenswood Spa Resort, Little River (page 114)
Reggie, at North Coast Country Inn, Gualala (page 124)

LODGINGS WITH MOST LEASH-FREE ACREAGE
Long Valley Ranch, Ukiah (page 118)
The Other Place, Boonville (page 122)

BEST FREE VEGGIE AND HERB PICKING
Mar Vista Cottages, Gualala (page 123)

BEST BONE PICKING
Mendocino Café, Mendocino (page 107)

that dog to have such patience and fascination, there must be magic in the air (or at least the smell of a few deceased fish).

NATIONAL FORESTS

The *National Forests and Wilderness Areas* resource at the back of this book has important information and safety tips on visiting national forests with your dog and has more background on the Mendocino National Forest.

Mendocino National Forest
🐾🐾🐾🐾🐕

Only a tiny section of this national forest rests in its namesake county. Some rangers prefer to have dogs off leash only in the two wilderness areas, neither of which is in Mendocino County. Others say it's OK for dogs to be leash-free everywhere but in camping areas.

Westport

Here's another New England look-alike. Westport is a tiny coastal town with a couple of inns and restaurants and a whole lot of charm. It's a wonderful place to visit if you like the appeal of Mendocino but prefer your sidewalks tourist-free and your beaches isolated.

PARKS, BEACHES, AND RECREATION AREAS

1 Westport–Union Landing State Beach
🐾🐾🐾🐾 (See Mendocino County map on page 96)

On one of the busiest weekends of the year, not a soul was using this beach. Only one of the 80 campsites was occupied. This is the kind of place you can pretend is your own almost year-round. You and your dog may well find yourself alone in the campgrounds and along the sandy beaches, but pooches are still supposed to be leashed.

One of the best times to visit is during the gray whale migration January–April. There are several good spots on the bluff tops where you can watch whales in comfort. Just set up a lawn chair, sit back with your binoculars, and wait. Even if you don't see a leviathan, at least you and your dog will have spent some good outdoor hanging-out time together. To make it even better, have a picnic.

Campsites are $10–15 and are first-come, first-served. The sites are all on the bluff tops, near the park road, and not far from Highway 1. You'll have no shade and no privacy unless you're the only camper (you camp just off the parking lots), but plenty of quiet. At night, it's easy to fall asleep to the gentle churning of the Pacific. The park has three entrances. We hear that the farther north you go, the better your chances of finding people. The beach is about

DIVERSION

Hang Around a Chandelier: The **Chandelier Tree** beckons all dogs and people who have ever stood with mouths agape at nature's awesome work. Sure, the 315-foot-high, 2,400-year-old tree has a painful-looking gaping hole in the center of its 21-foot-diameter base so cars can pass through. But of all the drive-through trees on California's north coast, this is the most spectacular: The thick limbs (some of which are eight feet in diameter) branch out about 100 feet above the ground in a most fascinating, chandelier-like way.

Dogs dig the tree, but they generally prefer the little nature trail that starts near the gift shop. It winds through a small section of fern-carpeted redwood forest. The short hike hits the spot after a long car ride.

The entry fee for the park is $5 per car. It's just south of Leggett, near the junction of U.S. 101 and Highway 1. Follow the signs. 707/925-6363.

2.5 miles north of the town of Westport. You can't miss the empty parking lots, but if you do, you'll still see the signs. 707/937-5804.

PLACES TO STAY

Howard Creek Ranch: This cozy, historic redwood inn, built in 1867, offers privacy, quiet, and 40 acres of coastal beauty. Each room at this working ranch is unique, with features so special it's hard to decide where to stay. Joe liked the old boat, which is now a miniature cabin, complete with wood-burning stoves and low wooden ceilings. He didn't have to duck here like his human companions often did, and he seemed to get a real kick out of hearing the thwack of a *Homo sapien*'s head against a thick beam. The redwood cabin is in the woods next to a stream that runs through the property, and it's oh-so-private.

For a truly relaxing weekend, stay in a room with a hot tub or sauna. After your own personalized spa treatment, take your best bud for a romp at the ocean, which is only about 300 yards away.

Rooms are $75–198. Dogs are $15 extra and are permitted only by prior arrangement. 40501 North Highway 1 95488; 707/964-6725; www.howard creekranch.com.

Fort Bragg

While Fort Bragg is now the commercial hub of the Mendocino coast, it once served as a fort built to "maintain order" for the Pomo Indian Reservation. The fort was abandoned in 1864, and it wasn't until 20 years later that Fort Bragg found its calling as a lumber town.

Now it looks like Fort Bragg has found a calling in the dog world: It's home to the first official off-leash dog beach in Mendocino County! People here worked really hard for years to make this happen. Dogs are crossing their paws that this will serve as a model for more off-leash havens on the Mendocino Coast.

Besides this new beach, our favorite part of town is the Noyo fishing village. Fishing fleets come in here with their catches and unload them at restaurants and processing plants. This is the real thing, not a San Francisco Fisherman's Wharf facade where selling T-shirts has come to replace the real business of fishing. And mmmm, it smells so fishy. Dogs are exhilarated just breathing the air.

PARKS, BEACHES, AND RECREATION AREAS

2 MacKerricher State Park

🐾🐾🐾🐾 (See Mendocino County map on page 96)

This eight-mile beach encompasses a few smaller beaches, including the secluded Pudding Creek Beach at MacKerricher's southern end. Unfortunately, dogs are forbidden at the strip of beach near the main parking lot, but all you have to do is walk north or south a few hundred yards and miles of beach are all yours.

Jake the Water Dog adores this seaweed-strewn beach, although his species is supposed to be leashed. There's a little of everything here, from headlands to forests to a small lake. For dog exercise, it's best to stick to the beach. You'll

DIVERSION

Plant Yourselves Here: When you and your leashed dog visit the exquisite **Mendocino Coast Botanical Gardens** in Fort Bragg, be sure to leave a lot of time for both of you to sniff around; this isn't the kind of place you want to rush through. The 47 acres of diverse plant and tree collections is right on the coast, and it's a combination that leaves people and dogs in a very relaxed and happy state of mind.

This is actually the only public garden in the continental United States that's right at the ocean. It's so close to the sea that you can even watch whales migrating from here at the right time of year. (Telescopes at the gardens' Cliff House help this feat.) Dogs are very lucky indeed to be able to come here.

While visiting, be sure to take a break at Cowlick's in the Garden, which offers great handmade ice cream as well as sandwiches and coffee drinks. General admission to the gardens is $10. Kids and seniors get discounts. Canines get in free—lucky dogs. 18220 North Highway 1, Fort Bragg; 707/964-4352; www.gardenbythesea.org.

run into fewer people and horses than you will in other park areas. Plus dogs aren't supposed to go on the unpaved trails in the wooded section of the park. Near the northern section of the beach, it gets so wide that you feel as though you and your dog are walking with Lawrence of Arabia. It may be tempting to walk on for what seems like eternity, but keep an eye on the time: It's tough walking back when it's dark.

Wildlife is everywhere. More than 100 species of birds inhabit the park, including the snowy plover. Because of the plover (who is endangered or threatened or maybe neither, but we'll leave that to the experts), certain areas are off-limits to doggies, and signage will steer your clear of these areas. But there are still plenty of places for our furry friends. Tidepools are rich with life, and harbor seals bask and breed on secluded rock outcroppings, sometimes even in the beach areas. But don't go anywhere near them, with or without your dog! They're shy creatures and will balk at the slightest disturbance, sometimes diving for long periods to avoid the possible threat.

It's fun to camp with your dog here. The 142 campsites are roomy, and many are surrounded by trees. Sites are $20–25. For reservations phone 800/444-PARK (800/444-7275) or go to www.reserveamerica.com.

The best place for doggy access to the beach is at the Ward Avenue entrance, about a half mile north of the main park entrance. This is also where the beach starts becoming an enormous sandy mass. But if you're camping in the main section, beach access is just a short walk north or south. If you're unsure of where you and the pooch can walk on the beach, ask a ranger. The areas are not clearly marked.

The main entrance is on the west side of Highway 1, about three miles north of Fort Bragg. It's marked by a large sign. You'll pass by a ranger kiosk, but

DOG-EAR YOUR CALENDAR

Dogs not only get to witness four days of people showing off their strength and logging skills when they attend Fort Bragg's **Paul Bunyan Days,** they actually get to participate. They can't take part in the ax throwing or the power-saw bucking. But if your dog is ugly—so ugly that cats laugh at him and babies scream when he walks by—he can enter the annual Ugly Dog Contest. It usually takes place on the Saturday of this four-day Labor Day weekend event. There are also contests for the largest dog, the smallest dog, the smartest dog, the prettiest dog, and the Frisbee-est dog.

The dog part of the festival takes place at the middle school fields, at the corner of Harold and Laurel streets. Phone the Chamber of Commerce for more information: 707/961-6300. Or go to www.paul bunyandays.com.

there's no fee for day use. An added bonus: If you're near the visitors center and just dying to see if you have email, you'll be able to check it here because there's free Wi-Fi these days. 707/937-5804.

❸ Noyo Beach Off-Leash Dog Area/Noyo Jetty Park

🐾🐾🐾🐕 (See Mendocino County map on page 96)

Drumroll! We are thrilled to announce that the Mendocino Coast finally has a leash-free beach. It took years of doing, and dogs say it was worth all the hard work. It's only about a quarter mile long, but "beggars can't be choosers," says Gail Brodkey, one of the people who made this happen. It's on the coast, near the Noyo Harbor—a working fishing harbor—and dogs think it's divine.

The rest of the beach is fine for leashed dogs. It's not heavily used; in fact, sometimes you may be the only ones on the beach.

Heading north on Highway 1, go right on North Harbor Drive and follow the road down the steep hill to the harbor. Continue on this road toward the jetty, where you'll find a parking area that's pretty much under the highway. There should be signs for the off-leash area by the time you read this. 707/961-2825.

❹ Jackson State Forest

🐾🐾🐾🐾 (See Mendocino County map on page 96)

Dogs are no longer allowed off leash at this 50,000-acre park. It's still a great place to visit with your dog, but it just isn't the same on a tether.

This is a demonstration area for forest management practices, with several self-guided educational nature trails and many miles of hiking available on old logging roads. Although it's getting a little worn out, we like to visit the Tree Identification Trail, just off Highway 20, about 11 miles east of Highway 1. It's one of the few areas of the forest that's actually marked from the highway, and it's a great place for you and your dog to learn the difference between madrone, hemlock, redwood, fir, and any other varieties that confuse you (including the oft-ignored wax myrtle). Dogs probably already know all about these trees, since the males of the species have made intimate acquaintances with so many in their lives. But they won't mind going along for the walk.

Critters abound, so leashes do make some sense. We've run into only the occasional quail and salamander during our sojourns, but we hear there are black bears and mountain lions around as well.

Sadly, the budget for the state forests has been cut so drastically that the forest is open to the public only from Memorial Day through Labor Day for now, and some trails might become neglected and some campgrounds may have to close. Call the forest before you visit to find out the status and obtain maps. As of press time, the forest had 44 campsites, available at no fee. You'll need to bring your own water (and don't forget your dog's) because the sites don't runneth over with amenities. You'll also need a camping permit and a campground map, which you can get from the camp host on site. Call 707/964-5674.

The forest stretches along Highway 20 from just east of Mendocino and Fort Bragg to about nine miles west of Willits.

PLACES TO STAY

Atrium: The woman who is in great part responsible for that off-leash beach you'll be enjoying while visiting Fort Bragg also happens to be the proprietor of this charming bed-and-breakfast. Be sure to let your dog shake Gail's hand. Dogs are welcome to stay in two of the cozy rooms—the ones with wood floors—at this lovely 1870s lodging. Each has a fireplace. Jake's favorite is The Lodge, with its beautiful wood walls, river rock fireplace, and outdoorsy decor.

The inn is conveniently located in the heart of historic downtown Fort Bragg. A full, tasty breakfast comes with your stay. Rates are $120–165. Dogs pay a $35 fee for the length of their stay. 700 North Main Street 95437; 707/964-9440 or 800/287-8392; www.atriumbnb.com.

Beachcomber Motel: Dogs love this place just a pinecone's throw from the beach and MacKerricher State Park. Rates are $59–149. Dogs are $20 extra. 111 North Main Street 95437; 707/964-2402 or 800/400-7873; www.thebeach combermotel.com.

Cleone Gardens Inn: It's hard to define Cleone Gardens: It has an older motel feel, but some of the rooms have a fireplace, some have a kitchen, and some have garden and forest views. Wherever you stay at Cleone, you're welcome to stroll around the inn's well-maintained five acres with your leashed pooch. (Bring a "doggy bag," of course.) Rates are $86–140. Dogs are $6 extra. 24600 North U.S. 1 95437; 707/964-2788; www.cleonegardensinn.com.

Coast Motel: Who needs a dog park with this place around? The owner permits dogs to run leashless on five tree-filled acres of land behind the motel! It's pretty safe from traffic. And if you want beach access, it's only a four-minute walk away. Rates are $55–219. Dogs are $15 extra. 18661 Highway 1 95437; 707/964-2852; www.mendocinocoastmotel.com.

Delamere Cottages: If you're looking to combine a romantic getaway with a blissful vacation for your dog, look no further. Admittedly, dogs and romance don't necessarily go hand-in-paw. Dogs somehow inevitably start chewing on their private parts or making strange noises during romantic moments. But at Delamere's two cozy oceanfront cottages, the combination somehow works.

The cottages are roomy enough so your dog can give you privacy, should you request it. Each cottage has a living room, a kitchen, a dining area, and of course, a bathroom and bedroom. One cottage has a fireplace. Beautiful gardens and gorgeous landscapes surround the cottages.

Two items Jake thought your dog should know: 1) There's a private path that leads down to a quiet beach and cove. It's gorgeous. 2) Dogs who stay here always get dog cookies. Rates are $175 nightly, and there's a two-night minimum. Cash or checks are accepted, but no credit cards. 16821 Ocean Drive 95437; 707/964-3175; www.delamerecottages.com.

Shoreline Cottages: What a treat for the dog-lover on a budget! The cute, yellow two-person cottages at this 1920s motor court each come with a full kitchen and have a downright friendly feel to them. And the price is right, just $70–90. Dogs are $10 extra per stay.

If you love dogs (you do, don't you?), you may want to stay in the dog-themed Dog Lover's Cottage. It has adorable pictures/paintings of dogs on the wall, dog/wolf-themed bedding, and even a bulletin board where you can leave a photo of your very own happy four-legged traveling companion. Your dog will feel very at home here. A big thanks to Lin Look and her sweet old Lab for cluing us in about the cottages. 18725 North Highway 1 95437; 707/964-2977 or 800/930-2977; www.shoreline-cottage.com.

Mendocino

Take your dog to New England and never leave the Golden State! Visiting this quaint village, which stood in as Angela Lansbury's fictional Maine seaside village in *Murder, She Wrote,* is like stepping across the country and back in time. (Dogs can actually stay in the inn that was supposed to be her home—the Blair House Inn.)

Sunset magazine declares Mendocino the "most picturesque town," and with its oceanside charm, beautiful boutiques, art galleries, and lovingly restored Victorians, it's easy to see why. But your dog doesn't care about pretty. She wants things friendly, perhaps with a bone thrown in for good measure. Fortunately there's plenty of friendly here. And of course, there's that mighty Pacific, which puts a smile on the snout of just about any dog.

The art galleries that help give Mendocino its flavor generally don't allow dogs. But at least you can window-shop with your favorite canine critic. If you see something you like, the artists and gallery owners tend to be very accommodating. One art collector we know ended up having tea and toast in a gallery where she was buying several small prints. Her mutt, Rosy, got her own piece of toast and was offered a pot of tea, which she couldn't drink because it was too warm. The artist obligingly found some ice.

PARKS, BEACHES, AND RECREATION AREAS

🐾 Russian Gulch State Park
🐾 🐾 🐾 (See Mendocino County map on page 96)

Your dog will enjoy this small, wild park whose streams drain Russian Gulch. You must leash up, though, and stay off some of the back trails here. But you can still enjoy exploring among the trees of the deciduous forest. And dogs of the leg-lifting persuasion like the fact that huge groves of willows line the gulch. In wet season, you'll have to wade across the gulch to reach the beach, a small one with cliffs at each end. The surf is ferocious; don't let your dog near it. Swimming in the fresh creeks is much more fun for her, anyway.

The day-use fee is $6. You and your dog can pitch a tent at the 30-site campground here for $20–25.

As you continue on Highway 1, about two miles north of Mendocino, watch for a small brown sign marking the turnoff. There's a dirt parking lot at the entrance. 707/937-5804.

6 Friendship Park
🐾 🐾 (See Mendocino County map on page 96)

If your dog is bursting at the seams, this is a decent place to pull off Highway 1. Otherwise, the Mendocino Headlands is a much better deal for dogs. The park is small, but friendly to leashed dogs. You'll find green grass, a playing field, and even some picnic tables in case your dog doesn't want to visit the local eateries after taking care of essential business here. Friendship Park is at Little Lake Road and School Street. 707/937-4133.

DIVERSION

Take Your Pooch for a Paddle: Here's a sure-fire way to get some vacation photos your friends will actually *want* to see: Take your dog for a canoe ride on the Big River. If your dog promises not to rock the boat too much, a canoe ride on the river can be a spectacular way to share your vacation time.

The dog-friendly **Catch-a-Canoe** rental shop, part of the Stanford Inn by the Sea, is home to a locally crafted redwood outrigger canoe, which is virtually untippable but still fast and easy to paddle. It's very popular with the doggy set. But if your doggy is more than 50 pounds, you'll have to sniff out another canoe. And you'll be in luck, because Catch-a-Canoe also rents out "the dog canoe," which is a bit wider and shorter than most canoes, thus a bit more stable. The shop will supply your dog with a doggy life vest, just in case. Be sure to call in advance to find out about tides and to reserve the dog canoe.

Rental rates are $20–25 per hour, or $60–75 per day. There's a two-hour minimum, so you may as well make a day of it. Other canoes are available for super calm dogs. You can call or go in and chat with the folks who run this place to figure out what's right for you. 44850 Comptche-Ukiah Road, Mendocino; 707/937-0273.

🐾 Mendocino Headlands State Park/Big River Beach

🐾🐾🐾🐾 (See Mendocino County map on page 96)

Mendocino's sculpted shoreline is a spectacular place for you and your dog to enjoy the sights, scents, and sounds of the Mendocino coast. Unlike most state parks, this one allows leashed dogs on the trails, which wind around the rocky bluffs and provide good views of wave tunnels and arched rocks. Fields extend along the cliff tops, so there's plenty of room for dogs who don't like to hover over the edge of promontories. It's cool year-round, so even malamutes can enjoy an August romp. A sandy beach at the mouth of the Big River near the southern headlands is a tempting place to let your dog off her leash, but watch out—the place can be heavily patrolled.

It's difficult to explore the tiny town of Mendocino without running into the headlands at every turn. Exit Highway 1 at Lansing Street and drive west. The park actually surrounds the little Mendocino peninsula, so just stop at any part that looks appealing. Parking won't be far away. To get to the sandy beach, exit Highway 1 at the sign for Mendocino Headlands State Park and Big River Beach. Follow the signs east. 707/937-5804.

PLACES TO EAT

Gray Whale Bar and Café: The attractive porch that wraps around the Mac-Callum House inn's main Victorian is a fun place to dine with your dog. The cuisine features seasonal vegetables (organic when possible), fresh fish, and organic meats, and the wine list showcases some excellent choices from wineries in the nearby Anderson Valley. Despite the epicurean cuisine, this is a very casual restaurant. Humans without dogs can eat inside, but on nice days, they prefer the porch tables, too. 45020 Albion Street; 707/937-0289 or 800/609-0492.

Mendocino Bakery: The food here is scrumptious and often even good for you. The bakery concentrates on vegetarian meals, and the pizza is out of this world. Dine with your dog at the many outdoor tables alongside the restaurant. 10483 Lansing Street; 707/937-0836.

Mendocino Café: Dogs love coming to this exquisite cafe, where everything is organic and delectable. They get treated beautifully, with a bowl of fresh water, lots of love (if it's not too busy), and, if you come at the right time, a beef bone (from grass-fed beef, no less). Owner Meredith and her superb chef offer a wide range of international choices, from light and healthful to sticky and sinful. Dine with your dog on the deck overlooking the water and a garden. 10451 Lansing Street; 707/937-2422.

The Ravens: Here's a first: Dogs who accompany their people to this outstanding organic vegan restaurant actually get to eat indoors. We all know that health departments ban all but assistance dogs from being inside restaurants, so how can this work? Since the restaurant is part of the magnificent Stanford

Inn by the Sea, and the inn allows dogs in its lobby, innkeepers have simply set up some little tables in the lobby, next to the main restaurant dining area. You will be served there just as graciously as you would be in the main restaurant. "We don't eat animals here, so it's an appropriate place for animals to be," says owner Jeff Stanford.

Eating with your dog at indoor tables is an exciting idea whose time has come in California. Who knows, maybe one day restaurant patrons around the state will be asked "dog, or no dog?" the same way they used to be asked "smoking, or nonsmoking?"

The cuisine here is delicious. Even nonvegans enjoy eating at the Ravens, although your dog may be left scratching her head about where all those meaty smells have gone.

Important note: If your dog is a cat-chaser, you should take your appetites elsewhere: A few of the Stanford Inn's cats make their living reposing around here. The Ravens is at the Coast Highway and Comptche-Ukiah Road; 707/331-8884; www.stanfordinn.com/ravens.html.

PLACES TO STAY

Abigail's: Stay here if you're on a budget but want to stay in town: Rooms at this house-turned-inn start at a mere $99—chicken feed for this area. The rooms and suites here are spacious and attractive, with big windows, wood blinds, and very comfy beds. Your stay includes a continental breakfast, and wine and cheese in the afternoon. And if your dog has been very good, you might want to consider the Pooch's Paradise Special, which includes dog treats, a $25 gift certificate to a local doggy boutique, and other goodies that will put a smile on your dog's snout. Rooms are $99–169. At $239–319, suites are not quite as easy on the wallet. Dogs are $25 extra. Inquire about Pooch's Paradise package rates. 951 Ukiah Street 95460; 707/937-4892 or 800/962-0934; www .abigailsmendocino.com.

Blair House Inn: The Blair House is one of the most well-known houses in Mendocino. If this Victorian mansion looks familiar to you and your dog, it's probably because it starred as the exterior of Jessica Fletcher's (played by Angela Lansbury) home in the TV series *Murder, She Wrote.* (And you thought she lived in Cabot Cove, Maine.)

The house really does make you feel as if you're in old New England. The simple, clean elegance here is rare these days. It's full of Swedish and American antiques, Oriental rugs, and all kinds of nifty things. But since you're staying here with your pooch, you can't actually stay in the house itself. That's OK, though, because you and your dog get to stay in your very own carriage house. The Blair cottage, a one-room carriage house, is more rustic than the main house, but it's still a charmer, with a queen-size bed, a little kitchen, a bathroom (with shower), and a small loft area up top.

The inn is a very short walk from the Mendocino Headlands. Rates for the carriage house are $150–175. Dogs are $10 extra. 45110 Little Lake Street, P.O. Box 1608 95460; 707/937-1800 or 800/699-9296; www.blairhouse.com.

MacCallum House: This is one of the most special, fun, welcoming, exquisite, first-rate places you'll ever stay with your dog. But don't let that scare you away: The prices are reasonable, and any size dog is warmly welcome—even large, drooling specimens such as Jake. "We've never, ever had any problems with dogs," says dog-loving co-owner Jed Ayres. "They are a joy to have around."

Just about any dog may end up drooling here: The dog-friendly attitude is so deep and firmly entrenched that even the dog-loving chef at the renowned MacCallum House Restaurant gets in on the dog-welcoming bandwagon with his delectable doggy treats made from organic goose livers. Dogs who stay here get these treats as part as a terrific dog package, which includes a fluffy plush dog bed, a towel, a sheet, soft bedding, and dog bowls. (Everything but the treats is a loaner.) Dog sitting is available, and the MacCallum House even sponsors a charity dog show on the property.

The MacCallum House itself—a Victorian mansion built in 1882—is about the only place dogs can't stay. But there are myriad rooms, suites, cottages, and even houses on the property and on nearby MacCallum property for dogs and their people. They're tastefully appointed—some could grace the best interior design magazines—and have a warm-yet-airy ambiance.

The barn, built in the 1880s, now houses several rooms with features that include decks, ocean views, hot tubs, and sumptuous river stone fireplaces. A handful of dog-friendly cottages dot the property. The most fabulous (and the most expensive) is the Water Tower, built in the late 1800s. It's a three-story vertical suite with to-die-for ocean views, a two-person tub, a dry sauna, and plenty of room. Water is still stored in a tank up top, and you can see a real working well below the tower via glass on the first floor. The tower has been lovingly restored, and it is one of the most attractive of these old structures in the area. Slightly less expensive is the Greenhouse cottage, with a beautiful trellised back dining area next to a hot tub.

As if these choices weren't enough, every suite in the four-star luxury MacCallum Suites, on a hill overlooking the village, is dog-friendly and stunning. The MacCallum-run vacation homes are also hits with people and their dogs: The Oceansong house is even fenced in, for extra-fun dog frolicking.

Prices for the range of accommodations are $110–395. The price includes a gourmet breakfast and a wine hour. (Dogs can join you on the wraparound porch of the main MacCallum House for these.) Dogs are $25 extra. 45020 Albion Street 95460; 707/937-0289 or 800/609-0492; www.maccallumhouse.com.

Mendocino Seaside Cottage: Don't be fooled by the name: This is no little cottage, but a large oceanside inn with four spacious suites and a separate cottage that's almost exclusively for pets and their people. How's this for a rule reversal: "People without pets may be able to stay, but only by special arrangement," jokes (we think) the inn's co-owner, Linda. Dogs wag their tails hard when they stay here: They get a gift basket with treats, a food bowl, and other goodies. Perhaps the best feature for dogs is that Mendocino Headlands State Park is pretty much the front yard here. It's a terrific place to explore with your leashed dog.

If you like an inn that caters to Romance (yes, with a capital R), this is the place for you: "You are a Special Valentine 365 Days a Year," touts the inn's website. The toll-free phone number even has the word "heart" in it. The suites have a honeymoon bent and a pretty feel that might not go well with a certain large yellow Lab I know (I shall mention no names, Jake), but dogs of the toy variety look perfect here. Actually, any size well-behaved dog is welcome at the inn. "We love all pets," says Linda. "As long as their people are well behaved."

Rates are $169–299. The inn is a few blocks from Mendocino's "business district," at 10940 Lansing Street, but correspondence should be sent to the inn's business address: 1050 Wallace Drive, Redwood Valley, CA 95470; 707/485-0239 or 800/94-HEART (800/944-3278); www.romancebythesea.com.

Mendocino Village Inn: If you love the exquisitely dog-friendly MacCallum House, you'll be smitten by the Mendocino Village Inn. This attractive 1882 Victorian has the exact same set of dog perks as the MacCallum House (from the MacCallum's wonderful pet basket to the gourmet treats), and the same extras the MacCallum offers humans (including a gourmet breakfast at the MacCallum House—just a short walk away—and wine and cheese). Is it coincidence? Copycatting? No, it's just the co-owners; they're the same for both properties. So we don't waste ink—heaven forbid in a 1,000-page book!—just back up a couple of listings to read the details of the extras.

Dogs are welcome to stay at any of the four beautiful Mendocino Village Inn rooms that have private entrances. Play games, read, or just relax in the attractive lobby area, or enjoy some sunshine on the inn's deck. If you simply must check emails, the inn has a computer with high-speed Internet you can use for free. Rates for the private-entrance rooms are $150–250. Dogs are $25 extra. The inn is on Main Street, but you check in at the MacCallum House, which is the address the owners prefer to give: 45020 Albion Street 95460; 707/937-0289 or 800/609-0492; www.maccallumhouse.com.

Retreat House: Got a few friends who want to stay in a beautiful old home in the heart of Mendocino but don't want to pay the prices of a bed-and-breakfast or inn? You can rent this sweet, spacious three-bedroom, two-bathroom house and its charming one-bedroom, one-bath cottage for a very affordable price. (Split four ways, it can be as low as $75 per room nightly, during slow season—not including taxes or a rather steep cleaning fee.)

The main house has a living room, dining room, and full kitchen. The master bedroom offers ocean views, so whoever gets to stay there might want to consider forking over a little extra. There's also a sauna and an indoor hot tub, for that pleasant sensation of home far away from home.

The retreat's pretty yard is fenced, but keep an eye on your dog, because it's definitely jumpable for pooches bent on escape. (Why a dog would want to escape from here is a mystery. Oh wait: Mendocino Burgers.)

A two-night minimum stay costs $590–790. Weekly rates are available. Dogs are $50 extra for the length of their stay, and there's a $170 cleaning fee. (This fee is for both the dogged and the dogless.) Don't be confused when you phone or check out the website: The rental is owned by the Whitegate Inn (not a dog-friendly place), and that's who answers the phone. 45130 Calpella Street 95460; 707/937-4892 or 800/531-7282; www.whitegateinn.com.

Sallie & Eileen's Place: The dog-friendly cabin here is for women only (sorry, men) and is so sweet you won't want to leave. You'll sleep in a cozy loft bedroom, relax in the rich-wood-walled, big-windowed living room, and gaze out the windows of the dining nook and the comfy bathroom to the woods beyond. The place has a great energy about it, according to guests like Angela Gardner, who visited with her dog Chico.

The cabin is in the woods, and there's a lovely path and pretty gardens on the property, which you'll share with one other cottage (that cottage doesn't allow dogs). Be sure to check out the swinging bench next to the tiny, fern-festooned pond. Bring a book and a cup of tea and stay a while.

The cabin, located about three miles from Mendocino, is $125 per night. Dogs are $5 extra, and children are $15 extra. (That's a switch!) There's a wooden hot tub here, and it's $5 per person per day. You may see Sallie's and Eileen's kitties, so if your dog is an incorrigible cat fiend, you should think twice about staying here. The mailing address is Box 409 95460. You'll get the actual street address when you make your reservation. 707/937-2028; www.seplace.com.

Stanford Inn by the Sea: Do you and your pooch love luxury, foresty surroundings, and the ocean? Have we got a place for you!

The Stanford Inn by the Sea has plenty of all three and has been dog-friendly for decades. There's luxury: The beds are big, furnished with comfortable antiques, and the rooms all have fireplaces and French doors leading to private decks. There's rustic scenery: The redwood inn is nestled in a grove of pines, surrounded by 11 acres. There's water: On one side of the property is the Pacific, and on the other is the Big River.

What more could you want? Red-carpet treatment for your dog? How's this: Dogs are provided doggy sheets so they can relax anywhere in your room and not leave it covered with their dogginess. Not enough? Okay, we'll tell all: Dogs get the canine equivalent of a pillow chocolate—dog biscuits wrapped with ribbons. (And humans get the real gourmet deal.) The inn also supplies pooches with Frisbees, bowls for water and food, and poop bags. The

staff here also will take your dog's photo for a
Very Important Pet photo album in the lobby.
Speaking of the lobby, dogs are even allowed
to join you at the indoor lobby tables of the
inn's superb vegan restaurant, The Ravens.

Humans get the royal treatment at the inn,
too. Guests get to use luxurious microfiber
robes, swim in the beautiful greenhouse's
heated pool or indulge in a spa or sauna there,
start the day with a gourmet breakfast, and
partake of wine and tasty snacks at the end of
a day of adventuring. Several different styles
of massage are also available, from standard
Swedish to hot rock massage, and the inn even
offers aromatherapy and facials. You can also take a yoga class here for just
$8–10. Try the downward-dog posture. You and your pooch will have some-
thing to talk about when you get back from class.

Rates are $195–305. (Suites are a bit pricier.) Your dog's entire stay will cost
him $25. Additional pooches are $12.50 each. The inn is at Comptche-Ukiah
Road and Highway 1. The mailing address is P.O. Box 487 95460; 707/937-5615
or 800/331-8884; www.stanfordinn.com.

Sweetwater Spa and Inn: If you and your dog want to sniff out a sweet
Victorian inn in the heart of Mendocino, sniff no further. The Sweetwater
is a joy for dogs and their people, and it's right across from dog-friendly Big
River Beach.

Dogs are welcome to lounge with you at the charming cottages that surround the inn. The cottages are graced by fireplaces or Franklin stoves, and
two have private hot tubs. Our favorite place to stay is the Redwood Tower,
one of two dog-friendly water towers. Dogs get to watch tourists and local cats
stroll by in all four directions from the rooftop deck. The tower (a real former
water tower) has a spiral staircase leading up to a wonderful master bedroom
with ocean and river views. Downstairs is a full kitchen and cozy, attractive
living room.

The cottages and water tower have access to a yard, so if your dog feels the
urge to visit the WC at 3 A.M., you don't have to get out of your jammies. Of
course, don't forget to scoop the poop.

The best part of the Sweetwater, in this human's opinion, is its big redwood
hot tub and its spa. Yummy professional massages and an oh-so-relaxing
atmosphere will melt the tension out of any visitor. Another feature that makes
it an ideal place to stay is its proximity to the ocean and town—and especially
its proximity to the terrific Cafe Beaujolais. Dogs aren't allowed there, but
there's nothing wrong with takeout.

If you prefer a vacation rental, the Sweetwater has charge of a few properties. In addition, the Sweetwater maintains a beautiful ocean-view lodging in Little River.

Rates are $120–225. Dogs are $15 extra. 955 Ukiah Street, 95460; 707/937-4076 or 800/300-4140; www.sweetwaterspa.com.

Little River

Lots of people consider this to be part of Mendocino proper. It's not, but with its seaside charm and dog-friendly abodes, it could be!

PLACES TO EAT

Restaurant at Stevenswood: The top-notch über-dog-friendly Stevenswood Spa Resort is where you'll find this five-star restaurant. It has no outdoor dining, so why is it in this book? Because the people here will set up well-behaved dogs and their people with a cozy table in the resort's lobby, immediately adjacent to the restaurant's entrance. The Ravens restaurant in Mendocino was the first place in all of California to create a setup like this, and Stevenswood—so close by—is the only other one we know of to bend over backward for their canine diners. Leave it to good old dog-friendly Mendocino County!

As for the food, prepare to be impressed. The menu, which changes daily, isn't long, but it's top-notch. The restaurant is within the Stevenswood Spa Resort, at 8211 North Highway 1. 707/937-4076.

PLACES TO STAY

Inn at Schoolhouse Creek: You and your dog can hunker down in one of the cozy cottages here, or at a room in a small lodge reminiscent of a 1950s motel. It's a fun place to stay, more of a bed-and-breakfast at heart than anything else. The inn, set on eight acres of meadows, gardens, and forest, provides a mouthwatering breakfast, and wine and hors d'oeuvres in the late afternoon. If your dog promises to watch, not participate, you can even head to the top of the meadow with her to soak in the inn's hot tub while you watch the sunset over the ocean.

On the more active side, you and the pooch can walk to Schoolhouse Creek, which runs through the eight-acre property, or cross the street and take a five-minute walk to a secluded ocean cove. This is most dogs' favorite thing to do, but here's one that comes in a close second: investigating the wonderful dog goodies they get upon arrival. Dog guests receive gourmet biscuits, a Frisbee, a towel, sheet, bowl, and poop bags. Such hospitality makes dogs feel utterly at home here.

Rates are $156–250. There's a $25–75 dog fee per stay, depending on your accommodation. The inn is at 7051 North Highway 1 in Little River. The mailing address is P.O. Box 1637 95460; 707/937-5525 or 800/731-5525; www.schoolhousecreek.com.

Little River Inn: Dogs who like deep dog-friendliness and wonderful lodgings with sumptuous views adore this seaside retreat. The inn rests on a hillside, and it is made up of many small buildings, most of which resemble elongated cottages. Dogs can stay in many of the inn's oceanview rooms (many have a fireplace or a whirlpool bath). Dogs aren't allowed in the rooms at the inn's main building, built in the 1850s, but that's OK because they won't have to doggyfoot around all the antiques.

The ocean is right across the road, and wonderful romping room is all around. The innkeepers will point you in the right direction. They love dogs. In fact, lucky dogs who stay here get a basket of pet treats, a food-and-water dish, poop bags, and special sheets to cover bedding and towels for muddy coats. If you'd like to go out for a while without your furry friend, the innkeepers will supply you with local pet-sitter referrals.

The owners aren't the only ones here who love dogs: The resident cat, Abby Rose, often comes out from the front office to greet canine visitors. If your dog is a chaser, best keep him elsewhere while checking in. (That said, we've been told that Abby Rose once took on two rambunctious great danes, so she can probably handle your pooch as long as he's not over the top with his cat obsession.)

Rates are $135–275. Dogs are $25 extra. 7901 North Highway 1 95456; 707/937-5942 or 888/466-5683 (which spells INN-LOVE, in case you were wondering); www.littleriverinn.com.

S.S. Seafoam Lodge: If your dog is a water dog, she'll take to this place in a snap. Each room has a nautical motif, and some provide views of the shoreline in the distance. You'll even have access to a secluded little beach. The cottages and small buildings are set in big tree territory, just a few miles south of Mendocino. With all this going for it, who could ask for anything more? OK, since you asked: The owners of the S.S. Seafoam Lodge love dogs, so your pooch will be a most welcome guest here. Rates are $110–225. Special winter rates are available. Dogs are $10 extra per stay (a good deal). The lodge is at 6751 North Highway 1 in Little River. The mailing address is P.O. Box 68, Mendocino 95460; 707/937-1827 or 800/606-1827; www.seafoamlodge.com.

Stevenswood Spa Resort: How would you like to be pampered in a beautiful resort in a forest near the ocean? Sign me up! This four-diamond resort is modern, cozy, tranquil, and surrounded on three sides by towering redwoods. The 10 suites (it's all suites here) are richly appointed, with the best of everything, from ultra luxe down comforters and premium 1,000-thread-count Egyptian bedding to imported cork floors and Italian espresso machines. Every suite has a woodburning fireplace, large windows, and all kinds of special touches. And speaking of touches, the Indigo Eco Spa here offers a very long list of wonderful treatments.

Lucky canine guests are not forgotten here. In fact, they get one of the best doggy VIP packages we've seen! Your dog gets a personalized bowl engraved with her name. You get to take that home as a souvenir. Dogs also get treats,

Italian bottled water (Jake prefers California pond water), a plush dog bed, and use of leashes, Frisbees, and balls. The resort will even supply tick spray so your dog won't give a free meal to those disgusting, blood-sucking creeps. (If you can't tell, ticks are not my favorite animal.)

There's plenty of room to run around—off leash!—on the resort's 14 acres, and the surrounding parklands. A resort rep says dogs are welcome at the adjacent parklands, but these are state parks, and we've been told by rangers that dogs can't officially go on the trails, so just keep an eye peeled if you venture there. If your dog is hankering to play with another dog, Zachary, the resort's friendly black lab, loves playing with other dogs and is usually up for a swim in some of the nearby rivers and beaches.

You can dine with your dog in your suite thanks to room service from the five-star Restaurant at Stevenswood, and your dog will get a special treat when your meal is delivered. Or you can take her to the restaurant itself. Read more about this dining experience under *Places to Eat.* A great breakfast comes with your stay. Suite rates are $149–875. Dogs pay a $50 fee for the length of their stay. 8211 North Highway 1 95456; 800/421-2810; www.stevenswood.com.

Sweetwater Inn: This is the cute little sibling of the terrific Sweetwater Inn in Mendocino. The inn is set on a sunny hill above Buckhorn Cove. You and your leashed pooch can saunter on down to that sheltered cove for some fine dog ambles along the water. Dogs are allowed in all the rooms here. Each has a fireplace and a fridge. Rates are $70–175. Dogs are $15 extra. You'll have to write to or call Mendocino's Sweetwater (a.k.a. The Big Sister) for reservations and more information. You check in at the Mendocino Inn and get directions to this one while you're there. The Mendocino Sweetwater is at 955 Ukiah Street 95460; 707/937-4076 or 800/300-4140; www.sweetwaterspa.com/lodging. (Click on "Little River lodging.")

Elk

PARKS, BEACHES, AND RECREATION AREAS

8 Greenwood State Park

🐾🐾🐾 (See Mendocino County map on page 96)

Leashed dogs enjoy a romp on the 0.25-mile-long beach here just about as much as their people do. The sea stacks alone are worth checking out, but with 47 acres of park set along coastal bluffs, there's more to do than just gawk. Admission is free. The park is conveniently situated beside the divine Greenwood Pier Inn. You'll see signs for the park once you're in the area. 707/937-5804.

PLACES TO EAT

Greenwood Pier Cafe: Dogs and their guests can sit at the outdoor tables among lettuce, herbs, and other plants growing for the scrumptious salads served here. Fresh local seafood is the specialty, but the place will tickle your taste buds no matter what you choose. The café is a new addition to the four-paw Greenwood Pier Inn. 5928 South Highway 1; 707/877-9997 or 707/877-3423.

PLACES TO STAY

Greenwood Pier Inn: I drool when I think of the Greenwood Pier Inn. It can't be helped. The place is a peaceful, spectacular work of art with one of the best locations of any inn we've ever come across. It's at the top of a magnificent ocean bluff. The views of the ocean are amazing, there's easy beach access, and the food is to die for. There's even a big outdoor hot tub perched on a bluff. (Sorry, water dogs, but the tub is for humans only.) The inn's cozy rooms are adorned with fireplaces, handmade quilts, and original, unique artwork. Rates are $110–325. Dogs and extra people (more than two) are an additional $15 each. 5928 South Highway 1, P.O. Box 336 95432; 707/877-9997, 707/877-3423, or 800/807-3423; www.greenwoodpierinn.com.

Philo

PLACES TO STAY

Highland Ranch: If you and your little dawgie (or big dawgie, though that doesn't really go with the old song) are hankering to git along out to the country and have a real ranch experience, complete with 20 horses and an Old West–style ranch dining area, you'll find no more beautiful or hospitable locale than the Highland Ranch.

Ranch owner George Gaines, a dapper and worldly rancher if ever there was one (he ran the international division of General Mills in Europe for many years, among his varied careers), has gone out of his way to make his 300-acre ranch super-welcoming for dogs and their dudes. (It is kind of a dude ranch, albeit an upscale one.) Dogs who stay here get a Doggy Pack with two towels, a doggy bedspread, chew toys, and a couple of dog biscuits. "We have several people who come here to give their dogs a vacation," he says without a wink.

Each of the eight large, homey guest cabins has a wood-burning fireplace, plenty of books to thumb through, vaulted beamed ceilings, and a big redwood deck. Dogs are welcome to explore the property off leash. And what a property it is: The ranch has four ponds, stocked with all kinds of fish for your angling pleasure. Water dogs love the ponds, especially on warm afternoons. There's plenty of shade from redwoods and firs, and, thanks to the ranch's land being adjacent to lumber company land, more than 100 miles of bridle trails. If you like to ride, you may have bowlegs by the end of your stay.

Human guests eat all their meals in the large dining room at the ranch's spacious, airy main house. With its high, beamed ceilings and simple Western decor, you wouldn't be surprised to see Hoss Cartwright ambling in for some chow. The food is fresh and tasty and always accompanied by a selection of Anderson Valley wines and locally brewed beers. (Hard to picture Hoss with a glass of chardonnay.) Cocktails are served in the living room. On cool evenings, you can sip beside a crackling fire.

At $300 per adult and $200 per child 6 and older (children under 6 are free), the rates aren't cheap, but they include your cabin, all meals, wine, beer, cocktails, riding, and taxes. (Extra charges apply only for private riding lessons, long-distance phone calls, and equipment if you want to shoot clay pigeons—a popular pastime here.) Weekly rates provide a slight discount. P.O. Box 150 95466; 707/895-3600; www.highlandranch.com.

Ukiah

PARKS, BEACHES, AND RECREATION AREAS

🐾 Cow Mountain Recreation Area

🐾🐾🐾🐾🦴 (See Mendocino County map on page 96)

How does 27,000 acres of leashless bliss sound? This rugged recreation area, run by the Bureau of Land Management, is heaven for dogs who need real, off-leash exercise. With elevations ranging 800–4,000 feet, a good-sized section of this land is probably off-limits for couch-potato dogs. But there are plenty of trails—31 miles, to be precise—that even the most sedentary dog/human pair can enjoy.

Dogs can be off leash everywhere but in developed areas such as the two small designated campgrounds, where pitching a tent at one of the 12 designated, first-come, first-served sites won't cost you a cent. Make sure that your dog is under voice control when he's off leash. Many mountain lions, deer, and bears (as well as human hunters in the right season) call Cow Mountain their home, and you don't want your dog tangling with any of them.

If you like nature-watching, you'll really enjoy it here. Quail, doves, rabbits, and feral pigs are common sights. Hunters also like it here for the same reasons. Anglers can fish the entire area, including the cold-water streams, which often brim with rainbow trout. Several of the small reservoirs have been stocked with sunfish.

The park is actually 52,000 acres, but about half of those acres in the South Cow Mountain Recreation Area are devoted to off-highway vehicles. If you venture on that acreage with your dog, do keep him on leash. But why go there when you can stay to the north, where the only forms of transportation you have to watch out for are horses and bicycles?

Other than the nearby Stornetta Public Lands, Noyo Beach Off-Leash Area, and little bits of Mendocino National Forest that sneak into this county, this is the only public land that allows dogs off leash in all of Mendocino County. Use it well, tread lightly, and pack out what you pack in.

Exit U.S. 101 at Talmage Road and drive east until you come to the City of 10,000 Buddhas (a Buddhist temple), where the road ends. Make a right onto East Side Road, and in about a half mile, go left on Mill Creek Road. The entrance to Cow Mountain will be on your left. For information and maps, call 707/468-4000.

🔟 Mill Creek Park
🐾🐾🐾🐾 (See Mendocino County map on page 96)

This 400-acre park directly across from Cow Mountain has everything dogs could want, except off-leash freedom. They can hike, splash in streams, fish and swim in two reservoirs, picnic, relax in the shade of bay trees, and draw deep dog breaths on ridge tops.

Exit U.S. 101 at Talmage Road and drive east until you come to the City of 10,000 Buddhas, where the road ends. Make a right onto East Side Road, and in about a half mile, go left on Mill Creek Road. After you pass the pond, you'll see signs for the park. Go right almost immediately, into a group picnic/playground area. Your dog can frolic in the meadow or hike with you on the trail that starts on the west end of the group picnic area. That trail branches off into several different trails, including a nature trail that follows the creek and a trail that leads you to the top of the southernmost ridge, where the views are unbeatable. Alternate entrances, in case the gate to the picnic area is shut, are available around the creek and pond, near the small, strategically situated parking lots. 707/463-4267.

PLACES TO STAY

Long Valley Ranch: Before you read this, tell your dog to sit. You will also want to sit when you learn about what you get at this spectacular property: Eight hundred acres! Yes, that's 800 leash-free acres. On this 800 acres of hills, valleys, and two ponds reside two exquisite houses, nowhere near each other.

The Glass House, which opened in 2006, is Jake's favorite because the Great Room (the living room/dining room/relaxing room) features a 36-foot-long glass wall. On the rare times he's inside, he can lie there steaming up any spot of window while looking out on a large pond (dubbed Piano Lake) and the surrounding mountains and dreaming of his next walk through *his* ranch. There's even a fireplace set into the glass wall (or sort of through it), so as you sit on the couch gazing at a starlit night, you can also gaze at the fireplace. This two-bedroom house has a very open feel, and is modern, yet cozy. If the house doesn't offer enough room, you can also rent the adjacent Madrone Studio building.

The Haiku House is a lovely, large (four-bedroom) recently remodeled home with lofty ceilings in the main area and a bright, airy demeanor. Dogs love to sit out on the wraparound porch and take in the views and smells of the surrounding land. (Just please have them respect the Japanese gardens when they go off for a potty break. Zen and dog wee don't go together.)

From either house you're welcome to hike the acreage and splash in the ponds. Long Valley Ranch is owned by the same folks who used to own the magnificent Sheep Dung Estates (and who also own The Other Place, in Boonville), and they know all about making the ideal getaway for you and your dog. Your stay comes with a bottle of local wine and a little assortment of breakfast goodies, including organic granola and milk.

There's a two-night minimum stay. Rates for the Haiku House vary, depending on how many people and dogs in your party. The price ranges from $175 for one bedroom (up to two people and two dogs, midweek price) to $425 for four bedrooms (up to eight people and four dogs, weekend price). The Glass House is $300–375 (for up to two people and two dogs), and an additional $100 if you use the Madrone Studio (for up to two more people). For either house, you'll pay an additional $25 for each extra pooch or person. Please note that Long Valley doesn't accept credit cards, so you may have to break into your pooch's piggy bank. You'll get directions upon reserving; the mailing address is P.O. Box 588, Boonville 95415; 707/895-3979; www.sheepdung.com.

Motel 6: Rates are $38–45 for the first adult, $6 for the second. 1208 South State Street 95482; 707/468-5404.

Point Arena

This little town that juts into the Pacific is best known for its historic lighthouse. With the great increase in ship traffic after the Gold Rush, mariners needed something to mark this significant point. The lighthouse, built in 1869, has served as a vital marker for mariners ever since. It's also recently become a beacon for dogs everywhere. So is a huge swatch of public coastal land just north of the lighthouse.

PARKS, BEACHES, AND RECREATION AREAS

11 Stornetta Public Lands

🐾🐾🐾🐾 ✕ (See Mendocino County map on page 96)

This 1,132-acre coastal wonderland is absolute dog heaven on earth! You and your voice-controlled dog are welcome to stroll on its two miles of coastline without a leash. It doesn't get better than this.

The property, managed by the way-cool (in the canine department) Bureau of Land Management, has everything a dog could wish for, including grassy fields, coastal bluffs, tidepools, rocky beaches, cypress and pine groves, wetlands, and cows. Yes, you read that right—cows. The property is home to many big, beautiful bovine, who like to graze here. (A ranger we spoke with wasn't sure if they're Stornetta dairy cows or actual cattle of the nondairy persuasion. Until I can see them close enough to take a look at their undersides, I'll just call them cows.) They're not necessarily going to be behind fences either, so for the sake of the cows and your dog, make sure your dog is truly under voice control if you let him off leash.

Even in this coastal paradise there are things you'll need to be aware of: Mountain lions have been spotted in the area, so don't let your dog wander off. The property also has some sinkholes and unstable cliffs, so watch your footing.

The off-leash status may not last forever. For the time being the property is under interim management rules, which do permit leash-free pooches. Dogs, keep your paws crossed that it stays that way! Humans, watch for signs that indicate any change in the leashless law here.

The property, which is right around the Point Arena Lighthouse, has a few access points; none of them are terribly straightforward. The easiest is to take Highway 1 to Lighthouse Road, go west, and drive in more than a mile, toward the end of the road, where you'll find some pullouts where you can park with your car fully off the road. For another access point, take Highway 1 just a little farther north, to Miner Hole Road. Drive west until you come to a gated road. There will be parking there, unless things change, which we're told they might. Park and walk in. Note that both areas can get very crowded during abalone season (in spring). There's also access from the Point Arena Lighthouse, but only if you're a guest of the lighthouse lodging. 707/468-4000.

PLACES TO STAY

Point Arena Lighthouse lodging: It used to take four men to keep the historic Point Arena lighthouse going, and these four men were each provided a good-sized home next to the lighthouse. Since there's no longer the need for this kind of upkeep, the homes, which have been rebuilt, are now rented out as vacation homes. And not just any vacation homes—very dog-friendly ones.

"We love pets, in fact we prefer dogs to kids most of the time," says Rae Radtkey, executive director of the nonprofit organization that now maintains the lighthouse. (Money from the house rentals is a major source of funding for the ongoing preservation of the lighthouse.)

The four houses, and the lighthouse, are set toward the end of a long, thin spit of land. The spit, being a spit, is surrounded by ocean on three sides. There's nothing like being lulled to sleep by the sound of the crashing ocean. The views are to drool for, as are the tastefully furnished homes, which all have three bedrooms, two bathrooms, wood-burning stoves (wood is supplied), full kitchens, and satellite TV, should you want to look at something other than some of the world's most stunning ocean scenery. Leashed dogs can join you to sniff out the 24 acres of surrounding land. Or check out Stornetta Public Lands, with access points very close by.

Rates are $200–225, plus a one-time cleaning fee of $50. (This fee is for people without dogs, too.) 45500 Lighthouse Road 95468; 707/882-2777; www.pointarenalighthouse.com. (Warning: Upon arrival at the website you'll be greeted by a loud foghornlike sound, which can be rather startling. Jake flew to the window looking terribly alarmed when I navigated to the site.)

Boonville

Fewer than 1,000 people live in this scenic Anderson Valley enclave. It's a low-key town that's home to a wonderfully eclectic bunch. You and your dog can imbibe the laid-back feel by staying at one of a couple of terrific lodgings that welcome dogs.

PARKS, BEACHES, AND RECREATION AREAS

12 Faulkner County Park

🐾🐾 (See Mendocino County map on page 96)

Since you and your dog probably each enjoy flowering shrubs for your own reasons, you'll have a pleasant stroll here. Of the two trails that wind through this 40-acre park, the Azalea Discovery Trail is the one nosy dogs like best. This is a 12-stop nature trail through a stand of azalea shrubs and redwoods. Difficult as it may be, try to prevent your dog from doing one-leg salutes to the azaleas.

The park also features a hiking trail to the top of the ridge. It's a short trail, but it gets the blood flowing after a long car trip. Kids enjoy the small play-ground near the entrance.

The park is on Mountain View Road, two miles west of Boonville. 707/463-4267.

PLACES TO STAY

The Boonville Hotel: This beautiful hotel was built in the 1860s, and from the outside you'd swear you were on a Hollywood backlot for old Westerns. But inside it's another story. It's up to date with clean lines, natural materials, and a very cozy-yet-hip feel. Local artisans created everything from the natural wood blinds in each room to various beds and armoires. As the people who run the lodging say, the Boonville Hotel celebrates the past without dwelling on it. (And in that spirit, rooms are free from phones and TVs.)

Dogs can't actually stay in the main hotel, but they're welcome to overnight in one of two rooms in an enchanting creekside building. Each room has a little yard and private entrance. At $275 per night, plus another $25 per pooch, these are the most expensive rooms, but they're also the largest. The hotel is on Highway 128 at Lambert Lane, P.O. Box 326, 95415; 707/895-2210; www.boonvillehotel.com.

The Other Place: Welcome to canine nirvana, dog heaven, pooch paradise! There are few other places like The Other Place. When you stay at The Other Place, you get 550 acres almost to yourself. The only folks you'll share the property with are the guests of the three cottages here. Your dog gets to be leash-free when you go for walks on all this rural gem! There's just one place you may want to consider leashing—around the few cows who live in the upper reaches of the property, should your hike take you that far. If you have any doubts about what your dog may do in a bovine encounter, please do leash up before you get to cow country.

Even if you choose to forgo exploring to stay in the comfort of your gorgeous cottage, your dog will still have the equivalent of a very, very large dog park in her own backyard. Each cottage is surrounded by three or four fenced acres. You can just let your dog out the door and not worry about her escaping! This amazing feature is the brainchild of owners Anne and Aaron Bennett, who once owned the hallowed Sheep Dung Estates (no longer available for rentals) in Yorkville. They created The Other Place for people who really want to get away from it all, and who want to do so with their dogs.

Actually, you don't have to get away from it all here because the cottages have TVs (with discreetly placed satellite dishes) and phones. You don't have to use them, but they're there. Speaking of cottages, they're exquisite. They're really more like small houses. They all have kitchens and wood-burning stoves, and are beautifully furnished and designed. The interiors should be featured in a magazine article on elegant simplicity. They're airy, with clean lines and a cozy, upscale feel. The cottages are good-sized, with one having two bedrooms. Our favorite is The Oaks, a one-bedroom studio under a canopy of very old oak trees. The view is to pant for. You can see vineyards in the valley, mountains in the distance, and Boonville. Your cottage comes with fixings for a healthful breakfast—and then some: Cottages are stocked with coffee, tea, milk, granola, organic apple juice, and locally grown and produced wine.

Enough slobbering. On to business: There's a two-night minimum stay. Rates are $150–350, and the price is good for up to two dogs and two people at the one-bedroom cottages and four dogs and four people at the two-bedroom cottage. Additional people or pooches are $25 each. Please note that the Bennetts don't do credit cards, so you can't put your vacation on plastic. You'll get directions when you reserve; the mailing address is P.O. Box 588 95415 707/895-3979; www.sheepdung.com.

Gualala

Gualala (gwa-LA-la for some, wa-LA-la for those who know) is a funny-sounding name for a cute little seaside town. The southernmost coastal town in Mendocino County, Gualala is the perfect place to visit if you're staying in Sea Ranch, just down the road in Sonoma County, and are getting tired of all that uninterrupted tranquility. Gualala also has a couple of beautiful dog-friendly lodgings of its own, and they're great places to stay, whether you're a dog or a dog's chauffeur.

PARKS, BEACHES, AND RECREATION AREAS

13 Gualala Point Regional Park

🐾🐾🐾 (See Mendocino County map on page 96)

This is the pristine, driftwood-strewn beach you can see from the town of Gualala, just over the Mendocino/Sonoma County border. The small, friendly visitor center offers displays of shore life, Pomo Indian artifacts, and old machinery. Outside is a sandstone replica of a bull sea lion. From there, it's a half-mile walk to the beach on a smoothly paved trail, where you and your leashed dog will stroll through mixed grasses, ferns, berries, dunes, and rows · of pines and cypresses. At the beach, you can take a trail through a marsh or along a coastal bluff. On the beach you'll find driftwood and piles of kelp bulbs, good for jumping on for their satisfying *pop*.

The day-use fee is $4. Campsites are $17 (for up to two vehicles), with overnight dogs costing $1. There are 26 sites. For reservations, call 707/565-2267. From U.S. 101, turn just south of Gualala at the sign announcing the park and the Sea Ranch Golf Links. 707/565-2041.

PLACES TO STAY

Mar Vista Cottages: A word of warning: Don't read this listing if your dog is under two years old. This charming retreat has experienced too much chewing damage from younger dogs, and the owners made a decision not to allow whippersnapper pooches under two. If your dog is older, read on! It's an absolutely heavenly place for the more mature set.

On a typical weekend at these 12 one- and two-bedroom cottages overlooking beautiful Anchor Bay, several dog guests cavort merrily around the property, sniffing each other, dipping their paws in a small pond, and generally enjoying life. "It's as much of a dog lover's paradise as you can get," says Suzanne Samuel, who alerted us to Mar Vista's wonders after she visited with Aleph Dog. (The human equivalent of a pond is the lovely Japanese soaking tub on the property. Go in and melt away your stress.)

People love Mar Vista as much as their dog companions. Mar Vista's friendly owners, Renata and Tom Dorn, bought these 1930s and 1940s cottages in 2000 and have done significant upgrading. The cottages are far enough from each other so there's sufficient privacy and quiet. Some of the cottages have fireplaces or wood-burning stoves, and all have full kitchens, hardwood floors, and country-style furniture. In addition, all are stocked with a big basket of dog towels, to keep pooches dry after a jaunt to the beach. The Dorns also offer bowls, dog rugs, and pooch beds upon request.

A big draw for human guests is the property's large fenced garden, where the Dorns grow all kinds of edible goodies and allow guests to self-harvest what they'd enjoy during their stay. Lettuce, herbs, and strawberries are generally available year-round, and you'll often come across potatoes, leeks, onions, zucchini, and a variety of other tasty veggies. Adding to the farmy atmosphere are pygmy goats, hens (whose eggs you're welcome to enjoy), and adorable rabbits. (They're all kept in areas that are pretty safe from dogs.)

Rates are $155–295. Dogs are $50 per stay for the first dog, $25 for a second. No more than two pooches per cottage, please. 35101 South Highway 1 95445; 707/884-3522 or 877/855-3522; www.marvistamendocino.com.

North Coast Country Inn: Reggie, described by his people as "a pure-hearted yellow Lab," is considered the vice-president of public relations here and will more than likely greet you when you arrive in the parking lot. He'll then escort you to the office, where he'll see that you and your canine companion are well taken care of. (For starters, he makes sure dog guests get treats immediately upon checking in.)

Reggie is lucky to live here. This inn is upscale but homey, with six comfy guest rooms in pretty redwood buildings that nestle into a ferny hillside under towering pines. Each guest room comes with a lovely sitting area next to a fireplace, as well as a dining area and a private entrance. Some have filtered ocean views. All are very cozy places to stay, with super comfortable beds (a few have canopies), cushy chairs, down comforters, down featherbeds, and high-quality sheets and towels.

The property was once part of a sheep ranch, and you can walk among the remaining fruit trees from the old ranch's orchard. The gardens and little paths here also beckon, and the inn features a very beautiful hot tub setup in a secluded tree-festooned area. A full, gorgeous breakfast in the breakfast room comes with your stay. Dogs aren't allowed in that room, so most people tie up their dogs to the railing just outside. Dogs don't seem to mind. "Reggie likes to keep them company," says proprietor Phil Walker.

Room rates are $195–225. Dogs are $25 extra. (Smaller dogs may only be charged $25 for the length of their stay.) The innkeepers prefer small dogs as guests, but as Phil says, "there are many, many exceptions. Lots of the dogs that stay here are big." In fact, the dog who recommended this inn is a big and beautiful golden retriever. Good dog, Nessie. (And your people, Denise and Eric, are good people, too, for emailing me your recommendation.) 34591 South Highway 1 95445; 707/884-4537 or 800/959-4537. www.northcoast countryinn.com.

Serenisea: Want to rent an attractive cottage or house on the exquisite Mendocino coast? Want good rates, a fireplace or woodstove, a full kitchen, and a hot tub? How about easy access to little beaches and tidepools? If your dog answered yes to any of these questions, check out the cottages and vacation homes offered to dogs and their people through Serenisea cottages and vacation rentals. (A couple of the vacation rentals have fenced yards, which we know is on your dog's list of priorities.)

Jake's favorite homes are Colt Cottage and the Anchor Bay house. The cozy wooden Colt Cottage has great views of the ocean and is on an acre of land, but it doesn't have beach access. The Anchor Bay house is very attractive, with excellent beach access, although less of its own land, which is really no big deal around here.

Marina, who helps run Serenisea, is a big dog lover who's involved in rescue and training. She's very accommodating to pooch guests and tries to supply the rentals with dog cookies when she knows they'll have canine visitors. Rates for the vacation rentals are $140–270. The five cottages owned by Serenisea start at $100 and have tidepool access. 36100 Highway 1 South 95445; 707/884-3836 or 800/331-3836; www.serenisea.com.

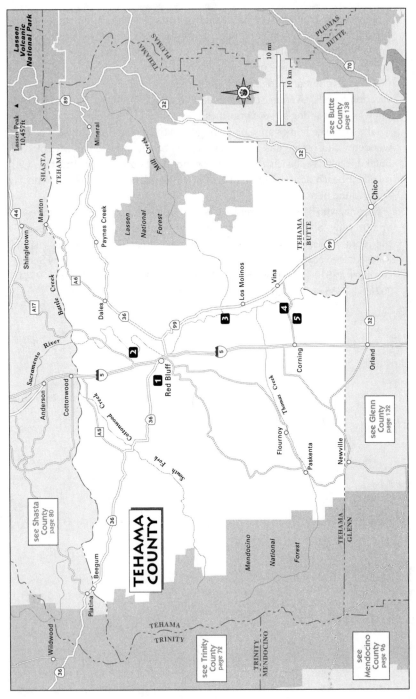

CHAPTER 9

Tehama County

This county can be described as a green sandwich. It has a little bit of Lassen National Forest on one side, a touch of Mendocino National Forest on the other, and lots of farmland in between. If you feel like doing your dog a favor, stop in Red Bluff and visit lush and lovely Dog Island. If it weren't for the leash thing—few off-leash opportunities—dogs would probably never want to go home.

NATIONAL FORESTS

The *National Forests and Wilderness Areas* resource at the back of this book has important information and safety tips on visiting national forests with your dog and has more background on the national forests listed below.

Lassen National Forest
🐾🐾🐾🐾🐾🐕

Mendocino National Forest
🐾🐾🐾🐾🐕

The Mendocino National Forest is full of campgrounds in the southwest part of the county.

PICK OF THE LITTER—TEHAMA COUNTY

BEST WOODSY WALKS
Dog Island Park/Samuel Ayer Park, Red Bluff (page 128)
Woodson Bridge State Recreation Area, Corning (page 130)

Red Bluff
PARKS, BEACHES, AND RECREATION AREAS

❶ Dog Island Park/Samuel Ayer Park
😺😺😺😺 (See Tehama County map on page 126)

Wow! A park named for the very creatures who most enjoy being here! Now if only dogs could legally run off leash, someone would have to change the name of this place to Dog Heaven Park.

This is a terrific place to take a dog. The park is lush, wild, and alive with riparian vegetation. You almost feel that somehow it's too verdant to be part of California.

Numerous nature trails wind throughout the park. One of them leads to a footbridge that takes you over to Dog Island, a big chunk of land nestled securely in the crook of a Sacramento River bend. The island is enchanting, but not super-quiet. I-5 crosses over the river close by.

From I-5, take the Red Bluff/Highway 36 exit west, cross the river, and turn right on Main Street. Follow Main Street to the sign for Dog Island Park, which will be on your right in a few blocks. 530/527-8177.

❷ William B. Ide Adobe State Historic Park
😺😺 (See Tehama County map on page 126)

This is a fun and historically interesting park to set paw in, but pooches can visit only under very restricted conditions—they're not allowed to visit the historic zone or the area where the animals hang out. (The chickens here are frequently mauled by marauding pooches, and the donkey was once attacked by three pit bulls, so the park's rangers are understandably protective.)

Leashed dogs join you for a 1.5-mile hike down by the Sacramento River Discovery Center, or they can plop down in the picnic area overlooking the Sacramento River. To most dogs, either option is better than staring blankly at an adobe memorial to a man who was president for 22 days during the infamous Bear Flag Revolt.

And in case you need access to something less historical, the park provides free Wi-Fi. The entry fee is $4 per vehicle. From northbound I-5, take the Antelope Boulevard exit and drive west a few blocks to Main Street. Turn right, drive about a mile to Adobe Road, and go right again. The park will be on your right in about one mile. 530/529-8599.

PLACES TO STAY

Cinderella Riverview Motel: You really can see the river from here, and there are plenty of balconies to prove it. Rates are $60–65. Dogs are $5 extra, and during dog shows at the nearby fairground this fee triples to $15. 600 Rio Street 96080; 530/527-5490.

Sportsman Lodge: This motel is so doggone animal-friendly that someone's pet camel stayed here one fine night. If you're heading for a dog show at the fairgrounds, this is a close, convenient place to stay with your pooch. Rates are $60–65. Dogs are $7 extra. 768 Antelope Boulevard 96080; 530/527-2888; www.rbsportsmanlodge.com.

Los Molinos
PARKS, BEACHES, AND RECREATION AREAS

🖻 Mill Creek Park
🐾🐾🐾 (See Tehama County map on page 126)
This park has great access to the Sacramento River for dogs who like to help you catch dinner or like to screw up your chances of catching it by wading in

all the fishy water. Since dogs are supposed to be leashed, you can usually control the situation.

Landlubbing pooches prefer the shaded meadows and the fenced-in ball fields. All in all, this is a peaceful, relaxing place to come with a dog.

From Highway 99, take Tehama Vina Road west, toward the Sacramento River. In a little under a mile, you'll start paralleling railroad tracks. You'll see River Road on your right, and immediately after that an unnamed road with a sign leading to Mill Creek Park. Turn right and follow it to the park. 530/528-1111.

Corning

PARKS, BEACHES, AND RECREATION AREAS

🎴 Woodson Bridge State Recreation Area
🐾🐾🐾🐾 (See Tehama County map on page 126)

You're in the middle of giant valley oak country here—a fact that sends many dogs into fits of happiness. Between all the oaks (*and* poison oak, so watch it!), walnuts, cottonwoods, elderberries, and willows, your boy dog will hardly be able to contain himself.

Wildflowers are abundant in this 428-acre park. With its location, flanking both sides of the Sacramento River, there's plenty of beauty, especially in spring. Autumn is also a spectacular and colorful sight. Just get on the nature trail and hike your city woes away.

During your visit, some of your neighbors may include Columbian black-tailed deer, bats, muskrats, hares, river otters, and skunks. If you're a bird-watcher, you'll love this place. If you're lucky, you may even spot the rare and endangered yellow-billed cuckoo. You'll know it when you see it.

The law requires that you keep your dog on a leash here and not use any unpaved trails. The day-use fee is $6. You can camp at any of the 37 campsites for $11. Reservations are only needed during the warmer months. Call 800/444-7275 or go to www.reserveamerica.com. From I-5, take the South Avenue exit and drive about eight miles east to the park. Park info: 530/839-2112.

5 Tehama County River Park

🐾🐾🐾 (See Tehama County map on page 126)

This park is almost directly across from the Woodson Bridge State Recreation Area. While it's not as large as the state park, there's no fee to use it, which makes it a very attractive alternative.

South Avenue bisects the park. The north side is grassy and fairly undeveloped, with great fishing access. When we visited, each of the three people fishing in the Sacramento had at least one dog. All the dogs were in and out of the river constantly. Of course, if the ranger had stopped by, everyone would have been fined for allowing their dogs off leash.

The section to the south of South Avenue is more developed, with playgrounds, a little store, and a picnic area. You can go back and forth between the two sections via a very short tunnel under the road.

From I-5, take the South Avenue exit and drive about eight miles east to the park. 530/527-4630.

PLACES TO STAY

Best Western Inn Corning: There's a big area to walk your pooch here. Rates are $65–90. Dogs are $10 per day. 2165 Solano Street 96021; 530/824-2468.

Holiday Inn Express: This is a quiet place, with a good continental breakfast and a relaxing steam room, sauna, pool, and whirlpool bath. Rates are $90–95. Dogs are $10 extra. 3350 Sunrise Way 96021; 530/824-2940.

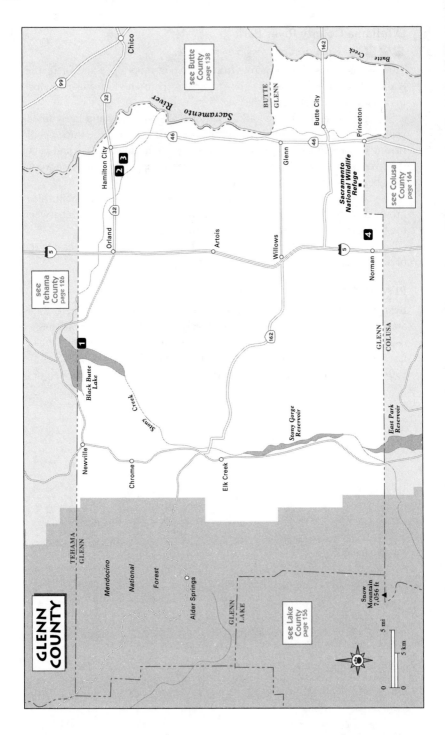

CHAPTER 10

Glenn County

There's not much in Glenn County that people or dogs would drive hundreds of miles to see. But several big wildlife areas can provide you and your dog with many memorable nature-watching hikes. Don't come here if you're seeking the bohemian café society life.

NATIONAL FORESTS

The *National Forests and Wilderness Areas* resource at the back of this book has important information and safety tips on visiting national forests with your dog and has more background on the Mendocino National Forest.

Mendocino National Forest
🐾🐾🐾🐾🐕

You'll find many rugged, attractive camping areas in the northwest corner of the county, where the land is about a mile above sea level.

PICK OF THE LITTER—GLENN COUNTY

WILDEST WALKS
Black Butte Lake, Orland (page 134)
Sacramento National Wildlife Refuge, Willows (page 136)

Orland

PARKS, BEACHES, AND RECREATION AREAS

◼ Black Butte Lake

🐾🐾🐾🐾 🐕 (See Glenn County map on page 132)

It's mighty secluded out here in the undeveloped parts of this big reservoir area run by the U.S. Army Corps of Engineers—so secluded, in fact, that you can hunt, if that's what you like to do. And if you hunt for birds, you can bring your dog along leash-free during the appropriate seasons.

Dogs don't have to be leashed in undeveloped areas, but they have to be under your control, even in the most remote acreage. The deer and rabbits appreciate it. If you're not going to be hunting, you might want to stay away from the very roughest land and enjoy any of three self-guided nature trails. You'll find nature at its best on these trails, without the brambles and burrs that take hours to pull out of your dog's coat. The Buckhorn Trail, an easy 1.5-hour walk, is at its freshest and most vibrant in the spring. You can pick up trail guides at the park headquarters or at the trailhead at the Buckhorn Campground.

The fishing at the lake is excellent in the spring and early summer. If some folks in your party aren't the angling types, they can hang out on land and picnic, visit the playground, or hike the nature trails. There are 40 miles of shoreline, and while dogs aren't allowed to swim at the Buckhorn Day-Use Beach, they can practice the dog paddle in most other places.

Camping with your dog is loads of fun, especially when the full moon slips over the lake and turns it a ghostly white. The 100 developed Class A camp-sites are $15; make reservations. Dogs must be leashed in camping areas. 877/444-6777.

Exit I-5 at the Highway 32/Black Butte Lake exit at Orland and drive west (the road will turn into Road 200) for about six miles. You'll come to a fork in the road. To get to the park headquarters, continue straight another couple of miles. That's also the way to the Buckhorn Recreation Area, with its nature trail and plenty of camping. To get to the other two nature trails, go left at the fork in the road, onto County Road 206. The Paul Thomas Trail is in the Orland Buttes Recreation Area. The Big Oak Trail is on County Road 200A, which continues from County Road 206. (Definitely bring a map.)

The most remote area is Grizzly Flat, which is barely accessible by car. Drive around the southernmost point of the lake on County Road 200A and you'll soon come to a rough gravel road, and then no road at all. You'll know you're there when you're still bouncing even though your car has stopped. For more info, you can write or call: Park Manager, 19225 Newville Road, Orland, CA 95963-8901; 530/865-4781.

PLACES TO STAY

Orland Inn: Rates are $52–72. Dogs are $5 extra for the length of their stay. 1052 South Street 95963; 530/865-7632; www.orlandinn.com.

Hamilton City

PARKS, BEACHES, AND RECREATION AREAS

🐾 Bidwell Sacramento River State Park

🐾🐾🐾 (See Glenn County map on page 132)

Sacramento River access at this 180-acre park is easy as one, two, wade. Fishing along the four miles of riverfront here is popular, but chances are you won't find too many people on the hiking trail. That's good news if you want to exercise your leashed dog before a day of angling together.

For a state park, the rules here are pretty laid-back—probably because until recently this was a state recreation area. At least for now, dogs can still go on unpaved trails. Be sure to check with a ranger before you set off on a hike with your dog, because this can change.

Dogs are now allowed at the gravel bar area of the Chico Creek Day-Use Area. You can also stop at the first section of park you come to, the Indian Fishery Day-Use Area, where there's a small picnic setting and an attractive wooded trail leading down to the river. It's usually very quiet here.

From Highway 32, go south on River Road. It's about 4.5 miles to the Indian Fishery Day-Use Area. 530/342-5185.

🐾 Mud Creek Levee

🐾🐾🐾🐾🦮 (See Glenn County map on page 132)

Mud Creek Levee doesn't sound like a place for dogs whose people need them to be well groomed. And indeed, it's not. But it's not always muddy, and dogs love a chance to come here. You and your dog can walk for miles and miles off

leash along a levee that follows Mud Creek. Your dog can even paddle around the creek, if she doesn't mind getting her feet wet. The creek eventually flows into the Sacramento River. It doesn't get much better than this for dogs, and it's a fun hike for people, too. Don't forget to pack towels in your car.

The levee is about 0.25 mile east of Bidwell-Sacramento River State Park, on West Sacramento Road. The rangers at the park know all about the walk and can answer your questions. 530/342-5185.

Willows

PARKS, BEACHES, AND RECREATION AREAS

4 Sacramento National Wildlife Refuge

🐾🐾🐾🐾🐾 (See Glenn County map on page 132)

Only hunting dogs are allowed off leash here, and only in specified areas during hunting season. But plain old average everyday pooches are allowed to explore along the 10,819 acres of marshy waterfowl territory, as long as they're leashed and stay on the walking trails.

More than 300 species of birds and mammals use the refuge throughout the year. It's a phenomenal place for wildlife observation. Bring your binoculars and a field guidebook, and you and your dog can learn all about the birds and the beasts here.

The refuge is open year-round. The entrance is about eight miles south of Willows. From Willows, take the Road 57 exit and drive south along the frontage road, Highway 99W (old Highway 99), about six miles to the entrance. 530/934-2801.

PLACES TO STAY

Motel 6: All you Saint Bernard owners, rejoice. The folks here have absolutely no rules at all about the size of the dogs who stay here. In this motel's previous incarnation as a Best Value Inn, the place even had an elephant as a guest once! (Although he didn't stay in a room.) Rates are $62–68. Dogs are $7 extra. Call ahead for the fee for elephants. 452 North Humboldt Avenue 95988; 530/934-7026.

Best Western Golden Pheasant: Springer spaniels and pointers drool at the name of this hotel. There's plenty of room on the hotel's grounds for your pooch to stretch her legs. Rates are $75–134. Dogs are $10 extra. 249 North Humboldt Avenue 95988; 530/934-4603 or 800/528-1234.

138

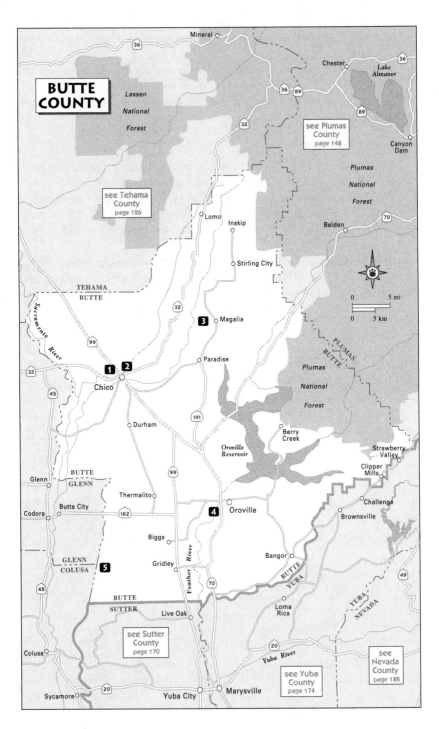

CHAPTER 11

Butte County

A couple of large off-leash parks, as well as the off-leash Plumas National Forest, make Butte County a fine place to take the four-footed beast in your life. So does Chico, the local dog-friendly university town.

NATIONAL FORESTS

The *National Forests and Wilderness Areas* resource at the back of this book has important information and safety tips on visiting national forests with your dog and has more background on the Plumas National Forest.

Plumas National Forest
😈😈😈😈🐾

A good-sized chunk of the northeast corner of the county is made up of this magical forest.

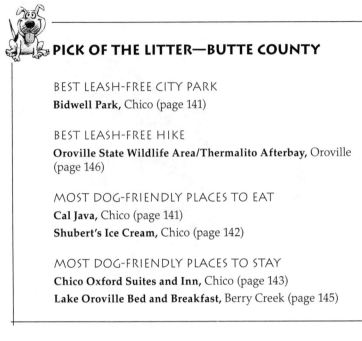

PICK OF THE LITTER—BUTTE COUNTY

BEST LEASH-FREE CITY PARK
Bidwell Park, Chico (page 141)

BEST LEASH-FREE HIKE
Oroville State Wildlife Area/Thermalito Afterbay, Oroville
(page 146)

MOST DOG-FRIENDLY PLACES TO EAT
Cal Java, Chico (page 141)
Shubert's Ice Cream, Chico (page 142)

MOST DOG-FRIENDLY PLACES TO STAY
Chico Oxford Suites and Inn, Chico (page 143)
Lake Oroville Bed and Breakfast, Berry Creek (page 145)

Chico

The laid-back atmosphere of California State University, Chico, helps make this community a relaxed, dog-friendly place. There's even a sweeping section of large Bidwell Park, which begins near campus, where dogs can run around off leash. And at press time, the city's first official dog park was in the works. Stay tuned for details in the next edition.

PARKS, BEACHES, AND RECREATION AREAS

1 Chico City Plaza
🐾🐾 (See Butte County map on page 138)

This is a sweet little park tucked in between municipal buildings in the center of town. Leashed dogs can hang out on the lawn area or near the benches. The park is in the heart of the old downtown area of Chico, so if you're going café-hopping or window-shopping with your pooch, you'll have a green spot for resting all your weary bones.

Concerts are held here during the summer, and as long as your dog doesn't disturb the peace, she's welcome to accompany you.

The park is on Main Street between East 4th and East 5th Streets. 530/896-7800.

2 Bidwell Park

🐾🐾🐾🐾🐕 (See Butte County map on page 138)

Some city brochures claim this is the third-largest municipal park in the United States. Others step the claim down a notch and call it the fourth-largest. Dogs don't care about such distinctions. They just know this 3,670-acre park is a happening place for dogs to trot around, do leg lifts, and get back to nature.

Most dogs we know prefer the rougher, untamed sections of Upper Park. And guess what? That's exactly where they're allowed to run around off leash. The entire huge area north of Upper Park Road is a leash-free swath of dog heaven. You can explore the terrain via miles of trails that run through here or just kick up your heels in a grassy field. Only the lakes are off-limits.

If you want your dog to be leashless in a more developed area, you'll have to get up early. The large section of park west of Manzanita Avenue permits leashless dogs from half an hour before sunrise through 8:30 A.M. You have to stay away from playgrounds, picnic areas, and swimming holes, but your dog can still have a great run here. There are plenty of trails and wooded sections that are well protected from traffic.

A fun addition to the park is a 37-acre parcel that was once a U.S. Forest Service tree nursery. A newly renovated half-mile trail, called the World of Trees Independence Trail, runs through the property. Dogs like the name, but they have to be leashed. In the 1890s, 16,000 trees from around the world were planted here to see which would do well in the climate. Many of those trees survived, and the trail has 20 "stops" where you can read about various trees. It's educational for humans and a good romp for dogs. It's even an excellent place for working companion and guide dogs, since the trail is accessible to the physically and visually challenged. Signs are in English and Braille. The trail is off Cedar Grove Road, near East 8th Street.

The park stretches 10 miles, from the university area all the way east to the rugged crags of Big Chico Creek Canyon. From Highway 99, exit at Highway 32 and head east to Bruce Road. Turn left on Bruce Road and drive north. The road will curve sharply to the right and become Chico Canyon Drive. Stay straight (Bruce Road becomes Manzanita Avenue) and drive on Manzanita about a half mile to Upper Park Road. Turn right and you'll be in the park. Watch for the dog area signs on your left. For the limited leash-free area, a good way to find a place with trails is to make a left turn from Manzanita Avenue onto Vallombrosa Avenue. Park on the road and walk in at any of several open areas in the wood fence. 530/896-7800.

PLACES TO EAT

Cal Java This micro-roastery not only serves up some smashing coffee but also welcomes dogs to its umbrella-topped patio tables. The friendly waitstaff

usually provides treats and water. (To dogs.) Thanks to Mercedes the Dog for writing to us to tell us about this place. It's at the Albertson Center, at 216 West East Avenue (really, W. East); 530/891-8935.

Shubert's Ice Cream: If your dog comes here at the right time, he'll be in for a snout-licking treat. Shubert's owners, Chuck and Kay Pullian, hate to see ice cream go to waste, and they love dogs, so when someone's ice cream falls off the cone and onto the floor here, the Pullians put it in a container, pop it in a special section of a freezer, and save it for the next dog customer. Same for ice cream that a customer licked but didn't like. These mishaps don't happen often, so you do have to be somewhat lucky to get one of these free dog delights. (Don't get the idea that this is a swell way to provide yourself with a free scoop of ice cream. A few bargain-hunting humans with little concern about prelicked ice cream already tried this trick, and the Pullians now require you to show a dog when you get the free ice cream.)

If you don't luck out, your dog can still enjoy Shubert's delicious ice cream at the outdoor benches here. "Lots of people buy their dog their own cone," says Kay. "Some people even buy one and share it with their dog. The person licks it, then their dog licks it, and they take turns. I don't know about that." Blech! I don't either, but Jake Dog says he's not so sure he wants to share a cone with me anyway.

Shubert's opened in 1938 and has been owned by the same family all these years, with the fourth generation now slinging the scoops. That alone makes it worth a visit. 178 East 7th Street; 530/342-7163.

PLACES TO STAY

Chico Oxford Suites and Inn: If you have to visit Chico, this is a terrific place to stay. Dogs love it here, but not just because of the clean and pleasant nature of the lodging, the refreshing pool, and the free breakfast and after-noon drinks and hors d'oeuvres. More likely it's because of the treats dogs get upon checking in, and because of the small outdoor swatch that's set aside for leashed dogs: It's only about 120 square feet, but it has a small tree, a fire hydrant, water, and poop bags. There's a fence, but it wouldn't keep even a baby mouse in: It's six inches high, just enough to set off the area. Another big draw: Burt, a manager here, has been described to me as "maybe the friendliest person on earth." Rates are $95–169. Dogs are $35 for the length of their stay. (There may be a preference for smaller dogs here, but if you have a good big dog, you probably won't have a problem.) 2035 Business Lane 95928; 530/899-9090 or 800/870-7848; www.oxfordsuites.com.

Holiday Inn of Chico: As long as your dog is "no bigger than a polar bear or a desk clerk," says the desk clerk, you and he (your dog, not the clerk) can cozy up together and watch satellite TV. Rates are $85–129. There's a $30 pooch fee per visit. 685 Manzanita Court 95926; 530/345-2491; www.holiday-inn.com.

Matador Motel: There are no bullfighters here, but an affable 140-pound bull mastiff named Chewy lives at the Matador with the motel's sweet man-ager, Irene. But Chewy is not behind the motel's name, either. The name probably comes from the 1930s mission revival style of the building. There are still wonderful painted tiles on the building facade and in the bathrooms. The rooms that allow dogs all have red-tile floors.

The Matador is nothing fancy, but it's a clean, interesting, inexpensive place to stay. What makes it an excellent place to bring a dog is Irene's love of dogs (if you have time, she'll gladly sit down and show you a photo album of her previous bull mastiff and listen to stories about your own dog), as well as the motel's proximity to decent dog-walking areas. It's on a frontage road where lots of other dogs stroll, and it's 10 minutes from Upper Bidwell Park.

A big tail-wag to Tapper the Traveling Dog and his chauffeur, Suzanne, for letting us know about the Matador. Rates are $42–66. 1934 Esplanade 95926; 530/342-7543.

Music Express Inn: This bed-and-breakfast inn consists of two 1970s ranch-style houses on four acres. The houses have nine rooms, all available to dogs and their people. All rooms have private baths, and most have pri-vate entrances and little fridges. Some have whirlpool baths. The inn gets its name from the children's music school on the premises. Rates (for rooms, not lessons) are $76–106. Dogs are $15 extra. 1145 El Monte Avenue 95928; 530/891-9833.

Safari Garden Motel: If you and your pooch stay here, you'll be only a mile from wonderful Bidwell Park. You'll also be staying in a smoking room. Dogs are $10 extra. Rates are $43–60. 2352 Esplanade 95926; 530/343-3201.

Magalia

PARKS, BEACHES, AND RECREATION AREAS

🐾 Upper Ridge Nature Preserve
🐾🐾🐾 (See Butte County map on page 138)

The soft dirt trails here are covered with pine needles, making this one of the cushiest parks around. Dogs enjoy winding along these nature trails while you stop at the numbered stations and learn all about this piece of pine and oak forest.

When you arrive at the preserve, go to the kiosk near the parking area, pick up a wonderfully detailed nature-trail map, and get your bearings. You can follow one of two mile-long trails. Both are lovely and will take you and your leashed pooch past streams, springs, and a whopping variety of trees. Dogs who like tranquility prefer the trail across the street from the parking area. It's a little more secluded.

The 80-acre park is leased from the Bureau of Land Management by a group of energetic, wilderness-loving retired men and women. They created the trails so people could learn about the natural environment here. Says Tom Rodgers, who helped get the group started in his mid-80s, "It's such a pleasure knowing that nature is a little better for what we've done, and that so are the people who nature helps educate."

From the Magalia area, follow Skyway to Ponderosa Way and turn left. Drive a little more than a mile and follow the signs to the preserve, which is just down the road on a gravel drive. The lessees have no phone number, but you can contact them by writing to Upper Ridge Wilderness Areas, P.O. Box 154, Magalia, CA 95945. The Bureau of Land Management may be able to help with questions. Call the office at 530/224-2100.

Paradise

As you enter town, a big wooden sign announces "PARADISE. To be all its name implies."

Sorry, Paradise. You failed the dog test. The Happy Hunting Grounds you are not. Dogs are banned at all municipal parks, and that gets their fur standing on end. (Besides, if you're going to have a sign like that, maybe you should put it in a place where the next thing you see is not a sign advertising duplexes, and then a Burger King, and then a tire shop and a wig store. It kind of takes the oomph out of a heavenly idea.)

Fortunately, the beautiful Upper Ridge Nature Preserve, just north of town in Magalia, has everything a leashed dog could want. And some of the scenery in the less-populated parts of Paradise really is beautiful. The town is surrounded by mountains, spectacular canyons, and tall pines.

PLACES TO STAY

Lantern Inn: This cozy 15-room motel is nestled in the pines, with a big vacant lot behind it. Dogs dig the location. There's even a great walking trail for leashed dogs and their people within a bone's throw. Water dogs quiver at the sight of the inn's attractive pool, but paws need to stay on terra firma. All the rooms have mini fridges and come with continental breakfast.

We found out about the Lantern Inn from Chewy, a 35-pound shepherd mix who had an extended stay here with his people. The motel's owners apparently went out of their way to make Chewy and his people feel at home. Rates are $65–75. Dogs are $10 extra. 5799 Wildwood Lane 95969; 530/877-5553.

Berry Creek

PLACES TO STAY

Lake Oroville Bed and Breakfast: This romantic, charming, cozy country inn is a treasure for pooches and their people. The six airy, antique-furnished bedrooms are so sweet that your dog's mouth might gape in awe that he's welcome here. Dogs are so welcome, in fact, that owners Ron and Cheryl Damberger provide tasty homemade dog biscuits wrapped in ribbon upon arrival of your pooch.

All the bedrooms come with private baths, and five have whirlpool tubs. Adding to the enchantment is an inviting parlor with a fireplace, a sunroom/reading room, a children's playroom, a warmly hued old-style billiard room, a wraparound porch, a barbecue area with great views, and a spectacular breakfast. Cheryl uses organically grown foods as much as possible and can cater to people with special diets, such as vegans or diabetics.

Dogs think all this is just keen, but most care much more about what's outside the big white doors. The inn is set on 40 acres of private property in the rolling hills overlooking Lake Oroville. Birds, butterflies, and wildflowers abound. Well-behaved pooches are even allowed to go leashless (which is a real blessing, especially considering that the nearby town of Oroville doesn't even allow dogs in its parks). But if your dog might chase deer or skunks, keep him leashed for everyone's sake.

Rates are $125–165. Dogs are $10 extra. 240 Sunday Drive 95916; 530/589-0700 or 800/455-5253; www.lakeorovillebedandbreakfast.com.

Oroville

PARKS, BEACHES, AND RECREATION AREAS

Dogs are not allowed in any Oroville city parks, nor in any Feather River Recreation and Park District parks. Oh boy, party on, dogs! The saving grace is the Oroville State Wildlife Area/Thermalito Afterbay.

4 Oroville State Wildlife Area/Thermalito Afterbay

😊😊😊😊 🐾 (See Butte County map on page 138)

Unlike at many other wildlife areas, if your dog isn't a hunting companion, she can still be off leash here as long as she's under voice control. There are about 5,000 acres of grasslands, marshlands, and riparian forests for you and your dog to explore. Where it's too wet to walk, take a levee.

Be sure to bring your binoculars if you enjoy bird-watching. More than 140 kinds of songbirds have been seen here. As you wander through the forests of cottonwoods, willows, and valley oaks, you may also spot other interesting fauna. If you're not certain your dog will stay close by, do the animals a favor and leash her.

From Highway 162, go south on Larkin Road (just east of the Oroville Airport). Follow the road a few miles to Vance Avenue and turn left. In 0.75 mile, you'll be at the wildlife area. Maps are usually available at the entry stations. 530/538-2236 or 916/358-2900.

PLACES TO STAY

Lake Oroville State Recreation Area There are more than 300 sites available. Campsites are $13–24. If you choose to stay on and around the paved roadways with your leashed pooch, you can enter the park for a $2 day-use fee. From Montgomery Street in the main part of Oroville, follow the green line down the road to the lake. For park information, call 530/538-2200 or 530/538-2219. For camping reservations, phone 800/444-7275.

Motel 6: Rates are $40–45 for the first adult, $6 for the second. 505 Montgomery Street 95965; 530/532-9400 or 800/466-8356.

Gridley

PARKS, BEACHES, AND RECREATION AREAS

5 Grey Lodge State Wildlife Area

😊😊😊😊 🐾 (See Butte County map on page 138)

Hunting dogs are the only ones who can be off leash in this spectacular wetland, and only during certain times of year. But this 8,400-acre wildlife area is a wonderful place to take well-behaved, leashed dogs the rest of the year.

Barkers and yappers should be left at home, especially during waterfowl season. Many of the birds have flown thousands of miles, and if they're disturbed, it could be detrimental to their health.

For most of the year, you can walk around on about 60 miles of hiking trails and levees. During waterfowl and nesting seasons, the hiking is very limited—to about four miles. But you don't have to walk a marathon to see amazing wildlife. Among some of the critters you may run into are sandhill cranes, hawks, river otters, egrets, waterfowl, deer, beavers, orioles, and black-shouldered kites.

From Highway 99, turn west on Sycamore Road and go six miles to Pennington Road. Turn left and continue three miles to the entrance on the right. The main parking lot is two miles to the west. The California Department of Fish and Game provides a handy little brochure with a decent trail map. You may be able to pick one up at the wildlife area, or order one by calling 530/846-7500.

PLACES TO STAY

Pacific Motel: "We take pains to make guests comfy, even dog guests," a friendly manager here told us. Nothing special here, just the basics conveniently situated on Highway 99. Three units at this small motel have kitchenettes, which is mighty handy given the dearth of dog-friendly eateries in the neighborhood. Rates are $55–68. Dogs are $5 extra. 1308 Highway 99 95948; 530/846-4580.

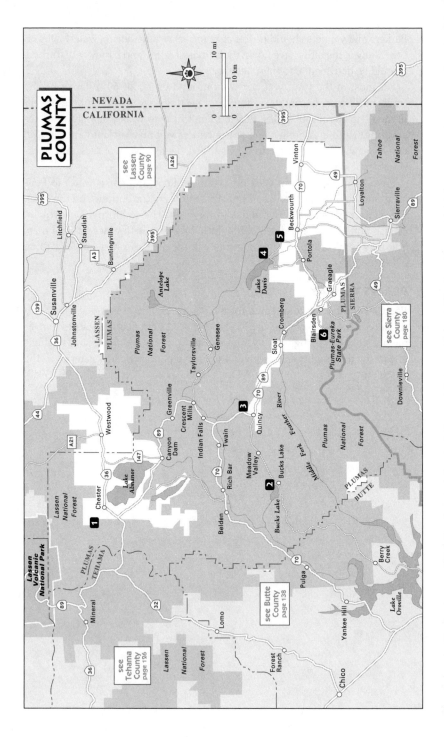

CHAPTER 12

Plumas County

Hidden between the ever-popular vacationlands of Shasta and Tahoe, Plumas County lives up to its publicity slogan, "California's Best Kept Secret." Even people in the next county asked, "Where's that?" when I told them where we'd just visited.

This county is 67 percent Plumas National Forest, which means there's natural beauty and off-leash dog heaven at almost every turn. It's Feather River Country here, with dozens of lakes and hundreds of miles of streams and rivers. That translates into endless good times hiking, fishing, swimming, wading, and cross-country skiing for you and your pooch.

Plumas is one of those counties so untouched by tourists that you can still find the best of rural life. And the country-style humor (watch for yellow road-side deer warning signs with the deer sporting big red noses) isn't bad either.

PICK OF THE LITTER—PLUMAS COUNTY

BEST LEASH-FREE HIKES
Plumas National Forest, (page 150)
Collins-Almanor Forest, Chester/Lake Almanor (page 150)
Bucks Lake, Bucks Lake (page 151)

MOST DOG-FRIENDLY PLACE TO STAY
Gray Eagle Lodge, Blairsden (page 154)

NATIONAL FORESTS

The *National Forests and Wilderness Areas* resource at the back of this book has important information and safety tips on visiting national forests with your dog and has more background on the national forests listed below.

Lassen National Forest
🐾🐾🐾🐾 🐕

Only a tiny part of this national forest falls in Plumas County. See the *National Forests and Wilderness Areas* resource for a complete description of this magnificent forest.

Plumas National Forest
🐾🐾🐾🐾 🐕

Chester/Lake Almanor
PARKS, BEACHES, AND RECREATION AREAS

🔲 Collins-Almanor Forest
🐾🐾🐾🐾 🐕 (See Plumas County map on page 148)

"Dogs love trees, and we love dogs," says a dog-loving forester here. That's why the Collins Pine Company rolls out the pine needle carpet for pooches in its 91,000-acre mixed conifer forest. Leashes can be shoved in your backpack, and you and your dog can hike unattached throughout this glorious working forest.

This is one of the most environmentally correct timber companies in the country, so you won't be seeing clear-cut patches that make the landscape look like a dog with mange. The family-owned company has been logging this forest since 1941, but with such a commitment to long-term sustainable forestry that it wins accolades even from environmentalists.

You'll love this place so much that you may want to spend a few days here. That means spending a few nights here. Many camping areas are available and the ones near streams are the best. There's no fee for any of them.

You'll want to stop in at the Chester office to get additional information about the best access routes for your level of hiking and to find out what areas of the forest are open. The office is at 500 Main Street. It's the one with the big green lawn (at least in the spring and summer). The phone number is 530/258-2111 or 530/258-4401.

PLACES TO STAY

Timber House: The folks here say they don't want Shetland ponies or Saint Bernards at this motel, but just about any other size pooch is OK. Rates are $79–100. Dogs are $20 extra per stay. Chester Park is nearby. 1st and Main streets, P.O. Box 1010, Chester, CA 96020; 530/258-2729.

Bucks Lake

PARKS, BEACHES, AND RECREATION AREAS

🐾 Bucks Lake
🐾🐾🐾🐾🐕 (See Plumas County map on page 148)

During warmer months, you and your dog can hike, swim, and fish till you drop. Campgrounds here are good places to drop, and the 49 undeveloped sites in Plumas National Forest are free. Twenty-nine of these sites are right along the lake's 14-mile shoreline, making for exquisite views. Sites are $18–20. They are first-come, first-served during certain times, but for reservations, phone 877/444-6777.

If trout fishing is your fancy, you'll have a hard time finding a much troutier lake. The lake is stocked annually with rainbow trout, so it's a great place to take young anglers and dogs who are entertained by fishing activity.

The lake is almost completely surrounded by Plumas National Forest, where dogs can run free in undeveloped areas. On the northeast side is the beautiful Bucks Lake Wilderness, where your obedient dog may also accompany you without a leash. From some of the peaks in this wilderness, you can see forever—or at least as far as Mt. Lassen.

During winter, the Bucks Lake area is a great spot for cross-country skiing. Dogs love going along for a little exercise, as long as the snow isn't too high.

From Highway 70 in Quincy, take Bucks Lake Road west about 12 miles to the lake. For information on campgrounds and the lake, call 530/283-5559; www.campwithus.com.

PLACES TO STAY

Bucks Lake Lodge: You and your pooch can stay at any of a dozen rustic housekeeping cabins at this lakeside resort. There's plenty of wilderness and open space around for you and your dog to explore on leash. The lodge has a restaurant, bar, and small store, so you can stay here for a while and never have to get into your car.

The road to the lodge is closed in winter, so plan ahead. If you really want to stay here in the cold months, you have to use a snowmobile or cross-country skis. (And unless your dog is bipedal, the ski option just isn't going to cut it.) Rates are $99–115. (The $115 cabins sleep up to 10 people. You can really get your money's worth with these if you're visiting with a big happy group.) Dogs are $10 extra. 16525 Bucks Lake Road, P.O. Box 236, Quincy, CA 95791; 530/283-2262; www.buckslakelodge.com.

Quincy

This is a Main Street community with restored and preserved buildings dating to the town's roots in the mid-1800s. If you whiz through town heading west, you'll barely get a glimpse of the downtown area, which is home to a couple of good, dog-friendly restaurants. Main Street goes only east and it's worth a gander.

PARKS, BEACHES, AND RECREATION AREAS

🐾 Gansner Park

🐾🐾🐾 (See Plumas County map on page 148)

Dogs enjoy bouncing around this long and luscious park. They're supposed to bounce around on leash, but if your dog happens to escape from your grasp, there's little danger: The park is almost entirely fenced. Generally, where there aren't fences, trees and brush are so thick that dogs would have a difficult time getting out. The grass is very green, the pines are very large, and the park generally is very uninhabited. You can picnic, barbecue, play tennis, or watch the kids at the park's small playground.

From Highway 70/89 just north of town, turn east on Gansner Park Road (there will be signs for the park). 530/283-6299.

PLACES TO EAT

Stoney's Country Burger: "Dogs? They're my favorite animals," says the kindly owner of this burger café. Try the Stoney burger. You'll love it, and if you don't, your dog will. 11 Lindan Avenue; 530/283-3911.

Portola

This old town is right on the Middle Fork Feather River, which is very accessible from many parts of town. Just bring your rod, reel, hiking shoes, and dog, and you can create a canine's dream day. Sadly, the wonderful Portola Railroad Museum no longer allows dogs on its trains.

PARKS, BEACHES, AND RECREATION AREAS

4 Lake Davis

🐾🐾🐾 🐕 (See Plumas County map on page 148)

This is the largest of the three Upper Feather River lakes, with 32 miles of shoreline, most of it in Plumas National Forest. The hiking right at the lake is limited, but you can manage to get in some exercise on trails and dirt roads that extend into the national forest from the lake area.

It's the perfect spot if you're vacationing with an avid angler. The hiking is excellent and off leash once you're out of the campgrounds and adjacent state game refuge and into the undeveloped areas of the Plumas National Forest. And there's plenty of nature to watch: Waterfowl, bald eagles, and bats are easy to see at various times of year.

Leashed dogs can choose from a total of 165 campsites. About half are available on a first-come, first-served basis. You'll need a reservation for the rest. Call 877/444-6777 to reserve a site. Sites are $18, except for an undeveloped overflow area, which is free. From Highway 70, take Grizzly Road or Lake Davis Road about seven miles north to the lake. For information on Lake Davis or to get maps of the forest near the other two Upper Feather River lakes, call 530/836-2575.

5 Portola City Park

🐾🐾🐾 🐕 (See Plumas County map on page 148)

Much more space is devoted to human activities than dog activities here, but there's still a decent little field, some trees, and a gazebo that leashed dogs seem to enjoy. The great news is that if your dog is under voice control, he can be leash-free here, as long as you keep him from the more developed spots. It's not far from the street, so think twice before you unleash. Either way, this is a nice little place to take a break with your dog.

From Highway 70, go south on South Gulling Street. The park will be on your left, across from City Hall, shortly after you cross over the bridge. 530/832-4216.

PLACES TO STAY

Sleepy Pines Motel: The owners of this homey motel have their own dog, and they'll often allow dogs as guests, but they want "nothing huge or dangerous." The lodging is very close to the Feather River. The owners can point you to the best fishing spots. Rates are $64–150. Dogs are $2 extra. (That's the lowest dog fee we've come across!) 74631 Highway 70 96122; 530/832-4291; www. sleepypines.com.

Blairsden

PLACES TO STAY

Gray Eagle Lodge: Many regulars say this is pooch paradise and human heaven. Glowing elysian comparisons are only natural when you stay at this extraordinary Sierra lodge, set in the middle of some of the best national forest land in the state. Reader Cynthia Harris says she and her then-new hubby brought their two basset hounds, Otis and Monroe, along on their honeymoon and had the time of their lives. "Our cabin had a deck that descended down to a stream, which was ideal for swimming bassets!" she wrote. Joe Dog (a.k.a. Mr. Water Is to Drink, Not to Swim In) was curious about how they wring all that water from their hush-puppy ears. (He was just jealous that they could float and he couldn't.)

A dozen Plumas National Forest trailheads start at the property. Well-behaved pooches can go leash-free on the trails, which lead to meadows, peaceful ponds, streams, and 40 alpine lakes where the fishing can be so good that the angler in you may never want to leave. If you catch a fish and clean it, the chef here will cook it for your breakfast. But the brochure admonishes, "Keep in mind, Chef's largest frying pan is ONLY 24 inches wide!" Those guests who tell a good fish story will be rewarded with a glass of champagne, so if you err on the side of exaggeration, this is your kind of place.

You can really get away from it all at the cozy TV- and phone-free wood cabins. But don't leave your taste buds behind, because the gourmet meals here (full breakfast and a four-course dinner are included in the room price) are wonderful. Picnic lunches are available for an additional charge. The ever-changing dinner menu includes terrific chicken, meat, fish, and vegetarian dishes, plus a notched-up comfort-food selection such as veal meatloaf with caramelized onion sauce.

Dogs can't go in the restaurant, but they can enjoy munching on their own delectable taste treats: The staff here provides pooch guests gourmet dog biscuits upon arrival! The owners love dogs and have their own friendly border collies, whom you'll likely meet during your stay.

After a long day of exploring and eating, relax by the big fireplace in the main lodge. (Dogs can no longer curl up beside that hearth. It's a health-code thing.) The lodge is open May–October. Rates are $235–265 per couple and include the sumptuous meals. Dogs are $25 extra. 5000 Gold Lake Road 96103; 530/836-2511 or 800/635-8778; www.grayeaglelodge.com.

Graeagle

PARKS, BEACHES, AND RECREATION AREAS

❻ Plumas-Eureka State Park

🐾🐾🐾🐾 (See Plumas County map on page 148)

Your dog isn't going to believe his pointy ears when you tell him the following news. (Before you tell him, make sure he's sitting.) Here it is: Dogs are actually allowed on a trail in this park. State parks pretty much ban pooches from trails, but because this is such a short trail and it leads to a very long and wonderful national forest trail, it's A-OK.

Dogs have to be leashed on the state park end of the trail. But it may be a wise idea to keep your dog leashed when you hit national forest land—even though leashes aren't mandatory—since there are bears in dem dar hills. We know this firsthand, because on our camping honeymoon, Mr. Bear visited our secluded campsite at Rock Lake. He hung out from midnight until about 3 A.M., when he probably realized he wasn't going to enjoy our dehydrated camping food any more than we did.

Back to state park grounds: Dogs are very limited in their activities in the historic 5,000-acre park surrounding the old mining town of Johnsville. But one thing they can do is camp with you at one of the 67 sites here. The fee is $20 a night. The campground can get crowded, so it's best to reserve during summer months. Phone 877/444-7275.

If you want to skip the more heavily used part of the park and get right to the Jameson Creek Trail (which leads to several isolated, pristine lakes), look for a sign for the trail on the left, about 0.12 mile before the park entrance. Follow the dirt road to the trailhead. You can also pick up the trail from the main part of the park. Just ask a ranger where it starts.

From Highway 89, take County Road A14 west a few miles to the park. 530/836-2380.

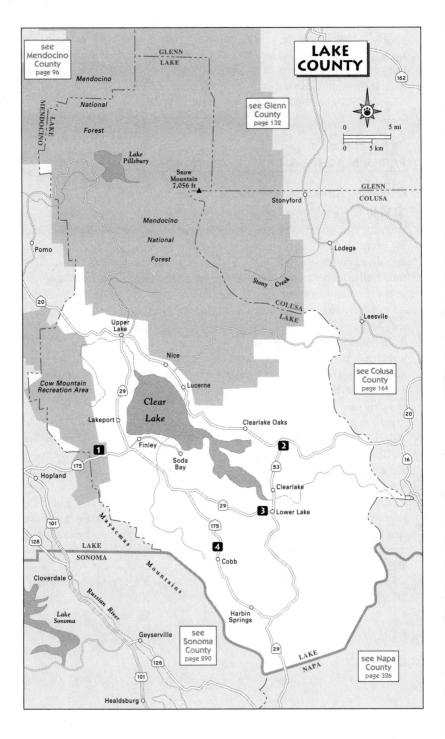

CHAPTER 13

Lake County

This is a county with an attitude about dogs—a bad attitude, with a few exceptions. Dogs aren't allowed in any county parks. Since parks in the small towns are county parks, that's a double dose of bad news. The major cities (Clearlake and Lakeport) also ban dogs from their parks, and dogs aren't permitted at public beaches around Clear Lake.

Signs throughout the county shout that dogs must be licensed and leashed and will be shot if they're caught molesting farm critters. Even the trash barrels in county parks are painted with big white "No Dogs" warnings. Looks as if you can't even walk your dog in a garbage can around here.

Welcome to Lake County, a major disappointment for our fine four-legged friends. The county slogan that occasionally pops up here is "Lake County: Dare to Explore." But that's a cruel joke for the canines in our midst. If they dare to explore too much, they're going to get socked with a big fine. And guess who has to pay?

What's a dog to do? She could start by thanking the Big Dog in the Sky for

PICK OF THE LITTER—LAKE COUNTY

BEST LEASH-FREE HIKES
Cache Creek Recreation Area, Clearlake Oaks (page 160)
Boggs Mountain Demonstration State Forest,
Cobb Mountain (page 162)

MOST DOG-FRIENDLY PLACES TO STAY
Edgewater Resort, Kelseyville (page 160)
20 Oaks Resort, Clearlake Oaks (page 161)

NICEST PLACE TO STAY
Rocky Point Cottages, Lakeport (page 159)

the national forests, the Bureau of Land Management, the California Department of Forestry, and (I never thought I'd say this) the state park system. If not for these, dogs would have to sneak around everywhere.

If your dog wants to hang out near the lake, you'll have to stay in one of the private resorts that has lakeside access. Something in the county's favor is that more lodgings here are dog friendly than in the past, and we've even sniffed out a beautiful one that's more upscale than anything we've seen around these parts. (See *Rocky Point Cottages,* in Lakeport.)

NATIONAL FORESTS

The *National Forests and Wilderness Areas* resource at the back of this book has important information and safety tips on visiting national forests with your dog and has more background on the Mendocino National Forest.

Mendocino National Forest
🐾🐾🐾🐾🐕

A huge section of this forest is in Lake County. It's a relief to dogs who aren't even permitted to set paw in county parks.

Lakeport

PARKS, BEACHES, AND RECREATION AREAS

1 Cow Mountain Recreation Area
🐾🐾🐾🐾🐕 (See Lake County map on page 156)

This is a great place to visit with your dog, who can run leash-free in many areas. The main entrance is on the other side of the county border, near Ukiah. Enter at Younce Road (Old Toll Road) from Lake County. (See the *Ukiah* section of the *Mendocino County* chapter for more details on this recreation area.)

PLACES TO EAT

Park Place: The fresh-made pasta here is delightful. Wash it down with your favorite local wine while you and your dog relax at the outdoor tables. The restaurant is next to a lakeside park, but since dogs aren't permitted at the park, all they can do is watch the ducks go by. 50 3rd Street; 707/263-0444.

PLACES TO STAY

Chalet Motel: This is your basic, lakeside, old-style motel. Jake and I don't see much chalet-ish about it. Rooms have a full, if small, kitchen. Rates are $79, and dogs are $20 extra. 2802 Lakeshore Boulevard 95453; 707/262-0999; www.chalet-motel.com.

Rocky Point Cottages: If you think you can't come to Clear Lake and stay in well-appointed, fairly upscale lodgings, think again. We bring you Rocky Point Cottages, dubbed by the owners as "the new spirit of Clear Lake." The lodgings consist of five lovely, tastefully furnished, cozy, airy cottages on a fenced lakefront property surrounded by big sycamores and oaks. The cottages, built in the 1920s, have been completely refurbished right down to impeccable wood floors. All have a deck or patio with a gas barbecue, fully equipped kitchens, lake views, and a selection of books and videos. Four feature fireplaces. And best of all, all are dog friendly.

Three cottages are three bedrooms and two baths. (They call these cottages?) Two (duplex style) are one-bedroom and one-bath affairs, which suits most dogs just fine. The friendly owners will accommodate requests to make your visit extra special, from preparing a picnic lunch for a day out, or a gourmet dinner.

Rates are $115–350. Each cottage has a one-time cleaning fee of $60–80, dog or no dog. So bring the dog and get your money's worth! 3884 Lakeshore Boulevard 95453; 707/263-5901; www.rockypointcottages.com.

Kelseyville

Kelseyville calls itself "a friendly little country town." (It also calls itself "pear capital of the world.") The Main Street area does, indeed, look a little like something out of *The Andy Griffith Show*—at least if you don't have your glasses on. Your happy hound will fit right in here.

PLACES TO STAY

Creekside Lodge: Rates are $50–110. Dogs are $10 extra, and you have to pay a $50 deposit (the kind you get back) and sign a waiver taking responsibility for dog damage. In addition, great big dogs aren't allowed. 7990 Highway 29 95451; 707/279-9258 or 800/279-1380; www.kitscorner.com.

Edgewater Resort: The resort's friendly and kindly resort owners, Sandra West and Lora Tell, adore dogs. They'll greet your dog with loving hugs and a dog biscuit if they're here when you check in. You and poochface can stay in a cabin by the lake or camp in your tent or RV. The cabins aren't the Taj Mahal, but they have real wood paneling and kitchens, and they're surrounded by lawn and big old trees. You can fish off a 230-foot fishing pier here or swim at the beach (humans can swim at the pool). Keep in mind that at the end of summer, heat and low water levels can lead to algae growth, which can turn the still water green.

Rates at the resort are $30–40 for tent or RV camping and $140–400 for a cabin. Dogs are $2.50 extra in tents or RVs, and $10 extra in the cabins. 6420 Soda Bay Road 95451; 707/279-0208 or 800/396-6224; www.edgewaterresort.net.

Clearlake Oaks

PARKS, BEACHES, AND RECREATION AREAS

🐾 Cache Creek Recreation Area
🐾🐾🐾🐾 ✖ (See Lake County map on page 156)

This 70,000-acre Bureau of Land Management area is a very welcome sight for dogs, who are banned from most parks in the county. Not only can they explore this huge and wild area, they can do so off leash, as long as they're obedient sorts. If you can't trust your dog not to wander away and get eaten, or not to wander away and eat another animal, then please keep him leashed.

Bring your binoculars, because you'll need them. You may see bald eagles, blue herons, tule elk, or even a black bear. A seven-mile trail (steep at times) provides you and the dog in your life with ample room to start an adventure. We like to visit in the spring, when the wildflowers open their blazing petals to a new year.

You can also camp here in primitive, fee-free sites. You'll need to get a campfire permit from any California Department of Forestry, Bureau of Land Management, or U.S. Forest Service office. The entrance to this patch of dog heaven is about eight miles east of town, on the south side of Highway 20. You'll see the signs. 707/468-4000.

PLACES TO STAY

Lake Haven Motel: This motel on a sheltered canal is owned by folks who love dogs and welcome leashed pooches (except rotties and pit bulls) to sniff out the surrounding area. Rates are $60–80. Dogs are $5 extra. 100 Short Street 95423; 707/998-3908 or 800/998-0106.

20 Oaks Resort: Kim and Steve, who own this one-acre property with four cottages and a few RV and camping sites, enjoy dog visitors. In fact, they like them so much that they provide them with treats, bowls, and bedsheets/blankets. Being the proud parents of two Westies, they know what makes a dog comfortable.

The cottages are duplex-style, and all have full kitchens. They're nothing fancy, but they make for a pleasant stay by the lake. And Kim and Steve are doing upgrades, both around the property and to the cottages themselves. You even get free Wi-Fi here. The lake is across the road, but you'll have access to the property's pier and dock, and to a good doggy swimming hole.

Cottages are $75–95. Tent camping amidst the oaks is $20, and you can overnight with your RV for $35. 10503 East Highway 20 95423; 707/998-3012; www.20oakscottages.com.

Lower Lake

PARKS, BEACHES, AND RECREATION AREAS

❸ Anderson Marsh State Historic Park

😺 😺 (See Lake County map on page 156)

For humans without dogs, this 870-acre park is a terrific adventure. Several miles of trails lead to remote bird-watching areas far from any roads.

But if you're lucky enough to be traveling with a dog, this park is just a leg-stretching zone. Dogs are not permitted on trails, but they're allowed at the picnic area at the ranch house. This is a pleasant place to plop down for a while. They're also permitted in the open fields behind the old Anderson barn. Since only the area adjacent to the barn is mowed, there's not much room to roam. The tall grass beyond the lawn can be full of ticks. At least your leashed dog will get to sniff an old outhouse or sit patiently outside the portable toilet while you explore its inner realms.

The park is open Wednesday–Sunday. The fee is $2 per car. The ranger is usually in the form of an iron post with a box on it, so if you'll be here only a few minutes, you might not need to pay. But real human rangers can come out of the woodwork (and there's quite a lot of wood around the barn), so be careful.

From Highway 53 just north of Lower Lake, turn west at Anderson Ranch Parkway and make an immediate right into the park. 707/994-0688 or 707/279-2267.

Cobb Mountain

PARKS, BEACHES, AND RECREATION AREAS

❹ Boggs Mountain Demonstration State Forest

😺 😺 😺 😺 🐾 (See Lake County map on page 156)

You and your blissfully leash-free dog can hike for days in a 3,500-acre forestry experiment. The forest is being studied as an example of how a forest that was nearly stripped can be brought back and managed for continuous forest production, public recreation, wildlife habitat, and a watershed.

It's working. You'll hike on miles of trails that wander through mixed conifer forests and grasslands. As long as your dog is obedient, you can let her off leash. But if she can't be trusted around deer and other critters of the woods, keep her leashed.

If your dog likes what she sees, she'll be happy to know she can go camping with you here! The forest has two campgrounds, with a total of 20 sites. The price? Free! It's fairly primitive camping, but there are tables, fire rings, and one outhouse per campground.

From Highway 175 about a mile north of Cobb Mountain, watch for a blue-and-white sign for the state fire station. At the first intersection past it, go east for about a quarter of a mile to the park's entrance. 707/928-4378.

PLACES TO STAY

Yogi Bear's Jellystone Park at Cobb Mountain: You and your little Boo-Boo can stay in your own tent or RV, or try one of the resort's tepees for a unique experience. It won't be a deep wilderness experience (tent sites have their own sink, water, and electricity), but there's a pond with rental kayaks and canoes, and enough room to stretch your paws. Rates are $20–25. If you like having a hard roof over your head, you can rent a simple cabin for $44–49. 14417 Bottle Rock Road, P.O. Box 49 95426; 707/928-4322 or 800/307-CAMP (800/307-2267).

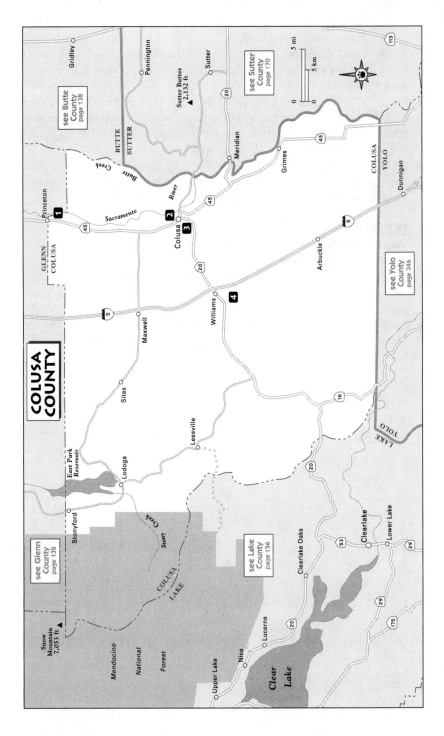

CHAPTER 14

Colusa County

This is a county of refuge. Actually, it's a county of a few refuges. Birds see the refuges on their little bird maps and flock here by the millions. It's an amazing sight to see with your leashed pooch during the winter.

Maxwell

PARKS, BEACHES, AND RECREATION AREAS

The Delevan National Wildlife Refuge is not open to the public, but the Sacramento National Wildlife Refuge is quite a special place to visit with a dog.

🟦 Sacramento National Wildlife Refuge

🐾🐾🐾🐾 🐕 (See Colusa County map on page 164)

The southern end of this magnificent refuge extends into northern Colusa County. (See *Willows* in the *Glenn County* chapter for an in-depth description.)

PICK OF THE LITTER—COLUSA COUNTY

WILDEST WALKS
Colusa-Sacramento River State Recreation Area, Colusa
(page 166)

BEST PLACE TO EAT
Granzella's, Williams (page 167)

Colusa

PARKS, BEACHES, AND RECREATION AREAS

2 Colusa-Sacramento River State Recreation Area

🐾🐾🐾 (See Colusa County map on page 164)

Primitive trails and mucky riverbeds are begging to be explored here. Dogs adore this place, but they're supposed to be leashed.

Our favorite trail starts right next to the boat-launch area. If you ignore some of the smaller trails that branch off it, the main trail will take you down to the sandy/muddy "beach" area along the Sacramento River. Some folks like to fish here, so if you want to get away, just head left and walk down the riverbed. You'll likely see dozens of beasty footprints from the night's activities. Dogs love to sniff at raccoon, deer, and bird prints.

The day-use fee is $6. It costs $12–15 to camp at one of the 14 sites. Campsite reservations are accepted from the middle of April through September. Highway 20 will take you directly to the park. Coming from I-5, Highway 20 changes its name to 10th Street once you enter Colusa. Follow 10th Street through town and into the park. For camping reservations, call ParkNet at 800/444-7275. For park information, call 530/458-4927.

3 Memorial Park

🐾🐾🐾 (See Colusa County map on page 164)

The park is in a really beautiful old section of town. It fits in well here, with graceful palms, stately trees, ultragreen grass, and plenty of places to sit. It's only a square block in area, but leashed dogs get plenty of fulfillment. Humans also enjoy the posh and relaxing surroundings.

The park is between Market and Jay streets and 9th and 10th streets. 530/458-5622.

Williams

Guys who wear cowboy hats for real hang out in Williams. So do oodles of people traveling on I-5. The latter folks don't stop because of any tourist attraction. They stop for gas and food. Fortunately, this town has much more ambience than most pit stops on the interstate.

PARKS, BEACHES, AND RECREATION AREAS

🛝 City Park

🐾 (See Colusa County map on page 164)

If you're stopping in Williams for gas, you may as well come here and give your pooch a quick walk. A few trees and a bit of grass will be welcome sights to the dog in your life, and a tiny playground seems to please any tots tagging along.

Exit I-5 at the main Williams exit, drive west to 9th Street, and turn left. The park will be on your left in a couple of blocks. 530/473-5389.

PLACES TO EAT

Granzella's: The food here is mahhvelous. Joe always drooled when he saw

anyone eating the special hot turkey and gravy sandwich. Best of all, the restaurant folks love dogs as much as dogs love the restaurant. "We're real animal lovers," says owner Linda Granzella. "We'll even go around the restaurant and find people who left their dogs in the cars with the windows rolled up." They're even happy to give your dog water. Eat at two picnic tables on the porch. 451 6th Street; 530/473-5583.

PLACES TO STAY

Comfort Inn: Rates are $70–80, and that includes a continental breakfast. Dogs are $5 extra. 400 C Street 95987; 530/473-2381 or 800/228-5150.

Stage Stop Motel: There's a fridge in every room here. It's not quite like a chicken in every pot, but it's not bad. The room rate is $45. Dogs are $5 extra. 330 7th Street 95987; 530/473-2281.

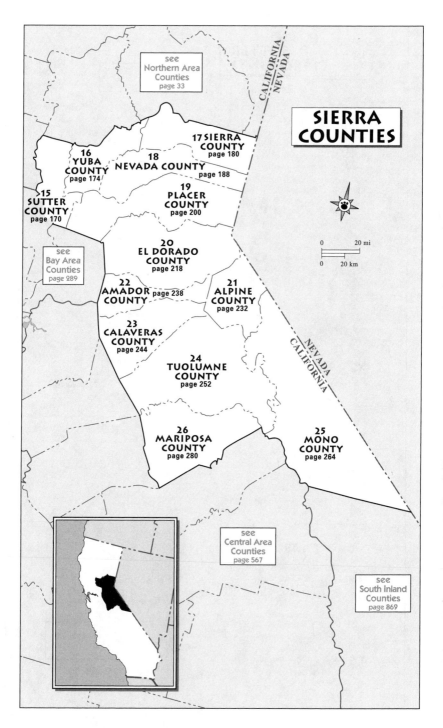

see
Northern Area
Counties
page 33

CALIFORNIA
NEVADA

SIERRA COUNTIES

17 SIERRA
COUNTY
page 180

16
YUBA
COUNTY
page 174

18
NEVADA COUNTY
page 188

15
SUTTER
COUNTY
page 170

19
PLACER
COUNTY
page 200

0   20 mi
0   20 km

see
Bay Area
Counties
page 289

20
EL DORADO
COUNTY
page 218

22
AMADOR page 238
COUNTY

21
ALPINE
COUNTY
page 232

23
CALAVERAS
COUNTY
page 244

NEVADA
CALIFORNIA

24
TUOLUMNE
COUNTY
page 252

26
MARIPOSA
COUNTY
page 280

25
MONO
COUNTY
page 264

see
Central Area
Counties
page 567

see
South Inland
Counties
page 869

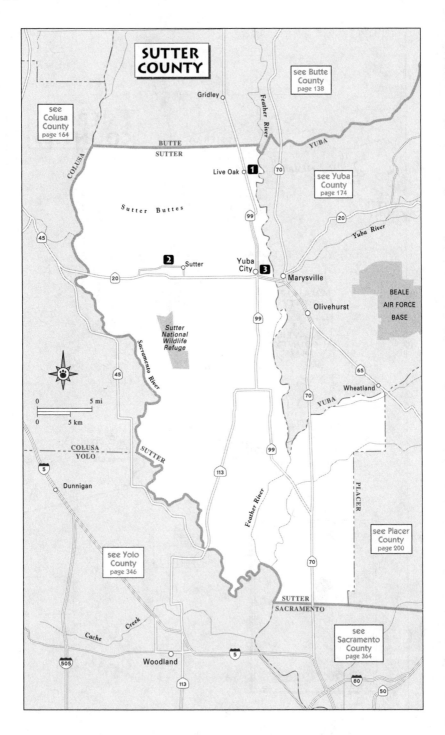

SUTTER COUNTY

see Butte County page 138

see Colusa County page 164

Gridley

Feather River

BUTTE
SUTTER

YUBA

Live Oak **1** 70

see Yuba County page 174

Sutter Buttes

99

20

45

Yuba River

2 Sutter

Yuba City **3** Marysville

20

BEALE AIR FORCE BASE

Olivehurst

Sutter National Wildlife Refuge

99

Sacramento River

45

65

Wheatland

70

YUBA

0   5 mi
0   5 km

COLUSA
YOLO

SUTTER

5

113

99

Dunnigan

PLACER

see Placer County page 200

see Yolo County page 346

Feather River

70

SUTTER
SACRAMENTO

Creek

Cache

505

Woodland

5

see Sacramento County page 364

113

80

50

CHAPTER 15

Sutter County

There's not much to do here with a dog, but where there's a full bladder, there's a way.

Live Oak

PARKS, BEACHES, AND RECREATION AREAS

🔢 Live Oak Recreation Park

🐾🐾🐾 (See Sutter County map on page 170)

This park doesn't have any big trails, but you and your leashed dog can hike around the dirt roads that wind through the park or just walk around the grassy fields. Feather River fans will appreciate the decent boat launch. People with pooches like to picnic under the oaks and willows before turning in for the night at the county's only campground. Small trails lead to the river, but it's a little rough at times and swimming is not allowed.

PICK OF THE LITTER—SUTTER COUNTY

BEST PARK
Live Oak Recreation Park, Live Oak (page 171)

The day-use fee is $5 per car. Camping at one of the 25 sites is $10 per car. You might be able to drive in and get a site, but if you don't want to take a chance that they'll all be gone, call 530/695-3823 for reservations. Exit Highway 99 at Pennington Road and drive east about a mile to the end of the road, where you'll find the park. 530/695-3823.

Sutter

PARKS, BEACHES, AND RECREATION AREAS

② Vera Carroll Park
☙ (See Sutter County map on page 170)

The huge orchard across from this tiny park may be tempting to visit with your dog, but if you don't own it or work on it, you can't set foot on it. The park has a fenced-in playing field, a few shaded picnic tables, and a swimming pool. As long as your dog is leashed and stays out of the pool, he'll be welcome here.

From Highway 20, go north on Acacia Avenue for about two miles. The park will be on your right, at College Avenue. It's run by the Sutter Youth Organization. 530/673-2495.

Yuba City

PARKS, BEACHES, AND RECREATION AREAS

"Our parks are for the people, not for the animals. We'd rather not be put in that book," a parks department staffer told me. But since dogs are permitted at all city parks on an eight-foot leash, we thought it would be nice for dogs to know their rights.

🖪 Sam Brannan Park

🐾🐾 (See Sutter County map on page 170)

The back area of this park is nicely fenced, so if your leashed dog makes a break for it, she'll be relatively safe. Otherwise, peruse the big grassy area, let your dog sniff the trees, or have a relaxing picnic at the many tables here.

From Highway 99, turn east on Bridge Street, drive a few blocks, and go left on Gray Avenue. The park is on your left in a few more blocks. 530/822-4626.

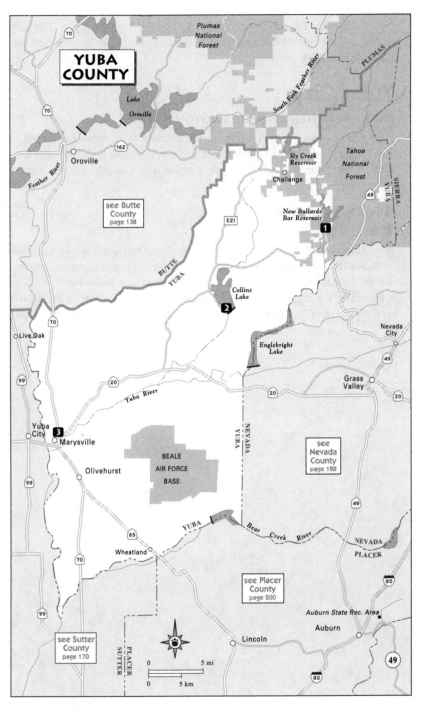

YUBA COUNTY

Plumas National Forest

South Fork Feather River

PLUMAS

Lake Oroville

162

Oroville

Feather River

see Butte County
page 138

Sly Creek Reservoir

Challenge

Tahoe National Forest

SIERRA
YUBA

49

New Bullards Bar Reservoir

1

E21

BUTTE
YUBA

Collins Lake

2

Englebright Lake

Nevada City

49

70

Live Oak

99

20

Yuba River

Grass Valley

20

NEVADA
YUBA

Yuba City

3

Marysville

Olivehurst

BEALE AIR FORCE BASE

see Nevada County
page 188

49

99

65

YUBA

Bear Creek River

NEVADA
PLACER

80

Wheatland

70

see Placer County
page 200

Auburn State Rec. Area

Auburn

99

see Sutter County
page 170

PLACER
SUTTER

Lincoln

0   5 mi

0   5 km

80

49

CHAPTER 16

Yuba County

If you're just passing through with a dog, you're doing the right thing. With the exception of a small piece of national forest land, Yuba County isn't exactly dog heaven. Besides, if you want to spend the night, you'll have to either camp, knock on a friend's door, or find the one lodging in the entire county where dogs are allowed.

NATIONAL FORESTS

The *National Forests and Wilderness Areas* resource at the back of this book has important information and safety tips on visiting national forests with your dog and has more background on the Tahoe National Forest.

Tahoe National Forest
🐾🐾🐾🐾🐕

A tiny section of this forest creeps into the eastern edge of Yuba County.

PICK OF THE LITTER—YUBA COUNTY

BEST SWIMMING HOLES
Bullard's Bar Reservoir, Dobbins (page 176)
Collins Lake, Oregon House (page 177)

Dobbins

PARKS, BEACHES, AND RECREATION AREAS

1 Bullard's Bar Reservoir

😈😈😈😈 🐕 (See Yuba County map on page 174)

This 16-mile-long crystal-clear lake is heaven to anglers and paradise to pooches. "You betcha, the fishing's the best and we like well-behaved dogs a lot," says a manager of the Emerald Cove Resort and Marina, the full-service concession at the southern tip of the lake.

While dogs must be leashed in campgrounds, developed areas, and at the Emerald Cove facilities, they're permitted to be leash-free in much of the land

DIVERSION

Make Like Cap'n Crunch: So, you're visiting **Bullard's Bar Reservoir** near Dobbins and you're overcome with the urge to hang out at the helm of a boat? If the closest thing you have to a water vehicle is your set of water wings, fret not. You're in luck: **Emerald Cove Resort and Marina** rents just about any kind of lake boat you and your dog may desire. You can rent patio boats, houseboats, pontoon boats, paddleboats, and even fishing boats for competitive prices. Call for a price list and brochure. When making a reservation, be sure to say you're bringing a pooch, because there are certain upholstered boats that need to stay dog-free. 530/692-3200; www.bullardsbar.com.

surrounding the eastern part of the lake. That's because the land is part of the mighty dog-friendly Tahoe National Forest. The Sierra foothills here are full of pine, manzanita, and oak. This makes boy dogs happy and also makes for some good-looking scenery.

The lake has 60 miles of shoreline and contains such goodies as black bass, kokanee salmon, and rainbow trout. If you've got the urge to wet a line, Bullard's Bar is a wise choice. If you need a boat to tote you around, Emerald Cove rents all kinds of fun water vehicles.

Camping is available at five main campgrounds, and there's even some shoreline camping. Sites are $22. A $7.50 reservation fee may be charged.

From Highway 20 about 12 miles east of Marysville, turn north on Marysville Road/County Road E21. Drive north about 15 miles on the narrow, winding road to Bullard's Bar Reservoir. When you pass by the tiny town of Dobbins (the closest town to the main resort area), you and your potentially carsick passengers will be glad to know you've got less than a mile to go. 530/692-3200; www.bullardsbar.com.

Oregon House

PARKS, BEACHES, AND RECREATION AREAS

2 Collins Lake

🐾🐾🐾🐾🐕 (See Yuba County map on page 174)

Good dogs who won't chase deer, skunks, and other critters are welcome to strip off their leashes and trot naked around the 600 acres of oaks and pines that surround 1,000-acre Collins Lake. Dog paddling is a popular pastime with unleashed pooches, so if you have a water dog, you couldn't ask for a more dog-friendly swimming hole. Dogs can't go swimming at the official swim beach, but there are plenty of other places to dip a paw. The fishing is terrific, too. Make sure your dog is leashed when you go anywhere near anglers or the developed area of the lake.

The lake has one developed campground and one undeveloped one. The latter is dog heaven. There are no barbecues or tables, but you won't have any neighbors, either. You'll be surrounded by trees and plenty of land. It's a first-rate way to get away from noise, loud kids, radios, and just about everything that reminds you of civilization. Both campgrounds require a leash.

You'll find 250 sites here, with nightly fees ranging $25–40. Reservations are recommended in spring and summer. Dogs are $2 extra. The park's day-use fee is $8–11 per vehicle, $16–19 per boat. From Marysville, take Highway 20 east for 12 miles and turn north on Marysville Road. The lake entrance will be on your right in about 10 miles. 530/692-1600 or 800/286-0576; www.collinslake.com.

Marysville

The historic district in Marysville is a real charmer—quite different from anything else you'll find in this sprawling, suburban-style county.

PARKS, BEACHES, AND RECREATION AREAS

🔳 Ellis Lake Park

😸😸😸 (See Yuba County map on page 174)

Swans, ducks, and geese enjoy this quaint park at least as much as people and their dogs do. Most of the park's 30 acres is taken up by a decent-sized lake, which was once a sprawling swamp. The swamp disappeared in 1924, when John McLaren, designer of San Francisco's Golden Gate Park, presented a local women's civic group with plans for transforming the muddy soup to its present pleasant state.

An attractive path encircles the lake, but you and your leashed pooch can also spend time at an old stone footbridge, a gazebo, and picnic tables. Dogs who like grass and dirt (and what dog doesn't?) enjoy lounging in the shade of the maples that dot the park.

Ellis Lake Park is between 9th and 14th streets and B and D streets. You won't want to hang out at the B Street side, because that's where all the car shops and convenience stores are. 530/749-3902.

PLACES TO EAT

Silver Dollar Saloon: This is a wonderful place with a big side patio for you and your dog. It's right next to Plaza Park's Chinese Bok Kai Temple. Just sit at the edge of the patio, near the gate, to keep your dog out of the bustle of this busy spot. The saloon has a pretty substantial menu, including steaks, sandwiches, and salads. 330 1/2 B Street; 530/743-1558.

PLACES TO STAY

Marysville Motor Lodge: Rates are $45–85. Dogs are $5 extra. 904 E Street 95901; 530/743-1531.

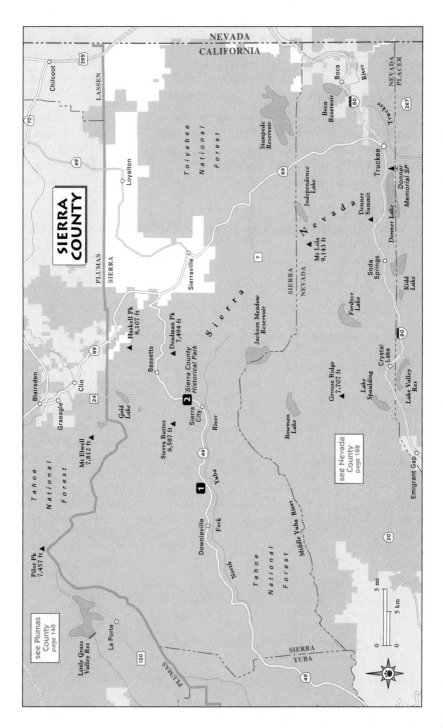

SIERRA COUNTY

NEVADA
CALIFORNIA

see Plumas County page 148

see Nevada County page 188

CHAPTER 17

Sierra County

Tahoe National Forest makes up a huge part of this mountainous county, causing dogs to give almost the entire county a four-paw rating. Peaks stretch to 9,000 feet above sea level and plunge into gigantic, serene meadows carpeted with wildflowers in the spring and snow in the colder months.

The North Fork of the Yuba River cuts through big rocks and mountains of tall pines and oaks. In summer, you and your dog can pull off Highway 49 and swim, fish (the fly-fishing is exceptional here), or pan for gold in the river. In autumn, bask in bright colors as the water maples and aspens prepare for winter.

Campgrounds are plentiful along Highway 49. They can be good places to start hikes, but there are actually only a few trailheads that begin near the road. Part of the Pacific Crest Trail passes between Bassett's Station and Sierra City. It's a great place to hike with an off-leash dog, because this section is on dog-friendly national forest land.

PICK OF THE LITTER—SIERRA COUNTY

BEST WAY FOR DOGS TO GET RICH QUICK
Gold panning, Downieville (page 183)

BEST EDUCATIONAL WALKIES
Sierra County Historical Park, Sierra City (page 185)

LODGING WITH MOST LAND
Herrington's Sierra Pines Resort, Sierra City (page 186)

MOST LUXE LODGINGS
My Sister's Cottage, Sierra City (page 187)
Sierra Solitude, Sierra City (page 187)

BEST INN FOR WATER DOGS
Riverside Inn, Downieville (page 185)

NATIONAL FORESTS

The *National Forests and Wilderness Areas* resource at the back of this book has important information and safety tips on visiting national forests with your dog and has more background on the Tahoe National Forest.

Tahoe National Forest
🐾🐾🐾🐾🐕

Calpine

This tiny Sierra enclave is not related to the San Jose–based Calpine Corporation, which operates about 90 power plants in North America. But it might help explain why the name sounds way too familiar for a place with a population of 200.

PLACES TO STAY

Sierra Valley Lodge: Dogs who like their vacations far from the hubbub of humans enjoy coming to the historic Sierra Valley Lodge. It's the only public-oriented business in this former logging town, and you won't get a TV or telephone in your room. A rustic lounge with a large rock fireplace adds to the peaceful flavor of this old-timey place—although on some weekends there's live music. If your dog's fur stands on end at the thought of this, please ask before booking a reservation. Dogs are allowed in two of the lodge's rooms. Rates are $60–70. Dogs are $10 extra. 151 Main Street 96124; 530/994-3367.

Loyalton

Loyalton is the only incorporated city within Sierra County, with a whopping population of nearly 900. There's a fun place to stay with a dog, should you need a place to rest your weary paws.

PLACES TO STAY

Golden West Saloon: This inn's lobby and bar date from about 100 years ago, but the room where you and your pooch are allowed to stay is merely a throwback to the 1970s. That's OK with Jake, who says any place that specializes in prime rib (served at the inn's restaurant, where the rule is no dogs) has got to be OK. A room here is $57. The mailing address is just Highway 49 (Main Street) 96118; 530/993-4467.

Downieville

While visiting this Old West gold town, you and your dog may feel as if some old miner might come running up behind you screaming he's hit the Mother Lode. It could happen. A while back, Joe and I ran into a prospector who was selling a chunk of gold big enough to pay his bills for two years. Granted, his bills were minimal since he lived out of a camper truck, but it was still impressive. He bought a drink for everyone within 100 feet and treated Joe to a piece of pizza.

Authentic is not the word for Downieville. Authentic implies that something has changed over time and then has been restored to be more like the original. But Downieville has barely changed since its heyday in the 1850s. Wood planks still serve as sidewalks and many buildings still have walls made of thick stones. The streets are narrow and jagged, just wide enough for a few stagecoaches (although cars do manage here nowadays). Ghastly green gallows stand next to the county jail, a grim reminder of the town's rowdy past. And gold miners still gather at the local assay office at dusk to weigh and sell the gold flecks and chunks they find in the North Fork of the Yuba River.

Inspired by this gold, Joe and I bought a $4 gold pan and a little red book that tells you how to pan for the stuff. (You can get panning supplies at at least a couple of stores in town.) We drove west of town a few miles on Highway 49 and stopped when we found what looked like a lucky spot on the Yuba River in Tahoe National Forest. We could feel our fortune in the air. We knew that after we spent a couple of hours sifting gravel and dirt, we'd find something that would let us retire early, or at least buy a bag of dog food. It was one of those things you could just sense.

Two hours later, I was still trying to get Joe to stop digging holes and covering up my freshly shaken gold pan with his freshly dug river dirt. It was bad enough that we had to watch the little red instruction booklet float away, then sink, after Joe crashed into me and knocked me into the river in a fit of canine glee within minutes of getting to our spot.

We left with soggy coats and unfulfilled dreams. That night, we bought a lottery ticket, won $5, and felt much better.

PARKS, BEACHES, AND RECREATION AREAS

1 Lion's Memorial Park

🐾🐾 (See Sierra County map on page 180)

If you like looking at old mining equipment, you'll enjoy this park. Several old, rusty gold mining relics are constantly on display here. The park is also a decent place to take a break from exploring town and relax on a bench with your dog.

The best part of this small, on-leash park is that it provides easy access to the Downie River, which runs right through town. The park is just next to Courthouse Bridge. 530/289-3201.

PLACES TO EAT

Indian Valley Outpost: Step inside and order a good home-cooked meal. While you wait (with someone staying by the picnic tables outside with your dog), shop the little store here for things such as handmade earrings and other local crafts. It's a fun place to spend a few extra dollars. Open during the warmer seasons (mid-spring to mid-autumn). Highway 49, about 12 miles west of Downieville; 530/289-3630.

Gallows Cafe: Dine at any of several rugged picnic tables in the front of the restaurant, or take your café cuisine back to Lion's Memorial Park and eat at the picnic tables overlooking the Downie River. 103 Nevada Street; 530/289-3540.

PLACES TO STAY

Camp Yuba's Sierra Streamside Cabins: The three rustic cabins and five RV spaces here are nestled in the Tahoe National Forest on the north fork of the Yuba River. The camp is about five miles east of downtown Downieville, so there's plenty of space for walking around with your best buddy. The owners here love dogs but have had a couple of bad experiences, so make sure your dog is really good here. And please keep him off the furniture. RV spaces are $30 nightly. Cabin rates are $500–550 per week. The cabins can be rented nightly only when available, and the rates are $120–200. 21792 Highway 49 95936; 530/289-3379; www.sierrastreamsidecabins.com.

Downieville Carriage House Inn: The folks here like to see your dog before they OK a stay here, but they'll settle for talking to you on the phone about your dog. "We just need to make sure a dog is well mannered," says John, who owns the inn. Your dog doesn't need to know which side of the plate the wine glass goes on; she needs only to be your basic good dog who won't tear the place apart or eat other guests or furniture.

The inn, built in 1938, is a simple nine-room lodging. Dogs love that it's a bone's throw to the Downie River. A new large suite (for six to eight people) opens right up to the river and a lawn area. Dogs dig this setup. Your room comes with fresh hot bread or muffins, and something to sip on, too. Rates are $60–175. 110 Commercial Street 95936; 530/289-3573 or 800/296-2289; www.downievillecarriagehouse.com.

Downieville River Inn & Resort: This beautiful Old West inn makes its home above the Downie River. The most scenic view of the inn is actually from the river itself, so if you want to take a postcard-perfect picture, you'll have to take a dip. (Your dog can be with you there, but not in the inn's sauna and heated pool.) If you stay on a Saturday night chances are you'll be treated to a bit of wine and cheese, and weekend guests also get a tasty continental breakfast. Rates are $69–195. 121 River Street 95936; 530/289-3308 or 800/696-3308; www.downievilleriverinn.com.

The Lure Resort: Dogs love to stay in the charming housekeeping cottages and the cozy log camping cabins at this riverside resort. But mostly, dogs love to be outside here. The resort is set on 14 acres along a half-mile stretch of the north fork of the Yuba River. Dogs are crazy about swimming in the river and hiking (on leash) around the property. People enjoy the outdoors too; the fishing is great, the gold panning is good, and the air smells oh-so-fresh. Rates are $65–250. Dogs are $20 extra. 100 Lure Bridge Lane, P.O. Box 95 95936; 530/289-3465 or 800/671-4084; www.lureresort.com.

Riverside Inn: Stay here and stay at the confluence of the Yuba and Downie rivers. Joe (a.k.a. Mr. Don't Get Me Wet) wouldn't have given a hoot, but it's Jake's dream come true. The 1940s-style motel has knotty-pine rooms with balconies overlooking the water below. It's a peaceful place to snooze the night away, since the sounds of the river can cover up the sounds of your snoring dog. Rates are $84–165. Dogs are $10 for the length of their stay. 206 Commercial Street 95936; 530/289-1000 or 888/883-5100; www.downieville.us.

Sierra City
PARKS, BEACHES, AND RECREATION AREAS

2 Sierra County Historical Park
🐾🐾 (See Sierra County map on page 180)

A restored hard-rock gold mine and stamp mill are the main attractions at this hilly, forested park a mile east of Sierra City. It's fascinating to learn about

DOG-EAR YOUR CALENDAR

The **Kentucky Mine Concert Series,** at Sierra County Historical Park, provides a summer of musical entertainment for you and your extraordinarily well-behaved dog. The concerts feature a wide variety of music, from Broadway to Celtic to Old West. Dogs who promise not to bark, howl, or stamp their feet are allowed to sit with you in the intimate outdoor amphitheater. For schedules and price information, write P.O. Box 368, Sierra City, CA 96125, or call 530/862-1310 or 530/862-1300.

how gold ore is mined, crushed, and has its gold extracted. While dogs are not allowed in the museum, they are sometimes permitted to go on a guided tour of the Kentucky Mine with you. Or you can take your own tour, looking into a restored miner's cabin or down a deep hole into the mine.

Leashed dogs enjoy the paved paths that lead to the attractions and the amphitheater. There are also some dirt paths above the amphitheater that lead you to the national forest, but rangers advice staying on pavement; rattlesnakes abound here.

The park is just east of the main part of Sierra City, on Highway 49. It's open Memorial Day–September or October, depending on what's going on. Hours vary. For more information phone 530/862-1310.

PLACES TO STAY

Bassett's Station Motel: This clean motel is utterly embraced by trees and sits near Howard Creek. Across the street is the Yuba River. Dogs love it. And you'll enjoy the convenience of staying in a motel room that's a housekeeping unit, as all the rooms are. You'll have a full little kitchen at your fingertips. None of that "let's get away from housework" vacation notion here! The hotel is open year-round. Rates are $80–85. Dogs are $10 extra. HCR2 Box 2, 100 Gold Lake Road 96125; 530/862-1297; www.bassetts-station.com.

Herrington's Sierra Pines Resort: This pretty, old resort is on the Yuba River, which is great for a good night's sleep. But it's even better for a good day's walk with your best pal, because well-behaved dogs are allowed off leash at the river's edge. And better yet, obedient dogs are allowed leash-free on the 55 acres of land surrounding the resort. For dogs whose people like to fish, there's a pond stocked with 3,000 rainbow trout. If the fish outwit you, you can enjoy a scrumptious meal at the resort's beautiful dining room, which has a cozy, log-cabin feel. The rooms are mostly motel-style, with wood paneling, and there are a few housekeeping units. The resort is closed Thanksgiving–

March. Rates are $69–130. 104 Main Street (Highway 49) 96125; 530/862-1151 or 800/862-9848; www.herringtonssierrapines.com.

Kokanee Kabins: These rustic buildings are in Tahoe National Forest, and just across the road is river access to the Yuba. Dogs dig it here because the land in the back of the cabins is great for doggy hikes and comes complete with fragrant pines and cedars. It also comes with bears, coyotes, foxes, and raccoons, so it's a good idea to keep your pooch leashed. Cabins are $65. One man runs this whole place, so it might take you a few tries to get the phone answered. The address is just Highway 49 96125; 530/862-1287.

My Sister's Cottage: This sweet cottage is filled with antiques and lace—not the kind of place you'd normally think would welcome dogs. But that's not the case. Far from it, in fact. "Everyone who comes has a dog. Dogs are great guests," said the owner, Lila. In the 15 years she's opened the cottage to people and their dogs, there's only been one problem involving a dog. That was a dog who shed so much there was even dog hair coating the fan. "It was a mess, but one incident in 15 years is a pretty good track record."

The house is very private, surrounded by a country garden, with a meadow across the way. It's on Highway 49, across from the Yuba River. Rates are $100. You'll get the physical address when you book the place. The mailing address is P.O. Box 485 96125; 530/862-1558.

Sierra Solitude: If you're longing to leave civilization behind, a visit to this beautiful three-bedroom, three-bathroom vacation home on three secluded acres is for you (and your dog). It's surrounded by woods on three sides so you won't see the neighbors, the magnificent Sierra Buttes tower above, and streams, forests, rivers, and trails are all within a bone's throw.

Inside the house you'll find a comfy mountain home aesthetic with an emphasis on luxuriously cozy furnishings. Even dogs have furniture, in the form of doggy beds scattered here and there. The owners of the house ask that your dog use the dog beds, and not the human furniture. And since the carpeting is light-colored, all muddy paws/bodies should be cleaned up before coming into the house. Rates are $195–255. Since this is a vacation home in a secluded setting, the owners prefer we leave addresses out of this listing. We can tell you it's located between Sierra City and Bassett's, just off Highway 49. 510/222-4138; www.sierrasolitude.com.

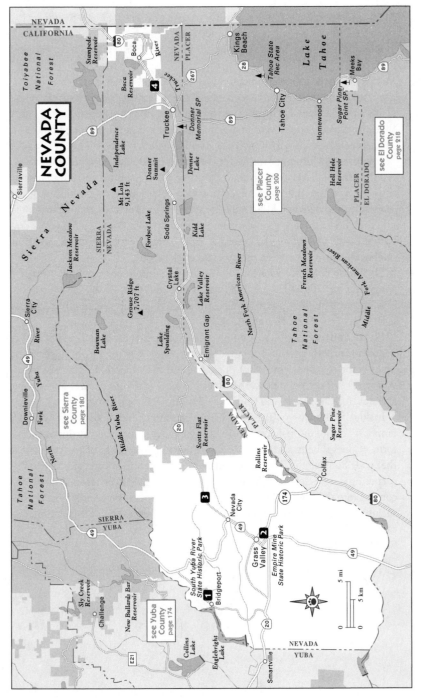

NEVADA COUNTY

CHAPTER 18

Nevada County

Do you have a digging dog? Buy yourself a plot of land and start scooping that dirt. Locals boast that more than half the gold that came out of California during the Gold Rush was found in Nevada City, Grass Valley, and other foot-hill areas of this county. Your hot-digged-y dog probably won't come up with much, but it's always fun to dream.

If you want to see where the riches really were, your best bet is to visit the Empire Mine State Historic Park (see the *Grass Valley* section), where hole-digging dogs can ooh and ahh at the mouth of the mine shaft that winds 5,000 feet below the surface.

Autumn in Nevada County is about as beautiful as autumn in New England. Much of the county, especially the Tahoe National Forest in the east, shows its true colors in the winter, when mountains are a crispy white. In Spanish, the very name *nevada* means "snow-covered." If you've always wanted a white Christmas, this is a spectacular place to watch the flurries fly. Some wonderful, dog-friendly lodgings in the eastern county are the perfect spots to enjoy all

PICK OF THE LITTER—NEVADA COUNTY

BEST LEASH-FREE RIVER WALK
Truckee River, Truckee (page 197)

MOST DOG-FRIENDLY PLACES TO EAT
Cousin Jack's Pasties, Grass Valley (page 192)
Joe Coffee, Truckee (page 197)

MOST HIP, DOG-FRIENDLY PLACE TO STAY
Cedar House Sport Hotel, Truckee (page 197)

COZIEST CABINS ON LOTS OF LAND
Shinneyboo Creek Cabin Resort, Soda Springs (page 195)

PRETTIEST OLD PLACE TO STAY
Swan-Levine House, Grass Valley (page 193)

BEST DOG SCENTS
Nevada City Carriage Company carriage ride, Nevada City
(page 194)

the seasons—especially winter. "I can only go there once a year," emailed Bob the Dog, of San Jose. "And there's no better time to go than winter, when it's like something in a glass ball."

NATIONAL FORESTS

The *National Forests and Wilderness Areas* resource at the back of this book has important information and safety tips on visiting national forests with your dog and has more information on the Tahoe National Forest.

Tahoe National Forest
🐾🐾🐾🐾🐕

Penn Valley

PARKS, BEACHES, AND RECREATION AREAS

🐾 South Yuba River State Park

🐾🐾🐾 (See Nevada County map on page 188)

This is one of the most interesting units in the state park system. For now, at least, leashed dogs are allowed to peruse the place. This is great news for pooches who like nature at its finest. The park is a patchwork of lands spread over a 20-mile length along the South Yuba River Canyon, from the top of Englebright Lake at Bridgeport to Tahoe National Forest above Malakoff Diggins State Historic Park.

The park has many access points, but our favorites are in the western section. For seclusion and serene beauty, try the westernmost access area. Driving north from Lake Wildwood on Pleasant Valley Road, you'll see a sign for the park and a small parking/pullout area on your left (there's space for only a few cars). If you're coming from Grass Valley or the town of Penn Valley, take Highway 20 west, turn right (north) on Pleasant Valley Road, and drive about six miles to the park.

As soon as you get out of the car, you and your leashed dog will hear the flowing river. Hike down the wide dirt path and when you come to a gravel section, go left. A few yards in, you'll come to one of the most beautiful sections of the South Yuba. The beach around it is sandy and the water in the river is a clear tropical blue (during nonrainy times of year). You'll want to stay forever.

Just a few hundred feet up Pleasant Valley Road is the Bridgeport Recreation Area, a much more widely used part of the park with bigger parking lots. Here's where you and your leashed dog can walk across the longest (243 feet) single-span covered bridge in existence. It's been around since 1862! Back then, it cost a whopping $5.50 to get across, but the fee included you, a loaded wagon, and six mules, oxen, or horses. These days, it's free.

You can also relax and picnic at a riverside table, swim in the crystal-clear Yuba, or hike a number of trails. One of the most rugged and scenic trails starts to the left of the covered bridge as you cross from the parking lot. The narrow trail takes you to Englebright Lake, about a mile away.

Please note that May 1–September 30, a couple of busy areas are off-limits to dogs (thanks to some negligent dog people in the past). You'll see the signs. And if you come in rainy season, be aware that this place can be tick heaven. 530/432-2546.

Grass Valley

Like Nevada City a few miles up the road, Grass Valley is a classic Old West town, only older and wester. But danged if it didn't ban dogs from city parks recently. Horsefeathers!

PARKS, BEACHES, AND RECREATION AREAS

🐾 Empire Mine State Historic Park
🐾🐾🐾 (See Nevada County map on page 188)

At one time, miners descended in cagelike trains deep into the earth here and rumbled the ground searching for gold in 350 miles of tunnels. The place was alive 24 hours a day—dirty, dusty, and dancing with gold. Miners extracted more than six million ounces of the precious ore during the mine's century of use.

Now, it's a quiet, calm 800-acre park with lush gardens and green meadows. While the mine and surrounding buildings are inactive, they're still fascinating to inspect. On hot summer days, a dog's favorite place is the shaft viewing area. It's a few dozen feet below ground, and the earthy scents are almost as relaxing as the cool, damp air. Leashed dogs are allowed on most trails, but not in the buildings.

The fee for adults is $3. From Highway 49, drive east on Highway 20/Empire Street about 1.5 miles. The park is on the right. 530/273-8522.

PLACES TO EAT

Cousin Jack's Pasties: British dogs go wild when they smell the Cornish pasties (yummy meat-and-potato pies) you can eat on the porch here. "Dogs are very welcome and may even get an extra snack," says a dog-loving manager. "Everything's homemade here, including the dog treats." 100 South Auburn Street; 530/272-9230.

PLACES TO STAY

Alta Sierra Village Inn: Your dog will like the views of the small lake you can see from your roomside deck. The lodging is on four acres, and no matter where you are, you'll have a view of the lake or the golf course. Rates are $59–175. Dogs are $10 for the length of their stay. 11858 Tammy Way 95949; 530/273-9102 or 800/992-5300.

Best Western Gold Country Inn: If you want your motel to be nestled in the pines, this is a good choice. If you want a pool and spa, it's a great choice. A continental breakfast comes with your room. Rates are $80–140. Dogs are $15 per stay. 11972 Sutton Way 95945; 530/273-1393.

Grass Valley Courtyard Suites: The rooms and suites here are spacious and attractive, with Tempur-Pedic beds, robes, and other niceties. The suites boast full kitchens and wonderful layouts. Humans can also use the heated pool, spa, and a decent little exercise area. By now your dog is probably looking at you and saying, "Yeah, yeah, but what's in it for me?" Good question, you clever canine. Waiting in the room or suite for your dog will be goodies such as tasty treats, a blanket, a dog bowl, and poop bags. "We love dogs staying with us," a late-night clerk told us. "They brighten our day—or night." (Note: This isn't a Courtyard by Marriott. It's independently owned and operated.) Rates are $140–325. Dogs under 40 pounds are $25 extra for the length of their stay. Bigger dogs pay $50 for their stay. (Large dog discrimination? Nah, just more dog hair to clean up, we're told.) The inn is conveniently situated within a block of historic Main Street, at 210 North Auburn Street 95945; 530/272-7696; www.gvcourtyardsuites.com.

Holiday Lodge: This is a popular accommodation for dogs on the show circuit. The hotel even has a little area for walking pooches, complete with poop bags. Humans get to use the pool when it's open during warmer months. Rooms come with a deluxe continental breakfast. Rates are $66–99. 1221 East Main Street 95949; 530/273-4406 or 800/742-7125; www.holidaylodge.biz.

Swan-Levine House: This big, airy house was built in 1880 and soon after was transformed into a small hospital. Now it's a magical inn, complete with an art studio (where you can try your hand at printmaking), brightly colored rooms furnished with antiques, and cozy fireplaces. Dogs who stay here should like cats—there are three on the property. In fact, if you're planning to visit with your pooch, call first and tell the owner about any cat-munching idiosyncrasies your dog may or may not have. Pooches stay at the discretion of the owner, so you'll need to have a chat first anyway. Rates are $100–115. Dogs are $15 for the length of their stay. 328 South Church Street 95945; 530/272-1873; www.swanlevinehouse.com.

Nevada City

Dogs are everywhere in this colorful Gold Rush town in the Sierra foothills. They dine with their owners, frolic off leash in Pioneer Park, and hang out with human friends on historic Broad Street. They sometimes even get to go shopping in some of the cutesy tourist-oriented stores.

The entire Old West/Victorian downtown is registered as a national historic landmark. On winter nights, when snow falls around the gaslit lamps in the narrow streets, it's classic Currier and Ives. Your dog trotting along will only add to the sweet scene.

DIVERSION

Get a Whiff of a Draft Horse: Dogs think being drawn along the historic streets of Nevada City in a carriage pulled by a hunky Percheron draft horse is one of the most riveting olfactory experiences ever. They thrill at the scent of horse heinie, their noses quivering perchance the horse does his horse business. And it's almost inevitable the horse will provide such canine entertainment—these big, calm beauties eat 20 pounds of grain and 30 pounds of hay daily. Fortunately for the carriage driver, no pooper-scooper is necessary.

The **Nevada City Carriage Company** offers terrific rides through historic downtown and the Victorian district. Rides for up to four people (and a dog) start at $40 for 15 minutes and go up to $120 for the one-hour grand tour. Dave, the dog-friendly manager, also offers special rides in more elaborate horse-drawn vehicles. Hours for regular rides vary by season, but the horses are out there daily year-round, weather permitting. Stable tours are also available.

You'll often find the carriages until 6 P.M. in front of the National Hotel downtown. In the evening, they'll be in front of Friar Tuck's Restaurant, at 111 North Pine Street. Look for the "Carriage for Hire" sign. For an information card, write 431 Uren Street (not Urine Street, tempting as that may be), Nevada City, CA 95959, or call 530/265-8778. The folks here are out and about on weekends, so you should phone during the week.

PARKS, BEACHES, AND RECREATION AREAS

🐾 Pioneer Park

🐾🐾🐾 (See Nevada County map on page 188)

Dogs love the tall pines that edge the park. These trees provide both shade and places for dogs to do their thing. Ball fields, a playground, a pool, and a shed with old firewagons are the major human interests here.

From northbound I-80, exit at Sacramento Street and go right immediately on Nile Street (at the sign for Pioneer Park). When the road comes to a T, go right. The park is on your left. You can either drive all the way in and park near the fountain, or park on Nimrod Street and walk down a paved road into the park's largest open field. 530/265-8223.

PLACES TO STAY

Outside Inn: What do you get when you take a 1940s-era motel and renovate it using loads of imagination and a love of the outdoors? You get the Outside Inn, situated under some sweet-smelling pines a short walk from downtown Nevada City. Most of the rooms at this fun inn have an outdoor theme. The Angler's Room is a fishing-fan's fantasy, while the Wildlife Room puts you in the company of critters who call Nevada County home (fear not, the critters are not real). The inn's staff is well versed in directing people and their pooches to some wonderful nearby hikes. (In addition, the outdoor-oriented staff can set up bike rentals and kayak lessons and point you to some choice swimming holes.) The inn even features a room with a climbing wall. That's not something many lodgings can boast. Rates are $75–180. Dogs are $10 extra. 575 East Broad Street 95959; 530/265-2233; www.outsideinn.com.

Soda Springs

PLACES TO STAY

Shinneyboo Creek Cabin Resort: If you've been hunting for dog heaven on earth, you've come to the right place. Shinneyboo Creek Cabin Resort (a.k.a. "the Boo") is paradise for pooches and people who like the great outdoors. Its eight enchanting, cozy, recently built cabins are set on 160 acres of Sierra beauty along the south fork of the Yuba River. And all this is surrounded on three sides by the dog-friendly Tahoe National Forest.

If you like going leashless, this is the place for you. You only need to leash up around the cabin area. The friendly Rogers family owns this piece of heaven and welcomes all well-behaved dogs. "They're part of the family, too," says Michael Rogers, a former thespian with a Masters of Fine Arts from Yale University, who left the theater business because his native Sierra drew him back.

In summer you and your dog can hike to your heart's content, get refreshed in pristine granite swim holes along the river, take an easy walk to a 30-foot waterfall, or just relax at the picnic table outside your door. You'll truly get away from the rigors of your busy life here. (No phones, no TVs, no Wi-Fi here.) Summer is also when you can stay at the Boo's large tent cabins. They're spacious (for tents), comfy, far from civilization and close to the river.

In winter, borrow some snowshoes or a sled from the Rogers family and enjoy that clean, fresh alpine scent as you have fun in the snow with your dog. Visit the resort's yurt, where you can cozy up to a fire, make some hot chocolate, read a book, and be on your way. When you return to your cabin, light your cast-iron fireplace and soak in your jetted bathtub. Ahh…

We've stayed here both seasons with Jake. We spent a few days around Christmas in a cabin, and we joined some friends in the summer in a tent cabin by the river. Jake has swum, hiked, gone on snowshoe treks, and even ended up on a sled a few times. He did not want to go home. Neither did we. You probably won't either.

Rates are $100–230 for the cabins, and $50–90 for the tent cabins. Dogs are $15 extra. A basket with breakfast fixings comes with your cabin. The resort is on Donner Summit, "on the quiet side of the Sierra," as Michael says. The mailing address is Box 38 95724; 530/587-5160; www.shinneyboocreek.com.

Truckee

If you want a preview of just what you're going to see when you visit this colorful old city, rent the silent Charlie Chaplin flick *The Gold Rush*. Some of the late-1800s architecture along Truckee's main street, Commercial Row, appears in the film. This enchanting Old-West street hasn't changed much since then, although the buildings now house some rather chichi businesses. We're surprised at the number of artsy, upscale shops that have sprung up here lately. We recently visited in our grungy camping duds with our dusty dogs, and got a few looks from the well-coiffed shoppers with their Coach bags. (Note to self: Next time, shower first.)

Truckee is home to Donner Lake, where many in the ill-fated Donner Party died in the winter of 1846 after running out of provisions during a "shortcut" leg of their journey from the Midwest. Their tragic tale is recounted at Donner Memorial State Park.

A more upbeat way to experience Truckee's freshwater wonders is to go hiking or trout fishing at the Truckee River. You'll find an access point just outside downtown. It's a great location if someone you're traveling with wants to shop while you and the dog get your paws wet.

PARKS, BEACHES, AND RECREATION AREAS

Truckee has a perfectly manicured regional park, but dogs don't feel welcome there. We prefer to drive another mile down the road and enjoy the wonders of Martis Creek Lake. The recreation area surrounding the lake straddles two counties (it's described in detail in the *Northstar* section of the *Placer County* chapter).

4 Truckee River

🐾🐾🐾🐾🐕 (See Nevada County map on page 188)

This beautiful, trout-filled river beckons hikers and anglers and their adventurous canines. The really good news is that dogs are allowed off leash along the river, since it's in Tahoe National Forest! Your pup can frolic while you catch and release all day. Use artificial lures and barbless hooks only.

Once you get past the first 200 feet or so along the riverbank, the trail can be narrow and rocky. If your dog is a klutz or has thin-skinned paws, you may not want to go any farther. She can still have plenty of fun sniffing around while you cast all day for the big one hiding behind the boulder.

From central Truckee, drive northeast on Highway 267 and go right on Glenshire Drive (it's about halfway between downtown and I-80). After 4.5 miles, you'll come to the Glenshire Bridge. Make a sharp right onto a dirt road after the bridge, and park in the flat, dirt area near the river. When choosing a fishing spot, be sure to head to the left as you face the river. If you walk to the right, you'll be in very private fishing grounds very quickly.

The folks at Mountain Hardware can give you fishing tips and updated regulations. Call them at 530/587-4844. The Truckee Ranger District of Tahoe National Forest wasn't very knowledgeable about this part of the river when we called but may be helpful with other information. 530/587-3558.

PLACES TO EAT

The places that allow dogs to join you for a bite here aren't fancy, but most dogs around here aren't in a fancy mood anyway.

Joe Coffee: Joe Dog would have loved this place and surely would have assumed it was named after him. This is a really friendly place to grab an excellent cuppa Joe and hang out with your dog. If you need Wi-Fi, you'll get it free here. The friendly waitstaff provides dogs with treats and water. Your dog is welcome to join you at the patio tables. Joe's is next to the old jailhouse, in the historic part of town, at 10120 Jibboom Street; 530/550-8222.

Old Gateway Deli: Eat tasty deli fare with your favorite dog at the outdoor tables here. 11012 Donner Pass Road; 530/587-3106.

Wild Cherries Coffee House: The coffee is great, the veggie chili is out of this world, and the soups, salads, and sandwiches are good and affordable. Your dog can join you at the outdoor tables here, or even on the grass. Your view will be a busy road and strip malls, but you're not here for the view, remember? 11429 Donner Pass Road; 530/550-0503.

PLACES TO STAY

Cedar House Sport Hotel: This new 42-room contemporary, hip-yet-cozy lodging is the most attractive, comfortable, and welcoming dog-friendly place to stay in this neck of the woods. Jake and I are thrilled that such a lodging now exists around here. The hotel's cedar exterior, "green" roof, and bold architecture usher you inside to rooms that are worthy of a design magazine's attention. They're modern and open and kind of organic-feeling, with micro-fiber/leather beds topped by Euro-style mattresses, down comforters from Germany, bent plywood furniture, and luxurious, white towels and linens. All rooms have a fridge, flat-screen TV, and free Wi-Fi.

Dogs are welcome in all the downstairs rooms. They love it here. The owner, Patty, enjoys dog guests ("in truth, we have more problems with kids than dogs," she said) and welcomes them with treats, special dog beds, and bowls. She said that insurance prevents her from allowing certain breeds, so call first to make sure yours isn't one of them. There's also a 100-pound limit, and a ban on dogs who are dribbly droolers. (Sorry on both counts, Saint Bernards.) The staff will be happy to point you and your dog to some "secret" fun spots that allow the hotel's canine guests, but not necessarily every dog that walks down the block. Rates are $140–295. Dogs pay a $50 per-visit fee. 10918 Brockway Road 96161; 866/582-5655; www.cedarhousesporthotel.com.

Donner Memorial State Park: Dogs aren't allowed on the trails or in the museum that tells the tragic story of the Donner Party, trapped here for the winter of 1846. But they can stay with you at any of the park's 150 campsites. And they can also accompany you to pay homage to the dozens of pioneers who perished here. A 22-foot-high monument rests on a stone base that's 16 feet high; 22 feet was the depth of the snow during that desperate winter. It's within doggy access. Sites are $25. The park is about two miles west of the town of Truckee, on Donner Pass Road. Phone 800/444-7275 for reservations, or call the park at 530/582-7892 for more information.

Grinnin' Bear Cabin: Stay at this cute vacation rental and here's what you get: a very dog-friendly three-bedroom, two-bathroom house that sleeps up to 12 people for a most reasonable price, nearby hikes, a securely fenced yard with a huge doghouse ("It's a mansion," says the house's owner, Andrea), a doggy door leading to the backyard, a wood-burning stove, and most of the other creature comforts. (The garage also sports a large kennel inside, in case you opt to go skiing or out on the town and don't want to bring your dog, but you also don't want to take the chance that he'll eat the house.) Because the home is in a planned community, you'll also have access to a large, private lake that allows dogs to do the dog paddle, and to a swimming pool, playground, and tennis courts.

Andrea says she decided to welcome dogs because she doesn't think people should have to leave their best buddy in a kennel when they go on vacation. "I have a terrific place for dogs. Why not invite them to stay, too?" she says.

Rates are $169–350. The house is four miles east of the historic part of Truckee. The mailing address: Box 10799 96162; 530/582-8703 or 800/289-1522; www.sierraviews.com.

Inn at Truckee: This is an attractive and comfortable place to stay—kind of a hybrid of hotel-motel, featuring a continental breakfast, in-room fridges, and a relaxing spa and sauna. The folks here love dogs and will direct you to a few secret dog areas, including some ponds that will put a smile on your water dog's snout. Actually, your dog won't have to go far to stretch her legs: There's a grassy fenced area and a creek just behind the inn.

Rates are $89–145. It costs $15 extra for as many dogs as you bring—a refreshing change from the usual per-pet charge. (Someone brought four dogs once, and that was pushing the limit a little. The only pack you should bring should be a backpack.) 11506 Deerfield Drive 96161; 530/587-8888 or 888/733-6888; www.innattruckee.com.

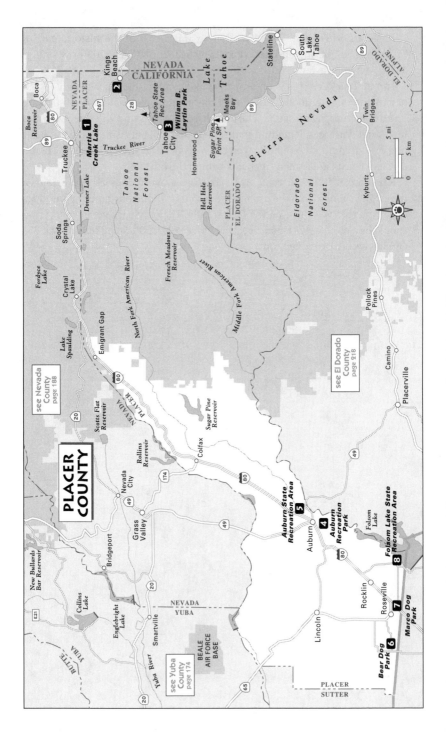

CHAPTER 19

Placer County

If your dog likes fresh mountain air, world-class ski resorts, and rivers rushing over hidden gold, Placer County is her kind of place. The county has a little of everything, and lucky dogs can experience its diversity.

Most dogs think the county gets better as they go from its more populated western end past the Mother Lode and into the magnificent mountains. Unless your dog likes to shop 'til she drops, the western valley region of Placer County probably won't be nearly as appealing to her as the high country. (But see the Diversion *Get Fruity with Fido* for a fun sojourn in the more rural parts of the western county.)

Part of the appeal of the eastern half of the county (the north and west Lake Tahoe region, essentially) is that much of it is Tahoe National Forest land, where dogs can shed their leashes everywhere except in campgrounds and developed recreation areas. And let's not forget that famous lake, with its sparkling blue waters surrounded by mighty mountains, cozy cabins, and ski resorts. Most dogs love the snow, and if your dog has never had a chance to

PICK OF THE LITTER—PLACER COUNTY

BEST HIKING
Tahoe National Forest (page 203)
Auburn State Recreation Area, Auburn (page 215)

BEST DOG BURGERS
Char Pit, Kings Beach (page 205)

BEST RIVERSIDE DINING
The River Grill, Tahoe City (page 211)

BEST LODGING WITH A BEACH
Holiday House, Tahoe Vista (page 208)

LODGING THAT'S BEEN DOG-FRIENDLY THE LONGEST
Rustic Cottages, Tahoe Vista (page 209)

MOST DOG-FRIENDLY PLACES TO STAY
Mother Nature's Inn, Tahoe City (page 211)
Tahoe Moon Properties, Tahoe City (page 213)
Tahoma Meadows B & B Cottages, Tahoma (page 214)

BEST NATURAL HIGH
Gondola rides at the ski resorts Northstar at Tahoe and Squaw Valley USA (page 204)

COOLEST SKIING
Tahoe Cross Country Ski Area, Tahoe City (page 210)

STORE THAT WILL LIGHT UP YOUR LIFE
Waxen Moon, Squaw Valley (page 206)

MOST FUN SHOPPING
Select stores at the **Village at Squaw Valley** (page 207)

DIVERSION

Get Fruity with Fido: The western half of Placer County is far from a suburban slumberland. In fact, a good part of it is heavily agricultural. You and your dog can experience the farming life firsthand by driving the **'49er Fruit Trail.** The trail passes by 100 farms, where you (and often your dog) can stop, look around, and buy very fresh farm goods—everything from apples to grapes to walnuts. There are even places to buy trout, sheep, and catfish! Before you let your dog out of the car, ask the farmer if it's OK. If it's not, and it's hot, drive on. Don't leave your dog in the car in warm weather even for a few minutes. For a map and list of all the farms, go to www.49erfruittrail andchristmastreelane.com.

romp around in it, this area of Lake Tahoe is a great place to introduce her. It's much more quiet and mellow than the South Lake Tahoe scene.

NATIONAL FORESTS

The *National Forests and Wilderness Areas* resource at the back of this book has important information and safety tips on visiting national forests with your dog and has more information on the Tahoe National Forest.

Tahoe National Forest
🐾🐾🐾🐾🦴

Northstar

The ski resort Northstar at Tahoe is undergoing some big changes, with construction of a much-needed ski village full of shops and restaurants, some of which will certainly allow good dogs. For now, Northstar invites dogs to ride its gondolas to great hiking areas during non-ski season. See the Diversion *A Fairly Natural High* for details.

PARKS, BEACHES, AND RECREATION AREAS

1 Martis Creek Lake
🐾🐾🐾🐾🦴 (See Placer County map on page 200)

This is a prime wildlife-viewing area, with great catch-and-release trout fishing and more than 1,400 acres of meadows, rolling sagebrush hills, and dense conifer forests. There's very little shade around the lake itself, so in hot weather

DIVERSION

A Fairly Natural High: During summer and autumn, you and your dog can be whisked halfway to the stars by gondolas at **Squaw Valley USA** and **Northstar at Tahoe** ski resorts. You'll dangle high above the mountains in these enclosed contraptions on the way up, so if you've ever felt like James Stewart in *Vertigo*, here's some advice: Don't look down, not even at your dog, who will probably be smiling and sniffing everyone's feet anyway.

Once the gondola drops you off, you can hike down the mountains on any number of trails. If you're just visiting for the view, you can turn around and go back on the next gondola. Dogs and their people think the hike is the best way to go, especially in early summer when it's still cool and the wildflowers are blooming.

The Squaw Valley USA gondola ride costs $17 per adult. After 5 P.M., it's $8. Dogs go for free. 530/583-6985. At Northstar, a lot of construction was going on at press time, and all gondola rides were free for humans and dogs. Things may change by the time you read this, but for now, that's quite a deal. 800/GO-NORTH.

don't plan to paddle around the lake all day while a friend and your dog watch from shore.

You and your dog will have a chance to gawk at all kinds of wildlife, including red-tailed hawks and chickadees. In spring, you can lie back in the meadows full of alpine wildflowers and watch life unfold. If your dog is truly under control, he doesn't have to wear a leash, except at the campground and developed areas.

Dogs and their friends enjoy the lake's campground. It's set in a prime wildlife-viewing area and is fairly quiet. The 25 sites are often filled with early-rising anglers or bird-watchers. Sites are $16. All sites but the two for campers with disabilities are available on a first-come, first-served basis.

The lake is halfway between Truckee and Northstar. From Northstar, travel about two miles northwest on Highway 267 to the park entrance. The campground is open May–September. Questions in summer? Call 530/587-8113. Questions in winter? Call 530/432-6427.

Kings Beach

A stinky law has dogs bummed out here. Dogs are no longer allowed at Coon's Beach. Granted, it wasn't exactly poochy paradise, but it was good for a little paw stretching. The problem? Poop. Or to be exact, the lack of scooping. You'd think dog people would learn…

PLACES TO EAT

Brockway Bakery: Got a hungry dog? Order her an organic dog biscuit while you order your own baked goods. Got a thirsty dog? There's a faucet where you can fill 'er up outside. Dine at the umbrella-topped tables. 8710 North Lake Boulevard; 530/546-2431.

Char Pit: No longer do dogs have to sit and wait and pray that you'll drop a bit of your lunch while dining with you at the outdoor tables here: Char Pit now sells a "Dog Burger." I did a double take when I first heard about the menu item, because "beef burger" means made from beef, "turkey burger" means made from turkey meat, so therefore "dog burger" means …. But fortunately, all it means is the owners love dogs, and for $1.50 your dog can enjoy a lovely beefy burger patty. 8732 North Lake Boulevard; 530/546-3171.

PLACES TO STAY

Waters of Tahoe Properties: This vacation rental agency has 21 super-dog-friendly, terrific, cozy houses scattered around North Lake. Some are chalets, some are big cabins, and some are luxury homes. Amenities at a few of the homes include hot tubs, swimming pools, tennis courts, and private beaches. Most just feature Mother Nature, which is what dogs really care about. Rates are $175–300 per night. Weekly rates are available. A few houses sleep up to 12 people. The rates are up to $1,000 nightly. 800/215-8904; www.watersoftahoe.com.

Squaw Valley/Olympic Valley

The world-famous Squaw Valley USA ski resort is home to the Village at Squaw. It's a good place to be a dog. As a concierge tells us, "The Village loves dogs." The Village has several dog-friendly restaurants, and some shops that welcome dogs. You can even make a candle with your dog. (See the Diversions *Life IS Good* and *Get Wick-ed*.) While Squaw itself offers no dog-friendly accommodations, there are plenty in nearby towns, plus a wide assortment of vacation rentals a bone's throw from the slopes.

Your dog can't ski here, but if she comes in summer, the hiking is marvelous. (Yes, another Diversion! See *A Fairly Natural High*, in the Northstar section.)

PLACES TO EAT

These eateries are among several dog-friendly eateries, all in the Village at Squaw. Since they all share basically the same address, we won't include addresses in the listings:

Auld Dubliner: You'll get hearty, tasty, traditional Irish "fayre" at this pub/restaurant. The boxty dishes—Irish potato pancakes stuffed with all kinds of fillings—are a real treat. Jake likes the smell of the corned beef and cabbage,

DIVERSION

Get Wick-ed: How's this for a whole new ball of wax? **Waxen Moon,** a make-your-own-candle studio in Squaw Valley, welcomes your well-behaved dog to join you as you create unique candles. It's a fun activity, and a great way to come up with some special holiday gifts while hanging out with your dog. You choose the size, shape, wax type, color, and scent. (You probably don't want your dog to help with choosing a scent, as you'd likely end up with a candle that smells like cow poo—or worse.) If you're too busy to make your own, the shop offers plenty of ready-made candles you can buy.

Waxen Moon is located in the Fountain Court at the Village at Squaw Valley, next to the dog-friendly Mamasake Sushi restaurant. 530/584-6006; www.waxenmoon.com.

and the beef stew. Wash it down with one of the Dubliner's fine Irish pints. (Dogs should stay away from the beers and ales. It makes it hard for them to drive home.) Dogs are welcome to dine with you at the outdoor tables. 530/584-6041.

Blue Coyote: This sports grill specializes in the kind of food dogs really appreciate: Burgers, steaks, and their kindred spirits. Your dog can join you at the dozen or so umbrella-topped tables at the restaurant's patio. Thirsty dogs get a bowl of water. 530/584-6080.

Fireside Pizza: We love the pizza here. It's not your everyday greasy pepperoni fare. This place offers up some truly gourmet pies, all on sourdough crust. For a culinary experience that will leave you looking at pizza with a newfound respect, try the grilled chicken bianco pizza, with grilled chicken, bacon, red onions, creamy house-made garlic sauce, and parsley. The pear and gorgonzola pizza is a signature dish, but I prefer these ingredients in a salad. Jake can recommend the Big Mountain: It's got every kind of smoked meat imaginable. (Well, no lox.) A friend got full and gave Jake his very own piece. If your dog gets thirsty—and Jake did after this slice of heaven—the restaurant has water bowls topped off with fresh water. Ahh. Dine with doggy at the 10 outdoor tables. 530/584-6150.

Mamasake Sushi: "Eat Raw at Squaw!" is the rallying cry at this popular sushi restaurant. (Is this why Mamasake is at Squaw, not, say, Northstar?) The sushi and sashimi are top-notch and fresh, but don't miss out on the delightfully different Calastan tapas. Dine with your dog at the patio tables. 530/584-0110.

PLACES TO STAY

Vacation Rentals By Owner (VRBO): Squaw Valley USA offers no dog-friendly accommodations, but thanks to this vacation rental agency, your dog won't be leaving tear marks in the snow. (Yellow marks, yes. Tear marks, no.) VRBO represents a few dog-friendly vacation rentals at Squaw, and many just down the pike. The homes are usually high-end (and often high-ceilinged) and tend to have a luxe mountain cabin style. With this rental agency you deal directly with the owner when you book, so phone numbers differ for every listing. To search for properties, go to www.vrbo.com.

DIVERSION

Life IS Good: Especially when you're in one of the most beautiful places on earth with your best friend at your side. Even though you can't hit the slopes together, there's one activity you can do here year-round: Shop. Several stores at the **Village at Squaw Valley** allow dogs to shop with their well-behaved people. Here are a few:

One of Jake's favorites is **Blue Sky,** which features the Life is Good brand of merchandise starring that dynamic duo, Jake (a happy human stick figure, not a dog, much to Jake Dog's disappointment) and his sidekick, Rocket the Dog. You can load up on great optimistic T-shirts, dog bowls, sleepwear, mugs, and all kinds of happy Life is Good-ies. 530/584-6074.

Another huge hit with Jake (the dog, not the smiling stick figure) is **Tails by the Lake,** a delightful specialty shop for dogs, cats, and their people. We wouldn't include it if it were simply a wonderful store for pet merchandise. (That's against the book's policy; this book would end up being 200 more pages if we added doggy stores, and my editors would want to throw me in the lake.) Tails by the Lake makes the cut because of all the items for humans. Robert, the store's friendly owner, offers all kinds of pet-related jewelry, art, little home furnishings, and clothing for enjoyment of the store's human customers. Of course, while you're shopping for yourself and your human friends, don't forget to buy some of the terrific dog treats and items the store is known for. ("Try the dog wine," Jake hiccups... er, says.) 530/583-9247; www.tailsbythelake.com.

Need a helping paw while figuring out what outfit looks especially fetching on you? Bring your dog with you to **Edin Boutique,** which specializes in women's clothing. "Good dogs are fun to have in the store," says a manager. 530/584-6145.

Tahoe Vista

PARKS, BEACHES, AND RECREATION AREAS

The Tahoe National Forest is right in your backyard here, but a local regional park makes for a more civilized outing.

◪ North Tahoe Regional Park

😸😸😸 (See Placer County map on page 200)

This kind of land is very rare in these parts. Leashed dogs are allowed everywhere except on the playing fields and bleachers in this 108-acre park. That means four miles of hiking trails are at their disposal. Better yet, some of those trails lead to Tahoe National Forest, where your dog can run untethered. The regional park is even fun in the winter because of its popular snow-play hill.

If you're shopping around for a companion for your dog, stop in at the county animal shelter, just a Frisbee's throw from the park. You can't miss the signs for it. The shelter has many sweet dogs who would much rather be romping around in parks with you than caged up and worrying about their fate. They're at 849 Shelter Road. 530/546-4269.

The park is at the corner of Donner Road and National Avenue. From Highway 28, drive inland a few blocks past the scenic cinderblock manufacturer and its neighboring mobile home park. Turn left at the sign for the park. 530/546-4212.

PLACES TO STAY

Holiday House: Dog-loving Alvina, who owns this wonderful lakeside lodging, has been welcoming dogs since 1986—well before it became the stylish thing to do. "People who have dogs are very good guests," she says. Her rescued German shepherd, Kyila, agrees.

Good guests and their people are welcome to stay at any of the Holiday House's seven lovely suites, all with decks, full kitchens, and free Wi-Fi. Six feature beautiful panoramic views of the lake and the surrounding mountains. Even more appealing, guests have full access to the lodging's beach! It's a rocky beach, with flat rocks that are quite walkable. In summer Alvina puts a float in the lake and some dogs end up swimming to it with their humans. "They have so much fun!" she says.

Alvina is no stranger to the water. She was the Nevada State Champion windsurfer for several years, and she teaches windsurfing at a nearby sandy beach in the summer. She's a good, patient, fun instructor. Your dog is welcome to accompany you to your lesson. In fact, your dog might be better than you are, if he decides to try his paws at it. Don't feel too bad. It has something to do with four feet and a low center of gravity.

Suite rates are $125–195. Dogs are $30 for up to three days, and $10 per day after. 7276 North Lake Boulevard 94168; 530/546-2369 or 800/294-6378; www.tahoeholidayhouse.com.

Rustic Cottages: This resort has been dog-friendly since 1925! It's a great place for a poochy vacation, and with plans for further improvements (the cottages are continually upgraded), it's going to be a doggone dynamite place. The owners, Janet and Marshall, are very nice folks, but they did a lot of work on the place, and they're a little wary about allowing dogs, so please let your dog inspire them to have confidence in their ilk.

The beds here are one of the biggest draws. One of the resort's owners handcrafts wrought iron and brass beds for a living, so his talent was put to use in each of the 18 cottages here. The linens are also first-rate, so the owners ask you not to let your dog on the bed unless you bring your own sheet to cover up the bed first.

The cottages even have TVs, which get a whopping 30 channels each, not that you want to be a couch 'tater when you're vacationing in Tahoe. But just in case, each TV has a VCR, so you can bring your own videos or borrow one of the hundred or so the resort lends out to guests, including *Dog Babysitter*. (My friend Denise Selleck tells me she is mesmerized by the video, but her dog falls asleep.) In the morning, you can grab some homemade muffins and waffles in the main lodge. (You can nab homemade cookies and/or brownies there all day.)

Better yet, though, is that the place is on two acres, with a small, semienclosed lot where your pooch can run leash-free if you stay with him and have a little faith that he won't escape. The lot isn't anything fancy, but dogs don't mind a little overgrown grass and a tree stump. In fact, most dogs prefer this decor to a perfectly manicured lawn. If you want quaint scenery, just look around the cottages. In the warmer months, fresh flowers adorn most cottage fronts. Lake Tahoe is across the street, though there's no beach access there for dogs. But some Tahoe National Forest land is behind the resort, and it's a four-paw adventure for dogs and their people. Reggie Dog and his people got rather lost on a trail here one day, but they eventually made it back to civilization.

Rates are $59–149. Dogs are $15 extra. 7449 North Lake Boulevard 96148; 530/546-3523 or 888/778-7842; www.rusticcottages.com.

Tahoe City

Tahoe City is a fun and scenic place to go for a bite to eat with your dog. During summer, there are so many eateries with outdoor tables in this lakeside village that you and your dog will drool just making the choice. It's an ideal place to bring your appetites after a long day of hiking in nearby Tahoe National Forest.

DIVERSION

Dashing Through the Snow: While you ski at the **Tahoe Cross Country Ski Area,** your happy, leash-free dog can trot along beside you on five miles of beautifully groomed dog-friendly trails. (Leashes are required only at the trailhead and parking lot.) It's a blissful experience for most dogs. In fact, Jake is so happy when he gets to ski with us that he leaves lots of cheery yellow marks all over the place.

For obvious reasons, dogs must be under voice control. The two dog-friendly trails are open to dogs 8:30 A.M.–5 P.M. Monday–Friday and limited hours on weekends and holidays. Humans pay $21 for a day of skiing. Dogs pay $4. Season passes are available. In fact, your dog's season pass will have his photo emblazoned on it!

The ski lodge is just as welcoming as the trails. Inside the cozy lounge you'll find plenty of dog biscuits. For humans, you'll find hot chocolate and cookies.

The ski area is at 925 Country Club Drive in Tahoe City; 530/583-5475; www.tahoexc.org. (A big woof of thanks goes to Alexandra, Deuce, and Jasper for letting us know about this terrific place.)

PARKS, BEACHES, AND RECREATION AREAS

🖪 William B. Layton Park
🐾🐾 (See Placer County map on page 200)

While dogs have to stay out of the park's most interesting feature, the Gate-keeper's Cabin Museum, they may stroll the 3.5 green acres of park on the shores of Lake Tahoe as long as they're leashed. Because of the park's picturesque gardens and ancient conifers, the place is often rented out for weddings and private parties. If your dog isn't invited, he has to stay away.

The park has picnic tables in the shade, but it's so close to many of the city's dog dining joints that you probably won't be hungry by the time you arrive here. The park is at 130 West Lake Boulevard. 530/583-1762.

PLACES TO EAT

You'll see lots of restaurants with patios in the warmer months, but unfortunately, most don't allow dogs. (Even Jake's by the Lake, as Jake was saddened to discover.) Here's a sampling of some that do:

Fiamma Cucina Rustica: This is a beautiful, romantic restaurant with some scrumptious pastas, chicken dishes, and pizzas. The smoked mozzarella and roasted eggplant pizza is out of this world. Dogs are allowed to dine with you at the lovely wooden tables outside, as long as it's not too busy. 521 North Lake Boulevard; 530/581-1416.

The River Grill: This is one of our favorite places around Tahoe to eat with Jake. That's because the gourmet American Bistro–style food is a real treat, and also because its heated patio is right on the north bank of the Truckee River, just downstream from Fanny Bridge. (So named because of all the fannies you see when their owners gaze over the side at fish. At least that's my theory.)

Rosie's Cafe: Eat steaks, burgers, and pasta on the charming porch. 571 North Lake Boulevard; 530/583-8504.

Sunnyside Market: It's not exactly the most elegant dining experience, but you and your pooch may eat on benches outside this little convenience store. The friendly staff makes up for the lack of tableside service (or tables, for that matter): "If we know you have a dog with you, we give them a treat!" said a manager. 1780 West Lake Boulevard; 530/583-7626.

Tahoe House Bakery and Gourmet Store: You and your dog can cool your paws under the awning-covered outdoor eating area here. Dogs can get water from a dog water station here, and in keeping with the theme of your doggy vacation, you (the human) can order a dog-paw–shaped cookie. The sandwiches and pastries are tasty, too. This is also where you can buy some quality gourmet meals that you can simply heat up when you get back to your lodging. 625 West Lake Boulevard; 530/583-1377.

PLACES TO STAY

Hauserman Rental Group: This is a very dog-friendly vacation rental agency, with many of the 300 rentals welcoming dogs. You can rent a condo, cabin, or luxurious lakeview home with your dog. You name the amenity, the agency will find it for you. Rates are $90–650, depending on the location and size of the rental. 475 North Lake Boulevard 96145; 800/20-TAHOE (800/208-2463); www.enjoytahoe.com.

Mother Nature's Inn: Each room at this renovated 1945 inn/very nice motel in the heart of Tahoe City features cozy lodge decor with wildlife and nature themes. The emphasis is on the great outdoors—very appropriate in these parts. This is Mother Nature at her best, especially where dogs are concerned: Dogs who come to this inn get treats, a doggy bed, poop bags, and a sheet for the bed, should your dog be interested in sharing your bed.

The owners love animals. According to Maizy Dog, who had her person, Sherry, write to us, they are "incredibly dog savvy and friendly... they treat people and dogs very nicely." In fact, Maizy Dog met the inn's owners alongside the highway after she got lost in a snowstorm. Despite her skittishness at being caught by strangers, with their own dog's help, the innkeepers managed to persuade her into their car. Back at the inn, they phoned Sherry (Maizy had tags, thankfully), who was much relieved to be reunited with her runaway. Maizy got treated royally there, with biscuits and lots of love.

If you want to shop for little gifty items or home furnishings, look no further than the inn's store, Cabin Fever. You're welcome to bring your dog, of course. Rates are $55–115. Dogs are $5 extra. 551 North Lake Boulevard 96145; 530/581-4278 or 800/558-4278; www.mothernaturesinn.com.

River Ranch Lodge: This century-old lodge sits on the banks of the Truckee River—a magnificent spot for dogs and their people. The rooms sport a rustic-yet-modern cabin feel, with lodgepole pine furnishings and updated interiors.

The lodge has a popular restaurant with a patio above the river, but alas, dogs aren't allowed. Conveniently for water dogs, one of the dog-friendly rooms—our favorite—has a balcony with a river view. Dogs are welcome to stay from April to November, but during snowy months, no dogs are allowed. Rates are $80–180. Dogs are $15 extra. The lodge is on the corner of Highway 89 and Alpine Meadows Road. The mailing address is P.O. Box 197 96145; 530/583-4264; 866/991-9912; www.riverranchlodge.com.

DIVERSION

Say Your Nuptials While Your Pup Chills: Calm, well-behaved, flea-free dogs are welcome to join you and your future spouse when you launch your lifetime of togetherness at **A Chapel at Lake Tahoe.** And fear not: The interior of the chapel is not gauche. "There's nothing plastic, glitzy, or Elvis about it," says a chapel owner. In fact, it's simple, with wrought-iron and wood benches and real live plants.

The basic wedding ceremony package is $295, which includes your wedding license. For more information, write to 3080 North Lake Boulevard, Tahoe City, CA 96154, or call 530/581-2757 or 800/581-2758; www.chapelatlaketahoe.com.

Tahoe Moon Properties: Of the 50 rental properties managed by this vacation rental agency, 47 permit pooches. "When I went into this business, I found that dog people are much better guests than nondog people," says Jill, who runs the agency. "Except for cleaning poop. Some aren't fantastic about that." (Picture a snowblower. Picture poop jettisoning through the snow blower. Not a pretty sight. Scoop the poop!)

Despite the poop problem, she decided that dog people are such good guests that the vacation rentals should offer something special. Now all dog-friendly rentals come with a bottle of wine for the humans, and a dog bowl, dog bed, dog biscuits, and even dog tags for canine friends. Many of the rentals have fenced yards, which make a dog's vacation even more heavenly.

Jill offers rentals throughout the Lake Tahoe area. Rates vary greatly, from $125 nightly for a modest one-bedroom home to $750 a night for a stunning and luxurious four-bedroom home. Tahoe Moon Properties' mailing address is P.O. Box 7521 96145; 866/581-2771; www.tahoemoonproperties.com.

Tahoma

If you're planning to ski at Homewood, you'll find some cozy lodgings a bone's throw away.

PLACES TO STAY

Norfolk Woods Inn: Dogs are "very welcome" to stay at the rustic cabins of this sweet bed-and-breakfast inn. "We love dogs," says a friendly manager. The cabins have two bedrooms upstairs and a kitchen downstairs. Fireplaces make the cabins extra cozy in the winter. A heated pool makes for a refreshing dip during the warmer months.

Rates for the cabins are $100–200. Dogs are $10 extra. 6941 West Lake Boulevard 96142; 530/525-5000.

Tahoe Lake Cottages: Dogs think this place is tops, but not necessarily because of the cozy cottages with full kitchens, knotty-pine interiors, and "old Tahoe" shingled exteriors. More likely it's because of the old-growth cedars and sugar pines that surround those cottages. "They get my leg a-twitchin,'" says Jake Dog.

The owners, the Lafferty family, adore dogs and kids. They used to have a gorgeous 110-pound dog named Brody, who liked to climb trees. He was a very good dog, beloved by guests and the Laffertys. Sadly, he passed away when we visited at Christmas. We were glad to have the chance to hug him good-bye. His old sidekick, a shelty named Leo, now greets guests.

There's a pool and a hot tub here, but no dogs, please, lest their fur gunk up the works. Rates for the cottages are $140–265. Dogs are $10 extra. Be sure to ask for the dog-lover's special discounts. They're available much of the time

in off-season. 7030 Highway 89 96142; 530/525-4411 or 800/852-8246; www
.tahoelakecottages.com.

Tahoma Lodge: Boyce, who owns these cabins, puts it simply: "I've been
allowing dogs here for 19 years. Let's say they're quite welcome." Cabins come
with a woodstove or fireplace. A pool is on the premises and so is a hot tub,
but only for critters of the human persuasion. Pets are welcome with prior
approval. Rates are $90–355. Dogs are $10 extra. 7018 West Lake Boulevard
96142; 530/525-7721; www.tahomalodge.com.

Tahoma Meadows B & B Cottages: Seven of the 15 wonderful cottages
here welcome dogs—and I do mean welcome. Lucky dogs who visit get
biscuits, a couple of tennis balls, a dog bowl (just a loaner, not a keeper), and
a list of favorite doggy hikes and outings in the area. "We really enjoy our dog
guests," says Dick, your host. Shasta, his big white Lab (perfect for camouflage
in the snow), likes to greet new visitors when possible.

The cozy cottages are surrounded by towering pines, with plenty of room
to roam around. Many cottages have fireplaces; most have kitchens. Those
that don't have kitchens are called bed-and-breakfast cottages, and your stay
includes a full breakfast at the main building. Guests of all the cottages can
head to the main building for a fun, relaxing wine-and-cheese hour every
afternoon. You'll enjoy an excellent lake view from the upper floor here.

Rates are $119–295. Dogs are $10 extra. If you stay for more than three nights,
you just pay a $25 dog fee for the length of your stay. 6821 West Lake Boulevard
96142; 530/525-1553 or 866/525-1553; www.tahomameadows.com.

Auburn

While this city has sprawled in so many directions that it looks like a giant
mall, there's still a fairly large, very historic downtown that looks like a big old
valuable antique. It's a great place to sniff out with your dog. And soon there
will be a real-deal dog park here: The Ashley Memorial Dog Park. Keep your
nose to the ground for details.

PARKS, BEACHES, AND RECREATION AREAS

🐾 Auburn Recreation Park

🐾🐾 (See Placer County map on page 200)

You can roll up your overalls and fish in the park's willow-shaded pond and
feel remarkably like Tom Sawyer. Except for the sports fields and playground,
this 62-acre park is a quiet one. Dogs may feel a little intimidated by the perfect
green meadows, but if you look hard, there are a couple of scruffier sections
around the edges. Leashes are a must.

Take the Dry Creek Road exit from Highway 49 and go west a few blocks to
Richardson Drive. 530/885-8461.

⑤ Auburn State Recreation Area

🐾🐾🐾🐾 (See Placer County map on page 200)

This 35,000-acre park lies along 30 miles of the North and Middle Forks of the American River. A few of the activities (and inactivities) available include fishing, gold panning, rafting, swimming, hiking, biking, horse-back riding, sunbathing, picnicking, and camping. Since dogs are supposed to stay out of the rivers and they don't ride bikes or horses, their selection is more limited.

On a quiet day when it's just you, your leashed dog, and the river, try to imagine 10,000 miners crowded into this area in hot pursuit of gold. It makes the occasional passerby seem less obtrusive.

If you and your dog have good hiking paws, 57 miles of trails await you. You can get maps and detailed info online at www.parks.ca.gov. The recreation area has about 25 campsites. They are first-come, first-served and cost $15 a night. A favorite for people who like to get away from the crowds is the Ruck-A-Chucky Campground. It's a quiet, primitive campground next to the Ruck-A-Chucky rapids on the Middle Fork of the American River. Ruck-A-Chucky has only five campsites, but it has a pleasant day-use area with picnic tables. 530/885-4527.

PLACES TO EAT

Awful Annie's: The name doesn't reflect the cuisine here, thank goodness. The food is tasty breakfast and lunch cuisine, with omelettes, soups, and salads. Vegetarians get to choose from a few dishes. Dogs get water if they're thirsty. Dine with your dog at two "dogs-allowed" tables on the attractive deck in Oldtown Auburn. 160 Sacramento Street; 530/888-9857.

Ikeda's Tasty Burgers: "A lot of people bring dogs. They have good taste," says Steve, Ikeda's co-owner. A local sheriff's official tells us Ikeda's has the "best burgers for a long ways," and we believe him. You can see Ikeda's from I-80, so it's a good place to come when you get the road-hungries. 13500 Lincoln Way; 530/885-4243.

La Bou: Eat yummy baked goods, sip stimulating coffee, do it all under the shade of La Bou's canopy. 2150 Grass Valley Highway; 530/823-2303.

PLACES TO STAY

Best Western Golden Key: This is a rosy place to stay: More than 120 rose bushes grace the gardens around the motel. There's plenty of lawn area for your dog to sniff out. Humans enjoy swimming in the year-round pool and relaxing in the spa. Rates are $89–119. Dogs are $15 extra. 13450 Lincoln Way 95603; 530/885-8611 or 888/201-0121.

Holiday Inn Auburn: Stay at this comfy, clean Holiday Inn and you'll get use of the heated outdoor pool, a spa, and little exercise facility. Rates are

$114–165. Dogs are $20 extra. 120 Grass Valley Highway 95603; 530/887-8787 or 800/814-8787.

TraveLodge: Rates are $69–79. Dogs are $10 extra. 13480 Lincoln Way 95603; 530/885-7025 or 877/885-7025.

Roseville

PARKS, BEACHES, AND RECREATION AREAS

For many years, dogs were banned from all Roseville parks. They couldn't set paw in them, even on leash. Eventually, this led dogs to convince their people that something should be done, so their people did something. They talked the city into giving dogs a park of their very own. And now there are two. Soon (maybe even by the time you read this) there will be three! The new park is going to be within William "Bill" Hughes Park. It will feature something I've never seen in a dog park: A special area where you can train your dog off leash and away from the normal hubbub of dog park life. Sounds interesting. Dogs are still verboten in all city parks except these.

The Roseville Dog Owners Group is behind the success of these dog parks. It's a good group to know about, especially if you and your dog are social creatures. They have many outings, including an annual sojourn to the wonderful Gray Eagle Lodge, in Blairsden. (See the *Plumas County* chapter.) For more on the outings or an update on the city's dog parks, see www.rosevilledog.org.

6 Bear Dog Park

🐾🐾🐾🐾🐕 (See Placer County map on page 200)

This two-acre fenced park is named after Bear "Baron Von Der Kristin," a heroic dog who was Roseville's first K-9 police dog. He would be proud of this park, which has all the usual dog-park accoutrements and a few extras, including an agility/obstacle course area, doggy showers, and pooch wading pools. The park has separate large and small dog sections. There's not much shade, but that may come soon.

The park is closed 6–10 A.M. Tuesday for maintenance. It's located within Mahany Park, on the park's north side (next to the baseball fields), at 1575 Pleasant Grove Boulevard. 916/774-5242.

7 Marco Dog Park

🐾🐾🐾🐾🐕 (See Placer County map on page 200)

Doggone it, this is one great place to be a dog. The park is a tail-waggin', leash-free kind of place. It consists of four fenced acres, with hills, flatlands, some shade trees, a doggy/human water fountain, and some small wading pools where your pooch can stay cool.

The park is immensely popular with dogs and their folks. Marco Dog Park would be a perfect park, except for one little problem: It was built on property

that's used as flood control land during the rainy months. That means that during much of the winter, the flat area is under about three feet of water and it's closed to dogs. But ducks love it, if that's any consolation. Thousands come to dip their little webbed toes and bob around for a bit. Duck Park is what locals call it then.

The park, like Petaluma's Rocky Memorial Dog Park (see the *Sonoma County* chapter), was named after a police dog who was killed in the line of duty during a drug raid. Maybe Rocky and Marco are romping around together in Dog Heaven right now with big grins on their snouts, comparing the parks that bear their names.

The park is closed dawn–3:30 P.M. Wednesday for weekly maintenance. Marco Dog Park is at Sierra Gardens Drive just north of Douglas Boulevard. It's in a ravine, several feet lower than the street and surrounding properties, so it's possible you might miss it if you're not looking carefully. 916/774-5242.

Granite Bay

PARKS, BEACHES, AND RECREATION AREAS

8 Folsom Lake State Recreation Area

🐾🐾🐾🐾 (See Placer County map on page 200)

An important entrance to this popular lake is in Granite Bay, just south of Folsom Road. Although most of this large park is in Placer County, we've listed it in *Sacramento County,* under its namesake, the town of Folsom.

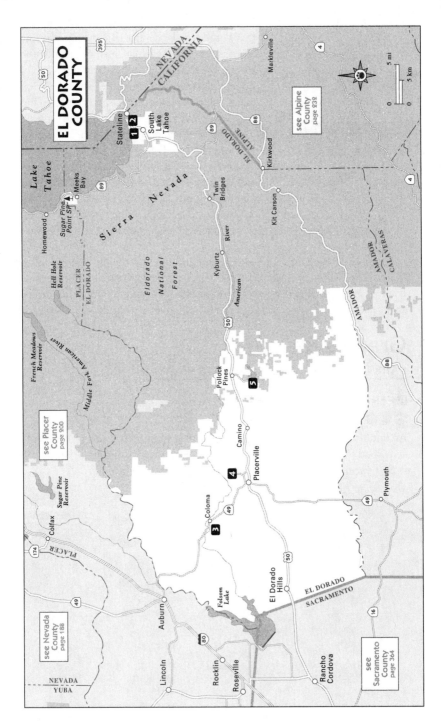

CHAPTER 20

El Dorado County

From Lake Tahoe to the lands east of the Mother Lode vein, this county is as attractive to dogs as it is to their people. The Eldorado National Forest is in your backyard almost everywhere you go. It's as scenic as it is dog-friendly. Lodgings that welcome dogs abound. Nevada's casinos are a bone's throw away. Wineries are plentiful, and many allow dogs in their picnic areas. Apple farms, Christmas tree farms, and even some fishing boats think well-behaved dogs make fine visitors.

When Jake first visited, he got to swim in Lake Tahoe, have a picnic at a winery, sleep at a dog-loving lodging, and run, run, run on many miles of National Forest trails. His tongue constantly hung out of his mouth like a slab of bologna, and he always had a huge smile on his snout. "That's one happy dog," someone observed. "Looks like he belongs in one of those dog food commercials." That's what this county can do to a dog.

PICK OF THE LITTER—EL DORADO COUNTY

BEST OFF-LEASH HIKING
Eldorado National Forest (page 220)

COOLEST RESTAURANT
FiRE+iCE, South Lake Tahoe (page 222)

MOST DOG-FRIENDLY PLACES TO STAY
Alder Inn and Cottages, South Lake Tahoe (page 223)
Fireside Lodge, South Lake Tahoe (page 225)

BEST LODGING FOR OFF-LEASH DOGS
Holly's Place, South Lake Tahoe (page 225)

MOST LUXURIOUS VACATION RENTALS
Stonehenge at Tahoe, South Lake Tahoe (page 227)

OVER-THE-BORDER WINNER
Montbleu Resort, Casino & Spa, South Lake Tahoe (page 224)

BEST CHARTER FISHING
Tahoe Sport Fishing, South Lake Tahoe (page 226)

NATIONAL FORESTS

The *National Forests and Wilderness Areas* resource at the back of this book has important information and safety tips on visiting national forests with your dog and has more information on the Eldorado National Forest.

Eldorado National Forest
🐾🐾🐾🐾🐕

The major part of Eldorado National Forest is in its namesake county. An exception to the off-leash policy of the national forests is in the Desolation Wilderness, where dogs are supposed to be leashed at all times.

South Lake Tahoe

With all its recreational opportunities, South Lake Tahoe can be a terrific place to be a dog. The biggest problem is when a dog's humans head for the ski slopes or casinos and leave their canine friends behind in their lodgings. As we've mentioned more than once, this is a big no-no. (A refreshing exception: At the Fireside Lodge, dogs are allowed to be in a kennel in your room if you're not there. That's a big plus, as long as your dog is used to being crated.) What's a dog to do? Fortunately, most hotels and inns have referrals to dog sitters and kennels. The phone book has loads, too, but it's best to go with a recommendation.

There's another solution: Stay in Stateline, Nevada, just over the border—literally spitting distance from South Lake Tahoe. The new Montbleu Resort, Casino & Spa (formerly Caesar's) has raised the bar on dog-friendly service. We've never listed anyone "over the border," but this one is so special, so close to California, and so important for dogs that we're making an exception. (See the Diversion, *Why Did the Dog Cross the Border?*)

PARKS, BEACHES, AND RECREATION AREAS

South Lake Tahoe has very few places to walk with your dog. Pooches are banned from city beaches and even from those federal beaches and federal parks that charge entrance fees. State parks here allow dogs only in camping and picnic areas. But there are a couple of places (both run by the folks who run the national forests) that dogs will be as excited to visit as humans.

◼ The Forest Service Taylor Creek Visitor's Center
😺😺😺😺 (See El Dorado County map on page 218)

This is among the most fascinating and well-developed wildlife-viewing areas in the state. You and your dog can spend the whole day here agog at Mother Nature while learning about this wet meadow area and the abundant life it supports.

A half-dozen trails with interpretive displays lead you over creeks, through aspen forests and grassy wetlands, and among wildlife you never dreamed you'd see so close to Harrah's and the Montbleu Resort. Among some of the critters you might spot are ospreys, beavers, Canada geese, kokanee salmon, trout, and, yes, hairy woodpeckers. There's even the possibility you'll see some deer and coyotes, so keep a tight hold on that leash.

The beach and undeveloped forestlands around the visitors center provide ample room to get away from the heavy summer crowds. If you plan to make a day of it, pack a lunch to eat at the comfortable picnic areas here.

From the junction of U.S. 50 and Highway 89, the center is about three miles north on Highway 89. The entrance is on your right. 530/543-2674.

◼ Tallac Historic Picnic Site/Kiva Beach
😺😺😺 (See El Dorado County map on page 218)

The huge swath of scattered pine trees that greets you as you enter this area is just as enticing for your leashed dog as the shoreline itself. There's some sage undergrowth, but it's fairly easy to navigate.

If you want to go directly to the water, just park and take the long dirt trail. The water's edge is a large and sandy area and provides a great panorama of

DIVERSION

Here Comes the Bride... and the Groom... and the Dog:
They've seen it all at the **Chapel of the Bells.** Dogs have worn tuxedos to weddings. They've been the best man, the maid of honor, the ring bearer, or the flower girl. They've given away the bride. "They've even cried," says employee Carolyn Lewis.

The chapel has a pooch-friendly indoor and outdoor facility in the heart of a woodsy but suburban neighborhood. The basic wedding costs $275, including the license but excluding the donation for the minister. For that kind of price, you can afford to bring the dog along on the honeymoon.

If you're in the Tahoe area and want to get married fast but this chapel doesn't ring your bells, just pick up a phone book and look in the Yellow Pages under Weddings. You're sure to find something the bride, groom, and pooch will all remember happily ever after.

The Chapel of the Bells is at 2700 U.S. 50. Its mailing address is P.O. Box 18410, South Lake Tahoe, CA 96151. 530/544-1112 or 800/247-4333; www.weddingtahoe.com.

Lake Tahoe. Apparently there have been some problems with off-leash dogs of late, so the pooch patrol is out in force. If you don't want a citation, don't forget to leash up and scoop up.

You can also have a picnic with your dog in the shady picnic area, or take him on a hike up the Tallac Historic Trail, which starts near the east end of the beach. There he'll be shaded from the sun and inundated with fascinating tidbits about the area's past. Poop-bag dispensers remind you to keep this historic area free of present-day dog reminders.

From the junction of U.S. 50 and Highway 89, take Highway 89 north about 2.5 miles. The entrance is on your right. 530/573-2674.

PLACES TO EAT

Colombo's Burgers A-Go-Go: You and your hungry dog can dine on burgers, chicken nuggets, and the like at the outdoor tables here. 841 Emerald Bay Road; 530/541-4646.

FiRE + iCE: This is one of the coolest (and hottest) dining experiences you'll ever have, with or without a dog at your side. It's right in the center of town, under the Heavenly gondola. Dogs can join you at the eight patio tables at the outdoor area, which has three fire pits for those chilly nights. (It's where the bar area is too, conveniently enough.) There is no menu at FiRE + iCE. It's strictly improv here. You choose the meats, seafoods, pastas, veggies, and sauces, bring it to the chefs at the grill, and watch it get cooked to perfection. That part takes place inside, but the staffers here say you're welcome to leave your dog tied up to your table outside while you're selecting your cuisine and watching it cook. If your dog doesn't like that idea, you and your human dining partner can take turns going inside.

The staff here is about as friendly and dynamic as they come. "I'm one of the biggest animal lovers on the planet!" exclaims bar manager Justin. "I've been known to see dogs and go back and make them a little beef and rice dish." He says other servers also love dogs and dole out occasional goodies. The restaurant is part of the Marriott Timber Lodge (which doesn't allow doggies to overnight, boo-hoo). 4100 Lake Tahoe Boulevard; 530/542-6650.

Grass Roots Natural Foods: This is a great place to visit for healthful, wholesome food. It even tastes delicious! Your dog can join you at the benches outside the big old blue house/store. If you want to make it an extra special dog day, buy some natural dog treats inside so your dog can eat with you. There's even a large grassy area to sniff around. 2040 Dunlap Drive; 530/541-7788.

Sprouts: As the name might imply, fresh, natural foods, not greasy onion rings and shakes, are the forte here. Eat at the picnic tables with your pooch. 3125 Harrison Avenue; 530/541-6969.

PLACES TO STAY

Please don't leave your dog alone in your room and go gamble across the state line! (See the introduction to the *South Lake Tahoe* section for more on this, and the Diversion *Why Did the Dog Cross the Border?* for a potential solution.)

Alder Inn and Cottages: If you feel like hitting the slopes but your dog just doesn't have the urge to don her skis, the inn, set on four wooded acres, can supply you with a dog-sitter and/or dog-walker for a decent fee. If you have more than one pooch, it will cost you a little extra. We've never used the service, but we've heard dogs get lots of tender loving care. In addition, the folks at the motel provide pooches with dog treats. Jake thinks that's a dog-gone decent thing to do. Rates are $54–125. Dogs are $10 extra. 1072 Ski Run Boulevard 96150; 530/544-4485 or 800/544-0056; www.alderinn.com.

Best Western Timber Cove Lodge: Dogs enjoy the courtyard here, and "we love dogs," says a manager. Room rates are $80–300. Dogs are $25 extra, and a $100 doggy deposit is required. 3411 Lake Tahoe Boulevard 96150; 800/972-8558; www.timbercovetahoe.com.

Big Pines Mountain House of Tahoe: Some of the rooms at this comfy motel have kitchenettes, and some even have fireplaces. You'll also get free Wi-Fi and a complimentary large continental breakfast. There's private beach access here, which is nice for water dogs, since all they can do at the motel's pool is stare at it longingly. Crated dogs are preferred, but not mandatory. Rates are $60–190. Dogs are $25 extra per room (the limit is two). 4083 Cedar Avenue 96150; 530/541-5155 or 800/288-4083; www.bigpinesmountainhouse.com.

Days Inn at Lake Tahoe: Bosco, a Mill Valley dog of the half-beagle persuasion, heartily recommends this Days Inn. "It's a great place, for a Days Inn," he writes. Rates are $70–169. Pooches are $10 extra and must be a year old before visiting here. Be sure to let the staff know ahead of time that you're bringing a pooch; otherwise the pooch-designated rooms might be booked with nondog people. 968 Park Avenue 96157; 530/541-4800; www.hotellaketahoe.com.

Emerald Bay State Park: Camping is available only in the summer. Although dogs are not allowed on the trails or the beaches, it's worth it to camp here just to be in this park's splendor. About 100 campsites are on the south side of the tranquil bay. Sites are $20. The park is on Highway 89, about eight miles north of the junction of Highway 89 and U.S. 50. Call park headquarters at 530/525-7277 for information. For reservations, call 800/444-7275.

Fallen Leaf Lake: This is a good place for dogs who enjoy socializing. In summer, chances are good that you'll be in close proximity to dozens of campers in

DIVERSION

Why Did the Dog Cross the Border? To get to the most dog-friendly place around. **Montbleu Resort, Casino & Spa** is just over the Nevada border, and we usually don't give space to businesses past the state line. But this one's so close, so convenient, and so dog-friendly we simply had to include it.

If you're going to be spending time and money at casinos, this elegant hotel—totally reworked and upgraded from its previous incarnation as Caesar's—is the perfect place to stay with your dog. Dogs are allowed to stay alone in the rooms. In fact, it's almost expected. You get a special doorknob tag for times when your dog is on her own, so a housekeeper doesn't walk in and get a surprise. As long as your dog isn't anxious when left alone in strange places, it's an ideal setup. You can gamble, check on her, gamble some more, take her for a walk and get some fresh air, and on into the night. Hopefully by the time you retire for the night you'll be celebrating your winnings, and not crying on her furry shoulder about that roulette ball that was just one little number away from making you rich.

Dogs get treated like royalty at the hotel. When you sign up for the hotel's Pet Package, your dog gets a doggy bed, water and food bowls, a biscuit or two, a keepsake pet tag, and access to a doggy room-service menu.

The staff is happy to point you toward the hotel's little dog-walking area (it's not fenced, so leashes are a must) and the dog-friendly Lam Watah Trail that leads to the lake. During winter, the hotel can arrange a horse-drawn sled trip for you and your dog. Room rates are $79–289. The hotel also has a variety of stunning suites available, should your pockets be deep. 55 Highway 50, Stateline, NV 89449; 775/588-3515 or 888/829-7630; www.montbleuresort.com.

this popular recreational lake area on U.S. Forest Service land. Anglers with dogs like to come here to take advantage of the hot bite the lake has in the summer.

There are 205 campsites. Fees are $20 a night. From the junction of Highway 89 and U.S. 50, go north about two miles on Highway 89 to the Fallen Leaf Lake turnoff. Go left and drive 1.5 miles to the camping area. Call 530/543-2600 for park information. For reservations, call 877/444-6777.

If you prefer to be away from the madding crowd, the Desolation Wilderness is accessible from here. There you can camp in peace, except for the occasional twittering of songbirds. Camping here costs $5 per person per night for the first two nights. After that, there's no charge. You must have a permit. And unlike in many other wilderness areas, dogs must be leashed.

Fireside Lodge: What used to be an old run-down motel is now a sparkling, fun, super-dog-friendly lodging. The rooms all sport a unique country mountain theme, with names such as the True West Room, the Angler Room, and the Bear's Den Suite (our favorite). The rooms are all cheery log-cabin style, with beautiful river-rock gas fireplaces and decor that lives up to the room's name. Each room also has a microwave and little fridge.

But wait! That's not all. Stay here and you get to go to the lodge's super-cozy Gathering Room for a wonderful cocktail hour and an expanded continental breakfast.

But there's still more! And this is the part your dog has been waiting for: The property backs up to national forest land, and you know how joyous national forests make dogs. In addition, use of the lodge's kayaks comes free with your room, and dogs are more than welcome to ride along. It's a 15-minute walk to the lake, so either someone at the lodge will drive the kayak to the lake for you, or you can do it yourself. (The staff will also tell you about some terrific paddling spots and beaches that swimming dogs adore.) And to top it off, all dogs who visit get dog cookies. Their people get doggy sheets to put on the beds and poop bags for those less-scenic moments.

Your dog can stay in your room while you're skiing or gambling as long as she's in a crate. This dogs-allowed-alone rule is a rarity in the area. Rooms are $99–169. Dogs are $20 extra and require a $100 deposit. 515 Emerald Bay Road 96150; 530/544-5515 or 800/MYCABIN (800/692-2246); www.tahoefiresidelodge.com.

Holly's Place: The wonderfully cozy cabins on this 2.5-acre property are nestled under fragrant pines, and the property is completely enclosed by a six-foot-high wall of stacked firewood. That means well-behaved dogs can be off leash here! And children enjoy the place too: Kids get to use the sandbox in summer, play outdoor games, try their hand at Ping-Pong, glide on sleds in winter, and even watch movies while eating hot popcorn. Please note that there are no in-room phones, and that maid service is available only by request during your stay. This is advertised as promoting much-sought privacy. Rates are $165–450. Dogs are $15 extra and must get prior approval. The mailing address is P.O. Box 13197, South Lake Tahoe, CA 96151; the street address is

DIVERSION

Will Your Doggy Get Soggy?: If you want to fish, sail, or motor around Lake Tahoe but don't want to leave your furry friend behind, there's good news: A few **boat-rental** businesses and **sport-fishing charters** allow well-behaved dogs who promise not to get the decks wetter than the lake will get them (if ya know what I mean).

You'll want a fairly calm dog who isn't so enticed by water that he'll jump in and paddle wherever his webbed paws will take him. Jake the Water Dog has been known to belly-flop out of a slow boat and swim oh-so-joyously around the lake, oblivious to the calls and enticements we were using to try to lure him back. I could just picture him thinking, "Hmm, swimming or stale crust of peanut butter sandwich? See ya later, Maria!"

Tahoe Keys Boat and Charter Rentals offers several types of boats, including sailboats, pontoon boats, and regular old fast motorboats. Rates are $105–170 per hour. Half-day and full-day rates are significantly discounted. 2345 Venice Drive East, South Lake Tahoe; 530/544-8888; www.tahoesports.com.

Dogs who wish for fish can join you in a chartered trout-fishing boat run by Tahoe Sport Fishing as long as the boat isn't crowded. Rates are $85–95 per person for a half-day trip. 900 Ski Run Boulevard, South Lake Tahoe; 530/541-5448; www.tahoesportfishing.com.

1201 Rufus Allen Boulevard 96150; 530/544-7040 or 800/745-7041; www.hollysplace.com.

Inn at Heavenly B&B Lodge: If you like mountains, trees, steam baths, saunas, and bed-and-breakfast inns, and if you really like your dog, come here! Dogs are welcome at this cozy bed-and-breakfast lodge, which is surrounded by a lovely wooded park. Most rooms have attractive river-rock gas fireplaces, patchwork quilts, and even log furniture. And unlike many other bed-and-breakfasts, each of the 14 rooms has its own bathroom and cable TV. (None of that business of sharing the WC with the neighbors while pining away for ESPN.) Rooms also have their own mini fridges and microwaves. Human guests get to use the spa room (hot tub, steam bath, and sauna) privately for one hour per day. Rates are $69–160. Dogs are $20 extra. 1261 Ski Run Boulevard 96150; 530/544-4244 or 800/692-2246; www.innatheavenly.com.

Motel 6: Too many people have left their dogs alone in their rooms here. This is a huge no-no. The motel has kennel and dog-sitter info available now to help eliminate this problem. (Many hotels around here do. It's an important service for this neck of the woods.) Rates are $39–105. 2375 Lake Tahoe Boulevard 95731; 530/542-1400.

Ridgewood Inn: Montana the Dog wrote to tell us about this cute, slightly upscale motel, with each room featuring a river-rock gas fireplace. The lodging's owners have a big, friendly yellow Lab (friendly, of course, is excess verbiage when describing a yellow Lab) who might greet you on your arrival. Rates are $62–89. Dogs are $10 extra. 1341 Emerald Bay Road 96150; 530/541-8589; www.ridgewoodinn.com.

South Lake Tahoe Reservation Bureau: Tired of motel roulette? Sick of toilet bowls with banners bragging about their sanitary conditions? You and your dog should consider phoning this reputable vacation rental bureau, where you can choose from dozens of dog-friendly cabins, condos, and houses. Many of the rentals even come with fenced-in yards. Rentals vary from studios to four-bedroom homes. Rates are $150–1,000. Dogs are $25 for the length of your stay. There may be a deposit as well. The agency works hand-in-hand with the Tahoe Keys Resort, but these rentals are in areas other than those of the Keys. 599 Tahoe Keys Boulevard 96151; 530/544-5397 or 800/462-5397; www.tahoevacationguide.com.

Spruce Grove: The cabins and suites here are really fun places to stay with a dog. All cabins are decorated in a vintage Tahoe theme. You'll find Field and Stream, billed as "the ultimate hideaway for the American angler," and the Bear's Den cabin, complete with a large river-rock fireplace. In addition, you and your pooch can stay at El Snowshoe, The Pioneer, and The Prospector, to name a few of the other theme cabins. While your dog may not give an arf about the decor, he'll be mighty happy to know that the whole property is fenced in. That means you can feel pretty secure in letting your pooch off leash if he's under voice control. Each cabin has a fully equipped kitchen and a gas fireplace. Gourmet coffee and tasty muffins are up for grabs in the morning. Rates are $150–295. 3597 Spruce Avenue 96150; 530/544-0549 or 800/777-0914; www.sprucegrovetahoe.com.

Stonehenge at Tahoe: Seven of the nine super-luxurious vacation rental homes offered by this agency welcome dogs. In one of the more unusual houses, guests have to enter a big stone cavern with a sod roof to get to the front door. Then there's another huge boulder in one end of the very large living room. (This one is aptly named Stonehenge, the agency's namesake.) The houses are so different and uniquely designed that it's hard to find any common words to describe them, except spacious and upscale. Rates range $200–1,000 nightly. For the budget-conscious, the agency offers a stunning cottage (really a house) on the Nevada section of the lake, for $200–275 nightly. The agency's mailing address is P.O. Box 9541 96158; 530/577-0732 or 800/822-1460; www.tahoestonehenge.com.

Tahoe Keys Resort: Dogs who like to have a home away from home, as opposed to a motel room away from home, will drool for joy when you spend your vacation here. And if your dog is a water dog, get out the drool bucket. The resort is a 750-acre community laced with 11 miles of inland waterways, right on the southern edge of Lake Tahoe. Each house is a waterfront home, situated on one of numerous lagoons. Rentals vary from studio condos to four-bedroom homes. Pooches are permitted in a bunch of the homes. Rates are $95–1,700 per night. Dogs require a $25 fee, which covers the length of your stay, and may require a deposit. 599 Tahoe Keys Boulevard 96151; 530/544-5397 or 800/462-5397; www.tahoevacationguide.com.

Tahoe Valley Campground: This is an attractive campground for such a large one, with a total of 413 camping and RV sites gracing the place. You'll find a rec room, a heated pool, laundry facilities, a tennis court, and a playground, to name a few of the amenities. There's even a free casino shuttle bus that will shuffle you off to the wonders on the other side of the state border. (No dogs allowed, but that's OK since most dogs don't understand crapshooting or blackjack.) The Truckee River is about 0.25 mile from the park, and there are plenty of trees surrounding the campground. A big surprise is that it's open year-round these days. Rates are $27–49. 1175 Melba Street 96158; 530/541-2222; www.rvonthego.com.

3 Peaks Resort and Beach Club: The logo of this motel-like resort is an adorable Saint Bernard dog wearing Hawaiian shorts. All the rooms have been remodeled of late. (Yay! No more carpeting on the walls!) They're reminiscent of cozy cabins, with pine paneling and pine furniture. A few have gas fireplaces, and some suites with kitchens are available. The grounds of the resort are a treat for dogs, with lots of grass and big trees to sniff out. Humans love the heated outdoor swimming pool and hot tub. People who stay here also get to enjoy a private gated beach nearby. Dogs have to remain on terra firma. Rates are $49–109, with suites running up to $229. Pets are $15 extra. 931 Park Avenue 96150; 800/331-3951; www.lake-tahoe-hotels.com.

Coloma

PARKS, BEACHES, AND RECREATION AREAS

🐾 Marshall Gold Discovery State Historic Park

🐾🐾🐾 (See El Dorado County map on page 218)

James Marshall, whose discovery of gold in John Sutter's mill here started the Gold Rush, died a penniless recluse. But at least he had a dog-friendly state park dedicated to him.

Dogs are allowed in more places here than at most state parks. While they're banned from American River beaches and most trails, they can hang out with you at picnic areas and walk with you in the meadow behind the visitors center. They can stroll along Main Street and peer at historic buildings, including a replica of Sutter's Mill. Dogs are even permitted to accompany you to the Munroe Orchard, where you can pick a piece of fruit and sit under a tree to while away the afternoon while your friends pan for gold in the river.

Rates are $5 per car. The park is on Highway 49 between Placerville and Auburn. 530/622-3470.

Placerville

When this city was one of the great camps of Gold Country, it was first known as Dry Diggins. The name lasted about a year. In 1849, after a number of lynchings, the place became known as Hangtown.

People had it tough back then. But dogs may have it even tougher here today, since there are very few parks. Open land has been replaced by strip shopping centers and new housing. The name Placerville may have been good for welcoming suburbia, but dogs should be sorely disappointed at the changes the decades have brought to this city on the east side of the famous Mother Lode vein.

Still, the historic downtown is a fun place to stroll with your dog. And you can even learn something about the old Gold Rush days if you visit Hangtown's Gold Bug Park.

PARKS, BEACHES, AND RECREATION AREAS

◪ Hangtown's Gold Bug Park
🐾🐾🐾 (See El Dorado County map on page 218)

Dogs dig it here. But it's not the gold they dig (lucrative as they may be, such terrierlike habits are discouraged). It's the park itself. Gold Bug is the city's largest park. While dogs aren't allowed to run around without a leash, it's a great place for them to stretch their legs while they explore a park that was once home to 250 mines.

If you're traveling with another human, one of you can walk around the park's dirt paths with the dog or picnic in the shade of oaks and pines while the other visits the Gold Bug Mine, which bans dogs. The mine is an educational experience for anyone who ever wondered what it was like inside one of these places. Admission to the mine is $4 for adults. Half-pints ages 7–16 are a buck. Quarter-pints (under seven) are free. An additional $1 will rent you a fascinating audiotape-guided tour.

The park is easily accessible from U.S. 50. Take the Bedford Avenue exit north for almost a mile and you're there. 530/642-5207; www.goldbug.org.

PLACES TO EAT

Noah's Ark: "Everybody should allow dogs!" exclaimed a dog-lovin' employee at the aptly named Noah's Ark. Buy your food inside this natural food market (doggy needs to stay outside) and eat it at the outdoor tables with your furry friend. You can buy soups, sandwiches, and all kinds of organic goodies. 535 Placerville Drive; 530/621-3663.

Sweetie Pie's: The owners describe themselves as "major dog lovers," so your dog will feel right at home at the umbrella-topped tables here. The muffins, fresh fruit, sandwiches, quiche, and homemade soups taste extra good when you know you're not getting the evil eye from the management. Sweetie

Pie's now features a dinner menu Thursday through Saturday. 577 Main Street; 530/642-0128.

PLACES TO STAY

Best Western Placerville Inn: You get a filling breakfast with your stay here. (Your dog won't.) You also get to dip your paws in the heated outdoor pool. (Your dog won't.) But it's a clean, convenient place to spend a night with the pooch. Rates are $99–189. Dogs are $25 extra. 6850 Green Leaf Drive 95667; 530/622-9100 or 800/854-9100.

Gold Trail Motor Lodge: There's plenty of shade on the well-landscaped grounds of this motel, a real plus in the hot summer months. Rates are $48–68. Dogs are $10 extra, and we're told they usually have to be small to stay here. 1970 Broadway 95667; 530/622-2906.

DIVERSION

Wine, Wine Everywhere: When you think of quality California wine, El Dorado County probably isn't the first vine-covered area that pops into your head. But the county's **vineyards and wineries,** small and family-operated, produce some surprisingly excellent wines. And the good news for your dog is that he doesn't have to be human to set paw on winery property: The majority of the 19 El Dorado Winery Association members permit well-behaved, leashed dogs to join you at their picnic areas. There's nothing like doing a little tasting (you'll have to split up your party so someone is always outside with the pooch), then a little buying, then a little picnicking.

Among the older and better-known wineries is the Boeger Winery, 1709 Carson Road, Placerville; 530/622-8094. Dogs are welcome at the picnic area here, as well as at several other Placerville wineries, including Holly's Hill Vineyards, 3680 Leisure Lane, 530/344-0227; Gold Hill Vineyard, 5660 Vineyard Lane, 530/626-6522; Lava Cap Winery, 2221 Fruitridge Road; 530/621-0175. Dog-friendly wineries can also be found in Camino, Fair Play, and Somerset. See www .eldoradowines.org for a list of area wineries.

One nearby winery that recently came to our attention is Busby Cellars, at 6375 Grizzly Flat Road, in Somerset. It's a family-owned vineyard and winery, with elegant wines and a dog-loving attitude. The winery's dog, Hank, often greets visitors. "We received the warmest welcome for Scooter," writes Rosie and Pat, whose fox terrier was invited to join them as they explored the vineyard. The winery's proprietors go out of their way for well-behaved dogs. There's even a water bowl for thirsty visitors of the canine persuasion. 530/344-9119; www.busbycellars.com.

DIVERSION

To the Trees, If You Please: El Dorado County is home to dozens of **Christmas tree farms** and **apple growers** that welcome dogs. (Please, no leg lifts on the host trees.)

Some farms do double duty and grow both Christmas trees and apples. Your dog can help you sniff out a tasty apple pie or fresh bag of apples at the Harris Tree Farm fruit stand and picnic area starting in August, and toward Christmas, he can watch as you choose and cut your own Christmas tree. (Dogs get all the easy jobs.) Harris is at 2640 Blair Road, in Pollock Pines; 530/644-2194. For a full listing of El Dorado County Christmas Tree Growers farms, see www.visit-eldorado.com/christmas.asp. Most permit leashed pooches.

Mother Lode Orchards has a big friendly black dog who welcomes visitors to the picnic tables, where you can feast on the 30 acres of orchards' peaches, plums, and apples. (You buy these already picked.) 4341 North Canyon Road, in Camino; 530/644-5101. A dog-friendly U-pick option is Hangtown Kid Apple Orchards, 2598 Mace Road, in Camino; 530/647-1810. A list of the county's many apple growers can be found at www.applehill.com.

Mother Lode Motel: Only little dogs up to 25 pounds can stay here. Rates are $54–78. Dogs are $10 extra. 1940 Broadway 95667; 530/622-0895.

Pollock Pines

PARKS, BEACHES, AND RECREATION AREAS

5 Sly Park Recreation Area

🐾🐾🐾 (See El Dorado County map on page 218)

Does your leashed dog like fun boating, terrific hiking, and watching people ride by on horses? Does she like camping but prefer to do it in a somewhat civilized fashion? If so, the Jenkinson Lake camping area is for her. There are 190 sites in this year-round campground, so she'll never feel alone. Alas, she'll feel very dry here: No dogs are allowed to set paw in the lake. (Thanks to Dina Savoroski's dog for letting us know this sad fact. Jake the Water Dog sobbed when he read her letter.)

Reservations are accepted March–September; otherwise, sites are first-come, first-served. Sites are $20–25 a night. Dogs are an additional $2 nightly for the first two pooches. More dogs than two? They're free. If you come here only for the day, the entry fee is $8. From U.S. 50, go south on Sly Park Road for about five miles. 530/644-2545.

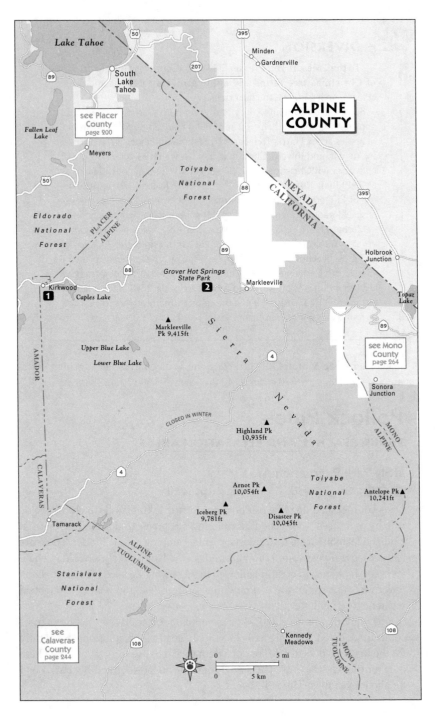

Lake Tahoe

Minden
Gardnerville

ALPINE COUNTY

South Lake Tahoe

Fallen Leaf Lake

see Placer County page 200

Meyers

Toiyabe National Forest

NEVADA
CALIFORNIA

Eldorado National Forest

PLACER
ALPINE

Holbrook Junction

Grover Hot Springs State Park

2

Markleeville

Topaz Lake

Kirkwood

1

Caples Lake

see Mono County page 264

Markleeville Pk 9,415ft

Sierra

Sonora Junction

Upper Blue Lake

Lower Blue Lake

Nevada

MONO
ALPINE

AMADOR

CLOSED IN WINTER

Highland Pk 10,935ft

CALAVERAS

Toiyabe National Forest

Antelope Pk 10,241ft

Arnot Pk 10,054ft

Iceberg Pk 9,781ft

Disaster Pk 10,045ft

Tamarack

ALPINE
TUOLUMNE

Stanislaus National Forest

MONO
TUOLUMNE

see Calaveras County page 244

Kennedy Meadows

0   5 mi
0   5 km

CHAPTER 21

Alpine County

More people live in one Los Angeles high-rise than in this entire county! With a population of only 1,200, Alpine County has plenty of room for a few good dogs. More than 90 percent of the land is public, most of it in the form of very dog-friendly national forests.

You'll find trailheads into the Eldorado, Stanislaus, and Toiyabe National Forests along Highways 88, 89, and 4. You can just pull over into a safe zone and hike with your dog if you know it's national forest land. As soon as you're away from roads and campgrounds, your dog can go leashless in nearly 800 square miles of meadows, alpine forests, and rocky mountains. There's one exception to this, just east of the county line in the Mokelumne Wilderness of Eldorado National Forest off Highway 88.

A drive along Highway 4 can be exciting as well as very scenic. The highway gets so narrow that eventually the stripes in the middle of the road disappear. It's steep and winding in parts, so tell your dog to look up if he's scared of heights. As you ascend to nearly 9,000 feet, the scenery becomes otherworldly.

PICK OF THE LITTER—ALPINE COUNTY

BEST DOGGY PHOTO ID
Kirkwood Ski and Summer Resort hiking, Kirkwood (page 235)

BEST HOT WATER YOU CAN GET INTO
Grover Hot Springs State Park, Markleeville (page 237)

BEST PLACE TO STAY
Sorensen's Resort, Hope Valley (page 236)

BEST KIT-BUILT LODGING
Carson River Resort's 1940s Sears and Roebuck cabins,
Markleeville (page 237)

BEST MUSHY TIME
Kirkwood Ski Resort skijoring lessons, Kirkwood (page 236)

Huge rock formations are everywhere. They're rounded from the passage of time, and some are stacked in impossible configurations.

NATIONAL FORESTS
The *National Forests and Wilderness Areas* resource at the back of this book has important information and safety tips on visiting national forests with your dog and has more information on the national forests listed below.

Eldorado National Forest
🐾🐾🐾🐾🐕

Stanislaus National Forest
🐾🐾🐾🐾🐕

Toiyabe National Forest
🐾🐾🐾🐾🐕

Kirkwood

Kirkwood, one of the best ski and summer recreation areas in California, is also quite accommodating to dogs. The town is split among three counties, but most people here consider Alpine County home.

PARKS, BEACHES, AND RECREATION AREAS

1 Kirkwood Ski and Summer Resort

🐾🐾🐾🐾 (See Alpine County map on page 232)

During summer and, these days, winter, you can't help but see dog after dog romping around this serene high Sierra playground. In summer, most of them have smiles on their slobbery faces because they're welcome to explore the resort's 12 miles of trails through meadows and up slopes and back bowl areas. They're supposed to be on leash, but it's a small price for your dog to pay to be able to tell his friends he vacationed here. In addition to wearing smiles, summer canine visitors can end up wearing a special mini-ski tag that serves as a hiking pass and doggy ID. "It's so cute!" said a dog-loving employee. And beyond cute, the passes are functional: Kirkwood takes a photo of any dog who gets a pass and keeps the photo on file for reference if your dog should get lost. (Of course, this won't likely happen if your dog is leashed, but...) The pass/ID is $5.

In winter, you can learn how to cross-country ski with your pooch! (Please see the Diversion *Get Mushy* for more on this very cool way to spend a vacation with your dog.)

The resort is about 60 miles northeast of Jackson, on Highway 88. You can't miss the signs for it. Once there, ask for a map of the trails from the general store/reservations desk. 209/258-6000; www.kirkwood.com.

PLACES TO STAY

Kirkwood Accommodations: From June through September, lucky dogs are allowed to stay in some of the lodges and condominiums at the Kirkwood Ski and Summer Resort. They're right across from the ski lifts, which won't matter to you in the summer. There's tons of hiking in the area, in addition to fishing, swimming, and general reposing in this peaceful Sierra setting. For more civilized relaxation, there are a pool and hot tub in the community center. Rates for the condos are $130–185 a night during summer. There's also a dog-friendly three-bedroom house available in summer. Rates are $450–600. Weekly and monthly rates are available for the condos and the house. Pooches require a $100 cash deposit and a $35 fee for their stay. The resort is about 60 miles northeast of Jackson, on Highway 88. You can't miss the signs. P.O. Box 1 95646; 209/258-8575 or 869/471-3932; www.kirkwoodaccommodations.com.

DIVERSION

Get Mushy: If you want to bone up on how to cross-country ski, you don't have to leave your pooch behind. Kirkwood Ski Resort actually hosts cross-country ski clinics for people who have dogs! You'll learn about the sport of **skijoring,** in which a rope is attached to a waist belt you wear and to your dog. It's a combination of cross-country skiing and mushing. You'll learn how to pick the right speed so you don't run over your dog or drag him along, or vice versa. You won't encounter real hills, so it doesn't get messy. When you're comfortable, you can take to the resort's skijoring trail! Call for prices and schedule. 209/258-6000; www.kirkwood.com.

Hope Valley

PLACES TO EAT

Sorensen's Resort Cafe: Sorensen's Resort houses a café that's open for breakfast, lunch, and dinner, and in all but the most chilly months, the patio is open and welcomes dogs.

PLACES TO STAY

Sorensen's Resort: This is a magical place to come with your dog. Six of the 33 cozy, nicely appointed cabins permit pooches, and some have gas log fireplaces for your happy dog to curl up in front of on a cold winter night. Several trails that start around the Sorensen property are ideal for hiking or cross-country skiing with your dog. You can just about ski right out your front door. There's an on-site dog-friendly café. Sorensen's is one-stop shopping for you and your smiling dog. Rates for the dog cabins vary seasonally, $155–400. Since not many places around here take dogs, these cabins are in high demand, so reserve well in advance of your stay. 14255 Highway 88 96120; 530/694-2203 or 800/423-9949; www.sorensensresort.com.

Markleeville

Jacob Marklee founded this Old West town in 1861 and spent the rest of his years—all three of them—here. In 1864, he was dead, the loser in a shoot-out with a fellow named H. W. Tuttle. Today, Markleeville has the distinction of being the county seat of the least-populous county in California.

PARKS, BEACHES, AND RECREATION AREAS

2 Grover Hot Springs State Park

😺😺😺😺 (See Alpine County map on page 232)

This is a rare bird for a state park—dogs are actually allowed to walk with you on trails. Leashed dogs can hike through ponderosa pine, incense cedars, and quaking aspen year-round. They're also allowed to camp with you in all four seasons. About the only thing they can't do is bask in the 105°F water in the pools or refresh themselves in the cold plunge area.

But that doesn't mean you have to deprive yourself of the possibly therapeutic effects of the waters. You and a friend can take turns. One can soak in the hot mineral water (it actually comes out of the ground at 148°F!) while the other takes the dog for a walk or on a mini fishing trip at the creeks and lakes here. Then switch. This way, everyone gets to enjoy the best this park has to offer.

The day-use fee, which covers pool use, is $5 per adult, $2 per child. Sleeping at one of the 76 campsites costs $25. The park is three miles west of Markleeville, off Highway 88 on Hot Springs Road. Call 530/694-2248 for information. For reservations, call 800/444-7275.

PLACES TO STAY

Carson River Resort: Dogs and their people are welcome to stay in six of the seven rustic, clean cabins set among the big pines by the east fork of the Carson River. One is an old miner's cabin, and the rest were built from Sears and Roebuck cabin kits from the 1940s. They're real classics. Most have kitchens, and all have a picnic table and barbecue grill. They like dogs here. "The manager was incredibly friendly to Lucky," writes Sara Peterson, who helped us sniff out this place. She also loved the "lovely quilts and warm blankets." The River Cabin has a woodstove, to add to the comfy feel. (If you're a fan of old, little-known novels, stay in this cabin. It's the backdrop for the 1927 romantic novel *The Looted Bonanza*.) Rates are $80–160. Dogs are $15 extra. You can also camp for $25–30. P.O. Box 457 96120; 877/694-2229; www.carsonriverresort.com.

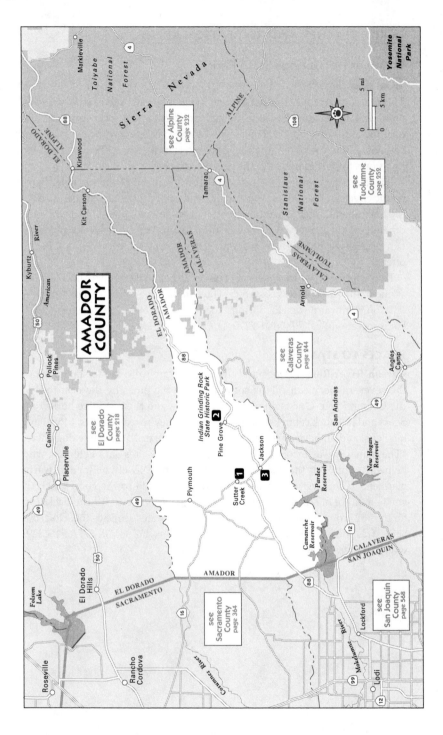

CHAPTER 22

Amador County

Amador County is a place too many people drive through without stopping to take a look around. Highway 88 makes it easy to cruise through this narrow county on the way to another destination. But if you drive past here with blinders on, not only are you missing some quaint old Gold Rush towns, you're also bypassing some of the most unusual vista points in California.

Among the sights you should try to take in is the rocky terrain of the Devil's Garden in the eastern part of the county along Highway 88 in Eldorado National Forest. Nearby are several trailheads leading into sections of this vast forest where dogs can usually prance about leashless. Eldorado National Forest is the only swath of public land in Amador County where dogs can experience this blissful freedom.

NATIONAL FORESTS

The *National Forests and Wilderness Areas* resource at the back of this book has

PICK OF THE LITTER—AMADOR COUNTY

BEST LEASH-FREE HIKING
Eldorado National Forest (page 240)

BEST DIGS IN A QUASI-GHOST TOWN
St. George Hotel, Volcano (page 241)

important information and safety tips on visiting national forests with your dog and has more information on Eldorado National Forest.

Eldorado National Forest
🐾🐾🐾🐾🏃

Sutter Creek

John Sutter, who owned the mill where gold was first discovered in the Mother Lode, also had his Midas-touch hand in a nearby creek. The creek was named after him, and the town came next.

PARKS, BEACHES, AND RECREATION AREAS

1 Minnie Provis Park
🐾🐾 (See Amador County map on page 238)

How often does a dog get to visit a park named after a city clerk? Minnie Provis Park, set in the heart of historic Sutter Creek, may be the only one with such a namesake. Minnie was Sutter Creek's first city clerk. She must have been a good one.

This small, green park is ideally situated if you and your leashed dog happen to be exploring the old downtown section of Sutter Creek. The park, which has its own poop-bag dispenser, is just behind City Hall. Exit Highway 49 at Church Street and go east a half block. Park on the street. 209/267-5647.

PLACES TO STAY

Days Inn Sutter Creek: After a day exploring Gold Country this is a fine place to kick up your heels. It's clean, nicely furnished, and rooms come with a mini-fridge, microwave, and decent continental breakfast. There's free Wi-Fi here, too, should your dog want to write home to tell his pals how much fun he's having on vacation. (You supply the laptop.) Rates are $69–139. Dogs are $10 extra. 271 Hanford Street 95685; 209/267-9177.

Volcano

The '49er miners thought a volcano had formed the bowl-shaped valley here, thus the name. But there is no volcano in Volcano. There is, however, a very picturesque semi–ghost town with some fine remnants of the Mother Lode days. Visit in early spring to view Daffodil Hill, which becomes a resplendent sea of yellow—a sight that may be lost on your dog if she really does see in only black and white.

PLACES TO STAY

St. George Hotel: Dogs come really close to staying in a National Historic Landmark hotel when they visit here. The main building of the hotel is a three-story brick structure built during the Gold Rush. Alas, dogs can't sleep there, but they're welcome to stay at the beautiful bungalow garden room annex, in an elegant room with hardwood floors, lace curtains, and an antique sewing cabinet. It'll remind your dog of Grandma's house. The bungalow is set behind the hotel and overlooks the inn's beautiful gardens. Rates are $107–112. Dogs are $20 extra. 16104 Main Street 95689; 209/296-4458; www.stgeorgehotel.com.

Pine Grove

PARKS, BEACHES, AND RECREATION AREAS

2 Indian Grinding Rock State Historic Park

😊 😊 (See Amador County map on page 238)

Dogs aren't permitted on trails here, but they are allowed on paved walkways and can visit bits of the reconstructed Miwok village and sniff at the old grinding rock. Leashed dogs can even read some of the petroglyphs around the park if they're of the erudite ilk.

Day-use visits cost $6 per carload. There are 23 campsites, available on a first-come, first-served basis. Sites are $15–20. The park is about halfway between Pine Grove and Volcano, on Pine Grove-Volcano Road. 209/296-7488.

Jackson

Jackson is one Old West town where there's still plenty of evidence of a rich and colorful heritage. The streets of downtown look as if they were pulled from a Hollywood back lot. You can even hear lively piano music pouring out of the classic old National Hotel (no dogs allowed).

Dogs are welcome to stroll through the historic downtown district with you. A couple of stores that sell goods reminiscent of the Gold Rush era might allow you in with your dog. These shop owners asked Joe not to tell anyone he shopped there, and we've yet to divulge the names.

The city has only a couple of parks, but there's no shortage of restaurants that will let your dog dine outside with you during good weather.

PARKS, BEACHES, AND RECREATION AREAS

3 Detert Park

😊 😊 (See Amador County map on page 238)

Does your pup like square dancing? Then dog-si-do on over to this pleasant community park's bandstand. Two local square dancing clubs practice here some enchanted evenings, and if you're lucky, you might get to watch (or take part in) some of the finest square dancing around.

If your dog prefers to stroll (on leash), the park has lush lawns and many shady trees. For the kids, there's a swimming pool and a unique playground. The park is an ideal stop if you're visiting the historic part of town. It's just east of Highway 49/88, north of Hoffman Street. 209/223-1646.

PLACES TO EAT

Mel and Faye's Diner: Down a burger and fries while at the "to go" patio with your dog. 205 North Highway 49; 209/223-0853.

PLACES TO STAY

Amador Motel: Dogs, if you want to feel mighty welcome, trot on over to this motel. "I'd rather have dogs here than children," says Mary, the owner. She'll even let pooches run free in the big backyard area here. All this made me realize Mary is a smart woman, but when she told me "your book is my favorite book," I realized she also has very good taste. Rates are $42–58. 12408 Kennedy Flat Road 95642; 209/223-0970.

Jackson Gold Lodge: Even though this lodge is just a bone's throw from Highway 49, it's tucked away on a steep incline so it's fairly well sheltered from traffic noise. Dogs feel perfectly at home in the basic motel rooms and duplex-style cottages here, and the pool provides welcome relief after a hot day of exploring in Gold Country. The lawn here is advertised as "perfect for letting your pets run around, or your kids." Rates are $65–150. Dogs are $10 extra. 850 North Highway 49 95642; 209/223-0486.

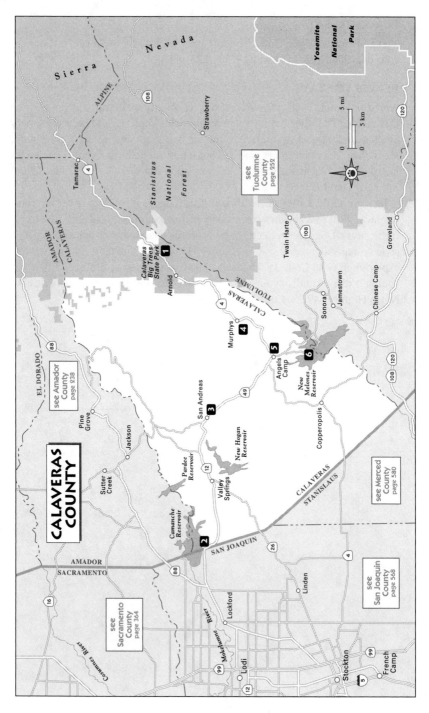

CHAPTER 23

Calaveras County

There are only four traffic lights in this entire Mother Lode county, and they're very new. Only one town (Angels Camp) is incorporated. If you want to mall-hop, you have to drive at least 70 miles. And just about every pickup truck has a dog.

"This is where dogs are still dogs, and there may be more of them than of us people," explained park caretaker Pat Mulgrew, of Murphys. "It's very old California. There's a leash law and it should be obeyed. But local dogs often choose to walk on their own, visit the park, and hang out with their friends. It's just that kind of place."

At least it's that way until the rest of the world moves in with all its ugly baggage. The folks at the Calaveras Lodging and Visitors Association boast that this is one of the fastest-growing counties in California. They're trying to attract more and more companies so they can bring in more residents. The real-estate business is booming. Visit while you can, before this historic land succumbs to suburban sprawl.

PICK OF THE LITTER—CALAVERAS COUNTY

BEST OFF-LEASH HIKING
Stanislaus National Forest (page 246)

MOST HAUNTED LODGING
Hotel Leger, Mokelumne Hill (page 246)

MOST ROMANTIC INN
Courtyard Bed & Breakfast, San Andreas (page 249)

BEST BONES TO PICK
Stories in Stones, Angels Camp (page 251)

NATIONAL FORESTS

The *National Forests and Wilderness Areas* resource at the back of this book has important information and safety tips on visiting national forests with your dog and has more information on the Stanislaus National Forest.

Stanislaus National Forest
🐾🐾🐾🐾🐕

About one-third of Calaveras County has the privilege of being part of Stanislaus National Forest.

Mokelumne Hill

Mok Hill, as it's referred to around here, figured pretty prominently in the wild days of the Gold Rush. (According to newspaper reports, the mining camp here was notorious for being big and bad: 17 people were killed in 17 weeks, and five more were shot the following weekend.) Come sniff out its history with your pup, and then stay at Hotel Leger, said to be haunted with the spirits of some interesting characters from the past.

PLACES TO STAY

Hotel Leger: The rooms of this Gold Rush–era hotel are filled with delightful antiques. Some rooms have fireplaces. And a couple may have ghosts. Interesting as they are to the old hotel's ambience, they're not an amenity you get charged for. So many guests and innkeepers claim to have seen or heard the ghost of George Leger (pronounced luh-ZHAY), the hotel's original owner, and a couple of others from long ago, that there's now a journal at the hotel for guests who want to leave accounts of their close encounters with the spirit world.

Being a historic inn, the walls are thin, and you can potentially hear street noise and sometimes your neighbors. Bring earplugs if this bothers you. Also bring your dog. Dogs enjoy it here, and if there's a ghost, chances are your dog will see it first. At the very least they'll see the hotel's nice yard, and the adjacent little park, where they can sniff around on a leash.

Rates are $55–175. The cheaper rooms share baths. (Not with ghosts, we presume.) Dogs are $20 extra. 8304 Main Street 95254; 209/286-1401; www.hotelleger.com.

Arnold

This is a fun Old West town that shares its name with the pig on *Green Acres*. Joe Dog discovered that it's not mere coincidence. If you're good and hungry, visit the dog-friendly restaurants he scouted out and you'll discover why.

PARKS, BEACHES, AND RECREATION AREAS

◱ Calaveras Big Trees State Park
🐾🐾🐾 (See Calaveras County map on page 244)

Dogs aren't permitted on the trails here, but nothing's stopping them from hiking along the fire roads and paved roads. "You and your dog might see more wilderness on these fire roads than you would on the regular trails," says interpretive ranger Joe Von Herrman.

The giant sequoias aren't accessible from the fire roads, but you'll probably pass by some of the largest sugar pines in existence. Depending on which roads you take, you could hike close to the Stanislaus River, pass by a historic logging railroad, or walk through chaparral-covered slopes and fir-filled forests.

For $1 you can buy a map of the fire roads and trails at the entry kiosk. The day-use fee is $6. There are 129 campsites. Sites are $19. The park is four miles northeast of Arnold, on Highway 4. Follow the signs. For camping reservations, call 800/444-7275. For park information, phone 209/795-2334.

PLACES TO EAT
Blue Coyote Cafe: Dogs feel a kinship with this place. Is it the water the servers give to dog visitors, or is it all in the name? Bring along your poochy dining companion and find out while eating great Southwest grub at the four outdoor tables. 1224 Oak Circle; 209/795-2872.

Giant Burger: Forget about Chez Panisse. Dogs like it plain and simple. And big. And beefy. Jake gives the food here his top rating: four paws and the big drool. Check it out with your dog at the 10 outdoor tables. 846 Highway 4; 209/795-1594.

PLACES TO STAY

Meadowmont Lodge: Huge dogs can't stay here, nor can dogs who shed a lot, but all others are welcome. (Big, shedding Jake had better look elsewhere.) Actually, if you bring a kennel or your dog's bed, you'll have a better chance of staying here with your large or shed-prone dog, especially if she's clean. Rates are $69–125. Dogs are $15 extra. It's at Country Club Drive and Highway 4. The mailing address is P.O. Box E 95223; 209/795-1394.

Sierra Vacation Rentals: Rent a cabin or mountain chalet to take your favorite canine companion and a few friends for an extra-special vacation get-away. All of the rentals have fireplaces or wood-burning stoves for those cold winter nights. Rates for up to eight people and a dog start at $225 per night. Weekly rates are available. Dogs require a $200 deposit. P.O. Box 1080 95223; 209/795-2422 or 800/995-2422; www.sierravacationrentals.com.

Valley Springs

PARKS, BEACHES, AND RECREATION AREAS

🐾 Lake Camanche

🐾🐾🐾 (See Calaveras County map on page 244)

Come here during the off-season, when it's not too hot or too inundated by water-skiers, and your dog will have a delightful visit. Pooches aren't allowed on trails here, but the land is very open, with scattered oaks on rolling hills and lakeside flats. Dogs can walk anywhere you do, as long as you stay off the trails.

Your dog can dip her paws in the water, but since she's supposed to be leashed, she can't pull an Esther Williams. The fishing is fantastic in the spring and early summer, and you can bring your dog along in the boat for good luck. If thoughts of catching bass, bluegill, or trout keep you awake at night, come here, fulfill your dreams, and rest easy.

There are 300 campsites, with rates of $25 a night. Dogs are $4 extra, and there's a two-dog limit per site. Sites are open year-round on a first-come, first-served basis, although reservations are available for holiday weekends. The day-use fee is $9 per car, with that extra $4 charge for hairy beasts. The lake is north of Highway 12 in the easternmost part of the county. Follow the signs seven miles to the entrance. 209/763-5178.

San Andreas

PARKS, BEACHES, AND RECREATION AREAS

❸ Nielsen Park

😺😺 (See Calaveras County map on page 244)

This is a fine place to stop with your leashed pooch during your Gold Country explorations. It's grassy, shady, and set along the refreshing San Andreas Creek.

The park is on Main Street, just east of Highway 49 and close to the local visitor center. There's no official phone number.

PLACES TO STAY

Courtyard Bed & Breakfast: This is a truly enchanting inn. Dogs, don't tell a soul about it. It's our little secret. One of the two rooms here is so romantic it could make a grown dog blush. It's the honeymoon suite, complete with a baby grand piano, private access, a private deck, and a fireplace. There's even a stained glass window over the bath, for those who like to watch Mr. Bubble in living color. The other room is also enchanting, with French blue highlights and oak and wicker furniture.

Hungry travelers like the fact that refreshments are served upon arrival. In the morning, fresh-brewed coffee is delivered to your room. Then you can amble down to the inn's cheery breakfast room, or in good weather, outside to the deck, where you can eat a big breakfast under the shade of a walnut tree. (Dogs prefer the latter option.) If your muscles are aching after a long drive, soak in the outdoor hot tub here. No dogs in the hot tub, though; they have to settle for a good back rub.

The rate for the suite is a mere $125. The other room is $90. 334 West Saint Charles Street 95249; 209/754-1518.

Murphys

"We have more dogs in Murphys than people," says Ron, who works for the park system here. Your dog is sure to love ambling through this sweet old Gold Rush–era town. And if you like wine, this is a great place to visit: Murphys has about a dozen wineries; it's fast becoming one of the wine regions of note in California.

PARKS, BEACHES, AND RECREATION AREAS

🐾 Murphys Park

🐾🐾🐾 (See Calaveras County map on page 244)

This is where the local dogs hang out. They like the shade, they enjoy the creek that flows through here year-round, and they appreciate each other's company. Many of them don't even wait for their owners to leash them up and walk them here. They head over by themselves. "It's breaking the rules, but they don't get themselves in trouble and they have real street smarts," says Pat Mulgrew, a park caretaker.

They also have good taste. The creek here is large, with a wooden footbridge you can cross to walk on the shadier, more secluded side of the park. It's at Main and South Algiers streets. For more info, call Ron at Murphy's Silver Company (that's how things like parks departments work in this neck of the woods). 209/728-2126.

Angels Camp

You can still check out the saloon in the Angels Hotel, on Main Street, where a barkeep told 29-year-old Mark Twain the tale that inspired his first published short story, "The Notorious Jumping Frog of Calaveras County."

Since the story was set in this dog-friendly land, it wouldn't have been complete without an interlude about a dog. The one in Twain's story was named Andrew Jackson, and he was apparently a bulldog. Twain's narrative could easily have been called "The Notorious Fighting Dog of Calaveras County," but publishers may not have jumped at it.

Fighting dogs aren't welcome here, but jumping frogs have never been forgotten. Each year, the town hosts the world-famous Jumping Frog Jubilee. As you may have guessed, dogs are not particularly welcome.

PARKS, BEACHES, AND RECREATION AREAS

🐾 Tryon Park

🐾🐾 (See Calaveras County map on page 244)

You and your gold-digging canine can pan for gold at Angels Creek, which runs right through this small park. It's a good place to take a rest if you're traveling on Highway 4. The park is on Highway 4 at Booster Way. 209/736-2181.

🐾 New Melones Reservoir

🐾🐾🐾 (See Calaveras County map on page 244)

When the lake is full, the five-mile trail that meanders around part of it may actually come close to the shore. But usually you and your leashed dog will

DIVERSION

Dem Dry Bones: Stories in Stones is an earth-science store that feels almost like a small museum. Fossils, rocks, shells, and minerals are labeled in a scientific way and set in cabinets. But unlike in a museum, you can buy almost anything you see here. You'll also find jewelry, educational books and kits, beads, and gift items, should old rocks not light your fire.

The owners and staff here adore dog visitors and welcome them inside. Even with all the tempting, ancient, crunchy items sitting around on the shelves, there haven't been many doggy faux pas here. Once, a little cocker spaniel came in, grabbed a preserved alligator head from a cabinet, and proudly paraded it around the store. When he finally spit out the gator head, it was undamaged, except for a little drool. "It was very funny," says a long-time employee.

The store is in the heart of old Angels Camp, at 1249 South Main Street; 209/736-1300; www.stories-in-stones.com.

have to be content wandering around the rolling foothills, among small scrub oaks that provide little shade. In the summer, it's probably not worth the visit. But the rest of the year, the hiking is pleasant—and the scenery is quite breathtaking in the spring.

Fishing isn't the best in the area, but in the spring the bass bite isn't bad, especially at the lake's northern arms. Your dog is welcome to wet his paws while you fish from shore or to join you on your fishing boat.

There are 300 campsites. They cost $16 a night. (Walk-ins are $12.) For reservations phone 877/444-6777. There's no day-use fee. From Angels Camp, head south on Highway 49 and follow the signs to the lake's north end. 209/536-9094.

PLACES TO STAY

Best Western Cedar Inn and Suites: "This is one of those places where the room is bigger than your house," wrote an impressed dog and his human. "You should check it out." Indeed we did, and it's a modern-yet-homey, clean place to stay when visiting this historic area. (The room size is impressive, and the suites could rival the size of some small houses. Some suites even have a gas fireplace.) People like the outdoor pool and whirlpool, and dogs like getting the crumbs from your continental breakfast. Rates are $89–184. Dogs are $15 extra. 444 South Main Street 95222; 209/736-4000 or 800/767-1127; www.bestwesternangelscamp.com.

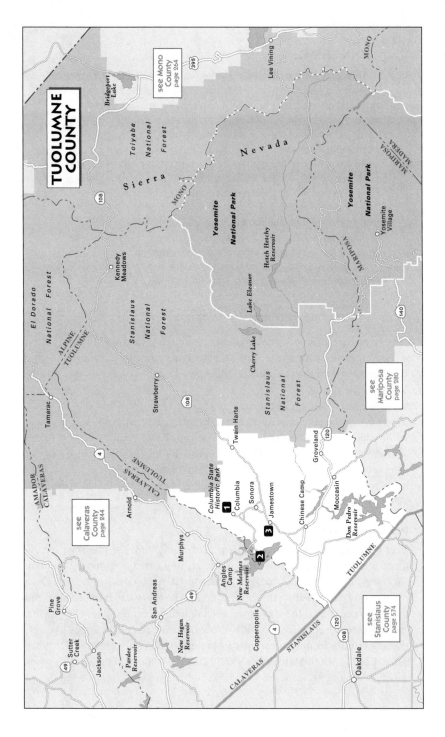

CHAPTER 24

Tuolumne County

For any dogs who don't know how to pronounce the name of this county, think of what you'd say if someone asked you, "To whom should I give this huge, rare steak?" You'd probably pipe up and shout, "To all o' me!" or something like that. And that's close enough.

Tuolumne is a colorful Mother Lode county, with many exciting adventures awaiting dogs and their people. Be sure not to miss Jamestown or the Columbia State Historic Park. Dogs adore these places (during off-season when they're not so crowded).

NATIONAL FORESTS

The *National Forests and Wilderness Areas* resource at the back of this book has important information and safety tips on visiting national forests with your dog and has more information on the Stanislaus National Forest.

PICK OF THE LITTER—TUOLUMNE COUNTY

BEST LIVING GHOST TOWN
Columbia State Historic Park, Columbia (page 256)

CATTIEST MAÎTRE D'
Garfield, of the National Hotel Restaurant (page 258)

MOST HISTORIC HAUNTED DOG-FRIENDLY INN
National Hotel, Jamestown (page 258)

MOST HISTORIC UNHAUNTED DOG-FRIENDLY INN
Groveland Hotel, Groveland (page 263)

BEST RIVERSIDE LODGING
Rivers Resort, Strawberry (page 255)

BEST EYEFUL FOR DOGS
Tom Fraser's Carriage Tours horse heinies, Jamestown (page 258)

BEST GOLD-COUNTRY ADVENTURE
Gold Prospecting Expeditions, Jamestown (page 259)

Stanislaus National Forest
🐾🐾🐾🐾🐕

There are plenty of places in this stunning forest where you can pull off along the northeast section of Highway 108 to hike or camp.

NATIONAL PARKS

Yosemite National Park
🐾🐾🐾

Yosemite has a bad reputation among dogs. Some of it's deserved, some isn't. (See the full listing in the *Mariposa County* chapter.)

Strawberry

PLACES TO STAY

Cabins at Strawberry: Chocolate Lab Reina loves to greet fellow canines as they arrive for their stay at these very upscale cabins. "She thinks she owns the place," says Mary, who really does.

Three of the 10 cabins allow dogs. They're actually not so much cabins as two-story houses with an airy cabin ambience. Each has three bedrooms, two bathrooms, a gas fireplace, very tasteful decor, a fully equipped kitchen, and a large fenced deck. Most overlook the river, which can be a deliciously torturous view for water dogs such as Jake, who sit there staring in anticipation at the flowing water, riveted... waiting... trembling. Normal dogs (sorry, Jake) simply enjoy the earthy scents and the surrounding pines, cedars, and firs.

Rates are $120–209. There's a $200 pooch deposit. 31888 Highway 108 95375; 209/965-0885 or 888/965-0885; www.strawberrycabins.com.

Rivers Resort: If you and your dog want to stay in cabins right on the Stanislaus River, rent one of the 14 very cozy cabins here. The cabins were recently upgraded (the place was formerly the Sparrow Resort), and they're better than ever. Humans drool over the large fireplaces in some cottages, and they love the quality wood interiors and the heated pool that's available in warmer months. Dogs go gaga over the fact that the national forest surrounds this resort. Joe Dog loved to fall asleep to the sound of the river. If you don't want to get away from it all, fear not—there's cable TV.

Cottages range in size 1–4 bedrooms, and rates are $120–209. Weekly rates are available. There's a $200 deposit for dogs. The deposit smarts, but you can use your credit card. There's no street address, but the resort is one of a few businesses on Highway 108 in Strawberry. The mailing address is P.O. Box 81 95375; 209/965-3278 for information, or 800/514-6777; www.gorrr.com.

Mi-Wuk Village

PLACES TO STAY

Mi-Wuk Village Inn and Resort: The country-style rooms at this nice little motel have VCRs, so if all the nature around here is just too natural for you, snuggle up with your dog in front of a campy old flick. Rates are $89–199. Pooches are $20 extra. 24680 Highway 108 95346; 209/586-3031 or 800/549-7886; www.miwukvillageinn.com.

Columbia

PARKS, BEACHES, AND RECREATION AREAS

1 Columbia State Historic Park

(See Tuolumne County map on page 252)

This park is actually a ghost town from the Gold Rush. But it's preserved in such a manner that it still has a pulse. It's alive. You can get a haircut at the state's oldest barbershop, sip sarsaparilla at a saloon, and buy old-style dry goods at one of the 1850s stores.

Be sure to bring a friend if you want to enter these establishments, because dogs have to stay outside (and be leashed), and you shouldn't leave them tied up, even for a few minutes. Just take turns dog-sitting.

But you don't have to go into the buildings to enjoy this town. The dogs and I like to saunter down the streets (no cars allowed!), kicking up dust as we amble along. We can stop and look inside these wonderful old buildings, but we get along fine without having to actually go inside. No shopping means no cash outflow. Since there's no admission fee at this "living museum," it's a very cheap date.

To give a dog a break from all the history here, go to the old schoolhouse and find the adjacent Karen Bakersville Smith Memorial Trail (named after a local teacher who died in a car crash). It's only a little over a half mile long, but it's wonderful to spy on nature as you hike through meadows and oak woodlands.

Please don't bring a dog here during the summer, unless it's raining or at least threatening to. It gets torturously crowded. We last visited in late fall, when the weather was perfect and the park almost empty.

Stop by the park headquarters and pick up a brochure outlining a 1.5-hour tour. From Highway 49, drive north on Parrott's Ferry Road/County Road E18. The entrance is in just over 1.5 miles, and it's on your right. 209/532-3184 or 209/588-9128; www.columbiacalifornia.com.

PLACES TO EAT

The Lickskillet: OK, we promise the name has nothing to do with the fact that this excellent restaurant welcomes dogs to dine at its outdoor tables. Dogs don't get to lick the skillets, but they do lick their chops over the unique cuisine and dog-friendly attitude here. "Dogs get water before their owners get a menu," says Peg, one of the dog-lovin' owners. The Lickskillet's 35 outdoor tables are a favorite hangout for local dogs and their people. The restaurant is open Wednesday–Sunday for dinner, and Thursday–Sunday for lunch. As with most other local eateries, the outdoor tables go south in the winter, so dogs are wise to come here in the warmer eight or nine months of the year. 11256 State Street; 209/536-9599.

PLACES TO STAY

Columbia Gem Motel: The "motel" name of this little gem, tucked under a canopy of pines and sequoias a bone's throw from Columbia State Historic Park, doesn't really do it justice. Only four units are of the motel persuasion. Seven are log cabins, with warm and cozy interiors (which, fortunately, are cool and cozy in summer).

The Gem (I can't in good conscience write "motel") is set on an acre of lovely manicured land, which leashed dogs are free to peruse as long as their humans promise to scoop the poop. Be aware that Baby, the owner's friendly cat, may be wandering around the property while you are. If your dog is like Jake, keep a tight hold of that leash.

Rates are $79–139, or $158 for a cabin that sleeps up to eight. 22131 Parrott's Ferry Road 95310; 209/532-4508 or 866/436-6685; www.columbiagem.com.

Jamestown

Jamestown was one of Bill Dog's favorite places to visit. During off-season, it's so uncrowded that he felt like one of the locals in this small Mother Lode town. That's when the town stops being quaint and becomes a real Old West hangout. Bill liked to sit on a bench outside one of the dusty buildings and listen to a couple of old natives tell their stories. But more than anything else, he enjoyed wearing his rust-colored bandanna around his shiny black neck. He knew he looked devastating.

Dogs can really have fun here. Between panning for gold, riding in a horse-drawn carriage, and exploring this colorful old town, they'll have enough entertainment to last them until their next vacation.

PARKS, BEACHES, AND RECREATION AREAS

2 New Melones Reservoir

🐾🐾🐾 (See Tuolumne County map on page 252)

Since the bulk of the lake (and the best fishing) is on the Calaveras County side, you'll find its description in the *Angels Camp* section of that chapter.

DIVERSION

Get Hot to Trot: Want a terrific way to experience Jamestown with your well-behaved pooch? Try **Tom Fraser's Carriage Tours.** You and your dog will ride in an antique carriage while a beautiful horse pulls you along the historic streets. But when you talk with your dog after your trip, you'll realize that the two of you had completely different experiences.

What humans see: antique shops, wooden sidewalks, great Old West buildings, old trains, and tourists taking pictures.

What dogs see: a horse's butt, a horse's butt, a horse's butt, a passing cat, and a horse's butt.

The price is right. A 20-minute ride is $6 per adult, $5 per child. Dogs have to sit on the floor, and they ride free. The carriages load at the park on Main Street. Rides are by reservation. 209/984-3125. (Owner Tom Fraser now also owns Coach Mountain Stage Lines, in nearby Columbia, should you want to explore that nifty area with your dog behind a horse.)

PLACES TO EAT

The Main Street Bar and Grill: You and your happy dog can enjoy some good pub grub together on the back patio here. The garlic fries alone are worth a stop. The patio is a pleasant place to spend a warm evening. A big thanks to Dixie and Bella, two big San Francisco dogs who first told us about this place. Good dogs! 18228 Main Street; 209/984-4830.

National Hotel Restaurant: Care for a little history with your Ruby Trout Amandine? Then dine at the vine-covered patio of this 1859 hotel's restaurant with your dog at your side. You may even see the hotel's resident ghost, but she pretty much stays in the hotel, from what we hear. (You can stay here too!) The food here is fresh and delicious. Lunch offers tasty salads and sandwiches (try the blackened chicken sandwich; it comes with bacon—need I say more?), and dinner expands to fancier fare. The mahi macadamia is a favorite. The brunch and dessert menus are also droolworthy.

If your dog is cat-crazy, make sure Garfield the cat, the resident "patio maître d'" is not on duty during your visit. (The hotel's website shows Garfield wearing a black bow tie. He is an elegant feline who does not look kindly on being on a dog's hit list.) 18183 Main Street; 209/894-3446.

PLACES TO STAY

National Hotel: Want some luxury with your history? Try this enchanting place. Built in 1859, it's one of the oldest continuously running hotels in California. The rooms are tastefully furnished with simple antique decor, and unlike in the old days, the hotel now provides private bathrooms and air-conditioning.

You may even run into Flo, the famed resident ghost. Apparently this harmless spirit favors the upstairs rooms but floats around here and there. We've heard from a guest who felt the room get chilly before she turned on the air-conditioning on a warm summer day, "and then Skitches (her dog) started twisting his head this way and that, obviously seeing something I couldn't see. He was scared at first but then started thumping his tail. I guess he met Flo!"

Ghost sightings or not, we think it's fantastic that dogs are allowed in such a historic lodging. Actually, well-behaved dogs are not just allowed here; they're welcomed with open arms! Dog guests get a nifty pet basket with treats, food and water bowls, towels, and poop bags. The owner, Stephen Willey, has dogs, loves dogs, and welcomes your good dog. "We will also accept well-behaved pet owners, if their pets can vouch for them," he writes on the hotel's website. Be sure to check out the hotel's dog-friendly patio restaurant. An excellent breakfast buffet comes with the cost of the room. Rates are $95–140. Dogs are $25 extra. 77 Main Street 95327; 209/984-3446 or 800/894-3446; www .national-hotel.com.

DIVERSION

Hit the Mother Lode: Cowabunga! No, er, Eureka! Aroooo! You and your dog will be hopping around like Yosemite Sam if you find a few specks of gold around here.

The folks at **Gold Prospecting Expeditions** say they've never met a dog who didn't like helping his owner pan for gold. You and your dog can take a walking tour guided by a prospector, and then get down to the business of panning. You keep what you find—and the folks here say you'll always find something in their special section of the Mother Lode.

If your dog can pan like Twinkles, the company's former resident poodle, you'll be rich. Twinkles used to stick her head underwater in a panning trough and come up with a gold nugget every time. Of course, she'd been trained, and the nugget was always there, so don't be too disappointed if your dog doesn't scoop up the down payment for your new house. (Sweet Twinkles is now panning for gold in Dog Heaven.)

Gold prospecting fun can run from one hour to five days. (The hour is cheaper, but the longer trips are really something to write home about.) Reservations for the longer trips are a must, and they're also appreciated for the one-hour version, even if just a day ahead of time. This will help ensure having enough guides. Prospecting Expeditions is at 18170 Main Street, Jamestown, CA 95327; 209/984-GOLD (209/984-4653) or 800/596-0009; www.goldprospecting.com.

Royal Carriage Inn: This Victorian/Western-style inn was built by a man named Royal H. Rushing, thus the name. ("Rushing Carriage Inn" would have created a rather odd image.) The main building here looks like something you'd see on a Hollywood backlot, but it's not where dogs get to stay. In back of the hotel's lovely garden are a few cute cottages. Dogs are welcome at one of these, which is actually half of a duplex. It's not a historic building like its tall, stately sister up front, and no one would ever want to shoot a scene for a Western here. But there is a Hollywood/Western link: According to the inn's owner, Dennis, Clint Eastwood once stayed in that very cottage. Who knows… your dog may still be able to detect his scent.

The humans in your party can enjoy the sumptuous parlor in the main building, because that's where continental breakfast is served. (You should probably take turns dining, because dogs mustn't be left alone in the cottage.) The cottage rate is $125–150. 18239 Main Street 95327; 209/984-5271; www .royalcarriageinn.com.

Sonora

This is the county seat of Tuolumne County and it's a real charmer. A stroll through the colorful downtown area with your leashed dog is a fun way to feel out the town's history of bullfights, bear fights, and gold camp justice. If you like an Old West town with an attitude, you'll enjoy Sonora.

PARKS, BEACHES, AND RECREATION AREAS

🐾 Woods Creek Rotary Park
🐾🐾🐾 (See Tuolumne County map on page 252)
Woods Creek runs through this pretty, shaded park. Dogs love to wet their paws in it on warm summer afternoons. Joe, the consummate landlubber, preferred to picnic at the tables set under shade trees, but Jake's preference would be to actually eat in the water. It's a great place to come to sample the tasty gourmet items you just bought downtown.

The park is just southwest of town, on Stockton Street and Woods Creek Drive (across from the Mother Lode Fairgrounds). 209/532-4541.

PLACES TO EAT
Schnoog's Espresso and Smoothie Bar: Enjoy imported espresso, locally produced coffee (coffee plantations in Sonora?), and fresh-baked goods from the house kitchen at the eight outdoor tables here. The manager here loves dogs, so your pooch will feel right at home. 1005 Mono Way; 209/533-2486.

PLACES TO STAY
Best Western Sonora Oaks: This is one of the more attractive, newer motels

DIVERSION

Tools of the Trail: When I first met Tonja Peterson, co-owner of the **Sierra Nevada Adventure Company,** she was running around the winter woods on snowshoes with her dog, Avery Mae, at her side. (Avery was sans snowshoes. "Too awkward," claimed the rottie-Australian shepherd mix.) We got to talking about Peterson's terrific outdoor store. "All genders, shapes, and sizes of dogs are welcome. We'd rate it four paws for dogs," Peterson said, taking her cue from a terrific California dog guidebook she stocks.

So we checked it out, and sure enough, it's doggone great. Dogs who visit here will get water, a dog treat, and some serious ear rubs if the place isn't too busy. Dogs can also pick from lots of dog bowls, dog books, collars, leashes, and dog backpacks. The outdoor equipment for humans is top-rate, too. 173 South Washington Street; 209/532-5621.

in the area. The outdoor pool is a big plus on hot summer afternoons. (It's a big covered ice patch on cold winter afternoons.) Rates are $99–175. Dogs are $25 extra. 19551 Hess Avenue 95370; 209/533-4400.

Sonora Aladdin Motor Inn: Dogs are welcome at this clean, modern motel. But they need to stay out of the refreshing pool and spa. The fur gunks up the plumbing. Rates are $70–110. Dogs are $15 for the length of their stay. 14260 Mono Way 95370; 209/533-4971 or 800/696-3969; www.aladdininn.com.

Sonora Days Inn: Dogs can stay only in the more modern, motel section of this partly historic inn. The lobby in the historic part of the inn is no longer off-limits: Any size well-behaved dog can join you here. Rates are $69–129. Dogs are $10 extra. 160 South Washington Street 95370; 209/532-2400 or 800/580-4667; www.sonoradaysinn.com.

Sonora Gold Lodge: This is a decent little motel not far from the main drag of Sonora. The rooms are clean, the pool is cool in the warm months, and you can even get a room with a little fridge and microwave for those home-away-from-home cats. Rates are $59–89. Dogs require a $100 deposit, which you'll get back if the room isn't a dog wreck when you leave. 480 West Stockton Street 95370; 209/532-3952 or 800/363-2154; www.goldlodge.com.

Twain Harte

Dogs enjoy strolling along the sidewalks of this charming little town, especially if they're of the literary persuasion. The town was named for writers Mark Twain and Bret Harte. It's a good thing that Aleksandr Solzhenitsyn and Michel Eyquem de Montaigne weren't big in the area when the place was named.

It's a very dog-friendly place. You never know where your dog will be invited in or given a treat. The Ace hardware store here allows well-behaved dogs inside and provides them little biscuits. Tellers at a bank's drive-up window have been known to slip a dog a treat in the little metal drawer. (Jake wants me to switch banks.)

PLACES TO STAY

El Dorado Motel: This is a decent place to stay, especially if you'd like a micro-wave and a fridge in your room. (This comes in handy when traveling with a dog.) Rates are $30–85. Dogs are $15 per visit. 22678 Black Hawk Drive 95383; 209/586-4479.

Gables Cedar Creek Inn: The eight enchanting cabins here have fireplaces/wood-burning stoves, antique furniture, and comfy beds with down comfort-ers. Most have little kitchens. This is all just peachy with dogs, but what really gets their tails wagging is the setting: a lush grassy area surrounded by tall pines and cedars. Jake's favorite cabin is the Hideaway, a spacious, creekside log cabin. Since it's across the creek from the other cabins (you have to cross a stone bridge to get there), it's quite secluded, really living up to its name.

The owners have enforced a 30-pound size limit for dogs for some time. The beef against dogs has primarily been their fur getting on everything. And the bigger the dog, the more fur is likely to be left behind. One Jake night would be equivalent to a dozen or so Chihuahuas.

Rates are $88–130. Dogs are $10 extra. A beautiful vacation home with sto-rybook charm is also available, with rates starting at $240. 22560 Twain Harte Drive 95383; 209/586-3008 or 888/900-4224; www.gocedarcreek.com.

Groveland

In 1849, when the town was founded, it was a rough-and-ready gold mining center. Today it's smoother around the edges, but you can't miss that Old West ambience.

PLACES TO STAY

Groveland Hotel: The suites at this Gold Rush–era inn come with a fireplace and a whirlpool bath so that you can have an evening of romantic relaxation. The place was chosen as one of the 12 Best Country Inns by *Country Inns* magazine. The hotel was originally built in 1849 but has subsequently been restored and refined. (You have use of a white terry robe with your room. It's that kind of place.) The Groveland Hotel is a top-notch inn as far as dogs are concerned and not because of the robes. Dogs who stay here get a treat, a snuggly quilt, and a dish. Lucky dogs! Rates are $145–275. Dogs are $15 extra. 18767 Main Street 95321; 209/962-4000 or 800/273-3314; www.groveland.com.

Sunset Inn: The three sweet housekeeping cabins here are set in a quiet meadow surrounded by the Stanislaus National Forest (dog heaven). The cabins are very cozy, comfy, and attractive. "This is really an ideal place for dogs," says friendly cabin owner Lauren. "We can't not have dogs here!" Each cabin has a kitchen and very useable porch/deck. If you want to visit Yosemite National Park, the cabins provide a fine place to start your adventure, since they're just two miles from the park's west gate. Rates are $130–160 for the double cabin, and up to $200 for the larger family cabin. Dogs are $20 extra. 33569 Hardin Flat Road 95321; 209/962-4360 or 888/962-4360; www.sunsetinnusa.com.

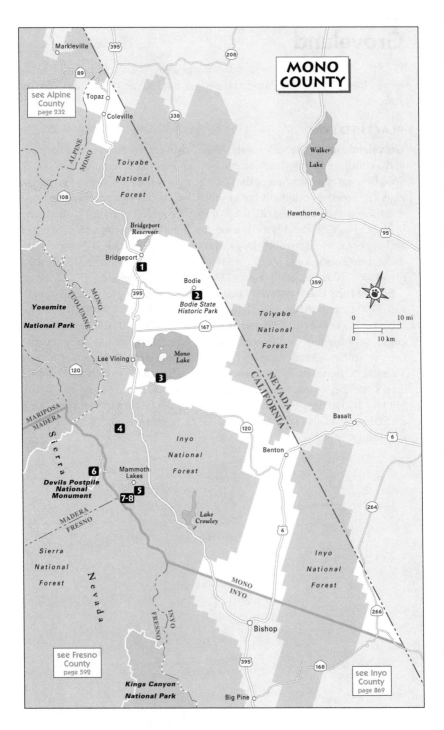

CHAPTER 25

Mono County

This is raw and rugged eastern Sierra country, where the cows graze amid such spectacular scenery that it's hard to believe they don't moo and ahh whenever we turn our backs.

When you contemplate the origins of the word "mono," you'll probably think of words such as "alone," "one," or "single." Certainly they capture the feel of this unique land. But in this case, the meaning of the word isn't so romantic. *Mono* is the Yokut Indian word for flies. Brine flies, abundant on the shores of salty Mono Lake, were an important source of protein for the Yokut, and they're still the most visible insect at Mono Lake. Fortunately, the flies don't bite, eat your picnic, or otherwise act tempestuously toward humans and their dogs.

In "Fly County," you can often just pull off the road into open public land and hike your heart out, especially in the county's northern reaches. As you drive along U.S. 395, you'll see so many signs for camping, fishing, and other outdoor recreation that you won't know where to turn first. This chapter describes a few of the more dog-friendly areas, but know that when you see

PICK OF THE LITTER—MONO COUNTY

BEST GHOST TOWN
Bodie State Historic Park, Bodie (page 269)

MOST OTHERWORLDLY PLACE
Mono Lake, Lee Vining (page 269)

BEST OFF-LEASH HIKES NEAR CIVILIZATION
Trails at Lake Mary and Horseshoe Lake, Mammoth Lakes (page 275)

FRIENDLIEST DINING
Base Camp Cafe, Mammoth Lakes (page 276)

BEST LUXURY TREATMENT
Double Eagle Resort and Spa, June Lake (page 271)

STEAMIEST SHOWERS
Convict Lake Resort, Mammoth Lakes (page 276)

MOST DOG-FRIENDLY PLACE TO STAY
Edelweiss Lodge, Mammoth Lakes (page 277)

EASIEST WAY TO RISE ABOVE IT ALL
Mammoth Mountain Ski Area gondolas, Mammoth Lakes (page 273)

signs for places such as Convict Lake, Crowley Lake, and Bridgeport Lake, generally you and your leashed dog will be welcome.

Lucky dogs who visit Mono County now get to stay at dozens of remarkable cabins in gorgeous settings. Some of these cabins are extremely luxurious, and some don't even have warm water. Most are somewhere between. "It's becoming doggy heaven in Mono County," writes canine correspondent Rexall, of West Hollywood. "I drag my human driver up here as often as I can."

NATIONAL FORESTS

The *National Forests and Wilderness Areas* resource at the back of this book has

important information and safety tips on visiting national forests with your dog and has more information on the national forests listed below.

Inyo National Forest
🐾🐾🐾🐾🐕

Toiyabe National Forest
🐾🐾🐾🐾🐕

Bridgeport

If you and your dog are film noir fans, you'll want to stop at this quiet little village and see if it looks familiar. Remember the movie *Out of the Past,* starring Robert Mitchum? Much of it was set right here in Bridgeport.

PARKS, BEACHES, AND RECREATION AREAS

1 Bridgeport Park
🐾 (See Mono County map on page 264)

This tiny county park is just a bunch of picnic tables on grass in the midst of a few pieces of old mining equipment. It's right next to the Mono County Museum, in case you're with someone who wants a little culture.

From U.S. 395, go east on School Street and left on Middle Street. 760/932-5248.

PLACES TO STAY

Best Western Ruby Inn: Stay here and you get a small area to walk your leashless pooch! Rates are $115–180. 33 Main Street 93517; 760/932-7241.

Twin Lakes Resort: The eight remodeled cabins here are set on a football field–sized lawn, and the lawn is surrounded by beautiful pine, aspen, silver maple, and cottonwood trees. It's enough to make a boy dog cry with joy. In summer, the trees of the surrounding Toiyabe National Forest are so lush that you may not be able to see nearby Lower Twin Lake. But it's still there. And it's very inviting for dogs and their people to take a swim, or even rent a boat and motor around the lake. (Boat rentals are available at the resort's marina and cost $65–180 per day. Dogs are welcome to join you.)

Winter is also a fun time to visit with a dog. "Dogs have so much fun in the snow here," says the very pleasant owner, Lori. "I watch dogs that have never seen snow before. They don't even know how to take a step in it at first. By the end of the visit, their owners can't even get them into the car they love the snow so much."

The cabins are basic but attractive. There are no phones and no TVs. "We've got lotsa nothin'" says Lori. Rates are $140–188. Dogs are $25 per stay. The two-night rates are a bit lower. The resort is 11 miles south of Bridgeport, but Bridgeport is the official address. P.O. Box 248 93517; 877/932-7751; www.lowertwinlakesresort.com.

Virginia Creek Settlement: This is a fun place to stay if you like casual Old West style and a friendly lot of people. It's part motel (the rooms look like the inside of a sparkling-clean log cabin), part campground, part housekeeping cabins, and part tent cabins. But the coolest part of all is the two old covered wagons. You and your dog can actually bunk overnight in them. You just provide the sleeping bag. The mattresses are already there. The wagons are kind of well worn, but that's part of their charm. (And they make for great photo ops with the pooch.) Much of this is set up as an old-fashioned Camp Town, which harkens to Gold Rush days. The folks here will even point you in the right direction to try some gold panning.

The Virginia Creek Settlement features its own cozy Italian/American–style restaurant. I don't know how many Italian restaurants were around during the Gold Rush, but I'm glad this one is. The food is most fulfilling after a day of adventuring.

Motel rooms are $65–85, cabins are about $89–130, and tent cabins and covered wagons are $25. Bring your own towels and soap for the more rustic accommodations, or pay an extra $1.50 per person. Tent sites are $14. You'll find it on U.S. 395 about five miles south of town, but the official address is still Bridgeport. It's one of the closest lodgings to Bodie State Historic Park. H.C.R. 62, Box 1050 93517; 760/932-7780; www.virginiacreeksettlement.com.

Virginia Lakes Resort: Some of the 19 housekeeping cabins at this very popular resort have views of beautiful Little Virginia Lake. The rest are on Virginia Creek. It's water, water everywhere, which makes Jake tremble with anticipation. (My fisherman husband trembles right along with Jake; trout fishing is hot here and at adjacent Big Virginia Lake.) The cabins vary from rustic to modern condo style, and our favorites have a fireplace and sundeck overlooking the lake.

The owners adore dogs. Carolyn, the owner, will provide you with info on local hikes and let you know when it's super-important to leash up on hikes. (Fawning season, for instance.)

The resort is open around May 20–October 15. It's about 13 miles south of Bridgeport, off U.S. 395 at Conway Summit. The mailing address: H.C. 62, Box 1065 93517; 760/647-6484; www.virginia lakesresort.com.

Walker River Lodge: This is a very dog-friendly motel. The kind owners here will show you a nearby little hike you can do with your furry friend. The lodge is right on the Walker River, a big-time trout area. Rates are $75–170. 1 Main Street 93517; 760/932-7021; www.walkerriverlodge.com.

Bodie

PARKS, BEACHES, AND RECREATION AREAS

2 Bodie State Historic Park

🐾🐾🐾 (See Mono County map on page 264)

This ghost town looks so much like *Gunsmoke*-land on a really bad day that it's hard to picture it as a thriving, raunchy, pulsating boomtown. But that's exactly what it was back in the 1870s during this area's gold rush. Dozens of saloons, a burgeoning red-light district, and murders nearly every day kept this lawless mining camp hopping.

These days, dogs can enjoy the 486 acres of this town-turned-historic park as long as they're law-abiding citizens on a leash. They're allowed to walk down the dusty streets with you and sniff at the 170 dilapidated buildings that remain, or they can kick up their heels in the more open areas of the park. Dogs seem to appreciate the wild and woolly luster that still shines through the educational veneer here.

From U.S. 395 just south of Willow Springs, take Highway 270/Bodie Road east about 13 miles. The last three miles are unpaved and can be impassable in winter. You'll pay $3 per adult, $1 per child. Dogs are free. 760/647-6445. A great website has lots of info on Bodie. It's not an official park service site, but it's well worth checking out: www.bodie.com.

Lee Vining

PARKS, BEACHES, AND RECREATION AREAS

3 Mono Lake

🐾🐾🐾🐾 (See Mono County map on page 264)

Spending the day at this strange and ancient lake is about the closest you and your dog will come to visiting another planet. You'll want to check your map and make sure you're still on Earth when you see the eerie volcanic formations, the old lake, and the tufa spires that look like giant, oozy sand castles.

This 700,000-year-old lake covers 60 square miles, but it's just a shadow of its former self. Since Los Angeles started using the fresh streams that fill Mono Lake, the lake has dropped 40 feet and its salinity has doubled. These days, the lake is nearly three times as salty and 80 times as alkaline as seawater. The salinity increase in this already salty lake seems to be creating some problems for the local environment, and studies on its effects are ongoing. But on the upside, it does make for buoyant swimming.

The alkaline water isn't a new phenomenon. Mark Twain wrote of Mono: "Its sluggish waters are so strong with alkali that if you only dip the most hopelessly soiled garment into them once or twice, and wring it out, it will be found as clean as if it had been through the ablest of washerwoman's hands." You may be tempted to toss your dirty dog in for a little cleansing splash, but the water can be irritating to the eyes.

The land surrounding the lake is run by different agencies. Fortunately, these agencies all have the same rules, which makes it easy to traipse from one part of the lake to the other without getting busted for a dog violation. Dogs are permitted, but they have to be on a leash, even in the Mono Basin National Forest Scenic Area. It's that simple.

Drive on U.S. 395 to the Mono Lake Visitors Center in Lee Vining and pick up some brochures about the geology of this fascinating area. Then look for signs for areas such as the Mono Lake Tufa State Reserve (there are areas on either side of the lake and the one on the south side is best) or the Mono Basin National Forest Scenic Area. Drive east until you're either in the middle of a dormant, pumice-covered volcano or standing on the shores of one of the oldest lakes in North America. It's ideal dog territory, with few souls venturing on the longer hikes.

The fee is $3 in the South Tufa area; the rest of the state reserve and the national forest are free. Call the reserve at 760/647-6331 or the national forest at 760/647-3044. You may actually have better luck reaching a real person at the Mono Lake Committee Information Center. 760/647-6595; www .monolake.org.

PLACES TO STAY

Lundy Canyon Campground: This county-run campground is set at 8,000 feet near Lundy Lake, just across the highway from Mono Lake. It's a barren, otherworldly dreamscape. Leashed dogs love it. They also seem to enjoy the county park where the campsites are. But if you want to take your dog for a long and fascinating hike, just take a quick ride to nearby Mono Lake. There are 60 sites, all first-come, first-served, and all are (are you ready?) free! (As in no charge!) From U.S. 395 about five miles north of Lee Vining, look for the signs for the campground, which is on the west side of the highway. 760/647-3044 or 760/647-6595.

Murphey's Motel: The attitude toward dogs at this fine little motel: "We love them!" Rates are $53–113. Dogs are $5 extra. The motel is directly on U.S. 395 in Lee Vining. You can't miss it. 51493 Highway 395 93541; 760/647-6316.

June Lake

PARKS, BEACHES, AND RECREATION AREAS

The June Lake Loop consists of four lakes west of U.S. 395. Dogs are permitted at all of them. Here we'll discuss only the two smaller lakes.

⁴ Silver Lake

🐾🐾🐾🐾🐕 (See Mono County map on page 264)

Leashed dogs may wag a tail or two when you catch trout after trout here. This 80-acre lake is stocked with many thousands of rainbows each year. But what really sets dogs off is that when you take them for a long hike up the magnificent trail that takes you far, far away from the bait store, the full-service resort, and the boat rental facility, they can be leash-free!

The trailhead is near the camping area, where dogs must be leashed ($13 per site; the rate will be going up soon). Once you start hiking, you and your leash-free dog may never want to return. The trail actually can loop you into Yosemite National Park, so you have to watch how long you tread, because dogs are banned from Yosemite's trails. But an exciting and not too strenuous hike will take you along the Rush Creek drainage, past Gem Lake and Agnew Lake and into the pristine Ansel Adams Wilderness. Bring a big lunch and lots of water, and you'll have a vacation your dog will remember into her old age.

The lake is about halfway on the June Lake Loop, so you can exit U.S. 395 at the north or south end of the loop (Highway 158), depending on the direction you're traveling. The campground, which has about 63 sites, is open May–September. All sites are first-come, first-served. 760/647-3045 or 760/647-6595.

PLACES TO STAY

Double Eagle Resort and Spa: So you think you'll be roughing it just because you're staying in the eastern Sierra Nevada? 'Tis to laugh! This is not a resort in the classic California lakeside sense of the word. It's a resort in the "ooh" and "ahhh" sense of the word. The Double Eagle has been listed by Forbes. com as one of the top 10 spas in world. It's an outstanding, upscale place, with amenities that will leave you and your dog drooling.

The two-bedroom cabins are new, luxurious, and exquisitely furnished. Wood-burning fireplaces and stoves, big decks, and fully equipped kitchens make you feel right at home in the quiet forest setting here. The resort is on 14 acres and bordered on two sides by National Forest land. This makes for some wonderful hikes.

The spa offers more than 50 specialty massages. Humans love the indoor swimming pool, whirlpool, and excellent fitness center. The resort's restaurant offers healthful, delicious cuisine. None of this interests dogs, but that's OK. It gets you there, which gets them there, and that's what counts. Dogs are allowed at nine of the cottages. Rates are $269–349, with dogs costing $15 extra nightly, or $50 per stay. 5587 Highway 158 93529; 760/648-7004; www .doubleeagleresort.com.

Fern Creek Lodge: It's kind of like a little village here. You've got 10 cabins (some are like big, two-story houses), four apartment units, a store that sells everything from groceries to fishing gear, and a large barbecue area. All the buildings are arranged in a semicircular fashion, with the main lodge and store in the center. Fern Creek has a very dog-friendly atmosphere, with many people either visiting with dogs or wanting to pet yours. Rates are $65–190. The biggest cabins sleep up to 16 people and cost $295. Dogs are $10 extra. 4628 Highway 158 93529; 760/648-7722 or 800/621-9146; www.ferncreek lodge.com.

Gull Lake Lodge: You're surrounded by forest at this *very* dog-friendly lodge. Owner Vikki Magee loves dogs and has a great theory about traveling pooches: "No bad dogs make it as far as the car," she says. It's been her experience that dogs who get to vacation with their people must be pretty darned special. And she's right. "Besides," she says, "they don't steal towels. And it's our experience that only the good dogs get to take their owners on vacation." Upon your arrival, you'll likely be greeted by her own two fabulously friendly pooches, Taco and Maggie.

The lodge, which is more of a nice, large, clean motel, has been remodeled and is looking good. The beds feature pillowtop mattresses and, in the cooler months, electric blankets. Rates are $70–165, and that includes fish-cleaning facilities, should you catch a fish around here. The lodge is between June and Gull lakes. Some rooms have lake views. 132 Leonard Street 93529; 760/648-7516 or 800/631-4081; www.gulllakelodge.com.

Mammoth Lakes

This charming resort town is a magical ski haven in the winter and an angler's dream in the summer. It's an excellent base for exploring the 200,000 surrounding acres known as Mammoth Lakes Recreational Area.

The lakes in this region are numerous and abound with great fishing and camping opportunities. The mountains and forests are rife with hiking and cross-country skiing areas for you and the pooch of your dreams. You can ski just about anywhere in the national forest, as long as you keep your dog off the groomed cross-country trails. And once you get away from people, you can unleash your obedient dog and bound through nature together.

Dog-friendly lodgings abound, but if you need extra help watching your dog (should you want to ski, for instance), many of the hotels and inns provide recommendations on good places for your dog to stay during the day, or reputable dog sitters. The phone book has quite a few listings, but we find it's best to get the poop from those in the know. For a super-dog-friendly lodging, where the owner has a side-business of dog-sitting and dog walking on the premises, sniff out Edelweiss Lodge.

PARKS, BEACHES, AND RECREATION AREAS

5 Shady Rest Trail

🐾🐾🐾 (See Mono County map on page 264)

This national forest trail is on the edge of the town of Mammoth Lakes, making it as convenient as it is splendid. Unfortunately, since the city officially runs this trail, leashes are the law.

During the summer, you and your pooch can walk or run on the six-mile forested trail that loops around Shady Rest Park (a Mammoth Lakes recreation park, where leashes are also the law).

In winter, it's a stunning place to take your dog on a little cross-country ski trip. Leashes can come in handy here. We've seen some people leash their dogs to their belts while skiing. When there's a little uphill slope, guess who's the engine? Most dogs wouldn't appreciate this and are happier gamboling through the woods than playing mush dog. Dogs aren't allowed on the groomed trails (there's nothing like paw holes to dampen a smooth cross-country adventure), but they can usually trot along on the left side of the trail.

DIVERSION

Rise Above it All: If the idea of dangling 11,000 feet above sea level doesn't faze you or your dog, hop aboard the **Mammoth Mountain Ski Area gondolas** for a lofty adventure.

Actually, during your 12-minute ascent from 9,000 feet to 11,000 feet on the Scenic Gondola Ride, you'll glide only a few dozen feet above the ground—spectacular views make it seem as though you're higher. You can sniff out a scenic spot about 0.2 mile away, or try your paw at descending the mountain. It's rather barren, and the trails aren't for the faint of heart: They're narrow and seem precipitous at times. (One very windy afternoon, I got several hundred yards down and decided that I'd better turn around. I felt as if I were going to blow off the mountainside. The gondola ride down was much less hair-raising, despite the high winds that made it feel like an amusement park ride.) The hike all the way down takes about 1.5–2 hours, depending on how you handle the trails.

The fee for adults is $16. Children 13–18 are $12, and ages 7–12 pay $8. Younger kids go free, as do dogs, as do humans over 80. To get here, exit U.S. 395 at the Mammoth Junction exit and drive west along Highway 203/Main Street through the town of Mammoth Lakes. Go right on Minaret Summit/Minaret Road. In about four miles you'll see the gondola station on your right. 760/934-2571 or 888/4-MAMMOTH (888/462-6668).

From U.S. 395, exit at Mammoth Junction and drive west along Highway 203/Main Street until the U.S. Forest Service Visitors Center, which will be before town on your right. You can stop in here and ask for additional trail information or proceed west on Highway 203 another 0.25 mile to Old Sawmill Road. Turn right and follow the road to Shady Rest Park. You'll see parts of the trail weaving around the park's perimeter and even along the entry road. Call 760/924-5500 for more information.

6 Devils Postpile National Monument

🐾🐾🐾🐾 (See Mono County map on page 264)

Although Devils Postpile is actually just over the border in Madera County, it is accessible only via its neighbor, Mammoth Lakes. If you're in the area with your dog, take advantage of this great exception to the national park system—dogs are allowed just about everywhere people can go, as long as they're leashed.

And what a place it is. If the devil ever did have a pile of posts, this would be it. The 60-foot wall of columnar basalt "posts" is truly awe-inspiring. Pick up a brochure and find out the fascinating geology behind these geometric (and geologic) wonders.

In addition to the postpile, this 800-acre park is also home to Rainbow Falls, where the Middle Fork of the San Joaquin River drops 101 feet over a cliff of volcanic lava. It's a remarkable sight. You can also get to some great backcountry trails from here: The Pacific Crest Trail and John Muir Trail are among the trails dogs love to sniff out.

Unless you plan on going up very early in the morning or after 8 P.M., or unless you're going to be camping or fishing one of the area's lakes with a boat, you'll have to take a fun shuttle bus a few miles down to the valley. On a recent trip, we met up with a little tiny mutt in a front carrier and a giant German shepherd from San Diego. The shepherd befriended my human child and shared a seat with her. (She said it was the best part of the trip. So much for Mother Nature.)

A great place to catch the shuttle is in front of the Mammoth Mountain Inn. Exit U.S. 395 at Mammoth Junction and drive west along Highway 203/Main Street through the town of Mammoth Lakes. Turn right at Minaret Summit/Minaret Road and drive about four miles. You can buy your ticket in the gondola building. The cost is $7 round-trip for adults, $4 for children. Dogs go free. The road is impassable in the winter, so the park is closed during snowy months (which can sometimes last into June, so call first). Call the U.S. Forest Service at 760/924-5500 for bus schedules and pickup locations. Phone 760/934-2289 for Devils Postpile information.

7 Lake Mary

😊😊😊😊🐕 (See Mono County map on page 264)

Dogs have to be leashed around developed and heavily used Lake Mary, but they can trot around leashless when they accompany you on the scenic trail that starts on the east side of the lake. Rangers ask that you wait until you're far from the lake to let your dog run free, and to do so only if she's under good control.

Lots of folks like to take their dogs on an early morning walk on the trail and then turn around and fish for dinner. The trout are planted, and it's hard not to catch one while trolling, or even fishing from shore. Most dogs seem to enjoy watching people fish, even if nothing is being caught. Some people don't even mind just walking around the lake with a leashed dog. There's also a gold mine at the very end of Coldwater Campground, next to the trailhead parking. You'll see the signs.

Other folks come here just for the off-leash hiking. The trail takes you many miles away. If your dog is a water dog, she'll love it. You pass by several quiet little lakes and one big one on the way to the Pacific Crest Trail. Consult an Inyo National Forest ranger at 760/873-2400 for maps and guidance.

June–November, 48 campsites are available here for $16 a night, first-come, first-served. Dogs must be leashed, but with the great views of the lake they get, they just don't seem to mind.

To reach the lake, exit U.S. 395 at Mammoth Junction and drive west along Highway 203/Main Street, through the town of Mammoth Lakes. The road curves to the left and becomes Lake Mary Road. Follow it about three miles to the lake. 760/924-5500.

8 Horseshoe Lake

😊😊😊😊🐕 (See Mono County map on page 264)

Most of the lakes in this part of the eastern Sierra are developed and popular among humankind. But although Horseshoe Lake is just a stick's throw from civilization, it's a refreshing exception. Not only is it breathtaking, it's quiet.

You really can get away from folks here. In summer, it's not as heavily fished as other local lakes, partly because it's not stocked with trout. But if you visit with a dog, chances are you'll have more on your mind than fishing anyway. And that's where this lake is a little piece of dog heaven. While your dog has to be leashed around the lake, he's allowed to romp leashless once he hits the connecting trails.

At the north end of the lake, you'll find a trailhead that leads you through magnificent landscapes, all set around 9,000 feet. The air is so clean you can almost feel yourself getting healthier with each step. Jake thinks it's the cat's pajamas. Eventually, the trail runs into the Pacific Crest Trail, where you can choose to venture off on longer or shorter treks. Consult an Inyo National Forest ranger at 760/934-2505 for maps and guidance.

To reach the lake, exit U.S. 395 at Mammoth Junction and drive west along Highway 203/Main Street, through the town of Mammoth Lakes. The road curves to the left and becomes Lake Mary Road. Follow it about seven miles. It loops by Lake Mary and eventually ends at Horseshoe Lake. 760/924-5500.

PLACES TO EAT

We last visited after a couple of dog-friendly restaurants had stopped allowing dogs, and after it started getting a bit chilly, and we didn't find much in the way of outdoor dining. We're told the pickings are getting slim here. (If you know otherwise, write to us at the address in the front of the book. Hungry dogs are counting on you!) Here are a few good bets in the meantime.

Base Camp Cafe: Dogs love this place. The waitstaff is super friendly, the food is down-to-earth delicious, and there's even a little bowl of water on the patio, where dogs dine. When Jake visited, a nearby diner ordered the Mountain Pot Roast, and Jake stared at every forkful the diner put in his mustache-topped mouth. He was lying near my chair (Jake, not the man), so I didn't think it was too obvious. The puddle of drool was somewhat pathetic, though, and when the man couldn't finish his generous portion, he asked, "Would your very good dog like this? I don't have a fridge in my hotel room." Jake will never forget him. (He has thrice been a leftover magnet at restaurants. Must be his big brown seal eyes.)

Everything from the salads to the burgers and special house-made soups is tasty here. There are plenty of vegetarian options, too. If you just want to come for a beverage, there's a great selection of hot and cold ones, with a respectable list of organic coffees and teas. And on Thursday evenings, you can carbo load at the all-you-can-eat pasta bar. Breakfast and lunch are served daily; dinner is served Thursday–Sunday. 3325 Main Street; 760/934-3900.

Giovanni's Restaurant and Lounge: Order a pizza to go and bring it to the outdoor tables to share with your dog. One of our favorite combos is the Gio special, with pesto, artichokes, mushrooms, and feta cheese. (Jake spits out the veggies oh-so-delicately but wolfs down the cheese and crust.) 437 Old Mammoth Road; 760/934-7563.

PLACES TO STAY

Convict Lake Resort: Dogs love coming to this terrific resort. Jake Dog thinks it's because they feel so welcome here. Says the owner: "We love all pets, even ostriches and tarantulas." Psst: The resort even takes cats.

Pets can stay at several deluxe cabins. The owners recently built four super-luxurious cabins, which come with fireplaces, double spa baths, and even steam showers. (A steam shower, should you be in the dark ages of pampering bathroom fixtures as I am, is a regular shower with a control that makes steam billow out any time you want. You don't even have to take a shower to get a steam. It's kind of like a spa steambath in your own cabin. Take that, Davy Crockett.)

In summer, dogs and their people can go out on the lake in a boat, help fish for supper, or just hike around the wilderness on the other side of the lake. Dogs like Jake have plenty of swimming options. The resort also has a wonderful restaurant, but you'll have to get takeout if you want your dog to partake. Horseback riding is another people-only option.

Rates range from $119 for regular (cute) cabins to $1,199 for a cabin that sleeps 34. (Yes, they call that a cabin here.) There are plenty of cabins in between, including a new super deluxe luxury unit with a gourmet kitchen. Ask about weekly rates and specials. Dogs are $20 for the length of their stay. Route 1, Box 204 93546; 760/934-3800 or 800/992-2260; www.convictlake .com.

Crystal Crag Lodge: Stay at this charming mountain resort on the shores of Lake Mary and you can wander around many acres of beautiful land with your leashed dog. But you'd better visit May–mid-October, because the lodge is closed in the winter. The rustic wood cabins are attractive and have full kitchens and baths. Most come with living rooms and fireplaces, too. Dogs like all that, but water dogs think it's truly the cat's meow that you can rent a small aluminum boat here and meander around the lake. Rates are $85–170. Dog rates are $10 extra for the first dog, $5 extra for each additional. 307 Crystal Crag Drive 93546; 760/934-2436; www.mammothweb.com.

Edelweiss Lodge: Has your dog been very good this year? If so, she deserves a visit to the rustic, cozy, super-dog-friendly cabins and apartments that make up the Edelweiss Lodge. The lodgings all have kitchenettes, wood-burning stoves, and access to a whirlpool bath.

"Yada, yada, yada," your dog may be saying right about now. OK, we'll cut to the chase: Edelweiss has everything a dog could dream of (except cats). Dog-adoring managers Keith and Marta want to make every dog feel at home, and they start out by providing pooches a Doggie Welcome Basket. This includes a dog bed/pad, blankets to protect the human bedding, gourmet dog biscuits, temporary ID tags, water and food bowls, and poop bags. "We even provide a dumpster to put the poop bags in, but you can't take it to your room," says Keith. (Whew!)

Marta even has her own doggy side business, Marta's Doggie Day Care. She'll walk your dog for you if you're off for a while and need to leave your dog in a kennel in your room. (This is allowed here.) If you want complete day care, your lucky dog gets to go to her home, where day-care dogs cavort about as if it's their home. She takes the dogs for walks and hikes and brings them on errands with her. She also houses dogs overnight, but that's probably not necessary given the breadth of dog-friendly lodgings here. Sometimes guests ask Marta and Keith if their dogs can just hang out with them at the lodge office for a while, and that can be worked out, too. Rates are about $30 daily for full day care or $15 for a good walk (a second dog in the same family is just $5 extra).

Lodging rates are $115–325. Dogs are $15 extra. 1872 Old Mammoth Road 93546; 760/934-2445 or 877/233-3593; www.edelweiss-lodge.com.

Motel 6: Rates are $70–95. It's one of the more expensive Motel 6s we've come across, but this one looks more like a giant ski lodge than a roadside motel. 3372 Main Street 93546; 760/934-6660.

Old Shady Rest Campground: Believe it or not, you're pretty much in town when you camp here, though you'd never know it by the scenery. You're in the woods, without a trace of civilization. Dogs are permitted on leash. There are 46 sites. Fees are $15, but they may be going up soon. For reservations, phone 877/444-6777. Sites are open year-round. From U.S. 395, drive west on Highway 203 for three miles to the Mammoth Visitor Center. Turn right and follow the signs to the campground. 760/924-5500. (There's also a New Shady Rest Campground nearby, with 87 sites. The same phone numbers apply for info and reservations.)

Rockcreek Lodge: If you like modern cabins, the lodge has got some attractive small and large ones. If you like your cabins rustic and old, it's got those, too. And if you like your rustic cabins with only cold running water, you can even get a couple of those here. (From the 1920s!) Dogs love coming here because the lodge is set on seven acres of lodgepole pines, with several trails leading from the property. The trails can take you on some magnificent hikes to lakes, remote forests, and peaceful meadows. A fishable creek is a quick walk from the lodge. (Come in the summer for a stunning wildflower display.) Stay here and you're on the edge of the John Muir Wilderness. After a long day of outdoor fun, settle back in with a delicious meal from the lodge's restaurant.

The lodge is only open for dogs in the warmer months. (Memorial Day through October, to be more precise.) Apparently snowy paw prints are frowned upon here. Rates are $110–170. Dogs are $15 extra. Route 1, Box 12 93546; 877/935-4170; www.rockcreeklodge.com.

Shilo Inn: All the rooms are mini-suites, and they're air-conditioned, which is a rare feature up here. Unnecessary in the winter, but it can be a real blessing in August. Rates are $150–250. Dogs pay a $25 fee for the length of their stay. The motel is a half block east of Old Mammoth Road, on Highway 203. 2963 Main Street CA 93546; 760/934-4500; www.shiloinns.com.

Sierra Nevada Rodeway Inn: Some rooms at this attractive Alpine-themed lodging have fireplaces and kitchens, for that home-away-from-home feeling. Suites and chalets are also available. Rates are $109–239. A continental breakfast comes with your stay. Dogs are $12.50 extra. 164 Old Mammoth Road 93546; 760/934-2515; www.mammothsnri.com.

Crowley Lake

PLACES TO STAY

Mono Sierra Lodge: This Eastern Sierra–style lodge (think a fusion of Western and Alpine) is surrounded by plenty of dog-friendly hiking areas. The folks here will be glad to point you and your pooch in the right direction. Stay at a comfortable motel room, a small housekeeping unit, or a deluxe housekeeping unit with a fireplace. Dogs can only stay here in the summer, so they don't get to see how beautiful this place gets when the nearby mountains are covered with snow. Rates are $95–150. Dogs are $15 extra. The lodge is on Crowley Lake Drive, just off Highway 395; the mailing address is Route 1, Box 88 93546; 800/723-5387; www.monosierralodge.com.

Tom's Place Resort: Dogs may stay at three of the 13 rustic housekeeping cabins here. Even though they're not fancy digs, dogs enjoy the cabins; they're surrounded by lots of trees, and there's a pleasant creek that runs through the property. The resort also has a fun old café on the premises, but dogs aren't allowed, even in the outdoor area. Oh well, you'll have to get room service. (This involves a human in your cabin walking over to the café, placing your order, and walking back with it.) Fortunately, the cabins all have little kitchens.

Rates are $60–70. It's one of the most affordable rates around. Dogs are $10 extra. The lodging address is HCR 79, Box 22A 93546; 760/935-4239; www.tomsplaceresort.com.

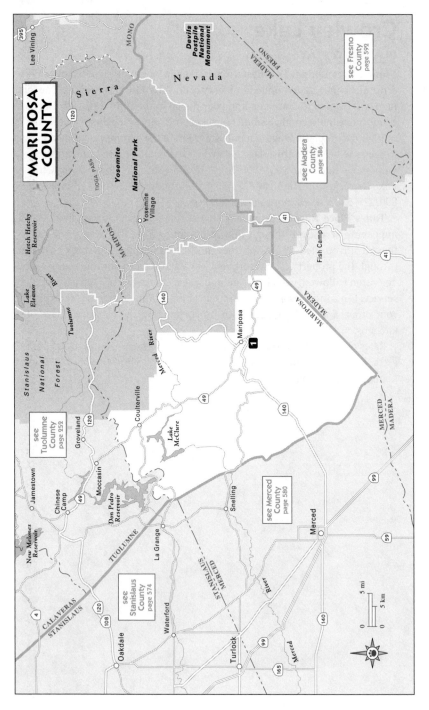

CHAPTER 26

Mariposa County

I've learned something about Yosemite National Park since the first edition of this book: While it's not a poochy paradise, it's not dog hell, either. When I first visited with Joe the Dog many moons ago, it seemed so restrictive, with its "dogs on pavement only and certain campgrounds" rules. But I've since discovered that pavement doesn't have to be Doggy Enemy Number 1, especially when there's so much of it. A bane for the natural beauty of Yosemite turns out to be a bonus for dogs. Paved paths and roads ribbon their way through the entire breathtaking valley, and you can see a great deal from them. In fact, if it makes your dog feel any better, let her know that many dog-free people spend almost their entire Yosemite vacation on asphalt.

The charming towns around Yosemite offer plenty of dog-friendly lodgings, and we're thrilled to report that the beautiful Tenaya Lodge is once again open for dog business. (No, not that kind of dog business.)

PICK OF THE LITTER—MARIPOSA COUNTY

BEST OFF-LEASH HIKES
Sierra National Forest (page 282)
Stanislaus National Forest (page 282)

MOST BEAUTIFUL, DOG-FRIENDLY PLACE TO STAY
Tenaya Lodge at Yosemite, Fish Camp (page 287)

BEST RIDE
Sugar Pine Railroad, Fish Camp (page 286)

NATIONAL FORESTS

The *National Forests and Wilderness Areas* resource at the back of this book has important information and safety tips on visiting national forests with your dog and has more information on the national forests listed below.

Sierra National Forest
🐾🐾🐾🐾 🏃

Stanislaus National Forest
🐾🐾🐾🐾 🏃

NATIONAL PARKS

Yosemite National Park
🐾🐾🐾

Ask just about everyone who's ever visited this park about what they've seen, and they'll gush about the impossibly beautiful geography, the dramatic waterfalls, the magnificent trails, the sheer cliffs, the pristine wildlife, and every other detail they can dredge up. It's not hyperbole. This fantastic park is bigger than the imagination, bigger than life. It inspires even the most jaded parkgoer to sing its praises.

Then ask the same question of people who've visited with dogs. They'll be able to tell you all about the lovely car campsites here. They can even expound on the glories of the commercialization of Yosemite Village, the clever way the parking lots are set up, and how toasty the blacktop gets at 2 P.M. in August.

But it turns out that Yosemite is not really such a doggy drag. You just have to know where to go. While dogs are not allowed on any trails, in meadows, or in the backcountry of Yosemite, they are permitted to explore the beautiful Yosemite Valley area via paved roads and paths. And for better or worse, there's a lot of pavement here. That means you and your leashed dog can peruse some absolutely stunning scenery from miles of flat, easy terrain. (More silver lining: The pavement will help keep your dog's nails trimmed.) We got a note and photos from Ansel the dog, whose people, Anne and Bill, brought him right on a paved trail that leads to the most popular sight in the valley—Yosemite Falls. Ansel, who was named after Mt. Ansel Adams, was a big hit around here and felt very welcomed wherever he went. (He only went on pavement, mind you.)

If you want to hit the real trails, you can have your dog stay at the park's kennel Memorial Day–Labor Day. (No, not the whole time. You know what we mean.) We're not talking luxury suites here. We're talking your basic cage-like contraptions that make you feel incredibly guilty for leaving the little guy behind. The kennel costs $8 per day, and space is limited. It's first-come, first-served, so get there early during busy times. Dogs are required to have all their shots, be more than 16 weeks old, and to be more than 10 pounds. (Sorry, teacup poodles!) The kennel phone is 209/372-8348.

Some folks think they can get away with leaving their dog tied up to their campsite for a few hours while they go exploring. But remember, if the ranger doesn't catch up with you, there's always the chance that a mountain lion or other cunning critter might catch up with your tethered dog. "We call one of these camping areas Coyote Point," a park employee told me. "You'd be a fool to leave your dog behind even for a little bit."

One clever reader wrote to us and told us how she and her husband get away with taking their smallish dogs through Yosemite. They tote them along on little doggy trailers attached to their bikes. Sometimes they strap a dog carrier to their chests and away they go. It probably isn't legal, so I won't use their names. But their truck's license plate is so wonderfully appropriate to the theme of this book that I can't help but mention it: CAB4K9S. (It sure be.)

Here are the campgrounds that permit pooches: In the valley, there's the Upper Pines Campground. Along Highway 120, you can stay at Hodgdon Meadow Campground, Crane Flat Campground (section A), White Wolf Campground (section C), Yosemite Creek Campground (front section), and the west end of the Tuolumne Meadows Campground. Along Glacier Point Road and Highway 41, you can stay at the Bridalveil Creek Campground (section A) and the Wawona Campground.

The campsites cost $14–20. Some are first-come, first-served; others are by reservation only. Call 877/444-6777 for reservation information, or 209/372-0299 for park information. Rates to enter Yosemite are $20 per car, and the pass you'll get is good for one week; www.nps.gov/yose.

PLACES TO STAY

The Redwoods in Yosemite: This group of lovely, privately owned mountain homes is by far the best thing that's ever happened to dogs in Yosemite. The Redwoods is nestled in the forest at 4,000 feet, where the air is so clean you can smell it. The homes range in size from cozy one-bedroom cottages to big five-bedroom spreads. They're all different, but they're attractive and woodsy, and most have decks and fireplaces.

Thirty of the Redwoods' 125 homes permit pooches. Some are really magical, with wide picture windows and huge stone fireplaces.

Dogs who stay here get to peruse the surrounding area on leash. They can sniff at trees and cruise by streams. This is much more than they can do in the rest of the park. There's even a little market, the Pine Tree, where dogs can often be seen waiting for their people to finish shopping.

Homes rent for a minimum of 2–3 days. Rates are $150–800 a night. Dogs are $10 extra. P.O. Box 2085, Wawona, Yosemite National Park, CA 95389; 209/375-6666 or 888/225-6666; www.redwoodsinyosemite.com.

Midpines

PLACES TO STAY

Homestead Guest Ranch: When you stay here, the house is all yours. It comes with a fireplace, a barbecue, and a well-stocked kitchen. Rates are $195 per couple plus $55 for each additional person. This is a wonderful place to stay, and the owners are sweet, dog-loving folks. They're happy to give you the good news that your dog can be leash-free on the ranch's 13 acres. Aroo! The ranch is about a half mile off Highway 140. The mailing address is P.O. Box 13 95345; 209/966-2820.

Mariposa

If you're on your way to Yosemite with your dog, take time to stop at this historic town. It's the county seat, but it looks nothing like most governmental centers we've seen. It's full of historic Gold Rush–era buildings and antique shops. The restaurants aren't bad either.

PARKS, BEACHES, AND RECREATION AREAS

🐾 Mariposa County Park

🐾🐾🐾 (See Mariposa County map on page 280)

This tiered park is like a wedding cake, with something delectable on every layer. Your dog will want to sink her teeth into it.

The top of the park is green and grassy, with picnic tables, a small playground, and excellent views of the town of Mariposa. A dirt road leads you to the lower levels, which have plenty of shade, picnic tables, and a decent walking path. Dogs must be leashed.

DIVERSION

Take a Sentimental Journey: If you're hankering to ride the old Logger Steam Train through some of Sierra National Forest's most magnificent scenery, you don't have to worry about waving good-bye to your dog. Leashed, calm dogs who can easily fit on your lap are welcome aboard the quaint old trains of the **Sugar Pine Railroad.** (In other words, 95-pound wiggly Jake Dog is not a good candidate.) Rates for the hour-long Logger ride are $17 for adults, $8.50 for kids. Dogs don't pay a cent, nor do tots under three.

If your dog is shy of loud noises, get as far back from the engine as possible, or simply take the railroad's "Model A"–powered trip on the Jenny railcar. It's quieter, shorter (30 minutes), and cheaper ($13 per adult, $6.50 per child, and still free for dogs and kids under three) than the Logger train.

For fairly obvious reasons, no dogs are allowed on the evening dinner ride. The train station is at 56001 Highway 41. It's about 12 miles past Oakhurst, two miles before the town of Fish Camp. And there's a terrific fringe benefit: It's right next to a couple of trailheads into dog-friendly Sierra National Forest. 559/683-7273; www.ymsprr.com.

From Highway 49/140 going south, turn right on 6th Street. In one block, jog right on Strong Street and make a quick left onto County Parks Road. 209/966-2498.

PLACES TO STAY

Best Western Yosemite Way Station Motel: A complimentary breakfast comes with your stay. Stoke up for a big day in Yosemite! Rates are $69–169. Dogs are $10 extra. 4999 State Highway 140 95338; 209/966-7545 or 800/321-5261.

Motherlode Lodge: Lucky dogs are allowed to be off leash in the back area here. That's great news for dogs who are weary of dainty little leashed walks while on a road trip. The owner, Lisa, adores dogs and will make your dog feel at home. Rates are $49–149. The physical address is 5051 Highway 140, and the mailing address is P.O. Box 986 95338; 209/966-2521 or 800/398-9770.

Fish Camp

PLACES TO STAY

Apple Tree Inn: Towering sugar pines surround the 18 new townhouse-like cabins that make up the Apple Tree Inn. It's tree city here, which is excellent news for dogs of the male persuasion. The Sierra National Forest is right across the street, and that's wonderful for all dogs. Yosemite National Park is just two miles down the road. This is a very peaceful place to stay, and the cabin rooms are beautifully designed. Dogs can't stay in the upstairs rooms (which are actually suites), but they're welcome at some of the first-floor rooms. Surprisingly, this serene resort is home to a delightfully unserene racquetball court, as well as an indoor pool and spa. Rates are $89–229. Dogs are $50 per visit. 1110 Highway 41 93623; 559/683-5111 or 888/683-5111; www.appletreeinn-yosemite.com.

Narrow Gauge Inn: Stay here and you're just a bone's throw from the dog-friendly Sugar Pine Railroad (see the Diversion *Take a Sentimental Journey*) and four miles from Yosemite National Park. This is an old-fashioned country-style inn. Most of the 26 guest rooms are on the small side, but they sport terrific mountain views, making them feel larger. The dog rooms are on the first level of the three-story inn, and all have balcony entrances. Dogs enjoy the property's tall trees, short trail, and seasonal creek. People like taking a dip in the heated outdoor pool or soaking in the hot tub. (Dogs would too, but they have to stick to the creek.) Rates are $79–170. Dogs are $25 extra per visit. 48571 Highway 41 93623; 559/683-7720; www.narrowgaugeinn.com.

Tenaya Lodge at Yosemite: When I got a letter from a dog named Maive claiming she had just had "the world's best vacation" at the Tenaya Lodge, I thought poor Maive was an aged dog confusing the good old dog-friendly days at Tenaya with the subsequent dark years of dogs being banned. Maive *is* an older girl (11) but it turns out her mental faculties are all in good working order: The Tenaya Lodge has lifted its many-year no-dogs-allowed rule and is now once again a fabulous place to go with your dog in tow!

This luxurious, relaxing, four-diamond (and four-paw) resort had been tops in my book (literally) for years, and now that it's dog-friendly once more, it's the cream of the crop again. In fact, it's even better than it had been. Its lobby—a grand Alpine beauty with an exposed-beamed cathedral ceiling, huge stone fireplace, and Native American floor designs—has always been droolworthy, but now it is radiant. And the 244 rooms have all been remodeled to the tune of $3 million. That means new furniture, earth-toned walls and decor, sumptuous bedding, and (this isn't luxurious, but it's convenient when traveling with a dog and needing to eat more in-room meals) in-room fridges.

Not only is the Tenaya Lodge allowing dogs again, it's positively welcoming them. The lodge prefers dogs that "aren't huge" but it's not an ironclad rule at this point. Dog guests are treated royally and get a Canine Companion package, with dog treats, poop bags, and a loaner plush pet bed and water bowl. Dog-sitting and dog-walking services are $10 per hour, and there's a three-hour minimum. Be sure to book this in advance.

You can get all kinds of spa treatments here, use the large indoor or outdoor pools, go ice-skating in winter, or get in shape at the fitness center. But since your dog can't do any of these activities with you, Jake and I recommend enjoying some of the 1.3 million acres of Sierra National Forest right outside the doors. You'll find miles of dog-friendly trails through lands some consider as attractive as nearby Yosemite. The concierge can point you in the right direction for a great five-mile roundtrip hike that takes you to a 20-foot waterfall. It's not exactly Bridalveil, but it's a fun excursion if you want to be able to actually hike on something other than pavement and concrete (à la Yosemite).

Rates are $169–435. Dogs are $75 for the length of their stay. 1122 Highway 41 93623; 888/514-2167; www.tenayalodge.com.

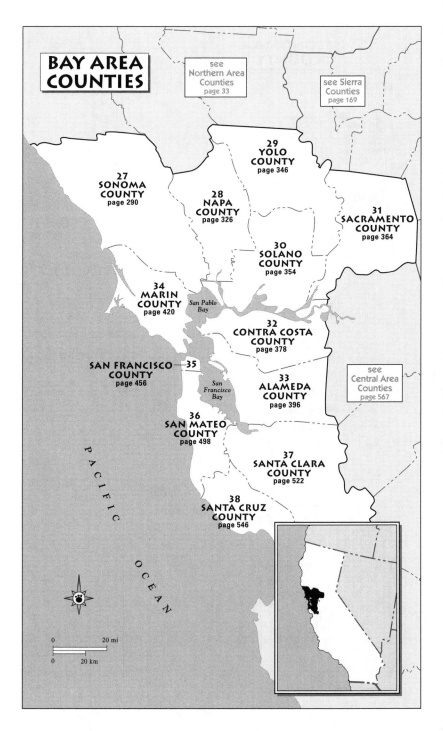

BAY AREA COUNTIES

see
Northern Area
Counties
page 33

see Sierra
Counties
page 169

29 YOLO COUNTY page 346

27 SONOMA COUNTY page 290

28 NAPA COUNTY page 326

31 SACRAMENTO COUNTY page 364

30 SOLANO COUNTY page 354

34 MARIN COUNTY page 420

San Pablo Bay

32 CONTRA COSTA COUNTY page 378

SAN FRANCISCO COUNTY—35 page 456

San Francisco Bay

33 ALAMEDA COUNTY page 396

see
Central Area
Counties
page 567

36 SAN MATEO COUNTY page 498

37 SANTA CLARA COUNTY page 522

38 SANTA CRUZ COUNTY page 546

PACIFIC OCEAN

0   20 mi

0   20 km

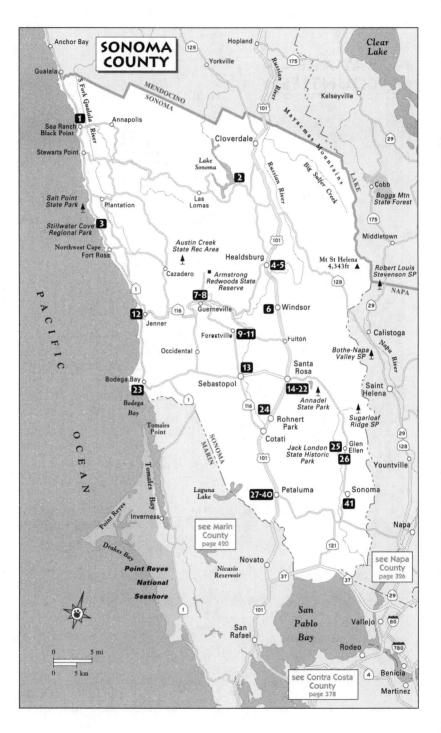

SONOMA COUNTY

Anchor Bay
Gualala
S Fork Gualala River
Sea Ranch
Black Point
Stewarts Point

1
Annapolis

Salt Point State Park
Stillwater Cove Regional Park **3**
Plantation
Northwest Cape
Fort Ross

Cazadero

Austin Creek State Rec Area

Armstrong Redwoods State Reserve

12
Jenner

7-8
Guerneville

Occidental

Forestville **9-11**

13

Bodega Bay **23**

Bodega Bay

Tomales Point

Sebastopol

24

Rohnert Park

Cotati

Tomales Bay

Inverness

Laguna Lake

27-40

see Marin County page 420

Nicasio Reservoir

Novato

Point Reyes

Drakes Bay

Point Reyes National Seashore

MENDOCINO
SONOMA

Hopland
Yorkville

128

Cloverdale

Lake Sonoma

2

Las Lomas

Russian River

101

Healdsburg **4-5**

6 Windsor

Fulton

Santa Rosa

14-22
Annadel State Park

116

Petaluma

Mayacmas Mountains

Russian River

Big Sulfer Creek

Mt St Helena 4,343ft

128

Clear Lake

175

Kelseyville

29

Cobb
Boggs Mtn State Forest

175

Middletown

Robert Louis Stevenson SP

NAPA

29

Calistoga

Bothe-Napa Valley SP

Saint Helena

Sugarloaf Ridge SP

29
128

Jack London State Historic Park **25**
26 Glen Ellen

Yountville

Sonoma **41**

Napa

121

see Napa County page 326

29

San Pablo Bay

San Rafael

101

37

37

Vallejo

Rodeo

Benicia

Martinez

80

780

4

see Contra Costa County page 378

PACIFIC OCEAN

SONOMA
MARIN

0   5 mi
0   5 km

CHAPTER 27

Sonoma County

Dog-friendly wineries. Off-leash parks galore. Sumptuous resorts and cute cottages that welcome dogs. French bistros and casual wine-country dining where dogs no one bats an eye at a dog, except to say, "Would you like some more water, pooch?"

Sonoma County is getting to be so dog friendly that dogs have become almost de rigueur here. "I visited Sonoma and felt naked without a dog," a reader, Kim, wrote me after she and her husband spent a romantic weekend exploring the region. (They'd been wanting a dog for years, and upon returning home they adopted a mellow malamute mix, Edna, who now travels with them regularly.)

Sonoma County has everything a dog's heart could desire, including the occasional ripe whiff of agriculture at its finest. Practically anything will grow here. It's the Bay Area capital for trees, flowers, and vegetables, as well as goats, sheep, cattle, chickens, pigs, and probably a few farm animals that are

PICK OF THE LITTER—SONOMA COUNTY

BIGGEST DOG PARK
Rocky Memorial Dog Park, Petaluma (page 319)

BEST BEACH
Sonoma Coast State Beaches, Jenner (page 304)

MOST DOG-FRIENDLY PLACES TO EAT
Willi's Seafood Restaurant, Healdsburg (page 298)
Charizma Wine Lounge & Restaurant, Guerneville (page 299)
Bistro des Copains, Occidental (page 306)
Animal House Cafe, Sebastopol (page 308)
Garden Court Cafe, Glen Ellen (page 316)

BEST PEOPLE WATCHING
Harmony Lounge, Sonoma (page 323)

COOLEST PLACE TO INSERT A DOLLAR
Russian River Resort's vending machine with dog treats, Guerneville (page 302)

BEST LODGING SWIMMING POOL THAT ALLOWS DOGS (ONLY ONE IN THE STATE!)
Casita Carneros' 20x40-foot pool, Sonoma (page 324)

MOST BEAUTIFUL OCEANFRONT HOUSE
Robinsong, rented through **Sea Ranch Vacation Homes,** Sea Ranch (page 293)

MOST DOG-FRIENDLY PLACES TO STAY
Creekside Inn and Resort, Guerneville (page 300)
Fern Grove Cottages, Guerneville (page 300)
Larissa House, Guerneville (page 301)
Dock Calm, rented through **Russian River Vacation Homes,** Guerneville (page 303)
Sheraton Sonoma County, Petaluma (page 322)
Casita Carneros, Sonoma (page 324)

MOST DOG-FRIENDLY WINE-TASTING
The Wine Room, Kenwood (page 296)
Wine Tasting of Sonoma County, Duncan's Mills (page 305)

BEST PLACE TO SHOP FOR OLD THINGS
Sparky's Antiques, Duncan's Mills (page 306)

being invented right now. Horticulturist Luther Burbank called the county "the chosen spot of all the Earth as far as nature is concerned." Dogs love this proximity to Mother Earth and Mother Cow Patty and Mother Chicken Manure. (See the Diversion *Sniff Out the Farm Trail* for ways to get close to this delightful aspect of Sonoma County.)

Sea Ranch

PARKS, BEACHES, AND RECREATION AREAS

1 Sea Ranch Beach Trails

🐾🐾🐾 (See Sonoma County map on page 290)

Sea Ranch is a private development, but seven public foot trails cross the property leading to the beach, which is also public property. The smooth, wide dirt trails are managed by Sonoma County Regional Parks, and they offer incomparable solitary walks through unspoiled grassy hills.

All the trails are clearly marked on Highway 1. Each trailhead has restrooms and a box where you are asked to deposit $4 for parking. No motorcycles, bicycles, or horses are allowed. Keep your dog on leash.

Here are the distances to the beach, listing trails from north to south: Salal Trail, 0.6 mile; Bluff-Top Trail, 3.5 miles; Walk-On Beach Trail, 0.4 mile; Shell Beach Trail, 0.6 mile; Stengel Beach Trail, 0.2 mile; Pebble Beach Trail, 0.3 mile; Black Point Trail, 0.3 mile. 707/785-2377.

PLACES TO STAY

Sea Ranch Vacation Homes beach rentals: The Sea Ranch Vacation Homes rental agency offers 12 beautiful, dog-friendly homes for rent in the glorious oceanfront community of Sea Ranch. Some homes are almost on the water, some are set in wooded areas, and some next to meadows. All are attractive, but our favorite is Robinsong, a stellar example of how a seaside home can live up to its landscape. The fireplace flanked by smartly cushioned "window seats" is worth the price of admission. You will love reading there, and your dog will adore snoozing on a blanket beside you. The look of the interior is clean and crisp, yet amazingly cozy. The spacious kitchen, which boasts an island, is set up for the chef in you.

Rates for the Robinsong are $260 nightly (there's a two-night minimum) and $1,560 for the week. It's one of the more expensive dog-friendly homes, but if you have it in your budget, it's worth it. Rates for the variety of dog-friendly homes are $120–270. Weekly rates are $720–1,620. Dogs are $10 extra nightly. For reservations and information, call 707/884-4235; www.searanchrentals.com.

Cloverdale

PARKS, BEACHES, AND RECREATION AREAS

2 Lake Sonoma Recreation Area

😾 😾 😾 (See Sonoma County map on page 290)

This is the only recreation site in the nine counties of the Bay Area run by the U.S. Army Corps of Engineers, and it's too bad. The Corps has a liberal attitude toward dogs, and this park is beautifully developed and managed, not to mention clean. It's also free. You must keep your dog on a six-foot leash, and he's not allowed on the swimming beach at the north end, but rangers told us there's no rule against dogs swimming anywhere else.

If you're the type who doesn't clean up after your dog, here's a warning: Change your act, or stay far from here. Rangers have been known to charge a cleanup fee for owners who ignore the deposits of their dogs.

A large lawn with picnic tables, some shaded, is at the visitors center. You can rent a boat from the private concession on the lake, which allows leashed dogs on all boats. Follow signs from the visitors center. To reserve a boat, call 707/433-2200. Waterskiing and camping are also popular here.

For a good dog hike, pick up a map at the visitors center and drive west on Dry Creek Road to the trailheads, which have their own parking lots. There are 40 miles of trails. Here are two of our favorites: There's a bit of shade at the Gray Pine Flat Trailhead. This smooth foot trail goes down to the lake through an unusual forest of foothill pines, madrone, manzanita, and blooming desert brush. The buzz of motorboats on the lake blends with the hammering of woodpeckers. You get a good view of the lake fairly quickly. If you'd prefer less of a climb back to the trailhead, take the Little Flat Trail, which starts lower down.

Horses are allowed on these trails, but bikes aren't—a plus for your dog's safety. Unfortunately, it gets bone-dry here in summer, and poison oak is common.

Camping is available at 113 sites at Liberty Glen Campground and several primitive boat-in sites on the lake. None of these sites has water. (Campers at Liberty Glen can stock up nearby.) Rates are $10–14. For reservations (advised in summer), phone 877/444-6777.

Take U.S. 101 to the Canyon Road exit. Go west to Dry Creek Road and turn right into the entrance. Take a right at the only fork. 707/433-9483.

Timber Cove
PARKS, BEACHES, AND RECREATION AREAS

🐾 Stillwater Cove Regional Park
🐾🐾🐾 (See Sonoma County map on page 290)

This is a tiny but delightful beach at the foot of spectacular pine-covered cliffs. Park in the small lot beside Highway 1, leash your dog, and walk down. There is a larger picnic area above the highway, where a $5 day-use fee is charged. From here, you have to cross the highway to get to the cove. Look both ways!

There are 23 campsites, available on a first-come, first-served basis. If you want to make a reservation, they're available through park headquarters. Sites are $18 per night. The turnout is about one mile north of Fort Ross State Park (where dogs are banned). 707/847-3245.

Healdsburg
PARKS, BEACHES, AND RECREATION AREAS

🐾 Villa Chanticleer Dog Park
🐾🐾🐾🐾🐾 (See Sonoma County map on page 290)

This 1.5-acre fenced dog park is a great place to take your dog whether you live here or you're just visiting. It's within a beautiful oak grove setting, so it's easy on the eyes, plus there's plenty of shade. Lucky dogs who come here have it all: trees, enough room to romp, and the smells of nature. It has all the good dog-park amenities, including benches and water. The ground cover is wood chips, which adds to the woodsy feeling here, but Jake thinks each wood chip is a delicacy and is content to plop himself down and gnaw away until an interesting dog or errant tennis ball catches his eye. Note that if you have an older or smaller dog, you might be better off at Badger Park.

The park is set within the larger Villa Chanticleer Park, which has buildings and backdrops that are popular for weddings. Be sure your dog is on leash if you explore beyond the dog area: You don't want your dog interfering with any nuptials. The address is 1248 Chanticleer Way.

DIVERSION

Merlot Over and Play Dead: I didn't make up this pun. (Mine are usually worse.) It's the name of a wine made by a Healdsburg vintner who owns the Mutt Lynch Winery. Other "doggone good wines," as Brenda Lynch calls them, are Canis Major and Portrait of a Mutt.

Sonoma County wineries are going to the dogs. Some have their own lines of dog-labeled wines. Several allow well-behaved dogs in their tasting rooms and at their picnic areas. I don't list which ones allow pooches in the tasting rooms because the health department doesn't necessarily approve, and I don't want to get anyone in trouble. Below is a taste of some of Sonoma's more dog-friendly wineries, listed by area. Phone the individual wineries for hours, prices, and dog-friendly specifics.

GEYSERVILLE
Stryker Sonoma, 5110 Highway 128; 707/433-1944; www.strykersonoma.com.

HEALDSBURG
Lambert Bridge Winery, 4085 West Dry Creek Road; 707/431-9600; www.lambertbridge.com.
Mutt Lynch Winery, 1960 Dry Creek Road; 707/942-6180; www.muttlynchwinery.com. This winery is all about dogs. Dog-labeled wines abound, and now you can even get custom labels featuring your very own canine. Open by appointment only.

KENWOOD
The Wine Room, 9575 Sonoma Highway; 707/833-6131; www.the-wine-room.com. Dogs have their own tasting bar (dog treats) at this multiwinery co-op tasting room. A new wine line, The Friendly Dog, has four "muttages" so far. If you hanker to pour from

5 Badger Dog Park
🐾🐾🐾🐕 (See Sonoma County map on page 290)

If your dog is small, old, or on the inactive side for whatever reason, this is the Healdsburg dog park to visit. Your elderly dog won't need an AARP card to enter, but if you have a dog like Jake (big, youngish, and very active), you should take your business to Villa Chanticleer Dog Park. Badger Dog Park is a lovely little fenced park, with one gorgeous large oak that people tend to congregate under. The ground is grassy, which dog paws appreciate. If only this park were bigger than a quarter acre we could give it an extra paw. It's set within Badger Park, which is at 750 Heron Drive. 707/431-3384.

a bottle that has your dog on the label, The Wine Room can arrange for custom canine labels.

SANTA ROSA
De Loach Vineyards, 1791 Olivet Road; 707/526-9111; www.deloachvineyards.com.
Hanna Winery & Vineyards, 5353 Occidental Road; 707/575-3371; www.hannawinery.com.
Martin Ray Winery, 2191 Laguna Road; 707/823-2404; www.martinray-winery.com.

SEBASTOPOL
Taft Street Winery, 2030 Barlow Lane; 707/823-2049; www.taftstreetwinery.com.

SONOMA
Sebastiani Vineyards and Winery, 389 4th Street East; 707/933-3230; www.sebastiani.com. Visiting dogs get to drink fresh water from the outside dog bowls.

DUNCAN'S MILLS
Wine Tasting of Sonoma County, 25179 Main Street; 707/865-0565; www.winetastingsonoma.com. See the full listing under *Duncan's Mills Places to Eat* for details.

WINDSOR
Martinelli Vineyards and Winery, 3360 River Road; 707/525-0570; www.martinelliwinery.com. Leashed dogs may sniff around the outside of this lovely property.

PLACES TO EAT
Costeaux French Bakery: Stroll around Healdsburg's good-looking town square, with its old buildings and benches for shady rest stops, and then drop in here for dinner or a wonderful pastry snack at an outdoor table. 417 Healdsburg Avenue; 707/433-1913.

Oakville Grocery: This gourmet grocer is the home of a terrific alfresco café where dogs are welcome. The outdoor café features a wood-burning fireplace, which makes for cozy evenings. Jake loves sniffing the rotisserie chicken, and the pizzas are to drool for. Wine is big here, too, but dogs should stick with water: There's always a doggy bowl here for thirsty pooches. 124 Matheson Street; 707/433-3200.

Willi's Seafood Restaurant: Like starters? This seafood restaurant is all about starters/tapas with a seafood bent. Blissfully, the seafood is oh-so-fresh. People who like ceviche say this is one of the best places to get it. The scallops wrapped in bacon are droolworthy. Chicken and other meaty dishes are also available, if you're not lured by fish. Nadia Stafford, who recommended this place to us, says the lobster rolls are to die for.

What really puts a smile on a dog's snout is that the waitstaff will bring your dog a little treat and a bowl of water. Dine together on the mostly shaded patio. 403 Healdsburg Avenue; 707/433-9191.

PLACES TO STAY

Best Western Dry Creek Inn: Rates are $115–199. Dogs are $20 extra. 198 Dry Creek Road 95448; 707/433-0300.

The Irish Rose Inn: This small, quaint inn in the heart of Dry Creek Valley is pink, and it's surrounded by 95 rose bushes. But even the manliest of dogs enjoys a stay here, thanks to owner Chris Matson's hospitality and a relaxed, friendly atmosphere. (Oh, and because dogs are fairly color-blind.) Dogs also get treats if their parents—you—are OK with that.) The two guest rooms in the main house are pleasant and airy. We like Michael's room for its mosquito-netting-draped king bed. There's also the Chateau Margi, a one-bedroom cottage with a small kitchen.

My favorite part of the Irish Rose is the pretty porch, where you can sit and relax in one of the wicker chairs after coming back from a day of wine-tasting. There's an afternoon wine and cheese social and a full, tasty breakfast. A big thank-you to Buster and Sage, who led us to this inn by having their favorite person, Juliann Bryan, write to us. Rates are $160–225. 3232 Dry Creek Road 95448; 707/431-2801; www.theirishroseinn.com.

Windsor

Until 1992, Windsor wasn't anything but an unincorporated county area. Then it became a town, thanks to the "d" word (development). In 1997, it spawned its very first park, and with that park came a fenced-in dog park. Dogs think Windsor's movers and shakers are very smart people, indeed.

PARKS, BEACHES, AND RECREATION AREAS

6 Pleasant Oak Park

🐾🐾🐕 (See Sonoma County map on page 290)

This is a fine example of how a fenced-in dog park can become a decent place, despite a rather austere start. In the park's early days, it was little more than a dirt lot surrounded by a very high fence with double gates. But now it's really something to wag about. It has water, grass, and enough trees to cast a cooling shade in the summer. Dogs from miles around come to socialize. Their humans have been known to follow suit. The park is at Old Redwood Highway and Pleasant Avenue. 707/838-1260.

Guerneville

Guerneville is the largest town on the Russian River. The river area is both a longstanding family vacation destination and a gay/lesbian-friendly resort area. What really counts, though, is that it's so dog-friendly. Behold!

PARKS, BEACHES, AND RECREATION AREAS

7 Armstrong Redwoods State Reserve

🐾🐾 (See Sonoma County map on page 290)

As is usual in state parks, you can take a dog only on paved roads and into picnic areas. But here you can give your dog and yourself an exceptional treat. The picnic grounds are a cool, hushed redwood cathedral. You can walk on Armstrong Woods Road, which winds along Fife Creek (usually lush, but dry in the heart of summer) all the way to the top of McCray Mountain, about three miles.

The drive is fairly terrifying, so you may prefer to walk anyway. Hikers, bicycles, and autos all share the road, so be very careful. Your dog must be leashed everywhere in the park. From Guerneville, go about 2.5 miles north on Armstrong Woods Road. The day-use fee is $6, but if you park out front you can walk in for free. 707/869-2015 or 707/865-2391.

8 Vacation Beach

🐾🐾🐾 (See Sonoma County map on page 290)

Vacation Beach is not really a beach, but an access point where the Russian River is dammed by two roads across it. It's one of several public spots where you and your dog used to be able to legally jump into the drink, but leashes seem to be the law here now. It's still fun. People and pooches picnic, swim, put in canoes, and cool their feet and paws in the cool river.

From Highway 116 between Guerneville and Monte Rio, turn south at the unmarked road where you see Old Cazadero Road veering north. You can park at the approaches to the dams but not on the crossing itself. 707/869-9000.

PLACES TO EAT

Charizma Wine Lounge & Restaurant: The home page of Charizma's website has a little picture of an adorable yellow Lab pup named Bella, whose people own this place. She won't be a pup anymore by the time you read this, but she still wields her influence: Dogs who come here get served treats. The inside of Charizma is cozy, almost living room–like. But dogs have to dine with you at the couple of sidewalk tables out front. It's OK. The food, from breakfast (we had killer oatmeal and Swedish pancakes) to dinner will keep your mind off the concrete and on your plate. 16337 Main Street; 707/869-0909.

Triple R Bar & Grill: You'll cluck for the chicken cobbler. You'll melt for the house-made mac and cheese (made with crispy onions). The home-style food here is great, and you can also get some lighter cuisine. The three R's in the Triple R stand for the dog-friendly Russian River Resort, of which the restaurant is part. Dogs can dine with you at the outdoor tables here.

The restaurant doesn't serve treats, but if your dog is hungry and you don't want to share, ask where the resort's vending machine is. Go there, put your money in, and press E-1 or E-8. Voilà! Treats for your dog! 16390 Fourth Street; 707/869-0691.

PLACES TO STAY

Creekside Inn and Resort: Dogs get to stay at three of several cottages and rooms at this fun inn near the Russian River. Bird dogs enjoy lounging in the Quail Cottage, a small, bright cottage with a fireplace. The Deck House, another poochy haven, is a little larger, with a sunny deck. The sweet one-bedroom Apple House is separated from the inn by a very old apple tree.

The real apple of your dog's eye will be the Dog Days Package. You and your dog will each get a tasty treat (gourmet chocolate for you, liver goody for your dog, and aren't you glad it's not vice versa?). You'll also receive a coupon for a little doggy gift and discounts on a grooming for your dog and a massage for you. The package entails staying a few nights, but it ends up being less expensive than doing a night-by-night tally. Other packages, such as the popular Gay Honeymoon package, are also available.

The inn's land is dotted with several large redwoods. The property spans three acres, and dogs are welcome to cruise around on leash. Human guests may hang out in the inn's main dining room and lounge, both of which have fireplaces. Humans can also swim in the pool here. Dogs have to be content to do the dog paddle in the Russian River, not too far away.

Rates are $105–165. Weekly rates are available. If you'd like to stay in a larger house, you can also rent the Summer Crossing, a small vacation home here. It goes for $285 nightly and sleeps up to four. 16180 Neeley Road, P.O. Box 2185 95446; 707/869-3623 or 800/776-6586; www.creeksideinn.com.

Fern Grove Cottages: Sleep in one of 20 charming cabins under 200-foot redwoods here! The friendly owners, Mike and Margaret Kennett, welcome good pooches. "We've had some great dogs stay here," says Margaret, who doles out biscuits at check-in and provides old blankets for your dog's sleeping pleasure.

The cottages are simple but cozy, with tasteful decor. Most have fireplaces, and some have kitchens. A delicious continental breakfast comes with your stay. The homemade granola and scones are divine. Rates are $89–259. Dogs are $15 extra. 16650 Highway 116 95446; 707/869-8105; www.ferngrove.com.

Dawn Ranch Lodge: The cottages on this 15-acre redwood-festooned property (formerly Fifes Guest Ranch) will melt your heart if you like older abodes. These were built in 1905, and they still have the charm of their day, updated with a simple, light, airy decor. They're super comfy, too. Dogs think they're the cat's meow, but truth be told, they really like walking around the ranch better. The meadows, the trees, the river, all speak to a dog's soul. And what's better for the soul of a dog than to be able to run around off leash in an apple orchard? Dogs under voice control are granted this fun privilege.

Cottages are $79–325. Dogs are $25 for the length of their stay. 16467 Highway 116, P.O. Box 45 95446; 707/869-0656 or 800/734-3371; www.dawn ranch.com.

Highlands Resort: If your dog has never been to a bar, ask to stay in the Highland's studio: The large room not only has a cozy fireplace, but it has its own wet bar. Teetotaling dogs might prefer the three larger cabins that allow dogs. The cabins have fireplaces, and some have kitchenettes, but no bar.

The Highlands, known as "a straight-friendly gay resort," is set on three wooded acres (which dogs can explore on leash) and has the feel of a country retreat. It has a swimming pool and outdoor hot tub—both clothing-optional. In the resort's brochure there's a bird's-eye–view picture of a fellow standing in the hot tub, with just a bit of bun showing. Joe Dog blushed and came back for another look.

Rates are $105–170. Dogs are $25 extra for the length of their stay. 14000 Woodland Drive 95446; 707/869-0333; www.highlandsresort.com.

Larissa House: This sweet one-bedroom home has a fenced garden/yard and private dock on the river. Nadia, the owner, lives next door and adores dogs. In fact, you pretty much have to have a dog to stay here. It's so doggone dog-friendly that the shower is designed so that you and your dog can shower at the same time (if your dog isn't too shy about these things). Nadia makes sure all dogs receive a welcoming bag of treats when they arrive. Dogs fall instantly in love when they meet Nadia, and the love-fest often continues year-round, when she sends them (note: *them,* not *you*) a Christmas card. Rates are $1,000 per week. 17798 Orchard Avenue 95446; 707/869-3651.

Russian River Getaways: If you and your dog want a home away from home while you vacation in the Russian River area, you've hit the jackpot. Russian River Getaways has dozens of beautiful dog-friendly homes for rent on a nightly or weekly basis. The homes are generally quite upscale, but the prices are fairly down to earth. (An aside that will put a smile on your dog's snout: The majority of the homes rented through Russian River Getaways permit dogs. "We tell them that if they don't allow dogs, they're not going to do such good business," says an employee. "They really can't compete.")

Most of the homes are very attractive, with wonderfully creative touches.

Just the names of some of the homes make you and your dog friend want to check them out: Bellagio, Bohemian Rhapsody, Jujube, The Bird Cage/La Cage aux Folles, the Luv Shack, and the Grand Prix (please don't pronounce the "x"—you'll embarrass your dog) are not your typical vacation home rental names. If you're looking to drop some dollars, check out Grandma's House (let's just say this must be some grandma with a billiard table in her 31-foot living room and a hot tub in her gazebo) and the River Queen, a fabulous manse on the river.

Rates for the homes range $185–1,100 nightly, and there's a two-night minimum. Weekly rates are available. For a brochure describing the homes, write Russian River Getaways at 14075 Mill Street, P.O. Box 1673 95446, or phone 707/869-4560 or 800/433-6673. The best way to check out the rentals is at www.rrgetaways.com.

Russian River Resort: This is a great place to meet a man, especially if you are a man. When we swung by for a peek at the resort, the saline pool was chock full of guys. Unlike at another clothing-optional dog-friendly resort down the road, everyone was wearing a swimsuit. Jake, who has been known to make friends with sunbathers who opt for no clothes (see *Baker Beach* in the *San Francisco County* chapter), may have been disappointed, but he didn't show it: Cheering him up was the dog-loving attitude of the guests and staffers. (Dogs aren't allowed in the pool area, but Jake had a peek.) "What a GORGEOUS dog!" was a refrain Jake frequently reveled in during his visit.

This is an adults-only resort, and a manager says that while most of the guests are gay or lesbian, everyone is welcome here. (Just not children of the human variety.) Jake wasn't the only visitor wearing a collar and a leash when we visited. "Looks like we have something in common," said a man whose outfit matched Jake's, except for the leather vest and chaps he was wearing. His big bear of a friend, who was holding the other end of the leash, gave Jake a friendly head rub and chest scratch, but I refrained from giving *his* leashed friend the same treatment.

The rooms have been attractively redone since a flood did a number on them, and they have comfy beds, microwaves, and little fridges, and some even feature pellet stoves. And here's a real boon for the canine set: There's a small lawn area at the rear of the property where dogs can exercise and play. An attractive restaurant with a dog-friendly patio is also part of the setup here.

I love unique dog-friendly touches, and the Russian River Resort has a special one: a vending machine that has two compartments with dog treats. Put in your money, and push the button for E-1 or E-8, and your dog will be amazed at what drops down. This is a first, to my knowledge, and we give a pat on the back to the person who thought of this.

Dogs aren't allowed at the resort on weekends or holidays. The good news is that it's less expensive here midweek. Rates are $65–175. 16390 Fourth Street

95446; 707/869-0691 or 800/417-3767; www.russianriverresort.com. Check out the Canine Corner page for some cute pictures of pet friends and the occasional amusing short video clip.

Russian River Vacation Homes: Spend your Russian River–area vacation in your own charming private house. This is an ideal way to vacation with your pooch. Russian River Vacation Homes offers 26 beautiful, quaint houses for pets and their people. From a one-bedroom rustic log cabin on the river to a three-bedroom riverside home complete with hot tub, you and your holiday hound will find the home of your dreams.

Scooter the Dog contacted us to tell us about a lovely two-bedroom rental home she co-owns with her people, Ed and Nancy. It's called Dock Calm, and sure enough, it has a river dock, and you'll feel very calm here. All rooms have river views. It's a very dog-friendly place, with nice furniture that's mostly fine for pooches. There's even a doggy door. Dogs also get to use a big doggy bed. Jake, a hearth dog if ever there was one, recommends putting it by the fire on a chilly evening. You could spend the day with your dog just lazing on the deck, with its outdoor couch and lounge chairs. A wonderful hot tub graces a second deck, and the river views from here are droolworthy. And speaking of drool, visiting dogs get complimentary dog treats with their stay.

Rates for the range of Russian River Vacation Homes are $145–535. Weekly rates are $750–2,450. Dock Calm falls somewhere in the middle. 707/869-9030, 800/310-0804 (California only), or 800/997-3312 (nationwide). Detailed info on rentals is at www.riverhomes.com.

Forestville

This beautiful town's motto is: "Where wine country meets the redwoods." This is Russian River country, and dogs love sniffing around some terrific beaches here. Be sure to visit the historic community's little "downtown." It's an eclectic charmer.

PARKS, BEACHES, AND RECREATION AREAS

If you have a dog who likes splashing in water, prepare for a very happy pooch: Forestville is home to three county beaches that permit leashed dogs. They're all Russian River havens, with good river access, old black walnut forests, German ivy, and lots of birds. Dogs need to be leashed, but there's plenty to enjoy, even tethered together. Since this pretty much describes all three river access locales, below we'll just list the pertinent info for each.

🐾 Steelhead Beach

🐾🐾🐾 (See Sonoma County map on page 290)

At 50 acres, with lots of picnic areas and flat grassy territory, this is the largest and most developed of the three county beach access areas in Forestville. If you drive in, you pay $5. Walk in and it's free. The park is at 9000 River Road. 707/565-2041.

10 Forestville River Access/Mom's Beach

😊😊😊 (See Sonoma County map on page 290)

It's 10 acres of on-leash fun here. This is an undeveloped area, at 10584 River Drive, off River Road, but it'll cost you $5 to enter, developed or not. 707/565-2041.

11 Sunset Beach

😊😊😊 (See Sonoma County map on page 290)

This is a wild and lovely river access location, with about 10 acres to explore with your leashed dog. Entry costs $5. 11057 Sunset Drive. 707/565-2041.

PLACES TO EAT

Russian River Pub: This log-cabin pub is known for its chicken wings ("Ain't no Thing but a Chicken Wing," read the t-shirts that adorn the servers), but much of the food here isn't typical pub grub; it's quality cuisine. You can order items like a seared ahi tuna salad, house-made pesto on a chicken sandwich, and meats that have been lovingly brined and coddled for hours. There are even some vegetarian options. Many regulars lovingly call the pub a dive, but you can't dive too deep with food like this.

If you come here with your dog, look for the server named Janice. She carries treats for her canine customers. Dine with your dog on the patio. 11829 River Road; 707/887-7932.

Jenner

PARKS, BEACHES, AND RECREATION AREAS

12 Sonoma Coast State Beaches

😊😊😊😊 (See Sonoma County map on page 290)

A string of beautiful, clean beaches runs south from Jenner to Bodega Bay, and you can't go wrong from Goat Rock Beach south to Salmon Creek Beach: Gorgeous bluff views, stretches of brown sand, gnarled rocks, and grassy dunes welcome you. Always keep an eye on the surf and a leash on your dog.

Dogs are not allowed on any of the trails that run on the bluffs above the beaches, on Bodega Head, in the Willow Creek area east of Bridgehaven, or in the seal rookery upriver from Goat Rock Beach. (Watch for the warning sign.) No camping is permitted on any of the beaches, except Bodega Dunes and Wright's Beach, which have campgrounds. These two also charge a $6 day-use fee. Day use of all other beaches is free. 707/875-3483.

The Bodega Dunes Campground has 99 developed sites, and Wright's

Beach Campground has 27 developed sites. Sites are $24 at Bodega, and $32 at Wright's. Reservations are highly recommended. Call 800/444-7275. For general beach info, call 707/875-3483.

PLACES TO STAY

Jenner Inn: This area is a black hole for cell phone reception, and only a few of the rooms and cottages have phones, and none have TVs, so this is a great place to visit if you really want to get away from it all. (That said, they do have Internet access in the parlor these days.)

There's so much relaxing to be done here that you'll scarcely notice that you're not doing anything. The early-20th-century rooms and cottages are comfy and furnished with antiques. Some have fireplaces, some have kitchens, and some have river views. The Russian River is just a bone's throw away, and it's a fairly quick walk to the ocean, should you want to see big water. The best part of staying here with a dog is the big three-acre meadow in the back: Pooches are welcome to trot around off leash! You won't need to worry about finding a local dog park if you stay here. Rates are $118–298. Highway 1, Box 69 95450; 707/865-2377; www.jennerinn.com.

Duncan's Mills

This cute little town on the Russian River is home to a general store, a candy store, a couple of restaurants, a wine-tasting store, several antiques shops, and a smattering of other sweet little places. It's a good, old-fashioned town that's had some new life breathed into it in recent years. Seventy percent of the 20 or so businesses here are run by women. Many of them are dog friendly.

PLACES TO EAT

Cape Fear Cafe: I hope this fun eatery is named for the beautiful Cape Fear coast of North Carolina, and not the disturbing movie where a dog gets poisoned (among other gruesome incidents). The people here are friendly, and the food—mostly of the American genre, mixed with some fun international renditions—is quite tasty. Dogs are welcome to dine with you at the umbrella-topped tables on the patio. Thank-you to Nadia Stafford, proprietor of the Larissa House in Guerneville, for letting us know about the café. 25191 Highway 116; 707/865-9246.

Wine Tasting of Sonoma County: If you're anywhere around the Russian River, you must bring your dog here. "We are super dog friendly!" says the kind, dog-loving owner, Prairie Silva. Not only do dogs get to join you at the three umbrella-topped tables or wraparound bench outside, but they get a delicious treat and cool water just for showing up. Plus they can catch things in the adjacent pasture ("things" being balls and Frisbees, not cows). Prairie goes the extra mile for canine visitors. You'll find out more when you visit.

DIVERSION

Like a Dog in an Antiques Shop: Your good, leashed dog is welcome to join you at **Sparky's Antiques,** as long as he's not like a bull in a china shop. Owner Carole Silva named the store after her beloved Jack Russell terrier, Sparky, a stray she and her family rescued. (He died recently, at the ripe old age of 18 or 19. Talk about antique!) She's only had one "bullish" experience, and that was more an owner error than a dog faux pas. A Cavalier King Charles spaniel got just a little too cavalier when his owner let him walk around the store on his own with his leash dragging behind. An antique statue of a horse went down. The owner graciously paid for the damages.

Like her daughter, Prairie, who owns Wine Tasting of Sonoma County just down the road, Carole loves dogs. She even supplies visiting dogs with biscuits and a bowl of water!

The store specializes in old jewelry, funky pieces from the 1950s (oh my goodness, is that considered antique already?), and Art Moderne. The store also is part of the Duncan's Mills Antique Merchants Society, which holds a huge antiques fair in town every Labor Day weekend. Antiques dealers come from everywhere, and leashed dogs are, indeed, invited.

The store is at 25185 Main Street, Duncan's Mills; 707/865-1022.

This place is all about Sonoma wine, cheeses, and other local products. You can taste wines and buy wine by the glass or bottle, cheese, grapes, and even get basic picnic supplies here. Since this isn't a restaurant or food-prep facility, Prairie says, "We can't physically cut the cheese." (She has a good sense of humor; she would like to see the health department relax a little about the cheese-cutting rule.) "But we can supply customers with what they need to have a great picnic." 25179 Main Street; 707/865-0565; www.winetasting sonoma.com.

Occidental

If you become an accidental Occidental tourist, you and your leashed pooch can enjoy a stroll through this historic landmark town, with its interesting assortment of shops and galleries. If you want to eat great food and/or spend the night, there's a dog-friendly restaurant and lodging.

PLACES TO EAT

Bistro des Copains: Ooh la la, dogs love this French bistro. Is it the *Bœuf en Daube à la Provençale* (for you non-French-speaking dogs, that's beef braised in red wine with lots of good stuff)? Is it the *Magret de Canard* (dog French lesson No. 2: duck breasts with more good stuff)? Who knows? It could even be the creamy risottos served with delectable ingredients. Maybe they just love it because they're welcome here, and they get biscuits and water when they join you on the pretty patio. The wine selection is lovely, too, but dogs don't generally care about this. 3782 Bohemian Highway; 707/874-2436.

PLACES TO STAY

Negri's Occidental Hotel: This is a very basic, although decent, motel. It's close to the village, and there's a pool, should you feel like doing the dog paddle. (Your dog needs to stay dry here.) Rates are $74–169. Dogs are $10 extra. 3610 Bohemian Highway 95465; 707/874-3623 or 877/867-6084; www.occidentalhotel.com.

Sebastopol

Dogs enjoy sniffing out this sweet semirural community. It's got oodles of little Farm Trails farms (see the Diversion *Sniff Out the Farm Trail*), should you be drooling for some fresh produce. (Some sell meat, too, should that interest your dog.)

PARKS, BEACHES, AND RECREATION AREAS

13 Ragle Ranch Regional Park Dog Park/ Animal Care Center Dog Park

🐾🐾🐕 (See Sonoma County map on page 290)

It's only a half-acre, but this simple little fenced park provides a welcome relief for dogs longing to run around without a leash. A doggy/human water fountain with a bone-shaped pad is a refreshing sight. Ground cover is hay—fitting for the area's rural feel. Trees, shrubs, benches, and other park accommodations will follow with more donations of time and money.

The park is within Ragle Ranch Regional Park, which has a lovely nature trail that will take you and your leashed dog to Atascadero Creek. Hang onto that leash, because this is a primo bird-watching area. Boy dogs love the oak grove that shades this area. From Highway 12, drive north on Ragle Road. The dog park is at 500 Ragle Ranch Road. 707/565-2041.

PLACES TO EAT

Ace in the Hole: This dog-friendly joint claims to be "America's First Cider Pub." And they don't mean the kind of cider you drank as a kid (unless you had a very interesting childhood). Several varieties of fermented cider come to life here, and all have unique flavors, from honey to berry. You can also get beer, ale, and English-Cal pub grub. Jake recommends the beef pot pie. Drink and dine with your dog at the big patio. Thank you to Marge and Homer pug

dogs for the heads up about this fun pub. It's at Highway 116 and Graton Road, about three miles north of the Sebastopol border. 707/829-1223.

Animal House Cafe: What a fitting name for a place that gives dogs treats. Yes, your dog gets a treat at the Animal House Cafe! What could be more appropriate? Admittedly, Animal House Cafe is an odd name for an Asian restaurant, but it was left over from its wilder deli days, and the current owner liked the name and likes dogs, so Animal House it is. You can get an assortment of Asian foods, from Chinese to Japanese to Thai. The curries are particularly tasty. Dogs are welcome to join you on the patio. 171 Pleasant Hill Avenue; 707/823-1800.

Santa Rosa

PARKS, BEACHES, AND RECREATION AREAS

This sprawling city has gone to the dogs, and dogs and their people couldn't be happier. It used to be that if you wanted to give your pooch a little off-leash exercise, you'd go out of town or sneak out to a park at night and hope no one was watching. But now the city has five very attractive off-leash dog parks and four parks that aren't fenced and have limited off-leash hours. That sound you hear is the sound of tails thumping. Hard. (Children's tails aren't wagging quite as quickly: Kids under 10 aren't allowed to set paw in any of the dog parks—not even on leash.)

For the most part, the dog parks are wonderful. And if you don't mind getting up early, the parks with limited off-leash hours offer even more room and more doggy-heaven scents. Dogs who visit these parks are allowed to run off leash 6–8 A.M. every day. The hours are strictly enforced, so be sure to bring a watch or cell phone. Dogs have to be under voice control, non-aggressive, spayed or neutered, and more than four months old. As always, be sure to scoop the poop.

We like the philosophy of the parks department people here. In a nutshell, if there's a rough part of a park where people are afraid to go, they put in a dog park because they believe "it brings positive activities into the parks. It makes it much safer and more comfortable for kids and others," according to Bill Montgomery, the department's now-retired deputy director. We hope other communities look to Santa Rosa as an example of how to incorporate dogs into the park scene so that it makes life better for everyone.

14 DeTurk Round Barn Park

🐾🐾🐾🐕 (See Sonoma County map on page 290)

This is one of the more interesting parks to peruse with your pooch. It's a smallish park in the historic west-side district of town, and it's home to a wonderful rare round barn that was built in the 1870s. Dogs have to be leashed to explore around the barn area.

What dogs like best about this park is a relatively small (9,000 square feet) dog park where they can throw their leashes to the wind. It's fenced with attractive white wood and has some young trees working to become shade trees. The dog park is actually called Maverick Park, in honor of a valuable member of the K-9 Corps of the Sonoma County Sheriff's Department who was killed in the line of duty in Santa Rosa. We won't forget you, Maverick.

The park is at Donahue and 8th streets. 707/543-3292 or 707/539-5979.

15 Doyle Park

🐾🐾🐾🐾🐕 (See Sonoma County map on page 290)

Doyle Park is a very stately place to take a pooch. A little stone bridge takes you over a stream and into the park's main entry area. The trees here have an elegant, deep-rooted look. The grass is like a cool, plush green carpet. At Doyle, even the squirrels don't look squirrelly.

Dogs think it's all grand. But what they think is even better is the fact that they can run around all this splendor without a leash 6–8 A.M., thanks to a great program run by the city. Dogs who can't make these hours don't have to mope around on leash, though: Doyle Park is graced not only with the off-leash program, but with its very own fenced doggy park. It's not as riveting as the rest of the park, but it's got water and some trees, and it's a very safe place to take even an escape artist. Like Rincon Park's dog run, Doyle's dog run closes during winter rains to keep the grass happy.

In addition to the rules mentioned in the beginning of this section, there's one that's a little tough if you're a parent of a dog and a young child: No children under 10 years old are allowed in the dog run, whether accompanied by a parent or not. The park users devised this rule, apparently meant to protect kids from getting mowed over by herds of dogs, and also to protect herds of dogs from lawsuits.

For the main entrance, take Sonoma Avenue to Doyle Park Drive and turn south, driving a few hundred feet over insufferable speed bumps to the parking area. The dog run will be way over to the left. To park closer to the dog run, take Sonoma Avenue to Hoen Avenue and turn south. The parking lot is on the right, and the dog run is on the other side of the ball field. 707/543-3292 or 707/539-5979.

16 Franklin Park

🐾🐾🦮 (See Sonoma County map on page 290)

Franklin is the smallest of the four parks that allow dogs off leash 6–8 A.M. It's green and slopey, with enough trees to make any boy dog happy. Be careful, because it's not as safe from traffic as some of the other parks (though it's not exactly Indy 500 territory around here).

The park is at Franklin Avenue and Gay Street. 707/543-3292 or 707/539-5979.

17 Galvin Community Park

🐾🐾🐾🦮 (See Sonoma County map on page 290)

Yahoo! This is yet another addition to Santa Rosa's growing legion of dog parks. The fenced dog park is where your pooch can run free here. It's about 0.75 acre. Amenities include benches for your tired tush and water for your thirsty pooch. The ground cover is mostly wood chips, and it smells so good when it's first brought in. Sometimes it can be a little hard to tell the poop from the wood chips, but you get used to it. Jake always poops in the grass, which is easy to see, but so hard to clean up. (This is more than you needed to know about Jake.)

The park is at Yulupa Avenue and Bennett Valley Road. 707/543-3292 or 707/539-5979.

18 Northwest Community Park

🐾🐾🐾🦮 (See Sonoma County map on page 290)

The fenced dog park within Northwest Park has doubled in size since its inception and is once again up and running—and so are the neighborhood dogs. (No, smarty, the dogs haven't actually doubled in size.)

The dog area is now an acre and has two sections, grass, some shade, and benches. The dog park is just northwest of Northwest Park's soccer fields. The park is on Marlow Road, behind Comstock Junior High School, north of Guerneville Road. 707/543-3292 or 707/539-5979.

19 Rincon Valley Community Park

🐾🐾🐾🐾🦮 (See Sonoma County map on page 290)

The fenced dog park here is one of the more attractive dog parks in these parts. That's mostly because it has grass. Real grass. Not just a few green sprigs fighting their way through the tough dirt, but good ol' carpety grass. That's not because the dogs here pussyfoot around. In fact, dogs are so happy to be here that they tear around with great gusto. We're not exactly sure why there's so much grass, but we do know that the dog run closes during the rainy winter months, so that could have something to do with it.

A few trees grace the dog-run area, and the views of the surrounding hills make it seem as if it's in the middle of the countryside. As of this writing, it's actually on the edge of the countryside.

The dogs who come to Rincon's dog run are a friendly lot, running to the fence and sniffing all newcomers, tails wagging exuberantly. The people who come here are much the same, except they chat rather than sniff. An interesting rule: No little kiddies under 10 allowed, even if they're with their parents. A parks department spokesman says park users made up the rule. So apparently if you've got a kid and a dog, you'll have to hire a sitter to bring your dog here. Boo!

But now here's something to cheer about: The dog park includes a little wading pond! This puts some big wag in a water dog's tail. There's also a separate section for large and small dogs. The park is on Montecito Boulevard, west of Calistoga Road. Don't forget that it's closed during rainy winter weather. 707/543-3292 or 707/539-5979.

20 Southwest Community Park

🐾🐾🐾🐕 (See Sonoma County map on page 290)

If your dog doesn't need a park in the hoity-toitiest part of town, this is a mighty convenient and friendly place to take him. First of all, it's relatively close to the freeway, so it's easy to get to if you're on the road. But better than that, it's big and green, with neatly paved paths that meander by cascading willows. It's also far enough from the road that the traffic danger is minimal. Why care about traffic? Because your dog can be off leash here 6–8 A.M., thanks to a program that's got dogs at its very heart.

From U.S. 101, take the Hearn Avenue exit and drive west for nearly a mile. The park is on the left, across from Westland Drive. 707/543-3292 or 707/539-5979.

21 Spring Lake Regional Park

🐾🐾🐾 (See Sonoma County map on page 290)

In winter, this county park doesn't offer dogs much more than a leashed trot around the lake. But in summer, it's leafy and full of the sounds of kids yelling and thumping oars. It's more fun here for people than dogs, who must be leashed. This is a good spot for a picnic, in-line skating, working out on a par-course fitness trail, a boat ride, or human swimming (no dogs allowed in the swim area). The path around the lake is paved for skaters, strollers, and bicyclists, and there are short dirt paths off into the open oak and brush woods. You can fish from the banks, where they're cleared of tules and willows.

The parking fee is $4 in winter, $5 in summer; the large lot has some shady spots. Campsites are $17, plus $1 extra for a dog. Most of the 30 sites are reservable, and a few are first-come, first-served. For reservations phone 707/565-2267. Dogs must have proof of a rabies vaccination. The campground is open daily May 1–September 30, weekends and holidays the rest of the year.

From Highway 12, on the Farmer's Lane section in Santa Rosa, turn east on Hoen Avenue. Take Hoen four stoplights to Newanga Avenue. Turn left on Newanga, which goes straight to the entrance. 707/539-8092.

22 Youth Community Park
🐾🐾🐾🐾🐕 (See Sonoma County map on page 290)

If you like oak trees, come here. Big oaks hang out all over the park. Some really big, really old oaks even have their own fences, so no one can do leg lifts or initial carving on their trunks.

The main attraction for dogs is the big green meadowy lawn area. Pooches love rolling on it and cantering over it. Your dog can be off leash here 6–8 A.M. thanks to a dog-friendly program.

A word of warning: Skateboarders abound here. A little skateboard area is in front of the park, and kids love skateboarding around the parking lot, too. Some dogs don't even notice them; others get nervous about the sound of board crashing on pavement.

The park is in the far west reaches of the city, on the west side of Fulton Road, about 0.25 mile south of Piner Road. 707/543-3292.

PLACES TO EAT

Flying Goat Coffee: Dine with your dog at the four umbrella-topped tables outside. There's usually a bowl of water out here, too. (For your dog, not your feet.) 10 4th Street; 707/575-1202.

Juice Shack: In the summer, come here with your hot pooch and cool off with a creamy smoothie or a fresh organic juice. In cooler months, you can enjoy hot juices here. Hmm… I'd rather go for the hot soup served here, or the wrap sandwiches. Dine with your dog at the outdoor area under the big pine tree. Thirsty dogs will get water on request. 1810 Mendocino Avenue; 707/528-6131.

PLACES TO STAY

Best Western Garden Inn: If you want to keep things cool and then nuke them, you'll be happy to know all rooms come with a mini-fridge and a microwave. Rates are $89–194. Dogs are $15 extra. 1500 Santa Rosa Avenue 95404; 707/546-4031.

Days Inn: Rates are $60–129. Dogs are $10 extra. 1985 Cleveland Avenue 95401; 707/545-6330 or 800/255-6330.

TraveLodge Santa Rosa: Rates at this TraveLodge are $55–139. Dogs are

$20 extra; a second pet will run you $10 more. 1815 Santa Rosa Avenue 95407; 707/542-3472.

Bodega Bay

PARKS, BEACHES, AND RECREATION AREAS

23 Doran Beach Regional Park

🐾🐾🐾 (See Sonoma County map on page 290)

This Sonoma County regional park offers leashed dogs access to marshland full of egrets, herons, and deer, as well as to the Pinnacle Gulch Trail. The plain but serviceable beach has almost no surf (which is great for dog swims), and there are picnic tables near the beach.

The fee for day use is $5 most of the year, and $6 Memorial Day–Labor Day. Campsites are $18 plus $1 for each dog. The campground, which has 134 sites, is on a first-come, first-served basis. The park is on Highway 1, one mile south of Bodega Bay. Phone 707/565-2041 for more info, or 707/565-2267 for camping reservations.

PLACES TO EAT

The Boat House: This restaurant in downtown Bodega Bay will allow you to sit with your dog as you eat fish-and-chips, oysters, and calamari at one of the six unshaded tables on its patio. If fish isn't your dog's wish, he can order a burger. 1445 Highway 1; 707/875-3495.

The Dog House: The name of the restaurant says it all. But if you need more, here are the words of one of the servers: "Dogs are treated better than people here." The Dog House is indeed a very dog-friendly place to dine. The food is unpretentious (hot dogs, burgers, etc.), and the servers love seeing a dog come to one of the eight outdoor tables. They often offer a bowl of water before the pooch even gets a chance to peruse the menu. 537 Highway 1; 707/875-2441.

Lucas Wharf: Your dog's nose will flare and drip with excitement as you dine at the outdoor tables here. That's partly because of the tasty deli specials, but it's mostly because your dog will be getting high on sea smells at this place right on the water. Speaking of water, the folks here love dogs and will provide your pooch with water, should she need to wet her whistle. 595 Highway 1; 707/875-3522.

Kenwood

PLACES TO STAY

Kenwood Oaks Guest House: This charming, comfortably appointed A-frame guesthouse is set on a two-acre horse ranch in the Sonoma Valley. Two friendly horses call the fields around the cottage home, and your dog will be so welcome she'll feel right at home, too. "I love dogs," says owner Joan Finkle, who is the proud mom of dogs Honey and Ella and who lives in a larger house across the property. "They're welcome off leash here, as long as they don't go in with the horses." (While the horses are friendly, some dogs don't know how to react when near these "giant dogs.")

The one-bedroom guesthouse is set back from the road about 300 yards, so there's ample buffer zone for fairly well voice-controlled dogs. It's fun to peruse the grounds, especially for boy dogs, who are agog at the giant valley oak by the house, and the other oaks nearby. A narrow, fenced doggy area sidles up to part of the length of the house and is accessible via a sliding glass door. It's about 20 feet long by six feet wide and has a gravelly ground cover. When the weather's right, guests sometimes use it if they want to hit the wineries or head to a restaurant and give their furry friends a break from touring.

You get free Wi-Fi here, should you need to get in touch with the non-rural world. Rates for the house are $195–275. There may be a cleaning deposit. The house is on Warm Springs Road. You'll get the address when you make your reservation. 707/833-1221; www.kenwoodoaksguesthouse.com.

Rohnert Park

PARKS, BEACHES, AND RECREATION AREAS

24 Crane Creek Regional Park

🐾🐾🐾 (See Sonoma County map on page 290)

Enjoy 128 acres of former grazing land and rolling hills with your pooch. There's some shade from oaks and their cousins, and a pleasant picnic area. Just keep your dog leashed at all times. When it was farmland, signs used to warn Dogs Caught in Livestock May Be Shot. The penalties aren't so harsh any more, fortunately.

From Rohnert Park, drive east on the Rohnert Park Expressway to Petaluma Hill Road. Turn south on Petaluma Hill Road to Roberts Road, and go east for two miles on Roberts Road. You'll find the park shortly after Roberts turns into Pressley Road. A machine is there to collect a $5 parking fee from you. 707/565-2041 or 707/823-7262.

PLACES TO STAY

Best Western Rohnert Park: This hotel is right next door to a huge veterinary center that is nationally renowned for its neurology department. If you find yourself taking your dog there, stay here. The manager, Johnny, loves dogs and brings his own pooch to work with him. According to Baron, a quesadilla-loving German shorthaired pointer who wrote to me, Johnny and the staff bent over backward making his stay as comfortable as possible when Baron was getting MRIs next door. Rates are $95–105. Dogs are $10 extra. 6500 Redwood Drive 94928; 707/584-7435.

Glen Ellen

PARKS, BEACHES, AND RECREATION AREAS

25 Jack London State Historic Park

😺😺😺 (See Sonoma County map on page 290)

The extensive backcountry trails here are off-limits to dogs, but the parts of historic interest are not. You're free to take your leashed dog the half mile to Wolf House, visiting Jack London's grave en route, and around the stone house containing the museum of Londoniana (open 10 A.M.–5 P.M., no pets inside). The trail is paved and smooth up to the museum, but then it becomes dirt and narrow.

Oaks, pines, laurels, and madrones cast dappled light, and the ups and downs are gentle. Signs warn of poison oak and rattlesnakes. The ruins of the huge stone lodge that was London's dream Wolf House are impressive and sad. A fire of unknown origin destroyed it in 1913. London planned to rebuild it, but he died three years later.

Dogs are also allowed in the picnic areas by the parking lot and the museum. From Highway 12, follow signs to the park. Turn west on Arnold Drive, then west again on London Ranch Road. The fee is $6 for day use. 707/938-5216.

26 Sonoma Valley Regional Park/ Elizabeth Anne Perrone Dog Park

😺😺😺😺🐕 (See Sonoma County map on page 290)

This large, welcoming park has a paved, level trail that winds alongside a branch of Sonoma Creek. Better yet for dogs who like to roll, it sports many dirt trails that head off into the oak woodlands above. Varied grasses, wildflowers, madrones, and moss-hung oaks make this a scenic walk. Dogs like to chew some of the grasses, roll on the wildflowers (don't let them do this!), and do leg lifts on the madrones and oaks. They may enjoy the park even more than you. If you start at the park entrance off Highway 12 and walk westward across the park to Glen Ellen for about a mile, you'll end up at Sonoma Creek and the old mill, with its huge working waterwheel.

Dogs need to be on leash for all that fun. But the big fenced dog park within the park is an exception. The Elizabeth Anne Perrone Dog Park is only about an acre, but it feels like more. It's totally landscaped, with grass and trees. "A dog lover's paradise," as reader Robin Domer and her furry children, Max and Oliver, wrote us. Pooper-scoopers, poop bags, and water are supplied.

The park is just south of Glen Ellen between Arnold Drive and Highway 12. The entrance is off Highway 12. The parking fee is $5. 707/539-8092.

PLACES TO EAT

Garden Court Cafe: This sweet café used to be right across the street from the leash-free Elizabeth Anne Perrone Dog Park, but it up and moved to downtown Glen Ellen. Fortunately it's every bit as dog-friendly as it used to be. Well-behaved dogs can join you on the patio, where they can drink from dog water bowls and even choose from a few items on a dog menu. Jake likes the Bleu Plate Special, a kind of egg scramble with burger, zucchini, and garlic. (His dog breath is rather interesting after such a meal.) If your dog hankers for something Italian, try the Babaloo pizza, which is a biscuit crust topped with ketchup, jack cheese, and fresh herbs. It's good-looking enough that you might be tempted to share it with your dog, but the human food here is tasty, too, and your dog will like you better if you order your own. If your dog doesn't feel like paying for one of these dishes, he can get a free house-made pooch biscuit. (Far from a consolation prize, judging by the blissful expression on Jake's face.) 13647 Arnold Drive; 707/935-1565.

Petaluma

Petaluma is a captivating Sunday afternoon stroll, with its tree-lined streets and pocket parks for your dog's pleasure. Victorian buildings, old feed mills, and a riverfront that remains mostly original, but not dilapidated, complete the charming picture. And let's not forget an added canine bonus: Depending on the wind direction, you can often smell fresh cow manure wafting in from the surrounding hills. Dogs thrive on this.

Best of all, dogs get to run leashless during set (if early) hours in a whopping 13 parks, and all day at their very own pooch park! No wonder they call this place PET-aluma.

PARKS, BEACHES, AND RECREATION AREAS

Dogs who live in Petaluma are lucky dogs indeed. A few years back, the enlightened Parks and Recreation Department decided that dogs needed places to run off leash and gave dogs who are under voice control the OK to be leash-free in a dozen parks during certain hours. Most of those hours have increased since then, but you should still watch your off-leash hours like a hawk—the fine for a first offense can be up to $100! Better to invest that money in a good watch.

Dogs also have their very own park, called Rocky Memorial Dog Park. It's not a real looker, but it's one of the largest dog parks in the state. Dogs are singing its praises ("Howl-elujah!").

27 Arroyo Park

🐾🐾🐾 🐕 (See Sonoma County map on page 290)

Most of Arroyo Park is very well groomed, with golf course–like green grass and a perfectly paved walking path running through its three acres. However, it seems many dogs prefer the seedier side of the park—the weedier, uncut area on the right as you face the park. We hope that area remains like this for dogs who like to walk a little on the wild side.

Dogs are allowed off leash here 6–11 A.M. weekdays and 6–8 A.M. weekends, and 8–10 P.M. every night. It's just a bone's throw from Wiseman Airport Park, though, which is a much safer place to run a dog, since you can get farther from the road. The park is at Garfield and Village East drives. 707/778-4380.

28 Bond Park

:: :: :: ⚡ (See Sonoma County map on page 290)

It's green here, so green that Joe couldn't help but run out of the car and throw himself down on the grass and start wriggling and writhing in ecstasy. I thought for sure he'd found something odorous to roll in, but underneath him was just clean, green grass. He rolled for about 10 minutes, got up, and heaved himself down in another spot, rolling and groaning and making the children in the playground giggle. The park is pleasant, with some shade from medium-sized trees. With six acres, it's a good size for dogs. And it's set in a quiet area, on Banff Way just south of Maria Drive, so traffic is minimal. Dogs are allowed off leash here 6–11 A.M. weekdays and 6–8 A.M. weekends, and 8–10 P.M. every night. 707/778-4380.

29 Del Oro Park

:: :: :: ⚡ (See Sonoma County map on page 290)

Del Oro is very suburban. It's got a nice little play area for kids. It's got green grass. It's surrounded by not-too-old suburban homes. It's got soccer goal posts. When we last visited, there were even two old Suburban sport utility vehicles parked in front.

Something not terribly suburban, a fire hydrant in one of the grassy areas, is probably the most coveted part of the park—at least for boy dogs. Well-behaved pooches can be off leash here 6–11 A.M. weekdays and 6–8 A.M. weekends, and 8–10 P.M. every night. The park is at Sartori Drive and Del Oro Circle. 707/778-4380.

30 Glenbrook Park

:: :: ⚡ (See Sonoma County map on page 290)

Who'd believe it? When we last visited, a great blue heron landed in this narrow park, which is surrounded by newish homes. This was a wonderful sight, because the land around here looks as if it's still in shock from all the development of the past decade.

The park is nearly four acres and is much longer than it is wide. It's directly across the street from Sunrise Park, but it's a little quieter and more attractive, with some medium-sized trees here and there. Its off-leash hours are generous on the hind end: 6–10 A.M. and 6–10 P.M. daily. The park is at Maria Drive and Sunrise Parkway. 707/778-4380.

31 Helen Putnam Regional Park

😊😊😊 (See Sonoma County map on page 290)

This 216-acre county regional park is, and will remain, a minimally developed stretch of converted cow pasture with oak trees. A wide paved trail shared by hikers and bicyclists runs between the main entrance and the Victoria housing development (to enter from that end, go to the end of Oxford Court). Dogs must be leashed. There's no shade from the scrub oaks, and it can get mighty windy. The paved trail has gentle ups and downs. Some other dirt trails give you steeper hill climbs. About 0.25 mile in from the main entrance is an old cattle pond good for a dog swim (if the dog stays on a leash—quite a feat).

Parking is $5. Next to the lot is a kids' playground and a picnic gazebo, set by a creek that's only a gully in summer. Drive south on Western Avenue and turn left on Chileno Valley Road. After a half mile, you'll see the turnoff to the park. 707/565-2041.

32 Lucchesi Park

😊😊😊🐕 (See Sonoma County map on page 290)

This is a well-kept, popular city park with a postmodern community center that impresses people but doesn't stir dogs much. Dogs prefer strolling through empty sports fields, picnicking at shaded tables, lounging under the weepy willows, watching ducks and the spewing fountain at the large pond, and trotting along the paved paths here. No dog swimming is allowed in the pond. It's a rule that makes it impossible to take Jake Dog near the pond, because he can't contain his excitement at the idea of being in the water. We've met other water dogs with the same affliction here.

Dogs are allowed off leash here 6–11 A.M. weekdays and 6–8 A.M. weekends, and 8–10 P.M. every night. Be sure to keep dogs away from the ducks and geese who like to lounge beside their pond, because feathers should not fly as a result of the city's kindly off-leash allowances. The park is at North McDowell Boulevard and Madison Street. 707/778-4380.

33 McNear Park

😊😊😊🐕 (See Sonoma County map on page 290)

McNear is an attractive seven-acre park, with green, green grass, plenty of shade, picnic tables, and a playground. But the part of the park dogs like best is the enclosed athletic field, where they're allowed to romp off leash 6–11 A.M. weekdays and 6–8 A.M. weekends, and 8–10 P.M. every night. The field is usually green and almost entirely fenced, but there are a couple of spots where a clever escape artist could slip out, so heads up. It's at F and 9th streets. 707/778-4380.

34 Oak Hill Park

😺😺😺😺 🐕 (See Sonoma County map on page 290)

Dogs love running up and down the gently rolling hills on this five-acre park set in the midst of beautiful old Victorian homes near downtown Petaluma. Oak Hill Park is hilly and oaky (surprise!), qualities dogs enjoy. Some good-sized oaks make their home in various parts of the park, and dogs appreciate their shade-giving arms.

Dogs are permitted to run off leash on the east side of the creek from Sunnyslope to Westridge Drive 6 A.M.–10 P.M. Monday–Friday. That's a lotta hours. But wait, that's not all! They can also visit the park off leash 6–11 A.M. and 5–10 P.M. on weekends. These are magnificent hours. The park is at Howard and Oak streets. 707/778-4380.

35 Petaluma City Hall Lawn

😺😺 🐕 (See Sonoma County map on page 290)

If you have business to conduct at city hall, your dog can conduct his own kind of business outside. (Unlike your business, your dog's will have to be scooped.)

The west lawn area permits off-leash dogs 6–8 A.M. every day, with evening hours 8–10 P.M. August–October, and 6–10 P.M. November–July. Petaluma City Hall is at 11 English Street. 707/778-4380.

36 Prince Park

😺😺😺😺 🐕 (See Sonoma County map on page 290)

Dogs are permitted off leash at this attractive 20-acre park during longer hours than they are at most other parks in the city, and they think this is just swell. On a recent visit, a springer-shepherd mix was running around drooling and panting and smiling like a dog in love. His person said when he comes here, he's ecstatic. "Willie loves the grass and the trees. I love the hours for off leash, and I love its safety from traffic," she said. (The park is set back quite far from street traffic.) Off-leash hours are rather confusing at first glance, but they're simple at second glance: 6 A.M.–3 P.M. weekdays September–May, 6–8 A.M. weekdays June–August, 6–8 A.M. weekends, and 8–10 P.M. every night. The park is across East Washington Street from the airport, just a little north of the airport sign. 707/778-4380.

37 Rocky Memorial Dog Park

😺😺😺 🐕 (See Sonoma County map on page 290)

The scenery isn't great, and the land has nary a tree on it, but it's one of the biggest dog parks we've ever encountered. And size does matter, at least when it comes to fenced dog parks.

This flat nine-acre piece of land is the best thing that's happened to Petaluma's dogs since the park system began allowing them off leash at certain parks during limited hours a few years back. Dogs enjoy the smell that can pervade the land; it's beside a marshy area next to the Petaluma River. Fortunately, it's well fenced so dogs can't chase the marsh birds or roll in the marsh muck. The fencing keeps the dogs from escaping to all areas but the parking lot, which leads to the park entrance, which eventually leads a busy road. So if you have a pooch who's prone to running away, be aware the place is safe, but it isn't foolproof.

Because it's so barren here, it can really roast on hot days. Be sure to bring water. A sign at the entrance says No Dogs in Heat, and I thought it was nice of them to be so concerned about the temperature for dog walking. It took me a few seconds and an eye roll from my husband to realize the sign's true intent.

On our first visit, Joe searched in vain for something to lift a leg on. He found only some garbage cans and a few big weeds, and they were right next to the parking lot. The next visit he just succumbed to the lack of leg-lift targets and took to relieving his bladder like a girl dog. But not, of course, until looking around to make sure no one was watching.

Rocky Park was named after a big-hearted police dog who died at the too-young age of 10 during a narcotics search. It was kidney failure that got him, not the wrong end of a dealer's pistol. Rocky had helped seize a few million dollars of narcotics in his career, but his greatest act came in 1992 when he saved the life of his beloved handler one night. A felon had escaped and the officer chased him to a creek, where the felon got the upper hand and was holding the officer's head underwater. The officer managed to hit a remote control button that opened the windows of the patrol car and released Rocky, who'd seen his friend in trouble. Rocky bolted to the creek and got the upper paw. He saved his friend and helped bag the bad guy. "It was the beginning of the era of Rocky," said Officer Jeff Hasty, a dog handler with the Petaluma Police Department. A bust of Rocky now graces the front lobby of the police department.

This is an easy park to visit if you're on U.S. 101 and your pooch is hankering to stretch his gams. Take the Highway 116 east (*not* west)/Lakeville exit and follow the street just over a half mile to Casa Grande Road, where you'll take a sharp right. Drive a few hundred feet past ugly storage bins and trucks and you'll soon hit the entrance to the park. Unlike most of the other city parks with off-leash times, this one has great hours: 6 A.M.–10 P.M. 707/778-4380.

38 Sunrise Park

😺 🐕 (See Sonoma County map on page 290)

If you're a real estate developer, there's a chance you might enjoy this park. It's very, very narrow, squeezed like an old tube of toothpaste by cookie-cutter

condos and townhouses. It's too close to traffic. It's not terribly attractive. But in its defense, it does have decent grassy areas and fun (for dogs) weedy patches. Another plus: Dogs can be off leash 6–10 A.M. and 6–10 P.M. daily. Those are some pretty long hours for a pretty slim park. It's at Marina Drive and Sunrise Parkway. 707/778-4380.

39 Westridge Open Space

🐾🐾🐾 🐕 (See Sonoma County map on page 290)

Dogs get to peruse the east side of this three-acre park off leash 6–10 A.M. and 6–10 P.M. daily. The park is long and narrow, with plenty of medium-sized trees, which turn a warm red in autumn. When we visited, a fluffy black cat teased Joe from the middle of the road. Another kitty was there when we recently sniffed out the park with Jake. Cat-chasers, exercise caution when off leash. The park is on Westridge Drive, near its intersection with Westridge Place. 707/778-4380.

40 Wiseman Airport Park

🐾🐾🐾🐾 🐕 (See Sonoma County map on page 290)

Plenty of pooches visit this park, and for good reason. Wiseman is 32 acres of well-kept playing fields, uncut grass, many shade trees, and comfortably wide walking paths. It's also a good place to watch little planes land and take off, because of its proximity to the airport. (They don't call it Airport Park for nothing.) Best of all, dogs can run off leash in the athletic fields during these hours: 6–11 A.M. weekdays and 6–8 A.M. weekends, and 8–10 P.M. every night. The best access is at St. Augustine Circle. 707/778-4380.

PLACES TO EAT

Apple Box: A store of antiques and housewares, this charmer also serves good desserts, teas, and coffee. There are 20 tables outside, right by the river. It's real olfactory bliss for your dog. 224 B Street; 707/762-5222.

Aram's Cafe: Dine on really good Mediterranean and Armenian food at the five outdoor tables. Aram's is in downtown Petaluma. 131 Kentucky Street; 707/765-9775.

PLACES TO STAY

Motel 6: Rates are $46–70 for the first adult, $3 for the second. 1368 North McDowell Boulevard 94954; 707/765-0333.

San Francisco North KOA: This is Jake's kind of camping. Upon arrival at this family camping resort, dogs get a little treat attached to a card that lists the doggy rules. The 60-acre campground is more attractive than most KOAs we've visited. The setting is rural, and there are trees everywhere. Like other KOAs, the campsites are drive-up and pretty doggone close to each other, but it's still a fun place to pitch a tent, especially if you like hot showers and cool pools as part of your camping experience. Better yet, try one of the cute log "Kamping Kabins." They're cozy, with a bunk bed and a queen-size bed. (You provide the bedding.)

Adding to its rural charm, this KOA even has a pen that houses several goats. Visit in the spring to see some adorable furry kids. At press time, an off-leash area was being planned, complete with an agility section. Jake can't wait to inspect it for the next edition. Until then, the managers here ask that you walk your dog on leash, either on camping roads or the designated field (which has poop bags!). The rule here, as it is at many KOAs, is no pit bulls. Rates are $29–45 for tent camping. Kamping Kabins are $56–85. 20 Rainsville Road 94952; 707/763-1492 or 800/992-2267; www.sanfranciscokoa.com.

Sheraton Sonoma County: Dogs are welcome to stay at this attractive hotel, as long as they weigh no more than 80 pounds. They're so welcome, in fact, that they'll get use of a big dog bed and doggy bowls. "We like to make their stay nice, too," says a hotelier. One of the more attractive features of this Sheraton is its location: It's close to Rocky Memorial Dog Park. Dogs who need a good run really appreciate the proximity. The hotel has a heated outdoor pool and a hot tub for the humans in your crew. Dogs must stay in first-floor rooms, and they mustn't smoke. (The entire hotel is nonsmoking.) Rates are $139–269. 745 Baywood Drive 94954; 707/283-2888.

Sonoma

Downtown Sonoma is a treat for people, and until the last few years, dogs had been banned from all the good spots—most city parks, Sonoma plaza, and the state historic park. But there's finally something to wag about: a new park just two blocks from the plaza. You can also find some great lodging not too far away.

PARKS, BEACHES, AND RECREATION AREAS

41 Ernest Holman Dog Park

🐾🐾🐾🐕 (See Sonoma County map on page 290)

Ernest was a good dog. So good that his person, Sue Holman, donated enough money for a dog park in his name. (Most of my human friends don't even have such formal-sounding names.) Opened in 1999, Ernest Holman Dog Park is a welcome addition to downtown Sonoma. It's small—a little under an acre—and the turf can be mushy in the wet season, but it's incredibly popular. Happy dogs of every ilk tear around this fenced area. When they need to catch their doggy breaths, they repose in the shade of the park's enormous redwood trees. People enjoy sitting on benches and chatting with other dog folks while watching their panting pooches. (There's water for when they—the dogs, not the people—need to wet their whistles.)

The park is two blocks north of the plaza, on First Street West, next to the police station. It's part of the Field of Dreams sporting field complex. 707/938-3681.

PLACES TO EAT

Harmony Lounge: For the best people- and pooch-watching in Sonoma, and some lovely food and drinks to boot, this is *the* place to be. The lounge is set in the gorgeous Ledson Hotel, right on the Sonoma plaza. It's the crown jewel of the plaza, with its ornate architecture and upscale old charm. The lounge's outdoor patio/sidewalk tables are right in front of the hotel, where you can watch the wine-country world float by.

Dogs don't have to be of the little frou-frou genre to eat here. "We've had a couple of Great Danes," says a manager. "There's plenty of room."

The food menu is short, the cuisine is upmarket and light, and the desserts have a decadent flair. Jake recommends the beef tenderloin carpaccio. For a real treat, try the black magic cake with a Sonoma port. Since dogs can't stay at the hotel, you may as well splurge at the lounge. 480 First Street East; 707/996-9779.

Sunflower Café: This is a peaceful haven for dogs and their people. The magnificent garden patio has a fountain that fascinates some dogs and makes others look as if they need to head to the nearest tree fast. Actually, a big, 160-year-old fig tree is in the middle of the patio area, but leg lifts are definitely not permitted.

The café is housed in the historic Captain Salvador Vallejo Adobe, which was built in the late 1830s. He would have loved the coffee here; many say it's the best in Sonoma. And the cuisine is of the delectable high-end-deli genre.

Bird dogs appreciate the idea of the smoked duck sandwich, but what sets Jake to drooling is the Sonoma Cheese Plate. The Sunflower is on the Sonoma Plaza, at 415-421 First Street West; 707/996-6645.

PLACES TO STAY

Best Western Sonoma Valley Inn: If you want to stay close to the town plaza, this hotel is just a little more than a block away. Rates are $149–329. Dogs are $25 extra. 550 Second Street West 95476; 707/938-9200 or 800/334-5784; www.sonomavalleyinn.com.

Casita Carneros: Here's a fabulous first: Dogs are allowed in the private pool here! The pool is huge—about 20 feet by 40 feet—and if your dog is a swimmer, he'll have the time of his life splashing around after a day in wine country. (If he's not a swimmer, the pool can be entirely covered so there's no danger of him becoming a soggy doggy—or worse.) How can a pool be so dog friendly? It's thanks to a heavy-duty sand filter that rids the pool of pet hair. Casita's owner, Cindy, loves dogs and wants them to be able to do the dog paddle in the pool. (For obvious reasons, dogs should stay out of the Jacuzzi.)

The guest cottage is an attractive, air-conditioned, one-bed affair with a fridge and microwave and other amenities of home. Cindy will happily provide your dog with creature comforts, like a doggy bed, should you need any extras. Your stay comes with a continental breakfast that comes right to your door, and you'll also get a bottle of Sonoma wine. The property is fenced and on a quiet rural road, on an acre that also has goats and ducks. It's all you need for a vacation in pooch paradise.

We thank Dog Friday and his person, Lori, for pointing us in the direction of the Casita Carneros. Rates are $225, and there's a two-night minimum. Dogs are $25 extra. 21235 Hyde Road 95476; 707/996-0996; www.casitacarneros.com.

The Lodge at Sonoma: This exceptional wine country resort is ripe with gorgeous rooms, top-notch furnishings, and super comfy beds with "clouds of pillows." Many rooms feature a fireplace, balcony, or patio, and all come with plush robes, bath salts, and a fridge. The Lodge also offers signature spa treatments to guests. Private cottages make up the majority of the lodgings here, and they're ideal for a doggy visit because they're large and many open onto a grassy or garden area. They're also on the pricey side, so a lodge room or suite is what dogs on more of a budget opt for.

The lodge, whose surname is "A Renaissance Resort & Spa," is actually in the Marriott bloodline, albeit top-of-the-line Marriott. You don't really say the "M" word around here. On the grounds is a popular tasting room, and a coffee and wine bar, but dogs aren't allowed inside. The humans in your party will also have access to the lodge's pool and decent fitness room.

Rates are $209–719. (The higher room rate is for a cottage in peak season.) There's a two-dog limit, and as with most Marriotts, dogs pay a $75 fee for the length of their stay. 1325 Broadway at Leveroni and Napa Roads 95476; 707/935-6600 or 888/710-8008; www.thelodgeatsonoma.com.

Stay Sonoma: Long to stay in a beautiful, spacious cottage on a small vineyard? The Bolen Vineyard Cottage could be just what you're looking for. It's set on three acres of Carneros vines and is a rural escape just five minutes from Sonoma's town plaza. Or maybe you'd prefer a larger house with an upscale Italian ambience, a gorgeous kitchen, and hardwood floors so perfect you could skate on them. Then you might want to sniff out Casa Luna, also just five minutes from the plaza. If you really want to stay close to the Sonoma plaza, two decent apartment units known as Furnished on First could do the trick; they're just five minutes away.

Stay Sonoma is a lodging service that helps put people in a variety of comfy lodgings for as little time as a two-night minimum stay. It's not really what you'd call a vacation rental service. The lodgings mentioned above are just a few of the dog-friendly abodes they represent. Since the downtown Sonoma area isn't exactly brimming with traditional dog-friendly hotels and inns, we're listing Stay Sonoma under the town of Sonoma, but the service also books for lodgings throughout the county and a little beyond the borders. Nightly rates for the lodgings above: Bolen, $225; Casa Luna, $525; Furnished on First, $205–$220. 866/647-8888; www.staysonoma.com.

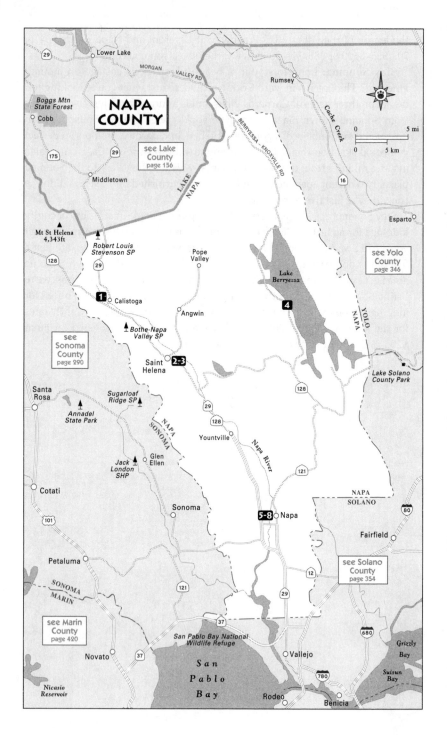

NAPA COUNTY

Lower Lake
MORGAN VALLEY RD
Rumsey
Cache Creek

Boggs Mtn State Forest
Cobb

see Lake County page 156

16

Middletown

LAKE NAPA

Esparto

Mt St Helena 4,343ft
Robert Louis Stevenson SP

128
29

Pope Valley

see Yolo County page 346

Lake Berryessa

BERRYESSA - KNOXVILLE RD

YOLO NAPA

1 Calistoga

Angwin

4

see Sonoma County page 290

Bothe-Napa Valley SP

Saint Helena
2-3

Lake Solano County Park

128

Santa Rosa
Annadel State Park

Sugarloaf Ridge SP

NAPA SONOMA

29
128

Yountville

Napa River

Jack London SHP
Glen Ellen

121

NAPA SOLANO

Cotati

Sonoma
5-8 Napa

80

101

Fairfield

Petaluma

see Solano County page 354

121

12

SONOMA MARIN

29

see Marin County page 420

Novato

37

680

San Pablo Bay National Wildlife Refuge

Grizzly Bay

37

Vallejo

Suisun Bay

Nicasio Reservoir

San Pablo Bay

780

Rodeo
Benicia

0   5 mi
0   5 km

CHAPTER 28

Napa County

Napa dogs don't whine. They wine. And since there are plenty of dog-friendly restaurants here (and some truly fabulous ones these days), they often wine and dine.

This is the home of the most famous wine-making valley in the United States, and dogs get to experience some of the fringe benefits of this productive area. Several attractive wineries invite well-behaved dogs to relax and sniff around with their owners; find details in the Diversion *Grape Expectations*. Just don't let your dog do leg lifts on inappropriate items, because Bacchus will get you. And your little dog, too.

More top-notch Napa Valley inns than ever before are opening their doors to dogs, but the county's parks still come up a little on the dry side (a unique state of affairs, with all this wine around). With the county's tremendous amount of lush, fertile, and inviting vineyards, you'd think there would also be plenty of parks for dogs to roam. But this isn't the case.

Only about a dozen public parks and a few miscellaneous sites in Napa

PICK OF THE LITTER—NAPA COUNTY

BEST DOG PARK
Alston Park/Canine Commons, Napa (page 339)

BEST RESTAURANTS FOR FOODIES
Cindy's Backstreet Kitchen, St. Helena (page 333)
Ristorante Tra Vigne, St. Helena (page 334)
Bouchon, Yountville (page 337)
Celadon, Napa (page 340)

MOST DOG-FRIENDLY PLACE TO EAT
Angele Restaurant, Napa (page 340)

MOST DOG-FRIENDLY PLACES TO STAY
Washington Street Lodging, Calistoga (page 331)
The Inn on First, Napa (page 343)
Napa River Inn, Napa (page 344)
Napa Valley Country Cottage, Napa (page 345)

MOST AWARD-WINNING B&B
Beazley House, Napa (page 342)

MOST UPSCALE "RANCH" ACCOMMODATIONS
Calistoga Ranch, Calistoga (page 331)

MOST DOWN-TO-EARTH
REAL RANCH ACCOMMODATIONS
RustRidge Bed & Breakfast Cottage, St. Helena (page 334)

BEST FUNKY ATTRACTIONS
Old Faithful Geyser, Calistoga (page 330)
Petrified Forest, Calistoga (page 332)

BEST PLACE TO TRY SOME BUBBLY
Mumm Napa Valley, Rutherford (page 335)

County allow dogs. The city of Napa has four parks where dogs are allowed, and all four permit them off leash in certain sections. You may incur the grapes of your dog's wrath if you don't take her to visit one of these leash-free lands next time you're in town.

Calistoga

PARKS, BEACHES, AND RECREATION AREAS

🖫 Pioneer Park

🐾🐾 (See Napa County map on page 326)

This is a small park, but its location, so close to the heart of Calistoga, makes it a great place to stop for a relaxing picnic with your leashed pooch. The two-acre park has plenty of shade trees and enough open area so your canine won't feel claustrophobic.

Going north on Foothill Boulevard, turn right on Lincoln Avenue. In two blocks, turn left on Cedar Street. The park will be on your right within a block. 707/942-2800.

PLACES TO STAY

Hillcrest II Bed and Breakfast: On the outside it's a good-looking, contemporary house. But on the inside, it's filled with antiques and other family heirlooms of the locally famed Tubbs family. Debbie O'Gorman, owner of Hillcrest II, is the last of the Tubbs family to live in the Napa area, and she's tastefully stocked the house with items from the family mansion, which burned down in 1964.

All this is well and good with dog guests, but what they *really* adore is that the house is set on 40 acres where they're allowed to romp on terrific trails without a leash if their humans are well behaved. This is a dog's dream come true, because there just aren't leash-free stomping grounds like these in Napa County, unless you own big property. It's at the base of Mt. St. Helena, and the house is on a hilltop (thus the name), so the views are breathtaking.

Humans enjoy using the gorgeous 40-foot-long pool. Dogs enjoy dipping their paws in the fishing pond. Humans can also use the kitchen and barbecue areas, which is convenient if you don't want to go out to eat every day. A delectable continental breakfast is served on weekends.

Debbie, who has two friendly dogs of her own, asks that you bring a bed for your dog, if he sleeps on the floor, or a blanket to place under him if he sleeps on human furniture. She even allows dogs to be left alone in the rooms if they promise to be good dogs. In addition—and better yet for many dogs—Debbie can sometimes pet-sit while you go out. "Whatever makes your dog happy," she says. Rates are $69–175. Dogs are $10 extra. 3225 Lake County Highway 94515; 707/942-6334; www.bnbweb.com/hillcrest.

DIVERSION

See Old Faithful in Your Own Backyard: You know you're in for a treat when a big sign greets you at the entry to **Old Faithful Geyser:** "Many Notable People Have Come to SEE HEAR AND LEARN the mysteries of this WONDER OF NATURE which captures the imagination. IT'S AMAZING."

And indeed, when dogs see the 350°F plume of water gushing 50 to 70 feet into the air, they generally stare for a few seconds with their mouths agape. But the sight of tourists jumping in front of the geyser for a quick photo before the eruption subsides quickly bores them. Dogs then try to wander to the snack bar and persuade the person on the other end of the leash to buy a couple of hot dogs. But even more fascinating is the scent of goat and pig in nearby pens.

If your dog is the brave sort, don't hesitate to bring him to visit Clow, the fainting goat. Clow butts her head against her fence at first, but she's only playing. After a few minutes, she was calming Joe's fears by licking him on the nose. Soon he was in love. Valentino, the Vietnamese potbellied pig who scared the heck out of Joe, is no longer here. (I hope he didn't go the way of so many of his oversized brethren.)

Old Faithful erupts every 40 minutes, and the eruptions last about two to three minutes. Picnic tables are plentiful, so bring a snack or buy one here between eruptions. A sign at the site warns that dogs aren't allowed in the geyser viewing area, but you can bring your dog—securely leashed—within a safe distance of the geyser and not get scolded or scalded.

The geyser and goats are between Highways 128 and 29 on Tubbs Lane in Calistoga and are open 9 A.M.–6 P.M. in summer, 9 A.M.–5 P.M. in winter. Admission is $8 for adults. 707/942-6463.

Meadowlark Country House: The simple elegance of this secluded 20-acre estate makes guests feel right at home. The house where dogs with people get to stay has a light and airy feel and attractive decor, but it's really the surrounding property that makes this place so special. Beware, though. Cats and guinea hens also make their home around the house, so if your dog is a chaser, hang on to that leash.

You and your pooch can hike on the estate's trails, past pastured horses, ancient oaks, and fields replete with wildflowers (and meadowlarks, thus the name). It's quiet here—a perfect place for a hilltop picnic with the pooch. If your dog can be trusted off leash, he can hike naked. It's "leashes optional" here, and that's a perfect match for the pool. If it's warm, the humans in your party can cool their heels (and knees and shoulders) in the beautiful swimming pool, which is surrounded by a cobblestone walk. The pool is clothing-optional, so if your dog blushes when he sees tushies, best wear your clothes. If all this isn't enough to fill your day, take a quick drive down the road and spend some time at the Petrified Forest.

Rates are $195–285. A delicious, large breakfast is included in the price, and your dog is welcome to join you (although you'll have to supply his chow). For those who need more paw room, guesthouses are available for $395–425. 601 Petrified Forest Road 94515; 707/942-5651 or 800/942-5651; www.meadow larkinn.com.

Pink Mansion: This enchanting old place is an 1875 Victorian—very picturesque and very pink. It's a frequent recipient of numerous awards for its charm and beauty.

Dogs are allowed in only one room—the Wine Suite (not the Whine Sweet, as some dogs may do to stay here)—so book ahead lest another dog beats you to the phone. It has a fireplace, a private entrance that leads to the garden, and a private sitting room with an extra bed upstairs. Dogs must be of the non-barking, clean, well-behaved variety, and they need to keep off the furniture and the beds.

Bird dogs enjoy the resident doves and parrots. Water dogs like watching their people splash around in the comfy heated indoor pool and adjacent hot tub, but they mustn't set paw in the water. Rates are $219. Pooches are $30 extra. 1415 Foothill Boulevard (Highway 128) 94515; 707/942-0558 or 800/238-7465; www.pinkmansion.com.

Washington Street Lodging: Relax in any of several cabins, each with its own little kitchen. You're just a couple of blocks from Calistoga's main drag here. Joan, the animal-loving owner, has a cat, but she says if the kitty doesn't like your pooch, or vice versa, she'll make herself scarce. Joan also has a happy basset hound who will probably become your fast friend when you visit. Cabins are $105–140, and dogs are charged a $15 fee per visit. 1605 Washington Street 94515; 707/942-6968 or 877/214-3869; www.washingtonstreetlodging.com.

Calistoga Ranch: When I think of a ranch, I think of horses and dirt and rustic lodgings and good hearty grub. Cowboys, too. Well, that was before I was married. But the Calistoga Ranch, an Auberge Resort, has none of the above. I can only guess that the ranch moniker must come from the 140 acres of secluded canyon land you can enjoy hiking on with your dog. Because it sure doesn't refer to the 46 gorgeous, freestanding, cedar-sided "guest lodges" that make up the place. Nor to the winemaking seminars, spa treatments, beautiful pool, state-of-the-art fitness center, yoga deck, or fine restaurant with artisan foie gras.

The name also couldn't have anything to do with how your "little dawgie" is treated. There's none of that sitting-around-the-campfire-waiting-for-some-vittles-to-drop-off-a-plate nonsense around here! No sir! Dog guests at *this* ranch get a room-service menu and organic dog treats. They also get a nutmeg-brown down-topped velvet dog bed custom-fitted with fine Italian linens

DIVERSION

Sniff Out a Petrified Forest: You and your leashed dog can roam among trees entombed by a volcanic explosion 3.4 million years ago. During a summertime visit, Joe found out why they call it the **Petrified Forest.** The sign announced in big bold letters, Once Towering Redwoods—Now the Rock of Ages. But Joe didn't know the true meaning of petrified until we encountered… the elves.

The Elves of Ages, that is. The ceramic kind you find on suburban lawns. They appeared everywhere Joe looked and at eye level for an Airedale. Every time he saw a new one, he backed away with his tail between his legs, checking periodically to make sure it wasn't following him.

Then came the petrifying elf. It didn't look any different from the others. But as soon as Joe laid eyes on it and its donkey companion, his tail went down. For about two minutes, he was too frightened to look at the elf, growling instead at a tree. Then, suddenly he decided enough was enough and bolted—leash and all. He was waiting by the wishing well when I finally caught up to him. He would have left the park if he could have negotiated the turnstile by himself. I couldn't help wondering how Airedales have remained so popular for frontline duty during wars.

The Petrified Forest is at 4100 Petrified Forest Road, off Highway 128. It's actually in the outskirts of Sonoma County, but its address is in Calistoga. The unpaved trail is a quarter-mile loop. Admission is $6 for adults. Dozens of tables are around the gift shop, so pack a picnic. The forest is open 9 A.M.–7 P.M. in summer, 9 A.M.–6 P.M. in winter. 707/942-6667.

by Rivolta Carmignani, a company known for its soft and luxurious sheets. (If you really like the bed, you can go online and buy one for $225–295, without the linens.) A housekeeper changes the dog sheets daily. (Please tip her well.) Hmm, nope, the ranch name definitely doesn't have anything to do with a dog's life here.

Maybe it's the fires. Your private lodge comes with a fireplace inside and outside. That's vaguely ranchy, in an upscale sort of way. We're getting warmer. And it's flanked by big trees. OK, that's also kind of ranchy. Warmer! Your lodge also comes with a mini-bar, down duvet, beautiful garden shower, and high-speed Internet access. Cold! Cold!

Is this the kind of place most dogs reading this book can afford? I wouldn't bet the ranch on it. The most basic accommodation is $550–845. (Per night.) You can get a super deluxe two-bedroom lodge for $3,850. Dogs pay $125 extra per stay. 580 Lommel Road 94515; 707/254-2888 or 800/942-4220; www.calistogaranch.com.

St. Helena

PARKS, BEACHES, AND RECREATION AREAS

② Lyman Park

🐾🐾 (See Napa County map on page 326)

You'll think you're on a movie set for some old-time village scene when you and your dog wander into this small, cozy park on historic Main Street. Leashes are mandatory, but the park has a gazebo, lots of trees and benches, and a lovely flower garden.

The park is nestled snugly between the police station and a funeral home, at 1400 Main Street, and is open dawn–dusk. 707/963-5706.

③ Baldwin Park

🐾🐾 (See Napa County map on page 326)

Baldwin Park has everything you could want in a park, except size. But what it lacks in acreage, it makes up for in dog appeal. Set off a small road, it's almost entirely fenced and full of flowering trees, oaks, and big pines. A dirt path winds through green grass from one end of the park to the other, passing by a water fountain and a conveniently placed garbage can.

Unfortunately, dogs must be leashed, but it's still a pleasant place to stretch all your legs after a tour through the wine country. The park is on Spring Street between Stockton Street and North Crane Avenue and is open dawn–dusk. 707/963-5706.

PLACES TO EAT

Cindy's Backstreet Kitchen: Chef, cookbook author, and restaurant entrepreneur Cindy Pawlcyn has another hit on her hands. The owner of the famed Mustard Grill and co-creator of several Bay Area restaurants has created a warm, fun, casual-but-upscale place to gather with friends and eat healthful, delicious, sometimes exotic versions of home-cooked food. As Cindy says on the brochure, this is "a local joint—hip, casual, not fussy. The food we serve is from our hearts, what we make at home and most like to cook."

We like to start with crispy Backstreet flatbread with local cheeses, roasted garlic, caramelized onions, and sun-dried tomatoes. Jake eyed a neighboring table's Mighty Meatloaf and spice-rubbed quails, but darned if they didn't drop a single bite. Your dog can dine with you on the brick patio under a 100-year old fig tree that offers gentle shade. 1327 Railroad Avenue; 707/963-1207.

Pizzeria Tra Vigne: The little sister of the more expensive and upscale Tra Vigne Ristorante, this pizzeria is just what the vet ordered if you have a pooch and a pedigreed palate but a more paltry pocketbook. Lots of families come here. The pastas, pizzas, and salads are delicious. Munch with your dog at the

DIVERSION

Grape Expectations: Dogs are welcome at so many wineries in Napa Valley these days that you may start wishing your dog could be your designated driver. (Don't try it: Dogs just don't have the opposable thumbs to operate those pesky steering wheels.)

Many of the wineries listed below allow dogs in their tasting rooms, but since health department officials aren't sure what to think about this, we're not going to point them out specifically. Most welcome dogs at their picnic areas. Some even allow pooches on vineyard tours. Phone the individual wineries for hours, prices, and dog-friendly specifics.

Here's a taste of some of Napa's most dog-friendly wineries, listed by area:

CALISTOGA

Cuvaison, 4550 Silverado Trail North; 707/942-6266; www.cuvaison.com.

Dutch Henry Winery, 4310 Silverado Trail North; 707/942-5771; www.dutchhenry.com. Winery Airedale Buggsy greets dog guests. Check out the website for a page dedicated to the winery pets.

Graeser Winery, 255 Petrified Forest Road; 707/942-4437; www.graeserwinery.com. Graeser has a line of dog-labeled wines named after various winery dogs. You may meet Graeser's pups during your visit.

---

four tables on the patio. Got a thirsty dog? The staff will provide her a bowl of water. 1016 Main Street; 707/967-9999.

Ristorante Tra Vigne: This is one of the most attractive restaurants with some of the best food in the Bay Area. The wood-burning oven gives even the most simple pasta, pizza, and meat dishes a taste that's out of this world. Your dog can dine with you at the 20 tables in the large, gardenlike lower courtyard. (The terrace is out because you have to go through the restaurant to get there, and that's a no-no.) The two of you are sure to drool over the gourmet cuisine. Thirsty dogs get a bowl of water. 1050 Charter Oak Avenue (you'll see the restaurant from Main Street, though); 707/963-4444.

PLACES TO STAY

El Bonita Motel: This little motel provides decent lodging at fairly reasonable prices for this area. Rates are $89–269. Dogs are $15 extra. 195 Main Street 94574; 707/963-3216 or 800/541-3284; www.elbonita.com.

RustRidge Bed & Breakfast: If you like wine, horses, or dogs, you need

RUTHERFORD

Mumm Napa Valley, 8445 Silverado Trail North; 707/967-7700; www.mummnapa.com. Dogs get royal treatment, with dog treats and water. Mumm Napa Valley even has its own line of logo doggy products.

Sullivan Vineyards, 1090 Galleron Road; 707/963-9646; www.sullivanwine.com. Open by appointment only.

ST. HELENA

Casa Nuestra, 3451 Silverado Trail North; 707/963-5783; www.casanuestra.com. A most mellow winery where dogs can stare at the resident goats who have a nonvintage table wine named after them. Dogs get tasty biscuits, too.

Markham Vineyards, 2812 St. Helena Highway North; 707/963-5292; www.markhamvineyards.com.

RustRidge Winery, 2910 Lower Chiles Valley Road; 707/965-2871; www.rustridge.com. Open by appointment only. Three big, friendly resident dogs welcome you and yours.

V. Sattui Winery, 1111 White Lane; 707/963-7774; www.vsattui.com.

YOUNTVILLE

Domaine Chandon, 1 California Drive; 707/944-2280; www.chandon.com.

---

to book a stay at this gracious ranch-style lodging. It's part of the 450-acre RustRidge Ranch & Winery, home of top-notch wine grapes, a great winery, and some mighty nice dogs and thoroughbred horses.

When you get to the ranch, you'll be greeted by dogs Tosca, Charlie, and Holly. "Our three dogs are always so happy to see other dogs," says proprietor Susan Meyer. If you plan to be a guest here, your dog should be a good socializer, because this trio sure is social. Their cat can be curious too, so no cat-killers allowed. Their horses also tend to be very friendly. In fact, Susan says they like to play with her dogs. But you need to keep yours out of their area because their tonnage to your dog's poundage just isn't a fair—or safe—match. (She worries when her dogs get in with them, but so far, so good.)

You and your dogs won't be staying at the main B&B: You'll have your very own, very cool one-bedroom cottage. It's hexagonal, with cathedral ceilings, windows overlooking the vineyards, a full kitchen, wood-burning stove, and a country-contemporary decor. The house is tucked in the trees and is very private. You even have your own Jacuzzi outside.

During your stay you're welcome to hike the land. It's big and beautiful and hilly and ripe with vineyards. You can also play tennis on the property, but most dogs can only be on the receiving end of the game, and that gets old.

Even though your cottage comes with a kitchen, your stay still includes the B&B benefit of a hearty farm-style breakfast of eggs, breads, coffee, and other goodies. In the evening, gather in the B&B's country kitchen to sample RustRidge's wines and enjoy some hors d'oeuvres. The cottage rate is $250. Dogs are $25 extra. 2910 Lower Chiles Valley Road 94574; 707/965-9353 or 800/788-0263; www.rustridge.com.

Lake Berryessa

PARKS, BEACHES, AND RECREATION AREAS

4 Lake Berryessa

🐾🐾 (See Napa County map on page 326)

Lake Berryessa, one of the largest man-made lakes in Northern California, offers 165 miles of shoreline for human and canine enjoyment. Most of the resort areas on the lake allow leashed dogs. Better yet, they allow them off leash to swim. The summer heat is stifling here, so your dog will want to take advantage of the water.

Most resorts rent fishing boats and allow dogs to go along on your angling adventure. The fishing is fantastic, especially for trout in the fall and black bass in the spring. It's cooler then, too, so you won't have to contend with so many folks riding personal watercraft, and your dog won't roast.

If you just want to hike and swim for an afternoon, explore the Smittle Creek Trail. The entrance is just north of the lake's visitors center, on Knoxville Road. The trail takes you up and down the fingers of the lake. In certain times of year, and more arid years, the lake can get so low that the trail is a dusty mile from the water. Grab a trail map or get advice from a concessionaire about best hikes for swimming dogs.

Dogs must be leashed, except when swimming. Plans have been in the works for years to create a 150-mile shoreline trail, which would provide much more romping room for dogs—even some off-leash areas. (See www .berryessatrails.org for more. A link will take you to a page called The Dog Owner's Vision for Lake Berryessa.)

To get to Lake Berryessa from the Rutherford area, take Highway 128 and turn left at the Lake Berryessa/Spanish Flat sign. It's a very curvy route, so take it easy if you or your dog tends toward car sickness. For more information about the lake, call the Bureau of Reclamation Visitor Information Center at 707/966-2111. For questions about lakeside businesses, call the Lake Berryessa Chamber of Commerce at 800/726-1256.

PLACES TO STAY

Here are a couple of places to pitch a tent, park an RV, or stay in a yurt (Spanish Flat only) on Lake Berryessa.

Rancho Monticello Resort: The "just basics" cabins here are just right for a Berryessa canine vacation. The 140-acre property also sports several dog-friendly vacation rentals. Rates for cabins and rentals are $75–350 (the expensive one sleeps 18). If camping is more your dog's style (or your budget's), you and your dog can pitch a tent or stay in your RV. There are 56 tent sites and 20 RV sites. Rates are $25–43. Dogs are $4. Day-use fee is $15. 707/966-2188. www.ranchomonticelloresort.com.

Spanish Flat Resort: Dogs really enjoy staying in the rustic log cabins by the lake. Rates are $100–130. There are also a couple of yurts you can stay in with your dog, and that's only $50. Camping is a crowded affair (pray your neighbors don't snore or party all night—or both) and will cost you $25–35. Dogs are $3 extra and love sniffing around the waterfront and walking on the meandering roads on leash. The very cool yurts are $45 nightly. Day-use fee is $12. 707/966-7700; www.spanishflatresort.com.

Rutherford

PLACES TO EAT

Rutherford Grill: The outdoor area is *the* place to eat at this wonderful restaurant (and of course, the only place to eat with a dog). It features a wood-burning fireplace, a fountain, and several attractive umbrella-topped tables. Try the "Knife and Fork Baby Back Barbecue Ribs," one of the most requested entrées. (Fear not: If you're not of the carnivorous persuasion, the restaurant offers several tasty dishes without meat.) 1180 Rutherford Road; 707/963-1792.

Yountville

Yountville town government bans dogs from its parks. Jake thinks dogs need to band together and do something about this.

PLACES TO EAT

Restaurants can get mighty crowded around here when tour buses offload, so if you see a bus coming, make sure your pooch is close at hand.

Bouchon: It's only natural that Bouchon would permit pups, because it's a French bistro, and a fabulous one at that. Bouchon, co-owned by renowned chef Thomas Keller (of French Laundry fame), serves absolutely delectable cuisine. If you've never ordered cheese with honeycomb, this is the place to try it. Jake suggests then moving onto a nice big plate of *gigot d'agneau* (roasted leg of lamb, served with a cocoa bean–based ragout), or maybe some *boudin noir,* which I, with all the French prowess I could muster, took to be a dish based on some sort of nice dark sourdough bread. (After all, isn't Boudin a San Francisco bread-baking company? And noir certainly means dark—I learned that in film class.) Upon closer reading, however, I discovered that *boudin noir* means blood sausage. I am grateful the menu was not entirely in French.

Dogs are welcome to join you at the marble-topped tables on the small but fetching patio here. It's set off from the sidewalk by flowers. 6534 Washington Street; 707/944-8037.

Compadres Mexican Bar and Grill: Tropical landscaping, intoxicating jasmine and honeysuckle, and umbrellas over tables make this one of the most pleasant restaurants for spending a lunchtime with your dog. Try the *pollo borracho,* a whole chicken cooked with white wine and tequila. 6539 Washington Street, at the Vintage 1870 complex; 707/944-2406.

Hurley's: The food here is a kind of melding of Mediterranean and California wine country cuisines. You can get everything from spicy vegetarian Moroccan plates to medallions of venison to squash blossom fritters. Enjoy your tasty food with your happy dog at the patio, which offers lots of shade on hot days and heat lamps for chilly nights. Thirsty dogs get water. 6518 Washington Street; 707/944-2345.

Napa Valley Grill: California cuisine reigns here, with fresh seafood as the focal point. Several outdoor tables with oversized umbrellas keep you and your dog cool. 6795 Washington Street; 707/944-2330.

PLACES TO STAY

Vintage Inn: Dogs who get to stay here are lucky dogs indeed. This inn ("inn" is an understated description of this place) puts dogs and their people in the lap of luxury, with a perfect blend of old-world charm and new-world design. The airy, beautiful, multilevel villas have fireplaces, and many have views of nearby vineyards. Dogs swoon over the grounds, which have pools, gardens, courtyards, and even a fountain.

This is a great place to stay if you're checking out the wineries on warm days and don't want to bring your dog along. The staff here can arrange for a pet-sitter to watch your pooch so he can keep cool and comfy while you sip your way through wine country.

Rates are $340–625 and include a California Champagne breakfast and afternoon tea. Dogs pay a $30 fee per visit. 6541 Washington Street 94599; 707/944-1112 or 800/351-1133; www.vintageinn.com.

Napa

The city of Napa has about 40 parks. Dogs are allowed in a whopping four, each of which has an off-leash section. You'll see dogs in some of the bigger parks, such as the Lake Hennessey Recreation Area, but they're not officially sanctioned, so we can't officially mention them.

PARKS, BEACHES, AND RECREATION AREAS

5 Alston Park/Canine Commons

🐾🐾🐾🐾 🐕 (See Napa County map on page 326)

With 157 acres of rolling hills surrounded by vineyards, Alston Park seems to stretch out forever. The lower part of the land used to be a prune orchard, and these prunes are just about the only trees you'll find here.

From there on up, the park is wide-open land with a lone tree here and there. Without shade, dogs and people can fry on hot summer days. But the park is magical during early summer mornings or any cooler time of year.

Miles of trails take you and your dog to places far from the road and the sound of traffic. Dogs are supposed to be off leash only in the lower, flat section of the park, known as Canine Commons. There's now a decent-sized fenced dog park there, complete with poop bags and drinking water.

From Highway 29, take Trower Avenue southwest to the end, at Dry Creek Road. The parking lot for the park is a short jog to your right on Dry Creek Road and across the street. It's open dawn–dusk. 707/257-9529.

6 Century Oaks Park

🧍🐕 (See Napa County map on page 326)

This park is a cruel hoax on canines. Dogs are restricted to a dangerous dog run—a tiny postage stamp of an area without fences, just off a busy street. And as for the park's name, which promises granddaddy oak trees, we're talking saplings here—maybe a dozen in the whole dog-run area. We don't know how many are in the rest of the park, because dogs aren't allowed there even on leash.

The dog-run area (we suggest keeping all but the most highly trained dogs on leash here) is on Brown's Valley Road, just off Westview Drive. Park on Westview Drive and walk around the corner to the dog run. The short walk to the park, with its shade and shrubs, is more enjoyable than the park itself. It's open dawn–dusk. 707/257-9529.

7 John F. Kennedy Memorial Park

🐾🐾🐾 🐕 (See Napa County map on page 326)

Throw your dog's leash to the wind here and ramble along the Napa River. Dogs are allowed in the undeveloped areas near the park's boat marina. The only spot to avoid is a marshland that's more land than marsh during dry times.

Dogs enjoy chasing each other around the flat, grassy area beside the parking lot. There's also a dirt trail that runs along the river. You can take it from either side of the marina, although as of this writing, the signs designate only the south side as a dog-exercise area. The scenery isn't terrific—radio towers and construction cranes dot the horizon—but dogs without a sense of decor don't seem to mind.

Dogs like to amble by the river, which is down a fair incline from the trail. But be careful if you've got a water dog, because riders of personal watercraft and motorboaters have been known to mow over anything in their path. There's no drinking water in the dog area and it gets mighty hot in the summer, so bring your own.

Take Highway 221 to Streblow Drive, and follow the signs past the Napa Municipal Golf Course and Napa Valley College to the boat marina/launch area. Park in the lot and look for the trail by the river. The park is open dawn–dusk. 707/257-9529.

🖥 Shurtleff Park
🐾🐾🐾🐕 (See Napa County map on page 326)

The farther away from the road you go, the better it is in this long, narrow park. It gets shadier and thicker with large firs and eucalyptus trees. Dogs are allowed off leash as soon as you think they're safe from the road.

The park is almost entirely fenced, but there are a few escape hatches. Two are at the entrance and two others are along the side that lead you into the schoolyard of Phillips Elementary School. This isn't normally a problem, unless your dog runs into the day-care center at lunchtime, as Joe once did. A teacher escorted him out by the scruff of his neck before he could steal someone's peanut butter sandwich.

You'll find the park on Shelter Street at Shurtleff, beside Phillips Elementary School. It's open dawn–dusk. 707/257-9529.

PLACES TO EAT

Angele Restaurant: Doggies who dine at this restaurant's riverfront tables get treats and water! "We love dogs!" says a server. The food is excellent—French with a Napa Valley flair. It can get a little tight here, and as Tera Dog, a rottie pup, wrote me, "Dog biscuits don't cut it when there is the smell of wild salmon and braised duck nearby!" Make sure your dog minds his manners with the neighbors. A big thanks to the aptly named Bacchus, another personable traveling rottie, for sniffing this one out for us. 540 Main Street; 707/252-8115.

Celadon: A woman once walked into this award-winning restaurant with four dogs and asked for a table for five. She was serious. So was the dog-friendly staff when they told her that one human could not take up a table for five at busy lunchtime.

You and your dog are welcome to dine at the spacious, gorgeous garden patio area here, but your dog will have to remain on the ground, not in his very own chair. Celadon's menu features "global comfort food," with a gourmet seasonal flair. The macadamia nut–crusted goat cheese with port-poached figs, apples, and crostini is delectable. 500 Main Street; 707/254-9690.

Napa Valley Traditions: Enjoy fresh baked goods and cappuccino at four outside tables shaded by two trees and an awning. Your dog will find as much to enjoy here as you will—inside, the shop also sells dog biscuits. 1202 Main Street; 707/226-2044.

Ristorante Allegria: Northern Italy meets California at this delightful find. The menu is seasonally influenced, with flavors that are out of this world. Your taste buds will be really happy here, and if you like wine (which chances are you do, since you're hanging out in Napa Valley), you'll love the wine list. You and your dog can dine together at the 12 umbrella-topped tables on the attractive brick-floor garden patio. 1026 First Street; 707/254-8006.

PLACES TO STAY

With more choices of dog-friendly lodgings than ever before, Napa is a heavenly place to stay with your furry friend.

The Carneros Inn: This gorgeous inn on 27 acres of Carneros grapes is a great place to stay if luxury and relaxation are at the top of your list, and budget concerns are on the bottom. Before reading on, know that you'll be paying a $150 pooch fee for your visit. That's a lot out of the dog-biscuit fund. Stay a while and get your money's worth.

All accommodations here are in the form of elegantly casual cottages. The cottages are grouped into little "neighborhoods," and people with dogs stay in a neighborhood consisting of seven enchanting garden cottages. They all feature wood-burning fireplaces, large windows, French doors, heated slate floors and limestone countertops in the bathrooms, a soaking tub facing your private garden, and a choice of indoor or heavenly alfresco shower.

You're welcome to peruse the property's vineyards and pretty apple orchards with your leashed dog, but no dogs at the patio area of the property's restaurant. Boo hoo! There's always room service.

The inn is a PlumpJack property. The PlumpJack group of wine, resort, and restaurant holdings is co-owned by San Francisco Mayor Gavin Newsom. So stay here, and you're helping keep him in his spiffy suits. Rates for the dog-friendly cottages are $480–520. Dogs pay that $150 fee per visit. Just one dog is allowed per cottage. 4048 Sonoma Highway 94559; 707/299-4900 or 888/400-9000; www.thecarnerosinn.com.

Beazley House: This cozy inn, which sits on a half-acre of verdant lawns and gardens, has been voted Napa's Best B&B by listeners of local radio station KVON every year for more than a decade. (As of press time, it was 11 years.) It makes me wonder: Are dogs the primary listeners of this station?

Dogs are warmly welcomed to the inn's two beautiful buildings by proprietors Jim and Carol Beazley, and sometimes by their friendly golden retrievers Tammy and Sissy. "I'd rather have dogs than some children," confesses Carol. (Watch out: Your dog may be trying to dial KVON to vote for Beazley House right now...)

The two buildings are imbued with a luxurious-but-casual wine country charm. Rooms have lovely furnishings, plush towels and robes, and even a little nip of chocolate. The Carriage House features rooms with direct garden access—something appreciated by many people with dogs—and The Mansion, circa 1900, sports slightly less expensive, smaller rooms. A scrumptious breakfast buffet comes with your stay, as does an afternoon refreshment hour, with tasty snacks that include Beazley House Chocolate Chip Cookies, beloved by repeat guests.

Rates are $185–309. ("We're a value, not a bargain," says Carol.) Dogs are $25 extra. 1910 First Street 94559; 707/257-1649 or 800/559-1649; www.beazleyhouse.com.

The Chablis Inn: Don't be fooled by the name of this place: It's not a darling wine country bed-and-breakfast inn. It's simply a decent motel with an enticing moniker. But it's striving to be more innlike, with some rooms offering down comforters and whirlpool tubs. All rooms come with bottled water, too. The motel has a couple of features that most charming inns don't, namely a pool and cable TV. Rates are $79–189. Dogs are $10 extra. 3360 Solano Avenue 94558; 707/257-1944 or 800/443-3490; www.chablisinn.com.

The Inn on First: This luxurious inn changed hands in 2007 (it was formerly The Daughter's Inn) and is fast becoming a favorite of pooches touring wine country. At check-in, dog guests get a dog toy, a treat, a souvenir pet tag, and bags for things you tend not to focus on at places like this. In the room your dog will find a custom doggy bed and food and water bowls. What a welcome!

Dogs can stay in three of five garden suites tucked under a 150-year-old oak tree. (Boy dog alert! Boy dog alert!) All three are on the ground floor and have their own private exterior entrances and decks. The suites are spacious and highly comfortable, with large spa tubs not languishing in the bathrooms, but as an integral part of the bedroom/sitting room. A full breakfast and complimentary afternoon snacks are part of your stay.

Rates are $295–339. Dogs are $35 extra (nightly), plus a one-time $50 cleaning fee per room. Do not let your dog sleep on your bed! As the website warns, "Evidence of dog hair on the bed will incur a minimum $100 extra cleaning fee." (They had a bad bed-shed experience once with a very nice but extremely sheddy Lab. No, not Jake, thank God.) 1938 First Street 94559; 707/253-1331; www.theinnonfirst.com.

The Meritage Resort at Napa: The Tuscan-inspired architecture and furnishings at the lovely Meritage Resort create a wonderful melding of northern Italian/Napa Valley ambience. Some rooms face vineyards, for a true wine-country experience. The rooms are luxurious, the pampering at the full-service spa exquisite, and the atmosphere decidedly dog friendly. "We appreciate a good dog," a manager told us.

Your dog can't go to the pool or spa, but she'll be able to accompany you to the wonderland that lies outdoors. The vineyard here has walking trails you can peruse with your leashed friend. Our faithful Napa Valley canine correspondent, Bacchus, brings his person, Karen, on a trail that leads to Napa's famed Grape Crusher statue. Try it—you'll like it. In the evening, bring some wine (possibly the free bottle you get at check-in) and head to the outdoor fire pit for the perfect end to a relaxing day in the Napa Valley. The resort also has an adjacent timeshare counterpart, Vino Bello Resort, should you and your dog want a kitchen, fireplace, living area, and just more space in general.

Rates are $249–700 (the pricier rates are for the timeshares; they're often available on a nightly basis). Dogs are $50 extra (yes, per night). 875 Bordeaux Way 94558; 866/370-NAPA (866/370-6272); www.themeritageresort.com.

The Napa Inn: If Queen Anne–style Victorians are your dog's cup of tea, sniff out this terrific 1899 bed-and-breakfast. Dogs are allowed to stay The Garden Cottage, which has a fireplace, mini-kitchen, and French doors that look out on a private flower garden. Dogs mustn't sleep on the beds, so BYOB. If the inn is really busy the innkeepers prefer small dogs, but they're open to well-behaved larger pooches at other times.

Your stay includes breakfast for two (humans) in the inn's sumptuous dining area. On cooler evenings, the humans in your party can sidle up to a fire in the relaxing parlor. Rates are $195–255. Dogs are $20 extra. 1137 Warren Street 94559; 707/257-1444 or 800/435-1144; www.napainn.com.

Napa River Inn: This dog-friendly, full-service luxury hotel doesn't just permit pooches: It showers them with goodies and services. You won't believe what this upscale boutique hotel offers dogs. Upon check-in, your dog gets use of a pet blanket embroidered with the inn's logo, a matching placemat, and attractive food and water bowls to put on the placemat. (If you want to buy these items, the gift shop sells them. The ones that come with your room are just loaners.) In addition, dogs get poop bags and locally made gourmet dog biscuits. As you may have guessed, unlike the aforementioned goodies, you don't have to give these items back when you're done with them. If you need a little assistance with dog duties, the bell staff here is often available to take your dog for a little walk along the inn's namesake, the Napa River. Dog-sitting can also be arranged through an outside service, but you'll have to give 72 hours notice. Dogs of any size are now allowed; this is great news for big dogs like Jake, since the old weight limit was just 40 pounds. In fact, the staff hosted a 150-pound mastiff not too long ago!

One of the three buildings that make up the inn dates from 1887. Its rooms are opulent but unpretentious, with fireplaces, clawfoot tubs, and canopy king-size beds. Rooms at the other two lovely buildings feature nautical themes or "contemporary wine country design." Included in your stay is a delicious

breakfast at Angele, the dog-friendly restaurant on this 2.5-acre property. Rates are $179–499. Dogs are $25 extra. 500 Main Street 94559; 707/251-8500 or 877/251-8500; www.napariverinn.com.

Napa Valley Country Cottage: A sweet patch of pooch paradise awaits you and the dog of your life here. This cozy cottage is surrounded by 12 acres of gardens, woods, walking paths, and open areas that are perfect for throwing a stick. Some of the acreage is fenced and gated, for that extra-secure leash-free romp. There's even a little vineyard, should you want some real wine-country ambience. A wooded area with a seasonal creek separates the cottage from the cottage-owners' house, so there's plenty of privacy.

The wood cottage itself is a very cute one-bedroom affair with a little kitchen and dining area, and a living room. (The futon in the living room folds out, should you be traveling with extra humans.) The large, sunny deck makes a great setting for dining alfresco with your dog friend. The cottage is perfect for pooches: It has Italian tile floors and is well stocked with doggy treats, doggy dishes, and a pooch bed.

Rates are $750–950 for one week, plus a $50 cleaning fee (even for nondog people). Dogs are $50 extra for the length of their stay. The cottage is on beautiful Mount Veeder. When you make your reservation you'll get the address. 707/226-6621; www.napavalleycasa.com.

Redwood Inn: Rates are $79–140. Dogs are $10 extra. 3380 Solano Avenue 94558; 707/257-6111 or 877/872-6272; www.napavalleyredwoodinn.net.

346

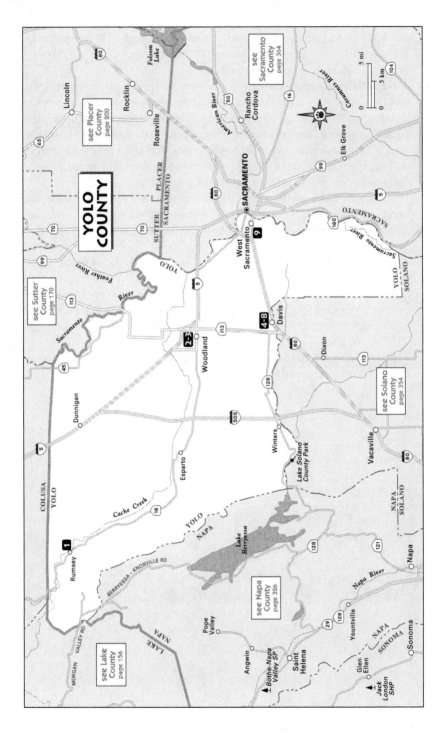

CHAPTER 29

Yolo County

The little towns along the winding Sacramento River haven't changed much since the early 1900s. That's good news for you, but it's not necessarily what your dog wants to hear. Restaurants with outdoor dining are rare, and dog-friendly parks are equally uncommon. You'll see mile after mile of wide-open land and dense forests, but most of it is privately owned and off-limits. For information on the one state wildlife area here (the Sacramento Bypass), call the California Department of Fish and Game at 530/355-0978.

The Sacramento River is so integral to life here that many of the county's parks are formed around public boat ramps that charge nominal launching fees. If you have a dog who loves to go angling for salmon, stripers, or shad, this is a great place to bring her to show off your fishing skills.

Davis is the only city with off-leash dog areas (and a terrific new one with this edition) and a fair number of outdoor dining establishments. Some of the parks are close to major highways, so they're a blessing when your dog starts moaning and getting that bulgy-eyed look on a long trip.

PICK OF THE LITTER—YOLO COUNTY

BEST HIKING
Cache Creek Canyon Regional Park, Rumsey (page 348)

BEST DOG PARKS
Toad Hollow Dog Park, Davis (page 351)
Sam Combs Dog Park, West Sacramento (page 353)

MOST DOG-FRIENDLY RESTAURANT
Sudwerk, Davis (page 352)

Rumsey
PARKS, BEACHES, AND RECREATION AREAS

🐾 Cache Creek Canyon Regional Park
🐾🐾🐾 (See Yolo County map on page 346)

This 700-acre park is flat in the developed sections and very hilly when you get away from people. Couch-potato canines enjoy picnicking at any of three car-accessible sites, as well as "ruffing" it at the campground. More adventurous dogs prefer hiking over the creek and into the woods with their human friends on a self-guided nature walk.

We've found that some park hosts don't know about the trails, so it's best to get a map of the nature walk before you go. Write for one from the Yolo County Parks Division at 292 West Beamer Street, Woodland, CA 95695.

Very feisty dogs may want to continue their treks onto federal land, where they're allowed to be off leash. More than 15,000 acres—some of it inaccessible because of the steep terrain—is out there for your leashless bliss. It can be tricky to find. Contact the Bureau of Land Management, Clear Lake Resource Area, 555 Leslie Street, Ukiah, CA 95482; 707/468-4000.

Camping at Cache Creek Canyon Regional Park costs $17–19. Dogs are $2 extra. There are 45 sites, all first-come, first-served. The day-use fee is $6. The first of the three park turnoffs is about six miles west of Rumsey on Highway 16. All sites are on the south side of the road. 530/666-8115.

Woodland

This little town has churches and saloons in unusually high numbers. You can do the sin-forgiveness-sin-forgiveness theme all week long here and barely walk (stumble?) a couple of blocks.

PARKS, BEACHES, AND RECREATION AREAS

The parks here used to allow dogs off-leash with a permit. Now leashes are the law for everyone. However, with any luck, Woodland dogs will soon have two fenced dog parks of their very own! Our paws are crossed that the dogs of Woodland will be able to run leash-free within the borders of their town and not have to make the sojourn to Davis, as so many do right now.

2 Woodside Park

🐾🐾 (See Yolo County map on page 346)

There's plenty of green, flat open space here for your dog's jogging pleasure. The park also has several shaded picnic tables for your dog's dining pleasure. The park is on the corner of Cottonwood Street and El Dorado Drive, just six blocks west of Crawford Park. 530/661-5880.

3 Crawford Park

🐾🐾 (See Yolo County map on page 346)

You and your dog will enjoy the year-round green grass and the abundance of shade trees here. This park is a great place to come to exercise your human and canine children at the same time. There's a pint-sized railroad village in the middle of the playground. Kids love it.

Exit I-5 at East Street and go south for several blocks. Turn right on Gibson Road. After a few blocks, go left on College Street and you'll find the park at the corner of College Street and El Dorado Drive. 530/661-5880.

Davis

Davis is home to a large University of California campus and a laid-back collegiate crowd. Many of the students miss their dogs and want to pet yours. It's also home to seven parks that have sections for leashless dogs. Davis is a nice place to be a dog.

PARKS, BEACHES, AND RECREATION AREAS

Davis is now home to Toad Hollow, a real-deal, good-sized fenced dog park! We describe five of the city's six leash-free areas below. Of the other two, one is a quarter-acre unfenced section of Walnut Park (the leash-free section is closest to Lillard Drive, just east of Cowell Boulevard). It's marked by signs. The other is a small section of the Aspen Greenbelt. It's on the north end of the greenbelt, near Glacier and Denali drives. (Ooh, sounds cold!). It's hard to see because it runs 100 feet from the quiet road and is separated by brush.

4 Community Park Dog Park

🐾🐾🐕 (See Yolo County map on page 346)

For many years, this was Davis's only fenced dog park. It got quite a bit of use, but it's been eclipsed by new Toad Hollow Dog Park. It's just a quarter acre, so it's truly a postage stamp–sized park, but it's a triangular stamp, so it's an interesting one. And it's not entirely flat, which is also a fairly unusual concept in dog parks. The park is a grassy area that's gently sloped, with a smaller flat area for dogs who prefer a more couch-potato approach. It has a green vinyl fence to match the grass (no, the grass isn't vinyl, smarty!) and a lot of shade from Chinese tallow trees. My area correspondent, Archie, had his person John McClure write to tell me that when Toad Hollow closes because of rain, this park gets overrun and can get a bit mucky. Thanks for the tip, Archie! The park is on F Street between 14th Street and Covell Boulevard. 530/757-5626.

5 Sycamore Park

🐾🐾🐕 (See Yolo County map on page 346)

If your dog won't be tempted to join in the fun and games of the playground on her right and the sports field on her left, the off-leash section of this park will suit her just fine. It's green, grassy, and fairly safe from traffic.

Park along Sycamore Lane between Villanova and Bucknell drives, not in the parking lot of West Davis Intermediate School. Go into the park's grassy field to the right of the school as you face it from Sycamore Lane. The dog-exercise area is to the left of the playground and is clearly marked. 530/757-5626.

6 Slide Hill Park

🐾🐾🐕 (See Yolo County map on page 346)

The off-leash part of this diverse community park is toward the back, protected from most traffic. It's also partly shaded and it has green grass, even in the middle of summer! What more could a city dog want? More room? Possibly, but this off-leash area is Davis's largest (although at a half-acre, it's not exactly a Goliath), so why be picky?

The park is also a great place to take kids. There are playgrounds and tennis courts, and there's even a decent-sized swimming pool in the front.

To get to the dog area, park in the lot at Temple Drive and walk into the park on the paved path, heading left past the tennis courts until you reach the back. The dog spot, under a small grove of trees, is marked by a garbage can and a sign. 530/757-5626.

7 Toad Hollow Dog Park

🐾🐾🐾🐾🐕 (See Yolo County map on page 346)

The dog people of Davis worked extremely hard to make this park a reality, often staying until after midnight at planning meetings with the city, and we're happy to say they've done a four-paw job of it. This 2.5-acre fenced park is just what Davis needed. Many people didn't feel comfortable taking their dogs to the small, unfenced off-leash areas offered by the city, and with Community Park's fenced area being so tiny, some dogs rarely got off-leash exercise. Thanks to Toad Hollow, this has changed.

The park is grassy, with trees lining parts of the outside of the chain-link fence. There's a slight grade on one side of the park, so it's not entirely flat. Dogs like that. The park has water, bag stations (for used grocery and newspaper bags, at this point), and some seating. We give it four paws even though it's still not at its ultimate planned goal yet. Within a couple of years, there should be more permanent seating, a walkway, new trees, and a section for small dogs. But for now, it's still a great place for dogs. Katharyn Hart, a U.C. Davis vet student who will probably be a vet by the time you read this, is among the very satisfied park users. She acquired two research dogs—hooray for her!—and was thrilled when Toad Hollow opened. "Even dogs like one of mine who does not come when called and pulls on the leash can enjoy themselves once there," she writes. Many echo her sentiments.

The only downside to Toad Hollow Dog Park is that it can be temporarily closed in winter months during and following heavy rains. That's because the park is located within a drainage basin that provides storage of stormwater runoff for all of downtown. You can call 530/757-5656 to check the status if you're not sure, or go to Davis' website and sign up for email updates. The city is also planning to put up a flag for when it's open, and a different one for when it's closed. That will leave no room for error. You don't want to be doing the dog paddle here.

An interesting aside: Toad Hollow Dog Park is very close to some frog tunnels built by the city so frogs could cross under the then-new six-lane Pole Line Road overpass, and not become roadkill while trying to get to and from their froggy wetlands. No one is sure whether frogs are using these six-inch-wide pipes. A must-see entrance features a miniature house/hotel (Toad Hall?) with little happy painted frogs looking out the windows, and some other little "buildings" that make up a mini frog village. Yes, it's called Toad Hollow, not Frog Hollow. It's more poetic, and what do the amphibians care? It's at 2020 Fifth Street. You'll see the little Toad Hollow sign. And now you know why the dog park has its name.

Toad Hollow Dog Park is at 1919 Second Street, between L Street and the Pole Line Road overcrossing. 530/757-5626.

8 Pioneer Park

😺 🐕 (See Yolo County map on page 346)

This park is good for kids, with playgrounds and basketball hoops, but the dog-exercise area is a little too close to the road for our comfort. It's also very small. If you have a very obedient dog who needs to stretch his legs off leash, but doesn't need to stretch them very far, this will do. It's clean, green, and has some shade. Fortunately, it's on a quiet road, so the danger from cars is low.

Pioneer Park is convenient for dogs traveling through on the freeway. Heading east on I-80, take the Mace Boulevard exit and go left on Chiles Road. Take a right on El Cemonte Avenue. Go left on Swingle Drive and you'll be at the park. The dog-walk area is just to the right, about halfway down the block on Hamel Street. 530/757-5626.

PLACES TO EAT

Redrum Burger: Murder Burger has reversed its first name (à la the mirror writing in *The Shining*), but the burgers are still to die for. They're big, hearty one-pounders you and your dog will drool for. You can also try an ostrich burger, if you want a red-meat alternative. The deep-fried veggie plate is a hit, as are the thick, real-ice-cream milk shakes. You and your dog can eat together at outdoor tables. Then go take a nice, long walk. 978 Olive Drive; 530/756-2142.

Sudwerk: Sudwerk is very conveniently located across from Toad Hollow Dog Park. Until recently, the food wasn't the draw for most people. (Greasy "taco pizza" gives you an idea of the previous cuisine.) But the menu recently completely changed, and the food is quite good now, with excellent gourmet-ish pizzas, flavorful chicken and meat dishes, and tasty salads and starters. Sudwerk is a microbrewery, so beers are still a big draw here, especially for the UC Davis students who favor this place.

Have a meal and a brew or two next to your favorite pooch at the large patio/beer garden. The servers like dogs and give visiting chowhounds a biscuit and bowl of water. (Thanks to reader Nhi Nguyen for the heads-up about Sudwerk.) 2001 Second Street; 530/758-8300.

PLACES TO STAY

Best Western University Lodge: When your dog needs to go see someone graduate or consult with a professor on some "arcanine" matter, this motel one block off campus (and a couple of blocks from Central Park, a good spot for leashed dogs) is a convenient place to stay. Rates are $75–105. 123 B Street 95616; 530/756-7890.

Howard Johnson Hotel: Reserve early: Dog rooms are limited. Room rates are $79–154. Dogs are $20 extra. 4100 Chiles Road 95616; 530/792-0800.

Motel 6: Rates are $40–60. There's a little grass on the premises for a wee stroll. 4835 Chiles Road 95616; 530/753-3777.

West Sacramento

PARKS, BEACHES, AND RECREATION AREAS

🛛 Sam Combs Dog Park

🐾🐾🐾🐾🐕 (See Yolo County map on page 346)

This fairly new dog park has many pooch fans. That's because it has plenty of shade from established trees, a separate small-dog area, benches, water, and all the other usual dog-park accoutrements. There's even a red fire hydrant. (Joannie, a friendly yellow Lab who had her person write to us about this park, says that while she can't use the hydrant, it's nice to see the boy dogs enjoying it.) It's about 1.5 acres, with tennis balls galore. The dog park is within the larger Sam Combs Park, at Jefferson and Stone Boulevards. It's a quick jaunt from Highway 50, should your dog need a rest stop. Exit the highway at Jefferson Boulevard, drive south about 0.75 mile, and turn right on Stone Boulevard, just after the railroad tracks. The park will be on your left. 916/617-4620.

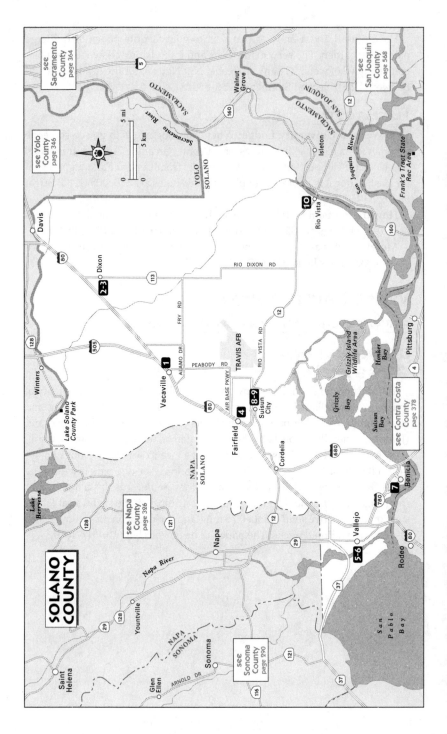

SOLANO COUNTY

see Sacramento County page 364

see San Joaquin County page 568

see Yolo County page 346

5 mi
5 km

Davis

Dixon

2-3

113

RIO DIXON RD

FRY RD

ALAMO DR

1

PEABODY RD

505

Vacaville

Winters

128

Lake Solano County Park

Lake Berryessa

128

NAPA SOLANO

see Napa County page 396

Napa

121

Yountville

29

128

Saint Helena

Glen Ellen

Sonoma

ARNOLD DR

NAPA SONOMA

116

121

see Sonoma County page 290

37

AIR BASE PKWY

TRAVIS AFB

8-9

4

Suisun City

Fairfield

Cordelia

RIO VISTA RD

12

Rio Vista

10

Isleton

Walnut Grove

160

5

SACRAMENTO

Sacramento River

YOLO SOLANO

SAN JOAQUIN

SACRAMENTO

12

San Joaquin River

Frank's Tract State Rec Area

160

Pittsburg

4

Honker Bay

Grizzly Island Wildlife Area

Grizzly Bay

Suisun Bay

680

see Contra Costa County page 378

Benicia

7

780

Vallejo

5-6

80

Rodeo

29

37

San Pablo Bay

Napa River

12

CHAPTER 30

Solano County

Solano County dogs are a happy lot these days, with some decent dog-friendly restaurants to dine in and parks to run around—a far howl better than it used to be here.

The marvelous 2,070-acre Rush Ranch Open Space permits leash-free pooches on a two-mile trail with views that are to drool for. This alone makes it absolutely worth the trip to Solano County. So does the Grizzly Island Wildlife Area, in the thick of the Suisun Marsh. As long as you visit when dogs can be off leash, your pooch will think she's in heaven. Mud heaven. Bring a towel.

Smaller leash-free areas (much smaller!) include dog parks in Vacaville and Benicia. A new four-paw dog park is finally open in Vallejo, which has a big need for off-leash romping room. Two parks in Dixon allow off-leash dogs, but if your dog isn't at perfect heel when you're at the parks, leash him fast, or you could find yourself paying a fine. The county is growing rapidly, and there's a real need for more leash-free areas.

If you find yourself at the famed Jelly Belly jelly bean factory in Fairfield, you'll be happy to know that while you wait for the rest of your crew to take the tour inside, you and your dog can have a decent time at the teeny little dog "relief" area beside the parking lot. You'll find some very green grass, some pretty ivy, poop bags, water, and a red fire hydrant ("This hydrant is here for your dog's pleasure," a big sign says. "Not a working hydrant.") If, God forbid, the Jelly Belly factory goes up in flames, at least the firefighters won't be fooled by the doggy decor.) It's not exactly Rush Ranch, but it's better than sitting in

PICK OF THE LITTER—SOLANO COUNTY

MOST TEMPTING HYDRANT
Jelly Belly dog "relief" area, Fairfield (page 355)
Janine Jordan Park for Dogs, Vacaville (page 356)

BEST LONG-AWAITED CANINE HOT SPOT
Wardlaw Dog Park, Vallejo (page 359)

BEST OFF-LEASH HIKING
Rush Ranch Open Space, Suisun City (page 362)

BEST PLACE TO HIKE WITH COWS
Rush Ranch Open Space, Suisun City (page 362)

MOST DOG-FRIENDLY PLACE TO EAT
Valley Cafe, Suisun City (page 363)

BEST GREASY SPOON
Babs Delta Diner, Suisun City (page 362)

MOST DOG-FRIENDLY PLACE TO STAY
Courtyard by Marriott, Vallejo (page 360)

your car the whole time watching tired, jelly bean–stuffed children having sugar-induced meltdowns on the asphalt.

Vacaville

PARKS, BEACHES, AND RECREATION AREAS

◼ Janine Jordan Park for Dogs

🐾🐾🐾 🐕 (See Solano County map on page 354)

Jake gives this park three paws despite its relatively small size of 0.7 acre. That's because it has friendly people, grass (although not always of the green variety), shade trees, and best of all: a golden fire hydrant (most dogs probably only dream of such idols) and a doggy drinking fountain made out of a decommissioned fire hydrant. The golden hydrant is a memorial to Panto, a dearly departed Vacaville Police K-9 partner. The fountain hydrant is an homage to all dogs.

The dog park is within Lagoon Valley Regional Park. If you're going to become a park regular, you should join its organizational group, PAWS (People Aware of the Well-being of the Speechless). The $25 membership fee goes toward park upkeep and supplies. (From what a visitor tells us, the park looks as if it's in need of some TLC lately. It wasn't when we saw it, though. Either way, your membership dollars will be put to good use.) Plus your membership will get you into the park without having to pay the $3 entry fee for the regional park. But if you're just passing through and want to check it out, it's worth the $3. (You'll also have to sign a waiver. They're available at the kiosk, or you can download one by going to the dog park's website, www.ourdogpark.org.)

The park may be moving to a location about a mile away, pending outcome of legal battles over a proposed development. But this wouldn't happen for a while, so we'll keep you posted in the next edition.

Exit I-80 at Pena Adobe Road/Lagoon Valley Regional Park. Go right at the stop sign (this is Riviera Road), and go left onto Pena Adobe. Follow the signs to Lagoon Valley Regional Park, which will be on your right. Drive 0.2 mile more and you'll come to the dog park. Lagoon Valley's number is 707/449-6122. The number to contact PAWS is 866/510-3681.

PLACES TO EAT

Pure Grain Bakery Cafe: Dine with your dog at the lovely outdoor patio area of this German-style bakery. The rye is to die for. The café's soups, salads, sandwiches, and coffees are tasty, too. And if your dog is like Gracie Autumn (our canine informant in the area), he might enjoy a taste of the café's creamy gelato. (Vanilla is Gracie's choice.) 11 Town Square/Main Street; 707/447-4121.

PLACES TO STAY

Best Western Heritage Inn: Small to medium dogs are allowed here. Don't try to pass your Saint Bernard off as a lapdog, even if he is your lapdog. Rates are $70–100. Pooches are $10–20 extra. 1420 East Monte Vista Avenue 95688; 707/448-8453.

Motel 6: If you want to shop at the famous outlet mall in Vacaville and you're traveling with someone who will watch your pooch, this is a convenient place to stay—it's about 1,000 feet from the mall. Shop 'til you drop, then drag yourself back here. Rates are $45–55 for the first adult, $6 for the second. 107 Lawrence Drive 95687; 707/447-5550.

Dixon

PARKS, BEACHES, AND RECREATION AREAS

❷ Northwest Park
🐾🐾🐕 (See Solano County map on page 354)
If your dog will stay very close at heel without a leash, she may go leashless at this grassy, 20-acre park. Otherwise, use your leash. With these fairly stringent rules, she probably wouldn't notice her freedom anyway.

The park is on West H and North Lincoln streets. 707/678-7000.

🔳 Hall Memorial Park

🐾🐾🐕 (See Solano County map on page 354)

If you have to conduct business with city government and you want your dog to conduct business, too, you couldn't have asked for a better location for a park. It's right behind City Hall.

There's not much in the way of shade here, but on cooler days this park proves a decent stroll for dogs, provided they're leashed or at very firm heel. The park also has a playground, a swimming pool, tennis courts, and picnic areas with barbecues, so it's even better for people. The park is at Hall Park Drive and East Mayes Street. 707/678-7000.

PLACES TO STAY

Best Western Inn: This is a convenient place to stay if you have to attend a University of California event and no rooms are available in Davis. It's just eight miles away, and a swift drive. Rates are $90–100. Dogs are $10 extra. 1345 Commercial Way 95620; 707/678-1400 or 800/528-1234.

Fairfield

If you're here on jelly bean business, you'll be happy to know your dog can do his business too. See the introduction to this chapter for more info on the dog relief area at the Jelly Belly factory.

PARKS, BEACHES, AND RECREATION AREAS

🔳 Rockville Hills Regional Park

🐾🐾🐾 (See Solano County map on page 354)

Hike, fish, and enjoy nature in this 630-acre park filled with trees and trails. The main trail is fairly steep and takes you to the top of the park, where you'll find two small ponds for fishing. After this hike on a summer afternoon, many dogs jump in when they reach the summit. A man told me that a small beagle once disappeared for several seconds and came up with a tiny fish flailing in her mouth. Could this be just another flagrant flailing fish story?

Once you enter the park, you're safe from traffic. But dogs are supposed to be leashed anyway, since the park is officially run by the city of Fairfield, which has a strict leash law. Check out the nature trail that a local Eagle Scout troop has created. A favorite of many dogs is the Mystic Trail. The 25 miles of trails are arranged in sort of stacked loop formations, so it's easy to get lost. Trail maps are available at the entrance. If in doubt, phone the number below for advice.

For the most vigorous workout, try the main trail. It's the one that bends slightly to the left and up a steep hill as you enter from the parking lot. The park is often desolate, so use judgment about hiking alone.

Exit Highway 80 at Suisun Valley Road and drive 1.5 miles (in the opposite direction from the myriad fast-food outlets) to Rockville Road. Go left on Rockville. In about 0.7 mile you'll come to a small brown sign for the park. In 1,500 feet you'll find a small parking area. The entry fee for humans is $2, and dogs are $1. 707/428-7614.

Vallejo

PARKS, BEACHES, AND RECREATION AREAS

Jake Dog and I crossed our fingers that there would be a dog park here by this edition of the book, and it paid off: Wardlaw Dog Park is a reality!

5 Dan Foley Park

🐾🐾 (See Solano County map on page 354)

You won't often see this at Six Flags Marine World—professional water-skiers practicing their acts over sloping jumps, then landing headfirst in the water when everything doesn't work out perfectly.

But you and your dog will be treated to this unpolished spectacle if you visit this park on the right day. The park is directly across Lake Chabot from Marine World, so you get to witness a good chunk of the goings-on there. Since dogs aren't allowed at Marine World, this is an ideal place to walk them if your kids are spending a few hours with more exotic animals. You still get to hear the sound of jazz bands and the roar of amazed crowds.

Dan Foley Park is so well maintained we initially were afraid it was a golf course. Willows and pines on rolling hills provide cooling shade, and there's usually a breeze from the lake. Leashed dogs are invited everywhere but the water. Even humans aren't supposed to swim in it. Picnic tables are right across from the water-ski practice area, so if your dog wants entertainment with his sandwich, this is the place.

The park is on Camino Alto North just east of Tuolumne Street. There is a $3 parking fee, $4 for nonresidents. 707/648-4315.

6 Wardlaw Dog Park

🐾🐾🐾🐾🐕 (See Solano County map on page 354)

Vallejo's first dog park is a testament to how to build a dog park right. It's a decent size, at 2.2 acres, which leaves plenty of room for your galloping dog to gather a good head of steam before having to avoid a fence or bench. Wardlaw has separate sections for large and small/fragile dogs, green grass, little trees that will grow and provide shade one day, attractive landscaping, an interior and exterior walking path, water, and five poop bag dispensers. Even with these dispensers, poop sometimes ends up orphaned. That's where the volunteer "Bark Rangers" step in (and hopefully not on). They help the city keep the park neat and safe and pretty. Bark Rangers are always needed. You can find out how to become one at the park's kiosk.

The non-dog-park area of the surrounding park (Wardlaw Park, to be exact) provides ample parking, a picnic area, bathrooms, and a two-mile walking path that permits leashed pooches. There's even a skate park. The park is fairly convenient from Highway 80, so we'll provide directions from there, should your dog need to stretch her gams on a road trip: Take the Redwood Street East exit and follow it for about a mile. After passing a large-looking park area, turn right on Ascot Parkway. You'll want to stay in the right lane, because you'll be going right again within a block, into Wardlaw. 707/648-4315.

PLACES TO STAY

Courtyard by Marriott Vallejo Napa Valley: While the kids are busy turning upside-down at unnerving speeds at Six Flags Marine World, located across the street, you and your dog can curl up, read a book, and enjoy the peace.

This former Holiday Inn is very dog friendly: It sports an outdoor pet area, allows well-behaved pets to be left in the rooms unattended (if you use the Do Not Disturb sign on the door), and provides old linen "for the use of furniture coverage so that your pet may enjoy the comforts of home," says the pet guideline sheet.

Rates are $119–269. Dogs are charged a $75 fee per visit. 1000 Fairgrounds Drive 94590; 707/644-1200.

Motel 6: This one's a mere two blocks from Six Flags Marine World. Rates are $46–50 for the first adult, $6 for the second. 458 Fairgrounds Drive 94589; 707/642-7781.

Quality Inn: Rates are $65–90. Dogs are $10 extra. 44 Admiral Callaghan Lane 94591; 707/643-1061.

Ramada Inn: Rates are $68–150. Dogs are charged a $50 fee per visit. 1000 Admiral Callaghan Lane 94591; 707/643-2700.

Benicia

PARKS, BEACHES, AND RECREATION AREAS

7 Phenix Community Dog Park

🐾🐾🐾🐾🐾 (See Solano County map on page 354)

Phenix Community Dog Park, named after a brave retired police dog, is a swell place for dogs. It's got a little more than an acre of grassy leash-free running room, and it's fenced, with water, picnic tables (which little dogs love to dodge under during chase games), poop bags, and small trees that are growing into shade-givers.

The park is in the northwest corner of the 50-acre Benicia Community Park. Enter the parking lot at Rose and Kearny drives and drive to the far west end. Then just follow the wide asphalt path with the painted paw prints to the dog park. Keep in mind that the rest of the park prohibits dogs, so don't let your dog talk you into visiting anywhere but the pooch park. If you enter the park elsewhere, the paw prints will still lead to Phenix. 707/746-4285.

PLACES TO EAT

Java Point: You and the dog of your choice are sure to enjoy the soups, sandwiches, bagels, and jammin' good java served here. This would be a terrific place to bring the pooch even if the food was just so-so. The folks here bring a fresh bowl of water to thirsty dogs. Dine with your smiling, well-quenched dog at the umbrella-topped patios. 366 1st Street; 707/745-1449.

PLACES TO STAY

Best Western Heritage Inn: Rates are $89–120. Dogs pay a $25 fee for the length of their stay. 1955 East 2nd Street 94510; 707/746-0401.

Suisun City

PARKS, BEACHES, AND RECREATION AREAS

🖪 Grizzly Island Wildlife Area

🐾🐾🐾🐾🐾 (See Solano County map on page 354)

This is what dogs have been praying for since they started living in cities: 8,600 acres of wide-open land where they can run—leashless—among the sort of wildlife you see only in PBS specials.

This sprawling wetland, in the heart of the Suisun Marsh, is home to an amazing array of fauna, including tule elk, river otters, waterfowl of every type, jackrabbits, white pelicans, and peregrine falcons.

Of course, walking in marshy areas has its pros and cons. It's muddy, and ticky. But you don't have to get muddy feet here; the landscapes are as varied as the animal life. Dry upland fields are plentiful. You can also canoe down a slough with your steady dog or hike on dozens of dirt trails. Many folks bring dogs here to train them for hunting, which brings us to the unfortunate subject of the park's schedule.

Because of hunting and bird-nesting seasons, Grizzly Island Wildlife Area is closed during fairly large chunks of the year. Be sure to phone first!

If your dog helps you hunt for ducks or pheasant, she's allowed to join you during some of the hunting seasons. Department of Fish and Game staff also occasionally open small sections to people during the off-season, but it's unpredictable from one year to another when and if they'll do it. Even when the park is open, certain sections may be off-limits to dogs. Check with staff when you come in. (Generally, dogs of the nonhunting variety are allowed February, July, and after elk season at the end of September.)

To get to the Grizzly Island Wildlife Area, exit I-80 at Highway 12 heading toward Rio Vista. Turn onto Grizzly Island Road at the stoplight for the Sunset

Shopping Center. Drive 10 miles, past farms, sloughs, and marshes, until you get to the headquarters. You'll have to check in here and pay a $2.50 fee unless you have a hunting or fishing license. Then continue driving to the parking lot nearest the area you want to explore (staff can advise you). Don't forget your binoculars. 707/425-3828.

🖅 Rush Ranch Open Space

😊 😊 😊 😊 🐾 (See Solano County map on page 354)

From freshwater and saltwater marshes to rolling grass-covered hills and meadowlike pastures, this 2,070-acre open-space parcel is home to some wonderfully diverse landscapes.

The to-wag-for news for dogs is that they're allowed to be off-leash on one of the three trails here if they're under voice control. (They're not allowed to even set paw on the other two.) Suisun Hill Trail is a big hit among canines. The two-mile trail takes you into hills with killer 360-degree views of the Suisun Marsh and the hills and mountains to the north. Rangers tell us that on a clear day, you can see the Sierra Nevada.

Cattle are in these here hills, so if your dog is a chaser, or a herder with an uncontrollable urge to do his job, keep him leashed. (Cattle dogs have been known to try to herd bevies of bovines. The cattle don't think this is cute. Neither do Rush Ranch rangers.) Plenty of wildlife is here, too. If in doubt, leash. (Bikes and horses aren't allowed, so those are two fewer distractions to worry about.)

It can be muddy and mucky here, even in dry season, so be sure to have a towel or two in the car. "It's definitely a three-toweler," warns Jessamy Fisher, who hiked here with dogs Gunther and Savannah. "But it was worth the wet dog/swamp smell in my Honda to see my little angels meet cows for the first time." Aww!

This is a special place, run by the Solano Land Trust. If you'd like to help support the educational and interpretive activities of the Rush Ranch Educational Council, or if you want more information, phone 707/432-0150. For details on Rush Ranch's history, flora and fauna, and other park info, see www .rushranch.org.

From Highway 12, exit at Grizzly Island Road and drive south for a couple of miles. To get to the trail, park near the entrance sign and cross Grizzly Island Road to the gate. Walk to the left and follow the trail markers.

PLACES TO EAT

Babs Delta Diner: Water dogs love Babs Delta Diner because it's right on the Delta waterfront, at the Suisun City Marina. But even landlubbing dogs and their people enjoy Babs' water views. The food is the hearty old-style Americana genre that you'll want to avoid if you're monitoring any of your body's statistics (cholesterol, for instance): Biscuits and gravy, thick-sliced ham, and corned beef hash are featured menu items. You can also get soup and salad, but your hungry, drooling dog will be praying you opt for the goopy meaty fare. Dogs are allowed at the patio seating. Thanks to Gracie Autumn and her person, Deborah, for leading us to Babs. 770 Kellogg Street; 707/421-1926.

Valley Cafe: Your dog will have a hard time forgiving you if you're on your way to Lake Berryessa and you don't stop at this cute eatery. That's because the owner loves dogs and makes 'em feel right at home. Next to the register is a jar of pooch treats that calls dogs from far and wide. If you cock your head just right, you can almost hear it in the breeze. "Oh dogggggyyyyy! Come eat us!!!! We're really yummmmmyyyyyy!!" Dogs also can wet their whistles with bowls of fresh water here. By the way, humans enjoy the café/diner cuisine. The BLT on grainy artisan bread is to drool for. Dine with your dog at the nine umbrella-covered tables outside. 4171 Suisun Valley Road; 707/864-2507.

Rio Vista

Humphrey the humpback whale visited this Delta town, and so should your dog. For now, this is a real, dusty Old West town—not one of those cute villages loaded with boutiques and "shoppes." It's refreshing to find a town with more bait shops than banks. However, in the name of "progress," Rio Vista is slowly becoming home to some major housing developments and all the shopping centers and other unsightly amenities that go with them. Get here now, and take some photos on the old streets with your smiling dog. In a few years, they could be collector's items.

Rio Vista isn't bursting with dog amenities. In fact, it's really appropriate to visit with your dog only if you're on a fishing holiday. Then you and your pooch can slip your boat into the water and take off on the Delta for a few hours. Come back with your catch and eat dinner at the county park as the sun goes down on another Delta day.

PARKS, BEACHES, AND RECREATION AREAS

🔟 Sandy Beach County Park
🐾🐾 (See Solano County map on page 354)

Take your dog to the very back of the park for a tolerable little hike, and he can even dip his paws in the Sacramento River! The closer day-use section is completely off-limits to dogs, so be sure you end up in the right area.

Your dog has another chance of getting wet if he follows you into the showers at the campground. Dogs are allowed at the campground. It's not terribly scenic and can get mighty dry at times, but hey, it's a place to stay on the river. There are 42 sites. Fees are $21 a night. Dogs are $1 extra. Half the sites are first-come, first-served. Reservations are recommended during summer.

Take Highway 12 all the way to Rio Vista; follow Main Street to 2nd Street, and go right. When the street bears left and becomes Beach Drive, the park is within a quarter mile. Bring proof of a rabies vaccination. 707/374-2097.

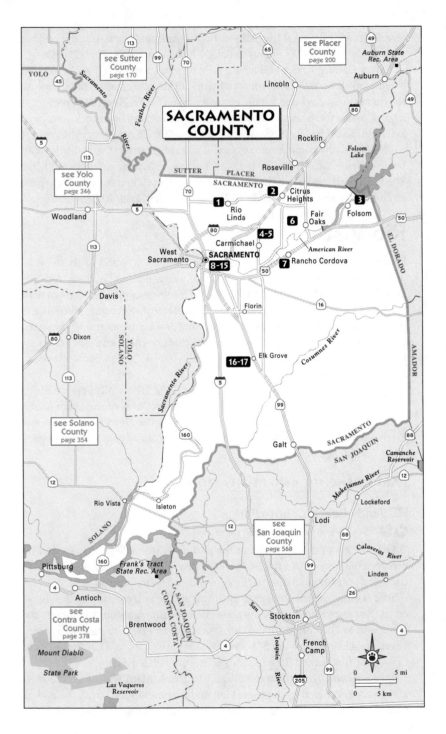

CHAPTER 31

Sacramento County

Capitol dogs can have a capital time around here. Sacramento County's dog parks are sprouting like foxtails on a warm summer's day. At last count, there were 11, and those that have been around for a while have seen terrific improvements. (The Wild West is back, judging by the names of a couple of them: The Canine Corral and C-Bar-C Dog Park.) By the next edition of this book, the city of Sacramento could have three more dog parks.

On the on-leash front, the American River Parkway is one of the finest county park systems we've come across. This riverside greenbelt extends 23 miles from Discovery Regional Park to Folsom Lake, encompassing 20 recreation areas and 5,000 acres. A multi-use trail connects it all, and you and your leashed dog are now welcome to peruse the trail! In fact, you'll find more than a dozen poop-bag stations along the way.

If you and your dog have a hankering to visit the state capitol building together, you'll get as close as the front door before you're ushered away. But it's more attractive from the outside anyway.

PICK OF THE LITTER—SACRAMENTO COUNTY

BEST HIKING
Folsom Lake State Recreation Area, Folsom (page 368)

BEST DOG PARKS
Phoenix Dog Park, Fair Oaks (page 371)
Partner Park, Sacramento (page 374)

BEST ART IN A DOG PARK
Pooch sport mural at Tanzanite Dog Park, Sacramento
(page 373)

BEST ART IN A DOG-FRIENDLY RESTAURANT
Danielle's Creperie and Gallery, Sacramento (page 376)

MOST TEMPTING TREES
Capitol Park, Sacramento (page 375)

MOST DOG-FRIENDLY PLACES TO EAT
Café Bernardo, Sacramento (page 375)
Bella Bru Cafe, Carmichael (page 370)

MOST DOG-FRIENDLY PLACE TO STAY
Sheraton Grand Sacramento Hotel, Sacramento (page 376)

BEST RIDE
Top Hand Ranch Carriage Company carriage rides,
Sacramento (page 372)

MOST POPULAR WATER DOG EVENT
Bark 'n' Splash Bash, Folsom (page 368)

The park surrounding the capitol (called Capitol Park, strangely enough) is an exquisite place, with hundreds of trees from around the world. If you're tired of high taxes and questionable politicians, you'll get vicarious pleasure watching your he-dog do leg lifts here.

Rio Linda

PARKS, BEACHES, AND RECREATION AREAS

1 Westside Park Dog Park

🐾🐾🐾🐕 (See Sacramento County map on page 364)

Here's the Westside story: It's your basic, decent fenced one-acre dog park with water, some small trees, and an attempt at grass. It's a popular place (you can tell by the condition of the grass) and gets a good workout with the after-5 pooch set. Some improvements will be in the works for the next few years, so keep your nose to the ground for changes. The park is at West 2nd Street and M Street. 916/991-5929.

Citrus Heights

PARKS, BEACHES, AND RECREATION AREAS

2 C-Bar-C Dog Park

🐾🐾🐾🐾🐕 (See Sacramento County map on page 364)

If your dog's a cattle dog, how could you not bring her here? C-Bar-C isn't a ranch, but it sure sounds as if it is. Here's what it looks like: More than two big, fenced acres with grass. (See? It could be a cattle stomping ground!) You won't find anyone mooing around here, but you will find some oohing and aahing by dog people who haven't seen it before. The trees here really set the park apart from so many; they're big, and they're plentiful. Oaks and pines predominate. Boy dogs keep very busy here.

The park has picnic tables, restrooms, water, and good parking. And now there's a separate section for little dawgies. It's on Oak Avenue, a little less than a mile east of Sunrise Boulevard. It's on the north side of Oak. 8275 Oak Avenue; 916/725-1585.

Folsom

Thanks in part to Johnny Cash, most folks who aren't from the area know of Folsom because of the imposing Folsom State Prison. But this is a charming Gold Rush town, which boasts in its motto that it's "Where the West Came and Stayed." A walk down historic Sutter Street will prove this slogan right. The wealth of antique shops, art galleries, and restaurants makes it a popular place for tourists. And we're keeping our paws crossed that soon it may be a more popular place for pooches: Dog people here have been working for years to get a dog park. Just when it looks as if it's going to happen, it doesn't, but now the park has the city's official blessing. Phone the city parks department at 916/355-7285 for updates, or check www.fidoinc.org, the website of Folsom Independent Dog Owners (FIDO). And if you have a swimming dog, be sure to check out FIDO's unique pool party. (See *Dog-Ear Your Calendar: Dive into a Pool Party* in this chapter.)

PARKS, BEACHES, AND RECREATION AREAS

3 Folsom Lake State Recreation Area

😾😾😾😾 (See Sacramento County map on page 364)

The bulk of this 12,000-acre reservoir is in Placer and El Dorado counties, but its Folsom entrance is popular and easy to find. With four million visitors every year, this park is one of the busiest recreational lakes in the state park system.

Fortunately, that doesn't stop the rangers from permitting leashed pooches on the 80 miles of trails here. The farther you get from the water, the better, at least during crowded months. It can get really crazy around the lake. The operative word here is *party*. But the hiking and horse trails that meander through the recreation area should give you and your dog a little peace.

You'll wander through valley oaks, oracle oaks, foothill pines, and toyon here. In the spring, wildflowers are everywhere. You'll see Indian paintbrush,

DOG-EAR YOUR CALENDAR

Dive into a Pool Party: This book is getting so big that we can only include the most interesting and unusual dog events. This is one of the chosen few. If you have a swimming dog, you will definitely want to catch the **Bark 'n' Splash Bash,** at the Folsom Aquatic Center. Dogs can swim and frolic in the center's Activity Pool, which is normally just used for pint-sized humans and their parents. They can play on the play structure, and enter and exit the water via the pool's easy-sloped ramps. Landlubbing dogs can also have lots of leash-free fun on the lawn, and there's ample opportunity for socializing.

You may be wondering how clean the pool could be after all this canine activity. Will there be hair and doggy flotsam and jetsam? There will, undoubtedly. But here's how the center can make this work: The bash is usually held around mid-October, right before the three pools are drained and sanitized.

To be admitted to the party, you have to provide written proof of your dog's current license. Leashes must be worn to the entry point. Humans enter for free, but dogs pay $10 each. The center is at 1200 Riley Street; 916/355-8318.

California poppy, and countless other colorful varieties. It's the best time to visit this park, because it's usually not too crowded or hot.

Bring your binoculars. You and your keen-eyed dog may come across such winged beauties as quail, grebes, red-tailed hawks, and eagles. Many are visible from the lake's edge. Dogs aren't allowed on the swimming beaches here, but with the lake's 75 miles of shoreline (when full), you're bound to find a few lakeside spots. You might even want to try your paw at fishing, which can be mighty good here.

The day-use fee is $7 per vehicle. Camping at one of the 182 sites costs $20. Sites are available on a first-come, first-served basis, except in summer, when reservations are highly recommended. Call 800/444-7275 to reserve a site. There are many ways to reach the park. To get to the park headquarters from the town of Folsom, go a couple of miles north on Folsom-Auburn Road. 916/988-0205.

PLACES TO STAY

Lake Natoma Inn: This large, attractive hotel nestles among the big trees that flank Lake Natoma and the American River. The location is enough to put the wag in any dog's tail. From here you can embark on some great hikes along the American River Parkway (see the introduction to this chapter). Rates are $119–299. Dogs require a $45 cleaning fee, plus they're $15 extra per night. 702 Gold Lake Drive 95630; 916/351-1500 or 800/808-5253; www.lakenatoma inn.com.

Carmichael

PARKS, BEACHES, AND RECREATION AREAS

◱ Carmichael Park Canine Corral

😻 😻 😻 🐾 (See Sacramento County map on page 364)

The showdown at the Canine Corral is over. At press time for this book's previous edition, it was the big dogs versus the little dogs. Actually, it was the big-dog people versus the little-dog people. Some people with small dogs had been requesting a separate fenced section within this one-acre park. All they wanted was one-tenth of the park space so their more delicate dogs didn't get mowed down. But a few big-dog folks bared their teeth over losing a chunk of land to the poochettes. The upshot: The little dogs have won the land grab, and now happily trot around their little parkette without fear of giant paws.

The park is about half grass, half dirt, with water, lights, and lots of shade from big oaks. It also has a concrete wash station for muddy paws, and there's even a delightful little wading pool. It's at Fair Oaks Boulevard and Grant Avenue. 916/485-5322.

5 Ancil Hoffman Park

🐾🐾🐾 (See Sacramento County map on page 364)

This 393-acre park is part of the grand American River Parkway. It has plenty of wooded areas for dogs who like to sniff trees and dozens of acres of open grassy land.

Our favorite part is toward the back of the park, near the picnic area. This section is full of shade trees and sports a wonderful dirt trail along the upper banks of the American River. It's also where you have easy access to the river. When we visited, a few folks were picnicking at the tables above, but not a soul (canine or human) was down by the river. If you don't mind walking on small, smooth rocks, you can have a good riverside hike. Dogs are supposed to be leashed, but water dogs have no problem taking a short dip. And as with all county parks, dogs are not permitted on any bike or horse trails.

A $4 vehicle entry fee is usually charged. You can park at an outside street and walk in fee-free if you don't mind a bit of a hike. From Fair Oaks Boulevard, drive east on Kenneth Avenue a few blocks, south on California Avenue one block, then east again on Tarshes Drive, into the park. 916/875-6961.

PLACES TO EAT

Bella Bru Cafe: Bring your dog to dine with you at umbrella-topped outdoor tables, and the folks here will throw in some pooch treats for your dog. 5038 Fair Oaks Boulevard; 916/485-2883.

Fair Oaks
PARKS, BEACHES, AND RECREATION AREAS

6 Phoenix Dog Park
🐾🐾🐾🐾🐕 (See Sacramento County map on page 364)

Dogs adore this 2-acre patch of pooch paradise. It has everything a dog could want, from a separate area for small or shy dogs to a swimming pool. Yes, a swimming pool. It's really a very sturdy, decent-sized wading pool, but it has water and it's a hit with dogs. (The littlest dogs can actually get a decent dog paddle going in it.) A hit with dog people is the paw-wash area—a concrete pad with a water faucet, which comes in mighty handy on muddy winter days. The park also has a separate section for small dogs, as well as drinking water, poop bags, and benches.

This is the kind of park you get when dog people and park people work well together. "The people in the dog group have been wonderful to deal with," said a parks department employee. The dog people say the same about the parks department. Check out the dog people website, www.fordog.org, for more on the park, or phone the city at 916/966-1036. The dog park is in the southwest corner of Phoenix Park. The main entrance to the park is at 9050 Sunset Avenue, a few blocks east of Hazel Avenue, but a good entry point for the dog park location is on Kruitof Way (about a block south of Sunset), just east of Hazel.

Rancho Cordova
PARKS, BEACHES, AND RECREATION AREAS

Rancho Cordova has 20 city parks, all of which permit leashed pooches. We list the best one below. For the last few years, dogs have been keeping their toes crossed about the possibility of having a little dog park to call their own in Rancho Cordova. So far, the city's decision-makers have just been discussing the idea—nothing concrete (or grassy) yet. It's been a long time, and dogs' toes are getting cramped. For information on the progress of the talks, or to find out how you can help the canine cause, call the city parks department at 916/362-1841.

7 Hagan Community Park
🐾🐾🐾 (See Sacramento County map on page 364)

Leashed dogs adore visiting this grassy 61-acre park, which adjoins the American River Parkway. Dogs can get their paws wet in the river or they can stare longingly at the ducks in the park's serene pond.

Dogs have to stay away from the park's fun little petting zoo, which contains such cuties as goats, rabbits, chickens, a sheep, a pig, and a very friendly

DIVERSION

A Moveable Beast: If you and your dog want to get a feel for Sacramento before you start exploring on your own, Jake highly recommends a carriage ride through the charming old part of town.

The folks who run the **Top Hand Ranch Carriage Company** are more than happy to take you and your well-behaved dog on a carriage tour around the more quaint section of Sacramento. As long as your dog doesn't interfere with the horse who's pulling this old-style carriage, he'll be welcome on any of the rides offered by Top Hand Ranch.

You'll find the carriage somewhere on the streets of Old Sacramento just about every day and on weekend nights. The price for a 10- to 15-minute ride is $10 for a small family (including a dog). A river park ride is $35 and lasts about a half hour. For a higher fee, you can arrange to go just about anywhere in the carriage. The capitol building is a frequent request. That tour takes roughly one hour and will cost you about $50. Call 916/655-3444 for locations and prices.

---

turkey. But they'll soon forget their disappointment when they learn that well-behaved pooches are permitted on the hand-built miniature train that travels on a quarter mile of track in the park.

A $4 vehicle entrance fee is in effect early April–Labor Day. From U.S. 50, exit at Mather Field Road and drive north a few blocks to Folsom Boulevard. Turn right at Folsom and in a few more blocks, head left on Coloma Road. In a few more blocks, go left on Chase Drive and follow it another nine blocks to the park. 916/362-1841.

PLACES TO STAY

AmeriSuites: Oh, Toto, there's no place like home. Actually, if your home is very clean, comfortable, quiet, roomy, and dog friendly, there *is* a place like home: the AmeriSuites hotel.

Every "room" at this hotel is actually a suite, with a living room (complete with sofa sleeper, easy chair, and desk area), separate bedroom, fridge, and cable TV with VCR player. It's a real boon to have all this space and all these amenities when traveling with a dog. Your suite comes with a complimentary extended breakfast buffet, as well as use of the heated outdoor pool and the fitness center. Rates are $69–139. Dogs are $35 per stay. 10744 Gold Center Drive 95670; 916/635-4799; www.amerisuites.com.

Days Inn: This inn is about a mile from the American River. Rates are $75. 12249 Folsom Boulevard 95670; 916/351-1213.

Quality Inn and Suites: Rates are $69–75. 3240 Mather Field Road 95670; 916/363-3344.

Sacramento

This is a capital place to be a dog. There are now five off-leash parks, with three more in the offing! The ones that have been around a while seem to get frequent face-lifts; the three upcoming parks are each slated to be a solid two acres. That's the way to do it, Sacramento!

PARKS, BEACHES, AND RECREATION AREAS

8 Tanzanite Dog Park

🐾🐾🐾🐾🐕 (See Sacramento County map on page 364)

Sacramento's newest addition to its fleet of dog-friendly parks is this lovely two-acre grassy, fenced park with all the usual dog-park amenities, including water, some trees, and benches. But it has something no other dog parks have: a mosaic mural of dogs playing sports. Very cute! Maybe it will help distract your dog from the off-limits pond just beyond reach of the dog park.

The park is within Tanzanite Community Park, at 2220 Tanzanite Way. It's just northeast of the intersection of I-80 and I-5, and fairly convenient if your dog is crossing his legs on a road trip. From I-80, exit at Truxel Road (east of I-5) and drive north about a half mile to Natomas Crossing Drive. Go left, and at the next block, Innovator Drive, go left again. Drive four blocks until the street dead ends at Tanzanite Way, turn right, and you'll see the park. 916/264-5200.

9 Discovery Regional Park

🐾🐾🐾 (See Sacramento County map on page 364)

Lots of leashed urban dogs stroll down here for their early evening walks, dragging their work-weary people behind them. The park has 275 acres of green open space, and although much of it is devoted to human activities such as archery and softball, there's more than enough room for your average dog to take an average walk. It's nothing your dog will write home about, but since he can't write anyway, it's no fur off his back.

This is a fine place to start a walk on the American River Parkway (see the introduction to this chapter for more on the parkway's new dog-friendly ways). Water dogs enjoy Discovery Regional Park because it's at the confluence of the American and Sacramento rivers. The banks are steep, so it's hard to reach out and touch the rivers. But they sure do look good.

Many people walk here with their dogs and avoid the $4 entry fee that is occasionally charged. If you're driving from the north end of the city, take I-5 to the Garden Highway, drive east, and take the first road to the right, Discovery Park Road. 916/875-6961.

10 Howe About Dogs Park

😾😾😾 🐕 (See Sacramento County map on page 364)

This was the very first dog park in Sacramento, and it helped pave the way for the others in the city. The park is on Howe Avenue, thus the name (actually, it's a longer story, but you can ask the folks there), and it has trees, a picnic table, benches, and quite a bit of grass.

Unfortunately it's small—a little over a quarter acre—which can make it a bit of a menagerie on weekends.

The park is within Howe Community Park, at Howe Avenue and Cottage Way (a few blocks north of Arden Way). 916/264-5200.

11 Bannon Creek Park Dog Park

😾😾😾 🐕 (See Sacramento County map on page 364)

At just over a half acre, Bannon Creek Park is one of the smallest of the city's dog parks. But it's a lovely one, with grass and mature shade-giving trees. Amenities include benches, a pooch drinking fountain, and poop bags. We like the comfortable, lush setting. (At least it was lush when we visited.) It's in Bannon Creek Park, on Bannon Creek Drive off Azevedo Drive. 916/264-5200.

12 Granite Park Dog Park

😾😾😾 🐕 (See Sacramento County map on page 364)

Dogs enjoy chasing each other around this two-acre fenced park almost as much as their people enjoy chatting with each other. This is a very social place to bring a pooch. The park's trees are in the sapling stage, so they don't give much shade, but there's water if your pooch gets thirsty. The park was recently remodeled and is looking even better. The park is in Granite Regional Park, on Ramona Avenue off Power Inn Road. 916/264-5200.

13 Partner Park

😾😾😾😾 🐕 (See Sacramento County map on page 364)

You and your pooch partner are sure to enjoy a romp at this 2.5-acre fenced park. It's an extremely popular place among people with pooches. The park is gorgeous, with rolling hills, green grass, and mature trees that give wonderful shade—definitely a cut above most fenced dog parks. A pathway wanders out to the hills, so if you want to get away from the cluster of dogs and people in the well-used part of the park, you can take a little hike. Amenities include water, poop bags, benches, and lights.

Partner Park is behind Belle Cooledge Community Center at 5699 South Land Park Drive. Parking is behind the center. 916/264-5200.

🐾 William Land Park

🐾🐾🐾 (See Sacramento County map on page 364)

As you enter this 236-acre park, you may be struck by the thought that it looks just like a golf course. Now hold on to that thought and look around very carefully. See those shiny sticks glimmering in the background and those people in white-and-green outfits walking forward at a determined pace or standing around scratching their heads? Those are golfers. Joe Dog, Nisha Dog, and I learned this the hard way one day when we bounded out of our car and directly into the line of fire of a golfer quite some distance away. Nisha immediately tried to eat the ball. It was not a walk I care to remember, nor, I'm sure, was it a game the golfer remembers fondly.

The golf course is not fenced off from most of the rest of the park, so you really do have to be careful here. A safe, shaded section of the park is at the north end. Since dogs must be leashed, it doesn't matter that a couple of little roads run fairly close. If you brought along the kids and someone to watch them, they can go explore the zoo and the amusement park on the other side of the park.

You can reach the park's north side by taking Riverside Boulevard (parallel to I-5) to 12th Avenue and turning east. 916/264-5200.

🐾 Capitol Park

🐾🐾🐾 (See Sacramento County map on page 364)

Your boy dog will be overwhelmed if you bring him here for the Capitol Park Tree Tour, a self-guided tour of this 40-acre park's magnificent assemblage of trees, which represent the continents and climates of the world. On the tour brochure, each tree is numbered, and its scientific and common names are given. So when your leashed dog sniffs at or does a leg lift on a dawn redwood tree, you can impress him by saying, "That's quite a *Metasequoia glyptostroboides*, eh, Spot?"

The park extends from the front of the state capitol building to several blocks behind it. It's a great excuse to get up close and personal with the capitol. Take a picnic and relax under the shade of a *Calocedrus decurrens* (incense cedar).

Warning: If your dog has any hint of terrier in him, you may not want to bring him here. Squirrels are everywhere. Joe Dog once pulled my arm so hard I thought I wouldn't be able to drive home. And the squirrels are probably still talking about the loud howling shrieks that emanated from that refined-looking Airedale's face.

The park runs from the capitol back to 15th Street, between L and N streets. Call 916/324-0333 to receive a tree-tour brochure.

PLACES TO EAT

Café Bernardo: The food at this midtown cafe is tasty and reasonably priced, and the service friendly—especially if you're a dog! "We make dog biscuits in house," a manager tells us. "And of course, we give bowls of water in case your dog is thirsty." This kind of dog-friendliness has led to the occasional impromptu "yappy hour" among people with dogs. As for human food, the café's salmon BLT has a stellar reputation around these parts. I was smitten by the rosemary chicken pizza, which is graced by just the right amount of goat cheese and caramelized onion. Dogs can dine with you at the covered outdoor patio area. A big thanks to California travel expert Barbara Steinberg for cluing us into this terrific eatery. 2726 Capitol Avenue; 916/443-1180.

Danielle's Creperie and Gallery: While Danielle's offers about 40 varieties of crepe, crepes are just one aspect of the delectable menu of Americanized French cuisine at this delightful restaurant. ("Americanized" means, in part, that you will be hard-pressed to find brains or organ meats on the menu.) The soups, salads, sandwiches, and appetizers are flavorful and fresh. The French onion soup is worth the price of admission. As Danielle's boasts, it "is the best you will ever taste."

Your dog is welcome to join you at the many umbrella-shaded patio seats. "Of course we allow dogs!" exclaimed a server. It wouldn't be a real French eatery if they didn't. If possible, take a peek inside the restaurant, where you'll find lots of intriguing art and sculptures—all of it for sale, and all of it displayed for just 45 days at a time. 3535-B Fair Oaks Boulevard; 916/972-1911.

PLACES TO STAY

Doubletree Hotel: Dogs under 50 pounds are welcome here. Rates are $99–395. Dogs are $50 for the length of their stay. 2001 Point West Way 95815; 916/929-8855.

Motel 6: Rates are $46–58. 1415 30th Street 95816; 916/457-0777.

Radisson Hotel: "We're very dog-friendly here!" says a front desk person, and she's right. During a recent stay, there were dogs walking up and down the lovely paths as if they owned the place. The rooms here are pleasant and clean, and it's nice because although the hotel has lots of rooms, it's only two levels (it's very spread out). Some rooms provide a water dog with views of the ultimate temptation—a little lake on the hotel's property. But sorry, dogs: No dog paddling is allowed here, or in the hotel's pool. Rates are $109–197. Dogs pay a $50 flat fee for their stay and require a $50 deposit. 500 Leisure Lane 95815; 916/922-2020.

Quality Inn: Dogs under 45 pounds are welcome here. Rates for humans are $50–70. Dogs are $25 extra. Be sure to declare your dog (as in "I have a dog with me," not "My dog is the best in the world, I do declare!") because if you sneak him in and get caught, you'll be charged $250. 3796 Northgate Boulevard 95834; 916/927-7117.

Sheraton Grand Sacramento Hotel: If you've never stayed in a restored Public Market Building, this is your chance. This historic marketplace has become a very attractive, dog-friendly hotel. All sizes of dogs are welcome, and they get treats upon arrival and use of a comfy dog bed and doggy bowls. Humans get use of the heated outdoor pool and decent fitness center. Rates are $99–349. Dogs require a $100 deposit. 1230 J Street 95814; 916/447-1700.

Elk Grove

This 130-square-mile service area (it's not really a city) now has two dog parks.

PARKS, BEACHES, AND RECREATION AREAS

16 Laguna Community Park Dog Park
🐾🐾🐕 (See Sacramento County map on page 364)

Dogs are loving this half-acre fenced park almost to death. "It's getting worn out," says a park worker. "It's overused." The grass is a bit on the worn-out side, and it's not the largest dog park in the world, but it's still a fine place to take a dog in need of leash-free romping room. The park has water, poop bags, a little shade, and benches. It's at Big Horn Boulevard and Bruceville Road. 916/405-7150.

17 Elk Grove Dog Park
🐾🐾🐾🐾🐕 (See Sacramento County map on page 364)

This dog park, the newer of Elk Grove's two, might help take the burden off Laguna's dog park. It's a lovely one, with two acres, shade from redwoods, and most of the other usual dog park amenities. The dog park is within the 127-acre Elk Grove Regional Park, which is at 8820 Elk Grove Boulevard. The dog park is on the park's west side. 916/405-7150.

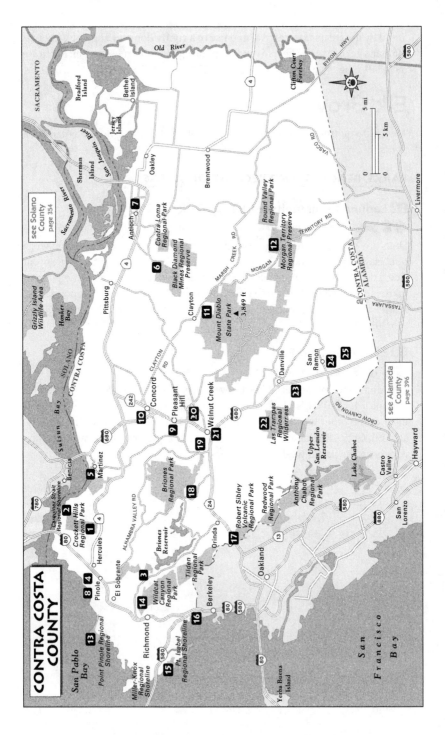

CHAPTER 32

Contra Costa County

Although much of Contra Costa County is considered a sleepy bedroom community for San Francisco, it's a rip-roaring frontierland of fun for dogs. From the renowned off-leash dog haven of the Point Isabel Regional Shoreline to the leash-free inland nirvanas of the East Bay Regional Park District (such as the Morgan Territory, in Clayton), this county enables every dog to have her day, day after day. (For more on the wonders of the East Bay Regional Park District, see the introduction to the *Alameda County* chapter.)

For dogs who like long hikes through highly diverse lands, 10 long regional trails lace Lafayette, Walnut Creek, and the other urban areas of the Diablo Valley. There are 60 miles of trails in all, linking a dozen towns and many beautiful parklands. Dogs must be leashed, but with all the horses and bikes that can visit here, it's a sensible rule.

The Briones to Diablo Regional Trail is one of the more popular trails. It's about 12 miles long and it snakes through some terrific parkland, including the off-leash wonderlands of the Acalanes Ridge Open Space Recreation Area and the Shell Ridge Open Space Recreation Area (both described in the *Walnut Creek* section). The trail, which is part paved/part dirt, starts at Briones Regional Park's Lafayette Ridge Staging Area, on Pleasant Hill Road just north of Highway 24.

PICK OF THE LITTER—CONTRA COSTA COUNTY

BEST OFF-LEASH HIKING
Crockett Hills Regional Park, Crockett (page 380)
Sobrante Ridge Regional Preserve, El Sobrante (page 382)
Black Diamond Mines Regional Preserve, Antioch (page 384)
Morgan Territory Regional Preserve, Clayton (page 387)
Briones Regional Park, Lafayette (page 392)
Las Trampas Regional Wilderness, Danville (page 394)

BEST DOG PARK
The Paw Patch, Concord (page 386)

BEST RESTAURANT NAME (DOG'S PERSPECTIVE)
The Dead Fish, Crockett (page 381)

BEST OFF-LEASH BEACH
Point Isabel Regional Shoreline, Richmond (page 390)

BEST CHURCH
**First Presbyterian Church of Richmond drive-in church
services,** Pinole (page 383)

The Contra Costa Canal Regional Trail is a good one for dogs who like to look at water but not set foot in it. We love this 12-mile trail, which follows the (off-limits) canal. For information and a trail map of all 10 regional trails, or for information on all the East Bay Regional Park District parklands, call 888/327-2757, or go to www.ebparks.org.

Crockett

PARKS, BEACHES, AND RECREATION AREAS

1 Crockett Hills Regional Park
😊😊😊😊🐾 (See Contra Costa County map on page 378)
This 2,000-acre beauty gets less paw traffic than many of the other East Bay Regional Park District lands, but it's probably because it's relatively new and word hasn't gotten out yet among the canine crowd.

Crockett Hills is excellent for well-behaved dogs who enjoy running around the great outdoors naked (without a leash). From shade-giving eucalyptus groves and oak woodland to rolling grasslands to rippling riverfront, the park has something for every dog's taste—unless their taste consists only of shopping at Saks. Late winter is a good time to visit if you like your hills soft and green rather than crunchy brown.

Several miles of trails—mostly fire roads, actually—run through the park. A four-mile segment of the Bay Area Ridge Trail cuts a path through. Views from some points along the way include Mt. Tamalpais, Mt. Diablo, and the Carquinez Strait. Jake likes visiting the staging area, where there's an old barn and a picnic area. Dogs have to be leashed in this section, but if they're under voice control, they don't need leashes in the rest of the park.

From northbound Highway 80, take the Port Costa/Crockett exit (Exit 27), turn left on Pomona Street, drive a few blocks, and go right on Crockett Boulevard, then turn right at the staging area. 888/327-2757.

PLACES TO EAT

The Dead Fish: The name alone is a draw for dogs. Jake has rolled in many a dead fish at the beach, and so have some of his best friends. But those dead fish stink. The dead fish at The Dead Fish don't. The cuisine here is all about fresh fish, but if you're not a fish fan, look around the menu a bit to find burgers, chicken, and some delectable side dishes, including a house favorite: garlic sage French fries.

How did this place get its moniker? Chef Andrea Froncillo explains that when he was a lad in Italy, his grandmother loved cooking the catch of the day. But whenever he asked her what kind of fish she was cooking, she never remembered. "She would shrug her shoulders and smile. *'It's a dead fish!'* Everyone laughed and had a great time."

The doggy dining area is top notch. Dogs are welcome to join you at the attractive large covered patio that overlooks the Carquinez Strait and the Carquinez Bridge. Dogs get a bowl of water if they're thirsty. 20050 San Pablo Avenue; 510/787-3323.

Port Costa

Port Costa is a sleepy, picturesque town of Victorian cottages. In the 19th century, it was a booming wheat export dock. Of course, if your dog remembers the Frank Norris book *The Octopus*, he already knows this.

PARKS, BEACHES, AND RECREATION AREAS

2 Carquinez Strait Regional Shoreline

😾 😾 😾 😾 🐕 (See Contra Costa County map on page 378)

This regional shoreline, run by East Bay Regional Parks, lies just east of Crockett. From the Bull Valley Staging Area, on Carquinez Scenic Drive, you can choose one of two leash-free hillside trails. The Carquinez Overlook Loop, to the right, gives better views of Port Costa, the Carquinez Bridge, and Benicia. We once surprised a deer here sleeping in the shade of a clump of eucalyptus.

The eastern part of the park, east of Port Costa, is contiguous with Martinez Regional Shoreline. But beware: You can't get there from here. (Carquinez Scenic Drive is closed at a spot between Port Costa and Martinez. You must turn south on twisty McEwen Road to Highway 4 instead.)

To get to the Carquinez Strait Regional Shoreline from I-80, exit at Crockett and drive east on Pomona Street through town. Pomona turns into Carquinez Scenic Drive, from which you'll see the staging area. 888/327-2757.

El Sobrante

PARKS, BEACHES, AND RECREATION AREAS

🖪 Sobrante Ridge Regional Preserve

🐾🐾🐾🐕 (See Contra Costa County map on page 378)

This 277-acre preserve brims with deer, coyotes, salamanders, and oodles of birds. Unless your dog is under perfect voice control, it's a good idea to use a leash here. From the Coach Way entrance, follow the dirt trail branching back to the left 100 feet from the entrance. This is the Sobrante Ridge Trail, which will take you through grass, dwarf manzanita, oaks, and coyote brush, up a half mile to views of both Mt. Tam and the top of Mt. Diablo. Branch off on the short loop, Broken Oaks Trail, for a picnic at one of the tables under cool oaks.

This 277-acre preserve is the habitat of the extremely rare Alameda manzanita. So that your dog knows what to watch out for, this manzanita is a gnarled, red-barked shrub that may have sprays of urn-shaped blossoms or clusters of red berries, depending on the time of year. The manzanitas cling to the hillsides. Don't let your boy dog do anything the manzanitas wouldn't want him to do.

From I-80 in Richmond, exit at San Pablo Dam Road and drive south to Castro Ranch Road. Turn left on Castro Ranch, then left at Conestoga Way, going into the Carriage Hills housing development. Take another left on Carriage Drive and a right on Coach Way. Park at the end of Coach and walk into the preserve. 888/327-2757.

Pinole

PARKS, BEACHES, AND RECREATION AREAS

🛽 Pinole Valley Park

🐾🐾🐾🐕 (See Contra Costa County map on page 378)

This city park is fortunate enough to be contiguous with Sobrante Ridge Regional Preserve. The paved bike path off to the right past the children's

DIVERSION

Drive Your Pooch to the Pulpit: Want to take your dog to church? If you don't think he's ready to pray in a pew, you can bring him along to attend a service in the comfort of your car. Since 1975, the **First Presbyterian Church of Richmond** has offered a drive-in service in a shopping mall parking lot. Held at 8:30 A.M. every Sunday outside the Appian 80 shopping center in Pinole, the ceremony attracts a few dozen worshippers every week.

Steve Niccolls, who taught junior high for almost 20 years and is a seminary student, is a popular preacher and "has a heart for the drive-in ministry," says his wife, Emily.

Steve transmits the service over shortwave radio from a mobile pulpit, complete with a sermon and choral music. On the first Sunday of each month, church elders bring communion around to each car on a silver platter. Parishioners honk and flash their headlights at Steve to say "Amen." It's quite a scene—and afterward you can go shopping. Dogs are as welcome to attend as anyone, and three dogs are there almost weekly. (They read about it in a previous edition of this book and dragged their people there.) Other animals are also welcome: Peepers the Duck usually makes a weekly appearance as well.

Exit I-80 at Appian Way. The shopping center is just north of the freeway, on the west side of Appian Way, Pinole. For more information, call 510/234-0954.

---

playground leads to Alhambra Creek—a good plunge for your dog if he can negotiate the banks wearing a leash. The path then becomes a fire trail and ambles through brush, oaks, and nicely varied deciduous trees. This trail is quite wild and litter-free. It ends at an outlet on Alhambra Road.

And joy of joys! There's a dog park within the park, between the baseball field and the barbecue pits. It's about an acre, with grass, benches, poop bags, water, and a separate section for small dogs. It's fun to mix a little off-leash romp with a leashed walk around the rest of the attractive park.

The entrance to the main park is at Pinole Valley Road and Simas Avenue. 510/724-9002.

Martinez

Martinez has a charming historic district right off the entrance to its regional shoreline park, so spend some time walking with your dog around the Amtrak station and antique shops. You'll see plenty of fellow strollers taking a break from the train.

PARKS, BEACHES, AND RECREATION AREAS

5 Hidden Lakes Open Space

😊😊😊😊 🐕 (See Contra Costa County map on page 378)

Although the city park called Hidden Valley Park doesn't allow dogs, the open space to the south of it does. It's crossed by one of the East Bay Regional Parks' trails (the California Riding and Hiking Trail) on its way from the Carquinez Strait Regional Shoreline to where it connects with the Contra Costa Canal Trail. Call 888/327-2757 or see www.ebparks.org for maps of the Contra Costa Regional Trails.

One entrance to Hidden Lakes is off Morello Avenue, where it intersects with Chilpancingo Parkway.

Antioch

Antioch is pretty much a desert for dogs, but south of town are two charming spots of relief.

PARKS, BEACHES, AND RECREATION AREAS

6 Black Diamond Mines Regional Preserve

😊😊😊😊 🐕 (See Contra Costa County map on page 378)

Leash-free dogs, especially leash-free dogs of the male persuasion, think this park is an excellent place to visit. The coal miners who worked and lived here in the 1860s and 1870s planted a variety of drought-tolerant trees not usually found in the East Bay, including something called "trees of heaven." Dogs who sniff these trees seem to know why they're called trees of heaven. Their noses just can't get enough as they press them deep into the bark.

The hills of Black Diamond Mines are jumbled and ragged, looking a lot like the Sierra foothills. From the parking lot, it's a moderate climb to the Rose Hill Cemetery, where Protestant Welsh miners (the tombstones bear the names Davis, Evans, and Jenkins) buried victims of mine accidents and many of their children, who died of diphtheria, typhoid, and scarlet fever.

Plenty of tunnel openings and piles of tailings have been preserved by the park for walkers to examine. A brochure marks mine sites. You should be alert for rattlers during warm seasons, although any rattler not actually snoozing will probably get out of your way before you even know he's near.

You can walk into this East Bay regional preserve from the Contra Loma Regional Park just below it. But from that direction, the trails are too hot and dry for a dog in summer. Instead, enter from the north by car via Somersville Road and park in the last lot, which has some shady trees.

It's $6 to park here. Dogs are $2 extra. Backpack camping is available for $5.

From Highway 4 at Antioch, exit at Somersville Road and drive south to the park entrance. Keep driving for a bit more than one mile if you want to park in the lot farthest in. You'll pass wonderful old mining-era houses and barns, now used as park headquarters and offices. 888/327-2757.

7 Contra Loma Regional Park

😺😺😺😺🐕 (See Contra Costa County map on page 378)

This 776-acre park is so well hidden amid the barren hills north of Black Diamond Mines that you might not ever know it is here. A few attractive trails, including a trail leading into Black Diamond Mines Regional Preserve, rise into the surrounding hills for you and your leash-free dog to explore. Dogs can be off leash in the backcountry. You'll know it when you see it.

Unfortunately, as in all regional parks, your dog may not accompany you in the swimming area, nor can he take an informal swim in the fishing areas, since park managers want to protect his feet from stray fishhooks. It's probably better not to bring your dog here on a hot day. Instead, save the trip for winter or spring, when the wildflowers burst open.

From Highway 4, take the Lone Tree Way exit. Go south on Lone Tree for a little more than a half mile, then turn right onto Bluerock Drive. Follow Bluerock along the park's east side to the entrance. The fee for parking is $6. The dog fee is $2. 888/327-2757.

Hercules

PARKS, BEACHES, AND RECREATION AREAS

8 San Pablo Bay Shoreline Park

😺😺😺🐕 (See Contra Costa County map on page 378)

This tiny, undeveloped East Bay Regional Park shoreline is just right if you happen to be in Hercules exploring the old Santa Fe Railroad yard. A paved trail runs about 0.12 mile along the tracks. New housing developments and interesting restored Victorian railroad workers' housing surround a small but pretty area of grass, swamp, and eucalyptus trees. Best of all, you and your dog can check it all out without a leash.

If you follow Railroad Avenue to its end, across the line into Pinole, there's a very small and beautifully landscaped city park behind the wastewater treatment plant (which smells fresh as a rose). You must keep your dog on leash here.

From I-80, exit at Pinole Valley Road and travel north. Pinole Valley Road becomes Tennent Avenue, then Railroad Avenue. Park somewhere around the Civic Arts Facility, a cluster of Victorian buildings in a grove of palms and eucalyptus. 888/327-2757.

Pleasant Hill

PARKS, BEACHES, AND RECREATION AREAS

9 Paso Nogal Park

😺😺😺😺🐕 (See Contra Costa County map on page 378)

This large open-space park has the best of both worlds: smooth dirt trails along gentle oak-dotted slopes, where leashed dogs can hike to their hearts' content, and a fenced park where they can throw off their leashes and run like the wind. The dog park has a small-dog section, benches, tables, water, and good parking. It's grassy and surrounded by trees. The trees within the park are nothing but glorified sticks right now, but they'll grow.

The dog park is open Monday–Saturday and is closed Sunday for maintenance. On Tuesdays it's closed until 1 P.M. To help preserve the lush grass, it's also closed when the ground is wet. (This can be weeks at a time during rainy season.) The park is at Morello Avenue and Paso Nogal Road. 925/682-0896.

Concord

PARKS, BEACHES, AND RECREATION AREAS

10 The Paw Patch

😺😺😺😺🐕 (See Contra Costa County map on page 378)

The grass truly is always greener on the other side of the fence at this wonderful 2.5-acre dog park. It's so green and lush that it has other dog parks green with envy. Dog parks with grass (a.k.a. turf) often struggle in vain against a tide of pounding paws. The grass can end up anything but green and rather downtrodden. But not the grass here—the park district folks work hard to maintain it. In fact, they recently won a coveted award for their turf management from the California Parks and Recreation Society.

There's more to this park than grass, though. It's got benches, water, poop bags, a smaller fenced area for small dogs, and lots of toys. The lucky dogs who come here get to sniff through a toy box set out by volunteers, and pick out a favorite toy to play with here, or they find toys scattered around the grass.

The park is within the lovely 126-acre Newhall Community Park. You can take your dog around the park on a leash. From the top of the hill you're rewarded with great views of everything from Mount Diablo to the Carquinez Straits. (This is where you'll also find a Vietnam War memorial.) The park is at Turtle Creek Road and Ayres Road. 925/671-3444.

Clayton
PARKS, BEACHES, AND RECREATION AREAS

🔟 Clayton Dog Park
🐾🐾🐕 (See Contra Costa County map on page 378)

Big oaks are adjacent to this dog park, but there's very little shade within. A dirt lot has wood chips, but dog people pine for grass. Yet for all its little foibles, this is a perfectly decent place to take a dog for an off-leash romp. It may not be the Ritz, but it's not a dive either. It has a picnic table, two benches, poop bags, and water, and it's along the Creek Trail, which makes for a fine leashed dog walk. The park is on Marsh Creek Road and Regency Drive, across from Clayton Park. 925/673-7300.

🔢 Morgan Territory Regional Preserve
🐾🐾🐾🐾🐕 (See Contra Costa County map on page 378)

Morgan Territory, named after a farmer who owned the land long before it became part of the East Bay Regional Parks system, is as far away from the Bay Area as you can get while still being in the Bay Area. From its heights, on a rim above the Central Valley, you see the San Joaquin River, the Delta, the valley, and, on a clear day, the peaks of the Sierra. Eagles and hawks soar above as you and your leash-free pooch explore ancient twisted giant oaks and lichen-covered sandstone outcrops below. Morgan Territory is close to the end of the earth and well worth the journey.

As the crow flies, Morgan Territory is equidistant from Clayton, Danville, San Ramon, Livermore, Byron, and Brentwood. And "distant" is the key word.

This 4,147-acre preserve has miles of hiking and riding trails. If you don't want to climb much but want great views of the Central Valley, try the Blue Oak Trail, which starts at the entrance. You'll even see the "back side" of Mt. Diablo. It's an unusual vantage point for Bay Area folks.

Most of the creeks are dry in the summer, though your dog can splash into cattle ponds, if he's so inclined. Watch for wicked foxtails in these grasses. These are the sticky wickets that help make veterinarians a well-off breed.

The easiest access is from Livermore in Alameda County. From I-580, take the North Livermore Avenue exit and drive north on North Livermore Avenue. Shortly after the road curves left (west), turn right, onto Morgan Territory Road, and follow it 10.7 miles to the entrance. From the Walnut Creek/Concord area, take Clayton Road to Marsh Creek Road, then turn right onto Morgan Territory Road. The entrance is 9.4 miles from Marsh Creek Road. 888/327-2757.

Richmond

Point Richmond, the Richmond neighborhood tucked between the Richmond-San Rafael Bridge and Miller-Knox Regional Shoreline, is a cheerful small-town hangout for you and your dog. Consider stopping by for a snack on your way to some of the magical, four-paw shoreline here.

Sit on a bench in the Point Richmond Triangle, the town center. You'll be surrounded by nicely preserved Victorian buildings, the Hotel Mac, and many delis and bakeries, some with outdoor tables. The Santa Fe Railroad rattles past periodically, blowing the first two notes of "Here Comes the Bride."

From I-580, on the Richmond end of the Richmond–San Rafael Bridge, exit at Cutting Boulevard and drive west to town. Bear right on Richmond Avenue. The Triangle is at the intersection of Richmond and Washington avenues and Park Place.

PARKS, BEACHES, AND RECREATION AREAS

13 Point Pinole Regional Shoreline

🐾🐾🐾🐾🐕 (See Contra Costa County map on page 378)

Of all the East Bay Regional Parks' shorelines, this is the farthest from civilization and its discontents, and thus the cleanest and least spoiled. It's also huge and a heavenly walk for dog or owner, with its views of Mt. Tamalpais across San Pablo Bay, and its docks, salt marsh, beaches, eucalyptus groves, and expanses of wild grassland waving in the breeze. Some of the eucalyptus trees are so wind-carved they could be mistaken for cypresses.

The park has fine bike paths, and your dog should be leashed for safety on these, but he's free on the unpaved trails—even on the dirt paths through marshes, such as the Marsh Trail. Just make sure he stays on the trail and doesn't go into the marsh itself. Dogs may not go on the fishing pier or on the shuttle bus to the pier.

From I-80, exit at Hilltop Drive, go west and take a right on San Pablo Avenue, then left on Atlas Road to the park entrance. There's a $6 parking fee and a $2 dog fee. 888/327-2757.

14 Wildcat Canyon Regional Park

🐾🐾🐾🐾🐕 (See Contra Costa County map on page 378)

This is Tilden Regional Park's northern twin. Tilden (see the *Berkeley* section of the *Alameda County* chapter) has its attractive spots, but it's designed for people. Wildcat seems made for dogs, because not much goes on here. Dogs really dig this. Who needs all those human feet passing by anyway? (Unless, of course, they're tracking eau de cow patty or some other savory scent.) Best of all, in many areas you can leave your dog's leash tucked away in your pocket.

DIVERSION

Foof 'Er Up: Is your pooch starting to smell like a dog? If you go to Point Isabel, you can give your dog both the walk of his life and a bath. **Mudpuppy's Tub and Scrub,** the park's very own dog wash, offers full- or self-service scrubbings in several elevated tubs. The cost is very reasonable, considering it includes shampoo, drying, and someone else to clean the tub afterward. And not only can your dog get unmuddy and downright gorgeous here, he can go home with some pretty doggone nice pooch items, too. Mudpuppy's offers a full line of dog toys, treats, and gifts. Owners Eddie Lundeen and Daniel Bergerac provide a fun, clean atmosphere. Call or stop by before your walk in the park to reserve your tub. (The earlier you do so, the better, especially on weekends.)

And here's some great news for your dog's best friend. (That would be you.) Mudpuppy's has a café next door, **Mudpuppy's Sit and Stay Café.** It has a walk-up window so you and your dog can get some delectable goodies for humans, including espresso, tasty pastries, warming soups (usually featuring one veggie variety and something hearty), chili, great sandwiches, and ice cream. The café makes this area one of the most dog-friendly and dog person–friendly around. Eat, drink, walk, talk, buy, suds, scrub, enjoy.

Mudpuppy's is in the first parking lot inside the park, off Isabel Road, Richmond. 510/559-8899; www.mudpuppys.com.

And you'll get a good dose of nature here: Large coast live oaks, madrones, bay laurels, chaparral, and all kinds of wildflowers thrive in this parkland.

At the main parking lot is Wildcat Creek, which gets low but usually not entirely dry in summer. Then you can follow the Wildcat Creek Trail (actually an abandoned paved road; dogs must be leashed on this trail); it travels gently uphill and then follows the southern ridge of the park. Or follow any of the nameless side trails, which are wonderfully wild and solitary. You can hear train whistles all the way up from Emeryville and the dull roar of civilization below, but somehow it doesn't bother you up here.

Other trails lead through groves of pines or follow Wildcat Creek. The park is roughly three miles long. Dogs are banned—even on leash—from wetlands, marshes, and ponds. And if you come to the boundary with Tilden, remember that dogs aren't allowed in the nature area across the line.

From I-80, southbound, take the McBryde exit and turn left on McBryde Avenue to the park entrance. If you're northbound, take the Amador/Solano exit. Go three blocks north on Amador Street and turn right (east) on McBryde to the entrance. 888/327-2757.

15 Miller-Knox Regional Shoreline

🐾🐾🐾🐾 🐕 (See Contra Costa County map on page 378)

Hooray! Wooooof! Yap! Although your dog must be leashed in developed areas, she can run free on the hillside trails east of Dornan Drive in this 259-acre park.

West of Dornan is a generous expanse of grass, pine, and eucalyptus trees with picnic tables, a lagoon with egrets (so there's no swimming), and Keller Beach (dogs are prohibited). It's breezy here and prettier than most shoreline parks by virtue of its protecting gentle hills, whose trails offer terrific views of the Richmond-San Rafael Bridge, Mt. Tamalpais, Angel Island, and San Francisco. Ground squirrels stand right by their holes and pipe their alarms. Although you can't bring your dog onto Keller Beach, there's a paved path above it along riprap shoreline, where your dog can reach the water if he's so inclined. In the picnic areas, watch for discarded chicken bones!

You can also tour the Richmond Yacht Harbor by continuing on Dornan Drive south to Brickyard Cove Road, a left turn past the railroad tracks. Or, from Garrard Boulevard, drive south till you see the Brickyard Cove housing development. The paved paths lining the harbor offer views of yachts, San Francisco, Oakland, and the Bay Bridge.

From either I-80 or I-580, exit at Cutting Boulevard and go west to Garrard Boulevard. Go left, pass through a tunnel, and park in one of two lots off Dornan Drive. 888/327-2757.

16 Point Isabel Regional Shoreline

🐾🐾🐾🐾 🐕 (See Contra Costa County map on page 378)

With so many Bay Area beaches either outright banning dogs or enforcing new leash demands, it not easy being a water dog around here these days. Thank goodness for this 21-acre patch of utter water-dog heaven! Dogs are so happy when they come here that some howl as they arrive in their cars. (Some owners do, too, but they're another story.)

Point Isabel is an exception to the East Bay Regional Parks' rule that dogs must be on leash in "developed" areas. This is a decidedly unwild but terrific shoreline park with plenty of grass and paw-friendly paved paths. It's swarming with dogs. In a census by the park district, 558,930 people and 784,370 pooches visited in one year. Fortunately, people here are generally very responsible, and the park looks pretty good, despite being assailed by more than four million feet and paws annually.

The large lawn area is perfect for fetching, Frisbee throwing, and chasing each other around. And the bay and the sand, ahh... these are a water dog's delight. The surf here is usually very tame, making dog paddling a joy.

There are benches, picnic tables, restrooms, a water fountain for people and dogs, and many racks full of bags for scooping. Cinder paths run along the riprap waterfront, where you can watch sailboarders against a backdrop of the Golden Gate and Bay Bridges, San Francisco, the Marin Headlands, and Mt. Tamalpais. On a brisk day, a little surf even splashes against the rocks.

After a wet and wonderful walk, you may want to take your pooch to Mudpuppy's Tub and Scrub, which is right here, for a little cleaning up. And after that, if you've been a very good human, you can treat yourself to a cuppa Joe and some café cuisine at the new Mudpuppy's Sit and Stay Café. Talk about a people and pooch paradise. (See the Diversion *Foof 'Er Up*.)

From I-80 in Richmond, exit at Central Avenue and go west to the park entrance, next to the U.S. Postal Service Bulk Mail Center. For more info on the park or its wonderful doggy user group, PIDO (Point Isabel Dog Owners and Friends—why isn't it called PIDOF?), see www.pido.org. 888/327-2757.

Orinda

PARKS, BEACHES, AND RECREATION AREAS

🔢 Robert Sibley Volcanic Regional Preserve

🐾🐾🐾🐾🐕 (See Contra Costa County map on page 378)

We're not exactly talking Mt. St. Helens here, but this 371-acre park has some pretty interesting volcanic history. Geologically inclined dogs can wander leashless as you explore volcanic dikes, mudflows, lava flows, and other evidence of extinct volcanoes.

The preserve is actually closer to Oakland than Orinda, but it lies in Contra Costa County. From the entrance on Skyline Boulevard, you can get on the East Bay Skyline National Recreation Trail and walk north to Tilden Regional Park (see the *Berkeley* section of the *Alameda County* chapter) or south to Redwood Regional Park (see the *Oakland* section of the *Alameda County* chapter). Or, for a shorter stroll, take the road to Round Top, the highest peak in the Berkeley Hills, made of volcanic debris left over from a 10-million-year-old volcano.

More attractive and less steep is the road to the quarries. It's partly paved and smooth enough for a wheelchair or stroller, but it becomes smooth dirt about halfway to the quarries. Both trails are labeled for geological features. (Pick up a brochure at the visitors center.) At the quarry pits, there's a good view of Mt. Diablo. This is a dry, scrubby, cattle-grazed area, but in the rainy season your dog may be lucky enough to find swimming in a pit near the quarries. In the spring, look for poppies and lupines.

From Highway 24 east of the Caldecott Tunnel, exit on Fish Ranch Road, drive north to Grizzly Peak Boulevard, and then take a left. Go south on Grizzly Peak to the intersection with Skyline Boulevard. Go left on Skyline. The entrance is just to the east of the intersection. 888/327-2757.

Lafayette

PARKS, BEACHES, AND RECREATION AREAS

18 Briones Regional Park

😺😺😺😺🐾 (See Contra Costa County map on page 378)

From both main entrances to this park, you can walk 0.25 mile and be lost in sunny, rolling hills or cool oak woodlands. Unless you stick to the stream areas, it's not a good park for hot summer days. But with a good supply of your own water, you and your dog, who may run blissfully leashless, can walk gentle ups and downs all day on fire roads or foot trails.

The north entrance requires an immediate uphill climb into the hills, but you're rewarded with a quick view of Mt. Diablo and the piping of ground squirrels, all of whom are long gone safely into their burrows by the time your dog realizes they might be fun to chase. If your dog is a self-starter, this end of the park is fine for you. The Alhambra Creek Trail, which follows Alhambra Creek, does offer water in the rainy season. Stay away from the John Muir Nature Area (shaded on your brochure map), where dogs aren't allowed.

When we're feeling lazy, we prefer the south entrance at Bear Creek, just east of the inaccessible (to dogs) Briones Reservoir. Here you have an immediate choice of open hills or woodsy canyons, and the land is level for a few miles. The Homestead Valley Trail leads gently up and down through cool, sharp-scented bay and oak woodlands.

Watch for deer, horses, and cattle. Some dogs near and dear to me love rolling in fresh cow patties—an additional hazard of the beasts existing in close proximity.

From Highway 24, take the Orinda exit; go north on Camino Pablo, then right on Bear Creek Road to Briones Road, to the park entrance. The parking fee is $6 and the dog fee is $2. 888/327-2757.

Walnut Creek

PARKS, BEACHES, AND RECREATION AREAS

At press time a full-time dog park was under construction in Heather Farm Park. This is great news for those who don't rise early enough to get to San Miguel Park during its leash-free hours.

19 Acalanes Ridge Open Space Recreation Area

😺😺😺😺🐾 (See Contra Costa County map on page 378)

In 1974, the city of Walnut Creek set aside a few open spaces for a limited-use "land bank." Dogs must be "under voice or sight command" (translation: off leash if obedient). The trails are open to hikers, dogs, horses, and bicycles, however, so on a fine day, your dog may have some competition.

Acalanes Ridge, close to Briones Regional Park (see the *Lafayette* section of this chapter), is crossed by the Briones to Diablo Regional Trail. Like the others, it lacks water.

A good entry point is from Camino Verde Circle, reached by driving south on Camino Verde from the intersection of Pleasant Hill and Geary Roads. For information on any of the open spaces, call 925/944-5766.

20 San Miguel Park

🐾🐾🐾🐾 🐕 (See Contra Costa County map on page 378)

Dogs who are early risers love waking up, throwing on their leashes, coming to this park, and then throwing off their leashes. This grassy four-acre park goes to the dogs 6–9 A.M. daily. It's positively poochy here during the morning canine commute. It's not a fenced area, and that's fine with dogs. Boy dogs and shade-seekers like the park's trees.

The park is a few minutes northeast of the I-680/Highway 24 interchange. From northbound I-680, take the exit toward Ygnacio Valley Road and turn right in 0.5 mile onto Ygnacio Valley Road. In about two miles, turn right on San Carlos Drive and in 0.3 mile, go left at San Jose Court. The park is at San Jose Court, off Los Cerros Avenue. 925/943-5855.

21 Shell Ridge Open Space Recreation Area

🐾🐾🐾🐾 🐕 (See Contra Costa County map on page 378)

This huge open space was under the ocean a long, long time ago, and it's home to many marine fossils, thus its moniker. Shell Ridge has 31 miles of trails through oak woodlands and grassy hills. Dogs salivate over this because if they're under "positive voice and sight command" they're allowed to be leash-free everywhere but in the developed areas (parking lots, picnic grounds, and the historic Borges Ranch Site). They also mustn't chase the cattle that graze on the rich grasslands. That's a big no-no. If in doubt, leash.

You can enter by the Sugarloaf-Shell Ridge Trail at the north edge. From I-680, take the Ygnacio Valley Road exit, go east on Ignacio Valley Road to Walnut Avenue (not Boulevard), turn right and right again on Castle Rock Road. Go past the high school, turn right, and follow the signs. 925/942-0225.

PLACES TO EAT

Lark Creek: Enjoy farm-fresh American cuisine with your dog at this popular downtown Walnut Creek gem, co-owned by famed chef Bradley Ogden. The produce, meat, and fish are locally grown/raised/caught when possible. I realize Jake longs for me to order the Yankee pot roast or bacon-wrapped meatloaf, but dishes like English pea risotto or wood-baked flatbread with spring onions, Yukon potatoes, and applewood bacon keep appearing at our table instead. Dine with dog at the sidewalk/patio tables. 1360 Locust Street; 925/256-1234.

Stadium Pub: This popular sports pub has 30 TVs, and you can even see some of them from the outside tables where you and your dog get to dine. Jake loves this, because anything with a ball is a ball for him. The staff is friendly, there are 22 beers on tap, and if you order the Chicago-style hot dog and give a bite to your dog, she'll be your best friend forever. (Oh wait, she already is!) 1420 Lincoln Avenue at Main Street; 925/256-7302.

Va de Vi: Located smack dab between Tiffany's and Tommy Bahama, this downtown Walnut Creek restaurant is a great place to go when your paws need a break from shopping. The food, which is mainly small plates, is superb, and the wine selection is huge. After all, Va de Vi means "It's about wine," in Catalan. Wine and dine with your dog at any of several lovely patio tables. 1511 Mt. Diablo Boulevard; 925/979-0100.

PLACES TO STAY

Holiday Inn: This comfy hotel has a pool, which humans enjoy, but what's really special about this place is its proximity to a hiking trail. The staff will tell you about it at the front desk. Rates are $99–164. There's a $25 fee for the length of your dog's stay. 2730 North Main Street 94598; 925/932-3332.

Danville

PARKS, BEACHES, AND RECREATION AREAS

22 Las Trampas Regional Wilderness

🐾🐾🐾🐾 🐆 (See Contra Costa County map on page 378)

This regional wilderness is remarkable for its sense of isolation from the rest of the Bay Area. You can experience utter silence at this 3,298-acre park, and the views from the ridge tops are breathtaking.

Rocky Ridge Trail (from the parking lot at the end of Bollinger Canyon Road) takes you and your leash-free pooch on a fairly steep 0.75-mile ascent to the top of the ridge, where you'll enter the East Bay Municipal Utility District watershed. Since dogs aren't allowed here and permits are required even for humans, it's better to head west on any of several trails climbing the sunny southern flanks of Las Trampas Ridge.

Creeks run low or dry during the summer, so bring plenty of water. Your dog should know how to behave around cattle, deer, and horses.

From I-680 about six miles north of the intersection with I-580, take the Bollinger Canyon Road exit and head north on Bollinger Canyon Road to the entrance. (Go past the entrance to Little Hills Ranch Recreation Area, where dogs aren't allowed.) 888/327-2757.

23 Hap Magee Ranch Canine Corral

🐾🐾🐾 🐕 (See Contra Costa County map on page 378)

This dog park is a pretty mix of grass and wood chips, with a little shade. It has all the usual dog park accoutrements, including a separate area for small or delicate dogs. From I-680 going north, exit at El Cerro Boulevard and turn right onto El Cerro at the light. At the second light, go right at La Gonda Way. The park is on the left after the stop sign. Park in the paved lot. 925/314-3400.

San Ramon

PARKS, BEACHES, AND RECREATION AREAS

24 Memorial Park Dog Park

🐾🐾🐾 🐕 (See Contra Costa County map on page 378)

Once a dog's paws get used to the decomposed granite that's on the surface of this park, this place is positively peachy for poochies. It's 1.3 acres, with a separate section within for dogs under 20 pounds. (These are the ones Jake would pick up and carry around a park in his mouth ever so gently when we first adopted him at six months.) There will be shade trees here one day, but until the young trees grow larger, man-made shade structures do the trick. The park has water, poop bags, benches, and picnic tables.

The park is on the northwest side of town. Exit I-680 at Bollinger Canyon Road and drive west 0.2 mile to San Ramon Valley Boulevard, where you'll find parking straight ahead on the south side of Bollinger. 925/973-3200.

25 Del Mar Dog Park

🐾🐾🐾 🐕 (See Contra Costa County map on page 378)

This one-acre fenced park is covered with cedar wood chips. Jake, unfortunately, is content to trot around a little and then settle down to see how many wood chips he can chew to smithereens before I can get him to start acting more like a dog, less like a termite. But normal dogs love gallivanting around here. The park has all the usual amenities, including water, benches, and shade structures (no shade trees yet). The park is on the south side of town, at Del Mar Drive and Pine Valley Road. 925/973-3200.

PLACES TO STAY

San Ramon Marriott at Bishop Ranch: The folks who run this attractive hotel are very friendly to creatures of the doggy persuasion. Rates are $89–239. Dogs pay a $75 fee for the length of their stay. 2600 Bishop Drive 94583; 925/867-9200.

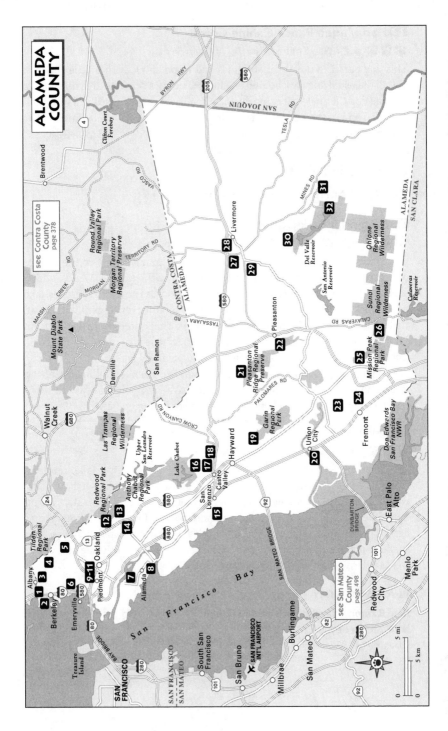

ALAMEDA COUNTY

CHAPTER 33

Alameda County

From the hallowed hippie havens of Berkeley's Telegraph Avenue to the pleasing suburban pleasantries of Pleasanton, Alameda County is like California in miniature: It has nearly every level of population density and type, and nearly every temperate natural environment. Somehow, it all works.

Dogs dig it here, whether they're rasta dogs or shaved shih tzus. The county is like the creek it's named after—it's been lined with concrete, filled with trash, and dammed into oblivion, yet it still manages to gush joyfully onward. Some of the wildest country in the Bay Area is in this county, full of hidden gems of nature. So many of these parks are off-leash havens that your dog may think he's dreaming.

The 12-mile Alameda Creek Regional Trail in Fremont is a favorite among dogs. They can run off leash on most of the trail, but where signs say leashes are required, heed the message.

As if all this weren't enough good news, your dog's hair will stand on end when he learns that unless he's a pit bull, he's allowed to run leashless on

PICK OF THE LITTER—ALAMEDA COUNTY

BEST BAYSIDE JUNGLE OF DOGS AND ART
Albany Bulb, Albany (page 399)

MOST MELLOW MUNICIPAL LEASH LAW
Berkeley (page 401)

BEST LEASH-FREE HIKES
Tilden Regional Park, Berkeley (page 402)
Redwood Regional Park, Oakland (page 409)
Chabot Regional Park, Castro Valley (page 412)
Sunol Regional Wilderness, Fremont (page 417)

MOST BONE-A-LICIOUS DOG PARK
Drigon Dog Park, Union City (page 414)

BEST PLACE FOR A DUCK TO EMBARRASS YOUR DOG
San Lorenzo Dog Park, San Lorenzo (page 411)

BEST TIKI BAR
Forbidden Island Tiki Lounge, Alameda (page 407)

MOST DOG-FRIENDLY PLACES TO EAT
Montclair Malt Shop, Montclair district, Oakland (page 411)
Noah's Bagels, Montclair district, Oakland (page 411)
Café Paradiso, Livermore (page 419)

MOST HOUND-HIP VIDEO STORE
Front Row Video, Berkeley (page 400)

MOST HOUND-HIP BOOKSTORE
Pegasus Books, Berkeley (page 400)

BEST POOCH CHOO CHOO
Tilden Park Steam Miniature Steam Train, Berkeley (page 403)

BEST HIKING BUDDIES
Sierra Club's Canine Hike Unit (page 404)

thousands of acres of park land within the East Bay Regional Park District. Some 59 parks and recreation areas and 29 regional interpark trails—95,000 acres in all—fall under the district's jurisdiction. Poop-bag dispensers are installed at the most heavily used areas, such as Point Isabel Regional Shoreline in Richmond (see the *Contra Costa County* chapter).

The only places where dogs must be leashed within the district's parks are in developed areas, parking lots, picnic sites, lawns, and in posted Nature Areas. They aren't permitted on beaches (Point Isabel Regional Shoreline is a major exception), wetlands, marshes, or in the Tilden Nature Area. In addition, dogs have to be leashed along Redwood Regional Park's popular Stream Trail. You can sniff out more details about this magnificent park system by going to www.ebparks.org and looking for the "Dogs" section. (Special rules and permits apply to anyone bringing more than three dogs. This was primarily designed for dog walkers, but if you have a gaggle of dogs yourself, you should check out the info on the site.) Or phone 888/327-2757.

Albany

PARKS, BEACHES, AND RECREATION AREAS

🔟 Albany Bulb

🐾🐾🐾🐕 (See Alameda County map on page 396)

By the time you read this, this wild bayside jungle of crazy public art and leash-free dogs may be on its way to becoming an environmentally correct habitat with no tolerance for off-leash dogs or outdoor sculpture or paintings that aren't government-approved. Your best bet is to run here as fast as your paws will take you if you want to see this spit of land in its current (at press time) fun, anarchic, freewheeling style.

This bulb-shaped peninsula used to be a dump, which was covered over and eventually became a home to the homeless. After most of the homeless were swept out in 1999, art and leash-free dogs flourished. The windy beach is a hit with dogs, who are by far the majority species on the beach. You'll drool over the million-dollar views of San Francisco Bay and the Golden Gate Bridge. The trails through the grasslands are also fun for a good romp, although it can feel a bit post-apocalyptic if the Bulb doesn't have many visitors when you're there.

Along your explorations you'll find unique works of art—most of it from found scraps of metal and construction material and flotsam in the vicinity. ("Trash art" is what some of the artists call it.) Some is quite awful, but much is truly enchanting, made by talented artists. Among the pieces: Life-sized people made of flotation foam, driftwood art of all forms, a striped concrete abode, a huge fertility goddess, a metal and wood arch featuring a dog and happy people, and a mixed media dragon.

DIVERSION

Stroll down Solano: A portion of Solano Avenue that runs through a bit of North Berkeley and Albany is a very friendly place to take your dog. People here truly enjoy pooches, and a few stores will let your leashed dog come in with you to browse.

One block in particular, the 1800 block in Berkeley, has a couple of super dog-friendly stores. The affable people at **Front Row Video,** 1831 Solano Avenue, will happily provide their dog customers with a treat. "Dogs can even come in on their own and look for films," joked an employee. (At least I think he was joking.) "Every once in a while, this happens." (Ah, apparently it's not a joke. It's Berkeley!) The store has a great selection of foreign and cult films, should your dog be tired of watching *Homeward Bound.*

A few doors down is **Pegasus Books,** 1855 Solano Avenue, a wonderful independent bookstore. (It has a sister bookstore on Shattuck Avenue in Berkeley, and a close cousin, Pendragon, in Oakland. We're not talking a major national chain here.) When you and your dog come in to look for books, the staff will give your pooch a biscuit. "We welcome dogs!" said a staffer. Canine correspondent Whomper, who told us about this place and the video store, has spent very agreeable nights here awaiting Harry Potter releases (back when Harry Potters were still being released).

Many staffers have their own pets, as you can see on the pet page of the website: www.pegasusbookstore.com. They're an understanding group, but please, no leg-lifts on the literature.

There's a big battle in the works as I write this, pitting park users and artists against environmentalists and others who want to see this become part of the adjacent Eastshore State Park. Right now it's owned by the city of Albany and managed in part by the East Bay Regional Parks District. It's a messy legal stew I won't get into here. Our paws are crossed for art and dogs, but the way the situation is going you'll definitely want to make sure leash-free is OK when you visit. (Thank you to Charlie and his person, Patti, for helping us sniff out this unbucolic gem.)

Exit Highway 80/580 or the Eastshore Freeway at Buchanan Street and head west. Park along the road at the far western end of Buchanan, and walk toward

the bay. The road will turn into a trail, which you'll follow out to the Bulb. If in doubt, look for other dog walkers. 510/528-5710.

Berkeley

You'll see a lot more unleashed dogs in Berkeley than in any other Bay Area city. That's because Berkeley, well known for its tolerance of eccentricity, has a fittingly liberal leash law: If your dog isn't wearing a leash but stays within six feet of you and is obedience trained, she'll be considered leashed! It's there in black and white in the city code. It's a very forward-thinking law, and it's been around for ages. Jake and I can't take advantage of this. (I can just picture myself explaining to the animal control officer: "Oh, six FEET. I thought it was six METERS!")

You also have to carry a poop bag at all times when your dog is out and about with you, leashed or not.

PARKS, BEACHES, AND RECREATION AREAS

2 César Chávez Park

🐾🐾🐾🐾🐕 (See Alameda County map on page 396)

Urban pooch paradise doesn't get much better than this. Dogs who come here get to feel the bay breeze blowing through their fur as they frolic with their

DIVERSION

Go Shopping in 1969: You and your dog can shop in the autumn of love when you stroll through the sidewalks of **Telegraph Avenue** near the UC Berkeley campus. Street vendors sell tie-dyed clothes, crystals, pottery, and T-shirts airbrushed with clouds. Street performers sing, juggle, beg for money, or do whatever else comes naturally. Incense and other herbaceous odors waft through the air, but dogs prefer the scents of all the nondeodorized humans.

Dogs who reminisce about the 1960s really dig it here. They're perceived as totally cool dudes and given major amounts of love from people who like to hug dogs hard. When we last visited, Jake was wearing his favorite psychedelic bandana, and he received a few "duuuudes" per block.

Some dogs—and humans—may find the weekend crowds a sensory overload. If your schedule allows, try a cool afternoon. From I-80, take the Ashby exit, go about two miles east to Telegraph Avenue, and turn left (north). The street-merchant part begins around the intersection of Dwight Way.

friends on 17 acres of prime land on the San Francisco Bay. Trails meander up and down the rolling hills and wind through a couple of quiet meadows. There's grass, grass everywhere.

The views of San Francisco, the Golden Gate Bridge, and the Bay Bridge are some of the best around. The park is equipped with plenty of poop-bag stations crammed to the gills. Use them. In fact, while you're at it, pick up an "orphan" poop if you see one lying around. Many people worked very hard for a very long time to get this park established, and the goal is to keep it beautiful and dog friendly.

This is also a great place to fly a kite, and there are plenty of instructions posted on how to do it safely around here.

Take University Avenue west past the I-80 interchange and follow the signs to the Berkeley Marina and César Chávez Park. 510/981-5150.

🐾 Ohlone Dog Park
🐾🐾🐕 (See Alameda County map on page 396)

For years after it opened as the first leash-free dog park in America in 1979, Ohlone provided a model for other cities considering opening a dog park. But sadly, the park is often in pretty bad shape these days, with mud happening before rainy season and in winter overtaking everything, including the mulch and woodchips used for covering the mud.

Still, it's a decent place for an off-leash romp in a safely fenced area. You'll find a water faucet, complete with a dog bowl set in concrete, and two picnic tables for owners who want to relax while their dogs socialize. The grass isn't always green here, but it's definitely better than what's on the other side of the fence. (Speaking of which, some of the park's neighbors are still making moves to limit hours or even to move the park out of the neighborhood. We'll update you about this sad situation in the next edition. This should not be happening to the nation's first dog park.)

The park is at Martin Luther King Jr. Way and Hearst Street. 510/981-5150.

🐾 Tilden Regional Park
🐾🐾🐾🐾🐕 (See Alameda County map on page 396)

Humans and dogs alike give Tilden a big thumbs-up (dewclaws-up). Leash-free dogs find the scents from its western ridge delectable and humans find the ridge's breathtaking views of the entire San Francisco Bay equally enticing.

Escapes from civilization are everywhere in this 2,078-acre park. Try the trails leading east from South Park Drive. They connect with the East Bay Skyline National Recreation Trail.

You can pick up the Arroyo Trail at the Big Springs sign and take it all the way to the ridge top. There's a great stream at the trailhead that you can follow

DIVERSION

Ride a Dog-Sized Train: If your dog's not an escape artist or the nervous type, he's welcome to ride with you on **Tilden Regional Park's miniature train.** The open-car train takes you for a 12-minute ride through woods and past stunning views of the surrounding area. Adventurous dogs like it when the train toots its whistle as it rumbles past a miniature water tower, a car barn, and other such train accessories. When Joe Dog appeared on KRON-TV's *Bay Area Backroads* riding the train, he was fine until we hit the little tunnel—then he decided he wanted to go home. He was relieved that part ended up on the cutting-room floor.

The Redwood Valley Railway Company runs trains 11 A.M.–dusk weekends and holidays (not Thanksgiving or Christmas) only, except during spring and summer school vacations, when it also runs noon–5 P.M. weekdays and until 6 P.M. weekends. Tickets are $2; kids under two and dogs ride free. You must keep the dog on a tight leash and make sure he doesn't jump out. It's in the southeast corner of Tilden Regional Park in Berkeley. From the intersection of Grizzly Peak Boulevard and Lomas Cantadas, follow the signs. 510/548-6100. www.redwoodvalleyrailway.com.

through laurel, pine, toyon, and scrub on your low-grade ascent. Your dog may want to take a dip in the stream for refreshment.

After the trail veers from the stream, it steepens and leads into cypress-studded meadows and eucalyptus groves. Eventually it feeds into the Skyline National Recreation Trail, also known as the Sea View Trail, offering vistas over the bay along the way.

Dogs aren't allowed in the large nature area at the northern end or in the Lake Anza swimming area. Leashes are required in all the developed areas, including picnic grounds and ball fields. Remember to watch your step in the areas frequented by dogs, as some owners neglect to clean up after their furry friends. There's nothing like stepping in a steaming pile of dog dung to put a damper on a day of exploring nature.

Speaking of steaming, be sure to check out Tilden's miniature steam train for a riveting good time. (See the Diversion *Ride a Dog-Sized Train.*)

From Highway 24, take the Fish Ranch Road exit north (at the eastern end of the Caldecott Tunnel). At the intersection of Fish Ranch, Grizzly Peak Boulevard, and Claremont Avenue, take a right on Grizzly Peak and continue north to South Park Drive. One more mile north brings you to Big Springs Trail. During peak season, continue on Grizzly Peak to the Shasta Gate. 888/327-2757.

DIVERSION

Take a Hike! East Bay dogs who enjoy the great outdoors are very lucky indeed. Berkeley is the home base for the San Francisco Bay chapter of the **Sierra Club.** The club holds several fun hikes for dogs each year, via its Canine Hike unit, and most of the hikes are in the East Bay. Dogs get to hike and play off leash, as long as they're well behaved and under voice control. Hikes are of varying difficulties and lengths. Some involve easy swimming (Jake is drooling), some involve camping, some even involve meeting the love of your life (when Sierra singles and their dogs come out to play). The folks who participate in the canine hikes are almost as friendly and fun-loving as their dogs. Phone 510/848-0800 for info on the dog hikes, or to find out how to join the Sierra Club. You don't have to be a member to do the hikes, but one of the benefits of membership is that you'll receive a schedule of all Sierra Club events—including doggy hikes—every two months.

5 Claremont Canyon Regional Preserve

🐾🐾🐾🐾🦮 (See Alameda County map on page 396)

This large park is full of steep hillside trails that lead to crests with stunning views of the university and the surrounding hills and valleys. If your dog likes eucalyptus trees and doesn't like leashes, take him here. It's one of those tree-filled, leashes-optional parks.

From Highway 13 (Ashby Avenue), drive north on College Avenue. Turn right on Derby Street, past the Clark Kerr Campus of UC Berkeley. The trailhead is at the southeast corner of the school grounds, near the beginning of Stonewall Road. 888/327-2757.

PLACES TO EAT

So many restaurants here have outdoor tables where dogs are welcome. Because of space, we list just a few.

La Mediterranée: This delicious and inexpensive Middle Eastern restaurant has built up quite a following; there's usually a line on weekends when Cal is mid-semester. The folks here will let your dog sit quietly at your feet at the outdoor tables, which have the added benefit of an outdoor heater on cool nights. You might want to tie your dog up on the sidewalk outside the fence separating the tables if it's especially crowded. 2936 College Avenue; 510/540-7773.

Rick and Ann's Restaurant: Dogs feel really at home here, because Rick and Ann and their staff love dogs. And dogs love that the food is delicious and all-American. Joe's favorites were meatloaf and creamy macaroni and cheese, and Jake feels the same way. It may take you a while to choose something from the imaginative menu, but just about anything you select will be great. 2922 Domingo Avenue; 510/649-8538.

Sea Breeze Market and Deli: Smack in the middle of the I-80 interchange, you won't even notice the traffic as you and your dog bask at sunny picnic tables, where crab claws crunch underfoot and begging is outstanding. Dogs are perfectly welcome so long as they don't wander into the store itself. You can buy groceries, beer, wine, classy ice cream, or a meal from the deli, including fresh fish and chips, calamari, prawns, scallops, chicken, and quiche. The deli serves croissants and coffee early; if you live in the East Bay, you can zip in for a quick croissant and a dog walk at César Chávez Park before work. It's at the foot of University Avenue, past the I-80 entrance. 598 University Avenue; 510/486-0802.

PLACES TO STAY

Beau Sky: This 1911 Victorian inn near the UC campus has a friendly staff and makes for a cozy stay for you and the dog in your life. It's a combination of boutique and Bohemian—and a fun place to spend a night with your dog. Humans get a free continental breakfast. Rates are $119–169. Dogs are $10 extra. 2520 Durant Avenue 94704; 510/540-7688 or 800/990-2328; www.beausky.com.

Golden Bear Inn: Rates are $77–100. Dogs are $10 extra. 1620 San Pablo Avenue, 94702; 510/525-6770; www.goldenbearinn.com.

Emeryville

PARKS, BEACHES, AND RECREATION AREAS

6 Emeryville Marina Park

🐾🐾 (See Alameda County map on page 396)

If you're a human, this is a fine park. If you're a leashed dog, it's just so-so. A concrete path follows the riprap shoreline past cypress trees and through manicured grass. A quick and scenic stroll down the north side will give you a fine view of the marina and a miniature bird refuge where egrets, sandpipers, blackbirds, and doves inhabit a tiny marsh. Dogs who like to bird-watch think it's cool here.

Dogs who like to fish don't have it so easy. Pooches aren't allowed on the fishing pier. But if you console them with an offer to picnic at tables with grand views of the Bay Bridge, they usually snap out of their funk.

From I-80, take the Powell Street exit at Emeryville and go west on Powell to the end of the marina. It has lots of free parking. 510/596-4395.

PLACES TO EAT

Kitty's: Your dog will want to bring you to this busy bar for the name alone. The food is pretty good, and you can eat it alongside your requisite drinks at the shaded patio area. 6702 Hollis Street; 510/601-9300.

Townhouse Bar & Grill: The exterior looks like a rustic old cabin a couple of grizzled miners might walk out of gripping their suspenders and carrying a flask of something strong and homemade. In fact, this place, built in 1926, was once home to a profitable bootlegging business and has been through many incarnations since. The current owners chose to keep the exterior charm of bygone days, but the rest of the Townhouse has been updated and glossed up a great deal.

Dogs are welcome to join you at the old wooden side patio. Some tables are shaded by umbrellas, so nab one of those on a hot day. The food is an eclectic blend of casual, somewhat upscale American specialties. 5862 Doyle Street; 510/652-6151.

Alameda

PARKS, BEACHES, AND RECREATION AREAS

7 Alameda Point Dog Run

😸 🐈 (See Alameda County map on page 396)

While this fenced park encompasses two acres along the Oakland Estuary, it's not much to look at—or to be in, for that matter. There are no trees. The ground is pretty much rock-hard, having baked in the sun and weathered through the years. Being just 100 feet back from this part of the estuary does provide a breeze, but the wind tends to be a bit strong here. Your dog's ears may flap in the breeze, but more likely they'll just stream straight back. There's no water, either. It's a good place to take a dog if you're near the ferry terminal, because it's on Main Street, adjacent to the terminal. It's better than nothing. 510/757-7529.

8 Alameda Dog Exercise Area

😸 😸 😸 😸 🐈 (See Alameda County map on page 396)

Wahoo! This is one of the bigger fenced-in dog parks we've encountered. It's nearly six acres, shaded here and there by some wonderful big cypress and pine trees. The ground wants to be grass, but it's pretty much packed dirt at this point. Dogs have a howling good time chasing each other around big brush patches here and there. Among the amenities: benches, a separate section for small dogs, water, and poop bags. But the best amenity here is a natural one: a fresh bay breeze. The park is right off the bay. You can see the masts of the boats in the harbor from the dog park.

The park is set beside Crown Memorial Beach, which bans dogs. The dog park is actually part of Alameda's largest park, Washington Park. That park has lots of great amenities for people, including wonderful playgrounds and ball fields. Leashed dogs enjoy the wide green expanses, the bike path, picnic area, and the edge of the marsh here. The dog park is at 8th Street and Central Avenue. It's to the left of Washington Park's tennis courts. 510/748-4568.

PLACES TO EAT

Aroma Restaurant: Any restaurant that has something about smell in its name is a sure-fire winner in a dog's book. And this places smells pretty good, with the scent of the basic Italianesque cuisine wafting out. (Must be the garlic.) It's right on a narrow bit of the Oakland Estuary, just a bone's throw from the Park Street Bridge. Dine with dog at the awning-topped outdoor tables. 2237 Blanding Avenue; 510/337-0333.

Forbidden Island Tiki Lounge: Humans have to be 21 or older to come here, but well-behaved dogs of any age can join you at the patio for a drink (or two or three or four, as it often goes here) at this fun, kitschy tiki bar. The drinks are tropical, large, and strong, and bear names like Suffering Bastard, Fugu for Two, the Combover, and Missionary's Downfall.

The lounge operates under a one-strike dog policy: "The first dog to fight with another dog or attack a patron will cause dogs to be permanently banned from Forbidden Island," warns lounge literature. My guess is that there's a reason this policy is so well defined. Well-behaved dogs and people only, please. 1304 Lincoln Avenue; 510/749-0332.

Piedmont

Piedmont is almost entirely residential, and very proper and clean. This means you won't be able to find a stray scrap of paper to scoop with, so be prepared. Its quiet streets are delightful for walking, offering views from the hills.

The parks below allow dogs off leash—but only if they have a permit from the city's police department. Licensed dogs from any city can get one, but it'll cost you more if you don't live in Piedmont, and more still if your dog is not spayed or neutered. The police department's animal services division issues these permits during limited hours on Thursdays only. Phone 510/420-3000 for details.

PARKS, BEACHES, AND RECREATION AREAS

9 Linda Off-Leash Area
😊 🐕 (See Alameda County map on page 396)

This is just a strip of pavement running down a dirt area (formerly grass) about the length of one city block. There's some shade. The "park" is set along a hill, but it's too close to a couple of roads for true off-leash comfort as far as my dogs are concerned. For some reason it gets tremendous use.

Beach Park is across from Beach School, at Linda and Lake avenues. You'll see the little doggy signs. A permit, issued only on Thursdays, is required for your off-leash use; phone 510/420-3000 for permit details. 510/420-3070.

10 Dracena Park
😊😊😊😊 🐕 (See Alameda County map on page 396)

Parts of this park are grassy, with tall shade trees here and there. But the part dogs long for is the off-leash section. It's a lovely area, with a paved path up and down a wooded, secluded hill. Tall firs and eucalyptus provide plenty of shade, and sometimes it's so quiet here you can hear several kinds of birds. The area isn't fenced, and at the top and bottom there's potential for escape artists to run into the road, so be careful and leash up at these points if you have any doggy doubts.

Poop bags are provided. The trail takes about 15 minutes round-trip, if you assume a very leisurely pace. We like to enter on Artuna Avenue at Ricardo Avenue, because it's safest from traffic and parking's plentiful on the park side of the street. But lots of folks enter at Blair and Dracena avenues. A permit, issued only during limited hours on Thursdays, is required for your off-leash use; phone 510/420-3000 for permit details. 510/420-3070.

11 Piedmont Park
😸😸😸😸 🐕 (See Alameda County map on page 396)

The huge off-leash section (allowed with permit only; phone 510/420-3000 for details) of this beautiful park is one of the best examples of a leash-free dog area in the state. A few salmon-pink concrete pathways lead you and your happy dog alongside a gurgling stream and up and down the hills around the stream. It's absolutely gorgeous and serene back here. (On our last visit, a hummingbird greeted us at the entrance and was back again when we left.) The park smells like heaven, with eucalyptus, redwood, acacia, pine, and deep, earthy scents wafting around everywhere. It reminds me of a serene Japanese garden, minus the Japanese plants.

The stream is fed year-round by a spring higher in the hills. This is pure bliss for dogs during the summer. The trails for dogs and their people run on the cooler side anyway, with all the tall trees. Almost the entire leash-free section is set in a deep canyon, so it's very safe from traffic. A leisurely round-trip stroll will take you about an hour, if you want it to. Poop bags are supplied at a few strategically located stations along the paths. Use them.

To get to the leash-free section of this elegant park, come in through the main entrance at Highland and Magnolia Avenues. You'll see a willow tree just as you enter. Continue on the path past the willow tree and follow it down to the left side of the stream. You'll see signs for the dog area. Be sure to leash up in other parts of the park, should you explore beyond the stream area. 510/420-3070.

Oakland

Oakland, the most urban city in the East Bay, is not the best place to be a dog: Only five city parks—the larger parks—allow dogs on leashes, and in restricted areas at that. A few others are in the contemplating stages. This is great news for dogs! As the Oakland Dog Owners Group motto says, Power to the Puppies!

The rest of the city's parks ban dogs outright. This is a very archaic law that needs to change, and we're glad there's some progress being made on behalf of our canine friends, who desperately need grassy places to romp.

If you're looking for a super dog-friendly neighborhood, look no further than Montclair. The bookstore, the florist, the pet store, and the hardware store have all been very kind to four-legged friends. In addition, a couple of dog-friendly Montclair eateries listed in this section really go all out for dogs.

PARKS, BEACHES, AND RECREATION AREAS

Dogs now have another place to run leash-free, and by the next edition you could be reading about at least one more, at Lakeview Park, near Lake Merritt. Still others are in the dream stages. It's a heartening state of affairs for dogs, who aren't permitted in most city parks at all. To check the status of the future parks, go to www.odogparks.org.

12 Redwood Regional Park

🐾🐾🐾🐾🐕 (See Alameda County map on page 396)

Although it's just a few miles over the ridge from downtown Oakland, Redwood Regional Park is about as far as you can get from urbanity while still within the scope of the Bay Area. Dogs who love nature at its best, and love it even more off leash, adore the 1,836-acre park. People who need to get far from the madding crowd also go gaga over the place.

The park is delectable year-round, but it's a particularly wonderful spot to visit when you need to cool off from hot summer weather. Much of the park is a majestic forest of 150-foot coast redwoods (known to those with scientific tongues as *Sequoia sempervirens*). The redwoods provide drippy cool shade most of the time, which is a real boon for dogs with hefty coats. Back in the mid-1800s, this area was heavily logged for building supplies for San Francisco, and it wasn't a pretty sight. But fortunately, sometimes progress progresses backward, and the fallen trees have some splendid replacements.

There's something for every dog's tastes here. In addition to the redwoods, the park is also home to pine, eucalyptus, madrone, flowering fruit trees, chaparral, and grasslands. Wild critters like the park, too, so leash up immediately if there's any hint of deer, rabbits, or other woodland creatures around. Many dogs, even "good" dogs, aren't able to withstand the temptation to chase.

Dogs have to leash up along the beautiful Stream Trail, which runs along the environmentally sensitive stream. Mud is inevitable if you follow the Stream Trail, so be sure to keep a towel in the car. Water dogs may try to dip their paws in Redwood Creek, which runs through the park. But please don't let them. This is a very sensitive area. Rainbow trout spawn here after migrating from a reservoir downstream, and it's not an easy trip for them. If you and your dog need to splash around somewhere, try the ocean, the bay, or your bathtub.

No parking fee is charged at Skyline Gate at the north end (in Contra Costa

County—the park straddles Contra Costa and Alameda counties). Entering here also lets you avoid the tempting smells of picnic tables at the south end. The Stream Trail leads steadily downhill, and then takes a steep plunge to the canyon bottom. It's uphill all the way back, but it's worth it. From Highway 13, exit at Joaquin Miller Road and head east to Skyline Boulevard. Turn left on Skyline and go four miles to the Skyline Gate.

If you prefer to go to the main entrance on Redwood Road, exit Highway 13 at Carson/Redwood Road and drive east on Redwood Road. Once you pass Skyline Boulevard, continue two miles on Redwood. The park and parking will be on your left. The Redwood Road entrance charges a $5 parking fee and a $2 dog fee. 888/327-2757.

13 Hardy Dog Park

😊😊😊🐕 (See Alameda County map on page 396)

This two-acre park in the Rockridge district has easy freeway access and plenty of shade. That's because it's under the freeway. But that's OK. It's a huge improvement from its previous incarnation as a fenced quarter-acre patch of dirt. Now it's big and grassy, with benches, water, and poop bags.

To get to the park from Highway 24, take the Claremont exit and follow Claremont Avenue back under the freeway. The park is under the freeway, at Claremont and Hudson Street. 510/238-3791.

14 Leona Heights Regional Open Space

😊😊😊🐕 (See Alameda County map on page 396)

Unmarked on most maps, and devoid of most amenities (water and restrooms, for instance), this 271-acre open space is good for dogs who like to get away from the crowd. You won't find many bikes or horses here. Since it's part of the East Bay Regional Park District, your dog need not be on leash.

The open space stretches from Merritt College south to Oak Knoll, and from I-580 east to Chabot Regional Park. A bumpy fire trail goes from Merritt College downhill to the southern entrance, just north of Oak Knoll. The best way to enter is to park at a lot off Canyon Oaks Drive, next to a condominium parking lot. Right at this entrance is a pond, but you won't see any more water as you ascend. It's a dry hike in warm weather.

The 2.7-mile fire trail leads gently uphill all the way to Merritt, through coyote brush and oak woodland. In spring, it's full of wildflowers and abuzz with the loud hum of bees. Watch out for poison oak.

From I-580, exit at Keller Avenue and drive east to Campus Drive. Take a left (north), then a left on Canyon Oaks Drive. 888/327-2757.

PLACES TO EAT

Oakland's College Avenue, in the Rockridge district, has a tolerant family atmosphere. Lawyers with briefcases buy flowers on the way home from the

BART station, and students flirt over ice cream. I've never seen anyone in this neighborhood who didn't love dogs.

The avenue is known to be a food lover's paradise, and among the attractions are a string of restaurants with outdoor tables, several of which follow. The Montclair district also has a couple of hits with the dog crowd.

Cafe Rustica: The pizza here is elegant. Eat it at the outdoor tables with your drooling dog. 5422 College Avenue; 510/654-1601.

Cole Coffee: This is a cheery and popular place with very good coffee (in the bean or in the cup), tea, and supplies. On weekend mornings, it's dog central. 307 63rd Street at College Avenue; 510/653-5458.

Montclair Malt Shop: Don'tcha just hate it when you go to an ice cream parlor and your dog's eyes almost tear up with the anticipation of a single drop of yummy cold cream falling from your cone to the ground so he can lap it off the sidewalk? You won't have to deal with those pleading eyes if you visit this delightful ice creamery: Dogs can order their very own special brew of pooch-friendly ice cream, known as Frosty Paws. Then you can dine together at the bench outside, or just stand around and talk with other dog people while your dog inhales his frozen treat. The place is known for its dog business; on a recent hot summer afternoon, 17 dogs were outside, downing their ice creams with delight. "We love dogs here," says super-friendly Diane, who makes the best malt this side of the bay. (She will be the first to tell you this, and she speaks the truth.) 2066 Mountain Boulevard; 510/339-1886.

Noah's Bagels: Not only do dogs get water in doggy bowls here, but they also get "floor bagels" when available. These are bagels that have been dropped on the floor, either by customers or employees. Do dogs care that their bagel has taken a little roll on terra firma? No! A little dirt only makes them more delectable. Dine with your dog at several outdoor tables here. 2060 Mountain Boulevard; 510/339-6663.

Oliveto Cafe: This café shares a building with the Market Hall, God's own food emporium. The food's the best, but for a dog, the atmosphere is congested. It's not for nervous dogs. Oliveto serves very classy pizza, tapas, bar food, desserts, coffees, and drinks, but alcohol is not allowed at the sidewalk tables. 5655 College Avenue, just south of Rockridge BART; 510/547-5356.

San Lorenzo

PARKS, BEACHES, AND RECREATION AREAS

15 San Lorenzo Dog Park

🐾🐾🐾🐕 (See Alameda County map on page 396)

It's just ducky with your dog if you want to take him to this pretty dog park: Part of it curves around a duck pond. The quackers sometimes waddle right by, somehow knowing that their canine friends can't get to them through the fence. It's almost like a cartoon at times, with a duck strutting his stuff while a dog looks on with almost embarrassed disbelief that there's no way on dog's green earth that he'll be having duck for dinner that night.

The dog park is only a half acre, but it has all the good pooch-park amenities, including water, benches, and poop bags. It's grassy with some decomposed granite. There's not much shade, although the back end has some big trees on the outside perimeter, which can provide shade at times.

The dog park is toward the back of San Lorenzo Community Park, at the very west end of Via Buena Vista. The address is 1970 Via Buena Vista. 510/881-6700.

Castro Valley

PARKS, BEACHES, AND RECREATION AREAS

16 Chabot Regional Park

🐾🐾🐾🐾🐕 (See Alameda County map on page 396)

You and your leash-free dog can throw your urban cares to the wind when you visit this 4,972-acre park filled with magnificent trails and enchanting woodlands. Except for the occasional sounds of gunfire, you'll scarcely believe you're in the hills east of metropolitan Oakland. But fear not—the guns you'll hear are merely being used for target practice at the park's marksmanship range.

The trails at Chabot (sha-BO) are so secluded that if no one is firing a gun, the only sounds you may hear are those of your panting dog and the singing birds. Adventure-loving dogs like to take the Goldenrod Trail, starting at the southern terminus of Skyline Boulevard and Grass Valley Road. It connects with the East Bay Skyline National Recreation Trail, which winds through Grass Valley and climbs through eucalyptus forests. Lucky dogs can be off leash everywhere but in developed areas.

Campsites are $18. Dogs are $2 extra. Reserve by phoning 925/373-0144. No reservations are taken October 1–March 31, when the 23 sites are first-come, first-served.

From the intersection of Redwood Road and Castro Valley Boulevard in Castro Valley, go north on Redwood about 4.5 miles to Marciel Gate. (The campground is about two miles inside the gate.) From Oakland at the intersection of Redwood Road and Skyline Boulevard, go about 6.5 miles east on Redwood to Marciel Gate. For general park info, call 888/327-2757.

17 Castro Valley Dog Park

🐾🐾🐾🐕 (See Alameda County map on page 396)

This is a fun place to take a dog for some leash-free exercise. It's about 0.6 acre and has water, poop bags, and benches. It's set within the beautiful Earl

Warren Park, whose walking path is worth sniffing out despite the on-leash requirement. The park is at 4660 Crow Canyon Road. Exit I-580 at Crow Canyon Road and head north several blocks. 510/881-6700.

18 Cull Canyon Regional Recreation Area

🐾🐾🐾🐕 (See Alameda County map on page 396)

Dogs may be off leash up on the grassy slopes laced with eucalyptus stands, but they have to wear their leashes in the areas designed for human fun. It's not such a bad fate, considering that there are plenty of grassy slopes away from developed areas.

In summer, fishing and swimming are popular here. But pooches may not go near the swimming complex, which includes an attractive pavilion and sandy beach. Leashed dogs may visit picnic areas, the Cull Creek area, and the willow-lined reservoir that sports a wooden bridge and a handful of ducks and coots.

From I-580, take the Center Street/Crow Canyon Road exit. Go left on Center Street and take a right on Castro Valley Boulevard. Follow it to Crow Canyon Road and take a left. Take another left on Cull Canyon Road. It's a half mile to the park entrance. 888/327-2757.

Hayward

PARKS, BEACHES, AND RECREATION AREAS

19 Garin Regional Park and Dry Creek Regional Park

🐾🐾🐾🐾🐕 (See Alameda County map on page 396)

Garin Regional Park is about one mile and one century away from one of the busiest streets in Hayward. It's a fascinating place for you and your dog to learn about Alameda County farming and ranching. The parking lot next to Garin Barn—an actual barn, blacksmith's shop, and tool shed that is also Garin's visitors center—is strewn with antique farm machinery.

A total of 20 miles of trails, looping among the sweeps of grassy hills, beckon you and your dog. Off-leash dogs are fine on the trails once you've left the visitors center. Dogs seem to like to think they're on their own farm here, looking for all the world as if they're strutting down their very own property and watching out for evil feline intruders.

Dry Creek, which runs near the visitors center, was a delightful small torrent one day when we were there after a March storm. There isn't much shade on hot days, though. That's when you might want to try cooling your paws at tiny Jordan Pond. It's stocked with catfish, should your dog care to join you on his kind of fishing excursion.

From Highway 238 (Mission Boulevard), Tamarack Drive takes you quickly up the hill to Dry Creek Regional Park. Garin Avenue takes you to Garin, or you can enter Garin from the California State University, Hayward campus. The parking fee is $5. Dogs are $2 extra. 888/327-2757.

Union City

PARKS, BEACHES, AND RECREATION AREAS

20 Drigon Dog Park

🐾🐾🐾🐾🐕 (See Alameda County map on page 396)

A dogbone-shaped walkway dotted with pawprints? Doggy tunnels, hoops, jumps, and other fun agility toys? Fire hydrants galore? A gated entrance featuring a giant dog bone and big concrete pillars with huge paw prints? What is this—dog heaven or something?

Yes! Drigon (DRY-ghin) Dog Park is pooch paradise that happens to be firmly planted on grassy terra firma. Its unique design is the brainchild of two dog-loving parks district planners—a $300,000 shining gem that's utterly to drool for. You drive by, you see it, you can't help but smile, even if you don't have a dog. It's real-world-meets-cartoon-fantasy—something you could find around the corner if you lived in Toontown.

The park is 1.5 acres, with a small section for wee dogs. It has water, poop bags, nicely designed benches, and shade in the form of a permanent awning. Everything here is doggy: The concrete around the newly planted trees has embedded paw prints. The hydrants are concrete (they can't rust or corrode from boy dog bladder activities) and have drainage. This helps keep the grassy area pretty green.

The park, named for a heroic police dog who is in a more ethereal dog heaven now, is closed Mondays for maintenance, and for 48 hours after inclement weather to keep it from becoming mud soup. It's in the middle of a residential suburban neighborhood, at 7th Street and Mission Boulevard. 510/471-3232.

Pleasanton

PARKS, BEACHES, AND RECREATION AREAS

21 Pleasanton Ridge Regional Park

🐾🐾🐾🐾🐕 (See Alameda County map on page 396)

This fairly recent and beautiful addition to the East Bay Regional Parks system is an isolated treat. Dogs may run off leash on all the secluded trails here as soon as you leave the staging area.

You can reach Pleasanton Ridge from either Foothill or Golden Eagle Roads. At the Foothill Staging Area, there are fine picnic sites at the trailhead. Climb up on the Oak Tree fire trail to the ridgeline, where a looping set of trails goes off to the right. The incline is gentle, through pasture (you share this park with cattle) dotted with oak and—careful—poison oak. Wildflowers riot in spring. It's a hot place in summer. At the bottom of the park, however, is a beautiful streamside stretch along Arroyo de la Laguna. There's no water above the entrance, so be sure to carry plenty.

From I-680, take the Castlewood Drive exit and go left (west) on Foothill Road to the staging area. 888/327-2757.

22 Muirwood Park Dog Exercise Area

😃 😃 😃 🐕 (See Alameda County map on page 396)

Dogs enjoy galloping around this very long, narrow park in part because it's so easy on their paws. The ground cover is affectionately known as "forest floor material," which is basically degraded wood chips mixed with leaf and branch litter. Much as you'd find in the real Muir Woods in Marin, the stuff makes for cushy walks and runs—it's great for the joints of older dogs.

If your dog likes chasing far-flung balls, this is a perfect place for it. The park is about 300 feet long by 40 feet wide, which means there's plenty of room to use your tennis ball launcher to its full capacity. The park has all the usual dog-park amenities, including benches, separate sections for small and large dogs, water, and poop-bag dispensers. There's ample shade from evergreen acacias—a popular food with giraffes. (You won't likely see any giraffes wandering through the dog park, but park workers have been known to collect leaves and branches for the giraffes at the Oakland Zoo.)

The park is at 4701 Muirwood Drive. The cross street is Las Positas Boulevard. 925/931-5340.

PLACES TO STAY

Crown Plaza: Rates are $69–179. Dogs pay a $25 fee for length of their stay. 11950 Dublin Canyon Road 94588; 925/847-6000.

Fremont

PARKS, BEACHES, AND RECREATION AREAS

23 Alameda Creek Regional Trail

😃 😃 😃 🐕 (See Alameda County map on page 396)

This 12.4-mile trail runs from the bayshore to the East Bay hills. The trail is actually two trails: The one on the southern levee of the Alameda Creek is paved, and leashes are the law here (understandably, with all the bikes passing by). The one on the northern levee is unpaved and permits dogs off leash for the entire length of the creek!

Dogs are sometimes disappointed to discover that 1) the creek is lined with concrete and 2) the trail doesn't just pass through farmland and greenbelt areas. It also runs alongside rail yards, industrial lots, and quarries. Junkyard dogs like it. Wilderness dogs just shrug their hairy shoulders.

A scenic stretch of trail is at the Niles Canyon end. Dogs find it especially interesting in winter after a storm, when there's actually water in the concrete-lined creek and ducks and coots splash around. Shinn Pond in Niles, and the Alameda Creek Stables in Union City are popular canine congregation sites.

You may enter this trail at many points near the creek's mouth—in the salt flats of the bay by Coyote Hills Regional Park. The trail officially begins in Fremont's Niles district, at the intersection of Mission Boulevard (Highway 238) and Niles Canyon Road (Highway 84). You can find an excellent map and more detailed info on the trail at www.ebparks.org. 888/327-2757.

24 Fremont Dog Park
😊😊🐕 (See Alameda County map on page 396)

A park with male-pattern baldness? That's what you get when you visit this fenced one-acre park. The surface is grass, but in the middle, there's a big bald patch. But dogs don't care about the aesthetics. They're just happy to be able to cruise around off leash. The park has benches, poop bags, and water. There's no shade, so it can get toasty at times.

The park is within the beautiful, 450-acre Central Park, which leashed dogs are welcome to explore. The dog section is on Stevenson Boulevard, just west of Gallaudet Drive, near the softball fields. 510/790-5541.

25 Mission Peak Regional Preserve
😊😊😊😊🐕 (See Alameda County map on page 396)

Smart Fremont dwellers take their dogs to this 2,596-acre park. It's a huge expanse of grass, dotted with occasional oak groves and scrub. Unfortunately for humans who get short of breath, the foot trails head straight up. Trails to the top rise 2,500 feet in three miles. (Pant, pant.)

Leash-free dogs love this place. The entrance at Stanford Avenue offers a gentler climb than the entrance from the Ohlone College campus. You'll pass Caliente Creek if you take the Peak Meadow Trail, but in hot weather, there won't be much relief from the sun. Be sure to carry water for yourself and your dog. The main point of puffing up Mission Peak is the renowned view stretching from Mt. Tamalpais to Mt. Hamilton. (On very clear days, you can see to the Sierra's snowy crest.) Your dog may not care much for the scenery, but she'll probably appreciate the complete freedom of the expanse of pasture here.

From I-680, take the southern Mission Boulevard exit in Fremont (there are two exits; the one you want is in the Warm Springs district). Go east on Mission to Stanford Avenue, turn right (east), and in less than a mile, you'll be at the entrance. 888/327-2757.

26 Sunol Regional Wilderness

🐾🐾🐾🐾 🐕 (See Alameda County map on page 396)

You and your leash-free dog will howl for joy when you visit this large and deserted wilderness treasure. It's like going to a national park without having to leave your poor pooch behind.

One of the best treats for canines and their companions is a hike along the Camp Ohlone Trail, which you reach via the main park entrance, on Geary Road. The trail takes you to an area called Little Yosemite. Like its namesake, Little Yosemite is magnificent. It's a steep-sided gorge with a creek at the bottom, lofty crags, and outcrops of greenstone and basalt that reveal a turbulent geological history. Its huge boulders throw Alameda Creek into gurgling eddies and falls. There's no swimming allowed here, much to Jake's dismay.

You can return via the higher Canyon View Trail or head for several other destinations: wooded canyons, grassy slopes, peaks with peeks of Calaveras Reservoir or Mt. Diablo. The park brochure offers useful descriptions of each trail. Dogs may run leashless on trails except for on the Backpack Loop.

Dogs are allowed only at the Family Campground site at headquarters and not at the backpacking campsites farther in. Sites are $12. The dog fee is $1. Dogs must be leashed in the campground or confined to your tent. (Anyone whose dog has ever chased off after a wild boar in the middle of the night understands the reason for this rule, and this park has plenty of boars.) Call 510/636-1684 to reserve. Reserved sites are held until 5 P.M. The day-use parking fee is $5, plus $2 extra for your dog.

From I-680, take the Calaveras Road exit, then go left (east) on Geary Road to the park entrance. The park may be closed or restricted during fire season, June–October. 888/327-2757.

PLACES TO STAY

Best Western Garden Court: Rates are $69–119. Dogs are $10 extra. 5400 Mowry Avenue 94538; 510/792-4300.

Livermore

PARKS, BEACHES, AND RECREATION AREAS

Livermore is barking up the right tree: It now has five dog parks!

27 May Nissen Dog Park

🐾🐾 🐕 (See Alameda County map on page 396)

At one-third of an acre, this is the smallest of Livermore's dog parks. But there's still enough room for dogs to have a decent time. There's water, some grass, and shade-providing trees. A double-gated entry helps prevent escape artist pooches from bolting when someone leaves or enters the park.

The dog park is set within May Nissen Park. It's on Rincon Avenue, just south of Pine Street. 925/373-5700.

28 Vista Meadows Park
😊😊😊 🐾 (See Alameda County map on page 396)

Your dog can't quite live out a favorite nursery rhyme and go 'round the mulberry bush here, but he can go under a mulberry tree (or do a leg lift on it, which is a popular pastime with some dogs here). This 0.75-acre fenced park has some mulberry trees on its back end. There's even a bench under them, should you feel like relaxing in their shade. The grass here is pretty worn down, but it can come back again with the help of the wonderful parks department. Amenities include water, poop bags, and a double-gated entry. The park is at Westminster Way and Lambeth Road. 925/373-5700.

29 Max Baer Dog Park
😊😊😊 🐾 (See Alameda County map on page 396)

This 0.6-acre, fenced-in dog park is level and grassy, with lots of shady trees. It's double-gated, for your dog's safety. Inside the park are poop bags, a water fountain and bowls, and chairs where people can hang out while their dogs romp. On summer evenings, as many as 25–30 dogs enjoy the park. "Everybody loves it," says veterinarian Martin Plone, who was behind the park's birth in 1993. "It's become a meeting place for people. While their dogs are playing, people form friendships."

The dog park is part of the popular Max Baer Park. It's at Murdell Lane and Stanley Boulevard. 925/373-5700.

30 Del Valle Regional Park
😊😊😊😊 🐾 (See Alameda County map on page 396)

This popular reservoir is best known for swimming, boating, fishing, and camping. Like Chabot Regional Park in Castro Valley, it's primarily a manicured and popular human recreation area, with neat lawns and picnic tables (where dogs must be leashed).

But, glory be to dog, the park sports several unspoiled trails for leash-free hiking in the surrounding hills. And, unlike at Lake Chabot, here you're permitted to take a dog on a rented boat. Every dog can have his day here.

From this recreation area, you can enter the Ohlone Wilderness Trail—29 miles of gorgeous trail through four regional parks.

The 150 sites at Family Camp allow dogs, but only on leash or confined to your tent. Sites are $18–20. Reserve by calling 510/636-1684.

From I-580, take North Livermore Avenue from downtown Livermore. It will become South Livermore Avenue, then Tesla Road. Take a right (south) on Mines Road, and then turn right on Del Valle Road. The parking fee is $5. The dog fee is $2. 888/327-2757.

🐾 Ohlone Wilderness Trail

🐾🐾🐾🐾🐕 (See Alameda County map on page 396)

Some of the area's most remote and peaceful wilderness areas are accessible only by way of this 29-mile trail. The trail stretches from Mission Peak, east of Fremont, through Sunol Regional Wilderness and Ohlone Regional Wilderness to Del Valle Regional Park, south of Livermore. You and your occasionally leash-free dog (signs tell you when it's allowed) will hike through oak and bay woods and grassy uplands that are carpeted with wildflowers in spring.

You'll also see abundant wildlife—if you're quiet and lucky, you might even see an endangered bald eagle. If your dog can't take the pressure of merely watching as tule elk and deer pass by, you should keep him leashed.

Because of some restrictions, you won't be able to do all 29 miles at once with your dog. That's OK. In fact, that's probably just fine with your dog.

A permit is required. Pick it up for $2 at the East Bay Regional Park District headquarters, the Del Valle or Sunol kiosks, or the Coyote Hills Visitors Center (Fremont). 888/327-2757.

🐾 Ohlone Regional Wilderness

🐾🐾🐾🐾🐕 (See Alameda County map on page 396)

The centerpiece of this magnificent parkland is the 3,817-foot Rose Peak—only 32 feet lower than Mt. Diablo. Leash-free dogs are in heaven on earth as they explore the surrounding 6,758 acres of grassy ridges. Wildlife is abundant, so if your dog isn't obedient, it's best to keep her leashed. The tule elk appreciate it, and your dog will appreciate it, too, should you run into a mountain lion.

The regional parks system shares the wilderness with the San Francisco Water District, which wants to limit the human presence here. Dogs may not stay overnight in the campgrounds.

To enter this wild and breathtaking area east of Sunol Regional Wilderness, you must pick up a permit (which includes a detailed trail map and camping information) for $2 at the East Bay Regional Park District headquarters or at the Del Valle and Sunol kiosks, and at the Coyote Hills Visitors Center (Fremont). 888/327-2757.

PLACES TO EAT

Café Paradiso: "Start your day in paradise," says a manager here. And the food here is heavenly. Try the Bird of Paradise sandwich for a real taste treat. The lucky dogs who dine at the umbrella-topped outdoor tables get not only water, but treats! 53 Wright Brothers Avenue; 925/371-2233.

PLACES TO STAY

Residence Inn Livermore: These are convenient little apartments/suites if you need more than just a room. Rates are $159–184, and there's a $75 fee per doggy visit, so you might want to stay a while. 1000 Airway Boulevard 94550; 925/373-1800.

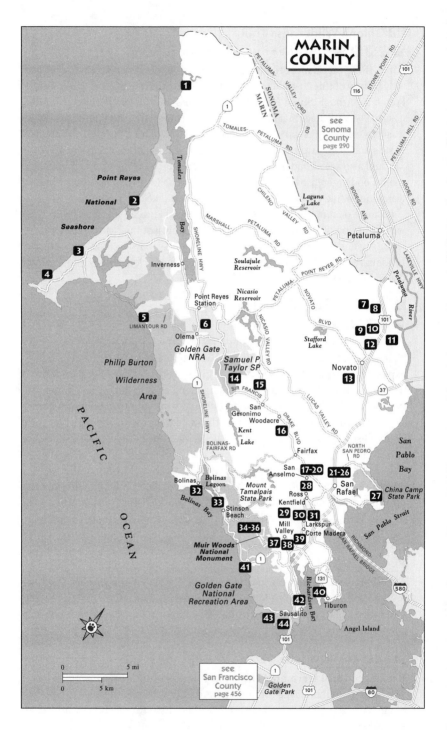

CHAPTER 34

Marin County

This is a good place to be a dog or a well-heeled human. For four-legged friends, it's got it all, from the bay to the ocean to the redwoods and hilly park-lands in between. Throw in some dog-friendly restaurants, inns, and cottages, and you've got the makings of a pooch paradise.

We have great news for your beast with this new edition of the book. The winds of change are blowing favorably for dogs again, and the leash law at Golden Gate National Recreation Area (GGNRA) lands that permits dogs in Marin is back to its friendly old ways: Dogs need only be under voice control on certain trails in the Marin Headlands, and at Muir Beach and Rodeo Beach! No leashes are necessary for well-behaved dogs. This is a huge victory for the canine set, and if they could clap, I'm sure they would give a standing ovation for the decision-makers who gave them back their freedom to run around in the buff again. (That said, this measure may only be temporary. Be sure to check out the GGNRA website before planning a hike here: www.nps.gov/goga.

PICK OF THE LITTER—MARIN COUNTY

BEST OFF-LEASH HIKE
Marin Headlands Trails (page 454)

BEST SOCIAL HOUR
Remington Dog Park, Sausalito (page 453)

BEST REMOTE BEACH
Kehoe Beach, Inverness (page 424)

BEST OFF-LEASH BEACHES
Muir Beach, Muir Beach (page 452)
Rodeo Beach, Sausalito (page 453)

PLACE TO HIKE OFF LEASH IN THE HEAT
Baltimore Canyon Open Space Preserve, Larkspur (page 443)

BEST BREAD
Bovine Bakery, Point Reyes Station (page 427)

BEST CHEESE
Cowgirl Creamery, Point Reyes Station (page 428)

BEST *DOSAS*
Table Cafe, Larkspur (page 444)

MOST DOG-FRIENDLY PLACES TO EAT
Christopher's, Novato (page 434)
Shaky Grounds, San Rafael (page 441)
Mama's Royal Cafe, Mill Valley (page 450)
Fish, Sausalito (page 455)

MOST MAGICAL LODGINGS
Manka's Inverness Lodge, Inverness (page 426)
Rosemary Cottages, Inverness (page 427)
The Old Point Reyes Schoolhouse Compound, Point Reyes
Station (page 429)
The Olema Inn, Olema (page 431)

OLDEST PLACE TO STAY
Smiley's Schooner Hotel, Bolinas (page 445)

The main page will provide a link to the dog issues pages. You can also phone the GGNRA dog-policy liaisons at 415/561-4732 for an update.)

Marin County operates 33 Open Space District lands. The landscapes include grassy expanses, wooded trails, redwood groves, marshes, and steep mountainsides. The idea is to set aside bits of land so that Marin never ends up looking like Santa Clara Valley. The Open Space parks are free and undeveloped.

Dogs used to be permitted off leash just about everywhere on Open Space lands. But now there are more restrictions than ever, and certain Open Space parks, like the beautiful Santa Margarita Island Open Space Preserve, now ban dogs outright. Others have gone to a leashes-only policy. The only areas dogs can run leash-free are on designated fire roads in the more dog-friendly parks. They must be leashed on trails. It's still a pretty good deal, since most dogs don't mind the wide berth. Speaking of wide berth, you're not allowed to bring more than three dogs at a time to Open Space lands. This rule keeps commercial dog walking at bay. Also, we've been told that too many people are parking illegally to use these lands. There are many complaints from neighbors on adjacent roads. Be sure to park legally. See www.marinopenspace.org for more park info, or phone 415/499-6387.

Life on a leash isn't the same as the untethered life. But it's not always a drag. Marin offers some real gems to leashed pooches. Most dogs are surprised to discover that if they wear a leash, they're even permitted to explore a bit of beautiful Mt. Tamalpais. Dogs' mouths also tend to drop open when you mention they can visit parts of the 65,000-acre Point Reyes National Seashore, home to 350 species of birds and 72 species of mammals, not including dogs. Because it's a delicate ecosystem and a national treasure, dogs are banned from campgrounds, most trails, and several beaches. But there are still some great places to explore. Where dogs are permitted, they must be on leash. It's a small price to pay to be able to peruse the place with the pooch at all. Kehoe Beach, Point Reyes Beach South, and Point Reyes Beach North are the seashore's most dog-friendly areas.

Dillon Beach
PARKS, BEACHES, AND RECREATION AREAS

🚹 Dillon Beach Resort
🐾🐾🐾🐾🐕 (See Marin County map on page 420)

Don't let the name fool you: This is a beach, not a high-end hotel with dozens of spa treatments. What really gets dogs excited is that not only are they allowed on the beach, but at a certain point that seems to confuse everyone we've spoken with there, they can throw their leashes to the wind. The rule says something to the effect that from the parking lot to the high tide line, dogs must be leashed, and from the tide line and into the water, dogs can be leash free. Check with the person at the kiosk when you drive in. Please make super-sure your dog is truly under voice control before letting her go, because this a rare privilege these days. (The next leash-free beach to the north is in Humboldt County; to the south it's in Pacifica.)

The beach is privately run and very well maintained. If you notice broken glass or anything that's not in keeping with a clean, safe beach, the staff asks you to report it.

There's a $5 fee per vehicle. It's worth the price. The beach is the north-ernmost beach in Marin County. So far north, in fact, that it has the Sonoma County area code. The address is One Beach Avenue; 707/878-2696.

PLACES TO STAY

Lawson's Landing and Resort: When you camp here, you camp in a grassy meadow along the sand dunes. There are no set campsites, just the open meadow. That's great, because sometimes you can have the whole place to yourself. Other times you have to share the meadow with lots of other out-doorsy sorts of folks. Camping is $20–22. Weekly rates are available. Lawson's Landing is easy to find once you're in Dillon Beach. The address is 137 Marine View Drive, P.O. Box 67, Dillon Beach, CA 94929; 707/878-2443; www .lawsonslanding.com.

Inverness

This sweet, quiet village on Tomales Bay is one of the most attractive in Marin. The dog-friendly beaches, cafés, and lodgings are to drool for. What's not to love about this place?

PARKS, BEACHES, AND RECREATION AREAS

2 Kehoe Beach

😾😾😾😾 (See Marin County map on page 420)

This is our favorite of the Point Reyes National Seashore beaches that allow dogs, since it's both the most beautiful and the least accessible. The only parking is at roadside. You take a half-mile cinder path through wildflowers and thistles, with marsh on one side and hill on the other. In the morning, you may see some mule deer. Then, you come out on medium-brown sand that stretches forever. Since the water is shallow, the surf repeats its crests in multiple white rows, as in Hawaii. Behind you are limestone cliffs. Scattered rocks offer tidepools filled with mussels, crabs, anemones, barnacles, snails, and sea flora.

In such a paradise of shore life, the leash rule makes sense. The chief reasons for leashing dogs (or banning them altogether) at the Point Reyes National Seashore beaches are the harbor seals that haul out onto the beaches. They're in no position to get away fast from a charging dog. The snowy plover, a threatened shorebird that nests on the ground, also appreciates your dog obeying the leash law. In fact, sections of this beach and the other Point Reyes beaches may become closed long-term because of these birds. Restricted areas will be posted so tell your dog to keep her eyes peeled.

From Inverness, follow Sir Francis Drake Boulevard to the fork. Bear right on Pierce Point Road and go about four miles; park beside the road where you see the sign and walk about a half mile to the beach. 415/464-5100.

🔳 Point Reyes Beach North

🐾🐾🐾🐾 (See Marin County map on page 420)

Point Reyes Beach North is a generous, functional beach. There's no long trail from the parking lot, no special tidepools or rocks, just a long, clean, beautiful running beach for the two of you. Officially, however, dogs must be leashed.

From Inverness, take Sir Francis Drake Boulevard. Follow signs for the lighthouse. Go about 10 miles. The turnoff for the beach is well marked. 415/464-5100.

🔳 Point Reyes Beach South

🐾🐾🐾 (See Marin County map on page 420)

Point Reyes Beach South is a little narrower and steeper than Point Reyes Beach North, and it has a few interesting sandstone outcrops with wind-carved holes. It has a bit less of that wide-open feeling. Leash the dog, and steer clear of dog-restricted areas.

Follow the directions for Point Reyes Beach North; it's the next beach southward. 415/464-5100.

PLACES TO EAT

Inverness Store: Lots of dogs visit this little grocery store, which has been around for more than 80 years. The folks here are kind to doggies and welcome them to munch a lunch at the picnic table at the dike here. They even invite dogs and their people to bring a blanket and make it a real picnic. (No ants, though.) 12784 Sir Francis Drake Boulevard; 415/669-1041.

Manka's Inverness Lodge: The main hall of this magnificent lodge burned down in December 2006. It is a tragedy for this beautiful lodge, but by the time you read this the restaurant should be reopened and look almost just like it used to. It's a mouth-watering restaurant, if wild game is the type of dish that makes your mouth water. (Your dog will surely love it.) P.O. Box 1110, Inverness, CA 94937; 415/669-1034 or 800/58-LODGE (800/585-6343); www.mankas.com.

PLACES TO STAY

The Ark: Don't expect 40 days and 40 nights of rain during your stay at The

Ark. But be assured that even if it's raining cats and dogs, you'll still have a wonderful time here. This two-room cottage is cozy and charming, with vast skylights, a soaring ceiling, a nifty loft, and a woodstove. The Ark is far removed from the hustle and bustle of downtown Inverness, and it's adjacent to a wildlife preserve, replete with trees. If you enjoy singing birds, open a window and let the songs stream in. Or walk outside to the beautiful, private area surrounding the cottage.

The Ark looks like something straight out of the 1970s. That's because it was built in 1971 by a class of UC Berkeley architecture students under the guidance of maverick architect Sim Van der Ryn. (It doesn't get much more '70s than that.) The class was called "Making a Place in the Country." As long as your dog doesn't take a stab at the subjects of "Making a Hole in the Yard" or "Making Pee-Pee on the Floor," he'll be as welcome here as the humans in his party.

The Ark sleeps up to six people. Rates are $215 for two people, $20 per additional person. Dogs pay a flat fee for their visit: $40 for one dog, $50 for two dogs. Delectable, healthful organic breakfast fixings (described in mouthwatering detail in the listing for the Ark's sister property, Rosemary Cottages) are $10 extra per person. Directions are available online, and the mailing address is P.O. Box 273, Inverness, CA 94937; 415/663-9338 or 800/808-9338; www.rosemarybb.com (click on The Ark).

Manka's Inverness Lodge: Often, humans and their dogs spend the night here, eat breakfast, and decide never to return home. It's an old hunting lodge and cabins, surrounded by woods and the beaches and mudflats of Tomales Bay—and the owners love dogs.

The lodgings are super-cozy, fun, luxurious, and unique. Features vary from one to the other and include fireplaces, huge tubs, antiques, and a variety of surprising decorative touches. Views are either of Tomales Bay or the surrounding woods.

Dogs can stay in any of the six cabins or the four rooms. The two-bedroom Boathouse is the largest and would be Jake's favorite, but water dogs aren't allowed there because it's right on the water and swimming dogs tend to make the place soggy—not really something the Boathouse needs. Rates for the cabins are $415–715. Dogs are $100 extra for the length of their cabin stay. Rates for the rooms in the lodge are $285–365, and dogs are $50 extra per stay.

The food here is exceptional. The lodge's restaurant has received many an award. The vegetarian and fish dishes are exotic and mouthwatering. But it's all the wild game dishes that make dogs vote it a four-paw restaurant. If dogs accompany you for a meal at the outdoor tables here, they'll drool over every mouthful you eat. (Note: At press time Manka's main hall, which housed the restaurant, had burned down. It's a sad event for this beautiful building, but by the time you read this it should have risen from the ashes and look as it did before—or even better, if that's possible.)

Look for the uphill turn off Sir Francis Drake Boulevard and take Argyle Way about 400 yards to the lodge. P.O. Box 1110, Inverness, CA 94937; 415/669-1034 or 800/58-LODGE (800/585-6343); www.mankas.com.

Rosemary Cottages: The two gorgeous cottages that share this spacious, wooded property are the kind of places you and your dog will not leave easily. The Fir Tree Inn and The Rosemary Cottage are set in a secluded spot, each with a wall of windows looking out at the stunning forest scenery of the Point Reyes National Seashore. A deck overlooks a sweet-smelling herb garden. Inside the cottages are cozy and beautifully crafted, with a full kitchen and many homey details. Snuggle up near the wood-burning stove on chilly evenings after a day of whale-watching and dog-walking at nearby beaches. Hearth-type dogs love it here.

There's plenty of privacy: Although the cottages share the garden and hot tub (which uses milder chemicals than chlorine and its harsh brethren), many guests spend their vacation here and never even know just where the other cottage is.

Owner Suzanne Storch wants your stay to be as restful and healthful as possible. She provides a "green" environment (only more-natural cleansers are used) and has been switching over to organic sheets and towels. Best of all, she provides the most delectable organic breakfast fixings, including a basket of oranges and other fruit, granola, yogurt, organic locally made bread and muffins, homemade jam, and eggs from her chickens. Even the coffee, tea, milk, and sugar are organic! The cost for these amazing breakfast baskets is only $10 per person.

The Rosemary Cottage is $245 for up to two people, and The Fir Tree is $265. Extra people are $20 each. If you have one dog, you'll pay a $40 flat fee. For two dogs you'll pay a $50 flat fee. Directions are available online, and the mailing address is P.O. Box 273, Inverness, CA 94937; 415/663-9338 or 800/808-9338; www.rosemarybb.com.

Point Reyes Station

This community is the commercial hub of West Marin. But that's not saying much, because it's not exactly Development Central out here. In fact, there are probably more cows than people. You'll find some terrific places to eat (two of them with names relating to cows, in fact) and to spend the night with your dog.

PLACES TO EAT

Bovine Bakery: The bread here will make you drool, which will make your dog embarrassed. Dine on bread or pizza or "killer monster cookies" at the bench in front. 11315 Highway 1; 415/663-9420.

Cafe Reyes: The patio on the café's side is big and very attractive, with

DIVERSION

If Only Dogs Could Read: Point Reyes Books once sent me a letter that ended like this: "We welcome genteel canines, whether a reading rover or a browsing bowser—or just a patiently waiting companion. *Se habla* milkbone." So of course, next time we found ourselves pawing around for a good book, Joe hounded me to drive with him to this wonderful little bookstore. He immediately fell in love with the place. Dogs get lots of loving and a crunchy biscuit. After a recent visit, his protégé, Jake, decided that instead of chewing books, he'd simply make dog-eared pages. Anything to go back.

This store really is a treat—for dogs and humans. It has a big selection of new and used books, with a strong outdoor book section. Combine a visit here with a hike and a lunch, and you've got yourselves a doggone great day. 11315 Highway 1, Point Reyes Station; 415/663-1542; www.ptreyesbooks.com.

excellent views of local scenery. Even dogs seem to enjoy its ambience. The food is great, too. Tasty wood-fired pizzas are the stars here. Bring yours to the 15 umbrella-topped tables and wolf it down with your pooch at your side. There's not really a street address. It's on Highway 1 and is big and wooden. You can't miss it. 415/663-9493.

Cowgirl Creamery at Tomales Bay Foods: No, this isn't related to the nearby Bovine Bakery, although they do sound good together. Cowgirl Creamery cheeses are so delectable they're worth the drive out to this end of the world. Sure, you can get these organic artisan cheeses around the Bay Area, but this is where they're born. On Fridays you can take a short tour of the cheese-making operation, still housed in an old barn.

Buy cheese, upscale deli items, organic produce, and baked goods inside (without your dog) and enjoy a restful meal together at the courtyard picnic tables. Note that the outside of the barn/store bears the name Tomales Bay Foods. 80 Fourth Street; 415/663-9335.

PLACES TO STAY

The Berry Patch Cottage: This garden cottage is surrounded by trees and has a private yard with plenty of berries (thus the name), fruit trees, and nut trees. The cottage's pleasant owners live next door, and they invite guests to share their vegetable garden. The cottage is basic, with furniture and appliances a couple of readers have said are a little run-down. If you expect luxury, you should probably look elsewhere. Rates are $100–150. Dogs are $5 extra. There's also a newer, smaller unit available now, and it has an enclosed patio with French doors. The mailing address is P.O. Box 712 94956. You'll get the physical address when you make a reservation. 415/663-1942 or 888/663-1942; www.berrypatchcottage.com.

The Old Point Reyes Schoolhouse Compound: The three glorious get-away cottages that make up the old schoolhouse area are the cat's meow for dogs and their people. On a serene stretch of rolling pastureland in Point Reyes Station, the cottages have a sweet country theme and seem perfectly at home in their surroundings. Dogs love it here, because each cottage is adorned with its own private enclosed patio. They're wonderful places to relax outside with your pooch.

The cottages have fully equipped kitchens that come with a real bonus: a lovely picnic basket and all the gear that goes with it (excluding the food). Now there's no excuse for not taking your pooch on a picnic. In addition, each cottage has a fireplace, as well as access to a secluded garden, hot tub, outdoor fireplace, and hammock.

Rates are $185–245. Dogs are $100 extra for the length of their stay. The cottages are on the historic Old Point Reyes Schoolhouse Compound. The mailing address is P.O. Box 56, Point Reyes Station, CA 94956; 415/663-1166; www.oldpointreyesschoolhouse.com.

Point Reyes Station Inn: Dogs are welcome to stay in one room at this recently built inn. It's a first-floor room with a private entrance, its own patio, a fireplace, and a whirlpool tub for two (that would be two humans, lest your water dog gets any ideas). Rates are $110–275. 11591 Highway 1 94956; 415/663-9372; www.pointreyesstationinn.com.

Seven Grey Foxes: These two plainly furnished apartments are tucked away on a quiet country road in a cozy neighborhood just outside the village. It's very peaceful here. The two-room apartment (a.k.a. the cottage) has views of attractive gardens, a kitchenette, and a Franklin fireplace. The one-room apartment is just a smaller version of the other except with no kitchenette. Rates are $85–95 for the smaller and $150 for the larger. You'll get the address when you make your reservation. 415/663-1089; www.sevengreyfoxes.com.

The Tree House: Lisa Patsel, Italian-born owner of this beautiful getaway perched on a ridgetop overlooking Point Reyes Station, loves dogs. In fact, she has seven of them—all bichon frises. That's a lot of white fluff. "Dogs are kids," she says. "Furry kids." You'd better believe she stops traffic when she rolls into town in her SUV full of canines.

Her bichons will greet you and your dog when you arrive on the 2.5-acre property. "They bark like hell when they see other dogs," she says. "But then I call them and they stop."

It's a little paradise here, with the postcard views, peaceful (except for occasional barking) surroundings, and cozy rooms. Dog guests can stay in three antique-furnished rooms, and by the time you read this, possibly a cottage. A filling breakfast comes with your stay. Be sure to visit the miniature llama,

Stella. She's a charmer. Be aware: Lisa also has kitties. She has parrots, too, but dogs don't usually see them as chaseable candy.

Rates are $125–155. The cottage, when it's ready for rent, will cost more. 73 Drake Summit, P.O. Box 1075 94956; 415/663-8720 or 800/977-8720; www .treehousebnb.com.

Olema

PARKS, BEACHES, AND RECREATION AREAS

5 Limantour Beach

🐾🐾🐾🐾 (See Marin County map on page 420)

This bountiful beach at Point Reyes National Seashore is most people's favorite, so it's often crowded. From the main parking lot, walk 0.25 mile through tule marsh, grasses and brush, and scattered pines, past Limantour Estero. Dogs are not permitted at the northwest end of the beach and must be leashed everywhere else.

Rules for leashed dogs are clearly marked—a refreshing exception to the obscure and contradictory rules in so many parks. For example, approaching Limantour Beach on the path, you'll see a sign that says dogs are prohibited to your right, allowed to your left. This beach is plenty big, so it's an excellent arrangement that keeps dog owners and dog avoiders equally happy. You may walk with your dog to Santa Maria Beach.

From Highway 1, look for the turnoff to Bear Valley Road, which runs between Olema and Inverness Park. Take Bear Valley from either direction to Limantour Road; turn south on Limantour all the way to the beach. 415/464-5100.

6 Bolinas Ridge Trail

🐾🐾🐾🐾 (See Marin County map on page 420)

This Golden Gate National Recreation Area trail, part of the Bay Area Ridge Trail, is not for sissies—canine or human. It climbs steadily for 11 miles from the Olema end, giving you gorgeous views of Tomales Bay, Bolinas, and the ocean, and ends up at the Bolinas-Fairfax Road below Alpine Lake. The GGNRA website proudly states that this is "the best trail in the area for walking a dog."

You must keep your dog leashed. One good reason for this is that there are cattle roaming unfenced along the trail. And the trail is very popular with non-sissy mountain bikers. (The trail is wide, but made of dirt and rock.) From the western end, you'll walk through rolling grassland with cypress clumps. Rock outcrops sport crowns of poison oak, so watch it.

You may be able to cope with 11 miles of this, but remember your dog's bare pads and don't overdo it. Also, it isn't much fun for man or beast to walk 11 miles attached by a leash.

Unfortunately, only the Bolinas Ridge Trail is open to dogs; you can't take any of the spur trails going south.

The western end begins about one mile north of Olema on Sir Francis Drake Boulevard. There's roadside parking only. 415/556-0560 or 415/663-1092.

PLACES TO STAY

The Olema Inn: This absolutely enchanting inn is exactly 100 years younger than our nation. It opened on July 4, 1876. That's a long, long time ago by California standards. The inn has obviously been revamped a bit since then, but it still retains the elegant charm of the era. The six beautiful rooms feature antique furniture mingling with up-to-date luxuries such as super-comfortable European Sleepworks mattresses topped with down comforters. (No dogs on the bedding, please.) A fresh breakfast of croissants, local artisan cheeses, fruit, and beverages comes with your stay. Eat it in the dining room or enjoy it in the pretty garden, the lush green grounds, or the big porch out front. Rates are $145–185. 10,000 Sir Francis Drake Boulevard 94950; 415/663-9559; www.theolemainn.com.

Novato

PARKS, BEACHES, AND RECREATION AREAS

7 Mount Burdell Open Space Preserve

🐾🐾🐾🐾🐕 (See Marin County map on page 420)

Mount Burdell is the largest of Marin's Open Space preserves. You'll share it with cattle, but there's plenty of room. There are several miles of trails, including part of the Bay Area Ridge Trail, that wind through its oak-dotted grasslands. Dogs have to be leashed on trails but are permitted to run leashless on fire roads here. Be sure to heed signs: Parts of the Open Space are off-limits to dogs because they're sensitive wildlife areas, and dogs aren't usually terribly sensitive to wildlife.

A creek is 0.15 mile up the trail starting at San Andreas Drive, but it's dry in summer. In winter, you might find the preserve's Hidden Lake. In summer, there are lots of foxtails and fire danger is high. No fires are ever allowed. Camping is allowed by permit, but there are no facilities.

From San Marin Drive, turn north on San Andreas Drive. Park on the street. 415/499-6387.

8 Miwok Park

🐾🐾🐾 (See Marin County map on page 420)

This is one of the best city parks we've visited. Dogs must be on leash, but it offers a great combination of dog pleasures and human amenities. Paved paths, good for strollers, wind through pine trees. You will find boccie ball courts, horseshoes, a kids' gym, and a lovely shaded picnic area with grills.

Outside the Museum of the American Indian in this park is an intriguing display of California native plants that the coastal Miwuk used for food, clothing, and shelter.

Best of all for canines, Novato Creek flows deep and 30–40 feet wide (even in summer). A woman we encountered with a golden retriever told us that the muddy bottom can sometimes be soft and treacherous, so keep a close eye on your dog if he goes swimming. The park is at Novato Boulevard and San Miguel Drive. 415/899-8200.

9 Indian Tree Open Space Preserve

🐾🐾🐾🐾🐕 (See Marin County map on page 420)

This is a great choice for a hike if the weather is hot: Your ascent to the top (and to terrific views) takes you through cool, shaded woodlands of oak, madrone, and bay. You'll also encounter redwoods and ferns along the way. At the top, the open area isn't parched and sun-baked like so many areas around here in summer: It's often cool and drippy with fog. Jake the dog, who lives in a foggy area of the city and can't take the heat, is very happy here. You needn't leash on fire roads here, but watch out for horses. Leashes are the law on the preserve's trails.

From U.S. 101, exit at San Marin Drive/Atherton Avenue; drive west on San Marin. After San Marin turns into Sutro Avenue, take a right onto Vineyard Road. Park along the dirt county road that begins at the trailhead. 415/499-6387.

10 Dogbone Meadow Dog Park

🐾🐾🐾🐾🐕 (See Marin County map on page 420)

Lucky dogs who visit here have two fenced acres of off-leash running room and all the "playground equipment" they could want. The park sports tunnels, ramps, jumps, hanging tires, and other fun agility equipment. Big dogs have big toys, and little dogs have littler toys. Everyone's happy here.

The park is a pretty combination of grass and landscaping bark, with the rolling hills of O'Hair Park in the background. (You can walk your dog on leash in this 100-acre city park.) The volunteers who worked so hard to make this park a reality have planted 35 trees, but it will take many years before they're shade-giving. Until then, people gather under shade structures on hot, sunny days. If your dog is dirty from all the romping around, you can use the dog-wash station near the entrance/exit. The park is at San Marin Drive and Novato Boulevard, on the left as you're heading west. 415/899-8200.

🐾 Deer Island Open Space Preserve

🐾🐾🐾🐾🐕 (See Marin County map on page 420)

This preserve is called an island because it's a high point in the floodplain of the Petaluma River, an oak-crowned hill surrounded by miles of dock and tules. You can easily imagine it surrounded by shallow-water Miwuk canoes slipping through rafts of ducks. The trail is a 1.8-mile loop of gentle ups and downs above ponds and marshy fields. There are some sturdy old oaks among the mixed deciduous groves, and lots of laurels. The trail is partly shaded and bans bikes. Dogs have to be leashed on the trails but are permitted off leash on fire roads here.

From U.S. 101, exit at San Marin Drive/Atherton Avenue; drive east about 1.5 miles and take a right on Olive Avenue, then a left on Deer Island Lane. Park in a small lot at the trailhead, by a small engineering company building. 415/499-6387.

🐾 Indian Valley Open Space Preserve

🐾🐾🐾🐾🐕 (See Marin County map on page 420)

Lots of dogs come here to trot around in leashless ecstasy on the fire road. On hiking trails, they have to trot around in leashed ecstasy. The hiking trails and fire roads are partly sunny, partly shaded by laurels, and much revered by canines. Take the Waterfall Trail if you love waterfalls and don't mind leashes. You'll be rewarded at the end, unless of course it's dry season.

From U.S. 101, exit at DeLong Avenue and go west on DeLong, which becomes Diablo Avenue. Take a left on Hill Road and a right on Indian Valley Road. Drive all the way to the end; park on this road before you walk left at the spur road marked Not a Through Street, just south of Old Ranch Road. Cross Arroyo Avichi Creek right at the entrance (dry in summer). 415/499-6387.

🐾 Loma Verde Open Space Preserve

🐾🐾🐾🐕 (See Marin County map on page 420)

This rugged Open Space connects to a couple of others, which makes for a vigorous hike if you and your dog aren't fair of paw. There are two access points to this Open Space, where dogs are allowed off leash on fire roads. One, south of the Marin Country Club, is a waterless, tree-covered hillside with a fire road. Bikes are allowed, so be sure to keep your leash-free dog under voice control. It's a good road if you like easily reachable high spots; there are fine views of San Pablo Bay. Exit U.S. 101 at Ignacio Boulevard. Go west to Fairway Drive and turn left (south), then left on Alameda de la Loma, then right on Pebble Beach Drive. Access is at the end of Pebble Beach.

The second access point is through the Posada West housing development. From Alameda del Prado, turn south on Posada del Sol. The trail opening is at the end of this street. 415/499-6387.

PLACES TO EAT

Christopher's: Christopher's is conveniently located next to the Marin Humane Society. Maybe that's why the restaurant has been taking out ads in local dog newspapers, focusing on its dog-friendly outdoor dining, and mentioning that "treats and fresh water await your best friend." They actually spend money to advertise this! Dogs, you've gotta love this place.

It's set in a business park in Bel Marin Keys, but the outdoor area is a good place to nosh together. The prime rib is on Jake's wish list. Vegetarian dishes are also available. 8 Commercial Boulevard; 415/382-8488.

PLACES TO STAY

Inn Marin: Any lodging that boasts three "dog pot stations" on the property has got to be doggone dog-friendly (and doggone clean, too). These stations are actually just waste cans coupled with plastic bag dispensers, but we appreciate the inn's discreet name for them. The 70-room inn is stylish, clean, and convenient to U.S. 101. It features excellent amenities for people traveling on business (data ports, two-line speaker phones, large desks) and people with disabilities (seven rooms have special features for wheelchairs, and for sight- or hearing-impaired guests). Rates are $99–169. Dogs are $20 total for the first six days, and then $40 per week after. (And get this: You can have up to four per room!) 250 Entrada Drive 94949; 415/883-5952 or 800/652-6565; www.innmarin.com.

TraveLodge: Rates are $69–99. Dogs are $10 extra. 7600 Redwood Boulevard 94945; 415/892-7500.

Lagunitas

PARKS, BEACHES, AND RECREATION AREAS

🔟 Samuel P. Taylor State Park

🐾🐾🐾 (See Marin County map on page 420)

An exception among the state parks: Dog access isn't too bad. You can take a dog into the picnic areas, and that's worth doing here. The main picnic area right off Sir Francis Drake Boulevard is cool and often lively with the grinding call of jays. It's an easy place to bring out-of-state visitors who may just want to eat a sandwich, hug a redwood, and go home. The park has hollow trees stretching 20 feet across that you can actually stand inside.

But best of all, you and your dog can peruse the beautiful Cross Marin Trail, which runs through the park. This is a paved trail popular with bikers, but it makes for a scenic, shady hike for you and your leashed friend. You can pick up the trail at the Redwood Grove Picnic Area.

The park has 60 campsites. Sites are $18–20. From April through October, call for reservations: 800/444-7275. The park's day-use fee is $6. The entrance is on Sir Francis Drake Boulevard about two miles west of Lagunitas. 415/488-9897.

PLACES TO EAT

Lagunitas Grocery: Grab a sandwich at the deli inside and feast on it at the outdoor tables with your dog. Thirsty dogs can ask for a bowl of water. 7890 Sir Francis Drake Boulevard; 415/488-4844.

Woodacre

PARKS, BEACHES, AND RECREATION AREAS

15 Gary Giacomini Open Space Preserve

🐾🐾🐾🐾🐾 (See Marin County map on page 420)

The most recent addition to Marin's Open Space lands is this 1,600-acre gem. The preserve stretches for seven miles along the southern edge of the San Geronimo Valley. Stands of old-growth redwoods shade the ferny lower regions of the park. The higher you go, the more grassy it gets. Dogs such as Jake (i.e., male) prefer the trees, but they can get the best of both worlds by following one of the wide fire trails and sniffing out various areas along the way.

Pooches may go leashless on the fire roads but not on the more narrow hiking trails. Come visit before the rest of the doggone world finds out about this hidden treasure.

From U.S. 101, take Sir Francis Drake Boulevard west to San Geronimo Valley Drive and turn left. You can park at the intersection of Redwood Canyon Drive, just west of Woodacre, and begin your hike at the nearby trailhead. This is a fun route to take with your dog, since it brings you from thick forest to the top of the ridge. 415/499-6387.

Fairfax

This small, friendly, progressive town is known as the birthplace of the mountain bike. That's not news that will put a wag in your dog's tail, but this will: Secret Agent Dog, a pooch with impeccable taste, had his person write to tell me that "Fairfax is… one of the most dog-friendly places we've ever lived." Mutt Mitt dispensers are placed strategically through town, and there are two drinking fountains (one by the baseball field, one by town hall) for both humans and dogs. People here love to see dogs with their people; some stores will welcome your dog if it's not busy, but we'll leave that on a case-by-case basis.

PARKS, BEACHES, AND RECREATION AREAS

16 Cascade Canyon Open Space Preserve
😸 😸 😸 (See Marin County map on page 420)

Doggone it. Dogs are no longer legally allowed to be leash-free on the fire road here. Jake doesn't like this slowly encroaching leashes-only rules at Marin Open Space lands, and neither does his human fellow hiker. Still, the fire road makes for a pleasant walk that leads all the way into the Marin Municipal Water District lands of Mt. Tamalpais (where leashes are the law, too).

The hiking trails at Cascade Canyon are even more enjoyable. The main trail sticks close to San Anselmo Creek, which is reduced to a dry creek bed in summer. A no-bicycles trail branches off to the right and disappears into the creek; the left branch fords the creek. When the water's high, you may be stopped right here. But in summer, you can walk a long way. Side trails lead you into shady glens of laurel and other deciduous trees, but there's lots of poison oak, too.

The park is at the end of Cascade Drive. The Town of Fairfax sign says Elliott Nature Preserve, but it's official Open Space. Please don't park at the end of Cascade. Spread out so the folks who live at the end of Cascade don't get so inundated with dogs. Pooches have been a problem for some residents, whose beautiful flowers and lawns have succumbed to dog feet and pooch poop. Be courteous, and think how you'd feel if the shoe were on the other paw. 415/499-6387.

San Anselmo

San Anselmo Avenue provides you and your mellow pooch a laid-back stroll, and you can both cool your paws in San Anselmo Creek, which runs through town. Your well-behaved pooch can even be off leash, provided she's under voice control.

PARKS, BEACHES, AND RECREATION AREAS

17 Red Hill "Park"
😸 😸 🐕 (See Marin County map on page 420)

For the last few editions of this book I've been writing in the introduction to San Anselmo that a group of local dog owners has been trying to get a dog park within this five-acre property behind the Red Hill Shopping Center. Part of the property has been a de facto dog park for years, very popular with pooches and their people. As of this writing, the property in Ross Valley isn't officially even a park for humans, but it's getting very close. Once that happens, and it could by the time you read this, the plan is for the dog park to get sanctioned along with it.

I usually don't give parks a listing unless they have the final handshake from government entities. But the dog area is included in San Anselmo government literature, people here—even city officials—refer to it as "the dog park," and it's been used by so many dogs for so many years, that Jake and I have decided that the time has come for a real listing. It's like when two people who have lived together for many years but never married start referring to each other as husband and wife. This park has now achieved a veritable "common-law" status in this book.

The doggy area of Red Hill isn't fenced (at this point), but it's far enough from traffic that most dogs are fine with this. When we visited it was cushy with green grass and brimming with leashless well-behaved dogs and their well-behaved people. Be sure your dog doesn't end up in the areas where people are playing ballgames. The park is between Shaw Drive and Sunny Hills Drive, behind the Red Hill Shopping Center in the Ross Valley area. 415/258-4640.

18 Loma Alta Open Space Preserve
🐾🐾🐾🐾🐕 (See Marin County map on page 420)
A little canyon amid bare hills, lined with oaks, bay laurel, and buckeye, this is an exceptional Open Space preserve. Shade is plentiful. The trail follows White Hill Creek, which is dry in the summer. Leashes are required on the trails, but obedient dogs can throw their leashes to the wind on the fire road.

You can park at the trailhead at the end of Glen Avenue, a turn north off Sir Francis Drake Boulevard. 415/499-6387.

19 Memorial Park
🐾🐾🐾🐕 (See Marin County map on page 420)
This pleasant and popular city park has tennis courts, three baseball diamonds, and a children's play area. Next to the diamonds is an area where leash-free dogs romp joyfully, fetching, chasing Frisbees, or socializing. Even a creek runs nearby. There's a hitch—dogs can be off leash only before 8 A.M. and from one hour before sunset to, well, sunset. The park is at Veterans Place, a quick jog east from San Francisco Boulevard. 415/258-4640.

20 Sorich Ranch Park
🐾🐾🐾🐾🐕 (See Marin County map on page 420)
The biggest and by far the wildest city park in San Anselmo is Sorich Ranch Park, an undeveloped open space soaring to a ridge top from which you can see a distant make-believe San Francisco skyline across the bay. From the very top of the ridge, you also can see Mt. Tamalpais and most of San Rafael, including

the one-of-a-kind turquoise and salmon Marin County Civic Center, designed by Frank Lloyd Wright. (Some Marinites are glad there's only one.)

The entrance from the San Anselmo side is at the end of San Francisco Boulevard, and the path is pretty much straight up. But if you aren't up to a 10-minute puffing ascent, you can just stroll in the meadows at the bottom. No leash is required, and the park is uncrowded and often pleasantly breezy. No water is available, and it can be scorching in summer. 415/258-4640.

PLACES TO EAT

Bubba's Diner: If you found an eatery by this name in many other towns, you might be inclined to stride by with nary a glance, lest you absorb grease and saturated fat just by looking at it. But being that this Bubba's Diner is in San Anselmo, grease is not the main ingredient of most dishes, and the saturated fat is at least upscale saturated fat.

Bubba's is a really fun, unpretentious place to bring a dog for some extra-tasty American-style eats. The cheery owner, Beth, likes to see well-behaved dogs dining at the two awning-shaded tables and benches in front of the restaurant. But she warns people not to tie dogs to the benches, lest the dog drag away the bench. (One small pooch actually went exploring the neighborhood, pulling the hefty pine bench behind him!) Take Beth's advice and hook your dog to the pay phone if you're dining alone and need to run in to place your order.

Choose from dozens of yummy dishes here. The food varies from healthful and delicious (oyster salad, grilled salmon with asparagus and sautéed spinach) to decadent and delicious (pot roast, fried chicken, burgers, mashed potato pancakes). If you're pining for some fried green tomatoes, look no further: Bubba's is famous for them. Thirsty doggies can get water here. 566 San Anselmo Avenue; 415/459-6862.

San Rafael

PARKS, BEACHES, AND RECREATION AREAS

21 Lucas Valley Open Space Preserve

🐾🐾🐾🐾 🐕 (See Marin County map on page 420)

This space of rolling, oak-dotted hills affords great views of Novato and Lucas Valley developments. The summit here is 1,825 feet—the second-highest in Marin. We like to take the scenic Big Rock Trail up to the Big Rock Fire Road. It's a gentle grade for beasts and their people.

The preserve has a dozen access points, most from Lucas Valley and Marinwood. One access point is reached by turning left (north) off Lucas Valley Road on Mount Shasta Drive, followed by a brief right turn on Vogelsang Drive. Park near this dead end and walk in. Keep in mind that all Marin Open Space

Preserves require pooches to be on leash except on fire roads. (Thanks to giant local golden retriever Duke, who set us straight on the preserve's exact location.) 415/499-6387.

22 Terra Linda–Sleepy Hollow Divide Open Space Preserve

🐾🐾🐾🐾🐕 (See Marin County map on page 420)

This ridgeline preserve has many entrances, but generally the best are the highest on the ridge. We'll describe the one that starts you at a good high point, so that you don't have to climb. From the entrance at the end of Ridgewood Drive, you can walk into Sorich Ranch Park in San Anselmo.

From this ridge, you can see the city of San Rafael, U.S. 101, the wonderful turquoise-roofed Marin County Civic Center, the bay, and the hills of Solano County. No leash is necessary on fire roads, unless you're worried about your dog's tangling with deer. But pooches must be leashed on trails.

Park near the very end of Ridgewood Drive. The entrance is unmarked, and you have to step over a low locked gate. 415/499-6387.

23 Field of Dogs

🐾🐾🐾🐾🐕 (See Marin County map on page 420)

We love the name, love the park. The people behind Field of Dogs worked really hard to make the park a reality. It took about six years. It's not only real now, but it's a great place to take a dog for off-leash exercise.

The one-acre park has little trees, big trees, a double-gated entry, benches, picnic tables, poop bags, and very nice park-goers—of both the pooch and people variety. Some trees are in the middle of the park, and we've heard about more than one head-on canine collision with a tree during chase games. After the swirling stars and tweeting birds wear off, the dogs are just fine.

The park is behind the civic center, at 3540 Civic Center Drive. It's an easy jaunt from U.S. 101. Exit U.S. 101 and continue east to Civic Center Drive, which is the first light. Turn left and the park will be on your right just past the post office and firehouse. 415/499-6405.

24 John F. McInnis County Park

🐾🐾🐾🐕 (See Marin County map on page 420)

This is an all-around, got-everything park for people. Among its riches are two softball fields, two soccer fields, tennis courts, a picnic area, a scale-model car track, a nine-hole golf course, miniature golf, batting cages, and a dirt creekside nature trail.

Best of all for trustworthy dogs, they can be off leash, so long as they're under verbal command and out of the golf course. This park isn't particularly pretty, but it's very utilitarian. From U.S. 101, exit at Smith Ranch Road. 415/499-6387.

25 San Pedro Mountain Open Space Preserve

😺😺😺 (See Marin County map on page 420)

A narrow footpath rises moderately but inexorably upward through a madrone forest. But if you make it up far enough, you'll be rewarded with terrific views of the bay and Marin's peaks. Unlike most other Open Space lands in Marin, this one doesn't permit pooches off leash on fire roads because the fire roads at the top are city property. This means dogs have to be leashed here. It's probably just as well since so many deer call this park home.

Park at the entrance at the end of Woodoaks Drive, a short street off North Point San Pedro Road just north of the Jewish Community Center of Marin. 415/499-6387.

26 Santa Venetia Marsh Open Space Preserve

😺😺😺😺 (See Marin County map on page 420)

Dogs are very lucky to be able to visit this saltwater marsh. Only leashed pooches on their best behavior should come here, because the preserve is home to an endangered bird, the California clapper rail. Keep your eyes peeled: It looks like a chicken (and apparently tastes something like one, too—it was heavily hunted during the Gold Rush, when its meat was considered a delightful delicacy), but it has a long beak.

Mmm, doggy, the scents can be mighty strong here sometimes. They're so doggone nose-flaring good your dog may not even notice he's wearing a leash. You may not feel the same about the odor, but, hey, just keep saying to yourself, "it's a natural smell."

It's cool and breezy here, but gentler than any San Francisco Bay shore park. The grasses and pickleweed make a pretty mixture of colors, and swallows dart above the ground hunting insects. Be sure to keep on the trails because this is sensitive marsh habitat.

Vendola Drive has two distinct parts, and you can get to the marsh from the end of either. 415/499-6387.

27 China Camp State Park

😺😺😺 (See Marin County map on page 420)

You shouldn't miss a drive through this lovely park, although it's not terribly hospitable to dogs except at Village Beach, the site of the 1890s Chinese fishing village for which the park is named. As you drive in, you'll see a rare piece of bay, marsh, and oak-covered hills as the Miwuks saw it. The hills, like islands, rise from salt-marsh seas of pickleweed and cordgrass. You'll see the No Dogs symbol at every trailhead, in case you're tempted. However, with your dog you may visit any of three picnic grounds on the way, via North Point San Pedro Road. Buckeye Point and Weber Point both have tables in shade or sun overlooking San Pablo Bay, mudflats at low tide, and the hills beyond the bay. Bullhead Flat lets you get right next to the water, but there's no shade at the tables.

Watch for the sign to China Camp Village, a left turn into a lot, where there's some shade. You'll see the rickety old pier and the wood-and-tin village. Park, leash your dog, and walk down to the village and the beach. On weekdays, this park is much less crowded. There are more picnic tables overlooking the water by the parking lot, an interpretive exhibit and, on weekends, a refreshment stand serving shrimp, crab, and beer. You can eat at picnic tables right on the beach—small, but pleasantly sheltered by hillsides, with gentle surf.

Swimming is encouraged here, and it's often warm enough. Derelict fishing boats and shacks are preserved on the beach. You can walk all the way to a rocky point at the south end, but watch out for the luxuriant poison oak in the brush along the beach. You may occasionally find broken glass.

There are 31 primitive walk-in campsites here. As in all state parks, dogs must always be leashed or confined to your tent. Sites are $20–25. To reserve (recommended April–October), call 800/444-7275. From U.S. 101, take the North Point San Pedro Road exit and follow it all the way into the park. (Don't go near McNears Beach County Park just south of China Camp. Dogs are strictly forbidden.) There's a $5 parking fee. 415/456-0766.

PLACES TO EAT

Le Chalet Basque: If you've never had Basque cuisine, this is a great place to try it. The portions are ample, tasty, and affordable, and your good dog can join you on the patio. The restaurant is well off the beaten path, in San Rafael's San Venetia neighborhood, but there's usually a good crowd. 405 North San Pedro Road; 415/479-1070.

Le Croissant Restaurant: With a name like this you'd expect California/French café cuisine, but don't let the name fool you: The food here is of the good old-fashioned 1960s diner genre. Breakfasts are heavy and delicious, or try the soups, salads, and sandwiches later in the day. Your dog can join you on the tree-shaded patio. Le Croissant is in the canal area of San Rafael, at 150 Bellam Boulevard; 415/456-0164.

Ristorante La Toscana: The Italian food here is basic and good. Enjoy pasta or several meaty dishes, including broiled lamb chops or New York minute steak, with your dog at the outside tables. The restaurant is across from the Civic Center and gets crowded when evening events take place. 3751 Redwood Highway; 415/492-9100.

Shaky Grounds: The shaky grounds here refer to coffee, not earthquakes (we think). If coffee isn't your cup of tea, you can order pastries, smoothies, soups, salads, and sandwiches. Dogs not only get water, but they're treated to treats here, too! 1800 4th Street; 415/256-2420.

PLACES TO STAY

Panama Hotel: Dogs are welcome to stay in three attractive rooms at this charming, funky, circa-1910 inn. These dog-friendly rooms are on the ground floor, have private sitting porches or patios, and tile or slate floors. In other words, they're easy maintenance and roomy enough for people with pets.

Pets feel welcome here. "We enjoy having dog guests," says one of the owners. To the point: Dogs get a couple of treats, two bowls, and pet towels upon check in. A continental breakfast comes with your room. Rates for the dog-friendly rooms are $135. Dogs are $15 extra, and there's a two-dog limit per room. A big thanks to Barbara Steinberg for the heads-up about this place. 4 Bayview Street 94901; 415/457-3993 or 800/899-3993; www.panamahotel.com.

Villa Inn: This is a pleasant and affordable place to spend the night with your dog. Rates are $69–125. 1600 Lincoln Avenue 94901; 415/456-4975 or 888/845-5246.

Ross

PARKS, BEACHES, AND RECREATION AREAS

28 Natalie Coffin Greene Park

🐾🐾🐾 (See Marin County map on page 420)

Leashed dogs are welcome at this enchanted mixed forest of redwood and deciduous trees. The picnic area has an old-fashioned shelter built of logs and stone.

The park borders generic Marin Municipal Water District land, and from the park, you can pick up the wide cinder fire road leading to Phoenix Lake, a five-minute walk. Bikers, hikers, and leashed dogs are all welcome on this road, but the lake is a reservoir, so no body contact is allowed—for man or beast.

The road continues, depending how far you want to walk, to Lagunitas Lake, Bon Tempe Lake, Alpine Lake, and Kent Lake (no swimming in any of them—sorry, dogs). Combined, the water district offers 94 miles of road and 44 miles of trail in this area, meandering through hillsides densely forested with pine, oak, madrone, and a variety of other trees. For a trail map, send a self-addressed, stamped envelope to Sky Oaks Ranger Station, P.O. Box 865, Fairfax, CA 94978, Attention: Trail Map.

At the corner of Sir Francis Drake Boulevard and Lagunitas Road, go west on Lagunitas all the way to the end, past the country club. You'll find a parking lot and some portable toilets. 415/453-1453.

Larkspur

PARKS, BEACHES, AND RECREATION AREAS

29 Baltimore Canyon Open Space Preserve

🐾🐾🐾🐾🐕 (See Marin County map on page 420)

If you don't like heat, this 175-acre Open Space is a fine place to come for a summer stroll. You have less chance of getting roasty-toasty here than at many other nearby parks: The big oaks, madrones, bays, firs, and even redwoods tend to keep things cool in the canyon. It even has a year-round creek and a seasonal 30-foot waterfall, Dawn Falls. It's worth the hike to the end of the canyon to see this cascade. It's about 2.2 miles round trip and has only a 300-foot elevation change—something most healthy dogs and people can easily manage.

Since it's a trail, not a fire road, dogs need to be leashed, as per Open Space District rules. Leashes aren't required on the fire roads, but bikes are also allowed on these trails, so be careful.

In the spring the place is verdant, lush, and full of wildflowers. That's our favorite time to visit. And unlike so many Bay Area locales, fall provides some real, live autumn colors, thanks to the maples here. When I'm missing the change of seasons, Baltimore Canyon beckons. On crisp, dewy mornings, I'm tempted to belt out the *Hairspray!* tune "Good Morning Baltimore," but for Jake's sake, I refrain.

From this Open Space you have good access to a lot of fire roads through the ridges connecting with Mt. Tamalpais (remember, though—no dogs at Mt. Tam State Park trails) and water-district lands.

Exit U.S. 101 at Paradise/Tamalpais Drive, and go west on Tamalpais Drive for about 0.8 mile. At the stop sign for Magnolia Avenue, turn right, and drive 0.6 mile. Turn left onto Madrone Avenue, just past the Lark Creek Inn. The road will be narrow and will eventually turn into Valley Way. In 0.8 mile, you'll find a small turnaround at the end of the road. Park only at the white-outlined roadside spaces, about 30 feet from the trailhead. 415/499-6387.

30 Blithedale Summit Open Space Preserve

🐾🐾🐾🐾🐕 (See Marin County map on page 420)

The access point at the end of Madrone Avenue—the north end of this Open Space—is a delightful walk in hot weather, through cool redwoods that let some light filter through. This isn't one of those really dark, drippy canyons; you're at a medium-high altitude on the slopes of Mt. Tamalpais. The trail follows Larkspur Creek, which retains some pools in summer. Cross the footbridge and follow the slightly rough foot trail. Unfortunately, leashes are now the law on these trails, but you can let your dog off his leash once you hit the fire road.

The drive up narrow Madrone Avenue is an adventure in itself; redwoods grow right in the street. According to a sign at the entrance, the part of this space belonging to the city of Larkspur requires dogs to be leashed. 415/499-6387.

🐾 Canine Commons

🐾🐾🐾🐕 (See Marin County map on page 420)

Canine Commons is popular with common canines. It isn't a very big dog park, but it was the first in Marin, opening its doggy gates in 1989. That's ancient history in the annals of dog parkdom. It's a basic dog park, with water, poop bags, and tennis balls.

Canine Commons is set within Piper Park, where you can play or watch softball, volleyball, tennis, and even cricket. Outside Canine Commons, dogs must be leashed. The park is between Doherty Drive and Corte Madera Creek. Canine Commons is at the west end of the park. 415/927-5110.

PLACES TO EAT

The Left Bank: Your dog doesn't have to be a poodle to enjoy dining at this terrific French restaurant. Because it's a French place, management knows that dogs and restaurants really do mix. But because they're in America, they have to abide by local health regulations and keep doggies from dining inside. That's OK, though, because there are plenty of outside tables. When it's crowded, managers ask that you tie your dog to the railing that surrounds the outdoor area. You can still dine right beside your pooch. Thirsty pooches can get a bowl of water. 507 Magnolia Avenue; 415/927-3331.

Table Cafe: You'd never guess such an amazing restaurant (formerly Tabla Cafe, until an upscale Manhattan restaurant with the same name threatened a lawsuit) could be tucked away in a shopping center known for its hardware store. But here it is. Table Cafe's food is extremely delicious, organic, and mostly locally grown or raised. The cuisine is best described as California-India fusion. Table is known for its *dosa,* a kind of Indian crepe filled with your choice of flavorful ingredients. Dogs are welcome to join you at the umbrella-topped outdoor tables. 1167 Magnolia Avenue; 415/461-6787.

Bolinas

Bolinas is famous for trying to hide from curious visitors—thereby drawing hordes of them. They keep coming, even though town citizens regularly take down the turnoff sign on Highway 1. So if you're coming from the east (San Francisco area), turn left at the unmarked road where Bolinas Lagoon ends. If you're coming from the west, turn right where the lagoon begins. Don't worry—if you succeed in finding the place, people are friendly.

Sometimes it seems as if half the inhabitants of Bolinas are dogs, most of them black. They stand guard outside bars, curl at shop owners' feet, snooze in the middle of the road. You'll find no city hall in Bolinas, an unincorporated area, and no chamber of commerce. Dogs are always welcome here, but cars, horses, bicycles, and too many unleashed dogs compete for space. Be thoughtful and keep your pooch leashed in town.

PARKS, BEACHES, AND RECREATION AREAS

Alas, dogs are no longer officially allowed on beautiful Agate Beach.

32 Bolinas Beach

🐾🐾🐾🦮 (See Marin County map on page 420)

At the end of the main street, Wharf Road, is a sand-and-pebble beach at the foot of a bluff. Dogs are free to run off leash. But watch for horses—with riders and without—thundering past without warning. It's animal anarchy here, and it's not the cleanest beach in Marin. We give it points for fun, though. 415/499-6387.

PLACES TO EAT

Coast Cafe: This is a very dog-friendly spot for breakfast, lunch, dinner, beer, wine, and ice cream. "Dogs are great!" has been the mantra of more than one waiter we've met here through the years. Dogs can dine with you at the street tables and sometimes the patio tables (ask first). A bowl of water is available on request, and in the morning, a coffee kiosk sells dog biscuits. Yum! 46 Wharf Road; 415/868-2298.

PLACES TO STAY

Smiley's Schooner Saloon & Hotel: No, you can't stay at the saloon (much as you might want to after a night of revelry with the fun-loving crowd here— besides, dogs can't go in the saloon, no matter how old they are in dog years). But you can stay with your dog at the Smiley's hotel. It's a very cool, funky, historic place, with rooms that are actually pretty decent for the price. (A friend told me her room was a little musty, but pleasant.) Smiley's really encapsulates the feel of Bolinas.

How old is Smiley's? I'll let a Smiley's ditty tell you: "Before Lincoln was president... Before baseball was a game... Before Jingle Bells was a song... There was Smiley's." Smiley's was established in 1851. That's Gold Rush–old. But don't let that stop you from bringing your laptop: Smiley's has free Wi-Fi. Rates are $100–115. Dogs are $10 extra. 41 Wharf Road 94924; 415/868-1311; www.coastalpost.com/smileys.

Stinson Beach

It's fun to poke around the town of Stinson Beach, which is swarming with surfers and tourists on beautiful days. You'll find a relaxed attitude toward dogs at the outdoor snack-shop tables. Bolinas Lagoon, stretching along Highway 1 between Stinson Beach and Bolinas, is tempting but environmentally fragile, so you should picnic along the water only if your dog is controllable. You'll also be taking a chance with muddy paws in your car. Don't go near Audubon Canyon Ranch, where herons and egrets nest.

PARKS, BEACHES, AND RECREATION AREAS

🐾🐾 Upton Beach ("Dog Beach")
🐾🐾🐾🐾 (See Marin County map on page 420)

Highway 1 to Stinson and Bolinas is worth the curves you'll negotiate. Don't be in a hurry. On sunny weekends, traffic will be heavy. Try it on a foggy day—it's otherworldly. Anyway, dogs often don't care whether or not the sun is shining.

The Stinson Beach area abounds with happy dogs, but the part of the beach that's run by the National Park Service bans the critters. They're allowed only at the picnic areas and parking lot there. Ooh, fun!

Fortunately, Upton Beach, the county-managed stretch of beach where private houses are built at the north end, does allow dogs on leash. This is itself a bit of a contradiction, because as you walk along with your obediently leashed dog, dogs who live in the houses lining the county stretch, and who don't have to wear leashes, come prancing out like the local law enforcement to check out the new kid.

Take the beach turnoff from Highway 1. Turn right at the parking lot and park at the far north end. Walk right by the sign that says, "No Pets on Beach"—you can't avoid it—and turn right. Where the houses start is the county beach. You'll see a sign dividing the two jurisdictions saying, "End of Guarded Beach." 415/499-6387.

PLACES TO EAT

Parkside: Dogs love dining at the patio tables with their people. The atmosphere is relaxed and thoroughly enjoyable. The food is tasty American-California cuisine. Sure, you can get yummy burgers and salads, but items like oven-roasted lemon-thyme polenta share the menu, and will make you glad you drove the extra distance to get here. *The San Francisco Chronicle* once wrote that Parkside's food "is some of the best in all of coastal Marin and Sonoma counties." 43 Arsenal Avenue; 415/868-1272.

Sand Dollar Restaurant: Enjoy a variety of good food and drinks at this café on Highway 1 that's been here forever—OK, since 1921. Seafood is the specialty. While dining at the heated patio with your dog, you might even catch some local musicians. 3458 Shoreline Highway; 415/868-0434.

PLACES TO STAY

Beachtime Beach House: This wonderful three-bedroom vacation rental puts the "Oh!!!" in ocean views. It's right on the dog-friendly beach, with sand truly just in front of the house. (The owners try to keep it there, and not inside, which is why they have an outdoor shower and hose, plus slate tile floors and hardwood floors—no carpeting.) It's an airy, attractive house, with three decks, a hot tub on the back deck, a great fireplace stove in the living room, and windows with views that are beyond droolworthy. If you like this one, you'll like the other properties the owners now rent out. Rates for the Beachtime Beach House are $280 per night, and $1,860–2,260 weekly. There's a $60 cleaning fee for the length of your stay. During winter you can rent the house on a monthly basis for a greatly reduced price. You'll get the address when you book the house. 415/577-4954; www.beachtime.org.

Redwoods Haus Bed and Breakfast: It's hard to categorize this place. It's funky, it's a little odd, it's clean, it's super-friendly, it's comfy, and it's cheap compared to most other West Marin lodgings. A very masculine boxer friend of Jake (a boxer dog, not the Muhammad Ali variety) stayed in what's called The Pink Room. With its pink bedspread, pink floral curtains, pink lamp, and other pink decorative touches and white girly furniture, it looks rather dollhouse-y. He didn't mind a bit, mostly because his people promised not to let anyone know that he stayed there. "Fergus would be so embarrassed," says Denise, his person. (Oops… Sorry, Fergus.)

Jake's favorite of the four guest rooms is The Crows Nest, which has soft but more masculine hues than The Pink Room and sports excellent ocean views. It's the biggest room, too, with a queen-size bed, a day bed, and a queen-size futon.

Here's an example of the funky nature of the Redwoods Haus: "All rooms come with…access to our piano, acoustic guitars, video library, charcoal barbecue, biergarten, and buffet area," its literature announces. That's quite a combination of amenities. It continues, "Cats are OK—purrr. Dogs are OK—wooof."

Rooms come with breakfast. It's not gourmet, but with eggs, ham, cereal, fruit, bread, and beverages, it hits the spot. Rates are $55–165. The Redwood Haus is at 1 Belvedere Street (at Highway 1) 94970; 415/868-9828; www.stinson-beach.com.

Mill Valley

PARKS, BEACHES, AND RECREATION AREAS

🐾 Mount Tamalpais State Park

🐾🐾🐾 (See Marin County map on page 420)

Generally, dogs are restricted to paved roads here. But dogs may stay in the campground, and there are also a few spots near the summit where you can take your dog (via the Marin Municipal Water District lands). The views from here are something you'll certainly appreciate on a clear day.

Stop for lunch at the Bootjack Picnic Area, west of the Mountain Home Inn on Panoramic Highway and about a quarter mile east of the turnoff to the summit, Pan Toll Road. The tables are attractively sited on the hillside under oak trees. The nearby Old Stage Fire Road is a water district road going almost the whole distance to the summit. You can also enter the Old Stage Fire Road right across from the Pan Toll Ranger Station, at the intersection of Panoramic Highway and Pan Toll Road. Pooches have special permission to cross the 100 feet or so of state park trail approaching water district trail.

The Bootjack Picnic Area parking lot charges $6 to park. (Once you pay in any state park lot, your receipt is good for any other spot you hit that day.) The park has 16 developed walk-in campsites that allow dogs. They're at the Pan Toll Station Campground. Sites are $15. All sites are first-come, first-served. 415/388-2070.

35 Mount Tamalpais Summit
😺😺😺 (See Marin County map on page 420)

The summit of Mt. Tam is worth the $6 fee that you're charged merely to drive here. But in addition to appreciating the magnificent views, you may also take your dog on one trail up here.

You'll find a small refreshment stand, restrooms, a visitors center, and viewing platforms. On clear days, you can see nine counties, whether you want to or not. In summer, white fingers of fog obscure a good part of your view as they creep between the "knuckles" of Marin's ridges.

It's too bad if your leashed dog doesn't care about views. But he will take eagerly to the smoothly paved Verna Dunshee Trail, about one mile long, running almost level around the summit. About three-quarters of this trail is also wheelchair-accessible.

From U.S. 101, take the Stinson Beach/Highway 1 exit. Follow Highway 1 to Panoramic Highway, which will be a right turn. Continue on Panoramic to the right turnoff to Pantoll Road; Pantoll soon becomes East Ridgecrest Road and goes to the summit, and then loops back for your trip down. 415/945-1455 or 415/388-2070.

36 Mount Tamalpais–Marin Municipal Water District Land
😺😺😺 (See Marin County map on page 420)

Your very best bet for a dog walk high on the mountain is to find one of the water district fire roads near the summit. Your dog must be leashed, but at least she can go on the trails with you, and you both can experience the greenness of this wonderful mountain. At this elevation, the green comes from chaparral, pine, and madrone.

Just below the summit on East Ridgecrest Boulevard, watch for the water district's gate and sign. This is the Old Railroad Grade Fire Road, which descends 1,785 feet from the entry point just west of the summit. On the way it intersects Old Stage Fire Road, then emerges at the Bootjack Picnic Area. En route, you'll cross three creeks. For obvious reasons, you'll be happier in warm weather taking this road down, not up; get someone to meet you in a car at the Bootjack Picnic Area.

Another spot to pick up a water district trail is off Panoramic Highway just west of the Mountain Home Inn. Look for the Marin Municipal Water District sign by the fire station. Park at the state park parking lot west of Mountain Home Inn and walk east along this fire road, called Gravity Car Road (though it's unmarked), through mixed pines, redwoods, fir, madrone, and scrub. Keep your eyes open for fast-moving mountain bikes. 415/945-1400.

37 Old Mill Park

🐾🐾🐾 (See Marin County map on page 420)

Refresh your dog under cool redwoods right in the town of Mill Valley. The old mill, built in 1834, was recently restored. A wooden bridge over Old Mill Creek leads to well-maintained paths that run along the creek. The creek is dog-accessible, though pooches are supposed to be leashed.

One picnic table here sits within the hugest "fairy ring" we've ever seen—40 feet across. Boy dogs like to imagine the size of the mother tree whose stump engendered this ring of saplings. The park is on Throckmorton Avenue at Olive Street, near the public library. 415/383-1370.

38 Camino Alto Open Space Preserve

🐾🐾🐾🐾 (See Marin County map on page 420)

In this accessible Open Space, your dog may run free on a wide fire trail along a ridge connecting with Mt. Tamalpais. You'll walk through bay laurels, madrones, and chaparral, looking down on soaring vultures and the bay, Highway 1, the hills, and the Headlands. A small imperfection is that you can hear the whoosh of traffic. Just pretend it's the wind. Dogs must be leashed on the regular hiking trails here. Park at the end of Escalon Drive, just west of Camino Alto. 415/499-6387.

39 Bayfront Park

🐾🐾🐾🐾🐾 (See Marin County map on page 420)

This good-looking park is well designed for every kind of family activity and for dogs. It has an exercise course, lawns are green and silky, and picnic areas are clean and attractive. The multiuse trails for bicycles, strollers, and whatnot may be used only by leashed dogs (there are bikes galore). But here's the canine payoff: It has a special dog run next to an estuary, where dogs are free to dip their paws. (Tioga, the dog of my freelance editor and researcher Caroline Grannan, learned to swim here. Or rather, she discovered swimming, because, as Caroline says, with labs like Tioga, there's really no learning curve for the dog paddle. It's instantaneous. In the other camp was my old Airedale, Joe, who lived for 13 years and never got the hang of staying afloat, poor beast.)

The dog-use area starts where you see the signs and all the other dogs.

Beware, owners of escape artists: The area is a big three acres, but it's not fenced. No scoops or water are furnished, but the Richardson Bay Estuary is right there to jump into.

At the end of the run there's even a marsh that dogs can explore, if you're willing to put a very mucky friend back into the car with you. Luckily, this marsh is all relatively clean muck (oxymoron alert!), free from the dangerous trash that fills many unprotected bay marshes.

For a dog park, this one offers an unparalleled view of Mt. Tam. Horses and bikes pass by harmlessly on their own separate trail in the foreground, and mockingbirds sing in the bushes.

The parking lot is on Sycamore Avenue, just after you cross Camino Alto, next to the wastewater treatment plant. Keep your dog leashed near the steep-sided sewage ponds; dogs have drowned in them. Also, be sure to keep your dog leashed until you've reached the grassy dog-run area; there's a fine if you're caught unleashed. 415/383-1370.

PLACES TO EAT

Grilly's Restaurant: If you order a chicken taco salad or the mixed veggie quesadilla here, chances are you'll never find their equals in another Mexican restaurant. They're that good. The rest of the food is decent, fast, and easy on the wallet. Dine with your dog at the small outdoor area. 493 Miller Avenue; 415/381-3278.

Mama's Royal Cafe: It's kitschy, it's divey, it's fun, and it's super dog friendly. Oh, and the food is fabulous too. The breakfasts are out of this world, and the crepes are to drool for. As for dogs, "We LOVE dogs here!" exclaimed a server. How much do they love dogs? "Sometimes we'll give them a little piece of bacon. And we always give them water." Dine with your dog at the umbrella-topped patio tables. The patio is next to the parking lot, but you'll hardly notice. Weekend brunch time can be very busy, but there's often live piano music to help pass the wait. 393 Miller Avenue; 415/388-3261.

PLACES TO STAY

Holiday Inn Express: Set on the edge of nature, this Holiday Inn Express is a good place to go with a pooch who likes to go for hikes. The rooms are attractive and comfortable. Rates are $129–189. Dogs pay a $75 fee for the length of their stay, so you might want to stay a few days to get your money's worth. 160 Shoreline Highway 94941; 415/332-5700.

Corte Madera

Dogs are banned from all parks here. But mope not, pooches, because at least you get to munch on café cuisine.

PLACES TO EAT

Book Passage Cafe: Whether your dog is illiterate or erudite, he's welcome to join you at the many shaded tables outside this bookstore/café. You can dine on sandwiches, muffins, and a few assorted hot entrées, as well as tasty coffees and healthful smoothies. Dogs aren't allowed inside the bookstore, so if you want to peruse (and who wouldn't—the bookstore is one of the best we've seen), bring a friend and take turns dog-sitting. 51 Tamal Vista Boulevard; 415/927-1503.

Twin Cities Market: Pick up a fresh deli sandwich (with your dog's favorite cold cuts, of course) and eat it with your pooch at the three tables outside. It's casual, but that's how most dogs like it. 118 Corte Madera Avenue; 415/924-7372.

PLACES TO STAY

Marin Suites Hotel: The guest accommodations here are mostly of the spacious suite variety, which works out great when traveling with a dog. You'll get a fully equipped kitchen and separate living room and bedroom. Traditional hotel rooms, with kitchenettes, are also available. Rates are $154–204. Dogs are $10 extra. 45 Tamal Vista Boulevard 94925; 415/924-3608 or 800/362-3372; www.marinsuites.com.

Tiburon

The town of Tiburon is almost too Disneyland-perfect, with its green lawns and fountains, brick sidewalks, and lack of smells. On a sunny day you can't beat the clean, safe street atmosphere for eating and strolling. Dogs, of course, must be as polite and well behaved as their owners. Tiburon did a good job of planning for parking: There's almost none except for one large lot with reasonable prices, which means that cars aren't driving around searching for a spot. Just give up and park there.

PARKS, BEACHES, AND RECREATION AREAS

40 Richardson Bay Lineal Park

🐾🐾🐾 (See Marin County map on page 420)

Generally known as the Tiburon Bike Path (and certainly rarely referred to with the odd "Lineal" in its name), this is a terrific multiuse park, unusual because it can be safely enjoyed by both bicyclists and dogs. It stretches two-thirds the length of Tiburon's peninsula and has parking at both ends. The larger lot is at the northern end. A dirt road, Brunini Way (no vehicles), leads into the park at the north end. You'll find a quiet, natural bay shoreline with a bit of marsh. There's some flotsam and jetsam, but only the highest quality, of course.

Keep walking and you'll enter McKegney Green, the wide bike path that runs for two miles along Tiburon Boulevard toward downtown. (It doesn't go all the way, though.) Your dog must be leashed. The path, marked for running trainers, swings past benches overlooking the bay and a kids' jungle gym.

Soon the path splits and goes past both sides of a stretch of soccer fields, fenced wildlife ponds (no dogs), and a parcourse fitness trail. You can take your dog on either side, but be aware that bicyclists use both. You'll also share this path, on a fair weekend day, with roller skaters and parents pushing strollers. On the green are sunbathers and kite fliers.

The view: Mt. Tamalpais and Belvedere, with the Bay Bridge, San Francisco, and the Golden Gate Bridge peeking out from behind. Bring a jacket—it can be breezy here—and carry water for your dog if you're walking far. The only fountains are for people. Going toward town on Tiburon Boulevard, turn right at the sign that says Blackie's Pasture Road. It leads to the parking lot. 415/435-7373.

PLACES TO EAT

Paradise Hamburgers and Ice Cream: This place furnishes bike racks and lots of outdoor tables. There's always a Fido bowl of water outside the door. The owners adore dogs and occasionally give a pooch a special treat. 1694 Tiburon Boulevard; 415/435-8823.

Muir Beach

PARKS, BEACHES, AND RECREATION AREAS

41 Muir Beach

😊😊😊😊🐾 (See Marin County map on page 420)

This beach is small, but a real gem, with rugged sand dunes spotted with plants, a parking lot and large picnic area, a small lagoon with tules, and its share of wind. Redwood Creek empties into the ocean here. Dogs are once again allowed off-leash here, which is as it should be.

You can reach Muir Beach via Highway 1. From Highway 1, watch for the turnoff for the beach. 415/388-2596.

Sausalito

Even if you live here, you should play tourist and stroll around Sausalito's harbor in the brilliant sea light (or luminous sea fog). On weekends, it's especially pleasant early in the day, before the ferries disgorge their passengers. The city's attitude toward dogs is relaxed. It's the perfect place to stop and sniff around for awhile.

PARKS, BEACHES, AND RECREATION AREAS

42 Remington Dog Park

🐾🐾🐾🐾 🐕 (See Marin County map on page 420)

Your leash-free dog can exercise his paws while you both exercise your social skills at this delightful park. Remington Park is named after the dog whose owner, Dianne Chute, helped raise the money to put the park together a few years back. It's more than an acre, all fenced, on a grassy slope with trees. Dogs have the time of their lives tearing around chasing each other, and humans have a great time chatting. The park comes complete with an informative bulletin board, a leash rack, benches, poop bags, and water. It even has a tent you can hide under in foul weather! Everything is cozy here.

Best of all, on Friday evening, about 100 human patrons and their dogs gather for cocktail hour, with wine, cheese, bread, and of course, doggy treats. It sounds very Marin, but it's really just very civilized. On a recent summer evening, the park was host to a Mexican happy hour. Margaritas, chips, and salsa made the atmosphere even more festive than the usual Friday night gathering.

From the day it was finished, Remington and his dog friends have made terrific use of this place. "It's the social hub of Sausalito," said the late cartoonist Phil Frank, "where the elite with four feet meet." What a boon to freedom-loving Sausalito dogs, who otherwise must be leashed almost everywhere in town.

From U.S. 101, take the Sausalito/Marin City exit, driving west to Bridgeway. Turn right on Bridgeway and drive south the equivalent of a long city block. Turn right at Ebbtide Avenue and park in the large lot at the end of Ebbtide.

43 Rodeo Beach and Lagoon

🐾🐾🐾🐾 🐕 (See Marin County map on page 420)

Yahoo and arrooo! Dogs are once again allowed to be leash-free here, as long as they're under voice control! Jake wags himself into a jiggling mass of happiness whenever we visit and take off his leash. Leashes were the law here for a few years—and may be again in the future—but dogs around the Bay Area are praying against this possibility. Meanwhile, enjoy, and be sure to check out the status of the leash law at www.nps.gov/goga.

Rodeo Beach is small but majestic, made of the dark sand common in Marin. Large rocks on shore are covered with "whitewash," birders' polite name for guano, which is the polite name for bird poo, which is the polite name for something we can't print here. Water dogs enjoy this beach, but letting your dog swim in Marin County surf is always risky—currents are strong, and trying to rescue a dog who is being swept away is to risk your own life. Don't turn your back on the surf here. Especially in winter, a "sneaker" wave can sweep you and your dog away.

If your dog promises not to bark and disturb wildlife, he can join you on an interesting walk around Rodeo Lagoon. The lagoon is lined with tules and pickleweed. Ocean water splashes into the lagoon in winter and rainfall swells it until it overflows, continually mixing saltwater and freshwater. Birds love this fecund lagoon. It can be almost too much for a bird dog to take. An attractive wooden walkway leads across the lagoon to the beach.

Heading north on U.S. 101, take the Alexander Avenue exit (the second exit after crossing the Golden Gate Bridge). Stay to the right on the exit ramp to get onto Alexander Avenue. Turn left on Bunker Road, where you'll see a brown sign for the Marin Headlands Visitor Center. Go through the one-way tunnel and drive about two miles. Turn left onto Field Road to reach the Marin Headlands Visitors Center—follow the signs for Rodeo Beach west from there. 415/331-1540.

🐾4🐾 Marin Headlands Trails

🐾🐾🐾🐾🐾 (See Marin County map on page 420)

From Rodeo Beach, you can circle the lagoon or head up into the hills, and your well-behaved dog can run naked (leash-free) beside you! You're in for a gorgeous walk—or a gorgeous and challenging walk, depending on the weather. Look at a map of the Bay Area, and it will be obvious why the headlands' trees all grow at an eastward slant. In summer especially, cold ocean air funnels through the Golden Gate, sucked in by the Central Valley's heat—chilling the headlands and the inhabitants of western San Francisco with fog and wind. The Bay Area may be "air-conditioned by God," but the headlands sit right at the air inflow, and it's set on "high." Never come here without at least one jacket.

Your dog will love the wind. The combination of fishy breeze and aromatic brush from the hillsides sends many into olfactory ecstasy. What looks from a distance like green fuzz on these headlands is a profusion of wildflowers and low brush. Indian paintbrush, hemlock, sticky monkeyflower, ferns, dock, morning glory, blackberry, sage, and thousands more species grow here—even some stunted but effective poison oak on the windward sides. (On the lee of the hills, it's not stunted.) Groves of eucalyptus grow on the crests. You hear a lovely low rustle and roar of wind, surf, birds, and insects—and the squeak and groan of eucalyptuses rubbing against each other. Pinch some sage between your fingers and sniff; if you can ever leave California again after that, you're a strong person.

The Golden Gate National Recreation Area (GGNRA), which oversees this 12,000-acre piece of heaven known as the Marin Headlands, permits dogs only on the Coastal Trail and the Miwok Trail these days, and if they're under voice control they can run leash-free. The trails are exquisite for humans and their sidekicks. Sights include the mighty Pacific Ocean, World War II gun emplacements, the Golden Gate Bridge, and San Francisco. As the trail rises and falls, you will discover a blessing: You'll be intermittently sheltered from the wind, and in these pockets, if the sun warms your back, it's pure paradise. (Except for the ticks. This is tick country, so search carefully when you get home.)

The most direct starting point for the dog-friendly trail access, should you not happen to already be at Rodeo Beach, is around the Marin Headlands Visitor Center. Heading north on U.S. 101, take the Alexander Avenue exit (the second exit after crossing the Golden Gate Bridge). Stay to the right on the exit ramp to get onto Alexander Avenue. Turn left on Bunker Road, where you'll see a brown sign for the Marin Headlands Visitor Center. Go through the one-way tunnel and drive about two miles. Turn left onto Field Road. The visitor center will be on the right side of the road, and you'll have access to trail maps, toilets, picnic tables, and other simple pleasures of the hiking life. 415/331-1540.

PLACES TO EAT

Just a few of Sausalito's pooch-friendly restaurants:

Fish: This fabulous eatery on the Sausalito waterfront is one of the most fun restaurants around. The fish is fresh, the harborside tables are to drool for, and the servers love dogs. Dogs get big bowls of water and samples of dog treats made with salmon! If your dog likes the treats (and she will), you can buy them here. The website is worth checking out: It's www.331fish.com. You can get the latest fish news and local bay and ocean-related activity schedules there, too. You can even click on the "fish.cam" to see what's happening at the restaurant at any given minute. What we especially love about the restaurant's location is that it's next to a dog-friendly point of land at Clipper Yacht Harbor. You'll see the Mutt Mitt dispenser. Dogs enjoy the bay views and the scents and sounds of the nearby harbor seals. The restaurant is at 350 Harbor Drive; 415/331-FISH (415/331-3474).

Northpoint Coffee Company: At a party for *Bay Area Backroads* host Doug McConnell's terrific website venture, OpenRoad.tv, I espied a water bowl in the back patio/garden area. Being the astute sort, I thought, "Hey, maybe they allow dogs here." And they do. The outdoor dining area has magnificent views of nearby Richardson's Bay and is graced by flowers and greenery—a great place for dogs and humans alike. The coffee here is tops. 1250 Bridgeway 94965; 415/331-0777.

Scoma's: Want fresh salmon and a magnificent view of the bay? Come to this waterfront eatery and dine with your well-behaved dog on the deck. 588 Bridgeway; 415/332-9551.

Tommy's Wok: This fun Chinese restaurant is just a bone's throw from Remington Park, so it's a great place to dine after your dog burns up all his energy. The food is delicious, leaning more toward Szechuan dishes but accommodating Cantonese-loving palates as well. Dine with your good doggy at the four outdoor tables. 3001 Bridgeway; 415/332-5818.

Rustico: Dogs can join you at the four sidewalk tables at this lovely restaurant that serves authentic Southern Italian cuisine. The Italian tapas are droolworthy. 39 Caledonia Street; 415/332-4500.

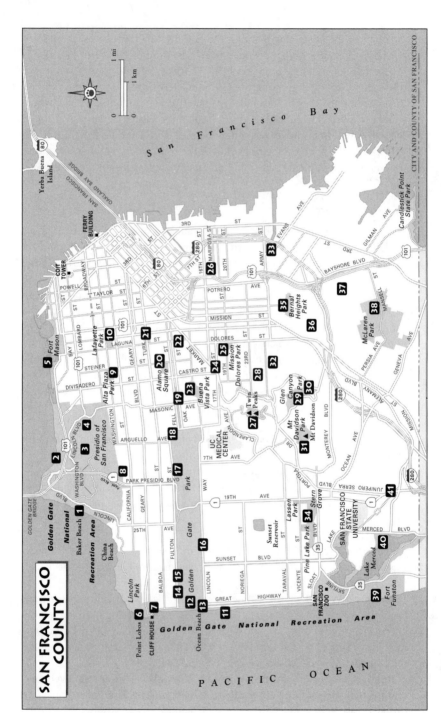

CHAPTER 35

San Francisco County

San Francisco is as beloved by dogs as it is by humans. From the Golden Gate Bridge to Fisherman's Wharf, from the Bay to the Breakers, this is one of the most dog-friendly cities on earth.

Dogs feel right at home here. Look at Jake. He feels incredibly at home here. OK, so San Francisco *is* his home. But even so, this is a city that makes its canine residents and visitors feel very welcome. The finest hotels here permit dogs, as do some of the most popular tourist spots, including Fisherman's Wharf, Pier 39, and the Golden Gate Bridge. Dog-friendly restaurants abound. No public transportation anywhere compares with San Francisco's, where canines can ride cable cars, streetcars, and buses. (Alas, ferries no longer permit pooches.) Dogs can go to a Giants ballgame, attend a Lutheran church every Sunday, and shop at swank stores in posh neighborhoods.

PICK OF THE LITTER—
SAN FRANCISCO COUNTY

MOST SPECTACULAR LEASH-FREE PARK
Land's End (page 465)

BEST LEASH-FREE BEACHES
Baker Beach (page 460)
Crissy Field (page 461)
Ocean Beach (page 467)

DOG HEAVEN
Fort Funston (page 484)

MOST DOG-FRIENDLY PLACES TO EAT
Calzone's Pizza Cucina (page 487)
Judy's Cafe (page 488)
Rose's Cafe (page 490)

MOST BUCOLIC OUTDOOR DINING
Park Chalet Garden Restaurant (page 489)

BEST POWER LUNCH
Absinthe Brasserie (page 486)

MOST DOG-FRIENDLY PLACES TO STAY
Hotel Monaco (page 493)
Harbor Court Hotel (page 494)
The Sir Francis Drake Hotel (page 495)
Westin St. Francis (page 496)
W Hotel (page 496)
Hotel Palomar (page 497)
Galleria Park Hotel (page 497)

BEST PLACES TO BUY FINE ATTIRE
Wilkes Bashford Company (page 468)
Saks Fifth Avenue (page 468)

BEST WALK WITH/AS A TOURIST
Golden Gate Bridge walk (page 461)

COOLEST CANINE CRUISE
Hornblower's Dog Day on the Bay (page 473)

MOST DOG-FRIENDLY CHURCH
St. Mary & St. Martha Lutheran Church (page 474)

BEST VIEW OF YODA
Letterman Digital Art Center (page 463)

BEST RIDE
San Francisco cable cars (page 485)

BEST DAY TO HAVE A BALL
San Francisco Giants' Dog Days of Summer (page 476)

BEST PLACE TO CATCH GREAT CONCERTS
Stern Grove Festival (page 481)

As for parks where dogs can run leash-free, the City by the Bay is replete with these gems. Some are diamonds, some are cubic zirconia, and a couple aren't worthy of a Cracker Jack box. The city runs about two dozen leash-free areas, known here as Dog Play Areas (DPAs). Golden Gate National Recreation Area (GGNRA) is in charge of such beauties as Fort Funston (Dog Heaven), Crissy Field, and Ocean Beach. At the moment, the dog situation at GGNRA lands is much better than it had been in the last edition of this book, and I have put the running-dog symbol (off leash) back in many GGNRA listings.

The roller-coaster ride of the GGNRA's leashes-on, leashes-off decrees isn't necessarily over. It's going through a protracted process called negotiated rule-making. For updates or to find out what you can do to help retain the leash-free lifestyle, go to the SFDOG website, www.sfdog.org. For official updates, check out the GGNRA's website at www.nps.gov/goga. The main page will provide a link to the dog issues pages. You can also phone the GGNRA dog-policy liaisons at 415/561-4732.

San Francisco

San Francisco is the only city in San Francisco County. When you have a city like this, who could ask for anything more?

PARKS, BEACHES, AND RECREATION AREAS

Dogs are allowed on-leash in any San Francisco park, and off-leash in portions of a whopping 24 city-run parks. The off-leash segments of these parks are known as Dog Play Areas and are often marked by brown signs. Many are being upgraded with poop-bag dispensers and triple-decker water fountains. This is a huge improvement from a few years ago, when many of the dog areas were in danger of closing or being severely restricted. At press time, well-behaved dogs are also allowed to be leash-free on many GGNRA properties, but this could change any time, so be sure to check signs or the GGNRA website, www.nps.gov/goga, before letting your dog run around in the nude.

1 Baker Beach

😼😼😼😼🐕 (See San Francisco County map on page 456)

This beach brings your dog almost within a bone's throw of the Golden Gate Bridge. And what a sight it is. Though in summer you shouldn't hold out much hope for a sunny day here, this sandy shoreline is ideal for a romp in the misty air. And dogs really appreciate Baker Beach in the summer. It's almost always cool and breezy.

If you like to sunbathe without a bathing suit and want to take your dog along, the very north end of the beach (closest to the bridge) is perfect. It's the only official nude beach in Northern California where dogs are welcome. (It's also the part of the beach that allows dogs to be leash-free. Go

DIVERSION

Saunter Across the Golden Gate: Like their people, dogs are thrilled to walk San Francisco's most famous landmark, spanning 1.9 miles from the city to Marin County. It's open 5 A.M.–9 P.M. daily to human and canine pedestrians, no fee.

The **Golden Gate Bridge** folks ask only that 1) if your dog can't contain his excitement over the views, you *please* pick up his poop (even if he's not so keen on the scenery and does his number, you'll need to scoop); and 2) your dog wear a leash. You both probably will want to wear sweaters, too—it can be a little nippy when making your way across.

You'll find vista points with parking lots on the northeast (Marin County) and southeast (San Francisco) sides of the bridge. These are the best embarkation points for your walk. The San Francisco side has meters that charge $0.25 for 10 minutes. On the Marin side you can park for free for up to four hours. (Ah, but they get you with the $5 bridge toll when you come back to the city.) For more info, call 415/921-5858.

figure.) Just make sure your dog doesn't get too up close and personal with exposed cobathers. Jake had cause to sniff out an interesting stick during a walk not long ago, and ended up sniffing out a man's bare tush too. Fortunately the owner of the tush took it in stride and told me that dogs seem to be drawn to him. I leashed Jake and walked away, red-faced, not sure how to respond beyond another apology while looking at an invisible object far in the distance. (The usual reply I give people who are flattered by Jake's attention, "Dogs know good people when they see them," seemed just plain wrong in this situation.)

The south end (of the beach) is also intriguing, with trails meandering through wooded areas and lots of picnic tables for leisurely lunches. Battery Chamberlain, with its 95,000-pound cannon aimed toward the sea, looms nearby.

From either direction, take Lincoln Boulevard to Bowley Street, and then make the first turn into the two parking lots. 415/561-4700.

🝰 Crissy Field

🐾🐾🐾🐾🦴 (See San Francisco County map on page 456)

There's nothing quite like Crissy Field at sunset. As the orange sun disappears behind the Golden Gate Bridge, you'll be viewing one of the most stunning blends of natural and man-made wonders in the world.

Crissy Field, part of the Golden Gate National Recreation Area, is a jewel of a park any time of day. Leash-free dogs can chase and cavort up and down the beach and jump into the bay any time of year in the eastern portion of

DIVERSION

Take Me Out to the Ballgame: Can't make it to the San Francisco Giants' Dog Days of Summer? Try a stroll around the outside of AT&T Park. A wide promenade flanks right field along **McCovey Cove.** At game time, you and the pooch can get a dog's-eye view of the game alongside other nonticketed folks.

Or make a day of it and walk the entire waterfront of San Francisco with your dog from here. Head west along the promenade, which turns into a sidewalk. You'll come to a grassy marina, complete with a poop-bag station. Continuing west, you'll pass the Embarcadero, Fisherman's Wharf, the Marina District, and, finally, beautiful Crissy Field. Keep walking west and you'll be under the Golden Gate Bridge. AT&T Park is at 24 Willie Mays Plaza. Call 415/972-2000 or visit the SF Giants' website: www.sfgiants.com.

Crissy Field. That's the majority of this area, from about 500 feet east of the Coast Guard station all the way east (away from the Golden Gate Bridge, in case you're from the other coast) to where most people park, and beyond. The far western portion requires leashes most of the year, thanks to our feathered friends, the snowy plovers, who have protected status. Leashes are the law in this Wildlife Protection Area from about July to May. Yes, that's a long time, and it can vary, depending on when the plovers return. Look for signage, or check the official status at www.nps.gov/goga.

Your dog will find the views here are to drool for. As you walk westward, you'll see the Golden Gate Bridge before you, Alcatraz and bits of the city skyline behind you. Sailboats sometimes glide so close you can hear the sails flapping in the wind. A 20-acre marsh lends a satisfying air of swampiness. (For its $25 million price tag, it should lend something.) Keep your dog out of it, by the way.

Enter on Mason Street in the Marina district and drive past the warehouses. Go right on Mitchell Street and through the parking lot. If you go too far east, you may run into a sea of sailboarders. On those days, try starting your walk close to the western edge of the parking lot. 415/561-4700.

3 Presidio National Park

😸😸😸😸 (See San Francisco County map on page 456)

Dogs and their people like to pretend that the Presidio is their very own country estate, complete with acre after rolling acre (1,480 in all!) of secret pathways, open meadows, and dense groves of eucalyptus and pine. It's truly a magnificent spread, and dogs, who must be leashed here these days, love it despite their tethers.

The park is on its way to becoming the only national park that's completely self sufficient (due to its stellar tenants like George Lucas's Letterman Digital Arts Center). Though the park is drawing more visitors than ever, there are still some out-of-the-way areas that even the most adventurous tourists and their dogs will have a difficult time finding. A hike that takes you away from it all starts when you park at the golf course parking lot just inside the Arguello Boulevard gate. Cross the street (carefully—it can get busy on this road) and follow the path down the hill. It will quickly widen and loop past wildflowers and seasonal sweet peas. Bear left at the first major fork and hike through a thick forest area, then bear right when that path gives you a choice. You'll hike up and down a gentle sequence of hills. Pull over and enjoy the larger hills to the west. Dogs thrill at dragging their people up and down them for no apparent reason. You'll run into a few more side trails along the way.

A slightly more tame walk starts to the west of Julius Kahn Playground on West Pacific Avenue. Again enter on Arguello, but immediately bear right. Parking will be on your right on the bottom of the hill. Cross the street and you'll see a plastic-bag dispenser for scooping the poop. Begin here and follow any number of paths.

The area near the park's Lombard Street entrance makes for a fun stroll in a more manicured setting. This is where you'll find Lucas's beautiful Letterman Digital Arts Center and the grassy 23-acre public park he created on the grounds. You and your leashed dog will be wowed by this creation, which includes a man-made stream and large pond, natural California boulders, comfy seating areas, and unbeatable views of the Golden Gate Bridge, the Palace of Fine Arts, and the bay. I have a scavenger hunt mission for you: Find the Yoda fountain. A clue: It's close to one of the buildings. Advice: You might have to ask a guard permission to see it, but it's worth it. Bring a camera. (Thank you to Carol Copsey and her notorious socialite dog, Bella Pearl, for introducing us to this heavenly part of the Presidio.) While in the area, sniff out the center's Perk Presidio Café for a convenient and attractive place to get some coffee and basic eats. 415/561-4700.

4 Palace of Fine Arts

🐾🐾🐾 (See San Francisco County map on page 456)

The glory of ancient Rome embraces you even as you approach this relic of the 1915 Panama-Pacific Exposition. From the huge colonnaded rotunda to the serene reflecting pool, the place drips with Romanesque splendor.

The Palace is especially grand under its night lighting. It's also an ideal place to take your dog while the kids go to the Exploratorium inside. Walk around the paved path that winds through the grand columns and around the pond. But keep your eyes peeled for people feeding the multitudes of pigeons, ducks, and geese. Dogs like to break up the feeding frenzy with an abrupt tug on the mandatory leash. Feathers fly and dried bread scatters everywhere.

The best place to enter for the full Roman effect is on Baker Street, between North Point and Jefferson Streets. Dogs are not allowed inside the buildings, although Joe did sneak into the Exploratorium one fine afternoon. (It's a long story.) He got as far as the tornado demonstration machine when he was nabbed and whisked away. 415/831-2700.

5 Fort Mason

🐾🐾🐾 (See San Francisco County map on page 456)

This park, perched high above the bay, is full of surprises. Depending on the disposition of your dog, some of the surprises are great fun. One can be downright frightening.

The best stands right in the middle of the wide-open field that constitutes the main part of the park. It's a fire hydrant, and it sticks out like a sore yellow thumb from its flat green surroundings. Joyous male dogs bound up and pay it homage time and time again.

The object that seems to take dogs aback, although people find it riveting, is a gigantic bronze statue of Phillip Burton, who helped secure the national park system, including the GGNRA. Several feet taller and broader than life (although even when alive, Burton was larger than life), with outstretched hand, it can send a dog fleeing as far as his mandatory leash will allow.

Lower Fort Mason is also interesting to investigate. You can walk alongside the piers and sniff the bay, or peer at the liberty ship *Jeremiah O'Brien.*

Enter the lower Fort Mason parking lot at Buchanan Street and take the stairs all the way up to upper Fort Mason. (Huff, puff.) Or park along Bay Street or Laguna Street and walk in. 415/556-0560.

6 Land's End

🐾🐾🐾🐾 🐕 (See San Francisco County map on page 456)

This is probably the most spectacular park in San Francisco. You won't believe your eyes and your leashed dog won't believe his nose. And neither of you will believe your ears—it's so far removed from traffic that all you hear are foghorns, the calls of birds, and the wind whistling through the pines and eucalyptus. One sound you won't hear if your dog is under voice control is the wind whistling past your leash. As of this writing, dogs can once again be leash-free in this piece of pooch paradise!

The towering cliffs, high above the crashing tide below, overlook virtually no civilization. At times, all you can see are ocean, cliffs, trees, wildflowers, and boats. It looks more like Mendocino did 100 years ago—at least until you round one final bend and the Golden Gate Bridge jars your senses back to semi-urban reality.

There are many entrance points, but we like to start from the parking lot at the end of Camino del Mar. Go down the wooden steps to the wide trail and turn right. As you hike, you'll come to occasional wood benches overlooking wildly beautiful seascapes. Take a moment to sit down. Your dog will appreciate the chance to contemplate the wondrous odors here.

The park service has made many improvements to Land's End in recent years, but despite some serious manicuring, most of it still retains its original wild feel. Some of its new features are fun for dogs and people. A very long wooden stairway leads from the main path all the way down to a beautiful rock-strewn beach with great views of the Golden Gate. The trip down is worth the rather rigorous hike back up. Other side trails will take you up hills, down hills, down to the beach, and up to clifftops. Try them all, but keep your eyes peeled for poison oak on the more narrow trails.

A very convenient entry point is at the parking lot on Point Lobos Avenue (which is what Geary Street turns into toward the ocean) just above the Cliff House and Louie's restaurant. But we like to park in the lot at the end of Camino del Mar, a little street just above that lot. You can take the wooden stairs down to a popular path, as described above, or amble along a wide trail that starts on the east end of the parking lot. 415/561-4700.

7 Sutro Heights Park

🐾🐾🐾 (See San Francisco County map on page 456)

This gem of a park set high on a cliff overlooking the Pacific Ocean is bypassed by most tourists. They just whiz by from one San Francisco coastal destination to the next, blissfully unaware that this lush green park houses the ruins of the stately home of former mayor Adolf Sutro, the renaissance man behind the Sutro Baths and other wonders of 1800s San Francisco.

The views of the ocean are spectacular, the Victorian-style gardens sweet, the statue of Diana still revered (with an ever-present scattering of flowers), and the path around the park is a must-visit for dogs who don't mind a little leash time. If you want to burn off steam first, visit Land's End for a leash-free hike. You can park at the lot on the south side of Point Lobos Avenue (what Geary Boulevard turns into when it gets out to the ocean), just up the road from the Cliff House. If that lot is full, the one across the street is a good alternative. For a little more exercise, try entering at the other end, at Balboa and La Playa streets, where you'll hike up a fairly long wooden staircase to the more manicured part of the park. 415/561-4700.

8 Mountain Lake Park
🐾🐾🐾🐕 (See San Francisco County map on page 456)

In this sociable park, your dog can cavort with other dogs while you shoot the breeze with other dog people. The off-leash area is between two signs on the east side of the park. You'll find a bench for humans and a pretty good safety net of trees and grass between dogs and the outside world.

The favorite game among dogs here involves a big green bush. One dog usually starts running around it for no apparent reason. Circle after circle, he'll attract more and more dogs into chasing him until almost every dog is swirling around in a dizzying loop. Watch too closely and you can get seasick.

Dogs find the rest of the park mildly entertaining, although they have to be leashed. The park's namesake lake is little more than a pond. Ducks and a couple of swans live here, and the temptation may be too much for your dog. We've seen dogs drag their owners ankle-deep into the muddy pond in pursuit of a duck dinner. The park is also home to an attractive playground and a decent heart parcourse fitness trail.

To reach the dog-run area, enter on 8th Avenue at Lake Street. 415/831-2700.

9 Alta Plaza Park
🐾🐾🐾🐕 (See San Francisco County map on page 456)

Smack in the middle of Pacific Heights, this park is where all the best breeds and most magnificent mutts gather daily. They flock to the hill on the north side of the park and conduct their dog business in the most discriminating fashion. It's not uncommon to see 25 dogs trotting around the park. Owners often address each other by their dogs' names—"Maggie's mom! How are you?"

For a real treat, visit here on the first Sunday of each month, when loads of pugs hold their monthly social gathering. It's a sight you must see at least once in your life. The gathering of pug mugs starts around 2:30 P.M. See www .geocities.com/pugsunday for more details.

The park's off-leash run is actually on the other side of the playground and tennis courts, on the second level up from Clay Street. Bushes line the paved walkway, and it's far enough from traffic that you don't have to worry too much about cars.

The park is bordered by Jackson, Clay, Steiner, and Scott streets. 415/831-2700.

10 Lafayette Park

🐾🐾🐕 (See San Francisco County map on page 456)

This four-square-block park gets lots of dog traffic. The park is hilly and green and studded with palm trees, pines, and well-trimmed bushes. The official dog-run area is near Sacramento Street, between Octavia and Gough streets. As you enter the park from the main Sacramento Street entrance, it's on your right. But most dogs gather atop the hill to the left, around two huge, smelly garbage cans.

The park is bounded by Laguna, Gough, Sacramento, and Washington streets. 415/831-2700.

11 Ocean Beach

🐾🐾🐾🐾🐕 (See San Francisco County map on page 456)

This broad, four-mile-long beach with a crashing surf isn't exactly Palm Beach. It's usually cold and windy and dotted with seaweed, jellyfish, jagged bits of shells, and less savory deposits from the Pacific. In other words, dogs think it's grand.

Ocean Beach is one of those places that's not usually on the radar of tourists. By the time they make it all the way out to this end of the world, they tend to spend their valuable time at the Cliff House or Beach Chalet restaurants. Only on the hottest days will you find a significant number of people here, and by significant I mean a smattering compared with beaches in the southern climes of the state. There's always plenty of room for running around without stepping over a sea of sun worshippers.

This is once again a pretty dog-friendly stretch of sand: Dogs can be off-leash year-round in the more populous section of the beach, from Stairwell 21 (just south of the Beach Chalet) all the way to the northern end of the beach, just below the Cliff House. (Basically Stairwell 1). The other year-round off-leash section goes from Sloat Boulevard south. In between these two areas is what's known as a Snowy Plover Protection Area, and unfortunately dogs are permitted off-leash only between May and July. To me, that sounds like June is the only month of leash-free bliss on this long segment of dune-lined beach, but GGNRA park officials say it varies and can be open to leash-free dogs as early as May. Oh boy, two months! It all depends on where the plover, a threatened bird, is hanging out at that time of year. So look for signs or go to the GGNRA website, www.nps.gov/goga, to get the official word.

DIVERSION

These Stores Are for the Dogs! Dogs who enjoy shopping with their people love San Francisco. Following are a few of the more pooch-friendly retail spots for the leashed and well behaved.

Beach Street: This isn't a store but a kind of outdoor tourist market where you can shop for baubles, bangles, and T-shirts with your leashed dog at any of dozens of little stands up and down this Fisherman's Wharf area street. The bulk of the stands on Beach Street are between Hyde and Polk Streets.

Neiman Marcus: Even jaded dogs can be agog when they visit this upscale store's beautiful atrium lobby. 150 Stockton Street; 415/362-3900.

Saks Fifth Avenue: Keep your dog under tight rein and she's welcome here. 384 Post Street; 415/986-4300.

Sports Basement: This doesn't really fit in with the high-end stores on this list, but outdoor-oriented dogs feel very comfortable visiting this fun, hip outdoor gear shop. The location south of Market Street is very dog friendly. (The store near Crissy Field has a no-dogs policy, alas.) The prices are lower than most outdoor outfitters, and you can even get yoga gear, stylin' shoes, and dog accoutrements (including canine backpacks). 1590 Bryant Street; 415/437-0100.

Wilkes Bashford Company: Pooches of any size are welcome to peruse this upscale Union Square store (it's to drool for), as long as they're clean and don't conduct any dog business. "I'm a nut about dogs," says Wilkes Bashford, the store's owner. "Dogs are a vital part of life." And he says all the dogs who've visited his store have been very well behaved. Bashford has been bringing his dogs to the store since 1968. Little Callie goes to work with Bashford just about every day. And even when Bashford is out of town on business, Callie makes her rounds at the store. Bashford's driver takes her there in the morning and drives her home in the afternoon. 375 Sutter Street; 415/986-4380.

You can park along the ocean, between the Cliff House and Balboa Street. Walk south on the sidewalk until you hit the beach. Or park in the spaces between Fulton Street and Lincoln Way. A parking lot is also at Sloat Boulevard, but beach access can be limited because of erosion. 415/561-4700.

12 Golden Gate Park

😊😊😊🐕 (See San Francisco County map on page 456)

This famed city park provides much dog bliss, but only in the places where dogs are supposed to be leashed. Four areas are set aside for leashless dogs, but dogs in the know like to avoid those places, for good reason. The following listings are for both leash and off-leash areas, from west to east, and north to south. For information about any area in the park, call 415/831-2700.

13 Golden Gate Park (Beach Chalet)

🐾🐾 (See San Francisco County map on page 456)

The paths in back of the Beach Chalet (near the soccer fields between the windmills near the ocean) run along the edge of the fields and can be a little unsavory at times, although they're looking better these days. To leashed dogs, they're full of good smells and interesting characters. The dog-friendly Park Chalet restaurant is right here, a perfect place to stop for some tasty chow after a little romp around the park (or vice versa).

This area also includes the hilly, piney area up behind the archery field. We haven't heard of any impalements up there, but be careful.

14 Golden Gate Park Dog Run

🐾🐾🐕 (See San Francisco County map on page 456)

This fenced-in dog exercise area has the dubious distinction of being right next to a field full of buffalo. Some dogs adore the location, especially when the wind is blowing in just the right direction. It's the only fenced-in dog run in the city, so it's really the only game in town for escape artists. But the park's fans aren't just dogs who walk on the wild side. All sizes and shapes of dogs come here for playtime. So many dogs use it that much of it is grassless and dusty.

The place can sometimes get a little rough around the edges when the usual dog crowd isn't around. People who like their dogs tough will occasionally drop in and hang out with something to swig while their dogs strut around. It's not usually a problem, though, especially during the normal dog rush hours (before work and after work for 9-to-5ers, and all day on weekends).

We've found more amorous dogs here than in any other park, so if your dog isn't in the mood (or you don't want her to be), this isn't the place to take her. For some reason, Jake, like dear Joe before him, gets accosted at almost every visit, so it's not one of his favorite places. He's flattered, but he's not that kind of dog.

The Dog Run is at 38th Avenue and Fulton Street. Park on Fulton Street and walk in, or take 36th Avenue into the park and go right at the first paved road. Drive all the way to the end, and there it is.

15 Golden Gate Park (by the Polo Grounds)

🐾🐾🐾 (See San Francisco County map on page 456)

Dogs who enjoy playing Frisbee go to the meadow just east of the polo field. It's known for wide-open dells, good bushes, and plenty of gopher holes for old sports. Leashes are mandatory, if you follow the law. Your best bet here is to come early in the morning. A walk around the dirt track above the grassy Polo Grounds is a favorite of many dogs and their leashed people, and the parcourse around the dirt track (on the other side of the trees and bushes) makes for a fun leashed walk with your furry friend. Jake likes to do the 6-inch-tall log hops but isn't a big fan of jumping jacks.

16 Golden Gate Park (South Side)

😺 😺 🐕 (See San Francisco County map on page 456)

Two areas set aside for leash-free dogs are slivers along the south end of the park. One is between 2nd and 7th avenues and bounded on the north and south by Lincoln Way and Martin Luther King Jr. Drive. It's a good length, but it's not terribly wide. The other is on the south side of the polo field, between 34th and 38th avenues and Middle and Martin Luther King Jr. drives. Bring your dog to these sections if he's very good off leash. They're too close to busy traffic for less disciplined dogs.

17 Golden Gate Park (Stow Lake/Strawberry Hill)

😺 😺 😺 (See San Francisco County map on page 456)

The summit of the man-made mountain at Stow Lake is truly a sniffer's paradise. Dogs who like to look at ducks will also enjoy the lake area. The path winds up Strawberry Hill to a breathtaking 360-degree view of the city. Unfortunately, dogs are not supposed to be off leash. It's best to avoid this walk on weekends, when bikers and hikers and wee ones are everywhere.

Stow Lake is between 15th and 19th avenues. From John F. Kennedy or Martin Luther King Jr. drives, follow the Stow Lake signs.

18 Golden Gate Park (Northeast Corner)

😺 🐕 (See San Francisco County map on page 456)

Dogs are allowed off-leash on one of the narrow fields at the northeast corner of the park, up by the horseshoe courts. It's a strange little area with hills and dales and dirt paths. Homeless people live here, and some don't keep good house. You'll see the campfire remains, old sleeping bags, and trash of every type. It's best to avoid this place, except in the middle of the day. Enter at Stanyan and Grove streets.

19 Golden Gate Park (The Panhandle)

😺 😺 😺 (See San Francisco County map on page 456)

That long, thin strip of park that extends eight blocks from the east end of the park to Baker Street is a great hangout for cool dogs. It's got a real Haight-Ashbury influence in parts, and although dogs must be leashed, they love to saunter around visiting other dogs wearing bandannas.

20 Alamo Square Park

😸😸😸🐾 (See San Francisco County map on page 456)

A postcard comes to life in this park for you and your leashed dog. This is where the famed Painted Ladies hold court over the city. These six brightly colored Victorian homes are even better in person than on a postcard.

Walk up the east side of the park, near Steiner Street, to enjoy the view of the old houses with the modern city skyline in the background. (Dogs need to be leashed in this half of the park.) Even if your dog doesn't care about architecture, she'll love the grassy hills that make up this park.

Dogs who like to run around all nudie (sans leash) are joyful these days because the city has given the OK to an official leash-free area on the park's west half. Hooray! (This had been a de facto leash-free area forever. Now it has the city's seal of approval.)

The park is bordered by Fulton, Hayes, Scott, and Steiner streets. 415/831-2700.

21 Jefferson Square Park

😸🐾 (See San Francisco County map on page 456)

It was a toss-up whether to give the tiny off-leash section of this park one paw or two paws, but in the end, Jake's pained look told me that a single paw was our rating. He was badly in need of a leash-free run, and I brought him here thinking he'd get to dash about. But the off-leash section here is so tiny and so close to busy streets that I'd have made even obedient Lassie stay on a leash. The park is attractive enough, with green grass, some trees, and even poop bags, but it doesn't make up for its kibble-sized leash-free area that's dangerously close to traffic. The doggy area is in the northwest corner of this rectangular park, at Eddy and Laguna streets. 415/831-2700.

22 Duboce Park

😸😸 (See San Francisco County map on page 456)

Even though Duboce Park isn't yet officially leash-free, it's been a leash-free park in practice for ages and is extremely popular with dog people. The official rule for the time being is that dogs are supposed to be leashed. When Jake and I visit, I keep him on the leash—not because I'm some kind of goody-two-shoes but because it's not a big area, and dogs are never more than a few fast steps from the nearest street. Jake isn't quite ready for being off leash here, but the dogs who come here seem to have no problem running free and staying off the streets.

A good 99 percent of dogs at this pleasant, grassy park are off leash. (The de facto dog park status here is widely known, so I'm not blowing any canine secrets.) Recently a football-field-sized portion of the park got the OK to become an official leash-free area! There's some debate about fences and no-dogs-at-all zones (besides the fenced playground here), so tune in next edition for details. The park is at Duboce Avenue between Steiner and Scott streets. 415/831-2700.

23 Buena Vista Park

🐾🐾🐾🐾 🐕 (See San Francisco County map on page 456)

The presence of vagrants who sometimes congregate at the front of the park has scared off lots of would-be park users, but it shouldn't. They're generally a friendly lot, posing no threat to folks exploring the park's upper limits with a dog.

This park is a real find for anyone living near the Haight-Ashbury district. Hike along the myriad dirt and paved trails winding through the hills, enveloped by eucalyptus and redwood trees. Some of the gutters are lined with pieces of tombstone from a nearby cemetery. The cemetery's occupants, who died in the 1800s, were moved to the oh-so-quiet town of Colma. The gutters give the park a historical, haunted feeling.

From the top of the park, you can see the ocean, the bay, the Marin headlands, and both the Golden Gate and Bay bridges. Birds sing everywhere, and there are lots of benches to rest on. Dogs are allowed off leash at the woodsy west side of the park, near Central Street.

A note: Sometimes people meet for assignations at the top of the park. Concealing shrubs and bushes have gotten haircuts of late, but this area is still a "hot spot," so to speak. If this bothers you or your dog, avoid this lovers' lane.

Enter at Buena Vista Avenue West and Central Street, or from Haight Street. 415/831-2700.

24 Corona Heights Park/Red Rock Park

🐾🐾🐾 🐕 (See San Francisco County map on page 456)

The rust-colored boulders atop this park cast long, surreal shadows at dawn. If you and your dog are early risers, it's worth the hike to the summit to witness this. And there's a fine view any time of day of downtown and the Castro district.

Unfortunately, dogs aren't allowed off leash on hikes up the hill. Until recently, the off-leash area was a roomy square of grass at the foot of the park. The leash-free section has now been made smaller (about 0.75 acre) and is completely fenced. It was a compromise between the dog people and the folks who like to sunbathe there without getting stomped upon and sniffed at. Because of heavy use, the fenced dog park is no longer grassy, but the surrounding area—leashes mandatory—is lush. (The grass truly is greener on the other side of this fence.)

After a bit of leashless playing, you can don a leash and take your pooch up the hill. Fences keep dogs and people from falling down the steep cliffs and from treading on native habitat. Keep in mind that there's virtually no shade, so if you have a black rug of a dog, think twice about climbing the hill on hot, sunny days.

The park is at Museum Way and Roosevelt Avenue. 415/831-2700.

DOG-EAR YOUR CALENDAR

Cruise with Your Canine: Now that the Blue & Gold Fleet no longer allows dogs on its ferries, what's a nautical dog to do? Well-heeled/well-pawed dogs do have an option: They can go on a **Dog Day on the Bay cruise** put together by Hornblower Cruises & Events to benefit the San Francisco SPCA.

For $125 per adult and $50 per child ages 4–12 (prices are subject to increase soon; younger kids and all dogs go free), this brunch cruise on San Francisco Bay isn't for every budget, but if you have the means, the cruise is worth the price of admission for the spectacle alone.

Dogs of every stripe and spot trot jauntily around the *River Bell,* a pretty, old riverboat casino, the largest of the Hornblower fleet. They sniff the salty breeze, they sniff each other, and they sniff around the dining room floor for errant bits of roasted sirloin, bacon, waffles, and other snout-watering human brunch items. They pose for pictures by the life ring that bears the day's name. They dine at the canine buffet, which features handmade treats, cheese trays, and some decadent dog "junk food." A non-alcoholic, yummy-to-dogs ale-like beverage is also offered, and comes in beer bottles, so your dog will think he is very cool.

But what happens when nature calls after all that beer and chow? No worries, Hornblower has that all figured out. Dogs go to the special sod-covered "poop deck," of course.

This festive cruise takes place in early May. It lasts two hours, but to take full advantage of the nautical setting, you can board an hour early. The cruise leaves from Pier 3 on the Embarcadero. For reservations or information, go to www.hornblower.com/dogdays or phone 888/HORNBLOWER (888/467-6256).

25 Dolores Park

🐾🐾🦴 (See San Francisco County map on page 456)

You can get a little history lesson while walking your dog here. A statue of Miguel Hidalgo overlooks the park, and Mexico's liberty bell hangs at the Dolores Street entrance.

History may not impress your dog, but a wide-open space for running off leash will. It's behind the tennis courts.

DIVERSION

Go to Church With Your Pooch! (Oh My Dog...): When Jake and I walked into **St. Mary & St. Martha Lutheran Church** in the Mission District one bright Sunday morning, the pastor smiled. None of the parishioners looked askance. The only churchgoers who stared were the other canines. We entered, appropriately enough, to the hymn "All Creatures of our God and King" and sat down in a row of this small, cheerfully colorful church, next to Bruce Engle and his shockingly calm Jack Russell terriers, Einstein and Emma Sue.

This wasn't a special service for pets. Dogs are welcome to go to Sunday services every week. Normally at least four or five dogs attend, but this was Labor Day weekend, and the only canines were Bruce's dogs and Jake. Bruce told me that a man named Alvin usually sits at the back of the church and plies the dogs with bits of turkey when they get restless, but it being a holiday, Alvin was gone, too.

About 10 minutes into the service, Jake started groaning and trying to leave. (No fault of Pastor Ron, who is an animated, kindly man.) To entice Jake to be quiet, I gave him one of the large treats I had brought for backup. It was too hard to break, so I gave it to him whole, and he started crunching away contentedly. It was at that very second—horror of horrors!—that Pastor Ron asked parishioners to pause for a moment of silence. The church went quiet, except for the CRUNCH, slurp, gruffle, CRUNCH that echoed off the tile floors and around the walls. There was nothing to do but pray that the moment of silence or the treat would be finished quickly. Mercifully the "silence" ended just as Jake started Hoovering the crumbs off the floor.

The service continued, and Jake eventually fell asleep on the cool tile floor (praise the Lord). But within a breath of this restful blessed event, Pastor Ron asked us all to rise, and up sprang energetic Jake. After a reading by a parishioner, Jake yawned one of those ridiculously loud, squeaky dog yawns. This drew an amused titter or two, including one from the reader.

The service lasted about an hour, and I'm relieved to report that Jake did very well overall. During communion, jazz pianist Richard

There are two problems with this area, though: 1) It's easy for your dog to run into the road—even if she's the voice control type, she could find herself in Church Street traffic just by running a little too far to catch a ball; and 2) you have to be on the lookout that your dog doesn't run over people who live in the park. Joe once slid into a sleeping homeless woman and scared her so bad she screamed and ran away.

Enter anywhere on Dolores or Church streets, between 18th and 20th

Daquioag played an uplifting Bill Evans–like tune that would have been equally fitting at a hip café, and Jake thumped his tail almost in time with the beat. Jake did eventually repose on the cool tile floor, he shook paws with a couple of churchgoers when Pastor Ron asked us all to offer each other a handshake of peace, he did no leg-lifts or barks, and he didn't even sneak a scone off the table at the coffee social that happens after each service. (Yes, dogs can join you for an after-service cuppa Joe!)

This is an embracing, friendly place. You don't have to be Lutheran to attend. The church offers shelter to the homeless, and daycare and food programs for the poor. Pastor Ron and Pastor Ed (who was gone that day because of the holiday; he came from another dog-friendly Lutheran church that had to close because of earthquake retrofit financial issues) love dogs and will make you and your well-enough-behaved one feel very welcome here.

You can choose from an English-language service at 10 A.M. or Spanish at 11. The first Sunday of October is the church's blessing of the animals for St. Francis Day. This is a most appropriate place to celebrate it. 1050 South Van Ness Avenue. 415/647-2717.

streets. The off-leash area is south of the tennis courts and north of the soccer field. 415/831-2700.

26 McKinley Square

🐾🐾🐾 (See San Francisco County map on page 456)

The view from this little patch of land is, shall we say, interesting. You can see for miles and miles, and the view includes several other leash-free parks, such as Buena Vista, Corona Heights, Mission Dolores, and Bernal Heights Parks. But you can also see such lovely sights as U.S. 101, with its cars rushing mad-cap-fashion just a couple of hundred feet down the hill from you. And if you ever craved a view of San Francisco General Hospital's most austere, Dickensian brick buildings, this is the place to come. If you had really long arms, you could almost reach out and touch them. Actually, depending on the direction of the wind, on some days they reach out and touch you—the steam from the hospital's huge chimneys has been known to slip right up to this hilltop park.

Dogs are permitted off leash in the back section of the park, between the playground and the community gardens. Signs will point you in the right direction. It's nothing beautiful, just a wide path with a little running room on a hillside dotted with brush and occasional trees.

The off-leash section is on 20th Street and San Bruno Avenue, just a few blocks from the heart of the Potrero Hill business district. 415/831-2700.

DOG-EAR YOUR CALENDAR

You won't strike out with your dog if you bring her to the **Dog Days of Summer** at AT&T Park. In fact, you'll score a home run. If you thought hot dogs and baseball go together, you should see just plain dog dogs and baseball. It's a match made in dog heaven!

At Dog Days of Summer, your pooch gets to join you for a baseball game on a set day in August. You'll sit together in "The Dog Zone" (a.k.a. the bleachers) and watch the San Francisco Giants pound the heck out of the visiting team (we hope). But that's not all. Before the game, you and your dog can take part in a poochy parade around the field! Not many dogs (or humans) can say they've cruised around a pro ballpark. There's also usually some kind of contest, be it a costume or "stupid pet trick" soiree. Cost for the day is about $40 for one human, and you can bring one dog. Additional humans in your party (sans dogs) are about $20. (Prices were scheduled to change around press time, so we can't get exact costs.) Dogs have to wear ID and rabies tags. 415/972-2000; www.sfgiants.com.

27 Twin Peaks

😺😺 (See San Francisco County map on page 456)

So dogs aren't allowed at the Top of the Mark. So what! The view from up here will put all those "No Dogs Allowed" establishments to shame, and it's cheaper to entertain guests up here—it's free, in fact.

The summits of the Twin Peaks are higher than 900 feet. It's usually cold up here, so bundle up. You can drive to the northern peak and park in the lot. It's very touristy, and on this peak, signs tell you what you're looking at—Tiburon, Nob Hill, Mt. Diablo, Japantown, and Mt. Tamalpais. Your dog won't get much exercise, though, since all he can do is walk around the paved viewing area on leash. And frankly, many dogs are bored by the marvelous vistas.

For your dog's sake, try exploring the other peak. It's a bare hill with wooden stairs up one side. While dogs must be on leash, it's not bad exercise. And the view—at almost 20 feet higher than the first peak—is *magnificent*. From here you can see other potential walks for you and your dog on the lower hills, where the views are almost as dynamic and the air is a little warmer. Be sure to keep him on leash, because the road is never far away.

The Twin Peaks are on Twin Peaks Boulevard, just north of Portola Drive. 415/831-2700.

28 Douglass Park

😺😺😺😺🐕 (See San Francisco County map on page 456)

The leash-free section at Douglass Park used to be a steep hillside with fences that were falling apart. It was so bad and difficult to get to (and to stay on!) that I decided not to waste space on it in previous editions. But now the city has changed the locale, and it's a completely different animal: a big, attractive, grassy field flanked by tall trees. It's actually a barely used softball field, so your dog can make like Barry Bonds and run the bases and then go out for a fly ball (of the lobbed tennis variety) to right field. There's plenty of room for dogs to run and play, and boy, do they.

Escape artist dogs are pretty safe here, although the park is not totally enclosed. The area near the entrance has no barrier. But the park is so big that you can keep your activities to a far-flung section of the field if escape is a concern.

The park has good views of downtown from the back fence area (it has some very tall fences in back from its softball days). If you want to sit and sip your coffee while your dog gallops around, you'll have to be a bump on a log: The only place to repose is a big log bordering the outfield. The leash-free part of the park is all the way at the top, on Douglass at 27th Street. 415/831-2700.

29 Glen Canyon Park

😊😊😊 (See San Francisco County map on page 456)

From the cypress forests to the streams and grassy hills, this 122-acre park was made for you and your dog. The nature trail in the middle of the park follows a muddy creek and is so overgrown with brush and bramble that at times you nearly have to crawl. It's as though the trail were blazed for dogs. There are so many dragonflies of all colors and sizes near the creek, and so much lush vegetation, that you may wonder if you've stepped back to the age of the dinosaurs. But it's not carnivorous giant reptiles you have to watch out for here—it's poison oak. There's a lot, so watch out, and tell your dog to do so, too.

Park at Bosworth Street and O'Shaughnessy Boulevard and walk down a dirt trail past a recreation center, through the redwoods and loud birds. Stay away from the paved road—it can look deserted for hours on end, and then a car suddenly whizzes by. Your dog is supposed to be leashed, but you should still be aware of the road. The area down the path a bit is swarming with kids year-round, since it houses a preschool during the school year and a day camp during the summer. (Additionally, kids also inundate the park's ball fields on weekends and on weekday afternoons after school, so you'd be best to make a sojourn here during earlier hours on weekdays, and again, make sure that leash is attached.) At this point, you can go left and up a hill for some secluded picnic spots or keep going and take the nature trail. When you finally emerge from the dragonflies and dense greenery, take any of several trails up the open, rolling hills and enjoy a panorama of the park. There are lots of options for side trails, too.

The part of the park that's easiest to access is at Bosworth Street and O'Shaughnessy Boulevard. There's only street parking, and it can get tight at times. If you'd like to avoid the paved road and all those kiddies for a bit longer, the best entrance is at the west end of Christopher Playground, just behind the Diamond Heights shopping center on Diamond Heights Boulevard, north of Goldmine Street. (Gotta love those rich street names.) A trail goes around Christopher Playground's ball field and leads down to Glen Canyon Park. 415/831-2700.

30 Walter Haas Playground

😊🐾 (See San Francisco County map on page 456)

No, even leashed dogs aren't allowed on the swings and slides at this charming playground, but just up the hill is a teensy-weensy fenced dog park where dogs can run leash-free. It's the most barren dog park I've seen, but it's on purpose: The clay ground with nary a sprig of grass is meant to be that way because it's easy to maintain. If your dog poops here, there's no way to ignore it. It sticks up off the flat earth in such an obvious manner that it's almost like it's waving a flag saying in a squeaky little voice, "Pick me up!"

If your boy dog needs a mark for a leg lift, his choices are the water fountain (bad idea, since a dog bowl is on the bottom level), the attractive low benches (bad idea, since people sit on them), or the few large-ish rocks that have been placed on the ground most likely with this purpose in mind (your best bet). Jake, however, chose none of the above the first time we visited. We threw the ball across the 0.3-acre enclosure a few times before he started looking desperate to get out. We leashed up and went on our way, and as soon as he was out he found the first tuft of grass and watered it for about 20 seconds.

My human child, Laura, asked me to mention that this seems like an excellent place to train a dog, and she's right. (Smarty pants kid!) With minimal distractions, especially when other dogs aren't around, you can really work on those stay and recall commands. The park is at the top of a windy hill that provides great views of the bay and the East Bay, including Mt. Diablo. You can also look down at the grass that surrounds the playground below. At this dog play area, the grass really is greener on the other side of the fence. It's at the intersection of Diamond Heights Boulevard and Addison Street. There are entrances on both streets. 415/831-2700.

31 Mount Davidson

🐾🐾🐾 (See San Francisco County map on page 456)

Hiking to the peak of this park can be a religious experience—literally. As you emerge from the tall pine and eucalyptus trees leading to the 927-foot summit, a concrete structure looms in the distance. As you get closer you'll see that it's a gigantic cross, 103 feet tall. It's so huge, and in such a prominent spot—at the end of a long, wide path surrounded by trees—that it can be a startling sight. On his first encounter, Joe backed out of his collar and collided with a tree. Since leashes are the law here, we had to quickly put him back together.

In 1934, President Franklin Delano Roosevelt became the first person to flick the switch and light the cross. These days it's only lighted the night before Easter and a couple of other holidays. There's been controversy about keeping the cross (a religious symbol) in the park (a city-run property). That church and state–mixing thing just wasn't making some folks happy. Thank God (so to speak), an Armenian group bought the property surrounding the cross. The cross, an intriguing landmark for generations—much more than a religious icon—will remain.

Since you enter the trails at such a high altitude, it's only about a 10-minute pilgrimage to the peak. But you can make it a much longer walk by experimenting with different trails. Note that 1) the trails can get very muddy, and 2) they're almost always nearly deserted. My wonderful research editor, Caroline Grannan, walks her trusty dog Tioga here and notes that this lack of hikers "is probably because it's practically impossible to find, even with GPS and a good map. The streets are like a plate of spaghetti."

You can bring your well-behaved dog to the legendary Easter Sunrise Service, an interdenominational affair that starts at around 5:30 A.M. One

DIVERSION

Sniff Out an Apartment with Your Dog: Looking for some digs with your dog? It's not always easy in San Francisco. But thanks to a wonderful program of the San Francisco SPCA, dog people are finding it easier to rent in the city. The **Open Door Program** helps landlords and potential tenants come together. This program has helped hundreds of canines and their people find housing since its inception a few years back. To see listings, and to get tips about how to make you and your dog more viable candidates for tenanthood, go to www.sfspca.org and click on Open Door.

mappable entry point for a good hike is at Dalewood Way and Lansdale Avenue. 415/831-2700.

32 Upper Noe Park

🐾🐕 (See San Francisco County map on page 456)

At last sniff, the leash-free section of this park was a tiny little area of compacted dirt. It was fenced and had water and two benches but no shade and no real appeal other than being an off-leash area. (To be fair, regular users say it's better than it used to be when the ground was a sandy, dusty mess.) The off-leash section is on Day and Sanchez streets, east of the ballfield. (You can enter only on Day Street at this point.) 415/831-2700.

33 Potrero Hill Mini Park

🐕 (See San Francisco County map on page 456)

If you value your safety, don't go to the designated off-leash part of this park, even if your dog is crossing her legs in need of an off-leash romp. A friend was mugged twice at gunpoint when she used to play tennis at the courts adjacent to the dog run. (For some reason she no longer plays tennis there.) The leash-free section of this tiny park is a postage-stamp-sized lawn next to a tiny, ancient playground. A steep, uncleared patch of land that stretches from the nearby housing projects to the lawn is also supposed to be part of the dog run. The city needs to rethink this whole setup. The park is at 22nd and Arkansas streets. 415/831-2700.

34 Pine Lake Park/Stern Grove

🐾🐾🐾🐾🐕 (See San Francisco County map on page 456)

These are two parks, but they're attached, have no line of demarcation, and share a common parking lot used by most park-goers, so we're putting them in one listing. But for reference's sake, this gorgeous 64-acre contiguous open space is made up of Pine Lake Park to the west and Stern Grove to the east. Now that your dog has his compass, let's talk a little about these beauties.

Dogs love it here, because it's a treasure of trees, hills, meadows, birds, fresh air, and leash-free areas. The best place for dogs to run off leash is just to the west of the parking lot (to the left, as you enter via the directions below—officially Pine Lake Park), where there's a wide-open meadow in a valley between two hills. It's not fenced (yay!) but thanks to its location it's safe from traffic, and a real treat with all the surrounding trees on the slopes. Many people come here to shoot the breeze with each other while their dogs run around, but the walk west on the meadow is a pleasant one. Note that during summer there's a city-run children's camp at the very west end of this meadow and beyond. Dogs need to stay away, even on leash. If you visit during other seasons, leash up here and you'll have a relaxing stroll around the lake that gives Pine Lake Park its name. (Actually, the lake is called Laguna Puerca, so if the park were named for it, it would be called Pig Lake Park. Nice moniker.)

The slopes on the north side have a couple of dirt trails dogs enjoy, but dogs are supposed to be leashed here. One of our favorite on-leash walks is to the east (right, as you enter) of the parking lot, where you start on a paved trail, cross over a grassy area to the dirt trails on the north slopes, and enjoy a super vista of the stage at the famed Stern Grove concert area. (See the Diversion *Groove at*

DIVERSION

Groove at the Grove: If you and your dog like music and don't mind crowds, a Sunday afternoon at **Stern Grove Festival** concert can be big fun. You can hear and see (if you get close enough) a variety of top performers at this beautiful outdoor concert area in dog-friendly Stern Grove. Recent concerts have featured Huey Lewis and the News, the Preservation Hall Jazz Band, and the San Francisco Symphony.

The festival runs through the summer, and there's no fee for admission. Dogs can't take in the performances from the main meadow, but they're allowed on the peripheral hills, on leash. (But if you want to bring vino, apparently you can't drink it on the hill. Maybe festival organizers are worried you'll get tipsy and roll down to the stage.) Another option is to go to the west meadow, which permits dogs and wine. Bring a picnic, a stuffed Kong, and, of course, a poop bag. You won't be able to see the performance from here, but you'll get an earful. Concerts start at 2 P.M. but get there significantly earlier for best seating. Keep in mind that your dog can run off steam before or after the concert in Pine Lake Park/Stern Grove's leash-free area to the west of the parking lot (the one west of the performance area). Stern Grove's main entrance is at 19th Avenue and Sloat Boulevard. 415/252-6252; www.sterngrove.org.

the Grove for more on these summer Sunday concerts.) We like visiting on non-concert days. We keep heading east on our choice of trails, and then descend and walk past the beautiful Trocadero Clubhouse to a thick grove of redwoods surrounding a small pond. It's a peaceful, meditative place, and you can enjoy the tranquility from a memorial bench under the trees. It's not necessarily as peaceful if you have a water dog obsessed with getting at a floating pinecone (I'll name no names, Jake), but it's still a great end to a loop hike here.

The official off-leash area for the Stern Grove end of the park is on Stern Grove's north side, on Wawona Street between 21st and 23rd avenues. It's a bit close to traffic, and the other meadow is a much better option. The two off-leash areas are now connected by a 0.2-mile trail where dogs can be off leash! The parking lot on which I've based all directions is just north of Sloat Boulevard, at Crestlake and Vale streets. 415/831-2700.

35 Bernal Heights Park

😺 😺 😺 🐕 (See San Francisco County map on page 456)

On one visit to this park, a dozen wolf-shepherds were the only dogs atop the amber hill. They ran and played in such pure wolf fashion that it was hard to believe they weren't the genuine item. The icy wind hit the power lines overhead and made a low, arctic whistle. The scene left an indelible impression that even in the middle of a city such as San Francisco, the wild is just beneath the surface. (To attest to this, a coyote has taken up residence here. Hardly anyone sees it, and it bothers no one, so fear not.)

The rugged hills here are fairly rigorous for bipeds, but dogs have a magnificent time bolting up and down. Humans can enjoy the view of the Golden Gate and Bay bridges. The vista makes up for the austere look of the treeless park. Dogs are allowed off leash on the hills bordered by Bernal Heights Boulevard. It can be very windy and cold, so bundle up.

Enter at Carver Street and Bernal Heights Boulevard, or keep going on Bernal Heights Boulevard until just past Anderson Street. 415/831-2700.

36 St. Mary's Park

😺 😺 🐕 (See San Francisco County map on page 456)

If it weren't for its teeny size, St. Mary's dog park would score three paws. It's an attractive place with friendly people and well-manicured grass that somehow withstands the pounding of paws day after day. It's totally enclosed and has three picnic tables and occasional shade from trees on a steep adjacent hillside. The leash-free section of St. Mary's is very close to I-280 (and the constant drone of traffic). From the park's main entrance on Murray Street at Justin Drive, walk immediately to the right and follow a paved path downhill past a playground and to the dog park, which will be on your left. A closer entrance is a block south, on Benton Avenue at Justin Drive. 415/831-2700.

❸❼ Crocker Amazon Playground

🐾 🐕 (See San Francisco County map on page 456)

You'd only want to bring your dog here for an off-leash romp if 1) you live near here; 2) a friend or loved one is playing a game at the adjacent ball fields; or 3) you enjoy run-down areas with power lines overhead. At this fence-free, leash-free area of the larger Crocker Amazon Playground (a misnomer, since most of this large park is not a playground), you'll walk on dirt and crunchy twigs under power lines and too close to a tiny playground and the ballpark for comfort unless your dog is über-good. In its favor, it sports many eucalyptus trees, which are appreciated by dogs of the male persuasion.

The leash-free area is on the northeast side of the park, between LaGrande and Dublin streets. Your best bet is to park on LaGrande and follow the paved path past the mini playground. You'll soon come to a rather ramshackle flat area with a poop bag dispenser, which is where you can unleash. You can also enter this section from the more findable Geneva Avenue. Drive into the parking lot on the 1600 block of Geneva, leash up, walk on the paved trail past the skateboard park (if devoid of boarders you could mistake it for an abandoned swimming pool) and up wooden stairs that bear the sign Dog Play Area. It'll be at the top of the stairs. 415/831-2700.

❸❽ McLaren Park

🐾 🐾 🐾 🐕 (See San Francisco County map on page 456)

In almost any other neighborhood, the 59-acre section of leash-free land on a hilltop with super views of the city would be a huge favorite with the canine set. It has everything dogs and their people love, including leash-free paved and dirt trails, tons of trees, grassy slopes, and killer vistas. But you won't usually find many dogs here, and it's most likely because of location, location, location: Part of the off-leash area is very close to the Sunnydale Housing Project, the largest housing project in San Francisco and one of the worst in the area in terms of living conditions and shootings. People who haven't been to this park say they'd never go. People who live nearby say maybe it's not a great idea.

That said, I've never had any problems when hiking here with Jake, and the few people we've passed have mostly been families, joggers, or dog walkers. Maybe we've just been lucky, maybe it's because Jake is 95 pounds of muscle (OK, there's a little fat and a lot of dewlap too), but I've talked with other park users and they say this underused park area is a safe (usually preceded by "as far as I can tell") and pleasant undiscovered gem.

The leash-free area is the hilltop bounded by Shelley Drive. Most of McLaren's trails run through remote wooded areas and windswept hills with sweeping views. This area is rife with trails, so you can park just about anywhere along Shelley Drive and begin your hike. One decent starting point is where Shelley meets Cambridge Street. There's even a stand with poop bags there. Bring water; we haven't found any. Dogs aren't allowed at the Greek-style Jerry Garcia Amphitheater or the picnic areas. 415/831-2700.

39 Fort Funston

🐾🐾🐾🐾 🐕 (See San Francisco County map on page 456)

Fort Funston is paws down Jake's favorite place to run around in San Francisco. He's not alone. This magnificent park, set on seaside cliffs that tower up to 200 feet above the Pacific, has everything it takes to make it dog heaven on earth. Trails wind through bluffs where you'll have stunning views of the ocean, some trails take you down to the beach itself, and happy leash-free dogs and their contented human counterparts abound.

As I write this, it's once again officially OK to be leash-free in all of Fort Funston except for a 12-acre section that's closed because it's bank-swallow nesting habitat. Some decisions are in the works about the fate of the rest of Fort Funston's wonderful off-leash designation, but our paws are crossed that the decision-makers do the right thing and continue the decades-old off-leash tradition here (and in other parts of the Golden Gate National Recreation Area).

This generously sized leash-free beauty is truly a mecca for dogs. What's so magical about Fort Funston is that humans enjoy it at least as much as dogs do. If you have a dog in the Bay Area and haven't visited Fort Funston, you haven't had one of the ultimate doggy experiences. So get your tail over here and see what real dog bliss is all about.

Fort Funston is located along Highway 35, south of the San Francisco Zoo. It's about 0.5 mile south of the turnoff to John Muir Drive. You'll see the signs. (If you get to the Daly City limits, you've gone too far south.) There's also some roadside parking near the John Muir Drive intersection. Use caution when parking here, though, because a few people I know have had their cars broken into in this area. 415/561-4700.

40 Lake Merced

🐾🐾 🐕 (See San Francisco County map on page 456)

As the city's largest body of water, Lake Merced is favored by Labrador retrievers, Portuguese water dogs, springer spaniels, and the like. An ideal spot to explore is the footbridge area near the south end of the lake. A couple of sandy beaches there are safe from traffic, but dogs are supposed to be leashed anyway. Once you cross the bridge, you'll find an inviting area with lots of little trees. This is where you'll find one of two double-decker drinking fountains for humans and their best friends. Lap up if you're going to hike around the entire lake: It's about a five-mile walk on paved trails and can be heavily used on weekends.

The off-leash section of Lake Merced is at the north lake area, at Lake Merced Boulevard and Middlefield Drive. Park on Middlefield and cross Lake Merced Boulevard at the light. You'll enter a small grassy/weedy section and come to a narrow dirt trail overlooking the lake's northeast bowl. We don't recommend

DIVERSIONS

Hop on a Bus: It's good to be a dog in San Francisco. Dogs are allowed on **Muni buses** and streetcars as long as it's not commute time (dog hours are 9 A.M.–3 P.M. and 7 P.M.–5 A.M.). Only one dog is permitted per vehicle. Dogs must be on a short leash and muzzled, no matter how little or how sweet. (There are many muzzles dogs barely notice. Shop around 'til you find one your dog doesn't despise.) Bus driver Tom Brown told us about the creative, but ineffective, ways some people muzzle their dogs. "This one man had a part–pit bull dog, and he put a little rubber band around its mouth," said Brown. "No way that dog was getting on my bus."

Dogs pay the same fare as owners. If you're an adult, you pay $1.50, and your dog does, too. Dogs of seniors pay the senior rate. Lap-sized dogs can stay on your lap, but all others are consigned to the floor. Keep your dog from getting underfoot and be sure he's well walked before he gets on. Call 415/673-MUNI (415/673-6864) for more information.

Ride Halfway to the Stars: Not many world-famous tourist attractions permit pooches. Can dogs ascend the Eiffel Tower? No. Can they visit the Vatican? No. Can they ride in a beautiful old **San Francisco cable car?** They sure can! (They can also go on the Golden Gate Bridge. See the Diversion *Saunter Across the Golden Gate* for details.)

Jake the Dog has mixed feelings about the cable car privilege. He doesn't mind the clanging of the bells, as his predecessor Joe did. But he's not too keen on wearing a muzzle (a requirement, along with a leash; the muzzle can be a gentle nylon one that most dogs, not including Jake, barely notice), and he really doesn't care for the hills. On a recent descent to Fisherman's Wharf, he tried to scramble from the floor to my lap, and we both slid down the bench and smack into the open newspaper of a surprised commuter. "Welcome to the sports section," he said with a bemused grin.

Opinions vary about whether dogs should ride inside or outside. Some drivers think the outside is better because the cable noise isn't so amplified, and dogs don't get so nervous. Others say the outside is too dangerous—that a dog could panic and jump off. I opt for inside, but if you have a small dog and can hold her securely on your lap, riding outside is the best way to get the full San Francisco experience.

Only one dog is permitted per cable car. Dogs aren't allowed during peak commute times (5–9 A.M. and 3–7 P.M.), and you should never take your dog on a crowded cable car. Off-season and away from touristy areas are your best bets. Dogs pay the same fare as their person. If you pay the full $5 adult rate, your dog does too. For more information, call 415/673-MUNI (415/673-6864).

letting dogs off leash until you're a bit into the park, because menacing traffic is so close by. There are birds galore and purple wildflowers in spring. The park is a tease, though, because there's no decent way to get to the lake from here—it's down a very formidable slope covered with impenetrable brush. Jake did once lead me on a journey down there to smell some duck guano coming from quackers nesting in trees above, and I lived to tell about it, but it's not high on my list of must-try-agains. 415/831-2700.

41 Brotherhood Mini Park

😺 😺 🐕 (See San Francisco County map on page 456)

This is a park built by a city that knows how to use its limited space. Weighing in at less than an acre, this relatively new fenced park along busy Brotherhood Way is squeezed onto a narrow tree-dotted slope at the southeast end of Brotherhood. It's a good place to let your dog run around if you're near the southwest part of the city and don't have time for Fort Funston. It's also conveniently located if you're on your way to Highway 101 or 280 from this neighborhood. It's very close to on-ramps for both.

Inside the fenced area you'll find poop bags, benches, really cool gnarled trees that like to grow horizontally, and some upright ones for shade. Dogs enjoy running up and down the slope and the wooden stairs near the Alemany Boulevard entrance. Got a thirsty dog? Head to the water fountain just outside the Alemany gate. It's got a doggy level bowl and levels for short and tall humans, too (sans bowls, of course).

There's an entrance along Brotherhood Way, the street known for its diversity of churches and religious schools; no houses or other businesses reside here. But since there's no parking on this section of Brotherhood, your best bet is the entrance on Alemany Boulevard, which parallels Brotherhood one narrow block to the south. Park along the street and go in through the double-gated entrance, making sure to shut the gates behind you so no other dogs escape into traffic. Be sure the double gates along Brotherhood are closed, too, because that traffic really gets busy. The Alemany entrance is just west of where Alemany Boulevard intersects with the east end of Brotherhood. (Just east of Arch Street.) 415/831-2700.

PLACES TO EAT

For a city known for its cool, foggy weather, San Francisco sure has a lot of sidewalk cafés. Here's a sampling:

Absinthe Brasserie: This elegant, forward-thinking restaurant with a Gallic bent is a power-lunch place for City Hall types. The lunch menu offers several varieties of oysters, caviar at $38 for a half-ounce, an interesting assortment of cheeses, and an upscale sandwich and main dish menu. Dogs dine at the outside tables. 398 Hayes Street; 415/551-1590.

Angelina's Caffe: Conveniently situated one-half block from Cal's Discount Pet Supply, Angelina's is a good place for you and your dog to take a break from shopping. It's got everything from soup to pine nuts, plus a large variety of coffees. Enjoy them at one of six sidewalk tables. You can also stock on up on Italian souvenirs here, but watch out for the red, white, and green hats. 6000 California Street; 415/221-7801.

Bistro Yoffi: It seems there's always a happy dog hanging out at the sidewalk tables in front of this colorful Marina district restaurant. The international and California-style cuisine here is marvelous. Jake Dog sends a thank-you to Matt Golden and his smiling dog for the tip. 2231 Chestnut Street; 415/885-5133.

Cafe Zoetrope: Dogs are welcome to join their people at any of 12 white-cloth–covered tables outside this upscale North Beach/Financial District restaurant owned by Francis Ford Coppola. Apparently if you come here enough, you're bound to run into the famous bearded director himself. 916 Kearney Street; 415/291-1700.

Calzone's Pizza Cucina: You and your dog can dine on wonderful pastas, pizzas, calzones, seafood, and steak at this North Beach restaurant. It has about a trillion outdoor tables to choose from. They're lovely, tiled works of art set under a canopy. On chilly evenings (or days) you'll be warmed by myriad heat lamps. This is a great place to watch the North Beach scene pass by.

Your dog will be happy to know that the waitstaff offers dogs treats and water! Jake would have preferred some of my fresh fettuccine with chicken, asparagus, roasted tomatoes, garlic, and other delicious ingredients, but the food was so good that I wasn't in the sharing mood despite his hungry brown eyes. 430 Columbus Avenue; 415/397-3600.

Cioppino's: Dogs love coming to this well-known Fisherman's Wharf seafood restaurant because they know they're more than welcome. The folks here always provide water to thirsty pooches. You can dine at any of oodles of plastic sidewalk tables here. 400 Jefferson Street; 415/775-9311.

Curbside Too: Want to have your dog at your side while you dine on tasty French cuisine? He'll lick his lips as you down your escargot at the attractive outdoor tables here. It's casual, but high quality. Just a bone's throw from the Presidio's western entrance. 2769 Lombard Street; 415/921-4442.

Dolores Park Cafe: Eat here and you're directly across the street from the off-leash area of Dolores Park. The food's OK and the servers have been overworked when we've visited on the weekend, but it's a decent place for a quick hot drink or smoothie (try the Chai Crush). Sit at the handful of sidewalk tables with your dog. 501 Dolores Street; 415/621-2936.

Duboce Park Cafe: This corner café with the logo of a dog running with a leash with no person attached is right across the street from the leash-free Duboce Park, so if you want a place to enjoy some tasty food or just a cup of coffee after a social excursion to the park, this is mighty convenient. Dogs dine at the sidewalk tables and are offered water. Treats are served "irregularly," says a server. This café is a first cousin of the Dolores Park Cafe. 2 Sanchez Street; 415/621-1108.

Fisherman's Pizzeria: If you and your salty mutt are sniffing around Fisherman's Wharf for pizza, you'll get a decent meal here. A sign above the entrance features a fisherman and his dog in a little boat, so you'll know you and your canine crew are welcome. Dine at the seven sidewalk tables. 2800 Leavenworth; 415/928-2998.

Ghirardelli Chocolate Ice Cream and Chocolate Shop: Here's where you can get some of that famous rich Ghirardelli ice cream with all the fixings. Just remember: The more your dog gets, the fewer sit-ups you have to do. Don't share your chocolate, though. It can be very bad for dogs, as you surely know by now. Dine at the outdoor tables. The restaurant is in the lower floor of Ghirardelli Square, one of the classiest tourist shopping centers we've seen. It used to be a chocolate factory, and if someone in your party holds your dog's leash, you can go inside the ice-creamery and still see some delectable milk chocolate being swirled about in a giant copper contraption that makes me want to dive into it every time I see it. 900 North Point Street. 415/474-3938.

Grove Cafe: This coffeehouse is so popular you might need a shoehorn to find room at the plentiful outdoor tables here. But if you and your dog like the Chestnut Street coffee scene, you'll enjoy sipping your Joe among the Marina District masses. You can wash down your coffee with some fine sandwiches, salads, and pastries. 2250 Chestnut Street, 415/474-4843.

Java Beach: After a morning of combing Ocean Beach, you can catch some rays and eat some lunch on one of the benches outside this über-popular yet mellow soup, sandwich, beer, and coffee café. 1396 La Playa at the Great Highway; 415/665-5282.

Judy's Cafe: Judy's is a beloved little weekend brunch hangout that offers great traditional brunch fare in huge portions. The omelettes are top contenders with the sourdough French toast (mmm). Dogs love Judy's because they're offered treats and water by the friendly waitstaff. Jake usually prefers fallen bits of human food, since he's a fan of syrup, of all things (and yes, I know he's not supposed to have any). Dine at the few outdoor tables with your happy dog. It's best to visit on a weekday. We send a thank-you to Elway, a West Highland terrier, and his mom, Tori, who told us about Judy's dog-friendliness after a trip here from their home in San Diego. 2268 Chestnut Street; 415/922-4588.

Kookez Cafe: Get a taste of "coast to coast" cuisine with your dog at Kookez's (pronounced Cookies) sidewalk tables, which are set off from foot traffic by an attractive wooden planter. This is a great place to come if you're hankering for American food that doesn't scream American: Recipes hail from all over the United States, with favorites from New Orleans, New York, Chicago, the West, and Texas. Thanks to Pooch Coach Beverly Ulbrich for telling us about this Noe Valley gem. 4123 24th Street; 415/641-7773.

La Mediterranée: Dog owners are lucky—there are two of these top

Mediterranean/Greek restaurants in the city; each puts tables outside in decent weather and has a dog-loving staff. Try the vegetarian Middle-East plate. Even meat-eaters enjoy it. The restaurant at 2210 Fillmore Street, 415/921-2956, has only a couple of tiny outdoor tables. (The area inside is fairly tiny, too.) The restaurant at 288 Noe Street, 415/431-7210, has several roomy sidewalk tables, some of which are covered by an awning.

La Terrasse: The food at this French restaurant is FAB-u-LOUS, as a friend describes it, and where better to eat it with your dog than at the restaurant's heated patio that seats 50? The Sunday brunch is a favorite; instead of waffles and their kin you're offered more substantial midday items like smoked salmon pizza made with crème fraîche. Lunch items include sautéed skate with brown butter and wood-roasted squab forestiere. La Terrasse is in the Presidio, close to the off-leash beach at Crissy Field. 215 Lincoln Boulevard; 415/922-3463.

Left at Albuquerque: The Southwest comes to San Francisco at this fun Union Street eatery. For an appetizer, try the cilantro-lime shrimp quesadilla. And if you want to make your dog very happy, order the Cowboy Mix Grill, a heaping plateful of ribs, chicken, and steak, with mashed potatoes. Your drooling dog may join you at the very attractive streetside dining area. 2140 Union Street; 415/749-6700.

Liverpool Lil's: You can see two wonderful sights from this fun English pub: 1) the Golden Gate Bridge; and 2) the western end of the Presidio. Enjoy a drink and fish and chips with your dog at your side at the six pleasant outdoor tables. 2942 Lyon Street; 415/921-6664.

Mocca on Maiden Lane: Now your dog can dine in one of the most posh streets of the Union Square area. Just a bone's throw from the finest stores in San Francisco, Mocca is a European-style café famed for its many types of salads. Dine at the zillions of umbrella-topped tables right on the street, which is closed to traffic. 174 Maiden Lane; 415/956-1188.

Mona Lisa Restaurant: This family-owned and -operated North Beach restaurant is our little secret, OK? We discovered it one day while roaming around without Joe Dog and had a most sumptuous feast inside. Everything we ordered, from salad to pasta to main dish to dessert, was wonderful. Plenty of insiders know about the Mona Lisa, but it's off the radar screen for most. We like that. But of course, after this appears, it will be on many a dog's radar. The pizza here has been called the best in North Beach by many a patron. Pooches get to join their people at four outdoor tables. 353 Columbus Avenue; 415/989-4917.

Park Chalet Garden Restaurant: If you could choose one restaurant in the Bay Area to visit with your dog, the Park Chalet should be high on your list, if not right at the top: This fabulous, dog-friendly restaurant resides in one of the most special locations of any restaurant Jake and I have visited: It's where beautiful Golden Gate Park meets the magnificent Pacific Ocean. In fact, it's right across the street from part of Ocean Beach that's leash-free year round, and it's officially within Golden Gate Park, next to some great on-leash walking areas.

The garden seating area is huge and grassy, graced by trees and gardens, and sided with lawns that kids tumble around in. It's truly a bucolic culinary experience. The flatbread pizzas are a real treat, and the rest of the menu is an eclectic mix of healthy international cuisine and standard American fare. Thirsty dogs get a bowl of water. The Park Chalet is behind and under its famed sister, the Beach Chalet restaurant (which has no outdoor seating), at 1000 Great Highway at the very west end of Golden Gate Park. 415/386-8439.

Perk Presidio Cafe: The outdoor seating area at this café on the campus of George Lucas's Letterman Digital Arts Center is surrounded by green and has breathtaking views of the Palace of Fine Arts. It's a relaxing, enjoyable place to grab a beverage (organic fair-trade coffee is the specialty), pastry, salad, or sandwich. Don't be surprised if you see Lucas himself here. You may even spy Darth Vader and a Storm Trooper or two walking by. It's just that kind of place. Dogs get a bowl of water. One Letterman Drive, Building C; 415/746-5456.

Pier 39: If your dog doesn't mind flocks of tourists, you'll find a wide selection of decent eateries with outdoor tables for the two of you here. Your dog gets to smell the bay and sniff at the sea lions below. Pier 39 is off the Embarcadero, near Jefferson Street. Here are a couple of the restaurants where you and your dog are allowed (and they're not allowed at all restaurants' outdoor tables, so ask before settling in with your dog). **Chowder's** has fried seafood and several types of chowder, making Pier 39 really feel like a pier, 415/391-4737; **Sal's Pizzeria** offers several special pizzas that will give you and your dog a real taste of San Francisco, 415/398-1198.

Sometimes it's fun to just grab a snack at one of a few walk-up windows on the pier as you stroll around. Jake highly recommends ordering a little bagful of hot and crispy-yet-gooey doughnuts from Trish's Mini Donuts, and then accidentally dropping one right in front of your dog.

Primo Patio Cafe: If you and the pooch need sustenance before or after a good sniff around AT&T Park, this casual Caribbean restaurant is a primo place to visit. It's just a block or so away from the San Francisco Giants' home, and the food is mouthwatering. Dine with your dugout dog at the two sidewalk tables here. (Sorry, no dogs in the garden section of the restaurant, since they would have to walk through the indoor section and past the kitchen.) 214 Townsend Street; 415/957-1129.

Rose's Cafe: As soon as you sit down to dine with your dog at this elegant Italian-Californian restaurant's lovely side patio, you'll know you've come to one of the most dog-friendly restaurants around. Your dog will almost immediately be greeted by someone from the staff (often the dog-loving manager, Matthew) and given a big bowl of water. Then comes the gourmet house-made dog biscuit, available for a fairly good price. Throughout the meal comes plenty of attention, often from other diners, sometimes from the folks who run Rose's.

My introduction to Rose's came a few years back, when I got a letter from reader Carol Copsey, and her dog, Bella, a flirty American Eskimo. She was a frequent patron and wanted to let Joe and me know about Bella's favorite restaurant. I phoned her, and we got together one cool summer evening for dinner at Rose's. Joe was immediately smitten by Bella's fluffy good looks, but he fell asleep somewhere between the second and third gourmet dog biscuit. Bella didn't know what to make of Joe's snoozing on their date, but she pulled through after another nibble of dog treat. We had a wonderful time dining under the cream-colored awning, heat lamps getting us warm enough to take off our wraps. More recently, Jake came here with Bella to celebrate her birthday, and she watched in muffled awe (or more likely shocked disgust) as he wolfed down three-quarters of the mashed-potato-frosting-topped ground turkey birthday cake in one breath. (We made this cake; it's not a menu item.)

The food here is superb. The menu changes frequently, but here are a few dishes to be sure to order if you see them listed: bruschetta with fresh tomatoes, garlic, and basil; peaches, kadota figs, and prosciutto; crescenza-stuffed focaccia; soft polenta with gorgonzola; sautéed sweet white corn; local albacore with tomato, fennel, romano beans, and tapenade. The desserts are every bit as delicious.

It can get pretty busy here at times, so try to come when it's less hectic, for your dog's sake as well as that of other patrons. A good bet is to phone for reservations and mention that you'll be bringing your well-behaved furry friend along. There are also a few tables along the front of the restaurant, but if you have a choice, the side area is the best. 2298 Union Street; 415/775-2200.

Sea Breeze Café: Come here for delicious comfort food with a European twist. If you're here for weekend brunch, try the brown sugar and vanilla cream oatmeal; the weather in the Outer Sunset district is usually just right for this kind of cozy dish. But what dogs like best is that the café owners love dogs and welcome them at the sidewalk tables with a bowl of fresh water. (You can get tasty, natural dog treats at the natural food store next door.) 3940 Judah Street; 415/242-6022.

Squat & Gobble: Dogs love visiting the Castro's Squat and Gobble café and crepery. Not only are the servers really friendly, but the sidewalk alfresco dining area is spacious and there's always a bowl of water for thirsty dogs. Try the Zorba the Greek crepe. It's to drool for. (Jake urges any dogs reading this to convince their people to order the Gobble Burger instead.) 3600 16th Street (at Market and Noe); 415/552-2125. Other Squat & Gobble locations with dog-friendly outdoor seating include: Lower Haight, 237 Fillmore Street, 415/487-0551; Marina, 2263 Chestnut Street, 415/441-2200; and West Portal (with only a couple of sidewalk tables), at 1 West Portal Avenue, 415/665-9900.

Steps of Rome: "Of course we allow dogs!" exclaimed a manager on a recent visit. "We love dogs!" This big and bustling North Beach restaurant is a really fun place for a meal or just coffee and people-watching. The staff is friendly, and the atmosphere is very Italian, in a modern kind of way. And the food—*delicioso!* I love it here because I'm a big risotto fan, and Steps features a different risotto daily. The sidewalk tables for you and your dog are plentiful and popular. 348 Columbus Avenue; 415/397-0435.

Universal Cafe: This charming little Potrero Hill restaurant is very popular with the pooch set. The very friendly staffers here love dogs and provide them water and kind words. The restaurant features a variety of magnificent dishes with a California twist. If it's on the menu, be sure to try the caramelized onion pizza with prosciutto, fontina, and ricotta. Dine with your happy dog at the five outdoor tables. (A big thank-you to Rosie Dog and her people, Melanie and Sandra, for letting us know about this gem.) 2814 19th Street; 415/821-4608.

PLACES TO STAY

The City by the Bay has some of the most wonderful dog-friendly hotels anywhere.

Campton Place: The European ambience and superb service make this a luxury hotel your dog will never forget. The rooms are magnificently comfortable, peaceful, elegant, and filled with extra touches that really make your stay here stand out. Some of the king rooms even feature sweet window seats with roman shades—the perfect place for relaxing with your furry friend. The weight limit for dogs is a bit like a yo-yo diet here: A couple of editions ago it was a scant 25 pounds. Last edition the sky was the limit. (Three cheers from 95-pound Jake.) This edition finds the weight limit at a middling 40 pounds, but if your dog is larger and very well behaved, you might be able to work something out. If not, check in again when we come out with the next edition to see if the limit has yo-yoed back up.

The hotel is just a half block away from Union Square. Rates are $325–2,000. Dogs are $100 extra for the length of your stay. 340 Stockton Street 94108; 415/781-5555; www.camptonplace.com.

Castro Suites: The owners of the two gorgeous apartments in this 1890s Italianate Victorian home advertise that they cater to gay, lesbian, and straight clientele. What they don't say right off is that they also cater to dog clientele. They welcome dogs. Dogs who dig gardens (not in the literal sense of the word, please) should stay at the delectable garden suite, with its open airy feel and its beautiful garden. Urban-oriented dogs enjoy the apartment with its views of downtown and the bay. Rates are $200. Weekly rates are available. You'll get the address when you make your reservation. 415/437-1783; www.castrosuites.com.

Hotel Beresford: This Union Square–area hotel bills itself as "the friendliest hotel in San Francisco." Is it true? We don't know, as we haven't done a personality survey of the city's hotel employees. But we can say that the staff members we've encountered here have been very friendly and helpful. When asked if there's a size limit on pet guests, a chipper front desk manager replied, "No, as long as you don't bring an elephant." We like the attitude.

The family-owned hotel features attractive rooms—nothing fancy, but comfortable and clean. You'll get a decent continental breakfast with your stay. Humans get to eat at the hotel's adjacent restaurant, the White Horse Tavern. It has a real English pub feel, but the food is actually delicious—and even healthful, if you order right.

Rates are $89–165. 635 Sutter Street 94102; 415/673-9900 or 800/533-6533; www.beresford.com.

Hotel Beresford Arms: The sister hotel of the Hotel Beresford, this one is bigger and more elegant, with a few extra amenities. The lobby, complete with pillars and a chandelier, is a bit grander. You and the pooch can stay in a standard room or a suite with a kitchen. A continental breakfast and a fun afternoon tea and wine social come with your stay. As an added attraction, the hotel advertises that its rooms feature whirlpool baths and bidets. (We aren't sure of the lure of the latter and assume that these bidets are not of the whirlpool bath variety.)

While this hotel is the prettier of the two, it's a little tougher on dogs. Pooches need to be in the smallish range (the front desk clerk or phone reservationist will help you decide if your dog is smallish), must stay on the third (smoking) floor, and are not allowed in the elevator. With this no-elevator rule, you might want to employ the porter to take up your bags, should they put the "lug" in luggage.

On the outside, the hotel looks like any of the many decent old brick-facade apartment buildings in the slightly-off-Union-Square neighborhood. It's not the Ritz, but it is a comfy place to stay with your wee dog. Rates are $119–299. Dogs are $20 extra. 701 Post Street 94109; 415/673-2600 or 800/533-6533; www.beresford.com.

Hotel Monaco: You and your dog will have *so* much fun at this upscale, sophisticated, whimsical hotel near Union Square. Upon entering the main lobby, you'll be wowed by the gorgeous two-story-tall French-style fireplace. (It's like the famed fireplace in *Citizen Kane,* only without the austere emotional surroundings.) Louis Armstrong hits and other sumptuous music floats around the high ceilings, which sport wonderful, light-hearted murals of the sky and hot-air balloons.

The rooms here are sumptuous, with opulent decor. You'll find a variety of furnishings, including canopied beds (with thick, rich material for the canopy), Chinese-style armoires, and cushy ottomans. If you need more room, you can stay in a gorgeous suite that comes with a big whirlpool tub and entertainment center with VCR.

The hotel's mission is to seduce and pamper, and dogs are not excluded from this noble cause. The Monaco offers something called the Bone A Petit Pet Package. It includes bottled water, poop bags, dog towels, quality chew toys, and gourmet dog cookies. You can also ask the front desk for Lassie, Babe, or Dr. Doolittle videos. The price for all this: $0! Yes, free! But you have to mention the Pet Package when you make your reservation. In addition, so that your furry friend won't be lonely if you need to step out, dog-walking or sitting services are available for a fee.

Rates are $179–650. Don't forget to ask for the Pet Package when making your reservation. The Monaco, a Kimpton hotel, is directly across from the Curran Theater. 501 Geary Street 94102; 415/292-0100 or 800/214-4220; www .monaco-sf.com.

Hotel Nikko: Dogs of all shapes and sizes are welcome to spend the night with you at this luxurious member of the exclusive JAL Hotels chain, near Union Square. It used to be that only small dogs were allowed here, so we applaud this new and gracious acceptance of larger dogs. Stay here and you get to sleep on a Subarashee Yume sumptuous pillow-top bed designed just for the Hotel Nikko. It's topped by Frette linens and a down comforter. It's best to bring your dog's own bed so the feathers won't fly.

Rates are $199–655. 222 Mason Street 94102; 415/394-1111; www.hotel nikkosf.com.

Hotel Triton: If you're hankering for a wonderfully unique, creative, fun, intimate, whimsical, sophisticated place to stay, hanker no more, and book yourself any of the 140 rooms at the Hotel Triton. It's as if Betty Boop, Salvador Dali, Pee-wee Herman, and Ub Iwerks somehow came together to create their dream lodging.

I normally consider it a sign of laziness when guidebook authors lift material straight out of a brochure, but I shall do this here with the noble purpose of letting the creative Triton folks speak for themselves: "Totally hip without the attitude, the Hotel Triton is not for your average Joe… " (I pause for a moment to say that Joe Dog tried hard not to take offense at this statement) "… but for guests with imagination and style. A tarot reading during nightly wine hour, whimsical sculptured furniture, and a twinkly eyed staff" (I pause again to attest to the fact that their eyes do, indeed, seem to sparkle a little more than those of most other hotel staffers) "await you at this fun and funky gem." Dogs are no longer allowed in the fun celebrity suites designed by the likes of Jerry Garcia and Santana, nor on the Eco-Floor, but there are still dozens of rooms where dogs are welcome.

Room rates are $150–389. The Triton, a Kimpton hotel, is right across the street from the Dragon Gate entrance to Chinatown, just east of Union Square. 342 Grant Avenue 94108; 415/394-0500 or 800/433-6611; www.hotel triton.com.

Harbor Court Hotel: The Harbor Court is homey and restful at the same time it's a happening place. Dogs who stay here can get the Pet Retreat package, which features a pet bed and pad, a rawhide bone, water and food bowls, bottled water, and poop bags. 165 Steuart Street 94105; 415/882-1300 or 866/792-6283; www.harborcourthotel.com.

Laurel Motor Inn: The owners love dogs, so many visiting dogs choose to stay here. It's conveniently situated in a lovely neighborhood just far enough from downtown to be able to get great views of it from some of the rooms. It's also just a bone's throw from the magnificent Presidio National Park. Rates are $169–219. 444 Presidio Avenue 94115; 415/567-8467; www.thelaurelinn.com.

The Marina Motel: This charming 1930s motel is a few blocks from two great places to walk your dog—Crissy Field and the Presidio. It has a bougainvillea- and fuchsia-festooned courtyard and little wrought iron balconies, which makes it feel less motelly and more Mediterranean. Some rooms have kitchens, and every room comes with free parking for one car. This alone is worth the room price in this neighborhood! Rates are $75–125. Dogs are $10 extra. 2576 Lombard Street 94123; 800/346-6118; www.marinamotel.com.

Ocean Park Motel: This art deco gem is San Francisco's very first motel. It was completed in 1937, one month before the Golden Gate Bridge. "When we took the place over (in 1977), deco was pretty much a lost art," says owner Marc Duffett. "But my wife and I put everything into this place to preserve the deco flair and at the same time make it homey."

Conveniently situated just a long block from Ocean Beach and the San Francisco Zoo, this pleasant motel provides a quiet, safe atmosphere away from the hectic pace (and price) of downtown. You can hear the foghorns from the motel's relaxing hot tub. You can also hear the streetcars, but it's not bad. And there's a special little play area for human kids. Accommodations range from rooms to suites, some with kitchens. Rates are $85–185. Dogs are $10–20 extra, depending on size. 2690 46th Avenue; 415/566-7020; www.oceanparkmotel.ypguides.net.

The Palace Hotel: Dogs at the Palace? I know what you're thinking: These must be those itsy-bitsy dogs you can't see until you step on them and they shriek, right? Wrong! This four-diamond luxury hotel welcomes any size dog to stay here, and it's thrilling to me that they're able to hunker down at this gorgeous old downtown hotel. Today the Palace, tomorrow the White House! Dogs can't have tea with you in the gorgeous tearoom, the Garden Court, but if you want a version of the famous Tea at the Palace, you can simply order room service. Jazz Brunch at the Garden Court is as famous as high tea, but the jazz musicians probably don't do room service. Rates are $249–679. 2 New Montgomery Street 94105; 415/512-1111; www.sfpalace.com.

San Francisco Marriott Fisherman's Wharf: Stay here and you and your pooch are just two blocks from all the T-shirt and souvenir shops that have taken over Fisherman's Wharf. Actually, some fishing boats still live at the Wharf, and some local crabs still frequent the restaurants, so it's not as commercialized as it looks at first (and second) glance. The rooms are decent, and your stay includes use of the hotel's health club and sauna. Dogs need to be under 50 pounds to stay here. Rates are $159–299. 1250 Columbus Avenue 94133; 415/775-7555 or 800/228-9290.

The Sir Francis Drake Hotel: This luxurious old Union Square hotel is famous for its Beefeater doorman who helps tourists and hotel guests alike.

Jake likes the Beefeater almost as much as he likes beef. So do other doggy visitors, who tend to get excited about this man in plush red and a cool hat.

This hotel has been a stylin' place since 1928, and since it's become a Kimpton hotel, it's also become a little more mod and super-dog-friendly. If you opt for the Bowzer Buddy Package during your stay, you can get a dog bowl with "in-room water service daily," a Sir Francis Drake Hotel chew toy, and a few other goodies. Rates for the package start at $189. You can choose a plain old stay at the hotel and it'll run you $139–419. Should you care to dance, the concierge will help you find a dog-sitter so you can cut a rug or two at the marvelous Harry Denton's Starlight Lounge, at the top of the hotel. 450 Powell Street 94102; 415/392-7755 or 800/795-7129; www.sirfrancisdrake.com.

TraveLodge by the Bay: Some rooms here have private patios. A few even have extra-length beds, should you find that you're tall. This motel is just three blocks from the part of Lombard Street that's known as "the crookedest street in the world." Rates are $65–169. Dogs are $20 extra. 1450 Lombard Street 94123; 415/673-0691.

Westin St. Francis: The cable car stops in front of this historic landmark, so there's no excuse for not taking your dog on it. (See the Diversion *Ride Halfway to the Stars* for more about dogs on cable cars.) After a day of sniffing around San Francisco, your relatively small dog (30 pounds is the max allowed here) can crash on the Heavenly Pet Bed supplied by the St. Francis. It's a miniature version of the delectably comfortable Heavenly Bed that humans get to sleep on here. Dogs love this, but they're also grateful that humans get one Heavenly item dogs don't: the Heavenly Bath. Rates are $219–749. 335 Powell Street 94102; 415/397-7000; www.westinstfrancis.com.

W Hotel: Need a dose of opulent optimism? Stay here, where the room types have names like Wonderful Room, Spectacular Room, Fabulous Room, and Extreme Wow Suite. All the rooms are the lap of luxury, with goose-down comforters and luxury spa goodies. And speaking of laps, it's not just lap dogs who can stay here. Any size dog is welcome!

Dogs have another reason for thinking this place is wonderful, spectacular, and fabulous: Pooches who stay here get use of a dog bed and bowls and are given swanky treats and signature waste bags (and there's nothing like a signature waste bag for picking up the poo). Walks can be arranged for a fee. Rates are $329–689. Suite fees start at $480. Dogs pay $100 for the length of their stay, "be it one night, or 101 nights," as the friendly concierge told me. I like a hotelier who thinks in dog movie terms. 181 3rd Street 94103; 415/777-5300; www.whotel.com.

Kimpton Hotels: There are several of these delightful, super-dog-friendly boutique hotels in San Francisco. Alas, there's not room to write about them all in detail. I've described three in my usual fashion in this section, but I don't want to ignore the others. They charge no dog fee except when a special dog package is offered. If you want to save money, you don't have to take the package, no matter how pleading your dogs' eyes.

Union Square Area

Hotel Palomar: It's sophisticated, it's luxurious, it's South of Market, and it's got an amazing dog package called the Woof for Wellness, which includes all-natural botanical spa sprays and treats, a cool leopard-print bed and "plateware," a toy, gourmet treats, and for those whiffy canine orifices, doggy breath drops and Sweet Smell Ear Care. 12 4th Street 94103; 415/348-1111 or 877/294-9711; www.hotelpalomar.com.

Monticello Inn: The only thing missing in this grand colonial-style hotel is Thomas Jefferson. The hotel is housed in a landmark 1906 building. 127 Ellis Street 94102; 415/392-8800 or 866/778-6169; www.monticelloinn.com.

The Prescott Hotel: Enjoy quiet luxury at this beautiful hotel. The rich color schemes in each room are perfect for a relaxing evening with your quiet dog. 545 Post Street 94102; 415/563-0303 or 866/271-3632; www.prescott hotel.com.

The Serrano Hotel: Dogs enjoy staying at this Spanish-revival hotel not because of the interesting architecture but because of the Pet Palace Package. It includes designer water, gourmet dog treats, poop bags, and complimentary valet parking. 405 Taylor Street 94102; 415/885-2500 or 866/289-6561; www .serranohotel.com.

Villa Florence Hotel: You like Italy? Stay at this lovely Italian-themed little hotel with your little dog. Small dogs only, per favore. 225 Powell Street 94102; 415/397-7700 or 866/823-4669; www.villaflorence.com.

Fisherman's Wharf

Argonaut Hotel: This luxurious, historic waterfront hotel provides great views of the Golden Gate Bridge, Alcatraz, and Ghirardelli Square. 495 Jefferson Street at Hyde Street 94109; 415/563-0800 or 800/790-1415; www .argonauthotel.com.

Best Western Tuscan Inn: Yes, Kimpton runs this Best Western, and you can tell by the nice touches, including a big fireplace in the lobby. 425 Northpoint Street 94133; 415/561-1100 or 800/648-4626; www.tuscaninn.com.

Financial District

Galleria Park Hotel: You'll find an urban oasis at this 1911 Art Nouveau–style hotel. Choose the Something to Bark About package and your dog will get a "doggy bag" filled with treats, a plush toy, bottled water, a bowl, and poop bags. 191 Sutter Street 94104; 415/781-3060 or 866/756-3036; www .galleriapark.com.

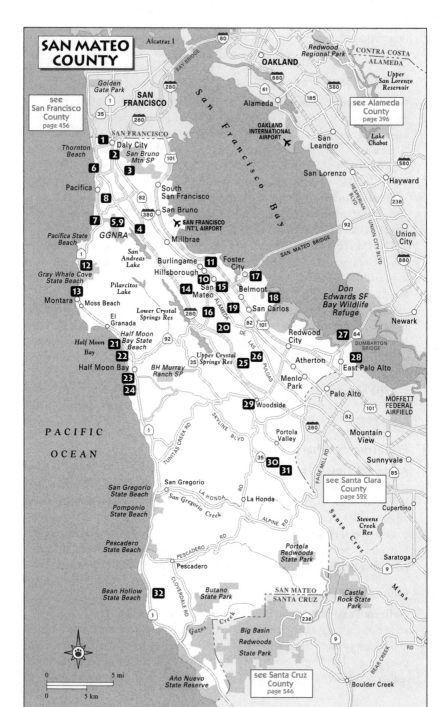

CHAPTER 36

San Mateo County

From the cool and foggy beaches of the coast to the warm and sunny inland communities, there's something for every dog's taste in San Mateo County. Sadly, the 15,000 acres of county parklands still ban dogs. Nothing has worked to change the county's ironclad law. (If it's any comfort to your dog, the county parks department is considering a ban on another human companion: cigarettes. Jake and his friends think when this ban takes effect, the county should eliminate the ban on dogs so there aren't too many rules. Good idea, dogs.)

Some state beaches have also tightened their rules and no longer allow dogs. But don't let your dog cry in her kibble. A few beaches (including one off-leash beauty in Pacifica) and plenty of parks still welcome your dog.

The Midpeninsula Regional Open Space District is a dog's best friend (second best, counting you), with four preserves in San Mateo County that allow dogs. One, Pulgas Ridge Open Space Preserve in San Carlos, even has a 17.5-acre off-leash area. Be sure to follow extremely good doggy etiquette at all the

PICK OF THE LITTER—SAN MATEO COUNTY

BEST OFF-LEASH BEACH
Esplanade Beach, Pacifica (page 504)

MOST PRIM AND TRIM DOG PARK
Foster City Dog Playground, Foster City (page 510)

BEST CHUNK OF LEASH-FREE LAND
17.5 acres within Pulgas Ridge Open Space Preserve,
San Carlos (page 516)

BEST LEASH-FREE PARKS BUILT ON A DUMP
Bayfront Park, Menlo Park (page 517)

SMALLEST DOG PARKS EVER
Mission Hills Park Dog Area, Daly City (page 501)
Palisades Dog Park, Daly City (page 501)

MOST DOG-FRIENDLY PLACES TO EAT
Cameron's Inn, Half Moon Bay (page 515)
City Pub, Redwood City (page 511)

MOST DOG-FRIENDLY PLACE TO STAY
Westin San Francisco Airport, Millbrae (page 505)

BEST SOCIAL HIKES
**Midpeninsula Regional
Open Space District
canine hikes** (page 502)

FRIENDLIEST
BOOKSTORE
Kepler's Books,
Menlo Park (page 517)

district's preserves, because there are a lot of antidoggers out there who would love to get the district to take away our privileges.

The district has unique rules about poop-scooping and six-foot leashes. Scooping the poop is required in places, but because of limited trash disposal sites, if you kick the poop off the trail, that's usually considered OK. (Helpful hint: Don't wear open-toed sandals.) And retractable leashes that go beyond the six-foot mark are allowed in many instances, which is a rare thing indeed. The exceptions: when you're within 100 feet of parking lots, roads, trailheads, picnic areas, and restrooms, and when you're within 50 feet of other people or any body of water, including creeks. It's a great policy—one other park districts should implement.

The district provides excellent park info and maps on its website, www .openspace.org. Or phone 650/691-1200 for doggy details.

Daly City

PARKS, BEACHES, AND RECREATION AREAS

1 Palisades Dog Park

🐾 🐕 (See San Mateo County map on page 498)

This is the second-smallest dog park I've ever seen. (For the smallest, see *Mission Hills*, the next listing.) It's not much bigger than many backyards in the area. It's fenced and has double gates for dog safety, but it's not signed, and there's nothing in it at all except for some petrified poops scattered around the thick grass.

The park is conveniently situated if you're on Highway 35/Skyline Boulevard and your dog starts crossing his legs. Turn west on Westridge Avenue and you'll see Palisades Park at the end of the road. Look to the right of the playground and you'll see the teeny dog park. 650/991-8006.

2 Mission Hills Park Dog Area

🐕 (See San Mateo County map on page 498)

Welcome to what is very likely the smallest dog park in California. I appreciate the fact that Daly City has tried to make a little something for dogs to run off leash, but this one's so small that a dog can barely trot before crashing into a fence. Jake just poked around for about 30 seconds, then stood at the gate looking plaintively to get out.

The park is about the size of a dining room and living room in a not-so-big house. The ground is dirt and weeds, and there's no water, and no place to sit. But there are two medium trees within, plus a double-gated entry, should you chance to encounter another dog here. (You probably won't.) The dog area is in Mission Hills Park, a small urban affair that has a little playground and a basketball court. It's at Frankfort and Gutenburg streets. Enter on Gutenburg on leash, walk past the playground, and you'll see a chain-link fence surrounding the postage stamp, er, dog park. 650/991-8006.

DIVERSION

Hike with Like-Minded Hounds: Want to take your dog for a hike but don't like the way the conversation kind of peters out after the first "How ya doin,' buddy? Are you a good boy?!" Sounds like it's time for a **docent-led dog hike.** These hikes, run by **The Midpeninsula Regional Open Space District,** provide a fun way to meet other dog people and to learn about your stomping grounds.

The hikes take place in some of the district's dog-friendly preserves a few times a year. They have themes like "fall hiking" or "day's end hikes." The day's end hikes are actually at night and loop by a pet cemetery. Dogs are not a requirement for any of the hikes, but you might want one at your side for that one.

The docent-led hikes are generally free, but reservations are necessary. Check out www.openspace.org/activities/ideas_for_dogs.asp for upcoming dog hikes, or phone 650/691-1200.

South San Francisco

PARKS, BEACHES, AND RECREATION AREAS

Psst, there's a rumor that the city is considering building its first dog park. Jake will sniff it out and give a full report in the next edition of our book.

🐾 Westborough Park

🐾🐾 (See San Mateo County map on page 498)

This is a hilly little park with many picnic tables, a tennis court, and a children's playground. Your best bet is to take the narrow, paved path along the back of the park. It's lined with trees and far from the madding baseball field below. Leashes are required. It's on Westborough Avenue at Galway Drive, just west of I-280. 650/829-3800.

PLACES TO STAY

Embassy Suites: The striking 9-story atrium here is home to palm trees, a delightful breakfast area, and a large koi pond filled with some real bruisers—one that must weigh in at 25 pounds. The rooms are all suites, with dark wood cabinetry that adds a luxurious touch.

Dogs are supposed to weigh less than 50 pounds to stay here, but that's only the weight of two giganto koi, and we hear there's some wiggle room. A grassy area off the parking lot is available for a late-night amble if your dog needs a toilet break. Rates are $189–249. Dogs pay a $50 flat fee for the length of their stay. 250 Gateway Boulevard 94080; 650/589-3400.

La Quinta Inn San Francisco Airport: Rates are $69–129. 20 Airport Boulevard 94080; 650/583-2223; www.laquinta.com.

San Bruno

PARKS, BEACHES, AND RECREATION AREAS

One of the state's original dog parks, the San Bruno Dog Exercise Area, has closed, but in its place—at another location—is a fresh addition, Commodore Dog Park.

4 Commodore Dog Park

🐾🐾🐾🐕 (See San Mateo County map on page 498)

The location of San Bruno's relatively new dog park is ideal for visitors passing by on the highway, as well as for dogs who have any business to conduct at San Francisco International Airport. The park is at the intersection of Highways 280 and 380, so close to the airport that you can almost feel the breeze of planes as they take off. (The noise level can be a little startling for noise-sensitive pooches and people. Old Airedale Joe would have had a heart attack. Jake, however, doesn't appear to even notice.)

It's a small but attractive park, set within the larger Commodore Park. The dog park has sufficient shade from mature trees, water (for people and dogs), separate areas for large and small dogs, benches, and enough grass to make it worth a roll.

The park is at Commodore and Cherry avenues, at the east end of Commodore Park. Traveling south on Highway 280, take the San Bruno Avenue exit. In about a half mile you'll come to San Bruno Avenue West. Turn left and drive 0.2 mile to Cherry Avenue. Go left on Cherry and drive 0.3 mile to the park. You'll pass under Highway 380, and the park will be on your right. 650/616-7195.

5 Sweeney Ridge

🐾🐾🐾🐾 (See San Mateo County map on page 498)

If your dog appreciates breathtaking vistas of the Bay Area, with a rainbow assortment of wildflowers in the foreground, this 1,000-acre park is a rare treat. But if your canine is like most, he can take or leave such a magnificent panorama.

Still, if you like stunning views and a vigorous uphill climb, take the Sneath Lane entrance. It may be toasty when you start, but bring a couple of thick wool sweaters if you plan to hike along the ridge—it's cold and often foggy up there. The furrier your dog, the more she'll take to the invigorating conditions.

The Skyline College entrance is ideal if you want a more moderate grade, but both trailheads will take you to the same place. The leash law here can come in handy if your dog is of the pulling mentality. Just say "mush" on those steep slopes.

From different parts of the ridge, you'll be able to see the ocean (and the Farallon Islands, on a good day), as well as Mt. Tamalpais in Marin, Mt. Diablo to the east, and Montara Mountain to the south. Judging by all the canines with flaring nostrils, the scents from all four directions must be as enticing as the views.

For the Sneath Lane entrance, take San Bruno's Sneath Lane all the way to the end. There's usually plenty of parking. The Skyline College entrance, off College Drive, is in the southeast corner of campus, near Lot 2. 415/239-2366 or 415/556-8371.

Pacifica

PARKS, BEACHES, AND RECREATION AREAS

6 Esplanade Beach

🐾🐾🐾🐾🐾 (See San Mateo County map on page 498)

Well-behaved dogs are welcome to throw their leashes to the wind then they set foot on this great beach! The beach is fairly wide (if it's not high tide) and long enough for a very good walk. Many people who come here bring tennis-ball launchers so their dogs can really go out for a fly ball.

At the top of the long staircase that leads to the beach you'll find an attractive grassy area right in front of some long, low apartments. Leashed dogs are welcome to sniff around this area. To get to the beach, exit Highway 1 at Manor Drive and head west on Manor toward the ocean. It will dead-end at Esplanade Drive. Turn right and follow Esplanade about 0.3 mile to where it makes almost a 90-degree curve to the right. (You'll see a large sign for the Land's End apartments.) The green park will be on your left, as will the staircase leading down the cliff to the beach. Park anywhere along the street. 650/738-7381.

7 Linda Mar Beach/Pacifica State Beach

🐾🐾🐾 (See San Mateo County map on page 498)

Even though this is a state beach, leashed dogs are welcome here. It's run by the city of Pacifica, so it doesn't have to follow the more stringent "no dogs" rules being enforced by most other state beaches in coastal San Mateo County. The setting alone warrants a visit. With green rolling hills in the distance behind you and the pounding sea before you, you and your dog won't regret stopping here. This is Surfer Heaven, so if your dog likes to see surfers doing their thing, this is the place to come.

The beach also provides an easy access point to a coastal multiuse trail that will take you north over bluffs with great views of the coastline, and all the way to Pacifica's jagged Rockaway Beach area. It's a decidedly more wild affair than Linda Mar, and dogs enjoy poking around. The trek from beach to beach about three miles.

Linda Mar Beach is also known as Taco Bell Beach in some circles, for its proximity to this long-surviving wood-clad member of the fast-food chain (the most attractive Taco Bell exterior we've seen, for what it's worth). You'll find the beach, and Taco Bell, on Highway 1. Park between Crespi Drive and Linda Mar Boulevard. 415/738-7381.

🛾 Milagra Ridge

🐾🐾🐾🐾 (See San Mateo County map on page 498)

Follow the trail up to the top of the tallest hill and you'll end up with both an incredible view of the Pacific and a perfect plateau for a picnic. You'll see hillsides covered with ice plant and even a few Monterey pines along the way. Visit in the spring if you want to be wowed by wildflowers.

Despite the leash law, dogs really seem to enjoy this park. Make sure to keep them on the trail, as the environment here is fragile. And keep your eyes peeled for the Mission Blue butterfly. This park is one of its last habitats. Milagra Ridge is especially magical at night. You've never seen the full moon until you've seen it from here.

Enter on Sharp Park Road in Pacifica, between Highway 1 and Skyline Boulevard. 415/239-2366 or 415/556-8371.

🛿 Sweeney Ridge

🐾🐾🐾🐾 (See San Mateo County map on page 498)

See the *San Bruno* section for this listing.

PLACES TO STAY

Pacifica Motor Inn: A very cute smiling dog on the inn's website has a cartoon bubble coming out of his mouth saying, "Dogs love the Pacifica Motor Inn… And a good bone!" So have no fear: Dogs are welcome here. And it's a bone's throw to Rockaway Beach and the dog-friendly coastal trail at Linda Mar Beach. The inn is pretty decent for a motel and has two floors, and some rooms have ocean views. It's set in a fun little seaside neighborhood.

Rates are $89–159. Dogs are $15 extra. 200 Rockaway Beach Avenue 94044; 650/359-7700 or 800/522-3772; www.pacificamotorinn.com.

Millbrae

Dogs are no longer allowed on trails surrounding Crystal Springs Reservoir, and they are howling. But they can still spend the night.

PLACES TO STAY

Clarion Hotel: Rates are $89–249. Dogs are $30 extra. 401 East Millbrae Avenue 94030; 650/692-6363; www.clarionhotels.com.

Westin San Francisco Airport: If you're traveling by air and need to stay somewhere with your dog, this is about the most convenient and luxurious place you can stay. It's only two minutes from the airport. Each of the 390 rooms is well appointed and has a very comfortable bed, known as the Heavenly Bed. So that dogs don't feel left out, dogs who stay here get their own Heavenly Pet Bed. Pooches we've talked with say the beds are dreamy. For humans, there are Mutt Mitts (not exciting, but very handy) and better yet, there's a fitness center and a yummy Mediterranean-style bistro. Rates are $129–379. 1 Old Bayshore Highway 94030; 650/692-3500 or 800/228-3000; www.starwood.com.

Burlingame

PARKS, BEACHES, AND RECREATION AREAS

10 Burlingame Dog Exercise Park

🐾🐾🐾 🐕 (See San Mateo County map on page 498)

Hooray! Burlingame's dog park is finally a reality. The half-grass, half–fine gravel park is a popular place, with a very different shape than most dog parks. It's very long, almost as long as two football fields end to end, and not extremely wide (anywhere from 30 feet to 70 feet). This lends itself very well to the park's name: It's a dog *exercise* park. With a shape like this, forward movement beckons. You and your dog can stand around and chat and sniff (as most do here), or you can really walk in this fenced park. In more typical squarish dog parks, you'd look kind of foolish taking a hike.

There are no decent-sized trees here yet. All are in the sapling stage, about waist-high at last check. But boy dogs still manage to do plenty of leg lifts on other spots they seem to find fascinating. Speaking of bodily functions, the one drawback to this park is that it's right next to a sewage treatment plant. This can make the park a little whiffy at times, depending on which way the wind is blowing, but it's usually not a problem. In fact, as far as dogs are concerned, the stinkier the better.

A nice bonus if you use this park: There's a great path you can follow. You can pick up the path behind the dog park. You have to leash up to use it, but it's a good walk. It's within Bayside Park, on the Old Bayshore Freeway between Anza Boulevard and Broadway. 650/558-7300.

11 Washington Park

🐾🐾 (See San Mateo County map on page 498)

This relatively small park has the look of an old college campus. Its trees are big and old and mostly deciduous, making autumn a particularly brilliant time. Bring a lunch and eat it on the thick, knotty old redwood picnic tables. They're something out of the Enchanted Forest. Joe Dog was always intrigued by the abundance of squirrels, but he never got too far with his pursuits, since leashes have been the law forever, and since the police station is around the corner.

The park is at 850 Burlingame Avenue below Carolan Avenue. 650/558-7300.

PLACES TO EAT

It's fun to stroll down Burlingame Avenue, between El Camino Real and California Drive. The stores are upscale, the people generally like good dogs, and there are plenty of restaurants where you can enjoy a tasty meal with your dog at an outdoor table. Here are three to get you started:

Cafe La Scala: The outdoor area at this exquisite Italian restaurant has dozens of tables, but it's still very romantic, with beautiful flowers, soft music, and pastoral murals. It's all very Florentine. Dogs need to sit at the edge of the patio area. In cooler months, the area is warmed by heat lamps. 1219 Burlingame Avenue; 650/347-3035.

Copenhagen Bakery & Cafe: We've enjoyed some magnificently rich, flavorful, top-notch baked treats here. But if you're hankering for a real meal, the café has a full menu of scrumptious dishes, from appetizers (try the soft polenta with wild mushrooms and gorgonzola) to salads to steaks (yes, steaks at a café, doggy). Enjoy them at a couple of lovely sidewalk tables. 1216 Burlingame Avenue; 650/342-1357.

Trapeze European Cafe: OK, this one's around the corner and down a half block from popular Burlingame Avenue, but your dog will thank you for the extra jaunt. The servers we've had here adore dogs, and Jake got a bowl of water and lots of pats when we dined at one of the few sidewalk tables. The fruits and veggies are pesticide-free, the meat is free-range, and the chefs know how to make the ingredients shine. 266 Lorton Avene; 650/344-4242.

PLACES TO STAY

San Francisco Airport Marriott: If you need to stay near the airport, and your dog appreciates good views of San Francisco Bay, you couldn't ask for a better hotel. Rates are $129–229, and dogs pay $75 for the length of their stay. 1800 Old Bayshore Highway 94010; 650/692-9100.

Vagabond Inn: With these prices, it's a wonder they still call it Vagabond Inn. Rates are $92–120. Dogs are $10 extra. 1640 Bayshore Highway 94010; 650/692-4040.

Montara

PARKS, BEACHES, AND RECREATION AREAS

🐾 McNee Ranch State Park

🐾🐾🐾🐾 (See San Mateo County map on page 498)

State parks usually ban dogs completely, or at least from all but paved roadways. But McNee is a refreshing exception to the rule. At McNee, you can hike at the same level as the soaring gulls and watch the gem-blue ocean below. The higher you go up Montara Mountain, the more magnificent the view. Hardly a soul knows about this park, so if it's peace you want, it's peace you'll get.

And if it's a workout you want, you'll get that, too. Just strap on a day pack and bring lots of water for you and your dog. If you do the full hike, you'll ascend from sea level to 1,898 feet in a couple of hours. As you hike up and away from the ocean and the road, you lose all sounds of civilization, and Highway 1 fades into a thin ribbon and disappears below.

As soon as you go through the gate at the bottom of the park, follow the narrow trails to the left up the hills. You may be tempted to take the wide and winding paved road from the start, but to avoid any bikers, take the little trails. Besides, they lead to much better vistas.

Eventually, you'll come to a point where you have a choice of going left or right on a wider part of the trail. It's a choice between paradise and heaven. Left will lead you to a stunning view of the Golden Gate Bridge and the Farallon Islands. Right will bring you to the top of the ridge, where you see Mt. Diablo and the rest of San Francisco Bay.

This was one of Joe's favorite parks, despite the leash law. Still, he always managed to slide down several steep grassy hills on his back, wriggling and moaning in ecstasy all the way.

It's easy to miss this park since there aren't any signs and there's no official parking lot. From Highway 1 in Montara, park at the far northern end of the Montara State Beach parking lot and walk across the road. Be careful as you walk along Highway 1, because there's hardly any room on the shoulder. You'll see a gate on a dirt road just north of you and a small state property sign. That's where you go in. A few cars can also park next to the gate on the sides of the dirt road. But don't block the gate or your car probably won't be there when you get back. 650/726-8820.

13 Montara State Beach

🐾🐾🐾🐾 (See San Mateo County map on page 498)

This long, wide beach has more nooks and crannies than your dog will be able to investigate. Around mid-beach, you'll find several little inlets carved into the mini-cliffs. Take your dog back there at low tide and you'll find all sorts of water, grass, mud, and beach flotsam. It's a good place for her to get her paws wet while obeying the leash law. The water at the inlets is as calm as pond water. This is where Joe first dared to walk in water. It was only a centimeter deep, but he licked his paws in triumph all the way home.

With the recent banning of dogs at other state beaches in the area, this one has been taking a pounding of late. I know it's hard, but please keep your dog on leash, or this beach could go the way of so many others.

Off Highway 1, park in the little lot behind the building that used to house the Chart House restaurant. There's also a parking area on the north side of the beach, off Highway 1. 650/726-8820.

PLACES TO STAY

Farallone Bed and Breakfast Inn: Two of the nine rooms in this homey Victorian inn have a private balcony and a small whirlpool bath. Some rooms have ocean views. A basic breakfast comes with your room. Rooms are $65–130. Dogs require a $25 deposit and are charged a $25 fee for the length of their stay. 1410 Main Street 94037; 650/728-8200 or 800/818-7319; www .faralloneinn.com.

Hillsborough

PARKS, BEACHES, AND RECREATION AREAS

14 Vista Park

(See San Mateo County map on page 498)

You can visit this park only if you live here, unless you choose to walk miles to get to it—there's no street parking for blocks, and no parking lot. And chances are that if you live in this town, your backyard is bigger anyway. A little section in the back has several tall eucalyptus trees that leashed neighborhood dogs call their own. It's good for sniffs when you can't get to a better park. Poop bags are provided.

The park is at Vista and Culebra roads. 650/579-3800.

San Mateo

PARKS, BEACHES, AND RECREATION AREAS

15 Central Park

(See San Mateo County map on page 498)

This is a lush, green, miniature version of Golden Gate Park. There's even a Japanese garden, and although no dogs are allowed inside, the Japanese ambience spills outside. The days we've visited, there was always something going on at the outdoor stage in back of the recreation center. A couple of large meadows are bordered by big shady redwoods. There's even a pint-sized railroad that takes up part of a small field. (Something not found in Golden Gate Park.) Someone told us that dogs have been known to chase the cars as they chug along the track. Leashes are a must.

The park is on East 5th Avenue at El Camino Real. 650/522-7420.

16 Laurelwood Park

😊😊😊 (See San Mateo County map on page 498)

A small, clear stream winds the length of this rural park in the suburbs. Joe Dog never wanted anything to do with the water and jumped from one side to the other without getting a toenail damp. But Jake, a.k.a. Mr. Water, delights in its fresh scents and enticing sounds. Follow the bike trail—heeding the leash law, as this is a popular spot for bikers—along the stream, and enjoy tree-covered hillsides in a virtually suburb-free environment. Only a few blocks from the Laurelwood Shopping Center, this park is an ideal getaway after a quick shopping trip. The kids can use the playground at the foot of the bike trail.

The park is at Glendora and Cedarwood drives. 650/522-7420.

PLACES TO STAY

Residence Inn by Marriott: There's a walking path not far from here, so it's a good place to stay with your pooch. Besides, it's a comfy lodging—not quite home, but it tries to come close. Rates are $99–199. Dogs are $10 extra, plus a $75 fee per visit. 2000 Winward Way 94404; 650/574-4700; www.marriott.com.

Foster City

PARKS, BEACHES, AND RECREATION AREAS

17 Foster City Dog Playground

😊😊😊🐕 (See San Mateo County map on page 498)

This tidy, neat, petite fenced park with artificial grass is a little like a Stepford Wife: Lovely to look at, but perfect to the point of being scary. When I visited with Jake, I spent the whole time silently praying that he'd poop on the refined gravel ground cover (formally known as decomposed granite), not on the carpetlike Field Turf. The turf is the modern version of Astroturf, and it's like a green rug that aspires to be golf-course grass. I asked a nice gent there what happens if a dog does go to the bathroom on it, and he pointed to a poop-bag dispenser (no problem), and also to a scrub brush and bucket of water near the water fountain (ah, the Cinderella routine).

Park fan Kirk Amspoker contacted me after reading the above description in the book's last edition, and told me that "non-Cinderellas are welcome .... The only time I've ever seen the water and brush used was for a dog with (how should I say) less-than-solid poop." So if your dog has firm poo, a bag will do. (Ah, the subjects we cover in this book.)

In the end, Jake didn't poop anywhere. He was having too much fun playing chase games with his new friends and learning to run through an agility tire and over an agility jump. Big dogs have their own section, which is great, because the small-dog section had really tiny, breakable dogs when we visited. (The small-dog section had the air of a casual country club, with the well-dressed dog people reposing on a variety of lawn chairs.) The entire park is less than a half acre, but dogs greatly enjoy themselves. There's shade from two large green shade structures, and water, scoops, picnic tables, and benches. A couple of very cute rusted-metal dog sculptures grace one end of the park.

Exit eastbound Highway 92 at Foster City Boulevard, go left at the offramp, and then right within a block at Foster City Boulevard. Travel about 0.7 mile and go right on Bounty Drive, and then left almost immediately into the parking lot. 650/286-3382.

PLACES TO EAT

Dogs dig dining at Foster City's lagoon-side restaurants. Here's one that welcomes dogs. Others do, too, but don't jump at the chance to advertise it.

Plaza Gourmet: Good dogs can dine with you on the attractive wood-planked deck. If your dog is thirsty, a fresh bowl of water is hers for the asking. 929C Edgewater Boulevard; 650/638-0214.

Redwood City

PARKS, BEACHES, AND RECREATION AREAS

18 Shore Dogs Park

🐾🐾🐾🐕 (See San Mateo County map on page 498)

This park is only 0.75 acre, but it doesn't matter. Dogs and their people are simply overjoyed just to have some legal off-leash romping room after so many years of being banned from all city parks. It can get mighty windy here, and it's quite a sight to see dogs joyously running around with their ears flapping, and then standing still only to have their ears continue to flap.

As its name may tell you, Shore Dogs Park is near the water. And what dog doesn't dig being able to sniff the odors wafting off of San Francisco Bay? During winter and fall, the park's location gives you and your dog a front-row seat to the shorebird migration. Your dog's jaw will drop as she watches an egret flap its gigantic wings. The birds have nothing to fear, as the park is fenced, and dogs can't fly.

Poop bags are provided, large and small dogs have separate sections, and there's a little "greeting area" where dogs can sniff each other out before entering. The park is off Redwood Shores Parkway, near the end of Radio Road, in Redwood Shores. 650/654-6538.

PLACES TO EAT

City Pub: Like pub food? Dine at the outdoor tables here at this charming hangout. If your dog is thirsty, the staff will happily provide a big bowl of water. And if treats are in stock, they'll supply a couple for your lucky dog. 2620 Broadway; 650/363-2620.

Milagro's: The outdoor tables at this upscale Mexican restaurant are warm and cozy year-round, thanks to some effective heat lamps. 1099 Middlefield Road; 650/369-4730.

Belmont

PARKS, BEACHES, AND RECREATION AREAS

19 Cipriani Park Dog Exercise Area

🐾🐾🐾🐕 (See San Mateo County map on page 498)

This 0.75-acre fenced park is a treat for leash-free pooches and their chauffeurs. That's partly because of all the social events that take place here: There are frequent potlucks, seminars on topics such as canine first aid, and even a couple of fairs a year. In addition, the park has all good dog-park amenities, including poop bags, water, picnic tables, attractive surroundings, and separate sections for large and small dogs.

The park is at 2525 Buena Vista Avenue, behind the Cipriani School. It's a little hard to find. From El Camino Real, go west on Ralston Avenue. In about 1.5 miles, you'll pass Alameda de las Pulgas. Drive another 0.75 mile, and be on the lookout for Cipriani Boulevard. It's a small street you can easily miss. Turn right on Cipriani and follow it a few blocks to Buena Vista. Turn left on Buena Vista and park near the school. You won't see the dog run from the street, but if you walk west and enter through the main park entrance, you'll soon see it. Whatever you do, don't take your dog through the school's playground when kids are present. The school really frowns on this. 650/595-7441.

20 Twin Pines Park

🐾🐾🐾 (See San Mateo County map on page 498)

This park is a hidden treasure, nestled among eucalyptus trees just outside the business district of Belmont. You'd never guess the dog wonders that await within. Your dog may hardly notice she's leashed. The main trail is paved and winds through sweet-smelling trees and brush. A clear stream runs below. In dry seasons, it's only about two feet deep, but in good years it swells to several feet. Dogs love to go down to the stream and wet their whistles. Past the picnic area are numerous small, quiet dirt trails that can take you up the woodsy hill or alongside the stream.

It's at 1225 Ralston Avenue, behind the police department. 650/595-7441.

El Granada

PLACES TO STAY

Harbor View Inn: Each of the 17 comfortable rooms at this upscale motel features a wonderful bay window seat, where you can get a very good view of the ocean and the harbor. You'll have to look over Highway 1, since you're on the east side of the road, but it's a nice touch you don't usually find at motels. The owners, Bob and Judy, have a little Yorkie, Joey, and they're mighty dog-friendly folks. They'll point you in the direction of a couple of hush-hush dog-walking spots nearby. Rates are $85–180. Bob and Judy will waive the pet fee for readers of this book, so be sure to mention you found them here! 51 Avenue Alhambra 94018; 650/726-2329 or 800/726-2329; www.harbor-view-inn.com.

Half Moon Bay

This is a delightful place to come for a day of sniffing around the enchanting old "downtown" and checking out the beautiful ocean views. It's a real treat on days that are scorching elsewhere: This area is air-conditioned by the god of woolly sheepdogs. No matter how steaming hot it is elsewhere, you can almost always count on cool weather here. It's often chilly and foggy in the summer, wet and windy in the winter, and moderate in the fall and spring.

PARKS, BEACHES, AND RECREATION AREAS

Dogs are no longer allowed on the sand at any of the four Half Moon Bay State Beach areas, but they're still welcome to take a stroll on the scenic blufftop paths that stretch almost from one end of Half Moon Bay to the other—Surfer's Beach, Half Moon Bay State Beach, and Bluff Top Park offer easy trail access.

Fortunately for sand-loving hounds, two city beaches permit leashed beasts.

21 Surfer's Beach

🐾🐾 (See San Mateo County map on page 498)

Water dogs dig being able to dip their paws in the water here. On almost any day, no matter how cold and gray it is, you'll find loads of surfers waiting for the perfect wave. The beach isn't big or wide, and it can be crowded at times, but it's a fun place to take a little stroll with your leashed dog. A trail that starts here takes you miles down the shore. It's a terrific, flat, easy, and very scenic hike. Jake highly recommends it.

Surfer's Beach is on Highway 1 and Coronado Street, just south of Pillar Point Harbor. 650/726-8820.

22 Half Moon Bay State Beach Trail

🐾🐾🐾 (See San Mateo County map on page 498)

This name is a misnomer. Thanks to the threatened snowy plover bird, and to people who abused the leashed-dog privilege, dogs are no longer allowed on the beach, even if they promise to wear their leashes and behave perfectly. But they are welcome on the paved blufftop trail here. The views are excellent, the sea air uplifting.

You can hook up with the trail here at several points. There's signage along different spots of Highway 1. At the very west end of Kelly Avenue you'll find Francis Beach and the entrance for the campground. At the west end of Venice Boulevard is Venice Beach (not to be confused with its radically different counterpart in Los Angeles County), and at the west end of Young Avenue you'll find both Dunes Beach and Roosevelt Beach.

This isn't the place to come for a 15-minute romp: If you park in the lots, it costs $6. You can park a little away on the street, or take your car down to the city-run Bluff Top Park, which has not only a paved trail, but a leashed-dog-friendly sandy beach—for free!

If you can ignore all the RVs and crowds of tents, the area above Francis Beach is a stunning camping spot. Perched on ice plant–covered dunes above the Pacific, it's one of the most accessible beach camping areas in the Bay Area. All of the 52 campsites are available on a first-come, first-served basis. Sites are $25 for the first vehicle, and $6 per additional vehicle.

From Highway 1, follow the brown and white signs to the appropriate beach. 650/726-8820.

23 Bluff Top Park
😺 😺 😺 (See San Mateo County map on page 498)

This is a splendid area to visit with a leashed dog. The beach is beautiful, long, and fairly wide, and the bluff top has a couple of fun and scenic trails. If you're hankering for a great walk, you can hoof it through other park and beach areas for several miles—almost all the way to the Half Moon Bay harbor.

From Highway 1, take Poplar Avenue west all the way to the end. A parking lot will be on your left. 650/726-8297.

24 Half Moon Bay Dog Park
😺 😺 🐕 (See San Mateo County map on page 498)

This 15,000-square-foot dog park is just "temporary" (and has been for several years now) until the long-awaited Coastside Dog Park is up and running. That one's been years in the planning and debating stages, so don't let your dog hold his dog breath. In fact, when I asked a former dog park coordinator about when the park might become a reality, he asked me if I was over 30. I said yes. "Not in your lifetime," he replied. Apparently there's been a lot of frustration about how the city has handled some issues.

The park is a disheveled mass of landscaping bark and scattered dog toys surrounded by temporary and not terribly attractive fencing. In other words, dogs love it here. Jake goes kooky when he arrives at this park, running around with every dog toy in his smiling face until we have to leave. And he never wants to leave. It goes to show that a dog park doesn't have to be fancy to be a hit with the canine crowd.

From Highway 1, turn west on Wavecrest Street (you'll find the super-dog-friendly eatery Cameron's at this intersection) and continue down the bumpy old road about 0.3 mile almost to the end. You'll see a brown sign that says all dogs must be on a leash. Immediately after that is a little dirt road to the right. Follow that past the horseshoe pits and you'll be there. For an update on the park situation, check out www.coastdogs.org. 650/726-8297.

PLACES TO EAT

Cameron's Inn: English pub grub and rich and creamy fountain treats are the specialty here, but burgers, pizza, and salads are big sellers, too. Dine with your pooch at the big outdoor patio. Dogs who are lucky enough to come to this funky, charming, British treasure get to sniff out a double-decker bus out front. (It makes for a very cute photo.) The folks here love dogs and provide them treats and water. Cameron's is a bone's throw from Half Moon Bay's temporary dog park. 1410 South Cabrillo Highway/Highway 1; 650/726-5705.

Casey's Cafe: The outdoor seating here is attractive, with several umbrella-topped tables in a pretty plaza. If you like to play games other than fetch, you'll be pleased to know that on warm evenings you can play your favorite board game at the outdoor tables while snacking with your dog at your side. (If he's a border collie you can even use him as your game partner.) Casey's is right next to the Zaballa House lodging, 328 Main Street; 650/560-4880.

Half Moon Bay Brewing Company: Good beer, good food, good dog-friendly ambience, and good sniffs from the waterfront. What else could a dog want? A bowl of water? It's yours for the asking. This fun eatery and drinkery is in nearby Princeton's Pillar Point Harbor, at 390 Capistrano Road; 650/728-BREW (650/728-2739).

Moonside Bakery: All the delicious treats here are baked daily, except for the soup, which generally isn't baked. (But it's still made fresh daily.) This is truly an exceptional bakery, featuring all kinds of crusty breads and delectable sweets but specializing in German baked goods. Dine with dog at the many attractive, wooden, umbrella-topped tables outside. 604 Main Street; 650/726-9070.

PLACES TO STAY

Holiday Inn Express: Just five blocks from Half Moon Bay State Beach, and a few blocks from downtown, this dog-friendly hotel is conveniently situated for adventure-seeking pooches and their people. Rates are $93–179. Dogs are $10 extra. 230 Cabrillo Highway 94019; 650/726-3400; www.hiexpress.com/halfmoonbay.

Zaballa House: Dogs and their human roommates get to stay in the attractive rooms and suites in back of this Victorian inn's main building—the oldest standing house in Half Moon Bay, built in 1859. Dogs don't mind the more modern digs. The rooms are spacious and very attractive, and all have fireplaces. Suites come with fireplaces, kitchenettes, whirlpool tubs, and private decks.

The owners of the inn really enjoy dog guests. "A lot of pets are nicer than their people," says one of the innkeepers. If you visit at the right time, the front-desk person might take a photo of you and your dog to put in the VIP Dog Guest photo album. The album is tucked away, and sometimes employees don't seem to know of its existence, but it's there.

The inn is right in beautiful downtown Half Moon Bay, next to some mighty dog-friendly eateries. Rates are $129–275. Dogs pay $10 extra. 324 Main Street 94019; 650/726-9123; www.zaballahouse.net.

San Carlos

PARKS, BEACHES, AND RECREATION AREAS

25 Heather Park
🐾🐾🐾🐕 (See San Mateo County map on page 498)

This is one of the few fenced-in dog parks we've ever seen that comes complete with rolling hills, wildflowers, old gnarled trees, and singing birds. Your dog will have the time of his life here, bounding up and down hills or trotting down the winding paved path to the bottom of the park—sans leash. You may be tempted to take some of the tiny dirt trails up the steep hills, but they tend to end abruptly, leaving you and your dog teetering precariously. The only thing the park lacks is water, usually a given at dog parks.

If you have a dog who likes to wander, watch out. There are a couple of potential escape routes near the two gates at the far ends of the park. The park is at Melendy and Portofino drives. 650/802-4382.

26 Pulgas Ridge Open Space Preserve
🐾🐾🐾🐾🐕 (See San Mateo County map on page 498)

A quick Spanish lesson: Pulgas means flea in Spanish, as my trusty researcher, Caroline Grannan, informed me. But don't let this park's moniker send you fleeing. There are no more fleas here than there are in other parks. In fact, Jake has never brought home extra vermin after a trip to Pulgas.

The name notwithstanding, dogs are thrilled to be here. Not only does this 293-acre Midpeninsula Regional Open Space District land permit leashed pooches, but on 17.5 acres in the middle of the preserve dogs are allowed to be leash-free.

The off-leash area is only for dogs under excellent voice control. That's always the case in off-leash, unenclosed areas, but it's particularly important here because of wildlife—and because of some vociferous folks who would love nothing better than to see leashes be mandatory here again. You know, *those* kind of people. The off-leash area is oak woodland and grassland, so dogs can explore a variety of landscapes. It's in the middle of the preserve and accessible via the Blue Oak Trail or the Cordilleras Trail.

Leashed dogs can explore the rest of this fairly flat, oak-chaparral area via three miles of trails that wind throughout. The best time to visit is in the spring, when the wildflowers come to life everywhere.

Exit I-280 at Edgewood Road and drive east almost a mile. Turn left at Crestview Drive and make an immediate left onto Edmonds Road. You'll see signs for the preserve. Roadside parking is limited here, but it's usually enough. 650/691-1200.

Menlo Park

PARKS, BEACHES, AND RECREATION AREAS

27 Bayfront Park

🐾🐾🐾 (See San Mateo County map on page 498)

This place used to be a dump—literally. It was the regional landfill site until it reached capacity in 1984. Then the city sealed the huge mounds of garbage under a two-foot clay barrier and covered it with four feet of soil, planted grass and trees, and voilà—instant 160-acre park!

Now it's a land of rolling hills with a distinctly Native American flavor. The packed dirt trails take you up to majestic views of the bay and surrounding marshes. There's no sign of garbage anywhere, unless you look down from the top of a hill and spot the methane extraction plant. Fortunately, very few vista points include that.

Our favorite part of the park is a trail studded with large, dark rocks arranged to form symbols, which in series make up a poem. The concept was inspired by Native American pictographs—a visual language system for recording daily

DIVERSION

Sniff Out a Good Book: Your dog doesn't have to be Mr. Peabody to appreciate fine books. In fact, even if your dog doesn't know his assonance from his alliteration, he could have fun accompanying you to **Kepler's Books**. Kepler's, one of the largest, very best, and most beloved independent bookstores around (it nearly went under not too long ago, but was rescued by community donations!), permits clean, leashed, well-behaved dogs to cruise the aisles with you. In fact, dogs who visit even get a tasty treat! Common sense and good manners apply. Please, no leg lifts on the merchandise; Kepler's frowns on yellow journalism. Dogs who lean toward the literary are welcome. Those who *jump* on the literature are not. After sniffing around the shelves, wander over to dog-friendly Café Borrone, right next door, for a tasty meal. 1010 El Camino Real, Menlo Park; 650/324-4321.

events. At the trailhead, you'll find a sign quoting part of the poem and giving a map of the trail, showing the meaning of each rock arrangement as it corresponds to the poem.

Although leashes are required, dogs seem really fond of this park, sniffing everywhere, their tails wagging constantly. Perhaps they can sense the park's less picturesque days deep underground. Or they may be touched by the Native American magic that imbues these hills.

The park starts at the end of Marsh Road, just on the other side of the Bayfront Expressway. To get to the beginning of the rock poem trail, continue past the entrance on Marsh Road to the second parking lot on the right. 650/858-3470.

PLACES TO EAT

Café Borrone: The motto here is "Because Europe is too far to go for lunch." You and your dog may well feel like you've headed across the big pond when you come here. At least 20 tables, many topped by shade umbrellas, grace the large open patio in front of the café. Dogs are welcome. The delicious soups, salads, and sandwiches are made with quality ingredients. Café Borrone is conveniently located right next door to the dog-friendly Kepler's Books, at 1010 El Camino Real; 650/327-0830.

Flea Street Cafe: Dogs would normally flee from a restaurant with the word "flea" in it, but not from this dog-friendly eatery. (It's named for the word Pulgas in its street name, which, again, means "flea" in Spanish.) You can get upscale organic food here. Jake nearly wailed with grief when I recently passed on the organic grass-fed Marin beef and instead ordered a delectable warm baby spinach salad and vegetarian bagna cauda. The restaurant serves dinner only. Dine with doggy at the outdoor tables. 3607 Alameda de las Pulgas; 650/854-1226.

Iberia Restaurant: This restaurant is among the finest dog-friendly restaurants in the state. It's so elegant you can eat like a Spanish king. Dine with your dog in a stately garden under the canopy of an enormous 400-year-old oak tree. Flaming dishes are big here, so if your furry friend fears fire, try ordering something a little less dramatic. (Fans of the Garden Grill, which occupied this space until 2000, will be happy to know that the owners, Jose Luis Relinque and his wife, Jessica, are the same—and so is the impeccable service and top-notch food.) 1026 Alma Street; 650/325-8981.

Rock of Gibraltar Comestibles: If you like what you've eaten at Iberia Restaurant next door, check out the gourmet Spanish food fixin's at this store/café. *Perros* need to stay outside while you shop, but they're welcome to join you at the outdoor tables for coffee and pastries in the morning or a variety of delicious sandwiches at lunch. The Rock is owned by the Relinques, who also own the Iberia Restaurant. 1022 Alma Street; 650/327-0413.

Atherton

PARKS, BEACHES, AND RECREATION AREAS

28 Holbrook-Palmer Park

🐾🐾 (See San Mateo County map on page 498)

Roses. Gazebos. Bathrooms that look like saunas. Trellises. Jasmine plots. Tennis courts. Buildings that belong in a country club. People in white linen love it here; dogs are often just plain intimidated. Joe never did a leg lift at this park when we visited. Jake has, but only after checking around to make sure no one—not even a songbird—was watching. Leashes are a must. Please note that on weekends, this is a prime spot for weddings with lots of dressed-up people, so you might want to steer clear.

Holbrook-Palmer Park is on Watkins Avenue, between El Camino Real and Middlefield Road. Leave your car at one of several lots in the park. 650/752-0534.

Woodside

PARKS, BEACHES, AND RECREATION AREAS

29 Thornewood Open Space Preserve

🐾🐾🐾 (See San Mateo County map on page 498)

This 141-acre preserve is a former estate, and the views of the valley from parts of this land are magnificent. Dogs can peruse the preserve on leash. Thornewood is the smallest of the Midpeninsula Regional Open Space District's preserves, but dogs dig the one-mile trail that runs through the oak woodland, chaparral, and redwoods here.

Dogs have to stay away from Schilling Pond because swans call it home, and dogs and swans don't mix. In fact, although the pond is almost entirely surrounded by dense vegetation, rangers have spotted dogs swimming after these beautiful birds. If this happens very much, the entire preserve could be off-limits to all dogs, so let's be careful out there.

From I-280, exit at Highway 84/Woodside Road and drive west into the hills, about five miles. The road will make several sharp turns, but keep following Highway 84. Go left at the narrow, signed driveway. It winds through the woods for 0.3 mile before reaching the small parking lot on the west side of the driveway. 650/691-1200.

PLACES TO EAT

Alice's Restaurant: You can get almost anything you want at this restaurant, including a table for you and your dog on the large porch. Weekends here are packed with bikers, especially for Alice's colossal breakfasts. If your dog rides in your motorcycle sidecar, this is the place for you. It's at 17288 Skyline Boulevard, on the corner of Highways 35 and 84, just two miles north of Portola Valley's Windy Hill Open Space Preserve; 650/851-0303.

Portola Valley

PARKS, BEACHES, AND RECREATION AREAS

30 Windy Hill Open Space Preserve

😺😺😺😺 (See San Mateo County map on page 498)

You can look out from the top of the first big hill you come to and see for miles all around—and though you're on the edge of the suburbs, you'll see hardly a house. This 1,130-acre preserve of the Midpeninsula Regional Open Space District has as many different terrains as it has views, including grassland ridges and lush wooded ravines with serene creeks and drippy redwoods.

There are more than three miles of trails that allow you and your leashed canine companion to hike together. But watch out for foxtails; the park is so dry that foxtails seem to proliferate all year.

Start at the Anniversary Trail, to the left of the entrance. The hike is a vigorous 0.75 mile uphill, and that may be enough, especially when it's baking. But you can continue down the other side of the hill and loop right, onto the Spring Ridge Trail. Near the end of this 2.5-mile path, you'll come to a wooded area with a small, very refreshing creek. This is a good place to sit a spell before heading back. These two trails are the only ones that permit pooches, so don't try your paw at any others.

Park at the lot on Highway 35 (Skyline Boulevard), 2.3 miles south of Highway 84 and five miles north of Alpine Road. You'll see the big sign for the preserve and three picnic tables. 650/691-1200.

31 Coal Creek Open Space Preserve

😺😺😺😺 (See San Mateo County map on page 498)

Jake loves visiting this 493-acre preserve in the winter because of the little waterfalls that gurgle along a couple of creeks. In fact, year-round, this is one of the best of the Midpeninsula Regional Open Space District preserves for dogs, because it's generally cooler than most. The dense oak and madrone forests offer a real respite from the hot summer weather.

Banana slugs like this climate as much as dogs do, so don't be surprised to see a few lurking on the trails. When Joe Dog happened upon a banana slug here, at first he looked disgusted. Then he barked at it a couple of times and sat down and moaned at it when it didn't respond. I tugged hard on his leash to get him away, because I knew his next move would be to make a banana slug appetizer out of it.

If rolling meadows are more your dog's style, this preserve has those, too.

The five miles of trails will take you through all kinds of landscapes. Let your dog choose his favorite, but make sure he's leashed.

The preserve has two entry points along Skyline Boulevard (Highway 35) in the southernmost part of the county (south of Portola Valley). One is about 1.2 miles north of Page Mill Road, at the Caltrans vista point, on the east side of the road. The other is at Skyline and Crazy Pete's Road, about two miles north of Page Mill Road, also on the east side of Skyline. This one has the closest access to the preserve, but there's only room for about three cars, and you'll need to walk down a fairly steep residential road to get to the trails. 650/691-1200.

Pescadero

PARKS, BEACHES, AND RECREATION AREAS

Beautiful Pescadero State Beach no longer allows pooches, even those with leashes and shamelessly pleading eyes. At least dogs still have Bean Hollow, and Arcangeli Grocery Company.

32 Bean Hollow State Beach

🐾🐾🐾 (See San Mateo County map on page 498)

This isn't a big sandy beach. In fact, it can be hard to find sand here at all. It's rocks, rocks everywhere, which is kind of fun. The rocky intertidal zone here is terrific for tidepooling, but only if you and your dog are surefooted. To get to the best tidepools, you must perform an amazing feat of team coordination—climbing down 70-million-year-old rock formations while attached to each other by leash. It's not that steep, just awkward. The pitted rocks can be slippery. This maneuver is not recommended for dogs like Jake, who goes deaf and senseless when the alluring ocean beckons him to swim. Besides, the surf can be treacherous in this area.

If you reach the tidepools, you're in for a real treat. But make sure your canine companion doesn't go fishing—we've seen a dog stick his entire head in a tidepool to capture a little crab. Fur and fangs aren't natural in the delicate balance of this wet habitat, so please keep dogs out of the tidepools. The mussels will thank you.

If you decide to play it safe and stay on flat land, you can still see the harbor seal rookery on the rocks below the coastal bluffs. Bring binoculars and you can really get a view of them up close and personal.

The beach is off Highway 1 at Bean Hollow Road. 650/879-2170.

PLACES TO EAT

Arcangeli Grocery Company: There's always fresh-baked bread here—still hot—waiting for you after a cold day at the beach. We like to buy a loaf of steaming herb-garlic bread and eat it at the picnic tables on the lawn in the back of the store. 287 Stage Road; 650/879-0147.

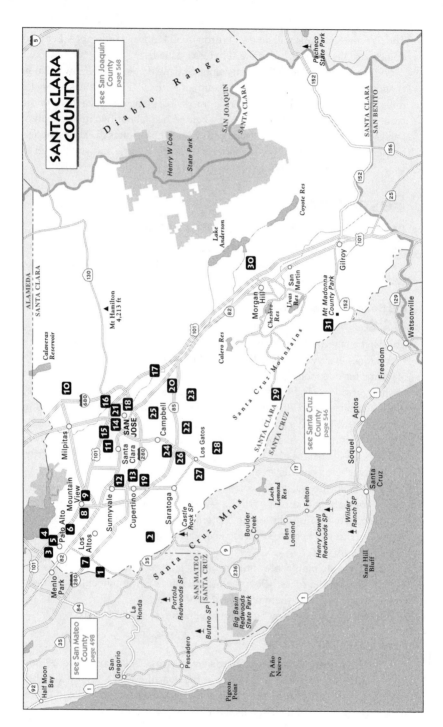

SANTA CLARA COUNTY

see San Joaquin County page 568

see Santa Cruz County page 546

see San Mateo County page 498

CHAPTER 37

Santa Clara County

While some parts of Santa Clara County are quite scenic, dogs have to face the facts: The place still revolves around Silicon Valley, and it's not a pretty sight. Cookie-cutter duplexes and townhouses abound. So do suburban-style office parks and strip shopping centers. Even dogs with questionable taste wince.

But if you get your dog out of the more populated areas and into the quieter county parks, you'll scarcely know you're in the middle of a megabyting, microchipping mecca. Some of the larger, wilder county parks may put your dog back in touch with the wolf inside herself. One dog we met on a trail at one park was sitting and howling every few hundred feet. Her person said she was just happy to be there. Joe Dog thought maybe the dog was just saying, "Get this leash off me!"

Fortunately, several leash-free parks now dot the county. And for dogs who don't mind leashed hikes, trails in most of the Santa Clara County's 45,000 acres of parklands (www.parkhere.org) welcome dogs more than ever before. "We've opened so much more of our park system to dogs. There are very, very

PICK OF THE LITTER—SANTA CLARA COUNTY

BEST NEW-ISH DOG PARK
Los Gatos Creek County Dog Park, Campbell (page 538)

COOLEST HIKE
Mount Madonna County Park, Gilroy (page 544)

MOST DOG-FRIENDLY PLACES TO EAT
Bill's Cafe, San Jose (page 537)
Rock Bottom Restaurant and Brewery, Campbell (page 538)
Classic Burgers of Los Gatos, Los Gatos (page 542)

MOST DOG-FRIENDLY PLACE TO STAY
Cypress Hotel, Cupertino (page 533)

BEST SHOPPING
Stanford Shopping Center, Palo Alto (page 526)
Santana Row, San Jose (page 526)

FRIENDLIEST PLACE TO BUY A PLANT
Yamagami's Nursery, Cupertino (page 532)

BEST SOCIAL GATHERINGS
Society Dog (page 539)

FRIENDLIEST PLACE TO BUY ART
Peabody Fine Art Gallery, Los Gatos (page 541)

few places where dogs are not allowed," says a park system representative. (Are you reading this, San Mateo County Department of Parks? Let this be a lesson to you!) We describe our favorite county parks in this chapter.

The Midpeninsula Regional Open Space District (www.openspace.org) is popular with pooches, with five dog-friendly Open Space preserves in the county. The district has unique rules about poop-scooping and six-foot leashes. (See the *San Mateo County* chapter for more on these rules, as well as the Diversion *Hike with a Like-Minded Hound* about the district's popular pooch hikes.) Its preserves are definitely worth sniffing out.

Palo Alto

For dogs, this town is the county's garden spot. Here, you'll find lots of other dog lovers and well-behaved dogs, enticing city parks—all of which allow dogs—and no fewer than three leash-free dog runs. At the Baylands, you and your leashed dog can watch birds and get a good workout at the same time. And many student-oriented restaurants with outdoor seating welcome your dog. If you're lucky enough to have a Palo Alto address, or a friend with one, you may bring your dog to the glorious Foothills Park on weekdays.

PARKS, BEACHES, AND RECREATION AREAS

Unless you have a working dog (and no, this does *not* mean a dog who is working on getting the dog treats out of your coat pocket—we're talking guide dogs and their ilk), you and your pooch can no longer walk together at the Stanford Dish. We know a good many dogs who have cried into their kibble because of this pooch ban. Fortunately, other pleasant Palo Alto areas still permit pooches to paw around.

1 Foothills Open Space Preserve

🐾🐾🐾 (See Santa Clara County map on page 522)

At 211 acres, this is the second smallest of the dog-friendly Midpeninsula Open Space District lands. It sports only a half-mile trail (one-mile roundtrip), but it's a fun place to take a dog who's happy with a moderate hike on leash. The trail leads up through chaparral-covered slopes to a ridge that leads to a grassy knoll with terrific views of the South Bay. It's not exactly an ocean or Golden Gate Bridge view, but it's rewarding. On temperate days we like to bring a little picnic along and plop down for some eats before heading back.

Trail access is at a two-car roadside pullout on the south side of Page Mill Road, 3.5 miles southwest of I-280. You'll see a brown pipe gate and wood rail fence there. Go over a step-over stile and follow the trail to the left. (The other trail quickly leads to a dead end.) 650/691-1200.

2 Long Ridge Open Space Preserve

🐾🐾🐾🐾 (See Santa Clara County map on page 522)

In order to hike here with a dog, you have to fill out a special permit, which is conveniently available at the Grizzly Flat parking area. You have to agree to keep your dog leashed and on restricted trails, namely the Peters Creek Trail, Ridge Trail, and a firebreak you'll see on the trail map there.

It's worth the tiny bit of extra effort to come to this 2,000-acre preserve. The trails make for many miles of superb hiking, and if you visit in spring, you'll be surrounded by a vast rainbow assortment of wildflowers, from purple lupines to cheery yellow buttercups. The dog-friendly trails take you through hilly grasslands as well as forests of oaks, bay, and Douglas firs that provide glorious shade. You may even encounter some wild turkeys along the way, so if you have a bird dog you'll be glad of your leash. (Nisha, the springer spaniel we had before she went to the happy hunting grounds in the sky, once brought Craig a live wild turkey in her mouth.)

The Grizzly Flat parking area is on Skyline Boulevard (Highway 35), 3.3 miles south of Page Mill Road and 3.6 miles north of Highway 9. (As a landmark, you'll see the Palo Alto city limits sign nearby if you're coming from the south.) 650/691-1200.

🖪 Palo Alto Baylands

🐾🐾🐾 (See Santa Clara County map on page 522)

This is the best-developed wetlands park in the Bay Area for adults, children, and dogs. It's laced with paved bike trails and levee trails. Along the pretty levee paths, benches face the mudflats. Don't forget your binoculars on a walk here. A cacophony of mewling gulls, mumbling pigeons, and clucking blackbirds fills the air. Small planes putt-putt into the

DIVERSION

Stop and Smell the Shopping Centers: Dogs are welcome to join you at **Stanford Shopping Center,** a 70-acre open-air mall that's disguised as a park. The grounds are home to 1,300 trees of 35 species, plus hundreds of hanging baskets and planters dripping with flowers. If a dog has to go shopping, this is one of the more pleasant places she could go. Many of the 120 stores allow dogs inside. Nordstrom and Neiman Marcus, two of the nation's most dog-friendly department stores, welcome dogs here. Rules at some of the others change frequently, so if you're interested in going inside with your dog, poke your head in and see if you can find someone to give your dog the thumbs-up. Chances are that not only will you end up sniffing out plenty of dog-friendly stores, but your dog will be offered some treats along the way. At El Camino Real and Sand Hill Road, in Palo Alto; 650/617-8200.

An intimate, slightly more trendy shopping center is the new **Santana Row** in San Jose. Charro, a San Jose pooch, wrote to tell us how much fun it is to be a dog there, and even though Jake isn't a shopping kind of dog, he enjoyed a trip there because he got so many pats from shopkeepers and fellow shoppers. (Plus there were plenty of palms and oaks to explore.) He was particularly interested in some leather shoes at Diesel (which only sometimes allows dogs), although he wasn't particular about which ones. Selecting shoes to chew is apparently a much quicker process than selecting shoes to wear. I quickly shooed him out of there. Santana Row is at Winchester Boulevard and Stevens Creek Boulevard, just off I-880 in San Jose. 408/551-4600.

nearby airport, and your dog will love the fishy smells coming from the marshes. This seems to be a popular spot for dog exercise. Keep your pooch leashed and on the trails.

Dogs shouldn't go near the well-marked waterfowl nesting area, but they're welcome to watch children feed the noisy ducks and Canada geese in the duck pond, as long as they don't think about snacks à l'orange.

From U.S. 101, exit at Embarcadero Road East and go all the way to the end. At the entrance, turn left for the trails, ranger station, and duck pond. A right turn takes you to a recycling center. 650/329-2423.

4 Greer Park

(See Santa Clara County map on page 522)

This is one of Palo Alto's parks with an off-leash dog run, but it isn't the largest (Mitchell Park holds that distinction). The park is green and pleasant, as are all the city's parks, but it's somewhat noisy because of nearby Bayshore Road. Dogs have to be leashed outside the dog run. There are athletic fields, picnic tables, and two playground areas. The dog run, near the Bayshore side, is small and treeless, but it's entirely fenced, if that's what your dog needs.

The park is at Amarillo Street and West Bayshore Road. The parking lot is off Bayshore, conveniently near the dog run. 650/496-6962.

5 Hoover Park

(See Santa Clara County map on page 522)

This park may be small, but dogs don't really care. It's home to a little-known dog park that's not as popular as the run at Mitchell Park, but that's part of the charm. There've been some improvements here recently, so if you haven't checked it out lately, it's worth a sniff.

The park is at Cowper Street between Colorado and Loma Verde avenues. 650/496-6962.

6 Mitchell Park

(See Santa Clara County map on page 522)

This generous, green park has some unusual amenities, including two human-sized chessboards and a roller-skating rink. The park is also a standout in the canine book: It has its own dog park that's completely fenced and has a row of pine trees on one side, water dishes on the other, and scrappy tennis balls everywhere.

The park has plenty of shade to delight a dog. Remember to leash outside the dog run. For kids, the playground area has sculptured bears for climbing and a water-play area (sorry, no dogs). The dog park is a short walk from the parking lot.

The park is on East Meadow Drive just south of Middlefield Road. 650/496-6962.

7 Arastradero Nature Preserve

☙☙☙ (See Santa Clara County map on page 522)

With 613 acres of rolling savanna grassland and broadleaf evergreen forest, Arastradero Preserve is one of the more peaceful and attractive parks in the area. Dogs dig it, but they have to be leashed. It's a good rule, because mountain lions, rattlesnakes, poison oak, and coyotes can be part of the scene here. And so can bikers.

Anglers are right at home in the preserve. A hike to Arastradero Lake takes only about 20 minutes from the main parking lot, and the fishing can be very good. (Sorry, no swimming, boats, or flotation devices.)

There are 6.25 miles of hiking trails. Jake Dog enjoys the hilly 2.8-mile Acorn Trail when he's in the mood to pant. Bring plenty of water; it can get toasty here.

From I-280, exit at Page Mill Road and go south. Turn right (west) on Arastradero Road (Refuge Road on some maps) and drive into the parking lot. 650/329-2423.

PLACES TO EAT

Palo Alto Sol: The friendly staff here will bring your thirsty pooch some water while he's drooling over your tasty Mexican food. The mole sauce is a must-order. 408 California Avenue; 650/328-8840.

Saint Michael's Alley: Dogs are welcome to join their people at the lovely shaded patio of this hidden gem. It's been around since 1959—ancient history in California! The California-classic cuisine here is delicious. I enjoy making a meal of starters here; they're too good to pass up. Thirsty dogs get a bowl of water if they bat their eyes nicely at their server. 806 Emerson Street; 650/326-2530.

Spalti Ristorante: Is your dog tired of being nearly trod upon when dining with you at sidewalk tables? If she's had one too many close calls with a fast-moving pair of Skechers, and if you enjoy delectable Northern Italian cuisine in an upmarket setting, come here for a relaxing, wonderful meal; the white-cloth-covered tables are set up in a roomy front entry alcove so you're off the sidewalk and have plenty of space around you to boot. (Just keep the boot off your dog's nose, lest she be reminded of her sidewalk experiences.) 417 California Avenue; 650/327-9390.

PLACES TO STAY

Sheraton Palo Alto: Rates are $132–329. Dogs must be under 80 pounds—a significant improvement over the former 20-pound pooch limit. "We're being flexible on weight," says a staffer. 625 El Camino Real 94301; 650/328-2800; www.sheraton.com.

Mountain View

PARKS, BEACHES, AND RECREATION AREAS

8 Rengstorff Park

🐾🐾🐕 (See Santa Clara County map on page 522)

This park is typically neat, green, and interesting for people, and it has another excellent feature: A sign reads, "Dogs must be on leash (except by permit)." This means that you can get a permit from the city that allows you to train a dog off leash, with the understanding that he'll be under control. Be forewarned, though: If you don't bring the permit along with you when training, you will be ticketed.

Rengstorff Park is at Rengstorff Avenue between California Street and Central Expressway. Call for details on getting a permit. 650/903-6331.

9 Mountain View Dog Park

🐾🐾🐾🐕 (See Santa Clara County map on page 522)

Ahh, this fenced park has redwood trees. They're Jake's favorite arbors. Other amenities in this 0.75-acre park include benches and a separate area for smaller or more timid dogs. The ground cover is mostly grass, so it's easy on the paws. It's an off-leash oasis, and dogs seem mighty happy to be here.

The park is on North Shoreline Boulevard at North Road. 650/903-6331.

PLACES TO STAY

Best Western Tropicana Lodge: No Ricky Ricardo band here, but it's a decent place to stay with your pup-a-loo. Rates are $70–110. 1720 West El Camino Real 94040; 650/961-0220; www.tropicanalodge.com.

Residence Inn by Marriott: You and your dog will feel right at home at the suites at this attractive hotel. They have kitchens and lots of other extras you won't find in a regular hotel. But better than that is the very dog-friendly attitude here. "We take all pets, from snakes to rabbits. We see them as part of the family and try to accommodate the owner's needs," one manager told us. The place even has a little fenced area for exercising dogs, and the staff is happy to point you to nearby trails. Rates are $99–239. There's a $75 doggy fee per visit, so it's best to stay for a while to get the most bang for your buck. 1854 West El Camino Real 94040; 650/940-1300.

Milpitas

PARKS, BEACHES, AND RECREATION AREAS

🔟 Milpitas Dog Park

🐾🐾🐾🐾🐕 (See Santa Clara County map on page 522)

The big-dog side of this terrific two-acre park has smallish trees. And the small-dog section has big trees. Go figure! But some of that small-dog shade leaks over to the large-dog side, so it's a win-win situation.

This is a great place to bring a dog who longs to run like the wind. It's mostly grassy, and it's a very generous size. Dogs can really work up a sweat while chasing each other or running after lobbed tennis balls. The dog park is flanked by the scenic rolling hills of the surrounding 1,539-acre Ed Levin County Park. (Dogs are allowed only on one short segment of the Bay Area Ridge Trail there, and in the picnic areas, so don't be too tempted to sniff out Ed Levin.)

The dog park has all the usual pooch amenities, from water to picnic tables to poop bags. And it has an interesting extra one: A tiny concrete-floored fenced area with a bench. No one was using it when we visited, but it looks like a decent place for a child who wants to feel protected from the pounding paws.

There's an entrance fee to get into the county park, and therefore to get into the dog park. It's a steep $6 per car. But annual passes are available, should you want to make this a regular stomping ground. The dog park is at the very end of the county park. (If you're not confident you'll find it, just ask the park ranger at the fee gate.) The county park is at 3100 Calaveras Road, about 2.5 miles east of I-680. For dog park inquiries, phone the City of Milpitas at 408/586-3210. For questions about Ed Levin County Park, phone 408/262-6980 or 408/355-2200.

PLACES TO STAY

Best Western Brookside Inn: Rates are $89–129. Dogs are $15 extra. 400 Valley Way 95035; 408/263-5566; www.bestwestern.com.

Santa Clara

PARKS, BEACHES, AND RECREATION AREAS

The original Santa Clara Dog Park is no longer with us. It's been replaced by the lovely Reed Street Dog Park.

🔟🔟 Reed Street Dog Park

🐾🐾🐾🐾🐕 (See Santa Clara County map on page 522)

This dog park is in a somewhat industrial part of town, but dogs don't mind a bit: Reed Street Dog Park has everything a dog could want in a pooch park: 1.5

DIVERSION

Go on a Pilgrimage: Mission Santa Clara, on the Santa Clara University campus, allows leashed dogs on its grounds. You might make it part of your walk if you're exploring the campus. The building, dating from 1929, is a replica of one version of the old mission, first built in 1777 but destroyed five times by earthquake, flood, and fire. Preserved fragments of the original mission and the old adobe Faculty Club are the oldest college buildings standing in the western United States. The mission is on campus, off El Camino Real, Santa Clara. 408/554-4023.

fenced acres, grass (some months more than others), little mounds/mini hills for adding interest to the ball chase, separate areas for small and large dogs, lots of shade from shade structures, benches, water, poop bags, and most of all, friendly people and dogs, even when it's crowded. While it's not the fanciest park we've visited, it gets plenty of points for the nice people and pooches who frequent the place.

Keep in mind that it can get muddy in rainy season, and it's closed for maintenance on Thursdays. The park is at 888 Reed Street, at Lafayette Street. 408/615-2260.

PLACES TO STAY

Quality Inn: Rates are $79–129. Dogs have to be less than 20 pounds to stay here, and they're $10 extra. 2930 El Camino Real 95051; 408/241-3010.

The Vagabond Inn: Rates are $69–99. Dogs are $20 extra. 3580 El Camino Real 95051; 408/241-0771.

Sunnyvale

PARKS, BEACHES, AND RECREATION AREAS

12 Las Palmas Park

🐾 🐾 🐾 🐾 🐕 (See Santa Clara County map on page 522)

With its paved paths, green grass, and beautiful pond, this park is the best in town for a walk among rolling hills. But dogs consider it a real gem because of the two-acre dog park within. It has all the usual helpful dog-park amenities, including shade, water, poop bags, and even a fire hydrant. It's a kind of

DIVERSION

Nursery Tail Wag: Dogs love visiting **Yamagami's Nursery.** Not only do they get to help you pick out some great plants and flowers for your home, but dogs get treats when they visit Yamagami's. The treats are located at the information desk, should your dog ask. "We're extremely dog friendly," says a Yamagami plant doctor at this old and popular family business. 1361 South DeAnza Boulevard, Cupertino; 408/252-3347.

fenced-in nirvana. Dogs get deliriously happy when they visit. Some spend so much time rolling in the cool grass that they miss out on hanging with their fellow canines. But do they care? A look at their smiling snouts and flaring nostrils will answer that question.

A quick note about that fire hydrant. Enough dogs have run headlong into it that there was some thought about removing it. So far, it's still here. Doggies, keep your eyes open!

The park is at Danforth and Russet drives. 408/730-7350.

PLACES TO STAY

Staybridge Suites: There's supposed to be a 50-pound pooch limit, but so many of the employees here love dogs that this rule is often bent. The suites are large and very livable, with kitchens and most of the amenities of home. Rates are $210–250. There's a $75 pooch fee per visit (this place caters to long-ish-term visitors). 900 Hamlin Court 94089, 408/745-1515 or 800/833-4353; www.wyndham.com.

The Vagabond Inn: Rates are $65–149. Dogs are $10 extra. 816 Ahwanee Avenue 94086; 408/734-4607; www.vagabondinn.com.

Cupertino

PARKS, BEACHES, AND RECREATION AREAS

13 Fremont Older Open Space Preserve

🐾🐾🐾 (See Santa Clara County map on page 522)

This 739-acre preserve smells sweet and clean, but that doesn't disappoint dogs. Pooches have enough trees and ground-level odors to keep them happily trotting along on their mandatory leashes.

Once you park in the small lot, you'll walk several hundred feet on a paved roadway, but be sure to turn right at the first sign for hikers. Otherwise you'll find yourself in the middle of a bicycle freeway. The narrow dirt trail to the right takes you on a three-mile loop through cool woodlands and rolling open hills up to Hunters Point via the Seven Springs Loop Trail. The view of Santa Clara Valley from the top of the 900-foot hill is incomparable. More trails may be open soon, so your dog's feet will be able to explore as never before.

Signs at the entrance warn of ticks, so be sure to give your dog (and yourself) a thorough inspection after your hike.

From U.S. 101 or I-280, take Highway 85 (Saratoga-Sunnyvale Road) south to Prospect Road. Turn right and follow the road to the park entrance. 650/691-1200.

PLACES TO EAT

Bobbi's Coffee Shop: Charro the Dog told us about this eatery, where every dog gets a bowl of water upon arrival at the outdoor tables. It's a convenient place to stop for a bite before or after a visit to the dog-friendly Yamagami's Nursery (see the Diversion *Nursery Tail Wag*), right next door. 1361 De Anza Boulevard; 408/257-4040.

PLACES TO STAY

Cypress Hotel: The word "Cypress" in a hotel name seems to confer ultra-dog-friendliness. Witness Doris Day's Cypress Inn in Carmel. The Cupertino Cypress, while larger and more hotelly than Doris Day's inn, makes dogs feel equally at home. They're not only welcome to join you at this fun boutique hotel, but they're encouraged to do so. There's even a package designed especially for pooches, called "See Spot at the Cypress." Included in your deluxe guest room or executive suite is a pet area with a dog bowl, biscuits, bottled water, chew toys, and a dog bed. Your dog will also get a dog tag stating, "I was pampered at the Cypress Hotel," and some other goodies, including free valet parking—something that comes in handy when you're traveling with luggage and a dog. The rate for the package is $129–299. If you want to simply stay here without the package but with your dog, your room will run you $89–229.

For a little more money, the concierge will arrange a pet massage, a grooming session, or even some time with a doggy psychic. (If a pet psychic were to read Jake's brain, she'd be hard-pressed to get beyond his ever-present thoughts of food, food, food.) 10050 South DeAnza Boulevard 95014; 408/253-8900; www.thecypresshotel.com.

San Jose

If you think San Jose offers little for dogs, think again. Okay, it's not dog heaven, but it does permit pooches in some decent parks, and now it even has six city parks where dogs can say good riddance to their leashes.

PARKS, BEACHES, AND RECREATION AREAS

San Jose's parks are slowly going to the dogs—in the best sense of the phrase.

The goal here is that each of the city's 10 districts will have at least one dog park. We're at six, and counting.

14 Watson Dog Park

🐾🐾🐾🐾🐾 (See Santa Clara County map on page 522)

The glorious centerpiece of this grassy, 1.25-acre park is an enormous Tree of Heaven, known among more scientific dogs as an *Ailanthus altissima*. It truly is a heavenly tree. It's where people and dogs congregate, which is a refreshing change from the common crowd-near-the-park-gate syndrome. While the park looks ethereal, the sound is that of the nearby freeway. Ah, well, now your dog has a great excuse not to hear you when you call her to go home. The park has all the usual amenities, from benches and picnic tables to water and poop bags. It also has a separate section for small dogs.

The dog park was closed for a while because of problems with contaminated water, but it's back up and running now. It's in the northeast corner of Watson Park, at East Jackson and North 22nd streets. It's just off U.S. 101. From northbound U.S. 101, exit at Julian Street/McKee Road, and turn left onto Julian Street. In a half mile, turn right onto North 21st Street, and in another half mile, make a right onto Jackson Street. The park will be within a block. 408/277-2757.

15 William Street Park

🐾🐾🐾 (See Santa Clara County map on page 522)

This park is a boy dog's dream come true. It's only about 15 acres, but it has 200 trees and 400 shrubs. The acreage-to-trees/shrubs ratio makes it easy for boy dogs to sniff out just about every arbor. The trees make it a really pleasant, attractive place to visit, even in the armpits of summer. Head for the shade and let your happy, leashed pooch loll and roll in the green grass.

The park is at 16th Street and East William Street. 408/277-2757.

16 Emma Prusch Park

🐾🐾🐾 (See Santa Clara County map on page 522)

This park, one of San Jose's most attractive working farms, is a museum. Like a symbol of the county, it lies in the shadow of the intersection of three freeways. Yet it's a charming place and, surprisingly, it allows your leashed dog to wander around the farm with you so long as he stays out of the farm-animal areas. A smooth paved path, good for strollers and wheelchairs, winds among a Victorian farmhouse (which serves as the visitors center), a multicultural arts center, farm machinery, a barn, an orchard, and gardens. Picnic tables are on an expanse of lawn with trees.

Ten more acres within the park are being developed, and there will soon be trails through demonstration gardens, row crops, pastures, and other agricultural areas. It's a great way to teach your dog about the origin of the ingredients for his dog treats.

The entrance is on South King Road, near the intersection of U.S. 101 and I-680/280. 408/926-5555.

17 Hellyer County Park

🐾🐾🐾🐕 (See Santa Clara County map on page 522)

This county park, which surrounds the two-acre Shadowbluff Dog Run, is a generous, rustic area, popular with bicyclists. The best deal for dogs is the El Arroyo del Coyote Nature Trail, which by some miracle allows dogs. Walk to the left at the entrance kiosk and cross under Hellyer Avenue on the bike trail to find the entrance to the nature trail. Cross the creek on a pedestrian bridge to your right; once across, take the dirt path to your left. Bikes aren't allowed, making it all the better for dogs.

Willows and cottonwoods are luxuriant here, and in spring, poppies bloom. Eucalyptus groves provide occasional shade. Watch out for bees and poison oak. Otherwise, this is heavenly territory for your dog.

The park is closed Wednesdays for maintenance. Access is very easy from U.S. 101. Exit U.S. 101 at Hellyer Avenue and follow prominent signs to the park. The dog area is about 100 yards past the entry kiosk. A parking fee of $6 is charged, and that can add up fast, since there's really no good parking nearby. So if you're planning to be a regular, your best bet would be to buy a park pass for the year. It's a small investment to make for your dog's happiness. 408/255-0225 or 408/355-2200.

18 Shadowbluff Dog Run

🐾🐾🐾🐾🐕 (See Santa Clara County map on page 522)

The two-acre enclosure within the large Hellyer County Park has just about anything a pooch could desire. You'll find shade from a few trees, water to slurp up, and lots of green grass. For humans, there are benches, poop bags, and garbage cans. (Seems the dogs get the better end of the deal.)

The park is closed Wednesdays for maintenance. From U.S. 101, exit at Hellyer Avenue and follow signs to the park. The dog area is about 100 yards past the entry kiosk. Parking fee is $6, so consider buying an annual pass if you're a regular. 408/255-0225 or 408/355-2200.

19 Saratoga Creek Dog Park

🐾🐾🐕 (See Santa Clara County map on page 522)

There's room in this fenced 0.3-acre park for only about 20 dogs, the ground cover is artificial turf and decomposed granite, and there's water, a poop-bag dispenser, and a bench. It's small, neat, and a needed addition to the neighborhood. Thanks to good dogs Rusty and Kalman for having their human, Walter, give me the heads up about this park, the latest to join the San Jose fleet. It's at Graves and Saratoga avenues. 408/277-2757.

20 Miyuki Dog Park

😊 😊 🐕 (See Santa Clara County map on page 522)

Dogs are happy to be at this tiny (0.37-acre) park without their leashes, even though the park isn't quite what it could be. The ground is covered with crushed granite, which can get a little dusty when everyone is running around. There's no water. The trees are small, but that will change. Meanwhile, many dogs enjoy sniffing and running around here. (Perhaps they haven't visited delightful Watson Dog Park yet.)

The park is at Miyuki Drive and Santa Theresa Boulevard. 408/277-2757.

21 Ryland Dog Park

😊 🐕 (See Santa Clara County map on page 522)

This tiny park really utilizes unused space: The whole thing is directly under a major overpass. I've never seen such a setup. Jake kept looking up and flinching, apparently not all that comfortable being under the rumble and bumble of thousands of tons of heavy traffic.

On a positive note, at least there's no need for the city to worry about erecting a shade structure or growing shade trees. And if you forget your sunscreen, no worries! The thick asphalt and concrete over you is better than any sunscreen money can buy.

Only a cool mural and great dog-themed fence prevent this from getting our lowest rating—the dreaded hydrant. The park is under the Coleman Street overpass, at San Pedro and Ryland streets. It's across the street from Ryland Park, which is green and sees sun. 408/277-2757.

22 Fontana Dog Park

😊 😊 🐕 (See Santa Clara County map on page 522)

This decent little fenced dog park is set in the larger Fontana park, named after San Jose police officer Jeffrey Fontana, who was shot to death in the line of duty not far from here.

It's quite a small dog park—about 0.3 acre, and that land is divided between large and small dog sections. But it has all the accoutrements that make for a pleasant dog park visit, including water, shade from trees, some little seating areas, and poop bags. The people are friendly, too, which definitely helps. The ground cover, formerly grass, was dirt when we visited, and dogs do tend to get a bit dusty if they're rambunctious here. The dog park section of Fontana is at Golden Oak Way and McAbee Road. 408/277-2757.

23 Almaden Quicksilver County Park

😊 😊 😊 (See Santa Clara County map on page 522)

This rustic, 3,600-acre park allows dogs on all 30 miles of trails. Some of these trails are popular for horseback riding, so watch out; although leashes are the law here, they don't always stop dogs who like to chase hooves.

In the spring, the hills explode with wildlife and wildflowers. Any of the trails will take you through a wonderland of colorful flowers and butterflies who like to tease safely leashed dogs. Speaking of insects, there's a down side to this park: Ticks seem to hang out here. "We got 20 off our dog, then three more when big welts developed," an unfortunate San Jose resident writes. Keep your pooch in the center of trails, and the bloodsucking pests will have to go elsewhere for dinner.

You can enter the park at several points. We prefer the main park entrance, where New Almaden Road turns into Alamitos Road, near Almaden Way. 408/268-3883 or 408/355-2200.

PLACES TO EAT

Bill's Cafe: You and your favorite dog can munch on simple café cuisine at this bistro with umbrella-topped tables. Lucky dogs who visit get water and a biscuit! 1115 Willow Street; 408/294-1125.

Left Bank: Of course your dog is allowed at this lively brasserie. What self-respecting French restaurant wouldn't welcome dogs? The large, attractive patio seats 80, so you'll never feel alone. Your dog would like you to order the steak tartare for a starter and the *carre d'agneau* (roasted rack of lamb) for your main dish, but there are less meaty options. The Left Bank is at 377 Santana Row; 408/984-3500.

Pizza Antica: This upscale pizza, pasta, and salad restaurant at Santana Row is a very dog-friendly place. Our canine correspondent Dakota reports that he's not only welcome here, but also he gets a bowl of water. A manager confirms: "We enjoy dog guests," she says. 334 Santana Row; 408/557-8373.

Siena Mediterranean Bistro: A lovely patio graced by a beautiful mural is where you and your dog get to dine when you eat at this hidden gem. The food is really good, creative, homey European cuisine with a Mediterranean lilt. I could eat the risotto with goat cheese, pumpkin, butternut squash and fresh sage every day. Jake, however, would prefer I order the rosemary venison medallions. 1359 Lincoln Avenue; 408/271-0837.

PLACES TO STAY

Doubletree Hotel: Rates are $99–329. A $50 dog deposit is required. 2050 Gateway Place 95110; 408/453-4000.

Homewood Suites: The suites here are comfy and much more like home than traditional hotels. Rates are $209. Dogs pay a $50 fee for the length of their stay, plus a deposit of $50. 10 West Trimble Road 95131; 408/428-9900.

Campbell

PARKS, BEACHES, AND RECREATION AREAS

Dogs aren't allowed in any Campbell parks except for one very suburban one that we won't spend time on here, and one great new dog park located within Los Gatos Creek County Park.

24 Los Gatos Creek County Dog Park

🐾🐾🐾🐾🐕 (See Santa Clara County map on page 522)

Jake seems to feel like a big man every time he enters this new, four-paw dog park. He trots right over to the sign that says Big Dogs, wags at it, and heads into the park with other large dogs. Some dogs that frequent this section are more like semi trucks, which probably makes Jake feel rather Toyota-ish, so he hangs with the medium-to-large dogs who make him look more sizeable.

The dog park (both the large and the small dog sections) is very well planned, with grass that is actually green, shade from trees and umbrellas, crushed granite pathways around the grassy areas, boulders and logs for adding interest for the human and canine set, water, benches, and poop-scoop areas. Jake particularly liked the logs and tried for minutes at a time to pry his jaws open wide enough so that he could carry around this prize stick of all sticks. Fortunately for everyone in the big dog section, his mouth wasn't big enough.

The park is located within Los Gatos Creek County Park, between the casting ponds (always a temptation for Jake) and the San Tomas Expressway. From Winchester Boulevard, travel east on Hacienda Avenue to the stop sign at Dell Avenue. The park is at the intersection of Hacienda and Dell. A $5 parking fee is charged in summer and on weekends and holidays, but if you want to avoid the fee, you can enter by paw on the beautiful Los Gatos Creek Trail. 408/355-2200.

PLACES TO EAT

The King's Head Pub and Restaurant: Want British food and drink, with a super-dog-friendly atmosphere? Come here for some fine brews and interesting food. Your dog can join you on the shady deck, and she'll get a big bowl of water if she's thirsty. We owe thanks to Jaz Dog and Trevor Dog for letting us know about this eatery. (They're the lucky dogs of the founders of Society Dog, a social group if ever there was one. See the Diversion *Drink Wine, Get Naked, Hop on a Bus.*) 201 Orchard City Drive; 408/871-2499.

Rock Bottom Restaurant and Brewery: The restaurant used to have a dog menu here, but most people were just ordering things such as bunless burgers for their dogs off the human menu (even before the low-carb craze), so it went back to human menus only. If you don't want to invest in your dog's carnivorous desires, you should know that the friendly servers here provide treats and water for pooches. For people, the signature microbrews are a big draw, as are tasty salads and interesting concoctions such as alder-smoked fish and chips. Dine at the full-service patio with your dog (it's even heated in the chilly months). It's at 1875 South Bascom Road, in the Pruneyard Shopping Center; 408/377-0707.

Yiassoo: Opa! The Greek food is tasty, inexpensive, and arrives quickly. Some call it Greek fast food. The servers here like dogs. "Absolutely, you come with your dog!" said a representative when I phoned about dog rules. I haven't made it down there yet, but friends reviewed it for me and gave it two paws up for friendliness. Dine at the patio with your pooch. 2180 South Bascom Avenue; 408/559-0312.

PLACES TO STAY

Residence Inn by Marriott: This is a convenient, comfortable place to stay when traveling with a dog. Residence Inns have only suites and apartments, and they all come with kitchens. Rates are $99–209. Extended stays get a discounted rate. Dogs have to pay a $75 cleaning fee. 2761 South Bascom Avenue 95008; 408/559-1551.

Saratoga

This beautiful little town has a couple of very dog-friendly restaurants.

PLACES TO EAT

International Coffee Exchange: This very dog-friendly café serves the best mochas around. They're made with Ghirardelli chocolate and fresh, house-made whipped cream. The café also serves pastries and sandwiches, should you want a little nosh with your pooch. Speaking of dogs and noshing, dogs

DIVERSION

Drink Wine, Get Naked, Hop on a Bus: If you and your dog like to socialize, have we got a group for you: **Society Dog.** It bills itself as "a social club for dogs and their people," and boy, is it social. When we attended a doggy Easter egg hunt at a Saratoga winery, people were sipping wine and making new friends, and dogs were sniffing each other's heinies and making new friends too.

It's just one of many gatherings throughout the year for this South Bay group. It has monthly "naked" dog walks where dogs can be leash-free, and "bark in the dark" group walks on certain evenings. Some get-togethers culminate in hanging out at an alfresco restaurant together. Special events include winery tours, group sojourns via bus to fabulously dog-friendly destinations such as Carmel, and a field trip to the San Francisco Giants' Dog Days of Summer event (see *Dog-Ear Your Calendar* in the *San Francisco County* chapter), also via bus. Basic membership is free, but you pay for special events. See www .societydog.com for more info and a schedule of upcoming events.

who visit get their very own treats! Dine together at the outdoor area's umbrella-topped tables. 14471 Big Basin Way; 408/741-1185.

Vienna Woods Restaurant and Deli: If you have an appetite for Austrian food, bring your dog here. You can get bratwurst, potato pancakes, and even apple strudel. The restaurant also serves sandwiches, quiches, lasagna, and other non-Austrian items. Dine with your pooch at the sheltered outdoor tables. 14567 Big Basin Way; 408/867-2410.

Los Gatos

Dogs like the super dog-friendly community of Los Gatos, but they think it needs a name change. Jake suggests "Los Perros."

PARKS, BEACHES, AND RECREATION AREAS

25 Los Gatos Creek Trail

🐾 🐾 (See Santa Clara County map page 522)

This nine-mile-long paved trail (and growing as funding becomes available) stretches from San Jose through Campbell and Los Gatos, along the Los Gatos Creek (for the most part). We like to explore it on cold, rainy days, because it's not crowded then, and you can get a good feel for the nature that lurks not far away. But on most days, it's a rather crowded affair, with lots of bikes and pedestrians—not an ideal place for a relaxing walk with your furry friend. You can pick up the trail in any number of spots along the route. Handy entry points around here are at Vasona Lake County Park, and downtown Los Gatos, at the Main Street Bridge. Since the trail is a multi-governmental affair, there's no phone contact number.

26 Vasona Lake County Park

🐾 🐾 🐾 (See Santa Clara County map on page 522)

This is a perfectly manicured park, with grass like that of a golf course. Dogs find it tailor-made for rolling, although they tend to get tangled in their leashes—which the county demands they wear here.

Several pathways take you through this 151-acre park and down to the lake's edge. But no swimming is allowed. And dogs aren't allowed to visit the children's playground either. You can picnic in the shade of one of the large willows or lead your dog up to the groves of pines and firs for a relief session. You can access the Los Gatos Creek Trail here, too, should you care to take a flat, paved walk with many other people.

From Highway 17, take Highway 9 (Saratoga-Los Gatos Road) west to University Avenue. Go right and continue to Blossom Hill Road. The park will be on your left. Enter at Garden Hill Drive. The parking fee is $6. 408/356-2729 or 408/355-2200.

🐾 St. Joseph's Hill Open Space Preserve

🐾🐾🐾 (See Santa Clara County map on page 522)

Want a quick escape from urban life? Visit this scenic, 173-acre preserve with your leashed pooch. Dogs are allowed on all four miles of trails here, but beware, it can get steep. The trails wind through oak woodlands and open grassland, and at the top of the 1,250-foot St. Joseph's Hill, you'll get magnificent views of the surrounding parklands. Joe used to love to sit here and let his nostrils flare.

From Highway 17, take the Alma Bridge Road exit and go across the dam. Public parking is available at Lexington Reservoir County Park. The trail to St. Joseph's Hill starts opposite the boat-launching area at the north end of the reservoir. 650/691-1200.

DIVERSION

A Nose for Art: When an art gallery is named after a dog, chances are that the owners might like dogs well enough to let them peruse the gallery. That's certainly the case with the **Peabody Fine Art Gallery** in Los Gatos. Its namesake, Mr. Peabody, is a five-pound Maltese. He's a cute white-haired little fellow who, like the brilliant polymath cartoon character he's named for, occasionally sports a bow tie (no thick round glasses, though). You won't see Mr. Peabody here too often these days, because he's getting older and has a heart condition that causes him to faint if he gets worked up. Seeing other dogs in "his" gallery tends do just that, so he's not as paws-on as he used to be.

Well-behaved dogs are welcome to help you sniff out the whimsical fine art that fills the Peabody. "Dogs have very good taste," says gallery director Ruth Bailey. (They certainly do—yours chose you, didn't he?) The gallery features fine art of a whimsical variety, from The Secret Works of Dr. Seuss (oh, to have one of his marvelous Unorthodox Taxidermy characters on our wall) to fun Disney fine art. With the exception of Dr. Seuss, all the artists represented here are alive, so when you buy at the Peabody, you're supporting a real live artist who may not have to wait tables forever.

This is a comfortable place to visit, with or without a dog. It's not like some galleries that make you feel like a troublesome flea. "We want people to be very much at ease here," says Ruth. Having your best furry friend at your side takes you a long way toward that goal.

There are two Peabody galleries. The super-dog-friendly one is in Los Gatos, at 11 North Santa Cruz Avenue; 408/395-3440. The gallery in Menlo Park also allows dogs. It's at 603 Santa Cruz Avenue; 408/322-2200. The Peabody website is www.peabodyfineart.com.

28 Sierra Azul Open Space Preserve (Kennedy-Limekiln Area)

🐾🐾🐾 (See Santa Clara County map on page 522)

The wildlife at this 5,000-acre preserve has it pretty good. There's so much steep, rugged terrain and dense chaparral that humans and their leashed doggy interlopers are pretty much forced to stay on the trails, out of critters' ways. Unfortunately for dogs and their people, mountain bikes seem to be everywhere on these trails, and they can go really fast. So on weekends especially, keep your eyes and ears peeled and be ready to dodge the traffic.

This is not a park for the fair of paw. A hike to the 2,000-foot ridge top can make even the fittest dog sweat. But the views from here or from the 1,700-foot Priest Rock are worth a little panting, at least on your part. Take it easy on your dog, though, and don't let him pant too much. It can get very, very hot here in the summer, and there's virtually no decent shade. The folks at the Midpeninsula Regional Open Space District beg you not to take your pooch here on summer afternoons.

Parking here is a real problem. If you visit on a busy day, have a contingency plan in case you don't get one of the coveted spaces. Also note that the two other sections of the Sierra Azul Preserve (Cathedral Oaks and Mt. Umunhum; really, I did not make up that name) don't permit pooches.

From Highway 85, exit at Los Gatos Boulevard and drive west a little more than two miles. At Kennedy Road, turn left and follow the road about two more miles to the parking spot at the trailhead. There's room for only two cars here. This is utterly inadequate, and the district is working to do something about this. In the meantime, there's room for about seven cars across Kennedy, on Top of the Hill Road. Please be considerate of the residents here, and keep noise to a minimum and don't litter. 650/691-1200.

PLACES TO EAT

Classic Burgers of Los Gatos: This dog-friendly eatery has fine burgers. Dogs drool over them at the four tables on the patio. In fact, they've drooled so much that the café's proprietors now offer dogs their very own ice cream for $0.50. Pooches can get water if thirsty, too. 15737 Los Gatos Boulevard; 408/356-6910.

Dolce Spazio Gelato: On warm days, this is the place to come. The homemade gelato is creamy and delicious. When there's a chill in the air, try something from the café's espresso bar. The good-sized patio has heat lamps, which helps dogs and their people cozy up to a winter visit. Thirsty dogs get water on request. 221 North Santa Cruz Avenue; 408/395-1335.

Johnny's Northside Grill: Barbecue is the specialty here, and dogs appreciate this deeply. Dine with your drooling friend at the outdoor tables. 532 North Santa Cruz Avenue; 408/395-6908.

Viva: Not to be confused with the Elvis hit of a similar name, Viva Los Gatos is a fun, upbeat place with friendly servers and a patio that welcomes dogs. The cuisine is generally of the World Food variety and is really tasty. 15970 Los Gatos Boulevard; 408/356-4902.

Morgan Hill

PARKS, BEACHES, AND RECREATION AREAS

Hooray! Morgan Hill is now home to its very own dog park!

29 Uvas Canyon County Park

🐾🐾🐾 (See Santa Clara County map on page 522)

This is a pretty, clean park of oak, madrone, and Douglas fir trees in cool canyons. The Uvas Creek Trail is a favorite trail. Dogs always appreciate a creek on a warm summer day, and this one doesn't dry up in hot weather. You might also try the wide, dirt Alec Canyon Trail, 1.5 miles long, within sight of Alec Creek, or the Nature Trail Loop, about one mile long, beside Swanson Creek. You may see some waterfalls in late winter and early spring. A ranger tells us that leashed dogs may now peruse all trails, even the Knibbs Knob Trail, which has a No Dogs sign (apparently left over from less-enlightened times). There's a $6 day-use fee.

Dogs are allowed in the campgrounds and picnic areas of Uvas Canyon. The park has 25 campsites, available on a first-come, first-served basis, for $18 a night. The campground is open daily April 15–October 31, and Friday and Saturday November–March. It's crowded on weekends during late spring and summer, so arrive early or camp during the week. Phone 408/355-2201 for reservations.

From U.S. 101, exit at Cochrane Road; go south on Business 101 to Watsonville Road, then right (west) on Watsonville to McKean-Uvas Road. Turn right on Uvas (past Uvas Reservoir) to Croy Road. Go left on Croy to the park. The last four miles on Croy are fairly tortuous. 408/779-9232 or 408/355-2200.

30 Morgan Hill Dog Park

🐾🐾🐾🐾🐕 (See Santa Clara County map on page 522)

This is how dog parks should be made. Morgan Hill Dog Park is a big three acres of rolling terrain. There's really room here for dogs to cut loose and for people to go for a stroll. (Compare its size to San Jose's three newest dog parks, which, when added together, total one-third of the acreage of this park.)

The park is grassy, fenced, and has separate sections for large and small dogs. There's water, and people like to bring their own dog bowls to prevent transmissible illnesses like kennel cough. If you just want to sit and rest while your dog sniffs about, you have your choice of plenty of benches. The park is the south section of the attractive Morgan Hill Community Park, where you can walk on leash. It's on Edmundson Avenue, just west of Monterey Road/Highway, and next to the Centennial Recreation Center. You'll see the big sign with the dog illustration that's reminiscent of a cave painting. Jake and I thank Marlys Warner-Hussey for giving us the heads up about this park. 408/782-0008.

PLACES TO STAY

Quality Inn: Rates are $70–100. Dogs are $15 extra. 16525 Condit Road, 95037; 408/779-0447.

Residence Inn by Marriott: This is an all-suites hotel, and the suites are spacious, with full kitchens and comfy beds. Your dog will have a choice of rooms for snoozing. A hot breakfast and afternoon social hour (Monday–Thursday) are included in the price. There's a decent little indoor pool and OK exercise room. Rates are $149–209. Dogs are $100 extra for the length of their stay. 18620 Madrone Parkway 95037; 408/782-8311.

Gilroy

PARKS, BEACHES, AND RECREATION AREAS

31 Mount Madonna County Park

😊😊😊😊 (See Santa Clara County map on page 522)

This magnificent 3,700-acre park is midway between Gilroy and Watsonville (in Santa Cruz County). No matter where you're coming from, it's worth the drive. The mountain, covered with mixed conifers, oak, madrone, and bay and sword ferns, is wonderfully quiet and cool—especially appreciated by San Jose dwellers, whose parks are almost never far from the roar of freeways. You may hear the screech of jays and little else.

Try driving on Valley View Road (to the right from the ranger station) to the Giant Twins Trail, where you can park in the shady campsite of the same name—at least when no one is camping there. (When we were there on a perfect Indian summer day in late September, the park was deserted.) Two huge old redwoods, green with lichen, give the trail its name. After half a mile, the trail becomes Sprig Lake Trail and continues for another two miles. Sprig Lake, really a pond, is empty in summer, but in spring it's stocked for children's fishing.

This walk isn't much of a strain. If you'd like more exercise, there are plenty of longer and steeper trails—18 miles in all, and as of this writing, your dog may enjoy every one of them. From the Redwood Trail or the Blackhawk Canyon Trail, you'll be rewarded with views of the Santa Clara Valley, the Salinas Valley, and Monterey Bay. For a walk almost completely around the park, try the Merry-Go-Round Trail.

The park's deer are only one of many reasons you should keep your dog securely leashed, tempting as it might be to let her off. "Dogs have instincts," a friendly ranger said.

Your dog might enjoy a camping vacation here. There are 113 large, private campsites. Sites are $16–25 per night. Phone 408/355-2201 for reservations. A $6 day-use fee is always charged on weekends and daily Memorial Day–Labor Day.

From U.S. 101, exit at Highway 152 west to Gilroy. Continue on 152 (Hecker Pass Highway) through part of the park. The entrance is a right (north) turn at Pole Line Road. 408/842-2341 or 408/355-2200.

PLACES TO STAY

Leavesley Inn: Rates are $65–75. Dogs are charged a $20 fee per visit. 8430 Murray Avenue 95020; 408/847-5500.

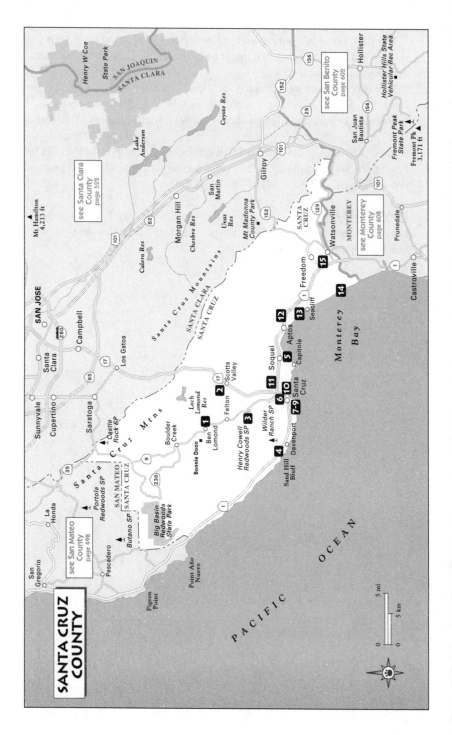

546

CHAPTER 38

Santa Cruz County

If you have a beach-loving dog, Santa Cruz County can be a decent place to take him. The beaches here rarely get too warm, and while some are packed beyond belief (dogs are generally not allowed at the popular beaches), most are on the quieter side. Unfortunately, there are only two official leash-free beaches in the county, and at press time, Lighthouse Field was in danger of becoming a leashes-only beach. Read about it in the Santa Cruz *Parks, Beaches, and Recreation Areas* introduction.

Jake, the ultimate Beach Dog Dude, is very happy whenever we visit Santa Cruz County. However on one trip, after a satisfying romp at Its Beach, we took him up to see a surfer statue, which is along the walkway there. After all, Jake is a dude, and I'm sure if he were human, he would surf. But the statue, a large and beautiful homage to surfers who have caught their last wave, scared the brave boy and he fluffed up and wouldn't go near it. In his attempt to escape, he even collided with a real surfer who was on his way down to the beach. It wasn't one of Jake's finer moments. He did enjoy a visit to the nearby

PICK OF THE LITTER—SANTA CRUZ COUNTY

BEST DOG PARK
Scotts Valley Dog Park, Scotts Valley (page 549)

BEST LEASH-FREE BEACH
Its Beach, Santa Cruz (page 558)

MOST DOG-FRIENDLY HIGH TEA
The Country Court Tea Room, Capitola (page 553)

MOST DOG-FRIENDLY ICE CREAM
Souza Cones Ice Cream and Candy, Capitola (page 554)

MOST DOG-FRIENDLY EATERY
Café Limelight, Santa Cruz (page 560)

BEST BET FOR A DOG HOUSE
A House in Santa Cruz owner-managed rentals (page 561)

MOST DOG-FRIENDLY PLACE TO STAY
Seashell Cottage Oceanfront Vacation Rental, Santa Cruz
(page 561)

BEST RIDE
Roaring Camp and Big Trees Narrow-Gauge Railroad,
Felton (page 550)

MOST FUN FLICKS
Skyview Drive-In Theatre, Santa Cruz (page 555)

Santa Cruz Surfing Museum (see the Diversion *Soak Up Some Surf Culture*), where nothing was nearly as discombobulating to him.

Dog Dudes have a couple of options for getting to the sand. They can convince you to drive or walk, of course. But if you're in midcounty, a far more interesting way to get to the beach is to take the turn-of-the-20th-century steam train run by the Roaring Camp and Big Trees Narrow-Gauge Railroad. The same company runs an 1880s narrow-gauge railroad through the redwoods. Both trips can be the thrill of a dog's life. (See the Diversion *Choo on This.*)

Jake's favorite beaches are the more desolate ones along the northernmost coast of Santa Cruz County. Only one, Bonnie Doon Beach, is detailed later in this chapter because there are so many of them and they're relatively small, with parking only on the shoulder of the road. But they're wonderful for getting away from the crowds, especially if you're also looking at getting away from day-use fees.

These beaches run from Scott Creek in the north to Wilder Ranch State Park in the south. Davenport is the midpoint. Many of the beaches are hidden from Highway 1, so sometimes the only way to tell if there's a beach at all is to look for a few other cars parked on the roadside.

Ben Lomond

PARKS, BEACHES, AND RECREATION AREAS

1 Quail Hollow Ranch

😻😻😻 (See Santa Cruz County map on page 546)

This 300-acre ranch-style park is the largest county park in Santa Cruz. It's also one of the least developed, making it a good area for a dog. There's plenty of wildlife around, so bring your binoculars and hold on tight to that leash. Deer and coyotes abound certain times of year. You'll also see a few quail, but don't get any ideas about dinner: No hunting is allowed.

From Highway 9, go east on Graham Hill Road and then north (left) on East Zayante Road. Turn left at Quail Hollow Road. The park is on the right. The official address is 800 Quail Hollow Road. 831/454-7900.

Scotts Valley

PARKS, BEACHES, AND RECREATION AREAS

2 Scotts Valley Dog Park

😻😻😻😻🐕 (See Santa Cruz County map on page 546)

It's only natural that, being in Santa Cruz County, there would be something in this park for water dogs: a little wading pool—and sometimes two, from what I hear. When Jake visited on a warm afternoon, he walked up to it as if he were going to take a drink, and then he suddenly plopped in and sat down, his blond tail wagging as fast as the water would allow.

The park is 1.2 fenced acres, with a smaller section for small or shy dogs. There are tennis balls galore, and water, poop bags, and plenty of seating. In summer, a temporary awning provides shade. The ground cover is a slightly softer version of the common wood-chip material found in many dog parks.

DIVERSION

Choo on This: Riding on the antique **Roaring Camp and Big Trees Narrow-Gauge Railroad** was one of Joe's favorite adventures ever—except whenever the engineer released loud bellows of steam. And whenever the railroad car moved.

Eventually he did get used to the chug-a-lug motion. Toward the end of the 1.5 hours, he was thoroughly enjoying himself, nose in the air, sucking in the smells of the primeval redwood forest from our open train car. But he still wouldn't leave my lap.

Most dogs are ecstatic on the train. Joe smiled the whole time and his tail never stopped wagging. When the steam let loose, he followed it with his eyes as if it were a beautiful white bird. He alternated between fascination, napping, and staring blankly at the sky, trying to sort out what had happened to him.

The railroad company offers another trip to the Santa Cruz city beach. But since dogs aren't allowed in that area, we recommend the excursion through the redwoods. Besides, halfway through the redwood trip, dogs and their people get to walk around the ancient forest a little before clambering back aboard.

At the end of either train journey, nothing beats spreading out a picnic at the old-fashioned depot's picnic tables. There's plenty of room for walking your leashed dog around the grounds. And humans have fun shopping at the antique general store. It's hard to leave the little shop without buying the kids a miniature train car, so if you don't want to spend extra money, you'd better not even go in.

Rates for the redwood trip are $19 for adults and $13 for children ages 3–12. Rates for the Santa Cruz beach excursion are $21 for adults and $16 for kids. Dogs get a free ride on both. Please note that dogs are now required to wear muzzles. It's not as bad as it sounds. We're not talking one of those Spanish Inquisition leather contraptions; just a simple nylon and Velcro muzzle will do. (When Joe Dog had to wear one, he didn't even seem to notice it was there.) If you don't have your own muzzle, it's likely there's one here you can borrow.

From Highway 1 in the Santa Cruz area, take Highway 17 north toward San Jose. Exit at the Scotts Valley/Big Basin exit and drive west on Mount Hermon Road 3.5 miles to Graham Hill Road. Turn left onto Graham Hill Road. Roaring Camp is 0.5 mile ahead on the right. Call for schedules and additional excursions. 831/335-4484.

Jake prefers grass, but this stuff makes scooping the poop a breeze and park maintenance pretty easy, too.

From Highway 17 in Santa Cruz, take the Mount Hermon Road exit and drive straight. You'll pass Scotts Valley Drive. Continue to the next street, Kings Village Road, and go right. The road ends in a T; go left (it's still Kings Village Road) and you'll quickly see the park and the parking lot. The address is 361 Kings Village Road. 831/438-3251.

PLACES TO STAY

Hilton Santa Cruz/Scotts Valley: Stay here and you and your dog can watch free movies from your spacious, comfortable room: Each room comes with a VCR and free access to the hotel's video library. Busy humans can work in a 24-hour business center and then work out in the fitness center or just take to the pool. Rates are $209–359. Dogs are $25 extra. 6001 La Madrona Drive 95066; 831/440-1000.

Felton

PARKS, BEACHES, AND RECREATION AREAS

🖪 Henry Cowell Redwoods State Park

😾😾😾😾 (See Santa Cruz County map on page 546)

Dogs are actually allowed on three trails here! This is a huge deal because state parks are not exactly known for their dog-friendliness. The main section of the park is 1,750 acres, and it's filled with things dogs love best: trees. Big trees. Redwoods. The largest is 250 feet tall and 16 feet wide. The oldest trees are between 1,400 and 1,800 years old. They've seen a lot in their lifetimes.

Dogs are permitted on Graham Hill Trail, Meadow Trail, and Pipeline Road. They can also dine with you at the picnic areas and camp at the 100-plus campsites. Dogs adore this, because the sites are surrounded by big old trees. The day-use fee is $6. Camping is $25. From Felton, take Graham Hill Road southeast about two miles to the park. The entrance is on the right. Phone 831/335-4598 for park information or call 800/444-7275 for campsite reservations.

PLACES TO EAT

Cowboy Bar and Grill: Mosey on over to this fun eatery and grab yourself some barbecued ribs, big beefy burgers, or buffalo patties with bacon. What more could a dog want in a dining partner? (Oh yes, he wants you to drop some of your food.) Your dog will get front-row seat on a large, shaded patio to watch you and all the happy customers snarfing down this chow. You can also get "cowboy libations" or a "cowpuccino," according to the menu. A big thank-you goes out to our canine correspondents Zoe and Sienna for letting us know about this restaurant. 6155 Highway 9; 831/335 2330.

Rocky's Cafe: This charming, funky café is located in a quaint old house set among the redwoods. The café has been around since 1972—ancient history in these parts. It's named after the beloved old dog of the café's original (and current!) owners George and Diane. Dogs are most welcome here. There's usually water on the wraparound veranda, where dogs can join their people for a meal. And inside the café is a wall of customers' dog photos. The food is standard tasty breakfast and lunch fare, very reasonably priced. 6560 Highway 9; 831/335-4637.

Bonnie Doon

PARKS, BEACHES, AND RECREATION AREAS

4 Bonnie Doon Beach
🐾🐾🐾🐾 (See Santa Cruz County map on page 546)

This beach, just north of Santa Cruz, is hidden from Highway 1 by bluffs, so few people know it exists. That's good news for dogs, even though they're still supposed to be leashed. Some days, you won't find a soul here. Other times, the crowd will consist of a couple of dozen folks picnicking and strolling. Still other times (sunny, warm days, usually), the crowd will consist of quite a few naked people. Naked men, to be exact. If your dog is an incorrigible sniffer of private places, it's best to steer clear of here on pleasant days. (Joe flunked the sniff test on two other nudie beaches, so we visited here in fog only.)

There are several other small unmarked beaches in this area, along the north coast of Santa Cruz County. Bonnie Doon Beach is at Highway 1 and Bonnie Doon Road. There's a small dirt parking lot on the side of the road. 831/454-7900.

PLACES TO STAY

Redwood Croft Bed and Breakfast: Stay in this beautiful country home with your dog and you'll feel as if you've gone to Grandma's house—only Grandma is very hip with a good eye for arts, antiques, and hot tubs. One of the two guest rooms here has a rock fireplace and a totally enclosed little yard with its own hot tub. You can soak while your dog sniffs around the place, and you won't have to worry about her wandering off. The house has big decks all around it, and it's sunny, even though it's surrounded by redwoods. The gardens here are to drool for—so are the breakfasts. Rates are $155–215. You'll get the address when you make reservations. 831/458-1939.

Davenport

This fun little coastal community is just a bone's throw from Bonnie Doon and its wonderful beach and dog-friendly lodging. The bakery below is a fun place to make a road stop.

PLACES TO EAT

Whale City Bakery, Bar and Grill: Sometimes known by its other name, Davenport Bakery, Bar and Grill, this is a fun and convenient place to stop on a trip between San Francisco and some far-flung destination to the south. The name of this restaurant—either name, actually—tells you just about everything you need to know about the cuisine. (Jake would like to add, however, that while the burgers here are to drool for, the fried calamari are truly a greaser-dog's dream come true.) Drink and dine at the tables out front, facing the ocean and Highway 1. They're wonderful in the cliffside fog or the bright sun. The new owner has added a dinner menu, so now you can enjoy a meal by moonlight. 490 Highway 1; 831/423-9803.

Capitola

This beautiful resort area's main beach, Capitola City Beach, is off-limits to dogs. But just down the road, New Brighton State Beach more than makes up for the loss.

If you feel like a beautiful stroll by Soquel Creek, take your leashed dog to the Esplanade, just off Opal Cliff Drive. It's the paved walk that usually has flowers at the entrance, east and inland of the Capitola Wharf (which also doesn't allow dogs).

PARKS, BEACHES, AND RECREATION AREAS

5 New Brighton State Beach

🐾🐾🐾🐾 (See Santa Cruz County map on page 546)

Dogs are free to enjoy this wide, arching beach, as long as they leave their leashes on. Dogs are also permitted on the little trails above the beach. If your dog is tiring of all the sand and surf on the beach, take her on the trail that leads up to big pines and eucalyptus trees. It starts to the left of the main beach entrance. If you walk along the forest/dune area, you'll be able to see Capitola as birds see it. Monterey Bay is also visible from spots here. Dogs like to sit and let their nostrils quiver over scents drifting in from around the world.

From Highway 1, take the New Brighton Beach exit west. Day-use fees are $6 per car. You'll find 112 campsites set on bluffs and surrounded by trees. Rates are $25–35 per night. For campground reservations (strongly recommended, as this is a mighty popular place), phone 800/444-7275. Call 831/464-6329 for beach information.

PLACES TO EAT

The Country Court Tea Room: This lovely English tearoom serves up a tantalizing variety of tea, and all the wonderful foods that accompany a good English tea. It also serves dogs! (No, get that gruesome thought out of your head.) On the menu, mixed in among items like The Queen Victoria Tea, King Henry VIII's English Trifle, and Sir Lawrence's Ploughman Plate, you'll find Sir L.G.'s Poochy Plate. This is a bowl of freshly baked light and dark chicken meat, created exclusively for lucky canines. It comes with a water bowl with ice and lemon—kind of a canine tea. After all, says owner Larry Waldrip, "Dogs are people too!"

The tearoom offers a better variety of foods than I've seen at most teahouses I've visited, and it's very good. Dogs get to join their people at the four umbrella-topped outdoor tables. A big thank-you to Jack Russell terrier Sophie Louise, who had her person, Karen, write to clue us in about this stellar find. 911 B Capitola Avenue; 831/462-2498.

Souza Cones Ice Cream and Candy: "Dogs are our best customers," a dog-loving staffer told us on our most recent visit. In fact, their best customers get a complimentary vanilla frozen yogurt! No wonder dogs love Souza's. If your dog is thirsty after that frozen treat, the staffers will provide a bowl of water. And should you be curious, the ice cream here is of the good, creamy ilk. Try a couple of scoops in a waffle cone. 200 Monterey Avenue; 831/475-9339.

PLACES TO STAY

Best Western Capitola by-the-Sea Inn and Suites: The list of amenities here is actually longer than the hotel's name. They include breakfast, a heated pool, morning paper, and some rooms with whirlpools, fireplaces, microwaves, and fridges. Rates are $129–300. Dogs are $10 extra. 1435 41st Avenue 95010; 831/477-0607; www.bestwestern.com.

Santa Cruz

Hey dogs, I'll bet you think this is a way laid-back town, don't you? You probably imagine you could roam around just about anywhere in this cool place, and that leashes would be viewed by city officials as a ridiculous contrivance, and that restaurants everywhere would welcome you with open, tattooed arms. Well, get that bandanna off your neck and get ready to wipe your doggy tears: The reality of Santa Cruz doesn't live up to the fantasy.

Forget the leash-free dream: Leashes can come off on just two small beaches, and only during limited hours. Further, at press time, the continued leash-free status of Lighthouse Field State Beach was in question. As far as being allowed everywhere, that's another doggy disappointment. Dogs are banned from Pacific Avenue, the main alfresco restaurant–filled street on the downtown mall area, and at such hangouts as Santa Cruz Beach, the Boardwalk, and the Municipal Wharf.

Some residents would like the city to follow in the footsteps of Carmel, whose parks, beach, restaurants, hotels, and other businesses are extremely welcoming to dogs. When resident Cathy Sutton is done fighting to keep the off-leash status of Lighthouse Field State Beach, she and a couple of other dog people plan to go around to restaurants to inform them of the myriad benefits of allowing well-behaved dogs at their outdoor tables. "They should see all the business they're missing out on," she wrote me, referring to the large number of dogs in the city (40 percent of residents have pets), many of whom would be excellent tableside companions. They plan to have this book in hand along the way. Jake and I applaud their cause and wish them the best of luck.

If this were any other city, the dearth of dog-friendly places wouldn't be such a disappointment. But this is Santa Cruz, land of the free, home of the unusual. Still, we've managed to sniff out some fun spots for dogs.

DIVERSION

Go to the Movies: Santa Cruz's **Skyview Drive-In Theatre** is one of those rare drive-in joints that dares to call itself a theater. In fact, these days, it's one of those rare drive-ins, period. We're thrilled it's still around. You'll need an FM radio to receive the soundtrack. The price is right: A double feature is just $6 per adult. Kids under 12, and dogs of all ages, are free. 2260 Soquel Drive. 831/475-3405; www.skyviewsantacruz.com.

PARKS, BEACHES, AND RECREATION AREAS

The fate of two of Santa Cruz's most beloved doggy areas, Its Beach and Lighthouse Field (which make up Lighthouse Field State Beach) was up in the air at this book's press time. Although the state owns Lighthouse Field State Beach, it has had a 30-year contract allowing the city of Santa Cruz to run it. Santa Cruz needed a place for its oodles of dogs to be off-leash and found this was a good area for off-leash activity (albeit during limited hours). But that contract is set to expire (it will have done so by the time you read this), and if the property goes back to state control, it's likely leashes will be the law. That would be really rotten.

A wonderful group, Friends of Lighthouse Field, has been working hard to help the city find alternatives to this jarring possibility. When this book went to press, the city had just offered to buy the 37-acre property from the state for $1 million. The state was weighing this offer. Sure, the property is worth millions more, but then the state wouldn't have to bear the cost of maintenance or deal with leash enforcement. By the time you read this, the fate of Lighthouse Field State Beach will likely have been decided. Before throwing your leash to the wind at your next visit, be sure to check the Friends of Lighthouse Field website (www.folf.org) for updates. Jake and I are crossing all our fingers and paws that this will work out for off-leash freedom. Dogs of Santa Cruz need and deserve no less.

As for the rest of the city, this edition brings a couple more leash-free areas, so that's good. And most city parks permit leashed dogs. San Lorenzo Park is a notable exception. So is Nearys Lagoon City Park, a popular wildlife sanctuary

DIVERSION

Hail a Water Taxi: Want that seafaring experience without the rolling waves or the expense? If it's Saturday or Sunday, and it's summer, and you're in Santa Cruz, you and your salty dog are in luck. The port district here runs free water taxis that motor around the **Santa Cruz Harbor,** making several stops to pick up and drop off passengers. The price? Zippo. Yes, a free taxi, and no crazy city taxi driver either. Such a deal! Even if your dog is prone to turning green at the mere sight of any water that's not in his bowl, he should be just fine on the water taxi. These flat-bottomed boats are stable, plus the harbor isn't exactly the Bering Sea. We're talking flat.

You can catch the taxi at several harbor spots. Our favorite is at Aldo's Harbor Restaurant, because there's decent parking around here and because there's nothing like waiting for a water taxi at a bustling, friendly dockside fish restaurant. (It's located at 616 Atlantic Avenue.) For more water taxi info, phone 831/475-6161.

you may be tempted to visit with your canine friend. But since dogs aren't part of the natural scenery here, they're not allowed.

6 University Terrace

🐾🐾🐾🐕 (See Santa Cruz County map on page 546)

This pleasant city park has a section in the lower area where dogs may be off leash during limited hours. It's a few unfenced acres of grass (or as the park supervisor, Jim, more accurately describes it, maintained weeds), with some small trees on the hillsides. A couple of big cypress trees give a little shade, not that you need shade much around these parts. You can get far enough from the street that you'll probably feel pretty safe from traffic.

The park is at Meder Street and Nobel Drive. The off-leash area is below the main park area (away from the playground). As you look at the park from Meder, the off-leash section is on the right, adjacent to a service road. Signs will point you in the right direction. Dogs are welcome to be off-leash here sunrise–10 A.M. and 4 P.M.–sunset. The rest of the time they need to be leashed. There's also another off-leash area on the south side of the tennis courts, with the same hours. Again, you'll see the signs. 831/420-5270.

7 Mitchell's Cove Beach

🐾🐾🐾🐕 (See Santa Cruz County map on page 546)

This is the place locals come with their dogs when they want to get away from the tourist scene. The beach is small, attractive, and not far from Its Beach. But for some reason, it's not nearly as well used.

Dogs may run off leash sunrise–10 A.M. and 4 P.M.–sunset. During the rest of the time they're permitted on leash (unlike the situation at Its Beach). The beach is between Almar and Woodrow avenues, along West Cliff Drive. It was unmarked last time we visited, but that may have changed. 831/420-5270.

8 Lighthouse Field

🐾🐾🐾🐾🐕 (See Santa Cruz County map on page 546)

Note: Be sure to read the introduction to the *Parks, Beaches, and Recreation Areas* section, above, for important information on the battle to keep Lighthouse Field off leash. By the time you read this, leashes may be the law. We sincerely hope not.

This is officially part of Lighthouse Field State Beach, but even though it's state parkland, it's run by the city, and dogs may run off-leash during certain hours. It's a great dog privilege. This is a terrific place with lots of shade via massive groves of trees. There are logs for dogs to go over (and under), little bridges, and plenty of room to run like the wind and chase balls. The view of the ocean from here is a winner. (Thanks to the dynamic duo, Zoe and Sienna Dogs, for updating me on the park's natural wonders. I hope they get to continue enjoying the park untethered.)

DIVERSION

Soak Up Some Surf Culture: Your well-behaved dog is welcome to join you in exploring more than 100 years of surfing in Santa Cruz, at the **Santa Cruz Surfing Museum.** If any museum is going to allow dogs, it's a surfing museum. "Sure, we allow dogs. We love dogs! Anyway, it's pretty mellow here," said a mellow employee. Just no leg-lifts on the boards, OK surfer dude doggies? These boards have seen their last wet days.

The small museum also features videos, photos, and surfing paraphernalia. It's housed in the Mark Abbott Memorial Lighthouse at Lighthouse Point (at 701 West Cliff Drive), overlooking the renowned Steamer Lane surfing spot. 831/420-6119; www.santa cruzsurfingmuseum.org.

Dogs can run off leash here sunrise–10 A.M. and 4 P.M.–sunset. The rest of the time they need to be leashed. Don't worry if outdated signs tell you only that dogs must always be leashed. The Lighthouse Field is on the nonocean side of West Cliff Drive, west of Point Santa Cruz. 831/420-5270.

9 Its Beach

🐾🐾🐾🐾🐕 (See Santa Cruz County map on page 546)

Note: Please read this section's introduction for important information on the battle to keep Its Beach off leash. The laws may have changed by the time you read this.

The beach is narrow and not nearly as heavily used by humans as other beaches in the area. It's surfer heaven here. Dogs seem to enjoy sniffing at surfers' neoprene-clad bodies as they jog toward the ocean with their boards. Jake once swam after a surfer and stayed near him until I was able to get his attention to call him back in. On his way back, a wave went over his head, scaring me to death and knocking some sense into him about safe swimming practices. He hasn't followed a surfer out since.

Even though this is part of Lighthouse Field State Beach, dogs are allowed to run leashless sunrise–10 A.M. and 4 P.M.–sunset. The rest of the time they're not supposed to even set paw on the sand, leashed or not. A big ticket can ensue. The beach is on West Cliff Drive, west of Point Santa Cruz and just west of the infamous Santa Cruz Surfing Museum. 831/420-5270.

🔟 Twin Lakes State Beach

🐾🐾🐾 (See Santa Cruz County map on page 546)

The beach here is wide and inviting for leashed dogs and their people. But unfortunately, even more inviting is a section that dogs should stay away from: Schwan Lagoon, a wildfowl refuge full of ducksch and geesch and, they say, even a few schwans.

Twin Lakes State Beach is on both sides of the Santa Cruz Small Craft Harbor, on East Cliff Drive and 7th Avenue. 831/427-4870.

🔟🔟 De La Veaga Park

🐾🐾🐾🐕 (See Santa Cruz County map on page 546)

Dogs need to be on-leash at this park except for the service road area into lower De La Veaga Park. And unlike Santa Cruz's other off-leash areas, this one allows dogs to be leash-free from sunrise to sunset—none of those pesky limited hours to worry about.

The service road into the lower park is at Market Street, past Gruenwald Court. There's a turnout where you can park for the off-leash area. You'll see the signs. The service road is part paved, part dirt, and only rangers really use it, so your dog is pretty safe from traffic here. It's not a long road, but at least it's off-leash, and it will take you a little uphill to an area about the size of half a football field where your dog can run among acacias and enjoy some leashless freedom! There's some talk about expanding this area to some green fields beyond, where dogs could run off leash during limited hours. "I'd like to see that happen," said Steve, the park's head of maintenance. We hope it does, too.

Lots of trails branch off the service road, but you do have to leash up. As for the rest of the park, it's an enjoyable place to explore, even on leash. When you get past all the golf courses, this large park (500-plus acres) and its trails are pretty remote and not that widely used. At the top of the park, you can see forever. Many trails lead you through fields, into woods, and back through lush meadowland. Just watch out for flying arrows at the archery range on the park's east side. 831/420-5270.

PLACES TO EAT

Santa Cruz has many restaurants with outdoor tables. Here's a sampling of a few dog-friendly ones—including one with its very own dog menu! You'll be able to sniff out plenty more on your own while you're exploring with your pooch. Just stay away from the alfresco restaurants on Pacific Avenue, the main drag downtown. It's a drag in more than one sense of the word: Dogs are banned from the entire strip. (So are skateboards, if that makes your dog feel any better.)

Aldo's Harbor Restaurant: Love fresh seafood? This is a great place to eat it. One selection is even called Aldo's Very Fresh Fish, literally the catch

of the day. The fish tacos are a treat, and we've heard great reviews of the coconut shrimp and the Australian lobster tail. If you don't like seafood, there are plenty of other options. Aldo's also offers a traditional breakfast menu. Dine with your dog at the wonderful harborside deck. 616 Atlantic Avenue; 831/426-3736.

Café Limelight: The hot panini sandwiches are a delight (try the roast turkey, brie, and pesto grilled on rosemary focaccia—it's out of this world), and the fresh soups and salads are also right on the money. But you will surely want to have your dog at your side when you visit the umbrella-topped patio tables here. Dogs get a complimentary little dog treat, and beyond that, dogs have their very own menu! Your dog can select from items like fresh roasted turkey, a roasted pig's ear, or a bully stick. If you don't know what a bully stick is, don't ask while you're eating. 1016 Cedar Street; 831/425-7873.

Kelly's French Bakery: This super-popular French Provincial bakery and organic farmers market café welcomes dogs at its front patio, "as long as their owners are leashed up," says a manager. The food's great, the bread is to die for, and the espresso is strong. A big thank-you to Sophie Louise, a happy local Jack Russell terrier, and to Zoe and Sienna Dogs, for turning us on to this great place. 402 Ingalls Street; 831/423-9059.

PLACES TO STAY

Continental Inn: This one's about five blocks from the water. Rates are $60–280. Dogs are $10 extra. 414 Ocean Street 95060; 831/429-1221; www.continentalinn.net.

Edgewater Beach Motel: No two rooms are alike at this attractive, dog-friendly haunt. Four of the rooms were built in 1886, although 1955 was the year a big chunk of the motel came into existence. You can get a room adorned with mahogany, redwood, or even a sunken fireplace, or a basic room with less character, but just as much comfort. (Face it—if you're traveling with your dog, you've probably got all the character you can handle anyway.)

Outside is a flower garden, a lawn area for kids, a picnic area with gas barbecues, and best for dogs, a big lot where they can do things doggies like to do. (Do clean up.) The lot is across the street from the wharf, where dogs are banned.

The owners love dogs and have three pooches themselves. "Pets make great guests. I'm more reluctant about having some people stay here than I am about dogs," says owner Win Alexander. Dog guests are supplied a dog sheet while they're here so they won't get fur on the bed. Rates are $89–359. Dogs are $10–30 extra, depending on their size. 525 2nd Street, 95060; 831/423-0440; www.edgewaterbeachmotel.com.

Guest House Pacific Inn: The rooms all have little fridges, so you and your dog can have some cool midnight snacks. The motel also has a heated enclosed pool, but no paw-dipping, please. Rates are $80–200. Dogs are $10 extra. 330 Ocean Street 95060; 831/425-3722.

A House in Santa Cruz: Looking for a pooch-friendly vacation rental by the ocean? This directory of owner-managed rentals features wonderful homes and cottages. Some are right across the street from the ocean, some are tucked away in quiet neighborhoods, and some have enclosed backyards for your dog friend. There's no agent to contact, so there's no central phone number. The website, www.ahouseinsantacruz.com/dogfriendly, has excellent photos and descriptions of each rental, plus phone numbers and rates for each.

Ocean Pacific Lodge: You're just a couple of blocks from beach action when you stay here. This is a clean, decent-looking place, with mini fridges and microwaves in all the rooms, which makes traveling with your canine troupe a bit easier. Humans enjoy the heated pool and continental breakfast. Rates are $75–275. Dogs must be under 25 pounds and pay a $20 fee for the length of their stay. 120 Washington Street 95060; 831/457-1234 or 800/995-0289.

Seashell Cottage Oceanfront Vacation Rental: "I give first priority to people with dogs," says friendly rental manager Susanna Eaton. "They make the best guests." The Seashell Cottage is the most popular of her eight beach rentals. It's an utterly enchanting one-room cottage perched over a secluded beach near the edge of a cliff. (Don't worry, it won't fall.) Enjoy a book on the window seat that faces the ocean, or relax in the small yard or deck, keeping off the chill with the outdoor fireplace.

Dogs truly feel welcome here. Treats are waiting for them when they arrive, and there's even a water dish and a spare leash, should you forget yours.

Rates are $225 nightly, or $1,500 weekly. For more on Seashell or Susan's other rentals, see www.beachnest.com, or phone 831/722-0202. You'll get the address of your rental when you make your reservation.

Aptos

If all suburbs could be like Aptos, this country would be a much better-looking place. While Aptos is falling victim to the suburban sprawl of its neighbors to the north, it still retains a core of grace in its old village section. Check out the rustic Redwood Village, whose quaint stores were originally built in 1928 with redwood hewn from trees on the property.

While exploring Aptos, if you run into Loma Prieta Drive, don't sit around with your dog and wonder why someone would name a street after the deadly 1989 earthquake. This is the area of the epicenter of that quake, which measured 7.1 on the Richter scale. If your dog starts acting restless, you may want to move on. It could be fleas. It could be boredom. It could even be gas. But why take a chance? Actually, people around here say the pressure along the fault line was relieved by the quake, so there's probably little chance that another big one could be centered here for a while.

PARKS, BEACHES, AND RECREATION AREAS

🔟 Aptos Polo Grounds Dog Park

😺😺😺🐾 (See Santa Cruz County map on page 546)

This one-acre fenced park seems bigger than it really is. It could be because it's a super-flat park with a wood-chip ground cover that blends in with the brownish grass (most of the year) behind it, creating the illusion of grandeur. Jake seems to have fallen prey to the illusion, becoming exhausted after a few quick passes from one side to the other while being chased by a friendly boxer. If reading all about these big dogs is intimidating your little dog, take heart: The park now has a separate section for small dogs.

The park is flanked on two sides by tall, beautiful trees, but no trees grace the park, so shade is limited to times when the sun is just right. The park has water, poop bags, benches, and a portable toilet right outside, in case you're hankering to do a leg lift yourself.

It's a quick trip from Highway 1 to the park, so it's handy if you need an exercise stop on a road trip. From Santa Cruz, take Highway 1 to the Rio Del Mar exit. Go left after the freeway and turn right on Monroe Avenue (the second traffic light). Monroe turns into Wallace Avenue. You'll come to a fork in the road, where you'll bear left onto Huntington Drive. The park entrance will be on your left after an area of houses. Drive in and you'll find the fenced doggy park. Please note that dogs are banned from the playing fields at Polo Grounds Park, but they're welcome to explore a fun trail near the dog park as long as they're leashed. A big thanks to Joan Fuhry for giving us the first heads up about the park. 831/454-7900.

PLACES TO EAT

Britannia Arms: We wouldn't characterize this restaurant and pub as English, as it serves mostly American-style food (plenty of barbecued dishes and burgers). But it's as dog-friendly as any English springer spaniel or Airedale could hope. When you step inside to order your food, you can attach your dog's leash to a dog hitch made especially for this situation. There's usually water for dogs, but if there isn't, it's yours for the asking. We've heard dogs get occasional treats, but it's not the official policy. Dine with your dog at several umbrella-topped patio tables. 8017 Soquel Drive; 831/688-1233.

Café Rio: If you wish for fish, try a dish from Café Rio. It's a primo fish restaurant with everything from abalone to smoked salmon. If your dog prefers aged beef, it's got that, too. The outdoor patio area here is big and leafy and welcomes well-behaved dogs. Café Rio is close to the Polo Grounds Dog Park. 131 Esplanade; 831/688-8917.

PLACES TO STAY

Apple Lane Inn: If you and your dog are hankering for simpler times—times when you could stroll out to the barn, collect a few eggs, pat the horses, mosey back to your Victorian farmhouse and have someone cook a gourmet breakfast for you, read a book under blooming wisteria on a pretty patio, pick a few apples from your trees, visit a goat and rabbits, go back inside and listen to the player piano while you play cards or games with your friends inside the parlor—you've found your nirvana. You can do all this and more—or much less, if you want to take it really easy—when you stay at this historic inn built on more than two acres.

Dogs can stay with their people in the large room called the Wine Cellar. I've heard mixed reviews from readers: Some say it's a great place to stay with a dog, others say it's got more of a chilly dungeon feel. It *is* dark, with only one window (and it's dark stained glass). And it *is* cool. The cooler air from its ground-floor location, and the full wine bottles that live in built-in wine racks on the walls, impart a kind of winery feel (or if you were raised Catholic, a churchlike feel). But don't drink that wine! It's old, and not in a good kind of way, apparently.

Rates are $100–200. Dogs are $25 extra. Oh, and if you bring a horse, he's $25 extra too, but he'll need to stay in the big barn or the field here, not in your room. 6265 Soquel Drive, 95003; 831/475-6868 or 800/649-8988; www .applelaneinn.com.

Seacliff

PARKS, BEACHES, AND RECREATION AREAS

13 Seacliff State Beach

🐾🐾🐾🐾 (See Santa Cruz County map on page 546)

Want to make your dog happy, even though he's officially supposed to be on a leash? Bring him here. A yearlong trial period showed that dogs and their well-behaved people should be allowed here. Before, the closest dogs could get to Seacliff State Beach was the RV campground perched above the beach. Somehow, looking down at a beach from your RV's picnic table isn't quite the same as trotting merrily down the beach with the breeze blowing through your fur.

The beach is about a mile long, so even though it can get pretty packed with pooches at the popular south end, there's plenty of space for some good exercise. And if you and your dog get hungry from all your beach activity, you can settle yourselves at the beach's picnic area. You can even nab one with a barbecue pit, if you feel like sharing a burger with your drooling canine.

Please remember to scoop the poop. Although there are plenty of garbage cans in which to toss your furry friend's feces (I couldn't help the alliteration), a park ranger tells us there's way too much poop left lying around. If this con-tinues, things could go back to the way they used to be, and that wouldn't be fun for anyone. The day-use fee here is $6, if you park in the lot. Exit Highway 1 at State Park Drive and head toward the ocean. 831/685-6442.

Watsonville

PARKS, BEACHES, AND RECREATION AREAS

The dog park Watsonville was considering when the last edition of this book went to press is now a reality. It's a tiny reality, but at least it exists.

🐾 Palm Beach

🐾🐾🐾🐾 (See Santa Cruz County map on page 546)

Dahling! What a mahvelous place! And not a sign of anyone rich and famous for miles!

This may not be the Palm Beach of rich Southern Floridians' fame, but it's a heavenly, remote place that has considerably more to offer down-to-earth dogs and their people. A trail takes you through a large eucalyptus grove where you and your dog can stop for a cool, relaxing picnic. Then it's onward to the large beach, where your dog has to remain leashed, but he can still have a jolly old time sniffing and walking and walking and sniffing. Even on perfect summer afternoons, this beach gets very little use, probably because of its location at the end of the county.

Fees are $6 per car. Exit Highway 1 at Riverside Drive/Highway 129 and follow the signs to Beach Road, past huge farms. The beach is at the end of the road. 831/429-2850 or 831/763-7064.

🐾 Watsonville Dog Park

🐾🐾🐕 (See Santa Cruz County map on page 546)

Dogs in this part of the county are happy to finally have a little something to call their own. And I do mean little. This fenced park is about 0.3 acre, with water, grass, benches, a small-dog section, and dogs that run like the wind—at least until they come up to a fence, which happens a lot in a park of this size.

Jake actually prefers to put on his leash and roam around the large county park that houses the dog park. Pinto Lake County Park has big trees, and a little lake where you can actually have a good chance of catching fish. Jake loves to watch people fish, and when they throw a fish back (which doesn't happen much around here), he is the sort of gentleman who will go and retrieve the fish for the person who "lost" it. Of course, this can't happen on a leash, but he tries, just the same.

The dog park is at 757 Green Valley Road. From southbound Highway 1, exit on Airport Boulevard, and make a left on Green Valley Road. From northbound Highway 1, take the Airport Boulevard exit, go left onto Airport Boulevard, and at Green Valley Road, go left. Note: You'll drive past Pinto Lake City Park before you see the county park. At the county park, turn left. 831/454-7900.

PLACES TO STAY

Motel 6: This one's only a couple of miles from Palm Beach. Rates are $78–130. The owners ask that you let them know ahead of time if you'll be bringing a dog. 125 Silver Leaf Drive 95076; 831/728-4144.

Santa Cruz KOA Kampground: The Santa Cruz KOA Kampground is one of the more attractive ones. Its cute log Kamping Kabins are set under big pines not far from the coast. If you prefer to camp, you can pitch a tent with your dog here too.

The KOA is a family-oriented place, with miniature golf, volleyball courts, a hot tub, a swimming pool, and fun summertime activities for kids. This is the priciest KOA in California, in large part because of the real estate values around here. Kamping Kabin rates are $78–130. (The upper end is for two-room Kabins.) Rates for the tent sites are $30–78. If you have an RV, you'll pay $62–110. The KOA is one mile from the coast, at 1186 San Andreas Road 95076; 831/722-0551 or 800/562-7701.

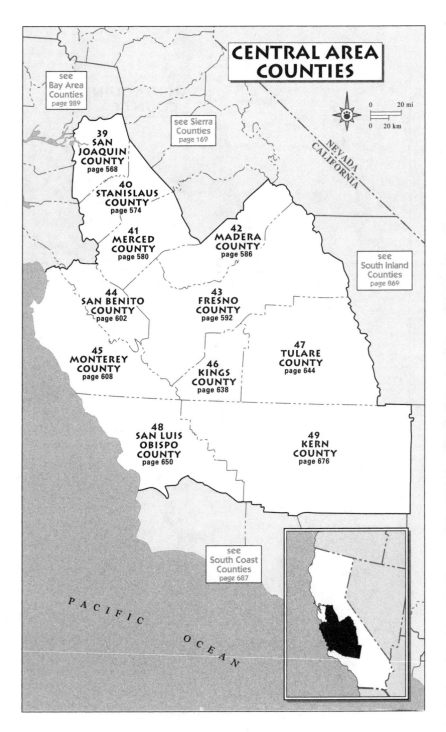

CENTRAL AREA COUNTIES

see Bay Area Counties page 289

see Sierra Counties page 169

see South Inland Counties page 869

see South Coast Counties page 687

NEVADA
CALIFORNIA

39 SAN JOAQUIN COUNTY page 568

40 STANISLAUS COUNTY page 574

41 MERCED COUNTY page 580

42 MADERA COUNTY page 586

44 SAN BENITO COUNTY page 602

43 FRESNO COUNTY page 592

45 MONTEREY COUNTY page 608

46 KINGS COUNTY page 638

47 TULARE COUNTY page 644

48 SAN LUIS OBISPO COUNTY page 650

49 KERN COUNTY page 676

PACIFIC OCEAN

0 20 mi
0 20 km

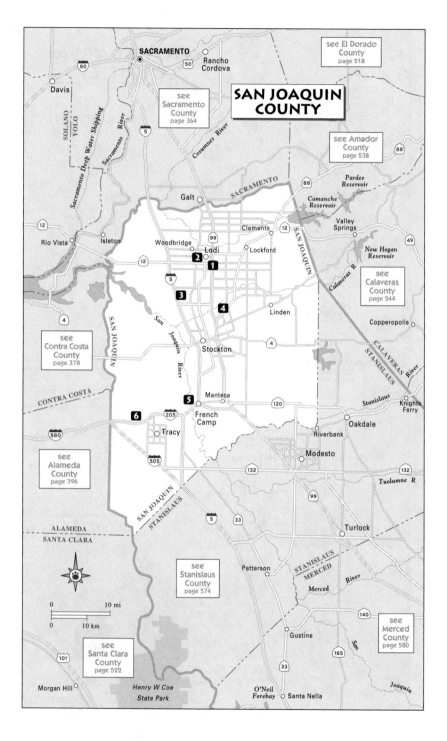

SAN JOAQUIN COUNTY

see El Dorado County
page 218

SACRAMENTO

Rancho Cordova

Davis

SOLANO
YOLO

Sacramento Deep Water Shipping

Sacramento River

see Sacramento County
page 364

Cosumnes River

see Amador County
page 238

Pardee Reservoir

Camanche Reservoir

SACRAMENTO

Galt

Clements

Valley Springs

New Hogan Reservoir

Rio Vista

Isleton

Woodbridge

2 Lodi **1**

Lockford

SAN JOAQUIN

Calaveras R

see Calaveras County
page 244

Copperopolis

3

4

Linden

San Joaquin River

see Contra Costa County
page 378

SAN JOAQUIN

Stockton

CALAVERAS River

STANISLAUS

Knights Ferry

CONTRA COSTA

Stanislaus

Manteca

5

6

Tracy

French Camp

Oakdale

Riverbank

Modesto

see Alameda County
page 396

ALAMEDA
SANTA CLARA

SAN JOAQUIN
STANISLAUS

Tuolumne R

Turlock

see Stanislaus County
page 574

Patterson

STANISLAUS
MERCED River

Merced

0   10 mi
0   10 km

see Santa Clara County
page 522

see Merced County
page 580

Morgan Hill

Henry W Coe State Park

Gustine

O'Neil Forebay

Santa Nella

Joaquin

CHAPTER 39

San Joaquin County

Chances are you won't be driving a few hundred miles just to vacation here with your dog. That's good. In fact, your dog is probably reading over your shoulder right now and slobbering in gratitude.

It's not that San Joaquin County is a terrible place for dogs. It certainly has its share of attractive parks. But since dogs aren't permitted off leash around here except in a couple of dog parks, and since this isn't exactly the wilderness capital of California, it's just not a great doggy destination.

Here's a good rule of thumb if you don't want to come away with a ticket for a dog offense: Tempting as it may be, don't let your dog walk on the paths and trails in the county-run parks. It's an offense punishable by a few dollars out of your dog bone fund. It's a ridiculous rule. What would have happened to Toto if he hadn't been permitted to walk on the Yellow Brick Road?

PICK OF THE LITTER—SAN JOAQUIN COUNTY

BEST PLACE FOR THE DOG PADDLE
Lodi Lake, Lodi (page 570)

BIGGEST OFF-LEASH DOG AREA
Vinewood Park, Lodi (page 570)

BEST WATERY ADVENTURE
Delta houseboat rentals, Stockton (page 571)

Lodi

PARKS, BEACHES, AND RECREATION AREAS

Lodi doesn't have dog parks, per se. "They're called Designated Dog Areas," a parks rep tells us. "They're not dog parks." And they're really not, in the traditional sense. (But a rose by any other name would smell as sweet.) Lodi has four not-dog parks. We write about our favorite two here.

🐾 Lodi Lake

🐾🐾🐾🐾 (See San Joaquin County map on page 568)

Water dogs love this 114-acre city park: They actually get to do the dog paddle—leash-free—in one section of the park's seven-acre lake. The swim area is only about 80 feet long, but that's plenty of splashing room. The park also features a very small fenced dog run. It has lots of trees, which boy dogs enjoy, and it's adjacent to the Mokelumne River. Dogs can take a stroll on paved paths around the rest of the park, but they must be leashed.

The doggy swim area is on the west bank of the lake, north of the dam, and bordered by the cemetery (it's fenced off—have no fear of your terrier going into dig mode). You'll see the signs. The dog run is on the lake's north side. The park address is 1101 West Turner Road, at Mills Avenue. 209/333-6742.

🐾 Vinewood Park

🐾🐾🐾🐾 (See San Joaquin County map on page 568)

The off-leash area within Vinewood Park is actually part of a retention basin/sump area. This means that it can close during rain or even threat of rain. But with four big acres of grassy, semifenced leash-free bliss, it's still a hot-diggety-dog place to go. The entire park itself is fenced, but the dog area is not separated by anything but signs and a wide strip of dirt (actually, a berm). Pay attention to the signs: The dog area is the south basin. Whatever you do, don't let your dog wander to the north basin off leash. There's a $270 fine for this offense. (That's a lotta dog food money.) Dog people here would like to see the dog area fenced off so this kind of thing doesn't happen.

The dog area has benches, poop-bag dispensers, and lots of trees, and it is wheelchair-accessible. Water is just outside the area. The park is at 1824 West Tokay Street, at Mills Avenue. From Highway 12, go north on Mills Avenue and drive about three stop signs. Go right on Virginia Street. 209/333-6742.

DIVERSION

Doggy Does Delta: There's really no better way to explore the Delta than on a houseboat. As your first mate steers the boat through the Delta's snaking waterways, you can prepare dinner, take a snooze on one of the boat's beds, catch some rays (and some fish), or just sit on the deck with your dog and sniff the brackish breeze. Just remember to park the boat occasionally (there's plenty of isolated, parkable land around) to let your pooch stretch his legs and tend to his business.

A dog-friendly **houseboat rental** company, Seven Crown Resorts, will rent you and your dog and some friends a houseboat for $750 for three days/two nights to $2,200 for a week. Phone 800/752-9669 for more information; www.houseboat.com. Other houseboat companies offer similar deals for Delta dogs and their people.

Stockton

PARKS, BEACHES, AND RECREATION AREAS

At press time, the city was hard at work on a dog park in Weston Park.

🐾 Oak Grove Regional County Park

🐾🐾🐾 (See San Joaquin County map on page 568)

This 180-acre park has more than 1,500 oak trees. If you want shade, or your boy dog wants a target for leg lifts, you've come to the right place.

You can easily get around the park without use of the wonderful 1.5-mile nature trail, and it's a good thing, because dogs aren't allowed to set paw on it. As with all San Joaquin County parks, dogs aren't permitted on trails or paths. But this park has enough open land so it won't matter much except on muddy days.

Dogs must be leashed. There's a $3 vehicle entry fee on weekdays, $5 on weekends and holidays. Dogs are $1. 209/953-8800.

🐾 Victory Park

🐾🐾🐾 (See San Joaquin County map on page 568)

Local dogs come to mingle at this attractive park, which is full of large oaks and conifers. There's a paved walkway around the park's 27 acres. A hike around it makes for an excellent exercise routine.

Weekdays after work are the best times to visit if you want your leashed dog to hang out with other leashed dogs. Too bad the city couldn't set aside a couple of acres as a fenced-in dog-exercise area so dogs could play as they really want to—sans leash.

The park is at Pershing Avenue and Picardy Drive. 209/937-8206.

PLACES TO STAY

La Quinta Inn: Rates are $79–119. 2710 West March Lane 95219; 209/952-7800.

Tiki Lagun Resort and Marina: This is kind of a fun place to come camping with your canine, especially if you're not into a big wilderness adventure. The 30 soft-grass campsites are set under tall shade trees, just a bone's throw from the Delta. Dogs dig it here. If you visit in an RV, there's a separate RV park, with 30 spaces and complete hookups. Compared to most RV/camp areas, it's small and secluded. Tiki Lagun even has launch ramps, should you bring a boat. Rates are $30–35. 12988 West McDonald Road 95206; 209/941-8975 or 800/338-7176; www.tikimarina.com.

Manteca

PARKS, BEACHES, AND RECREATION AREAS

All dog parks here permit pooches on leash. There are 46 parks here, but Northgate is where the local pooches hang out, and so can yours.

5 Northgate Park

🐾🐾 (See San Joaquin County map on page 568)

If your dog wants to meet the hounds of Manteca, come to Northgate Park, where Manteca dogs gather for long afternoons of leisure. The setting is grassy and fairly flat, with softball fields and picnic tables. It's not exactly Yosemite National Park, but dogs have more fun here.

Dogs are supposed to be leashed. The park is at Northgate Drive and Hoyt Lane. 209/239-8470.

Tracy

PARKS, BEACHES, AND RECREATION AREAS

6 El Pescadero Dog Park

🐾🐾🐾 (See San Joaquin County map on page 568)

Local canines are crazy for this fenced dog park. It's about an acre, with lots of grass for happy dogs to run around on, and even some dog agility toys, built by local, dog-loving Eagle Scouts. Park amenities include benches, water, and poop bags. The park is within El Pescadero Park, which is at Kavanagh and Louise avenues. The dog park is on the Kavanagh side. 209/831-6200.

PLACES TO STAY

Motel 6: This one's a trucker haven but it has plenty of dog guests. Rates are $43–53 for one adult, $3 extra for the second. 3810 North Tracy Boulevard 95376; 209/836-4900.

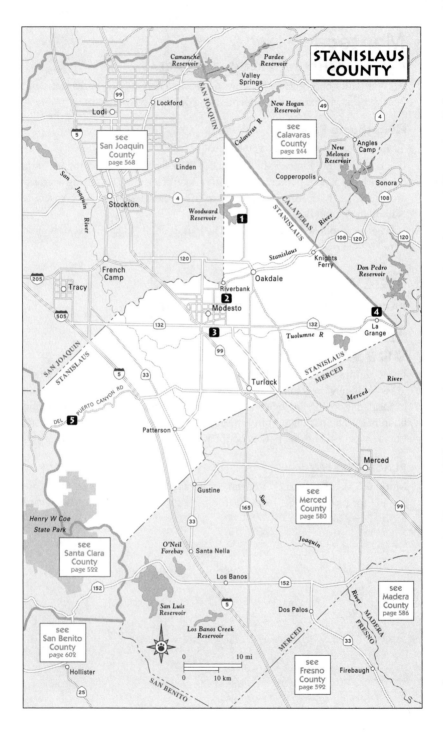

STANISLAUS COUNTY

Camanche Reservoir

Pardee Reservoir

Valley Springs

99

Lockford

Lodi

5

New Hogan Reservoir

49

4

see San Joaquin County page 568

see Calaveras County page 244

New Melones Reservoir

Angles Camp

Linden

Copperopolis

Sonora

108

4

Stockton

Woodward Reservoir

1

108

120

120

San Joaquin River

120

Stanislaus

Knights Ferry

Don Pedro Reservoir

205

French Camp

Oakdale

Riverbank

2

Modesto

4

La Grange

Tracy

505

132

3

132

Tuolumne R

99

SAN JOAQUIN

STANISLAUS

5

33

Turlock

STANISLAUS

MERCED

Merced

River

DEL PUERTO CANYON RD

5

Patterson

Henry W Coe State Park

Gustine

165

San

see Merced County page 580

99

see Santa Clara County page 522

152

O'Neil Forebay

Santa Nella

33

Joaquin

Merced

see Madera County page 586

MADERA

FRESNO

see San Benito County page 602

San Luis Reservoir

Los Banos

152

5

Dos Palos

0   10 mi

0   10 km

Los Banos Creek Reservoir

33

MERCED

see Fresno County page 592

Firebaugh

Hollister

25

SAN BENITO

CHAPTER 40

Stanislaus County

Chambers of Commerce in these parts boast that "Summer Lasts Longer" here. Longer than what? When we asked, they weren't too sure. But when it's late September and your dog's tongue is unfurled just as long and bologna-like as it was in July, you may find the answer yourself: Summer lasts longer than hell here.

Fortunately, there are plenty of decent parks near the county's rivers. Dogs like to cool their fuzzy heels in the water.

Director George Lucas grew up here, surviving one sweltering summer after another. In his film *American Graffiti* (inspired by his younger years in Modesto, but not set there), a drive-in diner played a key role in the lives of his characters. It was a cool place to go on hot summer nights. If you and your dog want to dine alfresco here, you'll find a respectable number of outdoor restaurants. The most fitting is Modesto's very own A&W Root Beer drive-in restaurant, where carhops on roller skates will take your dog's order lickety-split. Jake is partial to the poodle skirts some wear.

PICK OF THE LITTER—STANISLAUS COUNTY

BEST HIKES
La Grange Regional Park, La Grange (page 578)
Frank Raines Regional Park, Patterson (page 579)

BEST PLACE TO CATCH A POODLE (SKIRT)
A & W Root Beer, Modesto (page 578)

Oakdale

PARKS, BEACHES, AND RECREATION AREAS

🐾 Valley Oak Recreation Area

🐾🐾🐾 (See Stanislaus County map on page 574)

Some of the most pristine river woodland left in California lies along the Stanislaus River, and you should be able to see a sampling when you and your leashed dog visit this park. A hiking trail here offers a short tour of the lush river woodland. Moisture-loving trees such as cottonwoods, alders, and willows will keep you shaded while you dip your toes in the cool river.

This isn't a well-known park, so it doesn't get as crowded as some of the other riverside parks in the area. There are 10 boat-in campsites available for $8 per site. There is also one group site available, for $38. Reservations are required. From Highway 108/120, go north on County Road J9 and cross the river. Turn right at Rodden Road and follow it east to the park. For more info or reservations, phone 209/881-3517.

Modesto

All 20 Modesto parks allow dogs on leash, and soon the city may get its own dog park, in Dry Creek Regional Park.

PARKS, BEACHES, AND RECREATION AREAS

🐾 Dry Creek Regional Park

🐾🐾🐾 (See Stanislaus County map on page 574)

A well-maintained bike/pedestrian trail leads you and the leashed dog in your life for more than three miles along the south side of Dry Creek. This park is actually a few parks strung together, so you'll find different terrain as you stroll merrily along. If your dog likes sniffing big trees or meditating at a riverside, he'll be happy here. And soon, he may be ecstatic here, because the park is slated to be the site of Modesto's first dog park! Keep your nose to the ground for details.

The park runs between La Loma Avenue and Claus Road. The section from El Vista Avenue east to Claus Road is not used much because it's very undeveloped. You may want to stick with the western part of the park. 209/577-5344.

🖪 Tuolumne River Regional Park
🐾🐾🐾 (See Stanislaus County map on page 574)

It's rare to find a city park that's even a couple of miles long, but here's one that spans six miles. Dogs think it's the cat's meow.

It has just about everything a dog could want, except permission to run around off leash. It's mostly undeveloped, meaning few softball fields or playgrounds to get in the way of a dog's endeavors. It's on the banks of the Tuolumne River, so water-loving dogs can cool their paws where they're able to reach the river. And it has an appealing blend of wide-open meadows, oak knolls, and natural riparian land.

The park is on the north side of the Tuolumne River and runs from Ohio Avenue on the west to Mitchell Road on the east. It has a golf course where dogs are verboten. It's also broken up by the occasional road and some sections of parkland that aren't too appealing. Try the area east of Tioga Drive. 209/577-5344.

PLACES TO EAT

A&W Root Beer: It's not the same diner as the one in *American Graffiti,* made by native son George Lucas. But the carhops still come by on roller skates, and poodle skirts are still in. Come here on a summer afternoon and slurp down a root beer served in a frosted mug. Your dog can join you at the shaded patio. In the winter, the patio is heated. That's the time to try two piping-hot cheeseburgers—one for you, one for you-know-who. 1404 G Street; 209/522-7700.

Piccadilly Deli: You and your dog will enjoy the deli fare, and you'll be grateful for the covered patio area during Modesto's long, hot summers. 941 10th Street; 209/523-0748.

PLACES TO STAY

Red Lion Hotel: Rates are $79–109. The rate for dogs is pretty high for a Red Lion, $50 per visit. Stay more than a night to get your money's worth. 1612 Sisk Road 95350; 209/521-1612.

La Grange

PARKS, BEACHES, AND RECREATION AREAS

◢ La Grange Regional Park

😺😺😺😺 (See Stanislaus County map on page 574)

This 750-acre park has an undeveloped trail system that takes you along the Tuolumne River and through a delicate wilderness area. Woodpeckers, eagles, bobcats, deer, and all their friends make the park their home at different times of the year. Bring your binoculars and keep your dog leashed. (It's a real trick to bird-watch with a dog who's tugging on your arm to visit a nearby tree, but it can be done.)

The park is in the historic town of La Grange and contains ancient adobe buildings, an old jail, a schoolhouse, a cemetery, and an abandoned gold dredge. It makes for an interesting pit stop.

There are several parcels of La Grange Park, which has an $8 day-use fee. Dogs are $3 extra. We like to start at the Basso Bridge Fishing Access. Exit Highway 132 at Lake Road and follow the signs. You'll be there in a snap. Park in the lot and head upriver. You can continue walking for a few miles and have a pleasant riverside hike. Or you can cross the street when you see a sign for the wilderness area and pay a visit to a more pristine setting. La Grange even offers camping. The sites are undeveloped and cost $14. 209/525-6750.

Patterson

PARKS, BEACHES, AND RECREATION AREAS

5 Frank Raines Regional Park

🐾🐾🐾🐾 (See Stanislaus County map on page 574)

This 2,000-acre county park is remote, mountainous, and full of wildlife you don't see much around these parts anymore. Leashed dogs love to hike among junipers, oaks, and foothill pines on the many dirt trails that wind through the park.

Springtime is the best season for a visit. The wildflowers are fantastic and the creek looks splendid when it's full.

About 640 acres of parkland are set aside for off-highway vehicle use. There are signs to steer you away from this area, but if you hear a roar that's not your dog's stomach, hike to another area. You may have accidentally stumbled into OHV land. There are also 43 acres of lawn with barbecues, a baseball diamond, and a playground. Dogs actually seem to like this manicured section because of the enchanting little nature trail here.

Tempting as it may be to slip your dog's leash off in the backcountry, you really shouldn't. If I can't inspire you to listen to the law, perhaps the tarantulas, rattlesnakes, bobcats, and occasional mountain lions can.

The day-use fee is $8. Campsite fees range $14–16. Dogs are $3 extra. There are 54 sites available on a first-come, first-served basis. From I-5, exit at Del Puerto Canyon Road and head west. You'll reach the park in about 18 winding miles. Follow the signs. 209/525-6750.

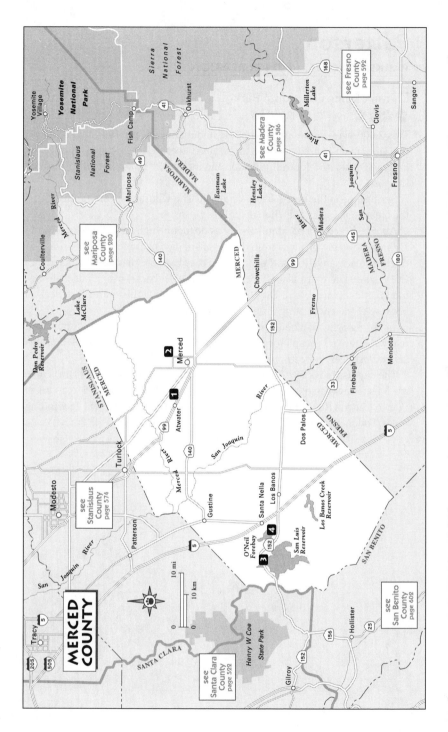

CHAPTER 41

Merced County

The county parks here ban dogs. The national wildlife refuges ban dogs. Even some of the smaller cities ban dogs from their parks. It can make a dog howling mad.

Atwater

PARKS, BEACHES, AND RECREATION AREAS

🔟 Ralston Park

🐾 🐾 (See Merced County map on page 580)

If you're window-shopping in the antique stores a few blocks away and need to rest your weary paws, try Ralston Park. It's got lots of lawn and plenty of trees.

Ralston Park is between Grove and Fir avenues, on 3rd Street. 209/357-6320.

PICK OF THE LITTER—MERCED COUNTY

BEST WALKS ON THE WILDLIFE SIDE
Los Banos Wildlife Area, Los Banos (page 584)

LODGING WITH COOLEST ARCHITECTURE
Ramada Inn Mission de Oro, Santa Nella (page 584)

Merced

Dogs of the male persuasion, rejoice! Merced is designated as a Tree City U.S.A. by the National Arbor Association. It's not exactly a forest, but the city does have an abundance of trees. It gives a dog plenty to sniff at, even if he's just accompanying you on a short walk. The city is planning its first dog park. We hope we'll be sniffing it out for you in the next edition.

PARKS, BEACHES, AND RECREATION AREAS

❷ Applegate Park
🐾 🐾 🐾   (See Merced County map on page 580)

More than 60 varieties of trees grace this lovely 23-acre park that borders Bear Creek. Boy, oh boy, do boy dogs adore Applegate Park! Kids like it, too. The park is home to a small zoo, as well as the Kiwanis Kiddieland mini-amusement park.

The city's 12-mile bike path runs through Applegate Park, so if you and your leashed dog want to saunter off to other parks, just follow the path to the next clump of greenery. Applegate is between M and R streets, on the south side of Bear Creek. 209/385-6855.

PLACES TO STAY

Merced Yosemite TraveLodge: Some of the spacious rooms here have tub spas, and you can swim in the motel's decent little pool, too. Water dogs have to be content to watch. Rates are $52–80. Dogs are $10 extra. 1260 Yosemite Parkway 95340; 209/722-6224.

Motel 6: Rates are $42 for the first adult, $6 for the second. 1410 V Street 95340; 209/384-2181.

Santa Nella

This town is alive because of I-5, which spews visitors into and out of town as quickly as they can get some gas and a bowl of Andersen's Split Pea Soup (which, in turn, can give folks enough of a different type of gas to last them clear to the Oregon border). If you want your pooch to have a sip of the delectable soup, go easy on it. Remember, you may be traveling in an enclosed vehicle together for many hours.

PARKS, BEACHES, AND RECREATION AREAS

🖪 San Luis Reservoir State Recreation Area

🐾🐾🐾 (See Merced County map on page 580)

The San Luis Reservoir is a water dog's dream. It's made up of three man-made lakes, and pooches have permission to do the dog paddle in all areas of the reservoir.

This park focuses on water activities, including fishing, swimming, and plenty of boating. It can get loud and crowded in the hot summer months, which always seem to attract fast boats. A better bet is in the spring, when it's cool and the fish are hungry. If you and the pooch are landlubbers at heart, you should probably find another park, since there's not much acreage outside of the picnic areas and campgrounds.

There are approximately 130 developed campsites and 400 primitive sites, many of which are along the water. Primitive sites are first-come, first-served and are free. Developed sites are $20–25. Exit I-5 at Highway 152 and drive west about four miles to the entrance road on the left. Call 800/444-7275 for reservations, or phone the park at 209/826-1197 for more information.

PLACES TO STAY

Motel 6: Rates are $40–49 for the first adult, $6.50 for the second. 12733 South Highway 33 95322; 209/826-6644.

Ramada Inn Mission de Oro: This hotel looks more like a Spanish mission than a place to spend the night with your dog. It's set on five acres of land that's terrific for leashed dog walks. Enjoy the fun outdoor pool here, but paws must stay on dry land. If you're here on a Sunday, you can attend a service at the on-site church. Your dog will have to say her prayers alone, because the church is for human animals only. Rates are $64–94. Dogs are $10 extra. 13070 Highway 33 South 95322; 209/826-4444.

Los Banos

PARKS, BEACHES, AND RECREATION AREAS

4 Los Banos Wildlife Area
🐾🐾🐾🐾🐕 (See Merced County map on page 580)

Dogs are allowed to roam leash-free here during certain times of the year, and the terrific news is that they don't have to be hunters' companions to do it. Unlike at so many other state wildlife areas, even dogs who just like to walk around and watch the birds fly by are permitted to experience this leash-free bliss.

The wildlife area is 5,568 acres of flat, grassy land with intermittent marshlands and ponds. You and your dog can walk just about anywhere on the dirt roads and levees here. With more than 200 species of birds, plenty of reptiles (including the rare giant garter snake), and many mammals, you'll have plenty to watch. Bring your binoculars and a good pair of walking shoes. Don't forget a towel for your dog. It can get muddy.

Camping is available February–mid-September. While there are no developed campsites, the Department of Fish and Game can suggest areas where you might find a good, very primitive site. There's no fee for camping. The day-use fee is $2.50, but that's waived if you have a valid hunting or fishing license or a California Wildlands Pass.

An important note: Dogs must be on leash April 1–June 30 because of nesting season. In addition, Los Banos is closed a few days every week in fall and winter, so be sure to phone the number below before venturing out here. From Highway 152, exit at Mercey Springs Road/Highway 165 and drive north for three miles to the wildlife area. 209/826-0463.

PLACES TO STAY

Best Western Executive Inn: This hotel looks more like a Federalist mansion than a Best Western. Some rooms even have a fireplace. Stay here and enjoy a pool, whirlpool, exercise room, and continental breakfast. Rates are $65–95. Dogs are $10 extra, and they prefer smaller dogs here. 301 West Pecheco Boulevard 93635; 209/827-0954.

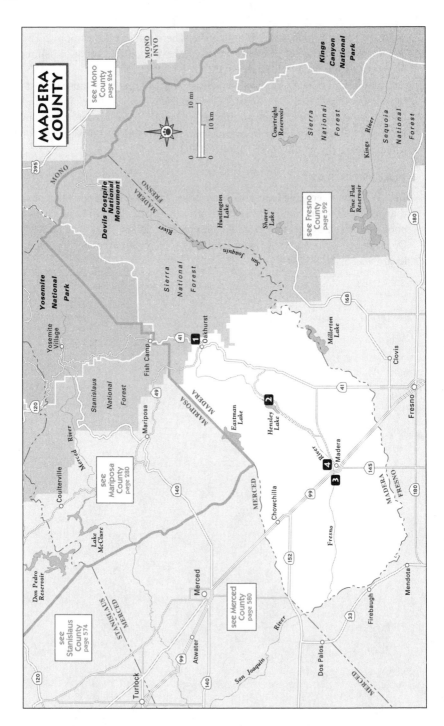

MADERA COUNTY

see Mono County page 264

see Fresno County page 592

see Mariposa County page 280

see Stanislaus County page 574

see Merced County page 580

CHAPTER 42

Madera County

Between the majestic Sierra National Forest and a couple of lakes where dogs can go leashless, Madera County is a hidden gem for dogs and their people. OK, so it's more like a tourmaline than a diamond. It still outshines many of the nearby areas.

NATIONAL FORESTS

The *National Forests and Wilderness Areas* resource at the back of this book has important information and safety tips on visiting national forests with your dog and has more information on the Sierra National Forest.

Sierra National Forest
🐾🐾🐾🐾🐕

PICK OF THE LITTER—MADERA COUNTY

BEST OFF-LEASH HIKE AND SWIM
Hensley Lake, Madera (page 590)

MOST BEAST-FRIENDLY PLACE TO STAY
Pine Rose Inn, Oakhurst (page 589)

NATIONAL MONUMENTS

Devils Postpile National Monument
☙☙☙

See the *Mammoth Lakes* section of the *Mono County* chapter for a description of Devil's Postpile. You can't get there from here, even though it's officially in Madera County.

NATIONAL PARKS

Yosemite National Park
☙☙☙

See the *Mariposa County* chapter for a detailed account of all the things dogs can and can't do at this wonderland.

Oakhurst

Many who live in this busy little foothills town consider Oakhurst the gateway to Yosemite. At about 15 miles from the south gateway to Yosemite National Park, it's certainly the closest town that has lots of amenities. Oakhurst is a good place to load up on dog treats, local crafts, fast food, and gasoline. It's also home to a couple of dog-friendly lodgings, should you care to spend the night here before (or after) your Yosemite adventure.

PARKS, BEACHES, AND RECREATION AREAS

■ Oakhurst Community Park
☙☙ (See Madera County map on page 586)

This is a really green, meadowy park that you can get to by crossing over a wooden footbridge from the Chamber of Commerce parking lot. It's very convenient for people on the go with a dog who's got to go.

A little dirt path encircles the park. You can walk around the park a few times to stretch all of your legs or relax in the gazebo or at a picnic table.

The park is just off Road 426 on Civic Circle. Follow the signs for the Chamber of Commerce. 559/683-7766.

PLACES TO EAT

Subway Sandwiches and Salads: Eat subs at the outdoor tables here. 425A Stagecoach Road; 559/683-3066.

PLACES TO STAY

Best Western Yosemite Gateway Inn: This inn is 17 miles from the south gate of Yosemite. Rates are $52–159. 40530 Highway 41 93644; 559/683-2378.

Pine Rose Inn: This bed-and-breakfast inn welcomes dogs as guests. "We love doggies and the people who come with them," says owner Anita Griffin. It's a beautiful place in a quiet mountain countryside setting just 12 miles from the south gate of Yosemite and two miles from Bass Lake. There's also plenty of hiking even closer to the inn.

Griffin has had some unusual guests. She once played hostess to a baby leopard so young his spots hadn't come out yet. A chimpanzee also made the inn his home for a few days while acting in a movie filmed in the area. "Obviously, good dogs are no problem at all," says Griffin.

You and your dog can stay in the main house or in one of five cottages. The rooms are full of country antiques, and some rooms even have fireplaces for those cold, wintry nights. A few rooms also have whirlpool tubs. This is the

perfect place to get away from it all. If the "it all" of the previous sentence means your dog for a while, the staff will be happy to arrange for a pet-sitter.

Rates are $79–169. The price includes a country breakfast. Dogs are $10 extra, as are children older than two. 41703 Road 222 93644; 559/642-2800; www.basslakeca.com/pineroseinn.

Madera

PARKS, BEACHES, AND RECREATION AREAS

As you'll note by the names of the two smaller parks, this is a very civic-minded area. I just want to know where the Shriners' park is—and what about those Masons?

☑ Hensley Lake

🐾🐾🐾🐾 🐕 (See Madera County map on page 586)

This 1,500-acre lake provides some choice fishing opportunities for you and your angling dog. With a launch fee of only $4, you can't lose, even if the bass aren't biting.

If you're the types who prefer to stick around terra firma, you'll be happy to know that the lake is surrounded by 1,500 acres of hilly land that you and your well-behaved dog can roam without a leash.

Visit in the springtime during the wildflower bloom if you really want a piece of paradise. If it's a tad warm, you'll find refreshing shade under the many oaks here. If it's still too warm for you, take a dip in the lake. Dogs are permitted to swim here, as long as they're not on the official beach areas. The day-use fee is $4. If you plan to go boating, the launch fee is $4. Dogs can also join you at the campground here. The rate is $14–20.

From Madera, drive northeast on Highway 145 for about six miles. Turn left on County Road 400 and drive 10 miles north to the lake. 559/673-5151.

For information on Eastman Lake, just northwest of Hensley Lake, call 559/689-3255. The setting, prices, and rules are pretty much the same as Hensley's. But apparently it's a trophy bass lake, should your dog really want to help you catch a lunker.

☑ Lions Town and Country Regional Park

🐾🐾🐾 (See Madera County map on page 586)

This charming park has lots of places to roam. The rolling hills and shaded meadows make it a fine park for an afternoon walk with your leashed dog.

A little canal runs through the park. Arched wooden footbridges take you over the waterway to more romping room. As long as there's not a baseball game going on, you won't have to worry about crowds.

The park is in the southwest part of town, at Howard Road, just east of Granada Drive. 559/661-5495.

🔵 Rotary Park

😺😺 (See Madera County map on page 586)

If you're cruising along Highway 99 and your dog starts crossing his legs and humming an unintelligible tune while avoiding direct eye contact with the bottle of water you've wedged between the seats, pull over here. The park has plenty of trees and lots of grass, even for the most discriminating dog's needs. If your kid happens to need a skate park at the same time, you're in luck.

Exit Highway 99 at Cleveland Avenue and drive east about a block to Gateway Drive (just before the railroad tracks). Turn right. The park will be on your right almost immediately. Snap on that leash and trot, don't walk, to the nearest tree. 559/661-5495.

PLACES TO STAY

Best Western Madera Valley Inn: Humans can enjoy the good-sized outdoor pool, the exercise room, and the continental breakfast here. Rooms come with a mini fridge, and some have a microwave. Rates are $56–85. Dogs are $15 extra. 317 North G Street 93637; 559/673-5164.

Days Inn: Rates are $65–75. Dogs are $5 extra. 25327 Avenue 16 93637; 559/674-8817.

Hensley Lake: See *Hensley Lake* for camping information.

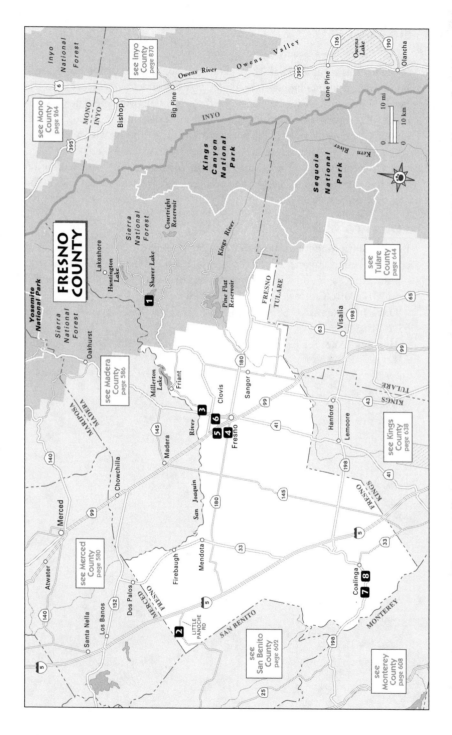

CHAPTER 43

Fresno County

At first glance, Fresno County seems like both an agricultural wonderland and a doggy wasteland. But your dog doesn't have to bite his toenails when he hears you're going to be spending some time exploring the area. The county has something for just about every dog's taste.

Rugged canines enjoy the leashless freedom they experience in the national forest and the Bureau of Land Management areas. And those with a more civilized bent enjoy the tinier, well-manicured city parks.

Dogs with a taste for olfactory offenses appreciate visits to the pungent section near the zoo at Fresno's Roeding Park and to the naturally stinky creek at Coalinga Mineral Springs. You may not be crazy about the odors, but it's worth a few moments of holding your breath to see that enraptured expression on your dog's quivering snout. Dogs who like to smell other dogs will be content with a visit to Fresno's two popular off-leash parks.

PICK OF THE LITTER—FRESNO COUNTY

BEST PLACE TO DOG-PADDLE
Shaver Lake, Shaver Lake (page 595)

BEST OFF-LEASH WILDFLOWER HIKE
Panoche Hills, Mercey Hot Springs (page 596)

BEST DOG PARK
El Capitan Dog Park, Fresno (page 598)

BEST STINKY PARK
Coalinga Mineral Springs Recreation Area, Coalinga
(page 600)

BEST PLACE FOR DOGS TO STAY
IF THE WIND IS JUST RIGHT
The Inn at Harris Ranch, Coalinga (page 601)

NATIONAL FORESTS

The *National Forests and Wilderness Areas* resource at the back of this book has important information and safety tips on visiting national forests with your dog and has more information on the Sierra National Forest.

Sierra National Forest

The cross-country skiing in some areas of this forest is first-rate. Leashless dogs love to bound along beside you as you slice through the snow.

NATIONAL PARKS

Kings Canyon National Park

See *Sequoia and Kings Canyon National Parks* in the *Tulare County* chapter for information on this not-so-dog-friendly park.

Lakeshore

A visit here will put you right on the shores of beautiful Huntington Lake. At an elevation of 7,000 feet, the lake is a great place to visit when it's roasty-toasty in the other parts of the state. It rarely gets too sizzling here.

PLACES TO STAY

Cedar Crest Resort: Depending on your style and mood, you and the pooch can stay at the resort's housekeeping cabins or floored tent cottages (concrete or wood floors with canvas sides and top and a bed inside). Joe Dog, who was not into roughing it, preferred the resort's higher-end cabins, which overlook Huntington Lake and have fireplaces and porches. Big pines surround most cabins here, and that was plenty of nature for a dog such as he was. You can even rent a "nonsinkable" boat here and putter around the lake with your pooch! Most dogs (unlike Joe the Landlubber) seem to enjoy a little cruise. Rates for the cabins are $105–170. The tent cottages are $35–40. Dogs are $5 extra. 61011 Cedar Crest Lane 93634; 559/893-3233; www.cedarcrestresort.com.

Lakeshore Resort: The managers at this 1920s-style mountain resort at Huntington Lake enjoy dog visitors. And if you have a pup-sitter and want to party, there's a saloon and dance hall on the premises. Rates are $85–150. Dogs are $15 extra. During certain times of year, the managers may ask that you sign a pooch release. 61953 Huntington Lake Road 93634; 559/893-3193; www.lakeshoreresort.com.

Shaver Lake

PARKS, BEACHES, AND RECREATION AREAS

1 Shaver Lake

🐾🐾🐾🐾 🐕 (See Fresno County map on page 592)

Although some of the land immediately surrounding this attractive lake is run by the county, even more of it is administered by the U.S. Forest Service. In fact, Sierra National Forest pretty much surrounds the lake. And you know what that means for dogs: No mandatory leashes on national forest land! (But be sure to leash up on county land.)

The lake is set at an elevation of 5,000 feet. There are 252 camping sites (at an area called Camp Edison), ranging $24–45 per site. Dogs are $4 extra. Reservations are highly recommended mid-June–mid-September. Call 559/841-3134 for reservations. Camp Edison is just one of several camping spots at Shaver Lake. Call the number below for info about the others, which are administered by another agency. Leashes are a must at the camping areas. From the town of Shaver Lake, follow Highway 168 north to the lake. 559/297-0706 or 559/855-5360.

Mercey Hot Springs

PARKS, BEACHES, AND RECREATION AREAS

2 Panoche Hills

🐾🐾🐾🐾 🐕 (See Fresno County map on page 592)

Panoche has panache! These 30,000 acres of rolling hills and grasslands are heaven to dogs who need more than just your average community park to make them feel like real dogs. Because the Bureau of Land Management operates it, obedient dogs are allowed to run around leashless. Keep a close eye on your dog, though, because the hills are home to endangered species such as the San Joaquin kit fox and the blunt-nosed leopard lizard.

Hilltops, some of which are more than 2,500 feet tall, give you great views of the lush San Joaquin Valley and the dramatic Sierra Nevada. And if you visit in the spring (by far the best time of year to come), you'll be treated to a spectacular wildflower bloom. The hilltops are also excellent for setting up a telescope and watching other worlds go by. Bring a hearty dinner and a blanket for your dog, and you couldn't ask for a better viewing station.

The hills are near Mercey Hot Springs, off County Road J1. You'll see the signs. Call before you visit so you can find out about any hunting that might be going on or closures due to fire danger. 831/630-5000.

Fresno

In the midst of the region's raisin growers and cattle rustlers lies Fresno, the heart of the Central Valley. And like all hearts that are anatomically correct (not like the kind you get on a Valentine's Day card), it's functional and essential but not too attractive.

Rest assured, there are some pretty good-looking parks in the midst of the malls and the cookie-cutter developments. Dogs are allowed on-leash in all city parks, and off-leash in three parks these days. If you have time to visit the charming Tower District, you may even start looking at Fresno in a different way. Or at least you'll start looking at Fresno.

PARKS, BEACHES, AND RECREATION AREAS

3 Woodward Dog Park and Woodward Park

🐾🐾🐾🐕 (See Fresno County map on page 592)

Situated within the beautiful and somewhat wild Woodward Park, this fenced one-acre dog park is a boon to dogs who want the best of both worlds. They need to be leashed when exploring regular parkland, but they can throw their leashes to the wind upon entering the dog park. When we last saw the park, it had just been reseeded with grass, so there was hope of greenery in the future. A couple of big trees provide some shade and some good aiming spots for boy dogs.

If you're going to pay the $3 parking fee to get into Woodward Park to get to the dog park, you might want to take advantage of Woodward Park itself. (Once again, leashes are the law outside the dog park.) With 299 acres of grassy meadows, rolling hills, big trees, trails, streams, lakes, and ponds, the park provides a much-needed refuge from life in Fresnoland. The park actually started out as a bird refuge. The sanctuary remains virtually untouched, but the surrounding parklands can be packed with people. It's not the kind of place your dog will want to visit on a weekend or just about any decent summer day. That's one reason the dog park is so handy—freedom from the masses and the leashes.

The parking fee February–October is $3 per car, but the rest of the year it's free. During the fee season, you can arrive before 9 A.M. to avoid the fee. You can also walk in and not have to pay. Driving north on Highway 41, exit at North Friant Road and drive northeast to East Audubon Drive. You'll be at the southeast corner of the park. Turn left and follow East Audubon Drive to the main entrance. You'll see signs for the dog park. 559/621-2900.

4 Kearney Park

🐾🐾🐾 (See Fresno County map on page 592)

People who visit this tree-filled 225-acre park may well think that the man for whom this park is named was a philanthropic sweetheart. After all, his huge mansion is in the middle of the park, and the land for the park was essentially his yard, surrounded by thousands of acres of his farmland. Anyone who would give that kind of property to the city must be a kindly gent, right?

But according to Dave Caglia, head of parks and grounds operations for the county, English-born Martin Kearney was an ornery, racist farmer who acquired his land through crooked deals. He was jilted by the love of his life and became ever richer and more bitter through the years. The raisin mogul turned into a woman-hating recluse and built this mansion, complete with 18-inch-thick walls.

When he died in the early 1900s (on a transatlantic ocean crossing, no less), he left some of the land to the University of California. In 1949, the university gave it to the county. It was the start of the Fresno County Park System.

The old guy may have been mean, but he sure knew how to make a pretty park. It's very popular—too popular for a dog's taste, at times. Don't come here with your dog on beautiful weekend afternoons unless you want to share it with the masses.

The park is filled with 100-year-old trees, including maples, palms, oaks, and eucalyptus trees that are seven feet across and 200 feet tall! Boy dogs can barely contain themselves. But they can't go too wild, because leashes are the law here.

There's a $5 day-use fee. The park is on Kearney Boulevard, seven miles west of Fresno. 559/488-3004.

5 Roeding Park Dog Park
🐾🐾🐾🐕 (See Fresno County map on page 592)

This decent-sized fenced park within Roeding Park has all the usual dog-park amenities, from water to poop bags to benches. It's a convenient place to come with your doggy if you're dropping off kids or friends at the Fresno Zoo, Playland, or Storyland—all of which make their home in the surrounding Roeding Park.

The part of 157-acre Roeding Park that's not the dog park or any of the attractions mentioned above is worth a sniff. Dogs have to be leashed, but they do enjoy the grass and trees in the sections where they're actually allowed. And ah, when the wind is right and they get a whiff of elephant or zebra poo, dogs are in olfactory heaven.

There's a $3 parking fee, or you can walk in free. Exit Highway 99 at Belmont or Olive Avenue and drive east to the park's main entrance. 559/621-2900.

6 El Capitan Dog Park
🐾🐾🐾🐾🐕 (See Fresno County map on page 592)

This is the kind of park dogs just drool to visit. It's fenced and tree-lined, with nearly 2.5 acres of grass. Dogs here have big smiles on their snouts as they run around and around and around.

On hot summer days, some folks bring plastic wading pools so dogs can cool their paws. The folks here are friendly, donating chairs to put under shade trees and making newcomers feel welcome. The park has wheelchair access, double gates for pooch security, lights, tables, poop bags, and water.

Please note that the park is actually built on land the city uses as an overflow area during heavy rains. The park can be closed at times during winter

because of flooding. When in doubt, phone the park department at the number below. The park is at El Capitan and Alamos streets, just off Shaw Avenue. 559/621-2900.

PLACES TO EAT

There seems to be an epidemic these days of Fresno restaurants saying no to dogs at their outdoor tables. We inquired in at least a dozen restaurants with outdoor tables and got only one that was OK with being in the book. Most told us, "It's against health regulations," or something along those lines. The health department may be a little too heavy handed here...

Bentley's Bistro: The salads and Cal-Med entrées here are fabulous. A friend recommends the slow roasted park tenderloin with caramelized apple and pear hash, roasted red potatoes, and seasonal veggies with a honey-brandy reduction. Dine with doggy at the patio. 9447 North Fort Washington; 559/892-4220.

PLACES TO STAY

Red Roof Inn: This one's located right off Highway 99. Rates are $49–74. The first dog is free, and the second is $20. 5021 North Barcus Avenue 93722; 559/276-1910.

TownePlace Suites: This all-suite Marriott hotel offers full kitchens and attractively furnished, comfortable suites. You'll also get free Wi-Fi, a tidy and quick breakfast, a pool, and even barbecue grills. It's clearly the kind of place that attracts business travelers staying more than one night. The dog fee will make you want to stay more than one night to get your money's worth: Room rates are $124–194, and dogs pay a $100 fee for the length of their stay. 7127 North Fresno Street; 559/435-4600.

Coalinga

PARKS, BEACHES, AND RECREATION AREAS

7 Coalinga Mineral Springs Recreation Area

🐾🐾🐾 (See Fresno County map on page 592)

Question: What smells like rotten eggs and attracts both man and beast? *Answer:* This park.

Leashed dogs love to come here because of the sulfur stench given off by the mineral-laden creek that runs through the park. Whenever Jake Dog starts staring at the ground as if he's just had an epiphany, I know we're either getting near one of these sulfur heavens or approaching a piece of roadkill.

Humans enjoy this flat 35-acre park because it's full of pines and surrounded by mountains. There are warnings against drinking the stinky creek water, but a local woman in her 80s has been drinking it for decades and at our last visit she looked mahhhvelous.

Camping here is secluded, primitive, and free. It's used mostly by hunters during wild boar season. You have to bring your own water and get prior written permission from the county parks department. You could stay back in the campground for a few days and never see a soul.

The day-use fee is $5. From Coalinga, drive northwest on Highway 198 for about 18 miles and turn right on Coalinga Mineral Springs Road. Continue five more miles to the park. 559/488-3004.

8 Coalinga Mineral Springs Scenic Trail

🐾🐾🐾🐾 🐕 (See Fresno County map on page 592)

Adjoining Coalinga Mineral Springs Recreation Area county park are 9,000 acres of open land run by the dog-friendly Bureau of Land Management. If the 35-acre county park doesn't satisfy you or your dog, continue to the adjacent BLM land and let the good times roll you through the grasslands. Just watch out for the occasional rocky outcropping.

The best part of this adventure is that if your dog is very obedient, you can let him run around leashless. But the 2.5-mile trail is also an equestrian trail, so if your dog thinks horses are giant dogs just waiting to be chased, keep him on his leash. Also be aware that deer live in the area surrounding the trail. If you aren't absolutely certain that your dog won't bound off after one, do everyone a favor and don't unleash him.

The hike is not for the fair of paw, since it can be steep. But if you and your dog are in good shape, it's worth the exertion. The trail leads you to Kreyenhagen Peak, where you'll have wonderful views of the southern Diablo Mountains. Come in the spring and watch the wildflowers go wild. In the warmer months, it can be mighty toasty and parched here.

We've heard that ticks can be a real problem at times. Call 831/630-5000 for information, advice, and a schedule of when hunters might be shooting at the deer and other critters you and your dog are trying to avoid. The trail starts where the county park leaves off. From Coalinga, drive northwest on Highway 198 for about 18 miles and turn right on Coalinga Mineral Springs Road. Continue five more miles to the park. 559/488-3004.

PLACES TO STAY

The Inn at Harris Ranch: Ahh, Spanish-style architecture and the smell of broiling beef wafting into your room from the famed steak-o-rama next door. What more could a dog want? The only smell that could make this place more appealing to dogs is that of the very whiffy Harris Ranch feedlot, but it's eight miles away. Unless the wind is just right, dogs are out of luck. Rates are $135–295. Dogs are $2 extra. It's just off I-5 at the Highway 198/Hanford-Lemoore exit. The location is 24505 West Dorris Street, and the mailing address is Route 1, P.O. Box 777 93210; 559/935-0717; www.harrisranch.com.

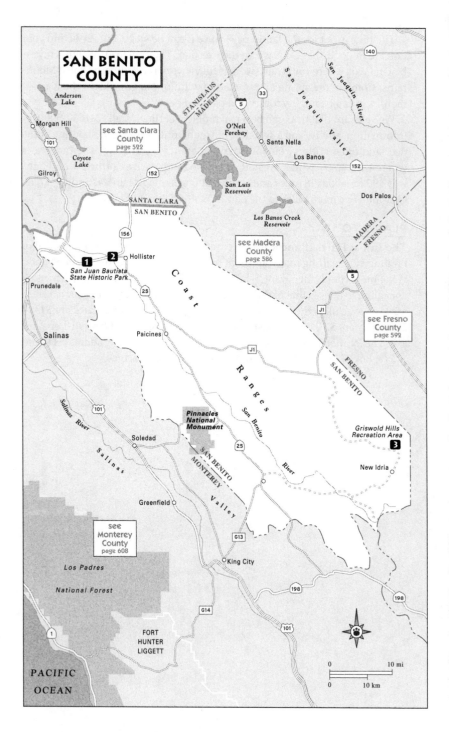

SAN BENITO COUNTY

Anderson Lake

Morgan Hill

101

Coyote Lake

Gilroy

152

STANISLAUS
MADERA

5

33

O'Neil Forebay

Santa Nella

San Joaquin River

San Joaquin Valley

140

Los Banos

152

see Santa Clara County page 522

San Luis Reservoir

Dos Palos

SANTA CLARA
SAN BENITO

156

1 2 Hollister

San Juan Bautista State Historic Park

Prunedale

25

Los Banos Creek Reservoir

see Madera County page 586

MADERA
FRESNO

5

J1

see Fresno County page 592

Salinas

Paicines

J1

Coast

Ranges

FRESNO
SAN BENITO

Salinas River

101

Pinnacles National Monument

Soledad

25

San Benito River

Griswold Hills Recreation Area 3

New Idria

Salinas

SAN BENITO
MONTEREY

Greenfield

see Monterey County page 608

Valley

G13

Los Padres

National Forest

King City

198

198

1

G14

FORT HUNTER LIGGETT

101

PACIFIC OCEAN

0   10 mi

0   10 km

CHAPTER 44

San Benito County

If you look at a map of this county, you may wonder, "What's a dog to do here?" Joe Dog looked as if he were being sent to purgatory the first time I told him we were going to visit San Benito County. He sat at the front door of the house and wouldn't budge. When I tried pulling him, he tugged back and slipped out of his collar. But since I had longer legs, a stronger body, and a box of desiccated liver treats, I won the battle. He gulped down the bait, frowned, and succumbed to his fate.

He must have remembered those vast stretches of privately owned nothingness we once drove across on the way from nowhere to not-much-of-anyplace-else. Even *I* wanted to be anywhere but there. But our last visit was different. It wasn't heaven, but it wasn't hell either.

PICK OF THE LITTER—SAN BENITO COUNTY

BEST EARLY CALIFORNIA LORE
San Juan Bautista State Historic Park, San Juan Bautista
(page 604)

BEST OFF-LEASH HIKE
Griswold Hills Recreation Area, New Idria (page 606)

San Juan Bautista

Be sure to swing by the Mission San Juan Bautista when you visit this town, especially if you and your dog are fans of Alfred Hitchcock. The mission (the largest of the old California missions) starred in the Hitchcock classic *Vertigo.* It's worth a peek, but dogs have to stay firmly planted on the ground outside. Jimmy Stewart would have envied the stance.

If you're hungry, don't let all the restaurants with outdoor tables fool you. We couldn't find any eateries that would permit pooches. But as the pendulum swings, we don't expect that to last for long.

PARKS, BEACHES, AND RECREATION AREAS

1 San Juan Bautista State Historic Park
🐾🐾🐾 (See San Benito County map on page 602)

Leashed dogs who like local history are welcome to accompany you as you tour this small state park. You'll see buildings such as the old Plaza Hotel, which was a popular stagecoach stop, and the Castro House, at one time the administrative headquarters of Mexican California. But since dogs must stay outside such buildings, they prefer to tour the livery stables, gardens, and orchards.

The park is on the plaza in the center of town. Admission is $2 per adult. Call 831/623-4881.

PLACES TO STAY

San Juan Inn: If you and your pooch are looking for a quiet spot to spend the night, stay here. Rates are $69–89. Dogs are $15 extra. 410 Alameda Street 95045; 831/623-4380.

Hollister

PARKS, BEACHES, AND RECREATION AREAS

There used to be one city park that had some decent room to walk around with a leashed dog, but now it's been developed into oblivion, like the rest of the city's parks. Sure, people need basketball courts and softball fields and barbecue areas, but there should be some room just to explore nature, too. Fortunately there's a county park here that does the trick.

🐾 San Justo Reservoir County Park

🐾🐾🐾 (See San Benito County map on page 602)

You and your leashed dog are free to hike on the dirt trail/fire road that encircles this 580-acre park. Many folks like to come here to fish at the 200-acre reservoir, but dogs generally prefer to amble through the open land. It's not the most attractive place in the world, but it beats the backyard.

The day-use fee is $5 per vehicle. You can launch your boat from here for a mere $2–3. You can also rent a boat here, if you don't have your own. The park is west of town. Exit Highway 156 at Union Road and drive south. The park will be on your right in a little less than a mile, at 2265 Union Road. Hours are limited, so call 831/638-3300 for a schedule.

Bitterwater

PLACES TO STAY

Pinnacles National Monument: Dogs are permitted only in picnic areas, parking lots, and paved roads, so they miss exploring all the fascinating pinnacle-shaped volcanic rock formations within. It's not much fun for your pooch, but you can console her with a good camping experience.

A privately operated campground, Pinnacles Campground (not to be confused with the Pinnacles National Monument campground, which is now closed), permits pooches, although it discourages them because the area is a wildlife preserve. The staff is diligent about dogs being on leash at all times. You can get to this 90-site campground from San Benito County, which leads into the east end of the park. Campsites are $10–30. Dogs are $3 extra.

Reservations are required for groups of 10 or more. Should you just want to explore around the park for the day, it costs $5 per vehicle, or $3 per person if you enter on foot. To get to this campground: From Highway 25 about 13 miles north of Bitterwater (32 miles south of Hollister), take Highway 146 southwest to the park. The Pinnacle Campground phone number is 831/389-4462. The number at the Pinnacles National Monument headquarters is 831/389-4485.

New Idria

PARKS, BEACHES, AND RECREATION AREAS

🖪 Griswold Hills Recreation Area

😊😊😊😊 🐕 (See San Benito County map on page 602)

Some small city parks I've explored are run by departments that tell you the parks' acreage down to the hundredth of an acre. When you're dealing with parks that are 3.21 acres, you want to count every square inch.

But then along comes the Bureau of Land Management. In its written material, it says Griswold Hills is "several thousand acres." We're not talking exact measurements here. But that's the charm of these off-leash BLM havens. Precision and rules are left at the gate (when there is a gate). Rules exist, but few restrict a well-behaved dog's good time.

This recreation area is made up of rugged canyons of scrub oak, juniper, and chaparral. Some trails take you to ridge tops for good views of the surrounding valleys. Others take you to the riparian zone at Griswold Creek. Not many people

know about this area, so if you and your dog need to get away from it all, there's a good chance you can.

The park isn't as big or as scenic as the BLM's nearby 50,000-acre Clear Creek Management Area. But we don't recommend that area for people who worry about things such as asbestosis, mesothelioma, or cancer. Because of naturally occurring asbestos, you and your dog are supposed to wear protective clothing and respirators when setting paw on much of the land. It's not worth it.

The main entrance to Griswold Hills is three miles south of Panoche Road on New Idria Road. Watch out for hunters during deer and quail seasons. Call 831/630-5000 for hunting dates and more information on local BLM lands.

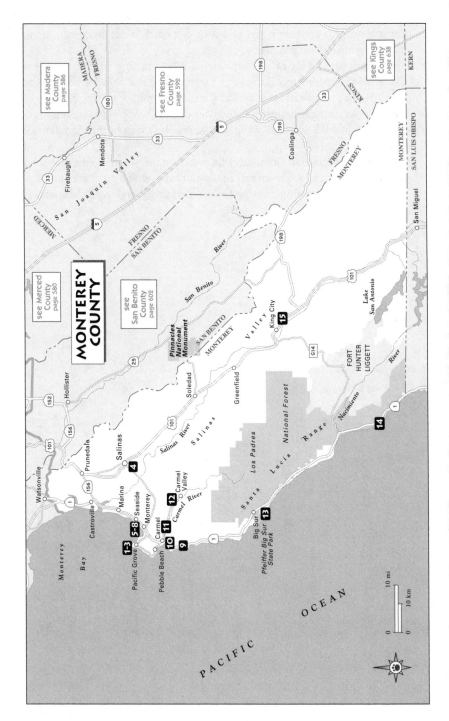

CHAPTER 45

Monterey County

Native son John Steinbeck and his fearless blue poodle, Charley, visited here during their cross-country journey recorded in the 1961 classic, *Travels with Charley*. The Gentle Reader is never sure what Charley did while his master paid homage to old bars and old memories in Monterey and Salinas, but wherever Charley went in this county, he probably felt as accepted as his human friend. Monterey County is as warm and welcoming as an old Italian aunt.

The Carmel area is one of the most dog-friendly places on earth. In fact, dogs are almost de rigueur here. With each edition of this book, it just keeps getting better. Dog-loving restaurants and inns abound. A couple of them offer dogs their own menus. Dogs are welcome at many theatrical productions at the Forest Theater. And there's Rodrigue Studio, which welcomes dogs by giving them biscuits in a crystal dish and letting them peruse the artwork.

If going leashless is your dog's fantasy, Carmel, Carmel Valley, and Pacific Grove are ideal stopping points. Their designated off-leash romping grounds are as picturesque as their cozy inns. And your dog would never forgive you if

PICK OF THE LITTER—MONTEREY COUNTY

BEST OFF-LEASH BEACH AND PARK
Carmel City Beach, Carmel (page 622)
Mission Trail Park, Carmel (page 623)

BEST DOGGY MENUS
The Forge in the Forest, Carmel (page 624)
Lenny's Deli, Carmel (page 625)

MOST DOG-FRIENDLY PLACES TO EAT
Trailside Cafe, Monterey (page 617)
Big Dog Sports Restaurant, Carmel (page 623)
Bubbly Fish Cafe, Carmel (page 624)
Le Coq d'Or, Carmel (page 625)
Portabella, Carmel (page 625)

MOST DOG-FRIENDLY PLACES TO STAY
Best Western Victorian Inn, Monterey (page 619)
Cypress Inn, Carmel (page 628)
Lamp Lighter Inn, Carmel (page 629)
Lincoln Green Inn, Carmel (page 629)
Sunset House, Carmel (page 630)
Carmel Valley Lodge, Carmel Valley (page 633)

BEST PLACE TO GET AWAY FROM IT ALL
Rosehaven Cabins, Big Sur (page 635)

COOLEST PLACE TO SCORE A PAINTING
Rodrigue Studio, Carmel (page 622)

BEST DOG-FRIENDLY THEATRICS
Forest Theater, Carmel (page 622)

TOP-NOTCH SHOPPING SPOT
Carmel Plaza, Carmel (page 621)

you forgot the northern segment of the magnificent Los Padres National Forest for a hearty leashless hike.

In addition, a two-hour walking tour welcomes dogs on its stroll through Carmel. Your dog will have a doggone great time, because part of the tour is devoted to the dogginess here.

I'm sad to report that dogs are now banned from several state beaches in the county. (The entire town of Moss Landing was wiped out of this book because the three beaches there now ban dogs. It's a sweet seaside community and worth sniffing out; just don't expect to be able to beach it there.) The blame has been placed squarely on the feathered shoulders of the questionably threatened bird, the snowy plover, but I've also heard it may have had something to do with other beach users getting annoyed at dogs whose people let them run around leashless despite the leash laws. Fortunately, enough beaches welcome dogs that you won't have to see yours cry in his kibble during your visit to magnificent Monterey County.

NATIONAL FORESTS

The *National Forests and Wilderness Areas* resource at the back of this book has important information and safety tips on visiting national forests with your dog and has more information on the Los Padres National Forest.

Los Padres National Forest
😺😺😺😺 🐕

This spectacular, rugged terrain in the Big Sur area is great for an outing with a spectacular, rugged dog. Actually, even spectacular couch-potato dogs can enjoy some of the hikes here in the Ventana Wilderness.

Pacific Grove

This quaint town on the rocky coast is a good place to get away from the crowds that can sometimes smother you and your dog during the peak tourist season in its neighboring city, Monterey. And if you like Monarch butterflies, Pacific Grove is your kind of town: It's known as Butterfly City, U.S.A., because of the millions of Monarch butterflies that winter here every year.

PARKS, BEACHES, AND RECREATION AREAS

1 Asilomar State Beach
😺😺😺 (See Monterey County map on page 608)

The beach here is great fun for leashed dogs. Not only do they get to romp on prime beach land, but they also can watch whales in the fall and winter and see what real tidepooling is all about year-round.

Tucked in and around this rugged shoreline are a vast variety of marine critters representative of the Central Coast. I've seen dogs try to eat the contents of tidepools—a dining activity that should be strictly forbidden. And for your dog's safety, don't take him on slippery rocks or let him get too close to the surf, where there can be hazardous rip currents.

Park along the shore on Sunset Drive, across from the Asilomar Conference Grounds. For sandy beach, park along the south end of Sunset Drive. 831/649-2836 or 831/372-4076.

🐾 George Washington Park

🐾🐾🐾 🐕 (See Monterey County map on page 608)

If you're dining at any of Pacific Grove's many outdoor eateries in the village center and your dog starts crossing his legs, have no fear, this park is near. And better yet, part of the park is devoted to off-leash dogs during certain times of the day.

Dogs may run leashless sunrise–9 A.M. and 4 P.M.–sunset. During winter, those hours can be a little restrictive, but it's better than nothing.

The segment of the park for leash-free canines is bounded by Short Street, Melrose Avenue, Alder Street, and Pine Avenue. Dogs are allowed on leash in the entire park (except developed areas like the ball field and playground) at any time during the day. 831/648-5730.

🐾 Lynn "Rip" Van Winkle Open Space

🐾🐾🐾🐾 🐕 (See Monterey County map on page 608)

This scrub oak haven near Pebble Beach is large enough so that even dogs who tend to wander out of sight aren't in much danger of wandering into the road. Dogs may be leashless sunrise–9 A.M. and 4 P.M.–sunset.

You'll find many a dog and many a dog person here during the off-leash hours. They tend to congregate near the park's entrance, but if your dog would prefer walking to talking, there are plenty of trails leading through the twisted scrub oaks and the small clear areas of the park.

The entrance can be hard to find. Follow the nontoll section of 17 Mile Drive south and go left on Sunset Drive, then right on Congress Avenue. Pass Forest Grove Elementary School on your left. Within a few hundred yards, you'll see a dirt parking area on your right. There's no sign, but this is the main entrance to the open space. 831/648-3100.

PLACES TO EAT

Bagel Bakery: It's bagels, bagels, bagels at this dog-friendly eatery. Get some bagel bones (twice-baked, extra hard bagels) for your dog while you nosh on a bagel sandwich, a bagel with schmear, or a plain old naked bagel. Dine together at the outdoor tables. 1132 Forest Avenue; 831/649-6272.

Goodies: The food here is fresh and tasty. Choose from any of about 10,000 sandwiches. (OK, 30 sandwiches, but what a variety—my favorite is the Mediterraneo, with feta, olives, spinach, cukes, and their ilk.) Thanks to Tracy and her dog, Chewbacca, for recommending Goodies to us. They have good taste. Dine with your pooch at several tables on the sunny patio. 518 Lighthouse Avenue; 831/655-3663.

PLACES TO STAY

Andril Fireplace Cottages: In these homey cottages, it's easy to get away from it all or to be on top of it all: All the separate cottages in this quiet area have cable TV, with VCRs for the asking. They also have wood-burning fireplaces, perfect for snuggling up with a human friend and a dog friend after a long day exploring the nearby beach. Rates are $80–190. Dogs are $14 extra. 569 Asilomar Boulevard 93950; 831/375-0994; www.andrilcottages.com.

Lighthouse Lodge and Suites: This used to be a Best Western, but now it's quite a lovely hotel, with upgraded rooms and a cool website. You'll get luxury (and very comfy beds) on a semibudget. Humans get to enjoy the pool, spa, and breakfast. Dogs get to enjoy sniffing the surrounding Monterey Pines. Rates are $89–164. Dogs are $25 extra. 1150 Lighthouse Avenue 93950; 831/655-2111 or 800/858-1249; www.lhls.com.

Olympia Motor Lodge: You and your dog can sit on your private balcony and contemplate life while staring at the ocean from a distance of about a quarter mile. This is a clean, decent lodge. Rooms come with down comforters. Rates are $88–180. Dogs are $30 extra. 1140 Lighthouse Avenue 93950; 831/373-2777; www.theolympialodge.com.

Salinas

The "Salad Bowl of the World" was one of Joe Dog's favorite places to visit on a Sunday drive. Most other city dogs we've talked to agree that it's a grand olfactory experience. When Joe smelled the chicken manure spread across great fields of green and saw horses readying for the rodeo, his nostrils shivered and his eyes bugged out, making him look very cartoony.

PARKS, BEACHES, AND RECREATION AREAS

4 Toro Regional Park

😾😾😾😾 (See Monterey County map on page 608)

This is the only park in the Salinas area where you and your dog can really take a hike. More than 4,500 acres of wilderness await leashed pooches. About 12 miles of hiking and horse trails are etched into the rolling foothills of Mt. Toro. As you climb, you'll occasionally be rewarded with shade from oak trees. It can be very hot in the summer, so be sure to bring extra water for you and your dog.

The views up high are spectacular. You can see both the Salinas Valley and the Monterey Bay, depending on where you hike. The park also features a self-guided nature trail adjacent to a gentle creek, as well as many picnic sites and play areas in the flat green valley near the parking lots.

Remember, as always when you travel with your dog, to have him wear his rabies tag or to bring along other proof of his rabies vaccination. Staff is going to ask to see it before letting your dog in. From Salinas, follow Highway 68 west about five miles to the signs for the park. The park's entrance is just a few hundred yards from the highway. Fees are $4 per vehicle on weekdays, $6 on weekends. 831/755-4899.

PLACES TO STAY

The lodgings that accommodate dogs here may not be fancy, but they're excellent places to relax and watch bad TV with your dog after a day of traveling.

Motel 6: Rates are $44–55 for the first adult, $6 for the second. 1257 De La Torre Boulevard 93905; 831/757-3077.

Vagabond Inn: Close to U.S. 101, this is where Joe and I once stayed and encountered at least five other dogs who were also guests. Rates are $59–189. (That upper limit seems like a lot of dough for a Vagabond Inn room.) Dogs are $10 extra. 131 Kern Street 93905; 831/758-4693.

Pebble Beach

PLACES TO STAY

The Lodge at Pebble Beach: Jack Lemmon brought his poodle here. Other golf-loving celebs still do. This magnificent lodge, adjacent to the Pebble Beach Golf Links, is as dog-friendly as it is distinguished.

The place is beautiful on the outside and like home (if your home is gorgeous and has spectacular views) on the inside. Most rooms have a fireplace, and all are lovely, with a wet bar, an honor-stocked fridge, and a patio or deck with to-drool-for views. In your bathroom you'll find an extra phone and a plush terry robe.

All this is fine with dogs, but what they really love about The Lodge is that it's a dog-adoring place. "We love doggies!" says the concierge, and she means it. The staff stocks treats at several strategically located points in the lobby, including the concierge desk, the bell desk, and the front desk. And even better than this, dogs get to explore the large, wooded area surrounding the inn. If they're really well behaved, you can let them be leashless! The paths here are splendid. Be forewarned, though, that you might be sharing the paths with horses, so if your dog is a chaser, keep that leash on.

Rates are $610–1,875. The lodge is on 17 Mile Drive. When you call for reservations, you can get directions. The address is simply 17 Mile Drive 93953; 831/647-7500 or 800/654-9300; www.pebblebeach.com.

Monterey

Although there's nowhere to legally let your dog off leash here just yet (it's in sight at El Estero Park, though), Monterey is still a grand stomping ground for dogs and their people. A few activities you can enjoy with your dog include taking in the sights of old/new Cannery Row, fishing off Municipal Wharf No. 2, and watching sea otters frolic about Monterey Bay.

PARKS, BEACHES, AND RECREATION AREAS

Leashed dogs are welcome on city beaches and county parks near Monterey but dogs are allowed to set paw in only five Monterey city parks. El Estero Park is the best of these, and there's really good news: It's slated to have its own dog park in the near future!

5 El Estero Park

🐾🐾🐾 (See Monterey County map on page 608)

Yahoo! At press time, plans were underway to create an off-leash park at this grand 45-acre centrally located park. It's going to be under a eucalyptus grove. Stay tuned for details in the next edition, when we hope the dog park is up and running.

Dogs are advised to stay away from this park's best feature, Dennis the Menace Playground (designed by the comic's creator, Hank Ketcham). But while the kids frolic on the playground's steam engine, roller slide, and giant swing ride, you and the dog can walk around El Estero Lake.

It's a fun walk for leashed dogs and their people. If you like bird-watching (and what dog doesn't?), you'll enjoy the ducks and migrating birds who hang out on the lake. Benches and picnic tables are scattered around this well-manicured tree-filled park, so you can really make an afternoon of it.

If you're heading from Highway 1 to the Cannery Row area of Monterey, you'll run right into the park. Exit Highway 1 at the Central Monterey exit. Stay in the right lane and go right on Camino Aguajito. The park will be immediately on your left. You'll get to the best parking area by going left on 3rd Street. 831/646-3866.

6 Jack's Peak Regional Park

🐾🐾🐾🐾 (See Monterey County map on page 608)

Some of the most stunning views of the Monterey Bay, Carmel Valley, and Santa Lucia Mountain Range can be seen from 1,068-foot Jack's Peak, the highest point on the Monterey Peninsula. You and your leashed dog will love the cool Pacific Ocean breezes that sweep through the pine-covered ridges and cathedral-like forests.

On the 8.5 miles of intersecting trails (including a self-guided nature trail), you and your dog can make a day of it or just take in a little fresh air for a half

DIVERSION

Take Someone Furry on a Surrey: Chicks and ducks and geese better scurry when you take your dog on a bicycle-powered surrey from **Bay Bikes,** on the famous Cannery Row. The surreys come complete with a fringe at the top. And so what if the dashboard isn't genuine leather? These surreys have baskets in the front, perfect for small- or medium-sized dogs. You and a friend can pedal up and down Monterey's scenic Recreation Trail while your dog just sits back and takes in the scents and sights. Folks who know recommend bringing a jacket or something soft and comfy for your dog to sit on. Wire baskets and dog tushies just don't mix.

Large surreys fit six adults and two children and cost $30 per hour. Smaller surreys fit fewer people, but they're only $20 per hour. 640 Wave Street (under the carousel); 831/646-9090.

---

hour. Jake enjoys the Pine Trail, which starts at the Jack's Peak parking area. This is also where you'll find one of the last three remaining native stands of Monterey pine in the world.

The best time to visit here is the spring, when the meadows are blanketed with wildflowers. But this park is worth a visit any time of year.

Fees are $3 on weekdays and $4 on weekends. Be sure to bring your dog's rabies tag or other proof of rabies vaccination, because it's required of all dogs. From Monterey, take Highway 68 east a couple of miles and go right on Olmstead Road. Then turn left on Jack's Peak Road and follow the signs to the park. 831/755-4899.

7 Monterey State Beach
😀😀😀 (See Monterey County map on page 608)
The entire state beach is actually made up of three segments spanning a few miles. But these days, dogs are permitted only at one section. If you're strolling along the Recreation Trail here and your dog needs to go roll in some sand, hit the beach at Del Monte Avenue, at the foot of Park Avenue. The official "dogs OK" area runs from just east of the Municipal Wharf to Seaside State Beach. 831/649-2836.

8 Recreation Trail
😀😀😀 (See Monterey County map on page 608)
Stretching five miles from Lover's Point in Pacific Grove (no dogs allowed in the little Lover's Point Park) past Cannery Row and into Seaside, this paved bike and walking path is a great way to see Monterey.

You and your leashed dog can get your fill of sightseeing and exercise here. You can sit on one of the many benches that dot the trail and watch some of the world's most fascinating marinelife. Jake the Dog likes to check out the mama otters wrapping their babes in kelp before they swim off to forage for food. He could stare for hours at the bobbing babes, but fortunately, the mothers return pretty quickly.

You can start the trail anywhere, but many folks like to start at Fisherman's Wharf. Although dogs aren't allowed on the wharf, this is where smaller dogs get to embark on one of the most fun adventures known to canines: riding on a bike, while you pedal.

PLACES TO EAT

Captain's Gig Restaurant: Ahoy, matey! Got a thirsty dog? Take him to the outdoor tables at this Fisherman's Wharf restaurant. Water is available upon request, as are some scrumptious fish burgers. 6 Fisherman's Wharf #1; 831/373-5559.

Tarpy's Roadhouse: When you and your good dog dine at the courtyard tables at this turn-of-the-20th-century roadhouse, you'll know why this is such a popular place. The wonderful California-American country cuisine, understated elegance, and beautiful gardens make it special indeed. If you're a fan of grilled food, your mouth will water over any food that comes from Tarpy's wood-burning grill. Something dogs like to dream about is the grilled Angus rib eye with herb au jus. Jake Dog gets weak in the knees even thinking about it. Tarpy's is right next door to the dog-friendly Monterey Stone Chapel, which makes Tarpy's a perfect place for a post-wedding dinner. 2999 Monterey-Salinas Highway; 831/647-1444.

Trailside Cafe: Tired of the crowds on Cannery Row, but hungry? Come here! It's just a short jog off the main drag, and the patio is a peaceful place to eat with a pooch. Dogs get treated like canine kings at the Trailside Cafe. The friendly folks here always give dogs a treat or two and make them feel right at home. Doggy water is always available for the asking. There's even a sign on the adjacent Recreation Trail that says Dogs Welcome on Patio. You can get breakfast or lunch here. Vegetarians like the grilled portobello burger. Meat eaters and their dogs slobber over the New York steak sandwich. And if you're in the mood to eat something whose cousin you've visited at the Monterey Bay Aquarium, try the Monterey sand dabs, which are lightly sautéed in a caper-lemon sauce. The café is a short walk from the Best Western Victorian Inn, at 550 Wave Street; 831/649-8600.

PLACES TO STAY

Bay Park Hotel: Plenty of trees surround this lodging, so dogs who like shade or leg lifts enjoy a stay here. Humans get use of the attractive pool and hot tub. Rates are $99–199. Dogs are $20 extra. 1425 Munras Avenue 93940; 831/649-1020 or 800/338-3564; www.bayparkhotel.com.

The Beach Resort: This Best Western is one of Jake's favorites. From his

DIVERSION

Tie the Knot, Bring Spot: If, while saying your wedding vows at the enchanting **Monterey Stone Chapel,** you begin to feel someone's cold nose nuzzling your ankle, don't blame a fresh guest or an eager spouse. It's just your dog. Probably.

The Monterey Stone Chapel is a terrific place to get hitched with your favorite pooch at your side. Owner Patt O'Brien loves dogs, especially dogs who don't mistake the green carpeting in the chapel for grass. The only dog who ever did that was her three-pound Yorkie, and he did it when he was only a puppy. When something that small does his business, you almost need a magnifying glass to clean it up.

O'Brien has been through it all with dogs at weddings. One time, a dapper Lab in a bow tie threw up all over his master's shiny shoes in the middle of the ceremony. Once a little Jack Russell bit one of the guests at his person's wedding. ("It was mayhem," she says.) But most of O'Brien's dog weddings go without a hitch (so to speak).

The chapel itself is a real looker. Unlike so many of its brethren, it's completely unkitschy, with a big stone fireplace, white lace curtains, and handmade wrought-iron candelabras. If you prefer to hold your ceremony in the chapel garden, the setting outside the chapel is a photographer's dream, complete with a little lake, redwoods (a boy dog's dream), and a wrought-iron archway. O'Brien can even set up your ceremony at one of many breathtaking outdoor coastal locations. Her business is called **A By-the-Sea Wedding,** and once you check out her favorite spots, you'll know why. Another real plus about getting hitched here: The terrific Tarpy's Roadhouse is right next door. It's a superb place to unwind after tying the knot.

The price is right, too. O'Brien will marry you with your dogs and a couple of friends at your side outside the chapel for $250. Three to 10 guests costs $300, and for 11 to 50 guests you pay only $400. For an additional $75, she can supply you the required license so you can get married as quickly as California law allows—and in some cases, that means lickety-split.

For more information, write to O'Brien at A By-the-Sea Wedding, 2999 Monterey-Salinas Highway, Suite 3, Monterey, CA 93940, or call 831/375-8574.

first-floor room (dogs are restricted to ground level) he can see the beach, gulls walking around, and girls in bikinis. But what he likes even more is the easy access to Monterey State Beach. Rates are $99–489. Dogs are $50 extra in ocean-view rooms, $25 extra elsewhere. (I still haven't figured out this price difference. Maybe dogs shed more when they see the ocean?) 2600 Sand Dunes Drive 93940; 831/394-3321 or 800/242-8627; www.montereybeachresort.com.

Best Western Victorian Inn: Dogs and their people are welcome to stay in the first-floor rooms of this charming hotel. You can't actually stay in the main beautiful Victorian house here. (That's for curling up with your dog in front of the marble fireplace and other such cozy activities.) But the simple country Victorian-style rooms in the more modern part of the hotel are just fine with the inn's happy dog and human guests. Many of the rooms have fireplaces, too, should you like to curl up in the comfort of your own room.

The best part of the deal for your furry roommate is that dogs who stay here get a Pooch Package with a dog bowl (with the inn's logo), tasty dog cookies, and bottled water. It's the dog's meow! People get to enjoy a good continental breakfast, and in the evening, a wine and cheese reception. All this is included with your room. Rates are $199–299. Dogs are $30 extra and they pay a $150 deposit (fully refundable). 487 Foam Street 93940; 831/373-8000 or 800/232-4141; www.victorianinn.com.

El Adobe Inn: Some of the 26 rooms at this clean motor lodge have bay views. Rates are $49–199. Dogs are $10 extra. A continental breakfast comes with your stay. 936 Munras Avenue 93940; 831/372-5409; www.el-adobe-inn.com.

Hyatt Regency Monterey: The hotel is made up of 26 three-story buildings with 30 rooms each. It takes 10 minutes to walk from one end of the well-manicured hotel property to the other, so it's not exactly an intimate place. Dogs are relegated to Building 16, which isn't known for its great views. But they don't care: The rooms are comfortable, and right outside the building is a big, grassy, tree-dotted area set aside for dogs. It's not fenced, and dogs need to be leashed, but they don't have to feel guilty going to the bathroom there, as they might in other parts of the hotel's landscaping. (Of course, scoop no matter where the poop happens.)

You can choose from many leisure-time activities. The hotel has a great golf course, a racquet club with several tennis courts, two outdoor pools with whirlpools, and a pretty decent poolside fitness center. Or you can just take your dog for a stroll on some nearby paths. (Your dog wants you to choose this exercise option.) Rates are $139–350. There's also a $10 resort fee per night. Dogs are $50 extra for the length of their stay. 1 Old Golf Course Road 93490; 831/372-1234 or 800/824-2196; www.monterey.hyatt.com.

Monterey Bay Lodge: Dogs like staying here because it's relatively close to Monterey Bay (less than two blocks). They can wake up and sniff the crabby breezes. Dogs of most sizes are welcome but the lodge staff prefers no "really huge dogs." Rates are $95–130. Dogs require a $100 deposit and are $15 extra. 55 Camino Aguajito Road 93940; 831/372-8057 or 800/558-1900; www .montereybaylodge.com.

Monterey Fireside Lodge: Stay here and your dog gets a treat that's almost as good as a dog biscuit: "I'll pet them and give them lots of love," says Steve, the innkeeper. The stipulation for dogs who stay here (besides being clean, well behaved, and never being left alone in the room or let on the beds): "The dog has to be cute," says Steve, who luckily thinks every dog is just the best.

The lodge is really a motel with pretty clothes. Every room has a gas fireplace, and many come with a fridge and microwave. The rooms are nothing fancy, but since when do dogs need fancy? Rates are $59–359. Dogs are $20 extra. 1131 10th Street 93940; 831/373-4172 or 800/722-2624; www.fireside monterey.com.

Motel 6: This is one of the most attractive Motel 6s we've ever seen: There's no trucker area, which makes for quieter nights, and the place has some tenderly cared-for landscaping, even around the little pool. It's very close to the heart of Monterey (albeit on cheapy motel row), so although it's one of the more pricey Motel 6s, it's a real deal. Rates are $50–130 for the first adult (that upper end seems like a lot for a Motel 6, even one as nice as this one), $6 for the second. 2124 North Fremont Street 93940; 831/646-8585.

Carmel

If a community could be dog heaven on earth, this picturesque village less than three hours south of San Francisco would be it.

"We invite our four-legged friends to enjoy Carmel and bring their two-legged friends to do the same," says Mayor Sue McCloud, whose own dog, a Dandie Dinmont terrier named Robbie, carries his own calling card (a real paper one, not the kind more frequently associated with dogs.)

Carmel is only one square mile in area, with just 4,081 residents. But while it's a bichon frise–sized town, the city government's devotion to dogs takes on Great Dane proportions.

Carmel spends $10,000 annually on biodegradable poop bags, placed strategically throughout town and on the beach. The village sponsors a swank dog calendar, where hundreds of pooches compete in front of local celebrity judges for dog-of-the-month status. And a big part of Carmel's website (www.carmel california.com) is devoted to dogs, with two of its seven short videos focusing on dog-friendly aspects of the village. In fact, Jake and I helped produce a 15-minute version of this video for Smiling Dog Films (www.smilingdogfilms .com). The screening at Carmel City Hall's council chambers was standing room only, packed with local dog lovers like the dapper Gene McFarland (a friend of the mayor's who babysat Jake at his lovely house during our filming; Jake had so much fun with his newfound "Uncle Gene" he wasn't sure he

DIVERSION

Shop with Class (Yes, and with Your Dog): Big dogs, little dogs, frou-frou dogs, and noodle-head dogs are welcome to join you as you shop at the high-end stores of **Carmel Plaza.** The motto here: "Where indulgence is encouraged." It's heavily upscale, with stores such as Louis Vuitton, Tiffany & Co., Georgiou, and Wilkes Bashford. (Dogs with a more casual bent can sniff around the likes of Chico's and Talbot's.)

They don't just tolerate dogs here. They welcome them with open, tennis bracelet–clad arms. Most of the stores have a canister with dog biscuits. Your dog can eat 'til he plops as you shop 'til you drop. A restaurant here, Lenny's Deli, even features a dog menu, in case the biscuits aren't fortification enough.

Be sure to stop by The Fountain of Woof, a wonderful creation that features a dog with water pouring out of his mouth and into a fountain base with a couple of little pools. Stop by and give your dog a guzzle. And if you want to guzzle, er, sip beside your dog, you're both welcome to attend a fun summer event. Every Friday night from July to September the plaza is home to wine and cheese tasting and live jazz. Many dogs bring their people.

Carmel Plaza is on Ocean Avenue between Junipero and Mission streets. 831/624-0137; www.carmelplaza.com.

wanted to leave when we came to pick him up that evening). About a quarter of the council chambers at the screening was filled with canines, who howled with laughter in all the right places. Carmel dogs obviously have good taste.

The majority of Carmel businesses strongly embrace the canine set. In fact, Carmel has more dog-friendly businesses per capita than any other community in California—possibly in the entire United States.

In recent years, lots of businesses across the country have gone dog-friendly as a way of attracting the vast market of dog people to their establishments. But Carmel isn't just riding a trend. Dogs have been a key part of life here for nearly a century, since professionals from urban areas and professors from Stanford started bringing their families—and their family dogs—to Carmel for vacations years before the city was incorporated in 1916. Dogs have been a big part of life here ever since. (In 1927, for instance, more dogs than people came to the formation of the volunteer fire department.)

Modern-day dogs adore visiting Carmel. Maybe there's an aura emanating from Doris Day's ultra dog-friendly Cypress Inn or the other gorgeous, super-dog-friendly inns here. Or perhaps it's the tantalizing dog burgers (that's burgers for dogs, lest a gruesome image flashed through your head) served at the wonderful Le Coq d'Or, or the water served in champagne buckets to dogs at the delightful Portabella restaurant, or the biscuits offered to art-loving pooches at the **Rodrigue Studio,** or the dog menus offered at the Forge in the Forest and Lenny's Deli. Maybe it's the fact that dogs are welcome to join you for productions at the **Forest Theater,** or that they get a treat just for going into the local branch of Wells Fargo with you. Of course, that welcome feeling could well come from knowing that Carmel City Beach, one of the most enticing beaches in California, lets pooches run leashless, as does the Mission Trail Park. And more well-read dogs might somehow know that the two local weekly papers have gone to the dogs—they feature regular columns about Carmel's canines—one is even "written by" a dog.

Whatever the case, your dog can't help but be happy in Carmel, which in these busy times still shuns the idea of street addresses. You won't have a problem finding your destinations, though, because the village is small enough and the people are friendly enough that it's very hard to stay lost for long—especially with a dog at your side.

PARKS, BEACHES, AND RECREATION AREAS

🮱 Carmel River State Beach
😸😸😸 (See Monterey County map on page 608)

Dogs can enjoy this large stretch of beach as far as their leashes will allow. It's convenient if you're stuck south of Carmel, but most dogs prefer Carmel City Beach because of its leash-free policy.

The state beach is accessible from many points, including Ribera Road, off Highway 1. 831/649-2836.

🔟 Carmel City Beach
😸😸😸😸🐕 (See Monterey County map on page 608)

The fine white sand crunches underfoot as you and your leash-free dog explore this pristine beach. It's the only beach for many, many miles that allows dogs off their leashes, so it's a real gem for dog travelers. Bordered by cypress trees and a walking trail, the beach is also popular among humans, especially on weekends. So if your dog is the type to mark beach blankets and eat things out of other peoples' picnic baskets, you may want to leash him until you find a less crowded part of the beach.

Poop bags are available at dispensers here, but it's a good idea to bring your own just in case doggy demand is high and they run out. From Highway 1, take the Ocean Avenue exit all the way to the end, where you'll find a large parking area that's not large enough on summer weekends. 831/624-3543.

🎗 Mission Trail Park

😺😺😺😺🐾 (See Monterey County map on page 608)

This 37-acre park, also known as the Mission Trail Nature Preserve, is lush with oaks, pines, toyon, willows, and other native vegetation, including various shrubs and wildflowers. There's really nothing else like this around here. The preserve's keepers say the park is actually the last remaining refuge of Carmel's natural flora. (Watch out for one of the natives—poison oak. It's abundant, so stick to the trails.)

It's a very appealing park, with five miles of trails for hiking and pleasant benches along the way for resting your weary paws or just relaxing while listening to the sounds of nature. What's particularly wonderful for the dog crowd is that dogs under voice control can be off leash here. Again, try to keep your dog on the trail to protect the native plants and protect yourself from poison oak. (Your dog can't get it, but if it gets on his coat and you touch him, you sure can!) During your visit, be sure to paw it over to the wooden footbridge here. It's a great spot for a photo opportunity.

There are several entrances to the park, but the most popular one is right across the street from the historic Carmel Mission, on Rio Road, a little east of Junipero Street. You won't miss the mission, and there's plenty of parking there. You'll find poop bag stations at the entrance. 831/624-3543.

PLACES TO EAT

There are so many dog-friendly restaurants these days that we may have to create a book just for them! Carmel definitely takes the cake (or rather, the dog treat) for pooch-pleasing dining.

Anton and Michel: Dine "fountainside" with your dog at the outdoor area of this yummy continental-style restaurant. The atmosphere is casual and elegant (these two adjectives pretty much define most of Carmel, by the way). The Italian and French food is delicious. Dogs get a big bowl of water here. The restaurant is at Mission Street and 7th Avenue. 831/624-2406.

Big Dog Sports Restaurant: Well here's a new one: Not only is your dog welcome to join you at the fun patio here, but if you bring in a photo of you and your dog together, you'll get a free pint of domestic beer or a free soda! (And no, if you bring in your dog's photo album, you can't drink the house dry. It's usually one freebie per visit or per customer.) The owners use the photos to cover some pictures that remain from the restaurant's previous incarnation as Sherlock Holmes Pub, so it's a win-win situation.

You don't have to bring your dog for the bonus beer, but how could you leave your dog behind when you go to a restaurant called Big Dog? (The moniker is a double hitter, paying homage to Carmel's dog-loving community and also to the avid golfers who call their drivers "big dogs.") The restaurant has burgers, upscale wraps, and other better–than–pub grub cuisine. It's at 3372 The Barnyard, upstairs in the Big Sur Barn. 831/625-0340.

Bubbly Fish Cafe: Celebrate the four big C's of the culinary world—caviar, champagne, cheese, and chocolate—with your very own big C at your side (for clarification, that would be your own canine, not your own cat or your own camembert). This is a decadently different restaurant with a narrow focus that seems to be working well, judging by the crowds that flock here. Dogs get a bowl of water and dog biscuits on the house! (Sorry, no caviar.) The restaurant is on San Carlos Street between Ocean and 7th Avenues. 831/626-8226.

Caffe Cardinale Coffee Roasting: Even if your dog doesn't have a taste for coffee, quiches, or tasty sandwiches, he'll like joining you at this dog-loving café. There's just one hitch. Really. There's a doggy hitch outside the café, so you can safely hitch your dog while you place your order. Then come back outside and dine with your pooch at the outdoor tables. Doggy diners get little biscuits for visiting. The café is on Ocean Avenue between San Carlos and Dolores streets. 831/626-2095.

Casanova Restaurant: Known around these parts as Carmel's most romantic restaurant, Casanova's is also surprisingly dog-friendly. It may take a little of the romance out of your evening when your dog starts grinding his chin into your date's lap in pursuit of a handout, but hey, it could also provide a much-needed icebreaker. Well-behaved pooches are welcome on the lovely front patio. The country French and Italian cuisine is superb. Casanova's is at 5th Avenue between San Carlos and Mission streets; 831/625-0501.

The Forge in the Forest: Dogs would give this wonderful restaurant five paws up if they had five paws. They get to dine with their humans at a delightful outdoor area, which is warmed by an outdoor fireplace when a chill sets in. Better yet, lucky dogs get to order from their very own dog menu! They get to choose from several dishes, including the Quarter Hounder (a burger patty, $4.95), Hot Diggity Dog (all-beef kosher hot dog, $3.95), and the Good Dog, which the menu announces is "for the very, very good dog." The Good Dog is six ounces of grilled juicy New York steak. The cost: $12.95. Several dogs have been treated to the Good Dog, according to dog-loving co-owner Donna. It's generally bought as a birthday treat, or when the dog's person is celebrating something special. If you don't feel like spending any money for your dog's dining, that's OK, too. All dogs get dog treats here. The price: the wag of a tail. Oh, did we mention that the food for humans is delicious too? You can choose from a very wide array of seafood, pastas, gourmet pizzas, sandwiches, soups, and salads. This heavenly eatery is on the southwest corner of 5th Avenue and Junipero Street; 831/624-2233.

Grasing's Coastal Cuisine: The seafood is so fresh here you'd swear it just jumped onto your plate from the ocean. The pastas and salads are tops, too. If your dog is thirsty, the staff will make sure she gets a snootful of water. It's at 6th Avenue and Mission Street. 831/624-6562.

Jack London's Bar and Grill: Dine on ribs, steaks, and other hearty foods while relaxing in the shade of the canvas canopy. Dogs may drool while watching you chow down on the meaty fare, but if you don't feel like sharing, don't feel too bad: The folks here make sure all dog diners get dog biscuits. The outdoor tables here are actually part of a shared courtyard, but dogs are more than welcome. At 6th Avenue and Dolores Street; 831/624-2336.

Le Coq d'Or: This intimate, delightful European country-style restaurant that serves only dinner is a paws-down favorite among dogs: Pooches who come here get a burger to call their own. The dog-loving restaurant owner, Annelore, serves her own special dog burgers, which consist of ground beef, rice, and garlic, with a dash of salt and pepper. "They smell so good I could eat one myself," she says. The burger comes with a dog bowl filled with fresh water. The cost for all this: $0. "I do it because I love dogs and I think customers like seeing their dogs eat at a restaurant," says Annelore, who also doles out cookies to dogs who are just passing by. (Jake the Dog will never forget the way he was greeted with a big dog biscuit when we were just poking our heads in to say hi one day. Whenever we've walked by since, he pulls hard to steer me to the restaurant.) The people food here is out of this world. Try the coq au vin or the Alsatian onion tart. We hear the sweetbreads are tasty, but you'll never get a firsthand review of them in this book unless Jake Dog takes over authorship. It's on the east side of Mission Street, between 4th and 5th Avenues; 831/626-9319.

Lenny's Deli: Get yourself some fine New York/California deli food (try the lox), and let your dog choose her lunch from her very own menu. Lucky dogs here can get anything from dog food to steak. If your dog can't read, just get whatever her nose points to when she sniffs her menu. Dog menu prices are just a tad above the prices on the kids' menu. (And kids don't get to choose kibble.) Dine at the umbrella-topped courtyard tables here. Lenny's is in Carmel Plaza, at the corner of Ocean Avenue and Junipero Street; 831/624-5265.

Portabella: If you love unique Mediterranean food, and if your dog loves being treated like the toast of the town, come to this elegant yet casual *ristorante*. Among the mouthwatering dishes are ravioli with pan-fried goat cheese and sun-dried tomatoes (my personal favorite). It's truly to drool for. You can get all kinds of Mediterranean-style dishes and fresh seafood here, but you can also get ye olde basic hamburger. Dogs think that's very cool. And they think it's even cooler that they're given water, and that the water comes not in a bowl but in a champagne bucket. It's enough to make even the most earthy mutt feel just a bit classy. Jake the Dog's first time with the champagne bucket was an embarrassingly noisy affair. The sound of his giant slurps echoed loudly off the walls of the semienclosed back patio, causing a bit of a titter among the patient diners. "Your dog was so good," said a fellow diner when we passed in the street later. "And so quiet, except when he drank." Many dogs come here and order from the children's menu. Portabella is on Ocean Avenue between Lincoln and Monte Verde streets; 831/624-4395.

Village Corner: Anyone who thinks California restaurants don't have staying power needs to pay a little visit to this fabulous California-Mediterranean bistro, which has been around as an eatery in one form or another for more than 60 years. It even has the original sign painted on the outside wall. The food is magnificent, and you can eat it next to your dog at the lovely, flower-rimmed patio that has its very own fireplace.

We came here for lunch once with Robbie, First Dog of Carmel, and his human, Carmel Mayor Sue McCloud. He was too tired from his busy day to enjoy the fresh water offered by the restaurant's manager, but he did take advantage of the sunny patio's excellent napping potential. Village Corner is at the corner of Dolores Street and Sixth Avenue, right across from one of the dog-friendly Rodrigue galleries. 831/624-3588.

PLACES TO STAY

The ever-growing number of wonderful dog-friendly lodgings here is a testament to Carmel's dog-friendly lifestyle.

Best Western Carmel Mission Inn: Want a comfortable, attractive, and reasonably priced place to stay in Carmel? With rates that start as low as $79, this Best Western is a good place to bed down in this pricey village if budget is a consideration. The rooms are fairly well appointed, and the folks here are friendly. If you like to wallow in water, check out the heated pool and two spas. (Dogs have to wait until they're at the Carmel City Beach to wet their paws.) Rates are $79–369. (The more expensive rooms are suites.) Dogs are $35 extra for the length of their stay. 3665 Rio Road 93923; 831/624-1841 or 800/348-9090; www.carmelmissioninn.com.

Carmel Country Inn: If you and your dog feel like a cozy room in a quiet setting, you'll enjoy a stay at this pretty 12-room inn. Fresh flowers adorn the rooms, which have a serene country feel. Suites have a balcony, a sitting room, and a fireplace. The inn is set around a cheerful garden, which dogs love to sniff around. But no doggy business there, please! Rates are $165–325. Dogs pay $20 extra. The inn is at 3rd Avenue and Dolores Street, and the mailing address is P.O. Box 3756 93921; 831/625-3263 or 800/215-6343; www.carmelcountryinn.com.

Carmel Garden Court Inn: The rooms here are light and airy, and the kind of "pretty" that beckons you to have a tea party. While you may not be able to get the *Alice in Wonderland* thing going, you can revel in another English tradition: evening port and sherry served by the fire at the inn's cozy little lobby. It's a great way to wind down after an active day of taking in the sights and smells with your dog.

Your day at the Garden Court starts with a yummy and fairly bounteous continental breakfast, complete with champagne (do we notice a little imbibement theme here?), which is brought to your room with the day's local newspaper. You can eat it (the breakfast, not the paper) in your PJs in your room or patio with poochy at your side. Or you can saunter out to the radiant fountain garden to partake in your eats.

Many of the rooms have fireplaces. Jake prefers the patio suites, which feature beautiful breakfast nooks and patios where he can sniff at life in Carmel. Rates are $150–245. There's a $50 charge for your dog for the length of his stay. The inn is at 4th Avenue and Torres Street. The mailing address is P.O. Box 6226 93921; 831/624-6926; www.carmelgardencourtinn.com.

Carmel River Inn: The 24 attractively furnished cottages here are sprinkled around 10 acres of lush, peaceful gardens. Dogs like it so much that many somehow convince their humans to keep coming here year after year. "We get lots of return guests with dogs," says an innkeeper. A few cottages are tiny; others are very generously sized. Many have fireplaces, which makes for a cozy picture if your dog likes to curl up in front of the hearth at night (as opposed to the sprawled-out-like-he's-been-shot-in-a-bad-Western-movie position Jake assumes in front of a crackling fire). Rates are $159–299. Dogs are $15 extra. The inn is at Highway 1 at the Carmel River Bridge. The mailing address: P.O. Box 221609 93922; 831/624-1575 or 800/882-8142; www.carmelriverinn.com.

Carmel Tradewinds Inn: The Pacific Rim–style hotel has an upscale but casual elegance, and its rooms and courtyard are so peaceful and perfect that your dog may scratch her head in wonder that the hotel allows dogs here at all. (As long as she's not scratching her head from fleas, you're all set.) Your dog might want to know that the inn has won accolades and awards for its stunning architectural design.

If your dog promises to be very quiet, you can take her to visit the secret garden, where you'll find a statue of Buddha. It's a very meditative garden, so don't bring a dog like Jake there. Water dogs tend to be mesmerized by the waterfall that cascades down one side of the plant-filled courtyard.

Rates are $195–550. (Some dog-friendly rooms are available with a fireplace and whirlpool tub.) Dogs are $25 extra. The inn is at Mission Street and 3rd Avenue. The mailing address: P.O. Box 3403 93921; 831/624-2776 or 800/624-6665; www.tradewindsinn.com.

Casa de Carmel: If you like wicker decor, light and cheery rooms, and a convenient location in the heart of the village, knock on the door of the Casa de Carmel. The exterior is an attractive blend of Spanish mission style and upscale motel. The rooms aren't terribly roomy, but do you really want to stay in your room very much when visiting one of the most dog-friendly places in the world? The rates are hard to beat around here: $155–325. The dog fee is $30 extra for one, $45 for two. On Monte Verde Street between Ocean and 7th Avenues. The mailing address is P.O. Box 2747 93921; 831/624-6046 or 800/328-7707; www.casadecarmel.com.

Coachman's Inn: This is a warm and fuzzy place to stay with your warm and furry friend. There's an air of Olde England here, with the inn's timbered stucco walls and comfortable decor. In the morning you'll get a danish (not an English, but that's OK), and in the late afternoon you can partake in sherry hour. Rates are $125–250. Dogs are $20 extra, and they must stay in one of the seven rooms on the ground floor. The inn is on San Carlos Street at 7th Avenue. The mailing address is P.O. Box C-1 93921; 831/624-6421; www.coachmansinn.com.

Cypress Inn: Dogs get the royal treatment here, in part because actress and animal activist Doris Day co-owns this sumptuous hotel. The stately Moorish Mediterranean–style inn is very elegant, with fine oak floors and delicate antiques, but you never feel out of place with your dog. The staff makes sure your dog feels especially welcome, right down to offering pet beds and pet food for your four-legged friend. The staff will help get you a pet-sitter, should you decide to venture out on your own without your dog. (We doubt your pooch will say *"que sera sera"* to this idea. Carmel is so dog-friendly you can easily do the whole scene with him. But some very friendly, excellent pet-sitters are available through the hotel if you can stand your dog's hound-dog look when you leave.)

No two rooms are the same here, and they're all enchanting, relaxing, and first-rate. The rooms come with extras not offered by most hotels, including fresh flowers, bottled water, fresh fruit, your very own decanter of sherry, and occasional chocolates. In addition, you can bring your dog to the hotel's lovely bar for a cocktail, and you can partake in a delightful afternoon tea at the inn's gorgeous lounge. It has a huge fireplace and luxe decor. I had the occasion to be here not long ago when the inn's co-owner, Denny LeVett, brought his standard poodle, Strutz, to join Carmel's Mayor Sue McCloud and her dog, Robbie, for high tea. When Denny was looking elsewhere, Strutz decided to plow his delicate but determined poodle nose into the cookies and scones. He Hoovered them up in seconds. Fortunately, Strutz knows the hotel's owner pretty well, and the tea party went on with quick replacements for all.

Rates are $145–575. It's $30 extra for one pooch, $50 for two. The inn is at Lincoln Street and 7th Avenue, and the mailing address is P.O. Box Y 93921; 831/624-3871; www.cypress-inn.com.

Happy Landing Inn: The exterior is pinkish-buff, but don't let that fool you: Inside is what the proprietors describe as a "Hansel and Gretel charm." (Not to be confused with the Lamp Lighter Inn's Hansel & Gretel Cottage.) OK, there's a bit of a pinkish theme even inside many rooms, but it's a very sweet place, with great old wooden ceilings that look like they're part of an old English cottage. Some rooms have stained-glass windows, and three have fireplaces.

Rates are $125–225. Dogs are $20 extra. Continental breakfast and weekend wine and cheese is included in the price. The inn is on Monte Verde Street between 5th and 6th avenues. 831/624-7917 or 800/297-6250; www.carmelhappylanding.com.

Hofsas House Hotel: This lovely boutique hotel has the intimate feeling of a bed-and-breakfast inn with the privacy afforded by a small hotel. The rooms are all decorated differently. One sports a beautiful Asian theme, while some have a light and airy upscale alpine cottage feel. Many of the 38 spacious rooms have excellent ocean views and fireplaces. All come with a tasty continental breakfast and free Wi-Fi. There are also a refreshing outdoor heated swimming pool and two dry saunas. Rates are $89–220. Suites run up to $300. Dogs are $20 extra. The hotel is on San Carlos Street between 3rd and 4th avenues, and the mailing address is P.O. Box 1195 93921; 831/624-2745; www .hofsashouse.com.

Lamp Lighter Inn: The two cottages and four big guest rooms here are some of the most enchanting lodgings around. When you see them on your jaunts down Ocean Avenue you feel as if you're looking at something straight out of a sweet old storybook. The accommodations are airy yet very cozy (and not at all cutesy), with an understated luxury. Dogs don't really care about all this, however. What they like is that it's just a bone's throw (about four short blocks) to the leash-free Carmel City Beach. That's about as close as you can get to it in a Carmel lodging. Dogs also enjoy the little treats they get at the front desk upon arrival. Plus they seem to think it's neat that a light, healthy breakfast is brought to your room each morning. (Jake likes the hard-boiled eggs, and since I don't, it's a match made in heaven.) Alternatively, you may ask for it to be served in the lovely garden area.

On a recent stay we were lucky enough to nab the popular Hansel & Gretel Cottage. It was truly a delight, with its cozy two bedrooms, fireplace, sitting area, little kitchen, and decanter of sherry just waiting to be sipped beside the fire. The second bedroom is a little loft affair with an old-timey railed lookout over the living room. Jake and our human child, Laura, spent the evening up there reading together and watching the blazing fireplace below.

Rates are $185–350. Dogs are $30 extra for one, $45 for two. The inn is at Ocean Avenue and Camino Real, and the mailing address is P.O. Box AF 93291; 831/624-7372; www.carmellamplighter.com.

Lincoln Green Inn: We love the four gorgeous, classy, old English–style cottages that make up this inn. Each white cottage, set in the inn's lush English country garden, is like its own little England—a touch of the Cotswolds—from the steep-pitched roofs to the forest-green shutters to the airy and cozy interiors with beautiful furnishings. Fireplaces are the rule here. The three one-bedroom cottages have kitchens, too, in case you feel like playing chef during your visit. (The fourth cottage, which has two bedrooms, sports an efficiency kitchen.) If you're longing for quiet, the Lincoln Green is for you. It's set in a restful part of town, far enough from the not-so-madding crowds in Carmel to afford real tranquility, and in the midst of the inn's sweet gardens. The inn is just a short walk to the Carmel River State Beach.

A continental breakfast, delivered to your cottage, comes with your stay. And so that dog guests don't feel left out, dogs who stay here get a little snack delivered with breakfast. Rates for the dog-friendly cottages are $295–350. Dogs are $30 extra. The cottages are on Carmelo Street between 15th and 16th avenues, and there's an actual street address here. (How did this happen in the land of no street addresses?) It's at 26200 Carmelo Street 93923; 831/626-4006 or 831/277-0337; www.lincolngreeninn.com. (The music on its home page is very appealing, in an old-timey newsreel-about-the-Cotswolds kind of way.)

Monte Verde Inn: You'll be right across from Carmel City Hall when you stay at this charming inn. Water dogs like Jake enjoy the ocean king suite on the second floor, which has a private little deck with an ocean view. The rooms here aren't über-upscale, but they're pretty, airy, and comfy. They come with a light continental breakfast delivered to your room and a decanter of cream sherry. (Generally not recommended for breakfast, though.) Rates are $185–650. Dogs are $30 extra. The inn is on Monte Verde Street between Ocean and 7th avenues. The mailing address is P.O. Box 2747 93921; 831/624-6026 or 800/328-7707; www.carmelmonteverdeinn.com.

Sunset House: The house was built in the 1960s to be a bed-and-breakfast inn, so all four of the rooms are large (600 square feet), with real brick wood-burning fireplaces that are match-ready, and private bathrooms. The rooms are airy, yet cozy, and are furnished nicely with a mixture of antiques and classic contemporary furniture. The two dog-friendly rooms have private entrances. Our favorite, the Porpoise Suite, has a whirlpool tub and canopy bed. The inn is in an attractive residential neighborhood, where it's a very short, two-minute walk to leash-free Carmel City Beach and the quaint shops of Carmel.

Now a little about the service: The staff welcomes canine and human guests with gift baskets. Humans get a smallish bottle of wine, some crackers, and other tasty treats. Dogs get treats of a different ilk, toys, and towels (for après-beach). In the morning fresh fruit, juice, coffee, and yogurt are delivered to your room. In addition, you'll get a breakfast certificate to be redeemed at one of four premier restaurants nearby.

Rates for the dog-friendly rooms are $175–215. Dogs pay a $30 fee for the length of their stay. The inn is on Camino Real, between Ocean and 7th avenues, and the mailing address is P.O. Box 1925 93921; 831/626-7100 or 877/966-9100; www.sunsethousecarmel.com.

Vagabond's House Inn: This is not a Vagabond Inn! Not by a loooong shot. Your dog will drool over this inn's beautiful courtyard with its ancient oak tree, little waterfall, and magical garden. (You may drool, too, but don't let your dog catch you or you'll never hear the end of it.) The humans in your party will fall in love with this English Tudor country inn. It's right in town, but you feel as though you're in merry old England here. When you sip the cream sherry that's comes in a decanter (no charge!) in your room in the afternoon, you may think you've died and gone to the British Isles.

The rooms have fresh flowers and are furnished with antiques. Most have fireplaces and designer bedding. Yummy! In the morning, continental breakfast is brought to the room. Your dog even gets his very own doggy biscuits with breakfast! (At least you won't have to share your pastries.)

Rates are $155–275. Dogs are $30 extra. (A second dog is $15 extra.) In case you have any nondog children, you should know that human children under 10 aren't allowed. (Now there's a twist.) The inn is at 4th Avenue and Dolores Street, P.O. Box 2747, 92921; 831/624-7738 or 800/262-1262; www.vagabonds houseinn.com.

Wayside Inn: Part inn, part motel, this is a charming old ivy-covered brick building well off the beaten path. What it lacks in divine exterior grace it makes up for inside, with comfortable country-style surroundings. Some rooms come with kitchenettes or fireplaces. Rates are $99–300. The inn is at Mission Street and 7th Avenue, and the mailing address is P.O. Box 1900 93921; 831/624-5336; www.innsbythesea.com.

Carmel Valley

Only 10 miles inland from Highway 1, this is one of the hidden jewels of the Central Coast. Carmel Valley boasts an average of 283 sunny days a year—quite a feat for any place so close to the ocean. The peaceful country setting isn't marred by the little Carmel Valley Village, the "city center" that's chock full of outdoor cafés that put out the welcome mat for dogs.

Jake, like Joe before him, was disappointed to learn that when Charley and John Steinbeck reached Carmel Valley in their travels, the human half of the team wasn't happy. In *Travels with Charley,* Steinbeck wrote of a conversation he had with his old friend Johnny Garcia in a Monterey bar: "I went to the Carmel Valley where once we could shoot a thirty-thirty in any direction. Now you couldn't shoot a marble knuckles down without wounding a foreigner. And Johnny, I don't mind people, you know that. But these are rich people. They plant geraniums in big pots. Swimming pools where frogs and crayfish used to wait for us."

Jake the Water Dog begs to differ about Steinbeck's comment about too many swimming pools. And he'll be the first to tell you that frogs and their friends still make Carmel Valley their home. You just have to visit Garland Ranch Regional Park to get a sampling of what was once wild and wonderful about the entire Carmel Valley area.

PARKS, BEACHES, AND RECREATION AREAS

12 Garland Ranch Regional Park

🐾🐾🐾🐾🐕 (See Monterey County map on page 608)

This 4,500-acre park is heaven for any dog who has ever dreamed of living in the country. From the maple-filled canyons to the dense oak woodlands to the willow-covered banks of the Carmel River, you can find almost any environment you and your dog like.

Nine miles of trails can take you and your leash-free dog from just above sea level to 2,000 feet. The wildlife here is plentiful. At the visitors center, you can pick up trail maps as well as species lists of common birds, mammals, and plants to look for while on the trails. Make sure your dog is kind to nature and doesn't disturb the creatures of the woods. Your dog should also know that this is horse country, so if he's thinking of spooking any equines, he'd better be leashed.

While the park has its wild side, it also can be downright civilized. You'll find restrooms and oodles of picnic tables near the visitors center.

Take Carmel Valley Road about 10 miles east from Highway 1. The park will be on your right. Park in one of the lots and follow any of the narrow trails over the Carmel River and to the visitors center, which is the convenient trailhead for all the park's trails. 831/659-4488.

PLACES TO EAT

The Corkscrew Café: This is a wonderful restaurant with a lovely outdoor seating area that has trees, a grape awning, and umbrella-topped tables. Dogs may not only join you there, but they also get treats and water. Try the cornmeal trout or the organic cheeseburger. 55 West Carmel Valley Road; 831/659-8888.

PLACES TO STAY

Blue Sky Lodge: The people who run this lodge/motel are super-friendly to humans and dogs. We've received rave reviews about the Blue Sky from a few of our readers, including Kerry Davis and her travel-lovin' dog, Sophie. It's not so much that it's a fancy place—it's really not. It's actually more of a basic motel from the 1950s. You can get anything from a motel room with a patio to a little townhouse. The friendly folks here and the nice nearby spots to exercise Spot (they'll point you to an attractive field, or you can take a short drive to Garland Park), combined with the lodge's very reasonable prices, make it an easy place to stay. Dogs are welcome just about anywhere at the lodge. They can even hang out with you beside the heated swimming pool (not in it, though, and they need to be leashed), or in the attractive and spacious lodge, complete with big fireplace and comfy old chairs. Rates are $79–159. P.O. Box 233, 10 Flight Road 93924; 831/659-2256 or 800/549-2256; www.blueskylodge.com.

Carmel Valley Lodge: This quiet, secluded country inn is a great place for dogs to get away from city life. The redwood buildings and cottages, some with fireplaces, kitchenettes, and private decks, are the perfect place to relax after a long day of hiking at Garland Ranch Regional Park. Humans get to enjoy the lodge's beautiful heated pool, sauna, hot spa, and fitness center. The place is as dog-friendly as it is beautiful. Its brochure and website feature a picture of "Lucky, the Lodge Dog," and some lodge literature states in bold: "Children and dogs are welcome as long as the kids are on a leash and the dogs are at least 12." The people who work here adore dogs and will point you and yours to some very nearby areas where your dog can get lots of exercise. In addition, dogs who stay here get treats upon arrival. Rates are $179–359. Dogs are $10 extra. A hearty buffet breakfast is included in the price. The lodge is at Carmel Valley and Ford roads. The mailing address is P.O. Box 93 93924; 831/659-2261 or 800/641-4646; www.valleylodge.com.

Los Laureles Lodge: What's good enough for a horse is good enough for you and your dog, right? Back in the 1930s, many of the 10 one-story buildings here were stables housing happy thoroughbreds owned by a wealthy family. Today they've been converted into comfortable guest rooms with knotty-pine paneling and simple country decor. There's no lingering equine odor, much to Jake's chagrin. Other rooms in other buildings are even older and have no horsey history. If you can afford a little extra, the king suite with a big stone fireplace and a white picket-fenced yard is a great place to stay with a dog. Dogs are happy staying anywhere at the lodge, because they get to trot around (leashed) on the property's 10 acres. People who like older saloons and newer pools enjoy the lodge's version of each of these, but dogs need to stay dry, in more ways than one. Rates are $79–650. Dogs are $20 extra. 313 West Carmel Valley Road 93924; 831/659-2233 or 800/533-4404; www.loslaureles.com.

Big Sur Area

As the two-lane ribbon of Highway 1 winds 90 miles up and down what many think is the most spectacular coastal scenery in the world, your dog may be praying for the end of the trip—or at least wishing for a dose of Dramamine.

Carsick dogs are not uncommon as mountains shoot up 1,000 feet over the crashing Pacific, only to curve and slope down again, roller coaster fashion. It's a good idea to take your time and stop at as many vista points as you can along the road. Your dog will thank you for it, and you'll get to breathe the exhilarating Pacific air and study the rugged shoreline.

A must-stop vista point is at the Bixby Creek Bridge, 260 feet high and more than 700 feet long. There are pullouts on either side.

Whatever you do when you're making these stops along Big Sur, make sure your dog is securely leashed and in no danger of stepping too close to the edge of the world. There's usually not much room between Highway 1 and the hazardous cliffs.

PARKS, BEACHES, AND RECREATION AREAS

13 Pfeiffer Beach
😊😊😊😊 (See Monterey County map on page 608)

You and your leashed dog will be stunned at the natural beauty of this white, sandy beach. Surrounded by sea caves, steep cliffs, and natural arches, you won't know what to marvel at first. Your dog will be so thrilled that he won't even notice he's leashed.

From the north, take the second right turn (Sycamore Canyon Road) off Highway 1 south of Big Sur State Park. It's a sharp turn. At the end of the narrow, two-mile road is a sandy trail under a canopy of cypress trees. It leads to the beach. The beach is dog-friendly because it's run by the good old U.S. Forest Service. 831/667-2423.

14 Sand Dollar Picnic Area and Beach
😊😊😊 (See Monterey County map on page 608)

Your dog will enjoy the romance of a picnic among the cypress trees here. After downing your French bread, brie, and white wine, take one of the trails across the field and follow it down to the beach. Although dogs must be leashed, it's a terrific spot. It's toward the southern end of Big Sur, so it's at a perfect place to take a break from driving.

The picnic area is about 11 miles south of Lucia, west of Highway 1. This is another beach run by the U.S. Forest Service, which explains its dog-friendly rules. 831/385-5434.

PLACES TO STAY

Here are just a few of the private and public campgrounds along the Big Sur coast, and one beautiful place with two magical one-bedroom cabins a little north of Big Sur.

China Camp: It's fun to camp here if you're planning on hiking in the Ventana Wilderness (see the *Los Padres National Forest* in the *Resources* section) but you're not quite sure about camping in the wilderness itself. A trail leads directly from the camp into the Ventana Wilderness. Dogs must be on leash at the campsite, but dogs under excellent voice control can put their leashes in their doggy backpacks once they're in the wilderness area. Six sites are available on a first-come, first-served basis. There's no charge for the sites. There's a two-dog maximum, and pooches must show proof of rabies vaccine. It's good for day adventuring, camping, or both. Keep in mind that there's no piped-in water, so bring plenty, or be ready to filter any you find in streams along the way. The campground is inland, about 20 miles southwest of Carmel Valley, on Tassajara Road. Call the Los Padres National Forest main office at 831/385-5434.

Fernwood Resort: Dogs enjoy a stay here because they have access to the Big Sur River. You and the pooch can stay only at the resort's campground, not the motel. It's conveniently situated right off Highway 1, but it's set far enough back so you don't feel as if the cars are right in your backyard. Tent sites start at $30, and RV sites start at $35. Dogs are $5 extra. There's no street address. It's just Highway 1, Big Sur CA 93920; 831/667-2422.

Kirk Creek Campground: You'll love the view from the bluffs above the beach here, and your dog will appreciate the cool Pacific breezes. You can bring your leashed dog down to the beach on a couple of steep trails, or you can take a trail from here that leads into the Ventana Wilderness. That's where your dog can legally remove his leash. Kirk Creek has 33 campsites, costing $22. The campground is west of Highway 1, about four miles south of Lucia. Call the Los Padres National Forest main office at 831/385-5434.

Rosehaven Cabins: These two beautiful cabins tucked away on 19 acres of Big Sur redwood forest are among the most enjoyable, lovely, welcoming, cozy, rustic-yet-luxurious places you can stay with a dog. One cabin, Serenity, is surrounded by a dense redwood grove. The other, Morning Lite, is built so high off the ground you feel as if you're in a tree house. Both cabins have wood interiors, well-stocked kitchens, pretty eating areas, comfy living rooms and bedrooms, and decks. The decks are where you'll find the bathrooms! Yes, you shower, bathe in a clawfoot tub, shave, and, er, read magazines on a secluded part of your deck while listening to the gurgling stream that flows nearby on the property. No one can see you, and you and your dog will have yet one more thing in common once you've experienced going to the bathroom in the great outdoors (in a flushable toilet, unlike your dog).

The cabins are less than 100 yards apart but truly secluded from each other and from the residence of the owners just down the little drive. You can hike on the property. A half-mile trail takes you to a 20-foot waterfall! The cabins have no phones or TVs, but you can get free Wi-Fi if you need to be in communication with the rest of the world. This is the kind of place I could live in while finishing writing an edition of one of these books.

Rates are very reasonable. Just $125, including taxes. Stay more than five nights and get the sixth night free. Stay more than that and you may be able to work out an even better deal with kindly, dog-loving owners Donna and Doug George. The cabins are 11.2 miles south of the Rio Road intersection in Carmel, and 15 miles north of the village of Big Sur. While closer to Carmel than Big Sur in distance, they're closer to Big Sur than Carmel in spirit, so we're listing them in the Big Sur section. You'll get the address and exact directions when you book your reservation. A huge woof of thanks to Chico Dog for having his person, Angela, write to us to tell us of this real find. 831/625-8682; www.rosehavencabins.com.

Pfeiffer Big Sur State Park: Though this state park has 821 acres of redwoods, some near Big Sur River, dogs are permitted only in the camping area. It's not so bad—each of the 218 campsites has a picnic table where your dog can join you for gourmet outdoor cooking, or he can sleep under it when the shade of the redwoods isn't enough. Sites are $20–35. The park is east of Highway 1, about 26 miles south of Carmel. Call park headquarters at 831/667-2315 for information. For reservations, call 800/444-7275.

King City

This is a fine place to stop with your dog, but a word of warning: It's also a good place to get caught speeding. The California Highway Patrol seems omnipresent on this stretch of U.S. 101, so watch yourself. The troopers don't take kindly to the old "my dog really has to go to the bathroom" excuse.

PARKS, BEACHES, AND RECREATION AREAS

15 San Lorenzo Regional Park
🐾🐾🐾 (See Monterey County map on page 608)

Conveniently situated just off U.S. 101 almost midway between San Francisco and Los Angeles, this is a great park for your dog to get out and stretch his legs on a long journey. The park is home to the intriguing Agricultural and Rural Life Museum, which tells the story of Salinas Valley agriculture. Although dogs aren't welcome in the buildings, humans are invited to enter a one-room schoolhouse and farmhouse. Day use is $4 per vehicle on weekdays, $6 weekends.

If you want to make a night of it, you can camp at any of the park's 99 campsites. Reservations are necessary only for group sites but are available for regular sites, too. Sites are $20–27. Dogs are $2 extra. Your dog must have proof of rabies vaccination. Exit U.S. 101 at Broadway and follow the signs. 831/385-5964.

PLACES TO STAY

Motel 6: Rates are $38–53 for the first adult, $6 for the second. 3 Broadway Circle 93930; 831/385-5000.

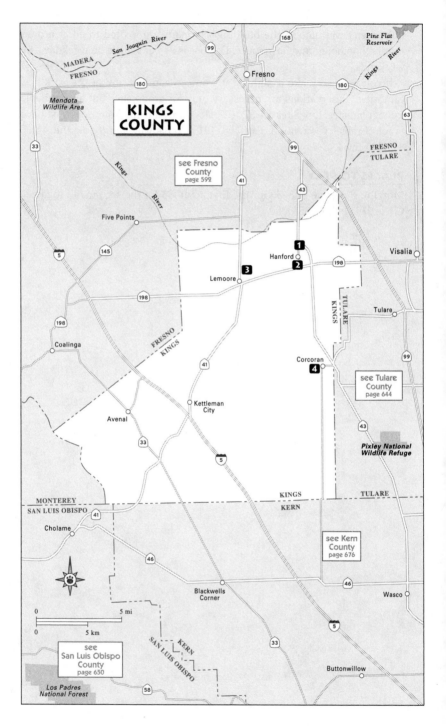

KINGS COUNTY

see Fresno County page 592

see Tulare County page 644

see Kern County page 676

see San Luis Obispo County page 650

Pine Flat Reservoir

Mendota Wildlife Area

Pixley National Wildlife Refuge

Los Padres National Forest

MADERA
FRESNO

San Joaquin River

Fresno

Kings River

FRESNO
TULARE

Five Points

Visalia

Hanford

Lemoore

TULARE
KINGS

Tulare

Coalinga

FRESNO
KINGS

Corcoran

Kettleman City

Avenal

MONTEREY
SAN LUIS OBISPO

KINGS
KERN

KINGS
TULARE

Cholame

Blackwells Corner

Wasco

SAN LUIS OBISPO
KERN

Buttonwillow

0   5 mi
0   5 km

CHAPTER 46

Kings County

This is farm country, the kind of land that drives dogs crazy around the time the fertilizer's being spread. But despite all the open fields and rural surroundings, it's tough to find a place to take a dog for a good time. Dogs would love to roll in the cow patties, but between your objections, the farmers' objections, and that killer look on Bessie's face, they quickly realize it's not the best idea in the world.

Interestingly, the most appealing areas for dogs are in the small cities, especially Lemoore and historic Hanford. There's just one dog park in the county but another is in the discussion stages. It was like this in the last edition, so apparently they're not talking very fast.

PICK OF THE LITTER—KINGS COUNTY

BEST OLD-FASHIONED PARK
Civic Center Park, Hanford (page 640)

Hanford

Anyone looking for a set for *The Music Man?* You couldn't find a more perfect one than the turn-of-the-20th-century town square in the middle of the old part of Hanford. It's got all the charm and permanence of River City, Iowa, and you won't have to put up with a freckle-faced kid with a bad lisp. The city has some of the grandest old buildings in California. Most of them are in or around Civic Center Park, where your leashed dog can enjoy green grass and big, stately trees.

PARKS, BEACHES, AND RECREATION AREAS

1 Civic Center Park

🐾🐾🐾 (See Kings County map on page 638)

If you were to find yourself in the middle of a park with huge shade trees, flowers, an antique carousel, a fire engine from 1911, and a neoclassical courthouse building, in what year do you think you'd be? 1920? 1930? It's hard to believe, but this old charmer exists today.

It must be something about the clock on the front of the Civic Auditorium across the street. The impressive classical revival building's big clock actually works. The whole thing is reminiscent of *Back to the Future*—clock, columns, and all. But the title of this ideal town square would have to be *Back to the Past.*

The place is very friendly to leashed dogs. The courthouse has been converted into quaint shops and offices. There's even a deli with outdoor tables.

Exit Highway 198 at 11th Avenue, drive north a few blocks, and go right on 7th Street. The park is at Irwin and 7th streets. 559/585-2500.

② Freedom Dog Park

🐾🐾🐕 (See Kings County map on page 638)

Welcome to the county's first dog park! It's a great name for a park where dogs can cast their leashes to the wind. Actually, the park is named for the park in which it's located—Freedom Park. Dogs do have freedom from leashes here, but it's not a big area, probably less than a quarter acre. But dogs who use it seem to be relieved to have anywhere to run off leash, and as the city's recreation director says, "It would be nice if we could make something bigger, but this is better than nothing." He hopes to build more dog park areas in the not-too-distant future.

The little grassy park has no shade, but it has other good dog-park amenities, like water and a separate section for small dogs. (As you can imagine, that one's really small.) The park is on 9 1/4 Avenue (yes, some streets here have fractional names), at Grangeville Boulevard. It's near the front of the bigger Freedom Park, in the southeast corner, near the parking lot. 559/585-2500.

PLACES TO STAY

Sequoia Inn: This is one of the nicest lodgings around these parts, and dogs are thrilled that they're welcome here. The decor is attractive, the rooms and suites comfortable, and the pool, spa, exercise room, and sauna are wonderful bonuses for the humans in your party. An expanded continental breakfast comes with your room. Rates are $66–123. Dogs require a $100 deposit. 1655 Mall Drive 93230; 559/582-0338.

Lemoore

Besides the gigantic Harris Ranch (a must-smell for dogs, described in the *Coalinga* section of the *Fresno County* chapter), Lemoore is the first civilization you come to driving east on Highway 198 from I-5. It's got a cute town center, lined with trees and antique stores. There's talk of a dog park here, but it's still in the early planning stages. It sure would be convenient for dogs on long road trips. Plus the dogs of Lemoore would like their own park. Many local dogs have to corral their people into the car to drive to Hanford's dog park if they're going to run off leash, and they're feeling guilty about wasting gas and global warming.

PARKS, BEACHES, AND RECREATION AREAS

🖪 City Park

🐾🐾 (See Kings County map on page 638)

This square-block park is usually green and grassy, which makes it ideal for dogs who like to roll. Willows and palms abound, so even in the heat of summer, you and your dog can survive. Kids like it here because of the special playground.

Take the Lemoore/Fresno exit (Highway 41) from Highway 198 and go north to West Bush Street. Go right on West Bush Street and drive for about 12 blocks. The park is on your left. 559/924-6767.

Corcoran

You'll see plenty of dogs here, but they're usually in the backs of big pickup trucks parked at local bars and convenience stores. The dogs like to bark, especially at each other.

To want to drive all the way out here with your dog, you probably have to have a loved one at the maximum-security Corcoran State Prison. Dogs aren't allowed to visit any of the prison's 5,500 inmates, so they'll be sorely disappointed if that's the only reason they came with you.

PARKS, BEACHES, AND RECREATION AREAS

4 Community Park
🐾🐾 (See Kings County map on page 638)

This is exactly what it sounds like—a park for the community, featuring picnic tables, ball fields, and children's playgrounds. It's the only game in town if your dog needs to relieve her bladder, and it can be quite crowded with local kids. The park is at Dairy and Patterson avenues. 559/992-2151.

Kettleman City

What can we say about Kettleman City, except that it's a good place to take a break while traversing the state on I-5?

PLACES TO STAY

Best Western Kettleman Inn and Suites: Stay here if you want comfort, an expanded breakfast, a little pool, and a whirlpool. The suites here are very roomy and well designed, and the rooms are spacious. Some of the rooms have whirlpools. It's the perfect place to stretch your legs during a long I-5 car trip. Rates are $70–169. Dogs are $5 extra. 33410 Powers Drive 93239; 559/386-0804.

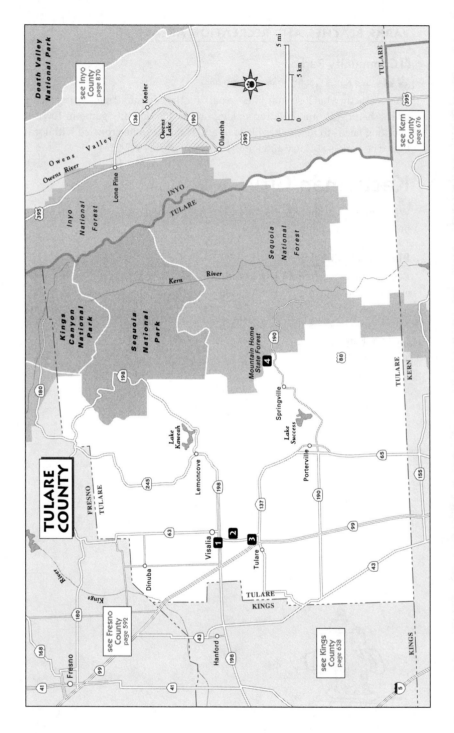

CHAPTER 47

Tulare County

Some people come here from other parts of the state and call this place "Tool-air" County. Others call it "Tool-ahh-ray." Don't do dat! You'll be pegged as an outsider immediately and your dog's credentials as a real dog will be questioned. When you're trying to remember how to say the name of this place, just think about the personality of a late-night CNN talk show host. If you say he's just too, too, "Too-larry" (King), you'll fit right in.

Don't worry if you don't find your thrills in the civilized parts of Tulare. About one-third of the county belongs to the U.S. Forest Service, the Bureau of Land Management (BLM), and the California Department of Forestry. In dog-speak, that translates to "Look, Ma, no leash!"

The BLM's dog-friendly Chimney Peak Recreation Area is split between Tulare County and its southern neighbor, Kern County. While Tulare County contains the best part of the recreation area, it's more easily reached from Kern County and is covered in that chapter.

PICK OF THE LITTER—TULARE COUNTY

BEST DOG PARK
Cody Kelly Bark Park, Visalia (page 647)

BEST HIKE AMONG THE TREES
Mountain Home State Forest, Springville (page 649)

NATIONAL FORESTS

The *National Forests and Wilderness Areas* resource at the back of this book has important information and safety tips on visiting national forests with your dog and has more information on the national forests listed below.

Inyo National Forest
😊😊😊😊🐾

Sequoia National Forest
😊😊😊😊🐾

NATIONAL PARKS

Sequoia and Kings Canyon National Parks
🚩

If you were a chocoholic, your idea of hell would probably include being chained to the middle of a small island surrounded by a sea of unreachable, creamy Ghirardelli, Godiva, and Guittard chocolates. If you were an ice skater, purgatory might include being relegated to gravel driveways for the rest of your life, never being able to set a blade on the ice that's all around you. And if you were a dog, your idea of hell would probably involve a visit to these two exquisite national parks.

Sequoia National Park contains the thickest concentration (and the biggest individual specimens) of giant sequoia trees in the world. And while Kings Canyon doesn't have the huge trees, it's wild and untamed, just begging to be sniffed at by an inquisitive dog snout. Dogs, however, must be cloistered in the car-camping areas and the little villages here, far from the trails and the madding trees. This is bad news. This makes boy dogs moan. This is hell.

A day-use pass is $20 per car, and this is good for a week. Fees for sites where

dogs can camp are $12–20. There are approximately 1,300 sites available on a first-come, first-served basis. The parks are connected and stretch for almost 60 miles from north to south. Because of their sizes, we can't provide specific directions here. Call the parks at 559/565-3134 for information on what areas might be best for you and your traveling dog. And if no one in your traveling party is going to be around to hang out with your dog while you explore the parks, leave him home with a friend. Too many dogs get stuck in cars here, and that can be dangerous as well as a crashing bore.

Visalia

PARKS, BEACHES, AND RECREATION AREAS

This relatively small community is now home to two pooch parks! Let that be an example to you larger towns that won't even consider them.

◻ Cody Kelly Bark Park

🐾🐾🐾🐾🐕 (See Tulare County map on page 644)

This is an attractive two-acre dog park, and it's got just about every possible dog-park amenity, including separate areas for large and small dogs, double gates, benches, poop-bag dispensers, doggy water fountains, faux fire hydrants, and plenty of trees. The park also has lights, and you can be in the park until 10 P.M., should your dog like nightlife. The park is named after a West Highland terrier whose generous human helped make the park possible. Thank you for inspiring your human, Cody.

The park is within Plaza Park, where you and your leashed dog can hike on a trail, relax under a big shade tree, or watch kids fish in a little pond. It's west of town, at Highway 198 and Plaza Drive, just east of Highway 99. If you know where the Visalia Airport is, you can't miss the park. (It's very conveniently situated if you're staying at the Holiday Inn Plaza Park, which is a bone's throw away.) For the official city word on the park, phone 559/713-4365. For info from the dog-park people, phone Amy at 559/280-3054.

🐾 Seven Oaks Bark Park

🐾🐾🐾🐕 (See Tulare County map on page 644)

This one is the younger, more diminutive sibling of Cody Kelly Bark Park. It's about an acre, and it has a bench, water, a picnic table, and poop-bag dispenser. There's not much shade, so it can be a scorcher on hot days. You may prefer to come here at night, and now you can, thanks to some new lights that stay on until 10 P.M. The park is on Tulare Avenue, just south of Ben Maddox Way. For official park info, phone the city at 559/713-4365. For info from the dog-park people, phone Amy at 559/280-3054.

PLACES TO STAY

Best Western Visalia Inn Motel: Rates are $79–96. Dogs must be under 25 pounds, and they're $15 extra. 623 West Main Street 93291; 559/732-4561.

Holiday Inn Plaza Park: Stay at this comfy, clean hotel and you're almost within Cody Kelly Bark Park. Rates are $135–145. Dogs are $25 extra. 9000 West Airport Drive 93277; 559/651-5000 or 800/465-4329.

Tulare

PARKS, BEACHES, AND RECREATION AREAS

🐾 Live Oak Park

🐾🐾 (See Tulare County map on page 644)

If you happen to be passing through town, this green park is worth sniffing out. Dogs like the combination of trees and fitness course.

The park is close to Highway 99. Take the Tulare Avenue exit east a few blocks and turn left on Laspina Street. In a few more blocks, you'll be at the park. It's right beside the Live Oak Middle School. 559/685-2380.

PLACES TO STAY

Best Western: Rates are $75–89. Dogs pay a flat $20 fee. 1051 North Blackstone Avenue 93274; 559/688-7537.

Springville

PARKS, BEACHES, AND RECREATION AREAS

◤ Mountain Home State Forest

😸😸😸😸🐾 (See Tulare County map on page 644)

If you and your leash-free pooch want to see the seventh-largest tree in the world, you'd better make nice with the rangers here. The tree isn't on any maps, and rangers prefer to point it out only to the folks they like.

If the ranger just doesn't dig you or your dog enough to let you check out that tree, don't worry. Plenty of other trees can make up for your loss. The forest's 4,800 acres are filled with trails that take you past other giant sequoias in addition to ponderosa pines, sugar pines, cedars, and firs.

Some of the rangers aren't keen on the forest's leash-free policy, and they recommend it only for the best-trained dogs. They say they've seen too many dogs get lost or chase down critters that are best left alone. But chances are if you and your dog aren't used to elevations around 6,500 feet, neither of you will be in the mood to run far. In the words of one ranger, "People just suck for oxygen until they get accustomed to the air up here."

Campsites are free, but dogs must be leashed. Sites are available June–October and are on a first-come, first-served basis. From Highway 190 in Springville, drive north on Balch Park Drive for three miles and then head east on Bear Creek Road for 15–21 miles, depending on your destination within the forest. Mobile homes should take an alternate route, continuing up Balch Park Drive for about 30 more miles to the park. Be sure to get a trail map and some ranger advice before venturing into the forest. 559/539-2855 in winter, 559/539-2321 in summer.

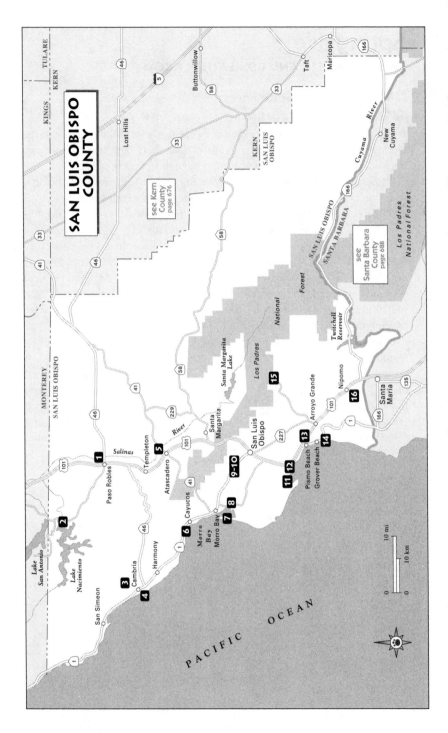

CHAPTER 48

San Luis Obispo County

Home of Hearst Castle, spectacular beaches, quaint seaside hamlets, and the mighty Pismo clam, this county is one of the state's most popular getaways. Dogs appreciate the olfactory beauty—the fishy piers, the farm-fresh soil, the smell of money—as much as their drivers enjoy the scenery and the history.

Dog activities are numerous. Your dog can dine with you at countless restaurants with outdoor tables. She can camp with you, fish with you, and tour wineries with you. She can stay with you at some decent digs, some of which are exceptionally dog friendly. (Dogs aren't allowed in Hearst Castle, or on its grounds, but that's no big surprise. Fortunately it's fairly easy to find a good pet-sitter or decent kennel around here.)

Thanks to Chevron (yes, Chevron), there's an off-leash beach just north of Morro Bay! Dog Beach is a truly bliss-inducing place to take a dog who needs to run like the wind. And dogs are welcome to be leash-free on 440 acres of coastside paradise, the Fiscalini Ranch Preserve in Cambria. These magnificent lands help make up for a dry spell going for dogs on at popular beaches:

PICK OF THE LITTER—
SAN LUIS OBISPO COUNTY

BEST BEACHES
Dog Beach, Morro Bay (page 666)
Oceano Dunes/Pismo State Beach, Pismo Beach (page 672)

BEST OFF-LEASH OCEANSIDE HIKING
Fiscalini Ranch Preserve, Cambria (page 659)

BEST DOG PARKS
Heilmann Dog Park, Atascadero (page 663)
El Chorro Regional Park Dog Park, San Luis Obispo
(page 668)

BEST COASTAL CANINE SOCIAL SCENE
Cambria Dog Park, Cambria (page 660)

COZIEST OUTDOOR EATING
Cambria Pines Lodge Restaurant, Cambria (page 661)

MOST DOG-FRIENDLY PLACE TO EAT
Mustache Pete's, Cambria (page 661)

RESTAURANT WITH BEST VIEWS
San Simeon Beach Bar and Grill, San Simeon (page 657)

Dogs are no longer allowed at most beaches throughout the county, thanks mainly to that seaside bird, the snowy plover. One beach in San Simeon, near the Best Western Cavalier Oceanfront Resort, still allows leashed dogs, as do Cayucos State Beach, a little area near Morro Rock, Dog Beach, and some beaches in the Pismo area.

Parks-4-Pups, a group of inspired, energetic dog lovers, led by the equally inspired and energetic Paula O'Farrell, is to thank for some of the leash-free parks and increased park access in the northern county in recent years. Thank you, Parks-4-Pups! To find out more about this group and how you can help with their efforts (including making sure dogs can continue to run leash-free at Dog Beach), go to www.tcsn.net/parks4pups.

MOST DOG-FRIENDLY ICE CREAM
The Scoop Ice Cream Parlor, Pismo Beach (page 673)

LODGING WITH BEST BEACH ACCESS
Best Western Cavalier Oceanfront Resort, San Simeon
(page 657)

MOST DOG-FRIENDLY PLACES TO STAY
Vine Street Inn, Paso Robles (page 656)
Cambria Shores Inn, Cambria (page 661)
Fogcatcher Inn, Cambria (page 662)
Cayucos Beach Inn, Cayucos (page 664)
Cottage Inn by the Sea, Pismo Beach (page 674)

BEST LODGING TO GET AWAY FROM IT ALL
Cambria Pines Lodge, Cambria (page 661)

BEST ASSORTMENT OF WINERIES
Paso Robles (page 654)

COOLEST EVENT
Dog Splash Days, northern San Luis Obispo County
(page 659)

MOST DOG-FRIENDLY SHOPPING
Prime Outlets, Pismo Beach (page 673)

NATIONAL FORESTS

The *National Forests and Wilderness Areas* resource at the back of this book has important information and safety tips on visiting national forests with your dog and has more information on the Los Padres National Forest.

Los Padres National Forest
🐾🐾🐾🐾🐕

Both the Santa Lucia Wilderness and the Manchesna Mountain Wilderness, east of the city of San Luis Obispo, are ideal for dogs who like their wilderness spelled with a capital W.

Paso Robles

PARKS, BEACHES, AND RECREATION AREAS

Until 2007, dogs weren't allowed in any Paso Robles parks. Yes, archaic but true. But thanks to some hardworking people in the local grassroots group, Parks-4-Pups, a couple of trails now permit dogs on leash—at press time, at least on a trial basis. And if all goes as hoped, this is just the proverbial paw in the door: Dogs may have their own off-leash park by the time the next edition of this book comes out. Stay tuned for exciting details! Meanwhile, a peek at other dog-friendly trails and areas.

🐾 Centennial Park Dog Walk

🐾🐾🐾 (See San Luis Obispo County map on page 650)

Woo hoo! Dogs are finally allowed to step paw in a Paso Robles park! This is a huge deal around this city. Until 2007, dogs were positively banned from all city parks here. That is an old, old, silly law, and we are very glad to see it changing. At press time, the trail was open to dogs on a trial basis, but all was looking rosy for the city council approving leashed dogs permanently.

The trail is a paved half-mile shaded loop that connects to a couple of pleasant, shaded bike trails for a total of about two miles of doggy romping room. You'll find poop bags along the way (always a good indicator dogs are allowed), and some picnic tables, should you want to enjoy a little food or rest along the way. From southbound U.S. 101, take the 16th Street exit, turn left on 13th Street, which turns into Creston Road. Go right on Nickerson Drive and follow signs to the park. You'll see signs for the walking trail. 805/237-3988.

DIVERSION

A Loaf of Bread, a Glass of Wine, and Thy Dog: Your dog may not have quite the nose for fine wines that you do, but he'd probably make an excellent companion when you visit some of the dog-friendly wineries of Paso Robles:

Le Cuvier Winery, 9750 Adelaida Road; 805/238-5706; www.lcwine.com.

Eberle Winery, 3810 Highway 46 East; 805/238-9607; www.eberlewinery.com.

Meridian Vineyards, 7000 Highway 46 East; 805/226-7133; www.meridianvineyards.com.

Sycamore Farms, 2485 Highway 46 West; 805/238-5288. There's an herb farm here, too. Thanks to Ruby Dog and Susan Brown for letting us know about this one!

DIVERSION

They're Charming and Slobbery and You Can Shop in their Store: When English Bulldogs Fanny and Winston hear the jingly bell ring at their sweet little home-furnishing/gift shop in downtown Paso Robles, they bustle over to the door to greet visitors. Their tongues hang out, they may slobber a bit, and they wag their bodies excitedly because they are so happy to see *you.* "At last, you're here!" they seem to say. It makes a body feel mighty welcome.

Fanny and Winston also enjoy seeing other dogs at their store, **Gibson and Company,** so your well-behaved doggy is invited to come along as you shop for attractive home furnishings and one-of-a-kind gifts. "I'd rather have dogs than children," says the shop's human owner, Jeanne Gibson.

Gibson and Company is at 1218 Pine Street, downtown. If you can't find it, ask just about any local where you can find Fanny and Winston Dogs and they'll point you in the right direction. They are legendary characters around here. 805/239-1979.

2 Lake Nacimiento

🐾 🐾 (See San Luis Obispo County map on page 650)

While this oak-lined lake has 165 miles of shoreline, only the section run by Lake Nacimiento Resort is open to the public. And with the resort's limited dog areas, that means just a so-so vacation for canines. Dogs are allowed on leash in the meadows and picnic areas. They're also allowed to camp with you at any of the resort's 350 sites. But unless your dog enjoys helping you fish for white bass and smallmouth bass from your boat, a visit here probably won't be the highlight of her year.

Dogs need to show proof of rabies vaccine. (I love the way rangers everywhere often state this: "They need to show proof of rabies." I've been tempted to answer, "Well, sir, he has been getting a little foamy around the mouth of late. Is that proof enough?" But I refrain, because I want to get into the park.) The day-use fee is $10 for the first two people, and $3 per additional adult. Kids are free. Dogs are $2–6 extra. Campsites are $30 per night per vehicle. Reservations are needed for RV sites. From U.S. 101, exit at Highway 46 and go west at the off-ramp. Follow this road, known for most of its span as Nacimiento Lake Road, for eight miles. When you get to County Road G-14, make a hard right and drive another eight miles. The resort is on the left. 805/238-3256.

PLACES TO STAY

Hampton Inn and Suites: The rooms here are spacious and clean, and they come with a little fridge, microwave, and access to the hotel's heated outdoor pool and whirlpool. Start your day with some good eats from the inn's breakfast bar. (Your dog must be content with her dog food, though.)

The folks who answer the phone say there's a 25-pound limit, but we are told that it's not strictly enforced at all. Rates are $120–169. A credit card deposit is required against doggy damage. 212 Alexa Court 93446; 805/226-9988.

La Quinta Inn & Suites: This is a pleasant, clean place to stay with a dog. You get free Wi-Fi here, and a good expanded continental breakfast. Pool access is for people only, not pooches. Rates are $109–179. 3446 Buena Vista Drive 93446; 805/239-3004.

TraveLodge: Rates are $59–159. The inn used to advertise that only small dogs were allowed, but now "We're more dog-friendly. As long as your dog's not an elephant," he's allowed, says the manager. (During a recent phone call the front-desk clerk told us there's a 10-pound limit—basically the size of Jake's head. This didn't seem right, based on the previous conversation with a manager. We then spoke with another manager, who said there's no size limit. Could be interesting at check in! Be sure to really nail this down before showing up with your dog.) Dogs are $10 extra. 2701 Spring Street 93446; 805/238-0078 or 800/578-7878.

Vine Street Inn: This charming inn was built in 1887 and word has it that it sits on land once owned by the uncle of Jesse James. (Yes, the lad who killed many a man, robbed the Glendale train, etc.) Enough history already! What's in it for your dog? A marvelous, dog-friendly cottage, and that's just the beginning.

Margot Van Horn, innkeeper/owner, tells us she doesn't have the correct lingo to write a description for dog guests, so she left it up to her personable little toy poodle, Hugo, to write something I can pass along to readers. (I hear a French accent when I read his writing. I think you will, too.):

"Woof Woof! I want to spread the word of how wonderful it is for all fellow dogs to come and visit. The first thing you get when you enter the cottage is of course a lot of hugs and pets from my gracious mistress, Madame Margot; face kissing from me; and you will find immediately a nice large bowl of water on the kitchen floor to quench your thirst. As well, your masters and mistresses will find large and small dog cookies and chewies in the refrigerator. There's a wonderful fenced yard where we can play. I hope you like to play because that's my FAVORITE thing. I hope to see you soon. Wooooof, whiff, wof, wif wifer (if pronounced correctly all dogs will understand this). Hugo."

I'd better watch out, because with writing like this, my publisher might consider having Hugo write the next edition of this book.

The cottage has its own private fenced patio under a spreading Blue Oak. It can sleep up to four people and has a full kitchen. The cottage is $243–270, and there's a two-night minimum. Longer stays qualify for discounts. Dogs pay a $200 deposit refundable once the cottage is given the all-clear. A huge thanks to Barbara Steinberg for giving us the heads up about this great little find! 1521 Vine Street 93446; 805/237-8463; www.vinestreetinn.com.

San Simeon

Dogs aren't trusted anywhere near the gilded towers of William Randolph Hearst's castle, so if you're thinking of visiting while your dog is with you, forget it. He'll have to wait in the car for at least three hours while you tour the castle, and that's a very bad idea.

But that doesn't mean you have to forgo this spectacular attraction. The Tail Wag's Inn, about nine miles south in Cambria, will board your dog for as long as your tour takes. With all the frills the inn provides your pet, she may come back thinking she should be living in Hearst Castle. Phone 805/927-3194 for info. There are also plenty of dog-sitters around. Ask your hotel for a recommendation.

Unfortunately, dogs are no longer allowed to amble on San Simeon State Beach (although you can still camp there), so your romping room here is rather limited. But if you stay at the wonderful Best Western Cavalier Oceanfront Resort, you'll be staying at the only beach around here where dogs are allowed. They have to wear leashes, but at least they get to enjoy themselves. (You can get to the beach even if you don't stay there, but it's sure nice to stay at a place where you can play on the beach.)

PLACES TO EAT

San Simeon Beach Bar and Grill: The panoramic ocean views from the outdoor tables (where dogs are allowed) make this a real destination restaurant for hungry dogs and their people. It can get windy here, though. Enjoy clam chowder, pizzas, and good grilled grub. 9520 Castillo Drive; 805/927-4604.

PLACES TO STAY

Best Western Cavalier Oceanfront Resort: This is San Simeon's only oceanfront hotel, and it's one of the most attractive and well-run Best Westerns we've ever checked out. (But don't let its brochure get your hopes up: The picture on the cover is not of the Best Western. It's Hearst Castle.) Many of the 90 rooms have a wood-burning fireplace, a stocked minibar, close-up ocean views, and a private patio. There's even room service, so you and your dog can dine together in the comfort of your own seaside abode. The humans in your party can keep in shape in the fitness room or at the two outdoor pools here (with ocean views to drool for). And if you stay here, you and your leashed pooch will have easy access to the long beach that backs up to the lodging. This is a huge deal right now, because no other beach in the area permits pooches.

Sunny Dog, a canine reader from Dayton, Ohio, had his person, Peggy, describe what they love most about their visits here: "It is quite delightful to sit on your patio and drink in that fabulous ocean view. The fire pits (surrounded by chairs) are lit at sunset and left burning through the night for those folks who want to enjoy the fire, the sound of the ocean, and the distant light from the Piedras Blancas Lighthouse." Nice writing, Sunny.

Many people are tempted to leave their dogs in their rooms when they go explore magnificent Hearst Castle, but this is a big no-no. The Cavalier makes it easy for you to do the right thing: It provides numbers for dog-sitters and for a wonderful kennel in Cambria. Be forewarned, though: At busy times, you need to make dog-care reservations well ahead of your visit.

Rates are $119–299. 9415 Hearst Drive 93452; 805/927-4688 or 800/826-8168; www.cavalierresort.com.

Motel 6: A Motel 6 in the same town as Hearst Castle? Go figure. This one started as a Holiday Inn, so it's a cut above many other Motel 6s. Rates are $39–99 for one adult (hey, it's San Simeon, where $100 Motel 6s aren't given a second thought), $6 for the second adult. The size limit of the past is history: "Just no horses," says a manager. 9070 Castillo Drive 93452; 805/927-8691.

Silver Surf Motel: The cover of the brochure for the Silver Surf has a picture of a magnificent mansionlike building with a cherub statue pointing to it. "Stay at Silver Surf Motel" it declares. And you thought Hearst Castle was gorgeous. Oh, wait, that *is* Hearst Castle on the cover. Ohhh, the brochure also says, "Visit Hearst Castle." Alas. The Silver Surf isn't exactly Hearst Castle, but then again, what is? This motel is pretty darned decent, with 72 rooms in a peaceful garden setting with plenty of trees to sniff, and a really attractive indoor pool and spa. Some rooms even have ocean views and fireplaces. Not bad for a motel, eh? Rates are $49–189. Dogs are $10 extra. 9390 Castillo Drive 93452; 805/927-4661 or 800/621-3999; www.silversurfmotel.com.

Cambria

Dogs love Cambria. It's a beautiful seaside haven that opens its sandy arms to dogs. Many restaurants here are dog friendly, and a number of hotels welcome dogs as well. Now that Cambria has its own dog park, it's the perfect place for a little pooch vacation on the Pacific. And while you're here, be sure to check out a real true-blue chunk of off-leash Dog Heaven: Fiscalini Ranch.

Unfortunately, two terrific beaches visitors once flocked to with dogs (Moonstone Beach and Shamel County Park's beach) are still off-limits, thanks to the snowy plover. But the boardwalk at Moonstone is dog friendly, and a very pleasant little 1.5-mile jaunt each way. There are even poop bags along the way (for your dog, in case you were wondering).

PARKS, BEACHES, AND RECREATION AREAS

Two popular beaches have closed to dogs, but—joy of joys—Cambria has a

DOG-EAR YOUR CALENDAR

Take Your Pooch to a Pool: Your dog will think you're all wet if you don't let her go to **Dog Splash Days,** a ridiculously fun event where dogs get to swim in outdoor community swimming pools. The pools are set up with ramps for easy entry and exit. Dogs have a choice of doing the pooch paddle in at least two local pools on the weekend after Labor Day.

Doesn't this muck up the water with hair and dog saliva? Probably. Does it matter? Not a bit: This is when the pools officially close to humans, and right before they're drained and super cleansed. Even if your dog doesn't swim, she'll have a great time just hanging out on the grass with you, perhaps joining you for a little picnic.

Dogs are $10, and humans are free. (The only humans you'll see in the pool are some dog trainers who help the dogs get in and out. They wear wetsuits to prevent scratches from all those paws paddling.) The event is a fundraiser for Parks-4-Pups, a local organization that has been instrumental in opening parklands to dogs and starting off-leash parks in Northern San Luis Obispo County. Contact Parks-4-Pups for details: 805/239-4437; www.tcsn.net/parks4pups.

dog park now! It's a much-needed addition to this very dog-friendly town. Best of all, dogs may go leash-free at the big, beautiful Fiscalini Ranch Preserve, a real coastal gem.

🐾 Fiscalini Ranch Preserve

🐾🐾🐾🐾🐕 (See San Luis Obispo County map on page 650)

You want to talk about dog heaven on earth? This 440-acre preserve that stretches along one stunning mile of oceanfront absolutely embodies that concept. Dogs are allowed to be leash-free everywhere except for one trail (the Bluff Trail), and oh the sights they'll see and the smells they'll smell. From the preserve's many trails, you can see rugged cliffs and tidepools below, and sometimes dolphins, otters, and whales. (Watch your dog's nose flare when a whale gets close. I think dogs can smell their powerful cetacean breath.) Above, you see the nearby hills and mountains. You can hike through cool Monterey Pine forests or enjoy a landscape full of wildflowers in spring. "It's simply wonderful there. There's something for everyone. It's an extremely special place," says Connie Davidson, who walked four or five miles most days with her beautiful friend, Buddha, a Great Dane/German shorthaired pointer/hound dog mix. (Sadly, Buddha has now gone from dog heaven on earth to the real deal. We hope it's as incredible as Fiscalini.)

How did this preserve get to be so dog friendly? Several years ago the property, then a ranch, was put up for sale. Housing developers were licking their lips and rubbing their hands at the opportunity to build hundreds of acres of residential developments along the coast. But local residents were horrified and stepped in to stop the development. They were instrumental in getting several agencies and enough resources together so that the land could be purchased and kept wild and natural. It was a huge accomplishment. Since citizens were behind this, they got to help decide how best to use the land, and they wanted dogs to be able to run leash-free. Dogs are deeply thankful. Without the people and the agencies, "we would have a sea of houses," says Davidson, who also works for one of the agencies that oversees the property (the Cambria Community Services District).

The property is split by Highway 1, and the best place for dogs is on the western part, which is a whopping 364 acres. To get there, take U.S. 1 to Windsor Avenue. If you're northbound, turn left, if you're southbound, turn right. Follow Windsor past a little park, and a residential area, Seacliff Estates. Just before the road ends, you'll find a few parking spots, or you can park in the residential area before that. You'll see two trails at the road's end. The one on your left allows off-leash dogs. The one on your right is the Bluff Trail, and dogs need to be leashed. Several other trails eventually branch off from these trails, and they're all good for well-behaved leash-free dogs! 805/909-1234 or 805/909-9794.

◳ Cambria Dog Park

🐾🐾🐾🐕 (See San Luis Obispo County map on page 650)

Dogs from all over the West use this park. That's because it's in an excellent location in the touristy part of Cambria. "I go by at 6:45 A.M. on my way to work, and that dog park is filled with people," says an employee of a local hotel. "I think to myself, 'Are you out of your minds?' But our guests with dogs love it. It seems to be THE happening place for dogs."

The Cambria Dog Park is indeed the place to come for socializing with your dog in Cambria. On any given day, you'll find plenty of tourist dogs here with their people, mixing with the friendly locals. "This park is a great source of happiness and sociability for dogs and people," says Joyce Heller, who was behind this park's inception.

As for the park's features, first of all, it's fenced, which apparently was a feat unto itself. Much of the park work was done by volunteers, and on fencing day, "it was pouring rain, and most of the people doing it were in their 70s, and the fence now is in kind of a funky line," says Heller. There are no trees, but there's a shade structure, should you want one in the usually clement weather here. The park also has a smaller section for small or delicate dogs, chairs, a hydrant, hauled-in water, and a good parking lot. The ground is bark, which always seems so appropriate for a dog park.

The park is at the very south end of Main Street, near its southern intersection with Highway 1. (Main Street loops around and hits Highway 1 at two points. You need the southern end.) 805/927-6223.

PLACES TO EAT

Here's a sampling of the dog-friendly eateries in Cambria:

Cambria Pines Lodge Restaurant: This is a truly unique outdoor dining experience. You and your dog get to dine in cozy little alcoves with glorious rock fireplaces. The alcoves kind of wrap you up and protect you from the elements. They're very popular, and there are only two of these alcoves with two tables each (that would be four tables, if Jake's math is correct), so if you want one you may have to wait a while. Reservations are highly recommended. Non-fireplace alfresco dining is also available, and if you're chilly you'll be given a blanket.

The food is upscale American fare, with produce that's mostly organically grown at the lodge's gardens. (The restaurant is part of the dog-friendly Cambria Pines Lodge.) 2905 Burton Drive; 805/927-4200 or 800/445-6868.

Mustache Pete's: Two dogs wrote to tell us about this fun eatery's covered patio area (which is heated when it gets chilly). Charlie Dog says he felt very welcomed because he got a biscuit upon arrival. And Copper Dog really lucked out: The server gave him a prime rib bone while his person, Kim, enjoyed her spaghetti. "I doubt Copper will ever be the same again after this gourmet snack," writes Kim. There's always a big bowl of water here, too. The gourmet pizzas are delectable, but Terry and Belle (Charlie's people) recommend the meatloaf.

These days, Mustache Pete's has two patios: One for people with dogs, and one for people without dogs. It's kind of like the old days when you'd be asked "Smoking or Nonsmoking?" only now, it's "Dogs or No Dogs?" Or something like that. 4090 Burton Drive; 805/927-8589.

PLACES TO STAY

Cambria Pines Lodge: You and your dog get to stay at one of nine rustic-yet-upscale cabins here that permit pooches. The 25-acre wooded property comes with oodles of Monterey pines and several trails for your dog's perusal. The gardens here are world class. This is a glorious place to visit if you want a little nature in your otherwise civilized vacation.

Your stay here comes with a full breakfast in the lodge. You can also eat at the lodge's wonderful restaurant with your dog. But no dogs are permitted in the great outdoor pool or day spa. The cabins are $99–399. Dogs are $25 extra. 2905 Burton Drive 93428; 805/927-4200 or 800/445-6868; www.cambria pineslodge.com.

Cambria Shores Inn: This charming and very dog-friendly little inn is just a bone's throw from the dog-friendly boardwalk at beautiful Moonstone Beach. Literally. You could throw a bone (OK, a tennis ball) from your room, and if you have a good arm, it will cross the street and end up down on the beach. Of course, this won't work if you don't have an ocean-view room, and it could get a little ugly in fact, but with three-quarters of the rooms here blessed with ocean views, your chances for a water landing are pretty good.

The innkeepers welcome dogs with open arms and with a VIP dog basket! The basket includes a beach towel (these can be replenished), a sheet to cover the bed if your dog sleeps there, a flashlight for nighttime outings, bowls, and custom dog treats. "Dogs are our niche," explains a friendly innkeeper. "We like to make them feel right at home." If only home were like this: Upon check-in, humans get homemade chocolate chip cookies. At "hors d'oeuvres hour" in the late afternoon, guests can relax after a long day of fun and eat all kinds of tasty treats, and in the future, drink a little wine. (The inn's lobby will be going through a remodel soon. After it's done, the owners hope to have a wine bar and appetizers to order.) A scrumptious continental breakfast, consisting of fresh fruit, croissants, a carafe of orange juice, and a dog biscuit (for the Very Important Pooch in your party), is delivered to your room in the morning. If you prefer, you can pick up your breakfast in the lobby.

Rates are $129–289. Dogs are $15 extra. 6276 Moonstone Beach Drive 93428; 805/927-8644 or 800/433-9179; www.cambriashores.com.

Creekside Inn: Want to stay really close to the local dog park? This charming, basic, clean, comfy motel is just 500 yards away and offers several dog-friendly rooms. A few of them have balconies overlooking a creek. Actually, there are so many trees and so much nature between the balconies and the creek that the creek isn't really that viewable. But it's the thought that a creek's back there that counts. You might even see some deer and other signs of nature in that area. Dogs like this. Rates are $59–169. 2618 Main Street 93428; 800/269-5212; www.cambriacreeksideinn.com.

Fogcatcher Inn: The inn has a lovely English country style, with vaulted ceilings and gardens that are to drool for almost all year-round. The rooms are spacious and well appointed, and each has a fireplace, microwave, and fridge. The heated outdoor pool has a decent ocean view, and a free hot breakfast buffet comes with your stay here. (No beasts at the buffet, please. We know how literally dogs take the phrase "all you can eat.")

What dogs like best is that they get a dog biscuit or two or three upon check-in. As for size limits, don't worry: "Last weekend we had a big German shepherd and a little Pekingese," said a manager, who loves doggy guests. "We take any good dog." Two rooms allow pets. Rates are $99–349. Dogs pay a $25 flat fee. 6400 Moonstone Beach Drive 93428; 805/927-1400 or 800/425-4121; www.fogcatcherinn.com.

Mariner's Inn: The owners here like dogs; they have a 132-pound English mastiff who's the sweetest thing around. Some of the rooms have ocean views. Rates are $55–210. Dogs are $10 extra. 6180 Moonstone Beach Drive 93428; 805/927-4624 or 800/344-0407; www.marinersinncambria.com.

Atascadero

PARKS, BEACHES, AND RECREATION AREAS

Atascadero now has its own dog park, thanks to the efforts of Paula O'Farrell and her inspired, energetic group, Parks-4-Pups, a nonprofit organization dedicated to promoting and protecting recreational opportunities for dog owners in north San Luis Obispo County. They are doing a four-paw job. Applause!

🐾 Heilmann Dog Park

🐾🐾🐾🐾 ✕ (See San Luis Obispo County map on page 650)

Sure, this attractive fenced dog park has the usual dog park amenities, like water, poop bags, and picnic tables (with umbrellas!). But it's also graced by sycamores and wine barrels planted with flowers. This is one pretty park. Dogs and their people love it here. The parking is excellent, and restrooms are nearby, to boot.

But what really sets this place apart is that it's so doggone social. It hosts Saturday coffee socials (known as Coffee and Canines) complete with doughnuts, it hosts Thursday evening socials during summer, and it's home to several events, including Wienerdog races and a visit from Santa Paws. If you want to exercise your dog in a lovely setting and be among a very friendly canine community, this park is the place for you.

The park is a quick jaunt from U.S. 101. From U.S. 101 take the Santa Rosa Road exit and follow the signs to Heilmann Regional Park. (It's east of the freeway.) Once at the park, drive to the end of the road (El Bordo Avenue). The dog park is at the end of the road. If you're coming from El Camino Real, turn east on El Bordo Avenue and follow it a couple of long blocks to Heilmann Regional Park. Continue to the end of the road, where you'll find parking and the dog park. 805/781-5930.

PLACES TO STAY

Motel 6: Rates are $52–66. 9400 El Camino Real 93422; 805/466-6701.

Cayucos

A funkier coastal community would be hard to find. Cayucos, about eight miles north of Morro Bay, provides a great escape from summer crowds. Even on holiday weekends, the place doesn't get packed. The Old West stores and saloons are a real find, but if you'd rather fish than shop and drink, try the old pier on Cayucos State Beach. It was built in 1875, and those in charge figure a few dogs aren't going to hurt it now. Besides, the fishing is great, and what dog wouldn't enjoy watching you reel in a mackerel or a salmon?

PARKS, BEACHES, AND RECREATION AREAS

6 Cayucos State Beach

😊😊😊😊 (See San Luis Obispo County map on page 650)

This beach is wide and wonderful, and dogs are actually allowed here on a leash! This is a big contrast to other state beaches in the area. Since the county actually runs the beach, and since there aren't big environmental issues at this one, dogs are still OK.

A couple of good greasy-spoon joints lurk nearby. We like to order lunch and bring it to the beach, where dogs pray hard that you'll drop a french fry in the sand.

The south end of the beach has fewer people and more seaweed—the stuff of fine dog outings. From Highway 1, go southwest on Cayucos Drive and turn left at Ocean Drive. You can enter almost anywhere between Cayucos Road and E Street, west of Ocean Drive. 805/781-5930.

PLACES TO STAY

Cayucos Beach Inn: This attractive, upscale, very dog-friendly motel is one block from the ocean, with easy beach access. Dogs love this. And they really love how they're treated here. Upon arrival, dogs get a Pet Package with dog treats, white towels (decorated with paw prints) for use after beach romps, and a dog blanket. The inn is so well set up for dogs that there's even a special hose outside for rinsing off wet, sandy dogs. Dogs don't like this, but it helps keep the place clean.

Room amenities for humans include fridges, microwaves, a wet bar, very comfy pillow-top beds, and a delicious continental breakfast. Many rooms have ocean views. Rates are $85–195. Dogs are $10 for the first night, $5 thereafter. That fee is good for up to three dogs! And it's not a per-pooch fee, but a per-stay fee. That's a doggone good deal, considering what they get. 333 South Ocean Avenue 93430; 805/995-2828 or 800/482-0555; www.cayucos beachinn.com.

Dolphin Inn: Frankly, I'd stay here just for the name, but the inn has other attractive features, such as its proximity to the water and a continental breakfast that comes with your room. Rates are $59–199. Dogs pay a flat fee of $10. 399 South Ocean Avenue 93430; 805/995-3810 or 800/540-4276; www .thedolphininn.com.

Estero Bay Motel: Just a half block from the ocean, this U-shaped motel is a fine place to spend the night with your dog. We like the owner's explanation for the motel's dog-friendly policy: "There are a lot of nice older women who have dogs they just can't part with. We want to help them stay together." *Awwww.* Rates are $59–129. Dogs are $10 extra. 25 South Ocean Avenue 93430; 805/995-3614 or 800/736-1292; www.esterobaymotel.com.

Shoreline Inn: If your dog longs for sand between his toes, stay here. This attractive inn is a few long steps from the beach, where leashed pooches are allowed. All rooms have a view of the strand and surf. The rooms are typical motel-style, but the suites are really lovely. They're light and airy, and all feature private balconies and TVs with extended cable channels. Our favorite two suites have fridges and fireplaces. All rooms and suites come with VCRs, which is a real plus when traveling with kids. Rates are $105–180. Dogs pay a flat $15 fee. 1 North Ocean Avenue 93430; 805/995-3681 or 800/549-2244; www.cayucosshorelineinn.com.

Morro Bay

The landmark Morro Rock draws more visitors to this seaside community than its beaches and quaint stores. This 576-foot-tall, 50-acre-wide extinct volcano peak juts into the Pacific and beckons anyone who gets a glimpse. In fact, in 1512 it attracted explorer Juan Rodríguez Cabrillo, who named the rock, which has become a landmark for ocean navigators and tourists. Dogs are no longer allowed to visit the rock, since it's part of the whole rotten deal with state beaches in the area. But they can come mighty close by visiting Coleman City Park.

And for pure doggy bliss, check out Dog Beach, a new discovery with this edition of the book.

PARKS, BEACHES, AND RECREATION AREAS

7 Dog Beach

😊😊😊😊🐕 (See San Luis Obispo County map on page 650)

Psst, dogs. I'll let you in on a little secret: If you don't know someone who knows about this beach, you'll never find out about it. So we're here to tell you about it, because you're a good dog.

This six-acre white-sand beach is adored by local dogs and their people, who get to throw their leashes to the wind once they're off the bluffs and on the beach. It's not just sand and surf here, either. Driftwood and rock make the landscape even more interesting for dogs. And the water itself is often so calm that even dogs who would never set a paw in most California surf might be tempted to do a little dog paddling.

This stretch of paradise comes to you courtesy of Chevron, which has been the overseer of this property for ages. Chevron will be decommissioning the land within a decade, but it looks like it's going to fall into dog-friendly hands, thanks to lobbying by pro-dog residents and groups like Parks-4-Pups. We'll keep our noses to the ground and keep you posted in future editions.

A big thanks to Sadie, a chocolate Lab who whines in anticipation when she's within a half mile of the beach, for letting us know about this sparkling gem. The beach is in the northernmost part of Morro Bay, about a mile north of Highway 41, a little south of the Cayucos border. From Highway 1, turn west on Yerba Buena Street, and make a quick right into the beach's parking lot. If

DIVERSION

Get Married, then Read a Book (or Vice Versa): Well-behaved dogs are welcome to go shopping with you at **Coalesce... A Bookstore & More,** in the old downtown section of Morro Bay. This independent bookstore offers a great variety of books, cards, and little gifties, and "as long as your dog doesn't do leg lifts like my old dog," you can bring your pooch along to help you select a title, says JoAnne, who has worked in the store for 20 years.

But wait! There's more! Should you want to get married with your pooch at your side, you can do that here, too. Talk about one-stop shopping. (Maybe this is what the "& More" part of the name means.) There's a charming little chapel tucked behind the store. Unlike buying books, however, you will have to make arrangements for your wedding ahead of time, and returns are discouraged.

We send a big arf to Susan Brown and Ruby for giving us the inside scoop on this fun place. 845 Main Street, Morro Bay; 805/772-2880.

you see poop bag dispensers at the parking lot, you'll know you're in the right place. Because the property is currently in a kind of no-man's-land, we're not able to list a contact phone number.

8 Coleman Park

🐾🐾 (See San Luis Obispo County map on page 650)

This is the park to visit if you forgot your sunscreen. At the right time of day, the shadow of Morro Rock will loom over you and protect you from those wrinkling rays. Walking through the dunes here while under the spell of the volcanic mound can be a hypnotic experience. Don't let the otherworldly quality of it all make you forget that your dog is supposed to be leashed.

There's a little area just north of the rock where dogs are allowed to wet their paws, since it's not state land. Water dogs, and any dog who is running a little warm, really appreciate this. The park is to the north of Morro Rock. For easy access, park in the Morro Rock lot, after Embarcadero turns into Coleman Drive. There's another lot for the park on the north side of Coleman Drive just before the rock. 805/772-6200.

PLACES TO STAY

Bayfront Inn: This place faces the waterfront and has terrific views of Morro Rock, a view the Bayfront Inn claims is the best view in Morro Bay. The rooms are small, but there's a pool and an attractive sunning area with a hot tub. Rooms have fridges and come with a continental breakfast. Rates are $69–159. Dogs are $12 extra. 1150 Embarcadero 93442; 805/772-5607 or 800/799-5607; www.bayfront-inn.com.

Econo Lodge: This 1960s-era inn is bright white with aqua doors—a real throwback to the glory days of motels. Rates are $59–149. Dogs are $15 extra. 540 Main Street 93442; 805/772-7503 or 888/900-3692.

Morro Strand State Beach: The beach gets much less use than many others around here, and it used to be heavenly for dogs. But now dogs are allowed only at the 104-site campground. The campground is nothing fancy or rustic. It's actually a converted parking lot. But it's right over the beach, so if sounds of crashing surf send you to sleep, you'll get your eight hours here. Camping costs $20–25. The beach/campground is west of Highway 1 between Atascadero Road and Yerba Buena Avenue. For camping reservations, call 800/444-7275.

San Luis Obispo

This city is the big jewel of the Central Coast. Some of the smaller gems such as Pismo Beach and Morro Bay can be more lustrous for dogs, but there's so much history here, and so much to do, that you're both bound to enjoy your visit.

If the past interests you at all, be sure to stop at the Chamber of Commerce and pick up a *Heritage Walks* pamphlet showing the fascinating buildings where much of California's history was shaped. Dogs may yawn as they trot by some of the ice cream–colored Victorians and whitewashed adobes, but when they arrive at Mission Plaza, the good times roll.

The plaza is the heart of the city and the home of Mission San Luis Obispo de Tolosa, built in 1772. Dogs aren't allowed inside, but it's the world outside that will interest them more anyway. That's where the beautiful Mission Plaza tantalizes with scents and sounds dogs love. A brick path follows a cool stream nestled in conifers full of songbirds and takes you by a few delicious-smelling restaurants with tables on the wood patios overlooking the stream.

But beware: The reason dogs like it here so much isn't necessarily for the food or ambience. They're wild about all the four-legged creatures who slink around here meowing for handouts of food and attention. If you have a cat-crazed canine, either avoid this area or keep a very tight hold on her leash.

PARKS, BEACHES, AND RECREATION AREAS

🟥 El Chorro Regional Park
😺 😺 😺 😺 (See San Luis Obispo County map on page 650)

For some reason, not that many people visit this 1,730-acre park, except on holidays and some summer weekends. You'll rarely find others on the four miles of trail here, but you may well run into deer, so keep your dog leashed except within the boundaries of the new dog park.

It's not even that common to see people using the many group picnic areas. There are 45 developed campsites, all with full hookups. Sites are $18–29. On weekends and holidays April–September, there's a $3 fee for dogs to get into the park, as well as a $2 per-vehicle fee. Driving south on U.S. 101, take the Santa Rosa Street/Highway 1 exit. Turn left on Santa Rosa (which turns into Highway 1 after Highland Drive). Continue about five miles. The park is on your right across from Cuesta College. 805/781-5930.

🔟 El Chorro Regional Park Dog Park
😺 😺 😺 😺 🐾 (See San Luis Obispo County map on page 650)

The fenced-in dog park at El Chorro Regional Park is a hot dog place, in more than one sense: It's a very popular dog park, and it has a huge, working barbecue pit in it. (It's about three feet by 10 feet. That's 30 square feet of dog heaven.) Cooking juicy burgers, hot dogs, and chicken in the center of a bunch of dogs who have worked up big appetites seems like an invitation to trouble, but apparently it's never been a problem here. (Then again, Jake has never been here during a cookout.)

Small and large dogs have separate areas (the grill is in the large-dog section). There's freshwater, plenty of trees, picnic tables, and tennis balls. Gus the Dog, who visits the park almost every day, wrote to tell us that he adores

DIVERSION

Catch a Fur Flick: The **Sunset Drive-In Theater** allows quiet dogs for no extra charge. Some pooches really enjoy a movie starring a dog, so be sure to bring your best friend if you notice one playing. Rates are $6 per human adult. Kids under 11 are free. 255 Elks Lane, San Luis Obispo; 805/544-4475.

the wood chips that cover the ground here. "It makes for great digging and chewing on sticks!" he wrote, via his translator, Erin.

The dog park is in the rear of El Chorro Regional Park, within the Lupine group picnic area. On weekends April–September and on holidays, there's a $3 fee for dogs to get in the larger park, as well as a $2 per-vehicle fee. Driving south on U.S. 101, take the Santa Rosa Street/Highway 1 exit. Turn left on Santa Rosa (which turns into Highway 1 after Highland Drive). Continue about five miles. The park is on your right across from Cuesta College. Follow signs to the dog park from the park entrance. 805/781-5930.

PLACES TO EAT

Country Yogurt Culture: Enter from the Mission Plaza side, where you and your dog can enjoy creekside tables and eight flavors of award-winning yogurt. The friendly service makes dogs feel right at home. 746 Higuera Street; 805/544-9007.

San Luis Fish and Barbeque: If you and Tex feel like good ol' barbecued anything, this is the place to get it. Slurp it down at the tables out front. 474 Marsh Street; 805/541-4191.

Uptown Espresso: Sip yours with a fresh bagel and your dog at your side on the large patio. You can even buy a pooch biscuit for a quarter. 1065 Higuera Street; 805/783-1300.

PLACES TO STAY

Best Western Royal Oak Motor Hotel: This is a terrific place to stay if your dog wants to stretch his legs. It's a quick walk to beautiful Laguna Lake Park, another great place to take your dog. When you're done walking, you can wash your sweaty clothes at the motel's laundry facility. Rates are $84–209. Dogs are $15 for the length of their stay. 214 Madonna Road 93405; 805/544-4410; www.royaloakhotel.com.

Days Inn San Luis Obispo: This newly remodeled Days Inn rates "5 Sunbursts," which is Days Inn lingo for super-duper. The rooms are big and airy, with furnishings that are a cut above those of most Days Inns. You'll get a fresh and fruity breakfast here. You'll also have access to a heated outdoor pool, hot tub, and exercise room. Your dog will have access to a nearby green strip. Everyone will be happy. Rates are $69–149. Dogs are $10 extra, and the management likes to keep them under 50 pounds, but that doesn't always happen. 2050 Garfield Street 93401; 800/544-7250.

Heritage Inn Bed and Breakfast: Very well behaved dogs who promise not to rile the owner's cat can stay with you on weekdays at this lovely, antique-furnished Victorian house. Advance arrangements are essential. The owner is careful about which dogs get to stay here. Joe would definitely not have been a welcome guest because of his tendency to try to make cats into eats. Dogs who get to stay are lucky indeed. The inn, while not in a rural area, is in a natural creekside setting. Pooches who do the dog paddle love it. Rates are $85–165 and include a full breakfast and a wine and cheese hour in the afternoon. Dogs pay a $35 flat fee. 978 Olive Street 93405; 805/544-7440; www.heritageinnslo.com.

Holiday Inn Express: Stay here and you can swim in the heated outdoor pool and have a free continental breakfast. Your dog can't, but don't feel bad: He's not paying the bill. Rates are $129–199. Dogs are $25 extra for the length of their stay. 1800 Monterey Street 93401; 805/544-8600.

Motel 6: There's a big field in back where dogs are allowed, at least for now. Rates are $44–105(!) for one adult, $3 for the second adult. 1625 Calle Joaquin 93401; 805/541-6992.

Avila Beach

This small coastal community is about the farthest north you'll find the Southern California beach lifestyle. And if you hear three siren blasts, prepare to have the beaches to yourself—the Diablo Canyon Nuclear Plant, which sits on a fault six miles north of town, just may have had a little boo-boo.

PARKS, BEACHES, AND RECREATION AREAS

🔟 Olde Port Beach

🐾🐾🐾 (See San Luis Obispo County map on page 650)

This lovely beach is secluded, with nary a soul around. Leashes are unfortunately now the law here, which seems a shame, since it's so far from the madding crowd.

It's still a much better beach for dogs than Avila Beach, and most state beaches in the county no longer even permit pooches. The name itself is picturesque, and so is the beach, looking out as it does on fishing boats moored offshore. If you have any salt in your blood, you'll enjoy the view from here. The occasional rider of personal watercraft can mar the tranquility, but if you visit in the cooler months, they are usually off doing more quiet activities.

From Highway 1/U.S. 101, take the Avila Beach exit west. Once in town, continue west, on Harford Drive. The beach is on your left. If you reach the Port San Luis Pier (not the modern, very long Union Oil Pier you'll come to first, but the woody old one in the harbor), you've gone too far. It's not so bad, though. You can either turn right around and find the beach or hang out at the pier and harbor area for a while. Dogs are fond of those fishy breezes and you'll enjoy looking at the old boats. 805/595-5400.

🔟 Avila Beach

🐾🐾 (See San Luis Obispo County map on page 650)

If you have images of strolling down the beach paw-in-hand with your dog all day long, change that image. Or at least change the hours. Dogs are permitted here, but only before 10 A.M. and after 5 P.M. You can understand the restrictions if you come here in the summer, when the place looks like Son of Jones Beach.

Dogs must be leashed. The beach runs along Front Street in the main part of Avila Beach. 805/595-5400.

Pismo Beach

The Chumash Indians, who lived here for at least 9,000 years, referred to this area as the place to find *pismu*, or tar. History has changed this once-pristine land to a busy seaside community, but your dog might show you that there's one thing that hasn't changed: This is still the place to find tar. Joe found it all over his paws when he was exploring one of the beaches. Later, despite cleaning his feet, I found it all over the inside of the truck. Even the dry cleaner found it—he found it amusing that the jacket I'd left inside the truck was covered with indelible paw prints.

This never happened again, and it has never happened to any other dogs we talked to on the beaches, so fear not. Pismo Beach is a good place for you and your dog to share some quality time. Most of the beaches here allow leashed dogs, who can be champion partners in clamming for the famous Pismo clams. They don't need a fishing license, but you will.

Pismo Beach is usually cool and foggy. It's ideal if you have a dog who melts in the heat. When we drive to Southern California, this is a must-stop area for whatever dog we're chauffeuring. Although there are no leash-free areas, they always appreciate land that is naturally air-conditioned.

PARKS, BEACHES, AND RECREATION AREAS

City parks here don't allow dogs. The 1,250-foot pier in the middle of the beach area also bans them. But there are a couple of beaches that more than make up for these places.

13 Oceano Dunes/Pismo State Beach

😺😺😺😺 (See San Luis Obispo County map on page 650)

It's hard to tell what dogs enjoy more here—exploring the long, wide beach or wandering through the great dunes above. Your leashed dog can get all the exercise he needs by trotting down the miles of trails on the unspoiled dunes. If he likes cold ocean spray, take him down to the beach for a romp among the gulls. (Dogs are allowed at both of these state beaches. This is a huge relief when you've come from the dog-verboten state beaches to the north.)

Camping is available at a couple of sections of the beach. Fees are $10 for the on-beach camping area south of the Pier Avenue entrance (four-wheel-drive vehicles are recommended) and $20–34 for camping among the trees at the Pismo State Beach North Beach Campground. There are a total of 185 campsites. For more info, call 805/473-7220. For reservations, 800/444-7275.

To avoid the $5 day-use fee at the Grand Avenue entrance, drive west from Highway 1 and park on Grand Avenue before the ranger kiosk. Once at the beach, head north. Walking south will put you in the middle of a busy off-highway vehicle area—not the best place for a dog. 805/773-7170.

14 Pismo Beach City Beach

😺😺😺 (See San Luis Obispo County map on page 650)

Does your dog like watching people in bathing suits play volleyball? Does she enjoy sniffing at bodies slathered with coconut oil? If so, this beach is for her.

DIVERSION

Give Your Dog an Outlet: Does your dog have a nose for bargains? Does he enjoy stores that welcome him inside? Does he desperately want to see you update your wardrobe without breaking into his dog-cookie fund? Then bring him to **Prime Outlets** in Pismo Beach, where dogs are welcome in most stores. Among the dog-friendly outlet stores: Geoffrey Beene, Izod, Jones NY, Polo, Tommy Hilfiger, and Van Heusen.

Prime Outlets' visitors desk/California Welcome Center reps provide shoppers with a list of dog-friendly stores and give visiting dogs a treat or two. "We have regulars who always come by for a snack while they're shopping," says an outlet manager. (I think he means dogs, not humans.) "It's always fun to see them."

Prime Outlets Pismo Beach is located at 333 Five Cities Drive; 805/773-4662; www.primeoutlets.com.

It's rarely so crowded that it's uncomfortable, but it's rarely so uncrowded that it's a bore for a social butterfly dog.

The farther north you walk, the fewer people you'll encounter. Dogs have to be leashed everywhere, but this shouldn't stop the digging breeds from helping you uncover prize Pismo clams (fishing licenses are required for the human half of the team). We once saw a dog who would thrust his entire snout into the wet sand and come up with a clam every time. His owner didn't even have to use his clam fork.

One of the many access points is west of Highway 1, at the foot of Main Avenue near the recreation pier. 805/773-4658.

PLACES TO EAT

Old West Cinnamon Rolls: This little café has some of the best cinnamon rolls we've ever laid teeth on. They're hot, sticky, and absolutely decadent. Enjoy them at the front bench and tables with your pooch at your side. 861 Dolliver Street; 805/773-1428.

The Scoop Ice Cream Parlor: When you say "The Scoop" to most dog people, they tend to think of the plastic bags, newspapers, or little shovels they use for scooping the, well, you get the picture. But this ice-cream parlor is so good that "The Scoop" might hold a whole new meaning to you after you visit with your pooch. And great news for dogs: When you buy yourself an ice cream, your dog gets a small doggy cone for free! The parlor no longer has outdoor seating—apparently because someone fell out of a chair and sued. (The nerve!) But dogs are still welcome to hang around while you enjoy your treats together. 607 Dolliver Street; 805/773-4253.

PLACES TO STAY

Cottage Inn by the Sea: Stay here and you get a very attractive, spacious, country-style room with a gas fireplace, a fridge, and a microwave. You also get a deluxe continental breakfast. You even get an ocean view. The best part for dogs is that most pet-friendly rooms are on the ground level, and each has a fenced area in back. This makes dogs smile. So do the biscuits they get at check-in. Rates are $99–329. Dogs are $20 extra. 2351 Price Street 93449; 805/773-4617 or 888/440-8400; www.cottage-inn.com.

Oxford Suites: From the attractive lobby with the tiled fountain and big fireplace to the guest suites, which include a work table (should you actually want to work while in Pismo Beach), sofa, microwave, and fridge, this place is a comfy home away from home. It's ideal for traveling with a dog, because you can do some kind of cooking here. Oxford Suites looks motelish from the outside, but once you're inside it doesn't really feel that way. Your stay here includes a full breakfast buffet and an evening reception with beverages and light hors d'oeuvres. There's even a year-round pool, but dogs have to keep their paws on terra firma. Rates are $99–239. Dogs are $10 extra. 651 Five Cities Drive 93449; 805/773-3773 or 800/982-7848; www.oxfordsuitespismo beach.com.

Sandcastle Inn: This whitewashed classic is elegant, modern, comfortable, and on the beach. Dogs enjoy an ocean view, but they especially appreciate the smells wafting in off the sea. Rates are $139–399. Dogs are $10 extra. 100 Stimson Avenue 93449; 805/773-2422; www.sandcastleinn.com.

Sea Gypsy Motel: If you're looking for a reasonably priced room or studio apartment on the beach, pull your caravan over to the Sea Gypsy Motel. It's conveniently situated a couple of blocks from "downtown" Pismo Beach, and it has a heated pool in case the ocean is a little too clammy for you. Rates are $65–175. Dogs are $15 extra. 1020 Cypress Street 93449; 805/773-1801 or 800/592-5923; www.seagypsymotel.com.

Spyglass Inn: This is a great place for the family, from the breakfast to the pool to the miniature golf course to the seaside setting. Dogs are allowed only in the downstairs rooms. Rates are $249–349. Dogs are $10 extra. 2705 Spyglass Drive 93449; 805/773-4855 or 800/824-2612; www.spyglassinn.com.

Arroyo Grande

PARKS, BEACHES, AND RECREATION AREAS

At press time, the city council here had voted unanimously to create a dog park at Elm Street Park. Tune in next time for details of the park, which should be up and running by then.

15 Lopez Lake Recreation Area

😊 😊 (See San Luis Obispo County map on page 650)

The rules at this county-run park are just like those at state parks: Dogs are not allowed anywhere but at campsites and paved areas. It's a restrictive, frustrating place for dogs. All the trailheads are marked by something that looks like a horse with a slash through it. Rangers swear it's a dog, though a big one. But if you sneak your dog onto a trail and get caught, don't try the old "I thought it meant 'No Great Danes'" excuse. They've heard it before and it didn't work then either.

The 940-acre lake is off-limits to dogs, unless they fish in your boat with you. In fact, most of the 4,200-acre park bans dogs. Plenty of dogs do camp here, though, at any of the 359 sites set in oak woodlands. Reservations are recommended. Leashes are mandatory, and dogs are supposed to sleep in your tent or camper at night. A bear is resident here, as are plenty of deer.

The entrance fee is $7 per car, $3 per dog. Campsites are $18–29. Call for reservations. As always, be prepared with proof of your dog's rabies vaccination. You'll probably need it here. Exit U.S. 101 at Grand Avenue and travel northeast, following the signs to Lopez Lake. 805/781-5930.

Nipomo

PARKS, BEACHES, AND RECREATION AREAS

16 Nipomo Regional Park Dog Park

😊 😊 😊 🐾 (See San Luis Obispo County map on page 650)

Tree-loving dogs enjoy sniffing out the scents of a few big pines here and even the woodchip ground cover. Jake tends to think the chips are bones, and he parades them around with a big grin on his snout as if to say, "Hey! Look what I got! Yup, and you don't!" to his dog pals. The dog park has the usual amenities, including poop bags and picnic tables. It's within the larger regional park, so if you want to take your dog around to watch a ball game or just stroll past picnickers (temptations to quiver for, for some dogs), you can do that, too.

It costs $2 per vehicle to enter the regional park on weekends April–September and on holidays. From U.S. 101, take the West Tefft Street exit and drive west. The park entrance is on the right, just past the Nipomo Library. The dog park area is on the West Tefft Street side, near the Pine day-use area. 805/781-5930.

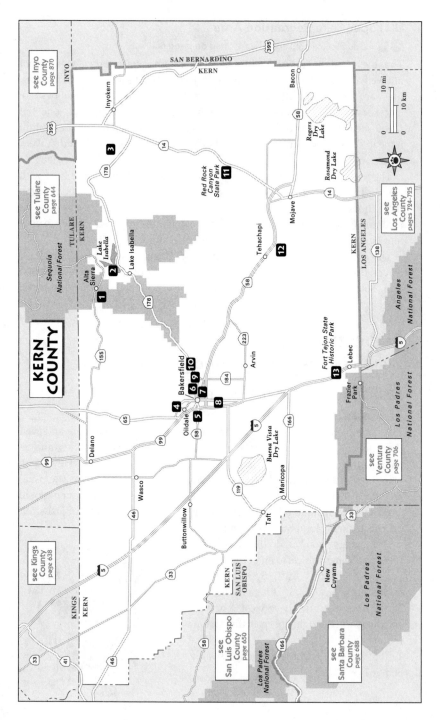

KERN COUNTY

see Inyo County page 870

see Tulare County page 644

see Kings County page 638

see Los Angeles County pages 724–725

see Ventura County page 706

see San Luis Obispo County page 650

see Santa Barbara County page 688

SAN BERNARDINO

INYO / KERN
TULARE / KERN
KINGS / KERN
KERN / SAN LUIS OBISPO
KERN / LOS ANGELES

Sequoia National Forest

Angeles National Forest

Los Padres National Forest

Red Rock Canyon State Park

Fort Tejon State Historic Park

Rogers Dry Lake

Rosamond Dry Lake

Buena Vista Dry Lake

Bacon

Inyokern

Alta Sierra

Lake Isabella

Lake Isabella

Bakersfield

Oildale

Delano

Wasco

Buttonwillow

Taft

Maricopa

New Cuyama

Frazier Park

Lebec

Arvin

Tehachapi

Mojave

10 mi
10 km

0

CHAPTER 49

Kern County

This large southern San Joaquin Valley county is a diverse land o' plenty. There are plenty o' farms, plenty o' deserts, plenty o' mountains, and plenty o' windmills—5,000 to be exact, enough to make Don Quixote quiver.

The county also has plenty o' fertilizer, and that fact will jump right out at you as you cruise down certain roads during certain fertilizer seasons. Bring a gas mask or forever hold your breath. When we drove through one fine October afternoon, the humans in the car turned green from the extra-ripe cow-patty smell. The dogs just sat there mesmerized, with big smiles on their snouts.

NATIONAL FORESTS

The *National Forests and Wilderness Areas* resource at the back of this book has important information and safety tips on visiting national forests with your dog and has more information on the national forests listed below.

PICK OF THE LITTER—KERN COUNTY

MOST INTERESTING USE OF DRAINAGE BASINS/SUMPS
City of Bakersfield dog parks (page 681)

BEST GOOD, CLEAN FUN
20 Mule Team Museum, Boron (page 686)

Los Padres National Forest
🐾🐾🐾🐾🐾

A sliver of this huge national forest pokes into the southwest edge of Kern County.

Sequoia National Forest
🐾🐾🐾🐾🐾

Only little segments of this grand forest dribble into Kern County from Tulare County.

Alta Sierra

PARKS, BEACHES, AND RECREATION AREAS

1 Greenhorn Mountain County Park
🐾🐾🐾 (See Kern County map on page 676)

This rugged park is surrounded by extraordinary Sequoia National Forest land. While the park itself is a speck compared with the forest, it resembles the wooded wonderland in every other way except one: Dogs must be leashed. Jake likes the place, but it's really easy to drive down the road a bit and start on a real wilderness hike in the national forest.

Greenhorn is slightly more civilized, if that's what your dog prefers. It's got a playground and a picnic area. But most of the undeveloped forest areas at Greenhorn are as wild as the surrounding national forest land. Its 160 acres are set at 6,000 feet. Trails run through thick cedar and white fir forests.

The park is on Highway 155, about six miles west of Lake Isabella. 661/868-7000.

Lake Isabella

PARKS, BEACHES, AND RECREATION AREAS

☑ Lake Isabella

🐾🐾🐾 (See Kern County map on page 676)

If what you want is a long hike with your leash-free dog, don't expect to find it right here. The land is surrounded by Sequoia National Forest, but there really aren't any trails around the lake. Just a short drive up the road, you'll find all the nude dog hiking you could imagine. Ask a ranger for directions to the national forest trails.

You can walk around some of the lake with your dog, but he's supposed to be leashed. With 38 miles of shoreline, this is the largest freshwater lake in Southern California, and it's worth taking a look around. The bird-watching is hot here, and so is the fishing for such goodies as largemouth bass. A day-use fee of $5 will get you into a popular beach area here. "We've seen dogs on kayaks, Jet Skis, and even at the helm of a ski boat, ears blowing in the wind," write Boomer and Bailey, two water-loving German shepherds who love coming to the lake.

There are nearly 800 campsites. Some sites are available on a first-come, first-served basis. Reservations are recommended for holiday weekends; call 877/444-6777. Campsites are $19; there are four no-fee primitive sites available. Some offer blissful seclusion. The lake is at Highways 155 and 178. From Bakersfield, head east on Highway 178 for about 30 miles. Call the ranger office for directions to your particular destination within the lake area. 760/379-5646.

PLACES TO STAY

Paradise Cove Lodge: Boomer and Bailey, who had their human, Jana Anderson, write to us about the fun beach at Lake Isabella, also turned us on to this motel. Good dogs! Paradise Cove Lodge is run by Shadow, a Siberian husky, and his person, Diane. It sits across the road and up a bit from beautiful Lake Isabella. You'll get stunning views of the lake from here. In addition, you'll have a grassy area with some trees, and picnic tables and benches outside the rooms make for great sunset viewing. (Boomer and Bailey say the squirrel-watching from here is pretty awesome, too.) The rooms are basic and clean. Rates are $70–85. Dogs are $10 extra. 10700 Highway 178 93240; 760/379-2719.

Inyokern

Friends who visited from New York could only call this town "Inyoface." It was amusing for at least a few seconds the first time they said it. But dogs find high amusement at the Chimney Peak Recreation Area, which lets them run around off leash and get rid of all that pent-up canine energy.

PARKS, BEACHES, AND RECREATION AREAS

3 Chimney Peak Recreation Area

😻 😻 😻 😻 🐕 (See Kern County map on page 676)

This 13,600-acre swath of land is not the Mojave Desert and it's not the Sierra Nevada. It's somewhere in between—a transition zone with less severe temperatures and an unusual mix of vegetation.

You and your well-mannered mutt will enjoy hiking leash-free through pinyon and juniper woodlands, foothill pines, sage, and desert needlegrass. In the spring, wildflowers explode with color and the place comes to life.

Speaking of coming to life, a brochure produced by the Bureau of Land Management describes another aspect of nature here: "Highlighting the wildlife attractions of the area are mule deer, black bear, mountain lion, bobcat... " If you don't think your dog can handle all this excitement, leash up.

The trails join with the surrounding dog-friendly national forest land, making this piece of dog heaven seem utterly vast. While there's plenty of good BLM turf in Kern County, the best section of the Chimney Peak Recreation Area is in Tulare County to the north. You can get there by taking Highway 178 to Canebrake Road and heading north. You may stop on the Kern side of the border if you wish, but the Tulare side has the good campgrounds and trails. (Dogs need to be leashed in campgrounds.) 661/391-6000.

Oildale

If you like oil (the expensive, inedible kind), you'll love this town. Grasshopper-like oil derricks are everywhere. Tanks, too. It's an interesting place to visit if you happen to be sick of forests and other forms of pristine landscapes.

PARKS, BEACHES, AND RECREATION AREAS

At press time, Oildale was in the process of installing its very own dog park. Stay tuned for details in the next edition, after we sniff it out.

4 Standard Park

🔥 (See Kern County map on page 676)

Old railroad cars and oil tanks clutter the area just east of the park. There's no mistaking where you are: You're in Oildale, land of much oil and many places named after the oil companies that have/had a stake in the town. This park is presumably named after the old Standard Oil company, a precursor to Chevron.

Standard Park is a flat 15-acre park edged with trees. If your leashed dog needs to get out of the car, it's a tolerable place for a little stretching and a few leg lifts. The park is a block south of Norris Road, just east of North Chester Avenue. 661/392-2000.

Bakersfield

This is the country music capital of California. You'll know it when you turn on your car radio. Find yourself a good country station, and as you cruise past oil derricks and the surrounding agricultural land, you'll feel right at home.

Bakersfield also happens to be the hub of the southern San Joaquin Valley. It doesn't draw many tourists, but whether you live here or just do business here (with your pooch, of course), you'll find enough decently dog-friendly parks to make your friendly dog happy.

PARKS, BEACHES, AND RECREATION AREAS

Bakersfield has gone to the dogs of late: There are now five grassy areas within larger city parks where dogs can run around without leashes, and at press time, a new real-deal dedicated dog park was on its way to becoming a reality. But don't call these fenced-in areas "dog parks." They're not strictly devoted to dogs. Soccer players and other park users can hang out in these areas. At this point it's kind of a first-come, first-served situation. So far, the easygoing policy has worked well. "If someone's there first and someone else wants to use it, they work it out," says friendly, helpful park supervisor Joe Gonzalez.

The dog areas have no amenities other than poop-bag stations and double gates. Their real purpose, and the reason they're fenced and gated, is that they're actually drainage basins. When it rains, excess rainwater has to go somewhere. It comes here. The areas can get pretty sumpy at times and often close for a few days after it rains. But being Bakersfield, as opposed to a soggier place such as Seattle, the areas dry out fairly quickly and are usually back in action within a few days of a heavy rain. The dogs of Bakersfield do lots of wagging when they see those gates unlock again.

5 Centennial Park Dog Area

🐾🐾🐾 🐕 (See Kern County map on page 676)

This is the largest of the city's four leash-free dog areas. Dogs here get to whiz around on nearly four acres. It's big enough so that even humans can get good exercise if they choose to go for a walk, rather than hang out and talk. (Please see the introduction to *Parks, Beaches, and Recreation Areas* for details on the city's four bare-bones off-leash areas.) This one is within Centennial Park, at Montclair Street and Marella Way. 661/326-3866.

6 University Park Dog Area

🐾🐾 🐕 (See Kern County map on page 676)

It's relatively small (1.5 acres), and it's bare, but it's a place to run off-leash. This city drainage basin has double gates and poop bags. This one's within University Park, at University Avenue between Camden and Mission Hills streets. 661/326-3866.

7 Hart Park/Kern River County Park

🐾🐾🐾 (See Kern County map on page 676)

Hart Park and Lake Ming make up the bulk of this 1,400-acre park. Hart Park, in a setting that's part golf course and part lunar landscape, is by far the better one for dogs. The bare rock mountain on one edge of the park gives way to huge green meadows, with shaded paths running throughout. And if you're a food hound, you'll be happy to know that you and your leashed dog are never more than a one-minute walk from a picnic table.

Down the road a bit is a huge soccer area. When no one's around, it's a terrific place to trot about with your pooch.

The easternmost section of the park is Lake Ming, a 100-acre lake with tolerable fishing in the cooler months and nothing in summer. At last look, only two tiny sections were open to anglers. Because of a parasite that can cause swimmer's itch, swimming and wading are often banned here. In all, it's not exactly a water dog's dream.

The 57 first-come, first-served campsites here are set in a remote, lush section of the Lake Ming area. Unlike the dry, dusty feel of most of the lake's shoreline, the camping here is a riparian escape. Sites are $11–22. Dogs are $4 extra.

From Panorama Drive in north Bakersfield, drive east to Alfred Harrell Highway and follow it as it curves by the Kern River. Eventually the road will lead you through the gates of the park. Follow the signs to the areas that most interest you and your dog. 661/868-7000.

8 Kroll Park Dog Area
😯😯🐕 (See Kern County map on page 676)

Dogs can throw their leashes to the wind in this 2.5-acre grassy fenced area that doubles as a city drainage basin. The only amenities are poop bags and double gates for safety. This one is at Kroll Way and Montalvo Drive, within Kroll Park. 661/326-3866.

9 Seasons Park Dog Area
😯😯🐕 (See Kern County map on page 676)

A word of warning before you set paw inside this fenced dog area with your medium or large dog: Don't! This off-leash area is dedicated to small dogs. There's not much to it, but it's a decent place for more diminutive doggies to congregate. Seasons Park itself has some lovely trees that were planted with actual seasons in mind. In other words, you'll see fall colors in fall, new little leaves in spring, and other seasonal feats in summer and winter. 661/326-3866.

10 Wilson Park Dog Area
😯😯🐕 (See Kern County map on page 676)

At two fenced acres, this is the second-smallest of the off-leash areas in Bakersfield. But it's also the most heavily used—these sometime city drainage basins are used by soccer players and other park users as well as free-running dogs. This one is at Wilson Road and Hughes Lane, within Wilson Park. 661/326-3866.

PLACES TO STAY

Bakersfield has so many dog-friendly lodgings that it puts many larger cities to shame. We'll mention just a fistful of them here.

Doubletree Hotel: This is one of the better Bakersfield accommodations, with large, attractive rooms, a pool, spa, and exercise area. Rates are $104–169. Dogs are $15 extra. 3100 Camino del Rio Court 93308; 661/323-7111; www .doubletree.com.

La Quinta Motor Inn: Rates are $75–85. 3232 Riverside Drive 93308; 661/325-7400.

Motel 6: There are five Motel 6s in Bakersfield. This is an amazing per capita number. Rates are $40–56. Call the national reservations number at 800/466-8356 or go to www.motel6.com for the location nearest your destination.

Residence Inn by Marriott: This is a convenient place to stay when traveling with a pooch. The rooms are all suites and apartments, and they all have full kitchens, so you don't have to worry about finding a pooch-friendly restaurant in these parts. The inn even provides dogs with their own poop bags and dog dish. Rates are $174–214. Dogs pay a flat $75 fee for the length of their stay. 4241 Chester Lane 93309; 661/321-9800; www.residenceinn.com.

California City

PARKS, BEACHES, AND RECREATION AREAS

No California City park permits pooches, and the Bureau of Land Management would sure appreciate it if you wouldn't take your dog to the Desert Tortoise Natural Area here. Even leashed dogs can pose a threat to the tortoise population.

🔢 Red Rock Canyon State Park

🐾🐾🐾 (See Kern County map on page 676)

This magnificent park is known as "the Grand Canyon of the West," and it lives up to the hype. The best time to be at this 10,384-acre park is at sunrise or at sunset. The low-lying sun dances with the red and white cliffs, and the results are magical. Dogs aren't permitted on the trails, but they can go along the small paved roads and seek out some of the stunning paleontological sites with you. Leashes are a must.

If you like borax, you'll be happy to know that this was a watering hole for the 20-mule team freight wagons on their grueling journey hauling the stuff.

The day-use fee is $5. There are 50 very primitive camping sites available on a first-come, first-served basis for $10–12 per night. The park is 25 miles northeast of the town of Mojave, on Highway 14. 661/942-0662.

Tehachapi

The Tehachapi area is home to thousands of windmills that supply more than one billion kilowatt-hours of electricity per year. Next time you're driving through some of the back roads with your dog, pull over and turn off your engine for a minute. The humming turbines provide an eerie contrast to the silence of the surrounding desert. Joe Dog loved the strange noises and would tilt his head every which way to try to figure out who was making them. When he ruled out the other passengers and the nearby rocks, he'd stare at me with an accusing look on his furrowed brow.

PARKS, BEACHES, AND RECREATION AREAS

🔢 Tehachapi Mountain Park
🐾🐾🐾🐾 (See Kern County map on page 676)

We love coming to this 490-acre park in late autumn, when there's a little nip in the pure, pine-scented air. With elevations of up to 7,000 feet and dozens of types of pines, firs, and oaks, this park provides a stunning contrast to the desert surroundings.

Bill and Joe slid around on their butts when we visited, because there was a good layer of slick snow in the upper reaches of the park. They had a great time slipping, sliding, and sniffing the mountain sage that was poking out of the snow. Leashes are the law here, but you can still have a terrific time exploring this beautiful park via the trails that run throughout. And you may never run into another soul.

The camping is some of the best we've seen in any county park. Many of the 61 sites are 200 feet away from each other. Tall trees add a little more privacy. Sites are $12–14 and are available on a first-come, first-served basis. Pooches are $4 extra.

From Highway 58, exit onto Highway 202 and drive south, continuing straight onto Tucker Road when Highway 202 veers west. In about another mile, at Highline Road, turn right, drive about 1.5 miles to Water Canyon Road, and turn left. The park is another 2.2 miles. 661/868-7000.

PLACES TO STAY

Best Western Mountain Inn: Rates are $69–91, and the inn asks for notice if you're coming with a pooch. 416 West Tehachapi Boulevard 93561; 661/822-5591.

Boron

Don't be surprised if your dog starts looking inquisitively at the empty sky here. Chances are that within a few moments the sky won't look so empty. This is the home of Edwards Air Force Base, and it flies some mighty odd-looking experimental aircraft up yonder. Dogs usually seem to notice well before their people. (See the Diversion *Call Out the 20-Mule Team* for one heckuva fun outing.)

DIVERSION

Call Out the 20-Mule Team: If your dog has fond memories of those puppyhood days when you sprinkled 20 Mule Team Borax on the rug almost daily to get out those "oops" odors, a trip to the **20 Mule Team Museum** will be a journey down olfactory memory lane.

The town of Boron is the home of U.S. Borax, whose open pit mine is one of the major sources of borate in the world. The museum pays homage to the days when 20-mule teams hauled 36-ton wagonloads of borax across 180 miles of desert to waiting railroad cars in Mojave. On the museum's grounds, you'll find the oldest house in Death Valley, built in 1883 by a borax miner. Other features of the rather small museum include an early Boron beauty shop and tons of mining equipment. If the "right" people are here during your visit, your dog may even be able to enter the museum. "All I ask is it's a nice dog," says one staffer. (Be sure not to let your dog do leg lifts on the displays. It's probably a good idea to take him for a walk before you get here.)

There's no fee, just a requested donation. From Highway 58, take the Boron Avenue off-ramp and drive south about 1.5 miles. 760/762-5810.

Lebec

PARKS, BEACHES, AND RECREATION AREAS

13 Fort Tejon State Historic Park

🐾🐾🐾 (See Kern County map on page 676)

The U.S. Army's First Dragoons established a camp here in 1854. Their mission was to protect white settlers and Native Americans in the Tejon Reservation from raids by other Native American groups, including the Paiutes, Chemehuevi, and Mojave.

The buildings here are all restored versions of structures that were the backbone of the fort back then. There's even a miniature museum to get you up to date with the past.

Dogs like it here, but their pleasure has little to do with the buildings and much to do with the land. There's plenty of land to peruse, on leash of course. If you get away from the main features of the fort and walk toward the back-country (past the outhouses), you're in for a treat. Large valley oaks, blue oaks, black willows, and cottonwoods are plentiful here, and critters such as deer, rabbits, quail, and several kinds of hummingbirds call the park home.

Admission is $3 for adults. Kids and dogs get in free. Exit I-5 at the Fort Tejon exit and follow the signs. It's just west of the freeway. 661/248-6692.

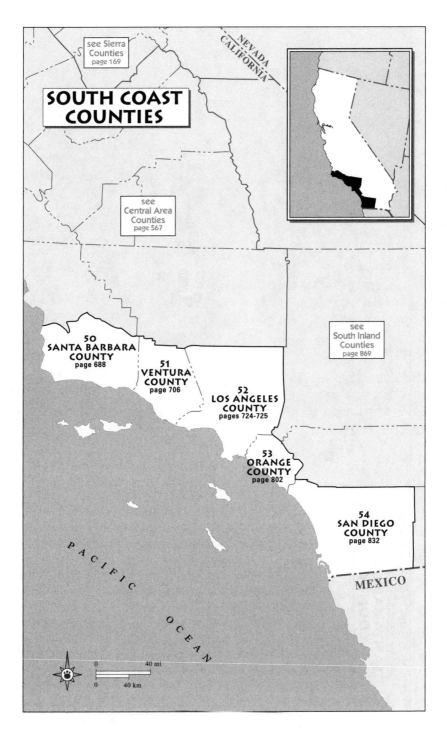

see Sierra
Counties
page 169

NEVADA
CALIFORNIA

SOUTH COAST COUNTIES

see
Central Area
Counties
page 567

see
South Inland
Counties
page 869

**50
SANTA BARBARA
COUNTY**
page 688

**51
VENTURA
COUNTY**
page 706

**52
LOS ANGELES
COUNTY**
pages 724-725

**53
ORANGE
COUNTY**
page 802

**54
SAN DIEGO
COUNTY**
page 832

MEXICO

PACIFIC

OCEAN

0   40 mi

0   40 km

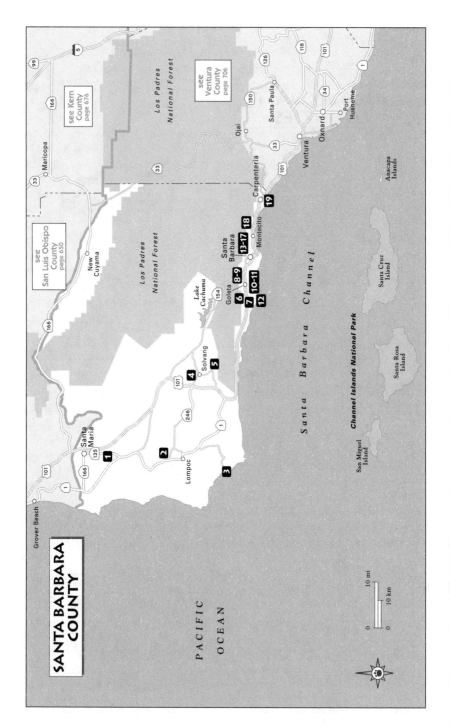

CHAPTER 50

Santa Barbara County

If you're like most folks, when you hear the words "Santa Barbara," you probably think of a sun-drenched vacation paradise on the central California coast. Images of whitewashed, Spanish-style buildings, palm-lined beaches, and big green resorts representing big green bucks may flash through your head. You can almost smell the sunscreen and feel the warm sand caressing your body.

On the other hand, if you're a dog, when you think of Santa Barbara County, you'll likely think of a leash that rarely comes off on beaches that are to drool for. Images of No Dogs signs on the most glorious beaches will flash through your furry head. You may even try to convey to your owner, "Hey, I've got a great idea. Let's go to Carmel!"

Well, at least there are lots of great restaurants with outdoor tables dogs can go to in Santa Barbara County, right? Well, yes and no: A few years ago, the Santa Barbara County health department decided to no longer allow dogs at the county's myriad restaurants with outdoor tables. It's a long and complicated story that I won't get into here. (Just know that it had nothing to do with

PICK OF THE LITTER— SANTA BARBARA COUNTY

BEST DOG PARK
WOOF PAC Park, Santa Maria (page 691)

BEST OFF-LEASH ROMPS
Douglas Family Preserve, Santa Barbara (page 697)
Elings Park, Santa Barbara (page 698)

BEST LEASH-FREE BEACH
Hendry's Beach/Arroyo Burro Beach, Santa Barbara (page 699)

MOST DOG-FRIENDLY PLACES TO STAY
Meadowlark Inn, Solvang (page 694)
Fess Parker's DoubleTree Resort, Santa Barbara (page 701)
Four Seasons Biltmore, Santa Barbara (page 702)
San Ysidro Ranch, Montecito (page 704)

BEST PLACE TO STAY IN A COVERED WAGON
Rancho Oso Guest Ranch and Stables, Santa Barbara (page 703)

BEST PLACE TO BE A POODLE
Bastille Day Parade, Santa Barbara (page 699)

health hazards.) This means dogs are officially not allowed at any restaurants with outdoor tables in the county. Restaurant owners can end up in court if they're too dog-friendly, and this can be costly.

We've heard the enforcement is difficult, but we've decided to exclude all Santa Barbara County restaurants from this edition, since to leave them in could be inviting legal trouble for them. Your dog may still be welcome at the outdoor tables of dozens of restaurants throughout the county, but we'll have to let you find them as you explore the area. (Putting them in the book is kind of like pointing a big flashing arrow at them for health officials.)

A very active group called Dog PAC of Santa Barbara, dedicated to the promotion of responsible dog ownership and preservation of Santa Barbara County dog owners' rights, is working on dealing with this problem, as well as on getting more doggy access to parks here. Check out Dog PAC at its website, www.dogpacsb.org. The group is behind most of the leash-free areas you'll read about in this chapter. If we rated dog groups the same way we rate parks, Dog PAC would get four paws.

NATIONAL FORESTS

The *National Forests and Wilderness Areas* resource at the back of this book has important information and safety tips on visiting national forests with your dog and has more information on Los Padres National Forest.

Los Padres National Forest
😺😺😺😺🐕

Sections of the forest are near the Santa Barbara coast. The off-leash trails provide a much-needed breather from the strict leash rules around this county.

Santa Maria

PARKS, BEACHES, AND RECREATION AREAS

🔳 WOOF PAC Park
😺😺😺😺🐕 (See Santa Barbara County map on page 688)

This three-acre fenced-in off-leash dog park is in the back of Waller County Park. (Which is a real gem itself.) It's a little hard to find, but once you see the entrance, you'll know you're in the right place: It looks like a giant red doghouse. Big dogs and bitty dogs have separate areas here, and there's plenty of water and poop bags. A fire hydrant graces each section. The grassy ground cover can turn to mud, but dogs don't mind a bit.

After your dog has had her leash-free fun inside the dog park, pop on a leash and stroll around the rest of Waller County Park. It's a beautiful 153-acre park with two duck ponds, quiet picnic spots, loads of trees, and sprawling lawn area. (Fun fact: WOOF stands for "Winners of Off-Leash Freedom.")

From Highway 135, go west on Goodwin Road and follow it to the park. 805/934-6123; for more info, www.woofpac.org.

Lompoc

It may be the home of a notorious federal penitentiary, but because of a few pooch-permitting parks, dogs don't feel imprisoned here.

PARKS, BEACHES, AND RECREATION AREAS

🐾 La Purisima Mission State Historic Park

🐾🐾🐾🐾 (See Santa Barbara County map on page 688)

This is a truly amazing place to bring dogs. Not only can they hike with you along 14 miles of trails here, but sometimes they're actually allowed inside the restored mission. They have to promise not to do leg lifts, bark, throw up, or any of those other activities not suited to the indoors. And they have to be on a leash at all times. (This policy seems to depend upon who's working here at the time, so it's not a guaranteed privilege.)

The original La Purisima Mission was founded in 1787, but an earthquake destroyed it in 1812. The mission was eventually picked up and moved across the Santa Ynez River to its present spot. During the 1930s, many of the mission's adobe buildings were restored. It was the largest mission restoration in California.

It's a treat to be able to take a dog inside such a historic place. But frankly, most dogs would rather be outside exploring this 967-acre park in their own doggy fashion.

The entrance fee is $4 per vehicle and it's good for up to nine people (and a dog). From Highway 1 in Lompoc, turn east on Purisima Road. The park entrance will be on your left in a couple of miles. 805/733-3713.

🐾 Jalama Beach Park

🐾🐾🐾🐾 (See Santa Barbara County map on page 688)

The park may be only 24 acres, but there are so many ways to enjoy nature here that it seems much larger. Bring your binoculars and you won't regret it. Gray whale–watching is excellent February–March and September–November. Bird-watching is hot year-round, but springtime attracts many rare birds.

Joe Dog's favorite activity was rockhounding, but he probably just liked the name. The beachcombing is great here, and since the park is within the Pacific Missile Range of the Vandenberg Air Force Base, you never know what you'll find. Wildlife-watching and surf fishing are also first-rate. As long as your dog shows proof of rabies vaccination and is on a leash and not harming the environment, she can accompany you anywhere here.

There's also camping at 110 campsites, some right by the beach. Sites are $16–25. Dogs are $3 extra. All sites are first-come, first-served. The beach is 15 miles off Highway 1, at the end of Jalama Road. The Jalama Road exit is about four miles south of the main part of Lompoc. 805/934-6123.

PLACES TO STAY

Quality Inn and Executive Suites: If you want a view of the Lompoc Airport, you've got it from the parking lot here. Joy of joys! Rates are $130–180. Dogs pay a $25 fee for the length of their stay. 1621 North H Street 93436; 805/735-8555 or 800/224-6530; qualitysuiteslompoc.com.

Super 8 Motel: There's a nice little grassy area on the premises. Rates are $70–140. (Who knew Super 8s could command such a price?) Dogs are $15 extra for up to two pooches. 1020 East Ocean Avenue 93436; 805/735-6444.

Solvang

Solvang is a sweet Danish village, with architecture as authentically Danish as its baked goods. The place was settled in 1911 by Danish folks who missed their homeland. They bought property and perpetuated all the Danish customs they could.

After an article about the small community appeared in the *Saturday Evening Post* in 1947, entrepreneurs rushed in from all over the country and created something of a Danish theme park atmosphere here. Still, the town retains its core of true Danish charm.

PARKS, BEACHES, AND RECREATION AREAS

4 Hans Christian Andersen Park

😻😻😻 🐾 (See Santa Barbara County map on page 688)

When you tell a dog that he's going to get to visit a park that's half developed and half rough, you know which half he's going to want to explore. This 52-acre park has a good undeveloped section for dogs who couldn't care less about refinement. And we recently discovered that it's OK to take a well-behaved dog off leash in this undeveloped area!

The area is full of brush, but there are enough trees and navigable walking areas for any dog to have a good time. If some human in your group insists on hanging out at the developed section of the park, your dog will get along just fine, as long as you leash up.

From Highway 246, take Atterdag Road north. The arched gateway to the park is about three blocks on the left. 805/688-7529.

5 Nojoqui Falls County Park

😻😻😻 (See Santa Barbara County map on page 688)

In nondrought springtimes, you'll be wowed by the Nojoqui (NAH-ho-wee) Waterfall, which plunges 100 feet. The rest of the year, you and your dog will still be in awe.

People often compare this 88-acre park with Yosemite National Park. It's kind of a miniature version, complete with thick forests and mini-mountains (also known as hills). Unlike in Yosemite, dogs are allowed to really explore the area. They have to be on leash, but they don't seem to mind.

From Solvang, go south on Alisal Road about 10 miles. After about six miles, the road will veer sharply to the right. Follow it for four more miles, and the park will be on your left. If you're on U.S. 101 south of Buellton, you can exit at the signed marker for the park and follow the signs for about two miles. The park will be on your right. 805/568-2461.

PLACES TO EAT

Since dogs are banned at all Santa Barbara County restaurants—inside and out—we haven't named any of Solvang's very dog-friendly eateries in this edition.

PLACES TO STAY

Meadowlark Inn: Good dogs are welcome at this lovely inn, which bills itself as a "wine country inn." Stay here and you get a comfy room and a small pool. Your dog gets big oaks and redwoods and two large lawns in front. Equally appealing for dogs: They now get dog treats when they stay here. Rates are $120–250. Dogs are $15 extra. 2644 Mission Drive 93463; 805/688-4631; www.meadowlarkinnsolvang.com.

Royal Copenhagen Inn: The rooms here are spacious and somewhat Danish in their decor. The exterior looks so much like a Danish village that it will leave you wondering if you're really in California anymore. You'll want to take a few photos here with your dog. It's the next best thing to visiting Copenhagen, and you don't have those cramped airplane seats to contend with. Guests get a free breakfast as well as an afternoon wine tasting. Rates are $79–219. 1579 Mission Drive 93463; 800/624-6604; www.royalcopenhageninn.com.

Viking Motel: Rates are $49–160. Dogs are $10 extra. 1506 Mission Drive 93463; 805/688-1337 or 800/695-8284.

Goleta

This cute seaside community is now home to four of the county's five off-leash-at-certain-hours parks. What a lucky town!

PARKS, BEACHES, AND RECREATION AREAS

6 Carneros County Park

🐾🐾🐾 (See Santa Barbara County map on page 688)

A beautiful lake is at the center of this wonderful county park and nature preserve. To protect the lake, no one except fish, birds, and little bugs are allowed to swim in it. But you and your leashed dog can explore the area on miles of trails (both dirt and paved). You'll likely see rabbits, squirrels, turtles, ducks, and geese. Please note: The name Los Carneros may or may not have its deep origins in *carne,* the Spanish word for meat, but please be sure your dog realizes the critters around here are not for his dining pleasure. If your dog is a chaser and you see this wildlife, keep a tight hold of that leash.

The park has a few picnic tables near the historic Stow House and even a miniature train ride for kids. (Open by special arrangement.) The area is undeveloped, with only one chemical toilet. But dogs don't care about that. They've got two Mutt Mitt stations, and if you use them, pooches will continue to be welcomed here.

Take Los Carneros Road north off Highway 101, cross over Calle Real, and you'll see the vehicle entrance to this park next to a county fire station on your right. If you're hiking to get here, you'll also have access to this park from Covington Way and La Patera Lane. 805/568-2461.

7 Girsh Park

🐾🐾🐾 (See Santa Barbara County map on page 688)

This lovely 12-acre park is an oasis amid developments. Leashes are a must, but it's still a dog-friendly place. Girsh is host to obedience trials, dog fairs, and pooch agility groups. This makes for lots of interesting doggy scents for your furry friend to investigate. The park is at 7050 Phelps Road, off Storke Road; 805/968-2773.

8 Patterson Park

🐾🐾🐕 (See Santa Barbara County map on page 688)

This is basically a giant lawn dotted with big trees. It's a 1.5-acre patch of county land in a residential neighborhood. It's a pleasant place to visit, but it wouldn't get space in this book if it weren't for one feature: Dogs are allowed to be leash-free here 8–10 A.M. Monday–Friday. That's mighty hospitable. There are no fences, so watch out if your dog is prone to darting into the street. Patterson's leash-free morning hours complement the evening off-leash hours of the nearby Tabano Hollow. Dogs in this neighborhood are lucky dogs indeed! From U.S. 101, exit on North Patterson Avenue. Drive north a few blocks, and turn right on University Drive. The park is in three blocks, at University Drive and the 500 block of Calle Aparejo. 805/681-5650.

9 Tabano Hollow

🐾🐾🐕 (See Santa Barbara County map on page 688)

Dogs are welcome to run off leash here every day from 4 P.M. to sunset. This is a grassy little area within a residential neighborhood. There are no fences, and it's only about an acre, but it has plenty of trees and is a pleasant place for an evening romp. And it's a happy respite from foxtails. From U.S. 101, exit on North Patterson Avenue. Drive north a few blocks, and turn right on University Drive. The park area is in five blocks, at the intersection of 5100 University Drive and Tabano Way. 805/681-5650.

🔟 Tucker's Grove County Park

😺😺😺😺 🐕 (See Santa Barbara County map on page 688)

Tucker's Grove has just about everything a dog could want in a park. Dogs who like the wild side dig this park's oak woodlands, brushy hills, popular trails, and pretty creek. More civilized sorts appreciate the open grassy lawn areas. And dogs who enjoy running leash-free have a real treat: From 8 A.M. to 10 A.M. and 4 P.M. to sunset Monday through Friday, dogs can run off leash in the upper part of the park known as Kiwanis Meadow. It's a major lawn area with lots of trees, and dogs really enjoy a good romp here. Please note that if this area has been reserved for a group picnic during these hours, leashes are the law.

From U.S. 101 take the Turnpike Road exit and drive north a few blocks. Once you cross Cathedral Oaks Road, the park entrance is straight ahead. 805/967-1112.

🔟🔟 Goleta Beach County Park

😺😺😺 (See Santa Barbara County map on page 688)

Leashed dogs enjoy strolling down the beach at this county park. You and your pooch can enjoy a relaxing picnic under pine and palm trees in the small park area, and then go get your paws wet as you saunter down the beach together. We prefer the section of beach near the Goleta Slough, which is wilder and more primitive.

From U.S. 101, go west on Highway 217. Just before you get to the University of California, turn left onto Sandspit Road and follow it to the beach. 805/568-2461 or 805/967-1300.

🔟🔟 Isla Vista County Park

😺😺😺 🐕 (See Santa Barbara County map on page 688)

Want to watch boats or whales or simply gaze at the surf below while your dog sniffs around an attractive grassy park? This pretty coastal park provides people with great vistas of the Pacific, and dogs with great oceanic smells. Noses really flare here.

Not only are dogs allowed, but 8–10 A.M. and 4 P.M.–sunset Monday through Friday, they may be off leash. It makes for a very special outing. While you're here, check out the fun sundecks, created as an "art in the parks" project. Just don't let your dog get too up close and personal with any sunbathers.

From southbound U.S. 101 take Glen Annie Road/Storke Road south to El Colegio Road and turn left. In one block you'll come to Camino Corto. Turn right and drive a few blocks to the park. From northbound 101 take the Glen Annie Road exit toward Storke Road, turn left onto Glen Annie Road and drive for a block. The road becomes Storke Road. Continue south, and bear left at El Colegio Road. In a block, go right on Camino Corto and take it a few blocks to the park. 805/681-5650.

Santa Barbara

The people behind this gorgeous oceanside city's publicity have dubbed Santa Barbara "The American Riviera®" and yes, that registered trademark symbol is meant to be there. (A bit commercial, but I suppose it wouldn't be good if some little pond town in South Dakota usurped the phrase.) While it's not quite as chic as its French counterpart, it's a beautiful, upscale, sunny vacation destination that's well worth the drive from Los Angeles—and beyond—with a dog.

Your dog may be reading this over your shoulder and saying, "Upscale, shmupscale! What's good about it for us dogs?" Well your erudite pup will be happy to know that dogs are welcome to run leash-free at three large and heavenly locations, including a stellar beach. People here are generally very friendly toward dogs, and some truly spectacular hotels and inns permit pooches.

Dogs can also stroll very close to a popular beach (non-dog, as most in the city are) on a wonderful palm-tree-fringed walkway that runs along a chunk of beach length at Cabrillo Boulevard. On Sunday and some holidays, the Santa Barbara Arts and Crafts Show makes its home here. It's a great opportunity to go shopping and take your dog along for advice on issues such as which scarf would look best on Aunt Edna. See www.sbaacs.com for more information.

An interesting way to spend a dog day is to walk around the historic sections of the city. While pooches aren't permitted inside buildings such as Mission Santa Barbara or the city's historic adobes, they love having their pictures taken outside so their friends at home can envy their worldly ways.

PARKS, BEACHES, AND RECREATION AREAS

13 Douglas Family Preserve

🐾🐾🐾🐾🐕 (See Santa Barbara County map on page 688)

This is one terrific chunk of leash-free land. The preserve is about 70 acres, and it's on a magnificent bluff overlooking the Pacific. Dogs drool over this place, and rightly so. The ocean breeze is cool, relaxing, and must contain some pretty fascinating scents, judging by the looks on dogs' faces as they sniff it in rapture. The park has great unpaved trails for perusing the preserve. It also has quite a few oaks, cypresses, and pines. To the north of the park is oak woodland, to the south is coastal sage scrub. An estuary and wetlands are below. Way below. Two hundred feet down the bluff, to be exact. Dogs have to stay away from there, because that's where some protected species hang out. There's really no access anyway, so it's almost a moot point.

Keep leashes on until you're well within the preserve so you don't ruffle the neighbors' feathers. From northbound or southbound U.S. 101, take Cabrillo Boulevard in the direction that's away from the mountains. Turn right on Cliff

DIVERSION

The Big Dog Is a Big Deal: The Santa Barbara–based casual clothing company, **Big Dogs Sportswear,** has a large factory outlet store right in town. Are dogs allowed? "Oh, by all means," a dog-loving manager told us. After all, the Big Dogs logo—a black-and-white Saint Bernard with a big smile and red tongue—is on every piece of clothing here. So what's another dog in the store? (Just don't let your own dog leave his own logo on any clothes, if you know what I mean.) 6 East Yanonali Street; 805/963-8728.

For more fun with the Big Dog, check out the chain's website, www.bigdogs.com. You can join the Big Dogs Club (no membership fee) and submit your dog's photo to be featured on the web page, send Big Dogs e-cards, play Big Dogs computer games (Jake's favorite is Chasing the Bone), or help with the Big Dogs Foundation's many worthwhile causes. And if you like discounts, you're barking up the right tree: The website offers Big Dogs members deals that are worth sniffing out.

Drive. You'll come to two stoplights within a block of each other. Turn left onto Mesa Lane (the second light) and then turn right onto Borton Drive. Turn left onto Linda Road and follow it to the end. There is on-street parking. (You can enter the park at Medcliff Drive, Borton Drive, or Mesa School Lane.)

14 Elings Park

🐾🐾🐾🐾🐾 (See Santa Barbara County map on page 688)

This 230-acre beauty is a privately run nonprofit, and for $60 a year, you and your dog can have one of 700 coveted permits to be leash-free here. (The office can grant you an exception if you're just visiting for the day.) Dogs must be under voice control and licensed, and their people need to pay strict attention to the rules here.

The park is a wonderland of hiking trails, big open fields, and fabulous ocean and mountain views. While the park has miles of trails, most people with dogs stay in the more landscaped areas. At least part of the reason is the lack of poison oak at these places. The popular-with-pooch spots include softball and soccer fields (when there's not a game), oak-grove-clad wedding areas (when there's not a wedding), and a well-maintained tree-lined 1500-foot walkway that pays homage to fallen soldiers. That path is on the side of a large cliff going to the upper part of the park. When you get to the top, where there's a monument to veterans, you'll see the oceans and mountains in the distance. It's a lovely area to sit with your dog and think about things like peace on earth.

From U.S. 101, exit at Las Positas and drive south toward the ocean. Go through two intersections, and you'll come to a small brown sign on your right that indicates the park is to your left. That little street is Jerry Harwin Parkway. Go left, and in 30 feet you'll be through the park's gate. Park parallel anywhere along the road or at the lots at the soccer fields or wedding areas. You'll be happy to know that if you're just visiting the area for the day, you can come here for free with your dog. Just check in at the office, and be sure to bring your dog's license. To find out how to obtain a permit, phone the park at 805/569-5611, or check out www.elingspark.org.

15 Hendry's Beach/Arroyo Burro Beach
🐾🐾🐾🐾🐾 ✂ (See Santa Barbara County map on page 688)

You can throw your good dog's leash to the wind here (don't forget to pick it up, though; they're not cheap these days) and take a little stroll on a sandy, crescent-shaped beach together. It's the only beach in the county that allows leash-free dogs, so enjoy! Along your way you'll see surfers, joggers, and loads of other happy dogs. What you won't see—at least if the beach's current leash-free status remains—is a ranger approaching you with ticket book in hand. (This is too common a sight at most beaches around here.)

But be careful where you tread: If you go in the wrong direction once you hit the sand, you could be in for a ticket. Here's how you get to the right place: The beach (signs will call it Arroyo Burro) is on Cliff Drive, just west of Las Positas Road. Park in the lot, walk to the beach, and turn left—*not* right! (You'll see the fun beachside restaurant, the Brown Pelican. Go to the left of it. You should also see a sign that points dogs in the right—that is, left—direction.) Dogs who are under voice control can shed their leashes east of the slough. The off-leash section starts there and goes almost to the steps at Mesa Lane.

The off-leash program here could change at any time, so be sure to check on its status. The city likes to say this is a county beach, and the county likes to say this is a city beach. The leash-free part appears to be a city-controlled section of a county beach. The city parks department number (where some people

DOG-EAR YOUR CALENDAR

If you're in Santa Barbara during the summer, keep your ears peeled for two delightful parades. **The Big Dog Parade,** which features at least 1,200 dogs (many in costume) and 16,000 spectators, is held the first Saturday of June. Check out www.bigdogs.com for more info, or phone 805/963-8727. And in mid-July, oodles of poodles and pseudopoodles take to the streets to celebrate **Bastille Day.** For more information on Bastille Day, check out www.french festival.com/poodle.html.

DIVERSION

Hi Ho, Surrey, Away!: Get your canine companion to hop up into your lap or onto the seat beside you and drive away in your very own surrey with the fringe on the top. Don't you hurry, though, because there are plenty of dog-friendly spots where you can rent one of these pedal-powered vehicles.

One of our favorites is **Beach Rentals,** at 23 East Cabrillo Avenue, Santa Barbara. The folks here want you to hang on to your dog, and for good reason: Cats and hamburgers are common sights on the oceanfront paths you're likely to use. Small surreys (for three adults and two small kids/one hefty dog) are $24 an hour. Large surreys are $34. 805/966-2282.

who answer the phone will tell you dogs aren't even allowed at the beach) is 805/564-5433, or check the website www.dogpacsb.org for updates.

16 Santa Barbara Botanic Garden

🐾🐾🐾 (See Santa Barbara County map on page 688)

As soon as you park your car, you'll be enveloped in the magical scents of lush vegetation and fresh earth. Dogs prefer to smell the compost heaps here, but what else would you expect?

This botanic wonderland is a rarity. Places such as this usually exclude dogs without a second thought. But the folks here actually like dogs. There's even a dedicated doggy fountain.

You and your leashed dog are welcome to explore this 65-acre garden on the 5.5 miles of trails that take you through the meadows, canyons, and ridges here. The garden features more than 1,000 species of rare and indigenous California plants. The entry fee for adults is $8.

Exit U.S. 101 at Mission Street and drive northeast. The road curves to the left after about 10 blocks (its name becomes Mission Canyon Road). Continue to Foothill Road, bear right, and then take a quick left on the continuation of Mission Canyon Road. The park will be on your left in about a half mile. The address is 1212 Mission Canyon Road. 805/563-2521.

17 Shoreline Park

🐾🐾 (See Santa Barbara County map on page 688)

Lots of dogs come here for their daily walks. Leashed dogs are allowed on the green area (not the beach). They walk the path, roll on the grass, and smell the ocean and the scent of the offshore oil rigs that dot the coast.

The park is on Shoreline Drive, between San Clemente Street and San Rafael Avenue, just south of Leadbetter Beach. 805/564-5433.

PLACES TO EAT

Many Santa Barbara restaurants have outdoor tables and, in the past, welcomed dogs. A few years ago, the Santa Barbara County health department stopped allowing dogs at restaurants' outdoor tables. Some might still serve you with a dog, but for their sakes, we can't name them in this edition.

PLACES TO STAY

Bacara: Not many dogs who read this are under 25 pounds, so we won't spend much time describing this understated but very luxurious resort. (Ninety-five-pound Jake wanted to keep it out of the book entirely, but in deference to his Chihuahua friend, Baby, he'll let it stay.) Suffice it to say that it's big yet intimate, and casual yet about as upscale as it gets. You can get any number of exquisite spa treatments here, and of course your room comes with the finest linens and softest robes. Rates are $450 to more than $2,600. Dogs need to weigh less than 25 pounds to stay here, and they pay $150 for the length of their stay. 8301 Hollister Avenue 93117; 805/968-0100 or 877/422-4245; www.bacararesort.com.

Best Western Beachside Inn: This clean, inviting hotel is across the street from the beach, but don't get your tail wagging too fast: It's a typical Santa Barbara beach—beautiful, warm, sandy, and dog-banning. Well, it doesn't hurt to look, anyway. Stay here and you get to use the cute little pool and indulge in the hotel's decent continental breakfast. Rates are $89–310. Dogs are $20 extra. 336 West Cabrillo Boulevard 93101; 805/965-6556 or 800/932-6556; www.beachsideinn.com.

Casa del Mar: Guests at this small Spanish-style inn get treated well for a decent price (at least decent for these parts). Stay here and you can partake in an extended continental breakfast in the morning, and a relaxing wine and cheese social hour in the evening. The inn is clean, quiet, and attractive, with a lush little garden, a sundeck with whirlpool tub, and cozy rooms. It's just a half block from the beach and two blocks from State Street. If you really want a home away from home, you can stay in a suite with a full kitchen and fireplace. Rates are $104–299. (Most regular rooms fall in the lower price range.) Dogs are $15 extra. 18 Bath Street 93101; 805/963-4418 or 800/433-3097; www.casadelmar.com.

Fess Parker's DoubleTree Resort: At first glance, the name "Fess Parker" and the word "luxury" make strange bedfellows. After all, Fess was the actor who brought American frontiersman Davy Crockett and Daniel Boone into millions of homes in the 1950s and '60s. But while Fess Parker's characters are synonymous with sweat and grit, the real Fess Parker, a longtime Santa Barbara County resident, is known for his good taste and good business sense. (He also owns a respected winery in the county.)

Fess, who hails from Texas, likes things big. The seaside resort has 337 luxurious guest rooms. It's set on a sprawling 24 acres. Standard rooms are a spacious 450 square feet. He also likes things first-class. The rooms are attractive and comfortable, with feather pillows (unless you're allergic), high-quality bath products, evening turndown service, and excellent views. Suites are especially spacious and attractive. The resort even has its own spa, billed as a "French sea spa."

We think Fess must also like dogs, because dogs get the royal treatment here. Fess Parker's dog guests don't have to watch hungrily as you chow down on your tasty room-service meal: They can order their own. The in-room pooch dining menu includes premium ground sirloin, a quality brand wet dog food, and gourmet dog cookies. And if you really want to treat your dog, canine massages are available. For $65, your dog can get a 40-minute in-room massage from a dog-knowledgeable massage therapist from the resort's spa. The massage is supposed to be especially good for arthritic dogs.

Although the resort is across from the beach, it's a beach you can't visit with your dog friend. Try the path that runs along the beach's edge, if being near the water is your wish. Otherwise, the 24-acre resort has ample room for romping with your leashed friend. Be sure to clean up after your dog.

Rates are $269–525. 633 East Cabrillo Boulevard 93103; 805/564-4333 or 800/222-8733; www.fpdtr.com.

Four Seasons Resort: The Biltmore Santa Barbara: This elegant oceanfront resort is renowned for its impeccable style, and its gracious, dog-friendly policy is the epitome of that style. Upon check-in, dogs get two dog bowls, a toy, tasty snacks, and their very own pooch menu with items like The Mighty Mutt, a filet mignon served rare. It's $10. (For that low price I'd probably order one for my husband, too.) Dog-walking is available, but who'd want someone else to walk his or her dog with nearby parks and the beautiful grounds of the Biltmore beckoning? Dog-sitting is also available. The Biltmore is made up of a gorgeous, top-drawer hotel surrounded by 30 private cottage rooms that are to die for. People with pooches have to stay at the cottages. If your budget is plump, it's well worth it to stay. The standard cottage rates are $550–1,035. Super-deluxe ones go up to $4,400. 1260 Channel Drive 93108; 805/969-2261; www.fourseasons.com/santabarbara.

Pacifica Suites: If you and your dog need more room than just a room, check out the luxurious Pacifica Suites. The Pacifica is an all-suites hotel, so no matter which room you stay in, you'll have a bedroom and a living room. Each room has a phone and a TV (this is convenient if *Lassie* is on at the same time as *Survivor*). Suites also have stereo-cassette players, VCRs, fridges, and microwaves. These extras make a real difference when traveling with a dog.

A full breakfast comes with the room, so don't worry about cooking your eggs in the nuker. People love the pool and spa, and leashed dogs dig walking around the Pacifica's grounds. The hotel is nestled in a peaceful grove of exotic plants and trees and century-old gardens. Sniff out the area via a meandering pathway. The hotel is right next to the Sexton House, a beautifully restored architectural landmark from the 1880s. Rates are $169–239. Dogs are $10 extra. 5490 Hollister Avenue 93111; 805/683-6722 or 800/338-6722; www.pacificasuites.com.

Rancho Oso Guest Ranch and Stables: Dogs and people who enjoy the Old West love staying at Rancho Oso. It's not historic, but it looks that way. You can stay in one of five rustic one-room cabins with knotty pine walls and bunk beds. Or if you really hanker for your pooch to be a "dawgie," try one of the 10 covered wagons here. You bring the sleeping bag; the ranch provides the army cots. They're loads of fun to stay in, and they make for great photo backdrops.

The ranch is on 310 acres of hills with enough trees for decent shade in the summer. You can walk your dog on the many trails, but keep her on a leash, because a lot of horses jog on the trails too. In fact, if you want to ride a horse yourself, you can set that up back at the ranch office. Guided trail rides are offered year-round. (Lots of folks come here to camp with their horses, but that's through a members-only camping organization, and that's a horse of a different color so we won't go into detail.)

Rates are $89–99 for cabins, $59–69 for wagons. Dogs are $7.50 extra. 3750 Paradise Road 93105; 805/683-5686; www.rancho-oso.com.

Secret Garden Inn and Cottages: Six of the nine pretty cottages and rooms here allow dogs. Since the dog ambience doesn't necessarily mix with the flowery romantic feel many guests come here for, dogs are asked not to peruse the pretty gardens and public areas around the inn and cottages. A great choice for a night or two is the Garden Room, which has French doors that open to a private little garden. It's your own little Secret Garden, with no nuzzling couples to annoy.

If you like to eat in a cozy setting, you'll never want to leave the inn. You get a full hot gourmet breakfast in the morning, a light snack with wine and cheese in the afternoon, and homemade brownies, cider, and tea in the evening.

Rates for the dog rooms are $255. Dogs require a $50 deposit. 1908 Bath Street 93101; 805/687-2300; www.secretgarden.com.

Montecito

PARKS, BEACHES, AND RECREATION AREAS

18 Toro Canyon County Park

🐾🐾🐾 🐕 (See Santa Barbara County map on page 688)

Dogs love being able to disconnect their leashes at this 74-acre park, but watch out where they strip down to their au naturel selves: Running nude (sans leash) is permitted only at the big meadow/picnic area here, and only 8–10 A.M. and 4 P.M.–sunset daily. The rest of the time, and at the rest of the park, leashes are the law.

The more wild parts of the park are worth sniffing out. They're tree-filled and hilly, with trails dogs love. But remember, they do have to be leashed. From southbound U.S. 101 take the Padaro Lane exit (exit 90). In a short block make a left onto Padaro Lane, and in 0.4 mile go right onto Via Real. Drive 0.6 mile to Toro Canyon Road and turn left (north). Continue driving north for about three miles. You'll see signs for the park. From here follow the signs about a mile to the park entrance. 805/969-3315.

PLACES TO STAY

San Ysidro Ranch: A word to the pooches who plan to come here: You lucky dogs! This top-notch 540-acre resort (where Laurence Olivier and Vivien Leigh wed and Jackie and John F. Kennedy honeymooned) is treat enough. But dogs who stay here get the truly royal treatment, also known as the Privileged Pet Program. The Ranch has been offering the program to pooches for more than a century. (Thus vastly preceding the more recent dog-friendly trend at upscale resorts.) Here's how it goes:

Upon registering at the Pet Register and wolfing down some tasty peanut butter biscuits, the guest dog goes to his cottage and finds his name and his accompanying human's name on a sign outside his cottage door. Inside, he'll be greeted by a basketful of VIP goodies, including a bowl filled with squeak toys, rawhides, tennis balls, cookies, and a two-liter bottle of Pawier water. His bed is soft and cedar-stuffed.

A room-service pet menu offers several dining items, including biscuits, ravioli, cheeseburgers, canned dog food, and even New York steak. If we could afford to stay here, Jake would surely check off every item on the list, vacuum it down, and wait patiently at the door for room service to deliver the next course.

Pooches who stay here can also get a luxury most people would drool for: a professional massage. A "slow and gentle" massage is said to increase circulation, help aches and pains, and soothe away fears. A half-hour massage costs $65. (Really.)

Dogs must stay in one of the Ranch's 21 freestanding cottages. Rates are $795–3,999. There's a $100 fee for the length of your dog's stay. Dog menu items are extra. You must let the staff know ahead of time that you'll be coming with your pooch so appropriate arrangements can be made. 900 San Ysidro Lane 93108; 805/969-5046; www.sanysidroranch.com.

Carpinteria

PARKS, BEACHES, AND RECREATION AREAS

The part of the city beach where dogs are permitted is fairly difficult to reach, and it pretty much bans dogs during the harbor seal birthing season in the spring. It's much easier to go to the Rincon Beach County Park, but if you really want to hit the small strip of city beach that permits dogs, call 805/684-5405 and find out its status.

🔟 Rincon Beach County Park
🐾🐾🐾 (See Santa Barbara County map on page 688)

A wooden stairway takes you from a green blufftop picnic area down to the sandy beach. It's not a huge beach, but the Beach Boys sang about it and surfer dudes love it.

The bluff provides an excellent view of the ocean. Even though nude bathing is illegal, naked people flock here. Just cover your dog's eyes as you pass by the fleshy masses. (The nudists really appreciate it if your dog obeys the leash law.)

The park is at Bates Road and U.S. 101, at the south end of Carpinteria. 805/654-3951.

PLACES TO EAT

As dogs are no longer officially allowed at outdoor tables of any restaurant in Santa Barbara County, no dog-friendly restaurants of Carpinteria are included in this edition. (One amazing coffee café provides a water bowl, doggy treats, and dog bagels. But I won't mention the name because I don't want to bring the most dog-friendly eatery in the county to the attention of the authorities.)

PLACES TO STAY

Holiday Inn Express: This one's cozy, clean, and conveniently situated. You get a pool, whirlpool, exercise room, and big continental breakfast when you stay here. Your dog gets, well… your dog gets to stay here. Rates are $105–192. Dogs are $10 extra. 5606 Carpinteria Avenue 93013; 805/566-9949.

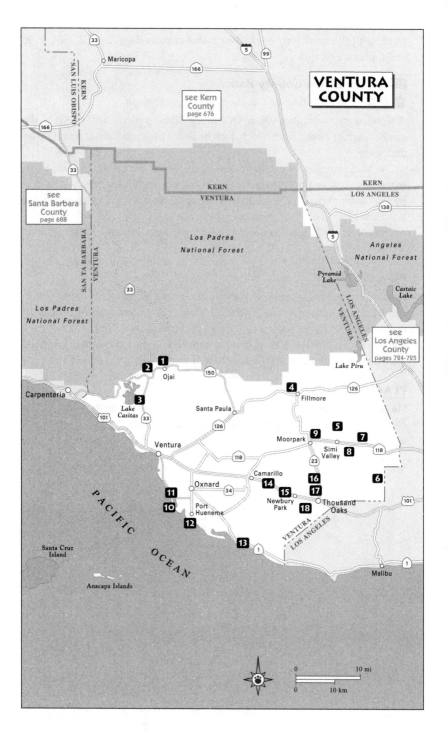

CHAPTER 51

Ventura County

This diverse coastal county is not a place to bring a dog who is seriously obsessed with swimming. All but a handful of beaches along the 42 miles of coastline here ban dogs, although a few allow them in their camping or picnicking areas.

Try not to let your dog visit Dog Hell here. You enter Dog Hell when you drive miles and miles to get to a county park, only to find Sir Ranger shaking his head at you, hands on hips, ready to do battle. County parks ban dogs from every inch of their terrain except campgrounds, which are generally not the most scenic spots in the world. Come on, Ventura County Parks system, it's time to venture into the 21st century.

Fortunately, between the Santa Monica Mountains National Recreation Area and the Santa Monica Mountains Conservancy, there's plenty of terrific land to explore. You and your dog can also have lots of fun while visiting the county's coastal communities, even though dogs are banned at most beaches. Some of these towns arc hard to pronounce, like Port Hueneme (pronounced

PICK OF THE LITTER—VENTURA COUNTY

COOLEST TRAIL
Ojai Valley Trail, Ojai (page 709)

BEST PARK FOR BOB HOPE FANS
Rocky Peak Park, Simi Valley (page 714)

BEST PARK FOR WESTERN FANS
Corriganville Park, Simi Valley (page 715)

MOST DIVERSE HIKE POSSIBILITIES
Happy Camp Canyon Regional Park, Moorpark (page 716)

BEST BEACHES
Hollywood Beach, Oxnard (page 717)
Sycamore Cove Beach, Port Hueneme (page 719)

COOLEST PLACE TO EAT
Deer Lodge, Ojai (page 710)

HIPPEST PLACE TO STAY
Blue Iguana Inn, Ojai (page 710)

MOST DOG-FRIENDLY PLACE TO STAY
Glen Tavern Inn, Santa Paula (page 711)

BEST BEACH HOTEL
Crowne Plaza Ventura Beach, Ventura (page 713)

MOST DOG-FRIENDLY SHOPPING
Simi Valley Town Center, Simi Valley (page 714)

BEST RIDE
Channel Islands Water Taxi, Oxnard (page 717)

"why-knee-me"), others you just don't even want to have to pronounce, like Oxnard. But they offer plenty of places to explore near or on the coast with your leashed dog.

NATIONAL FORESTS

The *National Forests and Wilderness Areas* resource at the back of this book has important information and safety tips on visiting national forests with your dog and has more information on Los Padres National Forest.

Los Padres National Forest
🐾🐾🐾🐾🐕

Ojai

Dogs enjoy a visit to this friendly, pleasant community, whose name is derived from a Chumash Indian word, *a'hwai*, which means both "nest" and "moon," according to town officials. Agriculture, nature, artists, and business live in fairly decent harmony here.

For a fun mini road trip, take your dog to the top of Dennison Grade (locals will point you in the right direction) and show him the view that was portrayed as Shangri-La in the film *Lost Horizon*—not the 1967 musical version (whose pop-music score by Burt Bacharach apparently I alone in the world happen to enjoy), but the 1937 classic. If you make a point to be there toward day's end, you may also be able to see the area's "pink moment," when the nearby mountains become a remarkable, unearthly shade of pink. Your dog may not appreciate this sight, especially if dogs really see only in black and white (I don't think this is the prevailing wisdom anymore), but he'll still enjoy being at the top of the world with you.

PARKS, BEACHES, AND RECREATION AREAS

1 Ojai Valley Trail
🐾🐾🐾 (See Ventura County map on page 706)

You and your leashed dog may have to share this 9.5-mile trail with a few fast bicycles and sweet-smelling horses, but don't let that stop you. It's a great way to get from Ojai to Ventura. Although most people start at the southern end and work their way northeast, it's an uphill climb that can get mighty toasty certain times of year. We recommend starting from Ojai. As they say, Go Southwest, young dog! (You can always meet up with a friend at the end who will drive you home.)

The trail is a "rails-to-trails" conversion of a more than century-old railroad line that hauled oranges and other goodies from local orchards to far-flung markets. It takes you and your leashed dog through little forested areas and quiet neighborhoods, past rolling hills and Christmas tree farms. Views of the surrounding mountains are to drool for at times. For the fair of paw, there are plenty of shaded, tranquil resting spots along the way. About midway there's a market and some fast-food-type restaurants—nothing you'd normally care to see on a nature hike, but a welcome oasis if you've worked up an appetite, or if you're crossing your legs for a pit stop. (There are no public restroom facilities on the trail at this point.)

Even if you walk only one segment of the trail, it's worth the trip. When the trail first opened, dogs were banned (it's a county parks thing), but the rule was so difficult to enforce that eventually pooches were given the OK. Take advantage of this! Rejoice! Take a hike!

The trail runs parallel to Highway 33. Its easternmost end just brushes Soule Park, but it's not well marked or as easy to access as it is just a few blocks to the west, on Fox Street, east of Libbey Park. Park at the Park & Ride lot at East Ojai Avenue and Fox Street and walk down Fox to the trail. There's also limited parking on residential streets. 805/654-3951.

PLACES TO EAT

Deer Lodge: This wood and stone landmark restaurant is one of the most cool, fun eateries where you can bring a doggy. You feel like you're at an old-West outpost, albeit a most civilized and attractive one, when you dine here. Deer figure prominently on the signage, decor (heads on old wooden walls), and the menu. You can get a venison salad, sample venison barley soup, or go for broke and try the "World Famous Deer Lodge Game Plate," which can include a selection of deer, wild boar, elk, antelope, kangaroo (oh god, no, say it's not true!—not cousins of Kanga and little Roo!), alligator, and pheasant. Your dog wants you to order this plate. Your dog is getting your car keys right now.

Best of all, the cowboy-hat-clad waitresses are mighty dog friendly, and dogs and their people have a choice of two patios. We prefer the lower patio, which is bigger, prettier, bamboo-covered, and warmed on cool evenings by an outdoor fireplace. 2261 Maricopa Highway; 805/646-4256.

Jim & Rob's Fresh Grill: Even though this sweet little eatery has only two outdoor tables, it gets a fair number of canine customers, according to servers (who will happily supply your dog with a bowl of water). 805/640-1301.

PLACES TO STAY

Best Western Casa Ojai: Enjoy this motel's heated outdoor pool and whirlpool (without your dog—sorry) and free continental breakfast (ditto). Room rates are $91–180. Dogs are $25 extra. 1302 East Ojai Avenue 93023; 805/646-8175.

Blue Iguana Inn: This old mission-style inn is "hip and stylish," according to *Sunset* magazine, which can now add the description, "dog friendly." The arched entrances, the ivy-covered trellises, the beautiful tilework and artwork, and the attractive pool make the Blue Iguana eye candy from the exterior. The rooms and suites themselves are just as wonderful, with a warm, cozy, sometimes colorful, sometimes muted natural ambience. You can also rent a lovely bungalow. Rates are $109–259. Dogs are $20 extra. (If you're reading this and know someone who wants to stay in a similarly outfitted place that doesn't allow dogs—heaven forbid!—point them to this place's sister, the Emerald Iguana Inn.) 11794 North Ventura Avenue 93023; 805/646-5277; www.blueiguanainn.com.

Santa Paula

PLACES TO STAY

Glen Tavern Inn: This Tudor-Craftsman hotel was built in 1911 and is a historic landmark. The lobby is beautiful, and the nondog rooms are kind of rustic and simple, with some antiques. But your dog won't have any encounter with the older rooms, because the dog-friendly rooms here are brand-new, very attractive, all very different from each other, and all with tile floors. Daisy Dog writes us that she stayed in Room 203 and loved its boutique-y feel.

The inn goes beyond just allowing dogs: It embraces them. Upon check-in, dogs get a bag of treats and two bowls to use. They're also given the OK to peruse the attractive green hotel grounds. The rate for this doggy package is just $99 and includes the normal $10 nightly fee for dogs. Such a deal! 134 North Mill Street 93060; 805/933-5550; www.glentavern.com.

Ventura

This seaside community is home to the ninth—and last—mission founded by Father Junípero Serra. Dogs can't go inside, but they're more than happy to smile at the camera for an exterior shot.

PARKS, BEACHES, AND RECREATION AREAS

2 Ojai Valley Trail

🐾🐾🐾 (See Ventura County map on page 706)

Please see the listing under *Ojai* for details about this 9.5-mile trail that goes from Ojai to Ventura. In case you want to go from Ventura to Ojai (if you like a vigorous uphill hike that leads you away from the ocean), Foster County Park is the trail's staging area. But keep in mind that dogs are allowed at that park only at the trailhead and the campsites. Exit Highway 33 at Casitas Vista Road and follow the signs. As you head northeast on the trail, you can also access it from points such as San Antonio Creek, Santa Ana Boulevard, Barbara Street, and Baldwin Avenue. 805/654-3951.

🖪 Camino Real Dog Park

🐾🐾🐾🐕 (See Ventura County map on page 706)

Annie Dransfeldt is a great local dog advocate. So great, in fact, that a few years ago this terrific little park was named after her. Well, apparently it was a little hard to pronounce or remember (kind of like naming a dog park after me), so it's now known by most as the name you see above, after the human park it's part of. It's two fenced grassy acres, with trees, double gates, a separate area for small dogs, a drinking fountain for dogs and their humans, and poop bags.

The park is within Camino Real Park, a 38-acre complex with lots of playing fields and courts and a refreshing eucalyptus smell. It's closed on city holidays. Unlike the other city dog park, this one's open 6 A.M.–dusk every day except Wednesday, when it opens at 9 A.M. because of park maintenance. It's at Dean Drive and Varsity Street. 805/652-4550.

PLACES TO EAT

Ventura restaurants are generous with doggy water bowls. As one server recently told us, "A dog can't order food. The least we can do is give them a free drink." A big thank-you to Colby and Dane Dogs, and their person, Annie Dransfeldt, for helping us sniff out a few of these eateries.

Andria's Seafood: The middle name here should be "and chips." You can get halibut and chips, Alaskan cod and chips, shrimp and chips, oysters and chips, ostrich burger and chips, krabby cake sandwich and chips, and really almost anything with chips. But wait! There's healthful stuff here, too. You can even get a veggie stir-fry or a charbroiled garlic sandwich. If that's just too virtuous, you can order a big side of chips. Dine with doggy at tables at the water's edge. 1449 Spinnaker Drive; 805/654-0546.

Duke's Griddle 'n' Grill: Your dog just might get a special treat from a waiter while you dine on the good grilled grub served at the outdoor tables here. At the very least, she'll get a bowl of water if she asks for one. 1124 South Seaward Avenue; 805/653-0707.

The Greek at the Harbor: The traditional Greek food here is scrumptious. Your dog would surely say *"Opa!"* if her little snouty mouth allowed. Even vegetarians delight in this lovely harborside restaurant. Dine at the patio tables with your dog. If she's thirsty, she can get a bowl of water. 1583 Spinnaker Drive; 805/650-5350.

The Habit: Dogs and their people rave about this hamburger haven. There's a reason it's called the habit. "I can't get enough of this place," writes Melvin Dog, who visits every time he's passing through town. "It's the best hamburger place we've ever eaten at and that's a lot of hamburger places. Oh, and the milk shakes are to die for." Dine with doggy at the outside tables. Thirsty dogs always get water. 487 East Thompson Boulevard; 805/667-2065.

PLACES TO STAY

For a city of this size, there's a disappointing dearth of decent doggy digs. We were at least able to find one pretty upscale place that allows dogs.

Crowne Plaza Ventura Beach: This 258-room hotel is the only hotel on the beach in Ventura. It's a super place to stay with a dog, because this particular beach allows leashed dogs! There's nothing more convenient at walkies time than strolling out of the hotel door and onto the sands of a beautiful Pacific beach.

The rooms are lovely. They're not super high-end (this used to be a Holiday Inn), but they're attractive, comfortable, and almost—but not quite—bou-tique-y. The rooms and suites with ocean views are worth the few extra dollars they may cost. Rates are $130–400. Dogs are $50 extra per stay. 450 East Harbor Boulevard 93001; 805/648-2100 or 888/233-0368.

Fillmore

This historic little city, nestled in the midst of flourishing citrus groves and with an attractive old downtown, was named one of "The West's Best Cities" by *Sunset* magazine. Fillmore, whose citrus was portrayed so elegantly on labels for wooden crates of fruit, is a fun place to sniff out with a doggy.

PARKS, BEACHES, AND RECREATION AREAS

4 Shiells Park

🐾🐾🐾 (See Ventura County map on page 706)

At just over eight acres, this park isn't huge, but it's a fairly attractive one, adjacent to Sespe Creek. Leashed dogs enjoy walking around the grass, pic-nicking, and watching kids play ball. But most of all, dogs (especially dogs of the male persuasion) enjoy the large trees.

When we're in the mood for a good walk, we leave the park (which has no real paths to speak of) and take a stroll on the paved bike path that runs adjacent to the creek. The path is about two miles long, so your dog should get all the exercise he needs. The park is at Old Telegraph Road and C Street. 805/524-1500.

Simi Valley

PARKS, BEACHES, AND RECREATION AREAS

The closest dog park is in Thousand Oaks, and residents are tired of making the trudge. At press time, the Rancho Simi Recreation and Park District had just allocated a whopping $500,000 for a three-acre dog park in Simi Valley. We look forward to sniffing it out for the book's next edition.

5 Las Virgenes Canyon Open Space Preserve

🐾🐾🐾🐾 (See Ventura County map on page 706)

Every acre of this spectacular 3,000-acre park is in Ventura County, but the only access is from Los Angeles County, so that's where you'll find its description in this book. See the *Calabasas* section.

6 Sage Ranch Park

🐾🐾🐾🐾 (See Ventura County map on page 706)

The 652 acres of wild parkland at Sage Ranch have the kind of diversity most parks can only dream of. Coastal sage scrub, the park's namesake, dominates, but along the park's 2.6-mile loop trail you'll also find grasslands, wildflowers (in spring), oak woodlands, an old orange grove, and a riparian area with sycamores, walnut trees, and ferns. The ferny fauna isn't far from some rocky outcroppings that look like they belong in an old Western flick. The contrast of environments makes for intriguing hikes. Even dogs seem to dig the varying scenery.

Exit U.S. 101 at Valley Circle Drive/Mulholland Drive. Drive north on Valley Circle Drive for about six miles. You'll come to a three-way stop at Woolsey Canyon Road. Go left and follow Woolsey Canyon Road to the end, where you'll head right on Black Canyon Road. The entrance to the park is about 200 yards north of the intersection. 1 Black Canyon Road; 818/999-3753 or 310/589-3200.

7 Rocky Peak Park

🐾🐾🐾🐾 (See Ventura County map on page 706)

If you and your dog want to pay homage to Bob Hope, watch some of his *Road* flicks one evening, then the next morning venture out to this sprawling

DIVERSION

Got a Canine Credit Card? Simi Valley Town Center, an open-air shopping mall, is a great place to bring your dog if you want to do more than window shop: The mall is very dog friendly, to the point that it even supplies poop bags—"just in case," says a mall employee. The mall has enough trees and plants to put a smile on your dog's snout. The best way to find out if a store will allow your dog is to pop your head in and point to your dog with a questioning look, eyebrows raised. If that doesn't work, just ask. There's no list of dog-friendly stores, and we're told they've been known to change rules pretty quickly, based on "incidents."

The mall's motto, "Always in Season," is amusing if you think about it from a doggy perspective. It's located at 1555 Simi Valley Town Center Way; 805/581-1430; www.simivalleytc.com.

4,815-acre park. Hope once owned the 4,400 acres of this land. Back then it was known as Runkle Ranch. Today it's an amazing place to hike through wide-open grasslands, oak savannahs, and gigantic sandstone boulder formations. If you visit in the spring, you'll be wowed by the wildflowers here. There's abundant wildlife, in addition to mountain bikes and equestrians, so leashes are the law.

Several trails that start at various points on the park's perimeter take you to vastly different parts of this huge park. Go to www.smmc.ca.gov if you want to make hiking plans before going, or just check out the trail map near the park entrance when you get here. A trail leading to a couple of popular trails starts here. The park entrance is across Highway 118 from Corriganville Park. From the east, exit Highway 118 at Rocky Peak Road. The park is on the north side of the off ramp. From the west, exit Highway 118 at Kuehner Drive. Turn right and follow it to the top of the pass (it will become Santa Susana Pass Road) and to the park entrance. 310/589-3200.

🐾 Corriganville Park

🐾🐾🐾🐾 (See Ventura County map on page 706)

If you're a fan of old Westerns, stop your stagecoach right here, pardner. And if you have a penchant for old jungle flicks, you also need to swing into this big park, which is named after actor and stuntman Ray "Crash" Corrigan, who bought the property in the 1930s.

Hundreds of movies were shot here from the 1930s into the 1960s. Back then, the property was as large as 2,000 acres, but now it's 220. That's OK. There's still plenty of room for you and your leashed little doggy (or big doggy) to git along and see some fun old movie backdrops. A few of the films that were shot here: *Fort Apache, Trail of the Vigilante, Mule Train, Rogues of Sherwood Forest, Escape from Fort Bravo, Skipalong Rosenbloom, Tarzan Escapes,* and even *The Inspector General.*

A stream cuts through an empty concrete-lined pool that was filled during Corriganville's movie days. It has windows in the side where cameramen were stationed to get underwater shots of the good guys fighting the bad guys in the "lake" or, in the case of the *Jungle Jim* movies (also shot here), wrestling an alligator.

There's a marvelous website about Corriganville, with a biography of its colorful namesake, information on all the former sets and present sites, and tons of old photos. The site name is a long and clunky one, with lots of slashes, so it's easier to just type "Corriganville" into a search engine. It will come up immediately. One piece of news it won't tell you is that the park has poop bag dispensers; this is something dogs with forgetful humans (the kind who leave the poop bags at home) like to know.

A huge thank you to Sheryl Smith and her dear English springer spaniel Gracie—who is now galloping around leash free in Dog Heaven—for their heads up about Corriganville and for their contribution to our description of this wonderful park.

From I-5 or I-405, head west on Highway 118 (the Ronald Reagan/Simi Valley Freeway), exit at Kuehner Drive (you'll be coming down out of the Santa Susana Mountains), and turn left. In about a mile, turn left at the signal at Smith Road. The entrance to Corriganville Park is at the end of the street. (Shortly before that entrance on the left you'll see the original entrance to the property.) 805/584-4400.

PLACES TO STAY
Motel 6: Rates are $60–70 for the first adult, $6 for the second. 2566 North Erringer Road 93065; 805/526-3533.

Moorpark

PARKS, BEACHES, AND RECREATION AREAS

🐾 Happy Camp Canyon Regional Park
🐾🐾🐾🐾 (See Ventura County map on page 706)

This 3,000-acre wonderland of lush forests, colorful shale outcroppings, and wide-open grasslands is a great place for a dog to bring a human. People love the splendid geological formations and the seasonal wildflowers. Dogs adore the variety of hiking possibilities in this vast wilderness area. The park has more than 12 miles of trails, but only some permit pooches. Signs will let you know what's OK and what's not. Dogs need to be on leash here; the park is home to sensitive wildlife habitats.

Exit U.S. 101 at Highway 23 and drive north to New Los Angeles Avenue. Go left (west) and at the third signal, Moorpark Avenue, turn right. Drive 2.6 miles (Moorpark Avenue will turn into Walnut Canyon Road) past the railroad crossing. You'll see a sharp 30 mph left curve at that point, but do not go left; continue straight and you'll almost immediately come to Broadway Avenue, where you'll make a right. Continue to the park, which has plenty of parking. 14105 Broadway; 310/589-3200.

Oxnard

What this city lacks in the appealing name department (you just can't say "Oxnard" so it sounds like anything remotely attractive) it makes up for with a couple of beaches that allow dogs, and a twice-monthly dog gathering that's a real gas.

PARKS, BEACHES, AND RECREATION AREAS

I had a scintillating conversation with a parks department employee about

🐕 DIVERSION

Be Harbor Hounds: The best way to see the sights of Channel Islands Harbor is from the water, and thanks to the **Channel Islands Water Taxi,** you don't have to rich or an angler to do the boat thing. You and your salty dog can hitch a ride on this 22-foot enclosed boat, which motors to five stops around the harbor, and it will barely make a dent in your dog food budget. The cost: $6 for a round-trip cruise (about 40 minutes), or $1–2 per hop. Dogs are free. During summer, the taxi runs most days noon–6 P.M. or 7 P.M. During the off-season, the taxi usually sets sail on weekends only. If you want to rent the boat for a private to-do, it will cost you $100 an hour, and you can bring up to 22 guests. (The captain is included with the fee.)

Our favorite place to catch the water cab is at Fisherman's Wharf, at 2741 South Victoria Avenue, Oxnard. (That's also where you'll find the Channel Islands Visitors Center, where you can pick up water taxi schedules and fun info about the area.) For other stops or more information, call 805/985-4677 or 805/985-4852.

---

the subject of dog doo-doo. He quoted from the scriptures (city code): "It says right here—'No person shall permit any dog to defecate on public property... without the consent of the person owning it.' That's the law."

"OK, so you have to fax the park commissioners, tell them your dog ate a whopper of a supper last night, and that you might be needing the use of their parks the next morning?" I asked. It took him a few minutes before he figured out that maybe there was more to this law than meets the eye. "Oh, right here it says that if you clean it up right away, you don't have to get permission," he said. "Whew!" said I. "Whew!" breathed my relieved dog.

Another city law says that you must always carry a pooper-scooper when with your dog. If you don't have one on hand, you could be fined. But what if your dog already did his business and you threw it out? "You'd better carry a spare just for show," another city employee told me.

The biggest park in the city, College Park, doesn't permit pooches because it's actually a county park (and we know how dog friendly those are). Fortunately, there are two beaches dogs can visit on leash and a terrific free dog club that welcomes any decent dog to cavort around leash-free every couple of weeks.

🔟 Hollywood Beach

🐾🐾🐾 (See Ventura County map on page 706)

You may not see silver-screen stars at Hollywood Beach, but your dog will still be dazzled as she joins you on a leashed walk on this beautiful chunk of sand and sea. Many dogs drag their humans here for a walk, and you may find some naked ones (sans leash) running around, but leashes are the rule. Unfortunately, a ranger recently told us that dogs aren't allowed here at all 9 A.M.–5 P.M.! That means some pretty limited walking hours. It's off Harbor Boulevard, at the corner of La Brea Street and Ocean Drive. 805/382-3007.

🐾 Oxnard Beach Park
🐾🐾🐾 (See Ventura County map on page 706)

This is a state park, but don't let that scare you off: It's run by the city of Oxnard, and dogs are welcome on leash. The park is less developed than many other beaches in the area. It covers about 62 acres and features dune trails and a picnic area. The beach is an extra wide one, and dogs really dig it here, even though they have to be attached to people.

The parking fee is $5 for the day. The beach is west of Harbor Boulevard, between Beach Way and Falkirk Avenue. 805/385-7950.

PLACES TO EAT

Big Daddy O's Beach BBQ: This meat-lover's paradise is a block from Silver Strand, an isolated beach dotted with surfers. Dogs can join you at the outdoor tables here while you dine on Big Daddy O's popular tri-tip sandwich, killer cheeseburger, or great barbecued chicken. Dogs love the alluring flame-cooked-meat scent of this place and have been known to pull their people for blocks in some cave-dog like urge to eat meat cooked on a fire. 2333 Roosevelt Boulevard; 805/984-0014.

Eric Ericssons: You and your dog will love eating here: The restaurant is right on the pier. Some of the outdoor tables face the pier, while some face the ocean. It's a great setup, with fabulous scenery. And the food's good to boot! Seafood is the main attraction, but lunch features a variety of tasty non-seafood items too. (Jake says come to dinner for the prime rib and drop some "accidentally" for your dog.) A big thank-you to Emily the coonhound for letting us know about this find. 668 Harbor Boulevard; 805/643-4783.

PLACES TO STAY

Casa Sirena: If you like boats, stay here. This pleasant, 176-room motel-like inn is right at a marina, with lots of boats and gulls. Many rooms have balconies or patios that overlook the harbor or the greener side of the inn. Rooms are of the basic clean motel variety. Get a suite and you won't have to sniff around for a restaurant, since they come with kitchenettes. It's convenient when staying with the pooch. Rates are $89–149. Dogs are $50 extra per stay. A light continental breakfast comes with your stay. Thanks to Angela Dog for having her person, Mark, write to us to tell us about this place! 3605 Peninsula Road 93035; 800/447-3529; www.casasirenahotel.com.

Residence Inn by Marriott: This is a convenient place to park it when traveling with a pooch. All the rooms are studios or apartments, and all come with full kitchens. Rates are $119–189 and include a full breakfast and complimentary afternoon beverages.

Dogs pay a $100 fee for the length of their stay. 2101 West Vineyard Avenue 93030; 805/278-2200; www.residenceinn.com.

Port Hueneme

Remember our little pronunciation lesson at the beginning of this chapter? This place is Port "Why-knee-me." No reason for you or your dog to be tongue-tied.

PARKS, BEACHES, AND RECREATION AREAS

Dogs are not allowed at this navy city's beaches, but they can peruse the parks here, in addition to Sycamore Cove, a terrific beach down the coast just a bit in Point Mugu State Park territory.

🐾 Port Hueneme Beach Park

🐾🐾🐾 (See Ventura County map on page 706)

Dogs can't go on the sand here, but it's still a pleasant place to visit with a canine. Leashed dogs are welcome to enjoy the big, grassy, landscaped part of the park and the walkway that runs through it along the length of the beach. They can sniff the palm trees and plop down under a picnic table while you enjoy the views and the sea breeze. It's a popular place for local dogs. The park is on Surfside Drive at Ventura Road. 805/986-6542.

🐾 Sycamore Cove Beach

🐾🐾🐾🐾 (See Ventura County map on page 706)

This big, beautiful beach welcomes leashed dogs to stroll on the sand, wade in the surf, and sniff around a grassy picnic area. It's the most dog-friendly part of the 15,000-acre Point Mugu State Park, which bans dogs from trails. You can even camp here; across the highway is a 55-site campground.

The day-use fee is a steep $10 per vehicle. The beach is about 11 miles south of Port Hueneme (about six miles north of the Los Angeles County line) on Highway 1/Pacific Coast Highway. 818/880-0350.

PLACES TO EAT

Anacappuccino: "We're dog friendly!" exclaims a server who loves dogs. Dine on traditional café food with your pooch at the four umbrella-topped tables outside. Thirsty dogs get water. 289 East Port Hueneme Road; 805/488-9580.

PLACES TO STAY

Point Mugu State Park Campgrounds: Dogs aren't permitted on the magical trails in this spectacular park, even with a leash. "They're a hazard to wildlife and other park visitors," a young ranger told me in a monotone, robotic voice. Creepy! But there are a few paved roads you can walk them on, if tar's your cup of tea.

At least dogs are allowed to help you pitch a tent at one of the 131 campsites. One of our favorite camping areas is at Thornhill Broome Beach. Dogs love camping beachside. (They can't visit the beach here, but they're welcome at Point Mugu's Sycamore Cove Beach.) Rates are $20. The park is about nine miles south of Port Hueneme Road, on Highway 1. For park info, call 818/880-0350. Call 800/444-7275 to reserve a site.

Camarillo

PARKS, BEACHES, AND RECREATION AREAS

It looks like Camarillo isn't going to stop at one dog park. Plans are in the works for a new one. We'll check it out and bring you details in the next edition.

14 Camarillo Dog Park

🐾🐾🐾🐕 (See Ventura County map on page 706)

If only dogs could see in color (and maybe they can, but that's another story)! The fire hydrant and drinking fountain in this one-acre, fenced dog park are so dazzling you almost need sunglasses to look at them. The hydrant is a bright fire-engine red, the fountain a brilliant green. They look especially colorful when surrounded by white dogs, black dogs, and Dalmatians.

The park has plenty of trees, which provide welcome shade in the warmer months. Dogs and their humans also have water fountains, benches, and a picnic table. It's a fun place to visit for a little relaxation and a lot of leash-free dog fun.

The dog park is in Camarillo Grove Park. There's a $3 fee to enter this park, but if you have a dog with you, it's free. (Dogs are like a bulky coupon.) You're relegated to the dog park, so don't go wandering off anywhere else once you're in. Exit U.S. 101 at Camarillo Springs Road. If you're coming from the north, go left at the stop sign at the bottom of the off-ramp and continue to the park. If you're coming from the south, keep heading straight from the off-ramp and you'll hit the park. The park is off Camarillo Springs Road at the base of the Conejo grade. 805/482-1996.

Newbury Park

PARKS, BEACHES, AND RECREATION AREAS

15 Rancho Sierra Vista/Satwiwa

🐾🐾🐾🐾 (See Ventura County map on page 706)

This 760-acre park is the westernmost parcel of the Santa Monica Mountains National Recreation Area. (See *Los Angeles County* for more on this terrific entity of the national parks system.) Its Satwiwa Native American Indian Culture Center and Chumash Demonstration Village are excellent places for learning about the history of the Chumash culture, whose people have lived in this area for thousands of years.

Dogs can't go in any buildings, but they're welcome on the park's four trails. Depending on which trail you take, you'll find yourself strolling on gentle hills, sweet-smelling grasslands, or possibly, if you go far enough, into a canyon shaded by sycamores and oaks. But don't go too far: Rancho Sierra Vista/ Satwiwa provides easy access to Point Mugu State Park and Boney Mountain State Wilderness—both of which ban dogs from their trails. Jake's favorite, because of its ban on horses and bikes, and its lack of connections to off-limits parks, is the Satwiwa Loop Trail, an easy 1.5-mile hike that takes you through the Satwiwa Native American Indian Natural Area. He's not much interested in the historical aspect of the area, but the apparently all-too-fascinating scents on the chaparral keep him from getting too bored.

Exit Highway 101 at Lynn Road and drive south 5.25 miles to Via Goleta. The park entrance is on your left. To get to the Satwiwa Native American Indian Culture Center, drive to the main parking area (you'll pass a couple of smaller ones) and walk 0.3 mile up a gravel road to the brown wooden building. The Satwiwa Loop Trail is a bone's throw away. 805/370-2301.

Thousand Oaks

PARKS, BEACHES, AND RECREATION AREAS

Zounds! The Thousand Oaks area is home to 13,000 acres of open space you can explore with a leashed dog. Most of these areas are difficult to access, but if you can find them, they're well worth the visit. We describe a couple of Open Space areas below. The Conejo Open Space Conservation Agency, which oversees these areas, can provide you with a general map and directions to other open space parks. 805/495-6471.

The city also has a dog park. Conejo Creek Dog Park has proven very popular with the pooch set.

The Thousand Oaks area is also home to some of the Santa Monica Mountains National Recreation Area (see the *National Recreation Areas* section of the *Los Angeles County* chapter). Dogs dig Thousand Oaks. As one very helpful local reader, Carolyn Greene, put it: "Although I enjoy living here myself, it's even better for dogs." Her beautiful 85-pound German shepherd, Jasmine, couldn't agree more.

A word of warning from another Caroline (my fabulous research editor, who knows what she's talking about): Coyotes live in the wilder parks and Open Space areas around here and have been known to lure dogs away—and not just to compare tails and fur color. Be careful, and keep those leashes firmly attached in the area's more undeveloped spaces. (It's the law, anyway.)

16 Conejo Creek Dog Park

😺😺😺🐕 (See Ventura County map on page 706)

Dogs who like to socialize dig this park. Every afternoon, dogs of all shapes, sizes, and backgrounds gather to sniff and chase around the three grassy acres here. (It's grassy in part because the park closes whenever it rains.) The dog park is divided into two sections: a smaller section for small or shy dogs and a bigger chunk for everyone else. There are three drinking fountains for dogs and their people, Mutt Mitt stations galore, and a few double-gated entries. But there's not much as far as trees. Lots of horses pass very close to the dog park to access popular trails, and trees could obscure their ability to see the dogs, which could lead to a startled horse and an injured rider. That said, all's not lost for dogs who like shade: By the time you read this, hot dogs (of the furry variety) and their humans should have some shade structures to hide out under.

The dog park is across the street from Waverly Park, a nice little community park, at 1350 Avenida de las Flores; 805/495-6471. A hotline for the dog park will tell you whether it's open or closed because of maintenance or mud; 805/381-1299.

17 Wildwood Park

😺😺😺😺 (See Ventura County map on page 706)

It's not every day you and your dog get to hike to a 60-foot waterfall, so take advantage of this amazing 1,700-acre park, run by the Conejo Open Space Conservation Agency. Joe Dog liked to walk to the waterfall and stand there in awe that such waterworks can actually exist in otherwise dry land.

Several trails wind through the coastal sage and xeric scrub-covered hills that make up most of the park. In the spring, the wildflowers go wild in a burst of intoxicating color and scent.

You'll have to keep your dog leashed as you hike the many miles of trails. The wildlife appreciates it. After all, there's not much habitat around here for these animals anymore.

From U.S. 101, exit at Thousand Oaks Freeway/Highway 23 and drive north about 2.5 miles to Avenida de los Arboles. Turn left and follow the road all the way to the end (about three miles). The parking area is on the left, next to the entry kiosk that holds maps and brochures of the park. 805/495-6471.

18 Los Robles Open Space

😺😺😺 (See Ventura County map on page 706)

If it's trails you want, it's trails you'll get at this terrific swatch of Open Space land run by the Conejo Open Space Conservation Agency (COSCA). The total trail system here is 15 miles! That's a lot of trail for you and your leashed, outdoors-loving pooch to peruse. Some of the trails are killer, with very steep grades, so avoid these for the sake of your dog's paws. The trail system is going to be a real wonder one day—there are plans to join the trails in Los Robles with trails in the Santa Monica Mountains National Recreation Area (see the *National Recreation Areas* section of the *Los Angeles County* chapter) to form a 40-mile trail system from Malibu to Point Mugu.

Before I continue, COSCA coordinator Mark Towne makes a plea for dogs to be leashed here:

> *We have a lot of problems with dogs off leash. It impacts the wildlife, and it could impact the dogs, too.... We've had dogs chasing rabbits, ground squirrels, and other wildlife. For a dog's sake, leashes are important because there are rattlesnakes and ticks.*

Got it? It's tempting to skip the leash, but leashes are the law here, and apparently for good reason. The trails at Los Robles are actually wide fire access roads, winding through chaparral country and coast live oaks. They're very well marked. If you start at the parking area at the end of Moorpark Road, you can connect to the Los Robles Trail. Take the trail west to the Spring Canyon Trail and follow it to Lynn Oaks Park and back for an easy three-mile round-trip hike. If you're in the mood for food, pack a lunch and take the Los Robles Trail due south (from Moorpark) for about a mile. You'll come to a pleasant little picnic area where you and your leashed beast can have a feast.

Dogs who like nature love the half-mile Oak Creek Canyon Loop. This is a self-guided nature trail detailing the area's indigenous plant life. You can get here by hiking from the Moorpark entrance, but you can also drive to this trail by following Green Meadow Avenue to the end.

From U.S. 101, take Moorpark Road south to the end (about a mile). The parking lot is on the right. 805/495-6471.

PLACES TO STAY

Motel 6: Rates are $53–73. 1516 Newbury Road 91320; 805/499-0711.

Thousand Oaks Inn: Stay here and you're next to Borders Books, which is great for literary dogs. You'll also get use of the hotel's free video library, which is great for couch-potato dogs. Your room comes with use of the hotel's heated pool and Jacuzzi, complimentary passes to a local workout joint, and a continental breakfast. Rates are $144–275. There's a $45 pooch fee per visit. 75 West Thousand Oaks Boulevard; 805/497-3701 or 800/600-6878; www.thousandoaksinn.com.

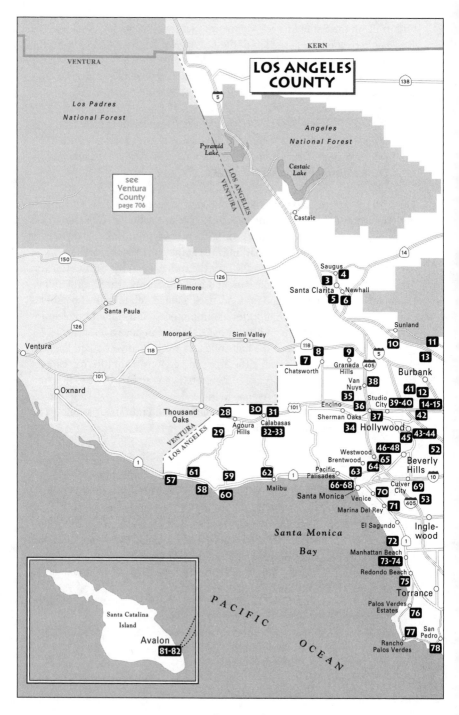

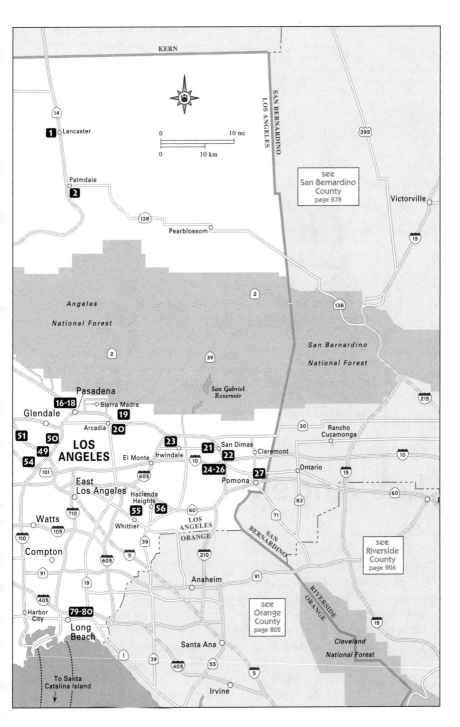

CHAPTER 52

Los Angeles County

Slowly but surely, Los Angeles County is going to the dogs, in the best sense of the phrase. This is a wonderful development if you're a dog or just someone who knows a dog.

When I started researching parks for *The Dog Lover's Companion to California* back in the early 1990s, there were only a couple of leash-free areas in the whole county. Today, there are 31, and counting. Most are fenced dog parks, but one, Westridge-Canyonback Wilderness Park in Encino, is a spectacular 1,500-acre swatch of wilderness. Go ahead, dogs: wag your tails, pant, let it all hang out. Look for the running dog symbol 🐕 in the pages that follow, and take your humans to a doggone great park.

Of course, there needs to be a much larger increase in the number of leash-free areas if L.A. County's hundreds of thousands of dogs are going to get the running room they deserve. If dogs had opposable fingers, they'd be crossing them hard for more places where they could just be their good old doggy selves and trot around naked. Many cities and park departments are working hand in paw with dogs and their people to help accomplish this mission. Jake and I hope we'll be sniffing out many more leash-free havens for the book's next edition.

The Los Angeles County Parks system is a good one, with dozens of large parks dotting the county. Most allow leashed pooches. So do most of the huge, wonderful parklands within the Santa Monica Mountains National Recreation Area and just about every inch of land operated by the Santa Monica Mountains Conservancy.

But not everything is to a dog's liking here. Dogs are still banned from all beaches except one in the Malibu area and a terrific leash-free beach area in Long Beach. The rest of the county's 74 miles of shoreline are off-limits, verboten, badlands. But that may one day come to an end if a couple of active dog groups get their way: A group called Unleash the Beach is working to get a chunk of Santa Monica Beach OK'd for off-leash use, and the long-entrenched group Freeplay is striving for the same thing at El Segundo's Dockweiler Beach. Jake and I applaud both groups for going beyond setting their sights only on leashed use. See www.unleashthebeach.org and www.freeplay.org.

Los Angeles is a huge county with oodles of dog-friendly activities. You can take your extremely well-behaved poochum-woochums shopping at certain exclusive Beverly Hills stores. You can spend the night at some of the world's finest hotels with your dog or take him to some super dog-friendly eateries. You can even go to clubbing with your dog. (OK, there's one club, and it only hosts events a few times a year, but it's worth checking out. See the Diversion *Drink, Dance, and Don't Forget Your Dog.*)

This chapter separates some of the districts in the city of Los Angeles into their own sections. For instance, Hollywood has its own heading. The city is too huge and diverse to lump all its districts together. Now, git along little doggy, and start sniffing out the tens of thousands of acres of urban and wild parks that welcome you and your ilk.

NATIONAL FORESTS

The *National Forests and Wilderness Areas* resource at the back of this book has important information and safety tips on visiting national forests with your dog and has more information on the Angeles National Forest.

Angeles National Forest
😺😺😺😺🐕

PICK OF THE LITTER—LOS ANGELES COUNTY

WHERE TO FOLLOW IN RIN TIN TIN'S PAWPRINTS
Garden of the Gods, Chatsworth (page 734)

MOST BEAUTIFUL NEW DOG PARKS
Alice Frost Kennedy Dog Park, Pasadena (page 741)
San Dimas Dog Park, San Dimas (page 744)

BEST BACKDROP
The Paramount Ranch, Agoura Hills (page 749)

BIGGEST VICTORY FOR NATURE
Upper Las Virgenes Canyon Open Space Preserve,
Calabasas (page 751)

BEST OFF-LEASH HIKE
Westridge-Canyonback Wilderness Park, Encino (page 752)

BIGGEST DOG PARK
Laurel Canyon Park, Studio City (page 755)

COOLEST NAME FOR A DOG PARK
The Boneyard, Culver City (page 785)

BEST LEASH-FREE BEACH (ONLY LEASH-FREE BEACH)
The Dog Zone at the Beach, Long Beach (page 794)

BEST TRAP FOR ICE-AGE ANIMALS
La Brea Tar Pits, Los Angeles (page 770)

NATIONAL RECREATION AREAS

Santa Monica Mountains National Recreation Area
😊 😊 😊 😊

Attention, smog-coated dogs and city-weary people: You can breathe a sigh of relief. Nature is only a stick's throw away from the crowded freeways and urban sprawl of one of the largest cities in the world.

Contrary to what some local dog people have heard, leashed dogs really

TOP DOG-FRIENDLY RESTAURANT
Quincy's BBQ, Encino (page 753)

ALSO VERY DOG-FRIENDLY PLACES TO EAT
All India Cafe, Pasadena (page 742)
Toast Bakery Cafe, West Hollywood (page 762)
Back Door Bakery, Los Angeles (page 772)
Java Man, Hermosa Beach (page 791)

MOST DOG-FRIENDLY PLACES TO STAY
Hotel Bel-Air, Bel-Air (page 760)
Beverly Wilshire, Beverly Hills (page 766)
The Peninsula Beverly Hills, Beverly Hills (page 767)
Raffles L'Ermitage, Beverly Hills (page 767)
Omni Los Angeles Hotel at California Plaza, Los Angeles (page 773)
W Los Angeles, Westwood (page 781)
Le Merigot, Santa Monica (page 784)
Loews Santa Monica Beach Hotel, Santa Monica (page 784)
The Turret House, Long Beach (page 797)

COOLEST RETRO HOTEL
Safari Inn, Burbank (page 738)

BEST CLUB SCENE
SkyBark, Los Angeles (page 770)

BEST RIDE
Catalina Express ferry, mainland–Catalina Island (page 798)

are allowed to explore portions of this 65,000-acre wonderland of mountains, canyons, woods, and fern glens. This national recreation area is a patchwork of county, state, and federal lands throughout the Santa Monica Mountains. While dogs are banned from trails on all state park lands and from most beaches within the recreation area, the majority of the recreation area's parks and open spaces welcome leashed dogs. Dogs need to wear a leash no longer than six feet (if it's retractable, measure carefully!) and be under control. (It seems like a redundant rule, but apparently the parks have had their share of out-of-control leashed dogs.) The most dog friendly of the national recreation area's lands are managed by the Santa Monica Mountains Conservancy. We describe many of these gems throughout this chapter and the *Ventura County* chapter.

The Mountain Parks Information Service provides a free map showing all the parks, delineating which permit dogs. You can also get free brochures of many of the dog-friendly parks, which show trailheads and give descriptions and directions. They're essential for planning any enchanting back-to-nature outing with your dog. Call 800/533-PARK (800/533-7275) to get your maps and brochures. For a map of the entire recreation area, go to www.nps.gov/samo. In a hard-to-navigate-to page within that site (www.nps.gov/samo/brochure/dogleash.htm), you'll also find a list of parks within the recreation area that allow dogs, along with the detailed dog rules. The people at the National Park Service Visitor Center can be very helpful in answering questions about the recreation area. You can reach them at 805/370-2301.

Spring is a terrific time to explore these lands. Wildflowers blossom white, yellow, orange, blue, red, and every other color your dog might not be able to see if he's as color-blind as scientists claim. Birds sing their hearts out. The grasslands, normally a dead tan-brown color, become as green as green gets.

But watch out in the warmer months: "A lot of people bring their dogs hiking in the 90-degree heat and don't give them as much water as they need," says Walt Young, chief ranger for the Santa Monica Mountains Conservancy. "The dogs get heat stroke and we have to be called in to help out." Take his advice and leave your dog at home if it's hot. If you must take your dog during the hot months, bring only fit, younger dogs, and be sure to offer water very frequently—even if she recently turned down a snootful.

Lancaster

PARKS, BEACHES, AND RECREATION AREAS

Lancaster finally has a dog park of its own! And it's doing so well that the city is strongly considering building others.

1 Lancaster Dog Park

🐾🐾🐾🐕 (See Los Angeles County map on pages 724–725)

The city's first dog park sprang up in late 2006, and it's very well used. "It's incredible how many dogs go there," said a city park official. So many, apparently, that you may be reading about more Lancaster dog parks in the next edition.

This is your basic fenced dog park, about an acre in size, with grass, benches, water, and a separate section for small dogs. The park is so new that there's no shade from the young trees, but one day they'll offer relief from the sun. The park is in western Lancaster, within the larger Hull Park, on 30th Street West at Avenue M. 661/723-6000.

PLACES TO STAY

Oxford Suites: The suites here are pleasant, clean, and roomy enough even for a big boy like Jake to stay here and not feel cramped. It's not fancy or boutique-y, but most dogs don't really care about decor. Thanks to reader Bob Pace and his dog for recommending this place. Rates are $119–169. Small dogs pay $25 extra per stay, large dogs pay $50 extra per stay. If your dog is medium, you'll have to figure it out with the hotel. 1651 West K Avenue 93534; 661/949-3423; www.oxfordsuiteslancaster.com.

Palmdale

PARKS, BEACHES, AND RECREATION AREAS

At press time, Palmdale was in the early planning stages for two dog parks. That's great news, because dogs around here need some space to run without a leash.

🐾 Ritter Ranch/Sierra Pelona Open Space

🐾🐾🐾🐾 (See Los Angeles County map on pages 724–725)

You and your dog can hike forever when you start hoofing it at this 4,200-acre open space. The park itself has many miles of trails, which take you and your leashed dog through beautiful open land, rolling hills, sage-covered expanses, and desert-like territory on the east end of the Sierra Pelonas. You won't find much shade here, so it's best to come in winter and early spring, when your dog won't bake in her coat like a potato in its jacket.

A variety of trails in the eastern portion of the park will take you to the Sierra Pelona Trail, which leads to the Angeles National Forest. Here, if your dog is under voice control, you may let her off leash. (Of course, by the time you get here, your dog may be too well exercised to really care about romping about all naked.)

Exit Highway 14 at Sierra Highway and drive north for about a mile until you get to Shannondale Road. Go right (north) on Shannondale, then right on Shannon Valley Road, driving east to Via Farnero Drive, where you'll go left and drive ever so briefly, going right on Shannon View Road (who is this Shannon, anyway?). Shannon View Road becomes Telephone Road. Follow it to the park entrance. 310/858-7272.

PLACES TO STAY

E-Z 8 Motel: We learned about this dog-friendly motel from Flint Dog and Serena Dog and their translator, Suzanne Stewart. They walked into the office and popped the question about whether or not dogs are allowed here, and the front-desk clerk smilingly told them, "We are a dog-friendly company." She says the first-floor room was very comfortable, with its own access to a landscaped area. At the time, there was a field of several acres next door for general dog romping, but this may not be the case when you visit. Time and developers march on. Rates are $46–56. Dogs require a $25 deposit. 430 West Palmdale Boulevard 93551; 661/273-6400.

Santa Clarita
PARKS, BEACHES, AND RECREATION AREAS
I've listed the Santa Clarita Woodlands Park under Santa Clarita because it's the closest real city to the park. While you're in the area, be sure to check out the former oil boomtown of Mentryville (see *Newhall*).

🖪 Santa Clarita Woodlands Park
😾😾😾😾 (See Los Angeles County map on pages 724–725)
Come here on a spring day and you and your leashed dog will swear you're nowhere near Los Angeles County. That's because this park is huge, with deep green (OK, seasonally green) hills of oaks and grasslands, hidden meadows, and a long, gurgling stream with banks of lush flora. We enjoy hiking here in the rain. After a long day in the valley, it's a refreshing way to wash away the dirt and stress of urban life.

The park, with its miles of trails and splendid views of the surrounding canyons and forests, opened to the public in 1997 after more than 100 years in the hands of the oil industry. It was actually the oil industry that kept this large swatch of land from succumbing to the rampant development of neighboring communities. Fortunately, the Santa Monica Mountains Conservancy got hold of the property before developers could. The result awaits the pitter-patter of your dog's paws.

Exit I-5 at Calgrove Boulevard and drive west a short jog to The Old Road; drive south until you see signs for the park, then head west again. The main entrance is at Ed Davis Park. 310/589-3200.

Saugus
PARKS, BEACHES, AND RECREATION AREAS

🖪 Vasquez Rocks Natural Area Park
😾😾😾 (See Los Angeles County map on pages 724–725)
This is Los Angeles County? It looks more like another planet. The slanted, jagged rocks and hidden caves are among the state's most famous geological wonders. They're so unusually beautiful that film crews routinely use them as a backdrop. When you call the park, chances are the answering machine will tell you how to get permission to make movies here. It's probably not the kind of information you and your dog need to know, but that's entertainment.

This smog-free 745-acre park, in the high desert near Agua Dulce, also features Tataviam Indian archaeological sites. Many trails branch off through chaparral and riparian plant communities. Make sure you bring drinking water; there's none in the park and you can work up a mighty thirst.

Dogs must be leashed, but back in the days of the bandit Tiburicio Vasquez, there were no such rules. If there had been, Vasquez, the park's namesake, would have found a way to break them. In the mid-1800s, Vasquez was a sort of Robin Hood character, robbing from the wealthy and giving the money to poor Mexicans. He used the caves and rocks as a hideaway from the sheriff's posses and vigilantes who were always on his trail. When you visit the park, stop at the entry kiosk and read about Vasquez's dramatic final days here. Then take your dog for a hike on the very trails Vasquez may have fled on, and let your imagination take you back to the days of the Wild West.

Exit Highway 14 at Agua Dulce Canyon Road and follow the signs to the park. 661/268-0840.

Newhall

PARKS, BEACHES, AND RECREATION AREAS

5 Mentryville

😾😾😾 (See Los Angeles County map on pages 724–725)

Once upon a time, there was oil in these hills. Mentryville was home to what's claimed to be the longest continually operating oil well in the world, running from the 1880s until 1990. The little town housed more than 100 families from its inception to about 1930, and some of it has been preserved and turned into a very cool park. You can see a handful of historic buildings and landmarks here, including a one-room schoolhouse, an old barn, the site of the famed oil well, and founder Charles Mentry's big old mansion.

Dogs can't go in the buildings, but they can check them out with you from the outside, as long as they're leashed. If this disappoints your dog, tell her that there's something even better for visiting pooches: They can join you on a wonderful hike through Pico Canyon, in the north end of Santa Clarita Woodlands Park. The trail takes you from Mentryville through chaparral-covered slopes and into a shaded, lush, riparian area near the headwaters of Pico Canyon and the Santa Susana Mountains. The trail continues but gets very rugged, so be prepared to turn around when your dog is tired. This isn't a loop trail.

From the San Fernando Valley, go north on I-5 and take the Lyons Road/Pico Canyon Road exit. Turn left at the off-ramp's stop sign (this will be Pico Canyon Road), cross over the freeway, and continue straight until you come to a Y intersection near the end of the road. Go left at the Y and continue to the end of that road, where you'll find a parking lot. 27201 Pico Canyon Road; 310/589-3200.

6 William S. Hart Regional Park

🐾🐾🐾 (See Los Angeles County map on pages 724–725)

If you and your dog are fans of the Old West, you must amble on down here. Coming to this park is like getting a personal invitation to the house and ranch of the silent Western movie hero William S. Hart. Unfortunately, Hart isn't around anymore to give you a personal tour, but feel free to peruse the property via a couple of trails. If you get a hankering to check out his hacienda, you can leave your dog at the shaded picnic area with your traveling pardner and take a guided tour.

Dogs have to be leashed at the park. Hart, a cowboy himself, might not have liked that rule, but it's a small price to pay to enjoy the hospitality of the ghost of these here hills. Besides, the property houses a little zoo with farm animals and a compost demonstration site. You don't want your pooch meddling with either.

Exit Highway 14 at San Fernando Road and follow the signs west to the park. 661/259-0855.

Chatsworth

PARKS, BEACHES, AND RECREATION AREAS

7 Garden of the Gods

🐾🐾🐾 (See Los Angeles County map on pages 724–725)

The huge sandstone rock formations at this 23-acre park have provided a dramatic background for many an old film. The Garden of the Gods is one of the last undeveloped remnants of the once thriving Iverson Movie Ranch, used by dozens of directors during its reign from the earliest days of film in 1912 all the way up through 1976. Movies and shows shot at the ranch include *Stagecoach, The Lone Ranger, Bonanza, Superman, Batman and Robin, Tarzan the Apeman, Little Bighorn,* and *The Fighting Seabees.* Even Laurel & Hardy and Shirley Temple filmed some scenes here.

If your dog's nose is very keen, he just might be able to sniff out where Rin Tin Tin once performed some scenes. We're not sure if the famous dog ever actually ventured to the Garden of the Gods during his time at Iverson, but he was definitely nearby.

A short trail takes you to some jaw-dropping rock formations. Exit Highway 118 at Topanga Canyon Boulevard and in less than a half mile make a right at Santa Susana Pass Road. In about another half mile you'll come to Redmesa Drive. Go right and follow it a few hundred feet to the park's entrance. (Redmesa bisects the park.) 310/589-3200.

8 Chatsworth Park South

🐾🐾🐾 (See Los Angeles County map on pages 724–725)

Joe Dog and Bill Dog had a rollicking good time roaming and rolling in this very spacious park one sunny afternoon. Other dogs were having the same grand old time, and when they joined together, it was a major pooch party.

The park's 81 acres provide lots of legroom for dogs, but the creatures are supposed to be leashed. An Elysian green meadow stretches as far as you care to run with your dog. If tiptoeing through the grass isn't your idea of a good time, you can walk along the park's wide dirt hiking trail. It's a wise idea to stick to the trails anyway: Rattlesnakes seem to enjoy living at this address.

The craggy mountains towering north of the park make for an impressive backdrop. Enough trees grace the park that you can lounge in the shade while you admire the scenery and the friendly dogs who frequent the place.

Exit Highway 118 at Topanga Canyon Boulevard and drive south for almost 1.5 miles to Devonshire Street. Turn right and drive a few blocks into the park. 818/341-6595.

PLACES TO STAY

Staybridge Suites Hotel: The suites are big and their fireplaces are awfully inviting. Rates are $156–186. Better plan on staying for a few nights, because the dog fees aren't cheap. You'll pay between $150 and $250 for the length of their stay, depending on the room size. If your dog is staying only one night, it's the same price as dressing him in a human disguise and getting him his own room! 21902 Lassen Street 91311; 818/773-0707 or 800/238-8000; www.summerfieldsuites.com.

Granada Hills

PARKS, BEACHES, AND RECREATION AREAS

9 O'Melveny Park

🐾🐾🐾 (See Los Angeles County map on pages 724–725)

This 672-acre park offers so many great hiking opportunities that your dog won't know which trail to try first.

Jake would like to suggest a fairly flat two-mile hike that takes you along a tree-lined creek at the bottom of the canyon here. It's often pretty green, and the creek actually has water in it, so it's not like so many dry L.A. County canyon parks.

Jake likes this park because he knows he's going to get a picnic after his leisurely hike. The picnic tables are plentiful, and they're at the beginning/end of this particular hike, so he knows if we don't eat upon entering, we'll definitely have a bite before leaving.

Exit I-5 at Balboa Boulevard and drive south about a mile to Orozco Street. Turn right and drive to the parking lot for the picnic area. The trail starts at the north end of the picnic area. For info on tougher hikes in this park, call 818/363-3556.

Lakeview Terrace

PARKS, BEACHES, AND RECREATION AREAS

10 Hansen Dam Recreation Area

😼😼😼 (See Los Angeles County map on pages 724–725)

This is 1,400 acres of hills, trees, shrubs, and grassy meadows. And the good news is that once again, it has a lake as its centerpiece. It disappeared for a few years during a long process of reclamation, but it's here to stay. Dogs enjoy sniffing around its perimeter and especially appreciate the horse trails here. They smell good to pooches, who may find an occasional munchie along the way (but try as your dog might, don't let him nibble these morsels).

From I-210, exit at Osborne Street and follow the signs for a couple of blocks. 818/899-4537.

Sunland

PARKS, BEACHES, AND RECREATION AREAS

11 La Tuna Canyon Park

😼😼😼😼 (See Los Angeles County map on pages 724–725)

Whether you're in the mood for an easy, cool, shady, wet hike; a more rigorous, steep, dry one; or something in between, you'll find what you're looking for at this 1,100-acre park on the north slope of the Verdugo Mountains.

If you and your leashed dog feel like taking it easy, head for The Grotto, a gorgeous, green cut in a canyon that seems to become more verdant and cooler as you walk along the trail. The trees and steep surrounding slopes provide plenty of shade. Before you know it, you'll be at a beautiful waterfall, if there's still enough water to fall when you're there. (In early spring, it can really flow.) It's mossy, cool, and relaxing.

Other trails take you through canyons full of oaks and sycamores. If you go high enough, things get sagey, and the views become magnificent, if you happen to like views of one of the world's biggest metropolitan areas. (Most people come here trying to forget the city, but it looks pretty good from the ridgetop.)

Exit I-210 at La Tuna Canyon Road and drive west. If you want to hit The Grotto, you'll find its parking and trailhead in a little under a mile, on the left. For the moderate La Tuna Canyon Trail, drive another half mile for parking, a picnic area, and the trailhead. This trail will lead you to other trails, which will take you out of the park and into other hiking areas—some steep and more demanding. 310/858-7272.

Burbank

PARKS, BEACHES, AND RECREATION AREAS

12 Johnny Carson Park

🐾🐾 (See Los Angeles County map on pages 724–725)

If you're of a certain age, you might remember all of Johnny Carson's lines about "beautiful downtown Burbank." Since the late *Tonight Show* host did his best to put Burbank on the map, the city decided to do the same for him. Just across from the NBC studios where he hosted his show year after year, there's a decent little park named after him.

The park, which used to be called Buena Vista Park, is a great place to visit with your dog if you're dropping off a friend at NBC or at the nearby Disney studios. It's well shaded and has many picnic tables and a footbridge that leads you to a fitness course. With Highway 134 roaring so close, it's not quiet, but who comes to this part of Burbank for tranquility?

A word of warning: Don't let your male dog lift his leg on the stone "sign" with Johnny Carson's mug engraved on it. We met a man who apparently sits on the grass all day watching for such indiscretions. He came running up to Joe after the dog did a quick leg lift. I thought perhaps he knew Joe or was running up to say Joe was a fine dog, but something about the way he was screaming "No, no pee on this! Bad dog!" led me to believe he had another mission.

Exit I-5 at Alameda Avenue and drive southwest for about 20 blocks. At Bob Hope Drive, turn left. The park will be on your left in about a block. 818/238-5300.

13 Wildwood Canyon Park

🐾🐾🐾 (See Los Angeles County map on pages 724–725)

The only way Jake would like this big park better than he already does would be if he could go leashless. It's beautifully manicured and surrounded by miles of forest. If he's in the mood to roll on the grass and enjoy a picnic near regal stone archways, we stay in the developed part of the park. If he's raring to explore nature and admire trees in his unique way, we take the myriad trails leading out from various points around the park.

His favorite kind of day involves a long hike through the hills, followed by a leisurely picnic at the serene, secluded, shaded picnic spots that dot the main area. You can't help but feel pampered in this lush park: It's run with such class that even the portable toilets are disguised to look distinguished.

Coming north on I-5, take the Olive Avenue exit and head northeast. Turn left at Sunset Canyon Drive. In six blocks, turn right on Harvard Drive, which will take you into the park. Make sure you bear right once you come to a fork in the road, or you'll end up on the adjacent golf course. 818/238-5300.

PLACES TO EAT

There are plenty of restaurants with outdoor tables in Burbank, but because of space constraints we're just listing the most dog-friendly one.

Priscilla's: If you and your pooch want to feel really welcome at a restaurant, come here. "We love dogs and would let them inside if we were allowed," says a manager. "We give them water, a little milk, whatever they want." You'll like the relaxed atmosphere on the patio with umbrella-shaded tables, as well as the gourmet coffees and tasty light fare. 4150 Riverside Drive; 818/843-5707.

PLACES TO STAY

Holiday Inn: Dogs stay in the lower floors of this 20-story hotel. Rooms are basic older hotel style, which dogs don't mind in the least. Rates are $159–195. Dogs are $10 and need to be under 50 pounds. 150 East Angeleno Avenue 91510; 818/841-4770; www.holidayinn.com.

Hotel Amarano Burbank: The rooms and suites at this boutique hotel are relaxing and luxurious without being over the top. You'll feel right at home here with your dog. It's not precious and chichi, but more of a sturdy modern European decor. If you have a yellow Lab like Jake, he'll look smashing with the muted mustard color scheme. (He might even momentarily camouflage away, as Jake did.) The beds have fine Italian linens and down comforters; the bathrooms feature marble and wood accents.

The double and king rooms all have a microwave and small fridge, but if you'll being staying a while, consider getting a suite. They're spacious and very comfy and come with a full, pretty kitchenette. Human guests get a welcome chocolate from Paris, and nightly turndown service is accompanied by a Belgian chocolate. (Nothing your dog can partake in, but you're footing the bill, so enjoy!) Rooms have free Wi-Fi. Rates are $209–320. Dogs are $75 per stay. 322 North Pass Avenue 91505; 818/842-8887 or 888/956-1900; www.hotelamarano.com.

Residence Inn Burbank Downtown: Suites are a good choice when staying away for a few days with a dog, and this all-suite hotel will make you feel right at home. The suites are attractive, spacious, and well appointed and have free Wi-Fi and full kitchens. And here's an amenity that's especially convenient for people traveling with dogs: Leave your grocery list in the morning, and you'll come back to a kitchen stocked with all your supplies!

Rates are $224–369. Dogs are $100 extra for the length of their stay, so stay a while and get your money's worth. 321 South First Street 91502; 818/260-8787 or 800/331-3131; www.marriott.com.

Safari Inn: Dogs who dig colorful retro chic love staying at the Safari Inn. This is a fully restored and renovated classic from the 1950s, complete with an ultra-retro 1960s neon sign announcing the motel to the world. The rooms here are bright, cheery, and well appointed—a few steps up from a typical motel. (How many motels offer room service from their very own decent restaurant?) You can even get a "groovy martini" at the inn's restaurant/lounge, if you really want to stroll (stumble?) down memory lane. Relax in the pool under a few tall palms and the bright lights of the neon sign.

Rates are $129–199. Dogs are $25 extra and have to sign off on a pet policy. (You can do it for your dog if he hasn't learned to write yet.) 1911 West Olive Avenue 91506; 818/845-8586; www.safariburbank.com.

Glendale

PARKS, BEACHES, AND RECREATION AREAS

Good news for all Glendale dogs who would rather not have to wear a leash everywhere they go. The city is in the early stages of planning a dog park! By the time the next edition of this book comes out, it might be a reality.

14 Brand Park

🐾🐾🐾 (See Los Angeles County map on pages 724–725)

If you feel as if you're on the estate of William Randolph Hearst when visiting this verdant park, you're not far off. It's actually the former property of the late real estate tycoon Leslie C. Brand, a.k.a. "The Father of Glendale."

Upon entering the park, you'll be greeted by a great white Moorish/Indian-style mansion. The mansion is now a library, surrounded by lush, shaded land. You and your leashed dog can pass an afternoon in perfect serenity here. Go ahead, pretend it's your estate. Relax, read, sniff the flowers, and have a little picnic.

If you prefer a little exercise with your lounging, a fire road takes you through the park and up to a ridge with a great view. This hike is not for the fair of foot: It's almost a six-mile round-trip, and, to put it mildly, it's not flat. But it's one of the more enjoyable hikes we found in the Los Angeles area. And if you want to keep going, there are ways to access the thousands of acres of open space that lie outside the park's perimeter. Unfortunately, the leash law applies in this area, too.

Exit I-5 on Western Avenue and go northeast about 1.5 miles. The road will take you to the park's magnificent library entrance. 818/548-2000.

15 George Deukmejian Wilderness Park

🐾🐾 (See Los Angeles County map on pages 724–725)

When we first heard the name of this park, we thought someone was making a joke. The words "George Deukmejian" and the word "wilderness" were often used in the same sentence when he was governor, but more like: "That George Deukmejian, he should have been more concerned about wilderness."

A couple of locals told us that back in the late 1980s, the Duke was against setting aside this large parcel of land for a park, but he was finally sold on it when a clever environmentalist came up with the idea to name the park after him. Whether this is true or just an urban myth, dogs can be grateful to the governor for making room for this 700-acre square of land.

This isn't what you'd call a breathtaking park. It can be very dry and dusty, with only an occasional tree to provide relief from the sun in these chaparral-covered hills. But the dogs we've seen cavorting around the park really love it here. They seem to smile as they accompany their leashed people up and down the canyon.

Maybe they're smiling because of the lack of people or the abundance of singing birds. Maybe it's the scents of strange fauna on the couple of miles of dirt road here. Or perhaps they know that if they walk far enough, they'll be in Angeles National Forest, where they can run around in leashless ecstasy. (It will be 100 percent easier to get there once some trails connecting the two areas are completed.) Whatever the case, this is a park that you might not find aesthetically pleasing, but your dog will.

Exit U.S. 101 on Pennsylvania Avenue. Go north a few blocks and turn left at Foothill Boulevard. Drive northwest about six blocks, then turn right on Dunsmore Avenue. The road will lead you into the park in about a mile, where you'll bear right after the sign for the park and drive up a narrow paved road to a dirt parking lot next to a horse corral. Start your hike at the wide, gated road just above the lot. 818/548-2000.

PLACES TO EAT

Sabor: The restaurant bills itself as a Latin fusion restaurant, and while it does have tasty dishes from other Latin nations, Cuban cuisine is really the focus here. It's authentic, delicious, and best accompanied by a mojito. You and your dog will be surrounded by an impressive wrought-iron fence as you dine at one of the umbrella-topped tables. 933 North Brand Boulevard; 818/247-6256.

PLACES TO STAY

Days Inn: Rates are $94–114. Dogs require a $50 deposit and must stay in smoking rooms. 450 West Pioneer Street 91203; 818/956-0202; www.days inn.com.

Vagabond Inn: Rates are $89–99. Dogs are $10 extra and are relegated to smoking rooms. 120 West Colorado Street 91204; 818/240-1700.

Pasadena

PARKS, BEACHES, AND RECREATION AREAS

After almost a decade of trying to get a dog park here, Pasadena residents finally got one. Alice Frost Kennedy Dog Park was worth the wait.

16 Brookside Park

🐾🐾🐾 🐕 (See Los Angeles County map on pages 724–725)

Brookside Park, home of the Rose Bowl, is a beautiful place, with roses hither and thither. The park has a playground, ball fields, trees, and acres of green grass. When there are no major games going on, it's a quiet park. There's even a trail you and your leashed pooch can take to get farther away from the madding crowd, in case you happen to be accompanying someone who has only one Rose Bowl ticket.

Dogs are allowed off leash here only for training purposes, and only at a designated area near the Rose Bowl. The hours for this training are 6 A.M.–10 P.M. weekdays and 6–10 A.M. weekends. (A word about training: We're not talking about training your dog to hike off leash or chase tennis balls. The training clause is for specific feats that don't cover a lot of ground, such as teaching your dog to come when called, to stay, and to heel. Be careful out there; park rangers know the difference between truly training your dog and walking around the park reading the newspaper with your dog. Most people who take advantage of this are in formal classes, by the way.)

Exit I-210 at Seco Street and follow the signs to the Rose Bowl. As you approach the Rose Bowl stadium, look for a big green meadow on your left. It's part of this large park complex. 626/744-4321 or 626/793-8824.

17 Eaton Canyon Park

🐾🐾🐾 (See Los Angeles County map on pages 724–725)

This wild and beautiful 184-acre park can be a little too enticing for dog folks: Many of the users allow their dogs off leash, according to rangers. This is something the rangers consider a big no-no, in part because of the wildlife here (many a deer has been chased, they say), in part because of the horses who share the trails (many a horse has been spooked, they say), and in part because of the rattlesnakes and poison oak here (many a dog has encountered both, the former with nasty results for the dog, the latter with nasty results for the dog's human).

Rangers have considered banning dogs in the past, but that's no longer a major possibility. Maybe the Alice Frost Kennedy Dog Park has taken some of the heat off the place.

Traveling east on I-210, exit at Altadena Drive and go north on Altadena. Drive 1.6 miles. The main park entrance is on the right. Follow the winding road to the park's nature center, where you can pick up a map and get your bearings. 626/398-5420.

18 Alice Frost Kennedy Dog Park

🐾🐾🐾🐾 🐕 (See Los Angeles County map on pages 724–725)

Alice Frost Kennedy was a zealous, influential Pasadena resident with a passion for beautifying the area. She was also a huge dog park advocate. If she were alive, she would surely be thrilled by the gorgeous dog park that now bears her name.

It's a beautiful four-paw affair with 2.5 acres of herbicide-free lush green grass, trees, separate sections for large and small dogs, water, poop-bag dispensers, and benches. It has a couple of fire hydrants that entertain the boy-dog set and is surrounded by a six-foot chain-link fence—much taller than most dog park fences. But it's not industrial in the least. Grape vines are growing up and around and through the fence. When the park is a bit more mature, you'll feel like you're in a lush vineyard. (Just don't eat those lower grapes.)

From eastbound I-210 take the San Gabriel Boulevard exit and make a left almost immediately onto North Sierra Madre Boulevard. Drive 0.4 mile north and make a right onto East Orange Grove Boulevard. The park is in a few blocks, within the seven-acre Vina Vieja Park (formerly Eaton Wash Park), at 3026 East Orange Grove Boulevard. 626/744-4321.

PLACES TO EAT

All India Cafe: The food here is utterly delicious. It seems every time you sneeze, it gets lavished with yet another "best Indian cuisine" honor. Vegetarians and meat-eaters alike love the delectable cuisine. Dogs would be content to laze at the sidewalk tables in the shade of an awning, but as a bonus they get their own doggy delight: cool water and a treat! 39 South Fair Oaks Avenue; 626/440-0309.

Jake's: Jake Dog loves visiting this Old Town Pasadena eatery and smelling the big burgers, chicken strips, and chunky fries. Humans can wash it all down with one of many brands of brews or something stronger from the full bar, and dogs get a bowl of water if they're thirsty. Dogs and their people can sit at several well-shaded outdoor tables. 38 West Colorado Boulevard; 626/568-1602.

Mi Piace: In Italian, the name of this restaurant means "I like it." And I do. The Italian food has a light and healthy California bent. Try the Chicken Mi Piace, which is white-meat chicken sautéed with mushrooms in a garlicky-herby white wine concoction. (A menu writer I'm not.) The little pizzas are zippy. Eat with your dog under the sidewalk awning. Dogs get fresh water if thirsty. In Old Town Pasadena, at 25 East Colorado Boulevard; 626/795-3131.

Malagueta: This restaurant advertises Brazilian cuisine with a Mediterranean flair. You can get everything from steak to little pizzas to a pretty big selection of churrasco. Dine with doggy at the sidewalk tables here. 43 East Colorado Boulevard; 626/564-8696.

PLACES TO STAY

Quality Inn Pasadena: Humans get a free expanded continental breakfast (you can even get waffles here) and use of the seasonal outdoor pool and indoor hot tub and sauna. Rates are $79–89. Dogs are $10 extra. 3221 East Colorado Boulevard 91107; 626/796-9291.

The Ritz-Carlton, Huntington Hotel & Spa: Remember all those times you've stayed at other hotels and shrugged off the postage-stamp-size towels or the paper-thin walls with a "Well, it ain't exactly The Ritz?" Well, this is exactly The Ritz. Only lucky dogs under 40 pounds get to experience this gorgeous, crème de la crème hotel. (The website says 30, but the front desk people say 40, so we're erring on the large side. Check before bringing your 40-pounder.)

This five-diamond hotel has been charming visitors since 1907. It is absolutely exquisite and regal. The Ritz has 393 rooms, including suites and some cottages, and most are dog friendly. Luxury guest room features and amenities include twice-daily housekeeping attention with evening turndown service, the best down comforters and pillows (with high-quality alternatives for the allergic), a marble bath, and über-comfy robes.

The hotel is set on 23 acres of gorgeous gardens, which you're free to peruse via myriad walking paths with your dog. (Just keep off the tennis courts and out of the pool.) Be sure to sniff out the historic 232-foot-long redwood covered bridge, complete with murals of California landmarks.

Rates are $230–410. (Suites can cost more than $3,000.) 1401 South Oak Knoll 91106; 626/568-3900; www.ritzcarlton.com/hotels/huntington.

The Westin Pasadena: If your dog is 40 pounds or under, he'll feel like a small human at this lovely hotel: Humans get the luxurious Heavenly Bed; dogs get the luxurious Heavenly Dog Bed. Humans get a fitness center; dogs get, well, free poop bags and some grass to peruse outside. Rates are $169–279. 191 North Los Robles 91101; 626/792-2727; www.starwood.com/westin.

Sierra Madre

19 Sierra Madre Dog Park

🐾🐾🐾🐕 (See Los Angeles County map on pages 724–725)

To visit this little dog park, you need to attend a tag sale of sorts. Dogs who come here need to wear a tag issued by the city. The tag is $25 for the calendar year, but the fee is prorated depending on the time of year you buy the tag. If you want to just check out the park for an afternoon, you're supposed to buy a daily pass for $5.

The park isn't even an acre, but it's got a separate fenced area for small or shy dogs, handicap access, lights, water, benches, and lots of dogs who are really fun to play with. It's within Sierra Vista Park, which has restrooms, should you need to heed nature's call after your dog does.

The park is at 611 East Sierra Madre Boulevard, south of the tennis courts in Sierra Vista Park. Call 626/836-8468 for park info. You can purchase tags at the city building at 232 West Sierra Madre Boulevard. The phone number there is 626/355-7135.

Arcadia

PARKS, BEACHES, AND RECREATION AREAS

20 Arcadia Dog Park

😸😸😸🐕 (See Los Angeles County map on pages 724–725)

This 0.75-acre park has lots of trees and bushes. Boy dogs are very content here. A concrete walkway helps keep the grass from being trampled by the feet of bipeds, but quadrupeds are taking a toll on the green grass, which does has a bit of scruffy dirt showing through. Still, the park is a pleasant place to visit and has all the major dog-park amenities, including a separate area for small dogs, benches, and water. From I-210, take the North Santa Anita Avenue exit and drive south about two blocks. Turn left at East Colorado Boulevard. Drive two blocks on Colorado and turn left on North Second Avenue. The park is immediately on your left, within Eisenhower Park. 626/574-5113.

San Dimas

PARKS, BEACHES, AND RECREATION AREAS

21 San Dimas Dog Park

😸😸😸😸🐕 (See Los Angeles County map on pages 724–725)

This is one pretty dog park. It's got gorgeous green grass, big leafy trees, shade gazebos, and two sections—one for big dogs and one for small dogs. It's kind of like a little country club that welcomes all well-behaved canines. It's only an acre, but it seems much bigger.

To keep the park so lush and green takes a bit of maintenance. The park is closed 1–3 P.M. Wednesdays and periodically closes for extended periods for turf maintenance.

Exit eastbound I-210 at San Dimas Avenue. Turn left and go north a few blocks to Foothill Boulevard. Go right on Foothill and drive 0.5 mile to San Dimas Canyon Road and turn left. In about 0.25 mile go left on Sycamore Canyon Road. At the first intersection, Horsethief Canyon Road, go left and drive about 0.5 mile to Horsethief Canyon Park, at 301 Horsethief Canyon Road. The dog park is within the park. 909/394-6230.

22 Frank G. Bonelli Regional Park

😸😸😸 (See Los Angeles County map on pages 724–725)

This is a great place to take a dog. Some 14 miles of trails can easily make you forget about your urban woes. The trails are rugged and geared toward equestrians, so be sure to keep that leash on your dog. You can hike up grassy hills and scrubby, weedy areas to majestic views of the region. The best spot we found to start one of these hikes was right across from the entrance to the east picnic valley. It's perfect; after a rigorous hike, you can hang out at a shaded picnic table and enjoy a little wine/water and cheese with your dog.

Puddingstone Reservoir is the centerpiece of the park, and the bass and trout fishing here is rumored to be pretty hot. But dogs aren't allowed to swim in it, nor go on the sandy beaches. Too bad, because it covers a whopping 250 acres when full. When we visited, humans weren't even allowed to swim in the lake because of bacteria. But you can still pull a bunch of fish out and eat them for dinner. Er, I think I'll stick with chicken.

The park is right next to the Raging Waters park, so it's a convenient place to take your dog if you don't feel like going home after you've dropped off the big kids at that exhilarating attraction. From I-210, exit at Raging Waters Drive/Via Verde and follow the signs east into the park. 909/599-8411.

Irwindale

PARKS, BEACHES, AND RECREATION AREAS

23 Santa Fe Dam Recreation Area
🐾🐾🐾 (See Los Angeles County map on pages 724–725)

When you're approaching this large county park, you'll find it hard to believe anything but industry could exist here. The area is fraught with unsightly evidence of rampant "progress."

But in the middle of it all is a big patch of green doing its best to fend off the onslaught of civilization. It's not the most attractive park in the world, but it's a commendable attempt.

The park's Santa Fe Reservoir is a decent place to share a picnic with your dog. You can also fish for trout or launch a boat here for a relaxing morning on the water. You won't exactly feel like you're in the middle of Wisconsin, but it's better than some water holes we've seen down here.

The best time you can have with your dog at this park is if you take a hike on the nature trail. Signs and pamphlets point out the flora and fauna you'll come across in the 1,000-acre nature area. The trail provides a good hike, but it's not without its sad side: As if the surrounding scenery were not enough of a reminder, signs tell you how humans have destroyed the habitat. Do your part to protect it, and make sure your dog is leashed and doesn't disturb the birds and beasts here.

There's an $8 fee per vehicle, which you can avoid by parking on a nearby street. (If you have the $8, keep in mind that the county park system is financially devastated and can use every penny to keep parks running.) Exit I-210 at Irwindale Avenue and go south about 1.5 miles. Turn right at Arrow Highway, and within a few blocks turn right again at the signs for the park. To get to the nature trail, bear to the right after the entry kiosk and follow the signs. 626/334-1065.

Claremont

Claremont is a good place to be a dog. The community has two dog parks and a huge park where leashed dogs love to roam (the Claremont Hills Wilderness Park).

PARKS, BEACHES, AND RECREATION AREAS

24 Claremont Hills Wilderness Park
😊😊😊😊 (See Los Angeles County map on pages 724–725)

The city obtained a beautiful 1,200-acre chunk of land and turned it into a beautiful 1,200-acre chunk of park. Pooches can explore this delightful acquisition, as long as they're on leash.

Claremont Hills is a hilly park (duh), with several miles of trails and fire roads leading through open land dotted with oaks and scrub. A creek runs through it during nondrought years. The park has cool, shaded canyons as well as terrific vistas of the surrounding valleys. All this makes it prime turf for mudslides. During rainy season, the entire park can close. Enter at the very south end of Mills Avenue. 909/399-5460.

25 Rancho San Jose Park Dog Park
😊🐕 (See Los Angeles County map on pages 724–725)

The entire Rancho San Jose Park, including its dog park, basketball courts, picnic area, and playground, is a wee 1.3 acres. The dog park itself is very tiny, but pleasantly green. It's a decent off-leash spot if you happen to be in the 'hood. It's not worth seeking out if you're closer to another place your dog can be leash-free. The park is on the 600 block of West San Jose Avenue, just a smidgen north of I-10. 909/399-5490.

26 Claremont Dog Park/Pooch Park
😊😊😊🐕 (See Los Angeles County map on pages 724–725)

Dogs are so happy to come here you can sometimes hear them baying from blocks away. It's the most popular park in Claremont, at least according to Ralph Dog and Zippity Dog, who are frequent visitors and can be trusted implicitly.

This 1.25-acre park is completely fenced, so dogs can run around to their hearts' delight. It's a long park, which is great for dogs who want to work up a full head of steam before having to turn around and run in another direction.

Pooches love the green grass and the old trees that grace a couple of sides of the park. There are benches galore for people and a water fountain for pooches and their people. Two fire hydrants sit in the middle of the park and garner adulation from male dogs. Pooch Park is within College Park, on College Avenue, just south of First Street and the Metrolink station. 909/399-5460.

PLACES TO EAT

Winston, a zippy little Jack Russell terrier who has a penchant for human food, helped us sniff out the dog-friendly restaurants below. Good boy, Winston!

The Danson-Espiau's: This is Claremont's original sidewalk café, with oodles of outdoor tables for you and your happy dog. The Mexican and American food here is very tasty. If you're in the mood for a hearty salad, try the Mexican salad. Too virtuous? Chase it with a side of house-made chips. 109 Yale Avenue; 909/621-1818.

Walter's Restaurant: Walter's has been a Claremont landmark restaurant since 1957, which is pretty much ancient history in these parts. You and your dog will lick your lips at the combination of California- and French-style cuisine using foods from around the world. "We have no boundaries," is how one manager describes the wonderful fusion foods. You'll find lots of terrific kabob dishes and menu items influenced by cultures from Afghanistan to India to Italy to Spain to Zaire. (Yes, that's A to Z.) Dogs are allowed at the sidewalk patio area but need to sit on the other side of the fence. (They can be pretty much at the feet of their humans; it's just that there's a little fence-y thing between you.) 308 Yale Avenue; 909/624-4914.

PLACES TO STAY

Ramada Inn and Tennis Club: This motel is so dog friendly that it even hosts dog shows. At times, all 121 rooms are taken up by dogs of the well-bred (literally) variety. The grounds have plenty of room for roaming with a leashed dog: The grassy courtyard alone is 31,000 square feet. "This is one of the MOST incredibly dog friendly places to stay in the world!" a Grass Valley dog, Addie, wrote me a while back. The staff agrees. "We love dogs! Adore them!" says a front-desk employee.

Every room comes with a fridge and a continental breakfast. Work it off in the pool or at the motel's eight tennis courts. Rates are $69–99. 840 South Indian Hill Boulevard 91711; 909/621-4831.

Pomona

PARKS, BEACHES, AND RECREATION AREAS

27 Ganesha Park

🐾🐾🐾 (See Los Angeles County map on pages 724–725)

If you don't feel like paying $8 to get into the nearby Frank G. Bonelli Regional Park (see the *San Dimas* section), try this fee-free park. It's a popular place, but most visitors congregate around the swimming pool, tennis courts, and playground. Leashed dogs can zip around the rest of the park without much fear of crashing into hordes of people. The grassy, rolling hills and flat meadows are perfect for a good romp.

The park is at White Avenue, just north of I-10 and south of the Los Angeles County Fairplex. 909/620-2321.

PLACES TO STAY

Motel 6: There's a decent grassy area on the grounds. Rates are $48–60 for one adult, $6 for the second adult. 2470 South Garey Avenue 91766; 909/591-1871.

Sheraton Suites Fairplex: "The bigger the dog, the better," a staffer here told us. That's the attitude we like to see. If you and your dog are going to be spending some time at the adjacent Fairplex Exhibition Center, this might be the place to stay. It's pretty exotic for this area. Rates are $100–299. 600 West McKinley Avenue 91768; 909/622-2220.

Westlake Village

PARKS, BEACHES, AND RECREATION AREAS

🐾 Triunfo Creek Park

🐾🐾🐾🐾 (See Los Angeles County map on pages 724–725)

Like wildflowers? Come here in the spring, when portions of this 600-acre park are blanketed with their beauty. Jake was really happy to learn that leashed dogs are allowed here, because the park is home to the *Pentachaeta lyonii*, an endangered yellow, daisy-ish flower you can find only in Southern California. Fortunately, I was able to successfully prevent him from making the flowers any more yellow than they are. (I don't know what happens when dogs do leg lifts on flowers that are listed as federally endangered, and I didn't want to find out.)

Some 90 species of wildflowers call the park home. Dogs who don't have a penchant for stopping and smelling the flowers can still enjoy a good romp on the trails, which take you through lush grasslands (in the spring) and oak woodlands. Jake liked the trees the best, partly because he's a boy dog, and

partly because he's a shade-seeking missile of a dog, even in the more temperate months.

Exit U.S. 101 at Lindero Canyon Road and drive south to Triunfo Canyon Road. The road pretty much dead-ends at the main trailhead. 310/589-3200. You can get an update on the wildflower situation here and at 40 other sites in Southern California by phoning the Wildflower Hotline at 818/768-3533.

Agoura Hills

PARKS, BEACHES, AND RECREATION AREAS

29 The Paramount Ranch

☙☙☙☙ (See Los Angeles County map on pages 724–725)

Want to take your dog around the U.S. without leaving California? A visit to this 436-acre ranch could fool your dog into thinking he's in Tombstone, Dodge City, New Mexico, the Ozarks, Colorado's Royal Gorge, or colonial Salem. The Paramount Ranch has been a convincing backdrop for hundreds of films since the 1920s. Among the stars who made movies here are John Wayne, Gary Cooper, Cary Grant, Basil Rathbone, Roy Rogers, Lucille Ball, Kirk Douglas, Jane Russell, and Cornel Wilde. Your dog may not be able to sniff out their scents any more, but if he has a keen nose, he can probably still track down Jane Seymour, whose popular series *Dr. Quinn, Medicine Woman* was filmed here for several years in the 1990s. (The ranch is still a working set, and it works pretty hard, judging by a look at a recent filming schedule.)

But chances are that your dog would be thrilled just to be allowed to join you at this fun park. The ranch is much smaller than it was in its heyday, but there's still plenty to see here, including an old Western town set complete with a saloon, a sheriff's office, and various stores. Several short trails, including the aptly named Backdrop Trail, take you past landscapes that will probably look very familiar thanks to their frequent use in films and TV shows.

Exit U.S. 101 at Kanan Road and follow it south for about 0.75 mile. Turn left on Cornell Road and drive about 2.5 miles to Paramount Ranch Road. Turn right and follow the road to the ranch. 818/597-9192.

30 Peter Strauss Ranch

☙☙☙ (See Los Angeles County map on pages 724–725)

This beautiful 65-acre property was once the home of actor and producer Peter Strauss, most noted for his role in the TV miniseries *Rich Man, Poor Man*. He needed a place for his myriad collection of cacti and other succulent plants (he'd had hundreds of them on his apartment roof), and what better locale than this oak woodland? Although he moved on (and protected the property from development by selling it to the Santa Monica Mountains Conservancy), some of his plants can still be seen in the cactus garden here.

A few remnants of Strauss's predecessor, a resort and amusement park known as Lake Enchanto, also remain. In the 1930s and 1940s, the property had many amusement rides and the largest swimming pool in the West, with a capacity of up to 3,000 people. You can still see the circular pool from the lush lawn here. (The pool is empty, but try to imagine it in its heyday.) You and your leashed dog can also sniff out the lovely imported Italian terrazzo tile dance floor near the lawn.

The ranch is a fine place to bring a dog, especially if you have a child in tow. Although the rides are gone, there's a sweet playground (for human kids, not dog kids) overlooking the remains of Lake Enchanto's dam. The Peter Strauss Trail is less than a mile long, and it's an easy, pretty hike. It's shaded by coast live oaks, and ferns are everywhere. (There's a little poison oak here, which we mention only because it's not something you'd expect at such a well-groomed place.) A shallow creek runs through the property and along the trail at times, making the setting even more tranquil.

Exit U.S. 101 at Kanan Road and drive south for 2.8 miles. Turn left on Troutdale Road, and at the end of the road the park will be in front of you. To reach the entrance, go left on Mulholland Highway, cross the creek, and bear right, into the ranch's parking lot. 805/370-2301.

③① Cheeseboro and Palo Comado Canyons

😸😸😸 (See Los Angeles County map on pages 724–725)

Some of the trails in these super-popular parks actually originated with the Chumash Indians, who lived here for several thousand years. Now it's hiker and mountain biker heaven, with leashed dogs getting a kick out of the place but always being on the lookout for the next passing bike.

Boy dogs thrill at the variety of trees, which include valley oaks, sycamores, coast live oaks, black walnut trees, and willows. The rolling grassy hills look so lush in the early spring, when they're actually green instead of the usual hue of dirty yellow Lab. (Jake blends right into the grass most times of year.)

Here's a bit of trivia that might be of interest to your dog if he's of the bird-watching bent. A ranger tells us that Cheeseboro Canyon has the largest concentrations of birds of prey nesting areas in the U.S. outside of Alaska. Jake was agog at the fascinating array of birds, although I think they all registered as "duck, duck, duck."

One of our favorite trails is the Cheeseboro Canyon Trail/Sulphur Springs Trail, an easy 4.6-mile hike with lots of shade from a valley oak savannah and a riparian coast live oak habitat. About 1.5 miles in, you'll come to a pretty picnic area next to a little stream. Have a bite and continue on—you may not want to eat when you get closer to stinky Sulphur Springs, although dogs go crazy for the scent. Jake couldn't get his nose off the ground as we approached. His schnoz flared and sniffed and snuffed as never before, and he looked positively devastated that he didn't find the dead animal that must have been causing that odor.

Take Highway 101 to the Chesebro Road exit and turn north, following Palo Comado Canyon Road (and the signs). Turn right onto Chesebro Road and continue to the end, where you'll find parking and picnic areas. 818/597-9192 or 805/370-2300.

Calabasas

PARKS, BEACHES, AND RECREATION AREAS

32 Upper Las Virgenes Canyon Open Space Preserve

🐾🐾🐾🐾 (See Los Angeles County map on pages 724–725)

Parts of *Gone with the Wind* were filmed on this stunning 2,983-acre wildland. But the land itself could have been gone with the wind a few years ago if Washington Mutual, Inc., had been able to proceed unimpeded: The corporation had planned a 3,050-home development here. Fortunately, the development was so contentious that the state ended up buying the land from Washington Mutual and will keep it as an undeveloped wildlife refuge and park. (It used to be known as Ahmanson Ranch, but an agreement was made not to call it that anymore. Shhh.)

This is great news for the environment and excellent news for people and pooches who like to hike on oak-studded rolling hills, wide-open mesas, and cool canyon bottoms shaded by sycamores. A few trails are already up and running, with many more planned for the future. (A big bonus, if you aren't fond of itching: There's no poison oak here.) Some endangered species that helped save the land from development reside here, so leashes are the law.

Although the property is located entirely in Ventura County, we list it here because Los Angeles County provides the only access at this point. Access from the Simi Valley area is likely at some time, but for now, this is the way to get here: Exit U.S. 101 at Las Virgenes Road and follow it north all the way to the end. There's also a parking lot at the end of Victory Boulevard. 310/589-3200.

33 Calabasas Bark Park

🐾🐾🐾🐾🐕 (See Los Angeles County map on pages 724–725)

This is the first dog park we've heard of that has a separate gated area not for small dogs, but for children! It's actually a good idea, because some children feel overwhelmed by big dogs running around. Apparently the area isn't used much. Most kids prefer to be with parents and canine siblings. But it's nice to know it's there. I know a few parents whose children would love to have their space separate from swirling dogs.

The park is two fenced acres of grass, with some shade trees, benches, poop bags, lights, and a dog drinking fountain. The park is at 4232 Las Virgenes Road, south of the Las Virgenes Municipal Water District. 818/878-4225 or 818/880-6461.

Encino

PARKS, BEACHES, AND RECREATION AREAS

34 Westridge-Canyonback Wilderness Park

🐾🐾🐾🐾 🐕 (See Los Angeles County map on pages 724–725)

Yes, that little running dog you see above really does belong there. It's not a typo—it's a miracle.

This is the only huge park (besides national forests and BLM lands) in the greater L.A. area where dogs under voice control are allowed off leash. Around these parts, dogs are usually relegated to fenced-in dog parks if they want to run around in the buff (sans leash). But thanks to the dog-friendly Santa Monica Mountains Conservancy, well-behaved dogs can be their doggy selves here and not be stopped by a fence in the face or a ranger with a citation book.

This 1,500-acre open space (and we're talking open—there's not much shade here, so bring lots of water for you and your dog) offers great views of the Pacific Ocean on clear days. The fire road along the north-south ridgeline is a popular hiking area, but it's also big with mountain bikers, so be careful with your off-leash pal.

At one point, the property had been slated for a 500-home development. It was also approved as a landfill (dump). Now that it's in the hands of the conservancy, it won't have to face those terrible fates again.

From I-405, take Mulholland Drive west 2.7 miles to the 17000 block. You can park in a 20-car roadside parking area and walk 10 minutes to the park entrance and the trail. 310/589-3200.

35 Sepulveda Basin Off-Leash Dog Park

🐾🐾🐾🐾 🐕 (See Los Angeles County map on pages 724–725)

It's big, it's fairly grassy, and it has four boy-dog toilets (OK, fire hydrants). What more could a dog want? Water? It's here at four mud-free drinking stations. Shade? There are enough small shade trees for comfort during the summer months. If those won't do, there are plenty of picnic tables. Dog friends? Yup. A section for small dogs? Yap! Sirloin strip? OK, the park doesn't have everything.

This is a heavenly place to visit if you're a dog who longs to be off leash, or if you're a dog person who longs to see your dog off leash. "It's been successful beyond our wildest dreams," says Ken Novak, a manager with the city of Los Angeles Recreation and Parks Department. Even the fencing is terrific here: It's green, so it matches the park. Ivy has been planted at its base, and it's starting to creep up toward its goal of becoming a wall of ivy. Outside the fence, there's a little more acreage for leashed dogs who want to lounge around on the grass and/or have a picnic with their people pals.

The park is at the corner of White Oak Avenue and Victory Boulevard;

818/756-8616 or 818/756-8191. For info on dog events at the park, phone 818/343-0013.

36 Balboa Park and Lake Balboa

🐾🐾🐾 (See Los Angeles County map on pages 724–725)

Balboa Park is completely recreation-oriented, which is good news for leashed dogs, for once. Pooches are allowed on the many playing fields that make up this large city park. And they're welcome on the big empty fields where no sports are played. If your dog likes to hike on forested trails, this place won't be his idea of heaven, since there are none. But if he enjoys a good roll in the grass, take him here at once. If no one is playing soccer or softball, he's in for a real treat.

Lake Balboa, across Balboa Boulevard from the park, is another story. It's officially considered part of the park, although people here seem to think of it as its own entity. Leashed dogs and the people they're attached to find it a more pleasant place, with a wide 1.3-mile walking path around the lake's edge. "It's more fun than a regular leash park," writes reader Sheryl Smith, mother of Gracie Dog. "There's an occasional fish flopping around to bark at, that some fisherman has just landed, and there are ducks and white and blue herons…. There must be lots of good smells there, because Gracie's nose is always to the ground there." If you ever run into Sheryl and Gracie, ask them about their collection of dog license tags from around the world. Their incredible collection numbers about 1,000, and some of the designs should be museum pieces.

Exit U.S. 101 at Balboa Boulevard, drive a couple of blocks north, and you'll be at Balboa Park's entrance. 818/756-9642.

PLACES TO EAT

Quincy's BBQ: This is one of the most dog-friendly, dog-loving places to eat in California. It's doggy to the bone. It's named after the owners' beloved family dog, who died but lives on through the restaurant. The menu features little walking cartoon dogs, and a cartoon drooling dog with a bowl of something delicious with a big "Q" on it. The motto is "The best BBQ under one woof." Inside the restaurant are pictures of Quincy and his friends, and there's a wall dedicated to photos of patrons' dogs. Cute doggy knickknacks line the shelves. There's a big barrel of peanuts, and while you're waiting for your food you can help yourself by filling a dog bowl—yep, a dog bowl—with them and eating them at your table. Your dog might get jealous, but fortunately, dogs who visit the fun patio picnic tables get water and treats.

As if all this weren't enough, in keeping with the owners' love of dogs, if you adopt a dog and show proof of adoption, lunch is on the house. That's right, you can have up to a $15 lunch (alcohol not included) for free because you've been so good and adopted your dog! This is a first, and we applaud this wonderful, innovative, generous gesture.

And what better place for a dog than a barbecue restaurant? Everything from the chicken to the tri-tip is utterly droolworthy. Your dog might not be satisfied with his little biscuits when there's a slow-cooked, wood-barbecued slab of meat calling his name on your table. We send a huge thank-you to our longtime correspondent friends Molly, the gorgeous springer spaniel, and her wonderful person, Sheryl, for writing to us about this fabulous find. It's at the Plaza de Oro, 17201 Ventura Boulevard; 818/784-6292 or 818/986-4099.

Sherman Oaks

PARKS, BEACHES, AND RECREATION AREAS

37 Dixie Canyon Park

😾😾 (See Los Angeles County map on pages 724–725)

If you like your urban walks on the wild side, take a hike at Dixie Canyon. This 20-acre park, donated to the Santa Monica Mountains Conservancy by Warren Beatty, is a pretty decent place to take a leashed dog. There's lots of shade from the California black walnut trees and coast live oaks, and the park's trail takes you by a year-round stream in the middle of the canyon. Watch out for poison oak: It's very thick on the canyon's east side. You should be OK if you stay on the trail.

From the intersection of Ventura Boulevard and Dixie Canyon Avenue, go south on Dixie Canyon Avenue for 0.8 mile and then turn left on Dixie Canyon Place. You'll quickly come to the end of the road (actually, a cul-de-sac). Park and take the stairs to the park's entrance. 310/589-3200.

Van Nuys

PARKS, BEACHES, AND RECREATION AREAS

38 Woodley Park

😾😾😾 (See Los Angeles County map on pages 724–725)

If you like your parks big and grassy, check out this one. Dogs really enjoy it here. There's ample shade, plenty of picnic areas, and a fitness course to keep you and the pooch in good condition. Unfortunately, there's also an unattractive water reclamation plant on the north side of the park, but they have to put them somewhere.

The park is between I-405 and U.S. 101. Take the Burbank Boulevard exit from I-405 and drive west into the park. Turn right on Woodley Avenue and drive past signs for the Japanese garden. The meadow area will be on your right. 818/756-8891.

Studio City
PARKS, BEACHES, AND RECREATION AREAS

39 Laurel Canyon Park
🐾🐾🐾🐾🐕 (See Los Angeles County map on pages 724–725)

Yee haw! Dogs, throw off your leashes and come here to be all the dog you can be! This is the biggest of the off-leash dog runs in Los Angeles County, and many consider it the best. It's nearly 20 acres, and there are sufficient trees and picnic tables to make everyone comfortable.

If you and your dog like to socialize, you couldn't ask for a better place. Canine rush hour (around 5 P.M., depending on the time of year) is a real scene. On a typical dog day afternoon, you'll find more than 100 dogs running like mad, sniffing each other in unmentionable places and pushing their noses to the ground in search of unusual odors. Their owners, meanwhile, chitchat about this and that (often, "this" being their dog and "that" being your dog).

People flock here from all over Los Angeles and the San Fernando Valley. There's plenty of water, plenty of poop bags, plenty of fence, and, most importantly, plenty of good dog fun. And for people who like to watch the stars, we hear that celebrities sometimes frequent the place on weekends.

Get here early so you can nab a parking space. The park is on Mulholland Drive, about 0.25 mile west of Laurel Canyon Boulevard. From Laurel Canyon Boulevard, go west on Mulholland and take the first left. The road winds down a hill and into the parking lot. 818/769-4415 or 818/756-8060.

40 Wilacre Park
🐾🐾🐾 (See Los Angeles County map on pages 724–725)

This scrubby, shrubby 128-acre park is the former estate of silent-movie star Will Acres. It's in the middle of one of Studio City's more posh neighborhoods, but once you're hiking, you'll feel like you're in the middle of nowhere. Dogs are welcome here, but so are horses and bikes, so be sure to leash. For a really fun hike, take the 2.7-mile loop trail to the very dog-friendly Coldwater Canyon Park (described under *Beverly Hills*), headquarters of a forest-friendly organization, TreePeople. If you hike up toward TreePeople's main building, you'll find a doggy drinking fountain along the way.

If it's toasty out, sniff out a narrow road at Wilacre that takes you to a shady canyon thick with big oak and eucalyptus trees. It's a popular spot for filming, so if you see a crew, you'll have to head back. The park is at the intersection of Laurel Canyon Boulevard and Fryman Canyon Road. The address is 3431 Fryman Canyon Road; 310/589-3200.

PLACES TO EAT
Aroma Cafe: This café is flanked by really lovely, dog-friendly garden patios.

The umbrella-topped tables are great places to relax and enjoy a super cup of aromatic coffee, or a good meal. The café serves breakfast, lunch, and dinner. You can get everything from a wild veggie breakfast burrito (delicious, but not for light appetites) to yummy salads and sandwiches to great big delectable desserts. Your dog is welcome to join you at the patio tables. You'll find water bowls in front of the café. A big thanks to Karen Whitaker and her three rescued dachshunds for letting us in on their find. The café shares space with Portrait of a Bookstore, a very cool place, at 4360 Tujunga Avenue; 818/508-0677.

Jumpin' Java: Don't let the name fool you. There's more than just coffee here. You can get breakfast, lunch, and dinner, too. The Mediterranean-style cuisine makes for tasty, light eating. Dine with your dog at the covered patio with six tables. 11919 Ventura Boulevard; 818/980-4249.

North Hollywood

PARKS, BEACHES, AND RECREATION AREAS

41 Whitnall Off-Leash Dog Park

😻😻😻🐕 (See Los Angeles County map on pages 724–725)

Before this park became a dog park, it had really gone to the dogs: It was a haven for drug dealing, gang activity, and illegal dumping. Then along came the dog park in 2002, and now it's clean as a whistle (a stray dog poop or two notwithstanding). Three cheers for the dogs and their people! (And for "Three-Dog Dave" Hepperly and Tamar Love Grande for giving us the heads up about this place.)

The park is a couple of grassy acres. It's got all the usual dog park amenities, including drinking fountains, shade umbrellas, benches, poop bags, double gates, and trees. Small dogs have a 100- by 200-foot section to call their own. Not bad for bitsy beagles. At the corner of Cahuenga Boulevard and Whitnall Highway; 818/756-8060.

Universal City

If you go to the exciting Universal Studios tour/theme park here, your pooch will be pleased to know that she can accompany you at least part of the way.

Universal Studios has a kennel, which dogs of visitors get to use for free. Bring a blanket and her favorite toy so she'll rest in comfort while you get jostled around a bit by King Kong or get the wits scared out of you at the Revenge of the Mummy ride. (Your dog should actually be glad she's not allowed on the rides.) The climate-controlled kennel is unattended but locked. Water is supplied. You can visit your dog any time by getting a key-bearing information booth employee to accompany you. A nearby bushy and grassy area serves as the squat spot.

To use the kennel, bring your leashed dog to the information booth just before the main entrance. 818/622-3801 or 800/UNIVERSAL (800/864-8377); www.universalstudios.com.

PARKS, BEACHES, AND RECREATION AREAS

42 South Weddington Park

🐾🐾 (See Los Angeles County map on pages 724–725)

Golf, anyone? This park is so green and trim that you can't help but think of Arnold Palmer. Joe Dog liked it because of its proximity to Universal Studios— it's right across the street. He enjoyed the kennels there because he knew a cat could end up spending the day just down the row from him.

The park is bordered by a couple of small side roads, so it's fairly safe from traffic. But since dogs are supposed to be leashed, that's not something you have to worry about.

Heading south on Lankershim Boulevard, go right on Bluffside Drive (directly across from the north gate of Universal Studios). 818/756-8188 or 323/923-7390.

PLACES TO STAY

Sheraton Universal Hotel: How often do you get to sleep on the back lot of a major motion picture studio with your dog? Stay here, and make it happen. (It's as close as your dog will come to Universal Studios, except for being in the kennel there.) The hotel is big, with cushy, well-appointed rooms.

Dogs love staying here. As part of their stay, they get to use a comfy dog bed (the Sheraton Sweet Sleeper Dog Bed, the smaller cousin of the Sheraton Sweet Sleeper Bed for humans) and get bowls for their food and water. Dogs need to weigh less than 80 pounds (Jake could get in by sucking in his belly). Rates are $209–329. 333 Universal Hollywood Drive 91608; 818/980-1212; www.starwood.com/sheraton.

Hollywood

Tinseltown just isn't what it used to be. The wealth of art deco architecture and grandiose theaters has faded. The half-mile Hollywood Walk of Fame is home to the homeless (although there are plans in the works to improve the area). But it's still worth visiting, for the myth and lure of Hollywood will never completely fade. (If you visit toward dusk, you may be glad you brought your dog.) Meanwhile, if you can foot the bill, a stay in the fabulous Chateau Marmont might restore a little of the old glow of Hollywood for you and your dog.

DIVERSION

Compare Paw Prints: On a visit to the forecourt of **Grauman's Chinese Theatre** in Hollywood, Joe Dog found out his paws were as big as the heels of Gene Autry's boots. Since he was an old Western movie buff (we'd caught him watching Westerns on TV), it was doubtless a thrill for him to see that he could, if necessary, walk a mile in Autry's boots. You and your dog can spend part of a fun-filled Hollywood afternoon measuring your feet and paws against the footprints of the stars. Be sure to bring a camera. Everyone else will have one, and your dog is likely to have his mug snapped more than once. The theater itself is at 6925 Hollywood Boulevard, Hollywood; 323/461-3331 or 323/464-8111.

When you're done comparing shoe sizes with the stars, take your feet for a stroll down the **Hollywood Walk of Fame.** It's on Hollywood Boulevard, between Gower Street and La Brea Avenue, and along Vine Street, from Sunset Boulevard to Yucca Street. More than 2,500 celebs are immortalized with stars planted into the sidewalk featuring their names. Your dog might be especially interested in seeing the stars for Rin Tin Tin and Lassie. The walk is free, but be prepared for a barrage of homeless people and scam artists with their paws out. For a list of the stars and their locations, go to www.hollywoodchamber.net.

PARKS, BEACHES, AND RECREATION AREAS

43 Trebek Open Space

🐾🐾🐾 (See Los Angeles County map on pages 724–725)

The category: Generous Gentlemen.

The answer: A 62-acre parcel of wilderness with fire roads for leashed dogs, mountain bikers, equestrians, and hikers was donated by this game show host who's always looking for life's questions, not answers. (Be sure to phrase your response in the form of a question.)

If you answered "Who is Alex Trebek?" you're right! (If you said only "Alex Trebek," your dog wins.) The popular, longtime *Jeopardy!* host donated this rugged, hilly area to the Santa Monica Mountains Conservancy, and even dogs who don't know a thing about his show are game for a vigorous romp here. It's adjacent to the leash-free Runyon Canyon Park, should your dog hanker to throw his leash to the wind and trot around naked. (Runyon is easier to find and easier to park at, so if you like convenience—and a leash-free romp—you're better off there.)

Exit U.S. 101 at Hollywood Boulevard and drive west for about two miles. Go right (north) onto Nichols Canyon Road. Roadside parking will be on your right in a little less than a mile. It's signed, but poorly, so keep your eyes peeled. 310/589-3200.

44 Runyon Canyon Park

🐾🐾🐾🐾 🐕 (See Los Angeles County map on pages 724–725)

Dogs are actually allowed to be their leash-free selves at this 125-acre undeveloped park. It's full of overgrown weeds and brush, but dogs don't care. In fact, they like it this way. Besides, there are plenty of trees to keep their interest while they walk up and down the hilly paths here.

And while it happened a long time ago, Jake thought you might want to know a little Hollywood lore a park ranger told us: This is the very same park where Errol Flynn was caught with a minor, causing a major public scandal. (Was this at the same time he was making the film *Assault of the Rebel Girls?*)

The park is on Fuller Avenue, north of Franklin Place. 323/666-5046.

PLACES TO EAT

Cat & Fiddle: Hey diddle, diddle! This British pub is a terrific place to take a thirsty dog, and to bring your thirsty self. Dogs get a bowl of water, and humans get a variety of beverages, including a good selection of on-tap lagers, ciders, beers, and ales. Dine on shepherd's pie (there's even a veggie version of this), Welsh rarebit, Cornish pasty, and their ilk alongside your dog at the pleasant outdoor table area. 6530 West Sunset Boulevard; 323/468-3800.

PLACES TO STAY

Best Western Hollywood Hills Hotel: Rates are $139–190. Dogs are $25 for the length of their stay and need to weigh less than 70 pounds. 6141 Franklin Avenue 90028; 323/464-5181 or 800/287-1700.

Chateau Marmont Hotel: This is that grand, white, castlelike building that makes you do a double take as you're driving on Sunset. Yes, dogs really are allowed to stay in this legendary Hollywood hideaway. Joe Dog was on his best behavior when we checked it out, walking rather regally and not even stopping to scratch his ears.

The chateau, which opened in 1929, is modeled after an elegant Loire Valley castle. You'll hear a lot of French around here. Actually, the staffers speak several languages, including "discreet." That last language has helped make the Marmont very popular with Hollywood's icons over the decades.

Huge suites and romantic bungalows offer privacy, and many are set among lush, peaceful gardens. There's something for nearly every robust budget, from a 400-square-foot room to a two-bedroom penthouse suite with two bathrooms, a dressing area, a large living room with hardwood floor and fireplace, a full kitchen, a formal dining room, and a 1,250-square-foot private terrace with great views of Hollywood. I think that was the room Joe Dog wanted, but we ended up elsewhere. (The Motel 6 in Long Beach, to be exact. Hey, you can't tell one place from the other when the lights are out. Well, not when there's no moon and you're sleeping. Deeply.)

If you and a human friend want to go out for a night on the town sans pooch, the concierge can help hook you up with a pet-sitter. Room and suite rates are $350–3,500. Dogs pay $100 extra per visit. 8221 Sunset Boulevard 90046; 323/656-1010 or 800/242-8328; www.chateaumarmont.com.

Bel-Air

PLACES TO STAY

Hotel Bel-Air: This gorgeous, legendary hotel hideaway puts the "l" in luxury and the "b" in bucolic, but it also takes the "$" out of your purse if you stay with a dog: You'll pay a $500 pet fee for the length of your stay. Yes, $500. Of all the hotels I've researched and stayed in, the Bel-Air holds the record for highest pet fees. I've never paid nearly this much for myself, much less a dog, but there are people who think nothing of dropping this kind of cash to be able to stay at this amazing place with their dog. In fact, a front-desk person I spoke with said it's not uncommon for guests to pay the fee and stay just one night.

If you don't mind the pet fee and if your dog is under about 30 pounds (30 pounds is the limit, but we're told there is some leeway: for $500, they should allow blue-whale-sized dogs.), a stay here is an unparalleled experience. I won't go into deep detail because most dogs reading this won't be able to talk their people into staying here, but suffice it to say that the rooms and suites are the height of classic luxury, with the best of everything. The grounds are a blissful 12 acres of lush gardens, with a swan-filled lake, a lovely old stone bridge, and a pool surrounded by bougainvillea, palms, and other tropical beauties. Lie on your chaise, over your plush pink signature beach pool towel, and you'll be bedazzled by your choice of poolside treats at your fingertips, including frozen grapes (I don't think anyone feeds them to you one at a time, though, and there probably aren't people who fan you with giant leaves, but around here you never know), house-prepared mini popsicles in sophisticated flavors like ginger and jasmine, and cold cloths.

Other niceties: You get a complimentary welcome tea delivered to your room upon arrival, twice-daily maid service, and free drop-off car service to Beverly Hills and other nearby communities. Dogs get a pet bed, bowls, poop bags, biscuits, and a bottle or two of water. Some of the rooms are less expensive than the pet fee, which is good news. Rates are $395–4,000. 701 Stone Canyon Road, Los Angeles 90077; 310/472-1211 or 800/648-4097; www .hotelbelair.com.

West Hollywood

Dogs love hanging around West Hollywood. It's an eclectic place with what seems like a higher-than-normal percentage of dog lovers. Jake simply loves all the attention lavished on him and others of his ilk here.

PARKS, BEACHES, AND RECREATION AREAS

45 William S. Hart Park

🐾🐾🐾🐕 (See Los Angeles County map on pages 724–725)

A Parisian pooch named Boo had his Parisian person Birgit write to tell me about this dear little park. "It isn't much bigger than an oversized handkerchief, but the dogs love it anyway," they wrote. And indeed they do. Lots of off-leash pooches trot around here with big smiles on their snoots. It's a very pretty little fenced park with trees and a doggy water fountain. Maintenance crews try to keep the park green, but with up to 100 thundering paws at a time, it's an onerous task.

It's easy to confuse this park with the big William S. Hart Regional Park in Newhall. They're both named for the same Old West movie star, but that's where the similarities end. While the Hart Park in Newhall is his 200-plus-acre former ranch, this Hart Park is essentially the yard of his former West Hollywood home. It's fitting that dogs are allowed to romp on both his country and his city property. He was a cowboy through and through, and he'd have liked this.

Dogs used to only be able to run off-leash during very limited hours, but now they can be leash-free any time the park is open! The park is at 8341 De Longpre Avenue, just off North Sweetzer Avenue, one block south of West Sunset Boulevard. 323/848-6400.

PLACES TO EAT

At press time, one of the last examples of architectural kitsch in L.A., the giant hot-dog shaped restaurant Tail O' the Pup, is temporarily closed while looking for a new spot to move to. It's a shocker that this tacky but beloved landmark, which has been in the same spot in West Hollywood since 1945, is looking for new real estate. By the time you read this, the owners plan to have found their new spot and opened their hot-dog window to customers once again. Check www.tailothepup.net or phone 310/652-4517 to find out the new location.

Comedy Store: Have a drink and an appetizer on a Friday or Saturday night with your best bud at the comedy palace of Los Angeles. As you sip your screwdriver and eat your little pizzas at the outdoor patio bar, you and your pooch can watch for your favorite comic. Sometimes comics do a little warm-up act on the patio. Your dog will be howling. 8433 West Sunset Boulevard; 323/656-6225.

Irv's Burgers: You and your dog can dine on great, meaty burgers and some healthier cuisine at this beloved eatery across from city hall. You sit on a stool at the counter while your dog looks on from below. 8289 Santa Monica Boulevard; 323/650-2456.

Joey's Cafe: Dine with your doggy at one of six shaded sidewalk tables here. The omelettes are droolworthy. Jake and I suggest the oven-roasted sun-dried tomato omelette with basil, spinach, and goat cheese. 8301 Santa Monica Boulevard; 323/822-0671.

Mel's Drive-In: This isn't a real drive-in, but you and your dog can park yourselves at the many umbrella-topped tables out front. Enjoy classically good burgers, fries, and shakes here. With all this decadent food floating around, the doggy drool can flow. Sneak yours a little bite of something and watch your dog smile. 8585 Sunset Boulevard; 310/854-7200.

Toast Bakery Cafe: This corner café has oodles of shaded outdoor tables and is a happening place for humans and canines. It always seems to be packed, but if you get here early your wait won't be so bad. Dogs get treats and water, and people get a variety of yummy breakfast and lunch items. The Belgian waffle with fruit was a hit with our table, and we've heard the house-made tomato-basil soup is to drool for. The baked goods are delicious, too. 8221 West Third Street; 323/655-5018.

PLACES TO STAY

The Grafton Balboa: The rooms at this gracious, first-rate hotel have a "Feng Shui reverential decor," according to the friendly manager. I think this means you and your dog will find it a peaceful place, but that could have more to do with the comfy beds and lovely furnishings than the fact that mirrors aren't facing the door. You'll adore the large, beautiful courtyard pool and Mediterranean gardens, but dogs need to keep their paws dry at the pool and down at the gardens (if ya know what I mean).

Rates are $199–350. Dogs pay a $100 fee for the length of their visit. The hotel is on the Sunset Strip, at 8462 West Hollywood Boulevard 90069; 323/654-4600; www.graftononsunset.com.

Le Montrose Suite Hotel/Hotel Gran Luxe: This attractive boutique hotel is hip, a bit retro, and fun, and it lays claim to being popular with A-list Hollywood celebrities. It's nestled in a lovely neighborhood away from the madding crowds, so if you and your dog want to escape the paparazzi (or just enjoy peace in a cool urban hotel), this is a fine choice.

All rooms are suites, with great color schemes involving espressos and creams with surprising dashes of brights. While definitely mod, they're also cozy. All rooms have fireplaces and some have kitchenettes. Rates are $225–550. Dogs pay a $100 fee for their stay. 900 Hammond Street 90069; 310/855-1115 or 800/776-0666; www.lemontrose.com.

Le Parc Suite Hotel: All rooms at this quiet, out-of-the-way hotel have kitchenettes and separate living/dining areas. Most come with a fireplace. While the 154-room hotel boasts that it has beautiful balconies, it doesn't matter to dogs, who need to stay in the first-floor (smoking) rooms during their visit.

While the rooms are comfy and spacious, the recreational areas are really terrific. The three-story hotel has a "rooftop oasis" consisting of a heated pool with rows of cabanas and lounge chairs overlooking the Hollywood Hills, a hot tub, and floodlit tennis court. Don't tell your dog about any of this, because he's not allowed to swim or play tennis. Rates are $219–259. There's a $75 fee for the length of your dog's stay. 733 North West Knoll Drive 90069; 310/855-8888 or 800/578-4837; www.leparcsuites.com.

Beverly Hills

This golden city offers dogs first-class treatment. "I never felt so at home as when I visited Beverly Hills," reports Shelby, a large chocolate Lab mix, via his translator Heidi. "I got to go shopping and eating and everyone was giving me pats on the head." What more could a dog want?

PARKS, BEACHES, AND RECREATION AREAS

Dogs aren't allowed in the stunningly beautiful Greystone Park. But then again, neither are cameras or picnics, so canines shouldn't feel too offended.

As for the rest of the parks, a woman at the parks department here had to double-check the dog rules with a supervisor when we called to update the book. When she came back to the phone, she had this answer: "I'm told we prefer the wind-up type, but we'll take the live ones." We give four paws for self-effacing humor in the land of 90210. If you want to sniff out a little wilderness in the land of opulence, Franklin Canyon Park and Coldwater Canyon Park offer big, wild chunks of dog heaven.

46 Coldwater Canyon Park

🐾🐾🐾🐾 (See Los Angeles County map on pages 724–725)

Los Angeles Magazine touted this 45-acre park as "one of the 300 best reasons to stay in Los Angeles," and dogs couldn't agree more. Although it's not one of the bigger Santa Monica Mountains Conservancy lands, it's one of the better ones for dogs who like a little socializing on their jaunts: It's rare to come here and not see several other people out hiking with their happy leashed dogs.

Boy dogs are especially tickled when they visit, because the park is headquarters for TreePeople, a grassroots group helping to keep trees in L.A., educating non-tree-people about the importance of urban forests, and planting oodles of arbors around L.A. (www.treepeople.org). There are plenty of trees along some of the trails here, and there's a trail for every hiking ability. The park is part of a 1,000-acre cross-mountain park, so you're not relegated to Coldwater property. Good trail maps can help you and your dog figure out where you want to hike. Before you head for the hills, top off your dog's tank with a swig from the doggy water fountain, near the TreePeople headquarters. (And as always when hiking in this region, don't forget to pack along plenty of water for you and your dog.) If you want to treat your dog to an extra special treat, take him on a full-moon hike here. They're out of this world. (See the Diversion *Give Your Dog the Moon*.)

The park is at Mulholland Drive and Coldwater Canyon Avenue. 12601 Mulholland Drive. 818/753-4600.

47 Franklin Canyon Park

🐾🐾🐾🐾 (See Los Angeles County map on pages 724–725)

Dogs dig this 605-acre park. It has everything dogs love, from lakes to woodlands to hilly grasslands. Most of all, it has space—a hot commodity in these parts. Dogs need to be leashed, but they still love sniffing around the park and trotting down the various trails. Jake's favorite is the Hastain Trail, a fairly arduous 2.3-mile round-trip that leads to an overlook with great views of the area. On a clear day, you can't see forever, but you can allegedly see the Pacific (we couldn't—the smog was rather thick when we checked it out).

The park is home to dozens of species of birds in the Pacific flyway, so bring your field glasses if you and your dog like bird-watching. It's also home to a

---

DIVERSION

Shop with a Canine Customer: If your dog enjoys shopping and is well behaved, many **Beverly Hills stores** will welcome your business (but not your dog's business, if you know what I mean—walk your dog first).

Dogs don't even have to be itsy-bitsy, or well-heeled, at many of these stores. "We've had cow-sized dogs shop here," says a sales clerk at the **Gap** store at 371 North Beverly Drive (310/274-0461). "As long as they're good dogs, they're welcome."

Sometimes this Gap even supplies canine customers with treats. Carol Martinez, media maven for the Los Angeles Convention & Visitors Bureau, says she once shopped here with her granddog, a seven-pound teacup terrier named Killer. "They had treats up on the counter, and he just stood there and ate them all up right out of the bowl," she says. "Of course, no one dared say anything when they found out his name."

Several small boutiques also allow the occasional pooch, but they asked not to be mentioned for fear of being besieged with giant dogs and dogs with bad bathroom habits.

One place you'll have to avoid with your dog is Neiman Marcus. A dog in another Neiman store bit a customer a few years back, and the Beverly Hills store has had to go along with a company policy banning all dogs. Instead, try **Saks Fifth Avenue** at 9600 Wilshire Boulevard (310/275-4211). Saks management prefers small dogs—the kind you can comfortably tuck under your arm—but I've seen some well-coiffed medium-sized dogs here.

nature center, amphitheater, and auditorium, but dogs need to steer clear of all these.

The best way to get there from U.S. 101 is to take the Coldwater Canyon Boulevard exit and drive south to the intersection of Coldwater Canyon and Mulholland Drive. Make a 90-degree turn onto Franklin Canyon Drive. (Note: There's no signage for the street.) At press time, there was also no signage for the park, but when you see a sign that says Road Closed 800 Feet and Sunrise to Sunset, you're at the park entrance. You can park in the north end of the park near the nature center or keep driving south to get to other areas to park and explore. 2600 Franklin Canyon Drive; 310/858-7272.

48 Will Rogers Memorial Park

🐾🐾 (See Los Angeles County map on pages 724–725)

Dogs and their elegantly clad people come to this lush park to lounge the afternoon away. Dogs have to be leashed here, and it's not a large park, but it is verdant and rich with the colorful sights and sounds of Beverly Hills. When Joe, Bill, and I visited, we witnessed a tiny bit of a dog being led out of a Rolls by a chauffeur who had the same air of noble servitude as if he were escorting the queen of England. He walked the little thing around once and said "Now, Emily." The dog did her little business on command. The chauffeur scooped and they sped off, no doubt to more pressing engagements.

The Will Rogers Memorial Park is a triangular chunk of fine real estate at the corner of Canon and Beverly drives and Sunset Boulevard, right across from the Beverly Hills Hotel. 310/285-2537.

PLACES TO EAT

The eateries listed on Beverly Drive are all near a free two-hour parking lot.

Café Rodeo: This restaurant is a rare breed: It's on Rodeo Drive. Not many restaurants are. And it has dog-friendly patio tables. Not many around here do. Dogs are welcome to join you for some fabulous people-watching from the pleasant sidewalk tables in front of this restaurant. The food is casual, with a vague nod to California cuisine. Mini kobe burgers and truffle fries are among the favorites here. Café Rodeo is within the Luxe Hotel (no longer a dog-friendly place to stay), at 360 North Rodeo Drive; 310/273-0300.

Jacopo's Pizzeria: Besides pizza, you can get chicken, seafood, and pasta at the outdoor tables here. Got a thirsty dog? Just ask for a bowl of water. 490 North Beverly Drive; 310/858-6446.

Subway: Yes, Virginia, there is a Subway in Beverly Hills. Dine with doggy at the outside tables. 279 South Beverly Drive; 310/278-7827.

Urth Caffe: All the coffees and teas here are organic and fair wage. There's a great selection. The sandwiches, salads, and house-made desserts are tasty. 267 South Beverly Drive; 310/205-9311.

DIVERSION

Give Your Dog the Moon: You and your dog will have a howl of a good time at the popular **full-moon walks** at Coldwater Canyon Park in Beverly Hills. **TreePeople,** a great group keeping trees in L.A., welcomes your good dog to accompany you on fun, one-hour hikes. You can choose from two or three hiking levels and topics of discussion. (The guides here aren't silent: You're going to learn something about insects or trees or the moon on their walks. Even your dog may come back more knowledgeable.)

The walks are given on the night of the full moon April through October. They start at sundown or, more precisely, moon-up. They're free to members of TreePeople and $5 for plain old people. Dogs are free. For details and schedules, check out www.treepeople.org or phone 818/753-4600.

PLACES TO STAY

Beverly Hilton: This elegant hotel has gone from allowing even the biggest moose of a dog to permitting pooches only if they're under 25 pounds. Even these wee dogs must sign a damage waiver. Rates are $170–345. Dogs are $25 extra. 9876 Wilshire Boulevard 90210; 310/274-7777; www.hilton.com.

Beverly Wilshire: This hotel puts the "E" in elegance and the "L" in luxury. Unfortunately, it also puts the kibosh on dogs who are barely larger than most cats. There's a 15-pound weight limit. Don't read any further if you don't want your larger dog to get tears all over your shoulder. Normally I wouldn't write much about a place that has such restrictive weight limit, but the Beverly Wilshire deserves the full treatment, despite its unfortunate pooch size limit.

Upon arrival, your tiny pooch will be presented with a silver tray containing two ceramic bowls. One has little treats and is accented by a sprig of fresh mint, the other bowl is for the bottle of Evian water your dog gets. Also on the tray are two white linen napkins, a rubber toy, and sometimes a vase with a long-stemmed rose. Your dog will also get a special pillow for napping. And all this is free! In addition, for a fee, the hotel provides dog-sitting and dog-walking. They'll even arrange for a vet or a groomer to come to your room, should you need one. Special gourmet meat selections are also at your dog's pawtips.

Oh, yeah, the hotel. Well, it's in the heart of Beverly Hills, at Wilshire Boulevard and Rodeo Drive, and it's exquisite. It's a historic hotel, built in 1928, and has 395 luxurious guest rooms, including 137 suites. All the rooms have a marble bathroom with deep-soaking bathtub, fully stocked private bars with fridges, the best of linens and down comforters, twice-daily maid service, and so on. You get the picture.

There's also a heated Riviera-style pool—but no dog-paddling pooches, please. For a real treat, rent a cabana for the day. Each lovely cabana comes with two chaise lounges, an overhead fan, a flat-screen television, two 15-minute foot massages, your choice of newspaper, a fruit basket, a split of champagne and a special "chef's creation." The hotel's acquisition by the upscale Four Seasons chain doesn't seem to have diminished the luxuries. In fact, if anything, there are more options than ever. The Red Carpet Ready package, for instance, comes with breakfast, a makeup consultation at Neiman Marcus, and two hours with a personal shopping assistant. And you can take your dog along, too.

The hotel has been home away from home to the rich and famous since 1927. It's well known as the setting for *Pretty Woman*. The more intimate scenes between Richard Gere and Julia Roberts took place in the hotel's Presidential Suite. For a mere $7,500 per night, you and your dog (and your human guests) can stay here, too. For the price, you get 4,000 square feet of space with gobs of rooms, two fireplaces, and lots of special touches (not the kind of touches in *Pretty Woman*, though). Some notables who really stayed in the Presidential Suite are Elvis Presley, the Dalai Lama, King Hussein and Queen Noor, Prince Andrew, Andrew Lloyd Webber, Elton John, and Mick Jagger.

If you want something a little simpler (cheaper), you can stay in a gorgeous room for as little as $500. 9500 Wilshire Boulevard 90212; 310/275-5200; www.fourseasons/beverlywilshire.com.

The Peninsula Beverly Hills: This five-star luxury hotel is one of the few upscale hotels around here that permit dogs of any size. "Even Great Danes are fine," says a front desk person. That's music to Jake's and my ears.

The hotel is top-drawer all the way, from its beautiful, classically designed rooms to its fabulous rooftop garden and cabana-clad lap pool and spa. The hotel offers suites and very private, glorious villas surrounded by lush tropical gardens.

Dogs get the royal treatment here. When you make your reservation you'll complete a Pet Preference form, in which you tell about your dog. When you get to the hotel, your dog will be greeted by some nice amenities tailored to her needs, including a dog bed and even some food, if that's OK with you. Rates are $599–4,000. Dogs are $35 extra. 9882 South Santa Monica Boulevard 90212; 310/551-2888 or 800/462-7899; www.beverlyhills.peninsula.com.

Raffles L'Ermitage Beverly Hills: If you can afford the first-class European elegance of this exclusive and very private five-star hotel, you won't regret a night or two here. You and your medium-to-small dog (40 pounds or less) will be pampered beyond belief. A chauffeur comes with your stay, so you and the pooch, who will be treated like anything but a pooch, can hitch a ride to nearby locales. A wonderful array of goodies awaits you daily and nightly in your suite. The marble bathrooms alone come complete with a steam room, phones, a TV, and a plush robe. And the pool area is gorgeous. (Sorry, no dogs.)

Dogs get a doggy bowl, a pooch bed, and a menu upon check-in. It's the most fascinatingly expensive and fancy pet room-service menu I've ever seen.

Some of the items: grilled filet of beef with organic rice and brown gravy ($28), poached salmon belly in frothed milk (for kitties, I imagine; $23), and the pièce de résistance, beluga caviar with a hard-poached egg ($155; again, it must be a rich cat thing—I've never spent that much on a dinner for four, much less on an appetizer for a pet).

Room rates are $495–785 ($1,000–$4,800 for suites). Dogs are charged a $150 fee for the length of their stay. 9291 Burton Way 90210; 310/278-3344; www.lermitagehotel.com.

Los Angeles

Many communities and districts within the city have their own headings. Check individual headings if you don't find the area you need here.

PARKS, BEACHES, AND RECREATION AREAS

49 Elysian Park
🐾🐾🐾 (See Los Angeles County map on pages 724–725)

The views of Dodger Stadium and downtown Los Angeles don't get much better than from this 585-acre park. The hills here often rise above the smog, and the Los Angeles skyline actually looks attractive from a couple of high-altitude picnic spots.

Angel's Point is a must-see for leashed dogs and baseball fans. Dogs like the breezes that blow in from the different sections of the city. Ball fans enjoy being able to peer into a little segment of Dodger Stadium. The park is conveniently nestled between I-5, U.S. 101, and I-110. To get to Angel's Point and the many roads and trails beyond, exit I-5 at Stadium Way and follow the signs to the park. Once you're in the park, take your first left, Elysian Park Drive. If you're on your way to drop off friends at a Dodgers game and your dog needs a quick walk, take your first right after you enter the park. It's a very green, tree-laden area that won't take you far off track from your destination. 213/485-5054.

50 Hermon Dog Park
🐾🐾🐾🐕 (See Los Angeles County map on pages 724–725)

The grass isn't always greener on the other side of the fence, especially if you're right outside the 1.3-acre Hermon Dog Park. The ground cover is decomposed granite, the stuff park paths are often made from. This is good news for the mud situation, since there won't be any, but it's not as scenic or pleasant to roll on as grass.

Still, there's greenery in the form of a large pine tree and two large sycamores in the park, and lots of newly planted trees on the park's outer perimeter. The park has benches, water, poop bags, and a separate section for little dogs. The park is at 5688 Via Marisol; 323/255-0370.

51 Griffith Park/Griffith Park Dog Park

😾😾😾😾 🐾 (See Los Angeles County map on pages 724–725)

This 4,017-acre park, badly scarred by recent fires but rising from the ashes, has something for dogs of every stripe (and spot), from dogs who need to run off leash to dogs who want to check out the famous Hollywood sign.

Since most dogs enjoy the leash-free life, we'll start with the dog park. It's a fenced-in 1.6-acre park, with a separate section for little or shy dogs. To get to the Griffith Park Dog Park, exit Highway 134 at Zoo Drive and follow Zoo Drive into the park. The dog park is next to the John Ferrar soccer field, on the right side of the road. (The freeway is on the left side.)

Anywhere else in this giant park, dogs must be leashed. Much of the acreage is taken up by such nondog attractions as the city zoo, an observatory and planetarium, a bird sanctuary, an outdoor theater, an equestrian center, golf courses, tennis courts, a swimming pool, a transportation museum, and a Western heritage museum. But fortunately, two-thirds of the park is wild and wonderful, straddling the eastern end of the Santa Monica Mountains. You can explore the undeveloped sections of the park via more than 57 miles of trails! This is the U.S.A.'s largest municipal park, and it can be quite an attractive place considering it's in the middle of three major freeways in the city that puts the "S" in sprawl. About 100 tree species thrive here, including oaks, pines, and even redwoods. Birds are abundant, which makes sense when you consider their alternatives in the urban realities beyond the park's perimeter.

With all the trails here (few are very developed), you have myriad choices about what kind of hiking you and your dog can do. Here are two suggestions to get you started:

1. Get a map before you arrive, so you'll have time to plan out your trek. Call the number below and the rangers will send you a free map showing all the trails.

2. Be careful. Because of the remoteness of some of the trail areas, they've become dumping grounds for bodies. And we're not talking bodies of literature, bodies of evidence, or even pigeon and squirrel bodies. Even with your dog at your side, you may not want to venture too far by yourself.

One fun hike you can take is the one that winds you as close as is legally possible to the famous Hollywood sign. From central Hollywood (Franklin Avenue and Beachwood Drive), go north on Beachwood Drive about 1.5 miles. At the street's northernmost end, it will come together with Hollyridge Drive. Park around here, and after walking about a block, you'll come to a wide trail on your left. It's not marked, but it will take you about 1.5 miles up Mt. Lee, where you'll be stopped by an ungracious fence. The fence is there at least in part because of the radio tower at the hilltop. (Maybe they also don't want dogs doing leg lifts on this oft-molested sign.)

One of the most entertaining activities you and your dog can share at Griffith Park is a train ride. U.S. 101, I-5, and Highway 134 surround the park. A popular entry is off I-5 at Los Feliz Boulevard. 323/913-4688.

DIVERSION

Drink, Dance, and Don't Forget Your Dog: The newest underground place to be seen is actually on a rooftop, at the hip, dog-friendly club **SkyBark.** SkyBark is the doggy version of SkyBar, one of the hottest nightspots for the L.A. elite. SkyBark is for the elite with four feet. Actually, dogs don't have to be elite at all to come here. Any well-behaved mutt who talks their person into buying a couple of tickets is welcome.

SkyBark is an occasional warehouse party of sorts, with fabulous 360-degree views of the downtown Los Angeles skyline, a full bar, ample dancing space, good food, and 3,000 square feet of leash-free space—also known as the "doggy dance floor." If someone (preferably a dog) can't get to a PETaPOTTY (the canine version of a Porta Potty) in time and has an accident, no problem: The turf/grass that covers much of the doggy dance floor can handle it—and so can the clean-team that's here to help with these matters.

There are cocktails galore, but dogs are the real social lubricants at these gatherings. You'll need nothing stronger than a Shirley Temple to feel right at home, even if you don't know a single person. With your dog at your side, the conversations happen naturally, the introductions are easy. Just watch where you step.

SkyBark events are held several times a year. They always benefit a charity, so it's a win-win-win situation. The club is on the roof of PETaPOTTY headquarters, in a very non-glam part of the city, at 1026 South Santa Fe Avenue. To find out about future events and ticket sales, call 213/891-1722 or go to www.skybark.com.

52 La Brea Tar Pits/Hancock Park

😾😾 (See Los Angeles County map on pages 724–725)

Take your dog to a tar pit that once trapped scads of Ice Age animals! What fun! The tar still bubbles up from its pond-like setting, but fear not: It's well fenced, so even the most ardent water dogs will be safe from the alluring mire. You can see how animals were drawn here thinking it was a place to splash around and guzzle some liquid refreshments. A few replicas of mammoths charging into the tar pit add a prehistoric air to the park.

The park itself has enough green grass for a pleasant stroll, but it's not big enough for a major exercise experience. There's a snack bar near the tar pit, but hanging around here probably won't give you an appetite, since on a hot day it can smell like roofing tar.

Hancock Park is alongside the George C. Page Museum, which houses skeletons and re-creations of formidable prehistoric animals trapped in the Rancho La Brea Tar Pits during the Ice Age. The Los Angeles County Museum of Art anchors the park's other side, so the park is convenient if you have to drop off a culturally minded friend.

The park is between Sixth Street and Wilshire Boulevard and Curson Avenue and Ogden Drive. Your best bet for free parking is along Sixth Street. 323/857-6311.

🐾🐾 Kenneth Hahn State Recreation Area

🐾🐾🐾 (See Los Angeles County map on pages 724–725)

Here's a Los Angeles–area park where the birds singing in the trees are actually louder than the drone of the freeways! The hilly section of this large park is a fascinating place to visit. Not only can you and your leashed dog do some intense hiking, you can also experience the world-uniting feel of the Olympics.

In 1932, the area was the site of the 10th Olympics. Then in 1984, Los Angeles again hosted the Olympics, drawing athletes from 140 nations. To serve as a continual (and growing) reminder of the events, 140 trees have been planted together on the hills where the 1932 events occurred. Each tree represents a nation that took part in the 23rd Olympics.

Watching their young leaves blowing in the breeze is enough to send patriotic shivers up your spine. It's also enough to make most male dogs stretch their leashes to pay their kind of homage to these saplings. But they can't. The trees are fenced in until they are big enough to withstand such assaults.

But there are many other trees to sniff in this large park. Several trails branch out from the parking lot at the Olympic Forest. Most take you up the hill, but you can also hike down by the lake and stream in the adjoining section of park.

Fees are $4 per vehicle on weekends and holidays. Driving north on La Cienega Boulevard in the Ladera Heights neighborhood north of Inglewood, you'll pass an oil-drilling site, then come to signs for the park. Although it's a state park, it's operated by Los Angeles County. 323/298-3660.

DIVERSION

You Can't Be Sirius: But you can check out this bright "dog star" and millions of other heavenly bodies when you attend a **Los Angeles Astronomical Society star party.** Well-behaved, nonklutzy canines are welcome to join you when you observe the universe with other astronomy buffs.

These nice folks who share their expensive equipment with the public deserve the utmost in consideration. If they ask you to take your pooch home because of crowds, or for whatever reason, please respect their wishes. For a schedule of upcoming star parties, or to ask about your dog attending, go to www.laas.com; 213/673-7355.

54 Silverlake Park Dog Park

🐾🐾🐾🐕 (See Los Angeles County map on pages 724–725)

It's hard to believe, but right in the middle of what has traditionally been the Land o' Leashes (that is, in the metro region of the city recreation and parks department) lies this fenced, 1.25-acre leash-free mecca.

The trees here are relatively wee, but dogs still are relatively happy weeing on them. Someday when the trees get big and strong, they won't mind so much. The park has water for pooches and people. The benches here make for more comfy human visits and also make a great place to sit down and talk to a new human acquaintance. (The park draws lots of singles from the surrounding community. We've heard there have been some matches made in heaven here.) Hit it off, and head to the nearby dog-friendly Back Door Bakery.

The park is on Silver Lake Boulevard, just south of Silver Lake and a bit north of Sunset Boulevard. 323/644-3946.

PLACES TO EAT

This is just a sampling of the eateries in Los Angeles proper. Some of the best dog-friendly restaurants are in surrounding areas.

Back Door Bakery: This is a major pooch hangout. Come here without a dog and risk feeling a bit naked. It's a bone's throw from Silverlake Dog Park and a great place to visit before or after your leash-free romp. Dogs get treats and water here, and humans can choose from a variety of yummy, casual food. Everything from soup to baked goods is house-made. Breakfast is droolworthy, with delicious omelettes and hefty quesadillas. 1710 Silver Lake Boulevard; 323/662-7927.

King's Road Cafe: The breakfasts here are to drool for, especially the omelettes. And if you like your coffee big, this is the place for you: The coffees here come in giant bowls. Boo the Parisian Dog originally raved so much about the atmosphere at the dog-friendly patio that we had to sniff it out for ourselves. Indeed, the wait staff here is super friendly, and the patrons are generally laid-back. There's a terrific newsstand just around the corner so you can have a good read while you eat good eats. It can get crowded here, especially on Sundays, so if you and your dog can make this a weekday destination, you'll probably enjoy it more. 8361 Beverly Boulevard; 323/655-9044.

Melrose Baking Company: If you want great baked goods at a fun outdoor setting, don't skip this place. 7356 Melrose Avenue; 323/651-3165.

Sante LaBrea: The outdoor area is lovely, they like dogs, and the food is healthful and very delicious. 345 North La Brea Avenue; 323/857-0412.

PLACES TO STAY

Please see other cities and communities (like Beverly Hills, Westwood, or West Hollywood) for nearby hotels.

Beverly Laurel Motor Hotel: You'll get a decent room for a decent price here. And it's in a great location, three blocks from CBS and near the farmers market. Cool off with a dip in the pool after a long day of exploring. The motel was built in 1964, and it looks it. Rates are $102–110. Dogs are $25 extra. 8018 Beverly Boulevard 90048; 323/651-2441.

Hyatt Regency Century Plaza: The only dogs who can stay here are dogs under 30 pounds. Boo-hoo for big Jake. This is a huge hotel, but the rooms are very comfortable and pleasant, with some of the best bedding money can buy. It may be hard for you to get out of bed in the morning with the fabulous mattress, down blankets, and über-soft sheets. Every room comes with a private balcony (called lanai here) facing either the mountains or the ocean. Marble baths and plush robes add to the upscale ambience.

Rates are $189–599. Dogs are $30 extra. 2025 Avenue of the Stars 90067; 310/228-1234; www.centuryplaza.hyatt.com.

Omni Los Angeles Hotel at California Plaza: This 17-story, 453-room hotel is big and has a big name, but only little dogs can stay here—25 pounds is the limit. That doesn't make sense to Big Jake and me. Rooms are lovely, with a comfortable neoclassical decor. The hotel offers several suites, fun kids' rooms adjoining parents' rooms, and some "Get Fit" guest rooms, featuring a treadmill, "get fit kit," and healthy snacks. (Who needs that when you have a dog to walk?) Dog-ettes get a bed, bowls, and treats.

The hotel is located in the heart of downtown. Rates are $219–499. Dogs are $50 extra per stay. 251 South Olive Street 90012; 213/617-3300; www .omnihotels.com.

Sofitel Los Angeles: "We love dogs here," more than one dog-happy manager has told us. This big, attractive, upscale hotel is near the best of Beverly Hills. Rooms have clean, simple, comfortable decor. Treat yourself to a spa visit while here. It's a lovely place to be pampered. Rates are $299–869. 8555 Beverly Boulevard 90048; 310/278-5444; www.sofitel.com.

Whittier

PARKS, BEACHES, AND RECREATION AREAS

🐾 Arroyo Pescadero

🐾🐾🐾🐾 (See Los Angeles County map on pages 724–725)

Jake Dog and I were excited when we planned our first trip to this Puente Hills wildlife corridor (former Chevron land), as it encompasses 1,700 acres—a really big chunk of wildland for these parts. But when we arrived, we found that there's just one trail here, a two-mile loop trail, which barely makes a dent in the vast acreage.

To our delight, however, our hike proved an excellent one, even with the mandatory leash. The trail starts out as an ADA-accessible interpretive path with some interesting displays and educational info about the park's flora, fauna, and importance as a wildlife corridor. Once Jake read the signs and got educated, we proceeded toward the hiking trail, which took us through a variety of environments, including coastal sage, chaparral, and a riparian community near a streambed. That was our favorite part, with plenty of greenery and relatively cool shade. He didn't want to leave, but we had more parks to sniff out, other Pescaderos to fry. (Jake made me write that ghastly pun.)

We hear that Arroyo Pescadero may get more trails in the future, but for now, this one really is all you'll need. The address is 7531 South Colima Road. Exit Highway 72 at Colima Road and drive north to the park entrance. Access is on the west side of Colima, across from the Murphy Ranch ballparks. 562/945-9003.

Hacienda Heights
PARKS, BEACHES, AND RECREATION AREAS

56 Hacienda Hills Open Space
🐾🐾🐾 (See Los Angeles County map on pages 724–725)

If your dog enjoys a hike on land dotted with trees (and more than dotted—at points, it's canopied), and you want to choose from different levels of trail difficulty, this 300-acre Open Space fills the bill nicely. It encompasses three canyons, which affords some strenuous hiking if you take the perimeter trail. Most dogs prefer the interior loop trail, which is shorter, flatter, and doesn't get quite so many mountain bikes.

Depending on where you hike, you and your leashed dog will see towering sycamores, oak woodlands, coastal sage scrub, sumac and toyon chaparral (in fact, one of the canyons here is the Toyon Canyon), and some riparian habitat. And if you go high enough, you'll have some fine views of downtown L.A. (not that this is what you came here for).

You can enter Hacienda Hills in two places in Hacienda Heights. Your best bet is to exit Highway 60 at South 7th Avenue and drive south to the end of the street, where you'll find the entrance. The address is 1600 South 7th Avenue. (The other entrance is at 14100 Skyline Drive, and that entails getting off the freeway at the same exit but taking a more circuitous route.) 562/945-9003.

Malibu

This mountainous oceanfront community is L.A.'s final frontier. Too remote for some, too expensive for others, it's one of the more natural and untouched areas in the county. Malibu's combined incorporated and unincorporated areas cover about 45,000 acres and are 27 miles long and up to eight miles wide. Only 28,000 people live here. Compared with the typical Los Angeles ratio of people to acres, this seems like the countryside. Here you'll find a few

magnificent parks where you and your happy pooch won't believe you could be within a bone's throw of one of the world's largest cities.

PARKS, BEACHES, AND RECREATION AREAS

Many of the Santa Monica Mountains National Recreation Area parks are found here. Malibu is also home to one of only two beaches in L.A. County where pooches are permitted. (The other is in Long Beach.)

57 Leo Carrillo State Beach

🐾🐾🐾 (See Los Angeles County map on pages 724–725)

Leashed dogs are allowed to trot around a portion of this 6,600-foot-long beach that straddles Los Angeles and Ventura counties. Dogs can sniff around the beach north of Lifeguard Tower 1 and south of Lifeguard Tower 3. Ask a ranger about this area's location when you park.

Dogs may also camp at one of the 136 sites here. Dogs prefer the campsites by the beach, but they go fast, so reserve ahead. Sites are $26. Call 800/444-7275 for reservations; 805/488-1827 for beach info. The beach entrance is on the 36000 block of Pacific Coast Highway, just south of the county border.

58 Zuma/Trancas Canyons

🐾🐾🐾🐾 (See Los Angeles County map on pages 724–725)

You and your leashed dog can take a short, easy hike or a rather arduous hike, but whatever you do, you're going to love this enormous patch of Santa Monica Mountains National Recreation Area land. At 6,229 acres, it's a biggie, with myriad choices for both the tenderpaw and the experienced canine climber.

Jake, being a dog who seeks shade above all else in life (except for leftovers), likes to stick to the more verdant expanses here. The streams that flow through the lands give rise to the "Zuma" part of the parkland's name. It's from a

Chumash word meaning abundance, and the streams do indeed provide abundant plant and animal life. Jake's favorite hike is the Zuma Loop Trail, along the base of Zuma Canyon. The two-mile loop features a hardwood riparian habitat, which is apparently a rare phenomenon. The shade provided by sycamores, willows, black walnuts, and oaks makes Jake a happy hiker. (More accurately, a happy reposer by the time he gets to this spot.) He especially likes this trail because it's easy and bans bikes.

We also enjoy a good jaunt on the Ocean View Trail and Canyon View Trail (which extend from the Zuma Canyon Trail). They wend through a chaparral environment with less shade, but the ocean views are worth the effort. It's a moderate three-mile loop that also doesn't permit bikes.

Duty-bound to sniff out a more challenging hike, we once made it to the Zuma Edison Road trail, which was a beauty, but as soon as we got to the most scenic part Jake started pulling on the leash to go back. Being rather pooped myself, I acceded to his request.

There are a couple of entrance options for the more popular trails. The simplest is to take the Pacific Coast Highway/Highway 1 to Busch Drive (near Zuma Beach, where dogs aren't allowed) and drive north on Busch until it ends. 805/370-2301.

59 Escondido Canyon Natural Area

🐾🐾🐾 (See Los Angeles County map on pages 724–725)

You don't have to drive all the way to Yosemite National Park to see one of California's most stunning waterfalls. Just drive to Malibu and take an easy 4.2-mile hike (round-trip) with your leashed dog. The Escondido Canyon Natural Area is home to a one-mile trail that takes you through grasslands, wildflowers (seasonally), and riparian woodlands, to the base of Escondido Falls—a 150-foot multi-tiered limestone waterfall that cascades over ferns and moss and is so beautiful it looks almost otherworldly. (Jake was frightened when he saw and heard the waterfall—his very first. He fluffed up, barked once, and decided it was time to pull me back to the car. With the aid of a couple of dog biscuits, he realized it was not, indeed, a car wash running amok and regained his rumpled composure.)

Late winter through spring is the best time to visit for the biggest flow. Come in August and you'll still have a decent hike, but you'll be looking at the Escondido Trickle.

Getting to this verdant nirvana on the one-mile trail is a joy. Getting to the trail itself is a unique experience. From the parking area you have to walk a mile or so through a very upscale Malibu neighborhood brimming with gorgeous homes. You may feel a little out of place with your hiking duds, but at least you'll have your dog at your side. From the main part of Malibu on Highway 1/Pacific Coast Highway, drive about five miles west to Winding Way (there will be a large sign for the Winding Way Trail). Turn right, and you'll almost immediately come to the parking lot. 310/589-3200.

60 Malibu Bluffs

🐾 🐾 (See Los Angeles County map on pages 724–725)

Want to watch some whales? Come to this six-acre park's whale-watching station with your leashed dog during the right time of year, and you may well see some. The park is of the community variety, and although dogs need to stay off the ball fields, they're welcome on the jogging path and the parcourse. 24250 Pacific Coast Highway; 310/317-1364.

61 Charmlee Wilderness Park

🐾 🐾 🐾 🐾 (See Los Angeles County map on pages 724–725)

If you and your dog don't like to sweat when you hike, but do like being rewarded with great ocean views on the trail, leash up and head to this 560-acre park. The Meadow Trail starts at a point high enough to see the Pacific from your very first steps. It's easy, often breezy terrain, and since the trail is actually a fire road, it's wide enough to accommodate you and your furry friend and any passing mountain bikes or horses. It's great for beginners or anyone not needing a big challenge. (It's a good choice for dogs getting on in years but still up for tackling something more than the corner hydrant.) You can loop around and come back for a bite to eat at the park's picnic tables. The park has a nature center (sorry, no dogs inside) and an informative native plant display. Come February through April and you'll be agog with all the wildflowers here.

There's a $3 fee per car. The park is at 2577 South Encinal Canyon Road. From Highway 1/Pacific Coast Highway in the Zuma Beach area, take Encinal Canyon Road north for four miles to the park. Turn left at the entrance and drive about a half mile to the parking area. 310/457-7247.

62 Corral Canyon Park

🐾 🐾 🐾 🐾 (See Los Angeles County map on pages 724–725)

We love this 340-acre park because it has such a variety of habitat, plus terrific views. You and your leashed dog can take a 2.5-mile loop trail that takes you through pristine wilderness, ancient marine terrace, sage scrub, coastal salt marsh, and a lush creek area with alders, oaks, sycamores, willows, and other trees that make boy dogs happy. At the top, you'll have terrific views of the Pacific and surrounding mountains.

The trailhead is conveniently located at 25623 Pacific Coast Highway, between Malibu Canyon Road and Kanan Dume Road. It's a civilized place to start a hike, with water, restrooms, picnic benches, and yes, even parking. (Note: Although a trail from here leads to Dan Blocker State Beach, dogs aren't allowed there, so don't even try it.) 310/589-3200.

PLACES TO EAT

Coogie's Beach Cafe: Enjoy gussied-up diner-style food with a few twists, including dishes like Italian-style egg rolls and charbroiled garlic turkey salad.

Dine with doggy at several outdoor tables. Palm plants try to shield you from the traffic at this fairly new shopping area. Coogie's is at Malibu Colony Plaza, 23750 Pacific Coast Highway; 310/317-1444.

Malibu Kitchen & Gourmet Country Market: The extra-good sandwiches and salads make this place a hit with dogs and their people. Sandwiches range from the sublimely vegetarian (warm seasonal roasted veggies with balsamic vinaigrette, goat cheese, and mixed greens) to the sublimely meaty. The "Better than Mom's Meat Loaf" sandwich, with ketchup, on homemade rustic bread, is a huge hit with dogs whose people tend to drop bits of food while eating. Dine at the seven outdoor tables. It's in the heart of Malibu, at 3900 Cross Creek Road; 310/456-7845.

PLACES TO STAY

Only one of the several lodgings in Malibu permits pooches. The good news for those on a budget is that it's one of the cheaper ones.

The Malibu Motel: This nice motel is retro without even trying. The rooms have been remodeled and have very comfy beds. All rooms feature a private ocean view deck. The motel is a half block from a beach, but the beach is not dog friendly so don't get your dog's hopes up.

Rates are $109–219—quite affordable for this pricey area. 18711 West Pacific Coast Highway 90265; 310/456-5486; www.themalibumotel.com.

Pacific Palisades

PARKS, BEACHES, AND RECREATION AREAS

63 Will Rogers State Historic Park

🐾🐾🐾 (See Los Angeles County map on pages 724–725)

"It's great to be great, but it's greater to be human," said humorist and actor Will Rogers, who made his home here during the 1920s and 1930s. Dogs may not exactly agree with this sentiment, but they do appreciate being able to peruse this 186-acre park.

Leashed dogs may explore along the trails that wind past a polo field, a roping ring, and Rogers's ranch house. Dogs can't go into the ranch house and should stay away from the stables and the polo fields on weekends, when polo matches are held.

A major warning: Heed the leash law. Rattlesnakes abound in the far reaches of the park, and nosy dogs who are allowed to romp off leash find them fairly frequently. Rangers here say about one dog a month gets bitten in the summer. Half survive it. Half don't. The trail here is wide, and if you stay toward the middle, you'll have no problems.

There's a $5 parking fee. The park is at 1501 Will Rogers State Park Road, off Sunset Boulevard. 310/454-8212.

PLACES TO EAT

A La Tarte Bistrot: Want a ménage a trois? You can order one right off the menu. After all, this is a French place! (The ménage is actually just a three-part salad. Sorry.) This chic French bistro has some delectable food. Dine at several shaded outdoor tables with your dear doggy at your side. (After all, this is a French place!) 1037 Swarthmore Avenue; 310/459-6635.

Jacopo's: My favorite pizza here is Max's Big Apple. It's about as close to real New York pizza as you and your dog will get in these parts, and you won't have to deal with airline hassles. 15414 Sunset Boulevard; 310/454-8494.

Brentwood

PARKS, BEACHES, AND RECREATION AREAS

64 Barrington Dog Park

🐾🐾🐾🐕 (See Los Angeles County map on pages 724–725)

This oddly shaped park (it looks kind of like a bow tie) features a separate area for small dogs. It's a couple of acres of grass and wood chips, with poop bags, water, tennis balls galore, and trees that offer pleasant shade for humans and pleasant leg-lift spots for boy dogs. People can rest their laurels on aluminum benches. (The folks here, the Friends of Barrington Dog Park, don't rest on their laurels long—they're always striving to make some kind of improvement in this fairly new park. In fact, new to this edition are shade structures and yet more trees.)

The park is closed for maintenance 6–10 A.M. Tuesday. It's at 333 South Barrington Avenue. Since it's close to I-405, here are directions from the freeway: Take the Sunset Boulevard exit and head west to Barrington Place. Go left on Barrington Place and drive past the entrance to Brentwood School. Go left immediately after the post office. The park is behind the post office. 310/840-2187.

PLACES TO EAT

Belwood Bakery: You and your pooch can dine on tasty baked goods and sandwiches at the three outdoor tables here. 11625 Barrington Court; 310/471-6855.

Westwood

This lively University of California community is a fun place to have a dog. People around here genuinely like them. A warning: If you're much above college age, you might feel a bit old here. But the energy is great, and when you're with a dog, you're young at heart anyway.

PARKS, BEACHES, AND RECREATION AREAS

65 Westwood Park

🐾🐾 (See Los Angeles County map on pages 724–725)

For a flat, squarish park, this isn't a bad place for a leashed dog. Long dirt paths wind their way through very green grass, past modern sculptures and many shaded picnic tables.

From I-405 take the Wilshire exit heading toward Westwood. Take your first right (on Veteran Avenue). The park will be on your right shortly after the federal building. Another section of the park is on Sepulveda Boulevard, just north of Ohio Avenue. 310/473-3610.

PLACES TO EAT

Le Pain Quotidien: This bakery/café chain originated in Belgium, where most of the franchises still reside. This one is quaint, on a fairly quiet street. You and your dog may think you're in Brussels or a Parisian side street. Enjoy the high-quality baked goods, and soups, salads, and special tartines with tasty fillings like gruyere cheese or imported French ham. The brunches are droolworthy. Try the goat cheese and asparagus omelette. Dine with your happy *chien* at the dozen or so umbrella-topped outdoor tables. 1055 Broxton Avenue; 310/824-7900.

Mr. Noodle: While not bearing the most dignified name in the world, this Asian fusion restaurant serves up some tasty food for an excellent price. Recently I got a big helping of yummy mint chicken (white meat, no less!), rice, egg roll, soup, and crunchy noodles for a mere $7.25. For that price, Jake could have ordered his own lunch. Dine with your dog at the four sidewalk tables. 1036 Broxton Avenue; 310/208-1730.

Stan's Corner Donut Shop: Lots of local cops hang out here, so it's got to be good. If you're in the mood for Indian food or a hot dog, Stan's serves this, too. Stan says, "I love dogs. I have a little French blood in me!" And dogs love the outdoor tables on this sunny corner and the water they'll get if thirsty. 10948 Weyburn Avenue; 310/208-8660.

PLACES TO STAY

The official mailing addresses of these two hotels are Los Angeles, but they're true Westwood glories.

Beverly Hills Plaza Hotel: With its koi ponds, terraced rooms, pretty gardens, little waterfall, and beautiful pool area, this is a very peaceful place to spend the night. The rooms are roomy (suites, really) and attractive, although perhaps needing a little updating. There used to be a 30-pound poochy size limit, but management is smart and now permits any size well-behaved pooch. There's a $200 cleaning fee for dogs and a $500 deposit, so bring the bankroll or the credit card if you decide to stay here. Rates are $195–625. 10300 Wilshire

Boulevard, Los Angeles 90024; 310/275-5575 or 800/800-1234; www.beverly
hillsplazahotel.com.

W Los Angeles: Dogs and their people really dig this luxurious, peaceful,
ultra comfortable and super-dog-friendly hotel. The beds have featherbed top-
pers and goose-down comforters and pillows (not that your dog should go on
the bed or anything). You can relax in your lush terry robe (hotel-supplied) on
your cushy sofa in your spacious room with your faithful, happy, furry friend
at your side.

The doggy details are just as splendid: Visiting pooches have to be under 40
pounds, which is unfortunate for Jake and his big ilk. But the lucky ones who
are small enough to stay here get a cozy bed, food and water bowl, floor mat,
and special treats at turndown. The W gives new meaning to the phrase, "It's
a dog's life." ("Not for me," mopes Jake.)

One of our favorite areas of this newly renovated hotel is the glorious poolside. The cabanas are fun, the chaise lounges uniquely comfy and cool, and the
people-watching is first-rate. The heated pool is great, too.

Rates are $389–499. Dogs are $25 extra. 930 Hilgard Avenue, Los Angeles
90024; 310/208-8765; www.starwood.com/whotels.

Santa Monica

Even though tourist dogs don't have many places to run around off leash (dogs
must be licensed Santa Monicans to use three of the four off-leash areas here,
and Los Angeles County residents with a special permit can join Santa Monica
dogs at the other), Santa Monica is a pretty great place to be a dog. It's laid-
back and, relatively speaking, down to earth. Dog-friendly eateries abound,
and the city is home to some of the most dog-friendly hotels around.

There's been a movement apaw for a few years to get a leash-free beach
here. It's had its ups and downs. It seems like a great idea, but many government entities are involved, and it's pretty complex. Not much progress has
been made since the last edition. To find out how to help (and help is greatly
needed), go to www.unleashthebeach.org.

PARKS, BEACHES, AND RECREATION AREAS

Leashed dogs are permitted in all city parks. (You must have a poop bag–type
implement showing, or you could get a ticket. It's best to carry an extra, in case
a cop comes after your dog goes.) If your dog is a tourist, the leashed parks here
are his only option: Three of the four dog parks here are open only to pooches
who are licensed Santa Monica residents. (We describe two of these three;
since the third, Memorial Park, is super tiny and open only to city residents,
we're not devoting space to it in this edition.) The city's fourth leash-free park,
Airport Park, allows only registered dogs from the county—but at least it's not
quite so exclusive as the others.

66 Airport Park Dog Park

😊😊😊 🐕 (See Los Angeles County map on pages 724–725)

If your dog is a resident of Los Angeles County and you've completed all the necessary paperwork, paid the $15.50, and obtained a permit from the Santa Monica Animal Control Division, you are entitled to use this dog park. That's a lot of work to go through to use a dog park, but at least Santa Monica has opened it to county residents. The other three dog parks here are for licensed Santa Monica dogs only. Unfortunately, if you're just in town visiting with your dog, you won't be able to use the park.

The park is the newest and the largest of Santa Monica's dog parks, but at 0.88 acre, it's not winning any prizes for size. It features a separate section for small dogs, and the usual dog-park goodies like water, benches, shrubbery, and little trees that will one day give shade. It's part of an eight-acre park built on a former runway of the Santa Monica Airport. The airport is adjacent to the park, and the little planes that taxi, land, and take off here make for fun plane-spotting. The park is on Airport Avenue at Bundy Drive and Centinela Avenue. To find out about obtaining a permit, phone 310/450-6179.

67 Joslyn Park Dog Park

😊😊😊 🐕 (See Los Angeles County map on pages 724–725)

At 0.83 acre, Joslyn's dog park may be small, but it's very attractive. It's set on a grassy hill with a few trees and great views of the city. It's completely enclosed, so those lucky pooches who get to go leashless are safe from traffic. It has poop bags, lighting, and a separate area for small dogs. Licensed Santa Monica dogs may run leashless 7:30 A.M.–8:30 P.M. on weekdays and 8:30 A.M.–8:30 P.M. on weekends. They must stay away from the playground and recreation area. All other dogs must be leashed, so it's best to keep them out of the dog run and explore other parts of the park. The park is at 7th Street and Kensington Road. 310/458-8974.

68 Pacific Park Dog Park

😊 🐕 (See Los Angeles County map on pages 724–725)

This fenced dog park, right next to a kennel, is less than a half acre and won't provide your pooch with endless miles of leash-free exercise. But it will provide her with endless leash-free socializing. If your dog is a social pooch, she could get all the exercise she needs here while engaging in faux wrestling matches and chase games. The park has water, a little shade, occasional grass, and benches to chase each other under. Licensed Santa Monica dogs may run leashless in the enclosed section west of the tennis courts 7:30 A.M.–8:30 P.M. on weekdays and 8:30 A.M.–8:30 P.M. on weekends and holidays. All other pooches have to be leashed, so it's best to stay outside the doggy area. The park is at Pacific and Main Streets. 310/458-8974.

PLACES TO EAT

If we listed all, or even most, of the restaurants in the popular eating parts of Santa Monica, we'd run out of pages in the book. So here are just a few.

Some of Santa Monica's most unusual and trendy restaurants reside on the **Third Street Promenade** between Wilshire and Broadway, and most have outdoor areas. That doesn't necessarily mean your dog is welcome at all of them, but your chances are better than when walking down a row of restaurants in Tahoe in January. You may want to watch your food, though, because a few of the homeless have been known to sneak up and grab it out from under you.

Restaurants along Santa Monica's **Main Street** are in a quieter setting than the restaurants in the Third Street Promenade. Unfortunately, we've found that most of the more upscale eateries won't allow dogs to dine with you outside.

Acadie Hand Crafted French Crepes: The crepes here are out of this world, with down-to-earth prices. My favorite is the Cevenol, with chestnut puree and crème Chantilly. Jake's favorite is anything that drops on the ground. The outside eating area houses several functional steel tables with plenty of room for pooches. 213 Arizona Avenue (at the Third Street Promenade); 310/395-1120.

Café Dana: We've been welcomed at this café's wonderful brick courtyard before and even offered a bowl of water (Jake has, I haven't), but we're now told dogs may have to be relegated to the sidewalk tables. Be sure to ask before you bring your dog to the enchanting courtyard. The house specials lean toward Greek food, but there's a wide variety of dishes here. If you like things English, try the afternoon tea, which comes with all the teahouse fixin's. 1211 Montana Avenue; 310/394-0815.

Interim Cafe: It used to be the Newsroom Espresso Café, but it's on its way to becoming another café. For several months it's been known officially as the Interim Cafe, an appropriate moniker if ever I heard one. Dine with your dog at the many umbrella-topped outdoor tables here. A must-try dish, even if you're not a vegetarian, is the Ultimate Maui Veggie Burger. 530 Wilshire Boulevard; 310/319-9100.

Joe's Diner: Joe Dog liked this one. He thought the name was in good taste but thought the good old-fashioned American cuisine was even tastier. Eat at one of two outdoor tables. 2917 Main Street; 310/392-5804.

PLACES TO STAY

Some of the most posh, dog-friendly hotels in California call Santa Monica home. The more affordable lodgings, like the local Best Westerns and Comfort Inns, don't allow dogs. If you want to stay in this beautiful coastal city, be prepared to dig deep in your wallet.

The Fairmont Miramar Hotel Santa Monica: You and your not-too-big dog can live in California-style casual elegance when you stay at this sprawling, lovely hotel. You can sleep in a 10-story tower with ocean views, a bungalow surrounded by beautiful gardens with little waterfalls, or a gorgeous six-story wing of the hotel. Everything is top-drawer here, from the pool to the bedding to the pampering service.

Dogs are OK "up to your knee," we're told. This is good for tall people with dogs that might otherwise not past the knee test. (It's probably not really knee-based. If your dog is above medium size, call and discuss the matter before reserving.) Rates are $339–1,300. 101 Wilshire Boulevard 90401; 310/576-7777; www.fairmont.com/santamonica.

Le Merigot: This opulent oceanfront gem has been described as "reminiscent of the fine hotels on France's Côte d'Azur," and also as "blending European elegance with the vibrant lifestyle of Southern California." *Brides* magazine describes the hotel as "Zen meets the millennium." You get the idea. It's cool, it's sleek, it's to drool for. Even the luxury spa here has won coveted awards. The rooms' ultra-cushy "Cloud Nine" beds—festooned with Frette linens, down duvets, and feather pillows—should win an award for comfort.

"Yada, yada, yada," your dog might be saying right about now. "But what's in it for me?" Well, doggy, Le Merigot has a marvelous program called "Club Meg," which allows dogs up to 100 pounds to be pampered guests at the hotel. (The brochure for the program features a dog who's the spitting image of Jake. Jake as the mascot for a luxury hotel pooch program is a funny thought, indeed.)

Dogs get pooch cookies, a dog magazine, and some other doggy amenities. They can also order dog-food room service. The kibble isn't as appealing as Loews's dog cuisine, but it's nothing to quibble about. There's also a grassy dog-walk area next to the hotel.

Rates are $319–610. Dogs pay $150 per stay, so stay a while. 1740 Ocean Avenue 90401; 310/395-9700; www.lemerigothotel.com.

Loews Santa Monica Beach Hotel: Everything about this elegant beachside resort is first-rate, from the gorgeous rooms to the sumptuous spa and health club. The lobby is to die for, too. It's also a great place to have a cocktail with your dog. Karen Dawn, founder of Dawn Watch, an animal rights media-watch organization, stayed at the hotel with her two dogs and significant other when they first moved to Los Angeles. "We'd come into the lobby's lounge area and order cocktails, and they'd put a little mat down for Paula and Buster and give them a bowl of water," she says. "They're incredibly dog friendly." Dogs are even allowed to check out the pool from the pool deck—not from the water, as Buster accidentally did one day. Buster, Karen's big mutt, trotted to the edge of the pool, leaned a little too far in to sniff at a ball, and tipped right in, much to his consternation.

Loews is, indeed, dog friendly. The "Loews Loves Pets" program considers all pet visitors VIPs (Very Important Pets) and starts their visit with a personal welcoming note from the hotel's general manager. Attached to the letter is a listing of pet-friendly places in the area. Dogs get a complimentary bag of biscuits, a toy, special placemats, and food and water bowls. Loews offers dogs gourmet room service with items like grilled lamb with rice, and even a vegetarian alternative should your dog be so inclined. Dog-walking or pet-sitting is available, too.

Rates are $309–1,250. Dogs are $25 extra. 1700 Ocean Avenue 90401; 310/458-6700 or 800/235-6397; www.loewshotels.com.

Culver City

Culver City has gone from a rather plain, forgotten place to a gentrified, hip community. As the New York Times put it so well, "Culver City, once considered a place to drive by on your way to somewhere else, has become Los Angeles's new stylish neighborhood, a magnet for lovers of the arts, good food, and culture."

Now that there's a great dog park here, you and your dog will have every reason to sniff it out for yourselves.

PARKS, BEACHES, AND RECREATION AREAS

69 The Boneyard

🐾🐾🐾🐕 (See Los Angeles County map on pages 724–725)

Great name for a dog park. It conjures up images of savory things dogs bury and dig up weeks later. But this isn't how it got its name. The park was built on an old oil field, which became a landfill after its usefulness was over. The landfill is where old, out-of-date oil-drilling equipment went when it died. It's a burial ground of sorts. Unfortunately for dogs, it's not a burial ground for giant steak bones.

The park is a little more than an acre, with water, benches, a separate section for small dogs, and something I've never heard of in a dog park: a time-out area. "It's a fenced-off area for dogs that get a little too excited and need a place to be on their own to calm down," explains Patty, with the Friends of the Culver City Dog Park. Apparently it's not used much, but it comes in handy from time to time.

There's not much shade in the park yet. The first trees that were planted didn't make it, but newer plantings hope to survive. And the temporary shade structure proved to be more temporary than anticipated when it blew away. But the park is a comfortable, friendly place, and if you don't mind a little decomposed granite in your shoes (no grass here), it's a fine place to take a dog. The Boneyard is within Culver City Park, on Duquesne Avenue and Jefferson Boulevard. 310/253-6470.

PLACES TO EAT

Several dog-friendly restaurants line Culver City Boulevard. Here's one we've heard great things about.

Ford's Filling Station: Acclaimed chef Benjamin Ford is the chef/proprietor of this terrific gastropub. The cuisine is fabulous upscale California-American with broad flavors of Italian, French, and whatever else Ford decides to include on a given week. It's comfort food for the epicurean.

The place is cozy and hip, popular with executives from nearby Sony Picture Studios. Ford's dad, Harrison, has been known to stop by for a visit on occasion. You and your dog are welcome to dine at the outdoor tables. (Your dog will want you to order the Kobe Beef Cheeks if he sees the menu, so try to keep it out of his reach.) A big thank-you to Bella Pearl and her mom, Carol Copsey, for letting us know about Ford's. 9531 Culver Boulevard; 310/202-1470.

Venice

Looking around Venice these days, you can see barely a hint of the dream of Abbot Kinney, the city's founder. In 1900, he began creating a city that was a near duplicate of Italy's Venice, complete with canals, Italian architecture, and imported singing gondoliers. He had hoped to create a cultural renaissance in America.

If he could see the scantily clad roller skaters, the punkers with metal in every conceivable body part, the homeless, and the body builders and religious zealots in action, old Mr. Kinney would shudder. But despite the wayward ways of those inhabiting his dream, the place has a wild charm, a playland quality. And what really counts is that dogs think Venice is cool.

There are plenty of dogs here. As of this writing, they're not allowed on the beach, but there's a big battle being waged about that. A terrific group, Freeplay, is working hard to get beach access and more off-leash parks. Freeplay started as an acronym standing for Friendly, Responsible, Environmentally Evolved Pet Lover's Alliance—Yes (not short, but the resulting acronym was worth it); www.freeplay.org.

PARKS, BEACHES, AND RECREATION AREAS

70 Westminster Dog Park

🐾🐾🐾🐾 🐕 (See Los Angeles County map on pages 724–725)

Since Freeplay helped open this fenced-in park several years back, beach-area dogs have joyously awaited their daily or weekly jaunts here. The park is more than an acre within very tiny Westminster Park, with plenty of shade and a few benches.

Small dogs have a choice of running with the big boys or playing in their very own smaller fenced-in dog run area. Most tiny canines we know would opt for the chance to be as big as they feel and not be set apart as a little dog. But it's a great feature for dogs in need of some protection from giant paws.

The park is at Pacific and Westminster avenues. The regional park office phone is 310/837-8116.

DIVERSION

Stroll to a Different Drummer: Since Venice's parks are so tiny, most people like to take their dogs for a jaunt along **Ocean Front Walk,** between Rose Avenue and Venice Boulevard. It's about as close to the beach as dogs are allowed, and for many, it's close enough. This is where you can consult a psychic; have your cards read by a tarot dealer; listen to street musicians; buy incense, T-shirts, or sunglasses; and watch skaters skate and lovers love.

If you like to check out bikini-clad babes—apparently one of Jake Dog's favorite pastimes—this is a hot spot. Jake smiles pantingly as cuties skate or jog or saunter by. Sometimes he even steps out into their path, urging them to stop with his big brown eyes. They often do, and they lavish him with pats and coddles. On a recent visit, a human dude saw the lovin' Jake was getting and asked if he could borrow him "just for 15 minutes." "Your dog gets more attention in five minutes than I got all week here," he said. Jake wanted to tell him that losing the nose ring and the nipple rings and covering his very hairy chest might help, but he remained politely silent.

You never know what you'll run into here. One day Joe Dog, Jake's predecessor, was trotting merrily along sniffing the air for all the great, cheap places to eat along the walk, when suddenly a hand appeared on the path before him. It wouldn't have been a big deal, except the hand wasn't attached to a body. It was writhing and doing sickening somersaults. Joe trembled and ran backwards right into a juggler. He stood there wrapped around the juggler's leg until the hand crawled away, back to the pile of motionless rubber hands from which it had strayed. He gave a shudder, unwrapped himself, and marched onward, never glancing back.

PLACES TO EAT

In addition to these restaurants, little eateries abound along Ocean Front Walk. Just grab a chair and table from the communal sidewalk restaurant furniture and enjoy one of the most scenic and unusual lunches you've ever experienced. See the restaurant listings for Marina del Rey for more super-close eateries.

Abbot's Habit: Your dog will want to make a habit of visiting this laid-back hangout, especially after he's offered a bowl of fresh water and you've bought him some of the crunchy dog treats sold here. Everyone from surfers to artists (often one and the same) comes here for the delectable baked goods and rich coffees. The sidewalk tables, where dogs are allowed, offer great people-watching opportunities. 1401 Abbot Kinney Boulevard; 310/399-1171.

Pasta Factory: The pasta and breads are made fresh right here every day. You'll give your crunchy boxed pastas at home the evil eye after you taste the difference. The pizzas and seafood are tasty, too. Dine with your dog at the outdoor tables. 425 Washington Boulevard; 310/823-9838.

Marina del Rey

PARKS, BEACHES, AND RECREATION AREAS

71 Burton Chace Park

🐾🐾 (See Los Angeles County map on pages 724–725)

Water dogs love this 10-acre park, because it's on a spit surrounded by water on three sides. But unless you visit via a boat (guest docks are available for a reasonable fee), dogs don't really get access to the water. It's Dock City here.

Leashed dogs of all ilks enjoy sniffing the salty breeze from this lovely, well-groomed park. The lawn can be golf-course-green, and the pathways are immaculate. This is a popular spot for weddings and group picnics, which you'll need to steer clear of, even if your dog loves parties. 13650 Mindanao Way; 310/305-9595.

PLACES TO EAT

The Cow's End: This is a fun coffeehouse where you can sip your stuff under a canopy. They're so doggone friendly here that your dog may even be offered a tasty dog biscuit if he plays his cards right. 34 Washington Boulevard; 310/574-1080.

Mercedes' Cuban Grill: The Cuban-Caribbean creations here are spicy and exotic. The ambience inside is cozy and creative, and outside, where dogs are allowed, it's pure fun in the sun. (Or in the moon, if you choose to have dinner here.) If you're thirsty for a unique drink, try the banana mojitos. Dogs get only a bowl of water if they're thirsty, but that's OK, because who wants a dog with banana breath? 14 Washington Boulevard; 310/827-6209.

El Segundo

Are you near the airport and looking for a place to run your dog off leash? Be sure to sniff out El Segundo's little off-leash gem. And if the dogs of L.A. County get their way, there could be an off-leash beach at Dockweiler Beach one of these days. A terrific group, Dog Beach Now, is trying hard to make this happen. Go to www.dogbeachnow.org for updates and info. For now, dogs have to be content to only camp there in an RV, on leash, and away from the water.

PARKS, BEACHES, AND RECREATION AREAS

72 El Segundo Dog Park

🐾🐾🐾🐕 (See Los Angeles County map on pages 724–725)

Like plane-spotting? Bring your furry pal to this dog park. It's on a grassy bluff that has views of nearby LAX, and you can watch the planes take off and land all day if you like. But chances are that your off-leash dog will have more important things to do at this long, 1.5-acre park, like sniff trees, sniff other dogs, run around a lot, and sniff more dogs. The park has water, benches, poop bags, double gates, and a separate section for small dogs.

It's on East Imperial Avenue between McCarthy Court and Sheldon Street, across from Imperial Avenue School. 310/524-2700.

PLACES TO STAY

Dockweiler Beach RV Park: Got an RV and an urge to cozy up to the ocean? Stay at one of the 118 sites here for a couple of nights. Pets must be leashed, and they can't officially go to the nearby beach. Rates are $28–32. Dogs are $2 extra.

From I-405 about 12 miles south of Santa Monica, exit at Imperial West Highway and drive four miles west to Vista del Mar. That's where you'll find the park. Call for reservations. 310/322-7036.

Summerfield Suites by Windham: You and your dog never have to leave your suite (except for the occasional potty break at the hotel's little dog-walk area… uh, for your dog) when you stay at this clean, comfortable lodging that's a favorite among people doing business near the airport. The suites all have a full kitchen, cozy living room, nice bedroom, and business-oriented features like high-speed Internet and a large, attractive working area. If you want your groceries delivered, that can be arranged for no extra fee (except the cost of the groceries).

Of course, you'll want to leave your suite so your dog can get some well-deserved off-leash exercise. And what better place than El Segundo Dog Park, which is a quick car ride away.

Dogs need to be under 60 pounds to stay here. Rates for suites are $189–219. There's a $150 fee per visit for dogs in the one-bedroom suites and a $200 fee per visit for dogs in the two-bedroom suites. 810 South Douglas Street 90245; 310/725-0100; www.wyndham.com.

Manhattan Beach

Dogs and people usually take an automatic liking to this seaside town. It's a friendly place, with people who stop you in the street to talk about how much they like your dog. This is not that common in these parts, so enjoy it. Unfortunately, the friendly attitude doesn't extend to the city's beaches or parks: Only one allows pooches.

PARKS, BEACHES, AND RECREATION AREAS

73 Live Oak Park

🐾🐾 (See Los Angeles County map on pages 724–725)

This is a jolly green continuation of Hermosa Beach's Hermosa Valley Greenbelt. It's skinny, dozens of blocks long, and it's the only public green in town that allows dogs. Leashes are a must, and don't even think about going on the beach with your pooch. Sorry, water dogs.

The park runs along Ardmore Valley Avenue for much of its length. 310/545-5621.

PLACES TO EAT

Hennessey's: Your dog can dine with you if you tie her to the other side of the railing at the patio area. Try the Cap'n Crunch French toast. Yum! 313 Manhattan Beach Boulevard; 310/546-4813.

Local Yolk: If you want a great breakfast, this place is just killer. (And this is not a reference to the cholesterol-raising dishes here.) A photo inside shows a man with a dog outside the restaurant. It says, "A safe place for dogs" (or something like that). And it is. Dogs are welcome to dine with you at the outdoor tables here. 3414 Highland Avenue; 310/546-4407.

Sloopy's Beach Cafe: Inside, this is a very funky place. It looks like a jungle or forest with tons of plants and tree-trunk tables. Outside there are just a few little tree-trunk tables with plastic chairs. Dogs can dine with you on tasty breakfast food and California lunch fare. 3416 Highland Avenue; 310/545-1373.

Uncle Bill's Pancake House: This is one of the more dog-friendly eateries around. "We love dogs!" says a manager. Uncle Bill's has been hailed as "the king of the South Bay breakfast eateries." Try the cheddar and bacon waffle. You'll be drooling as much as your dog. Thirsty dogs get a bowl of water. Dine with your furry friend at tables out front. 1305 Highland Avenue; 310/545-5177.

PLACES TO STAY

Residence Inn by Marriott: You and your dog can get a roomy apartment-style suite here. Some come with fireplaces, and all come with a kitchen, which is a mighty convenient feature when traveling with a pooch. Rates are $139–199. There's a $75 deposit and a $100 cleaning fee for the length of your stay when you visit with a dog. 1700 North Sepulveda Boulevard 90266; 310/546-7627 or 800/321-2211.

Hermosa Beach

PARKS, BEACHES, AND RECREATION AREAS

Dogs aren't allowed at any of Hermosa Beach's beaches.

74 Hermosa Valley Greenbelt

😊😊 (See Los Angeles County map on pages 724–725)

This long, narrow strip of green runs 30 blocks—the entire length of the city. It's got a pleasant soft dirt/chipped bark path down the middle, which leashed dogs really enjoy treading on. It's shaded in parts and can be fairly quiet, considering that it's sandwiched by two roads. But it's quite narrow, not ideal for a dog who likes to do heavy-duty exploring.

You can enter the park almost anywhere along Ardmore Avenue or Valley Street. The park continues north into Manhattan Beach. 310/318-0280.

PLACES TO EAT

As if to make up for the lack of poochy beach access, dog-friendly eateries abound here.

Good Stuff: This delightful eatery is right by the strand and the beach. Dine on everything from traditional (really yummy) breakfast dishes to burgers, from wraps to pretty darn good Mexican food. Dogs can join their people at the many outdoor tables. If it's busy, you have to sit at the side tables with your dog. 1286 The Strand; 310/374-2334.

Java Man: Dogs enjoy this old, funky sandwich/coffee/soup place. It's on a busy part of the street, but dogs don't seem to mind: The folks here give dogs treats and water, and the dogs don't notice the traffic passing by. 157 Pier Avenue; 310/379-7209.

Martha's 22nd Street Grill: They'll often let your dog sit beside you at the outside tables here, but if it's crowded, you'll be asked to tie your dog up to one of the poles on the side. The food is really good—and good for you, too. The menu includes apple pancakes, Monte Cristo sandwiches, and veggie burgers. Your dog can get a bowl of water if his whistle needs wetting. 25 22nd Street; 310/376-7786.

Redondo Beach

PARKS, BEACHES, AND RECREATION AREAS

Dogs are banned from all city parks, beaches, and Open Space lands, with one very special exception. When you're done getting down and dirty at the dog park, take a trip to the Ushampooch, a fun, clean self-serve dog wash just one block from the park, at 1218A Beryl Street; 310/798-7300; www.ushampooch.com.

🐾 Redondo Beach Dog Park

🐾🐾🐾🐾 🐕 (See Los Angeles County map on pages 724–725)

A few years ago, dogs were thrilled to have a 2.5-acre leash-free, fenced park to call their very own, even though there was no shade and much of the park ran under big power lines. After all, before that, dogs couldn't even set paw in any local parks. But now that the park has been expanded and gussied up a bit, dogs are positively ecstatic.

The park is now six big acres. It's divided into three parts—two big parks that switch off being open to give the grass a chance to grow, and one smaller park for small dogs. The park also has about 30 fairly new trees. The trees are still too small to give shade, but at least they give hope for shade in the near future.

The power lines over a swatch of the park don't do much for the place aesthetically, but dogs don't care. There's doggy drinking water, cool green grass, good sniffs, and lots of other dogs to pal around with. In fact, a survey shows that the dog park is the busiest park in the city, with about 1,500 visitors on some of the busy weekends.

The park is at Flagler Lane and 190th Street. Driving north on Highway 1/Pacific Coast Highway, go right on Beryl Street. In about 10 blocks you'll come to Flagler Lane. Go left on Flagler. Parking is on the right, before the stop sign on the top of the hill. 310/318-0610; www.rbdogpark.com.

PLACES TO EAT

Coffee Cartel: Buy books and a cuppa Joe at this older, fun place with a literary bent. Coffee Cartel sponsors everything from poetry readings to bluegrass bands. Dogs can join you at the outdoor tables. 1820 South Catalina Avenue; 310/316-6554.

Redondo Beach Brewing Company: The grilled food is great, and the ales are all that. For something different, try the Greek tacos or the scrumptious chicken adobo sandwich. Drink and dine with your dog at the shaded tables out front. 1814 South Catalina Avenue; 310/316-8477.

Zazou: This terrific restaurant offers a fun mix of California-Provençal cuisine. The dishes are flavorful and, for the most part, healthful. (Dogs long for the braised rabbit, but the butternut squash and ginger raviolini are truly droolworthy.) You can eat at the tables out front with your dog, but you can't drink alcohol out here. (Neither you nor your dog, to clarify.) 4810 South Catalina Avenue; 310/540-4884.

PLACES TO STAY

Best Western Redondo Beach Inn: Rates at this attractive Best Western, which features a pool and spa, are $89–109. Dogs are $50 extra for the length of their stay. 1850 South Pacific Coast Highway 90277; 310/540-3700.

Palos Verdes Estates

PARKS, BEACHES, AND RECREATION AREAS

76 Malaga Park

😺 (See Los Angeles County map on pages 724–725)

We mention this tiny park only because it's so close to a really lovely European-style part of this luxurious city. You and your leashed dog can catch a refreshing ocean breeze at Malaga Park, since it's high on a hill. Dogs like to relax on the small plot of lush grass and contemplate what it would be like if their backyard looked like this. People enjoy sitting on the stone benches and contemplating the same thing. In the spring, a little garden comes alive with color. Make sure your leashed dog doesn't think the park is larger than it is and accidentally wander into the flower beds.

From Palos Verdes Drive going west, go right on Via Corta. Park on the street. The park is immediately on your left. Don't blink or you'll miss it. 310/378-0383.

PLACES TO EAT

Rive Gauche: Elegance is the operative word at this four-star French restaurant. Yet the managers gladly permit pooches to dine with you at the patio tables. "We're very dog friendly here," they say. Some patrons have been bringing their dogs here for years, much as they would if this restaurant were in France. One regular told us that sometimes her dog manages to mooch a little something from her waiter. I don't think that's the norm here; still, maybe your dog will get lucky.

There's a canopy over the patio, so you and your *chien* can dine without the sun smacking you in the eyeballs. 320 Tejon Place; 310/378-0267.

Harbor City

PARKS, BEACHES, AND RECREATION AREAS

🐾 Ken Malloy Harbor Regional Park

🐾🐾 (See Los Angeles County map on pages 724–725)

This 210-acre park between Harbor City and Wilmington is right beside a huge oil refinery. Yum, yum. The air is often an otherworldly hue. It's not the most appetizing place, but you can manage to stomach a picnic here. To the park's credit, there's a good-sized lake along the east end. It may not be a prime fishing spot, but at least it's good old H_2O.

The best thing about this park is its proximity to I-110. If you have a dog who's in dire need during a Sunday drive, a jaunt to this park won't take you far off course. Exit I-110 at Highway 1/Pacific Coast Highway and drive west a short half mile. The entrance is on your left. 310/548-7728.

San Pedro

Stick close to the waterfront here and you'll have a great time. Los Angeles Harbor is a working harbor where you can see tankers, container vessels, cruise ships, and pleasure craft going about their business.

San Pedro is a point of embarkation for one of the ferry lines to Catalina. It's a fun excursion to take with a sea-loving pooch. (See the *Santa Catalina*

Island section for more on the ferry services.) For more on fun things to do in this town, check out www.sanpedro.com. The folks who run this site are very helpful and have a couple of dogs themselves.

PARKS, BEACHES, AND RECREATION AREAS

78 Knoll Hill Dog Park

🐾🐾🐾🐾 🐕 (See Los Angeles County map on pages 724–725)

This three-acre dog park has everything a dog could ask for, and something a dog would never think of asking for: great views of the Port of Los Angeles. Set on a hilltop above the hustle and bustle of the city, the park is a wonderful place to visit if your dog needs to burn off steam while you take a breather on one of the park's chairs or benches.

The park is divided into two sections: a two-acre section for all dogs and a one-acre section for small dogs. The parks have water stations, poop-bag dispensers, multiple fire hydrants, and some trees. There's ample parking, which is reason alone to visit in these parts.

This pooch paradise is on top of Knoll Hill—which announces itself in big white letters against the hillside—just north of the Vincent Thomas Bridge. Exit I-110 at Highway 47 and drive east. In less than a mile you'll come to the Harbor Boulevard exit, just before the bridge. Follow it north (it will actually be signed as Front Street once you exit) and make a left at the second Knoll Drive (the first Knoll Drive is a one-way street away from the hill) and head up the hill. The park is being managed and maintained by its users. They're hopeful that the city will take over one of these days. Meanwhile, if you have questions or want to contribute or help with upkeep, contact Peninsula Dog Parks, Inc., 310/514-0338; www.dogparks.org.

Long Beach

Joy, joy, joy! Dogs not only set paw on sand at a nice section of beach here, but they can do it off leash if they're under voice control! It's one of only two spots in the whole county where dogs can put their paws to the sand.

In other nautical news, Long Beach is where you can board a fast (about 75 minutes) ferry to beautiful Catalina. See the *Santa Catalina Island* section for details about the ferry service.

PARKS, BEACHES, AND RECREATION AREAS

79 The Dog Zone at the Beach

🐾🐾🐾🐾 🐕 (See Los Angeles County map on pages 724–725)

This three-acre chunk of sand and surf is the only beach in Los Angeles County that allows off-leash dogs—and one of only two beaches in the entire

🐕 DOG-EAR YOUR CALENDAR

If you like Easter, and your dog has a sense of humor, put the **Haute Dog Easter Parade** in Long Beach on your must-do list. As seen on Jay Leno, hundreds of leashed pooch participants trot down the street in their Sunday best. Prize categories include best Easter hat/bonnet, best Easter attire, most whimsical outfit, best kissin' canine, longest ears, shortest tail, dog-person look-alike, and best dog legs. The parade benefits local charities. For details and this year's dates, log on to the fabulous website of Justin Rudd's Haute Dogs: www.hautedogs.org. You'll also find info there on other terrific dog events, including the Haute Dog Howl'oween Parade (at a recent Howl'oween Parade, 500 dogs came in costume!) and an interfaith blessing of the animals. In addition, the lively and beautifully designed site features info on just about anything that involves dogs in the greater L.A. region.

---

county that allow dogs at all. Dogs and their people are extremely grateful for this 235-yard-long stretch of dog-friendly beach. Dogs run around with huge smiles on their snouts. People stand around with huge smiles on theirs.

This is not a dog beach: People are big users of this beach, so unless your dog is very good under voice control, keep her leashed. The dog zone has some unique rules. Most notably, only one dog per adult is allowed, and "children must be supervised by adults. Children are not permitted to run, shout, scream, or wave their arms or otherwise excite or antagonize dogs." I'm sure that went over big with local parents.

The Dog Zone is in effect 6 A.M.–8 P.M. daily. It's on the beach in the Belmont Shore area of Long Beach, approximately between Roycroft and Argonne avenues. You'll see the signs. Parking is available at the metered beachfront lot (enter off Bennett Avenue, from Ocean Boulevard). Bring plenty of quarters. There's also limited free parking along Ocean Boulevard.

A final note: If your pooch works up a powerful thirst during her escapades at the beach, be sure to visit the nearby Fountain of Woof, next to the restrooms at the end of Granada Avenue.

🞮 Recreation Park Dog Park

🐾🐾🐾🐾🐕 (See Los Angeles County map on pages 724–725)

Pooches passing through or living in Long Beach are extremely lucky dogs. This is an incredibly fun, attractive park for leashless dogs and their people.

The fenced park is about two acres with a few big old shade trees, 20 benches, several picnic tables, poop bags, doggy water fountains, and a small fenced area for small or shy dogs. Dogs tremble with excitement as they approach.

It's wonderful to watch their joy as they bound from one end of the park to the other, somersaulting and crashing into each other with gleeful abandon.

The park is also very human friendly, with bathrooms and a water fountain for people. It's not cheap to keep up a park like this, so if you feel like donating to the cause, please put some spare change in the parking meter at the park's gate to help keep the park in good working order.

Exit I-405 at Bellflower Boulevard and drive south about two miles to 7th Street. Turn right and drive about another mile to the sign for the park's maintenance yard and dog park. Turn right again and park in the lot next to the dog run. Dogs are allowed in other parts of Recreation Park, but they must be leashed. 562/570-3100.

PLACES TO EAT

Dogs are banned from the charming Shoreline Village shops and restaurants. Too bad, because it's the perfect atmosphere for well-behaved pooches and their people. But here are a few places that will make you forget about Shoreline's lack of doggy dining.

Polly's Gourmet Coffee: Sip fresh coffee and chow down on house-baked muffins and pastries at this café's patio with umbrella-topped tables. Polly's actually shares the patio with a couple of other restaurants (including Z Pizza), so your dog can smell everything from pizza to fried chicken while accompanying you for your meal. 4606 East 2nd Street; 562/433-2996.

Z Pizza: This pizzeria may be the last one in the phone book, but it's tops with dogs. You can get every kind of pizza imaginable here. Dine at the patio Z Pizza shares with a couple of other restaurants, including Polly's Gourmet Coffee. (Or if you're staying in a nearby hotel, Z will deliver, by bicycle.) 4612 East 2nd Street; 562/987-4500.

PLACES TO STAY

It's not easy being a medium-to-large dog who needs to stay in Long Beach. Only a couple of accommodations are accommodating. The rest are for the small-dog set.

GuestHouse Hotel: This one's close to California State University, Long Beach. Humans enjoy the outdoor "tropical" pool and attractive decor. Your stay includes a continental breakfast and passes to a health club nearby. Got kids? Try the bunk-bed rooms. Rates are $89–159. Dogs are $10 for the length of their stay. 5325 East Pacific Coast Highway 90804; 562/597-1341 or 800/990-9991; www.guesthouselb.com.

Hilton Long Beach Hotel: This used to be called the Long Beach Hilton at the World Trade Center, but 9/11 put an end to that. This is a beautiful hotel in a jazzy location. There's a big fitness center, too, in case walking your dog isn't enough exercise. (Then you can use the steam room or the pool for that spa feel.) Unfortunately, only small dogs (under 25 pounds) can stay here. Those little guys need a $100 deposit. Rates are $150–325. 701 West Ocean Boulevard 90831; 562/983-3400 or 800/445-8667; www.hilton.com.

Holiday Inn—Long Beach Airport: Rates at this retro round tower are $119–179. Dogs are $25 extra and require a $100 deposit, and they need to weigh less than 25 pounds. 2640 Lakewood Boulevard 90815; 562/597-4401.

Residence Inn by Marriott: You and your dog can have a very comfortable stay at this all-suite lodging. Condos and townhouses are also available. The hotel welcomes many dogs every week. It's a good place to stay if you're in town for a while, because your suite comes with many of the comforts of home, including a little kitchen area and a living room. Most rooms come with VCRs, and a few even have fireplaces.

Guests get a complimentary hot breakfast every day. Once a week the hotel hosts a fun barbecue by the pool. It's a great way to mix and mingle with other guests. The property even has two outdoor areas designated for leashed dogs to walk and do their thing. (Don't forget to scoop.)

Rates are $139–2199. Dogs are $100 for the length of their stay. 4111 East Willow Street 90815; 562/595-0909; www.residenceinn.com.

The Turret House: If your dog is looking for a delectably dog-friendly getaway, The Turret House should be very high on your list of places to stay. It's a painstakingly restored 1906 Victorian that's as dog friendly as it is beautiful.

Owners Brian and Jeff, career flight attendants who cut their bed-and-breakfast teeth on an inn in coastal Maine, are some of the most welcoming hosts you and your dog will ever come across. So are their two friendly English bulldogs, Waldo and Winston. "They love it when we have dog guests," says Brian. "They're very good hosts." The apple doesn't fall far from the tree.

The inn itself is gorgeous, with claw-foot tubs in every bathroom and fireplaces in each of the five bedrooms. But since your dog is probably reading over your shoulder right now, let's talk about the doggy extras: Dogs are given all-natural pooch treats upon arrival. The backyard is completely fenced, and dog doors lead from the house to the yard. Well-behaved dogs get to wander around and trot outside when they need to water the grass. What a treat! Some dogs have been known to wander out of the main house through a doggy door, across the backyard, and into Brian and Jeff's adjacent cottage through their doggy door. "We've had some fun surprise visits," says Brian.

Pet-sitting and dog-walking are available for an extra fee, should you decide to strike out sans dog for a while. Room rates are $99–125. The price includes an expanded continental breakfast buffet and snacks, sodas, beer, and wine. 556 Chestnut Avenue 90802; 562/624-1991 or 888/4-TURRET (888/488-7738); www.turrethouse.com.

Santa Catalina Island

Catalina is slowly becoming an easier place to vacation with your dog. Getting here with a dog has never been a problem, thanks to the ferries being so dog friendly (see the Diversion *Nautical Dog!*). It used to be that once you arrived on the island, there was no place to spend the night with your dog. But now two hotels permit pooches!

Neva Jennings, the personable former longtime president of the Avalon Humane Society, is hoping one day the island will have an official dog park. "I've been yapping and carrying on for 20 years to try to get this little space," she says. (Neva hopes the park will be named Bark Park. Jake and I think it should be named the Neva Jennings Bark Park—not just because she helped win this little patch of land for dogs, but also because of her 21 years as president of the humane society here.)

As far as stretching your dog's legs elsewhere, it's pretty restrictive. With the exception of the magnificent and wild Catalina Island Conservancy lands and a 10- by 10-foot patch of dog-dedicated dirt on the way from the ferry to town, and a little area behind the Nature Center at Avalon Canyon, dogs are not allowed at any parks, beaches, or along most of Avalon's main oceanfront drag, Crescent Avenue.

DIVERSION

Nautical Dog! Unless you have your own boat, you're going to have to rely on passenger ships to take you to Santa Catalina Island. Although dogs must be leashed and muzzled, most seem to enjoy the scenes, smells, and sounds they experience aboard these big boats. (Muzzles can be of the lightweight nylon and Velcro variety. Many dogs barely notice them.)

The *Catalina Express* is the fastest passenger boat to the island's only real town, Avalon. The excursion takes a little more than an hour. If it's foggy, however, the trip can last a long time, so the short cruise time is not a guarantee. Our last excursion to Catalina on this line took well over two hours because of the drippy September morning fog. Trips leaving from San Pedro and Long Beach cost $59 round-trip per adult, a little less for seniors and children. Trips leaving from Dana Point take a little longer and cost a bit more. Although you'll pay $6 to bring a bike, surfboard, or stroller on either excursion, dogs still go for free! Reservations are highly recommended. 310/519-1212; www.catalinaexpress.com.

If there's no room at the two dog-friendly hotels, or if you just want a little time to explore Avalon with the human you came with, Neva Jennings can help. In addition to all her other work on behalf of dogs and humans (she is very active in Meals on Wheels as well), she runs the Avalon Boarding Service. This is no kennel: This is Neva's own home. Happy dogs who stay with her get to make her home their home. Neva knows dogs, loves dogs, and will treat your pooch kindly and warmly. Even the most skittish dogs tend to feel content at her side.

Neva says she's "very elastic" about pick-up and drop-off times, and she'll meet you somewhere other than her home if it's easier for you. She'll even just board your pooch for the day, if that's all you need. Dog boarding starts at $15 for 24 hours, which includes high-quality pooch food and some exercise. How does she afford to do it at this incredibly low rate? "I'm not in it to make money," she says. You can phone her at 310/510-0852 or write her at P.O. Box 701, Avalon, CA 90704.

PARKS, BEACHES, AND RECREATION AREAS

If you don't know where to go, this place can be difficult for a dog. It seems like every time you find a decent spot of green or beach, you also spot a No Dogs Allowed sign.

But we're here to help you know where to go. Local water dogs know of a couple of spots where pooches can do the dog paddle: Casino Point and Pebbly Beach. These are not public beaches but decent little swimming holes. We've been implored not to include directions to these unofficial dog patches in our book, because last time we did there was a backlash against dogs using them. But any local can tell you where to find them.

The bulk of the island is undeveloped. Dogs are permitted on these natural lands if they have a permit and wear a leash.

81 Nature Center Dog Area

😾 (See Los Angeles County map on pages 724–725)

If this area weren't on Catalina—an island greatly in need of green spots to walk a dog—we probably wouldn't include it in the book. The area isn't for off-leash dogs, and it's not terribly big, but it's a grassy (and dirt-y) area dogs are allowed to explore. Poop bags and garbage cans attest to this. The doggy area is behind the old Interpretive Center, which is now The Nature Center at Avalon Canyon, at 1202 Avalon Canyon Road (about a mile or so from the main part of Avalon). There's a fence around it, but only for demarcation, not for keeping dogs fenced in. Leashes are the de rigueur outfit here.

Nobody seems to know who is in charge of the land, but since it's next to the Nature Center, we'll list its number: 310/510-0954.

82 Catalina Island Conservancy Land

🐾🐾🐾 (See Los Angeles County map on pages 724–725)

Catalina Island is 76 square miles. A whopping 85 percent of this land is maintained by the county and by the Catalina Island Conservancy, whose mission is to keep this beautiful terrain in its natural state.

Dogs are allowed to join you on the trails here. Leashes are the law, and for good reason: Conservancy lands truly are where the buffalo roam and the deer and the antelope play. (To be more precise, it's where the American bison roam and the mule deer and black buck antelope play. But let's not get carried away with details.) It's also home to the endangered island fox and some shrews, bats, and snakes that are considered California Species of Concern—a few steps below threatened or endangered, but nothing you want your dog trying to chase down anyway. Rattlesnakes also slither about, although you'll be unlikely to see any if you stay on the trails. And poison oak is among the 600 or so plant species here, quite common in the canyons and creek beds. Keep your eyes peeled and your dog leashed and you'll enjoy a terrific hike on any of several trails that loop around the island's wild lands. There's a trail for just about every level of hiker.

Dogs aren't allowed to stay at developed campgrounds, but if you have your own boat, you'll be happy to know that your dog can join you in the primitive boat-in campsites. (Primitive as in there's no water, no bathroom, and—hooray!—no tourists thronging about. You must bring your own water and your boat's portable toilet if you plan to go to the bathroom during your stay.) Rates are $12 per adult, $6 per child. Dogs are free but must be leashed or on a lead at all times. (This is a service not only to the delicate wildlife but to your dog. You might get a visit from some wild boars, and not of the crashingly so variety.) See www.campingcatalina.com for more important boat-in camping information. Phone 310/510-8368 for reservations, or reserve on the Internet to save the $10 reservation fee. Go to www.visitcatalinaisland.com.

You'll need a permit to hike anywhere but Avalon. The permits are free, and they can be obtained at the conservancy office in Avalon, 125 Clarissa Avenue; 310/510-2595. Two other locales on the island also offer permits. See www.catalinaconservancy.org for details or phone 310/510-1421. You can get a free hiking map by sending a self-addressed stamped envelope to the Catalina Island Conservancy, Attention Visitor's Services—Hiking Map, P.O. Box 2379, Avalon, CA 90704.

PLACES TO EAT

Casino Dock Cafe: This is the only restaurant on the island that openly welcomes dogs! Dine outside, overlooking Avalon Bay, at the base of the casino. The cuisine is of the burger-seafood-chicken variety. Thirsty dogs get a bowl of water. 2 Casino Way; 310/510-2755.

PLACES TO STAY

Best Western Catalina Canyon Resort: This 72-room hotel permits pooches under 40 pounds. It has a pool, a day spa, and a hot tub. Nice for humans, but dogs don't care that they can't get massaged or soak their paws. They're just happy to be here. It's more than a half mile to the water, and there's no ocean view, but dogs don't care about that either. There's a restaurant on the premises, but no pooches there, please. We think dogs do care about this, but you can always get a doggy bag. Rates are $190–250. 888 Country Club Road, Avalon, CA 90704; 310/510-0325; www.bestwestern.com.

Edgewater Beachfront Hotel: Any size dog is welcome to stay at this fun and funky harborside hotel. Carlton, a very cute cocker spaniel mix, is the official hotel greeter and can be found hanging out in the lobby most afternoons. Nothing makes you feel more at ease about bringing your dog to a hotel than having a friendly resident dog on hand. "It was like he was saying 'It's OK, come on in, we love dogs here!' when we visited," writes Jeannie, whose terrier, Smurfboy, felt utterly at home during his stay. (The people who run the hotel have this to say about Carlton: "Oh man, he owns us!")

The rooms are all different. Our favorite has a brick wall and a nautical theme, but there are big suites with Jacuzzi tubs and several other rooms to choose from. All rooms include dual-headed shower tubs, mini fridges, microwaves, and "electric" fireplaces (this just means there's no wood, but there is a flame). The ocean-view rooms are worth the higher price, if you don't get to view much ocean where you're from. Rates are $99–475. Dogs are $50 for the length of their stay. 415 Crescent Avenue, Avalon, CA 90704; 310/510-0347; www.edgewaterbeachfronthotel.com.

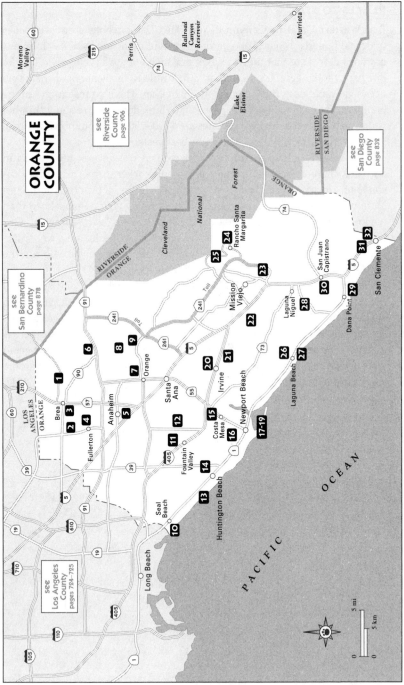

CHAPTER 53

Orange County

This is the amusement capital of America, and that's not an amusing thought to dogs. They're banned from such first-rate attractions as Disneyland and Knott's Berry Farm. But the county is also home to some dog-friendly places that just might put a grin on your pooch's rubbery lips and make a stay well worth his time.

The scent of money is unmistakable here—the land is some of the most expensive in the country. That ends up being a boon for dogs, since the communities can afford to support hundreds of parks.

Dogs are allowed at all county-run parks except wilderness parks. The only beaches that permit pooches are those of Huntington Beach, Newport Beach, and Laguna Beach. Huntington Beach's Dog Beach is a mile-long chunk of leash-free dog heaven, and a huge attraction for dogs of every spot and stripe. If you're visiting the area with your dog, he'll never forgive you if you don't stop here for a little sand and surf.

Orange County is now home to 11 dog parks which vary in nature from

PICK OF THE LITTER—ORANGE COUNTY

PRETTIEST NEW DOG PARK
Arbor Dog Park, Seal Beach (page 810)

BEST LEASH-FREE BEACH
Dog Beach, Huntington Beach (page 812)

LONGEST DOG PARK NAME
Sergeant Baron Von Willard Memorial Dog Playground,
San Clemente (page 830)

MOST SNOUT-LICKING-GOOD DOG MENU
Park Bench Cafe, Huntington Beach (page 814)

MOST WELCOMING RESTAURANTS
Britta's, Irvine (page 822)
Madison Square & Garden Cafe, Laguna Beach (page 826)

MOST DOG-FRIENDLY PLACES TO STAY
Sheraton Park Hotel, Anaheim (page 808)
Westin South Coast Plaza Hotel, Costa Mesa (page 816)
Fairmont Newport Beach, Newport Beach (page 820)
The Island Hotel, Newport Beach (page 820)
Casa Laguna Inn, Laguna Beach (page 827)
St. Regis Monarch Beach Resort & Spa, Dana Point (page 829)

BEST WATER ADVENTURES
Ferries and cruises, Newport Beach (page 818)

SWINGIN'EST POOCH POOL PARTY
Three Dog Bakery, Newport Beach (page 820)

spectacular to ho-hum. A few editions ago, there was nary a dog park, so even the ho-hum is terrific progress.

If you and your dog are salty sea dogs, make a beeline to Newport Beach's Balboa Pavilion. You can sail away with a few companies here. You won't go far— the shorter trip lasts three minutes, while the longer trip goes around the harbor for a couple of hours. But you will have a splashingly smashing good time.

NATIONAL FORESTS

The *National Forests and Wilderness Areas* resource at the back of this book has important information and safety tips on visiting national forests with your dog and has more information on the Cleveland National Forest.

Cleveland National Forest
🐾🐾🐾🐾🐕

Brea

PARKS, BEACHES, AND RECREATION AREAS

1 Carbon Canyon Regional Park
🐾🐾🐾 (See Orange County map on page 802)

This 124-acre park is nestled among the rolling foothills of the Chino Hill Range. It has the usual recreational facilities, including tennis courts, ball fields, and tot lots. But by far the favorite attraction for dogs and their people is a 10-acre grove of coastal redwoods near the Carbon Canyon Dam. Jake thinks I should mention that dogs can also check out the pepper trees, sycamores, eucalypti, and Canary Island pines. But be careful not to let the trails lead you into the adjacent Chino Hills State Park. Pooches are not permitted in most places there.

The entry fee here is $3 per car on weekdays, $5 on weekends, $7–10 on major holidays. Exit Highway 57 at Lambert Road and drive four miles east (Lambert becomes Carbon Canyon Road). The park entrance is one mile east of Valencia Avenue. 714/973-3170.

Fullerton

PARKS, BEACHES, AND RECREATION AREAS

2 Brea Dam Recreation Area
🐾🐾🐾 (See Orange County map on page 802)

Dogs love to cool their heels in the stream that winds through this 250-acre park. While there are plenty of trails throughout the park, not one runs by the stream for any significant length. But it's fairly open land with only occasional thick brush, so it's not too tough to get around.

For dogs who like trees (and what canine isn't an arborist at heart?), you'll find oaks and California bay laurel galore. When Joe Dog used to visit, he liked to picnic under a shady oak and sleep on his back, all four legs pointed straight up to the sky.

Enter at the Fullerton Tennis Center area, at Harbor Boulevard and Valencia Mesa Drive. 714/738-6300.

🔢 Craig Regional Park

😾😾😾 (See Orange County map on page 802)

This natural haven's undulating tiers of green slopes create an island of tranquility right next to the bordering Highway 57. A nature trail leads for 2.2 miles through the hills and flats of the park. Pick up a brochure at the ranger kiosk and learn about the multitude of plant and animal life that hides from civilization here.

For the humans in your crew, there are facilities for basketball, softball, volleyball, and racquetball. You can picnic with your pooch or have your dog help you watch your kids at the playground.

The parking fee is $3 per car on weekdays, $5 on weekends, $7–10 on major holidays. The entrance is on State College Boulevard, just south of Highway 90. 714/973-3170.

🔢 Fullerton Pooch Park

😾😾😾🐾 (See Orange County map on page 802)

The big eucalyptus trees that dot this dog park are a real boon on hot days, and lovely to behold. Boy dogs love 'em too. The park is nearly two acres, with three fenced sections. The largest is more than an acre, and it's for bigger dogs. The other two are for more petite pooches. One has wood chips, and the big dog area and the normal small-dog area has grass, which is struggling to survive under the stress of galloping paws.

The park is just a temporary park until the real deal gets approved and built, mostly likely by 2010. It has all the usual dog-park amenities, including benches and water. What we love about the park is that it's adjacent to the Hunt Branch Library, and the dog park community has been very involved in a program where kids read aloud to dogs. Hats off to you, Fullerton dogs and dog people.

The park is at 201 South Basque Avenue. It's at the very end of South Basque Avenue, just south of the railroad tracks, and north of Basque's intersection with West Valencia Drive. 714/738-6575.

PLACES TO STAY

Fullerton Marriott Hotel: If you and your pooch need to stay near California State University, Fullerton, this is the place for you. Rates are $179–209. Dogs pay a $35 cleaning fee for the length of their stay, plus a $100 deposit. 2701 East Nutwood Avenue 92631; 714/738-7800.

Anaheim

Anaheim is the home of the Disneyland Resort and is just a few miles from Knott's Berry Farm, Movieland Wax Museum, Medieval Times "dinner tournament," and Adventure City.

These attractions may be fun and laughs for humans, but they don't exactly make a dog howl with joy. "Who cares?" say the dogs. If humans were banned, you'd feel the same way.

If someone in your party is sick of Disneyland and has just come along for the ride, he can take the dog around while you play. Several dog-friendly parks make life a little easier for the canines among us.

Otherwise, if you go to Disneyland and don't have a dog-sitter, you can bring your dog to the Disneyland Kennel Club for the day. Rates are $20 per day (no dogs overnight). Bring your dog's favorite toy or blanket, and proof of rabies, distemper, and hepatitis vaccines (which seems like a lot of proof, but there you have it). The Kennel Club supplies food and water, but you can bring your own food if you prefer. You can take a break from Fantasyland, Tomorrowland, or any of the other happy lands and take your pooch for a leashed walk in the kennel's tiny exercise area (Poopland?) whenever you want. For details, call 714/781-7290.

PARKS, BEACHES, AND RECREATION AREAS

5 Boysen Park

🐾🐾 (See Orange County map on page 802)

Not only is this park attractive and green, it's also fairly close to Disneyland. Leashed dogs enjoy romping in the short grass, lounging under a big shade tree, and watching the kids ride in the faux rockets in the creative playground here.

From Harbor Boulevard around Disneyland, go north several blocks and turn right on Vermont Avenue. The park is on your right in about 1.5 miles. Park on the street, or turn right on State College Boulevard and make a quick right onto Wagner Avenue, which will take you to the parking lot. 714/765-5191.

6 Yorba Regional Park

🐾🐾🐾 (See Orange County map on page 802)

If you like suburban-style parks, this one's for you. There are tot lots, ball fields, and plenty of picnic areas in this 166-acre park. You can also fish at the little lakes and connecting streams or ride your bike or hike around the trails here.

The park can get very crowded, so try to visit on a weekday. Dogs must be leashed. The parking fee is $3 per car weekdays, $5 weekends, $7–10 on major holidays. From Highway 91 in the far east reaches of Anaheim, exit at Weir Canyon Road/Yorba Linda Boulevard, drive north to La Palma Avenue, and follow the signs. 714/973-6615.

PLACES TO STAY

Many of Anaheim's zillion or so hotels now permit pooches. Don't be tempted to leave your dog in your room when you go out to play for the day. It's not good for your dog, your room, or any unsuspecting housekeepers. Disneyland's kennel is a decent option and a good deal ($20 per day) if you're doing the Disney scene; 714/781-7290.

We don't go into much detail on the hotels here because there are so many. We'd rather give you a wide selection in this area, since rooms here can be scarce at busy times. Every hotel below has a pool, which is nice for humans but makes water dogs ache with desire.

Anaheim Plaza Hotel & Suites: Rates are $79–199. Dogs are $10 extra and must stay in a smoking room. 1700 South Harbor Boulevard 92802; 714/772-5900 or 800/622-6415.

Clarion Anaheim Resort: Rates are $69–199. Dogs pay $25 for the length of their stay. 616 Convention Way 92802; 714/750-3131; www.choice hotels.com.

Embassy Suites Hotel Anaheim North: This is one of the more attractive places to stay with a dog. The hotel's gardens, complete with waterfalls and koi pond, are a welcome relief from all the plasticized perfection of Disneyland. Rates are $129–229. Dogs are $50 extra per stay and must be under 50 pounds. 3100 East Frontera Street 92806; 714/632-1221.

Hilton Anaheim: This luxurious hotel allows dogs at its lovely rooms. Dogs must be under 50 pounds. Rates are $79–399. 777 Convention Way 92802; 714/750-4321 or 800/916-2221.

La Quinta Inn Anaheim: Rates are $99–179. 1752 South Clementine Street 92802; 714/635-5000.

Residence Inn by Marriott: You'll feel right at home in the comfy suites here. (And you won't be stuck eating Mickey Mouse–shaped pancakes. Each suite has a kitchen.) Rates are $139–450. Dogs pay a $75 fee. 1700 South Clementine Street 92802; 714/533-3555.

Sheraton Anaheim Hotel: If your dog has a long face because she can't go to Sleeping Beauty's castle in Disneyland, then stay here: This big, sprawling hotel on 13 acres has a castlelike look to it. (The lobby even features a huge stone fireplace.) Rates are $179–279. 900 South Disneyland Drive 92802; 714/778-1700; www.sheratonanaheim.com.

Sheraton Park Hotel: This one rates high with our dog readers, whose people love the pool, and whose dogs love the Sweet Sleeper pet bed, doggy bowls, and bag of goodies they get upon check-in. Dogs need to be under 40 pounds, and certain breeds aren't allowed. (Call for details.) Dogs must stay on the first floor, and they can peruse a grassy area on hotel grounds. Rates are $99–189. 1855 South Harbor Boulevard 92802; 714/750-1811.

Orange

PARKS, BEACHES, AND RECREATION AREAS

No dogs are permitted in any Orange city parks. Fortunately Orange has its very own dog park now, so dogs are no longer complaining about this archaic city rule.

7 Orange Dog Park

🐾🐾🐾🐕 (See Orange County map on page 802)

The City of Orange has long banned dogs from city parks, but at least now there's a place they can put their paws on a little dirt and grass. The big bonus here is that dogs can run leash-free as well. This two-acre dog park is a welcome respite for area dogs, who probably thought leashes were part of their bodies every minute they were outside their homes.

The park is grassy, but the turf has had issues of late and the ground cover is actually part-grass, part-dirt. It can get mighty dusty here in dry season, but with a little maintenance this could be remedied by the time you read this. A huge plus here is the shade from the big trees. It's very welcome on hot days. The park has a separate section for small dogs, and all the usual dog-park amenities, including water, benches, and poop-bag dispensers.

From Highway 55, take the East Chapman Avenue exit and drive east one long block to South Yorba Street (across from the Chapman Medical Center). Turn right on Yorba. Yorba Park (the park that houses Orange Dog Park) is immediately on your right, at 190 South Yorba Avenue. The dog park is in the southwest corner of Yorba Park. 714/744-7274.

8 Santiago Oaks Regional Park

🐾🐾🐾🐾 (See Orange County map on page 802)

This 350-acre wildlife reserve is dominated by majestic coast live oaks and California sycamores. Santiago Creek, the main tributary of the Santa Ana River in Orange County, runs through much of this park.

Dogs love it here, but they have to be leashed. Boy dogs seem to have a special fondness for the park, no doubt because there are thousands of ornamental trees on the north side of the creek.

Bring your binoculars. The wildlife-watching is terrific. More than 130 species of birds have been observed here. Coyotes, bobcats, and mountain lions have also been known to frequent the park. If you need any extra inspiration to keep your dog leashed, that should do the trick.

The parking fee is $3 per car on weekdays, $5 on weekends, $7–10 on major holidays. From Highway 55, take the Katella Avenue exit east about 4.5 miles to Windes Drive (Katella Avenue eventually becomes Santiago Canyon Road). Turn left on Windes Drive and follow its angular turns as it leads you north to the park entrance. 714/973-6620.

9 Irvine Regional Park

🐾🐾🐾🐾 (See Orange County map on page 802)

This 447-acre park is home to the Orange County Zoo, but since dogs aren't allowed at the zoo, they don't care much for it. They prefer to hike along the miles of equestrian and nature trails that run through the chaparral and forests of huge oaks and sycamores.

There's something for everyone here. You can rent a horse, a pony, a bicycle, or a paddleboat. You can walk by the creek, eat lunch at shaded picnic tables, play softball, throw horseshoes, or just do nothing and take a snooze with your dog under a big old tree. Dogs usually opt for the hike, the snooze, or both.

The parking fee is $3 per car weekdays, $5 on weekends, $7–10 on major holidays. If you walk in, there is no fee. From Highway 55, take the Chapman exit and head east for about five miles to the park entrance. 714/973-6835.

Seal Beach

This coastal city is the gateway to Orange County, and the home of the Seal Beach Naval Weapons Station, which makes up two-thirds of the land here.

PARKS, BEACHES, AND RECREATION AREAS

10 Arbor Dog Park

🐾🐾🐾🐾🐕 (See Orange County map on page 802)

This is one good-looking dog park. It's green and grassy, with mature trees that dole out shade. It's adjacent to the Navy Golf Course, which makes the area even greener. In the background are snow-capped Mt. Baldy and the San Bernardino mountains.

Dogs here are happy as can be, trotting around this spacious park's 2.2 acres, rolling in the grass, and enjoying the camaraderie of other happy, leash-free dogs. Small dogs have their own fenced area. The park also has water, poop bags, and benches. If watching all the dog action makes you thirsty, you can grab a soda from the vending machine just outside the park gate.

The park location is a little tricky to describe. It's just off Lampson Avenue, between Heather and Rose streets. Those two are small streets and hard to find, so most people around here describe the park as being halfway between Valley View Street and Los Alamitos Boulevard. The park is right behind the two-story WestEd building, which is at 4665 Lampson Avenue. 562/431-2527.

PLACES TO STAY

Pacific Inn: Dogs who are in the 35-pound range may stay at this 70-bedroom accommodation. (Management tells us there's definitely some wiggle room with the size constraints.) Some rooms are set up as suites; some have microwaves and mini fridges. The place has a decent little pool in an enclosed courtyard area, and a breakfast room where you can eat your complimentary morning meal. Rates are $130–175. Dogs are $75 per visit. 600 Marina Drive 90740; 866/466-0300; www.pacificinn-sb.com.

Fountain Valley

PARKS, BEACHES, AND RECREATION AREAS

11 Mile Square Regional Park

😊😊😊 (See Orange County map on page 802)

The park has many miles of scenic trails that leashed dogs love to explore. The trails go through 200 acres of grass, trees, and picnic areas. If your pooch is a sports enthusiast, take her to the fishing lakes, soccer fields, or ball fields. She's even permitted to watch from a suitable distance as folks in the large hobby area play with model rockets, remote-control airplanes, and model cars.

This is a welcome expanse of green for folks in the dense residential developments that surround the park. The parking fee is $3 per vehicle on weekdays, $5 on weekends, $7–10 on major holidays. The park is at Edinger Avenue and Euclid Street. There are entrances on both sides. 714/973-6600.

Santa Ana

It's refreshing to see that a few farm fields still thrive in the midst of this governmental center of Orange County. The downtown area is a charmer, but there's not much for a dog to do, unless he feels like soaking up history on a walking tour of the renovated district. Call the Orange County Historical Society at 714/543-8282 for information.

PARKS, BEACHES, AND RECREATION AREAS

12 Centennial Regional Park

😊😊😊 (See Orange County map on page 802)

If you want a real treat, get here early on a cool morning and watch the steam from the park's lake rising up through the surrounding willows. As the sun's rays turn the vapors a golden-orange hue, you'll swear you've never seen such a beautiful sight.

The sign on the lake says No Swimming, but the ducks just don't listen. You and your leashed dog should stay high and dry, though, no matter how tempting a little wade would be on a hot summer afternoon.

The park has many big green fields, most of which are sports fields. But if you visit during a nonathletic time, you'll just about have the whole place to yourself. Walkways run throughout the park, so you and your dog can cover lots of ground with ease.

The park's main entrance is at Centennial Park and Mohawk drives. 714/571-4200.

PLACES TO EAT

The Green Parrot Café: You and your dog will love eating and relaxing at this restaurant's enchanting Spanish-style courtyard, which features a fountain and even has ivy growing along the large arches. (Not the Golden Arches, thankfully.) The menu here changes frequently, but you're pretty much guaranteed excellent California bistro cuisine no matter what the chef is cooking that day. Thirsty dogs get a bowl of water. 2035 North Main Street; 714/550-6040.

PLACES TO STAY

Red Roof Inn: Rates are $55–70. 2600 North Main Street 92701; 714/542-0311.

Huntington Beach

Hey, dog dude! This is the surfing capital of the Orange coast. (It's known as Surf City USA,® complete with registered trademark.) And you're allowed off leash here! Dogabunga!

PARKS, BEACHES, AND RECREATION AREAS

⓭ Dog Beach

😸😸😸😸🐾 (See Orange County map on page 802)

This magnificent mile-long section of beach welcomes well-behaved dogs to run like the wind and splash in the surf—all without a leash. The beach gets about 100,000 dog visitors a year from all over the world. That's a lot of very happy pooches. (Some even speak only French, Italian, or Japanese.)

For a few scary years, dogs had been in danger of losing even their leashed pooch privileges here, because too many owners seemed to think their dogs had poop privileges. The poop on the beach was getting out of hand. The problem was actually that it was never getting *into* hand, or at least into poop bags.

A Dog Beach preservation group formed, started clean-up rallies and increased signage, as well as casual spot patrols for scofflaws, started bringing dogs back into good graces with the city. At various rallies, hundreds of people came to help scoop the poop. Newspapers and TV stations got the scoop and gave the group lots of coverage. "All my life I've done important things and haven't had a lot of public notice," says Huntington Dog Beach president Martin Senat, a dapper English gent. "All of a sudden I'm picking up dog feces and the world is watching."

To find out what you can do to help with Dog Beach, call 714/841-8644 or check out the Dog Beach website at www.dogbeach.org. This is a very active group, with fundraisers and fun items for sale to benefit beach maintenance.

Dog Beach is on the Pacific Coast Highway between 21st Street and Seaport Street. You'll recognize it by all the blissed-out dogs running around the golden sand and jumping into the ocean, and the blissed-out surfers behind them. Be sure to bring plenty of quarters, because the parking here is all meters. At a quarter for 10 minutes, an hour here will cost you $1.50. The phone number for more beach info is 714/536-5281.

14 Best Friend Dog Park

🐾🐾🐾🐾🐕 (See Orange County map on page 802)

Pooches here can let down their hair and run around like the dogs they were meant to be—happy and leash-free, sniffing anywhere they want to sniff without their people getting embarrassed. The dog park is two acres within 350-acre Central Park, with mulch ground cover (for mud-free romping), fledgling trees, running water, benches for people, poop-bag dispensers (they go through more than 52,000 bags a year!), and even an ocean breeze. You can see the ocean from parts of the park.

Small dogs love it here, because they have their own little fenced area. Of course, most small dogs think they're really huge dogs, so they don't need their own park. But for the more timid tiny pooch, this "park within a park within a park" offers a feeling of security.

There's even a Doggy Walk of Fame here. The sidewalk from the parking lot to the park's front gate is covered with more than 800 12-inch squares of cement on which dogs have impressed their own paw prints and people have written something about their dogs. Kind of a Grauman's Chinese Theatre of the canine world.

The dog park is in the west side of the park, on Edwards Street, a little north of Ellis Avenue and south of Slater Avenue. Call the Best Friend Park hotline for info on dog park activities: 714/536-5672.

Best Friend Dog Park is in the lovely 350-acre Central Park. Unless you visit the park on a sunny weekend day, it isn't hard to find a peaceful place where you can be away from people and just have a restful picnic with your favorite person, your favorite book, and your favorite dog. There are lots of trees, rolling hills, and all the natural settings dogs dig.

Central Park is divided in half by Golden West Road. It's almost as if there are two separate parks. Each half even has a truly wonderful restaurant chock-full of outdoor tables (read about and then visit Alice's Breakfast in the Park and the amazing Park Bench Cafe, a must-visit for dogs). Enter the east half of the park by heading east on the entry road, just across from Rio Vista Drive. The west half is accessible by driving west on Ellis Avenue. The dog park is on Edwards Street, at Talbert. 714/536-5431.

PLACES TO EAT

Alice's Breakfast in the Park: Many folks bring their dogs to this enchanting restaurant during a Sunday morning stroll. It's in the western half of Central Park, and it has plenty of outdoor tables. The cinnamon rolls are great. 6622 Lakeview Drive; 714/848-0690.

Hero's Pub: Dogs get treated like heroes here (not the edible kind, thankfully) and get water if they're thirsty and attention if it's not too busy. Dogs enjoy the grassy area outside, where they can dine with their humans. A server told us they're thinking about giving dogs some kind of extra-special treatment, but they hadn't figured out just what. 714 Adams Avenue; 714/536-1188.

Park Bench Cafe: This extremely dog-friendly eatery warrants a write-up in the *Los Angeles Times*. It deserves to be featured on NBC *Nightly News*. The BBC could even do a nice piece on it. In fact, these news organizations and many others have been drooling over this place since owner Mike Bartusick created a dog menu and added some picnic tables just for dogs and their people in 1994.

Now dogs can drool just like the media, thanks to some snout-watering culinary treats for dogs only. The motto here is "Every Dog Has His Day at the Park Bench Cafe." On weekends, the place is jammed with dogs having their days. "It's crazy busy," says Bartusick. "I love it." With Central Park's leash-free pooch park just a bone's throw away, this place is almost always hopping.

The Canine Cuisine menu items include the Hot Diggity Dog (a plain all-beef hot dog, sans bun, cut up in doggy-size bites), the Wrangler Roundup (a juicy lean turkey burger patty), and Anabelle's Treat (four chopped strips of bacon). As you can see, the dog menu is much like the human menu, only with the focus more on meat, less on accessories. All pooch items are served on disposable dishes, so don't worry about finding dog slobber on your plate when you're downing your own food here.

The Park Bench Cafe, located in the shade of pine trees at the edge of Central Park, has been a dog-friendly eatery for years. Thirsty canine cruisers were invariably offered a big bowl of water when their people stopped by for a bite during a long walk through this beautiful park. Bartusick saw that many of the people were also ordering food items for their pooches. "Eventually I thought, why not have a menu where dogs are as welcome as people?" he says. "It's very California, but, hey, what's wrong with that?"

The café is conveniently located at the entrance to the east side of Central Park. 17732 Golden West Street; 714/842-0775.

Pick Up Stix: The Chinese food here isn't exotic, but it's tasty and served by a friendly staff. Try the cream cheese wontons for something delightfully different. The restaurant shares outdoor tables with some other businesses, but the waitstaff is happy to serve you there if you just pop your head in and tell them you'd like outdoor tableside service. 5143 Warner Avenue; 714/840-0776.

PLACES TO STAY

Bolsa Chica State Beach: There's a small paved trail where you and your dog can go for a stroll. Sorry, pooches, but you can't set a paw on the beach itself. Fortunately, just down the sand a bit is Huntington's Dog Beach.

The state beach is on Highway 1, about three miles north of the main section of Huntington Beach. For information, call 714/846-3460. For reservations, phone 800/444-7275.

Extended Stay America: Three cheers for this all-studio-suites hotel! It's the first in Huntington Beach that allows dogs of a decent size. And it's convenient for dog people because you can cook your own meals here; each suite comes with a little kitchen. It keeps those restaurant bills down, too. Rates are $99–139. Dogs are $25 extra, not to exceed $75 per stay. 5050 Skylab West Circle 92647; 714/799-4887; www.extendedstayamerica.com.

Hilton Waterfront Beach Hotel: Dogs can only enjoy the Pacific views in the 290 well-appointed rooms here if they're under 20 pounds, so we'll keep the description short (kind of like the dogs who are allowed here). The park has tons of great recreational amenities, including a fabulous tropical-feel pool, a sand volleyball court, and lighted tennis court. Rates are $199–399. Dogs are $50 extra. (Yes, per day.) 21100 Pacific Coast Highway 92648; 714/845-8000; www.hilton.com.

Costa Mesa

PARKS, BEACHES, AND RECREATION AREAS

15 Costa Mesa Bark Park/TeWinkle Park Dog Run

🐾🐾🐾🐾🐾 (See Orange County map on page 802)

I met a woman who has trained her dog, Nadine, to go to the bathroom on command. The magic word is "Tinkle." It's not dignified, but it works just about every time. When she first took her dog to TeWinkle Park, a few people were talking about "TeWinkle," and sure enough, Nadine went tinkle just about every time.

Dogs can tinkle in TeWinkle, but they can also do plenty of other fun things. This 50-acre park has two acres fenced for dogs (with a separate area for smaller pooches), who cavort about the dog run sans leash for hours on end. It has all the usual dog park amenities, including water and a bit of shade from a few trees. The park is at Arlington Drive and Newport Boulevard. 714/754-5300.

PLACES TO EAT

Napa Valley Pizza and Pasta: Dine on tasty, basic pizzas and pastas with the doggy at the umbrella-topped outdoor tables. We're not sure why the restaurant has "Napa Valley" in the name. There's not a hint of goat cheese on the

DIVERSION

Take Your Lab to The Lab: Dogs are welcome to cruise around with you as you peruse **The Lab Anti-Mall** in Costa Mesa. The Lab is kind of the flip-side of malls. It's mellow. It's artsy. It's cutting edge. It's a dog's kind of place. "You're never going to see as many people with tattoos and pierced body parts as you'll see here," says Mary Bavry, who has frequented The Lab for years with her sweet dogs. "But dogs sure do feel welcome."

The stores are not what you'd find at the Fashion Island mall. The Lab has hipster and progressive clothing stores, edgy gift stores, and Dr. Freeclouds, a popular underground electronic music store. Many stores will let your pooch inside to shop with you. The **Gypsy Den** café permits pooches at its outside table.

The Lab is at 2930 North Bristol Street; 714/966-6660; www .thelab.com.

---

menu! Got a thirsty pooch? They'll give her a bowl of water. 2278 Newport Boulevard; 949/646-9399.

California Wrap & Grill: You can get just about anything in a wrap here, including steak and potatoes, Thai chicken and veggies, and salmon. Next on the menu should be the Dog Biscuit Wrap. Why not? Dogs are welcome at the 20 partly shaded outdoor tables and would love a wrap to call their own. 250 East 17th Street; 949/548-4403.

Gypsy Den Café: Located at the wonderfully different Lab Anti-Mall, the Gypsy Den serves up some great veggie food as well as "light carnivorous cuisine," as one employee puts it. Dine with your dog at the many outdoor tables, which come with heat lamps when needed. 2930 North Bristol Street; 714/549-7012.

Side Street Cafe: Want to dine on decadent, delectable food with your dear dog? Come to this café's four umbrella-topped tables for breakfast and order the stuffed French toast. "Cheapskates welcome," says a server. The prices are indeed good for what you get. 1799 Newport Boulevard; 949/650-1986.

PLACES TO STAY

La Quinta Motor Inn: Dogs must be under 25 pounds to stay here. Rates are $91–111. 1515 South Coast Drive 92626; 714/957-5841.

Westin South Coast Plaza Hotel: The rooms are spacious and well appointed, the beds are heavenly (truly—the Heavenly Bed is the cornerstone of the hotel's luxury comfort reputation), and the luxury amenities are top-rate. But what small-to-midsize model dogs (40 pounds or less is the rule here) dig most is that they get the royal treatment: Guest dogs receive treats upon check-in, plus use of dog bowls and the pooch equivalent of the Heavenly Bed: the Heavenly Dog Bed. After a restful night on the king of dog beds, your dog can stretch his gams at a park across the street. Rates are $139–309. 686 Anton Boulevard 92626; 714/540-2500; www.westin.com.

Newport Beach and Corona del Mar

If your dog enjoys the water-dog lifestyle, he's sure to love Newport Beach. Between the beaches, bays, and boats, many watery adventures await any dog who doesn't get seasick while watching you fill the bathtub.

The city encompasses several communities, including Balboa Island, Corona del Mar, and Mariners Mile. Balboa Island has its own section in this chapter.

PARKS, BEACHES, AND RECREATION AREAS

16 Upper Newport Bay Regional Park
🐾🐾🐾 (See Orange County map on page 802)

Upper Newport Bay is surrounded by shopping centers and suburban sprawl, but fortunately, this large park preserves the remaining sanctity of the once-pristine bayside. The myriad dirt trails in this open, hilly area provide you and your leashed dog with a great way to get around. Dog footprints are embedded in the trails—evidence of happy pooches on muddy days.

The park is made up of tall grasses and twiggy weeds. No trees get in the way of the bird-watching here. Bring your binoculars and try to ignore the

---

DIVERSION

Go Island Shopping: Dogs are a normal part of the scene at **Fashion Island,** Newport Beach's huge open-air shopping mall. There's plenty of walking room and even some grassy areas where your dog can rest her weary paws. Some of the mall's 200 stores permit pooches inside, but since they do it on a case-by-case basis, we'll let you explore for yourself. (FYI, should you be looking for lingerie, Victoria's Secret allows any well-behaved dog. "We've had our share of mishaps, but we still welcome dogs here," says a manager.)

Be sure to stop by the concierge desk with your dog. Most concierge staff love dogs and will supply your dog with a treat. As an added bonus, the mall is just a bone's throw away from Upper Newport Bay Regional Park, a great place to drop after you shop. Fashion Island is on the Pacific Coast Highway (Highway 1), between Jamboree Road and MacArthur Boulevard (Veterans Memorial Highway); 949/721-2000.

DIVERSION

A Three-Minute Tour: The historic **Balboa Pavilion/Balboa Fun Zone** in Newport Beach is where you and your dog can embark on nautical adventures on two unique boat lines. This is one of our favorite places to go with pooches because they're so welcome on these vessels. It's easy for your dog to feel like one of the family here. Best of all, pooches go for free on both excursions.

The smaller of these boats is the **Balboa Island Ferry,** which is open-hulled and fits only three cars and a few passengers at a time. The trip from Newport Beach to lovely Balboa Island takes only a few minutes, but it's a good way to test if your dog is up for a longer journey on the other dog-friendly boat line here. Fees range from $1 for a walk-on passenger to $2 for a car and passenger. The ferries run every few minutes during daylight hours.

Dogs with a more nautical bent can join you for a howling good time on a cruise of Newport Harbor—one of the nation's finest yacht harbors. The **Fun Zone Boat Company** offers a couple of grand tours. On one, you'll see the homes and yachts of celebrities and learn the history of the area. On the other tour, you'll cruise up to the haunts of the vocal, local sea lions. "The sea lions are fascinated by the dogs, and the dogs are fascinated by the sea lions," says Captain Mike. "It's quite a sight." Each tour is 45 minutes long and costs $14 per adult and $7 per child. Or take a 90-minute tour that combines both of the shorter jaunts. It costs $17 per adult and $7 per child. 949/673-0240; www.funzoneboats.com.

tall office buildings in the distance. You can also do some excellent, up-close bird-watching from Back Bay Road, on the east side of the bay. But it's easier to get to the regional park section, and it's less stress for the birds if you keep your dog far from them. The poor birds have enough on their minds with the onward march of malls and suburban subdivisions.

Traveling north on Irvine Avenue, turn right on University Drive. About the equivalent of a block down the road, turn around and park on the other side of the street (there's no parking on the south side), then walk back across the street and to the park entrance. 949/923-2290.

🐾 Balboa Beach

🐾🐾🐾 (See Orange County map on page 802)

Balboa Beach is wide and sandy enough for a dog to forget that it's a dog's life. The only reminders here are the mandatory leash attire and the restricted dog-access hours. Dogs are permitted year-round these days (a big improvement over the previous ban on dogs in summer), 6–9 A.M. and after 5 P.M.

The beach runs from around Main Street to the West Jetty area. You can enter the beach at the ends of many of the streets. 949/644-3717.

18 Corona del Mar State Beach

🐾🐾🐾 (See Orange County map on page 802)

Fear not! Although this is a state beach, dogs are permitted to peruse the place. That's because the city of Newport Beach maintains it and makes most of the rules. Dogs can sample the sandy life daily 6–9 A.M. and after 5 P.M.

If you happen to be east of the eastern jetty at the entrance to Newport Harbor, you'll be happy to know that this large and popular beach also permits leashed pooches. The beach starts at the eastern jetty at the entrance to Newport Harbor. 949/644-3717.

19 Newport Beach

🐾🐾🐾 (See Orange County map on page 802)

This beach starts out quite narrow at the northern border of Newport Beach and widens as it continues south to around Main Street. You'll have fun watching the surfers surf and the sun worshippers sizzle to a golden brown.

The only problem is that during the times when dogs are allowed, there's not a whole lot of sun to worship. Dogs, who must be leashed, can enjoy the beach 6–9 A.M. and after 5 P.M. daily.

Many dogs, including Jake, enjoy hanging out by the pier area and grabbing a bite from the nearby restaurants. Your dog will, too. (Jake asked me to write that on behalf of his pooch friends in the area.) 949/644-3717.

PLACES TO EAT

Alta Coffee: The large gazebo outside the restaurant is a terrific place for you and your pooch to sip the great coffee and dine on the café's tasty soups, pastas, and pastries. In fact, the gazebo is packed with lucky dogs every weekend, according to a manager. We've also heard it's a great place to sniff out potential romance (with your dog first introducing you to someone else's dog, and then, of course, the dog's person). If your dog is thirsting for something more quenching than love, a bowl of water will be provided on request. 506 31st Street; 949/675-0233.

Bluewater Grill Seafood Restaurant & Oyster Bar: Dine with your salty dog at this classic New England–style seafood house on the waterfront. The mesquite-charbroiled seafood is truly droolworthy. Your dog can join you at the patio tables, and if she's thirsty, she'll get a bowl of water. 630 Lido Park Drive; 949/675-3474.

Pacific Whey: The salads are nice, the fruits and oatmeals and organic nummies are tasty, but where this restaurant really excels is in the down-home

DIVERSION

Swimwear Optional: Visit the **Three Dog Bakery,** and you may find dogs in bathing suits (or naked—gasp!). Or they may be wearing board shorts. Or wacky Halloween costumes. Anything is possible. The bakery's owner, Sandy, and her Labs Storm and Jag, think up all kinds of fun events for their dog customers. Pool parties (three wading pools in the parking lot, a pet psychic, and a toenail-painting groomer were among the attractions at a recent pool party attended by 200 dogs), luaus, and various seasonal parties are the norm here. And now, once a month, the bakery is home to a pet adoption fair. On the best day so far, 21 lucky dogs and cats and an iguana found new homes.

The fresh-baked dog goodies at this bakery are so good, and the service so doggone dog friendly (read: they get a free treat), that dogs have been known to tear into here, leaving their people scratching their own heads about the location of their canine. The bakery is in Newport Beach's upscale Corona del Mar Plaza, 924 Avocado Street; 949/760-3647.

comfort food department. The chicken potpie is fabulously droolworthy, and Jake would like to suggest the filet mignon over biscuits (topped with red wine mushroom sauce) and the meatloaf with mushroom gravy. Dogs are welcome at the outdoor tables at both Newport locations: Crystal Cove Promenade, 7962 East Coast Highway, 949/715-2200; and Newport Hills Shopping Center, 2622 San Miguel Drive, 949/644-0303.

PLACES TO STAY

Fairmont Newport Beach: The hotel was recently vastly overhauled to the tune of $32 million, and with this incredible transformation came another: Dogs "up to golden retriever size" are welcome! In its previous incarnation as Sutton Place, dogs had to be 25 pounds or lighter. This is a thrilling improvement as far as dogs are concerned—beyond all the architectural redesign and upgraded rooms.

The 440-room hotel is luxury all the way, from the über-nice bedding to the big, beautiful spa. The design and decor are thoroughly modern, but also very comfortable. "Yada, yada," your dog is probably saying. "What about us dogs?" Well, lucky dogs who stay here get some treats (when available), doggy bowls, and smaller canines even get use of a pet bed. Dogs can peruse the pretty, green grounds, too. Rates are $149–399. Dogs are $25 extra. 4500 MacArthur Boulevard 92660; 949/476-2001; www.fairmont.com/newportbeach.

The Island Hotel: This glorious five-diamond hotel rolls out the plush red carpet for dog guests, who must be under 25 pounds: They get a little welcome card when they arrive and receive doggy biscuits and bowls. This sumptuous 295-room hotel is a breathtakingly luxurious urban oasis for humans (the motto here is "Where you are the center of attention"), but since the size limit rules out most dogs reading this book, we won't devote more space to the details. If you want to stay with your dog in luxurious accommodations with spectacular views of Balboa and Catalina, you can find out more at www.theislandhotel.com.

Rates are $225–499, with suites ranging up to $5,000. Dogs are $100 per stay. 690 Newport Center Drive 92660; 949/759-0808.

Irvine

PARKS, BEACHES, AND RECREATION AREAS

20 Central Bark

🐾🐾🐾🐾🐕 (See Orange County map on page 802)

With a whopping three acres of off-leash romping room, Central Bark is one of the largest dog parks in Southern California. It's a big fenced field with a smaller fenced area for small or shy dogs. There's not much in the way of trees here, but in the summer people bring a tarp and canopies for shade.

Central Bark is a very popular spot, and it includes all the dog-park accoutrements, including doggy fountains, lights, poop bags, and even faux fire hydrants. If your dog isn't the only one who has to lift a leg while you're at the park, you'll be happy to know that restrooms are available for humans, too.

The park is open every day except Wednesday, when it's closed for maintenance. It can get mucky and muddy here in the rainy months, and if it's bad enough, the park will close for the day or a few days. If in doubt, phone 949/724-MUDD (949/724-6833) for updates on park closures. The park is at 6405 Oak Canyon, one driveway past the Irvine Animal Care Center. 949/724-7740.

21 William R. Mason Regional Park

🐾🐾🐾 (See Orange County map on page 802)

If you're a local University of California dog and you need to get away from campus for a few hours, tell your owner about this county park. Three miles of hiking and biking trails wind through the park's eastern wilderness. It's a great escape from the urban realities lurking just outside the park's perimeter.

The park has the usual human recreational facilities, as well as one unusual one: a Frisbee golf course. It's a good thing dogs have to be leashed, or it would be pure, unbridled, ecstatic mayhem among the retrieving pooches here.

The parking fee is $3 per car on weekdays, $5 on weekends, $7–10 on major holidays. You don't have to pay a thing if you walk in. The park is at University and Culver Drives. 949/923-2220.

PLACES TO EAT

Britta's: Interestingly, we have a Brittany spaniel to thank for telling us about this super-dog-friendly spot. "My mom thought maybe it was named after me. You know, Britta-Brittany?" writes Brenda, an alliterating Brittany who adores Britta's. Dogs who visit Britta's partly shaded patio get pooch biscuits, and if thirsty, water. People who come here get delectable, seasonally inspired cuisine. 4237 Campus Drive; 949/509-1211.

Champagne French Bakery Cafe: The quiches, croissant sandwiches, French onion soup, and salad Niçoise are delectably Franco-American (not in the Uh-Oh SpaghettiO sense), but you'll also find a big variety of non-French foods here. If you're in the mood for a decadent pastry, look no further. The sweets are divine. Thirsty dogs get water when you dine at the patio. The café is at Woodbridge Center, at 4628 Barranca Parkway; 949/653-6828.

PLACES TO STAY

Candlewood Suites: If your dog needs plenty of room, the spacious suites here will fill the bill. There's even a walking trail around the hotel's property. This is an all-suites lodging, and rooms come with kitchens. That's handy when traveling with a dog. Rates are $130–210. Dogs must be under 70 pounds and are $75 extra for a stay of up to six nights, and $150 extra for more than that. 16150 Sand Canyon Avenue 92618; 949/788-0500 or 800/946-6200; www.candlewoodsuites.com.

Hilton Irvine/Orange County Airport: Rates at this attractive hotel are $119–309. Dogs are $50 extra per visit. 18800 MacArthur Boulevard 92612; 949/833-9999.

La Quinta Inn: Some of the rooms here are architecturally fascinating—one of the buildings used to be a lima bean silo! Really. You must see this place for yourself. Rates are $119–139. 14972 Sand Canyon Avenue 92718; 949/551-0909.

Laguna Woods

PARKS, BEACHES, AND RECREATION AREAS

🐾 Laguna Woods Dog Park

🐾🐾🐾 🐕 (See Orange County map on page 802)

This is a pretty little dog park with some shade trees (hey, it's Laguna Woods, after all) that provide welcome relief from the summer sun. Dogs are provided with water and poop bags. The list of rules on the park's website says that dog tags must be "worm and visible," which I hope is a typo.

If your big dog is a morning dog, you'll have to take her elsewhere for her early constitutional: The park is open only to small dogs 8 A.M.–1 P.M. Small and large dogs can run about here 1–7 P.M. The park is on Ridge Route between Moulton Parkway and Avenida de Carlotta. 949/452-0600 or 949/639-0500.

Mission Viejo

PARKS, BEACHES, AND RECREATION AREAS

23 Wilderness Glen Park

😊😊😊 (See Orange County map on page 802)

At certain times of year, a creek rushes through this narrow, two-mile-long wooded park and provides a refreshing escape from the surrounding suburbs. This is a hidden, unmarked park that most people just drive past without realizing it's there. It's in a narrow canyon, surrounded by lush foliage. A trail follows the creek, so you and your leashed dog can have a waterside sojourn. You can even dip all your feet in the water to cool off on a warm afternoon.

The park is bordered by Los Alisos Boulevard on the east side. You can enter the park at many points by turning left on any street that runs into the park. Our favorite is Via Noveno. Park around Atomo Drive and walk down the wooden stairs into the park. 949/470-3000.

24 O'Neill Regional Park

😊😊😊😊 (See Orange County map on page 802)

So close to suburbia, and yet so far, this is the paws-down favorite Orange County park for dogs who like wilderness. Dogs are not permitted in the county's true wilderness parks, but for some reason, this 1,700-acre piece of lush land doesn't fall into that category.

Dogs love to hike along the 6.5 miles of trails that go past streamside oak and sycamore woodlands. They have to be leashed, which is something the mountain lions here don't appreciate. Besides the woodlands, you can peruse grassy meadows and shrub-covered hillsides. And if you're in a hungry mood, the area near the entryway has plenty of picnic tables. You supply the food and the park will supply the ambience.

Camping is available along the creek and in the higher elevation Mesa Camp area. There are 90 campsites, all first-come, first-served. Fees are $13–15. Camping pooches are $2 extra. If you're just here for the day, you'll be charged a parking fee of $3 per car on weekdays, $5 on weekends, $7–10 on major holidays.

Follow El Toro Road (in the city's northernmost reaches) northeast. It eventually turns into Live Oak Canyon Road and veers to the south. About three miles past where the road changes names, you'll come to the park's main entrance. It's just south of the Rama Krishna Monastery, on the right side of the road. 949/923-2260.

Rancho Santa Margarita

PARKS, BEACHES, AND RECREATION AREAS

25 Rancho Santa Margarita Dog Park

🐾🐾🐕 (See Orange County map on page 802)

It's amazing just how much you can squeeze onto a half acre. This diminutive pooch park contains a section for large dogs, a section for small dogs, and a separate gated section where they can drink water after sniffing around the park. It's all a bit on the miniature side, but dogs who visit seem to enjoy themselves.

The tiny park has a wood-chip ground cover, and all the usual dog-park amenities, from poop bags to the water fountain. A shade structure helps keep things cool. The park is within Canada Vista Park, at 24328 Antonio Parkway, east of O'Neill Regional Park. 949/635-1800.

Balboa Island

This small Newport Harbor island is a bayfront wonderland. You can drive here from the mainland, but dogs prefer to take the ferry from Newport Beach. The island isn't exactly replete with big parks, but dogs enjoy strolling down Bayfront to the Grand Canal and back. When you've worked up a big hunger, head for the dog-friendly Park Avenue Cafe, not far away.

PLACES TO EAT

Park Avenue Cafe: Dogs are welcome to dine at one of the two tree-shaded patios with you, and boy do they like it here. It may have something to do with the thick steaks, steaming racks of lamb, and other assorted goodies. (Just a hunch.) 501 Park Avenue; 949/673-3830.

Wilma's Patio: This homey, attractive family restaurant is beloved for its breakfasts. You and your happy pooch will drool over the Balboa Belly Bomber, a warm French roll stuffed with an egg. ("This woman bought herself one and her dog one the other day," a server told us. "The dog ate his in, like, five seconds.") Dogs can't actually eat at the namesake patio at Wilma's Patio, but they can join you for a meal at the two shaded front tables. 203 Marine Avenue; 949/675-5542.

PLACES TO STAY

Balboa Inn: Got a little dog who doesn't mind if you fork over $50 per night for him to stay with you? Then this Spanish-style inn right on the sands of Balboa is a fine choice. The main building was born in 1929, but a new addition offers a bit more luxury and comfort, with ocean-view balconies, Jacuzzi tubs, and plush robes. Boy dogs enjoy the palm trees. Rates are $139–469. Dogs, as stated above, are $50 extra nightly. 105 Main Street 92661; 949/675-3412 or 877/BALBOA-9; www.balboainn.com.

Laguna Beach

Exclusive but friendly, Laguna Beach has an unmistakable Mediterranean feel, thanks to the mild seaside climate and all the fine art galleries and outdoor cafés. Dogs are happy here, especially because of a fine dog park.

PARKS, BEACHES, AND RECREATION AREAS

26 Laguna Canyon Dog Park
🐾🐾🐾🐾🐕 (See Orange County map on page 802)

People come from many miles away to take their dogs to this large dog park in the canyon. During pooch rush hour, it's not uncommon to see dozens of leashless, grinning dogs running and tumbling around in great joy.

Although there's no shade, there's plenty of doggy drinking water. Picnic tables add a dimension of comfort for the park's humans.

The park has to close periodically because of the danger of mudslides, so if you're traveling a long way to get here, call the city first to check on the situation. In addition, the park is closed Wednesdays for maintenance.

From Highway 1, go north on Broadway/Laguna Canyon Road. The park will be on your right in 2.6 miles, just before the GTE building. 949/497-0706.

27 Laguna Beach Beaches
🐾🐾🐾 (See Orange County map on page 802)

Leashed dogs can peruse the beaches, but June–mid-September, their visiting times are limited. During that period, pooches aren't allowed on the beach 8 A.M.–6 P.M.

Main Beach is a long, sandy beach with a playground and basketball courts in downtown Laguna. A good entry point is at Pacific Coast Highway and Broadway/Highway 133. If you want to get away from people, you may be better off at any of the pocket beaches dotting the city's coast. There are also several small, rocky pocket beaches you can reach via walkways off Cliff Drive. 949/497-0706.

PLACES TO EAT

Eva's—A Caribbean Kitchen: Good Caribbean food can be hard to find on this coast. Eva's has great food and a very dog-friendly attitude. It's a real gem. The food is outstanding, from the Callaloo soup to the jerks and curries and blackened fishes and meats. The Caribbean-inspired desserts are worth saving room for. Try the West Indian Key Lime Pie. Jake and I are drooling just thinking about it.

Eva loves dogs. Her own rat terrier, Elvis, sometimes pays a visit to the outdoor tables "when he feels like coming to the restaurant," she says. Dogs are welcome to dine with you at the umbrella-topped tables outside, but if you have a medium to large dog, please call ahead and let them know. It can get crowded here, and they'll do their best to save you a table with a little legroom. 1350 South Coast Highway; 949/376-1995.

Madison Square & Garden Cafe: John Madison, vivacious owner of this delightful garden café, is mad about dogs. So mad, he says, that "I built this place for dogs because I love animals. I would have 100 dogs if I could." Instead of owning them himself, however, he invites customers to bring their dogs. "If the dogs could come in with their own credit cards, I wouldn't need the people," he jokes. (He knows most dogs don't have good enough credit ratings to qualify for cards.)

The restaurant is totally dog friendly. No one needs to go inside the quaint old house where the kitchen is located. To order, you simply step up to the window, order, get a number, go to the tables in the gorgeously landscaped backyard, and await the food. The garden has oodles of tables and lots of plants and trees and prettiness. If it's cold, fear not: Many heaters are on hand.

Dogs who come here gets gobs of attention from John (if he's here, which he

often is), as well as water and dog treats. John doles out several pounds of treats a week and even has duck and rice treats for allergic dogs. Dogs revere this man.

Human customers enjoy the tasty, simple breakfasts and lunches. (No dinner here.) Menu headings like "Good Eggs, and Eggs That Must be Whipped," "Good Witch, Bad Witch… Sandwich!" and "Grill Me All You Want… I'll Never Tell" hint at John's quirky sense of humor. A couple of breakfast items really stand out: the rich ricotta pancakes and the cinnamon swirl French toast.

A big thank-you to Tiffany and Max, the clever cocker spaniels who originally wrote to tell us about this place. The café is at 320 North Coast Highway; 949/494-0137.

PLACES TO STAY

Carriage House: Only the most well-behaved dogs are welcome here, and only if you call ahead of time and get the OK. After all, it's not every day a dog gets to stay in a 1920s bed-and-breakfast that's a historic landmark. You'll get a carafe of wine, some fresh fruit, and other taste treats when you check in. The courtyard here is lovely and relaxing, but no leg lifts, please. Rates are $150–195. Dogs are $10 extra. The friendly folks here will help you arrange a pet-sitter if you find yourself in need of some pooch-free time. 1322 Catalina Street 92651; 949/494-8945 or 888/335-8945; www.carriagehouse.com.

Casa Laguna Inn: The Casa Laguna is an enchanting, romantic Spanish-style bed-and-breakfast that overlooks the mighty Pacific Ocean. Its 15 rooms, four suites, Mission House, and charming cottage are set on a terraced hillside. Surrounding the lodgings are luscious tropical gardens that include such goodies as banana and avocado trees and bougainvillea. Well-behaved dogs and their people love to relax on the aviary patio, beneath a family of glorious queen palms.

There are many little nooks and gardens to discover at the Casa Laguna, and your dog will enjoy helping you find them all. As the day ends, watch the sun set over Catalina Island.

Dog guests feel very welcome here: Upon check-in they get a doggy food bowl and a water bowl, some pooch treats, and a list of nearby dog-friendly parks. Rates are $250–590 and include an extensive buffet breakfast and afternoon wine with hors d'oeuvres. Dogs are $25 extra. 2510 South Coast Highway 92651; 949/494-2996 or 800/233-0449; www.casalaguna.com.

Vacation Village: Dogs love staying at this vacation oasis, because they're allowed on the beach, which is right behind the hotel. Leashed pooches can peruse the beach here anytime it's open to dogs (before 8 A.M. and after 6 P.M. June–mid-September). Humans like the fact that there's full beach service, complete with towels and lounge chairs. Usually, however, sunbathing and dogs don't mix. The hotel's restricted dog times (they're not allowed in from the last week of June through Labor Day) certainly decrease the temptation to get tan with your dog.

If you (the human in your party) want to swim but find the surf a bit rough, the hotel has two pools for your paddling pleasure.

Rates are $99–389. There's a $50 pooch fee per visit. 647 South Coast Highway 92651; 949/494-8566 or 800/843-6895; www.vacationvillage.com.

Laguna Niguel

PARKS, BEACHES, AND RECREATION AREAS

28 Pooch Park

🐾 🐾 🐾 🐕 (See Orange County map on page 802)

It's only a bit over one acre, and it has only three small trees, but to dogs who long to run unfettered by a leash, this fenced park is poochy paradise.

Pooch Park is gobs of fun for dogs on the go. It's at the top of a canyon, and it's got the coolest dog-watering area yet. If your dog is Lassie, or a Lassie wannabe, she can press a lever with her paw and drink the water as it streams several inches into the air. Or she can let the water fill a strategically placed water bowl. Of course, if she's like Joe Dog was, she can accidentally step on the paw-activated fountain, get splashed in the face, and have the heebie-jeebies for the rest of the afternoon.

No longer grassy, the park is filled with wood chips. It can be a little tough on tender paws, but it's easier to maintain than grass, and it's not as splintery as it sounds. Humans enjoy the shaded sitting areas under attractive canopies and sun umbrellas on hot days. Dogs do, too.

The park is on the west side of Street of the Golden Lantern, between Beacon Hill Way and Chapparosa Park Road (closer to Beacon Hill Way). My faithful correspondent "Three-Dog Dave" Hepperly tells me there are now signs stating Dog Park Parking, which make the entrance easier to find than it used to be. 949/362-4300.

Dana Point

PARKS, BEACHES, AND RECREATION AREAS

Dogs are not allowed in any beaches here or at any Dana Point city park. The city's adventure-loving namesake, Richard Henry Dana Jr., who wrote the high-seas novel *Two Years Before the Mast*, probably wouldn't have liked Dana Point's attitude. But he's been dead for more than a century, so there's little he can do about it.

29 Lantern Bay Park

🐾 🐾 🐾 (See Orange County map on page 802)

Since this is a county park, pooches are permitted. It's a beautiful stretch of grass and trees set high above the ocean. Paved walkways meander throughout and there are picnic tables galore. Leashed dogs love to sniff the sea breezes and watch the gulls.

From Highway 1, turn toward the beach on Harbor Drive and make a right onto Lantern Street. 949/248-3530.

PLACES TO STAY

St. Regis Monarch Beach Resort & Spa: Oh, to drool for! This five-diamond ultra-luxury resort hotel has everything you could want in a sumptuous seaside vacation, from to-die-for rooms to a private beach club to pampering spa treatments. There's no size limit for humans, but alas, dog guests here are limited to 30 pounds. Little dogs get treated well here and are provided with a doggy bed, cute little dishes, and bone treats. Rates are not cheap, with rooms starting at $595. Dogs are $150 for the length of their stay. One Monarch Beach Resort 92629; 949/234-3200 or 800/722-1543; www.stregismb.com.

San Juan Capistrano

The rebuilt version of the mission that was constructed by Father Junípero Serra in 1776 attracts some 300,000 visitors annually. Around March 19 every year, the swallows arrive from Argentina to nest in the valley. They used to flock to the mission, but with recent noisy renovations and hordes of visitors, they've taken to other parts of the valley. "They've gone to the suburbs, just like humans," says one docent.

Dogs aren't allowed on the grounds of the mission, but you can watch this annual migration from just about anywhere in town. It's not as dramatic as Alfred Hitchcock's *The Birds,* but it's still a great way to pass a lazy afternoon in one of the parks here.

PARKS, BEACHES, AND RECREATION AREAS

🐾 C. Russell Cook Park

🐾🐾🐾 (See Orange County map on page 802)

Big old trees line the perimeter of this park, where you and your leashed dog may choose to amble along the shaded path near the creek bed.

If your dog likes his paws to hit green grass with every step, hang out on the greenbelt area. You'll find ball fields and playgrounds, but you'll also find some open areas where you can get away from other folks.

The park is on Calle Arroyo and stretches for several blocks between Calle del Campo and Avenida Siega. 949/493-5911.

PLACES TO EAT

Cedar Creek Inn: You and your history-loving dog can dine at the lovely, big, tree-shaded patio that faces Mission San Juan Capistrano. The fresh fish is delicious, as are the house-made desserts. 26860 Ortega Highway; 949/240-2229.

PLACES TO STAY

Best Western Capistrano Inn: The hotel offers a complimentary breakfast to humans on weekdays. (Actually, it's a breakfast voucher for Denny's.) Rates are $70–149. Dogs are $25 extra. 27174 Ortega Highway 92675; 949/493-5661.

San Clemente

PARKS, BEACHES, AND RECREATION AREAS

31 Rancho San Clemente Ridgeline Trail

🐾🐾🐾 (See Orange County map on page 802)

The views from this three-mile trail are to drool for: At certain points you and your leashed dog can see the mighty Pacific, Catalina, and even some parts of San Diego. If you venture to the highest parts of the park (a 700-foot elevation), you can even see Los Angeles County, in all its smoggy splendor. You'll hike through brush and grass, with not much in the way of shade trees. Bring plenty of water.

Mountain bikes share the trail, so keep your eyes peeled and your leash ready to reel in your dog. There are several entrance points, including one at Avenida Salvador, from Avenida Presidio or East Avenida San Juan, and one at Calle Cordillera, off Calle Amanecer. If you happen to be going to the dog park and want to get a little exercise yourself, you can start at a fire road behind the dog park. 949/361-8278.

32 Sergeant Baron Von Willard Memorial Dog Playground

🐾🐾🐾🐕 (See Orange County map on page 802)

Residents of San Clemente should be glad there's just one dog park here. Now all they have to say is, "Coming to the dog park?" "Yeah, see you there!" But heaven forbid they have to differentiate dog parks and name this one. It's a mouthful. Will they call it Baron Playground? (Sounds empty and forlorn.) Will they call it the whole thing? I guess they'll cross that bridge when they come to it.

Sergeant Baron Von Willard was San Clemente's first K-9 police officer. The 130-pound black Alsatian German shepherd won many citations for outstanding, brave service and won the hearts of residents. The park is dedicated to this courageous beast, who is no longer with us. (It would have been easier on people here if his name were Ralph or Dave, but they're getting used to the name.)

The park is a respectable size, with two acres for the main part of the park, less for the section for little dogs. The bigger dog area has a surface of decomposed granite (they finally gave up on grass here), a shade structure, a few benches, water, and poop bags. The small-dog area is still grassy, those lucky little dogs! It's at Calle Extremo and Avenida La Pata; 949/361-8278 or 949/361-2264.

PLACES TO EAT

Antoine's Cafe: Dine on tasty French and American food (mostly American, with some Frenchish offerings like quiche) at several umbrella-topped sidewalk tables. Thirsty dogs get a bowl of water. 218 South El Camino Real; 949/492-1763.

Beach Garden Cafe: The views from the outdoor tables are gorgeous, and the breakfast and lunch fare is just as delectable. 6181/2 Avenida Victoria; 949/498-8145.

PLACES TO STAY

Holiday Inn San Clemente: If you're lucky, you might get a room with an ocean view here. Rates are $159–225. Dogs are $20 extra. 111 South Avenida de Estrella 92672; 949/361-3000.

Sea Horse Resort & Villa Del Mar: These two properties are super close to the Pacific, right off the San Clemente Pier. Choose from suites and studios. Many have panoramic ocean views. The decor isn't chic, but the places are comfortable and spacious and the views alone are worth the price of admission. Rates are $169–329. Dogs require a $100 deposit. (The real kind, that's actually refundable.) 602 Avenida Victoria 92672; 949/492-1720 or 949/498-5080; www.seahorsesanclemente.com or www.villasanclemente.com.

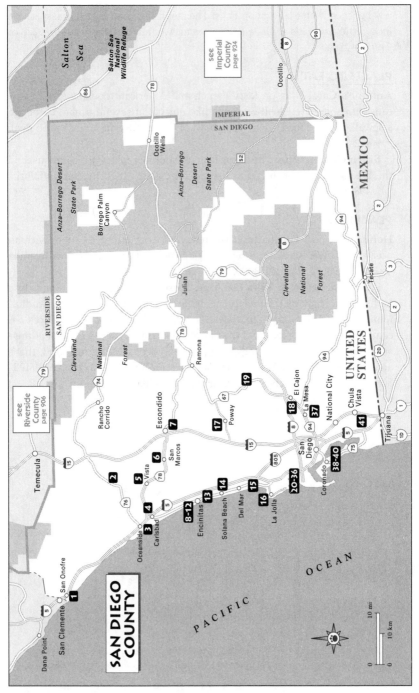

CHAPTER 54

San Diego County

Look at a map of the county and you'll see green blotches everywhere. But don't be fooled. Most of these verdant expanses are golf courses. Golf is the game of choice here, and since dogs don't play golf very well (their hair gets in their eyes), you can ignore all those areas.

But fear not: San Diego County isn't such a tough place for dogs. In fact, it's a great place for dogs. Most county-run parks permit them (although they're banned from trails at camping parks), but even better, several fabulous beaches and a couple dozen parks allow dogs to run in leash-free ecstasy. And there are so many dog-friendly restaurants and hotels, especially in the city of San Diego, that we could fill a book with them. My editor will not like this, so I won't.

The historic mining town of Julian, about 50 miles northeast of San Diego, is a great place to vacation with a pooch. If your dog is fond of apples, or if you're big on apple pie, visit during the fall: In October, more than 10,000 apple pies a week are baked here. If you don't visit, who's going to eat them? (It's a crusty problem.)

PICK OF THE LITTER—SAN DIEGO COUNTY

BEST LEASH-FREE HIKING
Elfin Forest Recreational Reserve, San Marcos (page 839)

BEST DOG BEACHES
Dog Beach, San Diego (page 854)
Fiesta Island, San Diego (page 855)
Coronado City Beach, Coronado (page 864)

BEST NEW DOG PARK
Rancho Bernardo Dog Park, San Diego (page 851)

BEST DOG AREA NEXT TO A
NUCLEAR POWER PLANT AND NUDE BEACH
San Onofre State Beach, San Onofre (page 836)

MOST DOG-FRIENDLY PLACES TO EAT
Stratford Court Cafe, Del Mar (page 843)
Froglander's Yogurt, La Jolla (page 845)
Point Loma Seafood, San Diego (page 859)
Terra, San Diego (page 859)
Cafe 1134, Coronado (page 866)
Market Cafe, Coronado (page 866)

The majority of the eastern half of the county is taken up by Anza-Borrego Desert State Park and Cleveland National Forest. The forest is heavenly for dogs. The 600,000-acre desert park, on the other hand, is a doggy drag. Pooches are permitted only in campgrounds and on roads. Granted, there are some dirt roads that aren't used much, but it's just not the same as hiking the trails here. And dogs are banned from walking on the desert itself.

Speaking of deserts, the coastal area from Oceanside all the way down to Cardiff is a virtual desert for dogs. They don't get to go near the water at all because beaches in this stretch ban the beasts.

Fortunately, once you get down to the Del Mar area, little bits of dog heaven pop up fairly frequently. You'll really hit pay dirt (pay sand?) when you venture onto San Diego's Dog Beach. Many adventures await you.

GREATEST
GOURMET GHETTO
Gaslamp Quarter eateries,
San Diego (pages 858-860)

MOST HIP
DOG-FRIENDLY
PLACE TO STAY
Hotel Solamar, San Diego
(page 861)

OTHER GREAT DOG-
FRIENDLY PLACES TO STAY
Pine Haven, Julian (page 847)
Westin Horton Plaza, San Diego (page 863)
Crown City Inn, Coronado (page 867)
Loews Coronado Bay Resort, Coronado (page 867)

BEST WAY TO PRETEND YOU'RE IN VENICE
A Gondola Company gondola ride, Coronado (page 865)

MOST DOG-FRIENDLY SHOPPING
(COMPLETE WITH COOL DOG PARK)
Otay Ranch Town Center, Chula Vista (page 868)

A special note: At press time, wildfires had devoured hundreds of thousands of acres of land in Southern California. San Diego County was the worst hit. Sadly, I can't guarantee all of the places in this chapter will be unscathed. I certainly hope so.

NATIONAL FORESTS

The *National Forests and Wilderness Areas* resource at the back of this book has important information and safety tips on visiting national forests with your dog and has more information on the Cleveland National Forest.

Cleveland National Forest
🐾🐾🐾🐾🐕

San Onofre

PARKS, BEACHES, AND RECREATION AREAS

1 San Onofre State Beach

🐾🐾🐾 (See San Diego County map on page 832)

This is one of the more dog-friendly state beaches we've come across. It can afford to be dog-friendly because it isn't exactly a coveted beach destination for most people: It's right next to the giant San Onofre Nuclear Power Plant. Ahhh, there's nothing like basking in some rays .... You just have to hope they're from the sun. Seriously, it's safe here, but it's not exactly Shangri-La. More on that later.

Unlike most state parks, this one actually allows dogs on a couple of trails. These wide trails lead from the 90-foot-high bluffs (where the campsites are) to the beach. Trail 1 and Trail 6, which bookend the three-mile-long campground, are the dog-friendly trails. Dogs must be leashed, but that's OK. They enjoy the adventure.

You'd probably find yourself using the trails only if you happen to be camping here. My ace correspondent "Three-Dog Dave" Hepperly first reported that camping here was a most interesting experience, and it wasn't exactly crowded. "There is a reason for this," he wrote. "1) People don't like to camp next to nuclear reactors. 2) The San Diego mainline Amtrak is about 100 feet away from the campsites, and 10 to 15 trains a day go by at 70 mph. 3) I-5 is about 200 to 300 feet away and there is a constant roar of big rigs. 4) Helicopters guarding the nuclear reactor fly by day and night." Still, Dave said he'd come back again and again because his dogs love the beach. And he has indeed been back. On his last trip, it was actually quite crowded. "The trail to the nude beach is jammed 'bun to bun,'" he wrote. Apparently you just never know what you'll find here.

About 500 feet of this beach is clothing-optional, by the way. (No wonder the Camp Pendleton choppers fly over so regularly.) The nude section is not far from the dog area, so watch out lest your dog end up sniffing out more than you bargained for.

Camping is $9–35. Call 800/444-7275 for reservations, even for the primitive sites. The day-use fee is $10 per vehicle. Exit I-5 at Basilone Road and turn south toward the ocean. Drive three miles, past the nuclear power plant. Basilone ends at the park entrance. For park info, phone 949/492-4872. If you're of the technical mindset and want to learn more about the nearby nuclear plant, go to www.nucleartourist.com and do a search for San Onofre.

Oceanside

PARKS, BEACHES, AND RECREATION AREAS

Dogs are banned from the city's beaches, as well as from the Oceanside Pier. Bummer, doggy surfer dudes. But you have the last laugh: There's now a dog park here!

2 Guajome Regional Park

🐾🐾🐾 (See San Diego County map on page 832)

Bring your binoculars and settle in for a day of bird-watching and hiking in one of the richest riparian areas in the county. Spring-fed lakes and a marsh are the centerpieces of this 569-acre park.

It's a little tricky to get around this place with a dog, because while there are miles of hiking trails, dogs aren't allowed on any of them. That's the general rule in San Diego County's camping parks and it's a doggy drag. But you can fish with your dog or picnic in the grassy hilltops here.

Humans like visiting the historic 22-room adobe ranch house on the park's eastern boundary. About 150 years ago, when this land was part of a vast Mexican land grant and the hub of the area's cultural life, the ranch house was the centerpiece of social activity.

Thirty-five campsites are available at $15–25 per site. Dogs are $2 extra. Some little cabins are available for $45. From I-5, take Mission Avenue east seven miles to Guajome Lakes Road, then south to the park's entrance. Call 858/565-3600 or toll-free 877/565-3600 for camping reservations. For park info, phone 760/724-4489.

3 Oceanside Dog Park

🐾🐾🐾🐾🐕 (See San Diego County map on page 832)

Despite that fact that the park is closed all April for yearly maintenance, and every Wednesday, Oceanside's dog park is a four-paw place to take a dog in need of leash-free exercise. (And what dog isn't in need of that?)

The fenced park was created on a beautifully landscaped hillside. The grass is lush and green, with decomposed granite walkways helping to keep it from being trampled too much by humans. A stately palm tree graces the entrance of one of the two sections (one section for large dogs, the other for petite pooches). The park has all the usual amenities, including water and benches. It's right next to the North County Humane Society, at 2905 San Luis Rey Road; 760/757-4357.

PLACES TO EAT

Beach Break Cafe: You and your dog can enjoy each other's company at the tables outside this daytime café. "Of course we allow dogs. We love them!" says a server. Dogs get free doggy bones here! (No need to break into their savings.) 1902 South Hill Street; 760/439-6355.

Carlsbad

It used to be that dogs weren't allowed in any city parks. Unfortunately, it's still that way, with one exception: a little off-leash park. If it were a little bigger, it would help put the "good" in Carlsbad. But for now, we'll have to just call it "CarlsOK." Some progressive park management people here are trying to make the parks more dog friendly. Then we can call it "Carlsgood." Phone 760/434-2826 for updates.

PARKS, BEACHES, AND RECREATION AREAS

⁴ Carlsbad Dog Park

🐾🐾🐕 (See San Diego County map on page 832)

This half-acre park is the only parkland dogs can visit in all of Carlsbad, since all other city parks ban poochies. So it's a pretty popular park, despite its size, and it smells decent for a dog park: The mulchy wood-chip ground cover is made from local eucalyptus trees, and it seems to absorb much of the dog-doo aroma. The park has some benches, scoop dispensers, water, and a little parking. It's in the northeast part of Carlsbad, on Carlsbad Village Drive, just east of El Camino. 760/434-2826.

PLACES TO EAT

Jay's Gourmet Restaurant: The locals know about this place and drool over it, and now you know, too. So drool! The pastas, pizzas, and Italian-style seafood are delicious. The attitude here is dog-friendly, with pooches who dine at the four outdoor tables getting lots of oohs and ahhhs and bowls of water from the staff. 2975 Carlsbad Boulevard; 760/720-9688.

Gregorio's: If you're in the mood for Italian food, this patio is for you (and your dog). Gregorio's even has handmade ravioli. If pasta makes your pooch thirsty, the servers will happily pour him a bowl of water. 300 Carlsbad Village Drive; 760/720-1132.

PLACES TO STAY

Quality Inn & Suites: This place overlooks the freeway, but the rooms are clean and comfy, and suites come with kitchenettes. That's handy when traveling with the pooch. Rates are $90–190. Dogs are $10 extra. 751 Raintree Drive 92009; 760/931-1185; www.innsofamerica.com.

South Carlsbad State Beach: Dogs aren't allowed on the beach here, but they're welcome to camp with you, even at the oceanside campground. There are 224 sites, with nightly fees of $20–35. For reservations, call 800/444-7275. For campground information, call 760/438-3143.

Vista

PARKS, BEACHES, AND RECREATION AREAS

5 South Buena Vista Park

🐾🐾🐾🐕 (See San Diego County map on page 832)

This pretty little neighborhood park is idyllically green, with maples shading the grassy areas and walkways you can peruse with your dog. Dogs are allowed to be off-leash here 7–9 A.M. and 4 P.M.–dusk. The rest of the time leashes are the law. You'll need to keep your dog out of the children's play area and basketball courts, but there's plenty of room to explore. Poop bags are provided, but if you want to water your dog, you'll have to bring a bowl and fill it at the human water fountain. The park is at 1851 South Melrose Drive. 760/726-1340.

San Marcos

PARKS, BEACHES, AND RECREATION AREAS

6 Elfin Forest Recreational Reserve

🐾🐾🐾🐾🐕 (See San Diego County map on page 832)

This 750-acre park is pure heaven for dogs and their people. It has 13 miles of trails that go past streams and little ponds, and through oak woodlands, riparian habitat, and coastal chaparral environs. Some points provide stunning mountain views to pant for.

Best of all, dogs may be off leash Monday through Friday at the top of the "Way Up" trail. You'll see the signs where it's OK to unclick your dog's leash and let her run like the wind. There used to be a lot more leash-free room at this park, but dogs are grateful to have this area.

The park is nestled between the communities of San Marcos, Del Dios, Escondido, and Carlsbad. Exit I-5 at Leucadia Boulevard, and drive east. It will turn into Rancho Santa Fe Road. Drive until you get to San Elijo, and go right. Go right again at Elfin Forest Road, which becomes Harmony Grove Road. Drive until you're between Mile Markers 6 and 6.5, and you'll be at the reserve. 760/632-4212.

Escondido

Dogs are banned from this city's parks. The only exception is an undeveloped service road in a section of Kit Carson Park, but it's generally just used by very local neighbors. Even the large Dixon Lake Recreation Area bans dogs, since it's operated by Escondido. Fortunately, the city has a place for dogs to romp, other than Escondido sidewalks: They have their very own park.

PARKS, BEACHES, AND RECREATION AREAS

7 Mayflower Dog Park/Escondido Dog Park

🐾🐾🐾🐕 (See San Diego County map on page 832)

Escondido dogs have a park they can set paw in, despite the city's ban on dogs in parks. And it's an off-leash one at that. Dogs love coming to this 1.5-acre grassy park. It has water, benches, fire hydrants, poop-bag stations, night lighting, and plenty of parking. It even has three different sections, so when one section gets worn down from the stampeding, it can take a breather while dogs gallop around another area. The third area is an agility course, should you have a dog who hankers for this kind of fun. A big thanks to Target and Marley, two marvelous English bulldogs, for sniffing out this park for us.

The park's address is 3420 Valley Center Road. It's between Washington Avenue and Lake Wohlford Road. 760/839-4691.

PLACES TO STAY

Castle Creek Inn Resort and Spa: This former Bavarian retreat has a cozy, quaint Hansel and Gretel feel—minus the cannibalistic witch. You and your dog can stay in one of 30 attractive suites here and you (the human, not the dog—sorry, pooch) can use the resort's tennis courts, pools, hot tub, and sauna and relax while luxuriating in one of many spa treatments. There's plenty of room to roam around the beautifully landscaped grounds with a leashed dog. Rates are $99–289. The higher price is for the inn's spacious three-bedroom villa. Dogs are $35 extra. 29850 Circle R Way 92026; 760/751-8787 or 800/253-5341; www.castlecreekinn.com.

Encinitas

Although this is the home of Paramahansa Yogananda's gold-domed Self Realization Fellowship Center, dogs are banned from Swami's Beach and all other municipal beaches. The beach that does allow dogs is a state beach in the charming Cardiff-by-the-Sea district of Encinitas.

Fortunately, most of the city's parks allow dogs. And best of all, there's now a leash-free dog park in Encinitas, a leash-free area, and three parks with limited leash-free hours. It's enough to make a dog howl with happiness. (And some dogs truly do—check it out sometime when there's a hound around.)

PARKS, BEACHES, AND RECREATION AREAS

The city has recently really gone to the dogs—in the best sense of the phrase. Not only is there one dedicated dog park, a dog-walk area, and three parks with off-leash hours, but the city was also strongly considering other pooch-park areas. Way to go, Encinitas! For info on the local dog park access group People and Dog Zones, go to www.padz.org.

8 Cricket's Corner Community Dog Park

🐾🐾🐾🐕 (See San Diego County map on page 832)

It's unusual to find such a green dog park. Somehow despite the park's popularity, its gorgeous grass keeps growing. (This can change at any time, of course, so don't be disappointed if you come here and find a big dirt lot.) Dogs have a little less than an acre of off-leash running room here. Small dogs get their own park within a park so they can stay away from the thundering paws of the big guys, but they're welcome in the big section. The park has water, trees, benches, and even a soda machine. (The latter is an odd amenity, but welcome on hot days.)

The park is on the property of the Rancho Coastal Humane Society and is open only when the society is open: 2–5 P.M. Tuesday and Thursday, and 11 A.M.–5 P.M. Saturday and Sunday. The address is 389 Requeza Street. From southbound I-5, take the Encinitas Boulevard exit and turn left onto Encinitas Boulevard. Go right on Westlake Street. At the stop sign turn right on Requeza Street. At the bottom of the hill go left into the driveway for the Rancho Coastal Humane Society. 760/753-6413.

9 Viewpoint Park

🐾🐾🐾🐕 (See San Diego County map on page 832)

This is a very green and pretty park. Dogs may be off leash in the lower part of the park (not the upper part with the great views) 6–7:30 A.M. and 4–6 P.M. Monday, Wednesday, and Friday. It's about 2.5 acres, and it's not fenced. Dogs love to run around on the grass, but keep 'em out of the tot lot. The park is at Cornish Drive and D Street. 760/633-2740.

10 Orpheus Park

🐾🐾🐾🐕 (See San Diego County map on page 832)

Dogs love to sniff around this 2.5-acre park, but they're not looking for Eurydice. They're joyously checking out the grass, the trees, and the eau de dog that's everywhere. This is a pretty hillside park with a decent ocean view. Dogs may be off leash 6–7:30 A.M. and 4–6 P.M. Monday, Wednesday, and Friday. 482 Orpheus Avenue. 760/633-2740.

11 Sun Vista Park

🐾🐾🐾🐕 (See San Diego County map on page 832)

Dogs must be very cognizant of where they go during the limited off-leash hours at this young four-acre park. They're allowed only on the east side of the creek/creekbed. The west side is the part where human kids cavort about. Signs warn against going over to the other side of the creek, but most dogs can't read, so keep an eye peeled.

Dogs may be off leash 6–7:30 A.M. and 4–6 P.M. Monday, Wednesday, and Friday. 2011 Avenida la Posta, at Rancho Santa Fe Road. 760/633-2740.

12 Village Park Trail and Off-Leash Area

🐾🐾🐾 (See San Diego County map on page 832)

This leash-free area is located right under the power lines, but if you don't look up, it's a pretty cool place. It's about a quarter mile long by 200 feet wide and has a trail that winds through it. But this is no grassy park. This is all natural, with dirt, chaparral, cactus, and other plantlife of its ilk. It's only partially fenced, so if your dog isn't under voice control, you may not feel comfortable letting her off leash. But once you're away from the roads and the entrances, it's a pretty safe haven for most off-leash pooches.

This area permits unleashed dogs every day, without the limited hours mandated at three other city parks. The park parallels Village Run West and runs from Mountain Vista Drive south to Encinitas Boulevard. There are four access points, but our favorites for easy access are on the south side, at either Encinitas Boulevard (although this spot has no parking) or where Village Run East turns north and becomes Village Run North. There's a helpful map at www.padz.org/sdge.html; 760/633-2740.

13 Cardiff State Beach

🐾🐾🐾 (See San Diego County map on page 832)

A while back, Joe Dog and I visited here during the highest tide of the year. Joe looked at me as if I were crazy for bringing him to a beach that was all ocean and no sand. He slowly shook his head, glared at me, and pulled me back to the car.

But normally there really *is* sand here, and quite a bit of it, too. It's a good place to bring a leashed dog, especially since it's the last beach area that allows dogs for many, many miles as you drive north.

If you're going to park your car here, it's $6. But you can walk in for free. There's camping here too, for $18. The beach is on Old Highway 101, directly west of the San Elijo Lagoon, in Cardiff-by-the-Sea. 760/753-5091.

PLACES TO STAY

Best Western Encinitas Inn and Suites and Moonlight Beach: Rates are $120–180. Dogs are $55 extra for the length of their stay. 85 Encinitas Boulevard 92024; 760/942-7455.

Del Mar

This stylish but sweet coastal community is mighty friendly to dogs. Within a few blocks, Jake got stopped and talked to by seven different pedestrians. One dapper old gent carried a zip-top bag filled with gourmet dog treats in his coat pocket. Jake fell in love, not wanting to leave his side, and looking back longingly as we parted company.

PARKS, BEACHES, AND RECREATION AREAS

14 Dog Beach/Del Mar City Beach

🐾🐾🐾🐾🐕 (See San Diego County map on page 832)

OK, dogs, get out your calendars and you can figure out when you can take off your leashes at this great beach. It gets a little confusing, so you might want to have your person help you figure it out.

Different segments of the beach have different rules regarding beach access and off-leash use. Here's a breakdown of the rules:

The part of the beach most dogs like to know about is the **north section.** Dogs congregate at the northernmost end, near the bluffs. It's not a long segment, but it's wide and very far from the road. Dogs have so much fun here that they usually collapse in ecstatic exhaustion when they get back to the car.

Leashes are the law June 16–September 14, but the rest of the year, your well-behaved dog can go sans leash! The entire off-leash area runs from 29th Street north to the Solano border. The best way to reach it from I-5 is to exit at Via de la Valle and drive west to Camino del Mar, where you'll go south for just about a block before you should start looking for street parking. It's across from the Del Mar Racetrack.

The **middle section** of the beach, from 29th Street down to Powerhouse Park/17th Street, prohibits dogs June 1–September 30. During the rest of the year, they can visit with a leash.

Dogs who visit the **south part** of the beach, from 6th Street up to Powerhouse Park/17th Street, can visit year-round, as long as they wear a leash.

A current dog license is required. And because too few people are cleaning up after their dogs, it may soon become mandatory to carry a poop bag in plain view. That way, you're telling the world (and any poop patrol police who pass by), "My dog doesn't need a toilet. He has *me*." 858/755-1556.

PLACES TO EAT

En Fuego Cantina and Grill: "We are the hottest place in San Diego. We're *en fuego!* On fire!" exclaimed an enthusiastic host. "We like dogs, too!" Dogs get a bowl of water while their humans dine on tasty Mexican food at the attractive patio. 1342 Camino del Mar; 858/792-6551.

Stratford Court Cafe: This place is a real charmer—a feast for the eyes and for your beast. You can eat your scrumptious food in a beautiful garden setting, next to the 1915 Cape Cod–style café. Try the Californian salad, with its caramelized walnuts and smoked gouda. And your happy dog will be offered a big bowl of water and even tasty dog biscuits made by Steve, the café's chef/owner. (The biscuits are $0.25 each. They're worth it.) 1307 Stratford Court 92014; 858/792-7433.

La Jolla

Back in the 1950s, Raymond Chandler wrote that La Jolla is "a nice place… for old people and their parents." He could have added two more categories to his description and it would have been more accurate. Something such as: La Jolla is "a nice place for old people, their parents, young people, and dogs."

Dogs, young folks, old folks, and older folks adore strolling along the seven miles of cliff-lined seacoast here. And they all equally love the impressive restaurant scene.

Unfortunately, your pooch won't be able to visit the parks and beaches of this stunning coastline 9 A.M.–6 P.M., but few dogs mind a nighttime stroll above the pounding Pacific. Luckily, cool cafés and elegant eateries abound. Many of them allow dogs to hang out with you as you dine at their outdoor tables.

La jolla means "the jewel" in Spanish. The name couldn't be more appropriate for this pristine, sparkling village. That's why, although it's actually part of the city of San Diego, it's being given its own listing here. It's like Monaco—a ravishing principality unto itself.

PARKS, BEACHES, AND RECREATION AREAS

15 La Jolla Shores Beach

😊😊😊 (See San Diego County map on page 832)

Just down the road from the famous Scripps Institution of Oceanography, this beach provides some breathtaking views of the La Jolla coast. But if you're visiting in the dark winter months, you might not get to see the views if you're with a dog. Dogs are banned 9 A.M.–6 P.M. April 1 to October 31, and 9 A.M.–4 P.M. the rest of the year. During their visiting hours, they must wear the mandatory leash.

The beach here is wide and lined with palms. Since you can't come here too much before dusk anyway, try to visit at sunset, when the gulls circle the bright gold sky and the orange waves crash on the distant cliffs. It's a stunning sight.

The beach is just west of Camino del Oro in the northern part of La Jolla. 619/235-1100.

16 Point La Jolla Cliffs and Beaches

😊😊😊 (See San Diego County map on page 832)

This is another one of those 9-to-6ers famous in the San Diego area. Dogs can visit the cliffs and beaches here only before 9 A.M. or after 6 P.M. April 1–October 31, or before 9 A.M. and after 4 P.M. the rest of the year.

What's great about this area is that there's access to the beach via stairs that take you down the cliffs, and there's also a grassy little park at the top of the cliffs. It's extremely beautiful and dramatic here. During the right tides, tidepooling is magnificent. Just make sure your dog doesn't stick his snout in the tidepools. The critters who call them home need all the peace they can get.

Enter on Coast Boulevard around Girard Avenue, and when you're done, go grab a bite to eat in any of the nearby mouthwatering restaurants. 619/235-1100.

PLACES TO EAT

La Jolla is a terrific place to grab a bite to eat with your dog. Many restaurants have lovely outdoor areas, and most of those happily permit pooches.

Elijah's Restaurant: Got a hankering for fabulous New York–style deli food? Except for the beautiful scenery, pleasant weather, and nearby ocean, you'll swear you're in New York when you sample the food here. The sky-high pastrami or corned beef sandwiches are droolworthy. Elijah's also features knishes and blintzes and a matzo ball soup people come here for when they're feeling a little run-down. Dinners are hearty, and salads and other healthy items are available too. Dine with doggy at the outdoor tables. 8861 Villa La Jolla Drive; 858/455-1461.

Froglander's Yogurt: The dog-loving owner here will gladly give your canine companion a free yogurt sample. 915 Pearl Street; 858/459-3764.

Sante Ristorante: The award-winning Italian food here is lovingly created, and absolutely delectable. Dogs enjoy sitting by their people at the totally covered patio area. A big *grazie* to Nico the Dog for writing to tell us about this gem. 7811 Herschell Avenue; 858/454-1315.

PLACES TO STAY

La Jolla Village Lodge: If you like to eat, stay at this 1950s-era motel. Not only does your room come with a fridge and microwave, but you get continental breakfast, and snacks are available all day. (It's not a great place for dieters.) Dogs like that the big sign out front usually says "Pets Welcome!" Rates are $150–250. Dogs are $20 extra for the length of their stay. 1141 Silverado Street 92037; 858/551-2001; www.lajollavillagelodge.com.

La Valencia Hotel: This historic, elegant hotel has been charming visitors and their happy dogs since 1926. It's exquisite, it's upscale, it's expensive, and it's for dogs who are less than 40 pounds. (Stop reading now if you have anything larger or a budget that matches your little dog's size.) Some rooms overlook the beautiful gardens, while others have breathtaking views of the ocean or La Jolla's village. You can also stay at a super-attractive villa here. Rates are $275–3,500. Dogs are $75 extra nightly. Hoo, that's a lot of dog-biscuit money. 1132 Prospect Street 92037; 858/454-0771 or 800/451-0772; www.lavalencia.com.

San Diego Marriott La Jolla: It's surprising to find such a large hotel in this little community, but it fits in fairly well with its lovely pools and nice landscaping. Rates are $189–259. Dogs are $75 extra for the length of their stay. 4240 La Jolla Village Drive 92037; 858/587-1414.

Poway

PARKS, BEACHES, AND RECREATION AREAS

🐾 Poway Dog Park

🐾🐾🐾🐾🐕 (See San Diego County map on page 832)

A visit to Poway Dog Park is like a stint on *Let's Make a Deal*. Dogs get to choose between Door Number One, Door Number Two, or Door Number Three. But unlike the old Monty Hall game show, no matter which door your dog chooses, she'll always be a winner. (No booby prizes of canned spinach here.) Poway Dog Park has three separate fenced areas for leash-free dogs, and they're all doggone great. Your dog can visit any or all of them in a given day. If the sniffs are boring in one area, try another. If there's a cute dog your pooch wants to meet in another fenced area, open the door for her mystery date and let the good times roll.

Each section of this nearly two-acre park is a poochie wonderland, with dog water fountains and even a fire hydrant for your dog's pee-rusal. There's some shade, but on hot days dogs the park could use a little more.

Exit I-15 at Poway Road and drive east about four miles. Turn right on Bowron Road. Park in the lot at the end of the road. Walk past the soccer and baseball fields to the pooch park, which is behind the swimming pool and baseball fields in Poway Community Park. 858/679-4342.

PLACES TO EAT

Chicken Pie Diner: This great 1950s-style diner boasts of "serving classic comfort food at family prices." Dogs dig it here, because even though they need to eat at the seven umbrella-topped tables outside, they still get the ambience of the place because the '50s jukebox music is piped out to this area. A big thank-you to Dyson Dog for letting us know about this place. 14727 Pomerado Road; 858/748-2445.

Julian

This entire old gold-mining town is a Designated Historic District. It's full of nifty old storefronts and dog-friendly folks. It's also full of tourists, especially if you visit during October, which is apple month in these parts. People here bake more than 10,000 apple pies a week in October—a fun time to visit if you like autumn leaves and crispy apples.

PLACES TO EAT

The Julian Grille: You and your dog can dine on tasty burgers, pastas, steaks, and salads at the restaurant's 15-table patio area. 2224 Main Street; 760/765-0173.

DIVERSION

Pick a Peck of Apples: What Peter Piper did with pickled peppers, you and your dog can do with apples, thanks to the dog-friendly folks at **Calico Ranch orchards** in Julian. From about mid-September through Thanksgiving, you and your leashed, cleaned-up-after dog can sniff out your favorite apples at the orchard's 30 acres of trees. Then take them home to make a to-drool-for apple pie or two (or 10). 4200 Highway 78; 858/586-0392.

Romano's Dodge House: The Italian food here is *buonissimo*. Dine with your dog at the six outdoor tables. 2718 B Street; 760/765-1003.

PLACES TO STAY

Angel's Landing: Angel's Landing is an appropriate name for this 53-acre chunk of pine-covered paradise. It's beautiful here and so secluded you won't even hear any traffic. The owners are some of the most animal-friendly people you'll ever encounter. They love dogs and even have an animal-rescue area on the property, with adopted chickens, bunnies, pigs, goats, and horses.

The Old Butterfield Stage Coach Route runs through the property and makes for a terrific hike with your leashed dog. (Leashes are a necessity here, because the place is also heaven for many deer and wild turkeys.) If it's a very clear day, you might be able to see the ocean from the meadows above Angel's Landing.

The rooms and suites at the lodge and smaller buildings are clean and pretty. The rates are $75–225. Dogs are $10 per stay. 2323 Farmer Road 92036; 888/253-7747; www.angelsresort.com.

Little Acorn Cabin: Many dogs have vacationed at this decent little housekeeping cabin. Dogs have to be preapproved, but there's no size limit. "We've had Great Danes and Saint Bernards stay here," says one of the owners. If you like to barbecue, you'll enjoy the cabin's grill and little picnic area. Rates are $85–125. 2142 Whispering Pines Drive 92036; 760/765-1611.

Pine Haven: This sweet, cozy cabin is one of the most pooch-friendly cabins we've come across. The entire 1.25-acre property is completely and securely fenced, so it's one big doggy playground! Not only that, but scattered around the tiered property are hidden "treasures" dogs revel in finding. (They're actually dog toys and tennis balls—no gold bullion or anything.) "The dogs love running around and suddenly finding a toy," says cabin owner Teresa, who adores dogs and is very involved with dog-rescue groups. In addition, dogs get a basket of toys they can play with and a doggy treat of their own. Plus, they can use the cabin's doggy beds and have a choice of two types of "tables" they can dine on. Jake loves slurping water and munching food from these raised bowl platforms. It really doesn't get more dog friendly than this. Teresa likes

DIVERSION

Get Carriaged Away: Ah! There's nothing like the smell of horse heinie to put a smile on a dog's face. Lucky dogs get to experience this olfactory bliss up close when they join you on a **Country Carriages buggy ride.** The carriage rides take you down quiet country roads around beautiful Julian. It can be romantic, but with your dog involved, it's just fun. Owner Wayne says some dogs are oblivious to the equines until partway through the ride. "Then it's like they go 'Hey! There's a horse in front of me!' and they let out a bark or two. The owners are embarrassed and try to make the dog be quiet. It's never been a problem," he says.

A half-hour ride is $30 for a couple with a couple of kids and/or a dog. The more people and the longer the ride, the more it costs. Wayne will even pick you up at your lodging, if it's not too far away, but he also picks up rides in front of the Julian Drug Store at Washington and Main Streets. Reservations are strongly recommended, especially during weekends. 760/765-1471.

dogs so much that she jokes that "People can't come if they don't have dogs." At least I think it was a joke.

With all these dog amenities, it's easy to brush past the cabin itself, but it's got loads of appeal. The living room is especially wonderful, with a floor-to-ceiling stone fireplace and views of a beautiful meadow. The cabin is on a small lane four miles from town and offers plenty of privacy. Rates are $160–180. Dogs are $30 extra for the length of their stay for the first dog, $10 for the second. You'll get the address when you make your reservation. 760/726-9888; the adorable dog-focused website is www.pinehavencabin.com.

El Cajon

PARKS, BEACHES, AND RECREATION AREAS

18 Wells Dog Park

🐾🐾🐾🏃 (See San Diego County map on page 832)

Work late? Got a night-owl dog? This 1.4-acre fenced park has lights so you can take your dog for a safe leash-free romp at night. It's part grass, part decomposed granite, and has water, shade canopies, picnic tables, and some shade-giving trees. Big dogs and little dogs have separate sections.

This is a city with more apartments than houses, so the dog park is a real boon for all the residents without yards. It's located in the southwest section of Wells Park, at 1153 Madison Avenue. 619/441-1680.

19 Louis A. Stelzer Regional Park

🐾🐾🐾 (See San Diego County map on page 832)

You and your favorite leashed pooch can walk in dreamy seclusion on most winter weekdays in this 314-acre park. A series of small meadows and a mile-long stretch of riparian woodland beg to be visited. If you hike up to Stelzer Ridge, you'll get spectacular views of the surrounding land.

If civilization is more your style, you can picnic under big, shady trees while the kids frolic at the two playgrounds. Louis A. Stelzer, who donated his ranch to create this park, specified in his will that he wanted the park to be developed for disadvantaged and disabled children. The results are commendable.

From Highway 67, exit at Mapleview Street and drive east about a half mile to Ashwood Street. Turn left and follow it for a couple of miles as it changes its name to Wildcat Canyon Road and leads you into the park. 619/561-0580.

San Diego

San Diego is both laid-back and exciting. You and your dog can stroll through the old Gaslamp Quarter, eating up the local history as well as the good food served at a few dog-friendly eateries. You can visit La Jolla's pristine shores for breathtaking scenery and clean-breathing air. You can even walk on historic land where California actually started (at the Presidio Park). If that's not stimulating enough, you can stroll down action-packed beaches together at sunset (on Mission Beach/Pacific Beach).

For dogs who like to run around in the nude (without a leash, that is), San Diego is a great place to be. The city is home to a couple of very dog-friendly off-leash beaches, and it's chock-full of dog parks—second only to San Francisco in number. This is a great place to be a dog, or to visit with one.

DIVERSION

Whatever Floats Your Boat: If you and your salty dog want to explore beautiful **San Diego Bay** by water, a couple of boat-rental companies are happy to accommodate you. You'll have your choice of sailing or motoring around the bay. The sailboats range 14–27 feet, with a price range of about $30–100 per hour. Powerboats come in a variety of sizes and horsepowers, with an hourly rate of $65–150.

Note: If your dog isn't a decent dog paddler, you should bring a doggy life jacket for her. Even if she's Esther Williams, it's not a bad idea. The smaller the sailboat, the better the chance you'll end up in the drink. Plus it can get busy in the bay, with Navy ships crossing here and there to make things interesting.

Seaforth Boat Rentals is on the San Diego waterfront at 333 West Harbor Drive (it shares the address with the San Diego Marriott Hotel and Marina, should you be looking for a place to stay on the water); 619/239-BOAT (619/239-2628). Action Sport Rentals is in Coronado and right next to the magnificent Loews Coronado Bay Resort, at 4000 Coronado Bay Road; 619/424-4466.

PARKS, BEACHES, AND RECREATION AREAS

San Diego is known for having a climate where things can really grow. Well, this city sure knows how to grow dog parks. A few years ago there were just a few. Now the city has raised a bumper crop. It's an absolutely terrific development, but it presents a bit of a problem for this book: space to write about them all! Rather than go into depth about each park, we'll save the longer descriptions for the more spectacular ones, and keep the typical dog park descriptions relatively brief.

20 Cadman Community Park

🐾🐾🐾🐕 (See San Diego County map on page 832)

If your dog's theme song is "Don't Fence Me In," she'll be happy here: The park's leash-free dog area—marked by signs—has no fences. But it does have grass, trees, park benches, and Mutt Mitt dispensers. It also has limited hours: It's open to off-leash dogs 7:30–10 A.M. and 4:30–7 P.M. during the school year. It's open 7–9:30 A.M. and 5–7:30 P.M. in summer. Leashes are mandatory on July Fourth, and on Saturdays March 1–June 15. 4280 Avati Drive, at Moraga Court. 619/525-8239.

21 Capehart Park Dog Park

🐾🐾🐾🐕 (See San Diego County map on page 832)

Small dogs who are worried about big dogs can take refuge in this fenced park's separate area for wee dogs. The entire park is about an acre, so there's not gobs of room to roam, but dogs enjoy it anyway. The park has water, picnic tables, and benches. It's at the corner of Felspar and Soledad Mountain roads. 619/525-8239.

22 Doyle Community Park Dog Park

🐾🐾🐾🐕 (See San Diego County map on page 832)

You won't find trees here, but in the warmer months you will find awnings where warm humans and hot dogs (the furry kind) take refuge. The fenced one-acre park has water, benches, and a separate section for small dogs. Doyle Park is at 8175 Regents Road, but the dog area is toward the back of the park, on Cargill Avenue south of Nobel Drive. 619/525-8239.

23 Dusty Rhodes Park Dog Park

🐾🐾🐕 (See San Diego County map on page 832)

At press time, this one-acre fenced park had no water, so be sure to bring your own. It's mostly grass, with some mulch ground cover. There's talk (among dog people) about expanding the park to five acres, which could make it a four-paw wonder. It's on Sunset Cliffs Boulevard between Nimitz and West Point Loma Boulevards, across Sunset from the wonderful Mission Bay Park. 619/525-8239.

24 Kearny Mesa Community Park Dog Park

🐾🐾🐕 (See San Diego County map on page 832)

Jake gives this park only two paws because even though it's a decent off-leash fenced area, there's no water, and parking can be problematic. If you want to fetch your dog a drink, you'll have to go to the adjacent restroom's drinking fountain, fill up a container (there are usually gallon milk containers at the park), and then pour it into a bowl you'll find here. Park users are hoping for a real doggy and human water fountain one of these days. Kearny Mesa Park is at 3170 Armstrong Street, at Mesa College Drive; you'll have to drive to the back of the park, past the pool and playing fields, to get to the dog area. 619/525-8239.

25 Maddox Park Dog Park

🐾🐾🐾🐕 (See San Diego County map on page 832)

Maddox Park is a small park surrounded by a residential area, so try to keep the barking to a dull roar. The fenced park within Maddox has about an acre of grass, with a picnic table and drinking fountain. It's at 7815 Flanders Drive, at Dabney Drive. 619/525-8239.

26 Rancho Bernardo Dog Park

🐾🐾🐾🐾🐕 (See San Diego County map on page 832)

This fenced park is the most recent addition to San Diego's great dog-park system, and it's a real winner. It has lots of running room, with 2.6 acres of

DIVERSION

Your Dog Wasn't Born with a Leash: And you weren't born yesterday. You know there's more to life than leashes and fenced urban dog parks. If you want to meet up with people who enjoy the great outdoors and love seeing their dogs run around like the leash-free creatures they're meant to be, sniff out the **San Diego Off Leash Dog Recreation Meetup Group.** This is a terrific bunch of friendly people and dogs who gather to explore the county's lakes, beaches, and glorious hiking areas. They welcome well-behaved newcomers and their dogs.

The leash-free get-togethers are a mere $1. This is an Internet-based group. You can find out more and check out the schedule at www.offleash.meetup.com (click on the San Diego group).

grass, and trees dogs love. (And not for their arboreal beauty, if you know what I mean.) There's a separate section for smaller pooches, and all the usual dog-park amenities, from water to poop bags. Both small and large-dog areas have a spigot with a "toxic-free" hose. (Now that's really taking care of our dogs.) It's one good-looking dog park, and dogs are very happy to be here.

The park was created with more than $800,000 from San Diego's portion of two state park bonds. No wonder it looks so good. Apparently there was none of that "let's scrape up some donations and see what we can manage," that so many dog-park founders go through. The park is at 18448 West Bernardo Drive. From I-15 take the West Bernardo/Pomerado Rod exit and go west. The Rancho Bernardo Community Park is about 0.25 mile in on the right. Drive to the southernmost end of the park, where you'll find the dog park. 858/538-8129.

27 Torrey Highlands Park Dog Park
🐾🐾🐾🐕 (See San Diego County map on page 832)

Dogs enjoy romping leash-free at this one-acre fenced dog park in the Carmel Valley area. The park has decent-sized trees along one side, and benches, water, and an adjacent restroom for humans. The ground cover is grassy with some mulch, and fairly easy on the paws. It's on Lansdale Drive off Del Mar Heights Road. 619/525-8239.

28 Balboa Park
🐾🐾🐾🐾🐕 (See San Diego County map on page 832)

This luxuriant semitropical park is one of California's best urban parks for people. Attractions include the San Diego Zoo, an enormous planetarium, several theaters, and a few world-class museums. But with the recent addition of three off-leash areas for dogs, Balboa Park is now one of the best urban parks for pooches, too.

Dogs used to be relegated to the lush, green center and the dirt paths on the east and west sides of this 1,200-acre park. Leashes were—and still are—a necessity in those areas. Dogs who wanted more freedom were out of luck until a kindly park official thought it might be nice to give them a chance to cavort about sans leash in a small area. The dogs all thought this was a mighty good idea, and they've been so well behaved that the park doubled their stomping grounds.

The two dog runs aren't fenced, but they're well marked with signs. The more popular dog area is Morley Field, which is the smaller of the two. It's lined by a grove of eucalyptus trees, so there's plenty of shade on hot days. You'll almost always find gaggles of pooches gallivanting about in high spirits. You can get to Morley Field from Morley Field Drive, off Florida Drive, in the north-central part of the park (northwest of the tennis courts). The second and larger of the areas is Nate's Point, on the northwest side of the park off Balboa Drive, just south of the Laurel Street Bridge. It's a picturesque place (nice for pooches with a sense of aesthetic beauty), with views of the famous old California Tower, Coronado, and even part of Mexico. It's about 1.5 acres, and like Morley Field, it's unfenced, so keep an eye peeled for signs for its boundaries.

To get to the park from I-5, exit at Park Boulevard and head north. Call the Balboa Park Visitors Center for more information and maps. 619/239-0512.

🐾 Black Mountain Open Space

🐾🐾🐾 (See San Diego County map on page 832)

It's utterly quiet here. So quiet you can hear your dog breathe when he's sitting still. So quiet you'll swear you hear his fleas gnashing their teeth. And except when people are shooting bullets through the signs that say No Liquor and No Firearms, it's almost always this silent.

A few miles of trails run through this mountainous, shrubby, completely undeveloped 200-acre park. It's not exactly Mt. Whitney, but from the top of Black Mountain (elevation 1,552 feet), you can get some good views of the surrounding hills and peaks.

The trek here looks complicated, but it's not bad. Exit I-15 at Rancho Peñasquitos Boulevard/Mountain Road and drive west about two miles to Black Mountain Road. Turn right and drive north about 2.5 miles, where the road will come to an abrupt end. Just before it does, turn right on the dirt road there. Follow the winding road up the mountain and eventually you'll come to a sharp right, where the road becomes paved. The road ends in a small parking lot. From here, you can see the start of the trail. 858/538-8082.

🔟 Dog Beach/Ocean Beach

🐾🐾🐾🐾🐾🐕 (See San Diego County map on page 832)

Welcome to Dog Beach! the sign announces at just about the same place that your dog charges out of the car to meet all his best buddies. Dogs truly do feel welcome here. They're free to run off leash at the north end of Ocean Beach, an area known far and wide as Dog Beach. Here they can really get down to the business of being a dog. As long as they listen when you call and don't get into trouble, they can hang out leashless all day. Many dog people bring a folding chair so they can relax while their dog experiences heaven on earth.

We've seen several folks visit here because, although they don't have a dog, they get great joy out of watching the footloose creatures tearing around. "They have such innocent happiness when they run about and play so gleefully," said dogless dog lover Maxine Chambers one gray morning. "It makes my day."

There are more dog footprints in the sand than human footprints, and not just because dogs have more feet. People come from many miles around, sometimes bringing their friends' dogs and their neighbors' dogs to participate in the whirlwind of excitement. (That said, the beach can have aggressive dogs at times, according to a couple of San Diego residents who have written to me. One of my correspondents had given up taking her dog there because of this. It's something to be aware of. I've never seen it myself, but I don't live here.)

The Dog Beach area of Ocean Beach is wide enough to be very safe from traffic. It's marked by signs. If you wander onto the other part of the beach, make sure you do so before 9 A.M. or after 6 P.M. April 1–October 31, or before 9 A.M. or after 4 P.M. during other times of year, and be sure to leash your dog.

DIVERSION

Wash That Sand Right Outta His Hair: After a long jaunt on Dog Beach, come to the **Dog Beach Dog Wash,** a wonderful place to keep your pooch looking as if he just strolled out of a dog-food commercial. If location is everything, this business has it all. It's only two blocks from Dog Beach. The owners say that some folks bring their dogs here almost every time they visit the beach. It's a great way to get rid of all that sand and dog slobber before getting back in your car. It's at 4933 Voltaire Street, Suite C, San Diego; 619/523-1700.

If you're nearer the Grape Street Dog Park with a dirty dog, be sure to check out the wonderful **South Bark Dog Wash.** It has a spalike ambience and very reasonable prices for what you get. It's at 2037 30th Street, San Diego; 619/232-7387; www.southbark.com.

Baths at Dog Beach Dog Wash are $11. South Bark baths cost $12. Blow-drys and medicated shampoos cost extra.

Exit I-5 at I-8. Drive west and follow the signs to Sunset Cliffs Boulevard. After several blocks, bear right at Voltaire Street. Follow Voltaire Street to its end and the entrance to Dog Beach. 619/235-1100.

31 Fiesta Island

🐾🐾🐾🐾🦮 (See San Diego County map on page 832)

Hey, dogs! You're going to find out just why they call this 1.5-mile-long island Fiesta Island. You can have a fabulous fiesta, then take a soothing siesta—and you can do it all off leash.

Yes, pooches, you can meet friends, swim in the bay, chase your shadow, and catch a stick without ever wearing that pesky old leash. As long as you listen to your people and don't cause any problems, this island is all yours. There's no development (as of this printing, anyway, although there's plenty of talk about it)—just dirt and sand and a little grass.

If you aren't very good at listening to your owners, ask them to take you to the far side of the island, where fewer cars cruise by. The perimeter of the island is a beach, and unfortunately, the road runs right behind the beach. It doesn't give water dogs a whole lot of room to run around, but it's enough for most.

If you choose to stay on the beach, you can avoid annoying little personal watercraft by staying away from the watercraft recreation sections of water, which are clearly marked. The interior of the island is made up of fields of dirt. Since this is a bigger area, you'll be farther from traffic here.

The views of downtown San Diego and Mission Bay Park are really spectacular from the south side of the island. Cameras come in mighty handy here. (Fiesta Island is actually part of Mission Bay Park, but the rules are so different that I prefer to list them separately.)

From I-5, take the Sea World Drive/Tecolote Road exit southeast to Fiesta Island Road, which is your first right. The road will take you onto the island. 619/235-1100.

32 Grape Street Park

🐾🐾🐾🐾🦮 (See San Diego County map on page 832)

Dogs love running on this attractive, grassy, unfenced five-acre area near downtown San Diego. There's shade, water, restrooms (for humans—dogs just use the trees), benches, and lights—everything you could want in a pooch park. There's talk about either fencing in a dog park here or making this unfenced area a full-time leash-free zone. Off-leash hours have greatly expanded since the last edition of the book. The hours dogs can now run around without leashes: 7:30 A.M.–9 P.M. Monday–Friday; 9 A.M.–9 P.M. weekends and holidays. Leashed dogs can visit any time. The park is at Grape Street and Granada Avenue. 619/525-8222.

33 Mission Bay Park

😾😾😾😾 (See San Diego County map on page 832)

Dogs are not allowed at this spectacular, huge park 9 A.M.–6 P.M. April 1 to October 31 (or 9 A.M.–4 P.M. the rest of the year). But even with these limited hours, and the mandatory leashes, it's a spectacular place to bring a dog. This is one of the nation's largest and most beautiful aquatic parks.

It's so big (4,600 acres, including the bay), with so many more entry points than signs, that you may make the same mistake many others have when seeing the park for the first time: "I thought it was a bloody golf course! Gawd! OK, Ginger, let's go for a walk," said Henry Miles, a British chap in his 70s. He was walking Ginger for his sister, who had told him about Mission Bay Park and how to get there. But when he saw the perfect grass, the gently rolling hills, and the sand, he figured he'd gotten the directions wrong. "They've got a lot of golf courses here, you know. Gawd, even their parks look like them. Ginger looks relieved, eh?"

I ran into Miles at the section of park near the San Diego Visitor Information Center. That section is particularly reminiscent of a golf course—in fact, it's just around the bend from a golf course that's a dead ringer for the park.

If you're on I-5 and your pooch wants to exercise while you get tourist information, exit at the Clairemont Drive/Visitor Center turnoff and follow the signs to the visitor center. Keep in mind that the visitors center and the pooch-walking hours rarely coincide, so it helps if you have a friend who can get the necessary tourist information while you walk your dog. You can park in the parking lot for only an hour, so if you're planning on a longer stay, there's street parking a little farther south.

The zillions of other access points are north of the San Diego River and south of Pacific Beach Drive. The east-west boundaries are East Mission Bay Drive (which parallels I-5) and Mission Boulevard (which runs a block east of the Pacific). You can also visit dog-friendly Fiesta Island, which is actually part of this park's territory (but listed separately, above). 619/235-1100, or to speak with a ranger, 858/581-7603.

34 Mission Beach/Pacific Beach

😾😾😾😾 (See San Diego County map on page 832)

The great thing about strolling down these two contiguous beaches with a dog is that no one seems to care if you don't have bulging biceps or a bikini-perfect body. Having a dog eliminates the need for physical prowess here. And on beaches that have built a worldwide reputation on how dazzling its bathers look, that's a mighty big plus.

On the downside, dogs are not allowed on these beaches 9 A.M.–6 P.M. April 1–October 31, or 9 A.M.–4 P.M. the rest of the year. The same hours hold for the paved promenade that runs behind the beaches. It's an understandable law during crowded summer days, but it would be a real boon for dogs if that rule could be eliminated during the winter. Since the poor pooches have to be leashed anyway, what's the harm?

To make the best of these restricted hours, try a visit to beautiful Belmont Park. The big attraction at this old-style amusement park is a restored 1925 roller coaster, the Giant Dipper. In addition, there's a quaint old carousel and historic indoor swimming pool. Dogs are required to be leashed and remain with all four feet planted firmly on the ground, but they can still have a good time watching the kids have fun. The park area is also home to dozens of shops and restaurants. It's at West Mission Bay Drive and Mission Boulevard. Its back faces Mission Beach. Call 619/491-2988 for Belmont Park hours and information.

Pacific Beach is north of Mission Beach. It starts around Tourmaline Street. The beach hooks up with Mission Beach and is one long, never-ending strip all the way down to the Mission Bay Channel. 619/235-1100.

35 Mission Trails Regional Park
😸😸😸 (See San Diego County map on page 832)

This is a really big chunk of green—5,109 acres, to be exact. Actually, it's a good deal greener on a map than it is in reality. Several miles of dirt trails wind through low brush and boulders, all in a rather desolate setting. Because this park is managed by the city (although owned by the county), dogs are permitted on the trails.

They love to bound up and down hill after hill with you tagging along behind them. There's a leash law here, so make sure that if they're bounding, you're bounding, too.

One good destination for your leaps and bounds is the Old Mission Dam Historical Site. Native Americans built it many decades back and it's still in good working order.

Good news for pooches: Dog-friendly rangers lead informative guided nature hikes for dogs and their people every other month. The hikes are not for the soft of paw or the fair of foot, but they're not usually terribly difficult, and we hear they're great fun. Call 619/668-3275 for more information.

Exit I-8 at Mission Gorge Road (one of the exits for the San Diego-Jack Murphy Stadium) and drive northeast past all the gas stations and fast-food marts. In about four miles, turn left on Father Junipero Serra Trail and you're in the park. Or if you want, you can park on Mission Gorge Road, at the trailhead off Jackson Road, just before you get to Father Junipero Serra Trail. 619/668-3275.

36 Presidio Park
😸😸😸 (See San Diego County map on page 832)

This is where California began. The hill here is known as the "Plymouth Rock of the West." Dogs are stepping on very historic land when they walk here.

Back in 1769, Father Junípero Serra dedicated his first of many California missions on this very same hill.

The mission has since moved, but a fascinating museum is a major draw here. Dogs don't have great interest in the Spanish furniture and historic documents in the museum, and they're not permitted inside anyway. They prefer the many wide dirt trails that run around the hill.

The trails are on rolling hills, shaded by plenty of trees. The views from here are incredible. On a clear day, you can see all of the city. Someone marching with a telescope said he could check out the beach scene from here, but I didn't confirm that.

From I-8, take the Taylor Street exit west. Go left at Presidio Drive, which will take you up to the park. You can park at the museum and get a map of the park. There's also a lower parking lot that has easy trail access. Call 619/297-3258 for the history of the area and general park information.

PLACES TO EAT

Costa Brava: It's garlic, garlic everywhere at this Pacific Beach tapas restaurant. If you're a vampire, stay away. Otherwise, this is a must-visit place. Here's what a *San Diego Magazine* food critic wrote: "The ocean breeze that sometimes blows like an exhaust fan through Pacific Beach has been put to the test by Costa Brava, above whose roof a cloud of garlic vapors collects day and night. It makes Garnet Avenue one of the more aromatic thoroughfares in town. At this new Spanish restaurant, garlic assumes a role similar to that of Virgil in *The Divine Comedy,* guiding diners through supremely pungent meals that some will regard as heaven." The tapas and paellas are so good you may have to ask your dog if you haven't been magically transported to Spain. Dine together at the outdoor tables. 1653 Garnet Avenue; 858/273-1218.

G5/Georges on Fifth: Want to eat at one of the most photographed buildings in the Gaslamp Quarter? If you like primo steak and seafood, pay G5 a visit. This popular place is located in the former home of Wyatt Earp's Gambling Hall & Saloon. Dogs can't go inside, but it's sure pretty outside, too. And if you're a steak buff, you may not be able to tell where your drooling begins and your dog's ends. The restaurant is known for its high-end—and high-priced—filet mignons and kobe steaks. (A 12-ounce top-quality filet mignon will run you $69.) Dogs dine at the half dozen tables out front. If it's too sunny, you'll have an awning. If it's cold, you'll have a heat lamp and your dog at your feet. 835 Fifth Avenue; 619/702-0444.

Kemo Sabe: The food at this Hillcrest restaurant is delicious and big fun. It's Pacific Rim fusion, and a real winner. Fabulous starters include smoked duck wonton soup and roasted nut-crusted fried brie with honey-roasted garlic and other tempting sides. The entrées are droolworthy. One of my favorites: The blackened satay chicken breast stack, which consists of jerk chicken layered with chili corn cake, melon salsa, and 10-spiced grilled plantain. Just writing about it is making my mouth water. Your dog may join you at the half dozen tables that run along the front of the building. Thirsty dogs get water. Thirsty people can get a choice of local microbrews and 50 varieties of wine. 3958 Fifth Avenue; 619/220-6802.

Lamont Street Grill: The cuisine at this lovely restaurant is hard to describe, so I'll let the restaurant's literature do it for me: It's "California comfort food, punctuated by bold and strange Mexi/Asian/Cajun flavors." (Given some time and a large dining allowance, I could have figured that out.) If you want a dish that sends a mixed message to your diet, try the boneless chicken breast (OK, healthy so far) topped with potato chips, seasoned sour cream, and green onions over pasta. (What was that about healthy?). Your dog can join you at the pretty brick patio area, which even has a few trees. If your dog is thirsty, she'll be given a bowl of water. A big thank-you to Red and his person, Andrew, for giving us the heads up about this restaurant. 4445 Lamont Street; 858/270-3060.

O'Bistro: This great little café has six things going for it: Location, location, location. And food, food, food. It's just a bone's throw from Dog Beach and has a dog-friendly patio with several tables. You can't beat the location if you're near Dog Beach and you're hungry. And the food is terrific. The lobster bisque is utterly revered by many of the regulars. I would have sampled it to let you know first-hand how good it is, but I may not have lived to write about it (shellfish allergy). Try the gorgonzola flatbread if you feel like a nontraditional pizza. The dog-friendly waitstaff gives dogs big bowls of fresh water. 4934 Voltaire Street; 619/223-2202.

Point Loma Seafood: You want a dog-friendly restaurant? Romp on over to Point Loma Seafood, where the dog-loving attitude is as yummy as the seafood. You and your dog can share a bayside table and the stuff memories are made of (that is, french fries). While you dine on such goodies as a shrimp sandwich or crab Louie, your dog will be eating and drinking his own restaurant food: free biscuits and fresh water. The only thing Joe Dog winced at here was the pickled squid cocktail. As it passed by our table, en route to some less fortunate soul, he sniffed the air and backed up as far as his leash would allow. That boy always had good taste. 2805 Emerson Street; 619/223-1109.

Royal India: The Indian cuisine at this lovely Gaslamp Quarter restaurant is first rate, with some unique Tandoori and curry dishes topping my list of favorites. Dogs get to join their people at the large, attractive deck. It seats 60 people and a few happy dogs. Thirsty dogs get water; chilly people get a heat lamp. This place is definitely worth sniffing out if you're in the mood for quality Indian cuisine. 329 Market Street; 619/269-9999.

Terra: This warm, sophisticated restaurant in the heart of beautiful Hillcrest serves some simply mouthwatering dishes. This upscale restaurant doesn't forget your canine companion. Indeed not. In fact, Terra has teamed up with the Original Paw Pleasers pet bakery to provide dogs some lip-licking choices from their very own menu. You may want to try the Puppy Pizza. Dogs can dine alfresco at the lovely patio. 3900 Vermont Street; 619/293-7088.

Trattoria La Strada: Enjoy a delicious Italian meal with your pooch at 12-table patio of this top-drawer Gaslamp Quarter restaurant. If you like fine Northern Italian cuisine, or a variety of carpacci, you'll love it here. There's also a steak number your dog will want you to dial: The Filetto "Ciao San Diego," a grilled filet mignon, wrapped with Italian cured pancetta and bay leaves, flambéed with cognac, sautéed in a light creamy peppercorn sauce, and served with bowtie pasta in a porcini mushroom sauce. I'm almost drooling right now, and I don't even eat beef. 702 Fifth Avenue; 619/239-3400.

PLACES TO STAY

Beach Haven Inn: Dogs have to be itsy-bitsy angels on their best behavior to stay here—25 pounds is the limit and they have to be "well behaved and well trained." Plus they can't stay here June 15–September 15. Cheez! This picky hotel is in the Pacific Beach area. Rates are $99–133. Dogs are $10 extra. 4740 Mission Boulevard 92109; 858/272-3812 or 800/831-6323. www.beachhaveninn.com.

Best Western Lamplighter Inn and Suites: If you and the pooch like your lodgings peaceful and palmy with plenty of flowering plants and trees, the Lamplighter is for you. The rooms are attractive, too. Suites have a breakfast bar and full kitchen. Some have a separate living area. Rates are $79–184. Dogs are $10 extra. (The dog-friendly folks here call it "pet rent.") 6474 El Cajon Boulevard 92115; 619/582-3088 or 800/545-0778; www.lamplighter-inn.com.

The Bristol Hotel: This is one of the cooler hotels to bring a canine in San Diego. It's contemporary, it's hip, it's a happenin' place in the Gaslamp Quarter. The lobby is jazzy, and the rooms are sleek, colorful, and comfortable. Stay here and you get use of a fluffy terry robe and free Wi-Fi. Your dog will have to be content with her coat. Rates are $129–289. The rule here is that dogs are supposed to be less than 50 pounds, "but the size limit is not enforced," someone here tells us. 1055 1st Avenue 92101; 619/232-6141; 800/662-4477; www.thebristolsandiego.com.

Casitas del Mar: This large, attractive duplex vacation rental is a quick two-minute walk to Pacific Beach in the north part of San Diego, bordering La Jolla. The size limit for dogs here is 50 pounds, so if you have a bigger pooch and want to stay in the neighborhood, try the Hohe House (see below). In addition, dogs can no longer stay here in the summer. They're limited to September 1 to May 15. If you're here off-season with a not-too-big dog, you're set.

Casitas del Mar has separate upstairs and downstairs units, each with two bedrooms and two baths. If you like sunsets over the ocean, choose the upstairs unit, "El Cielo." Rates are $1,800 weekly during the dog-friendly off-season. Dogs are $100 extra. You'll get the address once you make the reservation. 619/200-1242; www.casitasdelmar.com.

Doubletree Hotel San Diego/Mission Valley: Dogs need to stay on the hotel's third or fourth floor. At least you won't be paying for a penthouse. Rooms are very comfy and spacious. Rates are $159–309. Dogs are $50 for the length of their stay. 7450 Hazard Center Drive 92108; 619/297-5466.

The Hohe House: This two-bedroom, two-bath oceanview vacation rental (Hoy, not Hoe-Hee, as I was saying until Steven Hohe himself informed me of my errant ways) comes with everything you need for a fun beachside vacation, including bikes, boogie boards, beach chairs, beach towels, beach umbrellas, and coolers. It's a two-minute walk to Pacific Beach and a bone's throw from La Jolla. Dogs are welcome here as long as they're not huge—the 80-pound range is about the limit. The well-appointed house is usually rented by the week, for $1,400–2,400. There's a $350 security deposit and a $99 cleaning fee. Dogs are $10 extra daily. Off-season there's a four-night minimum at $220 nightly.

Next to the house itself is a very cozy little studio efficiency, where only small dogs are allowed. The Hohe Guest Studio rents for $129–149 a night, with a two-night minimum. Steven Hohe has a few other dog-friendly vacation rentals in the area. Phone for details. You'll get the Hohe House address when you make your reservation; 858/273-0324; www.10kvacationrentals .com/hohe/hohehouse.

Holiday Inn on the Bay: As long as you're willing to sign a contract stating that you will accept responsibility for any damage your dog may do and that you won't leave him alone in your room, you and your dog are welcome here. (Oh, and you have to pay a one-time $25 dog fee and a $100 deposit.) But don't try to sneak off and leave the pooch alone—the hotel will call the pound folks, who will arrive pretty quickly since they're just across the street. How convenient. Rates are $170–360. 1355 North Harbor Drive 92101; 619/232-3861.

Hotel Solamar: If you and your dog prefer hip, modern, almost sassy lodgings, this Gaslamp Quarter hotel is one you simply must sniff out. The 235 rooms in this four-star Kimpton hotel have a uniquely energetic decor and design. Since your dog may see only in black and white, I'll let the hotel's literature tell him about the color scheme: "Vibrant and playful tones of pink, green, and blue dance upon a rich, sensual backdrop of chocolate brown .... Imagine a palette by starting with fresh roasted espresso beans. Add a hot pink cosmopolitan, a juicy Granny Smith apple, and the captivating blue of a tropical aquarium." As Jack, a Jack Russell terrier who visited here recently wrote me, "It's totally cool!"

But what dogs think is really cool is the treatment they get here. Upon arrival they get treats, toys, and bowls. And there's no extra charge for all this! At press time the hotel was in the process of re-creating the pet package to include more goodies and services.

The hotel's fourth-floor outdoor pool, complete with bar, is surrounded by plush loungers like something you'd see in the French Riviera. The hotel offers several complimentary services to humans, including free Wi-Fi, evening wine hour complete with Buddha Art Boards (you'll see when you get there), and overnight shoeshine. The hotel also puts out an end-of-the-day "What's Flaring Up Tonight" newsletter. At press time for this book, the name was a little too close to home: The wildfires that burned hundreds of thousands of acres in the county were raging. In fact, the hotel concierge told us that at the moment the hotel had 50 dog guests and lots of cats, hamsters, and other pets (and their people) who had been evacuated from their homes. "Of course we're going to take them in. They have nowhere else to go," said the concierge. The hotel's welcoming of this many animals of all types gives the hotel huge points in my book (literally).

Rates are $136–609. (The high rate is for a suite.) 435 Sixth Avenue 92101; 619/531-8740 or 877/230-0300; www.hotelsolamar.com.

Ocean Beach Vacation Bungalows: How's this for dog heaven on earth? Lucky dogs who come here get to stay with their people at either of two adorable vacation rental bungalows that are just a half block from Dog Beach, where dogs can throw their leashes and their cares to the wind!

These two one-bedroom bungalows are next-door neighbors and have hardwood floors and fenced yards. They're basic-looking on the outside, but the interiors are attractive, comfortable, and cozy, with full kitchens, lovely furnishings and special extra touches. One is known as the Cape Cod bungalow, the other as the Bahamas bungalow. Rates are $775–1,500 for a week. Dogs are $50 per stay. You'll get the addresses when you reserve. 619/861-4262 or 619/443-0704; www.thebestcall.com.

Ocean Villa Inn: Here's a dog's dream come true: The adored, famed, revered, worshipped Dog Beach is right next door to this motel! It doesn't get any more convenient than this. Dogs are allowed in the downstairs rooms and the studios, which come with a mini fridge and microwave—very handy when traveling with a pooch. Rooms are clean and pleasant. Nothing fancy, but who needs fancy when you're a bone's throw from a magnificent dog-friendly beach?

Rates are $99–360. The inn allows up to four dogs per room! That's a real rarity these days. The dog fee is stepped: 1–2 dogs cost $25 per stay, 3 dogs cost $50 per stay, 4 dogs cost $75. A $100 deposit is also required. 5142 West Point Loma Boulevard 92107; 619/224-3481 or 800/759-0012; www.oceanvillainn.com.

Old Town Inn: The rooms at this Spanish-style motel are spacious but standard issue. The palms surrounding the inn make for a pretty picture. Rates are $60–180. Dogs are $10 extra. 4444 Pacific Highway 92110; 619/260-8024 or 800/643-3025.

San Diego Marriott Hotel & Marina: The people who work at this lovely waterfront Marriott have a great attitude about large dogs. Not only do they tolerate them, but they're happy to see them. "The size doesn't matter. It's often the small ones that bark a lot anyway," says one hotelier. (Smart man.)

This Marriott is on the water, right next to the dog-unfriendly Seaport Village. At least the views of the bay are to bark about—er, to write home about. The humans in your party can enjoy the heated outdoor pools and the sauna, whirlpool, and exercise room. If you like the boating life, you and your dog can rent a boat from a boat-rental company on the property and have a great day on San Diego Bay. (See the Diversion *Whatever Floats Your Boat*.) It's one of the more expensive Marriotts we've come across. Rates are $230–465. 333 West Harbor Drive 92101; 619/234-1500; www.marriott.com.

Vagabond Inn: This one's in the Mission Valley area. Rates are $69–99. Dogs are $20 extra. 625 Hotel Circle South 92108; 619/297-1691.

Westin Horton Plaza: It's modern, it's chic, it's a cool place to stay with a dog who's not too big. (Dogs need to be under 40 pounds.) Lucky dog guests will get use of a Heavenly Pet Bed (a smaller version of the Heavenly Bed human guests rave about) and bowls for water and food. "We like to see dog guests come in," says a friendly front-desk worker. "They are so much fun." This large, upscale hotel is downtown, right next to the famed Horton Plaza shopping center. Rates are $225–400. 910 Broadway Circle 92101; 619/239-2200; www.starwood.com/westin.

La Mesa

PARKS, BEACHES, AND RECREATION AREAS

37 Canine Corners

😊😊😊🐕 (See San Diego County map on page 832)

Dogs get two-plus acres of fenced fun here. It started nice and green, but that quickly turned to dirt. The ground cover is now mostly manufactured sand, which is better than dirt, but not much fun to roll on. (Or so Jake tells me.) The park has a separate section for small dogs, and all the usual dog park amenities including water, poop bags, benches, and shade structures. Add to this some well-established pines and eucalyptus, and tennis balls galore, and it's a good place to take a dog in need of a leash-free run. "It's trouble-free, with lots of very, very friendly dogs," says Becky Rice, one of the park's founders. "It's a very social environment for dogs and their people." Even guide dogs have their day here: Once a month it's Guide Dogs Day Out Program. Throughout the year the park hosts events such as costume contests and photo time with Santa.

The dog park is within the grassy, 53-acre Harry Griffen Park. The larger park is home to a pleasant little reservoir leashed dogs like to peruse. The park is in the easternmost section of the city, on the border of El Cajon. The main entrance is at 9550 Milden Street, in back of Grossmont High School. The official city number for the park is 619/463-6611, but if you have dog-park questions, you can phone the dog-park association at 619/469-3748.

Coronado

Folks traveling with dogs aren't allowed to take the ferry to this islandlike destination across the San Diego Bay. But a graceful 2.2-mile bridge will get you there just as fast—which is the speed your dog will want to go when she learns she can run off leash at one of the beaches here.

PARKS, BEACHES, AND RECREATION AREAS

38 Coronado City Beach/Dog Beach

😊😊😊😊🐕 (See San Diego County map on page 832)

The westernmost part of this beach is a nude beach for dogs, where they can strip off their leashes and revel in their birthday fur. And since few people know about it, even the shyest dog will feel at home running around flaunting her more natural self.

As long as your dog is under voice control, she can be leashless at a small segment of this little beach. Your dog has only a few hundred feet of shoreline to run along, but the area between the beach border and the water is fairly wide.

The off-leash section is marked by signs and runs along Ocean Boulevard from around the foot of Sunset Park (on Ocean Drive) to the border of the U.S. Naval Station. You'll see the doggy poop bags. (Not far down the street is a hose-off station, should you not want to go home with sandy paws.) From the bridge, continue straight. In a few blocks, turn left on Orange Avenue and drive through town all the way down to the traffic circle. Go around the circle to Loma Avenue and follow it south about a block to Ocean Boulevard. Drive northwest a few blocks and park on the street around Sunset Park. 619/522-7380.

39 Coronado Tidelands Regional Park

😊😊😊 (See San Diego County map on page 832)

Situated on San Diego Bay just north of the toll plaza, this is the largest of Coronado's parks and it's got a little of everything. From manicured golf course–like lawns to playing fields, walking paths, and terrific views of San Diego, the park suits the needs of just about any dog. There's even a small beach here. Dogs must be leashed, though, so there's no swimming back to San Diego!

After crossing the bridge, take your first right onto Glorietta Boulevard. Go right again into the park on Mullinix Drive. 619/686-6225.

40 Coronado Cays Dog Park

😊😊😊🐕 (See San Diego County map on page 832)

This wonderful park is one of the best-kept secrets around. (And with all the Naval operations nearby, that's saying a lot.) That's because it's within the

DIVERSION

Venice, Shmenice: When you and your dog share a private gondola that takes you through Coronado Cays's scenic canals and waterways, you'll feel almost as if you've been transported to Italy's famed land of canals. The only difference is that instead of your gondolier singing, he'll use a CD player for the Italian tunes. Oh, and there's no ancient architecture. And no magnificent Old-World charm. OK, it may not be just like Italy, but it's still a wonderful excursion, and the gondolas—which are very sizeable and waterway-worthy—are pretty much guaranteed not to tip over, even if your dog gets a case of the wiggles.

The **Gondola Company** can arrange all kinds of special cruises, some featuring a brunch or dinner excursion. A popular one, the Passport Cruise, lasts one hour and includes an hors d'oeuvre or dessert plate. Bring your own vino or bubbly; the gondolier provides the wine glasses and an ice bucket. You'll also get use of a blanket. The Passport Cruise is $85 for two people and a dog. (You can invite your friends for $20 extra each. The boat can hold up to six passengers.) Cruises are offered 11 A.M.–midnight. The most popular cruise, the Sunset Cruise, can be very romantic (despite your dog), and costs $99. The Gondola Company is right next to the ultra dog-friendly Loews Coronado Bay Resort, at 4000 Coronado Bay Road; 619/429-6317; www.gondolacompany.com.

gated community of Coronado Cays. You actually have to go past a security officer at the community's gate to get to the park. Most people think it's off-limits to anyone but residents, but that's not true. Anyone with a well-behaved dog is welcome.

It's a great place to bring a dog. It even attracts people who don't have dogs. Yayoi, a Cays resident with a penchant for dogs, says she just goes there "for a dog fix. I don't have a dog, but I love to watch them. They're so happy to be on this planet when they're there. I can almost hear them talking to each other about how excited they are to be here as they bound out of their cars."

The official dog park area of this 6.8-acre grassy park is along a walkway that follows a brick wall separating the park from traffic. You'll see signs and poop-bag dispensers. That's where you can let your dog off-leash. It's a pleasant walk past big green fields often used for soccer. In fact, most people who use the park assume the whole park (except the tennis courts and other developed areas) is for leash-free pooches. If there's not a game, we're told it's really not a big problem if your dog trots around the fields a bit. But during game times, keep to the official area. Another section dogs enjoy—particularly boy dogs—is over by a treed area.

From the Silver Strand Freeway/I-75, take the Coronado Cays exit and follow the road to the gate. Once past security you'll come to a four-way stop. Make a right, and park in the area closest to the brick wall. (You might want to just ask security where the dog park is when you enter. It's easier.) The park is run by the local homeowners association. 619/423-4353.

PLACES TO EAT

Cafe 1134: Pooches who keep you company at these outdoor tables while you dine on sandwiches and coffee are lucky dogs indeed: The staff here provides dog biscuits and a water bowl for your fine furry friend. 1134 Orange Avenue; 619/437-1134.

Crown Bistro: The breakfasts here have won Best Breakfast awards many years in a row. It's a mighty convenient place to dine if you're staying at the Crown City Inn, since it's part of the inn's property. Dine with your very good doggy on scrumptious California-style food at the bistro's six small shaded patio tables. This is an intimate place, and at times when it's busy, you may be asked to come back with your dog when there's a little more space. The folks here are really friendly to dogs, and they even provide water to thirsty pooches, but the space is small enough that the owners ask patrons with pooches to call ahead to see if it's a good time to come. Any size well-behaved dog is welcome, pending adequate space. Regulars here include a 170-pound rottweiler and a 15-pound miniature dachshund. 520 Orange Avenue; 619/435-3678.

Market Cafe: Dogs are welcome to join you at this gorgeous café set in Loews Coronado Bay Resort. The outdoor tables overlook the marina. It's a real treat. The food for humans is a fresh delight, with seasonal salads, great little pizzas, and tasty pastas. And heaven forbid your dog should feel left out. Dogs who come here not only get treats and a bowl of water, but if they request, they can choose an item from the Loews pet room service menu. Care for Bow-Wow Tenderloin of Beef? The tenderloin is mixed with eggs and rice and will cost you $19. (Jake has to stick with the free dog treats here.) 4000 Loew's Coronado Bay Road; 619/424-4444.

Tent City Restaurant: Tent City was a makeshift vacation community of large white tents set up in 1900 near all the sun and fun that comes with life in Coronado. Residents, presidents, actors, and writers enjoyed a little coastal R&R at this simple seaside spot. That's all gone now, but you and your dog might be able to imagine what it was like while you dine under the big umbrellas that shade the many patio tables outside the fun Tent City Restaurant. The food here is an eclectic mélange of California fresh and traditional surf and turf. 1100 Orange Avenue (at the Museum of History and Art); 619/435-4611.

PLACES TO STAY

Coronado Inn: This is a clean, decent motel with an attractive pool area and complimentary continental breakfast. If you have dirty laundry, you don't have to worry about walking around whiffy. Just use the coin-op laundry on site here. Rates are $109–269. Dogs are $10 extra. 266 Orange Avenue 92118; 619/435-4121 or 800/598-6624; www.coronadoinn.com.

Coronado Victorian House: In this gorgeous 1894 Victorian, all the beds in the seven bedrooms are from the 1800s and are topped with featherbed mattresses. The rooms at this bed-and-breakfast all have private bathrooms (some with claw-foot tubs) and are beautifully furnished, reflecting the tastes of Bonni Marie, the inn's dog-loving owner. Bonni Marie will proudly tell you about her three "monkeys" (cute little dogs, not really monkeys). She's a most friendly innkeeper, and a dance instructor to boot.

Sadly for dogs who weigh more than a large bag of dog food, 40 pounds is the size limit for pooches here. Rates are $300–500 nightly, with a two-night minimum stay. Dogs are $25 extra. An important piece of information to know when you make your reservation: You may not cancel your reservation, and your fee is nonrefundable. Ouch! 619/435-2200 or 888/299-2822; www.coronadovictorianhouse.com.

Crown City Inn: This sweet little hotel is as welcoming for dogs as it is for humans. People get free use of bicycles, and iced tea or hot chocolate and cookies every afternoon. Dogs get a food mat, water bowl, a treat bag with a toy, and info on pet-sitters and dog-friendly parks and eateries. Everyone who comes here is happy. Your room comes with a fridge and microwave, but with the Crown Bistro restaurant so close to your room, you may want to give your kitchenette skills a break. Rates are $100–249. Dogs are $8–25. 520 Orange Avenue 92118; 619/435-3116; www.crowncityinn.com.

Loews Coronado Bay Resort: Prepare to be impressed. This modern, luxurious hotel presides over a 15-acre peninsula, with the Pacific on one side and San Diego Bay on the other. The rooms are crisp and clean, yet super-comfy, with great waterfront views. The gardens are gorgeous, and the palm-lined three-pool area is to drool for (although no drool *or* dogs are allowed in the pools; pooches can take their dog paddle to the nearby Coronado City Beach/ Dog Beach). If you like the sporting life, you can play tennis at the hotel's three lighted courts or rent a boat and set sail on the bay, with your dog as first mate. (See the Diversion *Whatever Floats Your Boat* in the *San Diego* section.) Or you and your dog can hire a gondola for an enchanting cruise through the Coronado Cays. (See the Diversion *Venice, Shmenice.*)

Speaking of dogs, the treatment they get here is nothing short of red carpet, thanks to Loews' Very Important Pet Program. Your dog will be welcomed with a note from the hotel's general manager. It includes a list of nearby dog-friendly locales, as well as groomers, pet shops, and vets. In your room you'll find food and water bowls, treats, and toys. A doggy roomservice menu is also available, with items that sound so good you might be tempted to share them. If you forgot a leash or your pet's bed, you can borrow these from the concierge's "Did You Forget" closet. Dog-walking and petsitting can be arranged if the staff isn't too busy. If you opt for a pet-sitter, you'll get a Puppy Pager, which allows hotel staff to contact you in case of emergency.

Rates are $199–535. Dogs are $25 extra. 4000 Coronado Bay Road 92118; 619/424-4000; www.loewshotels.com.

Chula Vista

PARKS, BEACHES, AND RECREATION AREAS

Chula Vista now has two leash-free pooch parks. One is very small, and since we only have room for so many parks in this book, we'll describe the larger and more used of the two. Actually, Chula Vista also has a great little dog park run by a mall, not the city. (See the Diversion *Is It a Mall or a Doggy Funland?*)

41 Montvalle Dog Park

🐾🐾🐾 🐕 (See San Diego County map on page 832)

This good-sized fenced park is divided into two sections: one for dogs up to 20 pounds, the other for the less-petite set. The park has both grass and decomposed granite and is well landscaped, with bushes lining parts of the fence and some trees adding visual interest (or olfactory interest, if you're a boy dog). Water, poop bags, and benches are among the amenities. The park is within the 29-acre Montvalle Park, at 840 Duncan Ranch Road, in the Eastlake area of the city. 619/691-5269.

DIVERSION

Is It a Mall or a Doggy Funland? That's what dogs and their people ask themselves after visiting the **Otay Ranch Town Center** open-air shopping mall, which opened in late 2006. Every store has a water bowl in front of it. "There's plenty to drink," says a mall liaison. Many stores allow good dogs inside. And in the southwest corner of the mall, near REI and the conveniently located Otay Pet Vet (which provides very affordable pet-sitting for shoppers), is a 10,000-square-foot dog park! It was part of the mall's master plan to be very accessible to people with dogs and human kids. (Kids have fun diversions like popper fountains and chalk gardens.)

The grassy fenced dog park is divided into two sections: One for small dogs, one for large dogs. It's graced with big, fun dog-themed pieces, including a bone-shaped bench, a giant hydrant boy dogs worship, and a huge dog house. It's all very whimsical and fun.

The mall is at the corner of Olympic and Eastlake parkways, in Chula Vista. 619/656-9100; www.otayranchtowncenter.com.

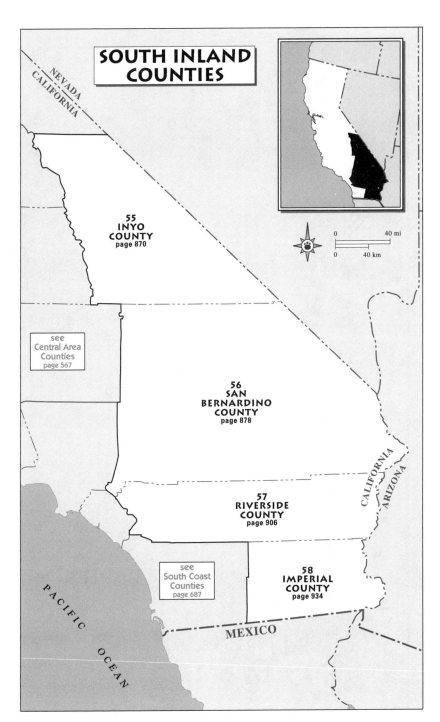

SOUTH INLAND COUNTIES

NEVADA
CALIFORNIA

**55
INYO
COUNTY**
page 870

see
Central Area
Counties
page 567

**56
SAN
BERNARDINO
COUNTY**
page 878

**57
RIVERSIDE
COUNTY**
page 906

CALIFORNIA
ARIZONA

see
South Coast
Counties
page 687

**58
IMPERIAL
COUNTY**
page 934

PACIFIC

OCEAN

MEXICO

0   40 mi
0   40 km

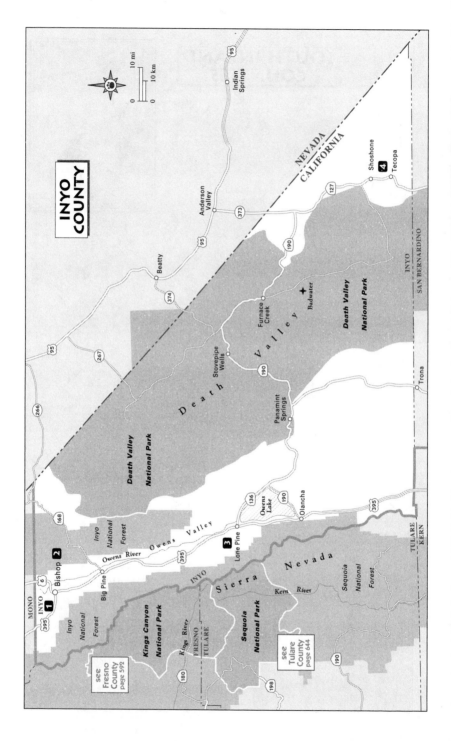

CHAPTER 55

Inyo County

The elevation: as low as 282 feet below sea level. Some of the hot spots to visit: Funeral Mountains. Chloride City. Death Valley. Furnace Creek.

It may sound like pure hell, but a visit to this county during the cooler months of the year actually might be one of the most interesting adventures you and your dog share in California.

Inyo County has an incredible variety of landscapes. The desert contains the lowest land in the United States, at 282 feet below sea level. The adjacent Sierra Nevada and the silver, knifelike pinnacles of towering Mt. Whitney make a strong contrast. In fact, Mt. Whitney, with its peak at 14,494 feet, is the highest point in the contiguous United States. Because its sheer eastern wall rises out of the low desert landscape of the Owens Valley, the effect is especially dramatic. In spring, wildflowers are everywhere. The sight of towering mountains against flowering desert makes dogs sniff the air in heavenly awe.

Warning: Don't bring your dog to the desert areas of the county in the summer or early fall. Dogs who aren't accustomed to the heat may not survive the average daily temperatures of 116°F, not to mention the perilously hot ground. It's not much fun for most humans, either.

PICK OF THE LITTER—INYO COUNTY

BEST HUGE PARK
Death Valley National Park (page 872)

PARK WITH OLDEST LIVING THINGS ON EARTH
Ancient Bristlecone Pine Forest, Big Pine (page 875)

BEST PLACE TO PRETEND YOU'RE IN A WESTERN
Alabama Hills, Lone Pine (page 876)

BEST PLACE TO STAY
Stove Pipe Wells Village, Death Valley (page 875)

BEST PLACE TO WATCH A WESTERN
Lone Pine Film Festival, Lone Pine (page 876)

NATIONAL FORESTS

The *National Forests and Wilderness Areas* resource at the back of this book has important information and safety tips on visiting national forests with your dog and has more information on the Inyo National Forest.

Inyo National Forest

Dogs love the 28,000-acre Ancient Bristlecone Pine Forest, part of this national forest northeast of Big Pine. The gnarled pines that look like living driftwood are thought to be the world's oldest living trees—and are probably the oldest living things on Earth! Tell your boy dog to be respectful of these aged arboreal wonders. Temperatures here are cooler than in much of the surrounding area because of the 10,000-foot elevation.

NATIONAL PARKS

Death Valley National Park

What's in a name? When I first thought about taking Joe to Death Valley, I pictured him ending up as a pile of bones in the sand while coyotes bayed and vultures licked their beaks. Taking a dog to Death Valley seemed like something rather, well, mean.

There *are* some hungry coyotes here. In fact, a spokeswoman says coyotes kill one to three dogs brought by visitors every season. My intrepid research editor, Caroline Grannan, recounts a close call she had with her now-late yellow Lab, Sally, after she let her off-leash:

> A coyote came flashing out of a little grove of date palms and shot across the golf course, and Sally took right off after it. They were out of sight over the berm in a minute, with me hopelessly running after then. Then a few minutes later, Sally happily trotted back over the berm toward me. At the time, it seemed kind of romantic, the pampered golden purebred taking off with the creature of the wild and then remembering her warm bed and designer kibble and changing her mind. Now I know how lucky we were, because it's typical coyote behavior to send a lone scout to lure dogs to where the hungry pack is waiting.

So why do we give this place a big four paws? Notice there is no running-dog symbol next to the paws. This park is a four-paw experience, but your dog absolutely needs to remain on leash here. And as long as you also stay away during the grueling months before, during, and after summer (April–September), you and your dog could have some of your best adventures ever.

This 3.2-million-acre park encompasses the former Death Valley National Monument, Eureka Sand Dunes National Natural Landmark, and several other federally run natural areas. In 1994, the Desert Protection Act merged these areas into one big, full-fledged national park. In most areas, that doesn't affect dog rules. But where dogs were once permitted to run around off leash at Bureau of Land Management lands here, they have to obey the new leash rules. And sadly, at the Eureka Sand Dunes area, whose centerpiece is a 700-foot-high mountain of sand, dogs can no longer cavort about on the dunes at all. It's a howling shame.

Fortunately, although dogs aren't permitted on trails at Death Valley, there are so few trails that it won't matter to you. What matters is that they're allowed to hike at your side on the more than 500 miles of roadway that stretch from one landscape to another within Death Valley. Most of these roads are unpaved and barely get used by vehicles, so chances are you can get plenty of pure desert solitude with pure desert air.

Keep in mind that dogs also aren't supposed to wander far off the road into backcountry. About 100 yards is the limit. Remember that with air as clean and land as flat as this, rangers are omniscient. Watch yourselves, because they are sure to be watching as well.

You'll see some of the most fascinating geologic formations on Earth here. Of course, most of the time it won't look like you're even on Earth, but don't let that bother you. The park's otherworldly nature is one of its charms. Much of the park is below sea level. The lowest point in the United States is here, in Badwater Basin. Within the park are elevations from 282 feet below sea level to 11,049 feet above sea level. Betwixt and between, you'll find vast salt flats, endless sand ridges, huge rocks, and twisting mountainsides.

When you get to the visitors center, pick up brochures on the history and geology of the place and decide which parts of Death Valley you and your dog would enjoy most. The park has nine campgrounds, six of which are open all year. There are about 760 campsites available on a first-come, first-served basis. Fees range from free to $18.

The entry fee for the park is $20 per carload, good for visits of up to a week. Being that the park is bigger than the state of Connecticut, there are many spots where you can enter it. To get to the main visitors center from U.S. 395, take either Highway 136 or Highway 190 east. Highway 136 will join Highway 190. From U.S. 395, the drive is a little more than 100 miles. Follow Highway 190 through all its confusing turns and you can't miss it. Even in the cooler months of the year, it's a good idea to bring extra water, just in case you break down and the temperature decides to do one of its soaring routines. 760/786-2331.

Bishop

Set between the state's two highest mountain ranges, Bishop has become the hub of this recreational wonderland. It's a small, laid-back town with only one thing that peeves pooches: Dogs are banned from the only city park here.

PARKS, BEACHES, AND RECREATION AREAS

❶ Pleasant Valley County Park
🐾🐾🐾 (See Inyo County map on page 870)

This park has the long, narrow Pleasant Valley Reservoir as its centerpiece. The reservoir is created by the Owens River, and fishing here is pretty hot (thanks in part to planted trout). Leashed dogs are allowed to cheer at your side as you catch supper from shore.

For dogs who aren't fishing fans, try the hiking trail on the reservoir's east side. The big rocky bluffs here are interesting, but the surrounding mountains topped with snow year-round are really impressive. However, dogs don't seem to care much for the visuals. Something about this place keeps their flaring nostrils pressed firmly to the ground. Since leashes are the law, you may feel some tugging when your dog decides to try to track one of these enticing smells.

There are 200 campsites, but they're pretty far from the lake. Sites are $10. Reservations are not necessary. Take U.S. 395 about seven miles north of Bishop, and then turn north on Pleasant Valley Road and drive about 1.5 miles to the lake. 760/873-5577.

PLACES TO STAY

Comfort Inn: This isn't just your average Comfort Inn. It's a mighty dog-friendly Comfort Inn. Hannah Dog (a husky-shepherd mix) and her folks were nice enough to write to let me know that the owner adores dogs, and that she "cheerfully takes dogs of all sizes." I called the owner to confirm, and indeed she's a doggy person. "Sure, we take all good dogs," she said. "We've even had Saint Bernards." The place even has a fish-cleaning station. I guess the owner likes fish, too. Rates are $79–229. Dogs are $5 extra. 805 North Main Street 93514; 760/873-4284 or 800/576-4080.

Thunderbird Motel: Rates are $50–80. Dogs are $5 extra. 190 West Pine Street 93514; 760/873-4215.

Vagabond Inn: This one comes with its own fish-cleaning facilities and a freezer. If you and your dog have a successful day angling, this might be the place for you. Rates are $90–110. Pooches are $5 extra. 1030 North Main Street 93514; 760/873-6351.

Big Pine

PARKS, BEACHES, AND RECREATION AREAS

❷ Ancient Bristlecone Pine Forest

🐾🐾🐾 (See Inyo County map on page 870)

This remarkable area is in Inyo National Forest (see the *National Forests* section at the beginning of the chapter for details), about 25 miles northeast of Big Pine.

There's a day-use fee of $3 per adult or a maximum of $5 per vehicle, and no fee for campsites. Winter usually makes the access roads impassable, but the forest is accessible early June–late October. From U.S. 395, turn east onto Highway 168 just north of Big Pine. Follow the highway east 13 miles to White Mountain Road. Turn left (north) and drive 10 miles to the Schulman Grove Visitor Center. The Bristlecone pines can be viewed from the parking area of the visitors center and along three trails. (Get outta the parking lot, for sure!) 760/873-2500.

PLACES TO STAY

Glacier Lodge: The main lodge here, built in 1917, burned down a few years ago. It will soon be rebuilt, and when it is, it's going to be an intriguing modern building with a full-service restaurant, a library, and a game room. Meanwhile, dogs and their people are welcome to stay at the mountain lodge's 10 rustic housekeeping cabins. You're surrounded by all kinds of recreational opportunities here, from fishing to hiking miles and miles of trails with your furry friend. Rates are $110–135. Dogs are $15 extra. The lodge is 11 miles west of Highway 395. The mailing address (there's really no street address) is P.O. Box 370 93513; 760/938-2837; www.sonic.net/~kwofford/glacier-lodge.

Death Valley

PLACES TO STAY

Stove Pipe Wells Village: Set on 100 acres of Death Valley National Park, this sprawling, rustic resort is mighty dog-friendly. Maggie the Wonder Dog, the canine companion of San Francisco's Kim Wonderly, wrote to us to tell us she gives it two paws up. You and your leashed dog are free to peruse the village's 100 acres and beyond. The lodging is a mere 10-minute walk from the most-photographed sand dunes in the world—if you love *Lawrence of Arabia,* you can pull a Peter O'Toole here and run around in your white robe. Rates for the hotel/motel are $71–111. Dogs require a $20 deposit, and your room may be checked for doggy damage before you leave. There's no street address. For information, write Stove Pipe Wells Village 92328; 760/786-2387; www. stovepipewells.com.

Lone Pine

This is a one-stoplight town—the gateway to Mt. Whitney. As Marilyn, an enthusiastic native who works at the Chamber of Commerce, put it, "We've got a real pretty town, real Western."

And real Westerns are what they've been shooting here for decades. Alabama Hills is a must-visit location for dogs and their people.

PARKS, BEACHES, AND RECREATION AREAS

🐾 Alabama Hills

🐾🐾🐾🐾 🐕 (See Inyo County map on page 870)

Pardner, if you like Western films and TV shows, you're gonna love this place. For more than 70 years, Hollywood has used Lone Pine's unique scenery in almost 300 films and countless TV shows.

This is where the *Lone Ranger* ambush was first filmed, where Roy Rogers found Trigger, where *Bonanza* became a bonanza. Giants such as Gene Autry, Roy Rogers, Hopalong Cassidy, Humphrey Bogart, Cary Grant, Gregory Peck, Spencer Tracy, and Clint Eastwood did their big scenes here. In fact, this is where Roy Rogers and Robert Mitchum filmed their first features.

DOG-EAR YOUR CALENDAR

Leashed dogs are welcome to attend all the outdoor segments of the three-day **Lone Pine Film Festival** celebrating the myriad Western flicks shot in the nearby Alabama Hills. Some of the most famous old cowboys and cowgals gather during this three-day festival, which is held on the second weekend of October, to talk with fans and even reenact a scene or two. If your dog is lucky, maybe he'll get to shake paws with one of the greats. See www.lonepinefilmfestival.org or call 760/876-9103 for information on this year's event.

Put a bandanna on your four-legged varmint and have a rip-roaring time exploring the rock formations, canyons, and barren flats that are the real stars here. Some photo markers are placed in the area showing which famous scenes were shot where. It's a real education for you and your dog. Be really careful where and if you allow your dog to be leashless, because dogs and the cars that wind around the park don't mix.

From U.S. 395, take the Whitney Portal Road about 2.5 miles west of Lone Pine and you'll find yourself on Movie Road. That's where your trek through movieland begins. Don't forget to bring a camera. 760/872-5000.

PLACES TO STAY

Dow Villa Motel: Rates at this basic, clean motel are $63–130. Dogs require a $50 deposit against dog deposits, if ya know what I mean. 310 South Main Street 93545; 760/876-5521; www.dowvillamotel.com.

Tecopa

The population is 99 as of a recent census. The neighboring community of Shoshone has a whopping 106 residents. These are fairly big numbers when you get this deep into the desert.

PARKS, BEACHES, AND RECREATION AREAS

❹ Tecopa Hot Springs County Park

🐾🐾🐾 (See Inyo County map on page 870)

The Paiute Indians used to bring their lame and sick ancestors to bathe in the hot mineral springs here, and now people from all over the world come for a soak. The 107°F waters are supposed to help alleviate the pain of arthritis, rheumatism, and other bodily woes.

While dogs can't take a dip, they are allowed to roam the 40-acre park with you. Switch off hanging out with the dog with a friend as you take turns rejuvenating yourselves in the baths.

Most of the park is taken up by a large, 250-site campground. Sites are $14–17. Many are available on a first-come, first-served basis, but you can also make reservations if that makes you feel better about driving all the way out here. The bathing is free. Make sure you don't come with your dog in the hot months. The temperature can climb to 118°F in some summer months, and that's hotter than the mineral baths.

From Death Valley Junction (Highways 190 and 127), follow the road about 36 miles to the park. 760/852-4481.

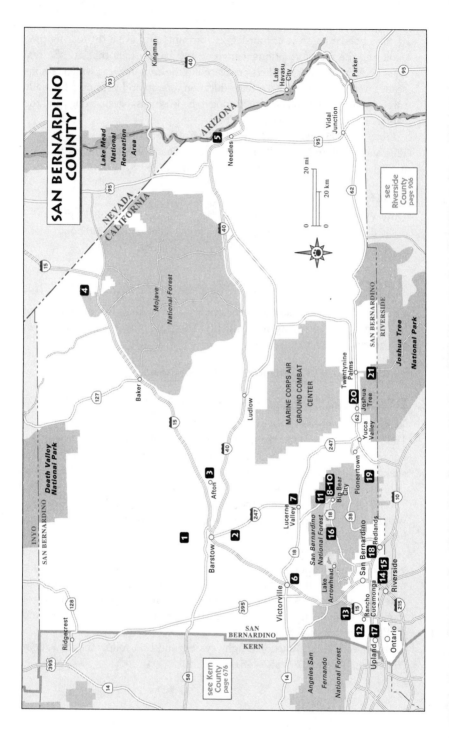

SAN BERNARDINO COUNTY

see Kern County page 676

see Riverside County page 906

CHAPTER 56

San Bernardino County

This is the Texas of California. It's just plain big. In fact, it's the biggest county in the nation, weighing in at more than 20,000 square miles.

That means you'll find a lot of variety here. This is where dogs can do just about everything they ever imagined a dog could do. They can ride the rails through a ghost town, roam around off leash on millions of acres of land, herd goats in Chino, take a horse-and-buggy ride in Big Bear, ride a rented boat around Big Bear Lake, and stay in some of the most wonderful cabins and resorts this side of the Rockies.

Try to visit the San Bernardino Mountains at sunset, when occasionally they play an optical trick. A few of the mountains will turn purplish pink, while others stay the same sandy brown and forest green. Then everything fades into a surreal orange mist. For people, it's a stunning sight. If dogs really do have black-and-white vision, they're probably not quite so thrilled.

PICK OF THE LITTER—
SAN BERNARDINO COUNTY

BEST OFF-LEASH HIKING
San Bernardino National Forest (page 881)
Rainbow Basin Natural Area, Barstow (page 882)
Stoddard Valley Open Area, Barstow (page 883)

BEST DOG PARK
Wildwood Dog Park, San Bernardino (page 896)

MOST DOG-FRIENDLY PLACE TO EAT
Wolfgang Puck Café, Ontario (page 899)

MOST DOG-FRIENDLY PLACES TO STAY
Cienaga Creek Ranch Mountain Cottages, Big Bear Lake
(page 890)
Eagle's Nest Bed & Breakfast Lodge, Big Bear Lake (page 891)
Golden Bear Cottages, Big Bear Lake (page 892)
Arrowhead Tree Top Lodge, Lake Arrowhead (page 898)
Rimrock Ranch Cabins, Pioneertown (page 903)

BEST GHOST TOWN
Calico Ghost Town, Calico (page 883)

MOST WELCOMING STORE
Big Dogs Sportswear, Lake Arrowhead (page 898)

BEST LIVE "THEATER"
Pioneertown Posse's Old West skits, Pioneertown (page 902)

NATIONAL FORESTS

The *National Forests and Wilderness Areas* resource at the back of this book has important information and safety tips on visiting national forests with your dog and has more information on San Bernardino National Forest.

San Bernardino National Forest
😾😾😾😾🐕

Much of the southwest corner of San Bernardino County is San Bernardino National Forest land. So far, dogs are allowed off leash in most parts of the forest, except for several times when they meet up with state parks. (Dogs aren't even allowed there *on* leash.) Unfortunately, local national forest rangers are facing the question of whether off-leash rules are appropriate in the forest. Complaints about dogs running up to frightened humans or fighting with each other have led to this dilemma. So make absolutely certain your dog is Mr., Mrs., or Ms. Obedience before taking off that leash.

On the way up to Big Bear Lake via Highway 38, you'll find numerous forest trailheads and picnic areas that make great rest stops on a long journey. See the *Big Bear Lake* section in this chapter for more on this popular resort area.

NATIONAL PARKS

Joshua Tree National Park
😾😾😾

Although most of this 794,000-acre park is in Riverside County, Twentynine Palms is where you'll find the visitors center and the gateways to some of the most beautiful areas in the park.

This is amazing land, with striking granite formations rising around dramatic desert plants and wildlife. In spring, it becomes a showcase of brilliant wildflowers. The giant Joshua tree plants are in the higher western half, and they're definitely worth a visit.

Dogs can be walked on paved and dirt roads, but not on hiking trails. They're permitted to wander on leash up to 100 yards from the road, and there are plenty of small dirt roads where you'll be far from most traffic. Leashes are the law here, but they're also a very good idea because of critters like mountain lions and bobcats. A bigger danger than those cats is actually the cactus. Dogs sometimes rub up against the prickly plants or try to bite them and end up with a major problem. One last warning: The ground here can get really toasty—sometimes too toasty for your dog's paws. If you wouldn't want to walk barefoot here, neither would your dog. Rangers report several cases of paw pad injury each year because of the hot ground. Come when it's cooler and you'll be better off.

There's a $10 entrance fee, and if you want to camp without water, it's free! Otherwise, sites are $10–12. There are 492 sites available on a first-come, first-served basis. However, the 100 sites at Black Rock Canyon require reservations. Always bring lots of water on your hikes here, and make sure your dog gets her fill. It doesn't usually get nearly as hot as in other parts of the desert, but don't take a chance. From I-10, exit at Highway 62 and drive northeast for about 39 miles to the town of Twentynine Palms. The visitors center is on Utah Trail, just south of the highway about a mile east of town. 760/367-5500.

Barstow

This is a mighty dog-friendly town. In fact, it's just the place for a bruised canine ego to go after stepping on one too many threadbare doggy welcome mats. The folks here generally like dogs at least as much as they like people.

PARKS, BEACHES, AND RECREATION AREAS

1 Rainbow Basin Natural Area

😻😻😻😻 🐕 (See San Bernardino County map on page 878)

If you and your dog like bones, faults, sediment deposits, or leash-free walks, don't miss this geological and anthropological wonder. Fossils of ancient animals are everywhere in the colorful sedimentary layers of the canyon walls (once a lake). Mastodons, camels, three-toed horses, rhinos, and dog-bears are among the animals whose remains have been discovered here. As you hike around, you'll see insect fossils that are among the best preserved in the world. You and your dog need to keep your paws off these fossils so they remain undisturbed for others to enjoy.

The geology of the place is also fascinating. Rainbow Basin's sediment deposits are textbook examples of folds, faults, and other disturbances of the earth's crust. If you're studying geology in school, this is the place to visit if you want to get the big picture.

Unfortunately, your dog probably doesn't give a hoot about bones she can't eat and sediment she can't wallow in. She knows what's important—being able to be at your side, off leash, while you peruse the area. The Bureau of Land Management, which operates the park, has some of the most lenient, dog-friendly rules in the state for obedient pooches.

The best place to take an off-leash dog is any flat area where she won't have much chance of disturbing this national natural landmark. There are no developed paths or trails, but since the place is nearly devoid of trees and thick underbrush, it's easy to navigate a course almost anywhere here. Be aware that you may run across desert kit foxes and bobcats. If you can't control your dog with critters like these around, keep her leashed. And make sure she goes nowhere near desert tortoises, the California state reptile (bet your dog didn't know that). Tortoises are easily traumatized, and contact with people or dogs could lead to their death.

For your pet's sake, don't visit in the summer. Our favorite time to hike here is in late autumn, when it's crisp but not freezing. Leashed dogs are allowed to camp with you at the 22-site Owl Canyon Campground (no hookups or even water). The fee is $6 per vehicle. No reservations are necessary.

From Highway 58 in Barstow, drive 5.5 miles north on Fort Irwin Road and turn left on Fossil Bed Road. It's a rough dirt road, and it will seem like an eternity of bouncing before you reach your destination, but it's actually just three miles. 760/252-6060.

🖾 Stoddard Valley Open Area

🐾🐾🐾🐾 🐕 (See San Bernardino County map on page 878)

Is your dog tired of those five-acre parks where leashes are a must? Does she long for wide-open desert ranges where she can tear around without a care in the world (except rattlesnakes and their friends)?

This 52,000-acre parcel of land just southeast of Barstow could be the answer to her poochy prayers. Not only are there mountains and endless open areas, there are also plenty of fascinating rock formations for you and your dog to explore.

To enter at the northern end, where there's a campground, exit I-15 at Sidewinder Road and drive the only way the road takes you. The campground has no developed sites, and no reservations or permits are required. The public land here is interspersed with private land, but Bureau of Land Management folks say unless an area is fenced off, posted, or developed, it's probably OK for hiking. 760/252-6060.

PLACES TO STAY

Econo Lodge: Rates are $40–60. Dogs are $8 extra. 1230 East Main Street 92311; 760/256-2133.

Holiday Inn Express: Rates are $122–212. 2700 Lenwood Road 92311; 760/253-9200 or 877/865-6578.

Quality Inn: The folks here really like dogs. Rates are $59–99. Dogs are $10 extra. 1520 East Main Street 92311; 760/256-6891.

DIVERSION

Go West, Young Pup: How many dogs can say they watched an Old West shootout on a dusty saloon-packed street? How many can brag they rode aboard a train through a ghost town?

Your leashed dog can be that lucky dog, if you take her to **Calico Ghost Town.** Calico thrived during the 1880s silver boom, and you can still roam around silver mines and stroll along wooden sidewalks on Main Street.

If you're a fan of this era, spend the night. Camping costs $18–33. There are about 260 campsites. Reservations are recommended in spring and fall. Or rent one of the six cabins in town. They're not haunted, but the price is so low you'll howl for joy: $28 for up to four people. A $25 deposit is required.

Admission to Calico Ghost Town Regional Park is $6, $3 for children ages 6–15. Train rides are $2.50, $1.25 for children. Dawgs are a buck. From Barstow, drive about six miles east on I-15 and exit at Calico Ghost Town/Ghost Town Road. Drive north three miles. When you see a yellow wagon, you'll know you're there. 760/254-2122; www.calicotown.com.

Afton

PARKS, BEACHES, AND RECREATION AREAS

🐾 Afton Canyon Natural Area

🐾🐾🐾🐾 (See San Bernardino County map on page 878)

Wow! Woof! How does 42,000 acres of land sound to you and your canine companion? If you don't demand lush green meadows to be part of your elysian ideal, this can be heaven on earth.

Afton Canyon is one of only three places where the Mojave River flows above ground year-round, so not only has it attracted visitors throughout history, it's also a water dog's delight. If you don't expect fine fishing here, no one will be disappointed.

Keep in mind that hundreds of bird, mammal, and reptile species call Afton Canyon their home, or at least their migratory hotel. It's a great place for wildlife-watching, and you need to keep your dog leashed.

Camping here isn't the prettiest, but it's a convenient place to spend the night. Sites (there are no hookups) are $6. There are 22 sites available on a first-come, first-served basis.

Afton is about 40 miles east of Barstow. From I-15, exit at Afton Canyon Road and drive three miles south to the park. 760/252-6060.

Needles

Named for the sharp peaks at the southern end of the valley, this Colorado River town is surrounded by some of the most fascinating desert landscapes in the world.

If all the wide-open territory near Needles makes you and your dog feel like insignificant specks in the universe, try a side trip to London Bridge, just down the road a bit in Lake Havasu City, Arizona. This is the same London Bridge that was sinking into the Thames River in 1962, until developers of this town bought it for $2.5 million and shipped it to the United States—granite block by granite block. Your dog can go back home and tell all his buddies that he visited London Bridge, and they'll be impressed (most of them think it's still in London). English springer spaniels get a misty, faraway look when they come here.

PARKS, BEACHES, AND RECREATION AREAS

🐾 Mojave National Preserve

🐾🐾🐾🐾 (See San Bernardino County map on page 878)

The next time your dog gives you one of those sideways glances that says "I gotta get outta the city," you might want to consider spending a few days exploring a desert environment that seems to go on forever. It actually does go on forever, or at least for 1.5 million acres to the west and north of Needles, whichever comes first.

Within this gigantic swath of land are volcanic cinder cones, booming sand dunes, old mines, new mines, mysterious petroglyphs, and dramatic cliffs. If you're a newcomer to desert life, you'll find the wildflowers, cacti, and yucca fascinating.

Dogs must be leashed here, now that the once leash-free land has been transferred from the dog-loving Bureau of Land Management to the National Park Service. Fortunately, the Park Service designated it a preserve rather than a park, so dogs are still allowed in many areas. They can join you for a jaunt along the many miles of old mining roads, but they're not permitted on the trails. And they're not allowed in the designated wilderness area unless they're hunting with you, and then they may hunt off leash. (Hunting just doesn't work well with leashes.)

Keep in mind that nearly 300 species of animals live here, including coyotes and Mojave green rattlesnakes. Since these rattlers are more aggressive than most other rattlers, and since dogs have been known to be a coyote delicacy, it's extra inspiration to keep your dog close at paw.

Camping ranges from no cost for wilderness camping to $12 for regular sites. Dogs must be leashed at the campgrounds. There are 65 campsites available on a first-come, first-served basis. The preserve can be entered at several points along I-40 and several points along I-15. Call 760/252-6100 to find out which entrance would best suit your travel plans.

5 Moabi Regional Park/Park Moabi

🐾🐾🐾 (See San Bernardino County map on page 878)

If your dog likes the water, tell her that the Colorado River runs through this park. If she's a landlubber, let her know that most of the park is lawns and desert land. There's something for most tastes at this 1,025-acre county park, but it's not always the quietest place in the world. Anglers can become frustrated with all the personal watercraft and fast boats that cruise around here. To have the run of the lake, try renting a houseboat from the park's marina. It's loads of fun, and all your dog has to do to go for a swim is hop out the back door.

There's a $10-per-vehicle day-use fee. Camping at the 130 sites is $15–25 (the pricier sites are on the river). Dogs are $1 extra. The park is at the intersection of I-40 and Park Moabi Road. 760/326-3831.

PLACES TO STAY

Best Western Colorado River Inn: Enjoy the hotel's heated indoor pool, the sauna, and a small exercise room (without your dog, of course). Dogs have to stay in the smoking rooms here, which is convenient if your dog smokes. Rates are $79–139. Pooches pay a $25 deposit. 2271 West Broadway 92363; 760/326-4552.

Victorville

PARKS, BEACHES, AND RECREATION AREAS

6 Mojave Narrows Regional Park

😊😊😊 (See San Bernardino County map on page 878)

This 840-acre park is by far the largest park in the area. It's kind of triangular, bordered on the left by railroad tracks and on the right by the Mojave River. The rangers tell that to people hiking with dogs, lest they get a little lost in their eagerness to get back to nature.

There are plenty of fields here, but the best place for walking around with your leashed dog is the more forested part of the park. If you're an angler with a dog who likes to cheer you on as you cast for supper, you'll be happy to know there's fishing year-round for $5 per day.

Camping costs $15–22. Dogs are $1 extra. There are approximately 65 campsites. Reservations are recommended, and there's a $5 reservation fee. The day-use fee is $3 per vehicle, $1 per dog. From I-15, take the Bear Valley Cutoff exit and drive east for five miles. When you come to the railroad track overpass, turn left at Ridgecrest Road. Drive three miles north to the park. 760/245-2226.

PLACES TO STAY

Red Roof Inn: This motel is conveniently close to Mojave Narrows Regional Park. Rates are $60–90. 13409 Mariposa Road 92392; 760/241-1577.

Lucerne Valley

PARKS, BEACHES, AND RECREATION AREAS

7 Johnson Valley Open Area

😊😊😊 (See San Bernardino County map on page 878)

If city life has your dog tied in knots, a visit to the Johnson Valley Open Area is bound to unkink him. There's nothing like 250,000 acres—including mountains, scrubby desert, dry lakes, sand dunes, and rock formations—to take the "d" out of "doldrums" and put it back in "dog."

While you may not run into any other people during your visit, keep in mind that much of this land is OK for off-highway vehicles to cruise. Coyotes aren't strangers to this place either. Keep your doggy leashed. You'll still have a fabulous time exploring this wild terrain.

There are many access points to this huge acreage. One good bet is to exit Highway 247 at Bessemer Mine Road and drive north a few miles. Big signs will show you the way. The public land here is interspersed with private land, but Bureau of Land Management folks say unless an area is fenced off, posted, or developed, it's probably OK for hiking. 760/252-6000.

Big Bear Lake

This lakeside mountain resort community isn't exactly Lake Tahoe, but that's part of its charm. It's generally more rustic, more natural, and far less crowded. The crisp, clean alpine air is a godsend any time of year.

The town's old-fashioned honesty and lack of smooth public relations pros is evident as soon as you approach the old village section. There, you'll see a road sign for skiing, with an arrow pointing to the left. Immediately below that is a sign for the hospital, with an arrow pointing to the right. It's not a joke.

This is a very dog-friendly community, complete with incomparable off-leash hikes, great restaurants, and charming lodgings where dogs are as welcome as their chauffeurs. Check out the old Big Bear Lake village. It gives a new meaning to old-style charm.

PARKS, BEACHES, AND RECREATION AREAS

Although this book doesn't normally go into detail on specific trails in national forests, we're mentioning a few here because they're so integral to your pooch having a doggone good time in the Big Bear Lake area. (These used to be off-leash trails, but, sadly, leashes are now the law.)

8 Cougar Crest Trail

😺😺😺😺 (See San Bernardino County map on page 878)

This two-mile trail goes through a mixed conifer section of San Bernardino National Forest. It's full of juniper, Jeffrey pine, and pinyon. Obedient dogs used to be able to go leash-free, but no more.

We like it best here in late autumn, when a dusting of snow rests on the pine needles and the air is crisp. We've never run into another person on the trail during this time of year. Cougar Crest Trail eventually connects with the Pacific Crest Trail, which traverses 39 miles of the Big Bear area. The scenery is outstanding.

From Big Bear Lake village, cross the lake at the Stanfield Cutoff and turn left on Highway 38. As you drive west, the trail is just over a half mile west of the ranger station, on the right side of the road. There's plenty of parking. 909/866-3437.

9 Pedal Path

😺😺😺😺 (See San Bernardino County map on page 878)

Here's one way to hike the Big Bear Lake area without roughing it too much. This six-mile paved path allows you and your leashed, lake-loving dog to hike along the scenic north shore of Big Bear Lake.

Sometimes bikers think they own the trail (it is called Pedal Path, not Four-Paw Path, after all), so make sure your dog is close to you. The trail starts at the north end of the Stanfield Cutoff. 909/866-3437.

DIVERSION

Whatever Floats Your Boat: A great way to explore **Big Bear Lake** with your dog is to do it by boat. A couple of marinas will rent you and your dog a variety of boats, with the proviso that you try not to let your dog have any little accidents on board. (Take frequent land breaks if your dog has a small bladder or has just eaten.) Pontoon boats are probably the most fun for dogs, because they're big, slow, and stable. Aluminum fishing boats are an option for fairly calm dogs who won't wriggle themselves into the drink with excitement when you land a big one. Very mellow dogs can even find out the answer to the age-old question: Can you canoe? (If your dog isn't a swimmer, she should wear a doggy life jacket on any boat. Even if she is a swimmer, it's not a bad idea, especially on a tippy canoe ride.)

Holloway's Marina (398 Edgemoor Road; 909/866-5706 or 800/448-5335; www.bigbearboating.com) rents fishing and pontoon boats. Big Bear Marina (500 Paine Road; 909/866-3218; www.bigbearmarina.com) rents fishing boats, pontoon boats, pedal boats, and canoes. You could also rent a Wave Runner water scooter with your dog, but don't.

10 Woodland Trail

🐾🐾🐾🐾 (See San Bernardino County map on page 878)

This 1.5-mile nature trail in San Bernardino National Forest has 20 stops where you and your well-behaved, leashed dog may learn about the flora and fauna of this mountainous region. It's especially glorious in an early-morning mist.

The trail rarely gets crowded, so it's a sure escape from the madding crowd. From Big Bear Lake village, cross the lake at the Stanfield Cutoff and turn left on Highway 38. Shortly after you turn, the trail is on your right. 909/866-3437.

PLACES TO EAT

Most of the restaurants listed below are in the old-style alpine village in the heart of Big Bear Lake. Whenever you visit here, you'll feel like it's Christmas.

The Mandoline Bistro: The food here is delectable and so diverse it's like choosing from the menus of several different restaurants. Entrées include Caribbean salmon (with grilled banana, lemon Dijon and chutney sauce, and sticky rice), cashew-crusted chicken breast (with wild mushroom bread pudding and tomato chutney), and filet mignon (with garlic mashed potatoes). The bruschetta appetizer is really wonderful, according to Tapper Dog, who sniffed this place out for us, but the menu warns that it's not for first dates. (In other words: Garlic City!) Dine with your dog at the umbrella-topped patio tables. 40701 Village Drive; 909/866-4200.

Nottinghams Restaurant & Tavern: If only your dog were allowed inside this restaurant, he'd get to see all the pretty antiques in the cozy dining rooms and bars. But dogs don't mind, because the courtyard area is a very welcoming place, with umbrella-topped tables and a peaceful fountain. The Cal-American menu offers something for everyone. The stuffed salmon and filet mignon are popular dinner dishes, and if you need a starter, try the caramelized brie. It's droolworthy! The restaurant is part of the dog-friendly Robinhood Resort. 40797 Lakeview Drive; 909/866-4644.

Sonora Cantina: This delightful restaurant boasts the best Mexican food in Big Bear. You can dine with your furry friend at the patio, where thirsty dogs get a nice bowl of *agua*. If you're very, very, very hungry, try the "Big Juan Burrito." If you can finish it in under 45 minutes, you get a T-shirt proclaiming your triumph. (No cheating by sharing it with your dog—you'd be sorry later, with the burrito's four meats, beans, and onions interacting in your dog's digestive tract.) 41144 Big Bear Boulevard; 909/866-8202.

PLACES TO STAY

Big Bear Lake is one of the best places in the entire state to spend the night with your dog. There are so many lodgings that accept dogs that you'll have a hard time choosing.

Big Bear Frontier Cabins & Hotel: If your dog wants to splash around the lake, this is a great place to stay. Most of the 33 cabins and 22 motel rooms are on the lakefront or just across the street. Dogs and humans can wet their paws at the private beach here, and humans (sorry, dogs) can also enjoy the lodging's heated pool and large hot tub. The lodgings are cozy, and even the motel rooms have beautiful wood paneling that's so shiny you could practically ice skate on it if gravity weren't an issue. All but a couple have wood-burning fireplaces.

It sounds like it's far off the beaten track, but Big Bear Frontier is just one block from the dog-friendly village of Big Bear Lake. Rates are $70–300. Dogs are $15 extra. (As for pet rates, the website also mentions that "birds fly free. Call about mules or horses." I asked if they really get mules and horses, and a front-desk clerk cheerfully told me, "No, but we love animals, so maybe we could work something out.") 40472 Big Bear Boulevard 92315; 800/457-6401; www.bigbearcabins.com.

Big Pine Flats Campground: This is one of the more out-of-the-way campgrounds in the Big Bear area. You and your dog can hike around the area and be fully enveloped by ravishing Mama Nature. Or you can drive a few miles and be in the heart of Big Bear Lake. There are 19 sites available on a first-come, first-served basis. The campground closes in winter. Sites are $18. From Fawnskin, follow Rim of the World Drive (its name will change) for seven miles to Big Pine Flat Station. The campground is on your right. 909/866-3437.

Black Forest Lodge: Everything here is Swiss chalet–style, from the cute motel to the cabins to the real chalets. A few of the cabins date back to 1895! These log beauties have been gutted, and couple of the old ones even have Jacuzzi baths inside. Many accommodations are graced by fireplaces, and all

DIVERSION

Get Hitched, with Your Dog's Help: The Big Bear **Hitching Post Wedding Chapel** is a dog's kind of marriage sanctuary. It's got a mountain/Western theme and no overly frilly frou frou.

Owners John and TraCee Green have played host to canine ring bearers, canine bridesmaids, and canine best men. A former owner said once he even helped a dog sign a marriage certificate (not the license, though). "We just put his paw on the ink pad, then stamped the certificate. He was a smart dog, but his penmanship wasn't good enough to sign his name," he said.

The Greens ask that dogs attend only midweek weddings. On busy days like Saturday, they don't have enough time to vacuum up dog hairs, and a few people visiting after dogs participated have complained about their allergies flaring up.

The fee for getting hitched here for the two of you and your dog(s) is $95 and includes the chapel. You can have up to 25 guests for just $120. The license, should you need one, is $85, and there's a suggested $50 donation for the minister. For more information, call 909/584-1030 or 800/828-4433 or write them at 604 West Big Bear Boulevard, Big Bear Lake, CA 92314; www.bigbearweddings.com.

---

are clean and attractive. The lodge's property has lots of trees for your pooch's perusal. Rates are $95–145. (And up to $225 for a chalet that sleeps 10.) Dogs can only stay in the cabins. 41121 Big Bear Boulevard 92315; 909/866-2166 or 800/255-4378; www.blackforestlodge.com.

Cienaga Creek Ranch Mountain Cottages: The five upscale-yet-rustic cottages here are set on 50 acres of forest where well-behaved dogs can say sayonara to their leashes. As if that's not enough, this tranquil acreage is surrounded by thousands of acres of dog-friendly national forest land. It's enough to make a grown dog cry with joy. And the giant pines, firs, and junipers that blanket the land are another dream come true for many boy dogs. Combine this with some pet treats at the beginning of your visit, and you'll surely have a dog who thinks he's found canine heaven on earth.

It's pretty heavenly for people, too. Everything is solar-powered, so ubiquitous utility lines don't mar the landscape. The cottages combine the rustic (log beds, log trim, wood wainscoting) with the divine (featherbeds, artisan tile, and marble in the spacious kitchen and bathroom). All have fireplaces; some have Jacuzzi spas. They're 100–200 feet away from each other, so there's plenty of privacy, too. And the little extras, including high-end toiletries and super-plush towels and robes, help guests feel extra pampered in the wilderness. Rates are $149–399. Dogs are $10 extra. There's no street address. P.O. Box 2773 92314; 888/336-2891; www.mountaincottage.com.

Cozy Hollow Lodge: This lodge deserves its name, since the simple cabins here have fireplaces and are definitely on the cozy side. It's a great place to stay after a long day on the slopes. In summer, a stream runs through the woods behind the lodge. Rates are $59–159. There's a $100 deposit for dogs and an additional $10 fee for each pooch, plus a one-time $25 cleaning fee. 40409 Big Bear Boulevard 92315; 909/866-8886; www.cozyhollowlodge.com.

Eagle's Nest Bed & Breakfast Lodge: Dogs are warmly welcomed here with a pet basket full of goodies including treats, a doggy toy, food and water bowls, and a towel for drying off wet paws. (The latter two are loaners.) They can stay at a charming two-room cottage suite with a fireplace or in the High-land Cabin, an absolutely wonderful, cozy, two-bedroom cabin with a wood-burning fireplace and even a deer head on the wall. (Jake is scared of it. This is embarrassing.) The cabin is rustic yet beautifully appointed. The exterior looks like it's straight out of a fairy tale in some woodland setting.

But dogs don't care about the decor or the storybook charm. What they want to know is: 1) Where can I go sniff out some nature and check out some trees? 2) What do I do while the humans are just sitting around reading and talking and watching TV? The answers will put a wag in any dog's tail: 1) The dog-friendly San Bernardino National Forest surrounds the cabin, and 2) You can curl up by the wood-burning fireplace or hang out in your completely fenced backyard. And don't forget to eat the treats they give you. Rates are $99–165. Dogs are $10 extra. 41675 Big Bear Boulevard 92315; 909/866-6465 or 888/866-6466; www.eaglesnestlodgebigbear.com.

DIVERSION

Catch a Stagecoach: If you and your little varmint have a hankerin' to be part of the Old West, hanker no longer! Michael Homan and his trusty **Bear Valley Stage Lines** in Big Bear Lake will take you and your dog and up to 12 other people on a 15-minute ride around town in a stagecoach so genuine it looks like John Wayne ought to be at the reins. Dogs will want to sit up front with Homan, who wears Western clothes. But it's not Homan they want to be near. It's the horses. Actually, the horses' rears, to be exact.

Enough of that. Adults are $10, children are $5. Dogs don't pay a cent. Homan says you'll need to be able to lift your dog up 3.5 feet to get him inside the stagecoach (it's a high entrance). The stagecoach stand is on Village Drive across from Chad's Place. No reservations are needed. Homan also can hitch a beautiful carriage to some beautiful horses, should you care to go on a more elegant, intimate ride. You'll need to make special arrangements for that, but dogs are also welcome. 909/584-2277; www.stagelines.com.

Golden Bear Cottages: There's an unmistakable bear theme going here. Most of the 28 cabins sport bear names. (Little Bear, Honey Pot, Snuggle Bear Manor, and Grizzly's Den are but a few of the cabins.) Dogs are invited to stay at half of the cabins. The proprietors here love dogs and want them and their people to enjoy their stay to the max. To that end, they've created a tall, fenced-in yard at each of the pet-friendly cabins. They're about 10-by-20 feet, give or take a little, depending on cabin size. "It gets cold around here, and when your dog needs to go to the bathroom early in the morning and you're still in your robe and slippers, it's really convenient to be able to just open up the kitchen door and say, OK, go ahead out!" says Don, who co-owns this lovely property. This is indeed a special touch, and one many guests are grateful for come winter.

You and your dog will have a beary good time at the interesting assortment of rustic cabins strewn over five acres. The prices are quite bearable, too. Rates are $79–299. Dogs are $10. 39367 Big Bear Boulevard, Highway 18 92315; 909/866-2010 or 800/461-1023; www.goldenbear.net.

Gold Mountain Manor: Dogs can't stay in the gorgeous, romantic log bed-and-breakfast manor, but they're welcome to stay at any of the six comfy, pretty cabins here. Rates are $150–750. 1117 Anita, P.O. Box 2027 92314; 909/585-6997 or 800/509-2604; www.goldmountainmanor.com.

Grey Squirrel Resort: These charming cottages are a half block from the lake, on 4.5 acres. Several of the cottages have fireplaces. For those achy muscles fraught with post-skiing-stress-disorder, the resort has a heated pool, which is enclosed in the winter (but pooches can't paddle here). Rates are $94–184. There's a $100 deposit for pets and an additional $10 fee per pooch. The cabins are on Highway 18, just west of town at 39372 Big Bear Boulevard 92315; 909/866-4335 or 800/381-5569; www.greysquirrel.com.

Lakewood Cabins: These homey cabins are 0.25 mile from the lake and skiing. Rates are $79–175, and dogs can stay in all rooms except the ones with Jacuzzis. 586 Main Street 92315; 909/866-7633.

Pine Knot Guest Ranch: Love llamas? Bonkers for bunnies? Stay at the comfy housekeeping cabins at Pine Knot and you can interact with animals other than your traveling companion (the one with dog breath). The two-plus-acre property is home to llamas you can join for a stroll or bunnies whose huge cage you can enter for a close encounter of the rabbit kind. It's also home to eight cabins, five of which allow dogs. All but one cabin has a wood-burning fireplace, and they all feature spa tubs for two. They're great to come back to after a long day on the slopes or on the lake. Rates are $89–159. The people who run the ranch also have six vacation home rentals not far away. Call to inquire about these. 908 Pine Knot Avenue 92315; 909/866-6500 or 800/866-3446; www.pineknotguestranch.com.

Quail Cove: "Pets are always welcome!" exclaims the lodge's brochure. The six cottages here are in a wooded, parklike setting by the water. All have wood-burning fireplaces, knotty-pine paneling, and full kitchens. Rates are $115–195. Dogs are $15 extra and require a $100 deposit. 39117 North Shore Drive 92315; 909/866-5957 or 800/595-2683; www.quailcove.com.

Robinhood Resort: The resort consists of several buildings with all kinds of wooden, attractive rooms and suites and cabins. Dogs can stay in only two rooms, and they're pretty basic motel-like no-frills affairs. They're popular rooms (dogs don't care about decor as long as they're with their people) and book fast, so reserve early. Rates are $79–169. Dogs are $10 extra. 40797 Lakeview Drive 92315; 909/866-4643 or 800/990-9956; www.robinhoodresort.info.

Serrano Campground: If you like rustic campsites and good hot showers, this San Bernardino National Forest campground is worth the $26–36 fee. The 132 sites are close to Big Bear Lake and the solar observatory (which is open to the public during certain days in the summer). The campground is on the north side of the lake, about two miles east of Fawnskin. It's very close to the Cougar Crest Trail. Call 877/444-6777 for reservations or 909/866-3437 for more information. The campground is closed in the winter.

Shore Acres Lodge: Does your dog love to swim and hike? If so, Shore Acres is a great place to stay, because it has lake access and is near some fun trails. This two-acre property has 11 comfortable housekeeping cabins, each with a fireplace, sundeck, and barbecue grill. Humans who enjoy outdoor recreation can also swim in the pool during warmer months, fish from the lodge's property, or embark on a boat trip from the lodge's own dock. Little humans enjoy the playground here. Soak in the year-round hot tub at the end of a long day of fun. Rates are $145–299. Dogs are $10 extra. 40090 Lakeview Drive 92315; 877/754-2327; www.shoreacreslodge.com.

Timberline Lodge: Like woods? You're in a little foresty area here. Like being close to the village? Stay here and you will be. How about lake views from cozy housekeeping cabins? The views are terrific. And the active life? The lodge has a seasonal heated outdoor pool, a children's playground, and volleyball, basketball, horseshoes, and tetherball (for humans only). The folks behind the front desk can tell you some fun nearby hikes your dog. "We love our puppy dogs up here!" says friendly manager Dave. Dogs dig Dave, too. Rates are $79–129. Dogs are $10 extra. 39921 Big Bear Boulevard 92315; 909/866-4141; www.thetimberlinelodge.com.

Wildwood Resort: When we inquired about whether dogs could stay at this wonderful four-acre resort, we were immediately and enthusiastically told "Oh, yes!" The woman we spoke with belongs to a Newfoundland dog club (actually, her dogs do), and she said that when the resort played host to the club's 50 Newfies, not a single pile of poop remained after their visit. It's stories like this that give dog people a good name and make dogs more welcome at other lodgings.

The resort has 25 sweet cabins that permit pooches. All have full kitchens, and most have fireplaces. You'll like it here. Rates are $120–265. Dogs are $10 extra. 40210 Big Bear Boulevard 92315; 909/878-2178 or 888/294-5396; www.wildwoodresort.com.

Fawnskin

This little town is near several dog-friendly lodgings and surrounded by the San Bernardino National Forest. But in case you're hankering for a more civilized park, we've sniffed out a sweet one for you.

PARKS, BEACHES, AND RECREATION AREAS

11 Dana Point Park

🐾🐾🐾 (See San Bernardino County map on page 878)

Swimming dogs adore this county park. It's along the north side of Big Bear Lake's Grout Bay, so it's somewhat off the beaten track. It's a fairly small park, but it has some romping room for leashed dogs, as well as a picnic area for hungry dogs and their people. Bird-watching is one of the big activities here, so be sure to bring your binoculars. November–March, you might see bald eagles roosting and feeding.

The park is just off the main part of this charming old village, on the south side of Highway 38. 909/866-0130.

Twin Peaks

PLACES TO STAY

Arrowhead Pine Rose Cabins: This five-acre property is three miles from Lake Arrowhead. Dogs like the fact that they can walk around the spacious land here and check out all the sweet-smelling pines. About half of the 17 cabins permit pooches. Some cabins have back patios where your dog can relax in a quasi-outdoor atmosphere without escaping. Rates are $69–450. Anything above $200 or so is in the three-bedroom-plus category, so you probably won't need to worry about that price. Dogs are $10 extra, and there's a $100 pooch deposit. 25994 Highway 189 92391; 909/337-2341 or 800/429-PINE (800/429-7463); www.lakearrowheadcabins.com.

Upland
PARKS, BEACHES, AND RECREATION AREAS

12 Baldy View Dog Park/Upland Dog Park
🐾🐾🐾🐾🦮 (See San Bernardino County map on page 878)
This fenced dog park is five grassy acres of fun, with lots of trees for your pooch's perusal. Small dogs have their own little area. Humans get to repose on benches. It's the de rigueur dog spot in Upland.

The people here know how to party. If they're not entering their dogs in the local Christmas parade, they're partaking in Valentine's festivities with their furry friends or hosting a "spring fling" party for them. You can get an idea of some of the events by checking out www.uplanddogpark.com.

The park is on 11th Street between San Antonio and Mountain Avenues. 909/931-4280.

Rancho Cucamonga
PARKS, BEACHES, AND RECREATION AREAS

13 Rancho Cucamonga Dog Park
🐾🐾🐾🐾🦮 (See San Bernardino County map on page 878)
This is one of the more attractive fenced dog parks we've come across. The park is about 30,000 square feet of grass, with great views of the San Gabriel Mountains. It's shaded here and there by beautiful jacaranda trees. When they bloom, their purple flowers are stunning. Bring a camera, and see if you can get your pooch to hold still long enough to get a photo of her under a canopy of purple blossoms.

The park has all the usual dog park amenities, including water and benches. There's a separate area for shy or tiny dogs (or both rolled into one) to get away from it all. Many more amenities, including a dog wash, are in the offing. Dogs are not necessarily smiling about this last addition.

This park is so close to a major freeway traveling dogs routinely find themselves on that directions are from I-15. Exit I-15 at Baseline Avenue and immediately take the option for heading north on East Avenue. The park, which is in Etiwanda Creek Community Park, is on your right within a few blocks, at the corner of Banyan Street and East Avenue. 909/477-2700.

San Bernardino

PARKS, BEACHES, AND RECREATION AREAS

14 Wildwood Dog Park

🐾🐾🐾🐾🐕 (See San Bernardino County map on page 878)

The grass is always greener on the other side of the fence here. That's because dogs use one side of this lush 3.5-acre park some days, and when the turf starts getting a little worn down, they switch to the other half to let the trampled half recover. It keeps it attractive and mud-free.

This is a super dog park in many ways. Small dogs have their own area, and there are restrooms, benches, poop bags, drinking fountains, lights, and even a building used for vaccination clinics. Enough trees provide shade to make some parts of the park more tolerable in summer.

The dog park is within 24-acre Wildwood Park, at East 40th Street and Waterman Avenue. If you feel like it's just your dog who gets exercise at the dog park (let's face it, it's not like humans get in great shape standing around talking and occasionally lobbing a tennis ball), you can pop on your dog's leash and head to the main park, where you can breeze along a fitness trail. 909/384-5233.

15 Glen Helen Regional Park

🐾🐾🐾🐾 (See San Bernardino County map on page 878)

This 1,425-acre park features two lakes that are regularly stocked with such goodies as trout and catfish. But if your leashed dog doesn't like to fish, she's sure to enjoy such goodies as the ecology trail and the grassy little hills that await her happy paws.

Rangers tell us that some dogs seem to get a kick out of watching kids zoom down the 300-foot, two-part water slide at the swim complex in the park's southeast corner. Dogs aren't allowed there, but the park has plenty of viewing spots for pooches and their people.

With all these activities, Glen Helen Regional Park is a great place for your dog to take the family. You can even camp here. There are 50 sites available on a first-come, first-served basis. The fee is $15, and dogs are $1 extra.

The day-use fee here is $5, plus $1 per dog. Fishing is $5 per person over six years old. Exit I-215 at Devore Road (just south of the I-15/I-215 junction) and follow the signs about 1.5 miles to the park. 909/887-7540.

PLACES TO STAY

Dog lodgings aren't exactly abundant here.

La Quinta Motor Inn: Dogs are allowed to stay in this motel's smoking rooms. Fortunately, there's a little grassy area outside where they can get some fresh air. Rates are $85–185. 205 East Hospitality Lane 92408; 909/888-7571.

Motel 6: There are two of these pooch-friendly motels in town. Rates are

$48 for the first adult, $6 for the second. In northern San Bernardino: 1960 Ostrems Way 92407; 909/887-8191. The other location is 111 West Redlands Boulevard 92408; 909/825-6666.

Lake Arrowhead

This attractive resort village in the mountains of San Bernardino National Forest has plenty for a dog to do. Dogs can lounge in lodges. They can hike the hillsides. They can do the dog paddle in the lake.

The Arrowhead district of the national forest has some terrific trails ranging in elevation 3,000–7,000 feet. Pooches are welcome to join you on a day hike or an overnighter. Contact the ranger station at 909/337-2444 for trail maps and advice on which hikes and campsites are better suited for your skill level and the time of year you'll be visiting. We've listed one of the popular trails and camp-grounds below (sadly, our favorite, the North Shore National Recreation Trail, is closed indefinitely), but there are plenty of smaller hike-in sites as well.

The lake itself is managed by an exclusive homeowners association, so public lake access is rather limited.

PARKS, BEACHES, AND RECREATION AREAS

16 Indian Rock Trail

🐾🐾🐾 (See San Bernardino County map on page 878)

If your dog's motto is "nice and easy does it," this trail will do it for him. It's an effortless half-mile hike through the San Bernardino National Forest to a former Serrano Indian encampment, where you'll still find the bedrock once used for grinding the area's abundant acorns into flour. (The stones were the answer to having to carry around heavy mortar and pestles.) Although this is national forest land, your dog should be leashed because it's a fairly well-used trail.

From Lake Arrowhead, drive north on Highway 173 to the Rock Camp Fire Station. The trail starts just east of the station. Parking is across the road. 909/382-2782.

PLACES TO EAT

Belgian Waffle Works: The waffles are crispy, the toppings are yummy, and you can enjoy them with your dog at the lakeside patio. The only hitch is that your dog needs to be on the other side of the fence. This isn't a big deal, since your dog can still be right beside you, but it's something Jake Dog thought you should know. The restaurant is dockside at the Lake Arrowhead Village, a cute little shopping area, at 28200 Highway 189; 909/337-5222.

Borderline Restaurant: This Mex-American restaurant offers two places where dogs can dine with their people: at a little two-table patio where you can dine side by side or in the solarium with your dog right outside and the doors

DIVERSION

Sniff Out Some Cool Clothes: A clothing store with the name **Big Dogs Sportswear** that has a giant Saint Bernard as its logo can't help but allow clean, well-behaved dogs to shop with their people. Most stores in the chain are dog friendly, but the folks at the Lake Arrowhead store go the extra mile and keep a bowl of fresh water handy for thirsty dogs, and even give biscuits to their canine customers. 28200 Highway 189; 909/336-1998.

open. (Barring bad weather or crowds.) "We bring them water and treat them good," a very pleasant waiter tells us. You can get shrimp, salmon, burgers, Mexican food, you name it. "The only thing we don't have is pizza," says the waiter. The restaurant is actually just a bone's throw from Lake Arrowhead, in the sweet town of Blue Jay, at 27159 Highway 189; 909/336-4363.

PLACES TO STAY

Arrowhead Tree Top Lodge: "We love dogs," says a kindly employee who also works for the local humane society. In fact, dogs get treats upon arrival.

Some of the rooms at this attractive lodge have kitchens and fireplaces, for that homey touch. The lodge is on five acres with a nature trail and creeks. Dogs dig that. It's a short walk to the village and to the lake from here. Rates are $69–189. Dogs are $8 extra. 27992 Rainbow Drive 92352; 909/337-2311 or 800/358-TREE (800/358-8733); www.arrowheadtreetop.com.

Prophets' Paradise Bed & Breakfast: This bed-and-breakfast is a real charmer. You and your dog will drool over the cozy antique-filled living room, which is especially inviting in winter when the fireplace is roaring. Take a dog here at Christmas for the best present you could give him. (And speaking of Christmas, the "Prophet" in Prophets' Paradise is the last name of the inn-keepers, not anything prophetic.)

The bed-and-breakfast is a five-level, 5,000-square-foot house on a hillside. Each room has its own floor. It's wonderfully private for a B&B. The pet rooms have decks and outside entrances. Rates are $120–185. 26845 Modoc Lane 92352; 909/336-1969 or 800/987-2231; www.prophetsparadise.com.

Saddleback Inn: Howard Hughes frequented this enchanting historic inn (although it wasn't quite so historic then, having been built in 1919), as did Charles Lindbergh and countless Hollywood icons, including Mae West.

In keeping with Mae West's famous line, now your dog can "Come up and see me sometime" at the Saddleback Inn. Many of the lovely cottages in back of the three-story inn welcome dogs. They're decorated in kind of a country, mountain-cabin style, and most have gas log fireplaces and Jacuzzi tubs. All come with a little fridge and microwave, should your dog hanker for a midnight snack. There's a fun restaurant on the premises, but your dog will have to be content with leftovers, as there's no outdoor dining. What dogs and their people usually like best about Saddleback is the gorgeous setting overlooking Lake Arrowhead, in the midst of big pines and cedars. The cottages are surrounded by these arbors, and that puts a smile on any dog's face.

Rates are $138–328. Dogs are $8 extra. 300 South State Highway 173 92352; 909/336-3571; www.saddlebackinn.com.

Ontario

PARKS, BEACHES, AND RECREATION AREAS

17 Cucamonga-Guasti Park

🐾🐾🐾 (See San Bernardino County map on page 878)

The park's name may not exactly roll off the tongue, but there's something for dogs of every stripe (and spot) here. Dogs who enjoy dipping their paws in the water like the fishing lake, where anglers catch bass, catfish, or trout. (Pooches aren't permitted in the swimming lake.) Dogs who like lazing in the grass under graceful shade-giving trees can snooze the afternoon away. And dogs who dig a good walk can amble along the park's lovely walking and bike paths.

The entry fee at this regional park is $5 per vehicle, except on holidays, when it's $10. If you walk in, it's $2 per person. Dogs are $1 extra whether you walk or drive in. You can buy fishing permits at the entry. The park is just north of I-10 on the Archibald Avenue exit. 800 North Archibald Avenue; 909/481-4205.

PLACES TO EAT

Wolfgang Puck Café: This wonderful café's food is half the price of Puck's more upscale Spago restaurants, so it's a great place to take a dog who's on a budget. Puck's delicious wood-fired pizzas, as well as pastas, salads, and terrific rotisserie chicken, are to drool for. Best of all, dogs feel very welcome; they get water and treats when they visit. 1 Ontario Mills Circle; 909/987-2299.

PLACES TO STAY

Best Western InnSuites Hotel & Suites: This is the best hotel for dogs who have to stay near the airport. Not only do you get a continental breakfast, but all the rooms are actually suites, complete with kitchenettes. And guess what else? Fire hydrants are pretty prominent outside the hotel. It's a boy dog's dream. People prefer the Jacuzzis, which grace half the rooms. Rates are $112–142. Dogs pay a $25 fee for their stay, in addition to a $50 deposit. 3400 Shelby Street 91764; 909/466-9600.

Country Inn & Suites: Stay at this all-suites hotel and get a complimentary breakfast, plus take part in a social hour. Rates are $84–194. Dogs are $50 extra for the length of their stay. 231 North Vineyard Avenue 91764; 909/937-6000; www.countryinns.com.

Residence Inn by Marriott: Staying in a one- or two-bedroom suite here is like staying at home, except you get regular maid service. It's a great place to stay if you like having a kitchen when you travel, along with a living room with a fireplace and access to a swimming pool (heated outdoor), whirlpool, and exercise room. The suites are comfortable, attractive, and located across from the Ontario Convention Center, which is convenient if your dog has an important convention to attend. A continental breakfast comes with your stay. Rates are $99–160. Dogs are $75 per stay. 2025 Convention Center Way 91764; 909/937-6788.

Redlands

Parts of this lush, resortlike town provide a breath of fresh air from smog-ridden and traffic-filled Southern California.

PARKS, BEACHES, AND RECREATION AREAS

18 Prospect Park

🐾🐾🐾 (See San Bernardino County map on page 878)

You'll be surrounded by exquisite views, towering palms, multitudes of orange trees, and flowers everywhere at this enchanting, verdant park. Prospect Park is out of a fairy tale. It's one big hill, with delicate wooden seats overlooking the surrounding orchards. At the top, you'll find an open-air theater, some peacocks, and a resident cat, so be sure to follow the rules and leash your dog.

This one's well worth the short trek from I-10. For the most scenic ride, exit the freeway at Orange Street and drive south, through the quaint downtown area. In about seven blocks, bear right at Cajon Street. The park is on your right in about one mile. Park on Cajon Street just after Highland Avenue (just past the orange grove and before the picnic area on your right). Walk back several feet to the wide paved path and embark on your wondrous journey. 909/798-7509.

PLACES TO STAY

Best Western Sandman Motel: With a name like this, it's got to be a good place to catch some winks. Enjoy the heated outdoor pool and hot tub. Room rates are $60–110. Dogs are $15 extra. 1120 West Colton Avenue 92374; 909/793-2001.

Yucaipa

PARKS, BEACHES, AND RECREATION AREAS

🔟 Yucaipa Regional Park

🐾🐾🐾🐾 (See San Bernardino County map on page 878)

This picturesque park is surrounded by the San Bernardino Mountains and Mt. San Gorgonio. But dogs who visit here have more important things on their minds than pretty scenery. First of all, they're not relegated to the usual six-foot leash—their leashes can be 10 feet long! Joy of joys. Then there's the size of this park—it's 885 acres, with enough grassy fields to tire even the friskiest hound dog.

Water-loving dogs enjoy accompanying their people to the three trout-stocked lakes, and water-loving kids get a kick out of the 350-foot water slides at the swim lagoon (no dogs allowed on the slides because they'd make the slides too hairy). Several campsites are available near the lake, so if you're in the mood for a little camping with your angling, you couldn't ask for a more convenient location. Sites are $18–27. There are about 35 campsites here. Reservations are recommended.

The day-use fee is $5 per vehicle on weekdays, $7 on weekends. On major holidays, it's $10 per vehicle. Dogs are $1 extra. Fishing permits are available for a small fee.

From I-10, take the Yucaipa exit and follow the brown Regional Park signs. It's about five miles from the freeway. 909/790-3127.

Angelus Oaks

PLACES TO STAY

The Lodge at Angelus Oaks: One day I got a letter written in silver ink and very big, childish handwriting, and signed with paw prints by Jake Dog (not my Jake Dog; this was before he was even a twinkle in his mother's eye) and Sadie Dog. They were writing to tell me about this wonderful place, which they call "a hidden secret."

Jake and Sadie are very smart dogs, indeed, because the lodge is one terrific place to stay with a dog. It's made up of several homey wooden cabins and is set on some prime acreage in the San Bernardino National Forest. It was built in the early 1900s as a stagecoach stop for pooped-out travelers, and it really hasn't changed much since. Each of the 12 cabins has a kitchen, bathroom with shower, and one or two bedrooms. The main lodge/office is very cozy, with a stone fireplace, a library, and an antique billiards table. But what dogs dig most is that it has lots of fun things to do outside. There's a snow play area (in winter) and a horseshoe pit and other fun nonsnow recreational opportunities.

DIVERSION

Woof for the Good Guys: Dogs can boo the bad guys, cheer for the good guys, and laugh at the drunk guys as they watch some amusing **Old West skits** with you on Pioneertown's scenic "Mane Street." (The good guys always win.) A dozen or so members of a local Western reenactment ensemble perform these lively sketches in this seemingly historic old movie town at 2:30 P.M. Saturday and Sunday April–November. The cost: free. You might even get to see some rope tricks and hear cowboy poetry. And you'll surely hear some loud gunfire (blanks, but loud—the opposite of silent-but-deadly). If your four-legged varmint is skittish of loud noises, it may be best to keep your distance. Afterward, you and your dog can have your photo taken with a gunslinger. For more information, phone the Pioneertown Posse at 760/228-0494 or check out www.pioneertown.com.

Best of all, the San Bernardino National Forest is everywhere. Some prime trails start just a short car ride away.

Rates are $85–115. Dogs are $5 extra. 37825 Highway 38 92305; 909/794-9523; www.angelusoakslodge.com.

Pioneertown

Everything on this town's "Mane Street" looked 100 years old from the moment it came to life in 1947. Pioneertown was built with two purposes in mind: as an Old West–style getaway for folks in the film business and a location for Hollywood Westerns. If it looks familiar, you may have seen it as a backdrop in a few Gene Autry films, including *On Top of Old Smokey* and *Whirlwind*. If you're a real buff of the genre, you may know it from lesser-known B-grade films such as *The Gay Amigo* and *The Daring Caballero*. (Gotta love those names.)

What separates this from your typical movie back lot is that it's a real town (albeit a tiny one). The storefronts aren't just propped up with lumber: They're the fronts of real working buildings, including the local post office.

P-town is a very cool place to visit with your dog, because dogs, like horses, fit in beautifully. Mane Street is unpaved and as casual as it gets. In fact, dogs who don't mind the sound of guns (shooting blanks) can watch some Old West skits here on Sundays (see the Diversion *Woof for the Good Guys*). For lots more details on this great, out-of-the-way place, check out www.pioneertown.com.

PLACES TO EAT

Pappy and Harriet's: What used to be a biker hangout (Harleys, not Schwinns) is now one happening restaurant and saloon. Its look fits right in with the Old West theme of Pioneertown, and so does the food (salads and veggie burgers notwithstanding). The steaks, chicken, and ribs are smoked and grilled over an outdoor mesquite fire, giving them a taste that will make your dog drool puddles. Dogs can join you at the picnic tables in the outdoor beer garden. "Horses, dogs, they're all fine with us," says friendly co-owner Robin. 53688 Pioneertown Road; 760/365-5956; www.pappyandharriets.com.

PLACES TO STAY

Rimrock Ranch Cabins: Like everything else in this pseudo–Old West town, the four cozy, spotless housekeeping cabins here were born in the 1940s as a place where the directors and stars of Western movies could kick off their boots and relax. Gene Autry and Roy Rogers were probably among the guests, say the owners, who are researching the history of the ranch. The cabins have a wonderfully funky charm, each with original knotty-pine paneling, attractive antique/Western decor, artisan tile floors, a well-equipped kitchen, and a private patio with outdoor fireplace. Guests get use of the wonderful mineral-water swimming pool, too. It's a delightful treat, and it seems to do wonders for skin and hair.

What dogs love is that the cabins are on 35 acres, and this acreage is backed by hundreds of acres of fairly new wilderness preserve. This is beautiful, pristine land with lots of fun hiking. (Keep it pristine and bring your poop bags.)

Dogs come here and never want to leave. "We're very dog friendly," says Szu (pronounced Sue) Wakeman, who owns the cabins with her Texas-born husband, Dusty. (Great name for these parts.) Dogs get tasty biscuits when they check in, along with a doggy bed and food and water bowls during their stay. You'll be greeted at the gate by Yellow Dog, a canine you'll never forget. He's a sweet, shaggy dog with piercing ice-blue eyes. "People come here and want to take him home. He's our canine ambassador," says Szu. He's been in hundreds of guest photos (they send them to Szu), and he apparently endears himself to guests so much that some even end up letting him sleep on their bed. (Not that he's pushy—just cushy.)

Please note: At press time, the cabins were temporarily closed because of the Sawtooth Fire, but they're scheduled to reopen by the time you read this. Before the "brief misunderstanding with nature," as the folks here call it, the rates were $103–157, with a 20 percent discount in summer. Dogs are $10 extra. Rates could change when the place reopens. The mailing address is P.O. Box 313 92268; 760/228-1297; www.rimrockranchcabins.com.

Yucca Valley

If you're on your way from Palm Springs to Joshua Tree National Park or Pioneertown, and if you like antiques or New Age paraphernalia, you'll want to leave a little extra time to peruse this funky community. It's also good for people who like appliance centers, but that probably won't be of interest since you can't fit a new fridge in the back seat with your dog.

PLACES TO EAT

Water Canyon Coffee Co.: You can get really good organic coffee drinks, sandwiches, and bagels here. And if you're visiting and they happen to have their homemade apple pie, you simply have to order a slice. It is some of the best we've ever had. (Jake didn't even get the crust, it was so good. Poor guy.) Dine at the nice covered little outdoor section. 66844 29 Palms Highway; 760/365-7771.

Joshua Tree

An entry point into Joshua Tree National Park (see the *Twentynine Palms* section) is just down the road from here, but there's a new entrance and visitors center here that's become our favorite.

PARKS, BEACHES, AND RECREATION AREAS

20 Joshua Tree National Park

🐾🐾🐾 (See San Bernardino County map on page 878)

You can find out more info on this intriguing national park at the beginning of this chapter, but Jake and I wanted to tell you a little about the west entrance to the park. It's very convenient to folks visiting Palm Springs, and now there's a new visitors center here, which really makes it an attractive place to enter the park. You can get all kinds of maps and info here, and you can watch videos and look at exhibits about the park's features. Dogs aren't allowed inside, but they can peruse the grounds. The visitors center is at 6554 Park Boulevard. From Highway 62/Twentynine Palms Highway, turn right on Park Boulevard and follow the signs to the center. 760/366-1855.

PLACES TO STAY

Joshua Tree Highlands House: You'll feel like Joshua Tree National Park is your very own backyard when you stay at this roomy, attractive vacation home on 10 acres. (The park is actually three short minutes away, but it looks like it's right here.) Dogs who like contemporary-yet-retro decor will brag to their furry friends about this clean, cool, sleek two-bedroom, two-bath home with a Jacuzzi tub, steam shower, full kitchen, and enclosed deck.

By day you get a jaw-dropping 360-degree view of the beautiful surrounding desert from this remote locale, and at night you get amazing stargazing. There's nothing like breathing in the sweet scent of desert night air while lying in your comfortable lounger looking up at Orion with your own down-to-earth Canis Major at your side.

The house's owners, Frederick and Jimmy, love dogs. In fact they have three of their own, and one regularly visits a children's ward at an L.A.-area hospital to give the kids a boost.

Rates for the house are $300 nightly, $1,500 weekly. Dogs are $35 extra. Frederick and Jimmy also own three other similarly fabulous vacation homes not too far away. They're a little smaller, a little less expensive, but equally chic. They don't give out the address for any of the houses until you reserve, but you can phone them to make arrangements at 760/366-3636 or 310/562-0511; www.joshuatreehighlandshouse.com.

Twentynine Palms

PARKS, BEACHES, AND RECREATION AREAS

21 Joshua Tree National Park

🐾🐾🐾 (See San Bernardino County map on page 878)

This town houses the headquarters and a good-sized swatch of this stunning park. See the *National Parks* section at the beginning of this chapter for details.

PLACES TO STAY

29 Palms Inn: Set on 70 acres of beautiful desert, this rustic resort is just what the vet ordered for you and your pooch. It's a stress-free environment, with a peaceful spring-fed shaded pond for toe-dipping, a pool (with a cute little bar) and hot tubs for lounging, hammocks galore, phone-free bungalows and adobe cottages, and a view of the heavens you don't want to miss. You can get a massage in your room, on your sun patio, or even in the great outdoors. The cooks at the delightful restaurant can pack a picnic lunch that you and your dog will drool for. Take it on a hike in Joshua Tree National Park, just down the road.

The cottage and cabins are unique, with a down-home, Old West, nouvelle-desert feel. Some have a fireplace and a kitchen. They all have evaporative coolers for hot summer days and heaters for cool winter nights. They also have cable TV, but the TVs are small and most are black and white. The resort's brochure says this is to help guests focus on more important things, but Jake Dog thinks it's because televisions are expensive. I love the lack of big Sonys, though, and I believe the brochure. Besides, snazzy new TVs just wouldn't fit in.

Rates are $85–280. There's a $35 dog fee per visit. 73950 Inn Avenue 92277; 760/367-3505; www.29palmsinn.com.

906

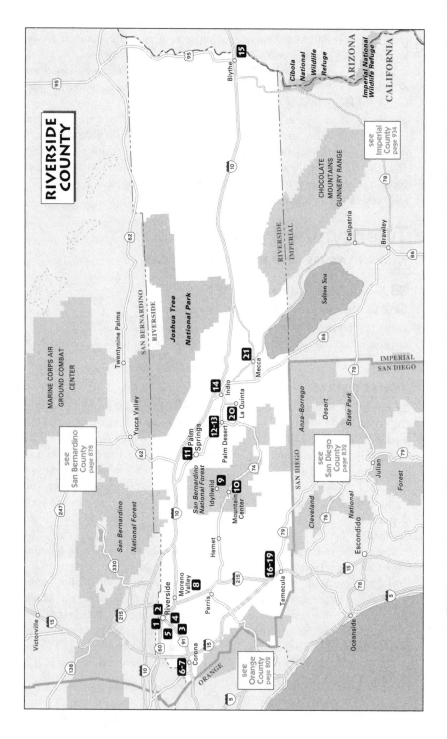

CHAPTER 57

Riverside County

Dogs are dancing with happiness in Riverside County these days, because they have so many dog parks to call their own. Dogs are no longer going to have to take to the desert to have a good time around here.

Actually, a trip to the desert during the more temperate months isn't a bad idea at all. In fact, dogs think it's a four-paws notion. But if it's hot or even warm outside, please forget it. The sand can be scorching even if the air isn't, and it can poach a pooch's paws.

Palm Springs has become quite the doggy destination of late. If you're in the mood for delectable desert oasis life, you'll find this resort town most amenable to dogs and their people. Palm Springs and surrounding resort communities are replete with super-dog-friendly inns and restaurants. Dogs are almost de rigueur here.

NATIONAL FORESTS

The *National Forests and Wilderness Areas* resource at the back of this book has

PICK OF THE LITTER—RIVERSIDE COUNTY

BEST DOG PARKS
Pat Merritt Dog Park, Riverside (page 909)
Riverwalk Dog Park, Riverside (page 910)
Palm Springs Dog Park, Palm Springs (page 920)

JUICIEST PARK
California Citrus State Historic Park, Riverside (page 912)

MOST SWINGIN' ALFRESCO DINING
Azul, Palm Springs (page 921)

MOST DOG-FRIENDLY PLACES TO STAY
Caliente Tropics Resort, Palm Springs (page 922)
Westin Mission Hills Resort & Spa, Rancho Mirage (page 925)

BEST PLACE TO SOAK YOUR WEARY BONES
Highland Spring Waters, Desert Hot Springs (page 914)

COOLEST UPDATED RETRO ATOMIC-AGE HOTEL
Del Marcos Hotel, Palm Springs (page 923)

COOLEST UPDATED RETRO 1970S HOTEL
The Mod Resort, Palm Desert (page 927)

FRANK CAPRA'S MUSE
La Quinta Resort & Club, La Quinta (page 931)

BEST HOMAGE TO MAN'S BEST FRIEND
March Air Field's War Dog Memorial, Riverside (page 910)

BEST RIDE
Orange Empire Railway Museum trains, Perris (page 916)

BEST PLACE TO SHOP
El Paseo, Palm Desert (page 925)

important information and safety tips on visiting national forests with your dog and has more information on the national forests listed below.

Cleveland National Forest
😺😺😺😺🐕

San Bernardino National Forest
😺😺😺😺🐕

NATIONAL PARKS

Joshua Tree National Park
😺😺😺

Although the bulk of this huge desert park is in Riverside County, the large visitors center area with easily accessible hikes is north of the border in San Bernardino County. Please see the *National Parks* section of that chapter for details.

Riverside

If your dog loves trees (Jake's ears just perked up), a jaunt along beautiful Victoria Avenue is a must. The seven-mile-long historic avenue is lined with more than 4,000 trees of 95 species. Male dogs think they've died and gone to heaven when they stroll down the avenue's walking path, past tree after tree after tree. To get a brochure that will help you identify the trees you and your dog admire here, call the visitors center at 951/684-INFO (951/684-4636).

PARKS, BEACHES, AND RECREATION AREAS

Riverside now has three great dog parks, and at press time, a new one—Tyler Doggie Bark—had just received the final go-ahead. We look forward to sniffing it out for the book's next edition.

1 Pat Merritt Dog Park
😺😺😺😺🐕 (See Riverside County map on page 906)

Dogs are ecstatic when they see this lush, green park—even if they can see only in black and white. The park is two terrific acres with great mountain views, and it's full of very happy dogs and their super-friendly people. The trees—once just glorified sticks—are growing and will provide nice shade here one day. The fencing—something I don't usually mention except to note that a park is fenced—is some of the most attractive dog-park fencing I've seen. Chain-link be damned! Stylish black wrought iron is what you'll see here. (The Palm Springs Dog Park fencing beats it out, but it's Palm Springs. What more can be said?) The park features two sections: one for all dogs, and one

DIVERSION

Pay Tribute to War Dogs and See Planes, Too: Back in the Vietnam War, thousands of specially trained dogs accompanied troops to the front lines in South Vietnam. Because their acute senses could detect danger in the form of ambushes, hidden trip wires, and explosives, and because of their dedication to their handlers, these amazing dogs are attributed with saving the lives of 10,000 soldiers. Nearly 300 dogs were killed in combat, and, tragically, the rest were euthanized after the war because the military thought they'd be too dangerous to return to civilian life.

These dogs are gone, but far from forgotten, at least by the veterans who accompanied them on their one-way trip. On a rainy afternoon in February 2000, some 2,000 people, many of whom were veterans from across the United States, attended a dedication of the **War Dog Memorial** outside the **March Air Field Museum.** Tearful veterans patted and hugged the bronze German shepherd depicted with his soldier in the striking 18-foot statue. The vets referred to their dogs as "America's forgotten heroes." They placed dozens of flowers at the statue's base.

Now you and your civilian dog can pay homage to these war dogs. Since the statue is outside (in the museum's front courtyard, to be exact), the folks at the March Air Field Museum say it's perfectly OK to bring your dog with you to visit. (Bringing a dog has provided at least one visitor with a convenient excuse about being a bit misty-eyed here: "I told my date sometimes I'm allergic to my dog," says the man, who was a hair too young for the war. "I don't think she bought it.") To find out more about the War Dogs association, call 877/WAR-DOGS (877/927-3647); www.wardogs.com.

While you're at March Air Field, you can have a more uplifting experience if you expand your visit to include the outdoor section of the museum's aircraft exhibit. About 40 historic aircraft are "parked"

---

for small or timid dogs. It has all the usual amenities, including benches and picnic tables (sleek and modern), water, poop bags, and lights. A huge thanks to my intrepid correspondent "Three-Dog Dave" Hepperly for the heads up about this terrific park (and photos).

The park is at Limonite Frontage Road and Emery Street, about a half mile north of the Santa Ana River. 951/826-2000.

❷ Riverwalk Dog Park

🐾🐾🐾🐾🦴 (See Riverside County map on page 906)

This is one good-looking dog park, considering how new it is. It has real-deal green grass, a cute stone walkway, and a fun kiosk that looks like a giant outside, and leashed dogs can accompany your exploration. You'll see everything from the Lockheed SR-71 Blackbird to the B-17 Flying Fortress and the B-25 Mitchell bomber. If you're an airplane buff, put this place on your must-see list. It's a good idea to take your dog for a thorough walk before your visit, because you really don't want him making his mark anywhere here.

If you're visiting with another human, you can switch off between being outside with the pooch and going inside to see more fascinating aircraft and related artifacts. The museum is a nonprofit organization, and a $7 donation ($3 for children 5–11) is requested. It's just off I-215, at the Van Buren exit. Its orange-and-white checkerboard roof is visible as you approach from the freeway. 22550 Van Buren Boulevard, Riverside; 951/697-6602; www.marchfield.org. (A special thanks to my invaluable correspondent "Three-Dog Dave" Hepperly for helping me sniff out this wonderful place.)

brown doghouse and bears a sign for the small dog portion of the park. Dogs enjoy tearing around this two-acre fenced park, and people enjoy visiting and socializing and watching their happy dogs from the benches. The park has water and poop-bag stations. The trees are small, but they'll provide shade one day. The park is in a convenient location to many dog people, including my intrepid correspondent, "Three-Dog Dave" Hepperly. He says that of the three dog parks in Riverside, this is the favorite of his canine committee. "The park has strong shrubs along the fence line, more places to sniff and pee," he writes. What more could a boy dog want?

The park is at the corner of Pierce Street and Collett Avenue, just west of the Riverwalk Parkway and a short hop north from Highway 91. 951/826-2000.

3 California Citrus State Historic Park

😺😺😺😺 (See Riverside County map on page 906)

Do you ogle oranges? Go ga-ga for grapefruit? Lust for lemons? If you're even remotely a citrus fan, this is a must-see park for your and your leashed dog. Dogs may not be as interested in citrus, but they love coming here anyway.

The park is a huge 377 acres, with a whopping 125 varieties of citrus trees. The citrus curious (and their canines) can learn more about these delights on a ranger-led or self-guided tour around the huge groves. Many of the trails are lined with palm trees, which add another level of the California Experience. In addition, there are miles of lush, landscaped trails and more rugged terrain. You'll learn so much about the history of oranges and their brethren that you'll never look at orange juice the same way again.

The people behind the park have big plans. They're now building a 6,000-square-foot visitors center, which will tell the story of California's earliest orange encounters. (The arrival of the orange in Southern California was like the gold rush in Northern California. These fruity beginnings led to the state's image as the Golden State—land of sunshine, opportunity, and plenty of sun-kissed eats.) The next phase of development involves the re-creation of a citrus-producing community circa 1880–1935. This will include an operating packing house, a workers' camp, a wealthy grower's home (which may serve as a restaurant), and an early citrus settlement with all kinds of neat old buildings.

Regular visitor Wendy and her dog Molly say they adore this park, and they inform us that dogs are not the only critters who visit here. "I have seen pet raccoons and pot-bellied pigs bring their owners to the park," says Wendy. Those animals have good taste! And unlike most dogs, they're not averse to a little citrus.

Bring a picnic and enjoy lounging on the park's large grassy lawn (complete with barbecue grills). Now orange you glad you took the time to read this? (Joe Dog made me write that.) The entry fee is $4 per vehicle. The park is in the heart of Riverside, one mile east of Highway 91, at Dufferin Avenue and Van Buren Boulevard. 951/780-6222.

4 Carlson Dog Park

😺😺😺🐾 (See Riverside County map on page 906)

This one-acre pooch park is in a really pretty spot, at the base of Mt. Rubidoux along the Santa Ana River. The dog park is fenced, with green grass, big shady trees, water fountains at human lip level and dog-slurping level, and poop mitts. My wonderful correspondent "Three-Dog Dave" Hepperly keeps me up to date on the goings on of this pooch park and other parks in the region, where he adventures with his dogs. He tells me there's now a separate section for little pooches here, which does come in handy.

The park is one mile west of downtown Riverside, on the east bank of the Santa Ana River, at Mission Inn Avenue near the bridge. 951/826-2000.

5 Rancho Jurupa Regional Park

🐾🐾🐾🐾 (See Riverside County map on page 906)

This huge county park encompasses a few others, including the Hidden Valley Wildlife Area. Stretching east to west for almost 10 miles, it more than makes up for all those smaller city parks that say "no way" to dogs.

Depending on which section you visit, you and your leashed dog can see lots of wildlife, fish for your supper, hike through fields and woods, or relax on the manicured grass of a shaded picnic area. Since our tastes are sometimes dictated by money, we like to go where we can avoid driving in and paying the $2 per person and $1 per pooch and kids fee—especially if we just need to stretch our legs. We've found a wonderful spot next to the park's nature center, where many interesting hikes originate.

To reach this fee-free area, exit Highway 60 at Rubidoux Boulevard, drive southwest a few blocks, and turn right on Mission Boulevard. In about six blocks, turn left on Riverview Drive/Limonite Avenue. In 0.6 mile, there should be a sign for a county park. That's where Riverview Drive veers to the left (Limonite continues straight). Follow Riverview for about another 1.5 miles. It will be smaller and more rural than the previous road. The park is on your left. Park in the lot near the nature center. Look for a trail and have yourselves a great hike.

If camping is your bag, you'll have to go to the fee area at Rancho Jurupa. From Highway 60, exit at Rubidoux Boulevard and drive south to Mission Boulevard. Turn left and drive about a half mile to Crestmore Boulevard. Follow Crestmore as it curves around the north side of the park. In about 1.5 miles, you'll be at the gate. Sites are $18. Dogs are $2 extra. There are approximately 70 sites available. For camping information, call Rancho Jurupa at 951/684-7032. For camping reservations, call 877/444-6777.

PLACES TO EAT

Check out the attractive pedestrian mall along Main Street for some doggone friendly eateries and some interesting history. These restaurants are a bone's throw from the Mission Inn, the city's premier historic and architectural landmark, located at 3696 Main Street. You can't go inside with your dog, but you can gawk from the outside.

Gram's Mission BBQ Palace: Dogs who visit the six outdoor tables here drool with delight at being so close to mouthwatering Cajun-style barbecued ribs, chicken, and other meaty delights. Thirsty dogs get a bowl of water. (And who wouldn't be thirsty after all that drooling?) 3527 Main Street; 951/782-8219.

Mario's Place: Trixie, Omar, and Hannah are dogs with impeccable taste. When they rave about a restaurant, you know it's a winner. And do they ever rave about this downtown Riverside gem. They're impressed by the lovely, long, narrow patio area that allows good dogs, and by the white tablecloths on the patio tables, and especially by the food: It's some of the best Italian food in the region. Try the butternut squash ravioli or the pear-gorgonzola wood-fired pizza. 3646 Mission Inn Avenue; 951/684-7755.

Riverside Brewing Co.: Thirsty dogs can enjoy a bowlful of water while you enjoy a stein full of fine house brew at the outdoor tables. Wash down a tasty burger or salad. 3397 Mission Inn Avenue; 951/784-2739.

Upper Crust Sandwich Shoppe: Dogs delight in this place because the folks here seem to delight in dogs. The meat loaf sandwich is one of the bigger draws, for humans and dogs alike. Dine with your dog at this downtown eatery's outdoor tables. Dog patrons get a big bowl of water. 3573 Main Street; 951/784-3149.

PLACES TO STAY

The county seat is not flush with places to stay, especially places of the dog-friendly variety. Here are two choices, should you need to bunk here overnight.

Best Western of Riverside: Rates are $75–150. Dogs are $20 extra. 10518 Magnolia Avenue 92505; 951/359-0770.

Motel 6: Rates are $51–55 for the first person, $6 extra for the second person. 1260 University Avenue 92507; 951/784-2131.

Desert Hot Springs

This little community is known for its naturally hot mineral water—and it doesn't smell like rotten eggs! Folks with aches and pains come to soak in pools and tubs full of the stuff, and they swear by it. Dogs do some swearing of their own around here, but for a different reason: Pooches aren't permitted in any city parks.

PLACES TO STAY

Highland Spring Waters: Need a good soak in natural hot springs mineral water? Come to this small hotel, where water is brought up to the pool and spa tubs from the hotel's well, 450 feet deep, nice and hot, and full of good-for-you minerals. And what's unique about the water here is that it doesn't smell, as mentioned above. The hotel's literature says that the water "has been recognized as one of the purest and most curative water in the world, many times compared to the famous Evian water." And the scenery from the outdoor pool is really lovely, with the oft-snowcapped San Jacinto Mountains as a backdrop.

Your dog won't care about all that curative water, because of course, dogs aren't allowed in it. But your dog is welcome to stay with you at this decent little inn. He's even allowed to sniff around the two native cactus garden courtyards, but watch out for his nose: You don't want him looking like some Warner Brothers cartoon, with a proboscis full of needles.

A variety of body treatments are also available for the humans in your party. Room rates are $110–275. 68187 Club Circle Drive 92240; 760/251-0189; www. highlanderlodge.com.

Corona

PARKS, BEACHES, AND RECREATION AREAS

6 Harada Heritage Dog Park

🐾🐾🐾🐕 (See Riverside County map on page 906)

This is a pretty basic dog park, as far as humans are concerned. There's no shade, and nothing to add interest to the flat 0.5 acre of fenced brown grass except a couple of picnic tables and, of course, their dogs. But the park has all the features dogs could want, including water, a separate section for small pooches, and decent running room. You can really lob a ball here. The park is in an unincorporated area just north of Corona. From Hamner Avenue, head west on 65th Street. The park is within the larger Harada Heritage Park, at the corner of 65th and Cleveland Avenue. 951/685-7434. (A big thanks to Riverside's "Three-Dog Dave" for cluing us in to this park.)

7 Butterfield Dog Park

🐾🐾🐾🐕 (See Riverside County map on page 906)

The dog people here worked hard for almost five years to make this fenced park a reality. The park's size, under an acre, is nothing to bark home about. But with its big old shade trees, cool green turf, benches, poop-bag dispensers, and friendly people and dogs, it's been a smash hit with dogs who dig the leash-free life. It's at 1886 Butterfield Drive. Exit Highway 91 at North Maple Street and follow it as it parallels the tracks for the Atchison, Topeka & Santa Fe (the railroad, not the song). Maple dead-ends into North Smith Street. Turn left on Smith, and go about three blocks to Butterfield Drive, where you'll go left again. The park is on your right, within the Butterfield Stage Trail Park. 951/736-2241.

Perris

PARKS, BEACHES, AND RECREATION AREAS

8 Lake Perris State Recreation Area

🐾🐾🐾 (See Riverside County map on page 906)

When people talk about this park, they generally focus on the lake. Comments I got when I asked friends about the park included the following: "You can catch some world-class fish there." "We had a great time swimming at the beach." And "I like to stand on the edge and watch for birds."

DIVERSION

Chug It Out with Your Dog: Dogs and railroads go together like love and marriage—or maybe even better. The **Orange Empire Railway Museum** is a great place to take a pooch. Jake Dog and I want to thank reader Marsden Chew MacRae for opening our eyes to this fun place. "On one memorable day, my golden retriever and I rode every single running exhibit, including the steam engine," writes Marsden Chew MacRae. (I use his three names again because he has such a great name.) "I also noted a rail fan with an attending German shepherd, who was much better trained than my dog and could actually get on and off without being lifted! Many dogs find the steps confusing and can't or won't navigate them, so bringing a dog small enough to lift might be important." That's some good advice from a man who knows his railroads. (He's traveled to many of the state's railroads with his faithful pooch.)

Leashed, well-behaved dogs can visit the museum's collection of streetcars, trolleys, a steam engine, and several diesels. They're not allowed in the buildings, but that's OK because the trains are much cooler. Speaking of cooler, it can get really hot here in summer, and this place can roast, so it's a good idea to bring your pooch here during other times of year.

Trolleys and trains operate 11 A.M.–5 P.M. Saturday and Sunday and major holidays. Special events are held throughout the year. An all-day ride pass is $12 for adults, $10 for children 5–11. Dogs and little kids don't pay a penny. Call or write for details. 2201 South A Street, P.O. Box 548, Perris, CA 92572-0548; 951/943-3020; www.oerm.org.

Great. Well, dogs, if you're into any of the above activities, forget it. You can't go near the lake, much less in it or on it. In fact, pooches have to stay at least 50 feet from the lake's edge. But fortunately, you are allowed to wear a leash and hike the trails. You'll be in sage scrub countryside, and there's not much shade, so go somewhere else if it's a hot day.

The day-use fee is $8 per vehicle. Camping costs $25–34. There are 167 tent-only sites and 265 RV sites. To reserve, phone 800/444-7275. From Highway 60, exit at Moreno Beach Drive and drive south a little more than three miles to the park. 951/657-0676.

Idyllwild

This sweet, year-round, mile-high resort is great for dogs on the go or for dogs who just like to sniff around artsy shops. Outdoorsy dogs can check out some marvelous hiking and cross-country skiing opportunities at nearby

San Bernardino National Forest (see the *National Forests and Wilderness Areas* resource at the back of this book). Indoorsy dogs can putter around the quaint alpine community's lovely village area.

With its myriad art galleries, visual art events, and music, dance, and theater productions, Idyllwild has been named one of the 100 Best Small Art Towns in America. Dogs are invited into some galleries and little shops on a case-by-case basis, so we won't go into specifics here. Just let your terribly cute and well-behaved dog sniff toward the door of one of these establishments, and she may well get an invitation to come in and help you select some merchandise.

If you and your pooch want to experience small-town types of events in this quaint alpine community, there's plenty to keep you busy. Dogs and their well-behaved people are invited to everything from outdoor pancake feasts (always benefiting a good local cause) to the July Fourth parade (complete with a greyhound contingent). The Idyllwild Chamber of Commerce website lists these and other to-do's: www.idyllwildchamber.com; 951/659-3259.

PARKS, BEACHES, AND RECREATION AREAS

9 Idyllwild County Park

😺😺😺 (See Riverside County map on page 906)

In the morning, the cool mountain air is delicately scented with fresh pines, and you may find yourself so invigorated that you actually want to get out of your tent and start the day early.

This is an attractive park, with scenic self-guided nature trails for you and your leashed pooch to peruse. Better yet, there's easy access to the wonderful, off-leash trails of San Bernardino National Forest. But you must check with a ranger before venturing out, because you could easily find yourself in the middle of Mount San Jacinto State Park—a major no-no for four-legged beasts of the domestic persuasion.

The day-use fee is $2 for adults, $1 for dogs, $1 for kids. Campsites cost $17, with dogs being charged the usual $1 county fee. Reservations are accepted for the 96 sites April 1–October 24. The rest of the year they're available on a first-come, first-served basis. The park is one mile north of Idyllwild, at the end of County Park Road; 951/659-2656. For reservations call 800/234-PARK (800/234-7275).

PLACES TO EAT

Cafe Aroma: Your schnozzle may not be as sensitive as your dog's, but come anywhere near here and you'll find that the Cafe Aroma really lives up to its name. The place smells simply *mahvelous!* The cuisine is a mixture of coffee-house and Italian. Cafe Aroma is famous around here for its morning scones and coffee. Later in the day, the café is full of wonderful garlicky, saucy, rich smells. Evening diners get to eat on white tablecloth-covered tables. It's lovely, but a bit perilous for the life of the tablecloth when you're downing your penne in spicy red sauce. 3596 North Circle Drive; 951/659-5212.

PLACES TO STAY

Fireside Inn: The seven duplex cottages here are oh-so-cozy. (Please don't let "duplex" conjure images of ugly 1970s-style housing units. The wood cottages here are just partnered together, but they're not cheap-looking. Of course, even if they were, your dog wouldn't care.) Each cottage has its own fireplace, a private bath with shower, a sitting room, and color cable TV complete with VCR. Real wood, stained in a warm golden hue, flanks cabin walls. Most cabins have kitchenettes, and a few have patios. If this isn't big enough for your needs, the inn's owners also have several larger rentals nearby where dogs are welcome. Rates for the Fireside Inn cottages are $65–135. Dogs pay a $20 flat fee. 54540 North Circle Drive, P.O. Box 313 92549; 951/659-2966 or 877/797-3473; www.thefiresideinn.com.

Knotty Pine Cabins: Dogs are welcome to stay at three of the eight wonderfully cozy, unique, well-appointed cabins here. (If you didn't already guess by the name, knotty pine figures heavily into the design schemes.) The cabins back up to a hill that's a fun place to give your dog some exercise.

Although the cabins are within walking distance of Idyllwild village, this is a peaceful place to vacation with your dog. In addition to the usual pines, oaks, and other flora, the grounds are blessed with lilac bushes! The scent of these glorious flowers is well worth planning a spring vacation around. Rates are $77–165. Dogs are $20 extra for the length of your stay. 54340 Pine Crest 92549; 951/659-2933; www.knottypinecabinsidyllwild.com.

Tahquitz Inn: Here's a dog rule you don't hear every day: No peeing on the totem pole! The eagle-topped totem pole here is a tempting target for many a boy dog, so steer clear. There's plenty of room on the grounds for a good walk, and plenty of trees for dogs who want to lift a leg. Most of the 16 cabins that make up the inn are attached in sort of a stepped pattern. This arrangement looks very much like a giant shallow staircase that winds around the inn's small pool. The cabins are pretty basic and somewhat motel-like inside, but they all have kitchens, and most have kind of funky fireplaces, so it's not so bad. The inn is 400 yards from Idyllwild's village. Rates are $78–115. Dogs are $10 extra. 25840 Highway 243 92549; 951/659-4554; www.tahquitzinn.com.

Mountain Center

While in town, stop by the Living Free animal sanctuary and see just how beautiful and livable an animal rescue facility can be. Living Free occupies 160 acres of scenic mountain country at the edge of the San Bernardino National Forest. You and your dog can visit together, and while you're on tour finding out about the many wonderful programs here, your dog will be cared for in a special pen. Your dog is guaranteed tender loving care while you learn about ways to help other animals get the same kind of love. For more information, call 951/659-4684.

🔟 Hurkey Creek Park

🐾🐾🐾🐾 (See Riverside County map on page 906)

At an elevation of about 4,500 feet and surrounded by 7,000-foot peaks, this meadowlike park stays cool even in the summer. Hurkey Creek flows through here, attracting lots of critters, so be sure your dog is leashed.

There are a couple of hiking trails, and dogs love them. They'd really like to be able to sneak into the adjacent San Jacinto Wilderness, but it's one of the few national forest wilderness areas that doesn't permit pooches (because of its intermingling with a state park that bans dogs).

The day-use fee is $2 for adults, $1 for dogs and kids. Camping is $17, with dogs paying $1 for the privilege. The park is four miles south of Mountain Center off Highway 74. There are 130 campsites available. For camping reservations, call 800/234-PARK (800/234-7275). The park phone number is 951/659-2050.

Palm Springs

First, the warning, straight from the Palm Springs Animal Shelter: "Our area can be quite warm (HOT!!!!) all year-round, so please, please, please be sure to warn travelers about the dangers.... Our visitors don't seem to realize how hot it is. With our low humidity, it doesn't feel as hot as it really is, and pets can't handle the hot cement sidewalks, hot desert sand, and hot asphalt without getting burned pads."

The shelter knows its stuff. Staffers have seen too many dogs whimper their last breaths because of heatstroke and other heat-related horrors. The municipal code forbids dogs to be left unattended in enclosed vehicles, no matter what time of year. The law is a good one. Since it was enacted in 1988, not a single pet has been lost to this disastrous practice.

Believe it or not, the entire posh desert playground city of Palm Springs is a wildlife preserve. You can routinely spot coyotes, bobcats, raccoons, snakes, lizards, and migratory birds around town. Occasionally, mountain lions and badgers have been sighted. Make sure your dog is leashed and that you hold the leash securely at all times.

The dog park here is renowned for its attractiveness and popularity. (Sounds like someone we all knew in high school.) Dogs flock here from all over to enjoy some much-needed off-leash time. Palm Springs is also home to a few natural areas around town where you can take your pooch for a good walk. In addition, you can also take your dog to some fun, if *un*natural, places.

Several spectacular lodgings (and several not-quite-so-spectacular ones) welcome well-behaved dogs. Many Palm Springs restaurants permit dogs to

DIVERSION

Who Needs Hollywood?: You and your dog can sniff out the sidewalk-embedded stars of more than 70 celebrities who have "lived, loved, and played" in Palm Springs. The **Palm Springs Walk of Stars** includes stars for Ralph Bellamy, Elizabeth Taylor, Frank Sinatra, Bob Hope, Ginger Rogers, Marilyn Monroe, and Marlene Dietrich. The Walk of Stars is on Palm Canyon Drive in the beautiful central village. You can get a complete list of celebrities and their stars' locations by visiting www.palmsprings.com/stars.

dine outside with you. In addition, dogs are welcome to attend a crowded but fun street fair every Thursday on Palm Canyon Drive. (See the Diversion *Take to the Streets.*)

PARKS, BEACHES, AND RECREATION AREAS

If you want to feel the desert in your paws when you and your dog go out for a walk, you'll be happy to know that Palm Springs is surrounded by land run by the Bureau of Land Management. Call 760/251-4800 for information on fun places to hike during the cooler months.

Dog owners in town frequently use the many local "wash" areas (dry streambeds) to run on leash with their dogs. You'll see them on the outskirts of town and beyond, but with the new park opening, you might not see them as much as you used to.

You can also take your leashed pooch to a nearby hiking area for an interesting desert romp. The Carl Lykken Hiking Trail starts at the extreme west end of Ramon Road. Don't forget your water. (There's some talk about banning dogs from the trail, so don't be surprised if you see one of those horrible signs with a slash through a dog silhouette during a future walk.) Unfortunately, our other favorite area for dogs, the 27,000-acre Indian Canyons, no longer allows dogs because of some very bad incidents with pit bulls and their people.

Of course, any trip to Palm Springs with a dog would not be the same without a visit to the beautiful Palm Springs Dog Park.

11 Palm Springs Dog Park

🐾🐾🐾🐾 🐕 (See Riverside County map on page 906)

Dogs of Palm Springs are panting, but not because of the heat (they all live in air-conditioned quarters, after all). They're panting with joy, because their dog park is so wonderful. This isn't just any ordinary dog park. Lest you've forgotten, this is Palm Springs, after all.

This 1.6-acre park is a real work of art, complete with an iron fence and double gates designed by sculptor Phil Evans. (How many dog park fences have dog paws and faces carved into them?) It's big compared with many dog parks, and it has everything a dog could want—and a lot more: It's green and grassy, with some trees, awnings for extra shade, a separate fenced area for pups or tiny dogs who are overwhelmed by the big dogs running around the main area, drinking fountains that have two levels so humans and their pooches can slurp together, picnic tables, lights at night, and plenty of poop bags. For your boy dog's aiming pleasure, the park also features 11 fire hydrants. Of course, these aren't your run-of-the-mill hydrants. These hydrants are of the beautiful antique variety. Your dog will do leg lifts in style. To that end, the park is also flanked by palms.

The park is directly behind City Hall, at 222 Civic Drive North; 760/322-8362.

PLACES TO EAT

Palm Springs is full of fine restaurants with outdoor areas where dogs are welcome. Most are along Palm Canyon Drive, the city's main drag.

Azul: The food is generally small plates, and a fun fusion of Asian, Spanish, American and other world cuisine. And the drinks are strong. But what's really great about Azul is its huge outdoor patio area. It's on a large, raised deck where you can check out the happenings on Palm Canyon Drive. You can sit at shaded tables, the outdoor bar, or—best of all—on wooden porch swings that glide on tracks. If you've had one too many mojitos you might want to stay off it, because it really can swing.

Last time we visited, a man with three fluffy little white dogs was buying drinks for a bunch of friends. They were all in white. They looked so clean and crisp with the white contrasting their tans. Then suddenly it dawned on me: We were here during the White Party, a huge circuit party with 20,000 gay men, most dressed in white. It was a fun time to be visiting this resort city, which was much more lively that week than I'd seen for ages. 369 North Palm Canyon Drive; 760/325-5222.

Hair of the Dog: As long as you don't find anything resembling this English pub's name floating in your appetizers or your beer, you'll enjoy it here. People

DIVERSION

Take to the Streets: On Thursday evenings, 7–10 P.M., well-behaved, leashed pooches may accompany you to Palm Springs' glamorous Palm Canyon Drive, where a street fair, **Villagefest,** will charm the spots off your dog. Musicians, food, arts and crafts vendors, and a certified farmers market make this street even more fun than it normally is. Villagefest takes place between Tahquitz Canyon Drive and Baristo Road. Parking is best behind the Desert Inn Fashion Plaza. 800/34-SPRINGS (800/347-7746); www.palmspringsvillagefest.com.

can sit at a half dozen outdoor tables with their pooches. 238 North Palm Canyon Drive; 760/323-9890.

Peabody's Coffee Bar & Jazz Club: You won't find Mr. Peabody here, but all other dogs, brainy or not, are welcome to dine and drink with you at the patio. (The listing for Sherman's, below, is pure coincidence. Either that, or someone's hiding a Wayback Machine somewhere in the desert.) 134 South Palm Canyon Drive; 760/322-1877.

Pomme Frite: The French and Belgian cuisine here is snout-licking good. Try the braised coq au vin for a traditionally delicious dish. If you're a mussel fan, you'll be happy to know that mussels are prepared nine different ways and always accompanied by crispy versions of the restaurant's name. Yum! Your dog can join you at the large, attractive, covered back patio. Watch out: The tablecloths are white! 256 South Palm Canyon Drive; 760/778-3727.

Sherman's Deli & Bakery: Dogs are welcome to join their people at the shaded tables in front of this New York–style eatery. And if your pooch is thirsty, she'll even get a big bowl of water. "We're dog friendly!" reports an equally people-friendly server. The brisket dinner is to drool for. A lunch that's no lighter on the meat is the double-combo pastrami sandwich that includes another meat of your choice. (Yes, it's filling.) Breakfasts are a delight, too. 401 East Tahquitz Canyon Way; 760/325-1199.

PLACES TO STAY

Palm Springs has oodles of quality canine accommodations. It used to be that they allowed only the itsy-bitsy-est of dog-ettes. Now most that permit pooches welcome any size good dog.

America's Best Value Inn: If you're traveling with more than one dog, this is a good place to bunk for the night: You can have up to three dogs per room, and the cost is only $10 extra per dog. Room rates are $52–90. 1900 North Palm Canyon Drive 92262; 760/322-3757.

Caliente Tropics Resort: If you like campy, retro, fun, attractive, super-dog-friendly accommodations, look no further than this fully renovated 1960s Polynesian-style motel. The rooms are tiki-boutique-y, tiki torches flank the pool and the grounds, and the signage is delectably 1964.

You and your dog can sniff out tiki god statues and other Polynesian artifacts throughout the resort. There's a tall, cylindrical, angry-looking god head outside that can scare the daylights out of more sensitive dogs. One pooch wrote to tell me he had a little accident when he sniffed it out, thinking it was a tree at first until he saw its glowering eyes and fierce mouth. He fluffed up, cowered two steps back, and "suddenly my owners found themselves wishing they had a pooper-scooper." This dog asked that I not use his name because he is embarrassed about this incident. Poor Frank. (Oops! Sorry, Frank.)

With the exception of a few rare incidents like Frank's, dogs absolutely adore this place. It's one of the more dog-friendly lodgings in this book. Dogs who come here get gourmet treats shaped like tiki heads, water and food dishes, blankets, poop bags, and cushy dog beds. Best of all, there's a fenced grassy area by the pool where well-behaved dogs are welcome to trot around leash free. In fact, there's even a fledgling Pet Star Walk of Fame right there. (One of the three concrete stepping stones has handprints of the late Anna Nicole Smith and her little dog. This might become a collector's item.)

In case you or your dog is interested in a little celeb history, you should know that long ago the Caliente had a private underground supper club where Elvis, the Rat Pack, and other big celebs could relax in peace. It was beautiful, with the popular colors of the time—purple and white—on the leather banquettes, white tablecloths, and a stage. Alas, a former owner concerned about earthquake proofing filled it with cement.

Rates are $65–225. Dogs are $15 extra. 411 East Palm Canyon Drive 92264; 760/327-1391 or 866/HOT-9595 (866/468-9595); www.calientetropics.com.

Casa Cody Country Inn: Dogs love this quaint, quiet historic country inn almost as much as their peace-seeking people do. The rooms are very attractively furnished, with tile floors and a relaxing, earthy decor. The suites and studios all have kitchens. Some have wood-burning fireplaces and private patios. The eight adobe hacienda-style buildings house 27 lovely accommodations, each around a beautiful courtyard resplendent with bougainvillea and citrus. The two small pool areas here are very pretty and tranquil.

Past canine visitors have caused some problems because irresponsible owners have left them alone in the room. Don't even think of doing this. Rates are $69–429. Dogs are $10 extra for the length of your stay. 175 South Cahuilla Road 92262; 760/320-9346; www.casacody.com.

Del Marcos Hotel: Stay at this fabulously retro hotel if you want a trip back in time to the Atomic Age. The hotel has been lovingly restored and exemplifies the cool, casual style of the best of the hip 1960s. It's the kind of place the Jetsons would have dug, if they could have lived a little closer to the ground. Happily, Astro would have been welcome here. The 16-room hotel is, of course, dog friendly.

The saltwater pool provides a refreshing change from all the chlorine you can soak up at other pools in the area. No dogs there, but they may peruse the grassy grounds. Rates are $149–259. 225 West Baristo Road 92262; 800/676-1214; www.delmarcoshotel.com. (The website's music will put you in the mood for your upcoming retro vacation.)

Doral Desert Princess Resort: This attractive, 285-room hotel is set on a golf course. Some of the rooms have great views of the big pool or the green. The rooms are generally large and have private patios. Rates are $79–329. Dogs pay a $75 flat fee. 67-967 Vista Chino 92234; 760/322-7000; www.doralpalmsprings.com.

Hilton Palm Springs Resort: "We are delighted to have dogs as guests. They find it very entertaining here," a vivacious, dog-loving staffer tells us. "That's why all the rooms have balconies. Dogs like to look out and see what's going on." From one side of this very comfortable, attractive hotel, dogs can look out at the mountains. From the other, they can look down at the swimming pool. Ask the concierge about nearby places to walk with your dog. "Lots of folks bring their pets here, and we've got some great places for them to walk," another staffer said. Rates are $95–400. Dogs require a $100 deposit, and they pay a $25 flat fee. 400 East Tahquitz 92262; 760/320-6868 or 800/522-6900; www.hiltonpalmsprings.com.

Motel 6: There are three of these motels in Palm Springs. Rates are $44–48 for one adult, $6 extra for a second adult. Phone 800/466-8356 for information and reservations.

Musicland Hotel: "Any pooch under 200 pounds is OK," says a dog-friendly staffer. The website confirms that "Musicland welcomes pets up to about 200 to 300 pounds." We like that attitude! The hotel is kind of basic, but it's clean, the prices are low, and your stay comes with continental breakfast. Rates are $33–99. Dogs are $5 extra. 1342 South Palm Canyon Drive 92264; 760/325-1326; www.funvacation.net/musicl.html.

A Place in the Sun: This is a fun place to stay if you like your immaculate room or larger bungalow surrounded by greenery and palms, backed by mountains. The two-bedroom bungalows (the largest accommodations) have a patio and fireplace, as well as a full kitchen. The pool and Jacuzzi are blissfully chlorine free! They're actually filled with mild saltwater (advertised as being only half as salty as your own teardrops). Any size good dog can stay here, "within reason," says a clerk. Rates are $79–309. Dogs are $15 extra. 754 San Lorenzo Road 92264; 760/325-0254 or 800/779-2254; www.aplaceinthesunhotel.com.

Quality Inn Resort: Rates are $49–189. 1269 East Palm Canyon Drive 92264; 760/323-2775 or 800/221-2222.

7 Springs Inn & Suites: Dogs and their people adore staying at this charming, affordable boutique hotel. The 50 rooms and suites are relaxing and beautifully designed, with tranquil earth tones, 500-thread-count sheets (the last motel we stayed at seemed to have 25-thread-count sheets—ouch!), goose-down pillows, marble floors, granite countertops, and views of the inn's little pool and garden area. Rates are $47–375. Dogs are $20 extra. 950 North Indian Canyon Drive 92262; 760/320-9110 or 800/883-0417; www.palmsprings.com/7springs/index.html.

Villa Rosa Inn: It's trees, trees everywhere at this lovely motel/inn, where all six accommodations are poolside. Dogs love the trees, and they enjoy the spacious Southwest-meets-Pier-1-Imports-style rooms and suites. Especially comforting to hot dogs are the cool terra cotta tile floors. Built in 1948, this inn is just as immaculate and crisp as the day it was born. (Except the flowers and arbors are a lot bigger now.) Rates are $99–175. Dogs are $20 extra and shouldn't be too big. "We try to keep them not major size," says an innkeeper. 1577 South Indian Trail 92264; 760/327-5915; www.villarosainn.com.

Rancho Mirage

PLACES TO STAY

Westin Mission Hills Resort & Spa: Dogs under 40 pounds are lucky dogs indeed. They get to stay at this first-class resort, in a choice of some 500 big, beautiful rooms with all the amenities humans could want. Dogs also get to use a comfy amenity: A Heavenly Pet Bed, a miniature version of the über-comfortable people beds that adorn all Westins.

All rooms come with a private patio. If you need more room, try one of the suites. They're fabulous and elegant. The inn is on 360 acres, which includes two championship golf courses, gorgeous pools, and a huge wellness spa. Rates are $159–409 for traditional guest rooms. 71333 Dinah Shore Drive 92270; 760/328-5955; www.starwoodhotels.com/westin.

Palm Desert

This desert resort town's motto, "Where the sun shines a little brighter," could use an addendum these days. We think it should read, "Where the sun shines a little brighter and dogs smile a little wider." See why.

PARKS, BEACHES AND RECREATION AREAS

You may think nothing grows in the desert, but two dog parks have popped right up out of the ground like miraculous desert flowers. Actually, it was a lot more work than just popping out of the ground. But the success of these dog parks has paved the path for more in the future. A city councilman told the *Desert Sun* newspaper that he doesn't foresee any parks being built in Palm Desert without having some kind of dog park facility. Oh, what a wonderful place to be a dog!

And if your dog enjoys shopping or eating or both, be sure to take her to **El Paseo**, Palm Desert's answer to Rodeo Drive. Many of its 300 stores and boutiques will invite your well-behaved dog inside. And the restaurants here are super dog friendly. The El Paseo shopping district is about a mile long and festooned with gorgeous flowers and palms.

12 Civic Center Park Dog Park

🐾 🐾 🐾 🐕 (See Riverside County map on page 906)

This luscious canine oasis is grassy, with trees, shaded seating, double gates, a beautiful iron fence, a separate area for small dogs who would rather not mess with the big guys, poop bags, and a big fire hydrant. The hydrant is so popular we've even heard about dogs lining up to make their mark.

The park is about a half acre, and dogs take advantage of their leashless freedom. They run and run, drink some water, run and run, sniff a newcomer, run and run, head for the hydrant, and run and run some more. Meanwhile,

DIVERSION

Make Tracks to Saks: Need a frock for that special occasion and just can't bear to leave your furry friend behind? Good news! If she's clean, flea-free, well-behaved, leashed, and promises not to leave puddles, you can bring her with you to shop at **Saks Fifth Avenue** on Palm Desert's upscale shopping street, El Paseo. (It's one of many places that allow people to shop with their dogs.) The woman we spoke with at Saks says that "maybe you wouldn't want to bring a Saint Bernard here." If you do bring a fairly large dog, please be sure to ask an employee if it's OK before you start sniffing around the couture. 73-555 El Paseo; 760/837-2900.

people have a grand old time socializing with each other. The park is within the attractive Civic Center Park, where there's a nice playground and lovely landscaping. If your dog is a night owl, he'll be happy to know the park has lighting and is open until 11 P.M. It's at Fred Waring Drive and San Pablo Avenue, near College of the Desert. 760/346-0611.

🔢 Joe Mann Park
🐾🐾🐕 (See Riverside County map on page 906)

The park is a wee 0.3 acre, but it has many good dog park amenities, including grass, benches, water, poop bags, shade cover, and even a fire hydrant. It's at Avenue of the States and California Avenue. 760/346-0611.

PLACES TO EAT

All but one of these (Sherman's) is part of the famed El Paseo, a mecca for shoppers and people-watching.

Armando's Dakota Bar & Grill: The patio here is much more popular than this Mexican restaurant's interior, partly because it's more attractive, and partly because of the great people-watching at this busy part of El Paseo. The patio is covered and has misters to cool you off. The Mexican food isn't gourmet, but it's tasty. The margaritas are worth ordering. 73-260 El Paseo; 760/776-7535.

BackStreet Bistro: Dogs enjoy joining their people at the alfresco tables at this California-cuisine restaurant. 72-820 El Paseo; 760/346-6393.

The Inn on El Paseo: The food at this very attractive Cal-American restaurant is snout-lickin' good. "Especially the meat loaf and the prime rib," Jake is telepathically telling me to write. This is a really popular place to grab a bite and cool your heels while doing the El Paseo shopping thing. The delicious salads and sandwiches are the perfect light option for a midday meal. Add some selections from the bar and you'll sail through the rest of your spree.

The two covered garden-patio areas are among the most inviting of El Paseo's alfresco choices, with cooling mist fans and, when needed, heating lamps. The patio area has a water bowl for thirsty pooches. 73-445 El Paseo; 760/340-1236.

Sherman's Deli & Bakery: If you like New York–style deli food, this place is a must-visit. For something delectably different, try the corned-beef sandwich with potato pancakes instead of bread. It's a house specialty. The house-baked goods are tasty, too. Best of all, dogs get water and doggy biscuits here. (Jake Dog likes these, but his sweet tooth makes him quiver for Sherman's wonderful cheesecakes.) Sherman's is in the Plaza de Monterey Shopping Center, at 73161 Country Club Drive. 760/568-1350.

PLACES TO STAY

The Mod Resort: Tiny, hip dogs who dig equally hip, cool mod digs will love this place. The new owner, Laura Slipak, bought it and revamped it, making it look so stylishly mod and 1970s that she says she thinks it's "the way the Rat Pack would have decorated it in the early '70s." The decor is a mélange of whites, silvers, and browns, punctuated with gleaming mirrors, shiny chrome, suede, and glistening metallic accents. It's not what you'd call cozy, but who needs cozy when you can channel Austin Powers? (That said, the beds are ultra comfortable—a feature not necessarily from the 1970s.)

The pool area continues the stylin' '70s motif, and you can hear tunes from Frank Sinatra and his brethren as you stroll the grounds. The resort is within walking distance of the high-end shops and restaurants of El Paseo shopping district.

Sadly for Jake and his big, cool friends, the only dogs who can stay here are those up to 15 pounds. "We'd rather have the Chihuahuas of the world," says Laura. (Admittedly, they do look better with the backdrop of this hotel than this giganto yellow Lab snoring at my feet.) Rates are $159–349. Most rooms here are suites and come with kitchenettes. The room rate includes a continental breakfast in the groovy lounge. 73-758 Shadow Mountain Drive 92260; 760/674-1966 or 800/MOD-1970 (800/663-1970); www.modresort.com.

The Inn at Deep Canyon: You and your dog can feast your eyes on the motel's palms, garden, pool, and hydrotherapy spa from most rooms here. You'll get a continental breakfast, too. Rates are $47–261. Dogs are $10 extra. 74-470 Abronia Trail 92260; 760/346-8061 or 800/253-0004; www.innadc.com.

Indio

It may look flat and boring, but this dry old town has the distinction of being the king of the only region in the United States that grows dates. And we're not talking a few trees—we're talking 4,000 acres' worth, making a semi-oasis out of an otherwise blah, depressing area.

PARKS, BEACHES, AND RECREATION AREAS

There's going to be a dog park around here in the near future. Keep your nose to the ground, and we'll update you in the book's next edition.

14 Miles Avenue Park

😾😾 (See Riverside County map on page 906)

If you're dropping someone off at the adjacent Coachella Valley Museum and Cultural Center, your dog might appreciate a little pause at this grassy, meadowy park. It looks like a golf course, but miraculously enough in this golf-inundated land, it's not. There are some deciduous trees, as well as palms, for the benefit of the boy dogs in the crowd.

The park is on Deglet Noor Street and Miles Avenue, about three blocks north of Highway 111. 760/391-4017.

PLACES TO STAY

Best Western Date Tree Motor Hotel: Rates are $60–120. Pooches are $10 extra. 81-909 Indio Boulevard 92201; 760/347-3421; www.datetree.com.

Palm Shadow Inn: This motel is truly a desert oasis. Its three acres of green grounds are ripe with flowers and date trees. There's a pool and hot tub, too. Not much here says "desert" except the sweet, dry air. Some of the rooms come with kitchens, which can make life easier when traveling with a pooch. Rates are $79–129. Dogs are $5 extra. 80-761 Highway 111 92201; 760/347-3476 or 800/700-8071; www.palmshadowinn.com.

Blythe

If you're traveling from the east on I-10 and vow that you'll stop in the first California town you hit, get ready to brake. Blythe isn't an exciting town, but it's a welcome sight if you've traveled across the country with the Golden State as your goal.

PARKS, BEACHES, AND RECREATION AREAS

15 Mayflower Park

😾😾😾 (See Riverside County map on page 906)

This park covers only 24 acres, but because it backs up on the refreshing Colorado River, it seems much bigger. The folks here are pretty laid-back about dogs when it's not crowded. Pooches should be leashed, but you can still let them do a little wading in the water. Just watch out for those pesky boats.

Mayflower Park is an excellent place to stop if you've been driving all day and feel like fishing for stripers or catfish, cooking your catch for dinner, and then camping by the river.

The day-use fee is $2 for adults, $1 for dogs, $1 for kids. Camping costs

$16–18, with dogs costing $1 extra. There are 180 sites available. The park is six miles northeast of Blythe, just north of 6th Avenue and Colorado River Road. Sites are first-come, first-served. For park info, call 760/922-4665.

PLACES TO STAY

Best Western Sahara Motel: Rates are $59–109. 825 West Hobson Way 92225; 760/922-7105.

Legacy Inn: Rates are $45–62. Small pooches are preferred, and they need to stay in smoking rooms. 903 West Hobson Way 92225; 760/922-4146.

Temecula

If cruising around the area makes you and your dog think it's all just one big subdivision after another, you need a visit to Old Town Temecula, with its attractive storefronts, antique shops, eateries, and host of fun events. While you're at it, take a trip to the area's Wine Country. You can drive while your dog drinks. Wait, your dog can drive while you drink. Hmm. Well, I'm sure you'll work it out between you (see the Diversion *Whine Not!*).

PARKS, BEACHES, AND RECREATION AREAS

For years, some people here were driving 80 miles round-trip to use Escondido's dog park—one of the closest around at that point. But now they can

DIVERSION

Whine Not! You can visit Temecula's fine wineries with your dogs, so there's no need to cry into your beer. Most of the 20 wineries here allow dogs to join you at their outdoor picnic areas. One of the humans in your party can go inside, do some tasting and touring, and perhaps bring out a bottle fresh from the cellars for your little picnic.

A very dog-friendly winery is **Bella Vista Cilurzo Vineyard & Winery** (41220 Calle Contento; 951/676-5250). "We love dogs!" says a winery rep who has a dog of her own. Equally dog friendly is **Keyways Vineyard & Winery** (37338 DePortola Road; 951/302-7888). "We allow horses," says a Keyways vintner. "Every week about 20 riders come up, park their horses, drink some wine, and ride away." (Now that's a new twist on drinking and driving.) "So of course we'll allow dogs." **Temecula Hills Winery** (47200 DePortola Road; 951/767-0677) also welcomes pooches at its picnic tables.

You'll find a helpful list and map of all of Temecula's wineries, their websites, and basic info at www.temeculawines.com.

save gas, help the environment, and make their dogs really happy: Temecula now has two dog parks of its very own! One more is on the drawing board.

16 Margarita Dog Park

🐾🐾🐾🐾🐕 (See Riverside County map on page 906)

Welcome to Temecula's first permanent dog park! It opened in late 2007 to the rave reviews of dogs, who loved the lush turf, the two sections, the trees, the water, and all the other dogs who were running around in leash-free bliss. It's a pretty good size, with plenty of room for chasing tennis balls.

A big thanks to my old Northwestern University pal Johanna Lack for letting us know about this great new park. From I-15, take Rancho California Road east 0.4 mile and turn left on Moraga Road. In one long block, the road will dead-end. Bear left on Margarita Road. Margarita Community Park, which is the home of the dog park, is immediately on your left. 951/694-6444.

17 Redhawk Dog Park

🐾🐾🐾🐕 (See Riverside County map on page 906)

This dog park is just temporary, but we're listing it because it's one of those temporary dog parks that's probably going to be around for a long time. Redhawk is the first dog park in Temecula and a very popular spot with local pooches. It's in two sections, one for large dogs and one the under-25-pound set. The total size is almost 1.5 acres. It doesn't have water or double gates or some of the other traditional pooch park amenities. A new, bigger, permanent park with all the works should be built here in 2009 or so, but in the meantime, this is a mighty good temporary park.

It's in the green and pretty Redhawk Park, which is very close to I-15. From the interstate, take Highway 79 east a little under a mile to Redhawk Parkway. Turn south (right) and drive a short distance to the park. The official park address is 44747 Redhawk Parkway. 951/694-6444.

18 Duck Pond Park

🐾🐾 (See Riverside County map on page 906)

Feel like breaking bread? Do it with the ducks! This pretty park has a duck-filled pond as its centerpiece and its raison d'être. They appreciate the bread, but they also appreciate you coming with a dog who isn't a duck-chaser. (Jake, who is a duck dog through and through, would go out of his bird here.) You can bring your calm leashed dog to the pond's edge or walk your normal leashed dog on a path that meanders through willows and other shady arbors.

This park doesn't have great scenery nearby: It's across the street from a big Target store and a slightly less unattractive place, the Tower Plaza shopping center. 28250 Ynez Road, at Rancho California Road; 951/694-6410.

19 Lake Skinner County Park

🐾🐾🐾🐾 (See Riverside County map on page 906)

So what if your dog can't swim in the lake or even hang out in your boat with you? Of the 6,040 acres of park, the lake makes up only about 1,200 acres. That means several thousand acres of hilly chaparral country are all yours. Leashed pooches are permitted to peruse the trails and run around the open turf areas.

During the rainy season, the trails may be closed. Call before you visit. The day-use fee is $2 per adult and $1 per child. Campsites are $12–18. Dogs are $2 extra. There are approximately 265 campsites. From I-15, take the Rancho California Avenue exit northeast and drive about nine miles to the park. Call 800/234-PARK (800/234-7275) for reservations. For park information, call 951/926-1541.

PLACES TO STAY

Motel 6: Rates are $45–67 for the first adult, $6 for the second. 41900 Moreno Drive 92590; 951/676-7199.

La Quinta

PARKS, BEACHES & RECREATION AREAS

La Quinta has its own pretty little dog park now. And by the time you read this, there should be one more—a bit bigger—at Center Point Park.

20 Fritz Burns Dog Park

🐾🐾🐾🐕 (See Riverside County map on page 906)

This is the kind of attractive dog park you'd expect in an upscale community like La Quinta. Its fence really sets it apart from other dog parks. It's wrought iron, tall, and stately. The bottom third of the fence has slats that are just two inches apart so the little guys can't get out, and the top two-thirds expands that distance to four inches. (No large dog worth his kibble will escape from that.)

The park itself is lush and green, with water for humans and dogs, separate sections for large and small dogs, a few trees, shade structures, and poop-bag dispensers. It's not a big place: The big dog section is about 6,000 square feet, and the little dog section has about half the running room. We'd give a less attractive park a lower rating. The park is within Fritz Burns Park, at the corner of Calle Sinaloa (Avenue 52) and Avenida Bermudas. 760/777-7090.

PLACES TO STAY

La Quinta Resort & Club: First, for all of you who have stayed at the La Quinta motel chain with your dog, this isn't one of those motels. Not by a long shot. This La Quinta is the mother of all La Quintas. This internationally famous resort is probably the most legendary of all the posh getaways in the Palm Springs area. The town of La Quinta was named after it, if that tells you anything. Built in 1926, it's the area's oldest resort. It quickly became a favorite retreat for the stars of the Golden Era of Hollywood. (Frank Capra wrote *It Happened One Night* in a casita here, and after its success, he declared it his good luck charm and returned frequently to write other screenplays.)

Before you read on, you should know that if your dog is more than 25 pounds, he can't accompany you here. Jake Dog cried in his kibble when he heard about this rule. I thought I'd spare you and yours the same disappointment and tell you up front. Actually, according to some unidentified sources, bigger dogs have been known to be allowed here. It may be worth a try, if your heart is set on this wonderland and your dog weighs more than his bag of dog food.

Everything here is top drawer. The 804 guest casitas, each a Spanish-style cottage, are beautifully furnished and offer real privacy and peace. Many have wood-burning fireplaces. The landscaping is lush, with gorgeous flowers and palms everywhere. The restaurants are magnificent (some allow doggies at their patios), and the shops at La Quinta's plaza are some of the finest around. Even the beauty parlor is special—a fun art deco style. For humans, there are 41 swimming pools, 34 spas, 23 tennis courts, and 90 famous holes of championship golf. You can get a massage in the sun, work out in the fitness center, and do a zillion other wonderful things. For dogs, there are a few little areas to ramble leash-free on the surrounding 45 acres, but you'll have to ask about those because we're not supposed to tell you where they are.

Dogs are relegated to the cottages with enclosed private patios. Rates for these are $225–445. Dogs pay a $100 fee for the length of their stay. 49-499 Eisenhower Drive, P.O. Box 69 92253; 760/564-4111 or 800/598-3828; www. laquintaresort.com.

Mecca

PARKS, BEACHES, AND RECREATION AREAS

🐾 Salton Sea State Recreation Area

🐾🐾🐾 (See Riverside County map on page 906)

If you ever wanted to explore the Salton Sea, this is a great place to start your observations. The park has 16 miles of shoreline, including five beaches. Dogs must wear the mandatory leash attire, but they manage to have a fabulous time anyway.

Unfortunately, dogs are not allowed on the trails that connect a couple of these areas together, but you can transport your pooch from one area to another by car. Try to spend at least one night. Three of the beaches are primitive, and they have campsites right at the seaside. While dogs must be leashed, they still love dunking their paws in the very buoyant water.

The day-use fee is $4. Camping costs $7–14. There are 149 developed sites. Call 800/444-7275 to reserve. Dogs generally prefer the cheaper, more primitive sites, which are $7. Take Highway 111 southeast of Mecca about 10 miles, and you'll find the park headquarters and visitors center on the west side of the highway. (About half of the park is in Imperial County. If you're approaching the lake from the southeast side and have a hankering to discover the Imperial section of the park, take Highway 111 to any of several entrances, including the popular Bombay Beach area.) 760/393-3059 or 760/393-3052.

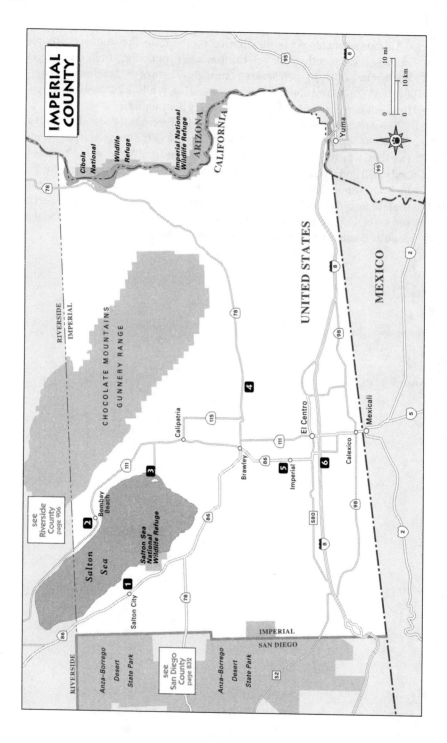

CHAPTER 58

Imperial County

Although this county is home to the Imperial Valley, one of the richest farming areas in the world, it's much more than just an agricultural wonderland. In fact, when you wander into the most dog-friendly areas, you'll wonder how land around here could be used for anything but sandboxes.

About 1.5 million acres of desert here is run by the Bureau of Land Management—those dog-friendly folks who rarely demand a leash. The dune areas are fascinating, and your dog will love racing up and down the sandy expanses.

Nearby is the strange and salty Salton Sea. At 36 miles long and 15 miles wide, it's one of the world's largest inland bodies of saltwater. Although officially considered a lake, it's got most of the qualities of a sea, including the fact that from most of its shoreline, you can look across and see vast, astounding nothingness.

The sea is situated at 234 feet below sea level (the "normal" sea level, that is), directly atop the San Andreas Fault. Millions of years ago, the valley region

PICK OF THE LITTER—IMPERIAL COUNTY

MOST MOONLIKE PARK
Red Hill Marina County Park, Calipatria (page 938)

BIGGEST SANDBOX
Imperial Sand Dunes, Brawley (page 939)

BEST BIZARRELY TEMPTING REAL ESTATE INVESTMENT
A house in Salton City (page 936)

here was filled with lakes and streams. But the lakes dried up as seismic activity caused the mountains to the west to grow, cutting off the moist, cool air from the ocean.

Then in 1905, the Colorado River flooded in Mexico and caused a two-year flood through the brand-new Imperial Valley irrigation system. It sparked the rebirth of the lake known as the Salton Sea.

Mixed with minerals left by earlier seas, as well as present-day evaporation and fertilizer runoff, the water is 10 percent saltier than an ocean. Dogs like to float around in it, but watch out for their eyes.

And if you smell a really foul stench while you're here, you may be tempted to drive away as fast as your four wheels will take you. The occasionally malodorous air is caused by an algae bloom and resulting fish die-off, and the operative expression here is *"Peeuuuw!"* But before you zip away, stop for a moment and let your dog take a few good, deep breaths of this wretched stink. She'll be on an olfactory high for the rest of the day.

Salton City

If you happen to have the *Twilight Zone* theme in your car, pop it in as you approach this land that time forgot.

After you notice the bright blue Salton Sea in the background, you'll become aware of lots and lots of lots. Empty ones. Many miles of curved, suburban-style roads wind in and out of this flat waterfront community, but no one is home. There should be thousands of houses on these paved grids, but there are only a smattering. It's as if Rod Serling went all out and made one of his eerie dollhouse-scale sets life-sized.

What really happened was an optimistic real estate sellout in the 1950s and 1960s. An extensive road system was developed and 20,000 lots were sold. But the folks who bought them generally just kept their investment without plopping down so much as a mobile home. So the roads essentially lead to nowhere. When you get lost on them, don't panic. Just remember that Rod Serling isn't around anymore, so this couldn't really be as strange as it seems, and you couldn't really be in the *Twilight Zone*. Could you?

Actually a savvy canine reader, Elmo, wrote to tell us that recently someone has come in, snagged a bunch of lots, and started to sell them to people looking for a cheap place to live. According to the website www.whysaltoncity.com, large lots are going for as little as $22,000. One selling point being used is that the lots are near the "cool waters of the Salton Sea." (Ah, yes, and fishermen don't even have to dip a line. They can just wait 'til the next algae bloom and watch those dead fish come floating to shore!) Well who knows? The way California real estate trends go, it might not be a bad investment at that.

PARKS, BEACHES, AND RECREATION AREAS

1 Martin Flora Park

🐾 (See Imperial County map on page 934)

Although the Salton City area is full of empty shoreline, community-service folks ask that you stick to the public parks with your dog. This isn't such a bad place to take a leashed pooch. It looks a little like a gravel parking lot, but never mind that. The Salton Sea is right here and so are plenty of picnic tables. The park is an unusual place to stop for lunch.

From Highway 86, turn northeast on North Marina Drive and follow it past all the empty streets. As the road approaches the sea, it will curve to the

right. In a few blocks, you'll come to Sea Port Avenue. Go left, and follow it a few more blocks to the park. Make sure you can figure out how to get back to Highway 86 before you leave, because many people have become mighty lost here, and there aren't many homes where you can stop and ask for help. And this park doesn't have any sort of a phone number we can refer you to. And about all we could come up with in a recent Internet search was a photo identified as the park, with a crude hand-lettered warning sign that reads: "YOU WILL GET STUCK." We talked to eight people at different entities, and they all know vaguely about the park, but no one has any idea who would be the contact. Perhaps the Twilight Zone isn't as far away as we think…

Bombay Beach

PARKS, BEACHES, AND RECREATION AREAS

2 Salton Sea State Recreation Area

😽😽😽 (See Imperial County map on page 934)

Since most people visit the north end of this 16-mile-long park that sits on the northeast section of the Salton Sea, you'll find its description, including camping information, in the *Mecca* section of the *Riverside County* chapter. But if you have a hankering to discover the Imperial County section of the park, take Highway 111 to any of several entrances, including the popular Bombay Beach area. "We love dogs, but they do have to be on leash," a friendly park employee says. 760/393-3052.

Calipatria

PARKS, BEACHES, AND RECREATION AREAS

3 Red Hill Marina County Park

😽😽😽😽 (See Imperial County map on page 934)

This peninsular park jutting into the southeast corner of the Salton Sea feels more like an island. The terrain is early moonscape and the 240-acre park is pretty much one big hill. You and your dog can see all the way to the Mexican border from here!

Dogs must be leashed, but at least they're allowed. They're banned from the neighboring Salton Sea National Wildlife Refuge.

The day-use fee is $2. Campsites are $7–12. There are 400 campsites available. No reservations are necessary. From Highway 111 just north of Calipatria, go west on Schrimpf Road, which is a graded dirt road. In about five miles, you'll be at the park. 760/482-4384.

Brawley

PARKS, BEACHES, AND RECREATION AREAS

4 Imperial Sand Dunes

🐾🐾🐾🐾 (See Imperial County map on page 934)

Before going on about how enthralling this enormous desert sandbox is, I want to play back something a local BLM staffer told me.

"Too often we get calls from someone who starts out crying, and when we ask what's wrong, they say they lost their poor dog in the desert," she said. "We hate those kind of calls. It's so sad. People let their pets wander too far sometimes, and they get disoriented and lost. Out here, there's not a good chance for survival, even when it's not extremely hot. We try to help them find their dog, but this is a big place. You feel so helpless."

She said this before leashes were the law here. Now that leashes are mandated, the BLM hopes dogs will be a bit safer. Keep that leash on, because it's not worth taking chances out here.

The Bureau of Land Management oversees 1.5 million acres in Imperial County. Much of the acreage is within this vast dune system, full of wind-sculpted crests and ripples that extend for more than 40 miles. The Imperial Dunes (also known as the Algodones Dunes) rise to 300 feet, and they're great fun to hike on or around with your sandy pooch.

Two-thirds of the dune area north of Highway 78 is closed to vehicles, so it's an ideal place for a dog hike. This is also where you may spot all sorts of desert wildflowers. An added bonus: You can set up your tent just about anywhere in the area, and there's no fee.

The BLM ranger station is a good place to start your adventure. No permit is necessary. From central Brawley, drive east on Highway 78 about 19 miles to Gecko Road. Turn right, and the ranger station is about a mile down the road. 760/337-4400.

PLACES TO STAY

Brawley Inn: This clean, comfortable hotel has a heated pool (they probably don't turn on the heat too much here) and is close to the town center. Rates are $79–156. 575 West Main Street 92227; 800/541-4567; www.brawleyinn.com.

Imperial

PARKS, BEACHES, AND RECREATION AREAS

At press time, Imperial was starting work on a dog park! It's needed here.

🖬 Eager Park

🐾 (See Imperial County map on page 934)

Stop here if your dog is longing to get out of the car or house and doesn't mind visiting a postage stamp–sized park. There are a few small trees and a small playground. Maybe the park should be reserved for Chihuahuas and Pekingese pooches, or at least dogs with small expectations. Dogs must be leashed.

From Highway 86, go west on 10th Street and left on H Street. 760/355-4371.

El Centro

PARKS, BEACHES, AND RECREATION AREAS

🖬 Sunbeam Lake County Park

🐾🐾🐾 (See Imperial County map on page 934)

This county park is filled with big old eucalyptus trees. That's not normally a selling point, but boy dogs who are tired of lifting their legs on desert boulders around this area seem to appreciate any kind of tree.

Sunbeam Lake itself is a fun fishing and swimming hole. Dogs must be leashed, so swimming is a bit restricted. The trails in this 140-acre park provide a fun walk for you and the leashed pooch.

It'll cost you $2 to use this park during the day. The park is seven miles west of El Centro. Exit I-8 at Drew Road and drive about a half mile north. 760/337-4557.

PLACES TO STAY

Brunner's Inn and Suites: Rates are $50–75. 215 North Imperial Avenue 92243; 760/352-6431.

Ramada Inn El Centro: It's comfortable and clean here, and you get use of a heated outdoor pool and a small exercise room. Rates are $72–90. Dogs are $10 extra. 1455 Ocotillo Drive 92243; 760/352-5152.

RESOURCES

National Forests and Wilderness Areas

Dogs of California, rejoice! If you really want to stretch those gams, the U.S. Department of Agriculture's Forest Service has a real treat for you. Instead of a walk in your friendly neighborhood park, how does an exhilarating, off-leash hike sound? You'll have your choice of millions of acres of national forests spread over a fascinating variety of terrain.

Most dogs call the forests "dog heaven." Those who don't speak English just pant with joy. There's something for every dog's tastes in national forests. Desert dogs are as happy as dogs who like waterfalls and forests. Most national forests have no entry fees, few leash rules, and plenty of free camping. And they all have some of the most beautiful land in California. (National Forests lay claim to 40 million acres around the state. That's 20 percent of California!)

If your dog is obedient enough to come when she's called, and you trust her not to wander off in pursuit of deer or other wildlife, she's more than welcome to be off leash in most of the forest areas. Be sure to talk with a ranger before planning your excursion, because rules change frequently, and areas that are OK for off-leash dogs today may not be tomorrow. Be aware that the front-line personnel at the forests might tell you that dogs must be on leash, but they're not always right. Ask for a supervisor or ranger if you have reason to think the leash laws are more lax.

Always carry a leash with you, just in case. It's a good idea to leash your dog on the trail when you see other hikers, or at least to pull your dog to the side so the others can pass by. "The leash law is still pretty loose (small joke)," says Matt Mathes, a dog-loving, very helpful representative of the U.S.D.A. Forest Service, but "believe it or not, not everyone loves dogs." Dogs must be leashed in developed campgrounds (which usually charge a small fee) and in developed recreation areas. But many areas of the forests are set up so that you can plop down a tent just about anywhere you please (for free). When you find that perfect, cool stream with a flat, soft area on the bank, your dog may not have to be leashed. But it's a bad idea to leave your dog leashless and outside your tent at night.

The Forest Service's California website, www.fs.fed.us/r5, offers excellent guides to every national forest in the state. Maps of specific national forests and wilderness areas are available for $9 each via www.nationalforeststore. com or at local forest headquarters. It's always a good idea to contact the forest rangers in the area you'll be visiting and ask if there are any exceptions to the leash-free policy where you're planning to hike, or if your forest destination is charging a small fee for use. More forest areas are charging fees these days, but the cost is nominal, and at least 80 percent of the fee goes back into upkeep and improvements of those forests.

Now for the obligatory poop paragraph. As far as bathroom etiquette goes, it's not necessary to pack out the poop. If you don't mind it squishing along in your backpack, that's great. But if you bury it, as you should bury your own, that's OK. Leave the forest as you found it. And please don't let your dog go to the bathroom near a stream. It can be a health hazard to anyone drinking the water later.

And dogs, if you come to really love your national forests, tell your people that because of severely reduced budgets, trail maintenance is suffering. Tell them that the trails could sure use a hand. Tell them that rangers would be thrilled to have teams of dog owners working together to help keep up the trails they use. Your people can contact a ranger to see how they can volunteer.

What follows is a very brief description of each forest in California. Again, be sure to contact a ranger before setting out so you can check on changing rules and portions of forests or trails that might be closed.

ANGELES NATIONAL FOREST

This 693,000-acre forest with more than 620 miles of trails covers about one-quarter of Los Angeles County and most of the San Gabriel Mountains. Forest Headquarters, 701 North Santa Anita Avenue, Arcadia, CA 91006; 626/574-5200.

CLEVELAND NATIONAL FOREST

This 566,000-acre chaparral- and conifer-covered land has 331 miles of trails, including a section of the Pacific Crest Trail that runs between the Anza-Borrego Desert and Mexico. Forest Headquarters, 10845 Rancho Bernardo Road, Suite 200, Rancho Bernardo, CA 92127-2107; 858/673-6180.

ELDORADO NATIONAL FOREST

Alpine meadows, rivers, streams, and glacial lakes are among the refreshing landscapes you'll come across in this forest, which encompasses 884,000 acres. This one's getting more "leashy," so talk to a ranger to get the scoop if you want leash-free hiking. Forest Headquarters, 100 Forni Road, Placerville, CA 95667; 530/622-5061.

INYO NATIONAL FOREST

This 1.8-million-acre forest stretches 165 miles from eerie, salty Mono Lake south past Owens Lake. It borders Mt. Whitney, the highest peak in the lower 48 states, and is home to hundreds of waterfalls and glacial lakes. Forest Headquarters, 351 Pacu Lane, Suite 200, Bishop, CA 93514; 760/873-2485.

KLAMATH NATIONAL FOREST

Tired of traffic, loud neighbors, and people snarling at your dog? Come here! (But don't tell anyone else about it.) This lovely 1.7-million-acre forest with 1,160 miles of trails is one of the least-used of California's national forests. Forest Headquarters, 1312 Fairlane Road, Yreka, CA 96097; 530/842-6131.

LAKE TAHOE BASIN MANAGEMENT UNIT

The bulk of this 205,000-acre unit of national forest is on the southern half of beautiful Lake Tahoe. Because it gets such heavy use, dogs are required to be leashed at all times. Forest Headquarters, 35 College Drive, South Lake Tahoe, CA 96150; 530/543-2600.

LASSEN NATIONAL FOREST

Wherever you and your dog tread at this 1.4-million-acre forest with 300 miles of trails is breathtaking. Volcanic craters and fascinating geologic features abound. Forest Headquarters, 2550 Riverside Drive, Susanville, CA 96130; 530/257-2151.

LOS PADRES NATIONAL FOREST

Ranging in elevations from sea level at Big Sur to nearly 9,000 feet at the crest of Mount Pinos, this spectacular forest is one of the most rugged and beautiful in the West. At 1.9 million acres, it's also one of the largest forests in the state. Forest Headquarters, 6755 Hollister Avenue, Suite 150, Goleta, CA 93117; 805/968-6640.

MENDOCINO NATIONAL FOREST

Many Bay Area residents come to this million-acre forest for quick day or weekend trips. This is the only one of California's national forests that is not crossed by a paved road or highway, so if you're looking to escape the world of wheels, you'll find your peace here. Forest Headquarters, 825 North Humboldt Avenue, Willows, CA 95998; 530/934-3316.

MODOC NATIONAL FOREST

This 1.9-million-acre forest in the far northeast reaches of the state is where the wild horses and the antelope play. The spartan chaparral- and juniper-covered Modoc Plateau and the surrounding evergreen lands are home to more than 300 species of wildlife. Forest Headquarters, 800 West 12th Street, Alturas, CA 96101; 530/233-5811.

PLUMAS NATIONAL FOREST

Canine hikers and other outdoors enthusiasts are attracted year-round to this 1.2-million-acre magical forest's streams, lakes, deep canyons, and lush mountain valleys. The forest has more than 1,000 miles of sparkling rivers and streams, along with about 100 lakes. Forest Headquarters, 159 Lawrence Street, Quincy, CA 95971; 530/283-2050.

SAN BERNARDINO NATIONAL FOREST

This forest is home to famed Big Bear Lake and Lake Arrowhead, popular Southern California resorts. It comprises 810,000 acres of land that vary from thick pine woods to rocky, cactus-filled desert. Forest Headquarters, 602 Tippecanoe Avenue, San Bernardino, CA 92408; 909/382-2600.

SEQUOIA NATIONAL FOREST

Giant sequoias, among the world's largest trees, grow in more than 35 magnificent groves on Sequoia National Forest's lower slopes. The park encompasses 1.1 million acres and has 830 miles of trails. Forest Headquarters, 1839 South Newcomb Street, Porterville, CA 93257; 559/784-1500.

SHASTA-TRINITY NATIONAL FOREST

Magnificent, massive Mt. Shasta is the most striking of many visual highlights within this 2.1-million-acre forest (the largest national forest in the state). Dogs can explore the less steep parts of this 17-mile-wide, 14,162-foot-high mountain, but the forest has a whopping 1,500 miles of other, more appropriate trails to try. Forest Headquarters, 3644 Avtech Parkway, Redding, CA 96002; 530/226-2500.

SIERRA NATIONAL FOREST

Surrounded by big, popular, restrictive-to-dogs national parks such as

Yosemite, the 1.3-million-acre Sierra National Forest is a joy for dogs. Forest Headquarters, 1600 Tollhouse Road, Clovis, CA 93612; 559/297-0706.

SIX RIVERS NATIONAL FOREST

Six major rivers (surprise!) are among the 1,500 miles of water in the forest. This long, narrow forest encompasses one million acres of Douglas firs, incense cedars, ponderosa pines, and dozens of other types of trees. Forest Headquarters, 1330 Bayshore Way, Eureka, CA 95501; 707/442-1721.

STANISLAUS NATIONAL FOREST

You and your dog can hike on 660 miles of trails that take you over volcanic ridges, through lush alpine meadows, and under tall pines and cedars in this million-acre forest. Forest Headquarters, 19777 Greenley Road, Sonora, CA 95370; 209/532-3671.

TAHOE NATIONAL FOREST

Lake Tahoe, the blue jewel of the Sierra, makes up this forest's southeast boundary. A hike on even a small part of the forest's 600 miles of trail will take you and your dog through a vast variety of vegetation, including mountain chaparral, mixed conifers, alpine plants, lodgepole pine, and pinyon juniper. Forest Headquarters, 631 Coyote Street, Nevada City, CA 95959; 530/265-4531.

TOIYABE NATIONAL FOREST

Although most of this 3.5-million-acre forest (the largest national forest in the lower 48) is spread throughout Nevada, a relatively small section of it crosses into California. You and your dog can peruse thundering waterfalls, clear streams, glacial lakes, and alpine meadows. Forest Headquarters, 1200 Franklin Way, Sparks, NV 89431; 775/331-6444.

INDEXES

Accommodations Index

Restaurant Index

General Index

C

G

YZ

Acknowledgments

Many tailwags to...

My fabulous, four-paw fact-checker/research editor Caroline Grannan. In a brilliant stroke of luck, I caught my dog-loving writer friend between gigs and she took kindly to my piteous (and pitiful) pleas for help. I am overwhelmingly grateful.

My husband extraordinaire, Craig Hanson, for getting me through both of my hard-drive crashes while I was working on this edition. I'm sure it's lots of fun being married to someone who loses 11 completed, backed-up chapters of a book close to deadline. His levelheadedness kept me focused on the end goal of somehow meeting deadline and also of somehow not chucking my sleek Apple laptop out the window—twice.

My lawyer, Karl Olson, for stepping in to stop a bum internet company from stealing my website, www.caldogtravel.com. Karl has the ferocity of a pit bull toward his opponents, but the demeanor of a lab to those he likes. Good Dog, Karl.

My faithful correspondent, "Three-Dog-Dave" Hepperly and his adorable motley crew for their innumerable and invaluable tips, photos, and articles.

My other longtime correspondents, Sheryl Smith and her dear Molly Dog, for helping me sniff out a few real beauties, including Quincy's BBQ in Encino—probably the most dog-friendly eatery in the state.

The legions of wonderful California canines who had their humans write to tell me about their terrific dog-friendly finds around the state. Wherever possible, I've noted you in the text, doggies.

And finally, to my talented editor, Shari Husain, who has been a lot of fun to work with, and who I know will find a way to cram all this material into a mere 1,000 or so pages.

Keeping Current

Note to All Dog Lovers:
While our information is as current as possible, changes to fees, regulations, parks, roads, and trails sometimes are made after we go to press. Businesses can close, change their ownership, or change their rules. Earthquakes, fires, rainstorms, and other natural phenomena can radically change the condition of parks, hiking trails, and wilderness areas. Before you and your dog begin your travels, please be certain to call the phone numbers for each listing for updated information.

Attention Dogs of California:
Our readers mean everything to us. We explore California so that you and your people can spend true quality time together. Your input to this book is very important. In the last few years, we've heard from many wonderful dogs and their humans about new dog-friendly places, or old dog-friendly places we didn't know about. If we've missed your favorite park, beach, outdoor restaurant, hotel, or dog-friendly activity, please let us know. We'll check out the tip and if it turns out to be a good one, include it in the next edition, giving a thank-you to the dog and/or person who sent in the suggestion. Please write us—we always welcome comments and suggestions.

The Dog Lover's Companion to California
Avalon Travel
1700 Fourth Street
Berkeley, CA 94710, USA
email: atpfeedback@avalonpub.com